1983
CATHOLIC
ALMANAC

Felician A. Foy, O.F.M.
EDITOR

Rose M. Avato
ASSOCIATE EDITOR

Our Sunday Visitor, Inc.
HUNTINGTON • INDIANA

ACKNOWLEDGMENTS: NC News Service, for coverage of news and documentary texts; *The Documents of Vatican II,* ed. W. M. Abbott (Herder and Herder, America Press: New York 1966), for quotations of Council documents; *Annuario Pontificio* (1982); *Statistical Yearbook of the Church* (1980); *The Official Catholic Directory* (P. J. Kenedy: New York 1982); *The Papal Encyclicals,* 5 vols., ed. C. Carlen (McGrath Publishing: Wilmington, NC 1981); The United States Catholic Mission Assoc. (1233 Lawrence St. N.E., Washington, D.C. 20017), for U.S. foreign-mission compilations and statistics; *Catholic Press Directory* (1982); *CCCB 1982 Directory* (Canadian Conference of Catholic Bishops: Ottawa, Ont. 1982), for Canadian Catholic statistics; other sources as credited in particular entries.

ISBN 0-87973-253-9
Library of Congress Catalog Card No. 73-641001
International Standard Serial Number (ISSN) 0069-1208

TABLE OF CONTENTS

3

MORALITY IN POPULATION POLICIES

The Vatican, reported NC News, told an international conference on demographics Sept. 21, 1982, that government population policies "should take into account not only scientific and political information but also ethical and moral perspectives."

The Holy See's position was stated to the European Population Conference by Father Jan Schotte, secretary of the Pontifical Commission for Justice and Peace, who headed the Holy See's delegation to the meeting.

The meeting, held Sept. 21-24 in Strasbourg and sponsored by the Council of Europe, had as its theme "Demographic Trends and Policy Responses."

The Vatican's position is that demographic information is important, said Father Schotte, "because it informs us about events and trends that touch on the lives and future security of living people and of future generations, and because it recognizes the importance of population growth and/or decline for strategies of social and human development."

But he said that policies which develop out of that information should be keyed to the "dignity and rights of the human person."

The First Human Right

"First among these human rights," Father Schotte observed, "is the right to life itself, which should be sustained by society and safeguarded by law and public policy."

"Thus, a population policy that respects human life cannot countenance abortion or euthanasia," he said.

"Instead," the Vatican delegate said, "governments should find ways to enable people — especially the young — to act responsibly in regard to parenthood and sexuality, and they should support and assist parents and their children throughout pregnancy and infancy."

On the exercise of responsible parenthood, Father Schotte observed that "decisions regarding the spacing of births and the size of the family should be worked out by the couple in light of their multiple responsibilities to God, themselves, their existing family and the society of which they are a part."

Recommendations to Governments

As specific recommendations, the Vatican proposed that governments:

• "establish social policies that support the family unit";

• "protect and preserve the value of the child from conception on";

• "ensure freedom from coercion in regard to decisions of responsible parenthood, including the somewhat subtle coercion invoked in some population policies and family planning programs";

• "strive to eliminate injustice and the causes of poverty, disease, hunger and economic dependence that have a serious effect on families and endanger their well-being and ability to function";

• "recognize the important contribution that women make to the welfare of society in the fulfillment of their maternal role, and establish policies that ensure financial equity for mothers who choose not to work during their child-rearing years";

• "protect couples from psychological pressure that favors only the childless or small family, and give appropriate encouragement and approval to those couples who choose to have even a relatively large family."

Responsibilities of Families

As responsibilities on the part of families, Father Schotte's testimony recommended:

• "engaging in social service activities";

• "assisting the underprivileged, the sick and the aging";

• "becoming involved in activities of political intervention so as to ensure that the laws and institutions of the state not only do not offend but support and positively defend the rights and duties of the family";

• "creating a positive influence on cultural, economic and juridical structures in order that the profound needs of specific family groups, such as migrant families and the families of those obliged to be away from home for a long period, be adequately met."

PUBLICATION HISTORY

The *Catholic Almanac* originated remotely from *St. Anthony's Almanac*, a 64-page annual with calendar, feature and devotional contents, published by the Franciscans of Holy Name Province from 1904 to 1929.

Completely revised and enlarged, the publication was issued under the title, *The Franciscan Almanac*, by *The Franciscan Magazine* from 1931 to 1933, and by St. Anthony's Guild from 1936 to 1971. From 1940 to 1969, its title was *The National Catholic Almanac*. The present title was adopted in 1969. The 1959 to 1971 editions were produced jointly by St. Anthony's Guild and Doubleday & Co., Inc.

The *Catholic Almanac* was acquired in 1971 by Our Sunday Visitor, Inc., Huntington, Ind. 46750.

POPE JOHN PAUL IN AFRICA

Following is an account of the principal events of Pope John Paul's second pastoral trip to Africa, Feb. 12 to 19, 1982.

During the trip, his 10th outside Italy since becoming Pope, the Holy Father traveled approximately 8,500 miles; visited four West African countries — Nigeria, Benin, Gabon and Equatorial Guinea; celebrated Mass before large and mixed gatherings of Catholics and non-Catholics, and delivered about 35 homilies and addresses on matters of pastoral and human concern, in English, French and Spanish.

─────── FEBRUARY 12 ───────

The Pope flew from Rome to Lagos, Nigeria, where he delivered an address at the airport, celebrated Mass at the National Stadium and attended a reception at the presidential residence in the evening.

On arrival at the Murtali Mohammed Airport late in the afternoon, the Holy Father was welcomed by a delegation headed by Nigerian President Alhaji Shehu Shagari and Cardinal Dominic Ekandem of Ikot Ekpene.

Reasons for the Visit

The Pope responded to their greeting with an address in which he stated the reasons for his pastoral visit.

"I have come in order to meet people of different religious persuasions ... and I earnestly hope that my presence among you will express the love and respect that I have for all of you, as well as my esteem for the worthy religious values that you cherish. I wish to show fraternal solidarity with all the people of this nation. ... It is my desire to pay tribute to Nigeria's contributions to justice, peace and development in Africa and beyond, and to support all efforts under way to build a society ever more fraternal and humane."

Addressing himself to Catholics, he said:

"I come to you in the name of Jesus Christ on a visit that is pastoral in nature ... to meet you, to listen to you, to celebrate the Holy Eucharist with you and for you ... to proclaim Jesus Christ ... to strengthen you in your faith and in your love for God and for all your brothers and sisters ... to support my brother bishops and priests in the work of evangelization and in their generous service to humanity."

He also addressed "words of friendship to all sectors of the national community," saying:

"In particular, my thoughts and affection go out to the sick, the old and the handicapped, and to all who are experiencing the burdens of suffering and sorrow. I hope to be able to be close to you in order to comfort you. I look forward to the opportunity to encourage and challenge the youth, and to honor all the citizens of Nigeria."

Results of Evangelization

At a Mass celebrated before a throng of about 85,000 persons in the National Stadium in Lagos, the Pope spoke glowingly of the evangelization of the country since the 1860s and of "the abundant harvest which we see today." He said "the acceptance of the Christian faith here in Nigeria has indeed been remarkable," so much so that "the Church in your land is now largely directed by Nigerian bishops and priests."

Among the works and results of evangelization, he called attention to preaching of the Gospel, sacramental ministry, Christian witness in ordinary life, action for peace and justice, and efforts toward Christian unity through dialogue with people of other churches.

Contributions of Catholics

"You Nigerian Catholics have not lived cut off from society," the Pope said. "You are indeed very much part and parcel of this country. ... You have contributed much to building up Nigeria into the great nation that it is." For example, the Church has promoted schooling, which in its turn has fostered all-around development: social, cultural, political and economic. You have also assisted your brothers and sisters by health care programs, mobile clinics in rural areas, maternity homes and hospitals. And you have not forgotten social services for orphans, the old, the handicapped and the poor.

"Also worthy of special mention are your efforts to help school-leavers to learn such important skills as carpentry, weaving, knitting, motor mechanics, shoemaking, baby care and homemaking. In this way you have equipped many young people to face the future with reason for hope. Through these many endeavors, you bear witness to Christ, who 'came not to be served but to serve' (Mt. 20:28)."

African Accomplishments, Potential

The accomplishments of African nations and the "human face" of development efforts were principal themes of a papal address at an evening reception at the residence of President Alhaji Shehu Shagari.

"I experience a deep joy in seeing how Nigeria, together with numerous other African nations, has acceded to full national sovereignty and is able to take its future in its own hands, according to the richness of its own genius, in respect for its own culture, and in consonance with its own sense of God and of spiritual values.

"It is my conviction that all of Africa, when allowed to take charge of its own affairs, without being subjected to interference and pressure from any outside powers or groups, will not only astound the rest of the world by its achievements but will be able to share its wisdom, its sense of life, its reverence for God with other continents and nations, thus establishing that exchange and that partnership in mutual respect that is needed for the true progress of all humanity."

Human Face of Development

"I wholeheartedly encourage all those entrusted with the well-being of their fellow men to make the human person the true criterion of all development efforts.

"Development projects must always have a human face. They cannot be reduced to a purely materialistic or economic endeavor. The human person must always be the ultimate measure of the feasibility and the success of an economic or social program. Progress can therefore not be separated from the dignity of the human person nor from respect for his or her fundamental rights.

"In the pursuit of progress, total progress, everything must be rejected that is unworthy of the freedom and the human rights of the individual and of the people as a whole. Thus are rejected such elements as corruption, bribery, embezzlement of public funds, domination over the weak, callousness toward the poor and handicapped.

"Participation in the political life of the country; freedom of religion, speech and association; the protection of a well functioning judiciary system; respect for and promotion of things spiritual and cultural; love of truth: these are the ingredients for progress that is truly and fully human."

————— FEBRUARY 13 —————

The Holy Father flew to Onitsha where he celebrated Mass, addressed a large gathering of young people, and visited the sick and aged at the St. Charles Borromeo Hospital. He then went to Enugu for an address to priests and seminarians before returning to Lagos for the night.

Family Values and Shadows

At a Mass celebrated in the morning in the outskirts of Onitsha, the Pope baptized, confirmed and gave first Holy Communion to 31 persons before a throng of about a million people. Family themes were the subjects of his homily.

"Brothers and sisters, your families have so many positive and praiseworthy values, based on your family traditions. You have strong family ties. Children are regarded as a blessing and are desired as the crown of marriage. The extended family system provides a loving, human environment for the care of orphans, the old and the poor.

"There are, however, some shadows. Traditionally, your culture did not exclude polygamy, even though most marriages were and are monogamous. Sometimes women were deprived of some of their rights. And the modern enemies of the family, the disturbing degradation of some fundamental values — divorce, contraception and abortion — have not spared your country."

Openness to Life

"Because the love of husband and wife is a unique sharing in the life of God himself, it should be genuinely and generously open to new life. It should be open to all those whose life is diminished or threatened by needs of one kind or another.

"Christian families of Nigeria, let your example shine before the whole world: stand up for life. Do not accept an anti-life mentality rooted in 'a corruption of the idea and the expression of freedom, conceived not as a capacity for realizing the truth of God's plan for marriage and the family but as an autonomous power of self-affirmation, often against others, for one's own selfish well-being' (Apostolic Letter, *Familiaris Consortio,* No. 6)."

"If you love your country, then love your family life. If you wish to avoid having a society that runs the risk of becoming more and more depersonalized and standardized and therefore inhuman and dehumanizing, then strengthen the structures of family life. Love your families. Respect them."

Discipline and Responsibility

The Pope spoke to 100,000 young people in the afternoon, citing the need they have for discipline in their lives and the responsibilities they have in society and the Church.

"You must be outstanding for discipline, strength and reliability. This will show itself in several ways. You will be chaste. You will resist all temptations which attack the sanctity of your body. You will bring your chastity to the priesthood, religious life or marriage. You will have many opportunities to express discipline through Christian temperance.

"The attractions and pressures of the world often lure young people into self-indulgence or escapism. Temptations to the excesses of drink and to drug abuse are all around you. Will power reinforced by humble prayer is essential to anyone who is trying to act in a fully human way."

He called on them to seek divine and human guidance in choosing their respective states of life, and reminded them of their responsibilities of citizenship.

"You should constantly strive to identify the ills of your society, such as bribery and corruption, the embezzlement of government or company funds, extravagant and unproductive spending, the parade of wealth, neglect of the poor and the friendless, nepotism, tribalism, political antagonism, denial of the rights of the poor, abortion, contraception and other evils which also ravage other countries. As true youth, you will see, judge and then act according to the criteria of the Gospel of Jesus Christ."

In conclusion, the Holy Father told his young listeners: "I have come to encourage you in the great mission you have to help build a better world, to advance Christ's kingdom of truth and life, of holiness and grace, of justice, love and peace. It is to him that I wish to direct your gaze."

Meaning of Suffering

This was the theme of the Pope's remarks during a visit with the sick and elderly at St. Charles Borromeo Hospital.

"Although God allows suffering to exist in the world, he does not enjoy it. Indeed, our Lord Jesus Christ, the Son of God made man, loved the sick; he devoted a great part of his earthly ministry to healing the sick and comforting the afflicted. Our God is a God of compassion and consolation. And he expects us to take the ordinary means to prevent, relieve and remove suffering and sickness.

"But . . . suffering and sickness still exist. A Christian sees meaning in suffering. He bears such suffering with patience, love of God and generosity. He offers it all to God, through Christ, especially during the Sacrifice of the Mass. . . . When suffering is associated with Christ's passion and redemptive death, then it has great value for the individual, for the Church and for society."

Priestly Life and Ministry

At Enugu after his visit to Onitsha, the Holy Father addressed priests and students for the priesthood at the major seminary, one of the largest in the world with an enrollment of about 700 students of philosophy and theology.

He called on priests to conform themselves to the model of the Good Shepherd in their ministries of proclaiming the Gospel, celebrating the Eucharist, sanctifying their people by word and sacrament, forming and building up the community of the Church, and providing their people with many forms of pastoral service.

Essential to the ministry of a priest, he said, is his life "in union with Christ."

"His life, like Christ's, must be marked by self-sacrifice, zeal for the spreading of the kingdom of God, unblemished chastity, unstinted charity. All this is possible only when the priest is a man of prayer and Eucharistic devotion. By praying the Liturgy of the Hours in union with the Church, he will find strength and joy for the apostolate. In silent prayer before the Blessed Sacrament, he will be constantly renewed in his consecration to Jesus Christ and confirmed in his permanent commitment to priestly celibacy. By invoking Mary, the Mother of Jesus, the priest will be sustained in his generous service to all Christ's brothers and sisters in the world.

"Yes, the priest must not allow the passing needs of the active apostolate to elbow out or eat into his prayer life. He must not be so engrossed with working for God that he is in danger of forgetting God himself. He will remember that our Savior warned us that without him we can do nothing. Without him, we can fish all night and still catch nothing."

The Holy Father sketched features of priestly ministry, saying:

"The priest must be a leaven in the Nigerian community of today. In a country in which many are over-concerned with making money, the priest by word and example must call attention to higher values. Man does not live by bread alone.

"The priest must identify with the poor, so as to be able to bring them the uplifting Gospel of Christ."

Observing that " 'evangelization would not be complete if it did not take account of the unceasing interplay of the Gospel and men's concrete life,' " the Pope added: "The priest will be deeply concerned with bringing the light of the Gospel and the power of God's word to touch the many different issues of family life, fundamental human rights and duties, justice and peace, development and liberation, culture and learning. He will endeavor to make Christ and the Church present in the fields of the arts and sciences, culture and the professions."

————— FEBRUARY 14 —————

The Pope flew to Kaduna in the morning, ordained 86 men to the priesthood, consecrated the people of Nigeria and other African countries to Mary, spoke before a gathering of lay persons, and delivered a brief address on Catholic-Moslem relations.

Address to New Priests

The Holy Father ordained 86 men to the priesthood during a Mass celebrated in Murtata Mohammed Square before a throng of 500,000 people. In an address to the new priests, he said:

"Ordination confers the authority and mandate to proclaim the Gospel and to preach in the name of the Church. As priests, you will preside at the celebration of the Eucharist, and in the name of Christ you will forgive sins in the sacrament of penance. In these and in the many other activities by which you will give the Church of God a shepherd's care, seek always to be regarded as one who serves."

Noting that "the anointed of the Lord are sent to the poor, to prisoners, to those whose hearts are broken, . . . to people who stand in special need of God's mercy," he said that these priests, like all others, had "a unique opportunity and responsibility to proclaim the mercy of God."

Consecration to Mary

The Pope consecrated Africans to Mary as he prayed the Angelus after the ordination ceremonies. He prayed:

"I desire to consecrate and entrust to you, Mother of the Church, in a special way the Church in the land of Nigeria. . . . In today's consecration, I entrust to you all those who live and work in the African continent, all of whom the heavenly Father has loved eternally in Jesus Christ and whom he wills to save through Christ's blood shed on the cross."

Apostolate of Lay Persons

Late in the afternoon, in the Cathedral of St. Joseph, the Pope addressed catechists and representatives of the National Laity Council and the Catholic Women's Organization.

"As lay people," he said, "you know that your special apostolate is to bring Christian principles to bear upon the temporal order," in marriage and family life, trade and commerce, the arts and professions, politics and government, culture, national and international relations.

He told his listeners they were called to be a "leaven for Christ" and "to promote justice, unity, honesty and public spiritedness," bringing "Gospel-inspired and concrete answers" to the problems of their society.

He spoke in praise of catechists and noted the substantial need of them in the ministry of the Church.

He also paid tribute to activities of Nigerian Catholic women, singling out for particular mention their "various initiatives in favor of the family" and their stance against abortion.

Catholic-Moslem Relations

A scheduled meeting with Moslem representatives at the Kaduna airport did not take place because of unresolved disagreement among leaders of local sects about who should attend. The Pope nevertheless made a brief statement on Catholic-Moslem relations before Alhaji Abba Musa Rimi, governor of Kaduna, and his aides.

"It is my earnest hope," the Pope said, "that our solidarity of brotherhood, under God, will truly enhance the future of Nigeria and all Africa. . . . I am convinced that, if we join hands in the name of God, we can ac-

complish much good. We can work together for harmony and national unity, in sincerity and greater mutual confidence."

-------------- FEBRUARY 15 --------------

The Pope flew to Ibadan where he celebrated Mass at the university and delivered an address to men and women religious at the seminary. He returned to Lagos in the afternoon. He met in the evening with members of committees who had made arrangements for his visit and with the bishops of the country.

Primacy of Spiritual Values

The Holy Father spoke about spiritual values and the service of people in a homily during Mass at the University of Ibadan. Before a congregation of faculty personnel, students and other members of the academic community, he said:

"I cannot fail to speak to you about the primacy of spiritual values in all the areas of the cultural environment in which you live and work, and to which you contribute so significantly. Without spiritual values, man is no longer true to himself, because without them he denies or ignores his essential relationship of dependence on the very source of his existence, his Creator, in whose image he was made and continues to exist.

"Like you, the Church is also at the service of man through the proclamation of the Gospel and its liberating and elevating influences. Science and religion are both gifts of God, the eternal Truth. . . . Science and religion are not only not opposed, but they understand each other, they work together, and they are both at the service of man and of truth."

Witness of Religious

In an address to men and women religious at the Ibadan seminary, the Holy Father called attention to their consecration to God by baptism and to the "special witness" they bear to Christ in the Church and in the world through their vows, life of prayer and commitment to "activities of the apostolate . . . in the cause of evangelization."

He stressed one point: "Even more important than the various works which you carry on is the life which you live; in other words, what you are. You are consecrated persons striving to follow Christ with great intensity of love."

A Word of Thanks

Back in Lagos, the Holy Father thanked members of the various committees who had organized arrangements for his stay in Nigeria. He told them:

"The arrangements you made have enabled me to exercise my pastoral mission as a servant of Christ's Gospel and as the universal shepherd of God's people. With your collaboration, I have been able here in Nigeria to proclaim Christ, the light of the world. . . . It is my hope that the pattern of collaboration and hard work that you have followed during the preparation of my visit will continue to inspire you in all your activities in your local churches and in the continued support you are asked to give to your bishops and priests."

Evangelization

Evangelization and inculturation were principal themes of the Pope's address to the bishops of Nigeria. Speaking in the evening at the apostolic nunciature in Lagos, he said:

"In anticipation of this pastoral visit, I expressed the hope that it would initiate a new era of evangelization. . . . Evangelization constitutes the essential mission of the Church; it is her vocatin, her deepest identity."

"In practice, the Church's vocation to evangelize means, above all, living the Gospel ever more deeply. It means accepting Christ's call to conversion and accepting the demands inherent in the faith preached by Jesus."

"Evangelization involves a process of purification and interior change that affects our local churches. It means conversion unto salvation: the ecclesial community becoming ever more a community of living faith; a communion of prayer; a center of charity radiating concern for the poor and the sick, the lonely, the abandoned, the handicapped, those with leprosy, those who are weak in faith, those who need support and are looking for someone to show them the love of Christ."

Inculturation

"An important aspect of your own evangelizing role is the whole dimension of the inculturation of the Gospel into the lives of your people."

"The Church truly respects the culture of each people. In offering the Gospel message, the Church does not intend to destroy or to abolish what is good and beautiful. In fact, she recognizes many cultural values and, through the power of the Gospel, purifies and takes into Christian worship certain elements of a people's customs. The Church comes to bring Christ; she does not come to bring the culture of another race. Evangelization aims at penetrating and elevating culture by the power of the Gospel."

"It is through the Providence of God that the divine message is made incarnate and is communicated through the culture of each people. It is forever true that the path of culture is the path of man, and it is on this path that man encounters the one who embodies the values of all cultures and fully reveals the man of each culture to himself. The Gospel of Christ, the Incarnate Word, finds its home along the path of culture, and from this path

it continues to offer its message of salvation and eternal life."

The Pope concluded with comments on authentic practice of the sacrament of penance and on the central sacramental significance of the Holy Eucharist.

———— FEBRUARY 16 ————

The first event of the day was a morning Mass for working people, celebrated in Holy Cross Cathedral, Lagos. Afterwards, the Holy Father met with and delivered addresses at gatherings of diplomats, members of the Polish community in Nigeria, foreign workers, Christian leaders and journalists.

Workers' Rights and Obligations

The rights and obligations of workers were the subject of comment by the Pope in a homily delivered at Mass in the Lagos cathedral.

"Each one has the right to proper pay and to reasonable working hours, including time for holidays. And work should never hinder the exercise of one's religious freedom. Work is for man, not man for work. So, work must not be allowed to dehumanize the person who does the work.

"Cases of misunderstanding (between employers and employees) are to be resolved not by violence, harsh words and antagonisms, but by mutual respect, willingness to listen and patient dialogue. Workers have the right to form unions and to ask for proper working conditions. But they also have the obligation to render loyal service, and employers have the right to receive the services for which they pay. Workers should not too readily have recourse to strikes . . . (which) remain extraordinary measures for the defense of human rights."

He called on workers and employers as well to "serve the country by vigorous efforts for economic development."

The Holy Father also urged systematic efforts by government and industry to cope with problems of rapid urbanization and industrialization, unemployment and rural underdevelopment.

Development Needs

At the second meeting of the day, with diplomats at the nunciature in Lagos, the Pope commented on the gap between rich and poor nations, and also on a tendency to have less regard for development than for "other matters."

"The plight of many Third World countries," he said, "remains a constant reminder that the development issue is not dead, although one sometimes gains the impression that it is no longer viewed with the priority that it continues to deserve. . . . Many of the world's governments today seem more preoccupied with other matters, such as inflation and military security. And yet, despite the impressive level of economic growth which some developing countries have achieved over the past decades, millions of people still remain caught up in a poverty that means not only low incomes but also malnutrition, hunger, illiteracy, lack of education, persistent unemployment and reduced life expectancy."

He urged a "leveling out" of the "disproportionate distribution of wealth and poverty" within and among nations, while emphasizing a kind of development "which respects the dignity and inalienable rights of the human person, and (which is) not merely a technological or economic development."

The Pope was critical of efforts by any nation to lord it over others, declaring: "Economic or monetary superiority, the possession of material goods and resources or technological capacity do not justify political or social, cultural or moral superiority of one people or nation over another. ... This further means that any position that seeks to justify such alleged superiority on an ideological or philosophical basis is not a valid position and must be rejected."

Sound international relations, the Pope also said, must begin by "making the dignity of the human person ... the basis and starting point."

The Pope spoke about respect for "the rights of nations and individuals" at a meeting with Poles at the nunciature.

Later, he urged foreign workers to repay the welcome given them in Nigeria with love for the country and respect for its laws.

Christian Witness and Dialogue

At a meeting with leaders of other Christian bodies, the Pope praised and encouraged activities of the Christian Association of Nigeria, founded in 1980, along with other efforts of dialogue and common witness at national and local levels.

He prayed that Christian churches would eventually receive "the gift of perfect unity in Christ. ... Meanwhile," he added, "it is necessary to continue your joint projects of Bible translation, dialogue and common witness to Christ."

The final event of the day was an unscheduled meeting with journalists, whom he urged to respect the principles of "sincerity, honesty and truth" in their work.

—————— FEBRUARY 17 ——————

The Holy Father left Lagos at about 9:00 a.m. on a flight to Cotonou, Benin. During a six-hour stay, he celebrated Mass and met with the president and bishops of the country. At his next stop, Libreville, Gabon, he addressed a gathering of priests, religious and lay persons, and met with President Omer Bongo.

At a Mass celebrated in the sports stadium at Cotonou before a congregation of some 20,000 people, the Pope spoke again about evangelization.

"Evangelizing means impregnating with the spirit of the Beatitudes ... the family, relationships among people and between them and God. ... And all this is meant to go so far as to mark the most intimate and most deeply rooted realities profoundly, from within, with the light and power of the Gospel. ... When grafted into the tree fed by African sap, the Gospel will make that tree bring forth new fruits. It will be then that men and women will acquire their authentic human and Christian personality, in coherence with themselves; that is to say, with their African soul."

Catholics and Marxism

Meeting with President Mathieu Kerekou after Mass, the Pope alluded indirectly to difficulties experienced by the Church because of the Marxist ideology in control of the country since 1972. He stressed the "important contributions" Catholics could make, if they were free to participate more actively, to the "economic, social and cultural uplifting of the nation."

He said the fruits of the Church's activities in Benin "are authentically African and Christian."

The Holy Father also declared, in veiled reference to the pervasive fact and influence of Marxist ideology, that Catholics "cannot accept teaching that might be in opposition to their conscience. They know that man does not live by bread alone, and their personal and communitarian relations with God are capital for them."

Suggestions to Bishops

To the bishops, the Holy Father suggested "three important points" for the guidance of their ministry in the face of adversity.

"First, favor the greatest possible unity among yourselves, unity without fault, among pastors and among all the Church's apostolic workers. That will be your strength, that will save your church.

"Then, go ahead with efforts enabling the faith to be strengthened, to be formed in depth, for it to be able to face up to atheistic ideologies, and for Christians to be able to take account of this.

"Finally, while always remaining within your solely spiritual missions, remain very attentive to human and moral problems which come to light in acute fashion in contemporary society, and train lay persons to take responsibility in this field.

"It will thus be manifest," he added, "that Christians are the first to contribute loyally to the good of society, to service of the country, particularly to development."

Mission of Priests

Late in the afternoon, the Pontiff addressed

an assembly of priests, religious, catechists and other lay persons at St. Mary's Cathedral in Libreville, Gabon. He had praise for them all, but the principal points of his talk concerned the identity and mission of priests which, he said, were under question in some quarters.

"Today, by saying that the priest ought to be a man like others, there is danger of relativizing the sacrament that he has received, of throwing a veil over that indelible character of priesthood of which traditional theology speaks and which was confirmed by the Council of Trent and the Second Vatican Council. In an authentic theological perspective, one is a priest for the whole of his life or he is not, just as one is either baptized or is not baptized."

He warned priests against "becoming authoritarian and blase functionaries" in the liturgy and against "sacrificing priestly ministry for the sake of non-priestly commitments."

"Giving up explicit proclamation of the Gospel in order to attend to social and professional tasks would mean crippling the apostolic and priestly ideal," he said. "I would add that the service of the sacraments is always an integral part of the priestly ministry."

Commitment of the Church

At a meeting in the evening with President Omer Bongo, the Pope called attention to the commitment of the Church to contribute to the "full development" of Gabon.

"Such progress," he said, "is actually based not only on riches and work but on other values as well, such as those of social justice, liberty, a sense of the common good, honesty and solidarity with the more deprived."

He thanked government officials for the freedom and respect enjoyed by the Church and for the high level of church-state cooperation in education, social services and other areas of public life.

———FEBRUARY 18———

The Pope took off from Libreville at about 7:30 a.m. on a flight to Malabo, Equatorial Guinea. He delivered two addresses at the airport there, one directed to the welcoming crowd and the other to the president. He was back in the air at 9:30 a.m. on the way to Bata, where he celebrated Mass in the Plaza Libertad. He left Bata at 3:30 p.m. and returned to Libreville where he had two meetings: one with young people, university students, professionals and workers in the Libreville stadium; the other with the bishops of Gabon.

Praise for Fidelity

The Pope stated the purpose of his visit to Equatorial Guinea in a brief address to a welcoming crowd at the Malabo airport.

"My trip has only an evangelical aim," he said. "I come to confirm your Christian faith and to encourage you in your loyalty to Christ and to the Church. I know very well that in the past you had to withstand many difficulties (during the 1968-79 repressive regime of Francisco Macias Nguema, the "Mad Man of Malabo"). Therefore, I now show you my pleasure in watching the firmness with which you gave witness to your support of Christ."

"May you always," he urged the large Catholic majority in the nation, "give example of harmony among yourselves, of mutual love, of capacity for reconciliation, of real respect for the rights of each citizen, family and social group. Respect and promote the dignity of all persons in your country as human beings and sons of God."

Assurance of Church Support

Addressing President Teodoro Obiang Msabogo, the Pope said: "I want to assure you . . . that the Church in Guinea desires to collaborate with loyalty in the common good, placing at your disposition its assistance for the moral elevation of persons, its work in favor of the reconciliation of minds, and its service in the educational and assistance fields.

"The Church wishes to serve the cause of dignifying man in all his aspects, without claiming anything but the proper climate of freedom, understanding and respect which makes possible the peaceful development of its spiritual and humanitarian mission. The well known and sorrowful occurrences of the past have not impeded its will to continue sowing good."

Tribute

Praise for Bishop Rafael Maria Nze Abuy, "who suffered so much for the Church" during eight years of exile and separation from his diocese, was one of the main subjects of the homily delivered by the Pope during a Mass celebrated in the Plaza Libertad in Bata. The Mass was attended by about 30,000 persons.

Mixed Messages

In his last evening in Gabon, the Holy Father directed appropriate remarks to a mixed gathering of professional people, university students and teachers, manual workers and young people.

• To professionals, he said: "The problem for you is not only to ensure that the process of (Gabon's) development will be continuous, but you have also and above all to assure mastery of it. . . . The time has come for you to enter into agreement for the concerted defense and promotion of fundamental ethical values . . . sacred respect for life, the inviolable dignity of every person, liberty of thought, of conscience, of religion, sharing of wealth in justice."

• To students and teachers, he said: The mission of a university is "to teach, not to indoctrinate; to show forth truth, not to hide it; to favor free confrontation of ideas, not to yield to the constraint of ideologies. . . . The purpose of university studies cannot be reduced to acquiring information, to obtaining diplomas, to winning lucrative posts. At the risk of being failures, (teachers) ought to lead students to total maturity of mind and of conscience."

• To workers, he declared: "The Church does not fear to stimulate workers to perform their tasks, but neither is it afraid to help them to obtain their legitimate rights . . . to work, to security, to hygiene, to human rates of production, to sufficient rest time, to just wages, to social protection, to respect for political and religious opinions, and for the liberty of worker associations."

• He urged youths to have enthusiasm for the values of true love and generosity.

Pastoral Worries

In an address to the bishops of Gabon, the Pope expressed his sympathy regarding their numerous "pastoral problems," which he described as follows: "lack of priests and women religious native to the country; difficulty of perseverance in vocations to the priesthood and religious life; lack of educators with sufficiently deep Christianity; the fact that many people have given up the practice of religion; hesitations regarding Christian marriage; the difficulty of making an impact upon the moral and social atmosphere; the still insufficiently indigenous character of your church."

Despite these problems, the Pope urged the bishops to carry out their ministry with hope and perseverance for the development of native vocations and the inculturation of the Church in Gabon.

——————FEBRUARY 19——————

The Pope started the last day of his tour with Mass before a large congregation in the President Bongo Stadium, Libreville. Immediately afterwards, he met with other Christian leaders. He departed for Rome early in the afternoon.

Local Church

The theme of the papal Mass and homily was the local church.

The Holy Father charged his listeners: "Set yourselves to building up the Church in Gabon . . . (which) must more and more depend on your responsibility." He said they must root the Church authentically, enduringly and vitally "so that it may touch the Gabonese soul deeply and bring forth fruits having the taste of this land." He called attention to the necessity for the communion of the Church in Gabon "with the other ecclesial

communities throughout the world and with . . . the successor of St. Peter."

The Pope stressed the role of the family, "the domestic church," in the development of the Church.

Finally, he said: "To conclude . . . and here I am announcing the peak of the good news to you: I ask the Lord for you to have a lively hope on the way of the sanctity of the Beatitudes."

The Pope told Christian leaders after Mass that he intended his meeting with them to show "the Catholic Church's will to go forward firmly with her commitment in the ecumenical movement, especially since the Second Vatican Council."

Impressions

The Pope gave an assessment of his pastoral trip on his arrival at Rome's Leonardo da Vinci Airport. He said, in summary:

"The more than 14,000 kilometers traveled in these days allowed me to come to direct understanding of the human and Christian reality of the nations visited in the cities of Lagos, Enugu, Onitsha, Kaduna, Ibadan, Cotonou, Libreville, Malabo and Bata; of the difficulties which are discussed in the respective countries; and also of the strong desire of those peoples to build a better tomorrow through a generous effort at the national level and through international cooperation. I was able once again to verify with deep pleasure that the foundations . . . of the African populations . . . are a spiritual vision of life, the idea of divinity as the primary cause of all things, the need for respect for the dignity of man, and the sense of the family. But what comforted me even more was to notice how the evangelical ferment manages ever more to bring alive the values of the African tradition and to assure at the same time its development, renewal and perfection. For this, much is owed to the work, often heroic, of the missionaries who have generously labored to scatter the seed of the kingdom of God and, above all, to bring a precious service to the local church. But no little credit goes also to the ready openness of the African soul, open more than ever to its sprouting and flowering."

MISSIONARY RESPONSIBILITY

"Our attitude today after Vatican II is that of service and cooperation. We aim at making local churches self-sufficient." So stated Father Raphael Ceffalo, provincial superior of the Comboni missionaries in southern Sudan, in an interview with the All African Press Service in July, 1982. He added: "Our responsibility has always been to make the people we work for responsible, committed and dedicated to their well-being as a group."

African countries are the special field of work for the Italian-based missionaries.

POPE JOHN PAUL IN PORTUGAL

Pope John Paul, on the 11th trip of his pontificate outside of Italy, made pastoral visits to six cities of Portugal between May 12 and 15, 1982.

Principal events of the trip were his visit to the Marian sanctuary at Fatima — in thanksgiving for Mary's intercession when his life was threatened a year earlier, and for the purpose of consecrating people of the world to Mary — and his celebration of Masses and delivery of homilies and addresses on significant subjects before gatherings of different types of people.

Following is an account of the trip and of a number of the 22 addresses delivered by the Holy Father.

(See separate entry, Fatima, under Apparitions of the Blessed Virgin Mary.)

——————— MAY 12 ———————

Before leaving Rome for Lisbon in the morning of May 12, the Pope told a throng of people in St. Peter's Square his reasons for making the trip.

Purpose of the Trip

"I go as a pilgrim of peace and fraternity to that soil which the Virgin chose and favored to launch to the world her heartfelt appeal for prayer, for conversion and for penance.

"It is actually not only in order to express my gratitude to Our Lady that I go to Fatima on pilgrimage. I go to that blessed place also in order to hear afresh, in the name of the whole Church, that message that echoed 65 years ago on the lips of our common Mother, concerned as she was for the destinies of her children. That message is revealed today as being more relevant and more urgent than ever. How can we not feel bewildered, in fact, at the sight of the spread of secularism and permissiveness which so gravely threaten the fundamentals of Christian morality?

"We are oppressed as well by the sad sight of so many brothers and sisters who are dying of hunger on this earth, dying of diseases and drugs. We are embittered by the sight of the dark fascination which the various forms of violence still exert over the human heart. In particular, we are distraught by having to face the fact that even today there is a yielding to the illusion that a just and lasting peace can arise from war. When will men come to understand that their dignity is degraded every time they fail to do everything possible for peace to triumph and reign among the peoples and nations?

"With these thoughts and this anxiety in my heart, I will kneel at the feet of Mary to implore her maternal intercession and at the same time to offer her promises of prayer, repentance and reparation in the name of all children of the Church. I nourish the hope that this gesture of mine will help to reawaken a fresh sense of responsibility in believers and induce each one to question himself honestly about his own coherence with the values of the Gospel."

On arrival at the Lisbon airport early in the afternoon, the Holy Father was welcomed by Cardinal Antonio Ribeiro of Lisbon and the President and Prime Minister of Portugal. To them and others who greeted him, he said:

"In this pastoral visit I would wish to enliven the community in union with my brother bishops and to confirm them. I would communicate Christ in humility and simplicity, announce his message and make known to all the 'human dimension' of the mystery of the redemption, wherein man can find the grandeur, the dignity and the essential value of his humanity."

Mission of Lay Persons

The Pope's first stop in the Portuguese capital was at the cathedral, where he addressed about 1,500 lay persons. He spoke about their mission in the Church and society.

"Your mission as lay persons is fundamentally one of sanctification of the world, through your personal sanctification and in service to restoration of the world. The Second Vatican Council had much to say about lay persons and their role in the Church. . . . It is a matter of Christians living in the world and being responsible for building up the temporal order in its various fields of politics, culture, the arts, industry, commerce, agriculture. . . .

"The Church has to be present in all sectors of human activity; nothing that is human can remain alien to her. It is you lay persons who must principally make the Church present there . . . I warmly appeal to you never to let the Church remain absent from any environment in the life of your beloved nation. Everything must be permeated with the leaven of the Gospel of Christ and lit by his light. It is your duty to do this" through individual apostolates of personal activities and through "associative forms of apostolate" with others.

In the church built over the birthplace of St. Anthony in Lisbon, the Pope told Franciscans that it was a "cause of satisfaction" for him to recall how the movement of their First, Second and Third Orders had "made a profound impression on the mind of the population of Portugal."

Before leaving Lisbon for Fatima, the Pontiff met privately with the President and attended a reception with political leaders.

At Fatima

During an evening prayer service at Fatima, the Holy Father spoke again about his reasons for visiting the shrine.

"I wished to submit my thanksgiving to the heart of the celestial Mother for having saved me from . . . peril (the attempt on his life of May 13, 1981). In everything that was going on, I saw . . . special maternal protection on the part of Our Lady. . . . I also saw an appeal, perhaps a call as well, to pay attention to the message that began from here 65 years ago by the intermediary of three children. . . .

"We are gathered here to entrust our hopes and anxieties with childlike confidence to the pure and maternal heart of Mary. We likewise wish to make a solemn expression of our readiness to set ourselves at the disposal of Christ's saving love, with our hearts and understanding and with all our strength, for the sake of salvation for ourselves and for all our fellow men, wherever they live."

Life Threatened

Just after recitation of the Rosary, as the Pope approached a small altar in front of the shrine, a knife-wielding young man shouting, "Down with the Pope and Vatican II," made a move toward him but was stopped in his tracks before he could get close.

The man was identified as Juan Fernandez Krohn, 32, a Spaniard ordained to the priesthood in 1978 at Econe, Switzerland, and a member of Archbishop Marcel Lefebvre's Fraternity of St. Pius X until 1980. He was charged with attempted murder.

——————— MAY 13 ———————

In an address to the bishops of Portugal in the morning, the Pope said they had a critical role to play in their country's transition into a modern society. He spoke about a wide range of pastoral problems in the country.

Critical Role of Bishops

"I am not surprised to find that in Portugal today there is a notable coexistence between a profound religious feeling and, on the other hand, an undeniable advance of what . . . may be called secularism. The multitudes here today in Fatima are an aspect of that former characteristic, which is manifest even more in parish life in certain parts of the country. The latter characteristic is to be seen in the agnosticism of most intellectuals, academics and large portions of youth, consisting in a certain concept of life or a certain humanism without God.

"Then there are the grave problems existing in the family environment, above all in what refers to the indissolubility of matrimony, the wearing away of moral conscience and consequent loosening of behavior, the search after well-being at any cost, and so on."

With these things in mind, the Pontiff cited the roles of bishops as pastors, guides and leaders of their people; as educators in the faith, seeking to make it "more conscious and less conditioned in your faithful, more rooted, less superficial, more committed, less individualistic, more practical and less inward-looking"; as "builders, guarantors and maintainers of ecclesial communion" among themselves and with their priests and people.

The Pope urged them to special efforts for the promotion of vocations to the priesthood and religious life, for effective religious education and training, and for pastoral concern "for the family and its authentic values."

The Call of Fatima

The Holy Father celebrated Mass before a throng of one million people in the morning on the 65th anniversary of Mary's first appearance at Fatima and the first anniversary of the nearly fatal attack on his life in St. Peter's Square.

One of those attending the Mass and receiving Holy Communion from the Pope was 75-year-old Carmelite Sister Lucia dos Santos, the only living member of the trio who witnessed the apparitions of Mary.

Fatima's call to conversion and penance, the Pope said in a homily, is even more relevant and urgent today than it was 65 years ago because so many people have rejected God. "My heart is oppressed," he said, "when I see the sin of the world and the whole range of menace gathering like a dark cloud over mankind."

He added, however, that his heart also "rejoices with hope" at the opportunity to reconsecrate the world to God whose redemptive love "is more powerful than evil. No sin of the world can overcome this love."

He said of the Fatima message:

"In the light of the mystery of Mary's spiritual motherhood, let us seek to understand the extraordinary message which began May 13, 1917, to resound throughout the world from Fatima, continuing for five months until Oct. 13 of the same year.

"The Church has always taught and continues to proclaim that God's revelation was brought to completion in Jesus Christ, who is the fullness of that revelation, and that no new public revelation is to be expected before the glorious manifestation of Our Lord. The Church evaluates and judges private revelations by the criterion of conformity with that single public revelation.

Summons to Conversion

"If the Church has accepted the message of Fatima, it is above all because that message contains a truth and a call whose basic content is the truth and the call of the Gospel itself.

"'Reform your lives and believe in the Gospel' (Mk. 1:15). These are the first words that the Messiah addressed to humanity. The message of Fatima is in its basic nucleus a call to conversion and repentance, as in the

Gospel. This call was ... addressed particularly to this present century."

"The message of Our Lady of Fatima is a motherly one (but) it is also strong and decisive. It sounds severe. It sounds like John the Baptist speaking on the banks of the Jordan. It invites to repentance. It gives a warning. It calls to prayer. It recommends the Rosary."

Consecration to Mary

At the end of Mass, the Pope re-consecrated the world to the Virgin Mary, asking that she intercede for its deliverance from hunger, sins against life, injustices in social, national and international life, and "from nuclear war, from incalculable destruction, from every kind of war."

Recalling Pope Pius XII's consecration of the world to Mary in 1942, he said he wanted "to include once more the hopes and anxieties of the Church in the modern world."

He prayed, in conclusion, for a "just and honorable solution" to hostilities between Argentina and Great Britain over the Falkland Islands.

Prayer, Soul of Apostolic Activity

Prayer as the soul of work for the Kingdom, was one of the main points of the Pope's address to priests, seminarians and religious. He said:

"The level of pastoral and apostolic results will always be in proportion with the degree of your fidelity to Christ, to your commitments to love. It is this fidelity which liberates the heart and inflames the spirit with total love for Christ and for his and your brothers and sisters in the world. ... And ... fidelity means cultivated union with the Lord through constant and profound self-renewal by means of prayer and sacramental life . . . . 'For without me, you can do nothing' (Jn. 15:5).

"Here ... I would indicate that this is the main point of my message to you today. Unless you have perfect equilibrium between your life with God and the activities that you carry out in service to mankind, not only will the work of evangelization in which you are engaged be compromised but so also will your personal condition as evangelized. Prayer is the soul of your work for the Kingdom: liturgical prayer centered on the Eucharist, received and lived with that purity of conscience that requires having recourse to the sacrament of reconciliation properly celebrated and not admitting palliatives."

Dedication of Center

Before leaving Fatima for the return to Lisbon, the Pope dedicated the Paul VI Pastoral Center for retreats and conferences; spent 45 minutes in prayer in the Chapel of Apparitions, at the actual site of Mary's six appearances to the three children in 1917; and delivered an address to sanctuary collaborators and workers on new construction at the shrine.

Back in Lisbon in the evening at a meeting with diplomats, the Pontiff observed that differences among people can sometimes "degenerate into local conflicts which are especially regrettable because of the loss of human lives, absurd destruction and sentiments of enmity" that can persist after the cessation of hostilities. He urged them to work for peace and justice.

MAY 14

At an early morning Liturgy of the Word in Vila Vicosa, Pope John Paul told tens of thousands of agricultural workers that the Church's teaching on the rights and dignity of the "man who works," while often framed in industrial terms, applies equally to those who work the land.

Farmers' Aspiration for Justice

His presence, he said, was meant as a "concrete sign that the Church recognizes and understands your rightful aspiration for justice, progress and peace. ... The Church, the Pope, the bishops of Portugal are with you to help you to overcome incomprehensions and injustices, to give a hand to the poorest and the most deprived."

Noting that the world "lives in terror of a great catastrophe which might invert its great successes if war came to prevail over peace," the Pope urged a reduction in arms spending so that countries might be guaranteed the minimum conditions necessary for development, particularly in agriculture and food production.

"The state of absolute poverty suffered by some countries with backward agricultural economies offends the dignity of millions of persons who are constrained to live in conditions of degrading penury," the Pope said.

"So, it is urgent to give workers of the land possibilities for concretely realizing their fundamental human rights." .

Christians, Moslems, Jews

Back in Lisbon, the Pope addressed a gathering of Christians, Moslems and Jews.

"We are rendered brothers in a certain way by faith and a commitment, similar in many ways among us, to demonstrate our respective religious positions with good works and by a desire that, as we honor the Creator of all things as Lord, our example may help others to seek God, to open to the transcendent, to recognize the spiritual value of the human person and, perhaps, to discern the foundation and permanent sources of human rights."

"These contacts of ours, dialogue, appreciation of the undeniable spiritual riches in each religion, Christian community and, when possible, prayer in common, can lead to a convergence of forces, so as to avoid the illusion of constructing a new world without God and the emptiness of a purely anthropocentric humanism. Without the religious dimension and ... without religious liberty, man is impoverished or defrauded of his basic rights. And we all desire to avoid this improverishment of man."

Higher Learning and Culture

Various subjects related to Catholic institutions of higher learning were covered by the Pope in a talk before a gathering of faculty members and students at the Catholic University of Lisbon.

"You well remember how I addressed an apostolic constitution, *Sapientia Christiana,* to the whole Church at the very beginning of my pontificate. It contains the definition of objectives and some guidelines for Catholic institutions of higher education. The activity of research and teaching at that level should be carried on within the life of the ecclesial community and integrated with the conditions of the world of today, the actual world, where rapid and profound transformations are going on. Such activity needs to turn toward constant rethinking of the scientific area, so as to shape culture in a Christian fashion."

Of faith-and-culture relations, the Holy Father said:

"There is no contradiction between culture and faith, as the Second Vatican Council insistently brought out. On the contrary, there may be reciprocal enlightenment and enrichment. From this derives a particular responsibility incumbent on Christian scientists and Catholic institutions of higher education. The responsibility is to contribute to eliminating the great disequilibrium between general culture and a deepening of faith.... In a Catholic university all activity, with the indispensable mark of intellectual honesty and academic seriousness, is located within the Church's evangelizing mission.... This evangelizing mission has the aim that 'modes of thinking, criteria of judgment and norms of action may be imbued with the virtues of the Gospel,' " as stated in *Sapientia Christiana.*

Challenge to Youth

The Pope met with several groups of people in late afternoon at the Lisbon nunciature. Afterwards, he addressed some 500,000 young people in Parque Eduardo VII.

He called youths "bearers of the great hope of humanity, of the Church and of the Pope," and urged them to respond positively to the call to salvation, to take part in the Church's mission of evangelization, and to be attentive to the divine call to their respective vocations.

He said that "evangelization is not effective without youthful enthusiasm, without youth in the heart, without a number of connected qualities: joy, hope, lack of guile, audacity, creativity, idealism."

———————— MAY 15 ————————

In the morning, the Pope traveled by train from Lisbon to Coimbra, where he met with intellectuals at the university of that name. Despite the advancement of civilization through science and technology, he said that modern culture appeared to be on the verge of a crisis of truth.

Crisis of Truth

"The meaning of truth has suffered a serious blow.... An objective vision of truth is often replaced by a more or less spontaneous subjective view. Objective morality gives way to individual ethics, where each one seems to set himself up as the norm of action." As a result, "man feels more and more insecure; he has the impression of living in a society ... without certainties and ideals."

While this may seem a desperate situation, he added, there are many reasons for hope for mankind of the year 2000 if people "commit themselves seriously to a profound renewal of culture."

The university plays a particular role in this, the Pontiff continued, because it is a "place for working on man's vocation to knowledge as well as where man's constitutive link with truth as the goal of knowledge can become a daily reality."

The Church and Culture

The Pope also described the relation of the Church to culture.

"In the Church's view, culture is not something coming as a stranger to the faith, but it can receive profound and beneficial influences from the faith. Nevertheless, it is necessary not to regard the relation of culture to the faith as a purely passive one.

"Culture is not only the subject of redemption and elevation; it can also have a role of mediation and collaboration. When God revealed himself to the Chosen People, he actually made use of a particular culture. Jesus Christ, Son of God, did the same in his time: his human incarnation in the course of time. The Church too has used in her preaching the discoveries of different cultures to spread and explain the message of Christ to all nations, to probe it, to more deeply understand it, and to give it better expression in liturgical celebrations.

"In our day, without renouncing her own tradition but in awareness of her universal mission, the Church tries to get into dialogue with the various forms of culture. She is concerned with discovering what unites within the magnificent patrimony of the human mind. Yet, harmony of faith and culture is not always achieved without difficulties. In spite of this, the Church does not cease trying to bring all cultures nearer, as well as all ideological concepts and all men of good will."

The Family

The Pope's second stop of the day was at Sameiro, where he celebrated Mass and preached before an assembly of some 400,000 persons at the local Marian shrine. The family was the theme of his homily, in which he covered key points of his apostolic exhortation, *Familiaris Consortio.*

His main appeal was for efforts to "maintain and preserve a situation favorable to the conjugal and familial community where, with the transmission of life, exists a very grave obligation to educate the offspring."

He also said:

"The future of man resides in the family and depends on the family more than on any other society, institution or environment."

"Matrimony is the cornerstone of the family, just as the family is the capstone of matrimony. It is impossible to separate one from the other. It is necessary to consider them together in the light of the future of man."

Industrial Workers

In Oporto, the last stop on the itinerary, the Holy Father addressed 350,000 industrial workers in a speech reminiscent of the contents of *Laborem Exercens,* his encyclical letter on work.

"Human work," he said, "can never be considered merely a function of capital. It transcends it absolutely. . . . Man is not made for the machine but the machine for man." Machines should not "enslave man to their rhythm, depriving him of a deserved employment and of a truly human standard of living."

The Pontiff defended the right of workers to form unions, but said they should never seek to resolve problems "with hate and violence."

Farewell Statement

Before leaving Oporto for Rome via Air Portugal at about 10:00 p.m., the Holy Father said in a farewell address:

"I leave a land where the glorious traditions of the past are joined by important achievements of our day, in courageous openness to the prospect of a future of hope. As I leave, I wish to renew my highest appreciation for the various elements giving dynamism to the social structures; and I express my best wishes that, thanks to their accord and loyal collaboration, continuous progress may become more and more a reality along the paths of justice, liberty and peace."

PASTORAL VISIT OF POPE JOHN PAUL TO GREAT BRITAIN

Pope John Paul, on the 12th pastoral trip outside of Italy since the beginning of his pontificate, became the first Bishop of Rome to set foot on British soil. He did so between May 28 and June 2, 1982.

Features of the visit included:

• visits to nine major cities of Great Britain (six in England, two in Scotland and one in Wales);

• the celebration of Mass seven times before large congregations;

• 26 addresses related to the seven sacraments, spiritual renewal in accord with the spirit and teaching of the Second Vatican Council, the quest for Christian unity (especially with the Anglican Communion), pleas for peace in the world and, especially, for an end to British-Argentine conflict over the Falkland Islands:

Following are accounts of each day's events and coverage under appropriate dates of a number of the Pope's homilies and addresses.

————— MAY 28 —————

The Pope left Rome early in the morning for the 3,000-mile flight to England. He arrived at London's Gatwick Airport at about 8:00 a.m.

He was greeted at the airport by Cardinals George Basil Hume of Westminster and Gordon Gray of Edinburgh. The leading Catholic layman in the welcoming party was the Duke of Norfolk, a descendant of a family faithful to the Church since the first days of British persecution of Catholics in the 16th century.

The Holy Father traveled by train to Victoria Station, London.

At Westminster Cathedral, he celebrated Mass and baptized five persons before a congregaton of about 3,000 people.

In the afternoon, he met privately with Queen Elizabeth for 30 minutes at Buckingham Palace.

Afterwards, he anointed the sick at a gathering of ill, handicapped and elderly persons at St. George's Cathedral in Southwark. In an address, he made one of many references during his visit to the British-Argentine conflict over the Falkland Islands.

"Let us pray," he said, "that negotiations may pave the way to a just and lasting peace. . . . As we speak of suffering, affliction and death, we cannot forget those who have suffered and died during the armed conflict in the South Atlantic. Let us . . . remember in our prayers the victims of both sides."

The last event of the day was an evening meeting with bishops of England at the residence of Cardinal Hume.

MEANING OF BAPTISM

The meaning of baptism was the theme of the Pope's homily during Mass at Westminster Cathedral.

He prefaced his remarks, however, with mention of the reasons for his pastoral visit. He said he was the first Bishop of Rome ever to set foot on British soil, and added: "I come among you in response to this command of the Lord ('Feed my lambs. . . . Look after my sheep,' Jn. 21:15-16). I come to confirm the faith of my brother bishops. I come to remind all believers who today inherit the faith of their fathers that in each diocese the bishop is the visible sign and source of the Church's unity. I come among you as the visible sign and source of unity for the whole Church. I come at the service of unity in love."

Bond of Unity

"Baptism creates a sacramental bond of unity, linking all who have been reborn by means of it. But baptism of itself is only a beginning, a point of departure, for it is wholly directed toward the fullness of life in Christ. Baptism is the foundation of the unity that all Christians have in Christ, a unity we must seek to perfect. When we set out clearly the privilege and the duty of the Christian, we feel ashamed that we have not all been capable of maintaining the full unity of faith and charity Christ willed for his Church."

In conclusion, the Pope paid tribute to the pride of British Catholics in their history, especially in the example of such heroic men as two martyrs of the 16th century, Sts. John Fisher and Thomas More, and Richard Challoner, bishop of the London District, in the dark years of the 18th century.

COLLEGIALITY

Episcopal collegiality and collaboration of bishops with others were subjects of a papal address to British bishops in the evening.

"In the principle of collegiality, the bishops find at one and the same time fraternal support and a criterion of accountability for their sacred mission."

In their ministry, bishops need good relations and collaboration with their priests, religious and lay persons.

Lay persons, "by fulfilling their own proper role, . . . are meant to offer a great service of loving support to their pastors in Christ."

Summarily, the Holy Father said: "With our clergy, religious and laity, and united one with another, let us proclaim the saving and reconciling message of the Gospel with a deep conviction that — like Jesus and with Jesus — we are not alone. In the collegiality of the Catholic episcopate let us find renewed strength and vigor to lead God's

people. And in Christ Jesus may we always realize that we are not alone."

--------- MAY 29 ---------

The Pope met before 8:00 a.m. with religious, men and women, Anglican as well as Catholic, at Digby Stuart Training College in London.

The ecumenical climax of the visit was the "celebration of faith" later in the morning at Canterbury Cathedral. The Pope and Anglican Archbishop Robert Runcie renewed their baptismal promises together and signed a "common declaration" announcing the establishment of a new commission for dialogue in quest of religious unity.

Ecumenical concern and desire were also the subjects of papal remarks to representatives of the British Council of Churches and the Free Church Federal Council after the conclusion of events at the Anglican cathedral.

The Holy Father celebrated Mass late in the afternoon before about 100,000 persons in Wembley Stadium and delivered a homily on the moral obligations of Christians.

In the evening, the Pontiff met with various groups of people at the residence of Cardinal Hume.

RELIGIOUS

The Pope told men and women religious that people want them to be signs of Christ's presence in the world.

"In you, the world wishes to see Jesus. Your public profession of the evangelical counsels is a radical response to the Lord's call to follow him. As a result, your lives are meant to offer a clear witness to the reality of the Kingdom of God already present in the affairs of men and nations."

"Believe in your mission within the Church. Let your faith shine before the world, as a lamp in the darkness. Let it shine as a beacon that will guide a confused society to the proper appreciation of essential values. May the spiritual joy of your personal lives and your communal witness of authentic Christian love be a source of inspiration and hope. Let your consecraton be known. Be recognizable as religious men and women. The secular city needs living witnesses such as you."

CELEBRATION OF FAITH

Pope John Paul and Anglican Primate Archbishop Robert Runcie joined in a "celebraton of faith," a service in Canterbury Cathedral during which they prayed together and led a large congregation in a renewal of baptismal promises.

The Pope called the renewal of vows a prayer that God will "heal the divisions introduced into the Church in the course of the centuries" and "a pledge to do all in our power to cooperate with the grace of the Holy Spirit, who alone can lead us to the day when we will profess the fullness of our faith together."

Archbishop Runcie said:

"If we remember our beginning in Jesus Christ Our Lord, if we can face the suffering involved in travelling his way, if we can lift our eyes beyond the historical quarrels (between the churches) . . . then we shall indeed enter a faith worthy of celebration, because it is able to remake our world."

New Dialogue Commission

Following the service in the cathedral, the Pope and Archbishop signed a common declaration in which they said:

"We are agreed that it is now time to set up a new international commission (replacing an earlier one which issued in March a Final Report on 12 years of dialogue).

"Its task will be to continue the work already begun: to examine, especially in the light of our respective judgments on the Final Report, the outstanding doctrinal differences which still separate us, with a view toward their eventual resolution; to study all that hinders the mutual recognition of the ministries of our communions; and to recommend what practical steps will be necessary when, on the basis of our unity in faith, we are able to proceed to the restoration of full communion."

The declaration urged Catholics and Anglicans throughout the world to join in "zealous prayer and fervent work" for reunion and to "grow in mutual understanding, fraternal love and common witness to the Gospel . . . in every country, diocese and parish in which our faithful live side by side."

The Pope and the Archbishop emphasized: "Our aim is not limited to the union of our two communions alone, to the exclusion of other Christians, but rather extends to the fulfillment of God's will for the visible unity of all his people."

MORAL DEMANDS

Moral demands of the Christian vocation were the subjects of the Pope's homily during Mass in Wembley Stadium.

At the beginning of his homily, the Holy Father said: "Together we shall renew our baptismal promises as an offering of ourselves to our heavenly Father, joined to the sacrificial offering of Christ in the Eucharist." He then proceeded to focus on the "moral demands of our Christian vocation."

"To be faithful to our alliance with God, we must be not just a people that prays, but also a people that does the will of the heavenly Father."

"We express our real acceptance of Christ's word by respecting the moral demands of our Christian vocation. And the fulfillment of these demands is an act of loving obedience to the Person of Jesus Christ, the Incarnate Word of God. If our faith is strong, the moral demands of the Christian life — although at times they are difficult to fulfill and although they always require effort and grace — will seem neither unreasonble nor impossible."

Conflict Unavoidable

"Certainly, our fidelity to the Gospel will put us at odds with the spirit of the present age. . . . The conflict between certain values of the world and the values of the Gospel is an inescapable part of the Church's life, just as it is an inescapable part of the life of each one of us."

"I have often spoken of the decline of respect for the fundamental moral values that are essential to the Christian life."

"The world has largely lost respect for human life from the moment of conception. It is weak in upholding the indissoluble unity of marriage. It fails to support the stability and holiness of family life. There is a crisis of truth and responsibility in human relationships. Selfishness abounds. Sexual permissiveness and drug addiction ruin the lives of millions of human beings. International relations are fraught with tensions, often because of excessive inequalities and unjust economic, social, cultural and political structures, and because of slowness in applying the needed remedies. Underlying all of this is often a false concept of man and his unique dignity, and a thirst for power rather than a desire to serve."

The Pope concluded with the exhortation: "Realize the greatness of your Christian vocation. Christ has called you out of darkness into his own wonderful light. Consider what God has done for you in baptism, and lift up your eyes and see the final glory that awaits you!"

—————— MAY 30 ——————

The Pope's first meeting of the day took place in London with members of Britain's Polish community. He told his countrymen that their homeland was "deeply furrowed by suffering."

He celebrated Mass and confirmed a group of young people later in the morning before a throng of 350,000 people at Bagington Airport, Coventry.

At Liverpool's Speke Airport in the afternoon, the Pope praised the generosity of the British in providing aid to the needy in developing countries and spoke about the critical problem of unemployment.

He visited the Anglican Cathedral before celebrating a second Mass in the early evening at the Cathedral of Christ the King. His homily focused on penance and reconciliation.

PLEA FOR PEACE

At Bagington Airport near Coventry, a city reduced to rubble in World War II, the Pope spoke of peace and war. At the same time, on the Solemnity of Pentecost, he spoke about and conferred the sacrament of confirmation on a group of young people.

"We are close to the city of Coventry, a city devastated by war but rebuilt in hope."

"Our world is disfigured by war and violence. The ruins of the old (Coventry) Cathedral constantly remind our society of its capacity to destroy. And today that capacity is greater than ever. People are having to live under the shadow of a nuclear nightmare. Yet people everywhere long for peace. Men and women of good will desire to make common cause in their search for a worldwide community of brotherhood and understanding."

"Peace is not just the absence of war. It involves mutual respect and confidence between peoples and nations. It involves collaboration and binding agreements. . . . Peace has to be constructed patiently and with unshakeable faith.

No Place for War

"Wherever the strong exploit the weak; wherever the rich take advantage of the poor; wherever great powers seek to dominate and to impose ideologies: there the work of making the cathedral of peace is undone, there the cathedral of peace is again destroyed. Today, the scale and the horror of modern warfare — whether nuclear or not — makes it totally unacceptable as a means of settling differences between nations. War should belong to the tragic past, to history; it should find no place on humanity's agenda for the future."

"The voices of Christians join with others in urging the leaders of the world to abandon confrontation and to turn their backs on policies which require the nations to spend vast sums of money for weapons of mass destruction."

"All people must deliberately and resolutely commit themselves to the pursuit of peace. . . . We must turn from domination to service; we must turn from violence to peace; we must turn from ourselves to Christ, who alone can give us a new heart, a new understanding."

CONFIRMATION

Turning to the young people about to be confirmed, the Pope said they, on reception of the sacrament, would take their places "among fellow Christians throughout the world as full citizens of the people of God."

"The Holy Spirit comes to dwell more fully in your hearts and to strengthen you for the struggle with evil. . . . The world of today needs you, for it needs men and women who are filled with the Holy Spirit. It needs your courage and hopefulness, your faith and your

perseverance. The world of tomorrow will be built by you.

"Today you receive the gift of the Holy Spirit so that you may work with deep faith and with abiding charity, so that you may help to bring to the world the fruits of reconciliation and peace.

"Strengthened by the Holy Spirit and his manifold gifts, commit yourselves wholeheartedly to the Church's struggle against sin. Strive to be unselfish; try not to be obsessed with material things. Be active members of the people of God; be reconciled with each other and devoted to the work of justice, which will bring peace on earth."

UNEMPLOYMENT

Unemployment was the subject of the Pope's address at Speke Airport, Liverpool, a city with one of the highest rates of joblessness in the British Isles.

He said the tragedy of unemployment affects every aspect of life, from the material and physical to the mental and spiritual. "It therefore very much concerns the Church, which makes her own the hardships and sufferings, as well as the joys and hopes, of the men and women of our time. It is a matter of vital importance, deserving the attention and prayers of all people of good will."

He said, in conclusion, that unemployment and other ills of society "could bring us to disillusionment and even despair if we were not a people of hope, if we did not have a deep and abiding confidence in the power and mercy of God."

RECONCILIATION

During a second Mass of the day, celebrated in Liverpool's Cathedral of Christ the King, the Holy Father delivered a homily on the sacrament of penance and reconciliation.

"In his consoling sacrament, she (the Church) leads each of the faithful individually to Christ; and, through the Church's ministry, Christ himself gives forgiveness, strength and mercy. Through this highly personal sacrament, Christ continues to meet the men and women of our time. He restores wholeness where there was division, he communicates light where darkness reigned, and he gives hope and joy which the world could never give. Through this sacrament the Church proclaims to the world the infinite riches of God's mercy, that mercy which has broken down barriers which divided us from God and from one another.

"On this day of Pentecost, as the Church proclaims the reconciling action of Christ Jesus and the power of his Holy Spirit, I appeal to all the faithful of Britain and to all the other members of the Church who may hear my voice or read my words: Dearly beloved, let us give greater emphasis to the sacrament of penance in our own lives. Let us strive to safeguard what I described in my first encyclical as Christ's 'right to meet each one of us in that key moment in the soul's life constituted by the moment of conversion and forgiveness' *(Redemptor Hominis,* No. 20).

'And, in particular, I ask you, my brother priests, to realize how closely and how effectively you can collaborate with the Savior in the divine work of reconciliation. For lack of time, certain worthy activities may have to be abandoned or postponed, but not the confessional. Always give priority to your specifically priestly role in representing the Good Shepherd in the sacrament of penance. And as you witness and praise the marvelous action of the Holy Spirit in human hearts, you will feel yourselves called to further conversion and to deeper love of Christ and his flock."

The Pope also spoke about the relationship of penance and reconciliation to the quest for Christian unity, and declared: "Restoration of unity among Christians is one of the main concerns of the Church in the last part of the 20th century."

——————— MAY 31 ———————

The Pope left Liverpool at about 7:00 a.m. for Manchester, the first of three stops on the day's itinerary.

Shortly after arriving in Manchester, he met with Sir Emmanuel Yocobovich, chief rabbi of the British Commonwealth, and other members of the Jewish community.

He celebrated Mass and ordained 12 men to the priesthood in Heaton Park. Before imposing hands on the ordinands, he told them:

"You must try to deepen every day your friendship with Christ. You must also learn to share the hopes and joys, the sorrows and frustrations of the people entrusted to your care. Bring to them Christ's saving message of reconciliation. Visit your parishioners in their homes. This has been a strength of the Church in England. It is a pastoral practice that should not be neglected. And do not forget those with special needs, especially those who are in prison and their families."

In the afternoon, at the Knavesmire Racecourse in York, the Pope spoke about marriage before a throng of about 200,000 people.

In Edinburgh, the Holy Father addressed 45,000 Scottish youths at Murrayfield Rugby Stadium; met with the Rev. John McIntyre, moderator of the General Assembly of the (Presbyterian) Church of Scotland at the Church's assembly hall; and addressed priests and religious in the cathedral.

MARRIAGE, FAMILY LIFE

"The hopes and ideals that sustain the Christian vision of marriage and family life" were the themes of the Pope's address at the Knavesmire Racecourse in York.

"Christian marriage is a sacrament of salvation. It is the pathway to holiness for all members of a family. With all my heart, therefore, I urge that your homes be centers of prayer; homes where families are at ease in the presence of God; homes to which others are invited to share hospitality, prayer and the praise of God."

The Pope recalled that in his apostolic exhortation on the family, *Familiaris Consortio,* he "underlined the positive aspects of family life today, which include: a more lively awareness of personal freedom and greater attention to the quality of interpersonal relationships in marriage, and greater attention to promoting the dignity of women, to responsible procreation, to the education of children.

"But at the same time, I could not fail to draw attention to the negative phenomena: a corruption of the idea and experience of freedom, with consequent self-centeredness in human relations; serious misconceptions regarding the relationship between parents and children; the growing number of divorces; the scourge of abortion; the spread of a contraceptive and anti-life mentality.

"Besides these destructive forces, there are social and economic conditions which affect millions of human beings, undermining the strength and stability of marriage and family life. In addition, there is the cultural onslaught against the family by those who attack married life as 'irrelevant' and 'outdated.' "

Broken Marriages

With warm and deep personal concern regarding broken marriages, the Holy Father said:

"We cannot overlook the fact that some marriages fail. But still it is our duty to proclaim the true plan of God for all married love and to insist on fidelity to that plan. . . . Let us not forget that God's love for his people, Christ's love for the Church, is everlasting and can never be broken. And the covenant between a man and a woman joined in Christian marriage is as indissoluble and irrevocable as this love. This truth is a great consolation for the world; and, because some marriages fail, there is an ever greater need for the Church and all her members to proclaim it faithfully.

"Christ himself, the living source of grace and mercy, is close to all those whose marriage has known trial, pain or anguish. Throughout the ages, countless married people have drawn from the paschal mystery of Christ's cross and resurrection the strength to bear Christian witness — at times very difficult — to the indissolubility of Christian marriage. And all the efforts of the Christian people to bear faithful witness to God's law, despite human weakness, have not been in vain. These efforts are the human response made, through grace, to a God who has first loved us and who has given himself for us."

"The Church is vitally concerned for the pastoral care of the family in all difficult cases. We must reach out with love — the love of Christ — to those who know the pain of failure in marriage; to those who know the loneliness of bringing up a family on their own; to those whose family life is dominated by tragedy or by illness of mind or body. I praise all those who help people wounded by the breakdown of their marriage, by showing them Christ's compassion and by counselling them according to Christ's truth."

YOUNG PEOPLE

The Pope addressed a large gathering of youths at Murrayfield Rugby Stadium, Edinburgh, his first stop in Scotland. He talked about their calling in life.

"It is not of primary importance what walk of life naturally attracts you — industry or commerce, science or engineering, medicine or nursing, the priestly or religious life, or the law, or teaching, or some other form of public service — the principle remains always the same: Hand the direction of your life over to Jesus and allow him to transform you and obtain the best results, the ones he wishes from you. Only Christianity has given a religious meaning to work and recognizes the spiritual value of technological progress."

"A correct understanding of the teaching of Jesus makes us react in a creative and cooperative fashion to the challenges that face us in life, without fear of acting mistakenly and alone, but under the guiding influence of his own Holy Spirit at every moment and in every circumstances, be it great or small.

"This extraordinary divine assistance is guaranteed to all who offer their lives to Jesus. God the Father's plan of salvation embraces all mankind. His one same Holy Spirit is sent as a gift to all who are open to receive him in faith. We each form a part of God's overall plan. An exclusively personal and private attitude toward salvation is not Christian and is born of a fundamentally mistaken mentality.

Responsibility toward Others

"Consequently, your lives cannot be lived in isolation and, even in deciding your future, you must always keep in mind your responsibility as Christians toward others. There is no place in your lives for apathy or indifference to the world around you. There is no place in the Church for selfishness. You must show a conscientious concern that the standards of society fit the plan of God.

"Christ counts on you, so that the effects of his Holy Spirit may radiate from you to others and in that way permeate every aspect of the public and private sector of national life."

PRIESTS

"In you I feel the heartbeat of the entire ecclesial community," the Pope told a gathering of priests, deacons and religious in the evening at the Edinburgh Cathedral.

He spoke about the nature of their respective ways of life and ministry, and addressed his remarks particularly to priests, whom he urged to recognize their ministry as a gift from God to the Church.

The priesthood, he said, is "not ours to do with as we please. We cannot re-invent its meaning according to our personal views. Ours it is to be true to the One who has called us."

In preaching the Gospel, priests "must not tamper with God's word" but should strive to apply it to changing world conditions while resisting "the temptation to alter its content or reinterpret it in order to make it fit the spirit of the present age."

He called on them to work closely with lay persons in a spirit of shared responsibility and authentic church renewal, saying:

"Let your people see that you are men of prayer. Let them see that you treat the sacred mysteries with love and respect . . . that your commitment to peace, justice and truth is sincere, unconditional and brave. Let everyone see that you love the Church and that you are of one mind and heart with her."

In conclusion, the Holy Father said:

"And to each priest and deacon, to each religious brother and sister, to each seminarian, I leave a word of encouragement and a message of hope. With St. Paul I say to you: 'This explains why we work and struggle as we do; our hopes are fixed on the living God' (1 Tm. 4:10). Yes, dear brothers and sisters, our hopes are fixed on the living God!"

—————— JUNE 1 ——————

Still in Edinburgh, the Pope met for the second time with the Rev. John McIntyre, moderator of the General Assembly of the (Presbyterian) Church of Scotland and other religious leaders.

The second event of the day was a visit to St. Joseph's Hospital in Rosewell, where the Holy Fther told handicapped patients that the reason for his visit was "to bear witness to the Church's mission from Christ to care for all God's people, especially those most in need."

In Glasgow by midday, the Holy Father addressed teachers, students and administrators at St. Andrew's College.

Late in the afternoon, the Pontiff celebrated Mass in Glasgow's Bellahouston Park before a throng of about 250,000 people, probably the largest gathering ever for a religious event in Scottish history.

At the cardinal's residence in the evening, the Pope reflected with the bishops of

Scotland on their episcopal ministry. He underlined the fact that "there is no doubt about it; our fidelity to the love of Jesus and our friendship with him are essential for all the apostolic works that are part of our daily lives."

FRUITFUL DIALOGUE

The Pope spoke about interfaith relations at a morning meeting with the Rev. John McIntyre, moderator of the Church's General Assembly, and other Christian leaders.

"I have been pleased to learn of the fruitful dialogues in which the Catholic Church in this country has been engaged with the Church of Scotland, the Episcopal Church in Scotland and other churches, and also of its collaboration with the Scottish Churches' Council in many aspects of its work. . . . Here we have an instance of that common witness which is both an expression of the degree of unity, limited but real, which we already enjoy through God's grace, and of our sincere desire to follow the ways by which God is leading us to that full unity which he alone can give.

"In following this road we have still to overcome many obstacles occasioned by the sad history of past enmities; we have to resolve important doctrinal issues. Yet, already our mutual love, our will for unity, can be a sign of hope to a divided world."

CATHOLIC EDUCATION

The value of Catholic education was the subject of a papal address to teachers, students and administrators at St. Andrew's College, Glasgow.

"In reflecting on the value of Catholic schools and the importance of Catholic teachers and educators, it is necessary to stress the central point of Catholic education itself. Catholic education is, above all, a question of communicating Christ, of helping to form Christ in the lives of others. Those who have been baptized must be trained to live the newness of Christian life in justice and in the holiness of truth. The cause of Catholic education is the cause of Jesus Christ and of his Gospel at the service of man."

FIDELITY TO FAITH

At a Mass celebrated before 250,000 persons in Glasgow's Bellahouston Park, the Holy Father called on his listeners to be true to their heritage of faith amid the struggles of daily life.

"We find it harder to follow Christ today than appears to have been the case before. Witnessing to him in modern life means a daily contest, not so quickly and decisively resolved as for the martyrs in the past. As believers, we are constantly exposed to pressures by modern society, which would compel us to conform to the standards of this secular age, substitute new priorities, restrict our aspirations at the risk of compromising our Christian conscience.

"The spirit of this world would have us capitulate on the most fundamental principles of our Christian life. Today, as never before, the basic doctrines of the faith are questioned and the value of Christian morality challenged and ridiculed. Things abhorred a generation ago are now inscribed in the statute books of society. These are issues of the utmost gravity to which a simple answer cannot be given; neither are they answered by being ignored. Matters of such magnitude demand the fullest attention of our Christian conscience.

"To provide the answers to such questions is a daunting task. It would be an impossible challenge for the majority of the faithful to attempt unaided. But you are not alone. The spirit of God is operative in the Church. Never before as in recent years has the teaching of the Catholic Church been so extensively reformulated, precisely with the issues that trouble the modern conscience in mind. It is sufficient to list the topics on which the Pope, the Ecumenical Council, the Synod of Bishops and the various national episcopal conferences, including that of the Scottish bishops, have given authoritative and clear statements of Catholic belief and practice for the guidance of the faithful in these perplexing times . . . I assure you that we are acutely aware of the problems you have to face in life, and of the anxiety which so often fills your hearts."

"Be loyal to the memory of your valiant forerunners in the faith. Be diligent in handing on intact the spiritual heritage committed to you. Be faithful to your daily prayers, to the holy Mass and the sacrament of penance, meeting regularly with Jesus as a loving and merciful Savior. Defend the sacredness of life and the holiness of matrimony. Understand your holy Catholic faith and live by its teaching. Face up to the difficult challenges of modern life with Christian fortitude and patience. Did not Jesus himself say to his disciples: " 'If anyone wants to be a follower of mine, let him renounce himself and take up his cross and follow me?' (Mt. 16:24; Mk. 8:34)."

——————— JUNE 2 ———————

The Pope flew from Glasgow to Cardiff, Wales, where he celebrated a late morning Mass and gave first Holy Communion to 30 children. About 100,000 people attended the Mass.

He addressed a large gathering of young people in the afternoon at Ninian Park.

He left the Cardiff Airport early in the evening and arrived at Rome's Ciampino Airport after 10:00 p.m.

THE EUCHARIST

The central significance of the Eucharist was

the theme of the Pope's homily during Mass at Cardiff's Pontcanna Fields.

The Holy Father reflected on the mystery of the Eucharist, which "holds such a central place in Christian life and ... is so closely linked to the mystery of the Church. For every generation in the Church, the food which nourishes the people of God is the Eucharist, the Body and Blood of Our Lord Jesus Christ."

In a simple direct address to 30 first communicants, the Holy Father said:

"Dear children: Jesus is coming to you in a new way today, in a special way. He wants to live in you. He wants to speak to you in your heart. He wants to be with you all through your day.

"Jesus comes to you in the Eucharist so that you will live forever. Holy Communion is not ordinary food. It is the bread of eternal life. It is something more precious than gold or silver. It is worth more than anything you can imagine. For this sacred bread is the Body and Blood of Jesus. And Jesus promises that, if you eat his flesh and drink his blood, you will have life in you and you will live forever.

"You come to the altar today with faith and prayer. Promise me that you will try to stay close to Jesus always, and never turn your back on him. As you grow older, go on learning about Jesus by listening to his word and by talking to him in prayer. If you stay close to him, you will always be happy."

INVITATION TO PRAY

The Holy Father's last important address of the trip was delivered in the afternoon of June 2 before a crowd of nearly 40,000 young people in Cardiff's Ninian Park. The subject was prayer, which he addressed after recapitulating the reasons for his pastoral visit.

"I have come to this land as a pilgrim pastor, a servant of Jesus Christ. I have come to proclaim Christ's Gospel of peace and reconciliation. I have come to celebrate his saving action in the sacraments of the Church. I have come to call you to Christ.

"Before I go away, there is something really important that I wish to emphasize. . . . It is prayer . . . something that is essential to your Christian lives."

"It is through prayer that Jesus leads us to his Father. It is in prayer that the Holy Spirit transforms our lives. . . . It is through prayer that we can clearly focus our attention on the Person of Jesus and see the total relevance of his teaching for our lives. . . . Prayer transforms our individual lives and the life of the world. . . . In prayer . . . you begin to breathe a new atmosphere."

"Through contact with Jesus in prayer, you gain a sense of mission that nothing can dull. Your Christian identity is reaffirmed and the meaning of your lives is forever linked to Christ's saving mission. . . . In prayer you will discover more fully the needs of your brothers and sisters. . . . Through prayer you will receive the strength to resist the spirit of the world. . . . Through prayer you will have a part in salvation history as it unfolds in your generation."

In conclusion, the Pope said:

"It is my hope today, as I return to Rome, that you will remember why I came among you. And, as long as the memory of this visit lasts, may it be recorded that I, John Paul II, came to Britain to call you to Christ, to invite you to pray."

PILGRIMAGE ON BEHALF OF PEACE

Pope John Paul made a hastily arranged visit to Argentina June 11 and 12, 1982, in an effort to do there what he had done just a few weeks previously in Great Britain — to plead for peace, to urge Argentina and Britain to negotiate an end to hostilities over the Falkland Islands, to express his sympathy for dead, wounded and grieving people, and to condemn "the absurd and always unjust phenomenon of war."

The Holy Father, on his 13th trip abroad, departed from Leonardo da Vinci Airport late in the evening of June 10 and arrived at about nine o'clock the following morning at the Buenos Aires Ezeiza Airport.

At the airport June 11, the Pope said he wanted his visit to be "simply a meeting of the father with his suffering children; a meeting with the brother in Christ, showing forth Christ anew as the way of peace, reconciliation and hope."

He also said he desired to show his "affectionate closeness to all the families mourning the loss of someone dear to them, to solicit from governments and the international community apt measures to avoid more damage, heal the wounds of war and facilitate the reestablishment of the climate for a just and durable peace, and a progressive calming of spirits."

Absurd Phenomenon of War

In the strongest statement made during his 31 hours in Argentina, the Pontiff declared:

"The sad spectacle of loss of human lives, with social consequences prolonged for no short time among peoples suffering war, makes me think with profound pain of the expanse of death and desolation which every armed conflict always provokes.

"We are not witnessing such frightening spectacles as Hiroshima or Nagasaki. But every time that we risk the life of people, we start up the mechanisms which lead toward these catastrophes; we walk down dangerous paths which are regressive and anti-human.

Because of this, humanity in this moment should once again question itself about the absurd and always unjust phenomenon of war, in its panorama of death and pain, in which the only thing left standing is the negotiating table that could have and should have avoided it.

"May it please God that this conflict which we lament, those existing between Iran and Iraq and in Lebanon, and others which trouble other parts of the world in more or less hidden ways, may be the last funereal examples of war, and may constitute a wholesome lesson whereby the world may learn to put respect for the sacredness of life above everything — always and in all circumstances — and may learn to relegate to oblivion the recourse to war, together with terrorism and methods of violence, and so decidely to follow paths of understanding, concord and peace."

Reconciliation and Patriotism

At the Cathedral of the Most Holy Trinity in Buenos Aires, the Pope told priests and religious:

"It is for you to exercise the 'ministry of reconciliation' by proclaiming the 'word of reconciliation' that has been entrusted to you. You will thus help your people to come together around the most authentic values of peace, justice, generosity and capacity for acceptance, values which lie at the basis of their Christian tradition and of the Gospel's teaching. You will serve the Church in this way by enabling the . . . Eucharist to bear fruit in you and in others. In this way you will nourish a climate of progressive serenity in society, in a hopeful vision of the future."

He urged his listeners to work for peace by teaching a "true patriotism," saying: "The authentic love for the fatherland, from which you have received so much, can lead to sacrifice, but at the same time it has to take into account the patriotism of others, so that in tranquillity there is intercommunion and enrichment within the perspective of humanism and catholicity."

In the afternoon, the Pope met for 30 minutes with President Leopoldo Galtieri and other members of the ruling junta at Casa Rosada, the presidential palace. No details of the meeting were reported.

Pilgrim of Difficult Moments

He celebrated Mass in the evening at the Shrine of Our Lady of Lujan, patroness of the nation, and told a throng of 500,000 people that he was with them "as the pilgrim of difficult moments." He spoke about "the mystery of the elevation of every man in Christ," through his cross. He prayed, as he had done earlier," for all those who have lost their lives because of the recent events (of the undeclared war with Britain). I recommend their souls to eternal rest in the Lord." He prayed also for "those who have lost their health and are in hospitals, that their minds may feel comforted in trial and in suffering."

The Pope had a two-hour meeting in the morning of June 12 with members of the Argentine Bishops' Conference and officials of other Latin American episcopal conferences.

He told them that "true and durable peace must be the mature fruit of an achieved integration of patriotism and universality." He urged them to be promoters of and witnesses to reconciliation, observing: "To be a bishop means to be always a handicrafter of harmony, of peace and of reconciliation."

Appeal to Young People

The Holy Father celebrated Mass at about 11:00 a.m. in Palermo Park and again, as at Lujan the previous evening, he spoke about the Eucharist. Toward the end of the homily, he addressed himself directly to young people in the congregation of more than a million. He said:

"I have seen in your eyes the ardent entreaty for peace arising from your spirit.

"Join with the young people of Great Britain who in recent days . . . were just as responsive to every invocation of peace and concord. . . .

"Do not let hatred erode the generous energies and capacity for understanding with all that you have within you. Join hands with the youth of Latin America . . . and form a chain of union stronger than the chains of war. In this way you will be youth preparing a better future. That is how you can be Christians."

The Pope left Ezeiza Airport at about 4:00 p.m. and arrived in Rome about mid-morning of June 13.

ADDRESS TO INTERNATIONAL LABOR ORGANIZATION

Pope John Paul flew to Switzerland June 15 for a 12-hour round of activities in Geneva which included 10 addresses, meetings with staff members of a number of international organizations and, finally, the celebration of Mass at the Palace of Expositions.

The trip, the third in 18 days, was the Pope's 14th outside of Italy since the beginning of his pontificate.

The principal event of the day was the papal address to 1,800 delegates attending the 68th annual conference of the International Labor Organization. In it, the Pope synopsized much of the contents of his encyclical on work, *Laborem Exercens,* dwelling on the dignity of the human person as the central value in any understanding or analysis of work.

He proposed solidarity among governments, employers and workers in pursuit of workers' rights, in line with ILO objectives. He also championed solidarity among workers themselves in defense of their rights.

The following topics were among major points of the address.

Union Freedom

"The right to labor union freedom is known as incontestably one of the more generally acknowledged basic rights, and Convention No. 87 (1948) of the International Labor Organization is evidence of this.

"Yet, it is a very threatened right. It is one that is often attacked both in its principle and in one or another of its substantial aspects, more often in such a way that labor union freedom comes out disfigured.

"It seems to be essential to recall that cohesion of the social forces is always desirable, and it ought to be the fruit of free decisions of those concerned — taken with full independence from political power — and worked out in full liberty to decide upon the internal organization, the way of functioning and the activities of labor unions."

Human Dignity

The Pope pointed to work as a central concern and theme of his pontificate, saying that in all its forms "work deserves a particular respect because it is the work of man, because behind all labor there is always a living subject, the human person. Labor takes its value and dignity from that."

He emphasized the need to humanize labor and to keep man at the center in all considerations of problems related to the world of work. "for not only does work bear man's mark, but it is in work also that man discovers the meaning of his existence."

Referring to the increasing sophistication of the means of production as one of the current causes of unemployment, the Pope defended "the principle of the primacy of human work over the means of production, and the primacy of the individual at work over production requirements or purely economic laws."

Because, he added, "the human person is the first and ultimate criterion in the planning of employment."

Solidarity

The Pope spoke on the theme of solidarity because of "the very nature of human labor. The problem of work has an extremely profound link with that of the meaning of human life. Work becomes a problem of spiritual life through that link, and so it really is. . . . The link between work and the very meaning of human existence always testifies that man has not been alienated by work, that he has not been brought into servitude. Quite the contrary, he confirms that labor has become the ally of his humanity."

The Pope urged worker solidarity as a response to injustice, stressing the fact that it is a struggle "for justice and for the truth of social life" rather than a mere "irreducible opposition in a struggle against others."

"Solidarity refuses to conceive of society in terms of struggle 'against' and to conceive of social relations in terms of irreducible class opposition," he said in a critique of the Marxist theory of class struggle.

He said solidarity must unite workers in all societies and regions in a single struggle against unemployment and other social ills.

APOSTOLIC EXHORTATION ON THE FAMILY

(Based on an article by Nancy Frazier, N.C. News Correspondent.)

(See additional entries on marriage.)

In the longest document of his pontificate, Pope John Paul called on Catholics to defend the rights and values of the family and to become "communities in communion" despite difficulties.

"The Church knows the path by which the family can reach the deepest truth about itself," he said in the apostolic exhortation, *Familiaris Consortio* ("Community of the Family"), on the role of the Christian family in the world.

"She (the Church) does not impose it but she feels an urgent need to propose it (this 'deepest truth') to everyone without fear and, indeed, with great confidence and hope, although she knows that the good news includes the subject of the cross," he added.

Synodal Background

The document, dated Nov. 22 and made public Dec. 15, 1981, was backgrounded by 43 propositions and related materials on the role of the family received by the Pope from the more than 200 bishops, 10 experts and 42 auditors who attended the 1980 assembly of the Synod of Bishops.

The Pope also accepted their proposal for the development of a Charter of Family Rights. He said such a charter would be prepared and "presented to the quarters and authorities concerned," noting that "the Church openly and strongly defends the rights of the family against the intolerable usurpations of society and the state."

Theological Synthesis

Observers called the exhortation the most complete synthesis to date on the theology of the family developed in centuries of church reflection, teaching and pastoral ministry.

Archbishop Jozef Tomko, secretary general of the Synod of Bishops, said Dec. 15 that "the Church has perhaps never before expressed in such a complete and articulated vision the four fundamental duties of the family."

Those duties, according to the document, are: "forming a community of persons; serving life; participating in the development of society; and sharing in the life and mission of the Church."

The exhortation restates in a systematic way the entire range of church teaching on marriage and family life, and rejects any suggestion that such teaching has become outmoded or undergone essential change.

"Not infrequently," the Pope said, "ideas and solutions which are very appealing, but which obscure in varying degrees the truth and the dignity of the human person, are offered to the men and women of today in their sincere and deep search for a response to the important daily problems that affect their married and family life."

Specific Subjects

The following are among subjects of church teaching covered in the document.

Contraception: Reaffirming the Church's ban on artificial contraception, the Pope urged theologians to "collaborate with the hierarchical teaching authority and to commit themselves to the task of illustrating ever more clearly the biblical foundations, the ethical grounds and the personalistic reasons behind this doctrine."

Catholic couples cannot look on the Church's birth control teaching "as merely an ideal to be achieved in the future. They must consider it a command of Christ the Lord to overcome difficulties with constancy."

Separated and Divorced Catholics: Those who do not remarry provide a witness to the Church and the world with "their example of fidelity and Christian consistency."

The Pope encouraged pastoral concern for those who do not remarry and those who do, but said that "the Church reaffirms her practice, which is based upon Sacred Scripture, of not admitting to Eucharistic Communion divorced persons who have remarried."

Because "their state and condition of life objectivley contradict that union of love between Christ and the Church which is signified and effected by the Eucharist," their admission to the sacraments could cause "error and confusion regarding the Church's teaching about the indissolubility of marriage."

The only exception would be in the case of a couple agreeing to live "in complete continence, that is, by abstinence from the acts proper to married couples."

The Pope told priests not to perform ceremonies of any kind for divorced persons who remarry, but also encouraged such persons "to make sure that they do not consider themselves as separated from the Church; for, as baptized persons, they can, and indeed must, share in her life."

Government Pressure: The document condemns pressures by government or other public authorities to take decisions on family matters out of the hands of the families themselves.

Government programs in favor of contraception, sterilization or procured abortion are "a grave offense against human dignity and justice."

Education: "The state and the Church have the obligation to give families all possible aid to enable them to perform their educational role properly."

Sex Education: "A basic right and duty of parents, it must always be carried out under their attentive guidance, whether at home or in educational centers chosen and controlled by them." The Church opposes sex education "disassociated from moral principles."

Role of Women: "The Church can and should help modern society by tirelessly insisting that the work of women in the home be recognized and respected by all in its irreplaceable value." At the same time, "there is no doubt that the equal dignity and responsibility of men and women fully justifies women's access to public functions."

Natural Family Planning: "Theological reflection is able to perceive and is called to study further the difference, both anthropological and moral, between contraception and recourse to the rhythm of the cycle. . . . Every effort must be made to render such knowledge accessible to all married couples."

Polygamy: "This directly negates the plan of God which was revealed from the beginning, because it is contrary to the equal personal dignity of men and women who in matrimony give themselves with a love that is total and therefore unique and exclusive."

Political Role of Families: "Families should be the first to take steps to see that the laws and institutions of the state not only do not offend but support and positively defend the rights and duties of the family."

NO TEMPORARY COMMITMENTS

Archbishop Pio Laghi, U.S. apostolic delegate, spoke against temporary commitments at a joint meeting of religious superiors Aug. 15 to 20, 1982, in San Francisco. He said: "Everything great is final. All life-determining commitments are irrevocable; not because they cannot be taken back (plainly, then can) but because, in making such commitments, we define ourselves as persons and so establish the parameters of success and failure, of generosity and selfishness, not merely for our lives but for our very selves. One of the worst aberrations of our times is the idea that one can be a religious — or a priest or a spouse — for a time. This is the very denial of the gift. Those who adopt this attitude lend themselves but they do not give themselves."

SYNOD OF BISHOPS: 1983 ASSEMBLY

Following are excerpts from the introduction to a document circulated among bishops of the world early in 1982 for the purpose of eliciting from them and others comments and suggestions relevant to "Reconciliation and Penance in the Mission of the Church," the theme of the sixth general assembly of the Synod of Bishops to be held in 1983, probably in the fall. The document, labeled "Lineamenta" ("Outlines") was issued by the Permanent Secretariat of the Synod to gather information useful for the drafting of a working paper for the assembly.

These excerpts are from the text circulated by the N.C. Documentary Service, Origins, Feb. 18, 1982 (Vol. 11, No. 36).

(See separate article, Synod of Bishops, for coverage of background and assemblies.)

The Theme

The proposed theme ("Reconciliation and Penance in the Mission of the Church") is of major interest for the internal life of the Church and also for all men of good will who seek the most profound meaning to their existence. For the Church the discussion of the theme is a moment of reflection and of discernment with respect to its own internal life and to its mission as laid out by Vatican Council II; for the world it is a pressing invitation to that peace which comes through conversion and reconciliation.

The title comprises three terms. The first two words express two profound interdependent aspects in the salvation event given by God. Reconciliation and penance are considered as a fundamental reality which takes place in the Church and, through the Church, in the world; that is, in relation to the mission of the Church.

The theme designated, therefore, is one only and unitary, even if it presents a wealth of aspects.

Right from its first announcement the theme gave rise to great interest in various parts of the world. Indeed, there exist reasons which render particularly urgent a treatment of this theme; and they are reasons pertaining both to the internal life of the Church and to her relation with the world.

Reasons of internal order:

• The need to take up again the teaching of Vatican II in order to attain a more profound change of mind and heart wished by that Council;

• The need to place oneself in a situation of advent, preparing oneself by means of a true interior renewal at the dawn of the third millennium;

• The need to live more profoundly the ecclesial communion, putting into effect ever more its fundamental condition: the conversion of the heart.

Reasons of external order:

• The ever more profound division of humanity demands of the Church an even greater commitment to root out the ultimate cause of this division, namely sin, by means of penance and reconciliation;

• The expectancy on the part of many, and of the poor in particular, of a peace that is the fruit of justice, on the one hand, and the collapse of many utopias which had trusted only in human strength, on the other;

• The Synod, therefore, inserts itself into the very heart of the drama of contemporary man and wishes to offer to that same man a message of well-founded hope.

Aim of the Lineamenta

The *lineamenta* are not a scheme or project of a future synodal document and have no pretense to completeness or perfection. They are provisional in character and limited, and thus it would be useless to make a critique of them or to attempt to perfect the text. It is important, however, to avail of them insofar as they are useful to the purpose. Intentionally, they remain at the generic and allusive level, leaving space for the more detailed and concrete considerations which will be put forward as experiences of faith and life in the ecclesial communities. In the replies account is to be taken of the fact that the Synod of Bishops follows pastoral aims, based, however, on a solid doctrinal foundation.

Finally, it is to be noted that the consultation that the *lineamenta* intend to promote is without limits and not reserved. The episcopal conferences, which are obviously the first and authoritative recipients, have complete freedom of action within the sphere of the chosen theme.

The Proposed Plan

The plan of the *lineamenta,* while having a unitary logic, is not the only one possible nor does it constitute an exhaustive study. Its outline is in three parts:

First part: "The World and Man in Search of Reconciliation" intends to recall attention to the situations of imbalance in the surrounding world and in the very heart of man which show the need and often also the innermost aspiration for renewal by means of reconciliation and penance.

Second part: "The Announcement of Reconciliation and Penance," primarily doctrinal in character, describes the initiative which, in the face of such situations, the merciful love of God has taken and to which man is called to respond with conversion and penance.

Third part: "The Church, Sacrament of Reconciliation," considers the pastoral work of the church as a place and mediator of reconciliation and penance.

NEW CODE OF CANON LAW

Publication of a new Code of Canon Law was expected possibly toward the end of 1982. In work for nearly 20 years under the direction of a commission set up by Pope John XXIII in 1963, it will replace the code promulgated in 1917 and in effect since 1918.

The principal purpose of the revision is not to break new ground in law but to put into one new code of general law developments — like decrees, declarations, constitutions and other official church documents — that have affected church law since 1917, especially since the Second Vatican Council.

The new code has fewer canons or norms than the old one, less than 1,800 compared with 2,414. It is also less detailed, more flexible, more clearly pastoral in spirit, and more based on theology "with a clear effort at decentralization," according to Jesuit Father Francesco Urrutia, a canonist on the faculty of the Pontifical Gregorian University.

Addressing a group of canon lawyers late in the summer of 1982 at Philadelphia's St. Charles Borromeo Seminary, Father Urrutia said that a much discussed *lex fundamentalis* or constitutional (fundamental) law of the Church — originally planned as a separate statement of basic principles governing church law — will not be promulgated but that features of it are incorporated directly into the new code itself.

Guiding Principles

Ten guiding principles for the new code were outlined by the 1967 assembly of the Synod of Bishops, he said. The Synod directed that the revised code should:

• be juridical in character, not just a set of broad moral principles;

• be intended primarily for the external forum (regarding determinable fact, as opposed to the internal forum or private conscience);

• be clearly pastoral in spirit;

• incorporate most of the faculties bishops need in their ministry;

• provide for subsidiarity or decentralization;

• be sensitive to human rights:

• state clear procedures for administrative processes and tribunals;

• be based on the principle of territoriality;

• reduce the number of penalties for infractions of law;

• have a new structure.

Seven books make up the structure of the new code, dealing with general norms, the people of God, the teaching mission of the Church, the sanctifying mission of the Church, temporalities, penal law and procedural law.

The code in effect since 1918 has five books covering: general rules or directives, ecclesiastical persons, sacred things, trials, crimes and punishments.

Features of the Code

The new code ratifies many changes already in place in the wake of the Second Vatican Council. It also introduces into prominence some new concepts and terms in church life.

One of them, along with the hierarchical constitution of the Church, is the underlying notion of the *communio* or community of all members of the Church.

It provides for greater participation by lay persons in the sanctifying, teaching and governing missions of the Church.

With respect to marriage, it emphasizes the covenant concept of the sacrament, stresses the pastoral responsibilities of the Church to couples preparing for marriage and in marriage, and recognizes the annulling effect of personality deficiency in verifiable cases. New norms regarding annulment proceedings in the U.S. require review by another tribunal before issuance of a decree of nullity.

Changes in law regarding censures limits the penalty of automatic excommunication to six offenses rather than 37 as in the existing code. The penalty is incurred when the offender has prior knowledge of the penalty and freely commits the crime of: obtaining or being party to an abortion; profaning the Eucharist; physically attacking the Pope; sacramental absolution of an accomplice; violation of the seal of confession; illegitimate consecration of a bishop.

The existing Code of Canon Law remains in effect until the new one is promulgated and made effective.

Father Francis Morrisey, O.M.I., dean of the canon law faculty of St. Paul University, Ottawa, Canada, has called the new code "the end of the beginning of the Vatican II era."

Cardinal John J. Krol told a group of canon lawyers during the summer of 1982 that Pope John Paul hoped to issue the new code of 1,776 canons or norms "at the earliest, on the first Sunday of Advent, or, at the latest, the first Sunday of Lent in 1983."

He emphasized the fact that the existing code, as modified since it became effective in 1918, would remain in force until the new code went into effect. He also said:

"The Church ... cannot exist without a body of laws. ... Some assumed that canon law had lost its binding force after the (Second Vatican) Council," despite clear papal statements to the contrary. "Some ... rejected objective norms ... and adopted subjective norms which led to disciplinary and doctrinal deviations ... and to disorder and disunity."

THE POPE AND THE JESUITS

Pope John Paul intervened in Jesuit affairs in October, 1981, with the appointment of a personal delegate to the Order to oversee its government and to prepare for the convocation of a General Congregation for the election of a successor to the ailing Superior General, Father Pedro Arrupe.

The compatibility of the intervention with the papal office and the relationship existing between the papacy and the Society of Jesus was described by the Pope Feb. 27, 1982, during a special meeting of Jesuit superiors near Rome. He said:

"The decision taken by the Holy See had its profound motivation and true source in the special love which it had and has for your great Order, well-deserving in the past and protagonist of the present and the future of the Church's history. On my part, this love is dictated by a special relationship of the Society of Jesus to my person and to my universal ministry."

The papal delegate and his coadjutor, or aide, were Fathers Paolo Dezza, 80, and Giuseppe Pittau, respectively; both were named in October, several weeks after Father Arrupe suffered a stroke on Aug. 7. Between the time he was stricken and Oct. 31, when they assumed their duties, the Order was under the administration of Father Vincent O'Keefe, vicar general of the Society.

Purpose of Papal Intervention

Father Dezza, in an Italian magazine article reported by NC News in January, 1982, said that his mandate was "to procure a deeper preparation" among Jesuits for a forthcoming General Congregation for the election of a new Superior General of the Order.

In the interview published in the Milan-based *Famiglia Cristiana,* Father Dezza said also that the Jesuits, although "healthy" as a religious Order, had some problems to resolve, including questions about theological positions and engagement in social and political activism.

Key Points

A number of such problems had been noted by Father Arrupe in a letter addressed to Jesuit superiors in October, 1979. Referring to a Sept. 21 papal audience with presidents of conferences of Jesuit provincials, he wrote:

"The points which the Pope expressly mentioned as requiring great attention by the superiors of the Society are the following: secularizing tendencies, austerity and discipline in religious and community life, fidelity to the teaching authority of the Church in doctrine, and the priestly character of our apostolic work. In addition, he mentioned the special attention which should be given to the spiritual, intellectual and apostolic formation of young Jesuits."

Meeting and Papal Counsel

These subjects were the themes of extended discussion during a meeting convoked by Father Dezza and held from Feb. 23 to Mar. 3, 1982, at Grottaferrata, near Rome. In attendance were 86 provincials along with assistants and councilors of the Jesuit General Curia.

Pope John Paul told the superiors of 26,662 Jesuits throughout the world what the Church expects of them. He said in an address Feb. 27:

'The Church today wants the Society to implement effectively the Second Vatican Council. . . .

"Allow me to insist once more and solemnly on the exact interpretation of the recent Council. It was and still is an ecclesial renewal under the guidance of the Holy Spirit. On this most important point the conciliar documents are absolutely clear.

"This renewal of fidelity and fervor in all sections of the Church's mission . . . must be welcomed and lived today according to the same spirit and not according to personal criteria or psycho-sociological theories."

In calling for fidelity to the teaching authority of the Church, the Holy Father cautioned against imprudent theologicial speculation and publication. He also warned against the unacceptable extremes of progressivism and integralism.

Priestly Service

Speaking of priestly service, the Pope quoted an address he delivered July 2, 1980, in Rio de Janeiro:

"Priestly service, 'if it is really to be faithful to itself, is essentially and *par excellence* spiritual. This must be even more emphasized in our times against the many tendencies to secularize the priest's work by reducing it to a purely philanthropic function. He is not a medical doctor, a social worker, a politician or a trade unionist. . . . Our service is always more precisely and specifically spiritual. . . . (Material assistance for people) must be a secondary service which must never obscure the principal service, which is to help souls to discover the Father, to be open to him and to love him in all things.' "

The Pope called for Jesuits to work effectively for promotion of the spiritual life of the faithful, with special reference to: the education of youth and scholarly pursuits; the formation of clergy and religious; missionary activity; engagement in ecumenical endeavors, relations with non-Christians, study and action with respect to atheism; the promotion of justice.

Several weeks after the meeting at Grottaferrata, Father Dezza addressed to Jesuits throughout the world a letter with a set of directives for carrying out the desires of the Pope for the Order's future. He made special note in his Mar. 25 letter of the high regard for the Society expressed by the Holy Father in his address of Feb. 27.

A Reassuring Experience

Father John J. O'Callaghan, president of the U.S. Jesuit Conference, said the Grottaferrata meeting was a "reassuring and satisfying experience" for the American participants.

"The positive tenor of the lengthy talk of the Pope, even in those passages where he referred to aspects of Jesuit religious life and apostolic endeavors about which we all have concern, confirmed our hopes that progress has been made toward the resolution of prob-

lems and misunderstandings," he said in a statement.

One sign of that progress, he observed, was the Pope's call for collaboration by the Society with him and the hierarchies of various local churches in the task of implementing enactments of the Second Vatican Council.

"The implementation of the grand directives of Vatican II, inevitably marked by a mix of successes and failures, has been an unusually difficult period in the life of the Society of Jesus," he said.

Noteworthy, Father O'Callaghan said, was the extraordinary degree of unity reached concerning the basically sound state of the Order "and on the significance we attach to the convocation of a General Congregation and the election of a successor to Father Pedro Arrupe, our Superior General, at the earliest possible time."

ANGLICAN-CATHOLIC FINAL REPORT

The Anglican-Roman Catholic International Commission of theologians officially published Mar. 31, 1982, a Final Report on 12 years of dialogue concerning subjects of belief and practice which have divided the two churches for more than 400 years.

The report included "Authority in the Church II," a new agreed statement, as well as earlier documents:

• the "Windsor Statement" on Eucharistic doctrine, published Dec. 31, 1971;

• the "Canterbury Statement" on ministry and ordination, published Dec. 13, 1973;

• the "Venice Statement" on authority in the Church, agreed to in 1976 and published Jan. 20, 1977;

• elucidations of these documents issued in 1979 and 1981;

• additional documentary material on the commission and related developments.

Key Issues

"Controversy between our two communions has centered on the Eucharist, on the meaning and function of ordained ministry, and on the nature and exercise of authority in the Church. Although we are not yet in full communion, what the commission has done has convinced us that substantial agreement on these divisive issues is now possible."

The "divisive issues," subsequently called "four difficulties," were "the interpretation of the Petrine texts, the meaning of the language of 'divine right,' the affirmation of papal infallibility, and the nature of the jurisdiction ascribed to the Bishop of Rome as Universal Primate."

Bishop Raymond W. Lessard of Savannah, chairman of the Anglican-Roman Catholic Consultation in the United States, said in a statement for publication Mar. 31:

"The Final Report maintains that, despite differences of vocabulary and theological em-

phasis, the Anglican Communion and the Roman Catholic Church are in fundamental agreement in the three areas on which, since the 16th century, Anglicans and Roman Catholics have maintained they differ from one another so sharply that in conscience their Christian communities would have to remain officially separated from each other."

Catholic Critique

The claim to fundamental agreement made in the Final Report was questioned by Cardinal Joseph Ratzinger, prefect of the Congregation for the Doctrine of the Faith, in a letter addressed to Bishop Alan C. Clark of East Anglia, England, co-president of the Anglican-Roman Catholic International Commission.

The claim was also questioned by the Congregation for the Doctrine of the Faith in the conclusion of a set of observations, dated Mar. 29, concerning the Final Report.

"At the conclusion of its doctrinal examination, the congregation thinks that the Final Report, which represents a notable ecumenical endeavor and a useful basis for further steps on the road to reconciliation between the Catholic Church and the Anglican Communion, does not yet constitute a substantial and explicit agreement on some essential elements of Catholic faith:

• "a) because the report explicitly recognizes that one or another Catholic dogma is not accepted by our Anglican brethren (for example, Eucharistic adoration, infallibility, the Marian dogmas);

• "b) because one or another Catholic doctrine is accepted only in part by our Anglican brethren (for example, the primacy of the Bishop of Rome);

• "c) because certain formulations in the report are not explicit enough to ensure that they exclude interpretations not in harmony with the Catholic faith (for example, that which concerns the Eucharist as sacrifice, the Real Presence, the nature of the priesthood);

• "d) because certain affirmations in the report are inexact and not acceptable as Catholic doctrine (for example, the relationship between the primacy and the structure of the Church, the doctrine of 'reception' — regarding the validation of doctrine by the acceptance of the people);

• "e) finally, because some important aspects of the teaching of the Catholic Church have either not been dealt with or have been only in an indirect way (for example, apostolic succession, the rule of faith, moral teaching)."

Recommendations

Regarding next steps to be taken, the congregation said "the results of its examination would recommend:

• "a) that the dialogue be continued, since there are sufficient grounds for thinking its continuation will be fruitful;

• "b) that it be deepened in regard to the points already addressed where the results are not satisfactory;

• "c) that it be extended to new themes, particularly those which are necessary with a view to the restoration of full church unity between the two communions."

Pope John Paul and Anglican Archbishop Robert Runcie, in a joint statement released May 29, 1982, at Canterbury Cathedral, announced the establishment of a new theological commission for a new phase of Catholic-Anglican dialogue.

THE BISHOPS SPEAK WITH THE VIRGIN: PASTORAL LETTER

"The Bishops Speak with the Virgin" is the title of the first-ever joint pastoral letter of the 14 Hispanic-American bishops of the United States. The letter, published July 22, 1982, was dedicated to the honor of Mary, the Lady of Guadalupe who appeared to the Indian Juan Diego near Mexico City in 1531. It is reflective of the origin, identity, culture and challenges of Hispanics in this country.

The following excerpts are from the text circulated by the NC Documentary Service, Origins, Aug. 12, 1982 (Vol. 12, No. 10).

Birth of a New People

At a unique moment in the history of this world, three radically different and totally unknown worlds met: indigenous America, Africa and Europe.

The clash carried many of the indigenous people to slavery and death, and made them strangers in their own land. The Africans were violently wrenched from their lands and transplanted to far-off countries as slaves. This initiated a shock whose reverberations are experienced even today. There also began at that time a *mestizaje,* an intertwining of blood and culture that in effect brought about the birth of a new people.

The roots of our Latin American reality are grounded in this threefold inheritance. It is our identity, our suffering, our greatness and our future.

Our Mestizaje

The Hispanic people of the United States of North America is a people of *mestizaje,* an interlacing of the blood and culture of the indigenous, African and European peoples. In the present reality of our people we find a new intertwining: that of the Latin American people and those of the United States. From this second *mestizaje,* the Hispanic-American people begin to emerge.

We are thus a new people, and within our very being we combine the cultural riches of our parents.

Our Reality

Much has been gained (from our history and heritage) but the suffering continues. We are conscious of the oppression and exploitation of our people. We have seen bodies disfigured by hunger and saddened by the fear of the law, we have heard the cries of abandoned children mistreated by their own parents. We sense the loneliness of the elderly ignored by their relatives and the depression of prisoners whose greatest crime has been the lack of money to pay someone to defend them in court. We have shared the pain and the heat of farm workers and domestic laborers, the invisible slaves of modern society. In the jails and the detention camps there are some who have come to our country in search of work and freedom, yet who have been considered criminals. We have seen our youth with empty eyes because they have nothing to look forward to in life. We have been with the countless victims of the violence that grows daily in our neighborhoods and even in our families. We will not rest until all injustice is eliminated from our life.

We have shared with our people the fear that comes from racism and discrimination. The knowledge that we might be rejected, ridiculed or insulted paralyzes us.

Our Identity

We are a people twice *mestizado.* We are in the beginning stages of our life as Hispanic Americans.

Every birth is at one and the same time joy and sadness. Our birth as a people has been the same. Constant rejection has been a part of our daily life.

Nevertheless, our parents taught us to love the United States, although the struggle has been difficult. Our people have always struggled to improve themselves. We love the peace founded on truth, justice, love and freedom. We have not taken up arms against our country but instead have defended it. We have fought to eliminate the injustices that rule our lives. The road has been long and difficult, littered with many obstacles, but we have made progress and will continue ahead with firmness and determination.

Our Accomplishments

Our people are beginning to count in society. Their voice is now being heard. Each day they are becoming more responsible for the religious and social structures that shape their life.

Your children (in direct address to Our Lady of Guadalupe) have already celebrated pastoral conventions on a national level.

The efforts of the farm workers have brought forth their fruits. Many of our people today enjoy a better life, thanks to the heroic efforts of our leaders.

Fourteen sons of our people have been called to be successors of the Apostles.

Vocations to religious life and to the priesthood are on the rise.

Catholic movements and associations have arisen, dedicated to the social and apostolic progress of our people.

We have pastoral centers dedicated to research, theological reflection, the production of materials and the formation of pastoral leaders.

The bishops have established national and regional offices to serve your people.

We give thanks to your Son for all that is being achieved. But we ask him to give us the strength and courage to continue facing the gigantic problems of our day. As John Paul II said in Mexico, "We want to be the voice of those who have no voice." The poor have the right to our love and special care.

Challenges

There are certain challenges in our society which we must meet.

Our betterment in social life does nt mean that we forget our roots — our Latin American *mestiza* tradition. The more we value our past, the more strength will we have to launch ourselves toward the building of our future.

Development of a more human life does not mean that we allow ourselves to be enslaved and destroyed by materialism, consumerism, social climbing, the desire for continuous pleasure and immediate gratification. All of this comes from the idolatry of gold. These values are the cancer of society.

The modernization of the family does not mean that we abandon the greatest treasure of our Hispanic culture. The family is in great danger today. Divorce is on the rise, the elderly are forgotten and even cheated, children are abandoned and young people make the street their home. The spirit of individualism is killing the spirit of community that is the core of the family.

Christian unity does not mean religious indifference. Ecumenism must not lead us to lose our identity as Catholics. Affirming ecumenism, we reject every type of active proselytizing which is anti-ecumenical and destructive to our people. The great diversity of fundamentalist groups and their anti-Catholic spirit divide our families and our peoples. Our response is not one of fighting against these groups nor one of speaking ill of them or their intentions, but rather we will take their activities as a challenge to us Catholics to live more authentically and apostolically the life of the Gospel.

(Under the heading, "Artisans of a New Humanity," the bishops reflected on the rediscovery of the Gospel, rebirth of the Church, the life of the Church, popular expressions of faith, catechesis, liturgy, theological reflection, vocations and a more authentic following of Jesus.)

Pilgrimage

We are heading into the 21st century!

Conscious of all that God has achieved through us, we call on our people to assume an attitude of leadership to create a more human society. We are all the Church, and together we can triumph.

We invite our people to be strong coworkers with us in ministry. Jesus told every one of us: "Go out and proclaim the good news." Christians, by nature, are evangelizers. The lay person, if Christian, evangelizes.

We invite young men and women especially to place their enthusiasm, their sense of commitment and their sincerity at the service of the Gospel. May they be young apostolic bearers of the Gospel to the youth of today.

We invite our brother priests to continue living their commitment. Do not be discouraged. We always walk with Jesus. We never go alone. He gives us the strength to be enduring guardians of the faith. May we also care for our traditions and language that are the means of spreading the Gospel. May we form the lay and religious ministers that God gives us, that they may be effective co-workers with us.

We congratulate them on all the good that has been done and we invite them to be the Good Shepherd with us. May they be men of prayer, devoted sons of the *Guadalupana*.

We invite our brother and sister religious to continue giving witness to the value of the life of poverty, chastity and obedience in a world that values riches, pleasure and power. We commend them because they have been a prophetic voice for justice and peace. We invite them, according to the particular charism of their community, to be united with the efforts of the local church in which they work so that in conjunction with the bishops and the people of God of that diocese they may build up the kingdom of God.

We invite the contemplative religious to continue offering to the Church the strength of their prayers and good example.

We invite our brother deacons to join our efforts and those of all the clergy in the apostolate. Faithful to their vocation as deacons, may they be men of service to the people. Let them not forget that the primary field of their apostolate is their home, their community and their place of work.

We challenge seminarians to commit themselves seriously to their studies and spiritual formation. Our people need compassionate priests with thorough knowledge of the sacred mysteries and a profound sense of the urgency of the social teachings of the Church.

Conclusion

O Mother of the Americas, just as you trusted Juan Diego, we beg you to trust in us, the Hispanic bishops. May you send us to places we are unaccustomed to visit; may you send us to proclaim your mandate: that a temple be built wherein we may feel the love and tenderness of our mother. We want to be the artisans and the builders of this new temple — a society in which all will be able to live as brothers and sisters. We want to build up the kingdom of God, where peace is found because hate, jealousy, lies, dissension and every kind of injustice will have disappeared.

Madre de Dios
Madre de la Iglesia
Madre de las Americas
Madre de todos nosotros
Ruega por nosotros.

BASIC CHRISTIAN COMMUNITY v. POPULAR CHURCH

The concept and operational model of basic Christian communities — *comunidades de base,* basic ecclesial communities — envision relatively small, basic communities of the faithful integrated for religious and secular life, with maximum potential for pastoral ministry, liturgical participation, apostolic activity and human, spiritual and social development.

Communities of this type originated mainly in Latin America, where it is estimated that they number more than 150,000. They have also developed in the United States and other places.

Ecclesial Communities

Basic communities were the subject of a message from the Pope to their leaders when he was in Brazil July 10, 1980. Its main theme was the need for such communities to maintain their sense of being church bodies.

He referred to the "enormous importance that basic communities have in the pastoral activity of the Church in Brazil." He warned, however, that it would be easy for a community to lose sight of its ecclesial or church-related base if it were formed and/or conducted for a political reason and purpose.

With respect to the leader of a basic community, the Pope said he "does not transmit his thoughts or doctrines but that which he learns and receives from the Church." He also said the leader should provide a "persuasive example of Christian life, of radiant and active faith."

Concern about Nicaragua

Papal concern about the nature and direction of basic communities surfaced again in 1982, in connection with developments in Nicaragua. Some communities there had been and still were deeply involved in the ongoing Sandinist revolutionary movement, to

such an extent that they rejected the authority of the Church and subordinated their ecclesial character to political purposes and activities.

With this background in mind, the Holy Father wrote a letter to the bishops of Nicaragua and they had it read Aug. 8 in parish churches throughout the country.

In the letter, the Pope wrote about "the absurd and perilous character of imagining oneself as being to one side of — not to say against — the Church built up about the bishop, as being another church conceived as 'charismatic' and not institutional, 'new' and not traditional, alternative and, as is envisaged lately, a 'popular' or 'people's' church.

"I am not unaware that an acceptable meaning may be attributed to such a nomenclature — regarded as synonymous with 'church born of the people.' By this would be meant that the Church arises when a community of persons — especially persons disposed by their littleness, humility and poverty to the Christian venture — opens to the good news of Jesus Christ and begins to live it in community of faith, love, hope, prayer, and celebration of and participation in the Christian mysteries, especially in the Eucharist.

Character of the "People's Church"

"But you know that the concluding document of the Third Episcopal Conference of Latin America at Puebla (in 1979) declared this name of *iglesia popular* to be 'scarcely a happy one.' It did so after mature study and reflection among bishops of the entire continent, because it was conscious that this name in general covers another reality.

"In its most common acceptance, which appears in the writings of a certain current of theology, 'people's church' means a church that arises much more from the presumed values of a portion of the population than from the free and gratuitous initiative of God. It means a church enjoying the autonomy of the so-called bases, without reference to the lawful pastors and teachers. Or it at least means that such a church sets the 'rights' of the aforementioned 'bases' over the authority and charisms that faith lets us see in the lawful pastors. Since the term 'people' easily takes on a markedly sociological and political content, it means a church incarnated in popular organizations, a church marked by ideologies placed at the service of their own causes and programs and opposed to groups considered not belonging to the people. It is easy to see — and the Puebla document explicitly says so — that the concept of 'popular church' scarcely escapes the infiltration of strongly ideological connotations along the lines of a certain political radicalization, of the class struggle, of the acceptance of violence for accomplishing determined ends, etc.

"When, in my opening speech to the assembly at Puebla, I myself raised serious res-

ervations about the term 'church born of the people,' I had the perils I have just mentioned in mind. Therefore, I still feel it a duty to repeat the same clear and affectionate pastoral warning by means of your voices. This is a call to your faithful through you.

Grave Deviation

"A 'people's church' opposed to the Church presided over by the lawful pastors is a grave deviation from the will and plan of salvation of Jesus Christ. It is so from the point of view of the Lord's and the apostles' teaching in the New Testament and in the ancient and recent teaching of the Church's solemn teaching authority. It is also a principle, a beginning, of fracture and rupture of that unity which he left as the characteristic sign of the Church itself and which he willed to entrust precisely to those whom 'the Holy Spirit established to rule the church of God' (Acts, 20:20).

"So, beloved brothers in the episcopate, I entrust you with the task of making this fundamentally important call to your faithful with patience and firmness."

NUCLEAR ARMS

Offensives for disarmament and peace, more vigorous than ever in 1982, created a great deal of concern, debate and movement, but the year ended with nuclear arsenals intact and additional production in progress. Meanwhile during the year, there was war with conventional weapons in Iran and Iraq, Afghanistan, the Falkland Islands, Lebanon and El Salvador.

The aims of opponents of the nuclear arms race were rather well summarized by Cardinal John J. Krol in an address Mar. 27, 1982, at a rally in Philadelphia.

"The arms race is not a secure way of maintaining true peace, and the balance of power is no sure plan to achieving it," he told thousands of participants in the interfaith demonstration.

Areas of Agreement

Citing Pope John Paul's call for a "moral about-face" away from nuclear weapons, he noted eight areas of general agreement among many people.

"1. We are opposed to all wars, both conventional and nuclear.

"2. We believe that peace is possible, but it must be pursued with the same energy and determination as is used in preparation for war.

"3. We acknowledge the right and duty of governments to legitimate self-defense, once all means of peaceful settlement have been exhausted.

"4. It is a primary moral imperative to prevent any use of nuclear weapons under any conditions.

"5. The deterrent effect of nuclear weapons

is as credible as the resolve to use them if deterrence fails. The use of such weapons is immoral.

"6. The possession of nuclear weapons in our policy of deterrence cannot be justified in principle but can be tolerated only if the deterrent framework is used to make progress on arms limitation, reduction and eventual elimination.

"7. It is an imperative for the superpowers to pursue meaningful arms limitaion aimed at substantial arms reduction and nuclear disarmament.

"8. The phasing out altogether of nuclear deterrence and the threat of Mutual Armed Destruction must always be the goal of our efforts."

Cardinal Krol also said:

"We recognize the right of legitimate self-defense, but this right is not a moral justification for unleashing massive destruction against innocent non-combatants. . . .

"We advocate disarmament, not unilateral but reciprocal or collective disarmament, proceeding at an equal pace according to agreement and backed up by authentic and workable safeguards."

Freeze Resolutions

The anti-nuclear movement generated a rash of weapons-freeze resolutions from grassroot levels to Congress. In Congress, 122 Representatives and 20 Senators co-sponsored (non-binding) resolutions Mar. 10 for a freeze, an end to the stockpiling of nuclear weapons and talks on weapon cutbacks. Anti-nuclear resolutions were voted in New England town hall meetings and the legislatures of several states. In Wisconsin, voters approved a state-wide referendum Sept. 14, calling on the U.S. and other nuclear powers to negotiate a reduction in nuclear weaponry.

Presidential Response

President Reagan's response to the anti-nuclear groundswell was a proposal announced Mar. 31 to "reduce nuclear weapons dramatically," but only after the United States has overcome the Soviet Union's "definite margin of superiority."

He committed his administration to "realistic arms control agreements on nuclear and conventional forces," but stressed that reductions would have to be on an "equal-force level."

The President reiterated his administration's position that the U.S. faced a strategic "window of vulnerability" because of massive Soviet weapon buildups unmatched by the U.S.

He backed a Jackson-Warner arms control resolution in the Senate, which backers of an immediate nuclear freeze characterized as a "build now, freeze later" approach to nuclear arms control. The resolution, endorsed by 58 Senators, was drafted as a counter-position to an immediate freeze resolution introduced Mar. 10 with the support of 20 Senators.

Bishops' Endorsement and Letter

The Nuclear Weapons Freeze Committee, based in St. Louis, reported in March that 69 U.S. Catholic bishops had endorsed the freeze. The number increased to 133 by April 25, according to Auxiliary Bishop Joseph Francis of Newark, speaking on behalf of Pax Christi-USA, the U.S. branch of an international Catholic peace movement.

Some months earlier, the National Conference of Catholic Bishops had set up a committee to draft a pastoral letter on war and peace, with major emphasis on nuclear weaponry. A first draft was produced, circulated among the bishops and others, and leaked to the press in June, 1982. Reactions and undisclosed comments were of such variety and depth that Archbishop Joseph L. Bernardin, committee chairman, notified bishops in July that the letter would be delayed for a period of six months to a year. Originally, plans called for debate and vote on the pastoral document at the November, 1982, meeting of the bishops' conference.

First Draft

The first draft of the letter judged two aspects of U.S. nuclear deterrence strategy as clearly immoral — the use or threat to use nuclear weapons first, and any use or threat to use such weapons against civilian populations.

The drafting committee did not condemn the possession of nuclear weapons under present conditions, but said that a nuclear deterrence policy, within defined limits, could be morally tolerated in the context of sincere efforts to achieve global nuclear disarmament.

Archbishop Bernardin issued the following statement when announcing the delay in writing the letter.

"1. The document is only a draft. Undoubtedly it will be revised considerably in light of the comments and suggestions made by the bishops and others. If it is approved, it will be a pastoral letter of the bishops, not the committee.

"2. In addition to the bishops, the Holy See and other episcopal conferences are being asked to react. The committee is especially anxious that the Holy See be involved in the process.

"3. The document attempts to give a moral analysis of a very complex topic. Therefore, it is important that the entire document be read carefully before a critique is given. Because it contains many interlocking ideas, it could be misleading to take a particular sentence or section out of context.

"4. The pastoral enunciates a number of principles contained in Catholic teaching and applies them to current realities. It clearly acknowledges that knowledgeable people of good will might well arrive at different conclusions. It provides, therefore, for a certain flexibility and avoids giving the impression that every position taken is necessarily definitive. The readers are invited to join the bishops in studying the issues and to form their consciences correctly so they can make their own decisions. The pastoral, in other words, seeks to contribute to the public debate about war, especially nuclear war, not close it off."

Just War Possible?

Debate about nuclear weaponry focused new and probing attention on the traditional just war theory, along with the question: Can there be a just nuclear war?

The elements of the just war theory are:

• It must be a war of defense against an unjust aggressor.

• It may not be fought to punish an offense or to recover a thing, but only to repel injury and aggression.

• All peaceful means of settling a dispute must have been exhausted.

• There must be a reasonable hope of success.

• There must be due proportion between the gravity of the injustice suffered and the damage the war would do.

• The war must be waged by legitimate authority.

• It must be limited war, in which the immunity of non-combatants is respected and the rules of morality apply.

Pope John Paul, talking with reporters June 2, suggested that the just war theory may no longer be applicable because of the destructive capability of weapons in contemporary arsenals.

"The right to self-defense cannot be denied," the Holy Father said. "But it is necessary to look for other solutions. Today it is necessary to exclude any war."

Appeal of Nobel Laureates

Nearly 100 Nobel Prize-winning scientists called for a freeze on the deployment and development of nuclear weapons and warned that "time is fast running out" to prevent a nuclear holocaust.

The appeal by 97 Nobel laureates, made Sept. 3, 1982, through the council of the Pugwash Conferences on Science and World Affairs, was distributed by the organization's executive office in Geneva.

More than half of the signers were from the United States, according to a list provided by the organization, a disarmament movement inspired by physicist Albert Einstein and philosopher and mathematician Bertrand Russell.

The statement said that "monstrously high levels of deployed nuclear arms must be reduced as soon as possible." The scientists endorsed a "standstill freeze" of weapons at prevailing levels.

"Such a freeze," they said, "should also include the development of new weapon technologies," and would be "an effective way of initiating the essential process of nuclear disarmament."

The statement said "disarmament is technically possible: all that is lacking is political will." It said the number of nations possessing nuclear weapons threatens "to increase greatly in the absence of a more effective worldwide non-proliferation arrangement."

Risks posed to mankind by the arms race "and by the dangerous confrontation between the major antagonists have, in recent years, grown more ominous," the statement said, and added: "Disarmament seems further away than ever."

The scientists urged governments to seek "a comprehensive international agreement aimed at eliminating the risk of nuclear war."

THE CHURCH IN TROUBLED COUNTRIES

(See additional Almanac entries for coverage of conditions and events troubling the Church in various countries.)

Bolivia: The Church was regarded with considerable reserve by the government because of its support for the poor and the rights of workers; also because of its criticism of policies of the regime regarded as prejudicial to the good of the country.

China: Catholics loyal to the Holy See comprise an underground church about which relatively little is known with certainty.

The church acceptable to the government — which is in fact, if not in law, schismatic — is the Patriotic Association of Chinese Catholics, with its own bishops, priests and limited freedom of ministry.

There appears to be no positive sign of possible reconciliation of the association with the Church.

Cuba: Two hundred aging priests and as many religious were carrying on a limited ministry in a climate of dominant atheism and materialism.

Czechoslovakia: Several priests were arrested in recent years on charges of subversive activity, the government's label for — among other things — anything having to do with religion that is not acceptable to the regime.

The government-controlled Pacem in Terris organization of priests protested late in the summer of 1982 a Vatican declaration against participation by priests in organizations and movements of a political nature. (See separate entry for coverage of the document.)

El Salvador: Civil strife was reported to have taken a toll of approximately 30,000 lives — mostly of civilians — between October, 1979, when a reformist junta took control of the government, and May, 1982. Parties to the conflict were government forces of one kind or another, rightist hit squads and guerrillas. Despite charges of communist involvement, the basic causes of struggle were internal — political and economic repression and corruption along with rampant injustice to the vast majority of the poverty-stricken population.

A leading symbol of the concern of the Church for the poor and the cause of justice in the country was Archbishop Oscar Romero of San Salvador who was shot to death while celebrating Mass Mar. 24, 1980.

Nine months later, four women missionaries from the United States were murdered.

Guatemala: Church personnel were among at least 13,000 persons, mostly civilians, killed in 1981 in fighting between government security troops, right-wing death squads and guerrillas.

More than 100 missionaries were forced to leave the country in recent years.

The Church is in a state of actual persecution by the government and right-wing groups because of its concern and work for the poor, especially Indians — many of whom have been massacred.

Nicaragua: Trends set in motion by the Sandinist government in control since the overthrow of the Somoza regime in July,

1979, appear to be threatening the freedom and influence of the Church. The Marxist-socialist orientation of the regime, along with its educational policies, control of the media and insistence on its version of fidelity to the ongoing Sandinist revolution, has already generated friction in church-state relations.

Pope John Paul, in a letter addressed to the bishops during the summer, warned against the danger of basic Christian communities *(comunidades de base)* losing their identity as church bodies and becoming instead cells primarily concerned with political issues.

Philippines: Cardinal Jaime L. Sin, in several public statements in 1982, was critical of the human rights policy of President Ferdinand Marcos.

Late in 1981 and continuing into 1982, a "climate of terror" persisted in Mindanao, according to the five bishops of the region. There and elsewhere, church personnel serving and siding with the poor were subject to harassment.

Poland: Archbishop Jozef Glemp, primate, and other churchmen spent most of 1982 in efforts to broker differences between the government and the Solidarity labor movement. Mediation efforts were generally fruitless, however, because of divergent lines firmly drawn by both sides. Lech Walesa, the origi-

nal sparkplug of Solidarity, was arrested and interned by the government with the declaration of martial law Dec. 13, 1981; he was still in detention at the time of writing.

Archbishop Glemp, in a homily delivered Sept. 3 during a Mass in Essen, West Germany, said the position of the Church in Poland is "extremely difficult, extremely dangerous and extremely full of responsibility." Praying that truth and justice would prevail rather than riots, he said "throwing rocks does not make sense."

The highlight of the year for Polish Catholics was the celebration of the 600th anniversary of the arrival in the country of the icon of Our Lady of Czestochowa (see separate entry). A big disappointment of the year was the refusal of the government to permit Pope John Paul to visit the country for participation in the jubilee ceremonies.

U.S.S.R.: Late in 1981, *Pravda* editorialized about what it called an irreversible extinction of religious belief in the Soviet Union. The official communist newspaper reported that, while 8 to 10 per cent of the population professed some form of religious belief, more than 70 per cent was atheistic.

There was evidence, however, of underground religious activity as well as of continuing practice of the faith in Lithuania.

BIOETHICS

Bioethics "can be defined as the systematic study, in the light of moral values and principles, of human conduct in the area of the life sciences and health care," according to Warren T. Reich, editor of the *Encyclopedia of Bioethics* published by Macmillan and Free Press (New York, 1980).

Subjects of study include: reproductive technologies, prenatal diagnosis, abortion, human experimentation, genetic intervention, behavior control, psychosurgery, definition of death, prolongation of life, euthanasia, right to privacy, allocation of scarce health resources, dilemmas in the maintenance of environmental health.

The Pope John XXIII Medical-Moral Research and Education Center is devoted specifically to examining the full range of emerging bioethical issues in the light of Catholic theology. Founded in 1973 by the Catholic Health Association and located in St. Louis, the center is supported by memberships, contributions and grants.

Similar research is the focus of the Institute for Theological Encounter with Science and Technology, located at St. Louis University and under the direction of Father Robert A. Brungs, S.J.

Need for Ethical Norms

Pope John Paul, in an address Oct. 27, 1980, to a group of Italian physicians, called

attention to the need for ethical rules in science.

"Science is not the highest value to which all others must be subordinated," he declared. Higher . . . is the right of individuals to their physical and spiritual life and to their psychic and functional integrity. . . . Scientific progress . . . cannot pretend to place itself in a sort of neutral ground. . . . Ethical rules, founded in the respect of the person's dignity, must illuminate and discipline medicine in the research phase as well as in the application of the results achieved."

The Pope said doctors are obliged to consider "the implicit danger to man's right to life of discoveries in the field of artificial insemination, birth and fertility control and hibernation, of retarded death, of genetic engineering, of the psychic drugs, of organ transplants."

While acknowledging that science has its "proper laws to follow," he said "it must recognize above all an insurmountable limit in the respect of person and in the protection of his right to live in a worthy way as a human being."

"The truth is that the technological development . . . suffers from a deep ambivalence. While it allows man to take control of his own destiny, it exposes him to the temptation of going beyond the limits of a reasonable control of nature, risking the survival and integrity of the human person."

In Vitro Fertilization

In vitro fertilization, artificial insemination and surrogate mothering are among subjects of serious ethical concern.

The first authenticated birth of a child fertilized outside a mother's womb occurred July 25, 1978, in Lancashire, England. (More than 30 children, seven of them in the United States, were born by this process by the end of the summer of 1982.)

Steps in the conception and birth were surgical removal of an egg from the mother, fertilization by sperm of the father in a laboratory vessel, and subsequent implantation and development of the fetus in the mother's womb.

The doctors who conducted the first successful procedure were Patrick C. Steptoe and Robert G. Edwards.

Praise for the scientific advance represented by the *in vitro* fertilization was matched with scientific and moral cautions. Pope Pius XII and traditional Catholic moral norms were quoted against the procedure because, among other things, of the divorce between normal marital intercourse and procreation.

"In vitro fertilization involves externalizing both sperm and ovum," stated Andre E. Hellegers and Father Richard A. McCormick, S.J., in an article published in the Aug. 19, 1978, edition of *America.* They continued: "It is, from the technological point of view, a step beyond artificial insemination that externalizes only the sperm. . . . Thus, at least some of the basic ethical considerations that surround *in vitro* fertilization are already present in the discussion of artificial insemination."

Moral norms relevant to both of these processes were stated by Pope Pius XII on two particular occasions.

Pius XII Statements

In an address to the Fourth International Convention of Catholic Doctors Sept. 29, 1949, he said:

"The practice of artificial insemination, when it is applied to man, cannot be considered exclusively, nor even principally, from the biological and medical viewpoint, while leaving aside the viewpoint of morality and law."

"Artificial insemination outside of marriage is to be condemned purely and simply as immoral."

"Artificial insemination in marriage with the use of an active element from a third person is equally immoral and as such is to be rejected summarily."

"With regard to the lawfulness of artificial insemination in marriage . . . the simple fact that the desired result is obtained by this means does not justify the employment of the method itself; nor does the desire of the marriage partners — most legitimate in itself — to have a child, suffice to prove the lawfulness or a recourse to artificial insemination for the fulfillment of that desire."

Speaking again, before the Second World Congress on Fertility and Sterility May 19, 1956, the Pope said:

"With regard to artificial fecundation, not only is there reason to be extremely reserved, but it must be absolutely rejected. In speaking thus, one is not necessarily forbidding the use of certain artificial means destined solely to facilitate the natural act or to achieve the attainment of the natural act normally performed."

"On the subject of the experiments in artificial fecundation *'in vitro,'* let it suffice for Us to observe that they must be rejected as immoral and absolutely illicit."

Unacceptable Eugenics

The Repository for Germinal Choice, a California sperm bank trying to produce high-I.Q. babies with sperm donated by Nobel prizewinners, was sharply criticized in August, 1982, by Jesuit Father Richard McCormick. News about the birth in April of the first child by artificial insemination of sperm from the bank prompted him to call the project "an isolated little symbol of a monstrous attitude."

Describing positive eugenics as "the preferential breeding of superior individuals to improve the eugenic stock of the human race," he said it reduces human beings to "animals" who are bred for "muscles or brain circumference."

"When we do that," he added, "we turn ourselves into shoppers and our children into purchases. A people that does that is on its way to doing a lot more than civilized people ought not do."

Surrogate Mothering

A surrogate mother is a woman who is artificially inseminated with sperm from the husband of another woman who cannot bear a child; she conceives the child, carries it to term and surrenders the baby to the couple after birth.

Father Robert Brungs, director of the Institute for Theological Encounter with Science and Technology, has called the surrogate arrangement "essentially adultery." Although he said he "can understand and sympathize with the reasoning some couples give for wanting this, the process is not an acceptable means to its ends. . . . You're giving a technological answer to a human problem."

Surrogate mothering represents not only an "intrusion of a third party into the psychophysical union of husband and wife," but also "creates all kinds of possible conflicts . . . where the child is tossed around like a plaything at the whims and desires of the people with power over it." So stated Father Richard McCormick, the Rose Kennedy professor of Christian ethics at Georgetown University's Kennedy Institute for Bioethics.

Father McCormick noted that many couples are attracted to the third-party process because parenthood "truly becomes an obsession." He insisted, however, that "it is still a flimsy reason for running the risks entailed in this."

Father Brungs likened the obsession to "falling in love with love rather than with a person. These couples seem to fall in love with motherhood."

The urgency of such couples is "understandable," stated Sulpician Father Philip Keane, associate professor of moral theology at St. Mary Seminary and University. He added, however, that parenthood remains "a good that is regrettably unavailable to everyone. None of us can have all of the good things we want, and in this instance the means of accomplishing creates more harm than good."

TUITION TAX CREDIT BILL

The Senate Finance Committee voted 12 to 6 Sept. 16, 1982, to pass a tuition tax credit bill with provisions that would delay the date tax credit legislation becomes effective until (1) either the Supreme Court reaches a decision in the Bob Jones University case (that no tax exempt status be given schools which discriminate racially), or (2) a Congressional statute on tax exemption has been passed.

Provisions

The legislation would give parents a tax credit for part of the tuition they pay to send their children to non-public schools.

The Finance Committee also voted to introduce a refundability provision on the Senate floor. Such a provision would mean that parents who do not have incomes high enough to require them to pay taxes would receive a refund for part of the tuition they pay.

President Reagan's tuition tax credit bill — the Educational Opportunity and Equity Act of 1982 — was sent to Congress June 22, 1982. It was similar to a bill proposed in 1981 by Sen. Daniel P. Moynihan (D.-N.Y.) and Sen. Robert Packwood (R.-Ore.)

The general rule of the Reagan bill was that, "in the case of an individual, there shall be allowed as a credit against the tax imposed . . . for the taxable year an amount equal to 50 per cent of the tuition expenses paid by the taxpayer during the taxable year to one or more educational institutions for any of his dependents who has not attained the age of 20."

The tax credit would not exceed $100 the first year, $300 the second year and $500 thereafter. Adjustments would be made for scholarships and financial assistance. The bill would phase out tax credits for parents with an adjusted gross income of more than $50,000.

Additional legislative action on the Reagan bill was pending at the time of writing.

Comments

Catholic educators and officials applauded announcement of the Reagan bill.

Msgr. Daniel Hoye, general secretary of the U.S. Catholic Conference, said shortly after the announcement that the result of the bill would be that "thousands of students, including many who are deserving but unable to meet the growing costs of parochial or private education, will benefit from this legislation because of the increased educational choices it helps make possible."

"At the same time," he added, "parents who are making heroic sacrifices on behalf of their children's education will receive some measure of much needed relief. Such relief is long overdue."

Another spokesman, Howard J. Fetterhoff, executive director of the Pennsylvania Catholic Conference, declared after action by the Finance Committee: "The tuition tax credit plan is necessary to guarantee educational freedom of choice. The plan would benefit significantly lower and middle income families as well as members of minority groups and the disadvantaged."

Albert Shanker, president of the American Federation of Teachers, and others — including officials of the National Education Association — were opposed to tuition tax credits, claiming they would have an adverse effect on public school education.

Additional opponents of the Reagan proposal were those who claimed that tax credits for the support of private education, especially in church-related schools, would be unconstitutional.

A Related Ruling

Two weeks after President Reagan spoke in favor of tuition tax credits at the convention of the National Catholic Educational Association in Chicago, a federal appeals court upheld the constitutionality of tax deductions for parents of public and private school students in Minnesota.

"We find that any benefit to religion or involvement between church and state is so remote and incidental that the challenged deduction does not violate the constitutional wall separating church and state," declared the 8th U.S. Circuit Court of Appeals in a 24-page ruling issued Apr. 30, 1982.

The court noted that the case had national significance and called on the U.S. Supreme Court to further resolve the constitutional issues.

VOLUNTARY PRAYER IN PUBLIC SCHOOLS

The following article by Joseph Duerr, news editor of "The Record," newspaper of the Archdiocese of Louisville, was written following the announcement May 17, 1982, of President Reagan's suggested wording for a constitutional amendment on voluntary prayer in public schools.

The suggested text reads:

"Nothing in this Constitution shall be construed to prohibit individual or group prayer in public schools or other public institutions. No person shall be required by the United States or by any state to participate in prayer."

If President Reagan looks to Catholics for support of his proposed constitutional amendment restoring prayer in public schools, he will find as much division among them as among the religious community at large.

Although a number of Catholic leaders spoke out strongly against the 1962 and 1964 U.S. Supreme Court decisions banning prayer and Bible reading in public schools, Catholics have lined up on both sides when amendments and other proposals on school prayer have come before Congress in the last two decades.

The Released Time Question

The Catholic bishops' conference, meanwhile, has approached the issue from a different perspective by injecting another matter — released time for religious instruction in public schools — into the debate.

The position of the bishops' conference is this: The problem did not begin with prayer and Bible reading decisions of the 1960s but with the 1948 court ruling which said that released time for religious instruction on public school premises was unconstitutional. Thus, it is necessary to reverse the 1948 decision in order to get to the root of the problem.

In accord with this stance, the Administrative Board of the U.S. Catholic Conference, the bishops' civil action arm, in 1973 called for a constitutional amendment to permit both religious instruction and prayer in public schools and other public institutions. "The U.S. Catholic Conference believes an amendment limited to allowing prayer would be inadequate to meet the national need," the board said. "The amendment which is needed must cover prayer and religious instruction."

This position was reaffirmed May 10 by Father Daniel F. Hoye, general secretary of the USCC, after Reagan had announced his support for the voluntary prayer amendment. Father Hoye said the USCC welcomed the president's proposal but also reiterated the call for passage of an amendment to deal with the "larger issue" of voluntary religious instruction in public schools.

School prayer amendments have been proposed in Congress since the Supreme Court decisions 20 years ago. Two amendments have reached the floor for a vote, but both failed to get the two-thirds vote required for passage.

Previous Amendment Proposals

In 1966, a voluntary prayer amendment backed by the late Sen. Everett Dirksen fell short by nine votes in the Senate (the vote was 49-37). Five years later, the House defeated an amendment to permit non-denominational prayer in schools and other public buildings (the measure was 29 votes shy of the two-thirds majority).

Congressional hearings on the Dirksen amendment saw Catholics lined up on both sides of the debate. In 1964 hearings, for example, nine Catholics spoke in favor of the proposal, 19 against.

In 1971 the USCC went on record opposing the non-denominational school prayer amendment. Archbishop Joseph L. Bernardin of Cincinnati, then USCC general secretary, said the amendment "would accomplish nothing on behalf of the goals it purports to serve and would represent a threat to the existing legality of non-denominational prayer."

Also, he explained, passage of the amendment "might lead many to think that something serious has been done about the problem of religious education of public school children. In fact, nothing of any moment would have been achieved."

Catholics also differed on a proposal before Congress several years ago to remove state school prayer cases from the jurisdiction of the Supreme Court and other federal courts. The measure passed the Senate 61 to 30 in 1979 but died in the House.

During hearings, Jesuit Father Robert F. Drinan, then a Democratic congressman from Massachusetts, opposed the bill, calling it "self-defeating." But William M. O'Reilly, executive director of the Maryland Federation of Catholic Laity, supported the measure, saying the best way "to protect the rights of everyone . . . is to let the matter be decided at the local level."

The USCC took no position on the school prayer jurisdiction legislation.

Divided Opinions

The religious community at large has also been divided over attempts to amend the constitution on school prayer, although many originally were critical of the 1962 and 1964 Supreme Court decisions.

Mainline Protestant and Jewish groups, for the most part, have in recent years defended the court decisions, while many evangelical Protestant groups have favored the voluntary school prayer proposals. Reactions to Reagan's endorsement of a constitutional amendment indicate these differences still remain.

For example, the Rev. Jerry Falwell, leader of the Moral Majority, hailed Reagan's announcement as the "light at the end of the tunnel we have all hoped and worked and prayed for."

But a group of Lutherans, Baptists, Methodists, Jews and Seventh Day Adventists opposed the president's proposal, saying, "We believe that the purpose of prayer is to praise and petition God, not to serve the secular purpose of creating a moral or ethical atmosphere for public school children."

HELMS BILL TABLED, HATCH DEBATE POSTPONED

(By Liz Schevtchuk, N.C. Correspondent.)

Two anti-abortion measures suffered severe setbacks in congressional action Sept. 15, 1982, when the Senate tabled the Helms bill, the target of an extensive filibuster by opponents, on a vote of 47-46, while action on the Hatch amendment to the Constitution was postponed until next spring on a decison of its sponsor and the Senate leadership.

Helms Filibustered

The Helms bill, which would have permanently restricted federal funding of most abortions and provided for speedy Supreme Court review of lower court decisions, suffered when its backers failed again to cut off a filibuster against the bill by its opponents. The Senate then voted to table the whole measure. It was attached to a debt ceiling bill being considered by the Senate and was sponsored by Sen. Jesse Helms (R.-N.C.).

Helms' bill was thwarted first by failure of an attempt in late afternoon to cut off the filibuster against the bill. The filibuster cutoff, a cloture vote, failed. The vote to table the bill entirely was then proposed by Sen. S.I. Hayakawa (R.-Calif.) and passed by 47-46, with Sen. Baker withholding his vote by pairing it with that of the absent Sen. Robert Stafford (R.-Vt.), who would have voted "aye" while Baker would have voted "nay."

Hatch Amendment

By agreement, Sen. Orrin Hatch (R.-Utah) and Senate Majority Leader Howard Baker (R.-Tenn.) postponed action on Hatch's amendment until February or later, when a new Congress has been convened. Hatch's proposed constitutional amendment would allow Congress and the states to outlaw abortion and declare that nothing in the U.S. Constitution guarantees a right to abortion.

Hatch said he was withdrawing the amendment from current Senate consideration because he feared it too would be the target of an extensive filibuster, because there was insufficient time to debate the measure, and because he lacked the two-thirds majority support needed to pass such constitutional amendments.

"It appears to me that the proposed constitutional amendment would not, in the present time context, in the remaining few days of the Senate, be given sufficient time," Hatch

said. Also, he added, "I do not believe that we have the requisite two-thirds votes on this constitutional amendment at this time."

Thus, proceeding with debate, "with the pressures that are on this body, would not be in the best interest of this amendment. It would be counterproductive. So, with that, I have chosen to withdraw the amendment," Hatch said.

Baker, in turn, said he agreed with Hatch "in making the commitment that we should have debate on the issue."

He said Hatch had been "very fair to me and I think the very least I can do and the Senate can do is to assure him that sometime early next year, meaning in the spring, shortly after we convene . . . that we will call up this or a similar amendment and deal with it."

Hatch, in withdrawing his amendment, added that he was "unwilling to demean this amendment. I am unwilling to go through a charade."

Senators' Comments

The Senate's actions prompted mixed comments from senators.

After the Hatch-Baker agreement, Sen. Charles Grassley (R.-Iowa) said he was "saddened that the events of today have dictated that the Senate will not be considering a constitutional amendment on the subject of abortion this year." He added that "this Congress has been able to go further in its efforts to protect that right (to life) than any other Congress since the Roe against Wade (Supreme Court) decision."

But Sen. Edward Kennedy (D.-Mass.) accused some anti-abortion senators of "hypocrisy" in favoring less government interference in people's lives except when it comes to abortion.

"With breathtaking hypocrisy they talk of taking government off people's backs — and then fight to put government into people's bedrooms," he said. They also have favored government budget cutbacks of services to pregnant women, those needing contraceptive assistance, children, the poor and others, he said.

"Congress will never resolve the issue of abortion by government fiat," Kennedy added. "But by defeating these amendments, Congress can begin to move beyond this issue and work for a better and more decent life for all citizens in our society."

Opposing Views

Pro-life organizations on Sept. 16 sounded discouraged about the Senate actions, while a pro-choice group sounded delighted.

"Obviously, we're not very pleased about it," said Dan Donehey of the National Right to Life Committee, who added that NRLC officials were preparing a more detailed response to the Senate activity. Despite the setbacks, however, pro-lifers are "absolutely not" giving up, he added.

Peter Gemma, executive director of the National Pro-Life Political Action Committee, said that the Senate actions at least indicated that votes on abortion issues can be close and will put senators, especially those facing re-election, on the record on abortion.

"The name of the game in politics is pressure. This gives us new momentum," said Gemma, who termed the current situation "the best of times and the worst of times" as far as anti-abortion legislation goes.

By contrast, Nanette Falkenberg, the executive director of the National Abortion Rights Action League, spoke of her group's victory.

"We won because we were organized, strong and powerful," she said. "The nation is turning the corner in its battle to keep abortion legal. The election in November will wrap up two years of growing strength and power for the pro-choice community and two years of dismal failure of the anti-choice groups."

ABORTION-RELATED COURT DECISIONS

Following is a chronological list of abortion-related decisions handed down by the U.S. Supreme Court and other courts since Jan. 22, 1973.

• In Roe v. Wade, the Court ruled, 7 to 2, Jan. 22, 1973: (1) During the first three months of pregnancy, a woman's right to privacy is paramount. Accordingly, she has an unrestricted right to abortion with the consent and cooperation of a physician. (2) In the second trimester, the principle controlling legislation on abortion is the health or welfare of the mother, understood in the widest possible sense. (3) In the "state subsequent to viability," the controlling principles are the State's "interest in the potentiality of human life" and "the preservation of the life or health of the mother." These rulings canonized the absolutely private right of a woman to have an abortion and denied to the unborn the right to life.

• In Dole v. Bolton, also decided Jan. 22, 1973, the Court ruled, 7 to 2, against restrictions on facilities that could be used in performing abortions.

• In Danforth v. Planned Parenthood, the Court ruled, 6 to 3, July 1, 1976, against the constitutionality of state laws requiring spousal (in the case of a married woman) or parental (in the case of a minor) consent for an abortion.

• The first of three versions of the Hyde Amendment was adopted by Congress Sept. 30, 1976, in an appropriations measure for the Department of Labor and the Department of Health, Education and Welfare. The amendment provided for limiting federal funding of abortions under Medicaid to cases of danger to the life of a mother and to cases of rape or incest reported in a required manner. (See below.)

• An injunction against the amendment was issued Oct. 22, 1976, by U.S. District Court Judge John F. Dooling, Jr., in a suit originally filed by Cora McRae.

• In Maher v. Roe, the Court ruled, 6 to 3, June 20, 1977, that the Constitution does not require states to pay for non-therapeutic (elective) abortions and does not require public hospitals to provide them.

• The Court set aside June 29, 1977, Judge Dooling's injunction against the Hyde Amendment and ordered him to restudy his ruling of the previous October in the light of its decision in Maher v. Roe.

• Funding restrictions of the Hyde Amendment went into effect Aug. 4, 1977, and the McRae case went back to the Dooling courtroom.

• The Court ruled, 6 to 3, Jan. 9, 1979, in Colautti v. Franklin against the constitutionality of a 1974 Pennsylvania law because of its vagueness about the timing of fetal viability. The decision had the effect of meaning that a woman exercising a legal right to have an abortion had the right to a dead fetus and that the doctor performing the abortion could not be charged civilly or criminally for the death of the fetus.

• In Bellotti v. Baird, the Court ruled, 8 to 1, July 2, 1979, against the constitutionality of a Massachusetts law requiring a minor to consult with her parents before having an abortion. In the absence of parental consent (which the Court ruled in 1976 was not required) or parental consultation (not required either), a court could clear the way for the abortion of a minor judged to be mature enough to have one.

• Judge Dooling ruled Jan. 15, 1980, against the constitutionality of the Hyde Amendment but stayed enforcement of his decision to permit an appeal to the Supreme Court.

• The Court responded Feb. 19, 1980, to Judge Dooling's action with a one-sentence order requiring federal and state governments to provide Medicaid funding for abortions deemed "medically necessary." The Court also ageed to rule on the constitutionality of the Hyde Amendment, in connection with another case (Williams v. Zbaraz) that originated in Illinois.

Hyde Amendment Constitutional

• In Harris v. McRae, the Court, with a 5-to-4 decision June 30, 1980, upheld the constitutionality of the Hyde Amendment and its restrictions on Medicaid abortion funding. The decision overturned the Dooling ruling of Jan. 15, 1980.

The conclusion of the Court's majority opinion declared:

"We hold that a state that participates in the Medicaid program is not obligated under Title XIX to continue to fund those medically necessary abortions for which federal reimbursement is unavailable under the Hyde Amendment. We further hold that the funding restrictions of the Hyde Amendment violate neither the Fifth Amendment nor the Establishment Clause of the First Amendment. It is also our view that the appellees lack standing to raise a challenge to the Hyde Amendment under the Free-Exercise Clause of the First Amendment."

While deciding that neither the federal government nor state governments are required to provide funding for "medically necessary" abortions, the Court noted that "abortion is inherently different from other medical procedures because no other medical procedure involves the purposeful termination of a potential life."

The Hyde Amendment provided: "None of the funds provided for in this paragraph shall be used to perform abortions except where the life of the mother would be endangered if the fetus were carried to term; or except for such medical procedures necessary for the victims of rape or incest, where such rape or incest has been reported promptly to a law enforcement agency or public health service."

Medicaid payment for "medically necessary" abortions continued for about two and one-half months after the decision of June 30, pending a ruling by the Supreme Court on petitions for reconsideration. The decision not to reconsider was announced Sept. 17 and payment was discontinued thereafter.

About two-thirds of the states dropped elective abortion funding from their Medicaid programs after the 1977 decision of the Supreme Court.

1981 Decisions

The Supreme Court, by a 6-to-3 vote in H.L. v. Matheson, upheld Mar. 23 the constitutionality of a Utah law requiring physicians to notify the parents of an unmarried, immature minor daughter seeking an abortion. The decision said: "Although we have held that a state may not constitutionally leg- islate a blanket, unreviewable power of parents to veto their daughter's abortion, a statute setting out a 'mere requirement of parental notice' does not violate the constitutional rights of an immature, dependent minor."

With another 6-to-3 vote in Gary-Northwest Indiana Woman v. Orr, the Court ruled Apr. 27 that states may outlaw the performance of abortions outside of hospitals for women more than three months pregnant. The Court declared that states may seek to protect a mother's health during the second trimester and may move to protect fetal life only during the final trimester.

None of the 1981 decisions dealt with the substance of abortion itself; rather, they concerned circumstances of performance without legal restraint.

No 1982 Decisions

The U.S. Supreme Court did not hand down any new decisions on abortion in its 1981-82 term but agreed May 24, 1982, to hear cases challenging the constitutionality of abortion laws in Virginia, Missouri and Akron, Ohio.

"The cases all deal with peripheral or procedural issues regarding the circumstances under which abortions are to be performed; and many of these issues have already been touched upon in one way or another by previous Supreme Court rulings," said Richard Doerflinger, legislative assistant for the Bishops' Pro-Life Committee.

"Even if the pro-life movement won every single case," he added, "abortion would still be legal throughout the United States for the entire nine months of pregnancy."

Pro and Anti Groups

Right-to-life supporters — of many different classes, income levels, religious faiths, political and philosophical persuasions — number in the millions. Some of their leading organizations and movements are the National Right-to-Life Committee, Americans United for Life, the Ad Hoc Committee in Defense of Life, the Right to Life Crusade, March for Life and Americans Concerned for Life.

Far out in front of the pro-abortion ranks are the National Abortion Rights Action League, the National Organization of Women and Planned Parenthood.

Statistics

Statistics on legal abortions performed in the U.S. each year from 1972 to 1978 provide reliable indices of the magnitude of the challenge facing right-to-life proponents. The numbers of abortions and years, as reported by the Center for Disease Control, U.S. Department of Health and Human Services, were: 586,760 (1972), 615,831 (1973), 763,476 (1974), 854,853 (1975), 988,267 (1976),

1,079,430 (1977), 1,157,776 (1978). The annual number since 1978 has been over one million.

The total number of abortions performed annually worldwide is estimated in the range of 30 to 35 million.

Charges Against the Church

The Catholic Church is the largest and strongest institutional opponent of abortion, because of its firm teaching and practice on the subject, and also because of the number of its members who are against it.

Because this is so in a cultural climate favoring abortion and moral liberalism, the Church has been accused and charged with:

• dominating the pro-life movement;

• trying to force its views on others who do not share its faith;

• violating a peculiar interpretation of the principle of separation of Church and state.

These accusations have been implicit and explicit in reporting of the abortion controversy ever since it began.

The Church insists, however, on its right to speak and act on moral issues on an equal basis with others who claim rights of conscience and freedom to influence others in a society which is subject not only to the laws of man but, above all, to universal moral law.

EQUAL RIGHTS AMENDMENT

Two weeks after the Equal Rights Amendment failed of ratification on its first try for want of approval by 38 states, it was reintroduced in Congress July 14, 1982, by a bipartisan group of 51 Senators and 201 Representatives.

In three sections, the amendment states:

• "Equality of rights under the law shall not be denied or abridged by the United States or by any State on account of sex."

• "The Congress shall have the power to enforce by appropriate legislation the provisions of this article."

• "The amendment shall take effect two years after date of ratification."

The First Time Around

The first passage of the amendment through the ratification process began with approval by the U.S. Senate (84 to 8) and House of Representatives (354 to 24). On Mar. 22, 1972, it was submitted to the states for ratification by the same date seven years later.

Twenty states ratified the amendment within three months of its passage by Congress, and two more by the end of 1972. Eight more ratified by the end of 1973, and five more by Jan. 18, 1977, when Indiana became the last, and 35th, state to ratify.

Fifteen states did not ratify the amendment: Virginia, North Carolina, South Carolina, Georgia, Florida, Alabama, Mississippi, Louisiana, Arkansas, Oklahoma, Missouri, Illinois, Arizona, Utah and Nevada.

Five states — Idaho, Kentucky, Nebraska, South Dakota and Tennessee — ratified but later voted to rescind approval.

As it became virtually certain that three more states — for the required total of 38 — would not ratify the amendment by the deadline of Mar. 22, 1979, moves were initiated for an extension of the ratification period.

Constitutional Questions

The constitutionality of an extension bill was upheld by a spokesman for the Justice Department during a hearing early in November, 1977, before the House Subcommittee on Constitutional Rights. John Harmon, assistant attorney general for the Office of Legal Counsel, said that Congress, which sets the time period for ratification, can extend it by a simple majority vote.

The first determination of a time limit was made by Congress in the ratification process of the 18th Amendment.

Harmon also said that the constitution, while giving states authority to ratify amendments, says nothing about a right to rescind ratification, although they are free to reject amendments in the first place.

The Justice Department's view of rescission was challenged by another subcommittee witness, Laurence Tribe, a Harvard Law School professor. He said that the Congress sitting at the time the 38th state ratifies an amendment would have the power to decide whether or not to honor a state's decision to rescind ratification.

The authority of Congress to extend the period for ratification was denied Aug. 3, 1978, by former Senator Sam J. Ervin, Jr. In testimony before the Senate Subcommittee on the Constitution, he said that Congress "has no power to amend the past. . . . The power to fix a reasonable time for state action on a proposed constitutional amendment must reside in the Congress that submits it. It cannot be determined retroactively by a subsequent Congress. The 95th Congress has power to legislate for the future. It has no power to amend the past."

Two weeks before the Ervin testimony, the House Judiciary Committee voted (19 to 15) July 18 to send to the House a measure recommending extension of the E.R.A. ratification period to June 30, 1982. At the same time, the committee defeated (21 to 13) a proposal that would have permitted states to rescind ratification already voted.

In October, both Houses concurred in (1) extending the time period for ratification to June 30, 1982, and (2) turning down a proposal that would have permitted states to rescind ratification.

The subsequent drive for ratification

stalled three states short of the 38 required for adoption of the amendment.

The new campaign for and against ratification has about the same cast of groups and the same basic scenario of issues.

Legislative Intent and Opinions

The legislative intent of the E.R.A., according to Senate and House reports issued in 1972, is to outlaw discrimination on the basis of sex, without affecting laws dealing with the unique characteristics of one sex.

The amendment could counteract discrimination against women and guarantee them equal rights with men, with respect to property and inheritance laws; opportunities for credit and in business, education and employment (for jobs, pay, potential for advancement); insurance and retirement programs, and in other areas.

Objections

E.R.A. opponents, however, focus objection on possibly adverse effects of the amendment on the quality of family life, divorce and alimony laws, military conscription, abortion and homosexual rights, and other matters. Many of them have not been convinced by a February, 1978, report of the U.S. Commission on Civil Rights which said that much opposition was based on "incorrect legal interpretations of the effect of the amendment." Their lack of conviction is related to doubt about the way in which courts might interpret the broad sweep of the amendment, given the vagaries of judicial decision and the manner in which litigation affects legislation.

Linkage of the amendment to abortion, homosexual and lesbian rights by the National Organization of Women and other groups has provoked the strongest objections of parties to the Stop-E.R.A. movement.

Some constitutional lawyers, like Professor Philip B. Kurland of the University of Chicago Law School, question the need for the E.R.A. They view as adequate guarantees of rights in existing provisions of the 14th Amendment, Title VII and other sections of the Civil Rights Act of 1964, state laws, and appropriate law enforcement. At least 16 states have E.R.A.-type measures in their constitutions.

Gallup Poll surveys indicate that majority opinion favors ratification by about 60 to 40 per cent, with more men in favor than women.

Catholics on Both Sides

Catholics of all ranks are on both sides of the E.R.A. debate, and it would be rash to estimate the numbers of those for or against it. The division of opinion is evident even among bishops.

On one side, the Administrative Committee of the National Conference of Catholic Bish-

ops voted May 1, 1978, not to authorize an endorsement of the amendment. They reject unanimously a document by their Ad Hoc Committee on Women in Society and the Church because of uncertainty about the impact of the amendment on "family life, the abortion issue and other matters." The Administrative Committee declared:

"While reaffirming our support for women's rights and our determinatinon to continue to work for them, we conclude that there are insufficient grounds for us as religious leaders to approve a change in our conference's policy first stated in 1972 and reaffirmed in 1975."

That policy concerned the possible effect of the E.R.A. on law and family life, and concluded: "The doctrinaire character and broad sweep of the amendment may very well destroy the unity essential to a stable family relationship."

On the other side, the ad hoc committee said: "Equality of rights for women is fully compatible with marriage and the family, and marriage and family will be enriched as women more fully develop their talents, exercise their capabilities, and gain recognition for their accomplishments."

The ad hoc committee argued that the E.R.A. would not inhibit efforts by pro-life advocates for passage of a constitutional amendment to safeguard the right of the unborn to life.

It was reported early in June, 1982, that 23 bishops had signed a statement in support of ratification of the amendment.

Groups and Pressure

Two mainline Catholic women's organizations, the National Council of Catholic Women and the Catholic Daughters of the Americas, and other groups are opposed to the E.R.A., for reasons similar to those stated by the bishops' Administrative Committee. Many pro-life advocates are also against the amendment.

On the other side, in favor of the amendment, are members of such groups as; the Quixote Center, Network, Priests for Equality, the Women's Ordination Conference, the National Coalition of American Nuns, the National Assembly of Religious Women, the Catholic Women's Seminary Fund, Christian Feminists, and the Baltimore Task Force on the Status of Women in the Church.

Political pressure for adoption of the E.R.A. had little effect from 1978 to the latter part of 1981. It was expected that such pressure would be stronger in the 1982 elections and subsequently.

Also expected is an increase in economic pressure as the result of resolutions enacted by scores of organizations not to hold conventions or other meetings in states failing to ratify the amendment.

VATICAN

Human Dignity, Creation, Research — All scientific research, whether it explores the origins of the universe or the effects of atomic bombs, must be based on concern for the dignity of the human person, Pope John Paul declared Oct. 3 in an address before a gathering of 150 scientists at Castel Gandolfo. He referred to "cosmology and fundamental physics, . . . the impact of modern biology on society" and other subjects under discussion during a study week sponsored by the Vatican.

In related developments:

• The Pope presented the Pius XII Gold Medal to Jean-Marie Lehn, of the College de France and the University of Strasbourg, for his research on the use of solar energy.

• Roger W. Sperry, a researcher at the California Institute of Technology and a member of the Pontifical Academy, was one of three American-based scientists awarded the 1981 Nobel Prize in medicine.

Beatifications — The Holy Father presided Oct. 4 at ceremonies for the beatification of three men and two women:

• Blessed Alain de Solminihac (1593-1659), bishop of Cahors, France, from 1636 until his death;

• Blessed Luigi Scrosoppi (1804-84), Italian priest, founder of the Sisters of Divine Providence;

• Blessed Riccardo Pampuri (1897-1930), Italian doctor and member of the Secular Franciscan Order and the Brothers of the Hospitaller Order of St. John of God;

• Blessed Claudine Thevenet (1774-1837), French nun, foundress of the Congregation of Religious of Jesus-Mary;

• Blessed Mary Repetto (1807-90), Italian member of the cloistered Sisters of Our Lady of Refuge.

The Pope, appearing in St. Peter's Square for the first time since he was shot May 13, was cheered by a throng of about 125,000 persons.

Lay Leadership and Witness — The Pope told the 26-member Pontifical Council for the Laity Oct. 5 that lay Catholics must be "witnesses to a new humanity" and must help to promote "a new international order." Reflecting on "the evangelizing presence of the laity in various fields of social life," he said: "At the heart of situations and problems where the future of man is at stake," lay persons must "give an example of generous sacrifice . . . to those who battle to open to Christ, Lord of history, the doors of the hearts of men, of culture and of peoples, of the future of nations, of a new international order."

Tribute to Sadat — The Pope, addressing a general audience Oct. 7, called assassinated Egyptian President Anwar el-Sadat "a great statesman" who will be remembered "for his courageous initiatives of peace" in the Middle East. On Oct. 6, the day on which Sadat was shot to death while watching a display of Egyptian armed forces, the Holy Father cabled a message of condolence to Vice President Hosni Mubarak: "In condemning this treacherous act of violence, I pray that almighty God may grant peace to this man of peace and bring to fulfillment his lofty vision of reconciliation among peoples."

His Brush with Death — Before a throng of 30,000 people attending a general audience Oct. 14, Pope John Paul said his brush with death the previous May 13 had made him more conscious of his own weakness and of the strength of God. He called his experience of suffering and convalescence a "special grace" and "a divine trial" which benefitted him and the Church.

Men and Women Religious — Religious communities, although distinctive in various respects, are linked together by their common spiritual basis, their commitment to human dignity and their importance to the local church. So stated the Pope Oct. 15 at a meeting with 1,000 participants in the first joint meeting of the Italian Conference of Major Superiors of Men and the Italian Union of Major Superiors of Women.

Need for Food — The Pope issued a strong call for a new international order "capable . . . of assuring sufficient food for every country in the world." He made the appeal in a letter addressed to Edward Saouma, director general of the United Nations Food and Agriculture Organization in connection with the celebration of World Food Day Oct. 16.

Vatican Radio reported Oct. 15 that more than 500 million persons were suffering from famine.

Values of Christian Marriage — The transcendent values of Christian marriage and the family can be adapted to local cultures but never abandoned, declared the Pope in an address Oct. 16 to members of the Congregation for the Evangelization of Peoples. He said: "At times the comparison between the ideal and reality can lead to an easy resolution, when the ethnic and ethical elements of native cultures are compatible with transcendent Christian values. . . . At other times the comparison brings to light an objective contrast, where clearly pagan traditions remain or where polygamy, the repudiation of spouses, the killing of unborn life are practiced."

Family and Work — The relationship between family and work was the theme of a papal talk Oct. 25. The Holy Father urged people in St. Peter's Square to pray that, through the intercession of Mary, "the fundamental link which exists between work and the life of every family may find its proper reflection in the entire social and juridical order, and also in the daily life of each person and each family."

Faith and Social Commitment — These were key points in an address delivered by the Pope Oct. 31 on the last day of a conference marking the 90th anniversary of publication of the encyclical letter *Rerum Novarum*. He said: "Consistency with one's faith does not impede the Christian from being present and committed in the building of society. This consistency — lived without compromises — assures . . . the presence of a light, of a truth, of a life in which social relations are born and are built on the recognition of human dignity."

The Pope Also:

• Was represented at celebrations marking: the eighth centenary of the birth of St. Francis Oct. 3 and 4 at Assisi, Italy, by Cardinal Agostino Casaroli; and the fourth centenary of the death of St. Teresa Oct. 14 at Alba de Tormes and Avila, Spain, by Cardinal Anastasio Ballestrero.

• Said that different liturgical, disciplinary and theological expressions can enrich the Church if they are "complementary rather than contradictory" to Catholic tradition, during a meeting Oct. 17 with Patriarch Abuna Telke Haimanot of the Ethiopian Orthodox Church.

• Ended a two-month stay at Castel Gandolfo Oct. 17.

Vatican Briefs:

• For the third year in a row, Christological themes were under study at the annual meeting, Oct. 1 to 7, of the International Theological Commission. Reconciliation and the sacrament of penance were the subjects chosen for study in 1981-82.

• The Pontifical Commission for the Revision of the Code of Canon Law completed the final review of its work at a meeting held Oct. 20 to 28 and passed its draft of proposals for a new body of church law on to Pope John Paul for final decision and promulgation.

• Vatican Radio called Oct. 27 for reassessment of "that authentic world calamity called the arms race," in connection with a report on the U.N. Week for Disarmament, Oct. 24 to 30.

• Tightened security measures for the protection of the Pope went into effect during the month as he resumed public appearances at the Vatican.

Papal Delegate to the Jesuits

Father Paolo Dezza assumed duties as the delegate of Pope John Paul to the Society of Jesus Oct. 31, eight days after the appointment was announced at the Rome headquarters of the Jesuits.

In an Oct. 5 letter to Father Pedro Arrupe, who had suffered a stroke Aug. 7, the Pope said Father Dezza would "represent me more closely in the society, look after the preparation of the general congregation — to be called in due time — and also, in my name and by my appointment, superintend the government of the society until the election of a new superior general."

Seventy-nine-year-old Father Dezza entered the Society of Jesus in 1918.

NATIONAL

Meeting of Catholic and Orthodox Bishops — Thirteen Roman Catholic and Orthodox bishops, meeting formally for the first time Sept. 30 and Oct. 1 in New York, reviewed ecumenical developments of recent years and discussed doctrinal and practical problems separating their respective churches. A Greek Orthodox spokesman said the bishops might consider the prospect of forming an Orthodox-Roman Catholic Council of Churches.

Catholic Charities — Delegates attending the 67th annual meeting of the National Conference of Catholic Charities Sept. 27 to Oct. 2 in Las Vegas resolved to "summon the President and our elected and appointed officials to a renewed dedication to a vision of economic justice for America, measured not solely in terms of the sum total of goods produced and wealth, but in terms of a just and equitable distribution of these benefits and of careful stewardship for future generations." Helen McDaniel, director of Catholic Social Services of Columbus, O., was elected president of the conference. Sister Ann Patrick, of the Missionary Servants of the Most Holy Trinity, was awarded the 1981 O'Grady Award.

Franciscan Anniversary — Thousands of Franciscan men and women commemorated the 800th anniversary of the birth of St. Francis of Assisi in ceremonies held early in the month in various cities of the country. Bishop Thomas C. Kelly told a congregation Oct. 4 in St. Patrick's Cathedral, New York: "The Francis we love is a man of passionate intensity, able, like few others, to . . clearly realize that there are only two things that really matter — to love the Lord and to love other people."

Rulings against O'Hair — The U.S. Supreme Court rebuffed Oct. 5 an effort by atheist Madalyn Murray O'Hair to force the city council of Austin, Texas, to end its practice of opening its meetings with a prayer. The Court also rejected her challenge to the annual display of a Christmas nativity scene and a Hanukkah menorah at the Texas Capitol in

Austin. Both practices had been ruled constitutional by lower courts.

NCCW Convention — Nearly 1,900 delegates attended the annual convention of the National Council of Catholic Women Oct. 5 to 9 in Orlando. Among resolutions passed were those on: abortion (for the Hatch Amendment), nuclear arms (for limitation and eventual abolition), the handicapped (for full participation in society, along with support for advocacy programs for the mentally ill and retarded), and women (commending bishops for "ongoing concern that women continue serving in a variety of ways in the Church").

TV Writers Criticized — Archbishop John R. Quinn, addressing a regional convention of the Catholic Press Association Oct. 15 in San Francisco, was critical of major TV writers whose attitudes "trivialize religion." He also said: "The mass media are in danger of becoming little more than transportation and marketing vehicles to deliver entertainment and 'supernews,' a blend of censorship, propaganda and 'public information.' "

World Food Day — In a statement for World Food Day, Oct. 16, leaders of the Interreligious Task Force on U.S. Food Policy called for establishment of an international system of grain reserves, adjustments of voting power in the International Monetary Fund and the World Bank, an increase in development aid and a sharp decrease in military aid to other nations. President Reagan, whose views differed from those of the task force, was on record to the effect that the U.S., which could not be blamed for the problem of world hunger, provided more food assistance annually to developing nations than all other nations combined.

1980 Marriage Decisions — Marriage tribunals of 161 U.S. dioceses reported decisions in 60,875 cases in 1980, according to findings of an unofficial survey released by the Canon Law Society of America. The report did not indicate types of decisions.

Refugee Policy — The bishops of Florida issued a joint statement in the middle of the month in which they called on the federal government to establish a refugee policy addressed to preparation for emergency situations, fair demographic distribution and fair sharing of tax burdens and social responsibility. They said: "Under the present administration even the inadequate grants made to entrants and refugees have been placed in jeopardy. A plan to eliminate relief programs . . . would place a nearly impossible burden" on state, church and other resources.

The Archdiocese of Miami had a remarkable record of service to thousands of refugees from Haiti, Cuba and other Latin American countries.

In a related development, Bishop Anthony J. Bevilacqua, chairman of the Bishops' Committee on Migration and Tourism, gave qualified endorsement Oct. 22 to a proposal of the Reagan administration that would grant amnesty to undocumented aliens.

National Briefs:

• Bishop Walter F. Sullivan called Oct. 5 for an end to Catholic-sponsored grade and high school football in the Diocese of Richmond after an eighth grader on a parish team died in a game.

• More than 1,000 women attended a rally sponsored by the National Organization of Women Oct. 12 at the Lincoln Memorial, Washington, to support a final drive to win ratification of the Equal Rights Amendment before the June 30, 1982, deadline.

• The wisdom and supernatural understanding of St. Teresa of Ávila should be "a reality in our lives and in our troubled world." So stated Oblate Father Joseph Chorpenning Oct. 14 during a Mass in Milwaukee marking the start of a year-long commemoration of the fourth centenary of her death.

• More than 600 persons attended the sixth National Workshop on Christian-Jewish Relations Oct. 26 to 29 in Milwaukee. The theme was "In the Image of God: The Challenge of Diversity."

• Criticism was reported of the decision of Bishop Glennon Flavin to authorize only men over the age of 21 to serve as lectors at Mass and other sacred celebrations in the Diocese of Lincoln. The limitation was scheduled to go into effect Jan. 1, 1984.

Hatch Amendment

Archbishop John R. Roach, president of the National Conference of Catholic Bishops, expressed support for an anti-abortion constitutional amendment introduced in the Senate by Sen. Orrin Hatch. In a column published Oct. 23, the archbishop said: "It is our best judgment that, while the amendment will not do all that those of us committed to the pro-life cause had hoped for and worked for, it does represent a significant advance in the fight for human life."

The amendment stated: "A right to abortion is not secured by this Constitution. The Congress and the several states shall have the concurrent power to restrict and prohibit abortions: Provided, that a law of a state which is more restrictive than a law of Congress shall govern."

INTERNATIONAL

End of Hunger Strike — Six Irish Republican Army inmates of Maze Prison near Belfast ended fasts to death Oct. 3 because, they said: "We have been robbed of the hunger strike as an effective weapon principally because of the successful campaign waged against our distressed relatives by the Catholic hierarchy." Termination of the strike, in protest against inmate status and prison conditions, came seven months after it had claimed 10 lives by starvation and 50 more in related acts of violence.

Guerrilla Involvement Denied — Jesuit officials and bishops denied early in the month allegations that church organizations were parties to "an infrastructure" of subversion in Guatemala. Such charges were made by Father Luis Eduardo Pellecer in a televised press interview Sept. 30. It was reported that the priest had disappeared June 9, had turned himself in to government security forces July 8, and had been held in custody until the time of the interview.

Requisites before Elections — "Respect for the basic rights of the human being," political dialogue and peace must precede" elections scheduled for March, 1982, in El Salvador, declared Bishop Arturo Rivera Damas, apostolic administrator of San Salvador, in a homily Oct. 4. He said: "The state of siege and martial law must be lifted, access to communications media must be secured. The left must curb its many abuses and attacks, and the right must end its no less grievous abuses."

Coptic Bishop Killed — Coptic Orthodox Bishop Samuel was killed in the burst of gunfire which took the life of President Anwar el-Sadat Oct. 6. He was one of five bishops appointed by the President to administer church affairs after Coptic Pope Shenouda III was denied recognition as head of the church and placed under virtual house arrest in a crackdown on alleged religious dissidents regarded as threats to national unity.

Criticism of Yugoslav Regime — In a statement issued after an Oct. 6 to 8 meeting, the bishops of Yugoslavia criticized the educational policy of the government, noting "with bitterness" that lessons and textbooks in all government schools presented atheism as "the only scientific conception of the world." The prelates also defended their right to protest hindrances to the free profession of faith and condemned the mass media for presenting a distorted view of the Church.

Nobel Prize to Refugee Agency — Awarding of the 1981 Nobel Peace Prize to the Office of the U.N. High Commissioner for Refugees (Poul Hartling), announced Oct. 14, focused attention on the importance of the agency as international refugee problems continued to increase. The office, honored with the same award in 1954, had 10 million refugees under its protective umbrella.

Resignations from Seminary Posts — Father Canuto Barreto resigned from the office of rector of the Managua Seminary, Nicaragua. He said he found it increasingly difficult to run the institution because seminarians were being adversely affected by religious and political tensions related to divergent attitudes toward the revolutionary government

in power since the summer of 1979. Three nuns engaged in administrative work at the seminary also resigned their posts.

Cancun Meeting — "The future of international cooperation for development and reactivation of the world economy" was the focus of discussions at the meeting Oct. 22 and 23 in Cancun, Mexico, of the heads of eight developed and 14 underdeveloped nations. The principal result was agreement to continue talks at future meetings. President Reagan was on record in favor of international economic reform and cooperation through the operation of private enterprise and the "magic of the marketplace."

Catholics a Minority Force — Despite the fact that they comprised 97 per cent of the nation's total population, Catholics had only a "minority force" in their influence on social, political and moral life in Italy. So declared the Italian Bishops' Conference in a statement released Oct. 23.

Opposition to U.S. Neutron Warhead — The Canadian Conference of Catholic Bishops condemned the decision of the United States to proceed with development of a neutron warhead. In a statement approved at a meeting held Oct. 26 to 30 in Ottawa, the bishops said: "We ask members of the Catholic community and the people of Canada to oppose vigorously the buildup of nuclear arms by all nations, and especially the United States and the Soviet Union. At some point we must say: Stop! That time is now."

International Briefs:

• Three Canadian Jesuits engaged in educational work in the northeastern Diocese of Darjeeling were expelled from India for undisclosed reasons.

• Vatican Radio reported Oct. 5 that inmates of Polish prisons had been given permission by the government to attend Mass on Sundays and major feast days.

• Statistics gathered by the Italian Association for Contraceptive and Sexual Education Centers indicated that 800,000 abortions were performed in Italy in 1980.

Terms for Reconciliation

Reconciliation of the government-sponsored Patriotic Association of Chinese Catholics with the Church "will depend on the Vatican, (which) should respect our right to govern ourselves." So stated Father Zi-Cheng Wang, a member of the association and vicar general of the Diocese of Yaoyang, during an international conference on religion held Oct. 2 to 7 in Toronto.

Hope of reconciliation was hard to come by in view of the association's outright rejection of papal authority and its commitment, in line with objectives of the Three Self-Help Movement, to absolute autonomy in the administration, propagation and support of the Church.

NOVEMBER 1981

VATICAN

Eliminate Poverty — The Pope urged representatives of 152 nations Nov. 13 to make the elimination of "absolute poverty" a priority in individual, national and international efforts. In his address to 850 participants in the 21st conference of the U.N. Food and Agriculture Organization, he also criticized costly development loans to countries unable to afford them. He described absolute poverty as "a condition in which life is so limited by lack of food, malnutrition, illiteracy, high infant mortality and low life-expectancy as to be beneath any rational definition of human decency."

Make Homes Domestic Churches — Pope John Paul appealed Nov. 15 to Catholics in Communist-ruled Hungary to make their homes "domestic churches" by teaching their children faith in God and service to people. His exhortation was contained in a letter commemorating the 750th anniversary of the death of St. Elizabeth of Hungary.

Migrant Workers — On Nov. 15, a day dedicated by the Church in Italy to migrant workers, the Pope said of their rights: "The right of the immigrant worker to leave his native land and establish himself in another country must be recognized, as also his right to live in a suitable house with his family, and his right to work and to receive equal treatment, both economically and in terms of social benefits, with the workers of the host country." The Pope made these and other remarks in an address to 60,000 persons in St. Peter's Square.

African Church Not under Foreign Domination — Pope John Paul, at a meeting Nov. 20 with the bishops of Ivory Coast, said they should not be swayed by persons claiming that the Church in Africa was subject to foreign domination. He told the prelates they should not let themselves "be influenced by those who, under the pretext of conserving and favoring African cultural traditions, accuse the local Church of being subjected to foreign tutelage."

Religious Are Subject to Bishops — "Religious, like all the faithful, are placed under the jurisdiction of the bishops" for the exercise of their ministry. So stated the Pope Nov. 20 in an address to participants in the plenary assembly of the Congregation for Religious and Secular Institutes. He criticized "an erroneous idea of exemption" leading some nuns, brothers and priests of religious institutes to "compartmentalize" the Church and to consider themselves separate from its structures. "Men and women religious," he said, "must develop their ecclesial sense for a better integration with the local Church and the universal Church."

Catholic Education — The Catholic school is "at the very heart of the Church," declared the Pope Nov. 21 before a gathering of more than 7,000 Christian Brothers, students and parents marking the 300th anniversary of the founding of the Brothers of the Christian Schools by St. John Baptist de la Salle. Addressing the brothers, he said: "Be faithful to your original vocation of being 'apostles of the school,'" a vocation which "is arduous and which demands renunciation and sacrifice, total dedication to the educative mission, an inexhaustible faith in young people and a great love of the Lord."

Concern for Earthquake Victims — Just before the first anniversary of the earthquake which claimed more than 3,000 lives in Southern Italy, the Pope celebrated Mass for 28 workers from one of the hardest-hit areas (Nov. 19), reminded the bishops of Italy of their responsibility for leadership in reconstruction efforts (Nov. 21), and made a general appeal for help for nearly 300,000 people facing a second winter without permanent housing (Nov. 22). In an address delivered before praying the Angelus at Collevalenza on the latter date, the Pontiff said: "Today . . . I feel the need to address a fervent invitation and pressing appeal to everyone in order that each . . . may make a generous contribution so that the legitimate expectations of those beloved peoples may not be further disillusioned."

Visit to Shrine — Pope John Paul proclaimed his belief Nov. 22 that "God's merciful love is stronger than every evil," in a homily during Mass at the Amore Misericordioso ("Merciful Love") Sanctuary at Collevalenza, 60-odd miles north of Rome. "In the course of the history of man," he said, "God's merciful love constantly makes its way through the barriers of indifference, of egotism, of inattention and of hate; through the barriers of lust of the flesh, of the eyes and of haughtiness; through the source of sin which each man carries within himself; through the history of human sins and crimes." The Holy Father was under heavy guard during this first trip outside of Rome since the attempt on his life the previous May 13.

A Gift from God — Pope John XXIII was "a great gift from God to the Church, because he brought the Church to life for people of today," the Holy Father said during a general audience Nov. 25, the 100th anniversary of the birth of his predecessor. He added: "We remember Pope John XXIII as one who pointed out to us the paths to renewal. . . . . We remember him because he spoke the words of Christ and told us about truth and justice, about love and freedom. . . . He offered hope to the whole world, placing his confidence in the young."

The Pope Also:

• Told a gathering of 6,000 persons that everyone should seek strength and inspiration from the saint after whom he was named, on Nov. 4, the feast of his patron, St. Charles Borromeo.

• Defended the rights of Catholics in Iran and urged its government "to work for the destruction of war and the abolition of hatred," as he received the credentials Nov. 14 of Iranian Ambassador Seyed Hadi Khosrovshahian.

• With 24 members of the College of Cardinals, concelebrated Mass Nov. 17 for two of their confreres — Egidio Vagnozzi and Stefan Wyszynski — who died during the previous year.

• Said the dialogue between the Catholic and Orthodox Churches should focus on achieving unity and must not get bogged down in consideration of secondary issues, in a letter presented Nov. 30 to Orthodox Patriarch Dimitrios I.

Vatican Briefs:

• Funds deposited in the Vatican Bank are not subject to the currency laws of Italy, according to a decision announced by the Rome prosecutor's office.

• Archbishop Giovanni Cheli, the Vatican's permanent observer at the United Nations, announced Nov. 18 that the Vatican was increasing its annual donation to the U.N. Relief and Works Agency from $2,500 to $12,500, for the benefit of Palestinian Refugees.

Hopes of the Pope

The Holy Father told an assembly of more than 200 German and Italian scholars Nov. 12 that he hoped they might help in saving Europe and the rest of the world from such catastrophes as atomic annihilation, totalitarian threats to democracy, explosive developments in the Third World and the spread of terrorism and violence.

Repeating a frequent theme of his three-year pontificate, the Pope also encouraged a search "for the spiritual foundations of Europe and of every nation, to find a meeting point among various tensions and various currents of thought, to avoid further tragedies."

NATIONAL

Canonizations — The Russian Orthodox Church Outside of Russia, in ceremonies held Oct. 31 and Nov. 1 in New York, canonized as "new martyrs" 8,500 persons killed during or after the Communist Revolution of 1917-18. Nicholas II, the last czar of Russia, and members of the royal family were among those so honored by the church, which is in-

dependent of the Russian Orthodox Church in the Soviet Union.

Family Needs Attention — "Ninety years ago it was the social question which was the first question of society. . . . Nowadays it is the family which needs the attention." This comment of Pope John Paul II was reported to participants in the National Consultation on Family Ministry by Bishop Paul J. Cordes, vice president of the Pontifical Council for the Laity. Attending the meeting Nov. 2 in Washington were representatives of Worldwide Marriage Encounter, National Marriage Encounter, Catholic Engaged Encounter, the Christian Family Movement, the Commission on Marriage and Family Life of the U.S. Catholic Conference, and the North American Conference of Separated and Divorced Catholics.

Tuition Tax Credit Downed — The D.C. Education Tax Credit Initiative was rejected by an 8-to-1 margin in the Nov. 3 election. The measure, supported by the National Taxpayers Union and sponsored by the D.C. Committee for Improved Education, would have enabled taxpayers to reduce their District of Columbia income taxes by up to $1,200-per-pupil for educational expenses at either public or private schools.

Aid for Philadelphia Schools — Protestant, Jewish and Catholic Business Leaders Organized for Catholic Schools were playing a leading role in community efforts to raise $77 million in aid to Catholic schools. Their interfaith fund-raising campaign, started in 1980 and scheduled to end in 1983, was said to be the first of its kind. Results to Nov. 9 amounted to $8 million in contributions from business leaders, trusts and business establishments.

Converts, Drop-Outs, Returnees — This was the title of a study sponsored by the U.S. Bishops' Committee on Evangelization. Findings reported by Archbishop Edward O'Meara at a press conference Nov. 17 in Washington included the following:

• Most Catholics who "drop out" of active church participation do so in their teens or early 20s.

• Nearly two-thirds of those who convert to Catholicism and more than two-thirds of Catholics who return to active practice of the faith after a period of inactivity do so in young adulthood, between the ages of 20 and 35.

• Highly significant in the decision of converts and returnees was the "human factor" of a friend, relative or priest who made them feel welcome and wanted in the Catholic community.

Sin and Reconciliation — These were the key subjects treated in a pre-Advent pastoral letter issued by 15 bishops in Texas. They said: "There is a legitimate concern that many Catholics are losing a sense of sin, which is leading to the disuse of the sacrament that gives them the rich and redeeming love of Christ. . . . Not only is there a lack of the sense of individual or personal sin, but there is an appalling disregard for the morality of the social issues of our day. . . . If we allow the diminishing sense of sin to grow, the result will be a practical denial of the need for God's mercy and the redeeming sufferings of Jesus would not be active for many."

Government Responsibility — "The Role of Government in Social Policy" was the title of a statement issued by the bishops of New York and circulated in the middle of the month among officials on all levels of government in the state. "In revising or terminating certain social programs and legislation, we must always strive to protect the human rights which those policies and programs were developed to serve," said the bishops. They also stated that national and state leaders may not leave the poor, immigrants and the handicapped "simply to their own devices."

Bishops' Meeting — Two hundred and eighty-four bishops attended the annual meeting of the National Conference of Catholic Bishops and the U.S. Catholic Conference Nov. 16 to 19 in Washington. (See separate entry.)

United Way Boycott — The United Way campaign in Berks County, Pa., failed to reach its $3.25 million goal partly because of a boycott led by priests, according to Samuel A. McCullough, county campaign chairman. Priests in the county had urged Catholics to refuse to donate to the local United Way because of its failure to abide by a 1974 pledge against support for Planned Parenthood abortion counseling.

Clothing Collection — More than 90 dioceses took part in the 31st annual Thanksgiving Clothing Collection for Catholic Relief Services. Bishop Edwin Broderick, executive director of CRS, said that "this year's collection will help clothe refugees, the handicapped and poverty-stricken families" overseas. More than eight million pounds of clothing and blankets were collected and distributed in the previous year to people in 32 countries in Latin America, Africa, Southeast Asia and the Mediterranean region.

National Briefs:
• Eight nuns formed the community of the first cloistered convent in the U.S. of the Benedictine Congregation of Solesmes, recently dedicated at Westfield, Vt.

• *Our Sunday Visitor* launched a "Turkeys for Poland" campaign for needy families in that beleaguered country.

• More than 2,000 young people from across the country attended the national convention of the Catholic Youth Organization Nov. 5 to 8 in Milwaukee.

• Threats to freedom of communications in

the 1980s were efforts to institute a "New World Information Order" and to exercise financial censorship over broadcasting, according to Thomas Leahy, a senior broadcast vice president of CBS. He was a featured speaker at the 10th annual assembly of Unda-USA, held Nov. 11 to 14 in New York. Paulist Father John Geaney was reelected to a three-year term as president of the Catholic broadcasters' association.

• National Bible Week was observed Nov. 15 to 22.

• Volunteer workers at Georgetown University Hospital in Washington were mounting a campaign to have Blessed Maximilian Kolbe identified as the patron of all volunteers. Conventual Father Kolbe suffered death as a volunteer in place of a condemned father of a family at Auschwitz, the Nazi concentration camp, during World War II.

Bishops and Nuclear Arms

The recent months' total of bishops commenting on nuclear arms reached more than 30 by Nov. 12. The following were representative of those who issued statements on the subject.

• Archbishop Philip M. Hannan of New Orleans: "The possession of weapons whose use is considered immoral may be justified if possession of such weapons is a deterrent to their use by the other side."

• Bishop Albert H. Ottenweller of Steubenville: "There is no way we can apply the 'just war' norms to machines with such destructive power (as nuclear bombs). We must say that their very use is madness and immoral."

• Bishop James D. Niedergeses of Nashville: Nuclear war is "folly of unbelievable dimensions."

• Archbishop John R. Quinn of San Francisco: "Current discussions about limited nuclear war and the possibility of exploding nuclear weapons as a warning to aggressive forces" are breaking down the barrier of the unthinkability of nuclear warfare.

INTERNATIONAL

Peace and Human Rights — "A peace without progress in respect for human rights will be an adulterated peace, because it will not be rooted in the spirit and the freedom of persons." So stated Dominican Father Paul Grossrieder, a Vatican representative at the Madrid conference reviewing results of the 1975 Helsinki Accords on European security. He recalled Nov. 3 a letter sent by Pope John Paul in September, 1980, to heads of the 35 signatory countries, in which the Pontiff said that religious freedom is a basis for other fundamental human rights and freedoms, and helps to promote them.

National Agreement Sought in Poland — In a move defiant of Marxist-Leninist doctrine, the leaders of Poland's Communist Party

(Gen. Wojciech Jaruzelski), Catholic Church (Archbishop Jozef Glemp) and Solidarity labor union (Lech Walesa) held an unprecedented summit conference Nov. 5 to try to form a "front of national agreement" to end the chaos troubling the country for more than a year. A communique issued by the government news agency said the three men "exchanged views on the possibility of setting up a front of national agreement and reconciliation, a permanent platform for dialogue and mutual consultation."

Two Priests Sentenced in Yugoslavia — Tanjug, the national news agency, reported that two Franciscan priests, Fathers Ferdo Vlasic and Jozo Krizic, were sentenced Nov. 11 to jail sentences of eight and five and one-half years, respectively, on charges of anti-state activities.

Refugee Quotas Biased — Ed Gale, supervisor of immigration services for Toronto's Catholic Family Services, charged that the 1982 refugee immigration quotas set by the Canadian government were "full of bias." New quotas reduced the number of government-sponsored refugees from Southeast Asia from 8,000 to 4,000, raised the Eastern European quota from 5,000 to 6,000, and limited to 1,000 the number of government-sponsored refugees from all of Latin America.

Anglicans Move toward Women Deacons — The General Synod of the Church of England voted Nov. 12 in favor of framing legislation that would provide for the admission of women, including those who were already deaconesses, to the order of deacon. Deaconesses, ordained in the Anglican Communion since 1862, were not considered to be in holy orders.

United Front Wanted — Forty representatives of the Catholic hierarchy and 40 leaders of Protestant and Orthodox churches in Europe called Nov. 19 for a united effort by European Christians against the arms race and world hunger. The churchmen, at the end of a four-day meeting at Logumkloster, Denmark, said in a statement: "We can never have peace as long as the world, beginning with our continent, can be the starting point and theater for a war which would destroy everything. We must commit ourselves to an organization of our society which favors peace and in which all men and all people may live in freedom, justice and mutual respect."

IRA Cooperation Condemned — So stated Cardinal Tomas O'Fiaich of Armagh Nov. 20 at a church in his see city: "Let me . . . state in simple language, with all the authority at my command, that participation in the evil deeds of this (IRA) or any other paramilitary organization which indulges in murder, wounding, kidnapping, destruction of property and other forms of violence is a mortal sin . . . To cooperate in any way with such organizations is sinful; and, if the cooperation is substantial, the sin is mortal."

Action against Discrimination — Late in the month, leaders of various churches asked their members to support urgent action to end racial violence in Great Britain. The call was sounded in a statement related to destructive riots which occurred the previous spring and summer in the Brixton section of London and in other urban areas.

Religious Suppression in Albania — Bishops of the Greek Orthodox Church issued an urgent appeal for religious freedom in Albania, which declared itself in 1967 to be the "first atheist state in the world." Their statement, reported in the Nov. 22 edition of *L'Osservatore Romano,* said: "Four hundred thousand Greek Orthodox believers of ancient Christian tradition have been brutally forced to live without God and without religion. Today, there is not even a bishop, all priests have been forced to leave their ministry, and churches have been converted into museums or amusement centers. . . . Thousands of faithful have been thrown in jail."

Declaration on Religious Freedom — Nineteen years after the start of work on the document, a Declaration on the Elimination of Religious Intolerance was approved by the U.N. General Assembly Nov. 25.

International Briefs:

• *Deo Gratias,* the publication of the Brazilian World Crusade for Thanksgiving, reported that special Masses of thanksgiving involving bishops, religious congregations and public officials were planned in 134 countries.

• The resignation of 70-year-old Bishop Donal R. Lamont, head of the Umtali Diocese for 24 years and an outspoken critic of white supremacy in Rhodesia (now Zimbabwe), was accepted by Pope John Paul.

Climates of Persecution

Conditions of persecution were reported in El Salvador and Guatemala.

• Jose Antonio Pastor Ridruejo, a special representative of the U.N. Human Rights Commission, reported Nov. 9 that there was "a general climate of persecution of the Catholic Church" in El Salvador. In support of the charge, he cited "blatant and illustrative cases of murder," such as mass killings of peasants, and attempts against priests and religious who acted to defend human rights.

• In Guatemala, where they had already denounced "a state of persecution of the Church" by the military government and paramilitary squads, the bishops declared in a pastoral letter in the middle of the month: "We do not hesitate to say that at the present time the whole social, political and economic foundations of the country are on the brink of collapsing in a bloodbath. Only the religious and moral values of our people can help to find a human and just solution to the grievous problems of our land."

DECEMBER 1981

VATICAN

Equality for Women Workers — Pope John Paul called for the adoption of "social legislation which recognizes the equality of men and women workers," in an address Dec. 6 to about 30,000 people in St. Peter's Square. He also said: "The true promotion of woman requires that work be structured in such a way that she must not pay for her own promotion with the abandonment of her own specific role and at harm to the family, in which she as mother has an irreplaceable role."

Educational Freedom — Freedom of education in a pluralistic society was the subject of an address delivered Dec. 7 by the Pope before a gathering of 200 Italian Catholic judges. He said: "The peaceful and respectful living together of all human groups within a pluralistic society does not mean that a philosophical and religious neutrality must be adopted in the school, because that would . . . arbitrarily impose on students an agnostic and escapist vision of the world." He said, in addition, that parents should be able to choose "the type of school which best corresponds to the model of education they desire for their children."

Plague of Abortion — The Pope condemned "the plague of abortion" and told people engaged in family ministry not to be silent or ambiguous about church teaching on artificial contraception. Addressing participants in two conferences Dec. 7, he said: "No human authority can declare legitimate that which divine law condemns. The life of every person, even the person conceived but not yet born, deserves an absolute and unconditional respect. . . . If this basic right is not respected, how is it possible to speak of the rights of man and the dignity of the human person?"

Tribute and Prayer to Mary — On the solemnity of the Immaculate Conception, the Holy Father paid tribute to Mary in the Piazza di Spagna, the site of a column and statue erected in Rome by Pope Pius IX to commemorate the proclamation of the dogma in 1854. He prayed there for Mary's help and intercession in the "great battle between good and evil" in the world.

Gap Must be Closed — The Pope criticized the increasing disparity between the rich and poor in Latin America and said Dec. 12 that Christians have the obligation to work to close the gap. Addressing Latin American diplomats and college students on the feast of Our Lady of Guadalupe, he appealed for "an urgent pledge in favor of justice, to seek seriously to even off the grave imbalances which exist in the economic, social and cultural fields."

Prevention of Nuclear War — "I am deeply convinced that, in light of the effects scientifically foreseen as sure in a nuclear war, the only morally and humanly valid choice is represented by a reduction in nuclear arms, in anticipation of their future total elimination, simultaneously effectuated by all sides, through explicit accords and with the commitment to accept effective controls." So stated Pope John Paul Dec. 13, a day after the Vatican announced he was sending delegations of scientists with an anti-nuclear war report to the United Nations and to the highest officials of the United States, Russia, Great Britain and France.

Threats to Peace — International terrorism and political crises in Poland, the Middle East and Central America were called major threats to world peace by the Pope in an address Dec. 22 to members of the College of Cardinals, staff members of the Roman Curia and lay employees of the Vatican. He also reviewed salient points of two of the weightiest documents he issued during the year — *Laborem Exercens,* the encyclical letter on work, and *Familiaris Consortio,* an apostolic exhortation on the family.

Christmas Message — The Holy Father's Christmas message "To the City and to the World" was keyed to the loss sustained by people who do not see their own humanity in Christ, who came into the world to reveal human beings to themselves and to make known to them their lofty vocation in and through himself. While calling for respect for the right to religious freedom, the Pontiff also said: "We cry out that Christ may have a place in the whole vast Bethlehem of the modern world; that the right of citizenship may be given to him who came into the time of Caesar Augustus."

After delivering his message, the Pope extended Christmas greetings in 42 languages to people throughout the world.

Martial Law in Poland — The Pope spoke out strongly Dec. 30 against the continuing state of siege in Poland and expressed anxiety about the condition of persons arrested and under detention since the imposition of martial law on Dec. 13. He said: "The fate of those who have been arrested and those who have been condemned to forced 'internment' arouses particular anxiety. . . . It is difficult for me, together with the Polish bishops, to refrain from expressing my trepidation, especially as these are my countrymen; the sons and daughters of the same homeland."

The Pope Also:

• Told an international group of about 70 canon lawyers Dec. 5 that the new Code of Canon Law would be "a pastoral and juridical instrument by which the fruits of the (Second Vatican) Council can acquire greater certainty and solidarity."

• Praised Mother Teresa of Calcutta for

her dedication to the "ideal of total giving" to "persons bearing in body and spirit the inflaming mark of suffering," in a letter read publicly Dec. 10.

• Called on the bishops of Sicily Dec. 11 to take steps to counteract the influence of the Mafia.

Vatican Briefs:

• The Pontifical Council for the Laity released Dec. 3 a 52-page study document entitled "Priests within Associations of the Faithful." Priests, it was said, should serve lay organizations as spiritual guides, "architects of communion, educators in faith, witnesses to God's absoluteness, true apostles of Jesus Christ, ministers of sacramental life." They should not be dominating figures or merely indistinct members of associations.

• "The use of Latin is neither frequent nor widespread" in the liturgy, according to responses of 1,750 bishops to a 1980 survey conducted by the Congregation for the Sacraments and Divine Worship. General disuse of Gregorian Chant was also reported.

• *L'Osservatore Romano* marked its 120th anniversary with a special supplement to its edition of Dec. 13.

Familiaris Consortio

Familiaris Consortio ("Community of the Family"), an apostolic exhortation on the theology of the family, was published Dec. 15. Called the longest document issued by Pope John Paul, the exhortation synthesized and enlarged upon the 43 propositions presented ot him by the 1980 assembly of the Synod of Bishops following their deliberations on the role of the Christian family in the Church and general society.

In addition to reaffirming traditional doctrine, the document cited four fundamental duties of the family, to:

• form a community of persons;
• serve life;
• participate in the development of society;
• share in the life and mission of the Church.

NATIONAL

Conference on Aging — The end of the four-day White House Conference on Aging took place Dec. 3 with passage by nearly 2,300 delegates of a package of more than 600 recommendations for the guidance of government policy for the next 10 years. Msgr. Charles J. Fahey, a delegate from New York, called the package "basically a good product." The major thrust of the recommendations reaffirmed the need for federal involvement in concerns of the elderly.

Nuclear Deterrence — "As long as our nation is sincerely trying to work with other nations to find a better way to maintain peace, the Church considers the strategy of nuclear deterrence morally tolerable; not satisfactory, but tolerable. ... The Church does not require, nor have the popes of the nuclear age or the Second Vatican Council recommended, unilateral disarmament." So stated Cardinal Terence Cooke, bishop for the armed forces, in a Dec. 7 letter addressed to Catholic military chaplains. More than 60 priests, religious and lay persons took exception to the cardinal's position, delcaring that the moral tolerance of which he wrote was based "on the fiction that 'our nation is sincerely trying to work with other nations to find a better way.'"

In a related development, Cardinal Cooke announced plans late in the month to establish a House of Prayer and Study for Peace in 1982 in the military vicariate.

Prayer Meeting Decisions — The U.S. Supreme Court handed down two decisions on the use of public educational facilities as places of meeting for prayer.

• In Widmar v. Vincent, the Court ruled 8 to 1 Dec. 8 that the University of Missouri at Kansas City could not deny student religious groups the use of campus facilities for worship services. The ruling was grounded on the free speech rights of the students, not on their rights to free exercise of religion.

• In Brandon v. Board of Education of Guilderland Schools, the Court declined without comment Dec. 14 to hear an appeal for reversal of lower court decisions denying a group of high school students near Albany, N.Y., the right to meet for prayer on public school property before the beginning of the school day. The ground of the decision was the No Establishment Clause of the First Amendment to the U.S. Constitution.

Prisoners of Conscience — "Deliberate cruelty threatens prisoners of conscience everywhere," according to Amnesty International's 426-page, 1981 report on conditions in 117 nations. The report, published Dec. 9, said that such prisoners "are held by governments in all the geographical regions of the world, in countries with the most diverse political, social and economic systems."

Film Ratings — The Department of Communications, U.S. Catholic Conference, announced changes in its film classification system, with addition of the word "recommended" to the classification of particularly praiseworthy films, and with the substitution of a single new category (O) for films previously labled condemned or morally objectionable in part for all. The changes, to go into effect Jan. 1, 1982, were designed to "clarify and strengthen" classifications and to make them "more useful to parents and others."

Racism in the Church — "The Church is not willing or interested . . . to put time, money and personnel into the black apostolate," declared Father Clarence Waldon of Indianapolis, one of several speakers who addressed a three-day workshop on Racism and the Church early in the month in Detroit. Racism still exists and is operative in the Church in subtle ways, he also said, and added that the Church needs to give blacks the same "opportunities that brought the immigrants out of the ghettos."

Test-Tube Baby Clinic and Birth — Bishop Edward D. Head and a spokesman for the local Catholic Physicians' Guild opposed the establishment by Erie County Medical Center, Buffalo, of an *in-vitro* fertilization clinic.

In a related development, the birth of the first test-tube baby in the U.S., Elizabeth Jordan Carr, was reported Dec. 28, at Norfolk, Va., General Hospital.

Setback for E.R.A. — U.S. District Court Judge Marion Callister ruled Dec. 23 in Boise that Congress acted illegally in extending the deadline for ratification of the Equal Rights Amendment and that states could rescind their ratifying votes. The decisions were handed down in a suit filed by state legislators of Idaho, Arizona and Washington after Congress voted in 1978 to move the deadline for ratification from Mar. 29, 1979, to June 30, 1982. Approval of three states were still needed for ratification of the amendment. Judge Callister's rulings were subsequently appealed to the U.S. Supreme Court.

Priest Murdered, Nun Attacked — Pallottine Father Patrick Ryan, pastor of a parish, was murdered in Texas and Sister of Charity Margaret Franks was sexually and critically injured in New York during the week before Christmas.

In another development, Leron Williams was sentenced in Columbia, Tenn., to die in the electric chair July 27, 1982, for the murder of Father Jay Jackson May 13, 1981.

National Briefs:

• Secretary of the Navy John Lehman rebuffed pleas to change the name of the U.S.S. Corpus Christi, a nuclear attack submarine.

• The first anniversary of the deaths of four U.S. women missionaries in El Salvador was marked with a day of remembrance Dec. 2. The women were Maryknoll Sisters Ita Ford and Maura Clark, Ursuline Sister Dorothy Kazel and lay volunteer Jean Donovan.

• The Reagan administration's belief that charitable organizations and volunteer groups could replace government programs aiding the poor was called "ludicrous" by Father Francis J. Giudice of Providence Dec. 7 in testimony before a committee of Congress.

• The Senate Subcommittee on the Constitution voted Dec. 6 to approve a constitutional amendment on abortion proposed by Sen. Orrin Hatch. (See separate entries.)

• Archbishop Edward A. McCarthy and Msgr. Bryan O. Walsh of Miami were among 17 civic leaders protesting against the "inhumane conditions" in which about 700 Haitians were being detained at the Krome Avenue Detention Center of the Immigration and Naturalization Service.

Leading News Stories of 1981

Editors of 37 Catholic newspapers selected the following as the 10 top news stories of 1981.

1. The attempt on the life of Pope John Paul and his subsequent recovery from wounds.
2. Violence in Central America.
3. The Solidarity-Church struggle for social change in Poland.
4. The attempt on the life of President Reagan, coupled with debate on violence.
5. Budget cutbacks by government and their effects on the poor.
6. Abortion developments, including the Hatch Amendment proposal.
7. Publication of *Laborem Exercens,* the papal encyclical on work.
8. Hunger strikers in Northern Ireland.
9. The assassination of President Anwar el-Sadat of Egypt.
10. The release of U.S. hostages from Iran.

Pope John Paul was voted the leading newsmaker.

INTERNATIONAL

Disabled Persons — They deserve "the practical concern of the world community" because of their numbers, "in excess of 400 million," and in view of their "particular human and social condition," declared Archbishop Giovanni Cheli, Vatican observer at the United Nations. In a statement issued early in the month on activities of the 1981 International Year of Disabled Persons, he said that efforts should be made for the integration, normalization and personalization of the disabled in society.

Delhi Declaration — The Delhi Declaration, issued by religious leaders at the conclusion of the Asian Conference on Religion and Peace in November, called on major powers to close down military bases in the Indian Ocean area, to keep nuclear weapons out of Asia and the Southwest Pacific, and to allocate at least one per cent of their gross national products to development projects in poor countries. The declaration also urged steps against caste and feminist discrimination. Signers of the declaration included Christian, Hindu, Moslem, Buddhist and Jewish leaders.

Missing Persons — Cardinal Raul Primatesta, president of the Argentine Bishops' Conference, asked the government to release information about persons who were missing after being abducted by pro-government paramilitary squads or groups of people claiming to be members of security forces. A U.N. report issued in January, 1981, estimated that 7,000 to 9,000 persons had disappeared in Argentina since the military coup of March, 1976.

Guadalupe Celebration — Five million persons, according to estimates, attended the celebration Dec. 12 in Mexico City of the 450th anniversary of the four apparitions of Mary to Indian convert Juan Diego between Dec. 9 and 12, 1531. Pope John Paul was represented by Cardinal Agostino Casaroli at ceremonies at the Basilica of Our Lady of Guadalupe. In a taped message to the throng of pilgrims, the Holy Father spoke in praise of Mary and her role as Mother of Christ. He also appealed for efforts for justice and peace in Latin America.

Jesuits — Worldwide Jesuit membership declined from 27,027 at the beginning of 1980 to 26,622 at the beginning of 1981, according to the 1982 yearbook of the Society of Jesus. During the year, however, there were increases of 201 Jesuits in India, 76 in Zaire and 54 in Portugal. Despite the loss of 143 members in 1980, the U.S. community remained the largest national group in the world, with 5,618 members at the beginning of 1981.

Human Rights in Nicaragua — The human rights record of the Nicaraguan government had "many deficiencies," declared Archbishop Miguel Obando Bravo in an interview published Dec. 16 in the Managua daily *El Nuevo Diario.* He also said: "The very leaders of the revolution have publicly maintained they are of a Marxist-Leninist orientation," but "you cannot rightfully say that they have fallen into totalitarianism or that the entire Sandinist government is Marxist."

A statement issued by five Christian groups in the country said that the existence of about 1,500 Christian communities showed that Christians had "full liberty to express our faith and the concrete possibilities to build the kingdom of God and his justice."

Causes of Bloodshed — Unjust conditions and political ambitions "have been responsible for the bloodshed that blocks the advent of peace" in El Salvador, said Bishop Arturo Rivera Damas in a pre-Christmas message. "The institutionalized violence under which we lived for so long has erupted in recent years with incredible cruelty amid base passions, selfishness, profit-seeking ambitions, revenge and hate," he added.

Christmas in China — More than 10,000 persons attended Latin Masses celebrated in two churches in Beijing by priests belonging to the Patriotic Association of Chinese Catholics, which was not in union with the Holy See. Protestant services were attended by several thousand persons. The papal midnight Mass, for the first time in 32 years, was broadcast to China by Vatican Radio.

Several weeks earlier, the Italian news agency ANSA reported the arrest Nov. 17 of four priests in Shanghai because of their refusal to join the Patriotic Association.

Canadian Bishops — The vigor of statements by the Canadian Conference of Catholic Bishops on concern for human rights at home and abroad was reported to be one of the more significant news developments of 1981. This was especially true of their support for the rights of native peoples in Canada and of their appeals for respect for human rights in El Salvador.

International Briefs:

• Five bishops in the Philippines condemned the "climate of terror" on Mindanao, in a pastoral letter reported by Vatican Radio Dec. 7.

• Caritas worker Lucio Aguirre was killed by Salvadoran security agents Dec. 7 at La Virtud refugee camp in Honduras.

• Pravda, the Soviet Communist Party newspaper, predicted the "irreversible extinction" of religious belief in the U.S.S.R., but warned of a continuing need for "committed anti-religious propaganda."

• A monument marking the Pope's visit to Hiroshima in February, 1981, was unveiled there Dec. 26.

• The Pope was among those expressing hope that Gen. James Dozier, who was kidnapped by Italian terrorists Dec. 17, would be released unharmed.

• Cardinal Franjo Seper, prefect of the Congregation for the Doctrine of the Faith, died of a heart condition Dec. 30 at Gemelli Polyclinic Hospital, Rome.

Martial Law in Poland

The government, seeking to break the back of the independent Solidarity labor movement, imposed martial law in Poland Dec. 13. The action resulted in the suspension of civil rights, the severing of direct communication between the bishops and the Vatican, and the arrest and detention of hundreds of unionists. Solidarity leader Lech Walesa, one of the first of those seized, was held incommunicado in an undisclosed place.

The Polish bishops issued numerous appeals for the end of what they called Dec. 16 a condition of being "terrorized by military force."

"We kneel before God," said Archbishop Jozef Glemp in an appeal read in all churches Dec. 20, "to implore him that no blood may be shed, since our nation has never known civil wars or fratricide. We implore you, in the name of God, not to raise a hand in hate against one another. Keep calm, do not cause our country to fall into a greater misfortune. Only self-control and the maintenance of calm can save the country and the Church which conducts its mission in the country."

Pope John Paul, along with several appeals, pleaded on Christmas Eve that Poles be permitted ot solve their own problems without outside interference.

JANUARY 1982

VATICAN

Catholic Press Necessary — "The Catholic newspaper is not a superfluous thing but a necessary instrument for evangelization," the Holy Father told a group of Italian bishops Jan. 4. "Today more than ever," he said, "one sees the importance of the formative work of the Catholic press, aimed at enlightening consciences, at dissipating false interpretations, insinuations and manipulations — in respect for the opinions of others and in faithful dialogue, backed by the conviction that each man, redeemed and loved by the Lord, is called to truth."

Concern for Poland — The Pope, in a letter addressed Jan. 4 to President Reagan, praised U.S. humanitarian concern for the people of Poland but took no stand on economic sanctions against the government proposed by the Reagan administration.

In an earlier letter to Gen. Wojciech Jaruzelski, written after the declaration of martial law Dec. 13, 1981, the Pope made "a pressing request and a warm appeal that further Polish blood not be spilled and that, by revoking the state of siege, the questions connected with the renewal of society, which from August of 1980 were being resolved through calm dialogue, might return to the same path, which is difficult but not impossible."

Epiphanies of God — While ordaining nine bishops on the solemnity of the Epiphany, the Pope urged them to "do everything of which you are capable so that the people to whom you are sent will be convinced that they are epiphanies of the living God." He said that persons recognizing themselves as manifestations of the Lord live a new life of fruitfulness in offering their activity as a gift to God.

Freedom of Religion in India — Pope John Paul told Indian Ambassador Narendra Singh Jan. 14 that his nation should ensure the rights of its citizens to freedom of conscience and freedom of religion. "I am confident," he said, "that (India's) praiseworthy traditions of respect for religious belief will ensure the continuation of these guarantees of freedom of conscience and of the right to freely profess, practice and propagate religion, without being discriminated against." Vatican sources said the Pope's remarks had reference to two issues of conflict between the Church and the government, namely, programs of sterilization and contraception, and legislative moves to approve a "patently anti-Christian" anti-conversion bill.

Diplomatic Relations with Britain — The Pope announced the establishment of diplomatic relations with Great Britain Jan. 16, nearly 450 years after they were broken during the reign of King Henry VIII. Archbishop Bruno Heim, apostolic delegate since 1973, was appointed apostolic pro-nuncio and head of mission.

Custodians of Hope — The Pope urged priests and students for the priesthood to become "custodians of hope" and "true teachers" during visits to two Roman colleges Jan. 16 and 17. At the Pontifical Athenaeum Antonianum, he said to Franciscan priests and students: "Like St. Francis, may you also be in today's world custodians of hope. . . . The recovery of certainty is urgent in today's world, furrowed by so many worries that are like a terrorist attack on the hope brought by Christ."

Prayer for Unity — The Week of Prayer for Christian Unity (Jan. 18 to 25) provides reason for joy and hope but also requires the participation of all Christians in the "great cause of Christian unity," declared the Holy Father at a general audience Jan. 20. While calling attention to ongoing interfaith dialogues and contacts, he said: "On the one hand, what we have in common in faith, doctrine and Christian life is clearly emerging; on the other hand, the divergences which still remain — and which dialogues must continue to confront and debate — are seen with greater clarity and are freed from the outlines of confusion which polemics of the past had created."

Chinese Catholics — The Pope, in a letter to bishops throughout the world, asked for prayers for Catholics in China who had undergone "hard sufferings" during the previous 30 years because of their fidelity to the Holy See. With an implicit reference to the separatist Patriotic Association of Chinese Catholics, he also said: "The link with the See of Peter and with its apostolic ministry is an indispensable condition for participating in union with the great Catholic family."

Parish Visits — The Pope's first parochial visit of the year in Rome, and the 47th of his pontificate, was to St. Teresa's Jan. 24. In a homily during Mass there, he said: "It is important that the parish become ever more a center of human and Christian gathering which realizes the full communitarian dimension."

On Jan. 31, he visited another parish of Rome, St. John Bosco, considered the largest in Italy.

Marriage and Annulments — In the sacrament of matrimony, "an indissoluble link unites the spouses, as Christ and the Church are united in one, single love." So stated the Pope Jan. 28 at a meeting with officials of the Sacred Roman Rota, the Church's high court of appeals. He also said, with reference to decrees of nullity, that the existence of a marriage bond "can be placed in doubt" and declared null "only for valid motivations for proven facts."

The Pope Also:

• Baptized 13 children Jan. 10.

• Named four auxiliary bishops Jan. 16 to the troubled leadership of the Church in The Netherlands.

• Thanked officials of the Pontifical Mission for Palestine Jan. 20 for their efforts to aid people in the Middle East.

• Was gratified at the rescue Jan. 28 of U.S. Brig. Gen. James Dozier from the hands of Italian terrorists.

Vatican Briefs:

• It was announced Jan. 18 that the 43rd International Eucharistic Congress would be held in Nairobi, Kenya; the dates of the congress were not reported.

• A document listing 27 questions related to the theme of the 1983 assembly of the Synod of Bishops was released Jan. 28. The document, addressed primarily to bishops throughout the world, dealt with the subject, "Reconciliation and Penance in the Mission of the Church." (See Synod of Bishops.)

Peace Day Message

"The Church supports and encourages all serious efforts for peace" and "wishes her children to join, through their witness and their initiatives, the first rank of those preparing peace and causing it to reign." So stated Pope John Paul in his message for the 1982 World Day of Peace, Jan. 1.

The Holy Father warned against "ideologies that hold up the prospect of a totally and permanently peaceful human society as easily attainable," declaring that "these deceptive hopes lead straight to the false peace of totalitarian regimes."

He also said that "Christians, even as they strive to resist and prevent every form of warfare, have no hesitation in recalling that, in the name of an elementary requirement of justice, people have a right and even a duty to protect their existence and freedom by proportionate means against an unjust aggressor." He added: "This right, which is very real in principle, only underlines the urgency for world society to equip itself with effective means of negotiations" for and in support of peace.

The theme of the 15th annual observance was "Peace, a Gift of God Entrusted to Us."

NATIONAL

Teaching of "Creation Science" Banned — After an historic nine-day trial in Little Rock, Ark., U.S. District Court Judge William Overton declared unconstitutional an Arkansas law that would have required the teaching of "creation science" as well as evolutionary theory in public schools of the state. In a decision handed down Jan. 5, he wrote that the law "was simply and purely an effort to introduce the biblical version of creation into the public school curricula" in violation of the principle of separation of church and state. "The argument that creation from nothing does not involve a supernatural deity has no evidentiary or rational support. Indeed, creation of the world 'out of nothing' is the ultimate religious statement because God is the only actor." One of several religious-leader plaintiffs was Bishop Andrew J. McDonald of Little Rock.

Postal Rate Increase Devastating — Robert Blum, board chairman of the National Society of Fund-Raising Executives, said that the combination of federal funding cuts and heavy increases in postal rates in effect as of Jan. 10 were a "double whammy" which might force the shutdown of 10,000 U.S. nonprofit agencies. The rate increases were "a major blow to the ability of the non-profit and religious press . . . to speak its mind and message," according to Archbishop Thomas C. Kelly, secretary of the U.S. Catholic Conference.

Anglican Clergymen — Bishop Bernard F. Law of Springfield-Cape Girardeau reported that 64 former Anglican clergymen seeking membership in the Catholic Church began in 1981 the initial process for admission to the Catholic priesthood. This development was a consequence of the permission granted by the Vatican in 1980 to the National Conference of Catholic Bishops to develop ways and means of receiving into the Church:

• members of the Anglican Communion who, "while wishing to retain some elements of Anglican tradition, fully accept Roman Catholic doctrine and the authority of the Pope and bishops";

• married Anglican clergymen, on the same terms and with the way open for them to become Roman Catholic priests and to continue in marriage after the validation of holy orders.

Ministry to Homosexuals — Establishment of a team ministry to homosexual men and women in the Archdiocese of Baltimore, with the approval of Archbishop William D. Borders, was announced in the middle of the month. A statement issued at the time said: "Obligations connected with sexual expression, arising as they do from the very meaning of human sexuality, bind all people, whether their orientation be heterosexual or homosexual."

Court Decisions — The U.S. Supreme Court ruled 5 to 4 Jan. 12 that Americans United for the Separation of Church and State had no legal standing to file suit against the constitutionality of the 1976 transfer by the federal government of a former Army hospital and other property to Valley Forge Christian College.

The Court also ruled Jan. 25 that a Louisiana law permitting voluntary prayer sessions in public schools was unconstitutional.

Stockholder Resolutions — Timothy Smith, director of the Interfaith Center on Corporate Responsibility, reported an increase in the number of stockholder resolutions filed by religious groups with corporations involved in the production of nuclear weapons. A typical resolution called on the American Telephone and Telegraph Co. to "study the moral, social, economic and national security implications of continued nuclear weapons production." The interfaith center had a membership of 14 Protestant denominations and more than 180 Catholic bodies, mostly religious institutes.

E.R.A. — With a "stay" order issued Jan. 25, the U.S. Supreme Court delayed the effects of E.R.A.-related rulings handed down the previous Dec. 23 by U.S. District Court Judge Marion Callister in Boise, Idaho. Callister ruled (1) that Congress had acted in an unconstitutional manner by extending for three years the period for ratification of the Equal Rights Amendment, and (2) that states could rescind ratification of the amendment.

New Federalism — President Reagan's State-of-the-Union proposal Jan. 27 for a massive shift of federal programs to the states was greeted with objections by church personnel concerned with the potential effects of such shifts on the poor. Funding shifts, without due safeguards, might not be used as intended for welfare and food stamp purposes, said Matthew Ahmann, staff member of the National Conference of Catholic Charities. Dr. Claire Randall, general secretary of the National Council of Churches, said that federal programs had become necessary after it became clear "that state and local governments lacked either the will or the ability to provide a minimum decent standard of living for all people." She added: "The systems that create poverty cross state lines, so state-by-state answers will not solve nationwide problems."

Tax Withholding in Protest — Archbishop Raymond G. Hunthausen of Seattle, in a pastoral letter published in the *Catholic Northwest Progress,* announced Jan. 28 that he would withhold 50 per cent of his federal income taxes as "a means of protesting our nation's continuing involvement in the race for nuclear arms supremacy."

Solidarity Day — Religious and labor leaders joined confreres at home and abroad Jan. 30 in Solidarity Day appeals for an end to what Cardinal Humberto Medeiros of Boston called the "sad, cold winter of oppression" in Poland. Demonstrations of protest against the imposition of martial law there were staged in most states as well as in Vienna, Tokyo, London, Brussels and several cities of West Germany.

National Briefs:

• Bishop Francis J. Mugavero of Brooklyn called for "increased sensitivity to the difficulties experienced by recent immigrants," in a statement marking the observance Jan. 3 to 9 of Migration Week, sponsored by the Migration and Tourism Committee of the National Conference of Catholic Bishops.

• The first national workshop on the rights of foreign seafarers was held Jan. 11 to 14 in New York under the sponsorship of the Seamen's Church Institute of New York and New Jersey and the Apostleship of the Sea.

March for Life

"Stick with the Life Principles" was the theme of the annual March for Life in Washington on Jan. 22, the ninth anniversary of U.S. Supreme Court decisions which overturned virtually all restrictive state laws on abortion. An estimated 25,000 persons took part in the demonstration in support of efforts to enact a constitutional amendment that would protect the right of the unborn to life. Similar demonstrations were held in a number of cities across the country.

President Reagan became the first Chief Executive to meet with pro-life leaders on the occasion of the march. At the White House, he reaffirmed his personal commitment to their cause but gave no indication concerning which of several proposed pieces of pro-life legislation he preferred.

INTERNATIONAL

Anti-Priest Actions in Czechoslovakia — *Avvenire,* the Milan-based Catholic daily newspaper, reported Jan. 2 that Dominican Father Jaroslav Duka was sentenced shortly before Christmas to 15 months in prison for "infractions of the norms on religious activity." The infractions consisted of the celebration of Mass and conferring of the sacrament of anointing of the sick.

Another source reported a raid in October on a home for elderly priests in Moravec. Also reported was the sentencing of Jesuit Father Frantisek Lizna to 27 months in confinement for damaging state interests abroad by writing about his ministry to his sister.

Apparitions? — Bishops in the region around Medjugorje, Yugoslavia, declined to comment on the nature or authenticity of alleged apparitions of Mary which six young people, aged 10 to 17 years, claimed they had experienced several times since June 24, 1981. The prelates said they could not make any official statement until enough time had passed for serious study of the claims and their consequences.

Task of Cuban Archbishop — Archbishop Marcos G. McGrath of Panama City, commenting on the installation Dec. 27 of Archbishop Jaime Ortega Alamino as head of the Archdiocese of Havana, said he faced a difficult task in the Communist-ruled country "where religion is discarded by the prevailing ideology." While noting some improvements in benefits to the Cuban people under the Castro regime, he said "it is regrettable that on fundamental matters, such as religious rights, there is no greater understanding."

Agreement on Baptism — The Church of Scotland (Presbyterian) and the Catholic Church in Scotland announced official acceptance of each other's administration of the sacrament of baptism. Father John Fitzsimmons, a member of the joint commission on doctrine, called the development "very welcome," declaring: "We feel that ecumenical contact between the two churches has been sealed by this mutual recognition of baptism."

Martial Law to Civil War? — The violation of freedom through the imposition and continuation of martial law could lead to civil war, said the Polish bishops in their first joint pastoral letter after the proclamation of martial law Dec. 13. The letter, approved at a meeting Jan. 19, called for the end of martial law, the "rapid release" of all prisoners, and the cessation of "coercion based on ideologies" and firings motivated by political reasons or union membership. The bishops also backed the re-establishment of free, self-governing labor unions and youth groups.

Persecution in El Salvador — The Salvadoran government was involved in a general persecution of the Church, according to a 273-page report released late in the month by the American Civil Liberties Union and the American Watch Committee. "Large numbers of Catholic religious and lay workers have been killed by the government in what appears to be general persecution of the Church," the report said.

Pope Criticized by Romanians — Patriarch Justin Moisescu and other leaders of the Romanian Orthodox Church, in a telegram to President Nicolae Ceausescu, protested against "attempts (by the Pope) to provoke dissent in the life of the Romanian Orthodox Church, to interfere in its internal questions and to sow discord among the faithful . . . in contrast with the ecumenical spirit constantly promoted by our church toward other cults, including the Romanian Catholic Church." At issue was a Jan. 6 address to Romanian visitors to the Vatican in which the Holy Father pleaded for the government to recognize "the freedom to adhere to a determined faith and to a corresponding confessional community," and the "freedom for the confessional communities to have their own internal hierarchies or ministers freely chosen, according to their institutional norms."

Vise-Like Relations — Bishop Jose Manuel Santos, president of the Chilean Bishops' Conference, was authority for the statement that church-state relations on issues of human rights in 1981 were "like a vise, always tense." In addition to this general remark, he said "there were attempts to expel 11 priests on charges of mixing in politics." The attempts were nullified because of a lack of evidence, reported Bishop Bernardino Pinera, general secretary of the conference.

Hiring Rights — Several Catholic leaders had praise for a new Ontario provincial human rights act guaranteeing the right of religious educational institutions to give preference in hiring to persons in accord with their beliefs. Under the act, which was expected to take effect within six months, educational institutions "primarily engaged in serving the interests of persons identified by their . . . creed" may "employ only, or give preference in employment to, persons similarly identified."

International Briefs:

• West German Catholics contributed nearly $450 million to Catholic assistance agencies in 1981, Vatican Radio reported Jan. 2.

• The Lutheran World Federation reported that the number of Lutheran communicants worldwide increased by 80,000 to 69,728,728 during 1981.

• Mehmet Ali Agca, convicted of the attempted murder of Pope John Paul, ended Jan. 9 a three-week hunger strike, his third, at the Marino Del Trono maximum security prison in Ascoli Piceno, Italy.

• Vatican Radio reported Jan. 14 that bible societies in three African countries had recently published translations of the Bible in local languages.

• Statistics released by the Polish bishops' office in Rome indicated that 688 priests were ordained and 6,714 seminarians were studying for the priesthood at the end of 1981.

Cooperation in Mozambique

The Marxist rulers of Mozambique were seeking the cooperation of the Church in developing a "new situation" for the people, said Bishop Manuel Vieira Pinto in an interview published in Lisbon. He said there had been considerable improvement in relations which had been strained and even bitterly hostile following the take-over of the government by the Front for the Liberation of Mozambique in 1975.

The bishop spoke of the help given by missionaries to public education and development projects, saying it "has increased credibility for the Church and has improved relations with the state."

He also said that "fundamental changes remain for the Church in Mozambique," including "how to form children and adults to be true Christians, and how marriage and general education, now under the exclusive guidance of the state, . . . can be supplemented with the Christian outlook."

FEBRUARY 1982

VATICAN

Protect the Unborn and Elderly — On the day the Church in Italy observed its fourth annual Day for Life, the Holy Father condemned abortion and called for greater attention to the needs of the elderly. "In a society that is sick with selfishness and intimately pervaded by the disquieting turmoil of death," he said Feb. 7, "it is necessary for Christians to maintain their attention to life at a high level. . . . Life is always a gift . . . because it springs from the love of a Father. In every life, even if just conceived, even if weak and suffering, the Christian recognizes the 'yes' that God has revealed to him once and for always. . . . I wish to confirm the very serious obligation to protect, respect, promote, defend life in all its phases, from that of conception to that of old age."

Solidarity a Constructive Force — Pope John Paul called the Solidarity trade union movement a "constructive force" in Poland and declared that its re-establishment was crucial to normalization of the "difficult situation" in the nation. Addressing about 30 international labor leaders Feb. 9, he said: "Along with you, I share the conviction that the re-establishment, in full and total respect, of the rights of workers, and especially their right to a union, already created and legalized, constitutes the only way out of this difficult situation" of martial law.

Progress toward Canonization — The Pope attended ceremonies Feb. 11 at which the Congregation for the Causes of Saints promulgated decrees on a miracle attributed to Spanish Sister Maria Angela Astorch (1592-1665) and on the heroic virtues of five other Servants of God: Queen Clotilde Saveria of Sardinia (1759-1802); Lebanese Sister Rebecca ar-Rayes de Himlaya de Bikfaya (1832-1914); Archbishop Guido Maria Conforti of Parma, founder of the Xaverian Missionary Fathers (1865-1931); Polish Sister Celina Chludzinska (1833-1913); Spanish Jesuit Father Francisco Garate (1857-1929).

Terrorism — Governments that support the "savage and inhuman" methods of terrorists should be condemned, stated the Pope in a message presented Feb. 18 at the meeting of the Congress of the World Christian Democratic Union in Rome. He called political terrorism "a sophisticated return to barbarism and anarchy," and said it is "always a manifestation of hatred, of ideological confusion, with the intent of sowing uncertainty and fear in national and international life."

The Church in Africa — In the first address to a general audience since returning from his second pastoral visit to Africa, the Pope said Feb. 24 that the Church there had entered "a new stage of evangelization." While not ceasing "to be missionary in these lands," he commented, the Church "has now also become African."

Lenten Penance — The Holy Father opened the lenten season with an Ash Wednesday procession between two of Rome's ancient basilicas and with a call for all Catholics to do penance. "Perhaps never does the word of God resound so directly for us" as it does on Ash Wednesday, he said in a homily at Mass Feb. 24 in the Basilica of St. Sabina. "Man is called to reconciliation with God in the death of Christ. . . . Man is called to penitence. 'Remember that you are dust and to dust you will return.' At the same time, hear the words, 'Do penance and believe in the Gospel.' "

Fratricidal War — Speaking of El Salvador Feb. 28 before about 30,000 people in St. Peter's Square, the Pope pleaded for an end to its "fratricidal war which shows no sign of lessening." He also said: "Nearly every day, hundreds of people are killed, and the sorrowful host of widows and orphans grows while a throng of refugees, which already exceeds hundreds of thousands, . . . seeks shelter in the mountains or in nearby nations. The guerrillas leave a trail of mourning in the cities and in the villages, . . . On the other hand, the action of the armed forces . . . is no less hard and severe." He expressed hope that "the people of El Salvador might resolve, without foreign interference, the grave problems that afflict them."

The Pope Also:
• Dedicated a new chapel at Rome's Leonardi da Vinci Airport to Our Lady of Loreto, just before leaving for his second pastoral visit to Africa Feb. 12.
• Began a six-day lenten retreat at the Vatican Feb. 28.

Concordat Concern — An editorial in *L'Osservatore Romano* early in the month expressed concern that a Jan. 23 ruling of Italy's constitutional court amounted to unilateral abrogation of Vatican-Italian pacts in force since 1929. The court ruled that declarations of nullity of marriage issued by church tribunals would no longer have automatic recognition in Italian civil law.

Vatican Briefs:
• Vatican Radio reported that "Jesus Christ, Life of the World," would be the theme of the 1983 Week of Prayer for Christian Unity.

Pastoral Trip to Africa

The Holy Father made his second trip to Africa from Feb. 12 to 19, with stops in Nigeria, Benin, Gabon and Equatorial Guinea. He celebrated eight Masses and delivered more than 30 addresses during the 8,500-mile tour, his 10th outside Italy since becoming Pope.

(See separate entry.)

NATIONAL

Racism — "Jesus Christ belongs to all people," said the bishops of the Santa Fe Province in a pastoral letter which decried racism as a "sinful, scandalous mentality." In "The Southwest: A Confluence of Cultures — A Challenge for Christians," they said: "Perhaps the most pressing demand the confluence of ethnic cultures will place upon us is our attitudes about racism. It has been said that we live in a racist milieu and that racism is a national plague. No one who is a poor, dark-skinned Hispanic needs to be told about the impact of living in a racist society. Nor does a Native American. We must also acknowledge racism's detrimental effect on the racist as well. Racism, like poverty, represents a sinful, scandalous mentality that must be a top priority for our pastoral ministry." The letter was dated Feb. 2.

Natural Death Act — Action was under way in the House of Representatives to disapprove the Natural Death Act passed by the City Council of the District of Columbia in October, 1981. The act provided that anyone over the age of 18 could sign a living will ordering doctors not to use artificial means to prolong life under certain circumstances. Opponents of the act claimed it amounted to "mandated euthanasia."

Ecumenical Dialogue Report — "Eucharistic Celebration: Converging Theology — Divergent Practice," was the title of a 19-page report on the official 1977-to-1981 Roman Catholic-United Methodist dialogue on the structure and doctrine of the Eucharistic celebration. Participants in the dialogue reported varying degrees of agreement, but substantial differences persisted regarding essential points of doctrine.

Asylum Denied Salvadorans — Donald Hohl, associate director of Migration and Refugee Services, U.S. Catholic Conference, expressed concern over the "almost blanket denial" of asylum for Salvadoran refugees brought to light by a United Nations study. According to an internal document of the Office of the U.N. High Commissioner for Refugees obtained by the *Washington Post,* a probe completed in the fall of 1981 disclosed that the U.S. had followed "a systematic practice" of returning Salvadorans regardless of the merits of their claims for asylum. Such a practice, it was reported, was in violation of the U.N. Protocol and Convention on the Treatment of Refugees, which prohibits deporting a refugee to a country where persecution is likely to occur. The U.N. report cited official U.S. statistics showing that asylum had been granted to only one of 6,000 Salvadorans apprehended for entering the country illegally in 1981. Hohl said the "U.S. Catholic Conference has asked the government to permit people to remain, not to turn them back."

Fetuses Found — Five hundred fetuses, some of them weighing up to four pounds, were discovered Feb. 4 in a metal container repossessed from the home of Malvin R. Weisberg, former operator of Medical Analytic Laboratoriees., Inc., of Santa Monica. Between 200 and 400 additional fetuses were found later in the month. The aborted fetuses had apparently been sent from hospitals to the Weisberg laboratories for medical tests.

Abortion Increasing — The Alan Guttmacher Institute reported in the January-February edition of *Family Planning Perspectives* that the number of legal abortions in the U.S. increased from 1.49 million in 1979 to 1.55 million in 1980. The institute is a population research affiliate of the Planned Parenthood Federation, one of the most aggressive organizational promoters of abortion on demand.

World Day of Peace — U.N. delegates from many countries attended a World Day of Peace celebration Feb. 10 at St. Patrick's Cathedral, New York. Cardinal Terence Cooke, military vicar for the U.S., quoted Pope John Paul in a keynote address: "Peace is of a rational and moral nature, the fruit of truth and virtue . . . is directed toward the common good . . . (and is) to be attained in truth, justice and love." He also announced the recent opening in New York of a center for prayer and study for peace, "in order to beg God's help to solve problems that are beyond our mere human powers, to bring an end to the sufferings of war."

Solidarity Peace Fund — Bishop Leroy Matthiesen announced Feb. 13 the establishment of a Solidarity Peace Fund to help workers wanting for reasons of conscience to resign from their jobs at the Pantex nuclear warhead assembly plant in the Diocese of Amarillo. "We who believe that we are stewards of life and creation, not its masters, must use all the religious and moral vision we have to prevent a threat to what God has created, what we could destroy but never re-create," the bishop said at a press conference in Omaha. The initial amount of the fund, donated by the central province of the Oblates of Mary Immaculate, was $10,000.

Hispanic Population Growth — A study conducted by the U.S. bishops' Secretariat for Hispanic Affairs indicated that the Hispanic population of the U.S. was increasing at a faster rate than both the general and Catholic populations. The total population of the nation, as of Apr. 1, 1980, was 226,504,825, an increase of 23,292,899 (11.5 per cent) from 1970. The Catholic population in 1980 was 47,502,152, an increase of 2,650,857 (5.9 per cent) from 1970. The Hispanic population in 1980 was 14,605,883, an increase of 5,037,440 (60.9 per cent) from 1970.

Media Grants — The Department of Communications, U.S. Catholic Conference, approved 32 projects for funding from the national collection of the Catholic Communications Campaign for 1982. The projects, funded with a total of $1,234,568, ranged from mini-TV spots to aid the elderly and handicapped, to a national Sunday magazine section for the Catholic press, TV news projects, training for journalists, aid to the Third World religious press, evangelization efforts and Hispanic TV programming. The largest grants were allocated to NC TV News, a weekly program for satellite transmission ($190,000); "Real to Reel," a weekly national Catholic magazine TV show ($163,400); and *"El Visitante,"* a national Catholic Hispanic magazine program ($142,500).

Policy on Homosexuals — Father Timothy S. Healy, S.J., in testimony before the Superior Court of the District of Columbia, defended Georgetown University's refusal to fund and give official recognition to homosexual rights groups. Doing so, he said, would be tantamount to endorsement and in contradiction to the teaching of the Church. Father Healy testified in a suit brought by two student organizations claiming that Georgetown was in violation of the D.C. Human Rights Act.

National Briefs:
• "By its very existence," the Catholic Church has a major impact on international affairs, declared former Secretary of State Henry Kissinger early in the month at a luncheon in Denver.
• Father Patrick Peyton, at the start of the 41st year of his Family Rosary Crusade, looked forward with confidence to an increase in devotion to Mary.
• "More than 400 religious leaders, including five Catholic bishops, appealed in a letter to Congress and the Reagan administration for an end to military aid to the government of El Salvador, charging that the regime was carrying out a campaign of indiscriminate repression and violation of human rights.
• Christopher Awards were presented Feb. 25 to a variety of persons for books, motion pictures, television productions and special accomplishments. (See separate entry.)

Monstrous Budget Cuts

Father William T. Cunningham told a Senate committee Feb. 25 that federal cuts in nutrition and food stamp programs were having a "monstrous" effect on elderly poor people.

Testifying before the Senate Special Committee on Aging, the director of Focus: Hope in Detroit, said that ensuring enough food for the health and well-being of the elderly poor "is not a matter of compassion. It is a matter of justice and wisdom. To deny adequate food is to break our contract with those who have labored and sacrificed to build the country."

As a society, he added, "we are coming to value only those who are economically productive. This nation proposes to . . . turn its back on the aged, to bankrupt the future and bury the past."

INTERNATIONAL

Protection for Child before Birth — Family Court Judge William Bradley of the Kenora, Ontario, Judicial District ruled that a child deserves protection before birth from such physical injury as fetal alcoholic syndrome. The decision, according to Don McPhee, secretary-treasurer of the Coalition for Life, could lead to far stricter application of abortion laws in Canada since, "if the fetus has a right to protection from abuse, that would include (protection from) abortion since it's the worst abuse. . . . The very fact of this ruling indicates the court's understanding of the humanness of the unborn child."

Absenteeism — Absenteeism from work without good reason is a moral evil that harms the dignity of the worker and, in the case of public employees, damages the entire community. So stated Franciscan Father Gino Concetti in an article published early in the month in *L'Osservatore Romano*. The article said that lack of commitment to one's job, incompetence, disloyalty and absenteeism insult the employer and "offend the worker's dignity as a person, frustrate and reduce his working capacity. . . . They also offend the dignity of his brothers, to whose promotion the fruits of his work are destined."

Hope for True Justice — The trial of five former Salvadoran National Guardsmen accused of the December, 1980, murders of four American churchwomen should be aimed at "true justice" and not at pleasing the United States to gain more military aid for El Salvador, declared Bishop Arturo Rivera Damas Feb. 14. "I hope this is not simply a gesture to gain publicity and promote further U.S. aid but, rather, a sign that justice is beginning to be applied impartially," said the apostolic administrator of the Archdiocese of San Salvador. He made the comment a day after a judge formally ruled that there was sufficient evidence to hold the five on suspicion of "aggravated homicide" in the deaths of Maryknoll Sisters Ita Ford and Maura Clark, Ursuline Sister Dorothy Kazel and lay missionary Jean Donovan.

Protest against College Closings — Catholics in Northern Ireland collected 295,000 signatures to a petition against a 1980 plan of the British government to close Ulster's only two Catholic teacher training colleges and to merge their programs with that of a state teacher training college. The bishops said the plan would jeopardize all Catholic education in Northern Ireland.

Cardinal Slipyi, 90 — In a pastoral letter marking his 90th birthday, Ukrainian Cardinal Josyf Slipyi praised Catholics in the Ukraine for their "courageous resistance to godless coercion" under Soviet rule since 1946. "Your suffering and persecutions," he said, "have aroused even the dormant conscience of the whole world, and this has led us to ponder upon human dignity and rights . . . Among these rights, the most important is the universal human right to profess belief in God and the right to freedom of religious convictions." The birthday of the cardinal, in exile since his release in 1963 from prison in the U.S.S.R., was the occasion for a six-day celebration by more than 500 Ukrainian-Rite Catholics in Rome.

Charismatics Strong — A late 1981 report issued during the month by the Rome office of the International Catholic Charismatic Renewal indicated continuing worldwide growth of the movement and said that the largest concentration of charismatics was in South America. There, "every nation has prayer groups, with some countries numbering their groups in the thousands," according to Father Tom Forrest, C.SS.R., author of the report.

Evangelization — "We can't evangelize individuals without evangelizing their environment," said Filipino Bishop Julio Labayen during a visit to Toronto. "What good does it do to put beautiful fish in an aquarium if you do not keep the water clean?" he said while commenting on why many bishops in the Philippines were engaging in social action projects and developing a "Church of the Poor." How is it possible, he questioned, to bring the "good news of the Gospel" to where social and economic structures promote "a world view that singles out the powerful and the wealthy as a privileged class, a world view that is shot through with materialism and profit for profit's sake?"

Persecution in Ethiopia — Coptic Archbishop Abba Matthias, at a news conference Feb. 26 in Houston, accused Ethiopia's military government of persecuting churches. The government, he said, was "planning what is officially called a 'War on the Cross.' . . . To a people clinging to our faith as our sole surviving hope, this is the bitterest blow. . . . We men of faith in Ethiopia — Orthodox, Catholic, Protestant or Moslem — are being wiped out simply because we wish to pray."

Martial Law, Criticism, Aid — The bishops of Poland called for a quick end to martial law in effect since Dec. 13, 1981, amnesty for political detainees and restoration of the Solidarity labor union, in a letter read Feb. 28 in churches throughout the country. The state-ment, drafted at a two-day meeting of the Polish Bishops' Conference, took on particular significance because it represented the hierarchy's first public commentary since its representatives met with Pope John Paul early in the month.

In other developments:

• Two criticisms aired Feb. 17 and 18 by Warsaw Radio were leveled against priests, accused of fomenting tension between the people and the government, and the Church, for publicly opposing the detention of Solidarity leaders.

• An unnamed priest from Kozalin Province was placed on trial for allegedly slandering the state and Gen. Wojciech Jaruzelski.

International Briefs:

• The U.N. Human Rights Commission reported an increase in the number of persons missing after abduction or arrest by government security forces. The report covered the cases of 2,100 persons missing in 22 countries.

• About 100 Jesuit officials gathered Feb. 23 at Grottaferrata near Rome for an extended meeting with Father Paolo Dezza, Pope John Paul's delegate to the Society of Jesus. (See separate entry.)

• The bishops of Portugal condemned as "iniquitous" a proposal by the Communist Party to legalize abortion.

• Amnesty International reported that more than 4,000 persons had been executed in Iran since the 1979 revolution and installation of an Islamic government.

• "True Freedom and Development in the Caribbean: Christian Perspective," was the title of a statement issued jointly by 16 bishops of the Antilles, in criticism of Communism and the evils of capitalism.

Brother Killed in Guatemala

Brother James Miller, 37, a member of the Winona, Wis., Province of the Christian Brothers, was shot to death by masked men in the afternoon of Feb. 13 while repairing a window at the Indian Center in Huehuetenango, Guatemala. It was thought his unidentified assailants were members of a right-wing death squad, and that he was murdered because of his identification and work with the poor as a teacher and director of a vocational farm project. Masses of Christian Burial were celebrated at the Indian Center Feb. 14 and at the Cathedral of St. Paul, Minn., Feb. 16. He was buried at Stevens Point, Wis.

Brother James was the third Catholic missionary from the U.S. to meet violent death in Guatemala since 1976. Maryknoll Father William Woods died in a plane crash caused by apparent sabotage. Father Stanley Rother of Oklahoma City was murdered by hooded men in July, 1981, in his rectory at Santiago Atitlan.

MARCH 1982

VATICAN

Relations with Jews — Although Catholic-Jewish relations have sometimes been marked by "misunderstandings, errors and even insults," they must now go forward "with understanding, in peace and in mutual esteem," declared the Pope Mar. 6 at a meeting with 40 churchmen and lay persons attending a five-day meeting sponsored by the Vatican Commission for Catholic-Jewish Relations. He said: "The terrible persecutions suffered by the Jews at various periods in history have opened eyes and disturbed many hearts. Because of this, Christians are on the right path of justice and fraternity when they seek, with respect and perseverance, to find themselves again with their Semitic brothers and sisters gathered around the common heritage."

Another Plea for End to Violence — "Ideas are not . . . imposed or made victorious with machine guns." So stated the Pope Mar. 7 before a gathering of 30,000 visitors in St. Peter's Square, as he echoed appeals of the bishops of Guatemala for an end to the "horrendous nightmare of death and destruction" afflicting their nation.

Visit to Assisi — The Holy Father paid a visit to Assisi Mar. 12 in what he called "an act of pilgrimage and communion" with the Italian Church's patron, St. Francis. While there, he delivered five addresses and paid tribute to St. Francis in one of many commemorations of the year-long celebration of the 800th anniversary of the saint's birth. He called on Franciscan priests, brothers and nuns to follow their patron's example of service "with courage, in total detachment from things of the world, as bearers of peace and announcers of the coming of the Kingdom." He told bishops they should be "opposed to traditionalism and immobilism," and that they were called to participate actively "in rebuilding the nation's civil texture on the basis of the ethical values of Christian humanism."

Workers' Rights — On his 25th visit within Italy since becoming Pope, the Holy Father made a 12-hour trip on the feast of St. Joseph, Mar. 19, to the Communist strongholds of Rossignano and Leghorn; en route, he stopped for prayer at the Montenero Marian shrine. In an address at a chemical plant in Rosignano, he supported the rights of workers to free association, a just salary and freedom from manipulation in an automated age.

Prayer for Chinese Catholics — The Pope, during a Mass broadcast directly to China Mar. 21, prayed that Catholics there might be able to "live their faith, remaining in the Catholic unity of Christ's holy Church." On the day before the Mass, he was the target of a bitter diatribe published by the New China News Agency, which expressed "indignation" at the claim that Catholics were being persecuted. Repression, as a matter of fact, was in force against Catholics not belonging to the dissident Patriotic Association of Chinese Catholics.

Praise for Cardinal Felici — Three days after the death Mar. 22 of Cardinal Pericle Felici, the Pope expressed "a debt of personal gratitude" to the prelate during a Mass concelebrated with 26 cardinals in St. Peter's Basilica. The 70-year-old cardinal had been prefect of the Apostolic Signatura and president of the Pontifical Commission for the Revision of the Code of Canon Law.

Role of the Holy Spirit — "Our Church is the Church of the Holy Spirit," the Pope told some 350 participants in the International Theological Congress on Pneumatology (study of the Holy Spirit). Addressing the ecumenical gathering Mar. 26, he said: "Faith in the Holy Spirit is the heart of the Christian faith. It is the Holy Spirit who is the heart of the sanctification of the disciples of Christ." The meeting marked the 1,600th anniversary of the First Council of Constantinople and the 1,550th anniversary of the Council of Ephesus, both of which contributed to development of the Church's understanding of the role of the Holy Spirit.

With the Handicapped — The Pope met Mar. 28 with 240 handicapped and incurable residents and out-patients of the Don Guanella Institute in Rome. He encouraged all of them to transform their "passion" of infirmity and trial into an act of redeeming love.

Celibacy — Celibacy as a supernatural gift and commitment was praised by the Pope at two general audiences during the month. Addressing 40,000 people in St. Peter's Square Mar. 31, he said: "Christ himself, by his teaching and example, showed us the value of continence embraced for the sake of the Kingdom of Heaven. He presented continence as something that is not only possible but particularly important."

The Pope Also:
• Made his 52nd visit to a parish of Rome, Most Holy Cross, Mar. 14.
• Voiced support Mar. 17 for the recent call of the Polish bishops for participation by Solidarity representatives in talks with the government to achieve national accord in Poland.
• Paid tribute to Archbishop Oscar Romero of San Salvador Mar. 21, three days before the second anniversary of his murder in El Salvador.
• Praised the Knights of Columbus for "important contributions to the Church's mission of proclaiming the gospel," in a message commemorting their 100th anniversary.
• Urged more than 8,000 university stu-

dents Mar. 30 to "learn to measure the problems of the world . . . by the yardstick of the cross and the resurrection."

Vatican Briefs:

• Plans were announced for the construction of an underground shelter, a 6,500-square-foot room with two and one-half miles of shelf space, designed to protect documents and manuscripts of the Vatican Library from nuclear attack, natural disasters and atmospheric pollution. It was also reported that the $1.5 million project would be paid for by an interest-free loan from the bishops of West Germany.

• A 15-member council of cardinals, meeting Mar. 16 to 18, received a report that the 1981 Vatican budget of $25.4 million had been balanced by increased contributions from Catholics throughout the world. The projected budget for 1982 amounted to $30 million.

Restrictions in Czechoslovakia

Continuing difficulties of the Church in Czechoslovakia were discussed by the Pope at a meeting Mar. 13 with Cardinal Frantisek Tomasek and four other bishops. Matters of particular concern were:

• the lack of bishops for more than half of the dioceses in the country, because of government policy;

• government restrictions on the number of priests and the scope of their activities, as well as on the number of students for the priesthood;

• government control of two seminaries and intimidation of students;

• parishes without priests.

The Pope said of parishes: "Many, a great many, parishes have for a long time already been without pastors, and everything leads us to fear, unfortunately, that their number will grow ever more in the future."

NATIONAL

Hatch Amendment to Full Senate — The Senate Judiciary Committee endorsed the Hatch Amendment Mar. 10, voting 10 to 7 to send the measure to the full Senate. The amendment would remove the right to abortion from the Constitution and would allow Congress and the states to pass restrictive legislation on abortion. Father Daniel Hoye, general secretary of the U.S. Catholic Conference, said the committee's action marked "the first time a constitutional amendment to protect unborn human life has reached this stage in the Congressional process." How far it might go toward eventual adoption, was open to serious question.

No Military Aid for El Salvador — Father J. Bryan Hehir, in testimony before the Senate Foreign Relations Committee Mar. 11, repeated an earlier appeal of the U.S. Catholic Conference against the Reagan administra-

tion's request for military aid to El Salvador. Instead, he urged economic assistance and stronger political efforts toward the solution of problems in the tortured nation.

In Vitro Fertilization Opposed — Medical and pro-life spokesmen voiced opposition during the month to a bill that would permit _in vitro_ fertilization programs in Massachusetts. Dr. Joseph R. Stanton, a fellow of the American College of Physicians, noted that the American College of Obstetricians and Gynecologists had said that technical and ethical issues of such fertilization remained unresolved. He also said that legalization of the procedure would lead to more induced abortions. Charles Dean, president of the Tidewater Chapter of the Virginia Society for Human Life, said "it would be a tragedy if that protection (of Massachusetts law against the procedure) were stripped away in order to accommodate the research interests of a small body of scientists."

Immigration Bill — A bipartisan immigration bill introduced in Congress Mar. 17 drew generally favorable comment from Catholic quarters. It was introduced in the Senate by Alan K. Simpson, Republican of Wyoming, and in the House by Representative Romano L. Mazzoli, Democrat of Kentucky.

Criminal Justice — In testimony prepared for a House subcommittee considering re-institution of capital punishment at the federal level, Msgr. Francis J. Lally said Mar. 17 that the U.S. Catholic Conference believed that, "under the conditions of contemporary American society, the legitimate purposes of punishment (reform, deterrence and retribution) do not justify the imposition of the death penalty." He called for a "comprehensive approach" to problems of violence, including elimination of social inequities, effective rehabilitation programs, greater assistance to victims of violent crime, and gun control.

Reagan Award Criticized — The National Conference of Christians and Jews presented its Charles Evans Hughes Gold Medal Mar. 23 to President Reagan "for courageous leadership in governmental, civic and humanitarian affairs." The decision of conference officials to make the presentation was hard to understand, according to some staff members and others, in view of the effects of the President's budget cuts on the poor and of his defense policies on international relations.

Sisters for Social Justice — Findings from a random sample of 3,780 sisters in 20 congregations in the U.S. indicated strong concern for social justice. Sixty-two per cent of the respondents said it should be the primary focus of the Church; 33 per cent considered themselves engaged in work for social change; 53 per cent thought the Church should be engaged in work directly alleviating the distress of the poor; 70 per cent felt the Church should cooperate with others in such action. The survey, designed by Notre Dame Sister Mary Augusta Neal, was conducted under the sponsorship of the National Assembly of Women Religious.

Knights of Columbus Centenary — The main event of the 100th anniversary celebration of the Knights of Columbus was a Mass celebrated Mar. 29 in St. Mary's Church, New Haven, Conn., where the fraternal society was founded by Father Michael J. McGivney. Resolutions honoring the Knights for "a century of dedication to the ideals of charity, unity, fraternity and patriotism" were introduced in the House of Representatives in February and in the Senate Mar. 17.

Congressional Chaplain — By a vote of 388 to 0 Mar. 30, the House of Representatives affirmed its right to have a chaplain to open its sessions with prayer and to perform pastoral duties, and to pay him a salary (of $52,000 under existing conditions). The practice of having a chaplain had been attacked in a law suit filed by atheist Madalyn Murray O'Hair, who charged that the use of tax funds to pay chaplains was a violation of the public's right to "freedom from religion."

Churches Can't Do It All — "The stark reality is that the resources of the churches and synagogues or of the entire private sector are simply not sufficient to replace the federal human-needs programs," slashed by the Reagan budget. So declared a group of Catholic, Protestant and Jewish officials in a statement released Mar. 31. "Government must fulfill its responsibility to ensure that the basic needs of all citizens are met," they said. "The charity of the religious community can only ease the burden of last year's budget cuts on the poor; it cannot resolve it."

National Briefs:
• Archbishop Peter Gerety of Newark announced Mar. 10 that he had given permission to Father James Pindar to work as an aide to Gov. Thomas Kean of New Jersey.
• Sisters of Social Service of Los Angeles opened a legal aid center for Salvadoran refugees in the Los Angeles area, to seek their release from detention by the Immigration and Naturalization Service.
• The U.S. Court of Appeals for the Seventh Circuit ruled Mar. 25 against the Archdiocese of Chicago by reversing the decision of a lower court which had dismissed a $1.5 million copyright infringement suit brought by F.E.L. Publications of Los Angeles.
• James C. O'Neill, former chief of the Rome bureau of NC News Service, was named representative of the International Catholic Union of the Press at the United Nations.
• Honored: Cardinal John F. Dearden, first U.S. bishop to receive the Laetare Medal of the University of Notre Dame, Mar. 21;

James V. Hitchcock, author and professor of history at St. Louis University, first recipient of the Cardinal Newman Lay Award of Cardinal Newman College, Mar. 26.

Offensive against Nuclear Arms

A springtime peace offensive against the nuclear arms race picked up momentum during the month. It had the support of:
• about 150 members of Congress who sponsored a resolution calling on superpowers to "pursue a complete halt to the nuclear weapons race";
• more than 80 organizations, from church groups to city councils;
• nearly 200 town meetings in three New England states;
• legislatures in Connecticut, Massachusetts and Oregon;
• 20 religious denominations;
• more than 130 Catholic bishops.
(See separate article.)

INTERNATIONAL

Cathedral Violated — Cardinal Emmanuel K. Nsubuga of Kampala accused members of the Ugandan army of inhuman behavior, charging that soldiers broke into the Kampala cathedral during Ash Wednesday ceremonies Feb. 24 and forced more than 1,500 worshippers into the street at gunpoint. "I hereby protest in the strongest terms against the godless and sacrilegious act of some members of the Ugandan army in violating my cathedral and using military force in expelling the congregation," he said in a statement issued Mar. 1.

Italian Priest and Parish Statistics — A report presented at a Mar. 1 to 3 conference in Rome indicated:
• 20.6 per cent of the Italian population belonged to 140 parishes with memberships of more than 20,000 people;
• nearly 10,000 of the country's 28,618 parishes had less than 500 members and often had to share priests for pastoral services;
• the number of diocesan priests declined from 40,431 in 1976 to 40,097 in 1981;
• 25.5 per cent of the priests were between 50 and 60 years of age, and 23.9 per cent were between the ages of 60 and 70.

Jesuits End Meeting — Nearly 100 Jesuit superiors from many countries ended a special assembly Mar. 3 after meeting with the Pope Feb. 27 at the Vatican and conferring with his personal representative about the state of the order. (See separate entry.)

Basque Appeal — Four Basque bishops, in a lenten pastoral letter, repeated a call for peace in the violence-prone region, saying that "the passion of the true Christian believer" demands respect for the human rights of others. In January, against the background of ETA terrorism, they said: "The life, liberty and safety of the human being cannot be manipulated by political and social interests. . . . We reaffirm our stand for peaceful means and denounce the contradiction of violence and the Christian conscience."

Halt the Arms Race — In a brief presented to Parliament's External Affairs Standing Committee, the Canadian Conference of Catholic Bishops called for the dismantling of the nation's military production system and for the exertion of pressure internationally for an end to the nuclear arms race. The brief said that over the previous 25 years the Catholic Church had emphasized "that the arms race is a scandal to humanity; that militarism is a cause of injustice; that injustice is a cause of war; that the true road to peace lies in integral development and liberation of peoples."

Birth Control in India and China — Vigorous birth control programs were continuing in operation in India and China, according to reports from New Delhi and Peking. In India, the government was providing contraceptive drugs and devices free of charge, along with incentives for the sterilization of women ($22) and men ($15). In China, couples living in cities were ordered ot have no more than one child, and additional steps were urged to halt what the New China News Agency called "the current tendency of rising population growth rate."

Madrid Talks Recessed — After 16 months of futile effort to broaden provisions on human freedoms, economic exchanges and the peaceful resolution of international disputes, representatives of 35 participating nations agreed Mar. 8 to recess until the fall the Madrid Conference on European Security and Human Rights. The purpose of the conference, which was frustrated by differences among Communist, Western and neutral nations, was to review compliance with accords agreed to at Helsinki in 1975. Vatican City was a signer of the accords.

Lack of Freedom in the Philippines — Vatican Radio reported Mar. 9 that Cardinal Jaime Sin of Manila criticized the government of President Ferdinand Marcos for viewing "society as a single, homogeneous structure in which there is space for just one ideology and just one power." In an address at Santo Tomas University, the cardinal also took exception to the regime's tendency to "politicize all social relations and, through its own unlimited control, to destroy all that is living, flexible and reconcilable in human life."

Abandon the IRA — Father Denis Faul, chaplain at the Maze Prison near Belfast, called on Catholics to abandon the outlawed terrorist Irish Republican Army. He did so at the funeral of IRA member Seamus Morgan who was killed by his colleagues for allegedly betraying them to the police. Father Faul angered some IRA members in 1981 by being instrumental in ending hunger strikes of IRA partisans seeking the status of political prisoners. Ten men starved themselves to death before the end of the strikes.

Civil Marriage in Greece — The Greek Parliament gave final approval during the month to legislation recognizing the legality of civil marriage ceremonies for the first time ever in the predominantly Orthodox nation. The new law gave citizens three options for marriage: a civil ceremony, an Orthodox Church ceremony or a religious ceremony performed in a Roman Catholic or other church. Until passage of the new measure, the only marriages recognized as valid in Greek law were those contracted with Orthodox ceremonies.

Doubts about Unity Plan — Cardinal George Basil Hume of Westminster praised the notion of interchurch covenants Mar. 24 but said he had "considerable hesitation" about a plan for four English churches to enter into a covenant aimed at church union. He specifically questioned the manner in which the Church of England (Anglican), the Methodist Church, the Moravian Church and the United Reform Church could work out problems connected with mutual recognition of their ministries and sacraments, and with future ordinations with use of a common ordinal.

International Briefs:

• A December edition of the underground *Chronicle of the Catholic Church in Lithuania,* delayed en route, reported that the Soviet KGB was responsible for the death in November of Father Bronius Laurinavicius, "an active defender of human rights."

• Bishop Jean Vilnet, president of the French Bishops' Conference, criticized government funding of abortions, saying that regulations announced Mar. 8 made "abortion a medical act like any other, trivializing it."

• Vatican Radio reported Mar. 24 that 681 Spanish diocesan priests were in missionary assignments in North and South America.

Ecumenical Dialogue Report

The Anglican-Roman Catholic International Commission of theologians officially released Mar. 29 a Final Report entitled "Authority in the Church II." The product of 12 years of high-level dialogue, the report included — along with the commission's previously published statements on the Eucharist, ministry and ordination, and authority in the Church — a new statement on church authority dealing with problems associated with the teaching and governing authority of the Pope.

Cardinal Joseph Ratzinger, prefect of the Congregation for the Doctrine of the Faith, called the report "a significant step toward reconciliation" between the two churches, but declared that substantial agreement on important doctrinal matters was still lacking.

APRIL 1982

VATICAN

Diplomatic Relations with Great Britain — Pope John Paul received the credentials Apr. 1 of Sir Mark Heath, Great Britain's first ambassador to the Vatican since King Henry VIII broke relations with Rome in 1534. At the same time, the papal representative to the Catholic Church in Great Britain, Apostolic Delegate Archbishop Bruno Heim, became a diplomatic officer, pro-nuncio or ambassador, to the country.

Moral Values, Sacrament of Penance — There seems to be "an idolatry which attaches itself today to money, to power, to sex," and which works "to the detriment of the values of the person and of truth, of interpersonal relationships and of communication," declared the Pope Apr. 1 at a meeting with a group of 11 French bishops. He also alluded to "a certain crisis with regard to the sacrament of penance," expressing concern about neglect of private confession and irregularities in the administration of general absolution.

New Global Economic Order — Pope John Paul called for the establishment of a new international economic order at the start Apr. 3 of a three-day symposium on social teaching embodied in papal encyclicals from *Rerum Novarum* (1891) to *Laborem Exercens* (1981). "Ever more frequently," the Pope said, "one hopes for a new international economic order which, overcoming the insufficient and inadequate economic models of the past, may assure humanity of a just participation in the goods of creation, with particular sensitivity to people in developing countries."

Mideast Appeal — The Pope opened Holy Week Apr. 4 with a strong and direct appeal to Israelis and Arabs to seek reconciliation "in the land of Jesus." He also defended the "legitimate aspirations" of West Bank Arabs in an address before 100,000 people in St. Peter's Square.

Understanding through Christ — The Pope, declaring that the "true content and value of every authentic human need" can be understood in and through Christ, urged 5,000 students Apr. 6 not to become cynical in their search for a "fuller and truer life." He did so in an address to participants in the 1982 International Congress of University Students.

Holy Week Ceremonies — The Pope took part in a full round of Holy Week ceremonies, beginning with the traditional Palm Sunday procession commemorating the entrance of Jesus into Jerusalem.

• Holy Thursday: He concelebrated the Mass of Chrism with 2,000 priests, whom he led in a renewal of their ordination vows. In the early evening, he celebrated the Mass of the Last Supper in the Basilica of St. John Lateran.

• Good Friday: He heard confession for an hour and a half, took part in the solemn liturgy of the day in St. Peter's Basilica, and joined 50,000 persons as their crossbearer during Stations of the Cross at the Colosseum in the evening.

• Easter Vigil: He baptized 26 persons during ceremonies of the vigil.

• Easter Sunday: He celebrated Mass on the steps of St. Peter's Basilica and at noon delivered his Easter message, offered greetings in 43 languages and imparted his blessing "To the City and the World" before a throng of 300,000 persons in St. Peter's Square.

Visit to Bologna — Respect for human dignity and sharing of wealth were among the subjects of addresses by the Pope during a 12-stop visit to Bologna Apr. 18. He told the mayor and other politicians of the showcase of Eurocommunism that social and political activity should be guided by "the positive interpretation of the ethical and religious dignity of man." At a Mass attended by 100,000 people in the city's largest square, he urged well-off societies to help those that are poor.

Falkland Islands in Dispute — Pope John Paul appealed for the sixth time Apr. 25 for peaceful resolution of the British-Argentine dispute over sovereignty of the Falkland (Malvinas) Islands. Addressing 20,000 people in St. Peter's Square, he said: "I call on you and all Catholics of the world, especially those living in the two countries involved, to join in my prayer that the Lord may inspire in the responsible leaders the decisiveness and courage to seek, in this perhaps decisive hour, the routes to agreement, with wisdom and generosity, at the service of the irreplaceable good of the peace of their peoples and for the tranquility of the American continent."

The Pope Also:

• Was represented by Cardinal Opilio Rossi at the National Eucharistic Congress in Panama Apr. 11 to 18.

• Received $38,500 from Brazilian Archbishop Helder Pessoa Camara Apr. 20 for the support of charities in Poland.

• Extended his condolences to Catholics of the Archdiocese of Chicago on the death Apr. 25 of Cardinal John Cody.

• Made his 54th visit to a parish in Rome, that of Sts. Marcellino and Pietro, Apr. 25.

• Praised efforts of South African bishops for "a just and peaceful solution to the problems of Namibia," the scene of continuing conflict between South African forces and guerrillas of the South West African People's Organization.

• Told 6,000 priests associated with the Focolare movement of the importance of devotion to Mary in their work, Apr. 30.

Pastoral Privileges for Travelers — The Pontifical Commission for Migration and

Tourism, in a decree issued Apr. 15, announced an expansion of privileges for travelers and priests engaged in their service. The major privileges concerned the celebration of Mass and the hearing of confessions.

Vatican Briefs:

• An editorial in the Apr. 22 edition of *L'Osservatore Romano* criticized Israeli bombings of southern Lebanon and expressed hope that "a sense of responsibility" would prevail in the region. At least 24 people were killed and another 500 wounded in air attacks Apr. 21.

• Cardinal Roger Etchegaray of Marseilles announced Apr. 24 his resignation as prelate of the Mission of France, an association of worker priests.

• Papal Nuncio Archbishop Angelo Rotta, with the knowledge and approval of the Vatican, issued more than 13,000 protective passes for Jews threatened with genocide in Hungary during World War II, according to Harvey Rosenfeld, author of *Raoul Wallenberg: Swedish Angel of Rescue.*

Easter Message

The Holy Father pleaded for "all victims of injustice" as he observed in his Easter message that the joy of the paschal mystery was "disturbed by situations of tension" in parts of the world.

Addressing 300,000 persons Apr. 11 in St. Peter's Square, he cited the suffering of "all the victims of injustice, of human cruelty and of violence, of exploitation and selfishness . . . (and of) all the millions and millions . . . threatened by the scourge of famine, which could be removed or diminished if humanity knew how to renounce even only a part of the resources which it foolishly consumes in armaments."

The Pope also said: "The joy of Easter is disturbed by situations of tension and of conflict . . . First of all, the consuming war . . . between Iraq and Iran has already brought much suffering to the people of the two countries. Recently, grave tension has developed between . . . Argentina and Great Britain, involving the loss of human lives and the threat of armed conflict and fearful repercussions in international relations. I express the fervent hope and the particularly pressing appeal to the parties involved to seek diligently . . . ways of peaceful and honorable settlement of the dispute while there is still time to prevent a struggle involving bloodshed."

The appeals for peaceful settlement of both disputes fell on deaf ears.

NATIONAL

Parental Consent and Contraceptives — "Contraceptives should not be provided to teen-agers as a matter of government policy," and "abortion and sterilization should be absolutely excluded from any government pro-

gram." So stated Father Daniel F. Hoye, general secretary of the U.S. Catholic Conference, Apr. 12 in comments related to a proposal by the Department of Health and Human Services that would require federally funded family planning agencies to notify parents within 10 working days that they had provided contraceptive drugs or devices to their children under the age of 18. In the absence of parental notification, Father Hoye said, "teen-agers are completely at the mercy of family planning operatives whose ideology of social engineering and population control blinds them to what is really in the best interests of the teen-agers themselves."

Ruling against Nuns — Rockingham County Superior Court Judge Joseph Nadeau ruled Apr. 13 against four Sisters of Mercy suing Bishop Odore Gendron over their dismissal from positions at Sacred Heart School in Our Lady of the Miraculous Medal Parish, Hampton, N.H. The judge said the court lacked jurisdiction to overrule the decision of the bishop when the diocese did not renew their contracts. The diocese contended that the sisters were not "present" to the parish community, ignored the school board, were cliquish, did not communicate with the parish staff, treated disdainfully legitimate questions raised by the parish or the school board, and harbored ill feelings. The breach-of-contract suit, the first of its kind ever brought by nuns against a bishop in the U.S., was filed Mar. 2 by Sisters Honora Reardon, Mary Rita Furlong, Catherine and Justine Colliton.

Treatment Withheld, Infant Dies — Right-to-life advocates and proponents of rights for the handicapped expressed dismay at the death Apr. 15 of a six-day-old baby with Down's Syndrome whose parents refused intravenous feeding for him as well as surgery for the correction of a defect which prevented him from being fed in a normal manner. The parents' decision was upheld by the Indiana Supreme Court in an Apr. 14 ruling, that they could not be forced to feed the child or have surgery performed on him. The infant was baptized three days before he died.

Encyclical Is Relevant but Disregarded — Pope John Paul's encyclical letter "On Human Work" *(Laborem Exercens)* is "very relevant" to conditions in the U.S. because of adverse public attitudes toward labor unions and problems confronting workers and unions, declared Msgr. George G. Higgins Apr. 22 in an address at Bellarmine College in Louisville. He added, however, that the encyclical had not received adequate attention in this country, where only about 25 per cent of the work force is unionized.

Religious Instruction — A study conducted by Andrew Thompson under the direction of Father Eugene Hemrick, director of research for the U.S. Catholic Conference, indicated that 56.45 per cent of Catholic boys and girls of elementary and secondary school age received formal religious instruction in 1980, in Catholic schools or in parish catechetical programs.

Arms Freeze — Auxiliary Bishop Joseph Francis of Newark announced at a press conference Apr. 25 in Washington that 133 U.S. bishops were on record in support of a bilateral, U.S.-U.S.S.R. freeze on nuclear weapons.

Earlier in the month:

• The U.S.-Europeace Tour, a two-week visit to 52 U.S. cities by 10 European peace advocates, ended Apr. 6.

• Nuclear disarmament and the quest for world peace were subjects of numerous homilies and statements by bishops and other people of the Church.

• It was estimated that by the end of the week of Apr. 18 to 25 one million persons had participated in Ground Zero programs in 650 towns, 350 colleges and 1,000 high schools, according to spokesman Ellis Woodward.

Women in the Church — The National Conference of Catholic Bishops released Apr. 27 a 13-page report on three dialogue sessions conducted between December, 1980, and August, 1981, by the Women's Ordination Conference and the Bishops' Committee on Women in Society and the Church. The bishops' committee said: "Let the focus (of concern) be women as persons and the gifts which they can bring to the ministry and pastoral needs of the Church. . . . Granted the traditional teaching excluding women from priestly ordination, there are significant levels of the Church's ministry which could be opened up to women, perhaps including the diaconate." A key question under discussion was: Is the rationale for ordained male leadership of the Church a matter of doctrine or sociology? It appeared that the report would be subject to serious scrutiny.

Name Change — A year-long controversy came to an end Apr. 28 when the White House and Department of Defense confirmed a name change for a nuclear attack submarine, from Corpus Christi to City of Corpus Christi. Objections had been raised, especially in Catholic circles, to use of the phrase, "Body of Christ," for the name of a warship.

Operation Jobs — Archbishop James V. Casey of Denver and his two auxiliaries were among signers of a statement highly critical of round-ups of undocumented aliens carried out by 400 agents of the Immigration and Naturalization Service in nine cities and resulting in 5,000 arrests during the last week of the month. Signers of the statement said: "We are outraged at recent mass round-ups of undocumented persons . . . that cause immense suffering to those arrested and to their families who are left behind. . . . The INS and the media have failed to inform the public that these raids subject American citizens of His-

panic ancestry and legal aliens to abuse at the hands of federal and local law enforcement personnel, and that a reign of terror has been created in many of our neighborhoods."

National Briefs:

• Philanthropist Louise M. Davies gave a $1 million endowment to the University of San Francisco to establish a forum to study and promote public awareness of moral and ethical values in American public life.

• The Knights of Malta opened a second free clinic for the poor in the Hispanic East Side section of Los Angeles; Cardinal Timothy Manning officiated at dedication ceremonies Apr. 2.

• Dale Francis, editor of the Washington archdiocesan *Catholic Standard* since October, 1978, resigned with publication of the Apr. 22 issue.

NCEA Convention

"Values and Vision" was the theme of the 79th annual convention of the National Catholic Educational Conference, held Apr. 12 to 15 in Chicago and attended by approximately 15,000 people.

The highlight of the convention was President Reagan's unveiling of a tuition tax credit proposal Apr. 15. Key elements of an Educational and Opportunity Equity Act, still in draft form, included a maximum tax credit of $500 per child for tuition paid to a non-public elementary or secondary school, an income cap "to insure the benefits go to working families" and a phase-in of credits beginning in 1983 and reaching completion in 1985.

The association's Teacher of the Year Award was presented to Shirley Joganic of St. Joseph's School, Tucson, Ariz.

INTERNATIONAL

Central American Refugees — Msgr. Giovanni Nervo, vice president of Italian *Caritas,* reported Apr. 1 that nearly two million of the 22 million inhabitants of six Central American nations were living the "anguished life" of refugees. Most seriously affected were one million persons displaced within Guatemala and 250,000 who had fled the country, along with 250,000 displaced persons within El Salvador and 350,000 who had fled. Other estimates were of 18,000 refugees in Nicaragua, 30,000 in Honduras, 20,000 in Mexico and 15,000 in Costa Rica.

Pledge in Guatemala — The bishops of Guatemala, after a meeting with military personnel in control of the government since Mar. 23, said they had obtained a pledge that the Church would be free to carry on its mission, and that the return of exiled church personnel would be studied by the regime.

In other developments:

• The Christian Brothers, concerned for the safety of about 150 young Indians, closed their center in Huehuetenango where Brother

James Miller was murdered in February.

• The bishops launched a relief campaign for an estimated one million victims of violence, casualties of "the cruelest fratricidal struggle in our history."

Warning in El Salvador — Bishop Arturo Rivera Damas, preaching on Palm Sunday in San Salvador, sounded a warning that more violence might replace euphoria in the aftermath of Mar. 28 elections in El Salvador. He called the massive turnout of voters "a vote in favor of peace, democracy and justice," but added that "the moment we are living in is full of dense, dark clouds, of uncertainties, as when a storm draws near." One of the main reasons for serious concern was the virtual certainty that a coalition of rightist parties would force the Christian Democratic Party of President Jose Napoleon Duarte out of effective participation in a new government.

Holy Week in Nicaragua — In Managua, crowds of Catholics filled churches for Holy Week services and close to 100,000 participated in a Good Friday outdoor procession of the Precious Blood. "It was a massive turnout," said Father Bismark Carballo, archdiocesan director of communications.

Bishops in Hungary — The appointment of two new Hungarian bishops and the promotion of three others were announced by the Vatican Apr. 10, a week after the return from Hungary of Archbishop Luigi Poggi, apostolic nuncio for special concerns. Vatican Radio said his talks with government officials had been "particularly useful and constructive," and that his visit had ended with "the resolution of several questions." Details were not disclosed.

Missile Testing in Canada — The decision of the Canadian government to permit U.S. testing of cruise nuclear missiles in northern Alberta and Saskatchewan was attacked in a telegram addressed to Prime Minister Pierre Trudeau by the chairman of the Social Affairs Commission, Canadian Conference of Catholic Bishops.

Release Interned Women in Poland — Archbishop Jozef Glemp appealed Apr. 18 for the release of all women interned since the imposition of martial law Dec. 13, 1981. He made the appeal in an address before a gathering of 30,000 persons taking part in a Marian celebration in Warsaw. "Let there be no more interned women during May," he said. "They should disappear as internees. We are asking authorities for this."

Euthanasia of Deformed Babies — "There is strong evidence for a significant increase in support among pediatricians for euthanasia of the newborn who are handicapped." This was the conclusion of a report — "Euthanasia and Clinical Practice: Trends, Principles and Alternatives" — released Apr. 15 by the Linacre Center in London. The report said that euthanasia of deformed babies had be-

come more overt since 1962, although it was often disguised by being described as "allowing babies to die. . . . To say one is 'letting a child die' is certainly a euphemism for killing when one is administering sedatives to the baby so that it shall be continuously sleepy, take little or no food and die within a few weeks." Increasing evidence was reported that this form of management was common and that the euthanasia of certain newborn babies was a systematic rather than an occasional occurrence in certain pediatric units. Infants with various abnormalities "are selected for non-treatment and 'custodial management,' " and this "regularly means: for sedation with a view to starvation and death," the report said. The Linacre Center was established by the bishops of England and Wales in 1977 to study questions of medical ethics.

Ukrainian Catholics — Cardinal Josyf Slipyi, exiled archbishop of Lwow, urged Ukrainian Catholics living in freedom to pray for their co-religionists suffering persecution under Communist domination in the Ukraine. Addressing several hundred persons attending Mass Apr. 18 at the Church of St. Sophia in Rome, he pleaded for prayers for those "who suffer under the yoke of atheism and who are deprived of the great gift of freedom which we who are outside the confines of the Ukraine are able to enjoy. . . . We turn ourselves in a special way to you, beloved people of the Ukraine, and to those who have been condemned and taken in chains to the cold and unfriendly lands of Siberia."

International Briefs:

• Columban Father Osmundo Bilbao Garamendi, 38, was shot to death Apr. 20 near Kampala, Uganda.

• The Israeli government presented its Medal of the Just posthumously to Salesian Father Bronius Paukstys who saved several hundred Lithuanian Jews, "with grave risk to his own life," during the Nazi occupation of Kaunas between 1943 and 1945.

Falkland Islands Conflict

Bishops on both sides appealed for peaceful settlement of the Argentine-British dispute over the Falkland (Malvinas) Islands while generally upholding the official stances of their respective governments. Their pleas, however, along with persistent diplomatic efforts of U.S. Secretary of State Alexander M. Haig, Jr., proved futile in the long run.

The conflict began Apr. 2 with the relatively bloodless occupation of the islands by Argentina, which claimed them as part of its territorial heritage from Spain despite British sovereignty since 1833. The issue was joined a little more than three weeks later when British forces seized South Georgia Island Apr. 25 and full-scale mobilization on both sides was in process.

MAY 1982

VATICAN

Dignity of Work and Workers — Addressing 3,000 persons on the feast of St. Joseph the Worker, May 1, Pope John Paul said: "My affectionate thoughts go in a special way to the workers here present and through them to all the workers of the world, exhorting them to become newly aware of the dignity that is theirs. With their daily labor they serve their brothers, they serve man and, through man, Christ. . . . In every type of work it is possible to serve Christ, fulfilling the advice of St. Paul and imitating the example of St. Joseph, guardian and servant of the Son of God."

Message on Vocations — "A vocation is a call to life, to receive it and to give it," declared the Holy Father in a message for the 19th World Day of Prayer for Vocations, May 2. He defined this life as that which "comes as a gift" through baptism. With special reference to the priesthood, he said: "The gift that excels above all, by virtue of holy orders, is the ministerial priesthood which shares in the one priesthood of Christ who offered himself on the cross and continues to offer himself in the Eucharist for the life and salvation of the world. . . . The living Church is the mother of life and, therefore, also the mother of vocations, which are given by God in order to give life." Vocations are both a sign of the Church's vitality and "a fundamental condition" for her life, development and mission.

Praise for Migration Committee — The Pope praised the American Committee on Italian Migration May 3 for its efforts to protect "the human dignity of each individual, universal brotherhood, the sanctity of the family and the family's need to be together." He said that "the Church cannot but praise everything that effectively promotes equality and justice for all people in the area of immigration, an area that so closely touches the good of the human person."

Missionary Cooperation — At a meeting May 7 with 90 of their national directors, the Pope said the four pontifical missionary societies were "the most effective and valid instruments of missionary cooperation." The fund-raising and disbursing societies were the Society for the Propagation of the Faith, the Society of St. Peter the Apostle for Native Clergy, the Society of the Holy Childhood and the Missionary Union of the Clergy.

Eucharist the Center — Pope John Paul told 35 U.S. priests May 7 that their lives and activities as pastors should be centered around the celebration of the Eucharist. "The essential mission of the priesthood is to be found in the Eucharist," he told participants in the Institute for Continuing Theological Education.

Threats to Peace — The Holy Father told about 80,000 persons in St. Peter's Square May 9 that threats to world peace had entered a critical phase. "The contemporary world is threatened in various ways," he said, "and perhaps more than ever before in the course of history." He did not mention any specific conflicts, but the timing of his remarks coincided with the continuation of fighting in the Middle East and South Atlantic.

Another Call for Peace — The Pope renewed his call "for peace between Argentina and England" May 19 during a general audience. Three days later, he concelebrated a Mass for peace with bishops from both countries as diplomatic efforts to mediate the Falkland Islands dispute seemed doomed to failure.

Council for Culture — The Pope, in a letter dated May 20, announced the establishment of a new Pontifical Council for Culture, to facilitate contact between "the saving message of the Gospel (and) the plurality of cultures." Cardinal Gabriel-Marie Garrone, retired prefect of the Congregation for Catholic Education, was named head of the council's presidential committee.

Needs of the Elderly — A "just pension" for the elderly is as much a matter of social justice as a "just wage" for workers, the Pope said in a message for World Communications Day, May 23. The message, which was related to the United Nations-sponsored 1982 World Assembly on Aging, focused on the place of the aged in society and the role of the media in shaping society's attitudes toward them. He called on media personnel to use the instruments in their hands to:

• "correct among the young modes of thinking regarding the old";

• remind the public of "the problem of a 'just pension' . . . as a demand of 'social justice' ";

• "communicate widely . . . a vision of old age as a gift of God to the individual, to the family and to society";

• provide programs and publications suitable for and helpful to the elderly;

Pastoral Trips — Pope John Paul completed a four-day trip to Portugal May 15 and began a six-day visit to Great Britain May 28. (See separate entries.)

The Pope Also:

• Expressed his condolences over the deaths of 39 mine workers in an explosion May 12, in a message addressed to Yugoslav President Sergej Kraigher.

• Marked his 62nd birthday quietly May 18.

• Met with: Mother Teresa of Calcutta May 17, Prime Minister Robert Mugabe of Zimbabwe May 22, and Director General Francis Blanchard of the International Labor Organization May 24.

Vatican Briefs:

• The Vatican was represented May 10 to 14 at a controversial peace conference in Moscow.

• In a letter dated May 27, the 1,800-member Association of Vatican Lay Employees requested direct negotiations with the Pope to resolve a contract dispute. The Holy Father subsequently agreed to meet with leaders of the association.

Beatifications

Pope John Paul advanced the canonization causes of two Canadians and three Europeans by beatifying them May 23 in ceremonies attended by about 20,000 people in St. Peter's Square. Servants of God called Blessed were:

• Holy Cross Brother Andre Bessette (1845-1937), prime mover in the building of St. Joseph's Oratory, Montreal;

• Sister Marie-Rose Durocher of Montreal (1811-1849), foundress of the Sisters of the Holy Names of Jesus and Mary;

• Dutch Redemptorist Father Peter Donders (1809-1887), missionary in Suriname for more than 40 years;

• Spanish Sister Maria Angela Astorch (1592-1665), member of the Capuchin Order of St. Clare;

• French Sister Marie Rivier (1768-1838), foundress of the Congregation of the Sisters of the Presentation of Mary.

In a related development, the Congregation for the Causes of Saints issued a decree May 11 acknowledging a miracle attributed to the intercession of the Servant of God Jeanne Jugan, foundress of the Little Sisters of the Poor.

NATIONAL

World's Fair Exhibit — An ecumenical exhibit portraying Christianity as "The Power," with Catholic participation, was opened May 2 on the grounds of the 1982 World's Fair in Knoxville.

Voluntarism Can't Do It All — Efforts by President Reagan to shift responsibility for the poor from government to churches and other private dispensers of charity were challenged by Archbishop Joseph L. Bernardin of Cincinnati in an address in Brooklyn, N.Y. "I am the first to admit that the church ought to do more," he said, "but government also has a responsibility from which it cannot escape. Voluntarism alone cannot solve the problem of poverty."

Misguided Prophets — Cardinal Silvio Oddi, prefect of the Congregation for the Clergy, warned students of St. Charles Borromeo Seminary, Overbrook, Pa., against a prediction "in some misinformed quarters that the Church of the future will become a sort of amorphous conglomeration of what are commonly, and ambiguously, termed basic Christian communities. ... We know that, while non-political, grassroot communities can indeed have a legitimate place in the organism of the body of Christ, they will not and may not appropriate to themselves the legitimate functions of the parish, the diocese or the universal teaching authority of the Church." He also said: "Still other misguided prophets suggest that the Church of tomorrow will become a sort of religious United Nations, so deeply inculturated in various civilizations of the globe that it will no longer be possible to accept a universal Pontiff. . . ."

Planned Parenthood — Bishop Sylvester W. Treinen of Boise and others involved in the pro-life movement praised the decision by United Way of Ada County to stop funding Planned Parenthood of Idaho in 1983. Reasons for the decision, according to Hal Bunderson, United Way board president, were the opposition of donors to Planned Parenthood's abortion policy and practices, and lack of the organization's need for funding.

Criticism of Dr. Graham — Father Casimir Pugevicius, executive director of Lithuanian Catholic Religious Aid, was among critics of comments on religious freedom in the Soviet Union made by Rev. Dr. Billy Graham who attended an international religious conferene on peace May 10 to 14 in Moscow. Father Pugevicius said the comments were contradicted by the plight of Pentecostalists who sought sanctuary in the U.S. embassy in Moscow, by the actions of demonstrators who tried to call attention to the condition of religious believers in the Soviet Union, and by documentation reaching the West from the U.S.S.R.

Care for Handicapped Infants — As the American Life Lobby and the Catholic League for Religious and Civil Rights involved themselves in the case of an Illinois baby born with a birth defect requiring surgery, the Department of Health and Human Services warned 6,800 hospitals May 18 that they must treat handicapped infants equally under the law or suffer possible loss of federal aid. The warning was circulated in a letter after President Reagan issued a directive Apr. 30 — following the death of a Down's Syndrome infant in Indiana — that hospitals should not discriminate in treatment against the handicapped.

Belief in God — More people in the United States and Ireland — 95 per cent — than in 14 other countries believe in God, according to a survey of 1,200 persons in each country conducted by the Center for Applied Research in the Apostolate in cooperation with the Gallup Organizations.

Investments for a Better Society — Through

"alternative investments" in minority-owned banks, community development projects, credit unions, cooperatives and similar programs, more than 30 Catholic religious orders and Protestant churches reported they were contributing to the economic development of disadvantaged people while also making a reasonable profit. The investing groups were associated with the Interfaith Center on Corporate Responsibility.

Anti-Abortion Measures — Gov. J. Joseph Garrahy of Rhode Island signed into law bills requiring: spousal notification of abortion; notification of a woman seeking abortion regarding medical dangers in both abortion and childbirth; parental or court approval for a minor seeking abortion. The bills were said to be modeled on laws already upheld by federal appellate courts.

National Briefs:

• The Citizens' Stamp Advisory Committee of the U.S. Postal Service announced that a 20-cent commemorative stamp marking the 800th anniversary of the birth of St. Francis of Assisi would be issued Oct. 7.

• Mercy Sister Arlene Violet announced May 14 that she would continue her campaign for election to the office of Rhode Island attorney general despite the declaration by Bishop Louis E. Gelineau of Providence that her candidacy was clearly in violation of Canons 139 and 592 of the Code of Canon Law.

• The U.S. Court of Appeals for the Seventh Circuit denied May 17 the petition of the Archdiocese of Chicago for a rehearing of a $1.5 million suit for copyright infringement brought by F.E.L. Publications of Los Angeles.

• The U.S. Supreme Court agreed May 24 to hear five abortion-related cases — from Virginia, Missouri and Akron, Ohio — dealing with peripheral or procedural issues regarding the circumstances under which abortions are to be performed.

Meetings

Meetings held during the month included those of the following organizations.

• The National Federation of Priests' Councils, in convention May 2 to 6 in Kansas City, Kan., condemned the use of anti-union firms by Catholic health and human service institutions, called for the direction or more resources and energy to ministry among Hispanics, and heard outgoing President Father Neil McCaulley urge support for bishops advocating strong action on social issues, especially the arms race. Father Robert Johnson, 31, of the Archdiocese of St. Paul and Minneapolis, was elected president of the federation.

• The Catholic Press Association Convention, May 12 to 15 in Scottsdale, Ariz., provided a forum for addresses on helping to harmonize differences among diverse peoples of the U.S. and on the Catholic press as a prophetic voice for the voiceless. The association presented its St. Francis de Sales Award posthumously to Allen C. Bradley, former office manager of *The Advocate* of Newark. Also honored was Paulist Father John B. Sheerin, on retiring his 25-year-old NC News Service syndicated column, "Sum and Substance."

• The annual meeting of the National Assembly of Women Religious, May 28 to 30 in Washington, was keynoted by Barbara Zanotti, who declared: "Let us be clear that feminism represents a historical shift — a movement away from structured male power and the norms of patriarchal systems. Feminism is a blessed politics for all of us if we women and men seize the courage to affirm those values which can initiate a new social order."

• The National Conference on the Charismatic Renewal in the Catholic Church, May 28 to 30 on the campus of the University of Notre Dame, was attended by about 13,000 persons from 10 nations.

INTERNATIONAL

Bishops Retain Authority — The Parliament of Ecuador modified a bill which would have replaced the authority of the bishops to appoint university presidents with an elective process involving faculty members, students and adminstrative personnel. Cardinal Pablo Munoz Vega of Quito said the proposed bill would have liquidated "the two institutions of higher learning sponsored at great sacrifice by the Church" — The Pontifical Catholic University in Quito and the Technological Institute at Loja.

Against Violence in Poland — Archbishop Jozef Glemp of Gniezno and Warsaw issued a new plea May 9 for dialogue after a week of violent clashes between police and Solidarity union supporters which left dozens of persons injured and imprisoned. Addressing 70,000 people at a Mass in Cracow commemorating the feast of St. Stanislaus, patron of Poland, he said: "In dialogue, and not in muscles, stands the strength of our spirit. . . . During a discussion, a rock is the weakest argument. . . . We ought to be wise, and wisdom is also prudence, the ability to carry forward a dialogue, the capacity to present just requests."

Bishops for Withdrawal — In a "Report on Namibia" issued May 14, the Southern African Catholic Bishops' Conference called "for the withdrawal of South Africa from a situation of violence that appears totally unacceptable to us." The bishops said most Namibians wanted a cease-fire between South African security forces and guerrillas of the South-West Africa Peoples' Organization, were in favor of elections under U.N. auspices, and were "prepared to live with whatever government emerges."

Steps toward Church Unity — Ways and means of bringing about union between the two churches were the subjects of study at the eighth plenary session of the international Lutheran-Roman Catholic Joint Commission, held May 10 to 15 in Venice.

Archbishop Not in Opposition Movement — Archbishop Miguel Obando Bravo denied assertions by Interior Minister Tomas Borge that he was involved in a movement seeking to overthrow the Sandinist government in Nicaragua. "A bishop's call is never to temporal power," the archbishop said in an interview published in the Managua daily, *La Prensa.* Borge had charged that the prelate was a member of a seditious "supreme directorate" of anti-Sandinist groups.

It was also reported that the bishops were critical of the regime's policies regarding freedom of the press, labor unions, religious holidays and Marxist influence. Many priests, religious and lay leaders were said to be active in support of the government.

Salvadoran Legal Aid — *Socorro Juridico,* the legal aid office of the Archdiocese of San Salvador, was closed and its work reorganized by Bishop Arturo Rivera Damas, apostolic administrator. He said, however, that its task of documenting abuses of human rights would be continued by the Office for Legal Protection, "because we find it now more needed than ever." *The Washington Post* reported May 15 that the decision to close *Socorro Juridico* was made because of differences between its staff and church leaders over its approach to handling tasks entrusted to it since it was established by Archbishop Oscar Romero in 1975.

Ecumenism among Religious — The Ecumenical Consultation of Religious, at its fourth annual meeting May 16 to 19 in London, decided to add to its Catholic-Anglican membership members of Lutheran religious orders and, eventually, of Orthodox monastic orders. Participants in the consultation also said in a joint statement that they had come to appreciate in a new way not only the profound union that binds them together, in sharing baptism and the religious vows of poverty, chastity and obedience, but also the differences in religious life as experienced in the Catholic Church and the Anglican Communion.

Use of Force Defended — As undeclared war between Great Britain and Argentina over the Falkland Islands continued to escalate, individual church leaders on both sides continued defending the use of force by their governments for what they considered to be serious reasons (rights to sovereignty and/or to resist aggression) proportionate to the evils of war. Among the prelates were Anglican Archbishop Robert Runcie, Cardinal George Basil Hume of Westminster and Bishop Desiderio Collino of Lomas de Zamora.

At the same time, two Argentine cardinals along with two British cardinals and two archbishops signed a peace-seeking statement May 22 after concelebrating Mass with Pope John Paul at the Vatican. They said: "We pledge ourselves to be witnesses of peace and reconciliation in the search for a just settlement of the conflict in the South Atlantic."

Christian Festival — More than 10,000 people came "Together in Hope" for the first national Christian festival in Ottawa May 21 to 24, ready to make a journey of faith with other Canadians of various denominations. The festival was sponsored by the Ontario Conference of Catholic Bishops, the Archdiocese of Ottawa and the Diocese of Hull, as well as by Lutheran, Anglican, Presbyterian, United Church, Baptist, Mennonite and Salvation Army groups.

Priests Convicted in Czechoslovakia — The Rome office of the Friars Minor reported May 26 that two Franciscans were convicted of anti-government activities in April as part of the Czechoslovakian government's intensified "anti-religious campaign." Father Jan Barta was sentenced to 18 months in prison. Father Ladislaw Kosmas Trojan received a 15-month suspended sentence.

International Briefs:

• The Rev. Dr. Billy Graham, Southern Baptist evangelist, was awarded the 1982 Templeton Foundation Prize for Progress in Religion May 11 in London; the prize was worth more than $200,000.

• Tullio Maiorino was ordained May 23 the first permanent deacon in the modern history of the Vicariate of Rome.

• The bishops of Zambia were reported worried that the government of President Kenneth Kaunda, despite his assurances that humanism remained the nation's official ideology, was leaning toward a form of socialism linked to communism.

Moscow Conference

Nearly 500 religious leaders from 80 nations assembled May 10 to 14 in Moscow for a Conference of Religious Workers for Saving the Sacred Gift of Life from Nuclear Catastrophe. They said in a final statement that mankind is "near the brink of total annihilation," and called on the Soviet Union and the United States to take urgent steps toward halting the arms race and dismantling their nuclear arsenals. Western clergymen called the statement a victory for balance over early efforts to turn the meeting into a pro-Soviet propaganda event.

Pope John Paul, in a letter to Russian Orthodox Patriarch Pimen of Moscow, host of the conference, spoke of his "desire to collaborate with your church in every field in which an authentic witness to the risen Christ and his Gospel can and should be given by Christians in today's world."

JUNE 1982

VATICAN

Pastoral Trips — The Holy Father completed three pastoral trips during the month: to Great Britain, June 2; to Argentina, June 13; to Switzerland, June 15. (See separate entries.)

Just War Theory? — Pope John Paul, interviewed June 2 during a flight from Cardiff, Wales, to Rome, suggested that the just war theory of St. Thomas Aquinas may no longer be applicable because of the destructive capability of modern weapons. "It cannot be denied, the right to self-defense," he said; "but it is necessary to look for other solutions. Today it is necessary to exclude any war."

Mission Day Message — "Neither isolation nor egoistical retreat" should keep local churches from fulfilling their duty of participating in the missionary task of the universal Church, declared the Pope in a message for the 1982 World Mission Day, Oct. 17. Missionary effort cannot be considered a "one way" system, he said, but is rather "a reciprocal and frutiful exchange of energies and goods, in the sphere of a fraternal communion of sister churches." While noting that there were "some signs of weariness" in missionary effort, he urged Catholics to resist the "temptation to retreat into oneself, to close oneself in on one's own problems, to exhaust the missionary impulse within oneself."

Ordinations to the Priesthood — The Holy Father ordained 80 men from 20 countries to the priesthood June 6 in St. Peter's Basilica. Six of the candidates were from the United States; 32 were members of Opus Dei.

Pope and President — The Pope and President Reagan, meeting for the first time June 7 at the Vatican, pledged that they would work for peace and justice in the world. In a statement read after the private, hour-long meeting, the Pope spoke about his concern for peace, especially in the South Atlantic, between Iraq and Iran, and in Lebanon; he also called for an end to the arms race and condemned "anything that wounds, weakens or dishonors human dignity." President Reagan called the Pope "one of the world's greatest moral and spiritual forces," criticized the martial law government of Poland, and said the U.S. would continue to work for peace and justice in the Middle East and Latin America.

Money for Health instead of Guns — While blessing a new cardiac unit for children at Rome's Child Jesus pediatric hospital June 8, the Pope said: "May it not happen that the most consistent spending of various countries should be applied to armaments ... while those works and initiatives are neglected that are necessary and cannot be delayed so that

the life of men, also from the health viewpoint, may be spent serenely and tranquilly in peace, justice and order."

Avoid Political Identification — While the Church must collaborate with civil authorities, it has to guard against losing its identity to a particular political party. So stated the Pontiff June 18 in an address to seven bishops of Zimbabwe. He said: "Pursuit of the common good of the whole of society calls for continued collaboration between the hierarchy and the civil authorities in an atmosphere of freedom and of respect for the different competencies of church and state. But (the Church) keeps her own identity, an identity based on the teaching of Christ, one that can never be confused with that of any political party. No political group can arrogate to itself the right to represent her."

The Polish Crisis — Addressing about 40,000 persons June 23 in St. Peter's Square, the Holy Father said that the contemporary crisis in Poland, like other situations in the nation's history, "places on trial the conscience, the heart and the will, not to be conquered by evil but to conquer evil with good."

Refugees — The Pope called the existence of 10 to 15 million refugees throughout the world "a shameful evil of our time," in a brief address June 25 to Poul Hartling, U.N. High Commissioner for Refugees. He praised the official for the work of his commission, and added: "The Catholic Church ... considers assistance to refugees as an essential work, in which she invites in a pressing manner her Christian children to collaborate, because the Bible in general and the Gospel in particular do not permit us to leave without help strangers who seek refuge."

Willing To Visit Lebanon — Twenty-two days after the June 6 invasion of Lebanon by Israeli armed forces, Pope John Paul told a gathering of cardinals and personnel of the Roman Curia: "I affirm ... publicly that I would be willing to go without delay to the martyred land of Lebanon, if that would be possible, for the cause of peace." The address was one of several appeals for peace made by the Pontiff.

Palestinian Homeland — The Pope told a gathering of about 20,000 people June 29 that the Palestinians had a right to a homeland. He said: "Let us pray that they may be able to see recognized their legitimate aspirations — the first of which is to be able to have a homeland — and that they may be able to live in tranquillity with all the peoples of the region."

The Pope Also:

• Took part in a Corpus Christi procession June 10 from the Basilica of St. John Lateran to the Basilica of St. Mary Major.

• Sent a message of sympathy to the new

king of Saudi Arabia following the death June 13 of King Khalid.

• Met privately June 17 with Ambassador Edward Rowny, head of the U.S. delegation to Strategic Arms Reduction Talks, 12 days before the start of a new round of negotiations.

• Told a group of Spanish bishops June 26 that "tourism can be depersonalizing, a font of hedonism and rampant consumerism."

Vatican Briefs:

• The number of Catholics in the world increased by nearly three per cent, to 784,660,000, in 1980, according to the latest edition of the *Statistical Yearbook of the Church.*

• In a statement commemorating World Environment Day, June 5, the Vatican Press Office called for increased attention to the care of natural resources, for the defense of mankind.

• Lay employees of the Vatican called off a strike scheduled for June 14 after the Pope agreed to give personal consideration to their demands.

Message to U.N. General Assembly

"Because peace is possible, peace is our duty, our grave duty, our supreme responsibility," declared the Pope in a message to the special session of the U.N. General Assembly on disarmament.

In the message read for him June 11 by Cardinal Agostino Casaroli, his secretary of state, the Pontiff said:

Armaments "are a consequence of an ethical crisis that is disrupting society in all its political, social and economic dimensions." True disarmament will come "only with the resolution of this ethical crisis. . . . To the extent that efforts at arms reduction and then of total disarmament are not matched by parallel ethical renewal, they are doomed in advance to failure."

NATIONAL

Catholic 1981 Statistics — *The 1982 Official Catholic Directory* reported 51,207,579 Catholics in the U.S. in 1981, an increase of 757,737 over the figure for the previous year. Reports indicated that:

• The number of students in Catholic elementary and secondary schools increased for the first time in 17 years.

• There were decreases in the numbers of bishops, priests, brothers and sisters, and an increase in the number of permanent deacons.

(See statistical tables.)

Church Membership — The 1982 edition of the *Yearbook of American and Canadian Churches* indicated that the membership decline of some mainline Protestant churches slowed between 1979 and 1980 while a number of small, conservative churches grew faster than the U.S. population. The reported

total of U.S. church membership in 1980 was 134.8 million, 58.7 per cent of the total population.

Bishops' Assembly — More than 200 bishops attended the Assembly of U.S. Bishops for Prayer and Reflection on Episcopal Ministry June 13 to 23 at St. John's University, Collegeville, Minn. (See separate entry.)

Abortion Control — Pennsylvania Governor Dick Thornburgh, after vetoing a similar abortion control measure six months earlier, signed legislation affecting the performance of abortions in the state. One of the measures prohibits abortion after viability and requires that a second doctor be present to care for a baby in cases where abortion could result in live birth.

Planned Parenthood Charged — Angelica Oliva, a needy mother, charged that she was denied after-childbirth medical care by tax-funded Planned Parenthood of Pasadena, Calif., because she refused to agree in writing to use a Planned Parenthood method of birth control.

In a related development, 25 taxpayers filed a suit against the city June 14 in which they charged that city-delegated Planned Parenthood was violating the rights of needy maternity patients to non-discriminatory medical care.

Free Education for Illegals — The U.S. Supreme Court, in a major expansion of the rights of illegal aliens, ruled June 15 that states providing free education in their public schools cannot exclude the children of illegal alien parents. The Court struck down a 1975 Texas law barring free education to illegal aliens. Also banned was the policy of the Tyler, Tex., school district of charging illegal alien children attending its schools a tuition fee of $1,000. The decisions were praised by Catholic churchmen in Texas and by officials of Migration and Refugee Services, U.S. Catholic Conference.

Human Development Funds Up — Contributions to the U.S. Bishops' Campaign for Human Development reached a 12-year high in 1981, with a total in excess of $9.3 million.

Survey of Seminary Professors — Catholic and Protestant seminary professors were more conservative on religious and moral questions than the general public but more liberal on certain political issues, according to a survey by the Roper Center at the University of Connecticut. Their differences on political issues, it was said, indicated that there is no clearly defined "Christian" position on many matters of public concern. Respondents to the survey numbered 1,112.

Voting Rights Act — Capping a year-long debate in which the U.S. Catholic Conference was an active participant, the Senate voted overwhelmingly June 18 to extend key provisions of the Voting Rights Act of 1965. The act, one of the most important civil rights enactments of the 1960s, bans discriminatory voting practices and requires states and localities with a history of voting discrimination to submit changes in voting procedures to the Justice Department or to the Federal District Court in Washington for approval.

K. of C. Funds to Charity — The Knights of Columbus gave more than $41.7 million to charitable and benevolent causes in 1981, according to a report from K. of C. headquarters in New Haven, Conn. Members also devoted 10.4 million hours in community service to youth, hospitals, orphanages and church activities.

Private School Enrollment — The Department of Education's National Center for Education Statistics reported that about five million of the 46 million elementary and secondary school students — one of every nine — attended a private school in 1980-81. Nearly 84 per cent of the private school students attended church-affiliated schools; 63 per cent of them were in Catholic schools.

Biblical School in Denver — Archbishop James V. Casey established a Catholic Biblical School in the Archdiocese of Denver because "more and more people are going to the Bible, reading it and wanting to understand it more fully," said Robert Borkovec, a member of the school's organizing committee. He said the school's program would be "designed for those people who have felt a hunger for the word of God and who specifically want a deeper understanding of holy Scripture ... and who want to carry back that understanding to other people in their parishes, communities and families."

Mother Teresa's Tour — Mother Teresa of Calcutta, near the end of a month-long tour of the U.S., said in Louisville June 22 that she thought women were attracted to her Missionaries of Charity because young people were seeking a life of prayer, poverty and sacrifice. Her community, founded in 1950, had 2,000 sisters, 300 novices and 213 missions in 52 countries. During her coast-to-coast tour, Mother Teresa spoke at several college and university commencement exercises, committed sisters of her order to staff a home for pregnant, unmarried women in Little Rock, visited houses of her sisters in Newark, N.J., and Appalachia, and promised to open a novitiate of the order in San Francisco.

Meetings — Meetings during the month included those of the:

• Association of Contemplative Sisters, June 1 to 8, in Cincinnati;

• Catholic Health Assembly, June 6 to 9 in Boston;

• Serra International, June 28 to 30 in Detroit.

National Briefs:

• Four Sisters of Mercy in New Hampshire, who lost a county court case against Bishop Odore Gendron after the Diocese of Manchester did not renew their teaching contracts, refused to leave the school convent until the State Supreme Court acts on their appeal.

• Catholic Relief Services launched June 8 a $300,000 emergency assistance program for victims of floods in Nicaragua and Honduras.

• The Metropolitan Museum of Art in New York received a $1 million check June 29 as the first installment by Philip Morris, Inc., of a $3 million grant to fund a U.S. tour of Vatican art treasures in 1983.

E.R.A. Not Ratified

The Equal Rights Amendment, hotly contested for 10 years, died June 3 for want of ratification by three states. Its status as of this date — with approval by only 35 states — was the same as in 1979, when the ordinary seven-year period for amendment ratification by three-fourths of the states was extended for three years.

Backers of the amendment indicated they would have it re-introduced in Congress for another passage through the ratification process. Opponents indicated no less determination to bring about its second defeat.

(See separate entry.)

INTERNATIONAL

Apartheid Rejected — One hundred and 23 Dutch Reformed ministers, in a joint letter, called for an end to strict racial separation in South Africa, declaring that a social order built on such separation "is unacceptable" and "cannot be defended scripturally." The letter was called one of the most important developments in the Afrikaans churches in decades.

End Sought to Sanctions on Poland — A joint committee composed of representatives of the Polish government and bishops of the nation said that economic sanctions of other nations were hindering Poland's recovery from its current crisis. Meeting June 8 in Warsaw, committee members said "normalization of social and economic life" in Poland depended on the country's achievement of a "social accord," which was impeded by sanctions imposed after the declaration of martial law Dec. 13, 1981.

Land Reform or Political Game? — The temporary suspension of a "land to the tiller" program in El Salvador prompted Bishop Arturo Rivera Damas, apostolic administrator of San Salvador, to say that leaders had engaged in political games. He said many people felt that the Constituent Assembly's announcement May 18 of a suspension of the program instead of abrogation, as first stated, was "a political game to shut the voice of protest by those deprived of its benefits, and at the same time leave the door open for further aid from the U.S. government." In Washington, U.S. Ambassador to El Salvador Dean

Hinton said June 11 that a key part of the program had been suspended but that, overall, it was still working. (The Constituent Assembly, formed several weeks after elections late in March, was under rightist control. Roberto d'Aubuisson was one of the more influential leaders of the extreme political right.)

Catholic West Bank University Closed — Nine-year-old Bethlehem University, a Catholic institution, was closed indefinitely by Israeli military authorities June 11 after students demonstrated against the Israeli invasion of Lebanon. Christian Brother Thomas Scanlon, vice president of the university, noting that the disturbances were mild and injury free, said he felt the rock-throwing incidents were provoked by military officers, in parking a jeep at the site where there had been no trouble at a previous demonstration.

End of Falklands Conflict — Hostilities in the Falkland (Malvinas) Islands ended June 15 with the surrender of Argentine forces to the British. But the underlying problem over sovereignty remained unresolved, and so did questions about the morality of massive armed conflict to settle such a relatively minor dispute. Pope John Paul, in addresses delivered personally in Great Britain and Argentina, pleaded for peaceful settlement of the matter — but in vain.

Massacres in Guatemala — Guatemala's Catholic Justice and Peace Commission demanded that the new military government "end the massacres and repression" of Indian peasants. It said that 450 Indians in 20 villages had been killed and the "entire populations" of seven other villages had been slain since the military took over the government in a coup in March. Supporting the committee was the 1,700-member Guatemala Conference of Religious Men and Women, which said in a statement early in the month that "the fact that some guerrilla activity goes on does not justify genocide, nor does the fact that people clamor for change in unjust social structures justify slayings." Church sources reported that more than 13,000 non-combatants were killed in 1981 in fighting between guerrilla forces and government troops.

Missionary Expelled from Honduras — French missionary Father Bernard Boulang, even though defended by the Honduran Bishops' Conference and the French ambassador, was forced to leave Honduras when immigration officials refused to renew his residency visa after security police accused him of subversive activity. The action was interpreted as one of a number of government moves against church personnel siding with the poor.

Third World Funding Policy — Cardinal G. Emmett Carter of Toronto announced a restructuring of archdiocesan funding to emphasize evangelization and pastoral projects over socio-economic programs in the third world. He said the usual contribution to the Canadian Catholic Organization for Development and Peace did "not take care of our responsibility for evangelization and pastoral projects."

Mozambique Missions — The Christian Council of Churches in Mozambique appealed to the government to reopen mission stations closed in the crackdown on church institutions soon after independence was won from Portugal in 1975. Mission stations, many of which had schools and hospitals, could play a significant role in the development of the country, said the Rev. Isaac Mahlalela, general secretary of the council.

Spread of Islam — A flurry of consultations among representatives of Moslem states and organizations in Africa were signs of a major effort to promote Islam throughout the continent, especially in Nigeria, according to C.O. Williams, general secretary of the Christian Council of Nigeria. He said: "We are not opposed to making the Koran available . . ., to the training of Islamic religious teachers, to the enlightenment of Moslems and all those who care to hear about Islam. Our concern is that some of the methods used are unorthodox, like ridiculing the (Christian) church, false allegations about the church, provocative pronouncements about the Bible and Christ, and forced Koranic studies in our schools that have been taken over."

International Briefs:

• In Nicaragua, more than 2,000 flood-victim families were being lodged temporarily in facilities provided by 20 religious orders.

• The prime concern of the churches in Namibia was "the huge swath of territory afflicted by poverty, suffering and insecurity," according to an unnamed staff member of the Washington-based Catholic Institute for International Relations.

• The steering committee of the Bolivian Bishops' Conference, in a statement issued June 20, was critical of the military government, charging that its economic policy "hurts the poor the most."

Peace for Galilee

An Israeli force of more than 20,000 men stormed across the southern border of Lebanon June 6 in the start of a "Peace for Galilee" offensive that resulted within two months in a siege of Beirut and the evacuation of forces of the Palestinian Liberation Organization from Lebanon.

Catholic Relief Services and other agencies for emergency assistance strained their personnel and resources to provide food, shelter and medical aid to beleaguered civilians and refugees. Meanwhile, appeals for an end to hostilities — from the Pope, other religious and civic leaders, and the United Nations — went unheeded amid the sounds of warfare.

JULY 1983

VATICAN

Weakening Effect of Materialism — Pope John Paul, addressing participants in a course on natural family planning July 3, said that materialism and the absence of an orientation toward God were combining to weaken the values and structure of the family. He also said that the regulation of fertility was "one of the most delicate and urgent problems for families today," and emphasized the need for natural methods based on observation of the characteristics of human sexuality and on respect for the teaching of the Church.

Prayer and Dialogue — Prayer and dialogue with Eastern churchmen were among subjects mentioned by the Pope July 4 before 10,000 people with whom he recited the Angelus in St. Peter's Square.

Prayer, he said, "is the first and fundamental condition of collaboration with the grace of God. One needs to pray to have the grace of God, and one needs to pray in order to be able to cooperate with the grace of God."

He also referred to a meeting under way of the international commission for dialogue between the Orthodox Church and the Roman Catholic Church. He called the dialogue "particularly important" and praised the late Orthodox Patriarch Athenagoras of Constantinople for helping to prepare for it. He said the Patriarch "ardently desired Eucharistic concelebration (still wanting) between Catholics and Orthodox."

Suffering in Lebanon — Suffering in Lebanon caused by Israeli-PLO armed conflict prompted several statements by the Pope during the month.

• On July 7, he said there was need for an early negotiated settlement of the Israeli siege of West Beirut because "every hour that passes is a new burden and a new threat of still harsher suffering which weighs on the defenseless population" of about 500,000 people.

• "We renew our prayers for our brothers in Lebanon," he said June 11. "The prolongation of the siege increases the threat of hunger and of epidemics and the nightmare of the victims, and brings even greater suffering."

• "We remember the suffering of the population of Beirut, besieged for several weeks, under frequent bombardments and deprived of necessities," he said July 18. "We pray to the Lord, through the intercession of Mary, to alleviate so many pains and to console those who are in anguish and danger."

New Name for Defense — "Peace is the new name for defense," declared the Pope in an address July 12 to 150 students of the NATO Defense College in Rome. "Peace is the only setting in which adequate defense is possible."

Human Rights in Poland — The Pope defended human rights in Poland and supported the nation's need to live its own life, in an address July 14 to a general audience. His statement was interpreted as criticism of the martial law regime in Poland and of Soviet interference in the nation's affairs.

Visit Postponed — Archbishop Jozef Glemp and General Wojciech Jaruzelski announced in separate statements July 21 that the Pope's hoped-for visit to Poland in August would be postponed because of social unrest connected with the conflict between the martial law government and the Solidarity labor movement.

Counsel for Palestinians — With hostilities in the Middle East in mind, the Pope told 20,000 people July 21 that "the Christians of Palestine are called to show that, in seeking the recogniton of their rights, they are inspired by thoughts of justice and of love, and not by hatred of others."

Hunger — The Holy Father, speaking July 25 at Castel Gandolfo, condemned the "scandal" of world hunger and called for "the victory of programs dedicated to development, nourishment and solidarity over those of hate, armaments and war. . . . The problem of world hunger arises today with tragic urgency, also because its solution, rather than becoming closer, with the passing of time seems to get even further away."

Opposition to Euthanasia — The Holy Father reaffirmed the opposition of the Church to euthanasia in a letter to the U.N. World Conference on the Third Age which opened July 26 in Vienna. Quoting a 1980 declaration by the Congregation for the Doctrine of the Faith, he said: "No one can in any way permit the killing of an innocent human being, whether a fetus or an embryo, an infant or an adult, an old person, or one suffering from an incurable disease, or a person who is dying."

Religion, Ethics and Culture — No discussing of culture can ignore religion and ethics, declared the Pope in a letter read July 30 at the Second World Cultural Conference, sponsored by the United Nations' Educational, Scientific and Cultural Organization, in Mexico City. "An authentic cultural policy," he said, "should see man in his totality, that is, in all his personal dimensions, without forgetting the ethical and religious aspects." He urged the conference to encourage "an unbiased search for truth and human values."

The Pope Also:

• Called the July 9 to 11 convention of Worldwide Marriage Encounter in Seattle "a privileged moment for reflection and commitment to the basic values of life and love," in a letter sent in his name.

• Condemned as "despicable acts of cold-blooded terrorism" July 20 bombings in London which left nine persons dead and 52 injured.

Vatican Briefs:
• Secretary of State Cardinal Agostino Casaroli announced July 13 the appointment of a panel of three banking experts to assist him in investigating the relationship between the Vatican bank and the finanically troubled Banco Ambrosiano. There was speculation in the press that the collapse of Banco Ambrosiano was triggered by the Vatican bank's refusal to back loans made by Ambrosiano subsidiaries on the strength of letters of patronage issued by the Vatican bank. The Vatican bank owned 1.58 per cent of Ambrosiano stock.
• Cardinal Joseph Ratzinger, prefect of the Congregation for the Doctrine of the Faith, reaffirmed to Swiss Bishop Pierre Mamie that the suspension from orders imposed in 1976 on dissident Archbishop Marcel Lefebvre was still in effect. He did so in a letter dated June 24 but not made public until July 15.

Lithuanian Bishops Appointed

The Vatican announced July 15 the appointment of two apostolic administrators in Lithuania — Bishop Vincentas Sladkevicius, 62, for the Diocese of Kaisiadorys and Father Antanas Vaicius, 56, for the Diocese of Telsiai. There was speculation that the appointments were signs of improved relations between the Church and the communist government.

In a message addressed to the people of Lithuania on the ordination of Father Vaicius as a bishop July 25, Pope John Paul said:

"May the whole Catholic community, whose faith has been tested by so many trials and difficulties, find in its pastor a defense, a zeal for souls and a strengthening for perseverance in the faith so that, strong in hope and grounded in charity, it may be able to cultivate the Christian dignity and virtues that complement the cultural heritage of the nation."

NATIONAL

Moon Marriages Criticized — The mass marriage of 2,075 couples in a Unification Church ceremony July 1 in Madison Square Garden drew criticism from representatives of the New York Archdiocese, the Brooklyn Diocese, the Jewish Community Relations Council of New York and the New York City Council of Churches. They said they felt a marriage ceremony for such a large number of people at one time negated the dignity and sanctity of what traditionally has been a highly personal and solemn rite.

Child Pornography Decision — A U.S. Supreme Court decision of July 2 allowing states to limit the production and circulation of child pornography was termed a landmark for children by Franciscan Father Bruce Rit-

ter, director of the Under 21 and Covenant House shelters for runaway teen-agers of New York City. "Many of our kids," he said "have been damaged by the child pornography industry, and I was shocked that there could be any controversy about a law which acted as an effective deterrent for those who prospered through the sale of children."

Fetus Has Right To Sue — U.S. District Court Judge T. Emmet Clarie ruled that a fetus has the right — equal to and independent of the mother's right — to sue the Hartford Police Department for injury allegedly sustained when police officers beat its mother during pregnancy. Gary Curran, legislative director of the American Life Lobby in Washington, commented: "If an unborn person has the right to sue," then it should also have "the right to life."

Cardinal Cody's Estate — The estate of Cardinal John Cody of Chicago, who died Apr. 25, was worth about $50,000, according to documents filed in Cook County Circuit Court, Ill. The money was to be used for the care of aged and infirm priests.

U.S. Attorney Dan K. Webb announced July 6 in Chicago that a federal grand jury probe into possible misuse of church funds by the Cardinal had been called off and that no indictments would be sought in the case.

No Unemployment Tax — The District of Columbia Court of Appeals, in the wake of a similar ruling by the U.S. Supreme Court May 26, declared July 8 that the parochial school system of the Washington Archdiocese did not have to pay unemployment compensation taxes for its employees. It was reported that the archdiocese was going to start its own unemployment fund in September for approximately 1,500 lay employees.

Adverse Effects of Budget Cuts — One hundred and four organizations funded by the Campaign for Human Development, responding to a survey conducted in the spring, indicated they had been adversely affected by the Reagan administration's budget cuts.

Ruling for Release of Haitians — A three-judge panel of the 11th U.S. District Court of Appeals upheld July 13 a ruling by U.S. District Judge Eugene P. Spellman to release about 1,900 Haitians detained in several centers around the country.

The U.S. Immigration and Naturalization Service began releasing detainees from Miami's Krome Avenue Detention Center July 23. Migration and Refugee Services, U.S. Catholic Conference, was one of five voluntary agencies arranging for their temporary resettlement and sponsorship.

Israeli Security, Palestinian Homeland — "The need to reconcile Israel's need for security with a Palestinian homeland remains at the heart of the Middle East problem. The United States should be committed to both." So stated Father J. Bryan Hehir July 13 in testimony delivered on behalf of the U.S. Catholic Conference before the House Subcommittee on Europe and the Middle East.

E.R.A. Reintroduced — Fourteen days after failing to achieve ratification, the Equal Rights Amendment was reintroduced in Congress by a group of 51 Senators and 201 Representatives.

Postage Relief — President Reagan gave the Cahtolic press and other non-profit mailers an unexpected gift July 18 by signing a $42 million postal subsidy measure that would help offset substantially higher postal rates for at least two months.

Certification Protested — Protests preceded and greeted the action of the Reagan administration in certifying July 27 that El Salvador was making progress in support of human rights and, therefore, deserved to receive continuing military aid, in the amount of $81 million for the rest of the fiscal year. Open to question and qualification was a State Department report claiming that there was a "downward trend" in political violence and a "demonstrable attempt" by the government to control its forces.

Basketball Dropped — Jesuit Father John Lo Schiavo, president of the University of San Francisco, announced July 29 that the school was ending its intercollegiate basketball program because of scandals which had damaged its "integrity and its reputation." Despite repeated efforts by the university to stop violations of National Collegiate Athletic Association rules, Father Lo Schiavo said "further deliberate and serious violations . . . have occurred, and the university cannot afford to pay the price the basketball program is imposing on it." In 58 years of competition, the Dons of the University of San Francisco compiled a record of 869 wins and 467 losses, and produced such stars as Bill Russell and K.C. Jones.

Meetings — Meetings during the month included the following.

• More than 6,000 people from 49 states and 14 foreign countries attended the Worldwide Marriage Encounter convention July 9 to 11 in Seattle.

• A highlight of the 10th annual Right to Life convention July 15 to 17 in Cherry Hill, N.J., was a message from President Reagan urging an end to legalized abortion.

• The third biennial convention of the Couple to Couple League, for the promotion of natural family planning, was scheduled July 28 to 31 at Creighton University, Omaha.

National Briefs:

• The Baltimore Archdiocese was answering Planned Parenthood newspaper ads backing legalized abortion with its own series of pro-life ads.

• Television is the greatest tool God has given to help nourish Americans suffering spiritual starvation, declared Mother M.

Angelica Francis, foundress and head of the Eternal Word Television Network, at the convention of the Catholic Daughters of the Americas in Chicago.

• Jacqueline Grennan Wexler was elected July 29 president of the National Conference of Christians and Jews.

Challenge to Hispanics

The 14 U.S. bishops of Hispanic ancestry, in their first joint pastoral letter, challenged Hispanic Americans to be "artisans of a new people" by developing their native cultural and religious values. "Conscious of all that God has achieved through us," they said, "we call on our people to assume an attitude of leadership to create a more human society."

The bishops said the outstanding assets of Hispanic Americans were faith, a culture permeated by the Gospel, extended family life and love for country and community. "the greatest strength of our people," they wrote, "comes from the rediscovery of the Gospel that is our truth, our way and our life."

The letter, honoring Our Lady of Guadalupe and entitled "The Bishops Speak with the Virgin," was published July 22.

INTERNATIONAL

Suffering in Lebanon — Said El-Azem, a UNICEF Worker, said that about 910,000 children and mothers in Lebanon's war zone had been severely affected by the fighting since the Israeli invasion of the country was launched June 6. He declined to estimate the numbers of dead and wounded in the absence of official statistics on casualties.

Report Criticized — The bishops of Honduras criticized a report by a committee of the Latin American Bishops Council which said that many Catholics, including priests, were influenced by Marxism. The report was poorly done and press comments based on it were an attempt to smear and divide the Church for political reasons, they said in a statement issued July 7. "We vigorously deny local media assertions that 'there are Marxists in the Catholic Church' and that 'many priests are committed to the armed struggle,' " they said. "The assertion follows the mentality of many who think the worst evil in Central America is Marxism and its ally is the Church. Yet we have said so many times that the Church condemns violence as anti-Christian and does not endorse extreme ideologies such as Marxism because they go against the Gospel."

U.N. Session Fruitless — The June 7 to July 10 special session of the United Nations General Assembly on disarmament came to a close without significant action on a comprehensive program for ending the arms race. The major products of the session were rhetorical fireworks, by President Reagan and Soviet Foreign Minister Gromyko, and a vague agreement to launch a "world disarmament campaign."

Favorable Attitude in Zimbabwe — The five Catholic bishops of Zimbabwe said the government had a "favorable attitude" toward the Church and that they were optimistic about the future, following the guerrilla war which brought the black-majority government of Prime Minister Robert Mugabe to power in 1980. Their views were published in the July 10 edition of *Fides,* the news service of the Congregation for the Evangelization of Peoples.

In a related development, the Catholic Justice and Peace Commission criticized new emergency regulations protecting Zimbabwe security officials from legal action against them.

Foreign Intervention Decried — Bishop Arturo Rivera Damas condemned foreign intervention for both sides in the Salvadoran civil war in two consecutive Sunday homilies during the month. He said on July 4: "The news is true that men from elsewhere, like Cuba and Nicaragua, are helping the guerrillas, but it is also true that other armies, like the Honduran soldiers, are cooperating from the border with the army of El Salvador. It becomes clear that foreign intervention is leading to the feared internationalization of the conflict."

Persecution in China — Chinese Catholics were in the same situation as English Catholics in the 16th century under Henry VIII "when Catholics, by being Catholics, were unconstitutional," said Father Joseph J. Spae in an interview for *The Tidings,* newspaper of the Archdiocese of Los Angeles. Father Spae was a consultor to the Vatican Secretariat for Non-Christians and a specialist in church relations with China. He said the attitude of the Chinese government toward the Church made reconciliation between the two all but impossible.

Changes Wanted in Brazil — The bishops of Brazil, making known their concerns as campaigns heated up for November elections, asked that security and immigration laws be eased as part of the military government's "political opening" aimed at fostering a wider civilian-role in national affairs. The prelates criticized the strictness of security laws and said immigration laws hampered the work of the Church, especially missionary activities, because they gave the government excessive control over who may enter the country.

Excommunication in Nicaragua — Santa Rosa Parish in Managua was placed under interdict July 22 and all parishioners involved in the beating of a bishop and his companions the previous evening were declared excommunicated by Archbishop Miguel Obando Bravo of Managua. He took the action, which included temporary closing of the church, because of what he called the "sacrilege and des-

ecration" which occurred when a melee broke out as Auxiliary Bishop Bosco Vivas Robelo went to the parish to retrieve the Blessed Sacrament. The incident was triggered by the transfer of the pastor to another parish.

Erosion of Rights in Guatemala — "Human rights in Guatemala are once again being eroded by a return to repressive measures of former regimes," according to a report on the four-month-old military government. The report was issued by a three-man, fact-finding team representing five U.S. science and health organizations. Despite the pledge of Gen. Efrain Montt to respect human rights, the report said, "the pattern now emerging is far different, with substantial violations of basic rights and a return to increasing brutality."

Sacred Heart Congress — More than 500 persons gathered July 24 to 28 in Toulouse to examine and discuss the roots of devotion to the Sacred Heart of Jesus and to mark the 25th anniversary of Pope Pius XII's encyclical on the subject, *Haurietis Aquas.* Cardinal Joseph Ratzinger, one of the speakers at the international congress, said that "in the heart of Jesus is found the center of the Christian faith."

International Briefs:
• The Catholic bishops of South Africa expressed support for the anti-apartheid statement made by 123 white Dutch Reformed leaders and reported in June.

• The bishops of Chile, in a statement issued in mid-July, urged the government and private enterprise to create more jobs in the economically troubled country.

Covenant Turned Down

The House of Clergy, unlike the House of Bishops and the House of Laity at the Anglican General Synod July 6 to 9, failed to approve by a two-thirds majority vote a proposal for a covenant among the Church of England, the Methodist Church, the United Reformed Church and the Moravian Church. The covenant would have involved mutual recognition of ministries (orders) and sacraments, the acceptance of bishops into the Methodist Church and United Reformed Church, and the conducting of joint ordinations. Defeat of the proposal meant the end of one of the more ambitious ventures toward church unity in England.

In other actions, the synod:
• gave provisional approval to a form of service "for the reconciliation of a penitent";

• asked for the preparation of draft legislation that would allow Anglican women priests from overseas to exercise their ministry on certain occasions when visiting England;

• committed itself to a policy of disengagement by Britain from the economy of South Africa.

AUGUST 1982

VATICAN

Peace Day Theme — The Vatican announced Aug. 3 that Pope John Paul had chosen "The Dialogue of Peace: A Challenge for Our Time" as the theme of the Jan. 1, 1983, observance of the World Day of Peace. "So many tragic events — wars, hostilities, and so many missed opportunities, fruitless negotiations or inconclusive international conferences — . . . point to the urgency of true dialogue as an instrument for peace in our day," the statement said. The statement called for "a true dialogue, not the pretense of empty discussions intended only to camouflage selfish intentions and to avoid honest communication, to resolve problems." The World Day of Peace observance was started by Pope Paul VI in 1968.

Violence in El Salvador Condemned — The Pope condemned military and guerrilla violence in El Salvador in a letter to the bishops there, issued Aug. 6 to coincide with celebrations honoring Christ, patron of the nation. The letter said: "The methodology of violence which has led to a fratricidal war — placing on the one side those who consider armed battle a necessary instrument for obtaining a new social order, and on the other side those resorting to principles of 'national security' to legitimize brutal repression — has no rational, and much less Christian, justification. . . . The discords and divisions that still disturb your country and cause new conflicts and violence have their true and deep root in situations of social injustice: a problem that has erupted with force at the political level."

Shooting in Paris — The Pope expressed "horror and indignation" Aug. 10 at the killing of six persons the day before at the Jo Goldenberg Restaurant in the Jewish Quarter of Paris. He did so in a message of sympathy to be relayed by Archbishop Jean-Marie Lustiger to families of the victims and the 22 persons who were wounded in the attack by unidentified terrorists.

Marriage Relationship — The Holy Father, addressing 20,000 people Aug. 11, continued his weeks-long discussion of St. Paul's view of the marriage relationship. Against the background of the Letter to the Ephesians, he said when St. Paul wrote that "wives should be submissive to their husbands as to the Lord," he did not mean "that the husband is 'boss' of the wife and that the inter-personal pact of matrimony is a pact of dominion of husband over wife. . . . There is to be no one-sided domination. Each is to be subject to the other from a sense of Christian piety, a piety that springs from awareness of the mystery of Christ and that finds its expression in love."

Meeting with Mother Teresa — The Pope met with Mother Teresa of Calcutta at Castel Gandolfo Aug. 19 after her return from a week-long visit to Beirut. She told the Pontiff that the people of the city, "despite being affected by a tragic situation in the middle of the destruction and deprivations of the long war, await with hope the definitive cessation of hostilities."

Nuclear Dissuasion Inadequate — You "are in a better position than others to gauge the apocalyptic effects of a nuclear war; in particular, the unheard of sufferings and the tremendous destruction of human lives and works of civilization. You can more easily ascertain that the logic of nuclear dissuasion cannot be considered a final goal or an appropriate and secure means for safeguarding international peace." So stated the Pope in a letter addressed to scientists attending an Aug. 20 to 23 seminar in Erice, Italy.

New Status for Opus Dei — Father Romeo Panciroli, director of the Vatican Press Office, announced Aug. 23 that the Pope had decided to establish Opus Dei as a personal prelature — a quasi diocese in its own right for Opus Dei members under their own bishop and exempt (in internal matters) from the jurisdiction of diocesan bishops. The prototype secular institute had more than 70,000 members in 80 countries. Father Panciroli said that the publication of documents implementing the Pope's decision had been postponed for technical reasons.

Two Visits outside the Vatican — The Pope made two trips Aug. 29, to the Republic of San Marino (his 15th foreign trip) and to the city of Rimini (his 28th trip within Italy).

• In San Marino, he celebrated Mass in the morning before about 30,000 people and spoke about "a Christian morality that is not just superficial and exterior." He said: "the Church can neither change nor lessen its own teaching on marriage and the family. It deplores every attempt both against the unity of matrimony and against its indissolubility." He also mentioned the Church's total opposition to abortion.

• Later, in Rimini, the Holy Father celebrated another Mass on an Adriatic beachfront before a throng of about 300,000 people. With a vacation theme in mind, he told young people attending a week-long Meeting for Friendship among Peoples: "To rest means to encounter oneself and to reconcile oneself with one's own depths. Only then do we truly rest."

The Pope Also:

• Prayed Aug. 4 that Poland would be saved from a destruction similar to that which occurred during insurrections against Nazi forces Aug. 1 and 2, 1944.

• Celebrated Mass for Pope Paul VI Aug. 6, the fourth anniversary of his death.

114

• Met with 100 African and Asian refugees Aug 12 at Castel Gandolfo.

• Spoke privately Aug. 18 with Ann Odre, one of the two American women wounded during the attempt on his life May 13, 1981.

• Met Aug. 24 with Archbishop Joseph Mercieca, a figure in church-state controversy in Malta.

Vatican Briefs:

• The establishment of diplomatic relations with Denmark, Norway and Sweden was announced Aug. 2.

• Msgr. Mario Peressin condemned the use of outer space for military purposes and called Aug. 10 for the formation of a "world conscience" to prevent the exclusion of poor nations from space exploration. Msgr. Peressin was head of a Vatican delegation to the second United Nations Conference on the Exploration and Peaceful Utilization of Extra-Atmospheric Space, Unispace '82, in Vienna.

• Artificial contraception is a "formidable enemy of youth and families today," declared Chilean Bishop Francisco Jose Cox Huneeus, secretary of the Pontifical Council for the Family, Aug. 10, in an address at the second Inter-American Congress on the Family in Acapulco, Mexico.

Churches, Priests in Nicaragua

A papal letter to the bishops of Nicaragua, condemning "popular churches" and warning against priests in government, was read Aug. 8 in churches throughout the country.

The "popular churches" meant were those which rejected church authority and were subject to conversion to political purposes.

What is expected of priests, the Pontiff said, "is the announcement of the Gospel, the proclamation of the Fatherhood of God, the dispensation of the sacramental mysteries of salvation.... It is not through a political role but through the priestly ministry that the people want to remain close to them."

NATIONAL

Repository for Germinal Choice — A leading Jesuit theologian sharply criticized the Repository for Germinal Choice, a sperm bank trying to produce high-I.Q. babies with sperm donated by Nobel prizewinners. News about the birth in April of the first child by artificial insemination from the bank prompted Father Richard McCormick, Rose F. Kennedy professor of Christian ethics at Georgetown University, to call the project "an isolated little symbol of a monstrous attitude." Calling positive eugenics "the preferential breeding of superior individuals to improve the genetic stock of the human race," he said it reduces human beings to "animals" which are bred for "muscles or brain circumference."

K. of C. Centenary — Knights of Columbus celebrated the 100th anniversary of their founding Aug. 3 to 6 in a round of activities attended by more than 7,000 Knights in Hartford and New Haven, Conn. Highlights of the convention were messages from the Pope, President Reagan, congratulations from various prelates, and resolutions which mirrored the President's support for tuition tax credits, school prayer and opposition to abortion. Cardinal Agostino Casaroli was the Pope's official representative at the celebration; also in attendance were about 150 cardinals and bishops. All paid high tribute to Father Michael McGivney, founder of the Knights, and the 1.36 million Knights in 7,200 councils in the United States and other countries.

Haitians on Parole — Barry University in Miami, near the Krome Avenue Detention Center, agreed to handle reporting procedures for Haitians on parole under an order issued June 29 by U.S. District Court Judge Eugene Spellman. He ordered that Haitian detainees who had entered the United States illegally be released from camps around the country while waiting for hearings to determine their status in this country.

Tekakwitha Conference — Members of more than 50 tribes — including 12 priests and more nuns — were among the 1,500 or more persons who attended the 43rd convention of the Tekakwitha Indian Conference Aug. 9 to 13 at Gonzaga University, Spokane. The theme of the meeting was "A Spiritual Journey and Healing Dialogue between Native Americans and Catholics." Ways and means of integrating Indian cultural practices into the liturgy were among subjects under discussion.

Coppola Execution — Bishop Walter F. Sullivan of Richmond and other religious leaders in Virginia appealed in vain to Gov. Charles S. Robb to halt the scheduled execution Aug. 10 of Frank J. Coppola, an ex-policeman convicted and sentenced to death in 1978 for the torture-murder of Muriel Hatchell. He was the first person executed in Virginia since 1962 and the fifth in the nation since 1967. Bishop Sullivan, while appealing for commutation of Coppola's sentence, said: "The death penalty contradicts our commitment to the value of all human life. It is simply an act of vengeance."

Chief Chaplains — Two priests were named chief military chaplains during the month: Father Patrick J. Hessian, promoted to the rank of major general, for the Army; and Redemptorist Father John A. Collins, also a major general, for the Air Force.

Immigration Act — The U.S. Senate, with an 81 to 18 vote Aug. 17, passed the Immigration Reform and Control Act of 1982 and sent it to the House of Representatives for debate. The act provided:

• Illegal aliens living continuously in the U.S. since before Jan. 1, 1977, would be eligible for permanent resident status and could apply for citizenship two years after obtaining it.

• Illegal aliens living continuously in the U.S. since before Jan. 1, 1980, would be eligible for temporary resident status and could apply for permanent status three years after obtaining it.

The act also provided for the fining of employers of illegal aliens, authorized the immigration of "guest" farm workers, and fixed the annual number of immigrants (exclusive of refugees) at 425,000.

The U.S. Catholic Conference, which supported efforts for immigration reform, took exception to restrictive amendments to the bill sponsored by Sen. Alan Simpson of Wyoming.

Payment for Abortions — The New Jersey Supreme Court ruled Aug. 18 that the state must pay for abortions for poor women for medical reasons even if the mother's life is not in danger. With its 5-to-2 ruling, the court overturned a 1975 state law which had restricted state funding to abortions in cases of danger to a mother's life. One commentator on the decision said: "Since the words, 'medically necessary,' are a euphemism for any abortion that an abortionist wants to perform, the practical effect of the decision is to force taxpayers to fund abortion on demand." The person making the comment was Richard Doerflinger, legislative assistant to the Committee for Pro-Life Activities, National Conference of Catholic Bishops.

Meetings — The following organizations were among those which held meetings during the month.

• Four hundred members of the National Black Catholic Clergy Conference, the National Black Sisters' Conference and the National Black Catholic Seminarians' Association met jointly Aug. 2 to 7 in Plymouth, Mich., a suburb of Detroit.

• Fourteen hundred members attended the international convention of the Daughters of Isabella Aug. 10 in Hartford, Conn.

• Two of three scheduled 1982 events of the Fourth Annual National Catholic Lay Celebrations of Evangelization were held in Minneapolis Aug. 20 to 22 and in Los Angeles Aug. 27 to 29. A third celebration was scheduled in Miami Oct. 22 to 24.

• The Cardinal Mindszenty Foundation held a conference Aug. 28 in West Lafayette, Ind., on "The Challenges of Communism to Faith, Family and Country."

National Briefs:

• Catholic Relief Services reported that Bishop Edwin B. Broderick would be leaving his post as executive director for new duties with the board of bishops which oversees CRS policy.

• Cardinal Agostino Casaroli, papal secretary of state, met with President Reagan Aug.

3 and with Secretary of State George Shultz Aug. 4.

• A nuclear freeze resolution supported by some Catholic and other organizations was narrowly defeated Aug. 5 by a 204-to-202 vote in the House of Representatives.

• Atlanta's oldest Catholic church, the Shrine of the Immaculate Conception, was destroyed by fire Aug. 6.

• Mass and a picnic in Grant Park, Chicago, Aug. 29 ended six days of events marking the installation of Archbishop Joseph L. Bernardin as head of the largest archdiocese in the United States.

• The Voice of America and Radio Free Europe broadcast to the Soviet Union an account of an Aug. 29 pilgrimage — at the Shrine of the North American Martyrs in Auriesville, N.Y. — for the suffering Church in Lithuania.

Meeting of Religious Superiors

About 800 members of the Conference of Major Superiors of Men and the Leadership Conference of Women Religious met jointly Aug. 15 to 20 to discuss ways to build bridges that can change the world.

One of the speakers, Archbishop Pio Laghi, apostolic delegate to the United States, warned against temporary commitments to religious life. Archbishop Augustin Mayer, secretary of the Congregation for Religious and Secular Institutes, told superiors that prayer, community life and respect for authority are necessary to achieve the goals of religious life.

INTERNATIONAL

A-Bombing Anniversaries — Observances Aug. 6 and 9 in the two target cities in Japan and other places marked the atomic bombing of Hiroshima and Nagasaki in 1945. More than 200,000 people were killed by just two bombs.

Assembly on Aging — The first World Assembly on Aging concluded a two-week session Aug. 6 in Vienna by adopting a plan of action calling for policies to enhance the lives of the elderly and to allow them to enjoy "in mind and body, fully and freely, their advancing years in peace, health and security." Delegates from 120 countries and representatives of 143 non-governmental organizations agreed that quality of life "is no less important than longevity," and that the elderly should therefore be able to enjoy in their own families and communities "a life of fulfillment, health, security and contentment, appreciated as an integral part of society." The Vatican was represented by a delegation headed by Bishop Francisco Jose Cox Huneeus, secretary of the Pontifical Council for the Family.

Restrictions in Bulgaria — Italy's national Catholic newspaper, *Avvenire,* reported Aug.

8 that the Bulgarian government had forbidden the teaching of religion to children under the age of 16. The report said the order was based on Article 20 of the Bulgarian law on teaching, which states that "the education and organization of children and youth are under the sole jurisdiction of the state." The paper said the order was the latest in a series of "numerous impediments placed on the activity of Catholics" since a communist regime came to power in 1947. The most serious impediment was the government's "strong resistance" to granting permission for the ordination of priests.

Anti-Mafia Effort in Sicily — The priests of Palermo joined forces in an effort to halt Mafia-related violence that had already taken a toll of 94 lives in the "triangle of death," the nearby towns of Bagheria, Casteldaccia and Altavilla. "Whoever favors the men of death in any way cannot remain tranquil before God," the priests said in a letter read in all churches of the archdiocese Aug. 15. They called on "the political parties, the parliament and the government to finally decide to end the inertia" by acting strongly against the Mafia.

Abortion in India — *Asiaweek,* a weekly news magazine published in Hong Kong, reported in its Aug. 20 edition that a trend toward routinely aborting female babies in India was causing "a nationwide furor among women's organizations." The magazine reported that "Feminist Amrita Chhachhi argues that the most disturbing facet of the sex tests (of the unborn, by amniocentesis) is the resultant sanction of abortion as a routine method of population control."

Vatican Accused — For the third time in three months, the official Soviet news media criticized Vatican policies in Eastern Europe and accused it of supporting anti-socialist activities. On Aug. 20, Tass reprinted an article from a Czechoslovakian weekly which charged the Vatican was trying to ban the Pacem in Terris organization of priests because it "supports the politics of peace of the Prague government and those of Moscow." At issue was a document published in the spring by the Congregation for the Clergy which reaffirmed the traditional ban on priests' associations for political purposes. Pacem in Terris was such an organization.

Swiss Dioceses Opposed — Swiss Protestant leaders were against a proposal by the Catholic bishops to establish three new dioceses, one of which would be in Geneva, once the capital of the non-Lutheran Reformation. Geneva has not had a Catholic bishop since 1535 when the celebration of Mass was prohibited in the city.

Freedom for Religious Sought in Hungary — Father Giuseppe Pittau, assistant to Pope John Paul's delegate to the Jesuits, asked the communist government of Hungary to ease restrictions on religious orders. While visiting members of his order in the country, he "presented to religious and government authorities the strong desire to receive permission, not only for the Jesuits but also for other religious, to be able to accept novices, open their own institutions, and thus aid in the ecclesial needs of the nation," according to a communique issued by Jesuit headquarters in Rome Aug. 31. Since 1950, Jesuits had not been allowed to "receive new recruits" and were "condemned to a slow extinction," the communique said.

Tension in Nicaragua — Tension between the bishops and the Sandinista government increased as both sides engaged in a war of words in which the bishops expressed concern for the future of Catholic schools, priests were accused of leading anti-government protests as part of a destabilization plot, and efforts were made to discredit an official of the Archdiocese of Managua on trumped-up allegations of immoral conduct.

International Briefs:

• A human rights monitoring group set up by religious orders in the Philippines said that the military had killed 62 persons and detained another 549 illegally this year.

• The Legal Aid Society of the Archdiocese of San Salvador reported Aug. 17 that government security forces and right-wing death squads in El Salvador had assassinated 3,258 people this year.

Celebration at Czestochowa

The coalescence of Polish religious and political sentiments was in strong evidence during the climactic celebration marking the 600th anniversary of the arrival in the country of the revered icon of Our Lady of Czestochowa. Two hundred thousand pilgrims assembled at the national shrine Aug. 26 not only to attend Mass but also to hear their Primate, Archbishop Jozef Glemp, voice their demands on the government.

The Archbishop appealed for: the relase of Lech Walesa, leader of the Solidarity labor movement; freedom for 600 persons interned under martial law; amnesty for several thousands convicted of martial law violations.

In other developments during the month:

• The bishops blamed the government for the postponement of the Pope's planned visit to take part in the anniversary celebrations.

• Warsaw's "flower war" of protest against martial law escalated in the middle of the month despite a decision by the city council to permit construction of a monument to the former Primate, Cardinal Stefan Wyszynski.

• The bishops again urged the government Aug. 30 to talk with Solidarity leaders.

• Strong anti-government demonstrations were mounted on Aug. 31, the second anniversary of the Solidarity movement.

SEPTEMBER 1982

VATICAN

Katholikentag — Pope John Paul told West German Catholics Sept. 1 to commit themselves to "the presuppositions of peace: truth, justice and freedom." In a message taped at the Vatican and broadcast during opening ceremonies of the Sept. 1 to 5 Catholic Day congress in Dusseldorf, the Pontiff commented on the arms race and the imbalance between rich and poor nations. "As the limits of growth and the strident disparity between North and South become ever more evident, develop a new life-style and a community of fraternal sharing," he said. "If the world situation, on account of totalitarian ideologies and a frightening competition for armaments, assumes ever more threatening forms, each one of you in his or her respective place must make an effort to find the peaceful solution to conflicts through politically responsible routes." More than 100,000 persons were expected to attend the congress, held semi-annually since 1848.

Deaths in Poland Deplored — The Holy Father, addressing a group of people Sept. 5 at Castel Gandolfo, deplored the deaths of six persons in street clashes in Poland Aug. 31. It was his first direct reference to violence which took place in dozens of Polish cities during demonstrations marking the second anniversary of agreements which led to the formation of Solidarity, the independent labor union. The demonstrations were mounted in protest against the suspension of many civil rights since the imposition of martial law Dec. 13, 1981.

Praise for Literacy Campaign — Attempts to achieve world literacy "should be considered not just as a type of assistance for the alienated but as a natural right of justice," declared the Pope in a letter to Amadou Mahtar M'Bow, director general of UNESCO. The letter praising the work of the agency marked the 16th annual World Literacy Day, celebrated Sept. 8 in the 157 member nations of the U.N. Educational, Scientific and Cultural Organization. UNESCO estimated that there were 815 million illiterate adults and 120 million illiterate school-age children in the world.

Meeting with Arafat

Pope John Paul met privately for 20 minutes Sept. 15 with Yasser Arafat, head of the Palestine Liberation Organization. The following communique was released by the Vatican Press Office after the meeting.

"This afternoon, Wednesday, Sept. 15, 1982, before the general audience, the Holy Father, moved by his constant concern for favoring the wearying process of peace in the Middle East, received Mr. Yasser Arafat, who had come to Rome to participate in the conference of the Interparliamentary Union.

"During the conversation, the Supreme Pontiff manifested his benevolence for the Palestinian people and his participation in their long suffering, expressing the hope that an equitable and lasting solution to the mideast conflict may be reached as soon as possible, which solution, excluding recourse to violence in any form, and especially to terrorism and revenge, may lead to the recognition of the rights of all people, and in particular that of the Palestinian people to their own homeland and of Israel to its security.

"Referring then to the drama of Lebanon, where many Palestinians still live, a drama aggravated by the tragic death of its President-elect, Bashir Gemayel (Sept. 14, in a bombing), the Holy Father, in heartily deploring the despicable act of terrorism, expressed the hope that the hoped-for process of reconstruction of the country will not, despite this, be interrupted, and that it may become a precious element of stability and peace for the Middle East."

The Pope's meeting with Arafat became a media event as soon as it was announced five days in advance. It also became the trigger for shrill, sharp, intemperate criticism of the Pope and the Church from high Israeli officials including, it was reported, Prime Minister Menachem Begin.

The Vatican made it clear in a communique issued Sept. 14 that there was no political significance to the meeting, "particularly as regards the character of representation for these (Palestinian) people as claimed by the PLO."

The meaning of this communique as well as the authentic purpose of the Pope in meeting with Arafat were misread, misinterpreted and maligned by the media, Israeli officials, spokesmen for about a half dozen leading Jewish organizations in the United States, some Catholic critics and others.

NATIONAL

Gay Rights Law Criticized — An editorial in the Sept. 2 edition of the *Catholic Standard and Times* called a new gay rights city ordinance in Philadelphia a "bad law, unnecessary law and a tragic precedent." The editorial commented: "It is certainly unreasonable and wrong to discriminate in hiring or housing solely on the basis of 'race, color, sex or national origin.' If, however, sexual orientation is defined as including homosexual, heterosexual or bisexual practice, one is adding to a list composed of involuntary conditions or states a new category which includes voluntary activity — a bad precedent indeed in the amendment of law."

Anglican-Lutheran Intercommunion — In one of several resolutions passed at the 67th general convention of the Episcopal Church, intercommunion was approved with three Lutheran bodies which had recently voted to merge — the Lutheran Church in America, the American Lutheran Church and the Association of Evangelical Lutheran Churches. The resolution said the move did not imply doctrinal agreement on the Eucharist and ministry. The convention was held Sept. 6 to 15 in New Orleans.

First New York Black Bishop — Msgr. Emerson J. Moore was ordained Sept. 8 the first black bishop in the history of the Archdiocese of New York. The new auxiliary bishop was to continue as pastor of St. Charles Borromeo Parish while serving also as the vicar for Central Harlem.

Ordained with Bishop Moore was Auxiliary Bishop Joseph T. O'Keefe, vicar general of the archdiocese.

Lutheran Merger — Archbishop John R. Roach, president of the National Conference of Catholic Bishops, hailed the decision of three Lutheran denominations to merge as a "significant step in the broader movement of ecumenism." In a statement issued Sept. 9, he said that "Roman Catholics join their Lutheran brothers and sisters in rejoicing at this new and important development." The previous day, the Lutheran Church in America, the American Lutheran Church and the Association of Evangelical Lutheran Churches had voted to form a new church of 5.5 million members that will be the third largest Protestant denomination in the United States. "Although it is of immediate concern to Lutherans," Archbishop Roach said, "I believe it represents another significant step in the broader movement of ecumenism. . . . I renew my prayers for the speedy coming to that full unity among Christians which Christ wills for his church."

The proposal to establish the new Lutheran denomination by Jan. 1, 1988, was overwhelmingly approved by the Lutheran Church in America at its convention in Louisville, by the American Lutheran Church at its convention in San Diego and by the Association of Evangelical Lutheran Churches at its convention in Cleveland. Results of the votes were announced simultaneously to the three conventions, which were linked by telephone.

Delegates to the three conventions voted to appoint a 70-member commission, headed by Dr. William A. Kinniston, president of Wittenberg University, to work out a constitution for the new church. A convention to approve the new constitution was scheduled for 1987.

Teresian Anniversary — Preparations were under way for the celebration Oct. 15 to 17 at the Catholic University of America of the 400th anniversary of the death of St. Teresa of Avila, Carmelite mystic and the first woman Doctor of the Church. Planned events included the world premiere to a cantata by Gian Carlo Menotti and a symposium on and an exhibit of the works of St. Teresa.

Italian Apostolate Conference — Establishment was announced of the Northeast Italian Apostolate Conference — a coalition of dioceses, religious communities and individuals — to assist bishops in ministry to Italian-speaking Catholics. Auxiliary Bishop Anthony J. Bevilacqua of Brooklyn was elected first president of the conference.

Tuition Tax Credit — The Senate Finance Committee voted 12 to 6 Sept. 16 to pass a tuition tax credit bill that would give parents a tax credit for part of the tuition they pay to send their children to non-public schools.

INTERNATIONAL

Canadian Maronite Eparchy — The Eparchy of St. Maron of Montreal for Maronite Catholics in Canada was established Sept. 6. The bishop named to head the new jurisdiction was a Lebanese-born American, Msgr. Elias Shaheen, pastor of the Maronite Cathedral of Our Lady of Lebanon, Brooklyn.

Tribute to Grace Kelly — Princess Grace of Monaco died Sept. 14 after an automobile accident in which she and her daughter were injured. Tributes to her character, talent, acting career and role as princess of Monaco were many and generous. Cardinal John J. Krol said of her: "She was indeed a gracious and gentle lady, a devoted and loving wife and mother, and a princess beloved by the people of Monaco. She was renowned as a talented actress, but her natural beauty was far exceeded by the spiritual beauty of her soul and of her living faith." Princess Grace was survived by her husband, Prince Rainier Grimaldi, two daughters and a son.

Negotiations To Continue — Argentina and Chile agreed to continue seeking a peaceful solution to their Beagle Channel dispute even if papal mediation fails, according to a Vatican communique issued Sept. 15. The two countries said they would abide by a treaty they signed in 1972, pledging that territorial disputes would be settled by peaceful means.

Moscow Group Disbands — The Moscow Helsinki Group, the leading human rights organization in the Soviet Union, said it had been forced to end its activities because of pressure from the government. "In this situation, the group cannot fulfill its duties and is forced under pressure of the authorities to end its work," said a statement issued Sept. 8.

World Anarchy — U.N. General Secretary Perez de Cuellar, in his first annual report to the General Assembly, said the world is "perilously close to a new international anarchy" and that current mechanisms of the U.N. may not be able to reverse the trend. He suggested, among other things, a U.N. summit meeting to discuss some of the problems besetting international relations.

POPE JOHN PAUL II

(See related entries under John Paul II in Index.)

Cardinal-Archbishop Karol Wojtyla of Cracow was elected Bishop of Rome Oct. 16, 1978, on the seventh or eighth ballot cast on the second day of voting at a conclave of 111 cardinals. He chose the name John Paul II and was invested with the pallium, the symbol of his papal office, Oct. 22 in ceremonies attended by more than 250,000 persons in St. Peter's Square.

The 263rd successor of St. Peter as Bishop of Rome and Supreme Pastor of the Universal Church, he is the first non-Italian Pope since Adrian VI (1522-23), the first Polish Pope in the history of the Church, and the youngest at the time of his election since Pius IX (1846-78).

Early Career

Karol Wojtyla was born May 18, 1920, in Wadowice, Poland.

He began higher studies at the age of 18, with major interests in poetry and theater arts. Forced to suspend university courses because of the outbreak of World War II, he went to work in a stone quarry and a chemical plant, thereby earning the later designation of himself as the "Worker Cardinal."

He started studies for the priesthood in 1942 in the underground seminary of Cracow, whose operations had been banned after the Nazi invasion of Poland.

Ordained to the priesthood Nov. 1, 1946, he was immediately sent to Rome for studies at the Angelicum University, where he earned a doctorate in ethics.

Back home in Poland, he worked as an assistant pastor in a village parish and as a chaplain to university students while continuing studies at the Catholic University of Lublin. He was awarded another doctorate there, in moral theology.

He began writing about this time, and eventually produced more than 100 articles and several books on ethical and other themes. Phenomenology was one of his fields of expertise.

University teaching came next, in 1953, with appointment in 1954 to the position of lecturer and later to the chair of ethics at the Catholic University of Lublin, the most prestigious institute of higher learning in Poland.

Bishop and Cardinal

He was ordained Auxiliary Bishop of Cracow Sept. 28, 1958, became vicar capitular in 1962 after the death of Apostolic Administrator Eugeniusz Baziak, and was appointed Archbishop Jan. 13, 1964. He was the first residential head of the see since the death of Cardinal Adam Sapieha in 1951. Between then and 1964 the archdiocese was run by administrators because the Communist government refused to permit the appointment and ministry of a residential bishop.

Archbishop Wojtyla attended all sessions of the Second Vatican Council from 1962 to 1965, and was one of the writers of the *Pastoral Constitution on the Church in the Modern World.* He also contributed input to the *Declaration on Religious Freedom* and the *Decree on the Instruments of Social Communication.*

His efforts to put into effect the directives of the council induced him to write a book, *Foundations of Renewal,* in 1972 and to start that same year an archdiocesan synod he saw concluded as Pope during his visit to Poland in 1979.

He was inducted into the College of Cardinals June 26, 1967, as one of the younger members, and subsequently served actively in the Congregation for the Sacraments and Divine Worship, the Congregation for the Clergy, and the Congregation for Catholic Education.

He also served as a theological consultant to Pope Paul VI.

He attended assemblies of the Synod of Bishops as a representative of the Polish Bishops' Conference and was a member of the synod's permanent council.

From the beginning of his priestly career, and especially during his episcopate, the Cardinal was vigorous in the defense of human and religious rights, the rights of workers, and rights to religious education.

Close to Cardinal Wyszynski and in company with his fellow bishops, he negotiated the tightrope of Catholic survival in a country under Communist control. With them, and as their spokesman at times, he was stalwart in resisting efforts of the regime to impose atheism, materialism and secularism on the people and culture of Poland.

Active Pope

Since the beginning of his pontificate, John Paul has been active as Bishop of Rome, with frequent visits to parishes and institutions of the diocese for the celebration of Mass and participation in other events. During these visits, as well as others to places of pilgrimage and historic significance in Italy, he has had perhaps more personal contact with the faithful than any other Pope. The number of attendants at weekly general audiences at the Vatican and Castel Gandolfo has been unprecedented.

Unprecedented also has been the attention focused on him during and in connection with his 15 pastoral trips to 29 foreign countries between January, 1979, and the end of August, 1982.

Extensive Travels

Pastoral Pilgrimages: His first three, in 1979, were to the Dominican Republic and Mexico, Poland, Ireland and the United States.

He traveled to Turkey at the end of November, 1979, to meet with Orthodox Ecumenical Patriarch Dimitrios I. With him, he announced the establishment of a joint commission of theologians to begin formal dialogue in quest of the union of Roman Catholic and Orthodox Churches.

He made four trips in 1980.

While touring six African nations in May, he spoke about Africanization of the Church, the cultural values of African peoples and the independence they should have from alien influences of other countries.

In France for an address before the United Nations Educational, Scientific and Cultural Organization also in May, he delineated with great clarity the stance of the Church on a wide variety of subjects, with special emphasis on its role in a secularized state, society and culture.

During a 13-city tour of Brazil in July, the Pope declared that the Church is on the side of the poor, appealed for across-the-board respect for human rights by governments and people of influence, called for measures of economic and social reform, and indicated his approval of non-violent social activism for the good of all peoples. He attended a plenary assembly of the bishops of the country and took part in opening ceremonies of a national Eucharistic congress.

His eighth and ninth pastoral pilgrimages were to West Germany, Nov. 15 to 19, 1980, and to the Philippines and Japan, Feb. 16 to 27, 1981. While in the Philippines, he beatified six 17th century martyrs of Japan.

Plans for additional trips in 1981 to Lourdes, for participation in the 42nd International Eucharistic Congress, and to Switzerland had to be cancelled because of the attack on the Pope's life in May.

The Pope made six trips outside of Italy by mid-September, 1982, to: the African nations of Nigeria, Benin, Gabon and Equatorial Guinea, Feb. 12 to 19; six cities of Portugal, May 12 to 15, as well as the shrine of Our Lady of Fatima where he consecrated the world to the Blessed Virgin Mary; nine major cities of Great Britain, May 28 to June 2; Argentina, June 11 and 12; Switzerland, June 15.

The 15th foreign trip of his pontificate was to the tiny Republic of San Marino, Aug. 29, when he also made his 28th pastoral visit to an Italian city other than Rome, Rimini.

Additional trips were in planning at the end of the summer of 1982. The next one, it appeared, would be to Spain in the fall for participation in events commemorating the 400th anniversary of the death of St. Teresa of Avila, Carmelite mystic and reformer, first woman Doctor of the Church.

Key Writings

Encyclicals: The homilies and addresses delivered by the Pope on these trips were the equivalent of doctrinal, pastoral and social encyclical letters on a wide variety of subjects, all related to the key document of the first year of his pontificate. That was the formal encyclical, *Redemptor Hominis,* a treatise on Christian anthropology dealing with the divine and human aspects of redemption and the mission of the Church to carry on a dialogue of salvation with all peoples.

Two other encyclicals published within less than a year of each other were *Dives in Misericordia* ("Rich in Mercy"), issued Dec. 2, 1980, and *Laborem Exercens,* on work as a "way of sanctification," whose publication was announced Sept. 13, 1981.

Apostolic Exhortation: The Pope published a lenghty exhortation on the family, *Familiaris Consortio,* in December, 1981. It is an extensive synthesis of the theology of the family based not only on traditional doctrinal background but also on recommendations that emanated from the 1980 assembly of the Synod of Bishops.

Various Items

Doctrinal Concern: In December, 1980, the Pope directly confronted the controversial writings of Father Hans Kung by giving his approval to a declaration by the Congregation for the Doctrine of the Faith that he could not be regarded as a Catholic theologian.

This action, along with various other statements and indications of attitude, mark John Paul as a pastor of decisive leadership for doctrinal orthodoxy and church discipline.

Canon Law: The Pope had the final draft of a revised Code of Canon Law under review in 1982.

Synods: The Holy Father convoked three of them in 1980.

With the Dutch bishops at the Vatican for a particular synod in January, he called for measures to cope with differences among the prelates, polarization among the people and action to remedy doctrinal and disciplinary irregularities. Later reports indicated that results of the synod were less than satisfactory.

Meeting with Ukrainian bishops in March, he named a successor to Cardinal Josyf Slipyi as the ranking Ukrainian bishop and turned down demands of some Ukrainians for a patriarchate.

With more than 200 delegates from episcopal conferences around the world, he held the fifth ordinary assembly of the Synod of Bishops.

He designated "Reconciliation and Penance in the Mission of the Church" as the theme of the 1983 assembly of the Synod, to be held most probably in the fall.

Cardinals: In June, 1979, the Holy Father inducted 14 new cardinals into the Sacred College, raising its membership at that time to 135.

There was speculation in 1982 that he might not create new cardinals until the expiration of current five-year terms of some cardinals in posts of the Roman Curia.

Meetings with Bishops: In relations with the hierarchy since becoming Pope, John Paul has met with groups of bishops making required *ad limina* visits to the Vatican, for first-hand reports and admonitions regarding conditions in dioceses all over the world. He has also met with assemblies of bishops in the countries he has visited.

Ecumenism: He met with Anglican Archbishop Robert Runcie at the Canterbury Cathedral during his visit to Great Britain in May, 1982. The two prelates prayed together, renewed their baptismal promises and issued a joint statement in which they announced the formation of a new joint Catholic-Anglican theological commission for a second phase of interfaith dialogue.

Audiences and Addresses: The Pope has delivered hundreds of addresses at general and private audiences and on special occasions. All of them have characteristically been grounded in doctrinal essentials coupled with relevance to the people being addressed or the events being commemorated.

Subjects of more than passing concern in 1982 were: marriage and the family; celibacy and the dedication of priests and religious; the call to all Catholics to participate actively in the mission of the Church; pleas for peace, especially in the Middle East, the Falkland Islands, El Salvador and Nicaragua; settlement of the Church-Solidarity-government crisis in Poland.

Near Tragedy: The Pope narrowly escaped death May 13, 1981, when he was fired upon at close range as he entered St. Peter's Square to address a general audience. Wounded more seriously than realized at first, he underwent emergency surgery and remained in Gemelli Polyclinic Hospital until June 3. On release, he stayed at the Vatican until June 20 when he was hospitalized a second time, until Aug. 14.

MUTUAL RECOGNITION NEEDED FOR PEACE

(By Father Kenneth J. Doyle,
NC News Correspondent)

Peace will never come to the Middle East until Israelis and Palestinians recognize each others' rights and identity, declared the Pope Sept. 15, 1982, shortly after meeting with PLO leader Yasser Arafat.

Addressing 20,000 people in St. Peter's Square, he called "barbarous" the assassination of Lebanon's President-elect Bashir Gemayel the previous day.

He said he "could not hide" his worries about the consequences for Lebanon of Gemayel's death and asked "all Lebanese, Christians and non-Christians, . . . to strengthen their bonds, to unite themselves for the good of the country, and absolutely not to yield to reactions of violence or of divisions."

To solve its problems, the Pope said, Lebanon needed to recover "sovereignty over all its territory," and this goal required the cooperation "of all its ethnic and religious components."

Despite the recent evacuation of PLO and Syrian troops trapped in West Beirut by Israeli soldiers, some PLO forces remained in other parts of the country, and Syrian and Israeli troops still continued to occupy parts of Lebanon.

Without mentioning specific proposals for mideast peace such as that offered by President Reagan, the Pope told the audience that recent weeks had been marked by "a flourishing of plans for re-launching negotiations and opening the way for a global solution to the conflict in the Middle East."

He added that "the Holy See is following with most attentive interest these initiatives and appreciates every effort which is made to favor dialogue and negotiations, in order to arrive finally at a settlement of the conflict."

The Pope said that "the Holy See is convinced above all that there will not be able to be true peace without justice; and that there will not be able to be justice if there are not recognized and accepted, in a stable manner, fair and equal, the rights of all the people involved."

Included in such rights, the Pontiff said, "is that of existence and security on one's own territory, in safeguarding the proper identity of each one."

He said that both Israelis and Palestinians had seen "simultaneously or alternately their rights assaulted or denied," and that "the Pope and the Catholic Church look with sympathy and consideration toward both these peoples."

The Pope suggested that the sad experiences of the previous several months in the Mideast might prompt the parties to hasten efforts at reconciliation and to "abandon every recourse to war, to violence and to all forms of armed struggle."

Dates and Events in Church History

First Century

Early 30's: First Christian Pentecost: gathering together of the Christian community, outpouring of the Holy Spirit, preaching of St. Peter to Jews in Jerusalem, baptism and aggregation of some 3,000 persons to the Christian community.

St. Stephen, deacon, was stoned to death at Jerusalem; he is venerated as the first Christian martyr.

34-64/67: St. Paul, formerly Saul the persecutor of Christians, was converted, baptized and joined to the college of Apostles. After three major missionary journeys, he was martyred in 64 or 67 at Rome.

39: The Gentile Cornelius and his family were baptized by St. Peter.

42: Persecution of Christians in Palestine broke out during the rule of Herod Agrippa; St. James the Greater, the first Apostle to die, was beheaded in 44; St. Peter was imprisoned for a short time; many Christians fled to Antioch and elsewhere.

At Antioch, the followers of Christ were first called Christians.

49: Christians at Rome, who were considered members of a Jewish sect, were adversely affected by a decree of Claudius which forbade Jewish worship there.

51: The Council of Jerusalem, in which all the Apostles participated under the presidency of St. Peter, decreed that circumcision, dietary regulations, and various other prescriptions of Mosaic Law were not obligatory for Gentile converts to the Christian community. The decree was issued in opposition to Judaizers who contended that observance of the Mosaic Law in its entirety was necessary for salvation.

64: Persecution under Nero: The emperor, accusing Christians of starting a fire which destroyed half of Rome, inaugurated the era of major Roman persecutions.

64/65: Martyrdom of St. Peter at Rome during the Neronian persecution. He established his see and spent his last years there after preaching in and around Jerusalem, establishing a see at Antioch, and presiding at the Council of Jerusalem.

70: Destruction of Jerusalem by Titus.

88-97: Pontificate of St. Clement I, third successor of St. Peter as bishop of Rome, one of the Apostolic Fathers. The *First Epistle of Clement to the Corinthians,* with which he has been identified, was addressed by the Church of Rome to the Church at Corinth, the scene of irregularities and divisions in the Christian community.

95: Domitian persecuted Christians, principally at Rome.

c. 100: Death of St. John, Apostle and Evangelist, marking the end of the Age of the Apostles and the first generation of the Church.

Second Century

c. 107: St. Ignatius of Antioch was martyred at Rome. He was the first writer to use the expression, "the Catholic Church."

112: Rescript to Pliny. Emperor Trajan instructed Pliny, governor of Bithynia, not to search out Christians but to punish them if they were publicly denounced and refused to do homage to the Roman gods. The rescript set a pattern of discretionary leniency for Roman magistrates in dealing with Christians.

117-138: Persecution under Hadrian. Many *Acts of Martyrs* date from this period.

c. 125: Spread of Gnosticism.

c. 155: St. Polycarp, bishop of Smyrna and disciple of St. John the Evangelist, was martyred.

c. 156: Beginning of Montanism.

161-180: Reign of Marcus Aurelius. His persecution, launched in the wake of natural disasters, was more violent than those of his predecessors.

165: St. Justin, an important early Christian writer, was martyred at Rome.

c. 180: St. Irenaeus, bishop of Lyons and one of the great early theologians, wrote *Adversus Haereses.* He stated that the teaching and tradition of the Roman See was the standard for belief.

196: Easter Controversy.

The *Didache,* written in the second century, was an important record of Christian belief, practice and government in the first century.

Latin was introduced in the West as a liturgical language.

The Catechetical School of Alexandria, founded about the middle of the century, increased in importance.

Third Century

202: Persecution under Septimius Severus, who wanted to establish one common religion in the Empire.

206: Tertullian, a convert since 197 and the first great ecclesiastical writer in Latin, joined the heretical Montanists. He died in 230.

215: Death of Clement of Alexandria, teacher of Origen and a founding father of the School of Alexandria.

217-235: St. Hippolytus, the first antipope. He was reconciled to the Church while in prison during persecution in 235.

232-254: Origen established the School of Caesarea after being deposed in 231 as head of the School of Alexandria; he died in 254. A scholar and voluminous writer, he was one of the founders of systematic theology and exerted wide influence for many years.

c. 242: Manichaeism originated in Persia.

249-251: Persecution under Decius. Many of those who denied the faith *(lapsi)* sought readmission to the Church at the end of the persecution in 251. Pope St. Cornelius had correspondence with St. Cyprian on the subject and ordered that *lapsi* were to be readmitted after suitable penance.

250-300: Neo-Platonism of Plotinus and Porphyry gained followers.

251: Novatian, an antipope, was condemned at Rome.

256: Pope St. Stephen I upheld the validity of baptism administered by heretics, in the Rebaptism Controversy.

257: Persecution under Valerian, who attempted to destroy the Church as a social structure.

258: St. Cyprian, bishop of Carthage, was martyred.

c. 260: St. Lucian founded the exegetical School of Antioch.

Pope St. Dionysius condemned teachings of Sabellius and the Marcionites.

261: Gallienus issued an edict of toleration which ended general persecution for nearly 40 years.

c. 266: Sabellianism was condemned and Paul of Samosata deposed.

292: Diocletian divided the Roman Empire into East and West. The division emphasized political, cultural and other differences between the two parts of the Empire and influenced the Church in the East and West. The prestige of Rome began to decline.

Fourth Century

303: Persecution broke out under Diocletian. It ended in the West in 306 but continued for 10 years in the East; it was particularly violent in 304.

305: St. Anthony of Heracles established a foundation for hermits near the Red Sea in Egypt.

c. 306: The first local legislation on clerical celibacy was enacted by a council held at Elvira, Spain; bishops, priests, deacons and other ministers were forbidden to have wives.

310: St. Hilarion established a foundation for hermits in Palestine.

311: An edict of toleration issued by Galerius at the urging of Constantine and Licinius officially ended persecution in the West; some persecution continued in the East.

313: The *Edict of Milan* issued by Constantine and Licinius recognized Christianity as a lawful religion and the legal freedom of all religions in the Roman Empire.

314: The Council of Arles condemned Donatism in Africa and declared that baptism by heretics was valid.

318: St. Pachomius established the first foundation of the cenobitic (common) life, as compared with the solitary life of hermits in Upper Egypt.

325: The Ecumenical Council of Nicaea (I), first of its kind in the history of the Church, condemned Arianism; see separate entry.

326: Discovery of the True Cross on which Christ was crucified.

337: Baptism and death of Constantine.

c. 342: Beginning of a 40-year persecution in Persia.

343-344: A local Council of Sardica reaffirmed doctrine formulated by Nicaea I and declared that bishops had the right of appeal to the pope as the highest authority in the Church.

361-363: Julian the Apostate waged an unsuccessful campaign against the Church in an attempt to restore paganism as the religion of the Empire.

c. 365: Persecution under Valens in the East.

c. 376: Beginning of the barbarian invasion in the West.

379: Death of St. Basil, the Father of Monasticism in the East. His writings contributed greatly to the development of rules for the religious life.

381: The Ecumenical Council of Constantinople (I); see separate entry.

382: The *Decree of Pope St. Damasus* listed the Canon of Sacred Scripture.

382-c. 406: St. Jerome translated the Old and New Testaments into Latin. His work is called the Vulgate Version of the Bible.

396: St. Augustine became bishop of Hippo.

397: A local Council of Carthage published the Canon of Sacred Scripture.

Fifth Century

410: Visigoths sacked Rome.

411: Donatism was condemned by a council at Carthage.

430: St. Augustine, bishop of Hippo for 35 years, died. He was a strong defender of orthodox doctrine against Manichaeism, Donatism and Pelagianism. The depth and range of his writings made him a dominant influence in Christian thought for many centuries.

431: The Ecumenical Council of Ephesus; see separate entry.

432: St. Patrick arrived in Ireland. By the time of his death in 461 most of the country had been converted, monasteries founded and the hierarchy established.

438: The *Theodosian Code,* a compilation of decrees for the Empire, was issued by Theodosius II. It had great influence on subsequent civil and ecclesiastical law.

449: The Robber Council of Ephesus, which did not have ecclesiastical sanction, declared itself in favor of the opinions of Eutyches who contended that Christ had only one nature.

451: The Ecumenical Council of Chalcedon; see separate entry.

452: Pope St. Leo the Great persuaded Attila the Hun to spare Rome.

455: Vandals sacked Rome. The decline of

imperial Rome dates approximately from this time.

484: Patriarch Acacius of Constantinople was excommunicated for signing the *Henoticon,* a unity law published by Emperor Zeno in 482 to end the turmoil associated with the Monophysite heresy. The document capitulated to the heresy. The excommunication triggered a 35-year-long schism.

494: Pope St. Gelasius I declared in a letter to Emperor Anastasius that the pope had power and authority over the emperor in spiritual matters.

496: Clovis, King of the Franks, was converted and became the defender of Christianity in the West. The Franks became a Catholic people.

Sixth Century

520 and later: Irish monasteries flourished as centers for spiritual life, missionary training and scholarly activity.

529: The Second Council of Orange condemned Semi-Pelagianism.

c. 529: St. Benedict founded the Monte Cassino Abbey. Some years before his death in 543 he wrote a monastic rule which exercised tremendous influence on the form and style of religious life. He is called the Father of Monasticism in the West.

533: John II became the first pope to change his name. The practice did not become general until the time of Sergius IV (1009).

533-534: Emperor Justinian promulgated the *Corpus Juris Civilis* for the Roman world. Like the *Theodosian Code,* it influenced subsequent civil and ecclesiastical law.

c. 545: Death of Dionysius Exiguus who was the first to date history from the birth of Christ, a practice which resulted in use of the B.C. and A.D. abbreviations. His calculations were at least four years late.

553: The Ecumenical Council of Constantinople (II); see separate entry.

585: St. Columban founded an influential monastic school at Luxeuil. He died in 615.

589: The most important of several councils of Toledo was held. The Visigoths renounced Arianism, and St. Leander began the organization of the Church in Spain.

590-604: Pontificate of Pope St. Gregory I the Great. He set the form and style of the papacy which prevailed throughout the Middle Ages; exerted great influence on doctrine and liturgy; was strong in support of monastic discipline and clerical celibacy; authored writings on many subjects. Gregorian Chant is named in his honor.

596: Pope St. Gregory I the Great sent St. Augustine of Canterbury and 40 monks to do missionary work in England.

597: St. Columba died. He founded an important monastery at Iona, established schools and did notable missionary work in Scotland.

By the end of the century, monasteries of nuns were common; Western monasticism was flourishing; monasticism in the East, under the influence of Monophysitism and other factors, was losing its vigor.

Seventh Century

613: St. Columban established the influential Monastery of Bobbio in northern Italy.

622: The Hegira (flight) of Mohammed from Mecca to Medina signalled the beginning of Islam, which, by the end of the century, claimed almost all of the southern Mediterranean area.

629: Emperor Heraclius recovered the True Cross from the Persians.

649: A Lateran Council condemned two erroneous formulas *(Ecthesis* and *Type)* issued by emperors Heraclius and Constans II as means of reconciling Monophysites with the Church.

664: Actions of the Synod of Whitby advanced the adoption of Roman usages in England, especially regarding the date for the observance of Easter. (See Easter Controversy.)

680-681: The Ecumenical Council of Constantinople (III); see separate entry.

692: Trullan Synod. Eastern-Church discipline on clerical celibacy was settled, permitting marriage before ordination to the diaconate and continuation in marriage afterwards, but prohibiting marriage following the death of the wife thereafter. Anti-Roman canons contributed to East-West alienation.

During the century, the monastic influence of Ireland and England increased in Western Europe; schools and learning declined; regulations regarding clerical celibacy became more strict in the East.

Eighth Century

711: Moslems began the conquest of Spain.

726: Emperor Leo III, the Isaurian, launched a campaign against the veneration of sacred images and relics; called Iconoclasm (image-breaking), it caused turmoil in the East until about 843.

731: Pope Gregory II and a synod at Rome condemned Iconoclasm, with a declaration that the veneration of sacred images was in accord with Catholic tradition.

Venerable Bede issued his *Ecclesiastical History of the English People.*

732: Charles Martel defeated the Moslems at Poitiers, halting farther advance by them in the West.

744: The Monastery of Fulda was established by St. Sturm, a disciple of St. Boniface.

754: A council of more than 300 Byzantine bishops endorsed Iconoclast errors. This council and its actions were condemned by the Lateran Synod of 769.

Stephen II (III) crowned Pepin ruler of the Franks. Pepin twice invaded Italy, in 754 and 756, to defend the pope against the Lombards. His land grants to the papacy, called the Donation of Pepin, were later extended by Charlemagne (773) and formed part of the States of the Church.

c. 755: St. Boniface (Winfrid) was martyred. He was called the Apostle of Germany for his missionary work and organization of the hierarchy there.

781: Alcuin was chosen by Charlemagne to organize a Palace School, which became a center of intellectual leadership.

787: The Ecumenical Council of Nicaea (II); see separate entry.

792: A council at Ratisbon condemned Adoptionism.

The famous *Book of Kells* ("The Great Gospel of Columcille") dates from the early eighth or late seventh century.

Ninth Century

800: Charlemagne was crowned Emperor by Pope Leo III on Christmas Day.

Egbert became king of West Saxons. He unified England and strengthened the See of Canterbury.

813: Emperor Leo V, the Armenian, revived Iconoclasm, which persisted until about 843.

814: Charlemagne died.

843: The Treaty of Verdun split the Frankish kingdom among Charlemagne's three grandsons.

844: A Eucharistic controversy involving the writings of Paschasius Radbertus, Ratramnus and Rabanus Maurus occasioned the development of terminology regarding the doctrine of the Real Presence.

846: The Moslems invaded Italy and attacked Rome.

847-852: Period of composition of the *False Decretals*, a collection of forged documents attributed to popes from St. Clement (88-97) to Gregory II (715-731). The *Decretals*, which strongly supported the autonomy and rights of bishops, were suspect for a long time before being repudiated entirely about 1628.

848: The Council of Mainz condemned Gottschalk for heretical teaching regarding predestination. He was also condemned by the Council of Quierzy in 853.

857: Photius displaced Ignatius as patriarch of Constantinople. This marked the beginning of the Photian Schism, a confused state of East-West relations which has not yet been cleared up by historical research. Photius, a man of exceptional ability, died in 891.

865: St. Ansgar, Apostle of Scandinavia, died.

868: Sts. Cyril (d. 869) and Methodius (d. 885) were consecrated bishops. The Apostles of the Slavs devised an alphabet and translated the Gospels and liturgy into the Slavonic language.

869: The Ecumenical Council of Constantinople (IV); see separate entry.

871-c. 900: Reign of Alfred the Great, the only English king ever anointed by a pope at Rome.

Tenth Century

910: William, Duke of Aquitaine, founded the Benedictine Abbey of Cluny, which became a center of monastic and ecclesiastical reform.

915: Pope John X played a leading role in the expulsion of Saracens from central and southern Italy.

955: St. Olga, of the Russian royal family, was baptized.

962: Otto I, the Great, crowned by Pope John XII, revived Charlemagne's kingdom, which became the Holy Roman Empire.

966: Mieszko, first of a royal line in Poland, was baptized; he brought Latin Christianity to Poland.

989: Vladimir, ruler of Russia, was baptized. Russia was subsequently Christianized by Greek missionaries.

993: John XV was the first pope to decree the official canonization of a saint (Ulrich) for the universal Church.

997: St. Stephen became ruler of Hungary. He assisted in organizing the hierarchy and establishing Latin Christianity in that country.

999-1003: Pontificate of Sylvester II (Gerbert of Aquitaine), a Benedictine monk and the first French pope.

Eleventh Century

1009: Beginning of lasting East-West schism in the Church, marked by dropping of the name of Pope Sergius IV from the Byzantine diptychs (the listing of persons prayed for during the liturgy). The deletion was made by Patriarch Sergius II of Constantinople.

1012: St. Romuald founded the Camaldolese Hermits.

1025: The Council of Arras, and other councils later, condemned the Cathari (Neo-Manichaeans, Albigenses).

1027: The Council of Elne proclaimed the Truce of God as a means of stemming violence. The truce involved armistice periods of varying length, which were later extended.

1038: St. John Gualbert founded the Vallombrosians.

1043-1059: Constantinople patriarchate of Michael Cerularius, the key figure in a controversy concerning the primacy of the papacy. His and the Byzantine synod's refusal to acknowledge this primacy in 1054 widened and hardened the East-West schism in the Church.

1047: Pope Clement II died. He was the only pope ever buried in Germany.

1049-54: Pontificate of St. Leo IX, who inaugurated a movement of papal, diocesan, monastic and clerical reform.

1055: Condemnation of the Eucharistic doctrine of Berengarius.

1059: A Lateran Council issued new legislation regarding papal elections. Voting power was entrusted to the Roman cardinals.

1066: Death of St. Edward the Confessor, King of England from 1042 and restorer of Westminster Abbey.

Defeat, at Hastings, of Harold by William I, who subsequently exerted strong influence on the life style of the Church in England.

1073-1085: Pontificate of St. Gregory VII (Hildebrand). A strong pope, he carried forward programs of clerical and general ecclesiastical reform and struggled against Henry IV and other rulers to end the evils of lay investiture. He introduced the Latin liturgy in Spain and set definite dates for the observance of ember days.

1077: Henry IV, excommunicated and suspended from the exercise of imperial powers by Gregory VII, sought absolution from the Pope at Canossa. Henry later repudiated this action and in 1084 forced Gregory to leave Rome.

1079: The Council of Rome condemned Eucharistic errors of Berengarius, who retracted.

1084: St. Bruno founded the Carthusians.

1097-1099: The first of several Crusades undertaken between this time and 1265. Recovery of the Holy Places and gaining free access to them for Christians were the original purposes, but these were diverted to less worthy objectives in various ways. Results included: a Latin Kingdom of Jerusalem, 1099-1187; a military and political misadventure in the form of a Latin Empire of Constantinople, 1204-1261; acquisition, by treaties, of visiting rights for Christians in the Holy Land. East-West economic and cultural relationships increased during the period. In the religious sphere, actions of the Crusaders had the effect of increasing the alienation of the East from the West.

1098: St. Robert founded the Cistercians.

Twelfth Century

1108: Beginnings of the influential Abbey and School of St. Victor.

1115: St. Bernard established the Abbey of Clairvaux and inaugurated the Cistercian Reform.

1118: Christian forces captured Saragossa, Spain; the beginning of the Moslem decline in that country.

1121: St. Norbert established the original monastery of the Praemonstratensians near Laon, France.

1122: The Concordat of Worms (Pactum Callixtinum) was formulated and approved by Pope Callistus II and Emperor Henry V to settle controversy concerning the investiture of prelates. The concordat provided that the emperor could invest prelates with symbols of temporal authority but had no right to invest them with spiritual authority, which came from the Church alone, and that the emperor was not to interfere in papal elections. This was the first concordat in history.

1123: The Ecumenical Council of the Lateran (I), the first of its kind in the West; see separate entry.

1139: The Ecumenical Council of the Lateran (II); see separate entry.

1140: St. Bernard met Abelard in debate at the Council of Sens. Abelard, whose rationalism in theology was condemned for the first time in 1121, died in 1142 at Cluny.

1148: The Synod of Rheims enacted strict disciplinary decrees for communities of women religious.

1152: The Synod of Kells reorganized the Church in Ireland.

1160: Gratian, whose *Decretum* became a basic text of Canon Law, died.

Peter Lombard, compiler of the *Four Books of Sentences,* a standard theology text for nearly 200 years, died.

1170: St. Thomas Becket, archbishop of Canterbury, who clashed with Henry II over Church-state relations, was murdered in his cathedral.

1171: Pope Alexander III reserved the process of canonization of saints to the Holy See.

1179: The Ecumenical Council of the Lateran (III); see separate entry.

1184: Waldenses and other heretics were excommunicated by Pope Lucius III.

Thirteenth Century

1198-1216: Pontificate of Innocent III, during which the papacy reached its medieval peak of authority, influence and prestige in the Church and in relations with civil rulers.

1208: Innocent III called for a crusade, the first in Christendom itself, against the Albigensians.

1209: Verbal approval was given by Innocent III to a rule of life for the Order of Friars Minor, started by St. Francis of Assisi.

1212: The Second Order of Franciscans, the Poor Clares, was founded.

1215: The Ecumenical Council of the Lateran (IV); see separate entry.

1216: Formal papal approval was given to a rule of life for the Order of Preachers, started by St. Dominic.

The Portiuncula Indulgence was granted by the Holy See at the request of St. Francis of Assisi.

1221: The Third Order of St. Francis for lay persons was founded.

1226: Death of St. Francis of Assisi.

1245: The Ecumenical Council of Lyons (I); see separate entry.

1247: Preliminary approval was given by the Holy See to a Carmelite rule of life.

1270: St. Louis IX, king of France, died.

Beginning of papal decline.

1274: The Ecumenical Council of Lyons (II); see separate entry.

Death of St. Thomas Aquinas, Doctor of the Church, of lasting influence; see separate entry.

1280: Pope Nicholas III, who made the *Breviary* the official prayer book for clergy of the Roman Church, died.

1281: The excommunication of Michael Palaeologus by Pope Martin IV ruptured the union effected with the Eastern Church in 1274.

Fourteenth Century

1302: Pope Boniface VIII issued the bull *Unam Sanctam,* concerning the unity of the Church and the temporal power of princes, against the background of a struggle with Philip IV of France; it was the most famous medieval document on the subject.

1308-1378: For a period of approximately 70 years, seven popes resided at Avignon because of unsettled conditions in Rome and other reasons; see separate entry.

1311-1312: The Ecumenical Council of Vienne; see separate entry.

1321: Dante Alighieri died a year after completing the *Divine Comedy.*

1324: Marsilius of Padua completed *Defensor Pacis,* a work condemned by Pope John XXII as heretical because of its denial of papal primacy and the hierarchical structure of the Church, and for other reasons. It was a charter for conciliarism.

1337-1453: Period of the Hundred Years' War, a dynastic struggle between France and England.

1338: Four years after the death of Pope John XXII, who had opposed Louis IV of Bavaria in a years-long controversy, electoral princes declared at the Diet of Rhense that the emperor did not need papal confirmation of his title and right to rule. Charles IV later (1356) said the same thing in a *Golden Bull,* eliminating papal rights in the election of emperors.

1347-1350: The Black Death swept across Europe, killing perhaps one-fourth to one-third of the total population; an estimated 40 per cent of the clergy succumbed.

1374: Petrarch, poet and humanist, died.

1378: Return of the papacy from Avignon to Rome.

Beginning of the Western Schism; see separate entry.

Fifteenth Century

1409: The Council of Pisa, without canonical authority, tried to end the Western Schism but succeeded only in complicating it by electing a third claimant to the papacy; see Western Schism.

1414-1418: The Ecumenical Council of Constance ended the Western Schism; see separate entry.

1431: St. Joan of Arc was burned at the stake.

1431-1449: The Council of Basle, which began with convocation by Pope Martin V in 1431, turned into an anti-papal forum of conciliarists seeking to subject the primacy and authority of the pope to the overriding authority of an assembly of bishops. It was not an ecumenical council.

1438: The Pragmatic Sanction of Bourges was enacted by Charles VIII and the French parliament to curtail papal authority over the Church in France, in the spirit of conciliarism. It found expression in Gallicanism and had effects lasting at least until the French Revolution.

1438-1443: The Ecumenical Council of Florence affirmed the primacy of the pope in opposition to conciliarism and effected a measure of union with separated Eastern Christians; see separate entry.

1453: The fall of Constantinople to the Turks.

c. 1456: Gutenberg issued the first edition of the Bible printed from movable type, at Mainz, Germany.

1476: Pope Sixtus IV ordered observance of the feast of the Immaculate Conception on Dec. 8 throughout the Church.

1492: Columbus discovered the Americas.

1493: Pope Alexander VI issued a *Bull of Demarcation* which determined spheres of influence for the Spanish and Portuguese in the Americas.

The Renaissance, a humanistic movement which originated in Italy in the 14th century, spread to France, Germany, the Low Countries and England. A transitional period between the medieval world and the modern secular world, it introduced profound changes which affected literature and the other arts, general culture, politics and religion.

Sixteenth Century

1512-1517: The Ecumenical Council of the Lateran (V); see separate entry.

1517: Martin Luther signalled the beginning of the Reformation by posting 95 theses at Wittenberg. Subsequently, he broke completely from doctrinal orthodoxy in discourses and three published works (1519 and 1520); was excommunicated on more than 40 charges of heresy (1521); remained the dominant figure in the Reformation in Germany until his death in 1546.

1519: Zwingli triggered the Reformation in Zurich and became its leading proponent there until his death in combat in 1531.

1524: Luther's encouragement of German princes in putting down the two-year Peasants' Revolt gained political support for his cause.

1528: The Order of Friars Minor Capuchin was approved as an autonomous division of the Franciscan Order; like the Jesuits, the Capuchins became leaders in the Counter-Reformation.

1530: The *Augsburg Confession* of Lutheran faith was issued; it was later supplemented by the *Smalcald Articles* approved in 1537.

1533: Henry VIII divorced Catherine of Aragon, married Anne Boleyn, was excommunicated. In 1534 he decreed the Act of Supremacy, making the sovereign the head of the Church in England, under which Sts. John Fisher and Thomas More were executed in 1535. Despite his rejection of papal primacy and actions against monastic life in England, he generally maintained doctrinal orthodoxy until his death in 1547.

1536: John Calvin, leader of the Reformation in Switzerland until his death in 1564, issued the first edition of *Institutes of the Christian Religion,* which became the classical text of Reformed (non-Lutheran) theology.

1540: The constitutions of the Society of Jesus (Jesuits), founded by St. Ignatius of Loyola, were approved.

1541: Start of the 11-year career of St. Francis Xavier as a missionary to the East Indies and Japan.

1545-1563: The Ecumenical Council of Trent formulated statements of Catholic doctrine under attack by the Reformers and mobilized the Counter-Reformation; see separate entry.

1549: The first *Book of Common Prayer* was issued by Edward VI. Revised editions were published in 1552, 1559 and 1662.

1553: Start of the five-year reign of Mary Tudor who tried to counteract actions of Henry VIII against the Roman Church.

1555: Enactment of the Peace of Augsburg, an arrangement of religious territorialism rather than toleration, which recognized the existence of Catholicism and Lutheranism in the German Empire and provided that citizens should adopt the religion of their respective rulers.

1558: Beginning of the reign of Elizabeth I, during which the Church of England took on its definitive form.

1559: Establishment of the hierarchy of the Church of England, with the consecration of Matthew Parker as archbishop of Canterbury.

1563: The first text of the *39 Articles* of the Church of England was issued. Also enacted were a new Act of Supremacy and Oath of Succession to the English throne.

1570: Elizabeth I was excommunicated. Penal measures against Catholics subsequently became more severe.

1571: Defeat of the Turkish armada at Lepanto staved off the invasion of Eastern Europe.

1577: The *Formula of Concord,* the classical statement of Lutheran faith, was issued; it was, generally, a Lutheran counterpart of the canons of the Council of Trent. In 1580, along with other formulas of doctrine, it was included in the *Book of Concord.*

1582: The Gregorian Calendar, named for Pope Gregory XIII, was put into effect and was eventually adopted in most countries: England delayed adoption until 1752.

Seventeenth Century

1605: The Gunpowder Plot, an attempt by Catholic fanatics to blow up James I of England and the houses of Parliament, resulted in an anti-Catholic Oath of Allegiance; the Oath was condemned by Pope Paul V in 1606.

1610: Death of Matteo Ricci, outstanding Jesuit missionary to China, pioneer in cultural relations between China and Europe.

Founding of the first community of Visitation Nuns by Sts. Francis de Sales and Jane de Chantal.

1611: Founding of the Oratorians.

1613: Catholics were banned from Scandinavia.

1625: Founding of the Congregation of the Mission (Vincentians) by St. Vincent de Paul. He founded the Sisters of Charity in 1633.

1642: Death of Galileo, scientist, who was censured by the Congregation of the Holy Office for supporting the Copernican theory of the sun-centered planetary system.

Founding of the Sulpicians by Jacques Olier.

1643: Start of publication of the Bollandist *Acta Sanctorum,* a critical work on lives of the saints.

1648: Provisions in the Peace of Westphalia, ending the Thirty Years' War, extended terms of the Peace of Augsburg (1555) to Calvinists and gave equality to Catholics and Protestants in the 300 states of the Holy Roman Empire.

1649: Oliver Cromwell invaded Ireland and began a severe persecution of the Church there.

1653: Pope Innocent X condemned five propositions of Jansenism, a complex theory which distorted doctrine concerning the relations between divine grace and human freedom. Jansenism was also a rigoristic movement which seriously disturbed the Church in France, the Low Countries and Italy in this and the 18th century.

1673: The Test Act in England barred from public office Catholics who would not deny the doctrine of transubstantiation and receive Communion in the Church of England.

1678: Many English Catholics suffered death as a consequence of the Popish Plot, a false allegation by Titus Oates that Catholics planned to assassinate Charles I, land a French army in the country, burn London, and turn over the government to the Jesuits.

1682: The four articles of the *Gallican Declaration,* drawn up by Bossuet, asserted political and ecclesiastical immunities of France from papal control. The articles, which rejected the primacy of the pope, were condemned in 1690.

1689: The Toleration Act granted a measure of freedom of worship to other English dissenters but not to Catholics.

This century is called the age of Enlightenment or Reason because of the predominating rational and scientific approach of its leading philosophers, scientists and writers with respect to religion, ethics and natural law. This approach downgraded the fact and significance of revealed religion. Also characteristic of the Enlightenment were subjectivism, secularism and optimism regarding human perfectibility.

Eighteenth Century

1704: Chinese Rites — involving the Christian adaptation of elements of Confucianism, veneration of ancestors and Chinese terminology in religion — were condemned by Clement XI. An earlier ban was issued in 1645; a later one, in 1742.

1720: The Passionists were founded by St. Paul of the Cross.

1732: The Redemptorists were founded by St. Alphonsus Liguori.

1738: Freemasonry was condemned by Clement XII and Catholics were forbidden to join, under penalty of excommunication; the prohibition was repeated by Benedict XIV in 1751 and by later popes.

1760's: Josephinism, a theory and system of state control of the Church, was initiated in Austria; it remained in force until about 1850.

1764: Febronianism, an unorthodox theory and practice regarding the constitution of the Church and relations between Church and state, was condemned for the first of several times. Proposed by an auxiliary bishop of Trier using the pseudonym Justinus Febronius, it had the effects of minimizing the office of the pope and supporting national churches under state control.

1773: Clement XIV issued a brief of suppression against the Jesuits, following their expulsion from Portugal in 1759, from France in 1764 and from Spain in 1767. Political intrigue and unsubstantiated accusations were principal factors in these developments. The ban, which crippled the Society, contained no condemnation of the Jesuit constitutions, particular Jesuits or Jesuit teaching. The Society was restored in 1814.

1778: Catholics in England were relieved of some civil disabilities dating back to the time of Henry VIII, by an act which permitted them to acquire, own and inherit property. Additional liberties were restored by the Roman Catholic Relief Act of 1791 and subsequent enactments of Parliament.

1789: Religious freedom in the United States was guaranteed under the First Amendment to the Constitution.

Beginning of the French Revolution which resulted in: the secularization of church property and the Civil Constitution of the Clergy in 1790; the persecution of priests, religious and lay persons loyal to papal authority; invasion of the Papal States by Napoleon in 1796; renewal of persecution from 1797-1799; attempts to dechristianize France and establish a new religion; the occupation of Rome by French troops and the forced removal of Pius VI to France in 1798.

Nineteenth Century

1809: Pius VII was made a captive by Napoleon and deported to France where he remained in exile until 1814. During this time he refused to cooperate with Napoleon who sought to bring the Church in France under his own control.

The turbulence in church-state relations in France at the beginning of the century recurred in connection with the Bourbon Restoration, the July Revolution, the second and third Republics, the Second Empire and the Dreyfus case.

1814: The Society of Jesus, suppressed since 1773, was restored.

1817: Reestablishment of the Congregation for the Propagation of the Faith (Propaganda) by Pius VII was an important factor in increasing missionary activity during the century.

1820: Years-long persecution, during which thousands died for the faith, ended in China. Thereafter, communication with the West remained cut off until about 1834. Vigorous missionary work got underway in 1842.

1822: The Pontifical Society for the Propagation of the Faith, inaugurated in France by Pauline Jaricot for the support of missionary activity, was established.

1829: The Catholic Emancipation Act relieved Catholics in England and Ireland of most of the civil disabilities to which they had been subject from the time of Henry VIII.

1832: Gregory XVI, in the encyclical *Mirari Vos,* condemned indifferentism, one of the many ideologies at odds with Christian doctrine which were proposed during the century.

1833: Start of the Oxford Movement which affected the Church of England and resulted in some notable conversions, including that of John Henry Newman in 1845, to the Catholic Church.

Frederick Ozanam founded the Society of St. Vincent de Paul in France. The society, whose objective was works of charity, became worldwide.

1848: The *Communist Manifesto,* a revolutionary document symptomatic of socio-economic crisis, was issued.

1850: The hierarchy was reestablished in England and Nicholas Wiseman made the first archbishop of Westminster. He was succeeded in 1865 by Henry Manning, an Oxford convert and proponent of the rights of labor.

1853: The Catholic hierarchy was reestablished in Holland.

1854: Pius IX proclaimed the dogma of the Immaculate Conception in the bull *Ineffabilis Deus.*

1858: The Blessed Virgin Mary appeared to

St. Bernadette at Lourdes, France; see separate entry.

1864: Pius IX issued the encyclical *Quanta Cura* and the *Syllabus of Errors* in condemnation of some 80 propositions derived from the scientific mentality and rationalism of the century. The subjects in question had deep ramifications in many areas of thought and human endeavor; in religion, they explicitly and or implicitly rejected divine revelation and the supernatural order.

1867: The first volume of *Das Kapital* was published. Together with the Communist First International, formed in the same year, it had great influence on the subsequent development of Communism and Socialism.

1869: The Anglican Church was disestablished in Ireland.

1869-1870: The First Vatican Council; see separate entry.

1870-1871: Victor Emmanuel II of Sardinia, crowned king of Italy after defeating Austrian and papal forces, marched into Rome in 1870 and expropriated the Papal States after a plebiscite in which Catholics, at the order of Pius IX, did not vote. In 1871, Pius IX refused to accept a Law of Guarantees. Confiscation of church property and hindrance of ecclesiastical administration by the regime followed.

1871: The German Empire, a confederation of 26 states, was formed. Government policy launched a Kulturkampf whose May Laws of 1873 were designed to annul papal jurisdiction in Prussia and other states and to place the Church under imperial control. Resistance to the enactments and the persecution they legalized forced the government to modify its anti-Church policy by 1887.

1878: Beginning of the pontificate of Leo XIII, who was pope until his death in 1903. Leo is best known for the encyclical *Rerum Novarum*, which greatly influenced the course of Christian social thought and the labor movement. His other accomplishments included promotion of a revival of Scholastic philosophy and the impetus he gave to scriptural studies.

1881: The first International Eucharistic Congress was held in Lille, France.

Alexander II of Russia died. His policies of Russification — as well as those of his two predecessors and a successor during the century — caused great suffering to Catholics, Jews and Protestants in Poland, Lithuania, the Ukraine and Bessarabia.

1882: Charles Darwin died. His theory of evolution by natural selection, one of several scientific highlights of the century, had extensive repercussions in the faith-and-science controversy.

1889: The Catholic University of America was founded in Washington, D.C.

1893: The US apostolic delegation was set up in Washington, D.C.

Twentieth Century

1901: Restrictive measures in France forced the Jesuits, Benedictines, Carmelites and other religious orders to leave the country. Subsequently, 14,000 schools were suppressed; religious orders and congregations were expelled; the concordat was renounced in 1905; church property was confiscated in 1906. For some years the Holy See, refusing to comply with government demands for the control of bishops' appointments, left some ecclesiastical offices vacant.

1903: Start of the 11-year pontificate of St. Pius X. He initiated the codification of canon law, 1904; removed the ban against participation by Catholics in Italian national elections, 1905; issued decrees calling upon the faithful to receive Holy Communion frequently and daily, and stating that children should begin receiving the Eucharist at the age of seven, 1905 and 1910, respectively; ordered the establishment of the Confraternity of Christian Doctrine in all parishes throughout the world, 1905; condemned Modernism in the decree *Lamentabili* and the encyclical *Pascendi,* 1907.

1908: The United States and England, long under the jurisdiction of the Congregation for the Propagation of the Faith as mission territories, were removed from its control and placed under the common law of the Church.

1910: Laws of separation were enacted in Portugal, marking a point of departure in church-state relations.

1911: The Catholic Foreign Mission Society of America — Maryknoll, the first US-founded society of its type — was established.

1914: Start of World War I, which lasted until 1918.

Start of the eight-year pontificate of Benedict XV. Much of his pontificate was devoted to seeking ways and means of minimizing the material and spiritual havoc of World War I. In 1917 he offered his services as a mediator to the belligerent nations, but his pleas for settlement of the conflict went unheeded.

1917: The Blessed Virgin Mary appeared to three children at Fatima, Portugal.

A new constitution, embodying repressive laws against the Church, was enacted in Mexico. Its implementation resulted in persecution in the 1920's and 1930's.

Bolsheviks seized power in Russia and set up a Communist dictatorship. The event marked the rise of Communism in Russian and world affairs. One of its immediate, and lasting, results was persecution of the Church, Jews and other segments of the population.

1918: The *Code of Canon Law,* in preparation for more than 10 years, went into effect in the Western Church.

1919: Benedict XV stimulated missionary work through the decree *Maximum Illud,* in which he urged the recruiting and training of native clergy in places where the Church was not firmly established.

1922: Beginning of the 17-year pontificate of Pius XI. He subscribed to the Lateran Treaty, 1929, which settled the Roman Question created by the confiscation of the Papal States in 1871; issued the encyclical *Casti Connubii*, 1930, an authoritative statement on Christian marriage; resisted the efforts of Benito Mussolini to control Catholic Action and the Church, in the encyclical *Non Abbiamo Bisogno*, 1931; opposed various Fascist policies; issued the encyclicals *Quadragesimo Anno*, 1931, developing the social doctrine of Leo XIII's *Rerum Novarum*, and *Divini Redemptoris*, 1937, calling for social justice and condemning atheistic Communism; condemned anti-Semitism, 1937.

Ireland was partitioned. All but two of the predominantly Catholic counties were included in the southern part of the country, which eventually attained the status of an independent republic in 1949.

1926: The Catholic Relief Act repealed virtually all legal disabilities of Catholics in England.

1931: Leftists proclaimed Spain a republic and proceeded to disestablish the Church, confiscate church property, deny salaries to the clergy, expel the Jesuits and ban teaching of the Catholic faith. These actions were preludes to the civil war of 1936-1939.

1933: Emergence of Adolf Hitler to power in Germany. By 1935 two of his aims were clear, the elimination of the Jews and control of a single national church. Persecution decimated the Jews over a period of years. The Church was subject to repressive measures, which Pius XI protested futilely in the encyclical *Mit Brennender Sorge* in 1937.

1936: A three-year civil war broke out in Spain between the leftist Loyalists and forces led by Francisco Franco. The Loyalists were defeated and one-man, one-party rule was established. A number of priests, religious and lay persons fell victims to Loyalist persecution.

1939: Start of World War II, which lasted until 1945.

Start of the 19-year pontificate of Pius XII; see separate entry.

1940: Start of a decade of Communist conquest in more than 13 countries, resulting in conditions of persecution for a minimum of 60 million Catholics as well as members of other faiths; see various countries.

Persecution diminished in Mexico through non-enforcement of anti-religious laws still on record.

1950: Pius XII proclaimed the dogma of the Assumption of the Blessed Virgin Mary.

1954: St. Pius X was canonized.

1957: The Communist regime of China attempted to start a national schismatic church.

1958: Beginning of the five-year pontificate

of John XXIII; see separate entry.

1962: The Second Vatican Council began the first of four sessions; see separate entry.

1963: Beginning of 15-year pontificate of Paul VI; see separate entry.

1978: Thirty-four-day pontificate of John Paul I; see separate entry.

Beginning of pontificate of John Paul II; see separate entry.

HERESIES

Heresy is the formal and obstinate denial or doubt by a baptized person, who remains a nominal Christian, of any truth which must be believed as a matter of divine and Catholic faith. Formal heresy involves deliberate resistance to the authority of God who communicates revelation through Scripture and tradition and the teaching authority of the Church. Obstinate refusal to accept the infallible teaching of the Church constitutes the canonical crime of heresy.

Formal heretics automatically incur the penalty of excommunication (Canon 1325 of the Code of Canon Law). Material heretics are those who, in good faith and without formal obstinacy, do not accept articles or matters of divine and Catholic faith.

Heresies have been significant not only as disruptions of unity of faith but also as occasions for the clarification and development of doctrine.

Heresies from the beginning of the Church to the 13th century are listed below.

Judaizers: Early converts who claimed that members of the Church had to observe all the requirements of Mosaic Law as well as the obligations of Christian faith. This view was condemned by the Council of Jerusalem held in 51 under the presidency of St. Peter (Acts 15:28).

Gnosticism: A combination of elements of Platonic philosophy and Eastern mystery religions which claimed that its secret knowledge-principle gave its adherents a deeper insight into Christian doctrine than divine revelation and faith. One Gnostic thesis denied the divinity of Christ; others denied the reality of his humanity, calling it mere appearance (**Docetism, Phantasiasm**).

Modalism: A general term covering propositions (**Monarchianism, Patripassianism, Sabellianism**) that the Father, Son and Holy Spirit are not really distinct divine Persons but are only three different modes of being and self-manifestation of the one God. Various forms of Modalism, which appeared in the East in the second century and spread westward, were all condemned.

Marcionism: A Gnostic creation named for its author, who claimed there was total opposition and no connection at all between the Old Testament and the New Testament, between the God of the Jews and the God of the Christians; and that the canon of Scripture consisted only of portions of Luke's Gospel and 10 Epistles of Paul. Marcion was excommunicated in 144 at Rome, and his tenets were condemned again by a Roman council about 260. The heresy was checked at Rome by 200 but persisted for several centuries in the East and had some adherents as late as the Middle Ages.

Montanism: A form of extremism preached about 170 by Montanus of Phrygia, Asia Minor. Its principal tenets were: an imminent second coming of Christ, denial of the divine nature of the Church and its power to forgive sin, excessively rigorous morality. Condemned by Pope St. Zephyrinus (199-217). Tertullian was one of its victims.

Novatianism: A heresy of excessive rigorism named for its author, a priest of Rome and antipope. Its principal tenet was that persons who fell away from the Church under persecution and/or those guilty of serious sin after baptism could not be absolved and readmitted to communion with the Church. The heresy, condemned by a Roman synod in 251, slowly subsided in the West and died in the East by the end of the seventh century.

Subordinationism, Adoptionism: Christological errors and logical antecedents of Arianism. The key tenet was that Christ, while the most excellent of creatures, was subordinate to God whose Son he was by adoption rather than by nature. First proposed at Rome late in the second century, it was condemned by Pope St. Victor in 190 and again in the following century, in 785 by Pope Adrian I, in 794 by a Council of Frankfurt, and in 1177 by Pope Alexander III.

Arianism: Denial of the divinity of Christ, the most devastating of the early heresies, authored by Arius of Alexandria and condemned by the Council of Nicaea I in 325. Arians and several kinds of **Semi-Arians** propagandized their tenets widely, raised havoc in the Church for several centuries, and established their own hierarchies and churches.

Macedonianism: Denial of the divinity of the Holy Spirit, who was said to be a creature of the Son. Condemned by the Council of Constantinople I in 381. Macedonians were also called **Pneumatomachists**, enemies of the Spirit; and **Marathonians**, after the name of one of their leaders, a bishop of Nicomedia.

Nestorianism: Denial of the real unity of divine and human natures in the single divine Person of Christ, proposed by Nestorius, patriarch of Constantinople. He also held that Mary could not be called the Mother of God *(Theotokos)*; that is, of the Second Person of the Trinity made Man. Condemned by the councils of Ephesus in 431 and Chalcedon in 451.

Monophysitism: Denial of Christ's human nature; also called **Eutychianism**, after the name of one of its leading advocates. Condemned by the Council of Chalcedon in 451.

Monothelitism: Denial of the human will of Christ. Severus of Antioch and Sergius, patriarch of Constantinople, were leading advocates of the heresy, which was condemned by the Council of Constantinople III in 681.

Priscillianism: A fourth century amalgamation of elements from various sources — Sabellianism, Arianism, Docetism, Pantheism, belief in the diabolical nature of marriage, corruption of Scripture. Condemned by a Council of Braga in 563 on 17 different counts.

Donatism: A development of the error at the heart of the third century **Rebaptism Controversy** (baptism conferred by heretics is invalid because persons deprived of grace are incapable of being ministers of grace to others). Followers of Donatus the Great asserted throughout the fourth century that sacraments administered by sinners were invalid. Condemnation of the heresy is traced to Pope St. Stephen I (254-257) and the principle that sacraments have their efficacy from Christ, not from their human ministers.

Pelagianism: Denial of the supernatural order of things, proposed by Pelagius (360-420), a Breton monk. Proceeding from the assumption that Adam had a natural right to supernatural life, the theory held that man could attain salvation through the efforts of his own free will and natural powers. The theory involved errors concerning the nature of original sin, the meaning of grace and other matters. St. Augustine opposed the heresy, which was condemned by the Council of Ephesus in 431. **Semi-Pelagianism** was condemned by a Council of Orange in 529.

Iconoclasm: An image-breaking campaign which resulted from an edict issued by Eastern Emperor Leo the Isaurian in 726, that the veneration of images, pictures and relics was idolatrous. The theoretical basis of the heresy was the Monophysite error which denied the humanity of Christ. It was denounced several times before its condemnation by the Council of Nicaea II in 787.

Berengarian Heresy: Denial of the Real Presence of Christ under the appearances of bread and wine, the first clear-cut Eucharistic heresy; proposed by Berengarius of Tours (c. 1000-1088). Condemned by various synods and finally by a council held at Rome in 1079.

Waldensianism: Claimed by Peter Waldo, a merchant of Lyons, to be a return to pure Christianity, the heresy rejected the hierarchical structure of the Church, the sacramental system and other doctrines. Its adherents were excommunicated in 1184 and their tenets were condemned several times thereafter.

Albigensianism, Catharism: Related errors based on the old **Manichaean** assumption that two supreme principles of good and evil were operative in creation and life, and that the supreme objective of human endeavor was liberation from evil (matter). The heresy denied the humanity of Christ, the sacramental system and the authority of the Church (and state), and endorsed a moral code which threatened seriously the fabric of social life in southern France and northern Italy in the 12th and 13th centuries. Condemned by councils of the Lateran III and Lateran IV in 1179 and 1215.

ECUMENICAL COUNCILS

An ecumenical council is an assembly of the college of bishops, with and under the presidency of the pope, which has supreme authority over the Church in matters pertaining to faith, morals, worship and discipline.

The Second Vatican Council stated: "The supreme authority with which this college (of bishops) is empowered over the whole Church is exercised in a solemn way through an ecumenical council. A council is never ecumenical unless it is confirmed or at least accepted as such by the successor of Peter. It is the prerogative of the Roman Pontiff to convoke these councils, to preside over them, and to confirm them" *(Dogmatic Constitution on the Church*, No. 22).

Pope Presides

The pope is the head of an ecumenical council; he presides over it either personally or through legates. Conciliar decrees and other actions have binding force only when confirmed and promulgated by him. If a pope dies during a council, it is suspended until reconvened by another pope. An ecumenical council is not superior to a pope; hence, there is no appeal from a pope to a council.

Collectively, the bishops with the pope represent the whole Church. They do this not as democratic representatives of their faithful in a kind of church parliament, but as the successors of the Apostles with divinely given authority, care and responsibility over the whole Church.

Council participants with a deliberative vote are: cardinals; residential patriarchs, primates, archbishops and bishops, even if they are not yet consecrated; abbots and certain other prelates, an abbot primate, abbot superiors of monastic congregations and heads of exempt clerical religious; titular bishops, on invitation. Experts in theology and canon law may be given a consultative vote. Others, including lay persons, may address a council or observe its actions, but may not vote.

Basic legislation concerning ecumenical councils is contained in Canons 222-229 of the Code of Canon Law. Basic doctrinal considerations were stated by the Second Vatican Council in the *Dogmatic Constitution on the Church.*

Background

Ecumenical councils had their prototype in the Council of Jerusalem in 51, at which the Apostles under the leadership of St. Peter decided that converts to the Christian faith were not obliged to observe all the prescriptions of Old Testament law (Acts 15). As early as the second century, bishops got together in regional meetings, synods or councils to take common action for the doctrinal and pastoral good of their communities of faithful. The expansion of such limited assemblies to ecumenical councils was a logical and historical evolution, given the nature and needs of the Church.

Emperors were active in summoning or convoking the first eight councils, especially the first five and the eighth. Among reasons for intervention of this kind were the facts that the emperors regarded themselves as guardians of the faith; that the settlement of religious controversies, which had repercussions in political and social turmoil, served the cause of peace in the state; and that the emperors had at their disposal ways and means of facilitating gatherings of bishops. Imperial actions, however, did not account for the formally ecumenical nature of the councils.

Some councils were attended by relatively few bishops, and the ecumenical character of several was open to question for a time. However, confirmation and de facto recognition of their actions by popes and subsequent councils established them as ecumenical.

Role in History

The councils have played a highly significant role in the history of the Church by witnessing to and defining truths of revelation, by shaping forms of worship and discipline, and by promoting measures for the ever-necessary reform and renewal of Catholic life. In general, they have represented attempts of the Church to mobilize itself in times of crisis for self-preservation, self-purification and growth.

The first eight ecumenical councils were held in the East; the other 13, in the West. The majority of separated Eastern Churches — e.g., the Orthodox — recognize the ecumenical character of the first seven councils, which formulated a great deal of basic doctrine. Nestorians, however, acknowledge only the first two councils; the Monophysite Armenians, Syrians, and Copts acknowledge the first three.

The 21 Councils

The 21 ecumenical councils in the history of the Church are listed below, with indication of their names or titles (taken from the names of the places where they were held); the dates; the reigning and/or approving popes; the emperors who were instrumental in convoking the eight councils in the East; the number of bishops who attended, when available; the number of sessions; the most significant actions.

1. Nicaea I, 325: St. Sylvester I (Emperor Constantine I); attended by approximately 300 bishops; sessions held between May 20 or June 19 to near the end of August. Condemned Arianism, which denied the divinity of Christ; contributed to formulation of the Nicene Creed; fixed the date of Easter; passed regulations concerning clerical discipline; adopted the civil division of the Empire as the model for the organization of the Church.

2. Constantinople I, 381: St. Damasus I (Emperor Theodosius I); attended by approximately 150 bishops; sessions held from May to July. Condemned various brands of Arianism, and Macedonianism which denied the divinity of the Holy Spirit; contributed to formulation of the Nicene Creed; approved a canon which made the bishop of Constantinople the ranking prelate in the East, with primacy next to that of the pope. Doubt about the ecumenical character of this council was resolved by the ratification of its acts by popes and the Council of Chalcedon.

3. Ephesus, 431: St. Celestine I (Emperor Theodosius II); attended by 150 to 200 bishops; five sessions held between June 22 and July 17. Condemned Nestorianism, which denied the real unity of the divine and human natures in the Person of Christ; defined *Theotokos* ("Bearer of God") as the title of Mary, Mother of the Son of God made Man; condemned Pelagianism, which reduced the supernatural to the natural order of things.

4. Chalcedon, 451: St. Leo I (Emperor Marcian); attended by approximately 600 bishops; 17 sessions held between Oct. 8 and Nov. 1. Condemned: Monophysitism, also called Eutychianism, which denied the humanity of Christ by holding that he had only one, the divine, nature; and the Monophysite Robber Synod of Ephesus, of 449.

5. Constantinople II, 553: Vigilius (Emperor Justinian I); attended by 165 bishops; eight sessions held between May 5 and June 2. Condemned the *Three Chapters,* Nestorian-tainted writings of Theodore of Mopsuestia, Theodoret of Cyprus and Ibas of Edessa.

6. Constantinople III, 680-681; St. Agatho, St. Leo II (Emperor Constantine IV); attended by approximately 170 bishops; 16 sessions held between Nov. 7, 680, and Sept. 16, 681. Condemned Monothelitism, which held that there was only one will, the divine, in Christ; censured Pope Honorius I for a letter to Sergius, bishop of Constantinople, in which he made an ambiguous but not infallible statement about the unity of will and/or operation in Christ. Constantinople III is also called the Trullan Council because its sessions were held in the domed hall, Trullos, of the imperial palace.

7. Nicaea II, 787: Adrian I (Empress Irene); attended by approximately 300 bishops; eight sessions held between Sept. 24 and Oct. 23. Condemned: Iconoclasm, which held that the use of images was idolatry; and Adoptionism, which claimed that Christ was not the Son of God by nature but only by adoption. This was the last council regarded as ecumenical by Orthodox Churches.

8. Constantinople IV, 869-870: Adrian II (Emperor Basil I); attended by 102 bishops; six sessions held between Oct. 5, 869, and Feb. 28, 870. Condemned Iconoclasm; condemned and deposed Photius as patriarch of Constantinople; restored Ignatius to the patriarchate. This was the last ecumenical council held in the East. It was first called ecumenical by canonists toward the end of the 11th century.

9. Lateran I, 1123: Callistus II; attended by approximately 300 bishops; sessions held between Mar. 18 and Apr. 6. Endorsed provisions of the Concordat of Worms concerning the investiture of prelates; approved reform measures in 25 canons.

10. Lateran II, 1139: Innocent II; attended by 900 to 1,000 bishops and abbots; three sessions held in April. Adopted measures against a schism organized by antipope Anacletus; approved 30 disciplinary measures and canons, one of which stated that holy orders is an invalidating impediment to marriage.

11. Lateran III, 1179: Alexander III; attended by at least 300 bishops; three sessions held between Mar. 5 and 19. Enacted measures against the Waldenses and Albigensians; approved reform decrees in 27 canons; provided that popes be elected by two-thirds vote of the cardinals.

12. Lateran IV, 1215: Innocent III; sessions held between Nov. 11 and 30. Ordered annual confession and Communion; defined and made first official use of the term "transubstantiation"; adopted measures to counteract the Cathari and Albigensians; approved 70 canons.

13. Lyons I, 1245: Innocent IV; attended by approximately 150 bishops; three sessions held between June 28 and July 17. Confirmed the deposition of Emperor Frederick II; approved 22 canons.

14. Lyons II, 1274: Gregory X; attended by approximately 500 bishops; six sessions held between May 7 and July 17. Accomplished a temporary reunion of separated Eastern Churches with the Roman Church; issued regulations concerning conclaves for papal elections; approved 31 canons.

15. Vienne, 1311-1312: Clement V; attended by 132 bishops; three sessions held between Oct. 16, 1311, and May 6, 1312. Suppressed the Knights Templar; enacted a number of reform decrees.

16. Constance, 1414-1418: Gregory XII, Martin V; attended by nearly 200 bishops, plus other prelates and many experts; 45 sessions held between Nov. 5, 1414, and Apr. 22, 1418. Took successful action to end the Western Schism; rejected the teachings of Wycliff; condemned Hus as a heretic. One decree, passed in the earlier stages of the council, asserted the superiority of an ecumenical council over the pope; this was later rejected.

17. Florence (also called Basel-Ferrara-Florence), 1438-1445: Eugene IV; attended by many Latin-Rite and Eastern-Rite bishops; preliminary sessions were held at Basel and Ferrara before definitive work was accomplished at Florence. Reaffirmed the primacy of the pope against the claims of Conciliarists that an ecumenical council is superior to the pope; formulated and approved decrees of union — with the Greeks, July 6, 1439; with the Armenians, Nov. 22, 1439; with the Jacobites, Feb. 4, 1442. These decrees failed to gain general or lasting acceptance in the East.

18. Lateran V, 1512-1517: Julius II, Leo X; 12 sessions held between May 3, 1512, and Mar. 16, 1517. Stated the relation and position of the pope with respect to an ecumenical council; acted to counteract the Pragmatic Sanction of Bourges and exaggerated claims of liberty by the French Church; condemned erroneous teachings concerning the nature of the human soul; stated doctrine concerning indulgences. The council reflected concern for abuses in the Church and the need for reforms but failed to take decisive action in the years immediately preceding the Reformation.

19. Trent, 1545-1563: Paul III, Julius III, Pius IV; 25 sessions held between Dec. 13, 1545, and Dec. 4, 1563. Issued a great number of decrees concerning doctrinal matters opposed by the Reformers, and mobilized the Counter-Reformation. Definitions covered the rule of faith, the nature of justification, grace, faith, original sin and its effects, the seven sacraments, the sacrificial nature of the Mass, the veneration of saints, use of sacred images, belief in purgatory, the doctrine of indulgences, the jurisdiction of the pope over the whole Church. Initiated many reforms for renewal in the liturgy and general discipline in the Church, the promotion of religious instruction, the education of the clergy through the foundation of seminaries, etc. Trent ranks with Vatican II as the greatest ecumenical council held in the West.

20. Vatican I, 1869-1870: Pius IX; attended by approximately 800 bishops and other prelates; four public sessions and 89 general meetings held between Dec. 8, 1869, and July 7, 1870. Defined papal primacy and infallibility in a dogmatic constitution on the Church; covered natural religion, revelation, faith, and the relations between faith and reason in a dogmatic constitution on the Catholic faith. The council suspended sessions Sept. 1 and was adjourned Oct. 20, 1870.

Vatican II

The Second Vatican Council, which was forecast by Pope John XXIII Jan. 25, 1959, was held in four sessions in St. Peter's Basilica.

Pope John convoked it and opened the first session, which ran from Oct. 11 to Dec. 8, 1962. Following John's death June 3, 1963, Pope Paul VI reconvened the council for the other three sessions which ran from Sept. 29 to Dec. 4, 1963; Sept. 14 to Nov. 21, 1964; Sept. 14 to Dec. 8, 1965.

A total of 2,860 Fathers participated in council proceedings, and attendance at meetings varied between 2,000 and 2,500. For various reasons, including the denial of exit from Communist-dominated countries, 274 Fathers could not attend.

The council formulated and promulgated 16 documents — two dogmatic and two pastoral constitutions, nine decrees and three declarations — all of which reflect its basic pastoral orientation toward renewal and reform in the Church. Given below are the Latin and English titles of the documents and their dates of promulgation.

• *Lumen Gentium* (Dogmatic Constitution on the Church), Nov. 21, 1964.

• *Dei Verbum* (Dogmatic Constitution on Divine Revelation), Nov. 18, 1965.

• *Sacrosanctum Concilium* (Constitution on the Sacred Liturgy), Dec. 4, 1963.

• *Gaudium et Spes* (Pastoral Constitution on the Church in the Modern World), Dec. 7, 1965.

• *Christus Dominus* (Decree on the Bishops' Pastoral Office in the Church), Oct. 28, 1965.

• *Ad Gentes* (Decree on the Church's Missionary Activity), Dec. 7, 1965.

• *Unitatis Redintegratio* (Decree on Ecumenism), Nov. 21, 1964.

• *Orientalium Ecclesiarum* (Decree on Eastern Catholic Churches), Nov. 21, 1964.

• *Presbyterorum Ordinis* (Decree on the Ministry and Life of Priests), Dec. 7, 1965.

• *Optatam Totius* (Decree on Priestly Formation), Oct. 28, 1965.

• *Perfectae Caritatis* (Decree on the Appropriate Renewal of the Religious Life), Oct. 28, 1965.

• *Apostolicam Actuositatem* (Decree on the Apostolate of the Laity), Nov. 18, 1965.

• *Inter Mirifica* (Decree on the Instruments of Social Communication), Dec. 4, 1963.

• *Dignitatis Humanae* (Declaration on Religious Freedom), Dec. 7, 1965.

• *Nostra Aetate* (Declaration on the Relationship of the Church to Non-Christian Religions), Oct. 28, 1965.

• *Gravissimum Educationis* (Declaration on Christian Education), Oct. 28, 1965.

The key documents were the four constitutions, which set the ideological basis for all the others. To date, the documents with the most visible effects are those on the liturgy, the Church, the Church in the world, ecumenism, the renewal of religious life, the life and ministry of priests, the lay apostolate.

The main business of the council was to explore and make explicit dimensions of doctrine and Christian life requiring emphasis for the full development of the Church and the better accomplishment of its mission in the contemporary world.

LIST OF POPES

(Source: *Annuario Pontificio*.)

Information includes the name of the pope, in many cases his name before becoming pope, his birthplace or country of origin, the date of accession to the papacy, and the date of the end of reign which, in all but a few cases, was the date of death. Double dates indicate times of election and coronation.

St. Peter (Simon Bar-Jona): Bethsaida in Galilee; d. c. 64 or 67.

St. Linus: Tuscany; 67-76.

St. Anacletus (Cletus): Rome; 76-88.

St. Clement: Rome; 88-97.

St. Evaristus: Greece; 97-105.

St. Alexander I: Rome; 105-115.

St. Sixtus I: Rome; 115-125.

St. Telesphorus: Greece; 125-136.

St. Hyginus: Greece; 136-140.

St. Pius I: Aquileia; 140-155.

St. Anicetus: Syria; 155-166.

St. Soter: Campania; 166-175.

St. Eleutherius: Nicopolis in Epirus; 175-189.

Up to the time of St. Eleutherius, the years indicated for the beginning and end of pontificates are not absolutely certain. Also, up to the middle of the 11th century, there are some doubts about the exact days and months given in chronological tables.

St. Victor I: Africa; 189-199.

St. Zephyrinus: Rome; 199-217.

St. Callistus I: Rome; 217-222.

St. Urban I: Rome; 222-230.

St. Pontian: Rome; July 21, 230, to Sept. 28, 235.

St. Anterus: Greece; Nov. 21, 235, to Jan. 3, 236.

St. Fabian: Rome; Jan. 10, 236, to Jan. 20, 250.

St. Cornelius: Rome; Mar., 251, to June, 253.

St. Lucius I: Rome; June 25, 253, to Mar. 5, 254.

St. Stephen I: Rome; May 12, 254, to Aug. 2, 257.

St. Sixtus II: Greece; Aug. 30, 257, to Aug. 6, 258.

St. Dionysius: July 22, 259, to Dec. 26, 268.

St. Felix I: Rome; Jan. 5, 269, to Dec. 30, 274.

St. Eutychian: Luni; Jan. 4, 275, to Dec. 7, 283.

St. Caius: Dalmatia; Dec. 17, 283, to Apr. 22, 296.

St. Marcellinus: Rome; June 30, 296, to Oct. 25, 304.

St. Marcellus I: Rome; May 27, 308, or June 26, 308, to Jan. 16, 309.

St. Eusebius: Rome; Apr. 18, 309 or 310, to Aug. 17, 309 or 310.

St. Melchiades (Miltiades): Africa; July 2, 311, to Jan. 11, 314.

St. Sylvester I: Rome; Jan. 31, 314, to Dec. 31, 335. (Most of the popes before St. Sylvester I were martyrs.)

St. Marcus: Rome; Jan. 18, 336, to Oct. 7, 336.

St. Julius I: Rome; Feb. 6, 337, to Apr. 12, 352.

Liberius: Rome; May 17, 352, to Sept. 24, 366.

St. Damasus I: Spain; Oct. 1, 366, to Dec. 11, 384.

St. Siricius: Rome; Dec. 15, or 22 or 29, 384, to Nov. 26, 399.

St. Anastasius I: Rome; Nov. 27, 399, to Dec. 19, 401.

St. Innocent I: Albano; Dec. 22, 401, to Mar. 12, 417.

St. Zozimus: Greece; Mar. 18, 417, to Dec. 26, 418.

St. Boniface I: Rome; Dec. 28 or 29, 418, to Sept. 4, 422.

St. Celestine I: Campania; Sept. 10, 422, to July 27, 432.

St. Sixtus III: Rome; July 31, 432, to Aug. 19, 440.

St. Leo I (the Great): Tuscany; Sept. 29, 440, to Nov. 10, 461.

St. Hilary: Sardinia; Nov. 19, 461, to Feb. 29, 468.

St. Simplicius: Tivoli; Mar. 3, 468, to Mar. 10, 483.

St. Felix III (II): Rome; Mar. 13, 483, to Mar. 1, 492.

He should be called Felix II, and his successors of the same name should be numbered accordingly. The discrepancy in the numerical designation of popes named Felix was caused by the erroneous insertion in some lists of the name of St. Felix of Rome, a martyr.

St. Gelasius I: Africa; Mar. 1, 492, to Nov. 21, 496.

Anastasius II: Rome; Nov. 24, 496, to Nov. 19, 498.

St. Symmachus: Sardinia; Nov. 22, 498, to July 19, 514.

St. Hormisdas: Frosinone; July 20, 514, to Aug. 6, 523.

St. John I, Martyr: Tuscany; Aug. 13, 523, to May 18, 526.

St. Felix IV (III): Samnium; July 12, 526, to Sept. 22, 530.

Boniface II: Rome; Sept. 22, 530, to Oct. 17, 532.

John II: Rome; Jan. 2, 533, to May 8, 535.

John II was the first pope to change his name. His given name was Mercury.

St. Agapitus I: Rome; May 13, 535, to Apr. 22, 536.

St. Silverius, Martyr: Campania; June 1 or 8, 536, to Nov. 11, 537 (d. Dec. 2, 537).

St. Silverius was violently deposed in March, 537, and abdicated Nov. 11, 537. His successor, Vigilius, was not recognized as pope by all the Roman clergy until his abdication.

Vigilius: Rome; Mar. 29, 537, to June 7, 555.

Pelagius I: Rome; Apr. 16, 556, to Mar. 4, 561.

John III: Rome; July 17, 561, to July 13, 574.

Benedict I: Rome; June 2, 575, to July 30, 579.

Pelagius II: Rome; Nov. 26, 579, to Feb. 7, 590.

St. Gregory I (the Great): Rome; Sept. 3, 590, to Mar. 12, 604.

Sabinian: Blera in Tuscany; Sept. 13, 604, to Feb. 22, 606.

Boniface III: Rome; Feb. 19, 607, to Nov. 12, 607.

St. Boniface IV: Abruzzi; Aug. 25, 608, to May 8, 615.

St. Deusdedit (Adeodatus I): Rome; Oct. 19, 615, to Nov. 8, 618.

Boniface V: Naples; Dec. 23, 619, to Oct. 25, 625.

Honorius I: Campania; Oct. 27, 625, to Oct. 12, 638.

Severinus: Rome; May 28, 640, to Aug. 2, 640.

John IV: Dalmatia; Dec. 24, 640, to Oct. 12, 642.

Theodore I: Greece; Nov. 24, 642, to May 14, 649.

St. Martin I, Martyr: Todi; July, 649, to Sept. 16, 655 (in exile from June 17, 653).

St. Eugene I: Rome; Aug. 10, 654, to June 2, 657.

St. Eugene I was elected during the exile of St. Martin I, who is believed to have endorsed him as pope.

St. Vitalian: Segni; July 30, 657, to Jan. 27, 672.

Adeodatus II: Rome; Apr. 11, 672, to June 17, 676.

Donus: Rome; Nov. 2, 676, to Apr. 11, 678.

St. Agatho: Sicily; June 27, 678, to Jan. 10, 681.

St. Leo II: Sicily; Aug. 17, 682, to July 3, 683.

St. Benedict II: Rome; June 26, 684, to May 8, 685.

John V: Syria; July 23, 685, to Aug. 2, 686.

Conon: birthplace unknown; Oct. 21, 686, to Sept. 21, 687.

St. Sergius I: Syria; Dec. 15, 687, to Sept. 8, 701.

John VI: Greece; Oct. 30, 701, to Jan. 11, 705.

John VII: Greece; Mar. 1, 705, to Oct. 18, 707.

Sisinnius: Syria; Jan. 15, 708, to Feb. 4, 708.

Constantine: Syria; Mar. 25, 708, to Apr. 9, 715.

St. Gregory II: Rome; May 19, 715, to Feb. 11, 731.

St. Gregory III: Syria; Mar. 18, 731, to Nov., 741.

St. Zachary: Greece; Dec. 10, 741, to Mar. 22, 752.

Stephen II (III): Rome; Mar. 26, 752, to Apr. 26, 757.

After the death of St. Zachary, a Roman priest named Stephen was elected but died (four days later) before his consecration as bishop of Rome, which would have marked the beginning of his pontificate. Another Stephen was elected to succeed Zachary as Stephen II. (The first pope with this name was St. Stephen I, 254-57.) The ordinal III appears in parentheses after the name of Stephen II because the name of the earlier elected but deceased priest was included in some lists. Other Stephens have double numbers.

St. Paul I: Rome; Apr. (May 29), 757, to June 28, 767.

Stephen III (IV): Sicily; Aug. 1 (7), 768, to Jan. 24, 772.

Adrian I: Rome; Feb. 1 (9), 772, to Dec. 25, 795.

St. Leo III: Rome; Dec. 26 (27), 795, to June 12, 816.

Stephen IV (V): Rome; June 22, 816, to Jan. 24, 817.

St. Paschal I: Rome; Jan. 25, 817, to Feb. 11, 824.

Eugene II: Rome; Feb. (May), 824, to Aug., 827.

Valentine: Rome; Aug. 827, to Sept., 827.

Gregory IV: Rome; 827, to Jan., 844.

Sergius II: Rome; Jan., 844 to Jan. 27, 847.

St. Leo IV: Rome; Jan. (Apr. 10), 847, to July 17, 855.

Benedict III: Rome; July (Sept. 29), 855, to Apr. 17, 858.

St. Nicholas I (the Great): Rome; Apr. 24, 858, to Nov. 13, 867.

Adrian II: Rome; Dec. 14, 867, to Dec. 14, 872.

John VIII: Rome; Dec. 14, 872, to Dec. 16, 882.

Marinus I: Gallese; Dec. 16, 882, to May 15, 884.

St. Adrian III: Rome; May 17, 884, to Sept., 885. Cult confirmed June 2, 1891.

Stephen V (VI): Rome; Sept., 885, to Sept. 14, 891.

Formosus: Portus; Oct. 6, 891, to Apr. 4, 896.

Boniface VI: Rome; Apr., 896, to Apr., 896.

Stephen VI (VII): Rome; May, 896, to Aug., 897.

Romanus: Gallese; Aug., 897, to Nov., 897.

Theodore II: Rome; Dec., 897, to Dec., 897.

John IX: Tivoli; Jan., 898, to Jan., 900.

Benedict IV: Rome; Jan. (Feb.), 900, to July, 903.

Leo V: Ardea; July, 903, to Sept., 903.

Sergius III: Rome; Jan. 29, 904, to Apr. 14, 911.

Anastasius III: Rome; Apr., 911, to June, 913.

Landus: Sabina; July, 913, to Feb., 914.

John X: Tossignano (Imola); Mar., 914, to May, 928.

Leo VI: Rome; May, 928, to Dec., 928.

Stephen VII (VIII): Rome; Dec., 928, to Feb., 931.

John XI: Rome; Feb. (Mar.), 931, to Dec., 935.

Leo VII: Rome; Jan. 3, 936, to July 13, 939.

Stephen VIII (IX): Rome; July 14, 939, to Oct., 942.

Marinus II: Rome; Oct. 30, 942, to May, 946.

Agapitus II: Rome; May 10, 946, to Dec., 955.

John XII (Octavius): Tusculum; Dec. 16, 955, to May 14, 964 (date of his death).

Leo VIII: Rome; Dec. 4 (6), 963, to Mar. 1, 965.

Benedict V: Rome; May 22, 964, to July 4, 966.

Confusion exists concerning the legitimacy of claims to the pontificate by Leo VIII and Benedict V. John XII was deposed Dec. 4, 963, by a Roman council. If this deposition was invalid, Leo was an antipope. If the deposition of John was valid, Leo was the legitimate pope and Benedict was an antipope.

John XIII: Rome; Oct. 1, 965, to Sept. 6, 972.

Benedict VI: Rome; Jan. 19, 973, to June, 974.

Benedict VII: Rome; Oct. 974, to July 10, 983.

John XIV (Peter Campenora): Pavia; Dec., 983, to Aug. 20, 984.

John XV: Rome; Aug., 985, to Mar., 996.

Gregory V (Bruno of Carinthia): Saxony; May 3, 996, to Feb. 18, 999.

Sylvester II (Gerbert): Auvergne; Apr. 2, 999, to May 12, 1003.

John XVII (Siccone): Rome; June, 1003, to Dec., 1003.

John XVIII (Phasianus): Rome; Jan., 1004, to July, 1009.

Sergius IV (Peter): Rome; July 31, 1009, to May 12, 1012.

The custom of changing one's name on election to the papacy is generally considered to date from the time of Sergius IV. Before his time, several popes had changed their names. After his time, this became a regular practice, with few exceptions; e.g., Adrian VI and Marcellus II.

Benedict VIII (Theophylactus): Tusculum; May 18, 1012, to Apr. 9, 1024.

John XIX (Romanus): Tusculum; Apr. (May), 1024, to 1032.

Benedict IX (Theophylactus): Tusculum; 1032, to 1044.

Sylvester III (John): Rome; Jan. 20, 1045, to Feb. 10, 1045.

Sylvester III was an antipope if the forcible removal of Benedict IX in 1044 was not legitimate.

Benedict IX (second time): Apr. 10, 1045, to May 1, 1045.

Gregory VI (John Gratian): Rome; May 5, 1045, to Dec. 20, 1046.

Clement II (Suitger, Lord of Morsleben and Hornburg): Saxony; Dec. 24 (25), 1046, to Oct. 9, 1047.

If the resignation of Benedict IX in 1045 and his removal at the December, 1046, synod were not legitimate, Gregory VI and Clement II were antipopes.

Benedict IX (third time): Nov. 8, 1047, to July 17, 1048 (d. c. 1055).

Damasus II (Poppo): Bavaria; July 17, 1048, to Aug. 9, 1048.

St. Leo IX (Bruno): Alsace; Feb. 12, 1049, to Apr. 19, 1054.

Victor II (Gebhard): Swabia; Apr. 16, 1055, to July 28, 1057.

Stephen IX (X) (Frederick): Lorraine; Aug. 3, 1057, to Mar. 29, 1058.

Nicholas II (Gerard): Burgundy; Jan. 24, 1059, to July 27, 1061.

Alexander II (Anselmo da Baggio): Milan; Oct. 1, 1061, to Apr. 21, 1073.

St. Gregory VII (Hildebrand): Tuscany; Apr. 22 (June 30), 1073, to May 25, 1085.

Bl. Victor III (Dauferius; Desiderius): Benevento; May 24, 1086, to Sept. 16, 1087. Cult confirmed July 23, 1887.

Bl. Urban II (Otto di Lagery): France; Mar. 12, 1088, to July 29, 1099. Cult confirmed July 14, 1881.

Paschal II (Raniero): Ravenna; Aug. 13 (14), 1099, to Jan. 21, 1118.

Gelasius II (Giovanni Caetani): Gaeta; Jan. 24 (Mar. 10), 1118, to Jan. 28, 1119.

Callistus II (Guido of Burgundy): Burgundy; Feb. 2 (9), 1119, to Dec. 13, 1124.

Honorius II (Lamberto): Fiagnano (Imola); Dec. 15 (21), 1124, to Feb. 13, 1130.

Innocent II (Gregorio Papareschi): Rome; Feb. 14 (23), 1130, to Sept. 24, 1143.

Celestine II (Guido): Citta di Castello; Sept. 26 (Oct. 3), 1143, to Mar. 8, 1144.

Lucius II (Gerardo Caccianemici): Bologna: Mar. 12, 1144, to Feb. 15, 1145.

Bl. Eugene III (Bernardo Paganelli di Montemagno): Pisa; Feb. 15 (18), 1145, to July 8, 1153. Cult confirmed Oct. 3, 1872.

Anastasius IV (Corrado): Rome; July 12, 1153, to Dec, 3, 1154.

Adrian IV (Nicholas Breakspear): England; Dec. 4 (5), 1154, to Sept. 1, 1159.

Alexander III (Rolando Bandinelli): Siena; Sept. 7 (20), 1159, to Aug. 30, 1181.

Lucius III (Ubaldo Allucingoli): Lucca; Sept. 1 (6), 1181, to Sept. 25, 1185.

Urban III (Uberto Crivelli): Milan; Nov. 25 (Dec. 1), 1185, to Oct. 20, 1187.

Gregory VIII (Alberto de Morra): Benevento; Oct. 21 (25), 1187, to Dec. 17, 1187.

Clement III (Paolo Scolari): Rome; Dec. 19 (20), 1187, to Mar., 1191.

Celestine III (Giacinto Bobone): Rome; Mar. 30 (Apr. 14), 1191, to Jan. 8, 1198.

Innocent III (Lotario dei Conti di Segni); Anagni; Jan. 8 (Feb. 22), 1198, to July 16, 1216.

Honorius III (Cencio Savelli): Rome; July 18 (24), 1216, to Mar. 18, 1227.

Gregory IX (Ugolino, Count of Segni): Anagni; Mar. 19 (21), 1227, to Aug. 22, 1241.

Celestine IV (Goffredo Castiglioni): Milan; Oct. 25 (28), 1241, to Nov. 10, 1241.

Innocent IV (Sinibaldo Fieschi): Genoa; June 25 (28), 1243, to Dec. 7, 1254.

Alexander IV (Rinaldo, Count of Segni): Anagni; Dec. 12 (20), 1254, to May 25, 1261.

Urban IV (Jacques Pantaléon): Troyes; Aug. 29 (Sept. 4), 1261, to Oct. 2, 1264.

Clement IV (Guy Foulques or Guido le Gros): France; Feb. 5 (15), 1265, to Nov. 29, 1268.

Bl. Gregory X (Teobaldo Visconti): Piacenza; Sept. 1, 1271 (Mar. 27, 1272), to Jan. 10, 1276. Cult confirmed Sept. 12, 1713.

Bl. Innocent V (Peter of Tarentaise): Savoy; Jan. 21 (Feb. 22), 1276, to June 22, 1276. Cult confirmed Mar. 13, 1898.

Adrian V (Ottobono Fieschi): Genoa: July 11, 1276, to Aug. 18, 1276.

John XXI (Petrus Juliani or Petrus Hispanus): Portugal; Sept. 8 (20), 1276, to May 20, 1277.

Elimination was made of the name of John XX in an effort to rectify the numerical designation of popes named John. The error dates back to the time of John XV.

Nicholas III (Giovanni Gaetano Orsini): Rome; Nov. 25 (Dec. 26), 1277, to Aug. 22, 1280.

Martin IV (Simon de Brie): France; Feb. 22 (Mar. 23), 1281, to Mar. 28, 1285.

The names of Marinus I (882-84) and Marinus II (942-46) were construed as Martin. In view of these two pontificates and the earlier reign of St. Martin I (649-55), this pope was called Martin IV.

Honorius IV (Giacomo Savelli): Rome; Apr. 2 (May 20), 1285, to Apr. 3, 1287.

Nicholas IV (Girolamo Masci): Ascoli; Feb. 22, 1288, to Apr. 4, 1292.

St. Celestine V (Pietro del Murrone): Isernia; July 5 (Aug. 29), 1294, to Dec. 13, 1294; d. 1296. Canonized May 5, 1313.

Boniface VIII (Benedetto Caetani): Anagni; Dec. 24, 1294 (Jan. 23, 1295), to Oct. 11, 1303.

Bl. Benedict XI (Niccolo Boccasini): Treviso; Oct. 22 (27), 1303, to July 7, 1304. Cult confirmed Apr. 24, 1736.

Clement V (Bertrand de Got): France; June 5 (Nov. 14), 1305, to Apr. 20, 1314. (First of Avignon popes.)

John XXII (Jacques d'Euse): Cahors; Aug. 7 (Sept. 5), 1316, to Dec. 4, 1334.

Benedict XII (Jacques Fournier): France; Dec. 20, 1334 (Jan. 8, 1335), to Apr. 25, 1342.

Clement VI (Pierre Roger): France; May 7 (19), 1342, to Dec. 6, 1352.

Innocent VI (Etienne Aubert): France; Dec. 18 (30), 1352, to Sept. 12, 1362.

Bl. Urban V (Guillaume de Grimoard): France; Sept. 28 (Nov. 6), 1362, to Dec. 19, 1370. Cult confirmed Mar. 10, 1870.

Gregory XI (Pierre Roger de Beaufort): France; Dec. 30, 1370 (Jan. 5, 1371), to Mar. 26, 1378. (Last of Avignon popes.)

Urban VI (Bartolomeo Prignano): Naples; Apr. 8 (18), 1378, to Oct. 15, 1389.

Boniface IX (Pietro Tomacelli): Naples; Nov. 2 (9), 1389, to Oct. 1, 1404.

Innocent VII (Cosma Migliorati): Sulmona; Oct. 17 (Nov. 11), 1404, to Nov. 6, 1406.

Gregory XII (Angelo Correr): Venice; Nov. 30 (Dec. 19), 1406, to July 4, 1415, when he voluntarily resigned from the papacy to permit the election of his successor. He died Oct. 18, 1417. (See The Western Schism.)

Martin V (Oddone Colonna): Rome; Nov. 11 (21), 1417, to Feb. 20, 1431.

Eugene IV (Gabriele Condulmer): Venice; Mar. 3 (11), 1431, to Feb. 23, 1447.

Nicholas V (Tommaso Parentucelli): Sarzana; Mar. 6 (19), 1447, to Mar. 24, 1455.

Callistus III (Alfonso Borgia): Jativa (Valencia); Apr. 8 (20), 1455, to Aug. 6, 1458.

Pius II (Enea Silvio Piccolomini): Siena; Aug. 19 (Sept. 3), 1458, to Aug. 15, 1464.

Paul II (Pietro Barbo): Venice; Aug. 30 (Sept. 16), 1464, to July 26, 1471.

Sixtus IV (Francesco della Rovere): Savona; Aug. 9 (25), 1471, to Aug. 12, 1484.

Innocent VIII (Giovanni Battista Cibo): Genoa; Aug. 29 (Sept. 12), 1484, to July 25, 1492.

Alexander VI (Rodrigo Borgia): Jativa (Valencia); Aug. 11 (26), 1492, to Aug. 18, 1503.

Pius III (Francesco Todeschini-Piccolomini): Siena; Sept. 22 (Oct. 1, 8), 1503, to Oct. 18, 1503.

Julius II (Giuliano della Rovere): Savona; Oct. 31 (Nov. 26), 1503, to Feb. 21, 1513.

Leo X (Giovanni de' Medici): Florence; Mar. 9 (19), 1513, to Dec. 1, 1521.

Adrian VI (Adrian Florensz): Utrecht; Jan. 9 (Aug. 31), 1522, to Sept. 14, 1523.

Clement VII (Giulio de' Medici): Florence; Nov. 19 (26), 1523, to Sept. 25, 1534.

Paul III (Alessandro Farnese): Rome; Oct. 13 (Nov. 3), 1534, to Nov. 10, 1549.

Julius III (Giovanni Maria Ciocchi del Monte): Rome; Feb. 7 (22), 1550, to Mar. 23, 1555.

Marcellus II (Marcello Cervini): Montepulciano; Apr. 9 (10), 1555, to May 1, 1555.

Paul IV (Gian Pietro Carafa): Naples; May 23 (26), 1555, to Aug. 18, 1559.

Pius IV (Giovan Angelo de' Medici): Milan; Dec. 25, 1559 (Jan. 6, 1560), to Dec. 9, 1565.

St. Pius V (Antonio-Michele Ghislieri): Bosco (Alexandria); Jan. 7 (17), 1566, to May 1, 1572. Canonized May 22, 1712.

Gregory XIII (Ugo Buoncompagni): Bologna; May 13 (25), 1572, to Apr. 10, 1585.

Sixtus V (Felice Peretti): Grottammare (Ripatransone); Apr. 24 (May 1), 1585, to Aug. 27, 1590.

Urban VII (Giovanni Battista Castagna): Rome; Sept. 15, 1590, to Sept. 27, 1590.

Gregory XIV (Niccolo Sfondrati): Cremona; Dec. 5 (8), 1590, to Oct. 16, 1591.

Innocent IX (Giovanni Antonio Facchinetti): Bologna; Oct. 29 (Nov. 3), 1591, to Dec. 30, 1591.

Clement VIII (Ippolito Aldobrandini): Florence; Jan. 30 (Feb. 9), 1592, to Mar. 3, 1605.

Leo XI (Alessandro de' Medici): Florence; Apr. 1 (10), 1605, to Apr. 27, 1605.

Paul V (Camillo Borghese): Rome; May 16 (29), 1605, to Jan. 28, 1621.

Gregory XV (Alessandro Ludovisi): Bologna; Feb. 9 (14), 1621, to July 8, 1623.

Urban VIII (Maffeo Barberini): Florence; Aug. 6 (Sept. 29), 1623, to July 29, 1644.

Innocent X (Giovanni Battista Pamfili): Rome; Sept. 15 (Oct. 4), 1644, to Jan. 7, 1655.

Alexander VII (Fabio Chigi): Siena; Apr. 7 (18), 1655, to May 22, 1667.

Clement IX (Giulio Rospigliosi): Pistoia; June 20 (26), 1667, to Dec. 9, 1669.

Clement X (Emilio Altieri): Rome; Apr. 29 (May 11), 1670, to July 22, 1676.

Bl. Innocent XI (Benedetto Odescalchi): Como; Sept. 21 (Oct. 4), 1676, to Aug. 12, 1689.

Alexander VIII (Pietro Ottoboni): Venice; Oct. 6 (16), 1689, to Feb. 1, 1691.

Innocent XII (Antonio Pignatelli): Spinazzola; July 12 (15), 1691, to Sept. 27, 1700.

Clement XI (Giovanni Francesco Albani): Urbino; Nov. 23, 30 (Dec. 8), 1700, to Mar. 19, 1721.

Innocent XIII (Michelangelo dei Conti): Rome; May 8 (18), 1721, to Mar. 7, 1724.

Benedict XIII (Pietro Francesco — Vincenzo Maria — Orsini): Gravina (Bari); May 29 (June 4), 1724, to Feb. 21, 1730.

Clement XII (Lorenzo Corsini): Florence; July 12 (16), 1730, to Feb. 6, 1740.

Benedict XIV (Prospero Lambertini): Bologna; Aug. 17 (22), 1740, to May 3, 1758.

Clement XIII (Carlo Rezzonico): Venice; July 6 (16), 1758, to Feb. 2, 1769.

Clement XIV (Giovanni Vincenzo Antonio — Lorenzo — Ganganelli): Rimini; May 19, 28 (June 4), 1769, to Sept. 22, 1774.

Pius VI (Giovanni Angelo Braschi): Cesena; Feb. 15 (22), 1775, to Aug. 29, 1799.

Pius VII (Barnaba — Gregorio — Chiaramonti): Cesena; Mar. 14 (21), 1800, to Aug. 20, 1823.

Leo XII (Annibale della Genga): Genga (Fabriano); Sept. 28 (Oct. 5), 1823, to Feb. 10, 1829.

Pius VIII (Francesco Saverio Castiglioni): Cingoli; Mar. 31 (Apr. 5), 1829, to Nov. 30, 1830.

Gregory XVI (Bartolomeo Alberto — Mauro — Cappellari): Belluno; Feb. 2 (6), 1831, to June 1, 1846.

Pius IX (Giovanni M. Mastai Ferretti): Senigallia; June 16 (21), 1846, to Feb. 7, 1878.

Leo XIII (Gioacchino Pecci): Carpineto (Anagni); Feb. 20 (Mar. 3), 1878, to July 20, 1903.

St. Pius X (Giuseppe Sarto): Riese (Treviso); Aug. 4 (9), 1903, to Aug. 20, 1914. Canonized May 29, 1954.

Benedict XV (Giacomo della Chiesa): Genoa; Sept. 3 (6), 1914, to Jan. 22, 1922.

Pius XI (Achille Ratti): Desio (Milan); Feb. 6 (12), 1922, to Feb. 10, 1939.

Pius XII (Eugenio Pacelli): Rome; Mar. 2 (12), 1939, to Oct. 9, 1958.

John XXIII (Angelo Giuseppe Roncalli): Sotto il Monte (Bergamo); Oct. 28 (Nov. 4). 1958 to June 3, 1963.

Paul VI (Giovanni Battista Montini): Concessio (Brescia); June 21 (June 30), 1963 to Aug. 6, 1978. (See separate entry.)

John Paul I (Albino Luciani): Forno di Canale (Belluno); Aug. 26 (Sept. 3) to Sept. 28, 1978. (See separate entry.)

John Paul II (Karol Wojtyla): Wadowice, Poland; Oct. 16 (22), 1978. to

ANTIPOPES

(Source: *Annuario Pontificio.*)

This list of men who claimed or exercised the papal office in an uncanonical manner includes names, birthplaces and dates of alleged reigns.

St. Hippolytus: Rome; 217-235; was reconciled before his death.

Novatian: Rome; 251.

Felix II: Rome; 355 to Nov. 22, 365.

Ursinus: 366-367.

Eulalius: Dec. 27 or 29, 418, to 419.

Lawrence: 498; 501-505.

Dioscorus: Alexandria; Sept. 22, 530, to Oct. 14, 530.

Theodore: ended alleged reign, 687.

Paschal: ended alleged reign, 687.

Constantine: Nepi; June 28 (July 5), 767, to 769.

Philip: July 31, 768; retired to his monastery on the same day.

John: ended alleged reign, Jan., 844.

Anastasius: Aug., 855, to Sept., 855; d. 880.

Christopher: Rome; July or Sept., 903, to Jan., 904.

Boniface VII: Rome; June, 974, to July, 974; Aug., 984, to July, 985.

John XVI: Rossano; Apr., 997, to Feb., 998.

Gregory: ended alleged reign, 1012.

Benedict X: Rome; Apr. 5, 1058, to Jan. 24, 1059.

Honorius II: Verona; Oct. 28, 1061, to 1072.

Clement III: Parma; June 25, 1080 (Mar. 24, 1084), to Sept. 8, 1100.

Theodoric: ended alleged reign, 1100; d. 1102.

Albert: ended alleged reign, 1102.

Sylvester IV: Rome; Nov. 18, 1105, to 1111.

Gregory VIII: France; Mar. 8, 1118, to 1121.

Celestine II: Rome; ended alleged reign, Dec., 1124.

Anacletus II: Rome; Feb. 14 (23), 1130, to Jan. 25, 1138.

Victor IV: Mar., 1138, to May 29, 1138; submitted to Pope Innocent II.

Victor IV: Montecelio; Sept. 7 (Oct. 4), 1159, to Apr. 20, 1164; he did not recognize his predecessor (Victor IV, above).

Paschal III: Apr. 22 (26), 1164, to Sept. 20, 1168.

Callistus III: Arezzo; Sept., 1168, to Aug. 29, 1178; submitted to Pope Alexander III.

Innocent III: Sezze; Sept. 29, 1179, to 1180.

Nicholas V: Corvaro (Rieti); May 12 (22), 1328, to Aug. 25, 1330; d. Oct. 16, 1333.

Four antipopes of the Western Schism:

Clement VII: Sept. 20 (Oct. 31), 1378, to Sept. 16, 1394.

Benedict XIII: Aragon; Sept. 28 (Oct. 11), 1394, to May 23, 1423.

Alexander V: Crete; June 26 (July 7), 1409, to May 3, 1410.
John XXIII: Naples; May 17 (25), 1410, to May 29, 1415.
Felix V: Savoy; Nov. 5, 1439 (July 24, 1440), to April 7, 1449; d. 1451.

Avignon Papacy

Avignon was the residence of a series of French popes from Clement V to Gregory XI (1309-77). Prominent in the period were power struggles over the mixed interests of Church and state with the rulers of France (Philip IV, John II), Bavaria (Lewis IV), England (Edward III); factionalism of French and Italian churchmen; political as well as ecclesiastical turmoil in Italy, a factor of significance in prolonging the stay of popes in Avignon. Despite some positive achievements, the Avignon papacy was a prologue to the Western Schism which began in 1378.

Western Schism

The Western Schism was a confused state of affairs which divided Christendom into two and then three papal obediences from 1378 to 1417.

It occurred some 50 years after Marsilius theorized that a general (not ecumenical) council of bishops and other persons was superior to a pope and nearly 30 years before the Council of Florence stated definitively that no kind of council had such authority.

It was a period of disaster preceding the even more disastrous period of the Reformation.

Urban VI, following transfer to Rome of the 70-year papal residence at Avignon, was elected pope Apr. 8, 1378, and reigned until his death in 1389. He was succeeded by Boniface IX (1389-1404), Innocent VII (1404-1406) and Gregory XII (1406-1415). These four are considered the legitimate popes of the period.

Some of the cardinals who chose Urban pope, dissatisfied with his conduct of the office, declared that his election was invalid. They proceeded to elect Clement VII, who claimed the papacy from 1378 to 1394. He was succeeded by Benedict XIII.

Prelates seeking to end the state of divided papal loyalties convoked the Council of Pisa which, without authority, found Gregory XII and Benedict XIII, in absentia, guilty on 30-odd charges of schism and heresy, deposed them, and elected a third claimant to the papacy, Alexander V (1409-1410). He was succeeded by John XXIII (1410-1415).

The schism was ended by the Council of Constance (1414-1418). This council, although originally called into session in an irregular manner, acquired authority after being convoked by Gregory XII in 1415. In its early irregular phase, it deposed John XXIII whose election to the papacy was uncanonical anyway. After being formally convoked, it accepted the abdication of Gregory in 1415 and dismissed the claims of Benedict XIII two years later, thus clearing the way for the election of Martin V on Nov. 11, 1417. The Council of Constance also rejected the theories of John Wycliff and condemned John Hus as a heretic.

20th CENTURY POPES

Leo XIII

Leo XIII (Gioacchino Vincenzo Pecci) was born May 2, 1810, in Carpineto, Italy. Although all but three years of his life and pontificate were of the 19th century, his influence extended well into the 20th century.

He was educated at the Jesuit college in Viterbo, the Roman College, the Academy of Noble Ecclesiastics, and the University of the Sapienza. He was ordained to the priesthood in 1837.

He served as an apostolic delegate to two States of the Church, Benevento from 1838 to 1841 and Perugia in 1841 and 1842. Ordained titular archbishop of Damietta, he was papal nuncio to Belgium from January, 1843, until May, 1846; in the post, he had controversial relations with the government over education issues and acquired his first significant experience of industrialized society.

He was archbishop of Perugia from 1846 to 1878. He became a cardinal in 1853 and chamberlain of the Roman Curia in 1877. He was elected to the papacy Feb. 20, 1878. He died July 20, 1903.

Canonizations: He canonized 18 saints and beatified a group of English martyrs.

Church Administration: He established 300 new dioceses and vicariates; restored the hierarchy in Scotland, set up an English, as contrasted with the Portuguese, hierarchy in India; approved the action of the Congregation for the Propagation of the Faith in reorganizing missions in China.

Encyclicals: He issued 50 encyclicals, on subjects ranging from devotional to social. In the former category were *Annum Sacrum,* on the Sacred Heart, in 1899, and nine letters on Mary and the Rosary.

Interfaith Relations: He was unsuccessful in unity overtures made to Orthodox and Slavic Churches. He declared Anglican orders invalid in the apostolic bull *Apostolicae Curae* Sept. 13, 1896.

International Relations: Leo was frustrated in seeking solutions to the Roman Question arising from the seizure of church lands by the Kingdom of Italy in 1870. He also faced anticlerical situations in Belgium and France and in the Kulturkampf policies of Bismarck in Germany.

Social Questions: Much of Leo's influence stemmed from social doctrine stated in numerous encyclicals, concerning liberalism, liberty, the divine origin of authority; socialism, in *Quod Apostolici Muneris,* 1878; the Christian concept of the family, in *Arcanum,* 1880; socialism and economic liberalism, relations between capital and labor, in *Rerum Novarum,* 1891. Two of his social encyclicals were against the African slave trade.

Studies: In the encyclical *Aeterni Patris* of Aug. 4, 1879, he ordered a renewal of philosophical and theological studies in seminaries along scholastic, and especially Thomistic, lines, to counteract influential trends of liberalism and Modernism. He issued guidelines for biblical exegesis in *Providentissimus Deus* Nov. 18, 1893, and established the Pontifical Biblical Commission in 1902.

In other actions affecting scholarship and study, he opened the Vatican Archives to scholars in 1883 and established the Vatican Observatory.

United States: He authorized establishment of the apostolic delegation in Washington, D.C. Jan. 24, 1893. He refused to issue a condemnation of the Knights of Labor. With a document entitled *Testem Benevolentiae,* he eased resolution of questions concerning what was called an American heresy in 1899.

St. Pius X

St. Pius X (Giuseppe Melchiorre Sarto) was born in 1835 in Riese, Italy.

Educated at the college of Castelfranco and the seminary at Padua, he was ordained to the priesthood Sept. 18, 1858. He served as a curate in Trombolo for nine years before beginning an eight-year pastorate at Salzano. He was chancellor of the Treviso diocese from November, 1875, and bishop of Mantua from 1884 until 1893. He was cardinal-patriarch of Venice from that year until his election to the papacy by the conclave held from July 31 to Aug. 4, 1903.

Aims: Pius' principal objectives as pope were "to restore all things in Christ, in order that Christ may be all and in all," and "to teach (and defend) Christian truth and law."

Canonizations, Encyclicals: He canonized four saints and issued 16 encyclicals. One of the encyclicals was issued in commemoration of the 50th anniversary of the proclamation of the dogma of the Immaculate Conception of Mary.

Catechetics: He introduced a whole new era of religious instruction and formation with the encyclical *Acerbo Nimis* of Apr. 15, 1905, in which he called for vigor in establishing and conducting parochial programs of the Confraternity of Christian Doctrine.

Catholic Action: He outlined the role of official Catholic Action in two encyclicals in 1905 and 1906. Favoring organized action by Catholics themselves, he had serious reservations about interconfessional collaboration.

He stoutly maintained claims to papal rights in the anticlerical climate of Italy. He authorized bishops to relax prohibitions against participation by Catholics in some Italian elections.

Church Administration: With the motu proprio *Arduum Sane* of Mar. 19, 1904, he inaugurated the work which resulted in the Code of Canon Law; the code was completed in 1917 and went into effect in the following year. He reorganized and strengthened the Roman Curia with the apostolic constitution *Sapienti Consilio* of June 29, 1908. While promoting the expansion of missionary work, he removed from the jurisdiction of the Congregation for the Propagation of the Faith the Church in the United States, Canada, Newfoundland, England, Ireland, Holland and Luxembourg.

International Relations: He ended traditional prerogatives of Catholic governments with respect to papal elections, in 1904. He opposed anti-Church and anticlerical actions in several countries: Bolivia in 1905, because of anti-religious legislation; France in 1906, for its 1901 action in annulling its concordat with the Holy See, and for the 1905 Law of Separation by which it decreed separation of Church and state, ordered the confiscation of church property, and blocked religious education and the activities of religious orders; Portugal in 1911, for the separation of Church and state and repressive measures which resulted in persecution later.

In 1912 he called on the bishops of Brazil to work for the improvement of conditions among Indians.

Liturgy: "The Pope of the Eucharist," he strongly recommended the frequent reception of Holy Communion in a decree dated Dec. 20, 1905; in another decree, *Quam Singulari,* of Aug. 8, 1910, he called for the early reception of the sacrament by children. He initiated measures for liturgical reform with new norms for sacred music and the start of work on revision of the *Breviary* for recitation of the Divine Office.

Modernism: Pius was a vigorous opponent of "the synthesis of all heresies," which threatened the integrity of doctrine through its influence in philosophy, theology and biblical exegesis. In opposition, he condemned 65 of its propositions as erroneous in the decree *Lamentabili* July 3, 1907; issued the encyclical *Pascendi* in the same vein Sept. 8, 1907; backed both of these with censures; and published the Oath against Modernism in September, 1910, to be taken by all the clergy. Ecclesiastical studies suffered to some extent from these actions, necessary as they were at the time.

Pius followed the lead of Leo XIII in promoting the study of scholastic philosophy. He established the Pontifical Biblical Institute May 7, 1909.

His death, Aug. 20, 1914, was hastened by the outbreak of World War I. He was beatified in 1951 and canonized May 29, 1954. His feast is observed Aug. 21.

Benedict XV

Benedict XV (Giacomo della Chiesa) was born Nov. 21, 1854, in Pegli, Italy.

He was educated at the Royal University of Genoa and Gregorian University in Rome. He was ordained to the priesthood Dec. 21, 1878.

He served in the papal diplomatic corps from 1882 to 1907; as secretary to the nuncio to Spain from 1882 to 1887, as secretary to the papal secretary of state from 1887, and as undersecretary from 1901.

He was ordained archbishop of Bologna Dec. 22, 1907, and spent four years completing a pastoral visitation there. He was made a cardinal just three months before being elected to the papacy Sept. 3, 1914, He died Jan. 22, 1922. Two key efforts of his pontificate were for peace and the relief of human suffering caused by World War I.

Canonizations: Benedict canonized three saints; one of them was Joan of Arc.

Canon Law: He published the Code of Canon Law, developed by the commission set up by St. Pius X, June 28, 1917; it went into effect the following year.

Curia: He made great changes in the personnel of the Curia. He established the Congregation for the Oriental Churches May 1, 1917, and founded the Pontifical Oriental Institute in Rome later in the year.

Encyclicals: He issued 12 encyclicals. Peace was the theme of three of them. In another, published two years after the cessation of hostilities, he wrote about child victims of the war. He followed the lead of Leo XIII in *Spiritus Paraclitus,* Sept. 15, 1920, on biblical studies.

International Relations: He was largely frustrated on the international level because of the events and attitudes of the war period, but the number of diplomats accredited to the Vatican nearly doubled, from 14 to 26, between the time of his accession to the papacy and his death.

Peace Efforts: Benedict's stance in the war was one of absolute impartiality but not of disinterested neutrality. Because he would not take sides, he was suspected by both sides and the seven-point peace plan he offered to all belligerents Aug. 1, 1917, was turned down. The points of the plan were: recognition of the moral force of right; disarmament; acceptance of arbitration in cases of dispute; guarantee of freedom of the seas; renunciation of war indemnities; evacuation and restoration of occupied territories; examination of territorial claims in dispute.

Relief Efforts: Benedict assumed personal charge of Vatican relief efforts during the war. He set up an international missing persons bureau for contacts between prisoners and their families, but was forced to close it because of the suspicion of warring nations that it was a front for espionage operations.

He persuaded the Swiss government to admit into the country military victims of tuberculosis.

Roman Question: Benedict arranged a meeting of Benito Mussolini and the papal secretary of state, which marked the first step toward final settlement of the question in 1929.

Pius XI

Pius XI (Ambrogio Damiano Achille Ratti) was born May 31, 1857, in Desio, Italy.

Educated at seminaries in Seviso and Milan, and at the Lombard College, Gregorian University and Academy of St. Thomas in Rome, he was ordained to the priesthood in 1879.

He taught at the major seminary of Milan from 1882 to 1888. Appointed to the staff of the Ambrosian Library in 1888, he remained there until 1911, acquiring a reputation for publishing works on palaeography and serving as director from 1907 to 1911. He then moved to the Vatican Library, of which he was prefect from 1914 to 1918. In 1919, he was named apostolic visitor to Poland in April, nuncio in June, and was made titular archbishop of Lepanto Oct. 28. He was made archbishop of Milan and cardinal June 13, 1921, before being elected to the papacy Feb. 6, 1922. He died Feb. 10, 1939.

Aim: The objective of his pontificate, as stated in the encyclical *Ubi Arcano,* Dec. 23, 1922, was to establish the reign and peace of Christ in society.

Canonizations: He canonized 34 saints, including the Jesuit Martyrs of North America, and conferred the title of Doctor of the Church on Sts. Peter Canisius, John of the Cross, Robert Bellarmine and Albertus Magnus.

Eastern Churches: He called for better understanding of the Eastern Churches in the encyclical *Rerum Orientalium* of Sept. 8, 1928, and developed facilities for the training of Eastern-Rite priests. He inaugurated steps for the codification of Eastern-Church law in 1929. In 1935 he made Syrian Patriarch Tappouni a cardinal.

Encyclicals: His first encyclical, *Ubi Arcano,* in addition to stating the aims of his pontificate, blueprinted Catholic Action and called for its development throughout the Church. In *Quas Primas,* Dec. 11, 1925, he established the feast of Christ the King for universal observance. Subjects of some of his other encyclicals were: Christian education, in *Divini Illius Magistri,* Dec. 31, 1929; Christian marriage, in *Casti Connubii,* Dec. 30, 1930; social conditions and pressure for social change in line with the teaching in *Rerum Novarum,* in *Quadragesimo Anno,* May 15, 1931; atheistic Communism, in *Divini Redemptoris,* Mar. 19, 1937; the priesthood, in *Ad Catholici Sacerdotii,* Dec. 20, 1935.

Missions: Following the lead of Benedict XV, Pius called for the training of native clergy in the pattern of their own respective cultures, and promoted missionary developments in various ways. He ordained six native bishops for China in 1926, one for Japan in 1927, and others for regions of Asia, China and India in 1933. He placed the first 40 mission dioceses under native bishops, saw the number of native priests increase from about 2,600 to more than 7,000 and the number of Catholics in missionary areas more than double from nine million.

In the apostolic constitution *Deus Scientiarum Dominus* of May 24, 1931, he ordered the introduction of missiology into theology courses.

Interfaith Relations: Pius was negative to the ecumenical movement among Protestants but approved the Malines Conversations, 1921 to 1926, between Anglicans and Catholics.

International Relations: Relations with the Mussolini government deteriorated from 1931 on, as indicated in the encyclical *Non Abbiamo Bisogno*, when the regime took steps to curb liberties and activities of the Church; they turned critical in 1938 with the emergence of racist policies. Relations deteriorated also in Germany from 1933 on, resulting finally in condemnation of the Nazis in the encyclical *Mit Brennender Sorge*, March, 1937. Pius sparked a revival of the Church in France by encouraging Catholics to work within the democratic framework of the Republic rather than foment trouble over restoration of a monarchy. Pius was powerless before the civil war which erupted in Spain in July, 1936; sporadic persecution and repression by the Calles regime in Mexico; and systematic persecution of the Church in the Soviet Union. Many of the 10 concordats and two agreements reached with European countries after World War I became casualties of World War II.

Roman Question: Pius negotiated for two and one-half years with the Italian government to settle the Roman Question by means of the Lateran Agreement of 1929. The agreement provided independent status for the State of Vatican City; made Catholicism the official religion of Italy, with pastoral and educational freedom and state recognition of Catholic marriages, religious orders and societies; and provided a financial payment to the Vatican for expropriation of the former States of the Church.

Pius XII

Pius XII (Eugenio Maria Giovanni Pacelli) was born Mar. 2, 1876, in Rome.

Educated at the Gregorian University and the Lateran University, in Rome, he was ordained to the priesthood Apr. 2, 1899.

He entered the Vatican diplomatic service in 1901, worked on the codification of canon law, and was appointed secretary of the Congregation for Ecclesiastical Affairs in 1914. Three years later he was ordained titular archbishop of Sardis and made apostolic nuncio to Bavaria. He was nuncio to Germany from 1920 to 1929, when he was made a cardinal, and took office as papal secretary of state in the following year. His diplomatic negotiations resulted in concordats between the Vatican and Bavaria (1924), Prussia (1929), Baden (1932), Austria and the German Republic (1933). He took part in negotiations which led to settlement of the Roman Question in 1929.

He was elected to the papacy Mar. 2, 1939. He died Oct. 9, 1958, at Castel Gandolfo after the 12th longest pontificate in history.

Canonizations: He canonized 33 saints, including Mother Frances X. Cabrini, the first US citizen-Saint.

Cardinals: He raised 56 prelates to the rank of cardinal in two consistories held in 1946 and 1953. There were 57 cardinals at the time of his death.

Church Organization and Missions: He increased the number of dioceses from 1,696 to 2,048. He established native hierarchies in China (1946), Burma (1955), and parts of Africa, and extended the native structure of the Church in India. He ordained the first black bishop for Africa.

Communism: In addition to opposing and condemning Communism on numerous occasions, he decreed in 1949 the penalty of excommunication for all Catholics holding formal and willing allegiance to the Communist Party and its policies. During his reign the Church was persecuted in some 15 countries which fell under Communist domination.

Doctrine and Liturgy: He proclaimed the dogma of the Assumption of the Blessed Virgin Mary Nov. 1, 1950 (apostolic constitution, *Munificentissimus Deus*).

In various encyclicals and other enactments, he provided background for the *aggiornamento* introduced by his successor, John XXIII: by his formulations of doctrine and practice regarding the Mystical Body of Christ, the liturgy, sacred music and biblical studies; by the revision of the Rites of Holy Week; by initiation of the work which led to the calendar-missal-breviary reform ordered into effect Jan. 1, 1961; by the first of several modifications of the Eucharistic fast; by extending the time of Mass to the evening. He instituted the feasts of Mary, Queen, and of St. Joseph the Worker, and clarified teaching concerning devotion to the Sacred Heart.

His 41 encyclicals and nearly 1,000 public addresses made Pius one of the greatest teaching popes. His concern in all his communications was to deal with specific points at issue and/or to bring Christian principles to bear on contemporary world problems.

Peace Efforts: Before the start of World War II, he tried unsuccessfully to get the contending nations — Germany and Poland,

France and Italy — to settle their differences peaceably. During the war, he offered his services to mediate the widened conflict, spoke out against the horrors of war and the suffering it caused, mobilized relief work for its victims, proposed a five-point program for peace in Christmas messages from 1939 to 1942, and secured a generally open status for the city of Rome. After the war, he endorsed the principles and intent of the United Nations and continued efforts for peace.

United States: Pius appointed more than 200 of the 265 American bishops resident in the US and abroad in 1958, erected 27 dioceses in this country, and raised seven dioceses to archiepiscopal rank.

John XXIII

John XXIII (Angelo Roncalli) was born Nov. 25, 1881, at Sotte il Monte, Italy.

He was educated at the seminary of the Bergamo diocese and the Pontifical Seminary in Rome, where he was ordained to the priesthood Aug. 10, 1904.

He spent the first nine or 10 years of his priesthood as secretary to the bishop of Bergamo and as an instructor in the seminary there. He served as a medic and chaplain in the Italian army during World War I. Afterwards, he resumed duties in his own diocese until he was called to Rome in 1921 for work with the Society for the Propagation of the Faith.

He began diplomatic service in 1925 as titular archbishop of Areopolis and apostolic visitor to Bulgaria. A succession of offices followed: apostolic delegate to Bulgaria (1931-1935); titular archbishop of Mesembria, apostolic delegate to Turkey and Greece, administrator of the Latin vicariate apostolic of Istanbul (1935-1944); apostolic nuncio to France (1944-1953). On these missions, he was engaged in delicate negotiations involving Roman, Eastern-Rite and Orthodox relations; the needs of people suffering from the consequences of World War II; and unsettling suspicions arising from wartime conditions.

He was made a cardinal Jan. 12, 1953, and three days later was appointed patriarch of Venice, the position he held until his election to the papacy Oct. 28, 1958. He died of stomach cancer June 3, 1963.

John was a strong and vigorous pope whose influence far outmeasured both his age and the shortness of his time in the papacy.

Second Vatican Council: John announced Jan. 25, 1959, his intention of convoking the 21st ecumenical council in history to renew life in the Church, to reform its structures and institutions, and to explore ways and means of promoting unity among Christians. Through the council, which completed its work two and one-half years after his death, he ushered in a new era in the history of the Church.

Canon Law: He established a commission Mar. 28, 1963, for revision of the Code of Canon Law. The work of this commission, still underway, will greatly influence the future course of Catholic life and the conduct of ecclesiastical affairs.

Canonizations: He canonized 10 saints. He also beatified Mother Elizabeth Ann Seton, the first native of the US ever so honored. He named St. Lawrence of Brindisi a Doctor of the Church.

Cardinals: He created 52 cardinals in five consistories, raising membership of the College of Cardinals above the traditional number of 70; at one time in 1962, the membership was 87. He made the college more international in representation than it had ever been, appointing the first cardinals from the Philippines, Japan and Africa. He ordered episcopal ordination for all cardinals. He relieved the suburban bishops of Rome of ordinary jurisdiction over their dioceses so they might devote all their time to business of the Roman Curia.

Eastern Rites: He made all Eastern-Rite patriarchs members of the Congregation for the Oriental Churches.

Ecumenism: He assigned to the Second Vatican Council the task of finding ways and means of promoting unity among Christians. He established the Vatican Secretariat for Promoting Christian Unity June 5, 1960. He showed his desire for more cordial relations with the Orthodox by sending personal representatives to visit Patriarch Athenagoras I June 27, 1961; approved a mission of five delegates to the General Assembly of the World Council of Churches which met in New Delhi, India, in November, 1961; removed a number of pejorative references to Jews in the Roman-Rite liturgy for Good Friday.

Encyclicals: Of the eight encyclicals he issued, the two outstanding ones were *Mater et Magistra* ("Christianity and Social Progress"), in which he recapitulated, updated and extended the social doctrine stated earlier by Leo XIII and Pius XI; and *Pacem in Terris* ("Peace on Earth"), the first encyclical ever addressed to all men of good will as well as to Catholics, on the natural-law principles of peace.

Liturgy: In forwarding liturgical reforms already begun by Pius XII, he ordered a calendar-missal-breviary reform into effect Jan. 1, 1961. He authorized the use of vernacular languages in the administration of the sacraments and approved giving Holy Communion to the sick in afternoon hours. He selected the liturgy as the first topic of major discussion by the Second Vatican Council.

Missions: He issued an encyclical on the missionary activity of the Church; established native hierarchies in Indonesia, Vietnam and Korea; and called on North American superiors of religious institutes to have one-tenth of their members assigned to work in Latin America by 1971.

Peace: John spoke and used his moral influence for peace in 1961 when tension developed over Berlin, in 1962 during the Algerian revolt from France, and later the same year in the Cuban missile crisis. His efforts were singled out for honor by the Balzan Peace Foundation. In 1963, he was posthumously awarded the U.S. Presidential Medal of Freedom.

Paul VI

Paul VI (Giovanni Battista Montini) was born Sept. 26, 1897, at Concesio in northern Italy.

Educated at Brescia, he was ordained to the priesthood May 29, 1920. He pursued additional studies at the Pontifical Academy for Noble Ecclesiastics and the Pontifical Gregorian University. In 1924 he began 30 years of service in the Secretariat of State; as undersecretary from 1937 until 1954, he was closely associated with Pius XII and was heavily engaged in organizing informational and relief services during and after World War II.

He was ordained archbishop of Milan Dec. 12, 1954, and was inducted into the College of Cardinals Dec. 15, 1958. He was elected to the papacy June 21, 1963, two days after the conclave began. He died of a heart attack Aug. 6, 1978.

Second Vatican Council: He reconvened the Second Vatican Council after the death of John XXIII, presided over its second, third and fourth sessions, formally promulgated the 16 documents it produced, and devoted the whole of his pontificate to the task of putting them into effect throughout the Church. The main thrust of his pontificate — in a milieu of cultural and other changes in the Church and the world — was toward institutionalization and control of the authentic trends articulated and set in motion by the council.

Canonizations: He canonized more saints, 84, than any other pope. They included groups of 22 Ugandan martyrs and 40 martyrs of England and Wales, as well as two Americans — Elizabeth Ann Bayley Seton and John Nepomucene Neumann.

Cardinals: He created more cardinals, 137, than any other pope and gave the Sacred College a more international complexion than it ever had before. He limited participation in papal elections to 120 cardinals under the age of 80.

Collegiality: He established the Synod of Bishops in 1965 and called it into session five times. He stimulated the formation and operation of regional conferences of bishops, and of consultative bodies on other levels.

Creed and Holy Year: On June 30, 1968, he issued a Creed of the People of God in conjunction with the celebration of a Year of Faith. He proclaimed and led the observance of a Holy Year from Christmas Eve of 1974 to Christmas Eve of 1975.

Diplomacy: He met with many world leaders, including Soviet President Nikolai Podgorny in 1967, Marshal Tito of Yugoslavia in 1971 and President Nicolas Ceausescu of Rumania in 1973. He worked constantly to reduce tension between the Church and the intransigent regimes of Eastern European countries by means of a detente type of policy called Ostpolitik. He agreed to significant revisions of the Vatican's concordat with Spain and initiated efforts to revise the concordat with Italy. More then 40 countries established diplomatic relations with the Vatican during his pontificate.

Encyclicals: He issued seven encyclicals, three of which are the best known. In *Populorum Progressio* ("Development of Peoples") he appealed to wealthy countries to take "concrete action" to promote human development and to remedy imbalances between richer and poorer nations; this encyclical, coupled with other documents and related actions, launched the Church into a new depth of involvement as a public advocate for human rights and for humanizing social, political and economic policies. In *Sacerdotalis Caelibatus* ("Priestly Celibacy") he reaffirmed the strict observance of priestly celibacy throughout the Western Church. In *Humanae Vitae* ("Of Human Life") he condemned abortion, sterilization and artificial birth control, in line with traditional teaching and in "defense of life, the gift of God, the glory of the family, the strength of the people."

Interfaith Relations: He initiated formal consultation and informal dialogue on international and national levels between Catholics and non-Catholics — Orthodox, Anglicans, Protestants, Jews, Moslems, Buddhists, Hindus, and unbelievers. He and Greek Orthodox Patriarch Athenagoras I of Constantinople nullified in 1965 the mutual excommunications imposed by their respective churches in 1054.

Liturgy: He carried out the most extensive liturgical reform in history, involving a new Order of the Mass effective in 1969, a revised church calendar in 1970, revisions and translations into vernacular languages of all sacramental rites and other liturgical texts.

Ministries: He authorized the restoration of the permanent diaconate in the Roman Rite and the establishment of new ministries of lay persons.

Peace: He instituted the annual observance of a World Day of Peace on New Year's Day as a means of addressing a message of peace to all the world's political leaders and the peoples of all nations. The most dramatic of his many appeals for peace and efforts to ease international tensions was his plea for "No more war!" before the United Nations Oct. 4, 1965.

Pilgrimages: A "Pilgrim Pope," he made pastoral visits to the Holy Land and India in 1964, the United Nations and New York City in 1965, Portugal and Turkey in 1967, Colombia in 1968, Switzerland and Uganda in 1969, and Asia, Pacific islands and Australia in 1970. While in Manila in 1970, he was stabbed by a Bolivian artist who made an attempt on his life.

Roman Curia: He reorganized the central administrative organs of the Church in line with provisions of the apostolic constitution, *Regimini Ecclesiae Universae,* streamlining procedures for more effective service and giving the agencies a more international perspective by drawing officials and consultors from all over the world. He also instituted a number of new commissions and other bodies. Coupled with curial reorganization was a simplification of papal ceremonies.

John Paul I

John Paul I (Albino Luciani) was born Oct. 17, 1912, in Forno di Canale (now Canale d'Agordo) in northern Italy.

Educated at the minor seminary in Feltre and the major seminary of the Diocese of Belluno, he was ordained to the priesthood July 7, 1935. He pursued further studies at the Pontifical Gregorian University in Rome and was awarded a doctorate in theology. From 1937 to 1947 he was vice rector of the Belluno seminary, where he taught dogmatic and moral theology, canon law and sacred art. He was appointed vicar general of his diocese in 1947 and served as director of catechetics.

Ordained bishop of Vittorio Veneto Dec. 27, 1958, he attended all sessions of the second Vatican Council, participated in three assemblies of the Synod of Bishops (1971, 1974 and 1977), and was vice president of the Italian Bishops' Conference from 1972 to 1975.

He was appointed archbishop and patriarch of Venice Dec. 15, 1969, and was inducted into the College of Cardinals Mar. 5, 1973.

He was elected to the papacy Aug. 26, 1978, on the fourth ballot cast by the 111 cardinals participating in the largest and one of the shortest conclaves in history. The quickness of his election was matched by the brevity of his pontificate of 33 days, during which he delivered 19 addresses. He died of a heart attack Sept. 28, 1978.

CANONIZATIONS BY LEO XIII AND HIS SUCCESSORS

Canonization is an infallible declaration by the pope that a person who suffered martyrdom and/or practiced Christian virtue to a heroic degree is in glory with God in heaven and is worthy of public honor by the universal Church and of imitation by the faithful.

Leo XIII
(1878-1903)

1881: Clare of Montefalco, virgin (d. 1308); John Baptist de Rossi, priest (1698-1764); Lawrence of Brindisi, doctor (d. 1619).

1883: Benedict J. Labre (1748-1783).

1888: Seven Holy Founders of the Servite Order; Peter Claver, priest (1581-1654); John Berchmans (1599-1621); Alphonsus Rodriguez, lay brother (1531-1617).

1897: Anthony M. Zaccaria, founder of Barnabites (1502-1539); Peter Fourier, cofounder of Augustinian Canonesses of Our Lady (1565-1640).

1900: John Baptist de La Salle, founder of Christian Brothers (1651-1719); Rita of Cascia (1381-1457).

St. Pius X
(1903-1914)

1904: Alexander Sauli, bishop (1534-1593); Gerard Majella, lay brother (1725-1755).

1909: Joseph Oriol, priest (1650-1702); Clement M. Hofbauer, priest (1751-1820).

Benedict XV
(1914-1922)

1920: Gabriel of the Sorrowful Mother

(1838-1862); Margaret Mary Alacoque, virgin (1647-1690); Joan of Arc, virgin (1412-1431).

Pius XI
(1922-1939)

1925: Therese of Lisieux, virgin (1873-1897); Peter Canisius, doctor (1521-1597); Mary Magdalen Postel, foundress of Sisterhood of Christian Schools (1756-1846); Mary Magdalen Sophie Barat, foundress of Society of the Sacred Heart (1779-1865); John Eudes, founder of Eudist Fathers (1601-1680); John Baptist Vianney (Curé of Ars), priest (1786-1859).

1930: Lucy Filippini, virgin (1672-1732); Catherine Thomas, virgin (1533-1574); Jesuit North American Martyrs (see Index); Robert Bellarmine, bishop-doctor (1542-1621); Theophilus of Corte, priest (1676-1740).

1931: Albert the Great, bishop-doctor (1206-1280) (equivalent canonization).

1933: Andrew Fournet, priest (1752-1834); Bernadette Soubirous, virgin (1844-1879).

1934: Joan Antida Thouret, foundress of Sisters of Charity of St. Joan Antida (1765-1826); Mary Michaeli, foundress of Institute of Handmaids of the Blessed Sacrament (1809-1865); Louise de Marillac, foundress of Sisters of Charity (1591-1660); Joseph Benedict Cottolengo, priest (1786-1842); Pompilius M. Pirotti, priest (1710-1756); Teresa Margaret Redi, virgin (1747-1770); John Bosco, founder of Salesians (1815-1888); Conrad of Parzham, lay brother (1818-1894).

1935: John Fisher, bishop-martyr (1469-1535); Thomas More, martyr (1478-1535).

1938: Andrew Bobola, martyr (1592-1657); John Leonardi, founder of Clerics Regular of the Mother of God (c. 1550-1609); Salvatore of Horta, lay brother (1520-1567).

Pius XII
(1939-1958)

1940: Gemma Galgani, virgin (1878-1903); Mary Euphrasia Pelletier, foundress of Good Shepherd Sisters (1796-1868).

1943: Margaret of Hungary, virgin (d. 1270) (equivalent canonization).

1946: Frances Xavier Cabrini, foundress of Missionary Sisters of the Sacred Heart (1850-1917).

1947: Nicholas of Flue, hermit (1417-1487); John of Britto, martyr (1647-1693); Bernard Realini, priest (1530-1616); Joseph Cafasso, priest (1811-1860); Michael Garicoits, founder of Auxiliary Priests of the Sacred Heart (1797-1863); Jeanne Elizabeth des Ages, cofoundress of Daughters of the Cross (1773-1838); Louis Marie Grignon de Montfort, founder of Montfort Fathers (1673-1716); Catherine Laboure, virgin (1806-1876).

1949: Jeanne de Lestonnac, foundress of Religious of Notre Dame of Bordeaux (1556-1640); Maria Josepha Rossello, foundress of Daughters of Our Lady of Pity (1811-1880).

1950: Emily de Rodat, foundress of Congregation of the Holy Family of Villefranche (1787-1852); Anthony Mary Claret, bishop, founder of Claretians (1807-1870); Bartolomea Capitanio (1807-1833) and Vincenza Gerosa (1784-1847), foundresses of Sisters of Charity of Lovere; Jeanne de Valois, foundress of Annonciades of Bourges (1461-1504); Vincenzo M. Strambi, bishop (1745-1824); Maria Goretti, virgin-martyr (1890-1902); Mariana Paredes of Jesus, virgin (1618-1645).

1951: Maria Domenica Mazzarello, cofoundress of Daughters of Our Lady Help of Christians (1837-1881); Emilie de Vialar, foundress of Sisters of St. Joseph "of the Apparition" (1797-1856); Anthony M. Gianelli, bishop (1789-1846); Ignatius of Laconi, lay brother (1701-1781); Francis Xavier Bianchi, priest (1743-1815).

1954: Pius X, pope (1835-1914); Dominic Savio (1842-1857); Maria Crocifissa di Rosa, foundress of Handmaids of Charity of Brescia (1813-1855); Peter Chanel, priest-martyr (1803-1841); Gaspar del Bufalo, founder of Missioners of the Most Precious Blood (1786-1837); Joseph M. Pignatelli, priest (1737-1811).

1958: Herman Joseph, O. Praem., priest (1150-1241) (equivalent canonization).

John XXIII
(1958-1963)

1959: Joaquina de Vedruna de Mas, found-

ress of Carmelite Sisters of Charity (1783-1854); Charles of Sezze, lay brother (1613-1670).

1960: Gregory Barbarigo, bishop (1625-1697) (equivalent canonization); John de Ribera, bishop (1532-1611).

1961: Bertilla Boscardin, virgin (1888-1922).

1962: Martin de Porres, lay brother (1579-1639); Peter Julian Eymard, founder of Blessed Sacrament Fathers (1811-1868); Anthony Pucci, priest (1819-1892); Francis Mary of Camporosso, lay brother (1804-1866).

1963: Vincent Pallotti, founder of Pallottine Fathers (1795-1850).

Paul VI
(1963-1978)

1964: Charles Lwanga and Twenty-One Companions, Martyrs of Uganda.

1967: Benilde, lay brother (1805-1862).

1969: Julia Billiart, foundress of Sisters of Notre Dame de Namur (1751-1816).

1970: Maria Della Dolorato Torres Acosta, foundress of Servants Sisters of Mary (1826-1887); Leonard Murialdo, priest, founder of Congregation of St. Joseph (1828-1900); Therese Couderc, foundress of Congregation of Our Lady of the Cenacle (1805-1885); John of Avila, preacher and spiritual director (1499-1569); Sts. Nicholas Tavelic, Deodatus of Aquitaine, Peter of Narbonne and Stephen of Cuneo, martyrs (d. 1391); Forty English and Welsh Martyrs (d. 16th cent.).

1974: Teresa of Jesus Jornet Ibars, foundress of Little Sisters of Abandoned Aged (1843-1897).

1975: Vicenta Maria Lopez y Vicuna, foundress of Institute of Daughters of Mary Immaculate (1847-1890); Elizabeth Bayley Seton, foundress of Sisters of Charity in the U.S. (1774-1821); John Masias, Dominican brother-missionary (1585-1645): Oliver Plunket, archbishop-martyr (1629-1681); Justin de Jacobis, missionary bishop (1800-1860); John Baptist of the Conception, priest, reformer of the Order of the Most Holy Trinity (1561-1613).

1976: Beatrice da Silva, foundress of Congregation of the Immaculate Conception of the BVM (1424 or 1426-1490); John Ogilvie, Scottish Jesuit martyr (1579-1615).

1977: Rafaela Maria Porras y Ayllon, foundress of Handmaids of the Sacred Heart (1850-1925); John Nepomucene Neumann, bishop (1811-1860); Sharbel Makhlouf, Maronite rite monk (1828-1898).

John Paul II
(1978-   )

1982: Crispin of Viterbo, Capuchin brother (1668-1750); Maximilian Kolbe, Conventual Franciscan priest (1894-1941); Marguerite Bourgeoys, foundress of Congregation of Notre Dame (1620-1700); Jeanne Delanoue, foundress of Sisters of St. Anne of Providence of Saumur, France (1666-1736).

English and Welsh Martyrs

Forty Martyrs of England and Wales, victims of persecution from 1535 to 1671, were canonized by Pope Paul Oct. 25, 1970.

The martyrs were prosecuted and executed as traitors for refusal to comply with laws enacted by Henry VIII and Elizabeth I regarding supremacy (the sovereign was proclaimed the highest authority of the Church in England, acknowledgment of papal primacy was forbidden), succession and the prohibition of native-born to study for the priesthood abroad and return to England for practice of the ministry.

John Houghton, prior of the London Charterhouse, was the first of his group to die (1535) for opposing Henry's Acts of Supremacy and Succession. Cuthbert Mayne (d.

1577) was the protomartyr of the English seminary at Douay. Margaret Clitherow (d. 1586) and Swithun Wells (d. 1591) were executed for sheltering priests. Richard Gwyn (d. 1584), poet, was the protomartyr of Wales.

Others in the group were:

John Almond, Edmund Arrowsmith, Ambrose Barlow, John Boste, Alexander Briant, Edmund Campion, Philip Evans, Thomas Garnet, Edmund Gennings;

Philip Howard, John Jones, John Kemble, Luke Kirby, Robert Lawrence, David Lewis, Ann Line, John Lloyd;

Henry Morse, Nicholas Owen, John Paine, Polydore Plasden, John Plessington, Richard Reynolds, John Rigby, John Roberts;

Alban Roe, Ralph Sherwin, Robert Southwell, John Southworth, John Stone, John Wall, Henry Walpole, Margaret Ward, Augustine Webster and Eustace White.

PAPAL ENCYCLICALS — BENEDICT XIV (1740) TO JOHN PAUL II

(Source: *The Papal Encyclicals* (5 vols.), Claudia Carlen, I.H.M.; a Consortium Book, © McGrath Publishing Co., Wilmington, N.C. Used with permission.)

An encyclical letter is a pastoral letter addressed by a pope to the whole Church. In general, it concerns matters of doctrine, morals or discipline. Its formal title consists of the first few words of the official text. A few encyclicals, notably *Pacem in Terris* by John XXIII and *Ecclesiam Suam* by Paul VI, have been addressed to "all men of good will" as well as to bishops and the faithful in communion with the Church.

An encyclical epistle, which is like an encyclical letter in many respects, is addressed to part of the Church, that is, to the bishops and faithful of a particular country or area. Its contents may concern other than doctrinal, moral or disciplinary matters of universal significance; for example, the commemoration of historical events, conditions in a certain country.

The authority of encyclicals was stated by Pius XII in the encyclical *Humani Generis* Aug. 12, 1950.

"Nor must it be thought that what is contained in encyclical letters does not of itself demand assent, on the pretext that the popes do not exercise in them the supreme power of their teaching authority. Rather, such teachings belong to the ordinary magisterium, of which it is true to say: 'He who hears you, hears me' (Lk. 10:16); for the most part, too, what is expounded and inculcated in encyclical letters already appertains to Catholic doctrine for other reasons. But if the supreme pontiffs in their official documents purposely pass judgment on a matter debated until then, it is obvious to all that the matter, according to the mind and will of the same pontiffs, cannot be considered any longer a question open

for discussion among theologians."

The following list contains the titles and indicates the subject matter of encyclical letters and epistles. The latter are generally distinguishable by the limited scope of their titles or contents.

Benedict XIV
(1740-1758)

1740: *Ubi Primum* (On the duties of bishops), Dec. 3.

1741: *Quanta Cura* (Forbidding traffic in alms), June 30.

1743: *Nimian Licentiam* (To the bishops of Poland: on validity of marriages), May 18.

1745: *Vix Pervenit* (To the bishops of Italy: on usury and other dishonest profit), Nov. 1.

1748: *Magnae Nobis* (To the bishops of Poland: on marriage impediments and dispensations), June 29.

1749: *Peregrinantes* (To all the faithful: proclaiming a Holy Year for 1750), May 5.

Apostolica Constitutio (On preparation for the Holy Year), June 26.

1751: *A Quo Primum* (To the bishops of Poland: on Jews and Christians living in the same place), June 14.

1754: *Cum Religiosi* (To the bishops of the States of the Church: on catechesis), June 26.

Quod Provinciale (To the bishops of Albania: on Christians using Mohammedan names), Aug. 1.

1755: *Allatae Sunt* (To missionaries of the Orient: on the observance of Oriental rites), July 26.

1756: *Ex Quo Primum* (To bishops of the Greek rite: on the Euchologion), Mar. 1.

Ex Omnibus (To the bishops of France: on the apostolic constitution, *Unigenitus),* Oct. 16.

Clement XIII
(1758-1769)

1758: *A Quo Die* (Unity among Christians), Sept. 13.

1759: *Cum Primum* (On observing canonical sanctions), Sept. 17.

Appetente Sacro (On the spiritual advantages of fasting), Dec. 20.

1761: *In Dominico Agro* (On instruction in the faith), June 14.

1766: *Christinae Reipublicae* (To bishops of Austria: on the dangers of anti-Christian writings), Nov. 25.

1768: *Summa Quae* (To the bishops of Poland: on the Church in Poland), Jan. 6.

Clement XIV
(1769-1774)

1769: *Decet Quam Maxime* (To the bishops of Sardinia: on abuses in taxes and benefices), Sept. 21.

Inscrutabili Divinae Sapientiae (To all Christians: proclaiming a universal jubilee), Dec. 12.

Cum Summi (Proclaiming a universal jubilee), Dec. 12.

1774: *Salutis Nostrae* (To all Christians: proclaiming a universal jubilee), Apr. 30.

Pius VI
(1775-1799)

1775: *Inscrutabile* (On the problems of the pontificate), Dec. 25.

1791: *Charitas* (To the bishops of France: on the civil oath in France), Apr. 13.

Pius VII
(1800-1823)

1800: *Diu Satis* (To the bishops of France: on a return to Gospel principles), May 15.

Leo XII
(1823-1829)

1824: *Ubi Primum* (To all bishops: on Leo XII's assuming the pontificate), May 5.

Quod Hoc Ineunte (Proclaiming a universal jubilee), May 24.

1825: *Charitate Christi* (Extending jubilee to the entire church), Dec. 25.

Pius VIII
(1829-1830)

1829: *Traditi Humilitati* (On Pius VIII's program for the pontificate), May 24.

Gregory XVI
(1831-1846)

1832: *Summo Iugiter Studio* (To the bishops of Bavaria: on mixed marriages), May 27.

Cum Primum (To the bishops of Poland: on civil disobedience), June 9.

Mirari Vos (On liberalism and religious indifferentism), Aug. 15.

1833: *Quo Graviora* (To the bishops of the Rhineland: on the "pragmatic Constitution"), Oct. 4.

1834: *Singulari Nos* (On the errors of Lammenais), June 25.

1835: *Commissum Divinitus* (To clergy of Switzerland: on Church and State), May 17.

1840: *Probe Nostis* (On the Propagation of the Faith), Sept. 18.

1841: *Quas Vestro* (To the bishops of Hungary: on mixed marriages), Apr. 30.

1844: *Inter Praecipuas* (On biblical societies), May 8.

Pius IX
1846-1878

1846: *Qui Pluribus* (On faith and religion), Nov. 9.

1847: *Praedecessores Nostros* (On aid for Ireland), Mar. 25.

Ubi Primum (To religious superiors: on discipline for religious), June 17.

1849: *Ubi Primum* (On the Immaculate Conception), Feb. 2.

Nostis et Nobiscum (To the bishops of Italy: on the Church in the Pontifical States), Dec. 8.

1851: *Exultavit Cor Nostrum* (On the effects of jubilee), Nov. 21.

1852: *Nemo Certe Ignorat* (To the bishops of Ireland: on the discipline for clergy), Mar. 25.

Probe Noscitis Venerabiles (To the bishops of Spain: on the discipline for clergy), May 17.

1853: *Inter Multiplices* (To the bishops of France: pleading for unity of spirit), Mar. 21.

1854: *Neminem Vestrum* (To clergy and faithful of Constantinople: on the persecution of Armenians), Feb. 2.

Optime Noscitis (To the bishops of Ireland: on the proposed Catholic university for Ireland), Mar. 20.

Apostolicae Nostrae Caritatis (Urging prayers for peace), Aug. 1.

1855: *Optime Noscitis* (To the bishops of Austria: on episcopal meetings), Nov. 5.

1856: *Singulari Quidem* (To the bishops of Austria: on the Church in Austria), Mar. 17.

1858: *Cum Nuper* (To the bishops of Sicily: on care for clerics), Jan. 20.

Amantissimi Redemptoris (On priests and the care of souls), May 3.

1859: *Cum Sancta Mater Ecclesia* (Pleading for public prayer), Apr. 27.

Qui Nuper (On Pontifical States), June 18.

1860: *Nullis Certe Verbis* (On the need for civil sovereignty), Jan. 19.

1862: *Amantissimus* (To bishops of the Oriental rite: on the care of the churches), Apr. 8.

1863: *Quanto Conficiamur Moerore* (To the bishops of Italy: on promotion of false doctrines), Aug. 10.

Incredibili (To the bishops of Bogota: on persecution in New Granada), Sept. 17.

1864: *Maximae Quidem* (To the bishops of Bavaria: on the Church in Bavaria), Aug. 18.

Quanta Cura (Condemning current errors), Dec. 8.

1865: *Meridionali Americae* (To the bishops of South America: on the seminary for native clergy), Sept. 30.

1867: *Levate* (On the afflictions of the Church), Oct. 27.

1870: *Respicientes* (Protesting the taking of the Pontifical States), Nov. 1.

1871: *Ubi Nos* (To all bishops: on Pontifical States), May 15.

Beneficia Dei (On the twenty-fifth anniversary of his pontificate), June 4.

Saepe Venerabiles Fratres (On thanksgiving for twenty-five years of pontificate), Aug. 5.

1872: *Quae in Patriarchatu* (To bishops and people of Chaldea: on the Church in Chaldea), Nov. 16.

1873: *Quartus Supra* (To bishops and people of the Armenian rite: on the Church in Armenia), Jan. 6.

Etsi Multa (On the Church in Italy, Germany and Switzerland), Nov. 21.

1874: *Vix Dum a Nobis* (To the bishops of Austria: on the Church in Austria), Mar. 7.

Omnem Sollicitudinem (To the bishopos of the Ruthenian rite: on the Greek-Ruthenian rite), May 13.

Gravibus Ecclesiae (To all bishops and faithful: proclaiming a jubilee for 1875), Dec. 24.

1875: *Quod Nunquam* (To the bishops of Prussia: on the Church in Prussia), Feb. 5.

Graves ac Diuturnae (To the bishops of Switzerland: on the Church in Switzerland), Mar. 23.

Leo XIII
(1878-1903)

1878: *Inscrutabili Dei Consilio* (On the evils of society), Apr. 21.

Quod Apostolici Muneris (On socialism), Dec. 28.

1879: *Aeterni Patris* (On the restoration of Christian philosophy), Aug. 4.

1880: *Arcanum* (On Christian marriage), Feb. 10.

Grande Munus (On Sts. Cyril and Methodius), Sept. 30.

Sancta Dei Civitas (On mission societies), Dec. 3.

1881: *Diuturnum* (On the origin of civil power), June 29.

Licet Multa (To the bishops of Belgium: on Catholics in Belgium), Aug. 3.

1882: *Etsi Nos* (To the bishops of Italy: on conditions in Italy), Feb. 15.

Auspicato Concessum (On St. Francis of Assisi), Sept. 17.

Cum Multa (To the bishops of Spain: on conditions in Spain), Dec. 8.

1883: *Supremi Apostolatus Officio* (On devotion to the Rosary), Sept. 1.

1884: *Nobilissima Gallorum Gens* (To the bishops of France: on the religious question), Feb. 8.

Humanum Genus (On Freemasonry), Apr. 20.

Superiore Anno (On the recitation of the Rosary), Aug. 30.

1885: *Immortale Dei* (On the Christian constitution of states), Nov. 1.

Spectata Fides (To the bishops of England: on Christian education), Nov. 27.

Quod Auctoritate (Proclamation of extraordinary Jubilee), Dec. 22.

1886: *Iampridem* (To the bishops of Prussia: on Catholicism in Germany), Jan. 6.

Quod Multum (To the bishops of Hungary: on the liberty of the Church), Aug. 22.

Pergrata (To the bishops of Portugal: on the Church in Portugal), Sept. 14.

1887: *Vi e Ben Noto* (To the bishops of Italy: on the Rosary and public life), Sept. 20.

Officio Sanctissimo (To the bishops of Bavaria: on the Church in Bavaria), Dec. 22.

1888: *Quod Anniversarius* (On his sacerdotal jubilee), Apr. 1.

In Plurimis (To the bishops of Brazil: on the abolition of slavery), May 5.

Libertas (On the nature of human liberty), June 20.

Saepe Nos (To the bishops of Ireland: on boycotting in Ireland), June 24.

Paterna Caritas (To the Patriarch of Cilicia and the archbishops and bishops of the Armenian people: on reunion with Rome), July 25.

Quam Aerumnosa (To the bishops of America: on Italian immigrants), Dec. 10.

Etsi Cunctas (To the bishops of Ireland: on the Church in Ireland), Dec. 21.

Exeunte Iam Anno (On the right ordering of Christian life), Dec. 25.

1889: *Magni Nobis* (To the bishops of the United States: on the Catholic University of America), Mar. 7.

Quamquam Pluries (On devotion to St. Joseph), Aug. 15.

1890: *Sapientiae Christianae* (On Christians as citizens), Jan. 10.

Dall 'Alto Dell' Apostolico Seggio (To the bishops and people of Italy: on Freemasonry in Italy), Oct. 15.

Catholicae Ecclesiae (On slavery in the missions), Nov. 20.

1891: *In Ipso* (To the bishops of Austria: on episcopal reunions in Austria), Mar. 3.

Rerum Novarum (On capital and labor), May 15.

Pastoralis (To the bishops of Portugal: on

religious union), June 25.

Pastoralis Officii (To the bishops of Germany and Austria: on the morality of dueling), Sept. 12.

Octobri Mense (On the Rosary), Sept. 22.

1892: *Au Milieu des Sollicitudes* (To the bishops, clergy and faithful of France: on the Church and State in France), Feb. 16.

Quarto Abeunte Esaeculo (To the bishops of Spain, Italy, and the two Americas: on the Columbus quadricentennial), July 16.

Magnae Dei Matris (On the Rosary), Sept. 8.

Inimica Vis (To the bishops of Italy: on Freemasonry), Dec. 8.

Custodi di Quella Fede (To the Italian people: on Freemasonry), Dec. 8.

1893: *Ad Extremas* (On seminaries for native clergy), June 24.

Constanti Hungarorum (To the bishops of Hungary: on the Church in Hungary), Sept. 2.

Laetitiae Sanctae (Commending devotion to the Rosary), Sept. 8.

Non Mediocri (To the bishops of Spain: on the Spanish College in Rome), Oct. 25.

Providentissimus Deus (On the study of Holy Scripture), Nov. 18.

1894: *Caritatis* (To the bishops of Poland: on the Church in Poland), Mar. 19.

Inter Graves (To the bishops of Peru: on the Church in Peru), May 1.

Litteras a Vobis (To the bishops of Brazil: on the clergy in Brazil), July 2.

Iucunda Semper Expectatione (On the Rosary), Sept. 8.

Christi Nomen (On the propagation of the Faith and churches), Dec. 24.

1895: *Longinqua* (To the bishops of the United States: on Catholicism in the United States), Jan. 6.

Permoti Nos (To the bishops of Belgium: on social conditions in Belgium), July 10.

Adiutricem (On the Rosary), Sept. 5.

1896: *Insignes* (To the bishops of Hungary: on the Hungarian millennium), May 1.

Satis Cognitum (On the unity of the Church), June 29.

Fidentem Piumque Animum (On the Rosary), Sept. 20.

1897: *Divinum Illud Munus* (On the Holy Spirit), May 9.

Militantis Ecclesiae (To the bishops of Austria, Germany, and Switzerland: on St. Peter Canisius), Aug. 1.

Augustissimae Virginis Mariae (On the Confraternity of the Holy Rosary), Sept. 12.

Affari Vos (To the bishops of Canada: on the Manitoba school question), Dec. 8.

1898: *Caritatis Studium* (To the bishops of Scotland: on the Church in Scotland), July 25.

Spesse Volte (To the bishops, priests, and people of Italy: on the suppression of Catholic institutions), Aug. 5.

Quam Religiosa (To the bishops of Peru: on civil marriage law), Aug. 16.

Diuturni Temporis (On the Rosary), Sept. 5.

Quum Diuturnum (To the bishops of Latin America: on Latin American bishops' plenary council), Dec. 25.

1899: *Annum Sacrum* (On consecration to the Sacred Heart), May 25.

Depuis le Jour (To the archbishops, bishops, and clergy of France: on the education of the clergy), Sept. 8.

Paternae (To the bishops of Brazil: on the education of the clergy), Sept. 18.

1900: *Omnibus Compertum* (To the Patriarch and bishops of the Greek-Melkite rite: on unity among the Greek Melkites), July 21.

Tametsi Futura Prospicientibus (On Jesus Christ the Redeemer), Nov. 1.

1901: *Graves de Communi Re* (On Christian democracy), Jan. 18.

Gravissimas (To the bishops of Portugal: on religious orders in Portugal), May 16.

Reputantibus (To the bishops of Bohemia and Moravia: on the language question in Bohemia), Aug. 20.

Urbanitatis Veteris (To the bishops of the Latin church in Greece: on the foundation of a seminary in Athens), Nov. 20.

1902: *In Amplissimo* (To the bishops of the United States: on the Church in the United States), Apr. 15.

Quod Votis (To the bishops of Austria: on the proposed Catholic University), Apr. 30.

Mirae Caritatis (On the Holy Eucharist), May 28.

Quae ad Nos (To the bishops of Bohemia and Moravia: on the Church in Bohemia and Moravia), Nov. 22

Fin dal Principio (To the bishops of Italy: on the education of the clergy), Dec. 8.

Dum Multa (To the bishops of Ecuador: on marriage legislation), Dec. 24.

Saint Pius X
(1903-1914)

1903: *E Supremi* (On the restoration of all things in Christ), Oct. 4.

1904: *Ad Diem Illum Laetissimum* (On the Immaculate Conception), Feb. 2.

Iucunda Sane (On Pope Gregory the Great), Mar. 12.

1905: *Acerbo Nimis* (On teaching Christian doctrine), Apr. 15.

Il Fermo Proposito (To the bishops of Italy: on Catholic Action in Italy), June 11.

1906: *Vehementer Nos* (To the bishops, clergy, and people of France: on the French Law of Separation), Feb. 11.

Tribus Circiter (On the Mariavites or Mystic Priests of Poland), Apr. 5.

Pieni l'Animo (To the bishops of Italy: on

the clergy in Italy), July 28.

Gravissimo Officio Munere (To the bishops of France: on French associations of worship), Aug. 10.

1907: *Une Fois Encore* (To the bishops, clergy, and people of France: on the separation of Church and State), Jan. 6.

Pascendi Dominici Gregis (On the doctrines of the Modernists), Sept. 8.

1909: *Communium Rerum* (On St. Anselm of Aosta), Apr. 21.

1910: *Editae Saepe* (On St. Charles Borromeo), May 26.

1911: *Iamdudum* (On the Law of Separation in Portugal), May 24.

1912: *Lacrimabili Statu* (To the bishops of Latin America: on the Indians of South America), June 7.

Singulari Quadam (To the bishops of Germany: on labor organizations), Sept. 24.

Benedict XV
(1914-1922)

1914: *Ad Beatissimi Apostolorum* (Appeal for peace), Nov. 1.

1917: *Humani Generis Redemptionem* (On preaching the Word of God), June 15.

1918: *Quod Iam Diu* (On the future peace conference), Dec. 1.

1919: *In Hac Tanta* (To the bishops of Germany: on St. Boniface), May 14.

Paterno Iam Diu (On children of central Europe), Nov. 24.

1920: *Pacem, Dei Munus Pulcherrimum* (On peace and Christian reconciliation), May 23.

Spiritus Paraclitus (On St. Jerome), Sept. 15.

Principi Apostolorum Petro (On St. Ephrem the Syrian), Oct. 5.

Annus Iam Plenus (On children of central Europe), Dec. 1.

1921: *Sacra Propediem* (On the Third Order of St. Francis), Jan. 6.

In Praeclara Summorum (To professors and students of fine arts in Catholic institutions of learning: on Dante), Apr. 30.

Fausto Appetente Die (On St. Dominic), June 29.

Pius XI
(1922-1939)

1922: *Ubi Arcano Dei Consilio* (On the peace of Christ in the Kingdom of Christ), Dec. 23.

1923: *Rerum Omnium Perturbationem* (On St. Francis de Sales), Jan. 26.

Studiorum Ducem (On St. Thomas Aquinas), June 29.

Ecclesiam Dei (On St. Josaphat), Nov. 12.

1924: *Maximam Gravissimamque* (To the bishops, clergy, and people of France: on French diocesan associations), Jan. 18.

1925: *Quas Primas* (On the feast of Christ the King), Dec. 11.

1926: *Rerum Ecclesiae* (On Catholic missions), Feb. 28.

Rite Expiatis (On St. Francis of Assisi), Apr. 30.

Iniquis Afflictisque (On the persecution of the Church in Mexico), Nov. 18.

1928: *Mortalium Animos* (On religious unity), Jan. 6.

Miserentissimus Redemptor (On reparation to the Sacred Heart), May 8.

Rerum Orientalium (On the promotion of Oriental studies), Sept. 8.

1929: *Mens Nostra* (On the promotion of Spiritual Exercises), Dec. 20.

Quinquagesimo Ante (On his sacerdotal jubilee), Dec. 23.

Rappresentanti in Terra (On Christian education), Dec. 31.

1930: *Ad Salutem* (On St. Augustine), Apr. 20.

Casti Connubii (On Christian marriage), Dec. 31.

1931: *Quadragesimo Anno* (Commemorating the fortieth anniversary of Leo XIII's *Rerum novarum:* on reconstruction of the social order), May 15.

Non Abbiamo Bisogno (On Catholic Action in Italy), June 29.

Nova Impendet (On the economic crisis), Oct. 2.

Lux Veritatis (On the Council of Ephesus), Dec. 25.

1932: *Caritate Christi Compulsi* (On the Sacred Heart), May 3.

Acerba Animi (To the bishops of Mexico: on persecution of the Church in Mexico), Sept. 29.

1933: *Dilectissima Nobis* (To the bishops, clergy, and people of Spain: on oppression of the Church in Spain), June 3.

1935: *Ad Catholici Sacerdotii* (On the Catholic priesthood), Dec. 20.

1936: *Vigilanti Cura* (To the bishops of the United States: on motion pictures), June 29.

1937: *Mit Brennender Sorge* (To the bishops of Germany: on the Church and the German Reich), Mar. 14.

Divini Redemptoris (On atheistic communism), Mar. 19.

Nos Es Muy Conocida (To the bishops of Mexico: on the religious situation in Mexico), Mar. 28.

Ingravescentibus Malis (On the Rosary) Sept. 29.

Pius XII
(1939-1958)

1939: *Summi Pontificatus* (On the unity of human society), Oct. 20.

Sertum Laetitiae (To the bishops of the United States: on the 150th anniversary of the establishment of the hierarchy in the United States), Nov. 1.

1940: *Saeculo Exeunte Octavo* (To the bishops

of Portugal and its colonies: on the eighth centenary of the independence of Portugal), June 13.

1943: *Mystici Corporis Christi* (On the Mystical Body of Christ), June 29.

Divino Afflante Spiritu (On promoting biblical studies, commemorating the fiftieth anniversary of *Providentissimus Deus*), Sept. 30.

1944: *Orientalis Ecclesiae Decus* (On St. Cyril, Patriarch of Alexandria), Apr. 9.

1945: *Communium Interpretes Dolorum* (To the bishops of the world: appealing for prayers for peace during May), Apr. 15.

Orientales Omnes Ecclesias (On the 350th anniversary of the reunion of the Ruthenian Church with the Apostolic See), Dec. 23.

1946: *Quemadmodum* (Pleading for the care of the world's destitute children), Jan. 6.

Deiparae Virginis Mariae (To all bishops: on the possibility of defining the Assumption of the Blessed Virgin Mary as a dogma of faith), May 1.

1947: *Fulgens Radiatur* (On St. Benedict), Mar. 21.

Mediator Dei (On the sacred liturgy), Nov. 20.

Optatissima Pax (Prescribing public prayers for social and world peace), Dec. 18.

1948: *Auspicia Quaedam* (On public prayers for world peace and solution of the problem of Palestine), May 1.

In Multiplicibus Curis (On prayers for peace in Palestine), Oct. 24.

1949: *Redemptoris Nostri Cruciatus* (On the holy places in Palestine), Apr. 15.

1950: *Anni Sacri* (On the program for combatting atheistic propaganda throughout the world), Mar. 12.

Summi Maeroris (On public prayers for peace), July 19.

Humani Generis (Concerning some false opinions threatening to undermine the foundations of Catholic doctrine), Aug. 12.

Mirabile Illud (On the crusade of prayers for peace), Dec. 6.

1951: *Evangelii Praecones* (On the promotion of Catholic missions), June 2.

Sempiternus Rex (On the Council of Chalcedon), Sept. 8.

Ingruentium Malorum (On reciting the Rosary), Sept. 15.

1952: *Orientales Ecclesias* (On the persecuted Eastern Church), Dec. 15.

1953: *Doctor Mellifluus* (On St. Bernard of Clairvaux, the last of the fathers), May 24.

Fulgens Corona (Proclaiming a Marian Year to commemorate the centenary of the definition of the dogma of the Immaculate Conception), Sept. 8.

1954: *Sacra Virginitas* (On consecrated virginity), Mar. 25.

Ecclesiae Fastos (To the bishops of Great Britain, Germany, Austria, Belgium, and Holland: on St. Boniface), June 5.

Ad Sinarum Gentem (To the bishops, clergy, and people of China: on the supranationality of the Church), Oct. 7.

Ad Caeli Reginam (Proclaiming the Queenship of Mary), Oct. 11.

1955: *Musicae Sacrae* (On sacred music), Dec. 25.

1956: *Haurietis Aquas* (On devotion to the Sacred Heart), May 15.

Luctuosissimi Eventus (Urging public prayers for peace and freedom for the people of Hungary), Oct. 28.

Laetamur Admodum (Renewing exhortation for prayers for peace for Poland, Hungary, and especially for the Middle East), Nov. 1.

Datis Nuperrime (Lamenting the sorrowful events in Hungary and condemning the ruthless use of force), Nov. 5.

1957: *Fidei Donum* (On the present condition of the Catholic missions, especially in Africa), Apr. 21.

Invicti Athletae (On St. Andrew Bobola), May 16.

Le Pelerinage de Lourdes (Warning against materialism on the centenary of the apparitions at Lourdes), July 2.

Miranda Prorsus (On the communications field: motion picture, radio, television), Sept. 8.

1958: *Ad Apostolorum Principis* (To the bishops of China; on Communism and the Church in China), June 29.

Meminisse Juvat (On prayers for persecuted Church), July 14.

John XXIII
(1958-1963)

1959: *Ad Petri Cathedram* (On truth, unity, and peace, in a spirit of charity), June 29.

Sacerdotii Nostri Primordia (On St. John Vianney), Aug. 1.

Grata Recordatio (On the Rosary: prayer for the Church, missions, international and social problems), Sept. 26.

Princeps Pastorum (On the missions, native clergy, lay participation), Nov. 28.

1961: *Mater et Magistra* (On Christianity and social progress), May 15.

Aeterna Dei Sapientia (On fifteenth centenary of the death of Pope St. Leo I: the see of Peter as the center of Christian unity), Nov. 11.

1962: *Paenitentiam Agere* (On the need for the practice of interior and exterior penance), July 1.

1963: *Pacem in Terris* (On establishing universal peace in truth, justice, charity, and liberty), Apr. 11.

Paul VI
(1963-1978)

1964: *Ecclesiam Suam* (On the Church), Aug. 6.

1965: *Mense Maio* (On prayers during May for the preservation of peace), Apr. 29.

Mysterium Fidei (On the Holy Eucharist), Sept. 3.

1966: *Christi Matri Rosarii* (On prayers for peace during October), Sept. 15.

1967: *Populorum Progressio* (On the development of peoples), Mar. 26.

Sacerdotalis Caelibatus (On the celibacy of the priest), June 24.

1968: *Humanae Vitae* (On the regulation of birth), July 25.

John Paul II
(1978-   )

1979: *Redemptor Hominis* (On redemption and the dignity of the human race), Mar. 4.

1980: *Dives in Misericordia* (On the mercy of God), Nov. 30.

1981: *Laborem Exercens* (On human work), Sept. 14.

ST. MAXIMILIAN KOLBE

Maximilian Kolbe, a Franciscan priest who volunteered to die in place of another man, was scheduled to be canonized Oct. 10, 1982.

He was born Raymond Kolbe Jan. 8, 1894, in Zdunska-Wola, Poland. He studied at the minor seminary of the Friars Minor Conventual in Lwow before receiving the Franciscan habit and the name Maximilian in 1911. Inspired by a deep and fervent devotion to the Blessed Virgin Mary, he founded the Knights of the Immaculate Movement in 1917 while still a student for the priesthood at the Seraphic College in Rome, for the purpose of mobilizing a spiritual army committed to Mary's life-giving mission in the Church. He was ordained to the priesthood in 1918 in Rome and was assigned to teach seminarians on his return to Poland the following year.

In 1927, near Warsaw, he founded the City of the Immaculate, a community dedicated to spreading the Gospel and serving the Church by means of publications which included a daily newspaper, a monthly magazine and other materials. He established another community of the same kind in Japan during a period of missionary assignment there from 1930 to 1936. Back in Poland, he resumed work at the original City.

Shortly after the Nazi invasion of Poland in September, 1939, he along with other friars was arrested and detained until Dec. 8. He returned to the City on release and turned it into a refugee center during a period of uncertain freedom before his second arrest on Feb. 17, 1941. He was consigned to the Auschwitz concentration camp where he, together with other interned priests, did whatever he could to provide pastoral care to fellow inmates.

Late in July, 1941, officers at the camp ordered the execution of 10 men in reprisal for the escape of one prisoner. Father Maximilian offered to take the place of one of the condemned men, Franciszek Gajowniczek, a Polish army sergeant and father of a family. The offer accepted, he was confined in a starvation bunker where he died Aug. 14 after being injected with a fatal dose of carbolic acid.

Father Maximilian Kolbe was beatified by Pope Paul VI Oct. 17, 1971.

It was expected that 81-year-old Franciszek Gajowniczek would witness the canonization of the priest who saved his life.

Papal Tribute

Pope John Paul paid tribute to Maximilian Kolbe in a homily delivered during Mass Aug. 26, 1982, the climactic day of celebration of the 600th anniversary of the arrival in Poland of the icon of Our Lady of Czestochowa (Jasna Gora). He said:

"I wish to express the conviction that this (canonization to come) is that particular gift which all of us bring to the Lady of Jasna Gora for the 600th anniversary. However, is not this perhaps in the first place her gift to us in the time of the jubilee? Yes, it is above all the Mother of Jasna Gora who gives us this saint, who has grown from Polish soil, who matured in the heroic sacrifice on the terrible pyre on which his nation burned, together with others, during the frightful years 1939-45.

"Yes, it is the Mother of Jasna Gora who gives him to us, Was he not, perhaps, in his days especially, the Knight of the Immaculate? Did he not persevere in a marvelous way until the very end in fidelity to his Lady, giving his life for a brother in the bunker at Oswiecim (Auschwitz)? . . .

"He showed solidarity with another man to the extreme limits, and he declared himself ready to go to death in his place. . . .

"May it speak to us and say that in Poland everyone must stand together . . . to reconstruct the common good through union with everyone and by means of dialogue with society. This good cannot be constructed by means of force and violence but with the eloquence of reason, which means respect for every man . . . Father Maximilian's deed in the concentration camp at Oswiecim invites and exhorts to such a union with everyone — to a union with the whole nation, already too much tried during many periods of its history."

ORGANIZATION AND GOVERNMENT

As a structured society, the Catholic Church is organized and governed along lines corresponding mainly to the jurisdictions of the pope and bishops.

The pope is the supreme head of the Church. He has primacy of jurisdiction as well as honor over the entire Church.

Bishops, in union with and in subordination to the pope, are the successors of the Apostles for care of the Church and for the continuation of Christ's mission in the world. They serve the people of their own dioceses, or local churches, with ordinary authority and jurisdiction. They also share, with the pope and each other, in common concern and effort for the general welfare of the whole Church.

Bishops of exceptional status are Eastern Rite patriarchs who, subject only to the pope, are heads of the faithful belonging to their rites throughout the world.

Subject to the Holy Father and directly responsible to him for the exercise of their ministry of service to people in various jurisdictions or divisions of the Church throughout the world are: resident archbishops and metropolitans (heads of archdioceses), resident bishops (heads of dioceses), vicars and prefects apostolic (heads of vicariates apostolic and prefectures apostolic), certain abbots and prelates, apostolic administrators. Each of these, within his respective territory and according to the provisions of canon law, has ordinary jurisdiction over pastors (who are responsible for the administration of parishes), priests, religious and lay persons.

Also subject to the Holy Father are titular archbishops and bishops (who have delegated jurisdiction), religious orders and congregations of pontifical right, pontifical institutes and faculties, papal nuncios and apostolic delegates.

Assisting the pope and acting in his name in the central government and administration of the Church are cardinals and other officials of the Roman Curia.

THE HIERARCHY

The ministerial hierarchy is the orderly arrangement of the ranks and orders of the clergy to provide for the spiritual care of the faithful, the government of the Church, and the accomplishment of the Church's total mission in the world. Persons belong to this hierarchy by virtue of ordination and canonical mission.

The term hierarchy is also used to designate an entire body or group of bishops; for example, the hierarchy of the Church, the hierarchy of the United States.

Hierarchy of Order: Consists of the pope, bishops, priests and deacons, by divine law. Their purpose, for which they are ordained to holy orders, is to carry out the sacramental and pastoral ministry of the Church.

Hierarchy of Jurisdiction: Consists of the pope and bishops by divine law, and other church officials by ecclesiastical institution and mandate, who have authority to govern and direct the faithful for spiritual ends.

Prelates: Clerics with the authority of public office in the Church — i.e., the authority of jurisdiction in the external forum. They are: the pope, patriarchs, residential archbishops and bishops, certain abbots and prelates, vicars and prefects apostolic, vicars general, certain superiors in clerical exempt religious communities. Titular archbishops and bishops without ordinary jurisdiction are not prelates in the strict sense of the term; neither are pastors, who have very limited jurisdiction in the external forum.

The Pope

His Holiness the Pope is the Bishop of Rome, the Vicar of Jesus Christ, the successor of St. Peter, Prince of the Apostles, the Supreme Pontiff who has the primacy of jurisdiction and not merely of honor over the universal Church, the Patriarch of the West, the Primate of Italy, the Archbishop and Metropolitan of the Roman Province, the Sovereign of the State of Vatican City, Servant of the Servants of God.

Cardinals
(See Index)

Patriarchs

Patriarch, a term which had its origin in the Eastern Church, is the title of a bishop who, second only to the pope, has the highest rank in the hierarchy of jurisdiction. He is the incumbent of one of the sees listed below. Subject only to the pope, an Eastern-Rite patriarch is the head of the faithful belonging to his rite throughout the world. The patriarchal sees are so called because of their special status and dignity in the history of the Church.

The Council of Nicaea (325) recognized three patriarchs — the bishops of Alexandria and Antioch in the East, and of Rome in the West. The First Council of Constantinople (381) added the bishop of Constantinople to the list of patriarchs and gave him rank second only to that of the pope, the bishop of Rome and patriarch of the West; this action was seconded by the Council of Chalcedon (451) and was given full recognition by the Fourth Lateran Council (1215). The Council of Chalcedon also acknowledged patriarchal rights of the bishop of Jerusalem.

Eastern Rite patriarchs are as follows: one of Alexandria, for the Copts; three of Antioch, one each for the Syrians, Maronites and Greek Melkites (the latter also has the personal title of Greek Melkite patriarch of Alexandria and of Jerusalem). The patriarch of Babylonia, for the Chaldeans, and the patriarch of Sis, or Cilicia, for the Armenians, should be called, more properly, *Katholikos* — that is, a prelate delegated for a universality of causes. These patriarchs are elected by bishops of their rites: they receive approval and the pallium, symbolic of their office, from the pope.

Latin Rite patriarchates were established for Antioch, Jerusalem, Alexandria and Constantinople during the Crusades; afterwards, they became patriarchates in name only. Jerusalem, however, was reconstituted as a patriarchate by Pius IX, in virtue of the bull *Nulla Celebrior* of July 23, 1847. In 1964, the Latin titular patriarchates of Constantinople, Alexandria and Antioch, long a bone of contention in relations with Eastern Rites, were abolished.

As of Aug. 1, 1982, the patriarchs in the Church were:

The Pope, Bishop of Rome, Patriarch of the West; Cardinal Stephanos I Sidarouss, C.M., of Alexandria, for the Copts; Ignace Antoine II Hayek, of Antioch, for the Syrians; Maximos V Hakim, of Antioch, for the Greek Melkites (he also has the titles of Alexandria and Jerusalem for the Greek Melkites); Antoine Khoraiche, of Antioch, for the Maronites; Giacomo Beltritti, of Jerusalem, for the Latin Rite; Paul II Cheikho, of Babylon, for the Chaldeans; Jean Pierre XVIII Kasparian, of Cilicia, for the Armenians.

The titular patriarchs (in name only) of the Latin Rite were: Cardinal Antonio Ribeiro, of Lisbon; Cardinal Marco Cé of Venice and Archbishop Raul Nicolau Goncalves of the East Indies (Archbishop of Goa and Daman, India). The patriarchate of the West Indies has been vacant since 1963.

Archbishops, Metropolitans

Archbishop: A bishop with the title of an archdiocese.

Metropolitan Archbishop: Head of the principal see, an archdiocese, in an ecclesiastical province consisting of several dioceses. He has the full powers of bishop in his own archdiocese and limited supervisory jurisdiction and influence over the other (suffragan) dioceses in the province.

Titular Archbishop: Has the title of an archdiocese which formerly existed in fact but now exists in title only. He does not have ordinary jurisdiction over an archdiocese.

Archbishop ad personam: A title of personal honor and distinction granted to some bishops. They do not have ordinary jurisdiction over an archdiocese.

Primate: A title given to the ranking prelate of some countries or regions.

Bishops

Residential Bishop: A bishop in charge of a diocese.

Titular Bishops: Have the titles of dioceses which formerly existed in fact but now exist in title only. They have delegated authority of jurisdiction, by grant in line with their assignments, rather than the ordinary jurisdiction of office which belongs to a residential bishop. An auxiliary bishop (titular) is an assistant to a residential bishop. A coadjutor bishop (titular) is an assistant bishop of higher status; some coadjutors have the right of succession to residential sees.

Episcopal Vicar: An assistant, who may or may not be a bishop, appointed by a residential bishop as his deputy for a certain part of a diocese, a determined type of apostolic work, or the faithful of a certain rite.

Eparch, Exarch: Titles of bishops of Eastern-Rite churches.

Nomination of Bishops: Nominees for episcopal ordination are selected in several ways. Final appointment in all cases is subject to decision by the pope.

In the U.S., bishops periodically submit the names of candidates to the archbishop of their province. The names are then considered at a meeting of the bishops of the province, and those receiving a favorable vote are forwarded to the apostolic delegate for transmission to the Holy See. Bishops are free to seek the counsel of priests, religious and lay persons with respect to nominees.

Eastern-Rite churches have their own procedures and synodal regulations for nominating and making final selection of candidates for episcopal ordination.

In some countries where concordat or other special arrangements are in effect, civil governments have specified privileges to express approval or disapproval of candidates for the episcopacy.

Ad Limina Visit: Residential bishops and military vicars are obliged to make a periodic *ad limina* visit ("to the threshold" of the Apostles) to the tombs of Sts. Peter and Paul, have audience with the Holy Father, consult with appropriate Vatican officials and present a written report on conditions in their jurisdictions. The most recent regulations concerning the formalities and scheduling of visits by bishops from various countries, generally every five years, were issued by the Congregation for Bishops in a decree dated Nov. 27, 1975.

Other Prelates

Some prelates and abbots, formerly called *nullius*, have jurisdiction over territories (abbacies, prefectures, prelatures) not under the authority of diocesan bishops.

Vicar Apostolic: Usually a titular bishop who has ordinary jurisdiction over a mission territory. A vicar apostolic could also serve as the administrator of a vacant diocese or a diocese whose bishop is impeded from the exercise of his office.

Prefect Apostolic: A prelate with ordinary jurisdiction over a mission territory.

Apostolic Administrator: Usually a bishop appointed to administer an ecclesiastical jurisdiction temporarily. Administrators of lesser rank are also appointed for special and more restricted supervisory duties.

Vicar General: A bishop's deputy for the administration of a diocese. Such a vicar does not have to be a bishop.

Honorary Prelates

Honorary prelates belonging to the Pontifical Household are: Apostolic Prothonotaries, Honorary Prelates of His Holiness, and Chaplains of His Holiness. Their title is Reverend Monsignor.

SYNOD OF BISHOPS

The Synod of Bishops was chartered by Pope Paul VI Sept. 15, 1965, in a document he issued on his own initiative under the title, *Apostolica Sollicitudo.* According to the document:

• The purposes of the Synod are: "to encourage close union and valued assistance between the Sovereign Pontiff and the bishops of the entire world; to insure that direct and real information is provided on questions and situations touching upon the internal action of the Church and its necessary activity in the world of today; to facilitate agreement on essential points of doctrine and on methods of procedure in the life of the Church."

• The Synod is a central ecclesiastical institution, permanent by nature.

• The Synod is directly and immediately subject to the Pope, who has authority to assign its agenda, to call it into session, and to give its members deliberative as well as advisory authority.

• In addition to a limited number of ex officio members and a few heads of male religious institutes, the majority of the members are elective by and representative of national or regional episcopal conferences. The Pope reserved the right to appoint the general secretary, special secretaries and no more than 15 per cent of the total membership. The numbers of members of ordinary assemblies of the Synod have varied between 197 and 210.

The Pope is president of the Synod.

The secretary general is Archbishop Jozef Tomko of Czechoslovakia.

First Meeting, 1967

The Synod met for the first time from Sept. 29 to Oct. 29, 1967, in Vatican City. Its objectives, as stated by Pope Paul, were "the preservation and strengthening of the Catholic faith, its integrity, its force, its development, its doctrinal and historical coherence."

One result of synodal deliberations was a recommendation to the Pope to establish an international commission of theologians to assist the Congregation for the Doctrine of the Faith and to broaden approaches to theological research. The commission was subsequently set up by Pope Paul in 1969.

In other actions, the Synod called for the formulation of a Code of Canon Law more pastoral than the one in force since 1918 and more in touch with the mentality, aspirations and needs of people in contemporary circumstances; favored the view that episcopal conferences should have major control over seminaries in their respective areas; suggested some changes in pastoral procedures with respect to mixed marriages, which were authorized in 1970; gave general approval to the New Order of the Mass which was promulgated and put into effect in 1969.

Extraordinary Session

The second Synod of Bishops, meeting in extraordinary session Oct. 11 to 28, 1969, opened the door to wider participation by the bishops with the Pope and each other in the government of the Church.

The business assigned to the meeting by Pope Paul was to seek and examine ways and means of putting into practice the principle of collegiality which figured largely in declarations of the Second Vatican Council on the Church and the pastoral office of bishops.

Accordingly, proceedings were oriented to three main points: (1) the nature and implications of collegiality; (2) the relationships of bishops and their conferences to the Pope; (3) the relationships of bishops and their conferences to each other. The end results were three proposals approved by the bishops and the Pope, and five times that number approved and placed under advisement by the Pope. All proposals pointed in the direction of more cooperative action by all the bishops with the Pope in the conduct of church affairs.

The three proposals which were approved and moved for action provided for regular meetings of the Synod at two-year intervals (later extended to three years), staff organization and operations of the general secretariat in the interim between meetings, and openness of the synodal agenda to suggestions by bishops.

Between the second and third meetings of the Synod, an advisory council of 15 members (12 elected, three appointed by the Pope) was formed to provide the secretariat with adequate staff for carrying on liaison with episcopal conferences and for drawing up the agenda of synodal meetings. The council, at its first meeting May 12 to 15, 1970, followed the lead of the second assembly by opening the agenda of the 1971 meeting to the suggestions of bishops from all over the world.

Synod '71

The ministerial priesthood and justice in the world were the principal topics of discussion at the third and longest meeting, the Second General Assembly of the Synod, Sept. 30 to Nov. 6, 1971.

Advisory reports on these subjects, compiled from views expressed by the bishops before and during the synodal sessions, were presented to Pope Paul at the end of the meeting. He authorized publication of the reports and said, in a letter made public Dec. 9, that he accepted conclusions reached by the bishops which "conform to the current norms" of church teaching.

The Priesthood

In its report on the priesthood, the Synod described difficulties experienced by priests, stated traditional doctrinal principles on the priesthood, and drew from these principles a set of guidelines for priestly life and ministry in the mission of Christ and the Church, and in the communion of the Church.

The report emphasized the primary and permanent dedication of priests in the Church to the ministry of word, sacrament and pastoral service as a full-time occupation.

The synodal Fathers — with 168 votes in favor without reservations, 21 votes in favor with reservations, and 10 votes against — supported the existing discipline of clerical celibacy. They favored leaving to the discretion of the Pope decisions regarding the ordination of already married men in special circumstances. They did not consider the question of permitting already ordained priests to marry. The majority voted against permitting priests who had left the ministry to resume priestly duties, although they said such priests could serve the Church in other ways and should be treated in a just and fraternal manner.

Justice in the World

In connection with "The Mission of the People of God To Further Justice in the World," a synodal report reviewed a wide range of existing injustices; cited the social-justice imperatives of the Gospel; called for the practice of justice throughout the Church and for greater efforts in education and ecumenical collaboration for justice; and outlined an eight-point program for international action.

Behind the Synod's recommendations were the convictions:

• "The Church . . . has a proper and specific responsibility which is identified with her mission of giving witness before the world of the need for love and justice contained in the Gospel message, a witness to be carried out in church institutions themselves and in the lives of Christians."

• "Action on behalf of justice and participation in the transformation of the world fully appear to us as a constitutive dimension of the preaching of the Gospel; or, in other words, of the Church's mission for the redemption of the human race and its liberation from every oppressive situation."

• "The present situation of the world, seen in the light of faith, calls us back to the very essence of the Christian message, creating in us a deep awareness of its true meaning and of its urgent demands. The mission of preaching the Gospel dictates at the present time that we should dedicate ourselves to the liberation of man even in his present existence in this world. For, unless the Christian message of love and justice shows its effectiveness through action in the cause of justice in the world, it will only with difficulty gain credibility with the men of our times."

Fourth Assembly

"Evangelization of the Modern World" was the theme of the fourth assembly of the Synod, Sept. 27 to Oct. 26, 1974. Its major product was a general statement on the subject, covering the need for it and its relationship to efforts for total human liberation from personal and social evil.

The statement reconfirmed "that the mandate to evangelize all men constitutes the essential mission of the Church," that "the duty to proclaim the Gospel belongs to the whole people of God," and that "this work demands incessant interior conversion on the part of individual Christians and continual renewal of our communities and institutions."

The bishops noted that evangelization is impeded by atheism, secularism, and the repression of religious liberty in a number of countries.

Communication of the Gospel was called "a dynamic process" which "takes place through word, work and life," and which needs "translation," expression and indigenization in terms of the religious and cultural patterns of people in different places.

The statement cited the need and intention for ecumenical collaboration with other Christians for the purpose of rendering "to the world a much broader common witness to Christ, while at the same time working to obtain full union in the Lord."

Liberation

Regarding the relationship between evangelization and human liberation, the bishops said:

"Faithful to her evangelizing mission, the Church, as a truly poor, praying and fraternal community, can do much to bring about the integral salvation or the full liberation of men. She can draw from the Gospel the most profound reasons and ever new incentives to promote generous dedication to the service of all men — the poor especially, the weak and the oppressed — and to eliminate the social consequences of sin which are translated into unjust social and political structures.

"The Church does not remain within merely political, social and economic limits (elements which she must certainly take into account) but leads towards freedom under all its forms — liberation from sin, from individual or collective selfishness — and to full communion with God and with men who are like brothers. In this way the Church, in her evangelical way, promotes the true and complete liberation of all men, groups and peoples."

Synod '77

"Catechetics in Our Time, with Special Reference to Children and Young People," was the theme of the fifth assembly, Sept. 30 to Oct. 29, 1977. Its major products were a "Message to the People of God," the first synodal statement issued since inception of the body, and two documents presented to Pope Paul — a set of 34 propositions and some 900 suggestions regarding the substance of the propositions and the message on catechetics.

The propositions covered six general subjects in considerable detail: the importance of catechetical renewal, the theme of authentic catechesis, the mode of authentic catechizing, the necessity of catechesis for all Christians, the community as the context and milieu of catechesis, attitudes and other factors affecting catechesis.

The "Message to the People of God" consisted of three parts, dealing with: the world, young people and catechesis; the manifestation of salvation in Christ; catechesis as the task of all people in the Church.

Sixth Assembly, 1980

"The Role of the Christian Family in the Modern World" was the theme of the sixth assembly, Sept. 26 to Oct. 25, 1980. Its major products were "A Message to Christian Families in the Modern World" and a proposal for a "Charter of Family Rights."

In the message to families, the bishops said: "Today the family is sometimes obliged to choose a way of life that goes contrary to modern culture in such matters as sexuality, individual autonomy and material wealth. In the face of sin and failure, it gives witness to an authentically Christian spirit."

The message criticized unjust structures which increase poverty in the world, the "spiritual emptiness" of materialistic cultures, and disregard for the rights of families by some governments and international agencies.

It reaffirmed the indissolubility of marriage and the contents of the encyclical *Humanae Vitae* (see separate entry), and urged those who find it hard to live up to "the difficult but loving demands" of Christ not to be discouraged.

The document called for the family to be a "domestic church," a "community of faith living in hope and love," which promotes the Christian formation of its members and others.

The bishops said the Christian family must not live closed in on itself but must be open to the community around it and, moved by a sense of justice and concern for others, must "foster social justice and relief of the poor and oppressed."

Family Rights

In addition to its message to families, the assembly drafted a proposal for a "Charter of Family Rights" consisting of two fundamental principles and 14 specific points. The proposal was forwarded to the Pope with the request that he develop and publish a similar charter.

The basic principles of the proposed charter were:

1. "The family is the basic cell of society, a subject of rights and duties, with priority over the state and any other community."

2. "The state by its laws and institutions must recognize and protect the family with respect to its liberty and assist it, not replacing it."

The draft stated that the family has rights:

• to exist and progress as a family; every person, especially of the poor, has the right to form a family and sustain it with appropriate assistance;

• to exercise its role in transmitting life right from its conception and to educate children;

• to intimacy of both conjugal and family life;

• to stability of the bond and institution of marriage;

• to believe and profess one's own faith and propagate it;

• to educate one's children according to one's own traditions and religious and cultural values, with the necessary instruments, means and institutions;

• to obtain physical, social, political and economic security, especially for the poor and weak;

• to habitation fit for leading a family life properly;

• to expression and representation before public authorities, economic, social and cultural, and those subject to them, either by oneself or through associates;

• to create associations with other families and institutions so that one may fulfill one's role fittingly and effectively;

• to protection for minors, with the help of adequate institutions and laws, against harmful drugs, pornography and alcoholism;

• to fruitful leisure which may foster family values;

• to dignified life and dignified death;

• to emigrate as a family to seek a better life.

Pope John Paul acknowledged the work of the 1980 assembly and gave it appropriate expression in *Familiaris Consortio,* his apostolic exhortation on the family, dated Nov. 22, 1981 (see separate entry). In the introduction to the exhortation he wrote:

"At the close of their assembly, the Synod Fathers presented me with a long list of proposals in which they had gathered the fruits of their reflections, which had matured over intense days of work, and they asked me unanimously to be a spokesman before humanity of the Church's lively care for the family and to give suitable indications for renewed pastoral effort in this fundamental sector of the life of man and of the Church.

"As I fulfill that mission with this exhortation, thus actuating in a particular matter the apostolic ministry with which I am entrusted, I wish to thank all the members of the Synod for the very valuable contribution of teaching and experience that they made."

Synod '83

"Reconciliation and Penance in the Mission of the Church" is the theme of the 1983 assembly, to be held probably in the fall. Preparations under way at the time of writing were related to a set of guidelines, made public by the Permanent Secretariat of the Synod early in 1982, designed to elicit comments and suggestions from bishops, theologians and others for use in preparing a working paper for the assembly.

The three main sections of the guideline document concerned social and world situations indicating a need for reconciliation, doctrinal background, and the pastoral mission of the Church in regard to penance and reconciliation. (See separate entry.)

ROMAN CURIA

The Roman Curia consists of the Secretariat of State, the Sacred Council for the Public Affairs of the Church, nine congregations, three tribunals, three secretariats, and a complex of commissions, councils and offices which administer church affairs at the highest level.

Background

The Curia evolved gradually from advisory assemblies or synods of the Roman clergy with whose assistance the popes directed church affairs during the first 11 centuries. Its original office was the Apostolic Chancery, dating from the fourth century. The antecedents of its permanently functioning agencies and offices were special commissions of cardinals and prelates. Its establishment in a form resembling what it is now dates from the second half of the 16th century.

Pope Paul VI gave the following short account of the background of the Curia in the apostolic constitution *Regimini Ecclesiae Universae* ("For the Government of the Universal Church"), dated Aug. 15, 1967.

"The Roman Pontiffs, successors to Blessed Peter, have striven to provide for the government of the Universal Church by making use of experts to advise and assist them.

"In this connection, we should remember both the Presbyterium of the City of Rome and the College of Cardinals of the Holy Roman Church which in the course of centuries evolved from it. Then, little by little, as we know, out of that office (Apostolic Chancery) which was set up in the fourth century to transmit papal documents, many offices developed; to these was added the Auditorium, which was a well-developed tribunal in the 13th century and which was more thoroughly organized by John XXII (1316-1334).

"With an increase in the volume of things to be dealt with, bodies or commissions of cardinals selected to treat of specific questions began to be more efficiently organized in the 16th century, from which eventually arose the congregations of the Roman Curia. It is to the credit of our predecessor Sixtus V that, in the constitution *Immensa Aeterni Dei* of Jan. 22, 1588, he arranged the sacred councils in an orderly manner and wisely described the structure of the Roman Curia.

"With the progress of time, however, it happened that some of them became obsolete, others had to be added, and others had to be restructured. This is the work our predecessor St. Pius X set out to do with the constitution *Sapienti Consilio* of June 29, 1908. Its provisions, a lasting testimony to that wise and ingenious pastor of the Church, were with a few changes incorporated into the Code of Canon Law" (Canons 242-264).

Reorganization

Pope Paul initiated a four-year reorganization study in 1963 which resulted in the constitution *Regimini Ecclesiae Universae.* The document was published Aug. 18, 1967, and went into full effect in March, 1968.

While the study was underway, the Pope

took preliminary steps toward curial reorganization by reorienting and changing the title of the Sacred Congregation of the Holy Office (to the Sacred Congregation for the Doctrine of the Faith) and by appointing a number of non-Italians to key curial positions.

The stated purposes of the reorganization were to increase the efficiency of the Curia and to make it more responsive to the needs and concerns of the Universal Church. The pursuit of these objectives involved various modifications.

Curial Departments

• The Office of the Pope, including the Papal Secretariat or Secretariat of State and the Council for the Public Affairs of the Church.

• Nine congregations, instead of twelve as formerly. The functions of the Sacred Congregation of Ceremonies were transferred to the Prefecture of the Pontifical Household; the duties of the Sacred Congregation for Extraordinary Ecclesiastical Affairs were taken over by the Sacred Council for the Public Affairs of the Church; the Sacred Congregation of the Basilica of St. Peter was reduced in rank. In 1969, the Sacred Congregation of Rites was phased out of existence and its functions were assigned to the Sacred Congregation for the Causes of Saints and the Sacred Congregation for Divine Worship.

In 1975 the Congregation for the Sacraments and Divine Worship was established to replace the Congregation for the Discipline of the Sacraments and the Congregation for Divine Worship.

• Three secretariats, the Council of the Laity and the Pontifical Commission on Justice and Peace.

• Three tribunals.

• Six offices, including the former Apostolic Chancery (abolished in 1973) and Apostolic Chamber, and the newly constituted Prefecture of Economic Affairs, Prefecture of the Pontifical Household, Administration of the Patrimony of the Apostolic See, and Central Statistics Office. Functions of the former Apostolic Datary and the Secretariats of State, of Briefs to Princes, and of Latin Letters were transferred to the Secretariat of State.

Operational Procedures

• The papal secretary or secretary of state has authority to take initiative in coordinating and expediting business through meetings and other cooperative procedures.

• Officials of departments have five-year terms of office, which may be renewed. Terms end automatically on the death of a pope. The five-year terms of consultors are renewable.

• Diocesan bishops as well as full-time curial personnel have membership in curial departments, in accordance with provisions of the decree *Pro Comperto Sane* of Aug. 6, 1967. Seven diocesan bishops hold five-year membership in each congregation, with full rights to participation in the more important plenary assemblies scheduled once a year. They are also entitled to take part in routine meetings whenever they are in Rome. Three general superiors of male religious institutes hold similar membership in the Sacred Congregation for Religious and Secular Institutes.

• Lay persons are eligible to serve as consultors to curial departments.

• Close liaison with episcopal conferences is required. They should be given prior notice of forthcoming curial decrees affecting them in any special way.

• In line with customary procedure, matters in which the competence of two or more departments is involved are handled on a cooperative basis, with mutual consultation and decision.

• Although Latin remains the official language of the Curia, communication in any of the widely known modern languages is acceptable.

• Informational and financial services are centralized in the Central Statistics Office and the Prefecture of Economic Affairs, respectively.

• Heads of curial departments are required to notify the pope before conducting any serious or extraordinary business.

• Authority to act and decide on many matters belongs to departmental officials in virtue of delegation from the pope. Some matters, however, have to be referred to the pope for final decision.

Internationalization

As of Aug. 1, 1982, principal officials of the Roman Curia (cardinals unless indicated otherwise) were from the following countries: Italy (Baggio, Caprio, Casaroli, Oddi, Palazzini, Paupini, Opilio Rossi, Abp. Casoria, Abp. Sabattani); Poland (Rubin, Abp. Deskur, Bp. Majdanski); Germany (Ratzinger, Msgr. Ewers, Bp. Cordes); United States (Baum, Abp. Marcinkus); Argentina (Pironio); Australia (Knox); Belgium (Abp. Jadot); Benin (Gantin); Brazil (Agnelo Rossi); France (Abp. Poupard); India (Abp. Lourdusamy); Netherlands (Willebrands); Scotland (Bp. Andrew); Venezuela (Abp. Castillo Lara).

The relationship between family and work was the theme of a papal talk Oct. 25, 1981. The Holy Father urged people in St. Peter's Square to pray that, through the intercession of Mary, "the fundamental link which exists between work and the life of every family may find its proper reflection in the entire social and juridical order, and also in the daily life of . . . each family."

DEPARTMENTS

Secretariat of State: Provides the pope with the closest possible assistance in the care of the Universal Church and in dealings with all departments of the Curia.

The cardinal secretary is the key coordinator of curial operations. He has authority to call meetings of the prefects of all departments for expediting the conduct of business, for consultation and intercommunication. He handles: any and all matters entrusted to him by the pope, and ordinary matters which are not within the competence of other departments; some relations with bishops; relations with representatives of the Holy See, civil governments and their representatives, without prejudice to the competence of the Council for the Public Affairs of the Church.

The cardinal secretary has been likened to a prime minister or head of government because of the significant role he plays in coordinating curial operations at the highest level.

The secretariat has two offices for preparing and writing letters for the pope (functions formerly performed by the Secretariat of Briefs to Princes and the Secretariat of Latin Letters), and a Central Statistics Office.

It also handles work formerly done by the Apostolic Datary (the dating and countersigning of papal documents, and the management of church benefices), and the Apostolic Chancery, abolished in 1973 (care of the pope's leaden seal and the Fisherman's Ring).

It has supervisory duties over the Commission for the Instruments of Social Communication, two Vatican publications, *Acta Apostolicae Sedis* and *Annuario Pontificio,* and the Vatican Personnel Office.

The Prefecture of Vatican City is answerable to the secretary of state.

OFFICIALS: Cardinal Agostino Casaroli, secretary of state, Most Rev. Eduardo Martinez Somalo, undersecretary and secretary of the Cifra.

Council for the Public Affairs of the Church: Handles diplomatic and other relations with civil governments. With the Secretariat of State, it supervises matters concerning nunciatures and apostolic delegations. It also has supervision of the Pontifical Commission for Russia.

OFFICIALS: Cardinal Agostino Casaroli, prefect, secretary of state; Most Rev. Achille Silvestrini, secretary.

BACKGROUND: Originated by Pius VI in 1793 as the Congregation for Extraordinary Affairs from the Kingdom of the Gauls; given wider scope by Pius VII, July 19, 1814; formerly called the Sacred Congregation for Extraordinary Ecclesiastical Affairs.

Kazimierz Szablewski, head of the Polish Government Delegation for Permanent Work Contacts with the Holy See since 1974, paid a farewell visit to Pope John Paul May 10, 1982.

CONGREGATIONS

Sacred Congregation for the Doctrine of the Faith: Has responsibility to safeguard the doctrine of faith and morals.

Accordingly, it examines doctrinal questions; promotes studies thereon; evaluates theological opinions and, when necessary and after prior consultation with concerned bishops, reproves those regarded as opposed to principles of the faith; examines books on doctrinal matters and can reprove such works after giving authors the opportunity to defend themselves.

It examines matters pertaining to the Privilege of Faith (Petrine Privilege) in marriage cases, and safeguards the dignity of the sacrament of penance.

It has working relations with the Pontifical Biblical Commission (see separate entry).

In 1969, Pope Paul set up a Theological Commission (see separate entry) as an adjunct to the congregation, to provide it with the advisory services of additional experts in theology and allied disciplines.

OFFICIALS: Cardinal Joseph Ratzinger, prefect; Most Rev. Jean Jerome Hamer, O.P., secretary.

BACKGROUND: At the beginning of the 13th century, legates of Innocent III were commissioned as the Holy Office of the Inquisition to combat heresy; the same task was entrusted to the Dominican Order by Gregory IX in 1231 and to the Friars Minor by Innocent IV from 1243 to 1254. On July 21, 1542 (apostolic constitution *Licet*), Paul III instituted a permanent congregation of cardinals with supreme and universal competence over matters concerning heretics and those suspected of heresy. Pius IV, St. Pius V and Sixtus V further defined the work of the congregation. St. Pius X changed its name to the Congregation of the Holy Office.

Paul VI, in virtue of the motu proprio *Integrae Servandae* of Dec. 7, 1965, began reorganization of the Curia with this body, to which he gave the new title, Sacred Congregation for the Doctrine of the Faith. Its orientation is not merely negative, in the condemnation of error, but positive, in the promotion of orthodox doctrine. The right of appeal, judicial representation, and the consultation of their proper regional conference of bishops, are assured to persons accused of unorthodox doctrine. The office for the censorship of books and the Roman Index of Prohibited Books were abolished.

Sacred Congregation for the Oriental Churches: Has competence in matters concerning the persons and discipline of Eastern Rite Churches. It has jurisdiction over territories in which the majority of Christians belong to Oriental Rites (i.e., Egypt, the Sinai Peninsula, Eritrea, Northern Ethiopia, Southern Albania, Bulgaria, Cyprus, Greece,

Iran, Iraq, Lebanon, Palestine, Syria, Jordan, Turkey, Afghanistan, the part of Thrace subject to Turkey); also, over minority communities of Orientals no matter where they live.

To assure adequate and equal representation, it has as many offices as there are rites of Oriental Churches in communion with the Holy See.

It is under mandate to consult with the Secretariat for Promoting Christian Unity on questions concerning separated Oriental Churches, and with the Secretariat for Non-Christians, especially in relations with Moslems.

It has a special commission on the liturgy and an Oriental Church Information Service.

OFFICIALS: Cardinal Wladyslaw Rubin, prefect; Most Rev. Mario Brini, secretary.

Members include all Eastern Rite patriarchs and the president of the Secretariat for Promoting Christian Unity. Consultors include the secretary of the same secretariat.

BACKGROUND: Special congregations for the affairs of the Greek and other Oriental Churches were founded long before this body was created by Pius IX Jan. 6, 1862 (apostolic constitution *Romani Pontifices*), and united with the Sacred Congregation for the Propagation of the Faith. The congregation was made autonomous by Benedict XV May 1, 1917 (motu proprio *Dei Providentis*), and given wider authority by Pius XI Mar. 25, 1938 (motu proprio *Sancta Dei Ecclesia*). John XXIII appointed six patriarchs, five of Eastern Rites and one of the Roman Rite, to the congregation and gave them the same rights as cardinals belonging to the body, in March, 1963. Paul VI named representatives of all Eastern-Rite bodies to serve as consultors of the congregation, in November, 1963.

Sacred Congregation for Bishops, formerly called the Sacred Consistorial Congregation: Has functions related in one way or another to bishops and the jurisdictions in which they serve.

Its concerns are: the establishment and changing of dioceses, provinces, military vicariates and other jurisdictions; providing for the naming of bishops and other prelates; studying things concerning the persons, work and pastoral activity of bishops; providing for the care of bishops when they leave office; receiving and studying reports on the conditions of dioceses; general supervision of the holding and recognition of particular councils and conferences of bishops; publishing and circulating pastoral norms and guidelines through conferences of bishops.

It supervises the Pontifical Commission for Latin America and the Pontifical Commission for Migration and Tourism.

OFFICIALS: Cardinal Sebastiano Baggio, prefect; Most Rev. Lucas Moreira Neves, O.P., secretary.

Ex officio members are the prefects of the Council for the Public Affairs of the Church, and of the Congregations for the Doctrine of the Faith, for the Clergy, and for Catholic Education. The substitute secretaries and undersecretaries of these curial departments are ex officio consultors.

BACKGROUND: Established by Sixtus V Jan. 22, 1588 (apostolic constitution *Immensa*); given an extension of powers by St. Pius X June 20, 1908, and Pius XII Aug. 1, 1952 (apostolic constitution *Exsul Familia*).

Sacred Congregation for the Sacraments and Divine Worship: Established in 1975 to replace the Congregation for the Discipline of the Sacraments and the Congregation for Divine Worship.

The congregation consists of two sections — for the sacraments and for divine worship. The former supervises the discipline of the sacraments without prejudice to the competencies of the Sacred Congregation for the Doctrine of the Faith and other curial departments. The latter has general competence over the ritual and pastoral aspects of divine worship in the Roman and other Latin Rites.

OFFICIALS: Most Rev. Giuseppe Casoria, pro-prefect; Most Rev. Luigi Dadaglio, secretary; Most Rev. Virgilio Noe, secretary (Divine Worship section).

BACKGROUND: The congregation was established by Paul VI Aug. 1, 1975 (apostolic constitution, *Constans novis studium,* dated July 11, 1975). Formerly its duties were carried out by the Congregation for the Discipline of the Sacraments (instituted by St. Pius X June 29, 1908) and the Congregation for Divine Worship (established by Paul VI, May 8, 1969, to replace the Congregation of Rites instituted by Sixtus V in 1588).

Sacred Congregation for the Causes of Saints: Handles all matters connected with beatification and canonization procedures, and the preservation of relics. These affairs were formerly under the supervision of the Congregation of Rites.

The congregation carries on its work through three sections or offices.

One section is a juridical office with supervisory responsibility over procedures and examinations conducted to determine the holiness of prospective saints. It includes a medical commission for the study of miracles attributed to the intercession of candidates for sainthood.

A second section, headed by the promoter general of the faith, who is popularly called the "Devil's Advocate," serves the purpose of establishing beyond reasonable doubt the evidence of holiness advanced in support of beatification and canonization causes.

Research and evaluation of documentary evidence figuring in canonization causes are the functions of the historic-hagiographical section.

OFFICIALS: Cardinal Pietro Palazzini,

prefect; Most Rev. Traian Crisan, secretary.

BACKGROUND: The functions and title of this congregation were determined by Paul VI May 8, 1969 (apostolic constitution *Sacra Rituum Congregatio*). Formerly, its duties were carried out by the Congregation of Rites, which was established by Sixtus V in 1588 and affected by legislation of Pius XI in 1930.

Sacred Congregation for the Clergy, formerly called the Sacred Congregation of the Council: Handles matters concerning the persons, work and pastoral ministry of clerics who exercise their apostolate in a diocese. Such clerics are diocesan deacons and priests, and religious who are engaged in ordinary parochial ministry in a diocese.

It carries on its work through three offices.

One office promotes the spiritual growth and formation as well as the professional competence of priests by encouraging the establishment and operation of pastoral institutes and other study opportunities; oversees the general discipline of the clergy, the establishment and conduct of pastoral councils and senates of priests, and resolves controversies among clerics; has a mandate to draw up a set of general principles to direct a better distribution of priests for pastoral service.

A second office, in view of its primary concern for preaching of the word of God, encourages effective apostolic programs and methods, with special emphasis on catechetical and other forms of religious training and formation for the faithful.

A third office has supervisory responsibility over church property and the temporalities of priestly life; among its functions are efforts to provide for the support of the clergy through suitable salary scales, pensions, security and health insurance programs, and other measures.

OFFICIALS: Cardinal Silvio Oddi, prefect; Most Rev. Maximino Romero de Lema, secretary.

BACKGROUND: Established by Pius IV Aug. 2, 1564 (apostolic constitution *Alias Nos*), under the title, Sacred Congregation of the Cardinals Interpreters of the Council of Trent; affected by legislation of Gregory XIII and Sixtus V.

Sacred Congregation for Religious and Secular Institutes, formerly known as the Sacred Congregation of Religious or for the Affairs of Religious: Has dual competence over institutes of religious, together with societies of the common life without vows, and secular institutes.

One section deals with the affairs of all religious institutes and societies of the common life, and their members. It has authority in matters related to the establishment, general direction and suppression of institutes; general discipline in line with their rules and constitutions; the movement toward renewal and adaptation of institutes in contemporary circumstances; the setting up and encouragement of councils and conferences of major religious superiors for intercommunication and other purposes.

A second section has the same competence over the affairs and members of secular institutes as the first has over religious.

OFFICIALS: Cardinal Eduardo Pironio, prefect; Most. Rev. Augustin Mayer, O.S.B., secretary.

BACKGROUND: Founded by Sixtus V May 27, 1586, with the title, Sacred Congregation for Consultations of Regulars (apostolic constitution *Romanus Pontifex*); confirmed by the apostolic constitution *Immensa* Jan. 22, 1588; made part of the Congregation for Consultations of Bishops and other Prelates in 1601; made autonomous by St. Pius X in 1908.

Sacred Congregation for Catholic Education, formerly known as the Sacred Congregation of Seminaries and Universities: Has supervisory competence over institutions and works of Catholic education.

It carries on its work through three offices.

One office handles matters connected with the direction, discipline and temporal administration of seminaries, and with the education of diocesan clergy, religious and members of secular institutes.

A second office oversees Catholic universities, faculties of study and other institutions of higher learning inasmuch as they depend on the authority of the Church; encourages cooperation and mutual assistance among Catholic institutions, and the establishment of Catholic hospices and centers on campuses of non-Catholic institutions.

A third office is concerned in various ways with all Catholic schools below the college-university level, with general questions concerning education and studies, and with the cooperation of conferences of bishops and civil authorities in educational matters.

The congregation supervises Pontifical Works for Priestly Vocations.

OFFICIALS: Cardinal William Wakefield Baum, prefect; Most Rev. Antonio M. Javierre Ortas, S.D.B., secretary.

BACKGROUND: The title and functions of the congregation were defined by Benedict XV Nov. 4, 1915; Pius XI, in 1931 and 1932, and Pius XII, in 1941 and 1949, extended its functions. Its work had previously been carried on by two other congregations erected by Sixtus V in 1588 and Leo XII in 1824.

Sacred Congregation for the Evangelization of Peoples (for the Propagation of the Faith): Directs and coordinates missionary work throughout the world.

Accordingly, it has competence over those matters which concern all the missions established for the spread of Christ's kingdom.

These include: fostering missionary vocations; providing for the training of missionaries in seminaries; assigning missionaries to fields of work; establishing ecclesiastical jurisdictions and proposing candidates to serve them as bishops and in other capacities; encouraging the recruitment and development of indigenous clergy; mobilizing spiritual and financial support for missionary activity.

In general, the varied competence of the congregation extends to most persons and affairs of the Church in areas classified as mission territories.

To promote missionary cooperation, the congregation has a Supreme Council for the Direction of Pontifical Missionary Works. Subject to this council are the general councils of the Missionary Union of the Clergy, the Society for the Propagation of the Faith, the Society of St. Peter the Apostle for Native Clergy, the Society of the Holy Childhood, and the *Fides* news agency.

OFFICIALS: Cardinal Agnelo Rossi, prefect; Most Rev. D. Simon Lourdusamy, secretary.

The heads of the Secretariats for Promoting Christian Unity, for Non-Christians, and for Non-Believers are ex officio members of the congregation.

BACKGROUND: Originated as a commission of cardinals by Gregory XIII and modified by Clement VIII to promote the reconciliation of separated Eastern Christians; erected as a stable congregation by Gregory XV June 22, 1622 (apostolic constitution *Inscrutabili*).

TRIBUNALS

Sacred Apostolic Penitentiary: Has jurisdiction for the internal forum only (sacramental and non-sacramental). It issues decisions on questions of conscience; grants absolutions, dispensations, commutations, sanations and condonations; has charge of non-doctrinal matters pertaining to indulgences.

OFFICIALS: Cardinal Giuseppe Paupini, major penitentiary; Msgr. Luigi de Magistris, regent.

BACKGROUND: Origin dates back to the 12th century; affected by the legislation of many popes; radically reorganized by St. Pius V in 1569; jurisdiction limited to the internal forum by St. Pius X; Benedict XV annexed the Office of Indulgences to it Mar. 25, 1917.

Apostolic Signatura: The principal concerns of this supreme court of the Church are to resolve questions concerning juridical procedure and to supervise the observance of laws and rights at the highest level. It decides the jurisdictional competence of lower courts and has jurisdiction in cases involving personnel and decisions of the Rota. It is the supreme court of the State of Vatican City.

OFFICIALS: Most Rev. Aurelio Sabattani,

pro-prefect; Msgr. Zenon Grocholewski, secretary.

BACKGROUND: A permanent office of the Signatura has existed since the time of Eugene IV in the 15th century; affected by the legislation of many popes; reorganized by St. Pius X in 1908 and made the supreme tribunal of the Church.

Sacred Roman Rota: The ordinary court of appeal for cases appealed to the Holy See. It is best known for its competence and decisions in cases concerning the validity of marriage.

OFFICIAL: Msgr. Heinrich Ewers, dean.

BACKGROUND: Originated in the Apostolic Chancery; affected by the legislation of many popes; reorganized by St. Pius X in 1908 and further revised by Pius XI in 1934.

SECRETARIATS

Secretariat for Promoting Christian Unity: Handles relations with members of other Christian ecclesial communities; deals with the correct interpretation and execution of the principles of ecumenism; initiates or promotes Catholic ecumenical groups and coordinates on national and international levels the efforts of those promoting Christian unity; undertakes dialogue regarding ecumenical questions and activities with churches and ecclesial communities separated from the Apostolic See; sends Catholic observer-representatives to Christian gatherings, and invites to Catholic gatherings observers of other churches; orders into execution conciliar decrees dealing with ecumenical affairs.

The Commission for Catholic-Jewish Relations is attached to the secretariat.

It has two offices, for the West and for the East. Each office is under the immediate direction of a delegate.

The prefects of the Congregation for the Oriental Churches and of the Congregation for the Evangelization of Peoples are ex officio members of the secretariat. Consultors include the secretaries of these two departments.

OFFICIALS: Cardinal Johannes Willebrands, president.

BACKGROUND: Established by John XXIII June 5, 1960, as a preparatory secretariat of the Second Vatican Council; raised to commission status during the first session of the council in the fall of 1962; this status confirmed Jan. 3, 1966.

Secretariat for Non-Christians: Is concerned with persons who are not Christians but profess some kind of religious faith. Its function is to promote studies and dialogue for the purpose of increasing mutual understanding and respect between Christians and non-Christians.

The Commission for Catholic-Moslem Relations is attached to the secretariat.

The prefect of the Congregation for the

Evangelization of Peoples is an ex officio member of the secretariat.

OFFICIALS: Most Rev. Jean Jadot, pro-president; Msgr. Pietro Rossano, secretary.

BACKGROUND: Established by Paul VI May 19, 1964.

Secretariat for Non-Believers: Studies the background and philosophy of atheism, and initiates and carries on dialogue with non-believers.

OFFICIALS: Most Rev. Paul Poupard, pro-president; Rev. Jordan Gallego Salvadores, O.P., secretary.

BACKGROUND: Established by Paul VI Apr. 9, 1965.

COUNCILS, COMMISSIONS

Laity, Pontifical Council for: Instituted on an experimental basis by Paul VI Jan. 6, 1967; given permanent status Dec. 10, 1976 (motu proprio *Apostolatus Peragendi*); its competence covers the apostolate of the laity in the Church and the discipline of the laity as such. Members are mostly lay people from different parts of the world and involved in different apostolates. The council is headed by a cardinal. The Council for the Family is attached to the Council while retaining its own identity. Cardinal Opilio Rossi, president.

Justice and Peace, Pontifical Commission: Instituted by Paul VI Jan. 6, 1967, on an experimental basis; reconstituted and made a permanent body Dec. 10, 1976 (motu proprio *Iustitiam et Pacem*). Holy See's organization for examining and studying (from the point of view of doctrine, pastoral practice and the apostolate) problems connected with justice and peace and awakening the sensitivity of the people of God to their responsibility in these areas. Cardinal Bernardin Gantin, president.

Revision of the Code of Canon Law: Instituted by John XXIII Mar. 28, 1963, to replace a former commission dating from 1917; Most Rev. Rosalio Jose Castillo Lara, S.D.B., pro-president.

Revision of the Code of Oriental Canon Law: Reconstituted by Paul VI in 1972 to replace a former commission dating from July 17, 1935, "to prepare ... the reform of the Code of Oriental Canon Law, both in the sections already published by ... four motu proprios" (1,950 canons concerning marriage; processes; religious, church property and terminology; Eastern Rites and persons), "and in the remaining sections which have been completed but not published" (the balance of a total of 2,666 canons); Cardinal Joseph Parecattil, president.

Interpretation of the Decrees of the Second Vatican Council, Commission:

Social Communication: Instituted on an experimental basis by Pius XII in 1948; reorganized three times in the 1950's; made permanent commission by John XXIII Feb. 22, 1959; name changed to present title Apr. 11, 1964; authorized to implement the *Decree on the Instruments of Social Communication* promulgated by the Second Vatican Council; under supervision of the Secretariat of State and the Council for the Public Affairs of the Church; Most Rev. Andrzej-Maria Deskur, president; Most Rev. Martin J. O'Connor, president emeritus; Most Rev. Agnellus Andrew, O.F.M., vice president.

Latin America, Commission: Instituted by Pius XII Apr. 19, 1958; placed under supervision of the Congregation for Bishops July, 1969; Cardinal Sebastiano Baggio, president.

Migration and Tourism, Commission: Instituted by Paul VI Mar. 19, 1970, for pastoral assistance to migrants, nomads, tourists, sea and air travelers; placed under the general supervision and direction of the Congregation for Bishops; Cardinal Sebastiano Baggio, president.

Cor Unum, Council: Instituted by Paul VI July 15, 1971, to provide informational and coordinating services for Catholic aid and human development organizations and projects on a worldwide scale; Cardinal Bernardin Gantin, president.

Family, Pontifical Council: Instituted by John Paul II May 9, 1981, replacing the Committee for the Family established Jan. 11, 1973, for "promoting the pastoral care of the family ... by putting into effect the teachings and directives of the ecclesiastical magisterium, so that Christian families may carry out the educative, evangelizing and apostolic mission to which they have been called"; has special relations with the Pontifical Council for the Laity. Cardinal James R. Knox, president.

Theological Commission: Instituted by Paul VI Apr. 11, 1969, as an advisory adjunct of no more than 30 theologians to the Congregation for the Doctrine of the Faith; Cardinal Joseph Ratzinger, president. (See separate entry.)

Biblical Commission: Instituted by Leo XIII Oct. 30, 1902; completely restructured by Paul VI June 27, 1971; Cardinal Joseph Ratzinger, president. (See separate entry.)

Abbey of St. Jerome for the Revision and Emendation of the Vulgate: Instituted by Pius XI June 15, 1933, to replace an earlier commission established by St. Pius X; Rev. Vincent Truijen, superior.

Sacred Archeology, Commission: Instituted by Pius IX Jan, 6, 1852; Most Rev. Gennaro Verolino, president.

Historical Sciences, Committee: Instituted by Pius XII Apr. 7, 1954, as a continuation of a commission dating from 1883; Msgr. Michele Maccarrone, president.

Ecclesiastical Archives of Italy, Committee: Instituted by Pius XII Apr. 5, 1955; Msgr. Martino Giusti, president.

Sacred Art in Italy, Commission: Instituted

by Pius XI Sept. 1, 1924; Most Rev. Giovanni Fallani, president.

Sanctuaries of Pompei, Loreto and Bari, Commission: Originated by Leo XIII for Sanctuary of Pompei, Loreto placed under commission in 1965, St. Nicholas of Bari, 1980; under supervision of the Congregation for the Clergy; Cardinal Umberto Mozzoni, president.

Russia, Commission: Instituted by Pius XI Apr. 6, 1930, to handle all ecclesiastical affairs of the country; placed under supervision of the Congregation for Extraordinary Ecclesiastical Affairs (now the Council for the Public Affairs of the Church) in 1934, with jurisdiction limited to clergy and faithful of the Roman Rite; under supervision of the Council for the Public Affairs of the Church; Most Rev. Achille Silvestrini, president.

Catholic-Jewish Relations, Commission: Instituted by Paul VI, Oct. 22, 1974, to promote and foster relations of a religious nature between Jews and Christians; attached to the Secretariat for Christian Unity; Cardinal Johannes Willebrands, president.

Catholic-Moslem Relations, Commission: Instituted by Paul VI, Oct. 22, 1974, to promote, regulate and interpret relations between Catholics and Moslems; attached to the Secretariat for Non-Christians; Most Rev. Jean Jadot, pro-president.

State of Vatican City, Commission: Cardinal Agostino Casaroli, president; Most Rev. Paul Marcinkus pro-president.

Protection of the Historical and Artistic Monuments of the Holy See, Commission: Instituted by Pius XI in 1923, reorganized by Paul VI in 1963; Most Rev. Giovanni Fallani, president.

Preservation of the Faith, Erection of New Churches in Rome: Instituted by Pius XI Aug. 5, 1930, to replace a commission dating from 1902; Cardinal Ugo Poletti, president.

Works of Religion, Commission: Instituted by Pius XII June 27, 1942, to bank and administer funds for works of religion; replaced an earlier administration established by Leo XIII in 1887; Most Rev. Paul C. Marcinkus, president.

Study of Organizational and Economic Problems of the Holy See: Council established in 1981 by Pope John Paul II; composed of 15 cardinals — residential archbishops — from countries outside of Italy.

Culture, Pontifical Council: Established in 1982 by Pope John Paul II to facilitate contacts between the saving message of the Gospel and the plurality of cultures. Cardinal Gabriel-Marie Garrone, head of presidential committee; Most Rev. Paul Poupard, president of executive committee.

Arrangements were made in 1982 for the exhibition of Vatican art works in several principal cities of the United States in 1983.

OFFICES

Prefecture of the Economic Affairs of the Holy See: A financial office which coordinates and supervises administration of the temporalities of the Holy See.

OFFICIALS: Cardinal Giuseppe Caprio, president; Msgr. Giovanni Angelo Abbo, secretary.

BACKGROUND: Established by Paul VI Aug. 15, 1967.

Apostolic Chamber: Administers the temporal goods and rights of the Holy See between the death of one pope and the election of another, in accordance with special laws.

OFFICIALS: Cardinal Paolo Bertoli, chamberlain of the Holy Roman Church; Most Rev. Ettore Cunial, vice-chamberlain.

BACKGROUND: Originated in the 11th century; reorganized by Pius XI in 1934.

Administration of the Patrimony of the Apostolic See: Handles the estate of the Apostolic See under the direction of papal delegates acting with ordinary or extraordinary authorization.

OFFICIALS: Cardinal Agostino Casaroli, president; Most Rev. Lorenzo Antonetti, secretary.

BACKGROUND: Some of its functions date back to 1878; established by Paul VI Aug. 15, 1967.

Prefecture of the Pontifical Household: Oversees the papal chapel — which is at the service of the pope in his capacity as spiritual head of the Church — and the pontifical family — which is at the service of the pope as a sovereign. It arranges papal audiences, has charge of preparing non-liturgical elements of papal ceremonies, makes all necessary arrangements for papal visits and trips outside the Vatican, and settles questions of protocol connected with papal audiences and other formalities.

OFFICIALS: Most Rev. Jacques Martin, prefect; Msgr. Dino Monduzzi, regent.

BACKGROUND: Established by Paul VI Aug. 15, 1967, under the title, Prefecture of the Apostolic Palace; it supplanted the Sacred Congregation for Ceremonies founded by Sixtus V Jan. 22, 1588. The office was updated and reorganized under the present title by Paul VI, Mar. 28, 1968.

Central Statistics Office: Compiles. systematizes and analyzes information on the status and condition of the Church and the needs of its pastoral ministry, from parish to top levels.

The office is one of the organs of the Secretariat of State.

BACKGROUND: Established by Paul VI Aug. 15, 1967.

Aid Office: Distributes alms and aid to the aged, sick, handicapped and other persons in need.

OFFICIAL: Most Rev. Antonio M. Travia, director.

BACKGROUND: The office originated as a charitable office in the time of Bl. Gregory X (1271-1276).

Vatican II Archives: Preserves the acts and other documents of the Second Vatican Council.

Personnel: Set up by Paul VI May 9, 1971, to handle personnel relations in the offices and other agencies of the Vatican.

OFFICIAL: Msgr. Michele Buro.

THEOLOGICAL COMMISSION

Establishment of a Theological Commission as an adjunct to the Congregation for the Doctrine of the Faith was announced by Pope Paul VI Apr. 28, 1969. The move had been recommended by the Second Vatican Council and was proposed by the Synod of Bishops in 1967.

The purpose of the commission is to provide the Doctrinal Congregation with the consultative and advisory services of theologians and scriptural and liturgical experts representative of various schools of thought. The international membership is restricted to 30, and the ordinary term of membership is five years.

Membership

The commission is headed by Cardinal Joseph Ratzinger, prefect of the Doctrinal Congregation. Msgr. Philippe Delhaye of Belgium is secretary. Members appointed to five-year terms in 1980 and listed in the 1982 edition of *Annuario Pontificio* were as follows.

Barnabas Ahern, C.P. (U.S.); Juan Alfaro, S.J. (Spain); Catalino Arevalo (Philippines); Hans Urs von Balthasar (Switzerland); Carlo Caffara (Italy); Giuseppe Colombo (Italy); Ives Congar, O.P. (France); Wilhelm Ernst (West Germany); Pierre Eyt (France); Ivan Fucek (Yugoslavia); Ferenc Gal (Hungary); Edouard Hamel, S.J. (Canada); Walter Kasper (West Germany); Hachem Elie Khalife, O.L.M. (Lebanon); Bishop Bonaventure Kloppenburg, O.F.M. (Brazil); Michael Ledwith (Ireland); Karl Lehmann (West Germany); Jorge Medina Estevez (Chile); John Onaiyekan (Nigeria); Carl Peter (U.S.); Candido Pozo, S.J. (Spain); Walter Principe C.S.B. (Canada); Ignacy Rozycki (Poland); Heinz Schurmann (West Germany); Bernard Sesboue, S.J. (France); John Thornhill, S.M. (Australia); Cipriano Vagaggini, O.S.B. (Italy); Christophe von Schonborn, O.P. (Switzerland); Jan Walgrave, O.P. (Belgium).

Meetings

The commission met for the first time Oct. 6 to 8, 1969, for organizational purposes and the assignment of subcommissions to studies on the priesthood, the theology of hope, unity of faith and pluralism in theology, the criteria of moral knowledge, and collegiality.

Week-long general assemblies, for discussion and decision on subjects of individual and group research have been held annually, except in 1978, since 1969.

Twenty-six members attending the second meeting, Oct. 5 to 10, 1970, discussed reports on the priestly ministry and collegiality. Views were exchanged about the question of ordaining married men, but marriage was ruled out for already ordained priests wanting to continue in the ministry. With respect to collegiality, no doubt was raised about the pope's authority to act independently in the Church; the consensus, however, was that he would be prudent to engage in wide consultation before acting.

By early 1971, the commission prepared the basis of a feasible working paper on the priesthood for the Synod of Bishops, which met for the third time in the fall. The ordination of women was one of the subjects covered, but it did not figure significantly in discussion by the commission because the issue was not considered urgent. Agreement was reported on two points: tradition militated against ordination but permitted a form of diaconal ordination with a rite and purpose distinctive and proper to women.

Various Studies

Pluralism in theology — concerning different ways of treating, presenting and expressing in practice the unity of faith — was the main subject under consideration at the fourth general assembly Oct. 5 to 11, 1972. The topic had been under study since the first meeting of the commission in 1969.

The October, 1973, meeting, attended by 21 members, completed work on a statement concerning apostolic succession and ordination to holy orders. The necessary sacramental sign of both, the statement said, is the imposition of hands by successors of the Apostles acting in accord with the intention of the Church.

The results of research on Christian morality were discussed at the 1974 meeting, and several articles on the subject were published in 1975.

The majority of members attending the Sept. 25 to Oct. 1, 1975, meeting approved a number of conclusions concerning the relationship between "the mandate given to the ecclesiastical magisterium (the teaching authority of the Church) to protect divine revelation and the task given to theologians to investigate and explain the doctrine of the faith." These conclusions were published by the U.S. Catholic Conference in April, 1977.

Christian salvation and human progress, centering on the nature of and relationship between evangelization and human liberation, was the subject of the meeting held Oct. 4 to 9, 1976. The subject was connected with earlier consideration of the matter by the Synod of Bishops, and also with the contents and tenor of the *Pastoral Constitution on the*

Church in the Modern World issued by the Second Vatican Council.

The meeting of Dec. 1 to 6, 1977, focused attention on pastoral aspects of Christian marriage and agreed on a summary of conclusions which: (1) reaffirmed the indissolubility of marriage and the stance of the Church against divorce; (2) declared that the Church should not witness the marriage of Catholics who have rejected the faith and the sacramental nature of marriage.

Various aspects of Christology were under consideration from 1979 to 1981.

The 1982 meeting was devoted entirely to the preparation of material related to the Sacrament of Reconciliation, the theme of the 1983 assembly of the Synod of Bishops. The theology of reconciliation was the main concern of the commission, whose findings were made available to the Permanent Secretariat of the Synod.

BIBLICAL COMMISSION

The Pontifical Biblical Commission, which has been instrumental in directing the course of Catholic biblical scholarship, was established by Leo XIII Oct. 30, 1902, with the apostolic letter *Vigilantiae Studiique,* at a time when biblical studies were open to great promise as well as to the serious threat of Modernism.

The commission was ordered to promote biblical studies; to safeguard the correct interpretation of Scripture, in the pattern of the rule of faith and against the background of sound scholarship; to state positions which had to be held by Catholics on biblical questions; to indicate questions requiring further study and/or those which were open to the judgment of competent scholars. The commission was also authorized — by St. Pius X in 1904, Pius XI in 1924 and 1931, and Pius XII in 1942 — to set up standards for biblical studies and to grant degrees in Sacred Scripture.

The commission issued 23 decrees or decisions between 1905 and 1953; letters on the scientific study of the Bible (1941) and the Pentateuch (1948); instructions on teaching Scripture in seminaries (1950), biblical associations (1955), and the historical truth of the Gospels (1964).

Pope St. Pius X stated the authority of decisions of the commission in the letter *Illibatae,* which he issued June 29, 1910, on his own initiative:

"All are bound in conscience to submit to the decisions of the Pontifical Biblical Commission pertaining to doctrine, whether already issued or to be issued in the future, in the same way as to the decrees of the Sacred Congregations (of the Roman Curia) approved by the Pontiff; nor can they avoid the stigma both of disobedience and temerity or be free from grave sin who by any spoken or written words impugn these decisions."

Decisions of the commission regarding points of doctrine are not infallible of themselves. They require religious assent, however, so long as there is no positive evidence that they are wrong. They do not close the door to continuing investigation and study.

The commission was reorganized June 27, 1971, in line with directives issued by Paul VI on his own initiative under the title *Sedula Cura.*

Fifteen new norms changed its structure from a virtually independent office of cardinals aided by lifetime consultors into a group consisting ordinarily of 20 biblical scholars with five-year terms (renewable) linked with the Congregation for the Doctrine of the Faith. Functionally, however, it remains the same.

The commission:

• receives questions and studies topics referred to it by a variety of sources, from the pope to Catholic universities and biblical associations;

• is required to meet in plenary session at least once a year and to submit conclusions reached in such meetings to the pope and the Congregation for the Doctrine of the Faith;

• is under directive to promote relationships with non-Catholic as well as Catholic institutes of biblical studies;

• is to be consulted before any new norms on biblical matters are issued;

• retains its authorization to confer academic degrees in biblical studies.

Cardinal Joseph Ratzinger, prefect of the Congregation for the Doctrine of the Faith, is president of the commission. The other members, as reported in the 1982 edition of *Annuario Pontificio,* are as follows.

Jose Alonso-Diaz, S.J.; Jean-Dominique Barthelemy, O.P.; Pierre Benoit, O.P.; Henri Cazelles, P.S.S.; Guy Couturier, C.S.C.; Msgr. Alfons Deissler; Ignace de la Potterie, S.J.; Jacques Dupont, O.S.B.; Joachim Gnilka; John Greehy; Pierre Grelot; Augustine Jankowski, O.S.B.; Archbishop. Carlo M. Martini, S.J.; Laurent Nare; Msgr. Jerome D. Quinn (U.S.); Matthew Vellanickal; Benjamin Wambacq, O.Praem.

Recent Meetings

Since its plenary assembly of April, 1980, the commission has focused attention on the hermeneutic problem in Christology, i.e., the interpretation of what Scripture says about the nature and mission of Jesus.

At its 1979 meeting, the commission initiated a study of acculturation in the Old and New Testaments. The purpose of the study, as stated by Pope John Paul, was "to establish the distinction" between what is culturally conditioned (language, manner of expression, historical circumstances) "and what must always retain its value" (truth relating to salvation) in the words and events used to communicate divine revelation in the Bible.

COLLEGE OF CARDINALS

Cardinals are chosen by the pope to serve as his principal assistants and advisers in the central administration of church affairs. Collectively, they form the Sacred College of Cardinals.

The college evolved gradually from synods of Roman clergy with whose assistance popes directed church affairs in the first 11 centuries. The first cardinals, in about the sixth century, were priests of the leading churches of Rome who were assigned liturgical, advisory and administrative duties with the Holy See, and the regional deacons of Rome.

For all cardinals except Eastern patriarchs, membership in the college involves aggregation to the clergy of Rome. This aggregation is signified by the assignment to each cardinal, except the patriarchs, of a special or titular church in Rome.

History of the College

The Sacred College of Cardinals was constituted in its present form and categories of membership in the 12th century. Before that time the pope had a body of advisers selected from among the bishops of dioceses neighboring Rome, priests and deacons of Rome. The college was given definite form in 1150, and in 1179 the selection of cardinals was reserved exclusively to the pope. Sixtus V fixed the number at 70, in 1586. John XXIII set aside this rule when he increased membership at the 1959 and subsequent consistories. The number of cardinals reached an all-time high of 145 under Paul VI in 1973. The number of cardinals entitled to participate in papal elections was limited to 120.

In 1567 the title of cardinal was reserved to members of the college; previously it had been used by priests attached to parish churches of Rome and by the leading clergy of other notable churches. The Code of Canon Law promulgated in 1918 decreed that all cardinals must be priests. Previously there had been lay cardinals (e.g., Cardinal Giacomo Antonelli, d. 1876, Secretary of State to Pius IX). John XXIII provided in the motu proprio *Cum Gravissima* Apr. 15, 1962, that all cardinals would henceforth be bishops.

Pope Paul VI placed age limits on the functions of cardinals in the apostolic letter *Ingravescentem Aetatem,* dated Nov. 21, 1970, and effective as of Jan. 1, 1971. At 80, they cease to be members of curial departments and offices, and become ineligible to take part in papal elections. They retain membership in the College of Cardinals, however, with relevant rights and privileges.

Three Categories

The three categories of members of the college are cardinal bishops, cardinal priests and cardinal deacons.

Cardinal bishops include the six titular bishops of the suburban sees of Rome and Eastern patriarchs.

First in rank are the titular bishops of the suburban sees, neighboring Rome: Ostia, Palestrina, Porto and Santa Rufina, Albano, Velletri, Frascati, Sabina and Poggio Mirteto. The dean of the college holds the title of the See of Ostia as well as his other suburban see. These cardinal bishops are engaged in full-time service in the central administration of church affairs in departments of the Roman Curia.

Four Eastern patriarchs, three of whom have since died, were made cardinal bishops by Paul VI in virtue of the motu proprio *Ad Purpuratorum Patrum* Feb. 11, 1965. Full recognition was given to their position as the heads of ancient liturgies and of sees of apostolic origin. Because of their patriarchal dignity and titles, which antedated the dignity and titles of cardinals, they were not aggregated to the Roman clergy and were not, like other cardinals, given title to Roman churches. The patriarchs were assigned rank among the cardinals in order of seniority, following the suburban titleholders. Patriarchs, at their request, were not included among cardinals inducted into the college in later consistories.

Cardinal priests, who were formerly in charge of leading churches in Rome, are bishops whose dioceses are outside Rome.

Cardinal deacons, who were formerly chosen according to regional divisions of Rome, are titular bishops assigned to full-time service in the Roman Curia.

The officers of the college are the dean and sub-dean, a chamberlain and a secretary. Pope Paul decreed Feb. 26, 1965, that the dean and sub-dean were to be elected by the cardinal bishops. He set this ruling aside in December, 1977, however, when he appointed Cardinals Carlo Confalonieri and Paolo Marella, respectively, as dean and sub-dean.

Selection and Duties

Cardinals are selected by the pope and are inducted into the college in a three-step process. Their nomination is announced and approved at a meeting (secret consistory) attended only by the pope and cardinals who are already members of the college; word of their election and confirmation is then communicated to the cardinals designate by means of a document called a *biglietto.* In successive and more public ceremonies, they receive the cardinalatial red biretta and ring, and concelebrate Mass with the pope and their fellow cardinals.

Cardinals under the age of 80: elect the pope when the Holy See becomes vacant (see Papal Election); are major administrators of church affairs, serving in one or more departments of the Roman Curia. All cardinals enjoy a number of special rights and privileges. Their title, while symbolic of high honor, does not signify any extension of the powers of holy orders. They are called princes of the Church.

A **cardinal in pectore** is one whose selection has been made by the pope but whose name has not been disclosed; he has no title, rights or duties until such disclosure is made, at which time he takes precedence from the time of the secret selection.

BIOGRAPHIES OF CARDINALS

Biographies of the cardinals, as of Aug. 1, 1982, are given below in alphabetical order. For historical notes, order of seniority and geographical distribution of cardinals, see separate entries.

An asterisk indicates cardinals ineligible to take part in papal elections.

Alfrink,* Bernard Jan: b. July 5, 1900, Nijkerk, Netherlands; ord. priest Aug. 15, 1924; professor of Sacred Scripture at Utrecht major seminary, 1933; consultor to Pontifical Biblical Commission, Rome, 1944; professor at Catholic University of Nijmegen, 1945; ord. titular archbishop of Tiana and coadjutor archbishop of Utrecht, July 17, 1951; archbishop of Utrecht, 1955-75; cardinal Mar. 28, 1960; titular church, St. Joachim. Former archbishop of Utrecht.

Antonelli,* Ferdinando Giuseppe, O.F.M.: b. July 14, 1896, Subbiano, Italy; solemnly professed in Order of Friars Minor, Apr. 7, 1914; ord. priest July 25, 1922; taught church history, 1928-32, and Christian archeology, 1932-65, at Antonianum; rector magnificus of Antonianum, 1937-43, 1953-59; definitor general of Friars Minor, 1939-45; held various offices in Roman Curia; secretary of Congregation of Rites, 1965-69, and Congregation for Causes of Saints, 1969-73; ord. titular archbishop of Idicra, Mar. 19, 1966; cardinal Mar. 5, 1973; deacon, San Sebastian (on the Palatine).

Aponte Martinez, Luis: b. Aug. 4, 1922, Lajas, Puerto Rico; ord. priest Apr. 10, 1950; parish priest at Ponce; ord. titular bishop of Lares and auxiliary of Ponce, Oct. 12, 1960; bishop of Ponce, 1963-64; archbishop of San Juan, Nov. 4, 1964; cardinal Mar. 5, 1973; titular church, St. Mary Mother of Providence (in Monteverde). Archbishop of San Juan, president of Puerto Rican Episcopal Conference, member of:
Congregation: Causes of Saints.

Aramburu, Juan Carlos: b. Feb. 11, 1912, Reduccion, Argentina; ord. priest in Rome, Oct. 28, 1934; ord. titular bishop of Plataea and auxiliary of Tucuman, Argentina, Dec. 15, 1946; bishop, 1953, and first archbishop, 1957, of Tucuman; titular archbishop of Torri di Bizacena and coadjutor archbishop of Buenos Aires, June 14, 1967; archbishop of Buenos Aires, Apr. 22, 1975; cardinal May 24, 1976; titular church, St. John Baptist of the Florentines. Archbishop of Buenos Aires, ordinary for Eastern Rite Catholics in Brazil without ordinaries of their own rites, member of:
Congregations: Oriental Churches, Catholic Education.
Office: Prefecture of Economic Affairs.

Arns, Paulo Evaristo, O.F.M.: b. Sept. 14, 1921, Forquilhinha, Brazil; ord. priest Nov. 30, 1945; held various teaching posts; director of *Sponsa Christi,* monthly review for religious, and of the Franciscan publication center in Brazil; ord. titular bishop of Respetta and auxiliary of Sao Paulo, July 3, 1966; archbishop of Sao Paulo, Oct. 22, 1970; cardinal Mar. 5, 1973; titular church, St. Anthony of Padua (in Via Tuscolana). Archbishop of Sao Paulo, member of:
Congregation: Sacraments and Divine Worship;
Secretariat: Non-Believers.

Bafile, Corrado: b. July 4, 1903, L'Aquila, Italy; practiced law in Rome for six years before beginning studies for priesthood; ord. priest Apr. 11, 1936; served in Vatican secretariat of state, 1939-59; ord. titular archbishop of Antiochia in Pisidia, Mar. 19, 1960; apostolic nuncio to Germany, 1960-75; pro-prefect of Sacred Congregation for Causes of Saints, July 18, 1975; cardinal May 24, 1976; deacon, S. Maria (in Portico); prefect of Sacred Congregation for Causes of Saints, 1976-80. Member of:
Congregation: Clergy;
Tribunal: Apostolic Signatura;
Commission: Revision of Code of Canon Law.

Baggio, Sebastiano: b. May 16, 1913, Rosa, Italy; ord. priest Dec. 21, 1935; ord. titular archbishop of Ephesus, July 26, 1953; served in Vatican diplomatic corps, 1953-69; nuncio to Chile, apostolic delegate to Canada, nuncio to Brazil; cardinal Apr. 28, 1969; archbishop of Cagliari, 1969-73; entered order of cardinal bishops as titular bishop of Velletri, Dec. 12, 1974. Prefect of Sacred Congregation for Bishops, 1973, member of:
Council for Public Affairs of Church;
Congregations: Doctrine of the Faith, Religious and Secular Institutes, Catholic Education, Evangelization of Peoples;
Commissions: Revision of Code of Canon Law, Latin America (President), Migration and Tourism (President), Sanctuaries of Pompei, Loreto, and Bari, Interpretation of Decrees of Vatican II;
Office: Patrimony of Holy See.

Ballestrero, Anastasio Alberto, O.C.D.: b. Oct. 3, 1913, Genoa, Italy; professed in Order of Discalced Carmelites, 1929; ord. priest June 6, 1936; provincial, 1942-48, and superior general, 1955-67, of Carmelites; author of many books on Christian life; ord. archbishop of Bari, Feb. 2, 1974; archbishop of Turin,

Aug. 1, 1977; cardinal June 30, 1979; titular church, S. Maria (sopra Minerva). Archbishop of Turin, president of the Italian Episcopal Conference, 1979, member of:
Congregation: Religious and Secular Institutes;
Commission: Revision of Code of Canon Law.

Baum, William Wakefield: b. Nov. 21, 1926, Dallas, Tex.; moved to Kansas City, Mo., at an early age; ord. priest May 12, 1951; executive director of U.S. bishops commission for ecumenical and interreligious affairs, 1964-69; attended Second Vatican Council as *peritus* (expert adviser); ord. bishop of Springfield-Cape Girardeau, Mo., Apr. 6, 1970; archbishop of Washington, D.C., 1973-80; cardinal May 24, 1976; titular church, Holy Cross (on the Via Flaminia). Prefect of Congregation for Catholic Education, 1980, grand chancellor of Pontifical Gregorian University, and member of:
Council for Public Affairs of the Church;
Congregations: Doctrine of the Faith, Bishops, Evangelization of Peoples;
Secretariat: Non-Believers;
Office: Administration of Patrimony of Holy See.

Benelli, Giovanni: b. May 12, 1921, Poggiole, Italy; ord. priest Oct. 31, 1943; entered diplomatic service of Holy See August, 1947, as attaché of secretariat of state; served in apostolic nunciatures in Ireland (1950-53), France (1953-60), Brazil (1960-62), Spain (1962-65); observer of Holy See at UNESCO, 1965-66; ord. titular archbishop of Tusurus, Sept. 11, 1966; pro-nuncio in Senegal and apostolic delegate to Western Africa, 1966-67; under-secretary of state 1967-77; app. archbishop of Florence, June 3, 1977; cardinal June 27, 1977; titular church, St. Prisca. Archbishop of Florence, member of:
Council for Public Affairs of the Church.
Congregations: Bishops, Catholic Education.

Beras Rojas, Octavio Antonio: b. Nov. 16, 1906, Seibo, Dominican Republic; ord. priest Aug. 13, 1933; founded national Catholic youth movement; ord. titular archbishop of Euchaitae and coadjutor archbishop of Santo Domingo, Aug. 12, 1945; archbishop of Santo Domingo, 1961-81; cardinal May 24, 1976; titular church, San Sisto. Former archbishop of Santo Domingo, military vicar of Dominican Republic, member of:
Congregation: Bishops.

Bertoli, Paolo: b. Feb. 1, 1908, Poggio Garfagnana, Italy; ord. priest Aug. 15, 1930; entered diplomatic service of the Holy See, serving in nunciatures in Yugoslavia, France, Haiti and Switzerland; ord. titular archbishop of Nicomedia, May 11, 1952; apostolic delegate to Turkey (1952-53), nuncio to Colombia (1953-59), Lebanon (1959-60), France (1960-69); cardinal Apr. 28, 1969; prefect of Congregation for Causes of Saints, 1969-73;

entered order of cardinal bishops as titular bishop of Frascati, June 30, 1979. Chamberlain (Camerlengo) of Holy Roman Church, 1979, member of:
Council for Public Affairs of Church:
Congregations: Bishops, Oriental Churches, Evangelization of Peoples;
Secretariat: Non-Believers;
Tribunal; Apostolic Signatura;
Commissions: Revision of Code of Canon Law, Latin America, State of Vatican City.

Brandao Vilela, Avelar: b. June 13, 1912, Vicosa, Brazil; ord. priest Oct. 27, 1935; professor and spiritual director at diocesan seminary at Aracaju; ord. bishop of Petrolina, Oct. 27, 1946; archbishop of Teresina, Nov. 5, 1955; established 20 social centers and a radio station; introduced agrarian reform of church properties; erected the Institute of Catechetics: archbishop of Sao Salvador da Bahia, Mar. 25, 1971; president of CELAM, 1967-72; co-president of Medellin Conference, 1968; cardinal Mar. 5, 1973; titular church, Sts. Boniface and Alexius. Archbishop of Sao Salvador da Bahia, member of:
Congregations: Clergy, Causes of Saints, Catholic Education:
Commission: Latin America.

Bueno y Monreal, Jose Maria: b. Sept. 11, 1904, Zaragoza, Spain; ord. priest Mar. 19, 1927; ord. bishop of Jaca, Mar. 19, 1946; bishop of Vitoria, May 13, 1950; titular archbishop of Antioch in Pisidia and coadjutor archbishop of Seville, Oct. 27, 1954; archbishop of Seville, 1957-82; cardinal Dec. 15, 1958; titular church, Sts. Vitus, Modestus and Crescentia. Former archbishop of Seville.

Caprio, Giuseppe: b. Nov. 15, 1914, Lapio, Italy; ord. priest Dec. 17, 1938; served in diplomatic missions in China (1947-51, when Vatican diplomats were expelled by communists), Belgium (1951-54), and South Vietnam (1954-56); internuncio in China with residence at Taiwan, 1959-67; ord. titular archbishop of Apollonia, Dec. 17, 1961; pro-nuncio in India, 1967-69; secretary, 1969-77, and president, 1979-81, of Administration of Patrimony of Holy See; substitute secretary of state, 1977-79; cardinal June 30, 1979; deacon, St. Mary Auxiliatrix in Via Tuscolana. President of Prefecture of Economic Affairs of the Holy See, 1981, member of:
Council for Public Affairs of Church;
Congregations: Bishops, Causes of Saints, Evangelization of Peoples:
Commission: Revision of Code of Canon Law.

Carberry, John J.: b. July 31, 1904, Brooklyn, N.Y.; ord. priest July 28, 1929; ord. titular bishop of Elis and coadjutor bishop of Lafayette, Ind., July 25, 1956; bishop of Lafayette, Nov. 20, 1957; bishop of Columbus, Ohio, Jan. 16, 1965; archbishop of St. Louis, Mo., 1968-79; cardinal Apr. 28, 1969; titular church, St. John Baptist de Rossi (Via

Latina). Former archbishop of St. Louis, member of:

Congregation: Evangelization of Peoples.

Carpino, Francesco: b. May 18, 1905, Palazzolo Acreide, Italy; ord. priest Aug. 14, 1927; ord. titular archbishop of Nicomedia and coadjutor archbishop of Monreale, Apr. 8, 1951; archbishop of Monreale, 1951-61; titular archbishop of Sardica, Jan. 19, 1961; assessor of Sacred Consistorial Congregation, 1961; pro-prefect of Sacred Congregation of the Council, Apr. 7, 1967; cardinal June 26, 1967; archbishop of Palermo, 1967-70; entered order of cardinal bishops as titular bishop of Albano, Jan. 27, 1978. Referendary of the Congregation of Bishops, 1970, and member of:

Council for Public Affairs of the Church;
Congregation: Causes of Saints;
Tribunal: Apostolic Signatura.

Carter, Gerald Emmett: b. Mar. 1, 1912, Montreal, Canada; ord. priest May 22, 1937; engaged in pastoral and teaching ministry in Montreal; founder and president of St. Joseph Teachers' College and co-founder and director of Thomas More Institute for adult education; ord. titular bishop of Altiburo and auxiliary bishop of London, Ont., Feb. 2, 1962; bishop of London, 1964-78; vice president, 1971-73, and president, 1975-77, of Canadian Conference of Catholic Bishops; archbishop of Toronto, Apr. 27, 1978; cardinal June 30, 1979; titular church, St. Mary (in Transpontina). Abp. of Toronto, member of:

Secretariats: Christian Unity, Non-Christians.

Casariego, Mario, C.R.S.: b. Feb. 13, 1909, Figueras de Castropol, Spain; ord. priest July 19, 1936; ord. titular bishop of Pudenziana and auxiliary bishop of Guatemala, Dec. 27, 1958; titular archbishop of Perge and coadjutor archbishop of Guatemala, Nov. 12, 1963; archbishop of Guatemala, Dec. 12, 1964; cardinal Apr. 28, 1969; titular church, St. Mary in Aquiro. Archbishop of Guatemala, member of:

Congregation: Causes of Saints.

Casaroli, Agostino: b. Nov. 24, 1914, Castel San Giovanni, Italy; ord. priest May 27, 1937; entered service of Vatican secretariat of state, 1940; undersecretary, 1961-67, of the Sacred Congregation for Extraordinary Ecclesiastical Affairs, and secretary, 1967-79, of its successor the Council for Public Affairs of the Church; ord. titular archbishop of Cartagina, July 16, 1967; chief negotiator for the Vatican with East European communist governments; missions included visits to Hungary, Yugoslavia, Poland, Czechoslovakia, Bulgaria; headed Vatican delegations to several UN conferences and the Helsinki Conference (1975); Pro-Secretary of State and Pro-Prefect of Council for Public Affairs of the Church, Apr. 28, 1979; cardinal June 30, 1979; titular church, the Twelve Apostles. Secretary of

State, July 1, 1979, prefect of Council for Public Affairs of the Church, July 1, 1979, president of Administration of Patrimony of Holy See, 1981, and of Pontifical Commission for Vatican City and member of:

Congregations: Doctrine of the Faith, Bishops;
Secretariat: Non-Believers;
Commissions: Institute for Works of Religion; Revision of Code of Canon Law.

Cé, Marco: b. July 8, 1925, Izano, Italy; ord. priest Mar. 27, 1948; taught sacred scripture and dogmatic theology at seminary in his home diocese of Crema; rector of seminary, 1957; presided over diocesan liturgical commission, preached youth retreats; ord. titular bishop of Vulturia, May 17, 1970; auxiliary bishop of Bologna, 1970-76; general ecclesiastical assistant of Italian Catholic Action, 1976-78; patriarch of Venice, Dec. 7, 1978; cardinal June 30, 1979; titular church, St. Mark. Patriarch of Venice, member of:

Congregations: Clergy, Catholic Education.

Ciappi, Mario Luigi, O.P.: b. Oct. 6, 1909, Florence, Italy; ord. priest Mar. 26, 1932; papal theologian from 1955, serving Pius XII, John XXIII and Paul VI; ord. titular bishop of Misenum June 18, 1977; cardinal June 27, 1977; deacon, Our Lady of the Sacred Heart (in Piazza Navona). Pro-theologian of pontifical household, member of:

Congregation: Causes of Saints.

Civardi, Ernesto: b. Oct. 21, 1906, Fossarmato, Italy; ord. priest June 29, 1930; assistant rector of Pontifical Lombard Seminary in Rome; held various curial offices; undersecretary, 1953-67, and secretary, 1967-79, of the Congregation for Bishops (known as the Consistorial Congregation until 1967); ord. titular archbishop of Sardica, July 16, 1967; secretary of College of Cardinals, 1967-79; filled office of secretary at 1978 conclaves which elected Popes John Paul I and John Paul II; cardinal June 30, 1979; deacon, St. Theodore. Member of:

Congregations: Causes of Saints, Evangelization of Peoples;
Tribunal: Apostolic Signatura.

Colombo, Giovanni: b. Dec. 6, 1902, Caronno, Italy; ord. priest May 29, 1926; rector of Milan Seminary, 1953; ord. titular bishop of Filippopoli and auxiliary bishop of Milan, Dec. 7, 1960; archbishop of Milan, 1963-79; cardinal Feb. 22, 1965; titular church, Sts. Sylvester and Martin (in Montibus). Former archbishop of Milan, member of:

Congregations: Sacraments and Divine Worship, Evangelization of Peoples, Catholic Education;
Commission: Revision of Code.

Confalonieri,* Carlo: b. July 25, 1893, Seveso, Italy; ord. priest Mar. 18, 1916; private secretary to Pius XI for 17 years, to Pius XII for two years; ord. archbishop of

L'Aquila, May 4, 1941; transferred to titular archbishopric of Nicopoli al Nesto, Feb. 22, 1950; cardinal Dec. 15, 1958; titular bishop of suburban see of Palestrina, Mar. 14, 1972, when he entered order of cardinal bishops, and Ostia, Dec. 12, 1977, when he was named dean of College of Cardinals; prefect of Sacred Congregation for Bishops, 1967-73; subdean of college of cardinals, 1974-77. Archpriest of Patriarchal Liberian Basilica, dean of College of Cardinals, Dec. 12, 1977.

Cooke, Terence J.: b. Mar. 1, 1921, New York, N.Y.; ord. priest Dec. 1, 1945; ord. titular bishop of Summa and auxiliary bishop of New York, Dec. 13, 1965; archbishop of New York, Mar. 2, 1968; military vicar for the U.S.; cardinal Apr. 28, 1969; titular church, Sts. John and Paul. Archbishop of New York, military vicar of U.S., member of:
Congregations: Bishops, Oriental Churches, Evangelization of Peoples;
Commission: Migration and Tourism.

Cooray,* Thomas B., O.M.I.: b. Dec. 28, 1901, Periyamulla Negombo, Ceylon (now Sri Lanka); ord. priest June 23, 1929; ord. titular archbishop of Preslavo, Mar. 7, 1946; coadjutor archbishop of Colombo, Sri Lanka, 1946-47; succeeded as archbishop of Colombo, July 26, 1947 (retired 1976); cardinal Feb. 22, 1965; titular church, Sts. Nereus and Achilleus. Former archbishop of Colombo, Sri Lanka.

Cordeiro, Joseph: b. Jan. 19, 1918, Bombay, India; ord. priest Aug. 24, 1946; served in educational and other diocesan posts at Karachi, Pakistan; ord. archbishop of Karachi, Aug. 24, 1958, the first native-born prelate in that see; cardinal Mar. 5, 1973; titular church, St. Andrew Apostle ("de Hortis"). Archbishop of Karachi, member of:
Congregation: Religious and Secular Institutes;
Secretariat: Non-Christians;
Commission *Cor Unum.*

Corripio Ahumada, Ernesto: b. June 29, 1919, Tampico, Mexico; ord. priest Oct. 25, 1942, in Rome, where he remained until almost the end of World War II; taught and held various positions in local seminary of Tampico, 1945-50; ord. titular bishop of Zapara and auxiliary bishop of Tampico, Mar. 19, 1953; bishop of Tampico, 1956-67; archbishop of Antequera, 1967-76; archbishop of Puebla de los Angeles, 1976-77; archbishop of Mexico City and primate of Mexico, July 19, 1977; cardinal June 30, 1979; titular church, Mary Immaculate al Tiburtino. Archbishop of Mexico City, member of:
Congregation: Sacraments and Divine Worship;
Commission: Latin America.

Darmojuwono, Justin: b. Nov. 2, 1914, Godean, Indonesia; ord. priest May 25, 1947; ord. archbishop of Semarang, Apr. 6, 1964 (resigned July 3, 1981, for health reasons); cardinal June 26, 1967; titular church, Most Holy Names of Jesus and Mary. Former archbishop of Semarang, military vicar of Indonesia, member of:
Congregation: Sacraments and Divine Worship.

De Araujo Sales, Eugenio: b. Nov. 8, 1920, Acari, Brazil; ord. priest Nov. 21, 1943; ord. titular bishop of Tibica and auxiliary bishop of Natal, Aug. 15, 1954; archbishop of Sao Salvador, 1968-71; cardinal Apr. 28, 1969; titular church, St. Gregory VII. Archbishop of Rio de Janeiro (1971), ordinary for Eastern Rite Catholics in Brazil without ordinaries of their own rites, member of:
Congregations: Bishops, Clergy, Evangelization of Peoples;
Commission: Social Communications.

Dearden, John Francis.: b. Oct. 15, 1907, Valley Falls, R. I.; ord. priest Dec. 8, 1932; ord. titular bishop of Sarepta and coadjutor bishop of Pittsburgh, May 18, 1948; bishop of Pittsburgh, Dec. 22, 1950; archbishop of Detroit, 1958-80; first president of the National Conference of Catholic Bishops and the United States Catholic Conference, 1966-71; cardinal Apr. 28, 1969; titular church, St. Pius X (alla Balduina). Former archbishop of Detroit, member of:
Congregation: Sacraments and Divine Worship.

De Furstenberg, Maximilien: b. Oct. 23, 1904, Heerlen, Netherlands; ord. priest Aug. 9, 1931; ord. titular archbishop of Palto and apostolic delegate to Japan, Apr. 25, 1949; internuncio, 1952, when Japan established diplomatic relations with the Vatican; apostolic delegate to Australia, New Zealand and Oceania, Feb. 11, 1960; nuncio to Portugal, 1962-67; cardinal June 26, 1967; titular church, Most Sacred Heart of Jesus (a Castro Pretorio); prefect of the Congregation for the Oriental Churches, 1969-73. Grand Master of Equestrian Order of Holy Sepulchre of Jerusalem, member of:
Council for Public Affairs of Church;
Congregations: Bishops, Causes of Saints, Evangelization of Peoples;
Commissions: State of Vatican City, Institute for Works of Religion.

Duval, Leon-Etienne: b. Nov. 9, 1903, Chenex, France; ord. priest Dec. 18, 1926; ord. bishop of Constantine, Algeria, Feb. 11, 1947; archbishop of Algiers, Feb. 3, 1954; cardinal Feb. 22, 1965; titular church, St. Balbina. Archbishop of Algiers, member of:
Congregation: Evangelization of Peoples;
Commission: Revision of Code .

Ekandem, Dominic Ignatius: b. 1917, Ibiono, Nigeria; ord. priest Dec. 7, 1947; ord. titular bishop of Gerapoli di Isauri and auxiliary bishop of Calabar, Feb. 7, 1954, the first Nigerian to become a bishop; first bishop of Ikot Ekpene, Mar. 1, 1963; cardinal May

24, 1976; titular church, San Marcello. Bishop of Ikot Ekpene, member of:

Secretariat: Non-Christians.

Enrique y Tarancon, Vicente: b. May 14, 1907, Burriana, Spain; ord. priest Nov. 1, 1929; ord. bishop of Solsona, Mar. 24, 1946; bishop of Oviedo, Apr. 12, 1964; archbishop of Toledo, 1969-71; cardinal Apr. 28, 1969; titular church, St. John Chrysostom. Archbishop of Madrid, 1971, member of:

Congregation: Bishops;
Commission: Revision of Code.

Etchegaray, Roger: b. Sept. 25, 1922, Espelette, France; ord. priest July 13, 1947; deputy director, 1961-66, and secretary general, 1966-70, of French Episcopal Conference; ord. titular bishop of Gemelle di Numidia and auxiliary bishop of Paris, May 27, 1969; archbishop of Marseilles, Dec. 22, 1970; prelate of Mission de France, 1975-82; president of French Episcopal Conference, 1979-81; cardinal June 30, 1979; titular church, St. Leo I. Archbishop of Marseilles, member of:

Congregation: Catholic Education;
Secretariat: Christian Unity;
Commission: Social Communications.

Flahiff, George B., C.S.B.: b. Oct. 26, 1905, Paris, Ont., Canada; ord. priest Aug. 17, 1930; professor of medieval history at the University of Toronto and Pontifical Institute of Medieval Studies in Toronto, 1934-54; superior general of Basilian Fathers, 1954; ord. archbishop of Winnipeg, May 31, 1961 (retired 1982); president of Canadian Conference of Bishops, 1963-65; cardinal Apr. 28, 1969; titular church, St. Mary della Salute (Primavalle). Former archbishop of Winnipeg, member of:

Congregation: Religious and Secular Institutes.

Florit,* Ermenegildo: b. July 5, 1901, Fagagna, Italy; ord. priest Apr. 11, 1925; taught Sacred Scripture at Lateran University from 1929; pro-rector of Lateran University and Institute of Civil and Canon Law, 1951-54; ord. titular archbishop of Hieropolis and coadjutor archbishop of Florence, Sept. 12, 1954; archbishop of Florence, 1962-77; cardinal Feb. 22, 1965; titular church, Queen of the Apostles. Former archbishop of Florence.

Freeman, James Darcy: b. Nov. 19, 1907, Sydney, Australia; ord. priest July 13, 1930; ord. titular bishop of Ermopoli minore and auxiliary of Sydney, Jan. 24, 1957; bishop of Armidale, 1968-71; archbishop of Sydney, July 9, 1971; cardinal Mar. 5, 1973; titular church, St. Mary Queen of Peace. (in Ostia Mare). Archbishop of Sydney, member of;

Congregation: Catholic Education.

Gantin, Bernardin: b. May 8, 1922, Toffo, Dahomey (now Benin); ord. priest Jan. 14, 1951; ord. titular bishop of Tipasa di Mauritania and auxiliary bishop of Cotonou, Feb. 3, 1957; archbishop of Cotonou,

1960-71; associate secretary (1971-73) and secretary (1973-75) of Sacred Congregation for Evangelization of Peoples; vice-president (1975) and president (1976) of Pontifical Commission for Justice and Peace; cardinal June 27, 1977; deacon, Sacred Heart of Christ the King. President of Pontifical Commission for Justice and Peace and the Pontifical Council *Cor Unum*, member of:

Council for Public Affairs of the Church;
Congregations: Bishops, Causes of Saints, Evangelization of Peoples, Oriental Churches, Religious and Secular Institutes, Catholic Education;
Secretariats: Non-Believers, Non-Christians;
Tribunal: Apostolic Signatura;
Commissions: Social Communications, Institute for Works of Religion.

Garrone,* Gabriel-Marie: b. Oct. 12, 1901, Aix-les-Bains, France; ord. priest Apr. 11, 1925; captain during World War II, cited for bravery, taken prisoner; rector of major seminary of Chambery, 1947; ord. titular archbishop of Lemno and coadjutor of Toulouse, June 24, 1947; archbishop of Toulouse, 1956-66; titular archbishop of Torri di Numidia and pro-prefect of Congregation of Seminaries and Universities, Mar. 24, 1966; cardinal June 26, 1967; titular church, St. Sabina; prefect of Congregation for Catholic Education, 1968-80. Former prefect of Congregation for Catholic Education, head of presidential committee of Pontifical Council for Culture.

Gonzalez Martin, Marcelo: b. Jan. 16, 1918, Villanubla, Spain; ord. priest June 29, 1941; taught theology and sociology at Valladolid diocesan seminary; founded organization for construction of houses for poor; ord. bishop of Astorga, Mar. 5, 1961; titular archbishop of Case Mediane and coadjutor of Barcelona, Feb. 21, 1966; archbishop of Barcelona, 1967-71; archbishop of Toledo, Dec. 3, 1971; cardinal Mar. 5, 1973; titular church, St. Augustine. Archbishop of Toledo, member of:

Congregation: Evangelization of Peoples.

Gouyon, Paul: b. Oct. 24, 1910, Bordeaux, France; ord. priest Mar. 13, 1937; ord. bishop of Bayonne, Oct. 7, 1957; titular archbishop of Pessinonte and coadjutor archbishop of Rennes, Sept. 6, 1963; archbishop of Rennes, Sept. 4, 1964; cardinal Apr. 28, 1969; titular church, Nativity of Our Lord Jesus Christ. (Via Gallia). Archbishop of Rennes, member of:

Secretariat: Non-Believers.

Gray, Gordon Joseph: b. Aug. 10, 1910, Edinburgh, Scotland; ord. priest June 15, 1935; ord. archbishop of Saint Andrews and Edinburgh, Sept. 21, 1951; chairman of International Committee for English in the Liturgy; cardinal Apr. 28, 1969; titular church, St. Clare. Archbishop of Saint Andrews and Edinburgh, member of:

Congregations: Evangelization of Peoples, Sacraments and Divine Worship;

Commission: Social Communications.

Guerri, Sergio: b. Dec. 25, 1905, Tarquinia, Italy; ord. priest Mar. 30, 1929; ord. titular archbishop of Trevi, Apr. 27, 1969; cardinal Apr. 28, 1969; titular church, Most Holy Name of Mary; pro-president of Pontifical Commission for State of Vatican City, 1968-81. Member of:

Congregations: Oriental Churches, Causes of Saints, Evangelization of Peoples.

Guyot, Jean: b. July 7, 1905, Bordeaux, France; ord. priest June 29, 1932; held various offices in Bordeaux diocese; ord. titular bishop of Helenopolis and coadjutor of Constance, May 4, 1949; bishop of Constance, 1950-66; archbishop of Toulouse, 1966-78; invested with Legion of Honor by French government; cardinal Mar. 5, 1973; titular church, Saint Agnes Outside the Walls. Former archbishop of Toulouse, member of:

Congregation: Catholic Education.

Hoeffner, Joseph: b. Dec. 24, 1906, Horhausen, Germany; ord. priest Oct. 30, 1932; ord. bishop of Munster, Sept. 14, 1962; titular archbishop of Aquileia and coadjutor archbishop of Cologne, Jan. 6, 1969; archbishop of Cologne, Feb. 23, 1969; cardinal Apr. 28, 1969; titular church, St. Andrew of the Valley. Archbishop of Cologne, member of:

Congregations: Oriental Churches, Religious and Secular Institutes, Evangelization of Peoples, Catholic Education;

Secretariat: Non-Believers.

Office: Prefecture of Economic Affairs.

Hume, George Basil, O.S.B.: b. Mar. 2, 1923, Newcastle-upon-Tyne, England; began monastic studies at Benedictine Abbey of St. Laurence at Ampleforth, 1941; made solemn perpetual vows as Benedictine, 1945; ord. priest July 23, 1950; abbot of Ampleforth, 1963-76; ord archbishop of Westminster, Mar. 25, 1976; cardinal May 24, 1976; titular church, S. Silvestro (in Capite). Archbishop of Westminster, member of:

Congregation: Religious and Secular Institutes;

Secretariat: Christian Unity.

Jubany Arnau, Narciso: b. Aug. 12, 1913, Santa Coloma de Farnes, Spain; ord. priest July 30, 1939; professor of law at Barcelona seminary; served on ecclesiastical tribunal; ord. titular bishop of Ortosia and auxiliary of Barcelona, Jan. 22, 1956; bishop of Gerona, 1964-71; archbishop of Barcelona, Dec. 3, 1971; cardinal Mar. 5, 1973; titular church, San Lorenzo (in Damaso). Archbishop of Barcelona, member of:

Congregations: Sacraments and Divine Worship, Religious and Secular Institutes;

Commission: Revision of Code.

Kim, Stephan Sou Hwan: b. May 8, 1922, Tae Gu, Korea; ord. priest Sept. 15, 1951;

ord. bishop of Masan, May 31, 1966; archbishop of Seoul, Apr. 9, 1968; cardinal Apr. 28, 1969; titular church, St. Felix of Cantalice (Centocelle). Archbishop of Seoul, apostolic administrator of Pyeong Yang, president of Korean Episcopal Conference (1981), member of:

Congregation: Evangelization of Peoples;

Secretariat: Non-Christians.

Knox, James Robert: b. Mar. 2, 1914, Bayswater, Australia; ord. priest Dec. 22, 1941, at Rome; forced to remain in Rome because of World War II; chaplain and later vice rector of Pontifical Urban University; secretary of apostolic delegation in Japan; ord. titular archbishop of Melitene, Nov. 8, 1953; apostolic delegate to British Africa, 1953-57; internuncio to India and apostolic delegate to Burma and Ceylon (Sri Lanka), 1957-67; archbishop of Melbourne, Australia, 1967-74; cardinal Mar. 5, 1973; titular church, Santa Maria (in Vallicella). Prefect of Sacred Congregation for the Sacraments and Divine Worship, 1974-81. President of Pontifical Council for the Family, 1981, member of:

Council for Public Affairs of Church;

Congregations: Bishops, Oriental Churches, Evangelization of Peoples, Catholic Education;

Commissions: Revision of Code of Canon Law, Interpretation of Decrees of Vatican II, Revision of Oriental Code of Canon Law;

Office: Administration of Patrimony of Holy See.

Koenig, Franz: b. Aug. 3, 1905, Rabenstein, Lower Austria; ord. priest Oct. 28, 1933; ord. titular bishop of Livias and coadjutor bishop of Sankt Poelten, Aug. 31, 1952; archbishop of Vienna, May 10, 1956; cardinal Dec. 15, 1958; titular church, St. Eusebius; president of Secretariat for Non-Believers, 1965-80. Archbishop of Vienna, ordinary for faithful of Byzantine Rite living in Austria, member of:

Congregation: Bishops;

Commission: Revision of Code.

Krol, John Joseph: b. Oct. 26, 1910, Cleveland, Ohio; ord. priest Feb. 20, 1937; ord. titular bishop of Cadi and auxiliary bishop of Cleveland, Sept. 2, 1953; archbishop of Philadelphia, Feb. 11, 1961, installed Mar. 22, 1961; cardinal June 26, 1967; titular church, St. Mary (della Merced) and St. Adrian Martyr; vice-president, 1966-72, and president, 1972-74, of NCCB/USCC. Archbishop of Philadelphia, member of:

Congregation: Oriental Churches;

Commission: Revision of Code of Canon Law;

Office: Prefecture of Economic Affairs.

Landazuri Ricketts, Juan, O.F.M: b. Dec. 19, 1913, Arequipa, Peru; entered Franciscans, 1933; ord. priest Apr. 16, 1939; ord. titular archbishop of Roina and coadjutor

archbishop of Lima, Aug. 24, 1952; archbishop of Lima, May 2, 1955; cardinal Mar. 19, 1962; titular church, St. Mary (in Aracoeli). Archbishop of Lima, member of:
Congregations: Clergy, Religious and Secular Institutes, Catholic Education;
Commission: Revision of Code.
Leger, Paul Emile, S.S.: b. Apr. 26, 1904, Valleyfield, Quebec, Canada; ord. priest May 25, 1929; rector Canadian College, Rome, 1947; ord. archbishop of Montreal, Apr. 26, 1950; cardinal Jan. 12, 1953; titular church, St. Mary (of the Angels); resigned as archbishop of Montreal (Apr. 20, 1968) to become missionary to lepers, retired 1979. Former archbishop of Montreal, member of:
Congregation: Evangelization of Peoples;
Commission: Revision of Code of Canon Law.
Lekai, Laszlo: b. Mar. 12, 1910, Zalalovo, Hungary; ord. priest Oct. 28, 1934; professor of philosophy and dogmatic theology at major seminary at Veszprem; arrested and imprisoned by Nazis during World War II; engaged in pastoral work and held diocesan offices after the war; ord. titular bishop of Girus Tirasii and apostolic administrator of Esztergom, Mar. 16, 1972; archbishop of Esztergom and primate of Hungary, Feb. 12, 1976; cardinal May 24, 1976; titular church, S. Teresa (on the Corso d'Italia). Archbishop of Esztergom, member of:
Congregation: Catholic Education.
Lorscheider, Aloisio, O.F.M.: b. Oct. 8, 1924, Linha Geraldo, Brazil; received in Franciscan Order, Feb. 1, 1942; ord. priest Aug. 22, 1948; professor of theology at the Antonianum, Rome, and director of Franciscan international house of studies; ord. bishop of Santo Angelo, Brazil, May 20, 1962; archbishop of Fortaleza, Mar. 26, 1973; president of CELAM, 1975-79; cardinal May 24, 1976; titular church, S. Pietro (in Montorio). Archbishop of Fortaleza, member of:
Congregations: Religious and Secular Institutes, Clergy;
Secretariat: Non-Christians.
McCann, Owen: b. June 29, 1907, Woodstock, South Africa; ord. priest Dec. 21, 1935; ord. titular bishop of Stettorio and vicar apostolic of Cape Town, May 18, 1950; first archbishop of Cape Town, Jan. 11, 1951; opponent of apartheid policy; cardinal Feb. 22, 1965; titular church, St. Praxedes. Archbishop of Cape Town, member of:
Congregation: Evangelization of Peoples.
Macharski, Franciszek: b. May 20, 1927, Cracow, Poland; ord. priest Apr. 2, 1950; engaged in pastoral work, 1950-56; continued theological studies in Fribourg, Switzerland, 1956-60; taught pastoral theology at the Faculty of Theology in Cracow; app. rector of archdiocesan seminary at Cracow, 1970; ord. archbishop of Cracow, Jan. 6, 1979, by Pope John Paul II; cardinal June 30, 1979; titular

church, St. John at the Latin Gate. Archbishop of Cracow, member of:
Congregations: Clergy, Catholic Education;
Secretariat: Non-Believers.
Malula, Joseph: b. Dec. 17, 1917, Kinshasa, Zaire; ord. priest June 9, 1946; ord. titular bishop of Attanaso and auxiliary bishop of Kinshasa, Sept. 20, 1959; archbishop of Kinshasa. July 7, 1964; cardinal Apr. 28, 1969; titular church, Ss. Protomartyrs (Via Aurelia Antica). Archbishop of Kinshasa, member of:
Congregation: Evangelization of Peoples.
Manning, Timothy: b. Nov. 15, 1909, Ballingeary, Ireland; completed studies for the priesthood at St. Patrick's Seminary, Menlo Park, Calif.; ord. priest June 16, 1934; became American citizen, Jan. 14, 1944; ord. titular bishop of Lesvi and auxiliary of Los Angeles, Oct. 15, 1946; first bishop of Fresno, 1967-69; titular archbishop of Capri and coadjutor of Los Angeles, May 26, 1969; archbishop of Los Angeles, Jan. 21, 1970; cardinal Mar. 5, 1973; titular church, Santa Lucia. Archbishop of Los Angeles, member of:
Congregations: Evangelization of Peoples, Religious and Secular Institutes.
Marella,* Paolo: b. Jan. 25, 1895, Rome, Italy; ord. priest Feb. 23, 1918; aide in Congregation for Propagation of the Faith; on staff of apostolic delegation, Washington, D.C., 1923-33; ord. titular archbishop of Doclea, Oct. 29, 1933; apostolic delegate to Japan, 1933-48, to Australia, New Zealand and Oceania, 1948-53; nuncio to France, 1953-59; cardinal Dec. 14, 1959; entered order of cardinal bishops as titular bishop of Porto and Santa Rufina, Mar. 14, 1972; president of Secretariat for Non-Christians, 1967-73. Archpriest of St. Peter's Basilica, sub-dean of College of Cardinals, 1977.
Marty, Francois: b. May 18, 1904, Pachins, France; ord. priest June 28, 1930; ord. bishop of Saint-Flour, May 1, 1952; titular archbishop of Emesa and coadjutor archbishop of Rheims, Dec. 14, 1959; archbishop of Rheims, May 9, 1960; archbishop of Paris, 1968-81; cardinal Apr. 28, 1969; titular church, St. Louis of France. Former archbishop of Paris, member of:
Congregations: Oriental Churches, Clergy, Sacraments and Divine Worship;
Commission: Revision of Code.
Maurer,* Jose Clemente, C.SS.R.: b. Mar. 13, 1900, Puttlingen, Germany; ord. priest Sept. 19, 1925; assigned to Bolivian missions, 1926; became a Bolivian citizen; ord. titular bishop of Cea and auxiliary bishop of La Paz, Apr. 16, 1950; archbishop of Sucre, Oct. 27, 1951; cardinal June 26, 1967; titular church, Most Holy Redeemer and St. Alphonsus. Archbishop of Sucre.
Medeiros, Humberto S.: b. Oct. 6, 1915, Arrifes, S. Miguel, Azores; came to U.S. at age

of 15; became American citizen, 1940; ord. priest June 15, 1946; ord. bishop of Brownsville, Tex., June 9, 1966; archbishop of Boston, Sept. 8, 1970; cardinal Mar. 5, 1973; titular church, Santa Susanna. Archbishop of Boston, member of:

Congregations: Bishops, Catholic Education.

Miranda y Gomez,* Miguel Dario: b. Dec. 19, 1895, Leon, Mexico; ord. priest Oct. 28, 1918; ord. bishop of Tulancingo, Dec. 8, 1937; titular archbishop of Selimbra and coadjutor archbishop of Mexico City, Dec. 20, 1955; archbishop of Mexico City, 1956-77; served as president of the Latin American Bishops' Council (CELAM); cardinal Apr. 28, 1969; titular church, St. Mary of Guadalupe (Montemario). Former archbishop of Mexico City.

Motta,* Carlos Carmelo de Vasconcellos: b. July 16, 1890, Bom Jesus do Amparo, Brazil; ord. priest June 29, 1918; ord. titular bishop of Algiza and auxiliary bishop of Diamantina, Oct. 30, 1932; archbishop of Sao Luis do Maranhao, Dec. 19, 1935; archbishop of Sao Paulo del Brasile, 1944-64; cardinal Feb. 18, 1946; titular church, St. Pancratius. Archbishop of Aparecida (1964).

Mozzoni, Umberto: b. June 29, 1904, Buenos Aires, Argentina; holds Italian citizenship; ord. priest Aug. 14, 1927; professor of theology and canon law at Macerata seminary, Italy; served on Vatican diplomatic staff in Canada, England and Portugal; ord. titular archbishop of Side, Dec. 5, 1954; nuncio to Bolivia, 1954-58, Argentina, 1958-69, Brazil, 1969-73; cardinal Mar. 5, 1973; deacon, St. Eugene. Member of:

Congregations: Oriental Churches, Clergy, Religious and Secular Institutes, Evangelization of Peoples, Causes of Saints;

Tribunal: Apostolic Signatura;

Commissions: Sanctuaries of Pompei, Loreto and Bari (President), Institute for Works of Religion.

Munoz Duque, Anibal: b. Oct. 3, 1908, Santa Rosa de Osos, Colombia; ord. priest Nov. 19, 1933; ord. bishop of Soccoro y San Gil, May 27, 1951; bishop of Bucaramango, 1952-59; archbishop of Nueva Pamplona, 1959-68; titular archbishop of Cariana and coadjutor archbishop of Bogota, 1968; archbishop of Bogota, July 29, 1972; cardinal Mar. 5, 1973; titular church, St. Bartholomew. Archbishop of Bogota, military vicar, member of:

Congregation: Sacraments and Divine Worship.

Munoz Vega, Pablo, S. J.: b. May 23, 1903, Mira, Ecuador; ord. priest July 25, 1933; ord. titular bishop of Ceramo and auxiliary bishop of Quito, Mar. 19, 1964; archbishop of Quito, June 23, 1967; cardinal Apr. 28, 1969; titular church, St. Robert Bellarmine. Archbishop of Quito, member of:

Congregation: Religious and Secular Institutes.

Nasalli Rocca di Corneliano, Mario: b. Aug. 12, 1903, Piacenza, Italy; ord. priest Apr. 9, 1927; ord. titular archbishop of Anzio, Apr. 20, 1969; cardinal Apr. 28, 1969; titular church, St. John the Baptist. Member of:

Congregations: Sacraments and Divine Worship, Causes of Saints;

Secretariat: Non-Believers.

Nsubuga, Emmanuel: b. Nov. 5, 1914, Kisule, Uganda; ord. priest Dec. 15, 1946; ord. bishop of Kampala, Oct. 30, 1966; cardinal May 24, 1976; titular church, S. Maria Nuova. Archbishop of Kampala, member of:

Congregation: Evangelization of Peoples.

O'Boyle,* Patrick A.: b. July 18, 1896, Scranton, Pa.; ord. priest May 21, 1921; executive director of War Relief Services, NCWC, 1943; ord. archbishop of Washington, Jan. 14, 1948 (retired, 1973); cardinal June 26, 1967; titular church, St. Nicholas (in Carcere). Former archbishop of Washington.

Oddi, Silvio: b. Nov. 14, 1910, Morfasso, Italy; ord. priest May 21, 1933; ord. titular archbishop of Mesembria, Sept. 27, 1953; served in Vatican diplomatic corps, 1953-69; apostolic delegate to Jerusalem, Palestine, Jordan and Cyprus, internuncio to the United Arab Republic, and nuncio to Belgium and Luxembourg; cardinal Apr. 28, 1969; titular church, St. Agatha of the Goths. Pontifical legate for Patriarchal Basilica of St. Francis of Assisi, prefect of Sacred Congregation for the Clergy, 1979, member of:

Council for Public Affairs of Church;

Congregations: Bishops, Oriental Churches, Causes of Saints, Evangelization of Peoples;

Tribunal: Apostolic Signatura;

Commissions: Revision of Code of Canon Law, State of Vatican City, Sanctuaries of Pompei, Loreto and Bari.

O'Fiaich, Tomas: b. Nov. 3, 1923; Crossmaglen, Ireland; ord. priest July 6, 1948; lecturer, 1953, and professor, 1959, of modern history at Maynooth College; vice president, 1970, and president, 1974, of Maynooth; prolific author of scholarly works; recognized authority on early Irish Christianity; ord. archbishop of Armagh and primate of All Ireland, Oct. 2, 1977; pledged to work for the cause of peace in Northern Ireland; outspoken in his condemnation of violence; president of Irish Episcopal Conference; cardinal June 30, 1979; titular church, St. Patrick. Abp. of Armagh, primate of All Ireland, member of:

Congregations: Clergy, Catholic Education;

Secretariat: Christian Unity.

Otunga, Maurice: b. January, 1923, Chebukwa, Kenya; son of pagan tribal chief; baptized 1935, at age of 12; ord. priest Oct. 3, 1950, at Rome; taught at Kisumu major semi-

nary for three years; attaché in apostolic delegation at Mombasa, 1953-56; ord. titular bishop of Tacape and auxiliary of Kisumu, Feb. 25, 1957; bishop of Kisii, 1960-69; titular archbishop of Bomarzo and coadjutor of Nairobi, Nov. 15, 1969; archbishop of Nairobi, Oct. 24, 1971; cardinal Mar. 5, 1973; titular church, St. Gregory Barbarigo. Archbishop of Nairobi, military vicar of Kenya, 1981, member of:
Congregations: Sacraments and Divine Worship, Religious and Secular Institutes.

Palazzini, Pietro: b. May 19, 1912, Piobbico, Pesaro, Italy; ord. priest Dec. 6, 1934; assistant vice-rector of Pontifical Major Roman Seminary and vice-rector and bursar of Pontifical Roman Seminary for Juridical Studies; professor of moral theology at Lateran University; held various offices in Roman Curia; secretary of Congregation of Council (now Clergy), 1958-73; ord. titular archbishop of Caesarea in Cappadocia, Sept. 21, 1962; author of numerous works on moral theology and law; cardinal Mar. 5, 1973; deacon, St. Jerome. Prefect of Congregation for Causes of Saints, 1980, member of:
Congregations: Oriental Churches, Clergy;
Tribunal: Apostolic Signatura;
Commissions: Revision of Code of Canon Law, Interpretation of Decrees of Vatican II.

Pappalardo, Salvatore: b. Sept. 23, 1918, Villafranca Sicula, Sicily; ord. priest Apr. 12, 1941; entered diplomatic service of secretariat of state, 1947; ord. titular archbishop of Miletus, Jan. 16, 1966; pro-nuncio in Indonesia, 1966-69; president of Pontifical Ecclesiastical Academy, 1969-70; archbishop of Palermo, Oct. 17, 1970; cardinal Mar. 5, 1973; titular church, St. Mary Odigitria of the Sicilians. Archbishop of Palermo, member of:
Congregations: Oriental Churches, Clergy.

Parecattil, Joseph: b. Apr. 1, 1912, Kidangoor, India; ord. priest Aug. 24, 1939; ord. titular bishop of Aretusa for Syrians and auxiliary bishop of Ernakulam, Nov. 30, 1953; archbishop of Ernakulam (Chaldean-Malabar Rite), July 20, 1956; vice-president of the Indian Bishops' Conference, 1966; appointed one of seven members of Pope Paul VI's advisory council for Eastern Rite churches, 1968; cardinal Apr. 28, 1969; titular church, Our Lady Queen of Peace (Monte Verde). Archbishop of Ernakulam of the Chaldean-Malabar Rite, member of:
Congregation: Oriental Churches;
Secretariat: Non-Christians;
Commissions: Revision of Code, Revision of Oriental Code (President).

Parente,* Pietro: b. Feb. 16, 1891, Casalnuovo, Monterotaro, Italy; ord. priest Mar. 18, 1916; director of Archiepiscopal Seminary at Naples, 1916-26; rector of Pontifical Urban College of Propagation of the Faith, 1934-38; Consultor of the Congregations of the Holy Office, Council, Propaga-

tion of the Faith, and Seminaries and Universities; ord. archbishop of Perugia, Oct. 23, 1955; titular archbishop of Tolemaide di Tebaide, Oct. 23, 1959; assessor (1959-65) and secretary (1965-67) of Congregation of Holy Office (now Doctrinal Congregation); cardinal June 26, 1967; titular church, St. Lawrence (in Lucina).

Paupini, Giuseppe: b. Feb. 25, 1907, Mondavio, Italy; ord. priest Mar. 19, 1930; ord. titular archbishop of Sebastopolis in Abasgia, Feb. 26, 1956; served in Vatican diplomatic corps, 1956-69; internuncio in Iran, 1956-57; nuncio to Guatemala and El Salvador, 1957-58, nuncio to Colombia, 1959-69; cardinal Apr. 28, 1969; titular church, All Saints Church. Major penitentiary 1973, member of:
Congregation: Causes of Saints;
Commission: State of Vatican City.

Pellegrino, Michele: b. Apr. 25, 1903, Centallo, Italy; ord. priest Sept. 19, 1925; ord. archbishop of Turin, Oct. 17, 1965 (resigned 1977); cardinal June 26, 1967; titular church, Most Holy Name of Jesus. Former archbishop of Turin, member of:
Congregation: Catholic Education.

Philippe, Pierre Paul, O.P.: b. Apr. 16, 1905, Paris, France; entered Dominican Order, 1926; ord. priest July 6, 1932; professor at Angelicum, Rome, from 1935; founded Institute of Spirituality for masters of novices at Angelicum, 1950, and school for mistresses of novices, 1953; apostolic visitor of various religious institutes, 1951-56; commissary of the Holy Office, 1955; consultor of various pontifical commissions and congregations from 1958; secretary of Congregation for Religious, 1959; ord. titular archbishop of Heracleopolis Magna, Sept. 21, 1962; secretary of Congregation for Doctrine of Faith, 1967-73; cardinal Mar. 5, 1973; deacon, St. Pius V; prefect of Congregation for Oriental Churches, 1973-80. Member of:
Congregations: Religious and Secular Institutes, Causes of Saints, Evangelization of Peoples;
Commission: Revision of Code.

Picachy, Lawrence Trevor, S.J.: b. Aug. 7, 1916, Lebong, India; ord. priest Nov. 21, 1947; dean, 1950-54, and then rector, 1954-60, of St. Francis Xavier University College, Calcutta; ord. bishop of Jamshedpur, Sept. 9, 1962; archbishop of Calcutta, May 29, 1969; cardinal May 24, 1976; titular church, Sacred Heart of Mary. Archbishop of Calcutta, president of Indian Episcopal Conference, 1975, member of:
Congregation: Evangelization of Peoples.

Pironio, Eduardo: b. Dec. 3, 1920, Nueve de Julio, Argentina; ord. priest Dec. 5, 1943; taught theology at Pius XII Seminary of Mercedes diocese, 1944-59; vicar general of diocese 1958-60; attended Second Vatican Council as *peritus*; ord. titular bishop of Ceciri, May 31, 1964; apostolic administrator of diocese of Avellaneda, 1967-72; secretary general 1967-72, and president, 1973-75, of CELAM; bishop of Mar del Plata, 1972-75; titular archbishop of Thiges and pro-prefect of Sacred Congregation for Religious and Secular Institutes, Sept. 20, 1975; cardinal May 24, 1976; deacon, Sts. Cosmas and Damian. Prefect of the Sacred Congregation for Religious and Secular Institutes, 1976, member of:

Council for Public Affairs of the Church.

Congregations: Bishops, Sacraments and Divine Worship, Catholic Education, Oriental Churches;

Commissions: Council for the Laity, Revision of Code of Canon Law, Latin America, Interpretation of Decrees of Vatican II.

Poletti, Ugo: b. Apr. 19, 1914, Omegna, Italy; ord. priest June 29, 1938; served in various diocesan offices at Novara; ord. titular bishop of Medeli and auxiliary of Novaro, Sept. 14, 1958; president of Pontifical Mission Aid Society for Italy, 1964-67; archbishop of Spoleto, 1967-69; titular archbishop of Cittanova, 1969; served as second viceregent of Rome, 1969-72; pro-vicar general of Rome, 1972, following the sudden death of Cardinal Dell'Acqua; cardinal Mar. 5, 1973; titular church, Sts. Ambrose and Charles. Vicar general of Rome, 1973, archpriest of Patriarchal Lateran Archbasilica, 1973, grand chancellor of Lateran University, member of:

Congregations: Clergy, Sacraments and Divine Worship, Oriental Churches, Religious and Secular Institutes;

Commission: Council for the Laity.

Poma, Antonio: b. June 12, 1910, Villanterio, Italy; ord. priest Apr. 15, 1933; ord. titular bishop of Tagaste and auxiliary bishop of Mantova, Dec. 9, 1951; bishop of Mantova, Sept. 8, 1954; titular archbishop of Gerpiniano and coadjutor archbishop of Bologna, July 16, 1967; archbishop of Bologna, Feb. 12, 1968; cardinal Apr. 28, 1969; titular church, St. Luke (a Via Prenestina). Archbishop of Bologna, member of:

Congregations: Clergy, Education.

Primatesta, Raul Francisco: b. Apr. 14, 1919, Capilla del Senor, Argentina; ord. priest Oct. 25, 1942, at Rome; taught at minor and major seminaries of La Plata; contributed to several theology reviews; ord. titular bishop of Tanais and auxiliary of La Plata, Aug. 15, 1957; bishop of San Rafael, 1961-65; archbishop of Cordoba, Feb. 16, 1965; cardinal Mar. 5, 1973; titular church, St. Mary Sorrowful Virgin. Archbishop of Cordoba, Argentina, member of:

Congregations: Bishops, Religious and Secular Institutes, Sacraments and Divine Worship;

Quintero,* Jose Humberto: b. Sept. 22, 1902, Mucuchies, Venezuela; ord. priest Aug. 22, 1926; ord. titular archbishop of ·Acrida and coadjutor archbishop of Merida, Dec. 6,

1953; archbishop of Caracas 1960-80; cardinal Jan. 16, 1961; titular church, Sts. Andrew and Gregory (al Monte Celio). Former archbishop of Caracas.

Ratzinger, Joseph: b. Apr. 16, 1927, Marktl am Inn, Germany; ord. priest June 29, 1951; professor of dogmatic theology at University of Regensburg, 1969-77; member of International Theological Commission, 1969-80; ord. archbishop of Munich-Freising, May 28, 1977 (resigned Feb. 15, 1982); cardinal June 27, 1977; titular church, St. Mary of Consolation (in Tiburtina). Prefect of Sacred Congregation for Doctrine of the Faith, 1981, member of:

Council for Public Affairs of the Church;

Congregation: Bishops;

Secretariat: Christian Unity;

Commissions: Biblical (President), Theological (President).

Razafimahatratra, Victor, S.J.: b. Sept. 8, 1921, Ambanitsilena-Ranomasina, Madagascar; entered Society of Jesus, 1945; ord. priest July 28, 1956; rector of Fianarantsoa Minor Seminary, 1960-63; superior of Jesuit residence at Ambositra, 1963-69; rector of Tananarive Major Seminary, 1969-71; ord. bishop of Farafangana, Apr. 18, 1971; archbishop of Tananarive, Apr. 10, 1976; cardinal May 24, 1976; titular church, Holy Cross in Jerusalem. Archbishop of Tananarive, president of Madagascar Episcopal Conference, member of:

Congregation: Evangelization of Peoples.

Renard, Alexandre Charles: b. June 7, 1906, Avelin, France; ord. priest July 12, 1931; ord. bishop of Versailles, Oct. 19, 1953; archbishop of Lyons, 1967-81; cardinal June 26, 1967; titular church, Most Holy Trinity (at Monte Pincio.) Former abp. of Lyons, member of:

Congregations: Religious and Secular Institutes, Evangelization of Peoples.

Ribeiro, Antonio: b. May 21, 1928, Gandarela di Basto, Portugal; ord. priest July 5, 1953; professor of fundamental theology at major seminary at Braga; ord. titular bishop of Tigillava and auxiliary of Braga, Sept. 17, 1967; patriarch of Lisbon, May 10, 1971; cardinal Mar. 5, 1973; titular church, St. Anthony of Padua (in Rome). Patriarch of Lisbon, military vicar, member of:

Congregation: Catholic Education;

Commission: Social Communications.

Righi-Lambertini, Egano: b. Feb. 22, 1906, Casalecchio di Reno, Italy; ord. priest May 25, 1929; entered service of secretariat of state, 1939; served in diplomatic missions in France (1949-54), Costa Rica (1955), England (1955-57); first apostolic delegate to Korea, 1957-60; ord. titular archbishop of Doclea, Oct. 28, 1960; apostolic nuncio in Lebanon, 1960-63, Chile, 1963-67, Italy, 1967-69; France, 1969-79; while nuncio in France he also served as special envoy at the Council of Europe, 1974-79; cardinal June 30, 1979; deacon, St. John Bosco in Via Tuscolana. Member of:

Council for Public Affairs of the Church;
Congregations: Bishops, Causes of Saints;
Secretariat: Non-Christians;
Commission: Sacred Art in Italy (Honorary President).

Rosales, Julio: b. Sept. 18, 1906, Calbayog, Philippines; ord. priest June 2, 1929; ord. bishop of Tagbilaran, Sept. 21, 1946; archbishop of Cebu, 1949-82; cardinal Apr. 28, 1969; titular church, Sacred Heart of Jesus (a Vitinia). Former archbishop of Cebu, member of:

Congregation: Clergy;
Commission: Revision of Code of Canon Law.

Rossi, Agnelo: b. May 4, 1913, Joaquim Egidio, Brazil; ord. priest Mar. 27, 1937; ord. bishop of Barra do Pirai, Apr. 15, 1956; archbishop of Ribeirao Preto, 1962-64; archbishop of Sao Paulo, 1964-70; cardinal Feb. 22, 1965; titular church, Mother of God. Prefect of Congregation for Evangelization of Peoples, 1970, grand chancellor of Pontifical Urban University, member of:

Council for Public Affairs of Church;
Congregations: Clergy, Doctrine of Faith, Bishops, Oriental Churches, Causes of Saints, Religious and Secular Institutes, Catholic Education;
Secretariats: Christian Unity, Non-Christians;
Commissions: Revision of Code of Canon Law, Revision of Oriental Code of Canon Law, Institute for Works of Religion.

Rossi, Opilio: b. May 14, 1910, New York, N.Y.; holds Italian citizenship; ord. priest for diocese of Piacenza, Italy, Mar. 11, 1933; served in nunciatures in Belgium, The Netherlands and Germany, 1938-53; ord. titular archbishop of Ancyra, Dec. 27, 1953; nuncio in Ecuador, 1953-59, Chile, 1959-61, Austria, 1961-76; cardinal May 24, 1976; deacon, S. Maria Liberatrice (on the Monte Testaccio). Member of:

Council for Public Affairs of the Church;
Congregations: Bishops, Oriental Churches, Sacraments and Divine Worship, Religious and Secular Institutes, Evangelization of Peoples;
Commission: Council for Laity (President).

Roy, Maurice: b. Jan. 25, 1905, Quebec, Canada; ord. priest June 12, 1927; chief of chaplains of Canadian Armed Forces during World War II; ord. bishop of Trois Rivieres, May 1, 1946; military vicar, 1946-81; archbishop of Quebec, 1947-81; primate of Canada, Jan. 25, 1956; cardinal Feb. 22, 1965; titular church, Our Lady of the Most Holy Sacrament and the Holy Canadian Martyrs; president of Council for the Laity and the Pontifical Commission for Justice and Peace (1967-76). Former archbishop of Quebec, member of:

Congregations: Clergy, Catholic Education;
Commission: Revision of Code of Canon Law.

Rubin, Wladyslaw: b. Sept. 20, 1917, Toki, Poland; seminary studies interrupted during World War II when he was arrested and deported to labor camp; completed studies at St. Joseph's University in Beirut; ord. priest in Beirut June 30, 1946 and served Polish community there; sent to Rome for further studies, 1949; chaplain for Polish refugees in Italy, 1953-58; rector of Polish College in Rome, 1959-64; ord. titular bishop of Serta, primate of Poland's delegate for emigration and auxiliary of Gniezno, Nov. 29, 1964; established contact with Polish emigrants throughout the world; secretary general of Synod of Bishops, 1967-79; cardinal June 30, 1979; deacon, St. Mary in Via Lata. Prefect of Congregation for Oriental Churches, 1980, member of:

Congregations: Doctrine of the Faith, Causes of Saints;
Tribunal: Apostolic Signatura;
Secretariat: Christian Unity;
Commissions: Revision of Code of Oriental Canon Law, Interpretation of Decrees of Vatican II.

Rugambwa, Laurean: b. July 12, 1912, Bukongo, Tanzania; ord. priest Dec. 12, 1943; ord. titular bishop of Febiano and vicar apostolic of Lower Kagera, Feb. 10, 1952; bishop of Rutabo, Mar. 25, 1953; cardinal Mar. 28, 1960; titular church, St. Francis of Assisi (a Ripa); bishop of Bukoba, 1960-68. Archbishop of Dar-es-Salaam, 1968, member of:

Congregation: Causes of Saints;
Commission: Revision of Code.

Salazar Lopez, Jose: b. Jan. 12, 1910, Ameca, Mexico; ord. priest May 26, 1934, in Rome; instrumental in building of new seminary at Guadalajara, the largest in Mexico; vice-rector and later rector of seminary; ord. titular bishop of Prusiade and coadjutor bishop of Zamora, Aug. 20, 1961; bishop of Zamora, 1967-70; archbishop of Guadalajara, Feb. 21, 1970; cardinal Mar. 5, 1973; titular church, Santa Emerentia. Archbishop of Guadalajara, member of:

Congregations: Sacraments and Divine Worship, Clergy.

Samore, Antonio: b. Dec. 4, 1905, Bardi, Italy; ord. priest June 10, 1928; served in apostolic nunciatures at Lithuania and Switzerland; worked in Vatican secretariat of state during World War II; assigned to apostolic delegation in Washington, D.C., 1947; nuncio to Colombia, 1950; ord. titular archbishop of Tirnovo, Apr. 16, 1950; secretary of Congregation of Extraordinary Ecclesiastical Affairs, 1953-67; cardinal June 26, 1967; entered order of cardinal bishops as titular bishop of Sabina and Poggia Mirteto, Dec. 12, 1974;

prefect of Congregation for Discipline of Sacraments, 1968-74. Librarian and archivist of Holy Roman Church, 1974, member of:
Council for Public Affairs of Church;
Congregations: Oriental Churches, Bishops, Evangelization of Peoples;
Commission: Revision of Code.

Satowaki, Joseph Asajiro: b. Feb. 1, 1904, Shittsu, Japan; ord. priest Dec. 17, 1932; served in various pastoral capacities in Nagasaki archdiocese after his ordination; apostolic administrator of Taiwan (then a Japanese possession), 1941-45; director of Nagasaki minor seminary, 1945-57; vicar general of Nagasaki, 1945; ord. first bishop of Kagoshima, May 3, 1955; archbishop of Nagasaki, Dec. 19, 1968; president of Japanese Episcopal Conference, 1979- ; cardinal June 30, 1979; titular church, St. Mary of Peace. Archbishop of Nagasaki, member of:
Congregation: Evangelization of Peoples;
Secretariat: Non-Christians.

Scherer, Alfred Vicente: b. Feb. 5, 1903, Bom Principio, Brazil; ord. priest Apr. 3, 1926; ord. archbishop of Porto Alegre, Feb. 23, 1947 (retired Aug. 29, 1981); cardinal Apr. 28, 1969; titular church, Our Lady of La Salette. Former archbishop of Porto Alegre, Brazil.

Schroeffer, Joseph: b. Feb. 20, 1903, Ingolstadt, Germany; ord. priest Oct. 28, 1928; studied at the Gregorian University, Rome, 1922-31; returned to Germany 1931; professor at Higher Institute for Philosophical and Theological Studies at Eichstatt; vicar general of diocese of Eichstatt, 1941-48; ord. bishop of Eichstatt, Sept. 21, 1948; app. titular archbishop of Volturnum and secretary of Sacred Congregation for Catholic Education, 1968; cardinal May 24, 1976; deacon, San Saba. Member of:
Council for Public Affairs of the Church;
Congregations: Doctrine of the Faith, Bishops;
Tribunal: Apostolic Signatura;
Commissions: Council for Laity, Revision of Code of Canon Law;
Office: Administration of Patrimony of Holy See.

Sensi, Giuseppe Maria: b. May 27, 1907, Cosenza, Italy; ord. priest Dec. 21, 1929; entered Vatican diplomatic service; served in nunciatures in Hungary, Switzerland, Belgium and Czechoslovakia, 1934-49; ord. titular archbishop of Sardes, July 24, 1955; apostolic nuncio to Costa Rica, 1955; apostolic delegate to Jerusalem, 1956-62; nuncio to Ireland, 1962-67, and Portugal, 1967-76; cardinal May 24, 1976; deacon, SS. Biagio e Carlo (ai Catinari). Member of:
Congregations: Oriental Churches, Causes of Saints, Evangelization of Peoples;
Commission: State of Vatican City.

Shehan,* Lawrence J.: b. Mar. 18, 1898,

Baltimore, Md.; ord. priest Dec. 23, 1922; ord. titular bishop of Lidda and auxiliary bishop of Baltimore and Washington, Dec. 12, 1945; bishop of Bridgeport, 1953-61; titular archbishop of Nicopolis ad Nestum and coadjutor archbishop of Baltimore, July 10, 1961; archbishop of Baltimore, 1961-74; cardinal Feb. 22, 1965; titular church, St. Clement. Former archbishop of Baltimore.

Sidarouss, Stephanos I, C.M.: b. Feb. 22, 1904, Cairo, Egypt; ord. priest July 2, 1939; ord. titular bishop of Sais, Jan. 25, 1948; auxiliary to the patriarch of Alexandria for the Copts, 1948-58; patriarch of Alexandria, May 10, 1958; cardinal Feb. 22, 1965. Patriarch of Alexandria for the Copts, member of:
Congregation: Oriental Churches;
Secretariat: Christian Unity;
Commissions: Revision of Code of Canon Law, Revision of Code of Oriental Canon Law.

Silva Henriquez, Raul, S.D.B.: b. Sept. 27, 1907, Talca, Chile; ord. priest July 3, 1938; ord. bishop of Valparaiso, Nov. 29, 1959; archbishop of Santiago de Chile, Mar. 14, 1961; cardinal Mar. 19, 1962; titular church, St. Bernard (alle Terme). Archbishop of Santiago de Chile, member of:
Commission: Revision of Code.

Sin, Jaime L.: b. Aug. 31, 1928, New Washington, Philippines; ord. priest Apr. 3, 1954; diocesan missionary in Capiz, 1954-57; app. first rector of the St. Pius X Seminary, Roxas City, 1957; ord. titular bishop of Obba and auxiliary bishop of Jaro, Mar. 18, 1967; apostolic administrator of archdiocese of Jaro, June 20, 1970; titular archbishop of Massa Lubrense and coadjutor archbishop of Jaro, Jan. 15, 1972; archbishop of Jaro, Oct. 8, 1972; archbishop of Manila, Jan. 21, 1974; cardinal May 24, 1976; titular church, S. Maria (ai Monti). Archbishop of Manila, member of:
Congregations: Evangelization of Peoples, Catholic Education;
Secretariat: Non-Christians;
Commission: Social Communications;
Office: Prefecture of Economic Affairs.

Siri, Giuseppe: b. May 20, 1906, Genoa, Italy; ord. priest Sept. 22, 1928; ord. titular bishop of Liviade and auxiliary bishop of Genoa, May 7, 1944; archbishop of Genoa, May 14, 1946; cardinal Jan. 12, 1953; titular church, St. Mary (della Vittoria). Archbishop of Genoa, member of:
Congregations: Clergy, Catholic Education;
Commission: Revision of Code of Canon Law.

Slipyi or Slipyj,* Josyf (Kobernyckyj-Dyckowskyj): b. Feb. 17, 1892, Zazdrist in the Ukraine; ord. priest Sept. 30, 1917; ord. titular archbishop of Serre, Dec. 22, 1939; coadjutor archbishop of Lwow for the Ukrainians, 1939-44; archbishop of Lwow,

Nov. 1, 1944; imprisoned 1945-63 for unspecified crimes; released by Soviets and allowed to go to Rome in February, 1963; named major archbishop by Paul VI, 1963; cardinal Feb. 22, 1965; titular church, St. Athanasius. Major Archbishop of Lwow of the Ukrainians (not permitted to exercise his office; he resides in Vatican City).

Suenens, Leo Josef: b. July 16, 1904, Brussels, Belgium; ord. priest Sept. 4, 1927; ord. titular bishop of Isinda, Dec. 16, 1945; auxiliary bishop of Mechelen, 1945-61; archbishop of Mechelen-Brussels, 1961-79; cardinal Mar. 19, 1962; titular church, St. Peter in Chains. Former archbishop of Mechelen-Brussels, member of:
Congregations: Evangelization of Peoples, Causes of Saints;
Commission: Revision of Canon Law.

Taofinu'u, Pio, S.M.: b. Dec. 9, 1923, Falealupo, W. Samoa; ord. priest Dec. 8, 1954; joined Society of Mary, 1955; ord. bishop of Apia (now Samoa and Tokelau), May 29, 1968, the first Polynesian bishop; cardinal Mar. 5, 1973; titular church, St. Humphrey (on the Janiculum). Bishop of Samoa and Tokelau, member of:
Congregation: Causes of Saints.

Thiandoum, Hyacinthe: b. Feb. 2, 1921, Poponguine, Senegal; ord. priest Apr. 18, 1949; studied at Gregorian University, Rome, 1951-53; returned to Senegal, 1953; ord. archbishop of Dakar, May 20, 1962; cardinal May 24, 1976; titular church, S. Maria (del Popolo). Archbishop of Dakar, president of Senegal-Mauretania Episcopal Conference, member of:
Congregation: Religious and Secular Institutes;
Commission: Social Communications.

Tomasek,* Frantisek: b. June 30, 1899, Studenka, Moravia, Czechoslovakia; ord. priest July 5, 1922; professor of pedagogy and catechetics at the theology faculty of Olomouc, 1934-39; resumed academic activity after liberation in 1945; author, *Catechism of the Catholic Religion;* ord. titular bishop of Butus and auxiliary of Olomouc, Oct. 13, 1949; only Czech bishop to attend Second Vatican Council; apostolic administrator of Prague, Feb. 18, 1965; cardinal May 24, 1976 (*in pectore*); solemnly proclaimed at June 27, 1977, consistory; titular church, Sts. Vitalis, Valeria, Gervase and Protase. Archbishop of Prague, 1978, member of:
Congregation: Clergy.

Trinh van-Can, Joseph-Marie: b. Mar. 19, 1921, Trac But, Vietnam; ord. priest Dec. 8, 1949; held various offices in Hanoi archdiocese; ord. titular bishop of Ela (with personal title of archbishop) and coadjutor archbishop of Hanoi, June 2, 1963; archbishop of Hanoi, Nov. 27, 1978; cardinal June 30, 1979; titular church, St. Mary in Via. Archbishop of Hanoi, member of:

Congregation: Evangelization of Peoples.

Ursi, Corrado: b. July 26, 1908, Andria, Italy; ord. priest July 25, 1931; vice-rector and later rector of the Pontifical Regional Seminary of Molfetta, 1931-51; ord. bishop of Nardo, Sept. 30, 1951; archbishop of Acerenza, Nov. 30, 1961; archbishop of Naples, May 23, 1966; cardinal June 26, 1967; titular church, St. Callistus. Archbishop of Naples, member of:
Congregation: Catholic Education.

Volk, Hermann: b. Dec. 27, 1903, Steinheim, Germany; ord. priest Apr. 2, 1927; professor of dogmatic theology at University of Muenster; ord. bishop of Mainz, June 5, 1962; cardinal Mar. 5, 1973; titular church, Saints Fabian and Venanzio (at Villa Fiorelli). Bishop of Mainz, member of:
Secretariat: Christian Unity.

Willebrands, Johannes: b. Sept. 4, 1909, Bovenkarspel, The Netherlands; ord. priest May 26, 1934; ord. titular bishop of Mauriana, June 28, 1964; secretary of Secretariat for Christian Unity, 1960-69; cardinal Apr. 28, 1969; titular church, St. Sebastian (alle Catacombe). President of Secretariat for Christian Unity, 1969, Archbishop of Utrecht, 1975, military vicar of The Netherlands, member of:
Congregations: Doctrine of Faith, Sacraments and Divine Worship, Oriental Churches, Catholic Education, Evangelization of Peoples;
Commissions: Revision of Code of Canon Law, Revision of Oriental Code.

Zoungrana, Paul, P.A.: b. Sept. 3, 1917, Ouagadougou, Upper Volta; ord. priest May 2, 1942, in the Missionaries of Africa; ord. archbishop of Ouagadougou at St. Peter's Basilica by John XXIII, May 8, 1960; cardinal Feb. 22, 1965; titular church, St. Camillus de Lellis. Archbishop of Ouagadougou, member of:
Congregation: Evangelization of Peoples.

CATEGORIES OF CARDINALS
(As of Aug. 1, 1982.)

Information below includes categories of cardinals and dates of consistories at which they were created. Seniority or precedence usually depends on order of elevation, except in the case of cardinal bishops whose seniority depends on date of appointment to suburban see.

Three of these cardinals were named by Pius XII (consistories of Feb. 18, 1946, and Jan. 12, 1953); 10 by John XXIII (consistories of Dec. 15, 1958, Dec. 14, 1959, Mar. 28, 1960, Jan. 16, 1961, and Mar. 19, 1962); 95 by Paul VI (consistories of Feb. 22, 1965, June 26, 1967, Apr. 28, 1969, Mar. 5, 1973, May 24, 1976, and June 27, 1977); 14 by John Paul II (consistory of June 30, 1979).

Order of Bishops
Titular Bishops of Suburban Sees: Carlo

Confalonieri, Dean (Dec. 15, 1958); Paolo Marella (Dec. 14, 1959); Antonio Samore (June 26, 1967); Sebastiano Baggio (Apr. 28, 1969); Francesco Carpino (June 26, 1967); Paolo Bertoli (Apr. 28, 1969).

Eastern Rite Patriarch: Stephanos I Sidarouss, C.M. (Feb. 22, 1965).

Order of Priests

1946 (Feb. 18): Carlos Carmelo de Vasconcellos Motta.

1953 (Jan. 12): Giuseppe Siri, Paul Emile Leger, S.S.

1958 (Dec. 15): Jose M. Bueno y Monreal, Franz Koenig.

1960 (Mar. 28): Bernard Jan Alfrink, Laurean Rugambwa.

1961 (Jan. 16): Jose Humberto Quintero.

1962 (Mar. 19): Juan Landazuri Ricketts, O.F.M., Raul Silva Henriquez, S.D.B., Leo Josef Suenens.

1965 (Feb. 22): Josyf Slipyi, Thomas B. Cooray, Maurice Roy, Owen McCann, Leon-Etienne Duval, Ermenegildo Florit, Paul Zoungrana, Lawrence J. Shehan, Agnelo Rossi, Giovanni Colombo.

1967 (June 26): Gabriel Garrone, Patrick O'Boyle, Maximilien de Furstenberg, Jose Clemente Maurer, C.SS.R., Pietro Parente, John J. Krol, Corrado Ursi, Justin Darmojuwono, Michele Pellegrino, Alexandre Renard.

1969 (Apr. 28): Alfredo Vicente Scherer, Julio Rosales, Gordon J. Gray, Silvio Oddi, Miguel Dario Miranda y Gomez, Giuseppe Paupini, Joseph Parecattil, John F. Dearden, Francois Marty;

George Flahiff, Paul Gouyon, Mario Casariego, Vicente Enrique y Tarancon, Joseph Malula, Pablo Muñoz Vega, S.J., Antonio Poma;

John J. Carberry, Terence J. Cooke, Stephan Sou Hwan Kim, Eugenio de Araujo Sales, Joseph Hoeffner, Johannes Willebrands, Mario Nasalli Rocca di Corneliano, Sergio Guerri.

1973 (Mar. 5): Antonio Ribeiro, James Robert Knox, Avelar Brandao Vilela, Joseph Cordeiro, Anibal Muñoz Duque, Luis Aponte Martinez, Raul Francisco Primatesta, Salvatore Pappalardo, Marcelo Gonzalez Martin, Louis Jean Guyot, Ugo Poletti, Timothy Manning, Maurice Otunga, Jose Salazar Lopez, Humberto S. Medeiros, Paulo Evaristo Arns, James Darcy Freeman, Narciso Jubany Arnau, Hermann Volk, Pio Taofinu'u.

1976 (May 24): Octavio Beras Rojas, Juan Carlos Aramburu, Hyacinthe Thiandoum, Emmanuel Nsubuga, Lawrence Trevor Picachy, Jaime L. Sin, William W. Baum, Aloisio Lorscheider, Laszlo Lekai, George Basil Hume, O.S.B., Victor Razafimahatratra, Frantisek Tomasek, Dominic Ekandem.

1977 (June 27): Giovanni Benelli, Joseph Ratzinger.

1979 (June 30): Agostino Casaroli, Marco Ce, Joseph-Marie Trinh van-Can, Ernesto Corripio Ahumada, Joseph Asajiro Satowaki, Roger Etchegaray, Anastasio Alberto Ballestrero, O.C.D., Tomas O'Fiaich, Gerald Emmett Carter, Franciszek Macharski.

Order of Deacons

1973 (Mar. 5): Umberto Mozzoni, Pierre Paul Philippe, Pietro Palazzini, Ferdinando Giuseppe Antonelli.

1976 (May 24): Opilio Rossi, Giuseppe Maria Sensi, Corrado Bafile, Joseph Schroeffer, Eduardo Pironio.

1977 (June 27): Bernardin Gantin, Luigi Ciappi.

1979 (June 30): Giuseppe Caprio, Egano Righi-Lambertini, Ernesto Civardi, Wladyslaw Rubin.

Ineligible To Vote

As of Aug. 1, 1982, fifteen of the 122 cardinals were ineligible to take part in a papal election in line with the apostolic letter *Ingravescentem Aetatem* effective Jan. 1, 1971, which limited the functions of cardinals after completion of their 80th year.

Cardinals affected were: Alfrink, Antonelli, Confalonieri, Cooray, Florit, Garrone, Marella, Maurer, Miranda y Gomez, Motta, O'Boyle, Parente, Shehan, Slipyi, Tomasek.

Two more cardinals were due to become ineligible to vote by the end of 1982: Jose Humberto Quintero, after Sept. 22; Giovanni Colombo, after Dec. 6.

Cardinals completing their 80th year in 1983: Alfred Vicente Scherer, Feb. 5; Joseph Schroeffer, Feb. 20; Michele Pellegrino, Apr. 25; Pablo Munoz Vega, May 23; Corrado Bafile, July 4; Mario Nassali Rocca di Corneliano, Aug. 12; Leon-Etienne Duval, Nov. 9; Hermann Volk, Dec. 27.

DISTRIBUTION OF CARDINALS

As of Aug. 1, 1982, there were 122 cardinals from more than 50 countries or areas. Listed below are areas, countries, number and last names.

Europe — 62

Italy (33): Antonelli, Bafile, Baggio, Ballestrero, Benelli, Bertoli, Caprio, Carpino, Casaroli, Cé, Ciappi, Civardi, Colombo, Confalonieri, Florit, Guerri, Marella, Mozzoni, Nasalli Rocca di Corneliano, Oddi, Palazzini, Pappalardo, Parente, Paupini, Pellegrino, Poletti, Poma, Righi-Lambertini, Rossi, Samore, Sensi, Siri, Ursi.

France (7): Etchegaray, Garrone, Gouyon, Guyot, Marty, Philippe, Renard.

Germany (4): Hoeffner, Ratzinger, Schroeffer, Volk.

Spain (4): Bueno y Monreal, Enrique y Tarancon, Gonzalez Martin, Jubany Arnau.

Netherlands (3): Alfrink, De Furstenberg, Willebrands.

Poland (2): Macharski, Rubin.

One from each of the following countries: Austria, Koenig; Belgium, Suenens; Czechoslovakia, Tomasek; England, Hume; Hungary, Lekai; Ireland, O'Fiaich; Portugal, Ribeiro; Scotland, Gray; Ukraine (now in USSR), Slipyi.

Asia — 10

India (2): Parecattil, Picachy.

Philippines (2): Rosales, Sin.

One from each of the following countries: Indonesia, Darmojuwono; Japan, Satowaki; Korea, Kim; Pakistan, Cordeiro; Sri Lanka, Cooray; Vietnam, Trinh van-Can.

Oceania — 3

Australia (2): Freeman, Knox; Pacific Islands (Samoa), Taofinu'u.

Africa — 12

One from each of the following countries: Algeria, Duval; Benin, Gantin; Egypt, Sidarouss; Kenya, Otunga; Madagascar, Razafimahatratra; Nigeria, Ekandem; Senegal, Thiandoum; South Africa, McCann; Tanzania, Rugambwa; Uganda, Nsubuga; Upper Volta, Zoungrana; Zaire, Malula.

North America — 17

United States (9): Baum, Carberry, Cooke, Dearden, Krol, Manning, Medeiros, O'Boyle, Shehan.

Canada (4): Carter, Flahiff, Leger, Roy.

Mexico (3): Corripio Ahumada, Miranda y Gomez, Salazar Lopez.

Puerto Rico (1): Aponte Martinez.

Central and South America — 18

Brazil (7): Arns, Brandao Vilela, De Araujo Sales, Lorscheider, Motta, Rossi, Scherer.

Argentina (3): Aramburu, Pironio, Primatesta.

One from each of the following countries: Bolivia, Maurer; Chile, Silva Henriquez; Colombia, Munoz Duque; Dominican Republic, Beras Rojas; Ecuador, Munoz Vega, S.J.; Guatemala, Casariego (b. Spain); Peru, Landazuri Ricketts; Venezuela, Quintero.

Cardinals of U.S.

As of Aug. 1, 1982, U.S. cardinals, years of elevation and sees.

Lawrence J. Shehan, 1965, Baltimore (retired 1974); Patrick A. O'Boyle, 1967, Washington (retired 1973); John J. Krol, 1967, Philadelphia; John F. Dearden, 1969, Detroit (retired 1980); John J. Carberry, 1969, St. Louis (retired 1979); Terence J. Cooke, 1969, New York; Timothy Manning, 1973, Los Angeles; Humberto S. Medeiros, 1973, Boston; William W. Baum, 1976, Washington, D.C. (1973-80); prefect of Congregation for Catholic Education, 1980.

Deceased cardinals of the United States,. Data: years of elevation, sees, years of birth and death.

John McCloskey, 1875, New York, 1810-1885; James Gibbons, 1886, Baltimore, 1834-1921; John Farley, 1911, New York, 1842-1918; William O'Connell, 1911, Boston, 1859-1944; Dennis Dougherty, 1921, Philadelphia, 1865-1951; Patrick Hayes, 1924, New York, 1867-1938; George Mundelein, 1924, Chicago, 1872-1939; John Glennon, 1946, St. Louis, 1862-1946; Edward Mooney, 1946, Detroit, 1882-1958;

Francis Spellman, 1946, New York, 1889-1967; Samuel Stritch, 1946, Chicago, 1887-1958; James F. McIntyre, 1953, Los Angeles, 1886-1979; John O'Hara, C.S.C., 1958, Philadelphia, 1888-1960; Richard Cushing, 1958, Boston, 1895-1970; Albert Meyer, 1959, Chicago, 1903-1965; Aloysius Muench, 1959, Fargo (and papal nuncio), 1889-1962; Joseph Ritter, 1961, St. Louis, 1892-1967; Francis Brennan, 1967, official of Roman Curia, 1894-1968; John P. Cody, 1967, Chicago 1907-1982; John J. Wright, 1969, prefect of Congregation for Clergy, 1909-1979.

REPRESENTATIVES OF THE HOLY SEE

Papal representatives and their functions were the subject of a document entitled *Sollicitudo Omnium Ecclesiarum* which Pope Paul VI issued on his own initiative under the date of June 24, 1969.

Delegates and Nuncios

Papal representatives "receive from the Roman Pontiff the charge of representing him in a fixed way in the various nations or regions of the world.

"When their legation is only to local churches, they are known as apostolic delegates. When to this legation, of a religious and ecclesial nature, there is added diplomatic legation to states and governments, they receive the title of nuncio, pro-nuncio, and internuncio."

[An apostolic nuncio has the diplomatic rank of ambassador extraordinary and plenipotentiary. Traditionally, because the Vatican diplomatic service has the longest uninterrupted history in the world, a nuncio has precedence among diplomats in the country to which he is accredited and serves as dean of the diplomatic corps on state occasions. Since 1965 pro-nuncios, also of ambassadorial rank, have been assigned to countries in which this prerogative is not recognized.]

(Other representatives, who are covered in the Almanac article, Vatican Representatives to International Organizations, are clerics and lay persons "who form . . . part of a pontifical mission attached to international organizations or take part in conferences and congresses." They are variously called delegates or observers.)

"The primary and specific purpose of the mission of a papal representative is to render ever closer and more operative the ties that bind the Apostolic See and the local churches.

"The ordinary function of a pontifical representative is to keep the Holy See regularly and objectively informed about the conditions of the ecclesial community to which he has been sent, and about what may affect the life of the Church and the good of souls.

"On the one hand, he makes known to the Holy See the thinking of the bishops, clergy, religious and faithful of the territory where he carries out his mandate, and forwards to Rome their proposals and their requests; on the other hand, he makes himself the interpreter, with those concerned, of the acts, documents, information and instructions emanating from the Holy See."

Service and Liaison

Representatives, while carrying out their general and special duties, are bound to respect the autonomy of local churches and bishops. Their service and liaison responsibilities include the following:

• **Nomination of Bishops:** To play a key role in compiling, with the advice of ecclesiastics and lay persons, and submitting lists of names of likely candidates to the Holy See with their own recommendations.

• **Bishops:** To aid and counsel local bishops without interfering in the affairs of their jurisdictions.

• **Episcopal Conferences:** To maintain close relations with them and to assist them in every possible way. (Papal representatives do not belong to these conferences.)

• **Religious Communities of Pontifical Rank:** To advise and assist major superiors for the purpose of promoting and consolidating conferences of men and women religious and to coordinate their apostolic activities.

• **Church-State Relations:** The thrust in this area is toward the development of sound relations with civil governments and collaboration in work for peace and the total good of the whole human family.

The mission of a papal representative begins with appointment and assignment by the pope and continues until termination of his mandate. He acts "under the guidance and according to the instructions of the cardinal secretary of state and prefect of the Council for the Public Affairs of the Church, to whom he is directly responsible for the execution of the mandate entrusted to him by the Supreme Pontiff." Normally, representatives are required to retire at the age of 75.

"L'Osservatore Romano" reported Feb. 10, 1982, that representatives of the Holy See attended 216 international meetings in 1981.

NUCIOS AND DELEGATES

(Sources: *Annuario Pontificio, L'Osservatore Romano,* NC News Service.)

Data, as of Aug. 1, 1982, country, rank of legation (corresponding to rank of legate unless otherwise noted), name of legate (archbishop unless otherwise noted) as available.

Delegate for Papal Representatives: Archbishop Giovanni Coppa. The post was established in 1973 to coordinate papal diplomatic efforts throughout the world. The office entails responsibility for "following more closely through timely visits the activities of papal representatives ... and encouraging their rapport with the central offices" of the Secretariat of State and the Council for the Public Affairs of the Church.

Africa, Southern (Botswana, South Africa, Namibia, Swaziland): Pretoria, South Africa, Apostolic Delegation; Edward Cassidy (also Pro-Nuncio to Lesotho).

Algeria: Algiers, Nunciature; Gabriel Montalvo, Pro-Nuncio (He is also Pro-Nuncio to Tunisia and Apostolic Delegate to Libya.)

Angola: Luanda, Apostolic Delegation; Giovanni De Andrea.

Antilles: Apostolic Delegation; Paul Fouad Tabat (resides in Port of Spain, Trinidad).

Argentina: Buenos Aires, Nunciature; Ubaldo Calabresi.

Australia: Canberra, Nunciature; Luigi Barbarito, Pro-Nuncio.

Austria: Vienna, Nunciature; Mario Cagna.

Bahamas: Nunciature; Paul Fouad Tabat, Pro-Nuncio (resides in Port of Spain).

Bangladesh: Dacca, Nunciature; Luigi Accogli, Pro-Nuncio (also serves as Apostolic Delegate to Burma.)

Barbados: Nunciature; Paul Fouad Tabat, Pro-Nuncio (resides in Port of Spain, Trinidad).

Belgium: Brussels, Nunciature; Igino Cardinale (also Nuncio to Luxembourg).

Benin (formerly Dahomey): Nunciature; Ivan Dias, Pro-Nuncio (resides in Accra, Ghana).

Bolivia: La Paz, Nunciature; Alfio Rapisarda.

Botswana: See Africa, Southern.

Brazil: Brasilia, Nunciature; Carmine Rocco.

Burma: See Bangladesh.

Burundi: Bujumbura, Nunciature; Bernard Jacqueline, Pro-Nuncio.

Cameroon: Yaounde, Nunciature; Donato Squicciarino, Pro-Nuncio (also Pro-Nuncio to Gabon Republic and Equatorial Guinea).

Canada: Ottawa, Nunciature; Angelo Palmas, Pro-Nuncio.

Cape Verde, Republic of: Nunciature; Luigi Dossena, Pro-Nuncio (resides in Dakar, Senegal).

Central African Republic: Bangui, Nunciature; Giovanni Bulaitis, Pro-Nuncio (also Pro-Nuncio to Congo and Apostolic Delegate to Chad).

Chad: Apostolic Delegation; Giovanni Bulaitis (resides in Bangui, Central African Republic).

Chile: Santiago, Nunciature; Angelo Sodano.

China: Taipei (Taiwan), Nunciature.

Colombia: Bogota, Nunciature; Angelo Acerbi.

Congo Republic: Brazzaville, Nunciature; Giovanni Bulaitis, Pro-Nuncio (resides in Bangui, Central African Republic).

Costa Rica: San Jose, Nunciature; Lajos Kada (also Nuncio to El Salvador).

Cuba: Havana, Nunciature; Giuglio Einaudi, Pro-Nuncio.

Cyprus: Nicosia, Nunciature; William A. Carew, Pro-Nuncio (also Apostolic Delegate to Jerusalem).

Denmark: Relations established in 1982.

Djibouti: See Red Sea Region.

Dominica: Nunciature: Paul Fouad Tabet, Pro-Nuncio (resides in Port-of-Spain, Trinidad).

Dominican Republic: Santo Domingo, Nunciature; Blasco Francisco Collaco (also Apostolic Delegate to Puerto Rico).

Ecuador: Quito, Nunciature; Vincenzo Farano.

Egypt: Cairo, Nunciature; Achille Glorieux, Pro-Nuncio.

El Salvador: San Salvador, Nunciature; Lajos Kada (also Nuncio to Costa Rica).

Equatorial Guinea: Santa Isabel, Nunciature; Donato Squicciarino, Pro-Nuncio (resides in Yaounde, Cameroon).

Ethiopia: Addis Ababa, Nunciature; Raymond Etteldorf, Pro-Nuncio.

Fiji: Nunciature; Antonio Magnoni, Pro-Nuncio (resides in New Zealand).

Finland: Helsinki, Nunciature; Luigi Bellotti, Pro-Nuncio.

France: Paris, Nunciature; Angelo Felici.

Gabon Republic: Libreville, Nunciature; Donato Squicciarino, Pro-Nuncio (resides in Yaounde, Cameroon).

Gambia: Nunciature; Johannes Dyba, Pro-Nuncio (resides in Monrovia, Liberia).

Germany: Bonn, Nunciature; Guido Del Mestri.

Ghana: Accra, Nunciature; Ivan Dias, Pro-Nuncio (also Pro-Nuncio to Benin and Togo).

Great Britain: London, Nunciature; Bruno Heim, Pro-Nuncio (also Apostolic Delegate to Gibraltar).

Greece: Athens, Nunciature; Giovanni Mariani, Pro-Nuncio.

Grenada: Nunciature.

Guatemala: Guatemala City, Nunciature; Oriano Quilici.

Guinea: Conakry, Apostolic Delegation; Johannes Dyba (resides in Monrovia, Liberia).

Guinea-Bissau: Apostolic Delegation; Luigi Dossena (resides at Dakar, Senegal).

Haiti: Port-au-Prince, Nunciature; Luigi Conti.

Honduras: Tegucigalpa, Nunciature; Andrea Cordero Lanza di Montezemolo. (also Nuncio to Nicaragua).

Iceland: Nunciature; Luigi Bellotti, Pro-Nuncio.

India: New Delhi, Nunciature; Agostino Caccavillan, Pro-Nuncio.

Indonesia: Jakarta, Nunciature; Pablo Puente, Pro-Nuncio.

Iran: Teheran, Nunciature; Pro-Nuncio.

Iraq: Baghdad, Nunciature; Antonio Del Giudice, Pro-Nuncio (also Pro-Nuncio to Kuwait).

Ireland: Dublin, Nunciature; Gaetano Alibrandi.

Italy: Rome, Nunciature; Romolo Carboni.

Ivory Coast: Abidjan, Nunciature; Justo Mullor Garcia (also Pro-Nuncio to Niger and Upper Volta).

Jamaica: Nunciature; Paul Fouad Tabat, Pro-Nuncio (resides in Port of Spain).

Japan: Tokyo, Nunciature; Mario Pio Gaspari, Pro-Nuncio.

Jerusalem, Palestine, Jordan, Israel: Jerusalem, Apostolic Delegation; William A. Carew (also Pro-Nuncio to Cyprus).

Kenya: Nairobi, Nunciature; Giuseppe Ferraioli, Pro-Nuncio (also Apostolic Delegate to Seychelles Is.).

Korea: Seoul, Nunciature; Luciano Angeloni, Pro-Nuncio.

Kuwait: Al Kuwait, Nunciature; Antonio Del Giudice, Pro-Nuncio (resides in Baghdad, Iraq).

Laos and Malaysia: Apostolic Delegation; Renato Raffaele Martino (resides in Bangkok, Thailand).

Lebanon: Beirut, Nunciature; Carlo Furno.

Lesotho: Maseru, Nunciature; Edward Cassidy, Pro-Nuncio (resides in Pretoria, S. Africa).

Liberia: Monrovia, Nunciature; Johannes Dyba, Pro-Nuncio (also Pro-Nuncio to Gambia and Apostolic Delegate to Guinea and Sierra Leone).

Libya: Apostolic Delegation; Gabriel Montalvo (resides in Algiers, Algeria).

Luxembourg: Nunciature; Igino Cardinale (resides in Brussels, Belgium).

Madagascar: Tananarive, Nunciature; Sergio Sebastiani, Pro-Nuncio (also Pro-Nuncio to Mauritius and Apostolic Delegate to Reunion).

Malawi: Lilongwe, Nunciature; Georg Zur, Pro-Nuncio (resides in Zambia).

Mali: Nunciature; Luigi Dossena, Pro-Nuncio (resides in Dakar, Senegal).

Malta: La Valletta, Nunciature.

Mauritania: Nouakchott, Apostolic Delegation; Luigi Dossena (resides in Dakar, Senegal).

Mauritius: Port Louis, Nunciature; Sergio Sebastiani, Pro-Nuncio (resides in Tananarive, Madagascar).

Mexico: Mexico City, Apostolic Delegation; Girolamo Prigione.

Morocco: Rabat, Nunciature; Pro-Nuncio.

Mozambique: Maputo, Apostolic Delegation; Francesco Colasuonna. (also Pro-Nuncio to Zimbabwe).

Namibia: See Africa, Southern.

Netherlands: The Hague, Nunciature; Bruno Wustenberg, Pro-Nuncio.

New Zealand: Wellington, Nunciature; Antonio Magnoni. (He is also Pro-Nuncio to Fiji and Apostolic Delegate to Pacific Islands).

Nicaragua: Managua, Nunciature; Andrea Cordero Lanza di Montezemolo (also Nuncio to Honduras).

Niger: Niamey, Nunciature; Justo Mullor Garcia, Pro-Nuncio (resides in Abidjan, Ivory Coast).

Nigeria: Lagos, Nunciature; Carlo Curis, Pro-Nuncio.

Norway: Relations established in 1982.

Pacific Islands: See New Zealand.

Pakistan: Islamabad, Nunciature; Emmanuele Gerada, Pro-Nuncio.

Panama: Panama, Nunciature; Blasco Francisco Collaco.

Papua New Guinea: Port Moresby; Nunciature; Francesco De Nittis, Pro-Nuncio. (He is also Apostolic Delegate to western and southern Solomon Islands.)

Paraguay: Asuncion, Nunciature; Joseph Mees.

Peru: Lima, Nunciature; Mario Tagliaferri.

Philippines: Manila, Nunciature; Bruno Torpigliani.

Portugal: Lisbon, Nunciature; Sante Portalupi.

Puerto Rico: See Dominican Republic.

Red Sea Region (Somalia, Djibouti, part of Arabian Peninsula): Apostolic Delegation; Giovanni Moretti (resides in Khartoum, Sudan).

Reunion: See Madagascar.

Rhodesia: See Zimbabwe.

Rwanda: Kigali, Nunciature; Thomas White.

Senegal: Dakar, Nunciature; Luigi Dossena, Pro-Nuncio (also Pro-Nuncio to Cape Verde Islands and Mali; Apostolic Delegate to Guinea-Bissau, and Mauritania.)

Seychelles Islands: See Kenya.

Sierra Leone: Apostolic Delegation; Johannes Dyba (resides in Monrovia, Liberia).

Singapore: Nunciature; Renato Raffaele Martino, Pro-Nuncio (resides in Bangkok, Thailand).

Solomon Islands: Apostolic Delegation;

Francesco De Nittis (resides in Port Moresby, Papua New Guinea).

Somalia: See Red Sea Region.

South Africa: See Africa, Southern.

Spain: Madrid, Nunciature; Antonio Innocenti.

Sri Lanka: Colombo, Nunciature; Nicola Rotunno, Pro-Nuncio.

Sudan: Khartoum, Nunciature; Giovanni Moretti, Pro-Nuncio (also Apostolic Delegate to Red Sea Region).

Swaziland: See Africa, Southern.

Sweden: Relations established in 1982.

Switzerland: Bern, Nunciature; Ambrogio Marchioni.

Syria (Syrian Arab Republic): Damascus, Nunciature; Angelo Pedroni, Pro-Nuncio.

Tanzania: Dar-es-Salaam, Nunciature; Gian Vincenzo Moreni, Pro-Nuncio.

Thailand: Bangkok, Nunciature; Renato Raffaelo Martino, Pro-Nuncio (also Pro-Nuncio to Singapore and Apostolic Delegate to Laos and Malaysia).

Togo: Lome, Nunciature; Ivan Dias, Pro-Nuncio (resides in Accra, Ghana).

Trinidad and Tobago: Port of Spain, Trinidad, Nunciature; Paul Fouad Tabat, Pro-Nuncio (also Pro-Nuncio to Bahamas, Barbados, Dominica, Jamaica and Apostolic Delegate to Antilles).

Tunisia: Tunis, Nunciature; Gabriel Montalvo, Pro-Nuncio (resides in Algiers, Algeria).

Turkey: Ankara, Nunciature; Salvatore Asta, Pro-Nuncio.

Uganda: Kampala, Nunciature; Pro-Nuncio.

United States of America: Washington, D.C., Apostolic Delegation; Pio Laghi.

Upper Volta: Ouagadougou, Nunciature; Justo Mullor Garcia, Pro-Nuncio (resides in Abidjan, Ivory Coast).

Uruguay: Montevideo, Nunciature; Franco Brambilla.

Venezuela: Caracas, Nunciature; Luciano Storero.

Vietnam and Cambodia: Apostolic Delegation.

Yugoslavia: Belgrade, Nunciature; Michele Cecchini, Pro-Nuncio.

Zaire: Kinshasa-Gombe, Nunciature; Giuseppe Uhac, Pro-Nuncio.

Zambia: Lusaka, Nunciature; Georg Zur, Pro-Nuncio (also Pro-Nuncio to Malawi).

Zimbabwe: Nunciature; Francesco Colasuonno, Pro-Nuncio (is also Apostolic Delegate to Mozambique).

Apostolic Delegate to U.S.

The representative of the Pope to the Church in the United States is Archbishop Pio Laghi, apostolic delegate. Archbishop Laghi was born May 21, 1922, in Castiglione, Italy. Ordained to the priesthood Apr. 20, 1946, he entered the Vatican diplomatic service in 1952. He served in Nicaragua, the U.S. (as secretary of the apostolic delegation, 1954-61) and India. He was recalled to Rome and served on the Council for the Public Affairs of the Church. He was appointed to the titular see of Mauriana and received episcopal ordination June 22, 1969. He was apostolic delegate to Jerusalem and Palestine, 1969-74, and apostolic nuncio to Argentina, 1974-80. On Dec. 10, 1980, he was appointed apostolic delegate to the United States and permanent observer to the Organization of American States.

The U.S. Apostolic Delegation was established Jan. 21, 1893. It is located at 3339 Massachusetts Ave. N.W., Washington, D.C. 20008.

Archbishop Laghi's predecessors were Archbishops: Francesco Satolli (1893-1896), Sebastiano Martinelli, O.S.A. (1896-1902), Diomede Falconio, O.F.M. (1902-1911), Giovanni Bonzano (1911-1922), Pietro Fumasoni-Biondi (1922-1933), Amleto Cicognani (1933-1958), Egidio Vagnozzi (1958-1967); Luigi Raimondi (1967-1973); Jean Jadot (1973-1980).

DIPLOMATS AT VATICAN

(Sources: *Annuario Pontificio, L'Osservatore Romano,* NC News Service. As of July 15, 1982.)

The dean of the diplomatic corps at the Vatican is Ambassador Luis Valladares y Aycinena of Guatemala, who has held the post since 1966.

Algeria: Anisse Salel-Bey, Ambassador.
Argentina: Jose Maria Alvarez de Toledo, Ambassador.
Australia: Lloyd Thomson, Ambassador.
Austria: Johannes Proksch, Ambassador.
Bahamas: Ambassador.
Bangladesh: Mohammed Sultan, Ambassador.
Barbados: Algernon Washington Symmonds, Ambassador.
Belgium: Eugene Rittweger de Moor, Ambassador.
Benin (formerly Dahomey): Douwa David Gbaguidi, Ambassador.
Bolivia: Ernesto Ruiz Rada, Ambassador.
Brazil: Antonio Correa do Lago, Ambassador.
Burundi: Ambassador.
Cameroon: Ambassador.
Canada: Yvon Beaulne, Ambassador.
Cape Verde, Republic of: Ambassador.
Central African Republic: Albert Sato, Ambassador.
Chile: Hector Riesle Contreras, Ambassador.
China (Taiwan): Chow Shu-Kai, Ambassador.
Colombia: Jose Manuel Rivas Sacconi, Ambassador.

Congo Republic: Jean-Pierre Nonault, Ambassador.
Costa Rica: Carlos Alberto Serrano Bonilla, Ambassador.
Cuba: Jose Antonio Portuondo, Ambassador.
Cyprus: Polys Modinos, Ambassador.
Denmark: Relations established in 1982.
Dominica: Ambassador (relations established in 1981).
Dominican Republic: Carlos Dobal Marquez, Ambassador.
Ecuador: Manuel De Guzman Polanco, Ambassador.
Egypt: Mostafa Kamal El-Diwani, Ambassador.
El Salvador: Prudencio Llach Schonenberg, Ambassador.
Equatorial Guinea: Ambassador (relations established 1981).
Ethiopia: Ambassador.
Fiji: Ambassador.
Finland: Bjorn-Olof Alholm, Ambassador.
France: Louis Dauge, Ambassador.
Gabon: Ambassador.
Gambia, The: Abdullah M.K. Boygang, Ambassador.
Germany: Walter Gehlhoff, Ambassador.
Ghana: Joseph Quao Cleland, Ambassador.
Great Britain: Mark Evelyn Heath, Ambassador.
Greece: Stephanos Stathatos, Ambassador.
Grenada: Ambassador.
Guatemala: Luis Valladares y Aycinena, Ambassador.
Haiti: Jean-Claude Andre, Ambassador.
Honduras: Alejandro Banegas, Ambassador.
Iceland: Niels P. Sigurdsson, Ambassador.
India: Narenda Singh, Ambassador.
Indonesia: Raymond Toto Prawira Supradja, Ambassador.
Iran: Seyed Hadi Khosroshahian, Ambassador.
Iraq: Anwar Sabri Abdul Razzak, Ambassador.
Ireland: Francis A. Coffey, Ambassador.
Italy: Claudio Chelli, Ambassador.
Ivory Coast: Joseph Amichia, Ambassador.
Jamaica: Keith Johnson, Ambassador.
Japan: Masami Ota, Ambassador.
Kenya: John Kamau Kimani, Ambassador.
Korea: Kim Joa Soo, Ambassador.
Kuwait: Essa Ahmad Al-Hamad, Ambassador.
Lebanon: Antoine Fattal, Ambassador.
Lesotho: Julius Nako Ts'oanamatsie, Ambassador.
Liberia: Ambassador.
Lithuania: Stasys Lozoraitis, Jr., first secretary.
Luxembourg: Jean Wagner, Ambassador.
Madagascar: Salomon Rahatoka, Ambassador.
Malawi: Ambassador.
Mali: Yaya Diarra, Ambassador.

Malta: Paolo Farrugia, Ambassador.
Mauritius: Leckraz Teelock, Ambassador.
Monaco: Cesar Charles Solamito, Ambassador.
Morocco: Youssef Ben Abbes, Ambassador.
Netherlands: Josef Laurentius Hubertus Ceulen, Ambassador.
New Zealand: John Vivian Scott, Ambassador.
Nicaragua: Ricardo Agustin Peters Silva, Ambassador.
Niger: Alzouma Tiecoura, Ambassador.
Nigeria: Isaac Jemide Sagay, Ambassador.
Norway: Relations established in 1982.
Order of Malta: Christophe de Kallay, Minister.
Pakistan: Ambassador.
Panama: Jose Manuel Watson Diez, Ambassador.
Papua New Guinea: Peter Ipu Paipul, Ambassador.
Paraguay: Juan Livieres Argana, Ambassador.
Peru: Jorge Nicholson Sologuren, Ambassador.
Philippines: Antonio C. Delgado, Ambassador.
Portugal: Goncalo Caldeiro Coelho, Ambassador.
Rwanda: Callixte Hatungimana, Ambassador.
San Marino: Dr. Giovanni Galassi, Minister.
Senegal: Paul Ndiaye, Ambassador.
Singapore: Chiang Hai Ding, Ambassador.
Spain: Jose Joaquin Puig de la Bellacasa y Urdampilleta, Ambassador.
Sri Lanka: Nadarajan Balasubramaniam, Ambassador.
Sudan: Bashir Bakri, Ambassador.
Sweden: Relations established in 1982.
Syria (Arab Republic): Adib Daoudy, Ambassador.
Tanzania: Nicholas J. Merinyo Maro, Ambassador.
Thailand: Varachit Nitibhon, Ambassador.
Togo: Vigniko A. Amedegnato, Ambassador.
Trinidad and Tobago: Ambassador.
Tunisia: Hedi Baccouche, Ambassador.
Turkey: Veedi Turel, Ambassador.
Uganda: Ambassador.
Upper Volta: Ambassador.
Uruguay: Carlos Maria Romero, Ambassador.
Venezuela: Luciano Joguera Mora, Ambassador.
Yugoslavia: Zvonimir Stenek, Ambassador.
Zaire: Tshimbalanga Shala-Dibwe, Ambassador.
Zambia: Peter Dingiswayo Zuze, Ambassador.
Zimbabwe: Ambassador.

Tightened security measures for the protection of Pope John Paul went into effect in October, 1981.

U.S. — VATICAN RELATIONS

Official relations for trade and diplomatic purposes were maintained by the United States and the Papal States while the latter had the character of and acted like other sovereign powers in the international community.

Consular Relations

Consular relations developed in the wake of an announcement, made by the papal nuncio in Paris to the American mission there Dec. 15, 1784, that the Papal States had agreed to open several Mediterranean ports to U.S. shipping.

U.S. consular representation in the Papal States began with the appointment of John B. Sartori, a native of Rome, in June, 1797. Sartori's successors as consuls were: Felix Cicognani, also a Roman, and Americans George W. Greene, Nicholas Browne, William C. Sanders, Daniel LeRoy, Horatio V. Glentworth, W.J. Stillman, Edwin C. Cushman, David M. Armstrong.

Consular officials of the Papal States who served in the U.S. were: Count Ferdinand Lucchesi, 1826 to 1829, who resided in Washington; John B. Sartori, 1829 to 1841, who resided in Trenton, N.J.; Daniel J. Desmond, 1841 to 1850, who resided in Philadelphia; Louis B. Binsse, 1850 to 1895, who resided in New York.

U.S. recognition of the consul of the Papal States did not cease when the states were absorbed into the Kingdom of Italy in 1871, despite pressure from Baron Blanc, the Italian minister. Binsse held the title until his death Mar. 28, 1895. No one was appointed to succeed him.

Diplomatic Relations

The U.S. Senate approved a recommendation, made by President James K. Polk in December, 1847, for the establishment of a diplomatic post in the Papal States. Jacob L. Martin, the first charge d'affaires, arrived in Rome Aug. 2, 1848, and presented his credentials to Pius IX Aug. 19. Martin, who died within a month, was succeeded by Lewis Cass, Jr. Cass became minister resident in 1854 and served in that capacity until his retirement in 1858.

John P. Stockton, who later became a U.S. Senator from New Jersey, was minister resident from 1858 to 1861. Rufus King was named to succeed him but, instead, accepted a commission as a brigadier general in the Army. Alexander W. Randall of Wisconsin took the appointment. He was succeeded in August, 1862, by Richard M. Blatchford who served until the following year. King was again nominated minister resident and served in that capacity until 1867 when the ministry was ended because of objections from some quarters in the U.S. and failure to appropriate funds for its continuation. J. C. Hooker, a secretary, remained in the Papal States until the end of March, 1868, closing the ministry and performing functions of courtesy.

Personal Envoys

Myron C. Taylor was appointed by President Franklin D. Roosevelt in 1939 to serve as his personal representative to Pope Pius XII and continued serving in that capacity during the presidency of Harry S. Truman until 1951. Henry Cabot Lodge was named to the post by President Richard M. Nixon in 1970, served also during the presidency of Gerald Ford, and represented President Carter at the canonization of St. John Neumann in 1977. Neither Taylor nor Lodge had diplomatic status.

Miami attorney David Walters, a Catholic, served as the personal envoy of President Jimmy Carter to the Pope from July, 1977, until his resignation Aug. 16, 1978. He was succeeded by Robert F. Wagner, also a Catholic and former mayor of New York, who served from October, 1978, to the end of the Carter presidency in January, 1981. William A.

Wilson, a California businessman and Catholic, was appointed by President Ronald Reagan in February, 1981, to serve as his personal envoy to the Pope.

None of the personal envoys had diplomatic status.

President Harry S. Truman nominated Gen. Mark Clark to be ambassador to the Vatican in 1951, but withdrew the nomination at Clark's request because of controversy over the appointment.

None of Truman's three successors — Dwight D. Eisenhower, John F. Kennedy or Lyndon B. Johnson — had a personal representative to the Pope.

At the time of Walters' designation for the non-diplomatic post, the House of Representatives had under consideration an amendment, already passed by the Senate, that would have lifted an 1867 prohibition against funding for diplomatic relations with the Vatican.

Any initiative for the establishment of formal diplomatic relations would have to be undertaken by the U.S. government.

VATICAN CITY

The State of Vatican City (Stato della Citta del Vaticano) is the territorial seat of the papacy. The smallest sovereign state in the world, it is situated within the city of Rome, embraces an area of 108.7 acres, and includes within its limits the Vatican Palace, museums, art galleries, gardens, libraries, radio station, post office, bank, astronomical observatory, offices, apartments, service facilities, St. Peter's Basilica, and neighboring buildings between the Basilica and Viale Vaticano.

The extraterritorial rights of Vatican City extend to more than 10 buildings in Rome, including the major basilicas and office buildings of various congregations of the Roman Curia, and to the Villa of Castel Gandolfo 15 miles southeast of the City of Rome. Castel Gandolfo is the summer residence of the Holy Father.

The government of Vatican City is in the hands of the reigning pope, who has full executive, legislative and judicial power. The administration of affairs, however, is handled by the Pontifical Commission for the State of Vatican City. The legal system is based on Canon Law; in cases where this code does not obtain, the laws of the City of Rome apply. The City is an absolutely neutral state and enjoys all the rights and privileges of a sovereign power. The Secretariat of State (Papal Secretariat) maintains diplomatic relations with other nations. The citizens of Vatican City, and they alone, owe allegiance to the pope as a temporal head of state.

Cardinals of the Roman Curia residing outside Vatican City enjoy the privileges of extraterritoriality.

The normal population is approximately

1,000. While the greater percentage is made up of priests and religious, there are several hundred lay persons living in Vatican City. They are housed in their own apartments in the City and are engaged in secretarial, domestic, trade and service occupations. About 4,000 persons are employed by the Vatican.

Services of honor and order are performed by the Swiss Guards, who have been charged with responsibility for the personal safety of popes since 1506. Additional police and ceremonial functions are under the supervision of a special office. These functions were formerly handled by the Papal Gendarmes, the Palatine Guard of Honor, and the Guard of Honor of the Pope (Pontifical Noble Guard) which Pope Paul disbanded Sept. 14, 1970.

The Basilica of St. Peter, built between 1506 and 1626, is the largest church in Christendom and the site of most papal ceremonies. The pope's own patriarchal basilica, however, is St. John Lateran, whose origins date back to 324.

St. Ann's is the parish church of Vatican City.

The vicar general of the pope for Vatican City, which is part of the diocese of Rome, is Most Rev. Peter Canisius Van Lierde, O.S.A., titular bishop of Porfireone.

The Vatican Library, one of five in the City, has among its holdings 70,000 manuscripts, 770,000 printed books, and 7,500 incunabula.

The independent temporal power of the pope, which is limited to the confines of Vatican City and small areas outside, was for many centuries more extensive than it is now. As late as the nineteenth century, the pope ruled 16,000 square miles of Papal States across the middle of Italy, with a population of over 3,000,000. In 1870 forces of the Kingdom of Italy occupied these lands which, with the exception of the small areas surrounding the Vatican and Lateran in Rome and the Villa of Castel Gandolfo, became part of the Kingdom by the Italian law of May 13, 1871.

The **Roman Question,** occasioned by this seizure and the voluntary confinement of the pope to the limited papal lands, was finally settled with ratification of the Lateran Agreement on June 7, 1929, by the Italian government and Vatican City and provided a financial indemnity for the former Papal States, which became recognized as part of Italy. The Lateran Agreement became Article 7 of the Italian Constitution on Mar. 26, 1947.

Papal Flag

The papal flag consists of two equal vertical stripes of yellow and white, charged with the insignia of the papacy on the white stripe — a triple crown or tiara over two crossed keys, one of gold and one of silver, tied with a red cord and two tassels. The divisions of the crown represent the teaching, sanctifying and ruling offices of the pope. The keys symbolize his jurisdictional authority.

The papal flag is a national flag inasmuch as it is the standard of the Supreme Pontiff as the sovereign of the state of Vatican City. It is also universally accepted by the faithful as a symbol of the supreme spiritual authority of the Holy Father.

In a Catholic church, the papal flag is displayed on a staff on the left side of the sanctuary (facing the congregation), and the American flag is displayed on the right.

Vatican Radio

The declared purpose of Vatican Radio Station HVJ is "that the voice of the Supreme Pastor may be heard throughout the world by means of the ether waves, for the glory of Christ and the salvation of souls." Designed by Guglielmo Marconi, the inventor of radio, and supervised by him until his death, the station was inaugurated by Pope Pius XI in 1931. The original purpose has been extended to a wide variety of programming.

Vatican Radio operates on international wave lengths, transmits programs in 35 languages, and serves as a channel of communication between the Vatican, church officials and listeners in general in many parts of the world. The station broadcasts about 240 hours a week throughout the world.

The staff of 300 broadcasters and technicians includes 32 Jesuits and is directed by Father Robert Tucci, S.J. Headquarters are located in Vatican City. Studios and offices are at Palazzo Pio, Piazza Pia, 3. The transmitters are situated at Santa Maria di Galeria, a short distance north of Rome.

1982 Vatican Stamps

The Vatican Philatelic Office scheduled the following issues of stamps and postal stationery for 1982. (Issue date is given where available.)

• Series commemorating the seventh centenary of the death of Bl. Agnes of Prague. Issued Feb. 16, 1982, in two values (700 and 900 lire) featuring two subjects..

• Series commemorating the fifth centenary of the death of the sculptor Luca della Robbia. Issued May 21, 1982, in three values of 1,000 lire each, joined in triptych.

• Series commemorating the fourth centenary of the death of St. Teresa of Avila.

• Series commemorating the fourth centenary of the reform of the Gregorian calendar.

• Series celebrating the Christian solemnity of Christmas.

• Air letter. Issued May 21, 1982.

• Illustrated stamped post cards.

Vatican Coins

The Vatican Numismatics Office issued a series of coins Mar. 22, 1982, for the third year of the pontificate of Pope John Paul II. The set consisted of six coins (10, 20, 50, 100, 200 and 500 lire).

Papal Audiences

General audiences are scheduled weekly, on Wednesday.

In Vatican City, they are held in the Audience Hall on the south side of St. Peter's Basilica. The hall, which was opened in 1971, has a seating capacity of 6,800 and a total capacity of 12,000.

Audiences are also held during the summer at Castel Gandolfo when the pope is there on a working vacation.

General audiences last from about 60 to 90 minutes, during which the pope gives a talk and his blessing. A résumé of the talk, which is usually in Italian, is given in several languages.

Arrangements for papal audiences are handled by an office of the Prefecture of the Apostolic Household.

American visitors can obtain passes for general audiences by applying to the Bishops' Office for United States Visitors to the Vatican, Casa Santa Maria, Via dell'Umilita, 30, 00187 Rome.

Private and group audiences are reserved for dignitaries of various categories and for special occasions.

Publications

Acta Apostolicae Sedis: The only "official commentary" of the Holy See, was established in 1908 for the publication of activities of the Holy See, laws, decrees and acts of congregations and tribunals of the Roman Curia. The first edition was published in January, 1909.

St. Pius X made *AAS* an official organ in 1908. Laws promulgated for the Church ordinarily take effect three months after the date of their publication in this commentary.

The publication, mostly in Latin and Italian, is printed by the Vatican Polyglot Press.

The immediate predecessor of this organ was *Acta Sanctae Sedis*, founded in 1865 and given official status by the Congregation for the Propagation of the Faith in 1904.

Annuario Pontificio: The yearbook of the Holy See. It is edited by the Central Statistics Office of the Church and is printed in Italian, with some portions in other languages, by the Vatican Polyglot Press. It covers the worldwide organization of the Church, lists members of the hierarchy, and includes a wide range of statistical information.

The publication of a statistical yearbook of the Holy See dates back to 1716, when a volume called *Notizie* appeared. Publication under the present title began in 1860, was suspended in 1870, and resumed again in 1872 under the title *Catholic Hierarchy*. This volume was printed privately at first, but has been issued by the Vatican Press since 1885. The title *Annuario Pontificio* was restored in 1912, and the yearbook was called an "official publication" until 1924.

L'Osservatore Romano: The daily newspaper of the Holy See. It began publication July 1, 1861, as an independent enterprise under the ownership and direction of four Catholic laymen headed by Marcantonio Pacelli, vice minister of the interior under Pope Pius IX and a grandfather of the late Pius XII. Leo XIII bought the publication in 1890, making it the "pope's" own newspaper.

The only official material in *L'Osservatore Romano* is that which appears under the heading, "Nostre Informazioni." This includes notices of appointments by the Holy See, the texts of papal encyclicals and addresses by the Holy Father and others, various types of documents, accounts of decisions and rulings of administrative bodies, and similar items. Additional material includes news and comment on developments in the Church and the world. Italian is the language most used.

The editorial board is directed by Valerio Volpini. A staff of about 15 reporters covers Rome news sources. A corps of correspondents provides foreign coverage.

A weekly roundup edition in English was inaugurated in 1968. Other weekly editions are printed in French, Spanish, Portuguese and German. Publication of a monthly Polish edition was begun in February, 1980.

Vatican Press Office: The establishment of a single Vatican Press Office was announced Feb. 29, 1968, to replace service agencies formerly operated by *L'Osservatore Romano* and an office created for press coverage of the Second Vatican Council. Rev. Romeo Panciroli is the director.

Vatican Polyglot Press: The official printing plant of the Vatican.

The Vatican press was conceived by Marcellus II and Pius IV but was actually founded by Sixtus V on Apr. 27, 1587, to print the Vulgate and the writings of the Fathers of the Church and other authors. A Polyglot Press was established in 1626 by the Congregation for the Propagation of the Faith to serve the needs of the Oriental Church. St. Pius X merged both presses under this title.

The plant has facilities for the printing of a wide variety of material in about 30 languages.

Activities of the Holy See: An annual documentary volume covering the activities of the pope — his daily work, general and special audiences, discourses and messages on special occasions, visits outside the Vatican, missionary and charitable endeavors, meetings with diplomats, heads of state and others — and activities of the congregations, commissions, tribunals and offices of the Roman Curia.

Statistical Yearbook of the Church: Issued by the Central Statistics Office of the Church, it contains principal data concerning the presence and work of the Church in the world. The first issue was published in 1972 under the title *Collection of Statistical Tables, 1969*. It is printed in corresponding columns of Italian and Latin. Some of the introductory material is printed in other languages.

VATICAN REPRESENTATIVES

(Sources: *Annuario Pontificio;* NC News Service.)

The Vatican has representatives to a number of quasi-governmental and international organizations.

Governmental Organizations: United Nations (Abp. Giovanni Cheli, permanent observer); UN Office in Geneva and Specialized Institutes (Abp. Edoardo Rovida, permanent observer); International Atomic Energy Agency (Mario Peressin, permanent representative); UN Organization for Industrial Development (Msgr. Mario Peressin, permanent observer); UN Food and Agriculture Organization (Bp. Agostino Ferrari-Toniolo, permanent observer); UN Educational, Scientific and Cultural Organization (Msgr. Renzo Frana, permanent observer);

Council of Europe (Msgr. Fortunato Baldelli, special envoy with function of permanent observer); Council for Cultural Cooperation of the Council of Europe (Msgr. Fortunato Baldelli, delegate); European Community (Abp. Igino Cardinale, apostolic nuncio); Organization of American States (Abp. Pio Laghi, permanent observer); International Institute for the Unification of Private Law (Prof. Pio Ciprotti, delegate); International Committee of Military Medicine and Pharmacy (Adolphe Vander Perre, delegate), World Organization of Tourism (Rev. Giovanni Arrighi, O.P., permanent observer).

Universal Postal Union; International Telecommunications Union; International Council on Grain; World Organization of Intellectual Property; International Union for the Protection of Literary and Artistic Works; International Union for the Protection of Industrial Property; International Organization of Telecommunication via Satellite (Intelsat); European Conference of Postal and Telecommunication Administration (CEPT).

Non-Governmental Organizations: International Committee of Historical Sciences (Msgr. Michele Maccarrone); International Committee of Paleography (Msgr. Jose Ruysschaert, delegate); International Committee of the History of Art (Prof. Carlo Pietrangeli, delegate); International Committee of Anthropological and Ethnological Sciences;

International Committee for the Neutrality of Medicine (Rev. Michel Riquet, S.J., permanent observer); International Center of Study for the Preservation and Restoration of Cultural Goods (Prof. Carlo Pietrangeli, permanent observer); International Council of Monuments and Sites (Prof. Carlo Pietrangeli, delegate); International Alliance on Tourism; International Astronomical Union; International Institute of Administrative Sciences; International Technical Committee for Prevention and Extinction of Fires; World Medical Association.

The Church of Santa Susanna was established as the national church for Americans in Rome Feb. 28, 1922; it was entrusted to the Paulist Fathers who have served there most of the time since then.

ASSOCIATIONS FORBIDDEN TO THE CLERGY

Membership by the clergy in organizations supporting particular political ideologies or in union-like associations are banned, according to a "Declaration on Some Associations and Movements Forbidden to the Clergy," released by the Congregation for the Clergy Mar. 8, 1982.

The following excerpts are from the text circulated by the NC Documentary Service, Origins, Mar. 25, 1982 (Vol. 11, No. 41).

"The sacred hierarchy never permitted, nor can at present permit, that the right of association of the clergy, either in the ambient of the ecclesial community or in the civil arena, be exercised by taking part in associations or movements of any kind which by their nature, aims or methods of action are an impediment to the hierarchical communion of the Church, or which cause harm to the priestly identity and to the fulfillment of the duties that priests, in the name of Christ, exercise at the service of the people of God."

Irreconcilable Associations

"Undoubtedly irreconcilable with the clerical state, and therefore prohibited to all members of the clergy, are those associations of clerics, even if erected or constituted only civilly, which directly or indirectly, in a manifest or underhanded manner, pursue aims relating to politics, even if presented under the external aspect of wanting to favor humanitarian ideals, peace and social progress. Such associations or movements, in fact, causing divisions and discord within the people of God, both among the faithful and among the presbyters in relations among themselves and with their Ordinaries (bishops), undoubtedly place in shadow the priestly mission and infringe on the ecclesial communion — the mission and communion which constitute an essential element in the life and ministry of the priest."

No Clergy Unions

"Similarly irreconcilable with the clerical state, and therefore prohibited to all members of the clergy, are those associations which intend to unite deacons or presbyters in a type of 'union,' thus reducing their sacred ministry to a profession or career, comparable to functions of a profane character. Such associations, in fact, conceive of the exercise of the functions of the ministerial priesthood as a relationship of work, and thus can easily place the clerics in opposition to their holy pastors who become considered only as givers of work."

While banning membership in organizations like these, the declaration acknowledges the right of clerics to form or join associations "for reasons consistent with the nature of the ministerial priesthood."

An unnamed official of the Congregation for the Clergy said that the declaration, while "meant for the whole Church," had little, if any, immediate application in the United States.

Targets

Following release of the document, several Italian newspapers said it was directed specifically against such organizations as Priests for Peace in Hungary, Christian Reality in Yugoslavia and Pacem in Terris in Czechoslovakia — all of which were said to collaborate closely with Communist governments and to be in frequent conflict with the bishops of their respective nations.

An unnamed Czechoslovakian bishop, according to one daily newspaper of Rome, expressed concern that the declaration might lead to worse relations between the bishops and government of his country.

Doctrine of the Catholic Church

Following are excerpts from the first two chapters of the *Dogmatic Constitution on the Church* promulgated by the Second Vatican Council. They describe the relation of the Catholic Church to the Kingdom of God, the nature and foundation of the Church, the People of God, the necessity of membership and participation in the Church for salvation.

Additional subjects in the constitution are treated in other Almanac entries.

I. MYSTERY OF THE CHURCH

". . . By her relationship with Christ, the Church is a kind of sacrament or sign of intimate union with God, and of the unity of all mankind . . ." (No. 1).

". . . He (the eternal Father) planned to assemble in the holy Church all those who would believe in Christ. Already from the beginning of the world the foreshadowing of the Church took place. She was prepared for in a remarkable way throughout the history of the people of Israel and by means of the Old Covenant. Established in the present era of time, the Church was made manifest by the outpouring of the Spirit. At the end of time she will achieve her glorious fulfillment. Then . . . all just men from the time of Adam, 'from Abel, the just one, to the last of the elect,' will be gathered together with the Father in the universal Church" (No. 2).

"When the work which the Father had given the Son to do on earth (cf. Jn. 17:4) was accomplished, the Holy Spirit was sent on the day of Pentecost in order that He might forever sanctify the Church, and thus all believers would have access to the Father through Christ in the one Spirit (cf. Eph. 2:18). . . .

"The Spirit dwells in the Church and in the hearts of the faithful as in a temple (cf. 1 Cor. 3:16; 6:19). . . . The Spirit guides the Church into the fullness of truth (cf. Jn. 16:13) and gives her a unity of fellowship and service. He furnishes and directs her with various gifts, both hierarchical and charismatic, and adorns her with the fruits of His grace (cf. Eph. 4:11-12; 1 Cor. 12:4; Gal. 5:22). By the power of the gospel He makes the Church grow, perpetually renews her, and leads her to perfect union with her Spouse. . . ." (No. 4).

Foundation of the Church

"The mystery of the holy Church is manifest in her very foundation, for the Lord Jesus inaugurated her by preaching the good news, that is, the coming of God's Kingdom, which, for centuries, had been promised in the Scriptures. . . . In Christ's word, in His works, and in His presence this kingdom reveals itself to men. . . .

"The miracles of Jesus also confirm that the kingdom has already arrived on earth. . . .

"Before all things, however, the kingdom is clearly visible in the very person of Christ, Son of God and Son of Man. . . .

"When Jesus rose up again after suffering death on the cross for mankind, He manifested that He had been appointed Lord, Messiah, and Priest forever (cf. Acts 2:36; Hb. 5:6; 7:17-21), and He poured out on His disciples the Spirit promised by the Father (cf. Acts 2:33). The Church, consequently, equipped with the gifts of her Founder and faithfully guarding His precepts . . . receives the mission to proclaim and to establish among all peoples the kingdom of Christ and of God. She becomes on earth the initial budding forth of that kingdom. While she slowly grows, the Church strains toward the consummation of the kingdom and, with all her strength, hopes and desires to be united in glory with her King" (No. 5).

Figures of the Church

"In the Old Testament the revelation of the kingdom had often been conveyed by figures of speech. In the same way the inner nature of the Church was now to be made known to us through various images. . . .

". . . The Church is a sheepfold . . . a flock . . . a tract of land to be cultivated, the field of God . . . His choice vineyard . . . the true Vine is Christ . . . the edifice of God . . . the house of God . . . the holy temple (whose members are) . . . living stones . . . this Holy City . . . a bride . . . 'our Mother' . . . the spotless spouse of the spotless Lamb . . . an exile. . ." (No. 6).

"In the human nature which He united to Himself, the Son of God redeemed man and transformed him into a new creation (cf. Gal. 6:15; 2 Cor. 5:17) by overcoming death through His own death and resurrection. By communicating His Spirit to His brothers, called together from all peoples, Christ made them mystically into His own body.

"In that body, the life of Christ is poured into the believers, who, through the sacraments, are united in a hidden and real way to Christ who suffered and was glorified. Through baptism we are formed in the likeness of Christ. . . .

"Truly partaking of the body of the Lord in the breaking of the Eucharistic bread, we are taken up into communion with Him and with one another . . ." (No. 7).

One Body in Christ

"As all the members of the human body, though they are many, form one body, so also are the faithful in Christ (cf. 1 Cor. 12:12). Also, in the building up of Christ's body there is a flourishing variety of members and functions. There is only one Spirit who . . . distributes His different gifts for the welfare of the Church (cf. 1 Cor. 12:1-11). Among these gifts stands out the grace given to the apostles. To their authority, the Spirit Himself subjected even those who were endowed with charisms (cf. 1 Cor. 14). . . .

"The head of this body is Christ . . ." (No. 7).

Mystical Body of Christ

"Christ, the one Mediator, established and ceaselessly sustains here on earth His holy Church, the community of faith, hope, and charity, as a visible structure. Through her He communicates truth and grace to all. But the society furnished with hierarchical agencies and the Mystical Body of Christ are not to be considered as two realities, nor are the visible assembly and the spiritual community, nor the earthly Church and the Church enriched with heavenly things. Rather they form one interlocked reality which is comprised of a divine and a human element. For this reason . . . this reality is compared to the mystery of the incarnate Word. Just as the assumed nature inseparably united to the divine Word serves Him as a living instrument of salvation, so, in a similar way, does the communal structure of the Church serve Christ's Spirit, who vivifies it by way of building up the body (cf. Eph. 4:16).

"This is the unique Church of Christ which in the Creed we avow as one, holy, catholic, and apostolic. After His Resurrection our Savior handed her over to Peter to be shepherded (Jn. 21:17), commissioning him and the other apostles to propagate and govern her (cf. Mt. 28:18, ff.). Her He erected for all ages as 'the pillar and mainstay of the truth' (1 Tm. 3:15). This Church, constituted and organized in the world as a society, subsists in the Catholic Church, which is governed by the successor of Peter and by the bishops in union with that successor, although many elements of sanctification and of truth can be found outside of her visible structure. These elements, however, as gifts properly belonging to the Church of Christ, possess an inner dynamism toward Catholic unity.

". . . the Church, embracing sinners in her bosom, is at the same time holy and always in need of being purified, and incessantly pursues the path of penance and renewal.

"The Church, 'like a pilgrim in a foreign land, presses forward . . .' announcing the cross and death of the Lord until He comes (cf. 1 Cor. 11:26) . . ." (No. 8).

II. THE PEOPLE OF GOD

"At all times and among every people, God has given welcome to whosoever fears Him and does what is right (cf. Acts 10:35). It has pleased God, however, to make men holy and save them not merely as individuals without

any mutual bonds, but by making them into a single people, a people which acknowledges Him in truth and serves Him in holiness. He therefore chose the race of Israel as a people unto Himself. With it He set up a covenant. Step by step He taught this people by manifesting in its history both Himself and the decree of His will, and by making it holy unto Himself. All these things, however, were done by way of preparation and as a figure of that new and perfect covenant which was to be ratified in Christ. . . .

". . . Christ instituted this new covenant, that is to say, the new testament, in His blood (cf. 1 Cor. 11:25), by calling together a people made up of Jew and Gentile, making them one, not according to the flesh but in the Spirit.

"This was to be the new People of God . . . reborn . . . through the Word of the living God (cf. 1 Pt. 1:23) . . . from water and the Holy Spirit (cf. Jn. 3:5-6) . . . 'a chosen race, a royal priesthood, a holy nation, a purchased people. . . . You who in times past were not a people, but are now the people of God' (1 Pt. 2:9-10).

"That messianic people has for its head Christ. . . . Its law is the new commandment to love as Christ loved us (cf. Jn. 13:34). Its goal is the kingdom of God, which has been begun by God Himself on earth, and which is to be further extended until it is brought to perfection by Him at the end of time. . . .

". . . This messianic people, although it does not actually include all men, and may more than once look like a small flock, is nonetheless a lasting and sure seed of unity, hope, and salvation for the whole human race. Established by Christ as a fellowship of life, charity, and truth, it is also used by Him as an instrument for the redemption of all, and is sent forth into the whole world as the light of the world and the salt of the earth (cf. Mt. 5:13-16).

"Israel according to the flesh . . . was already called the Church of God (2 Ezr. 13:1; cf. Nm. 20:4; Dt. 23:1, ff.). Likewise the new Israel . . . is also called the Church of Christ (cf. Mt. 16:18). For He has bought it for Himself with His blood (cf. Acts 20:28), has filled it with His Spirit, and provided it with those means which befit it as a visible and social unity. God has gathered together as one all those who in faith look upon Jesus as the author of salvation and the source of unity and peace, and has established them as the Church, that for each and all she may be the visible sacrament of this saving unity . . ." (No. 9)

Priesthood

". . . The baptized, by regeneration and the anointing of the Holy Spirit, are consecrated into . . . a holy priesthood. . . ."

(All members of the Church participate in

the priesthood of Christ, through the common priesthood of the faithful. See Priesthood of the Laity.)

"Though they differ from one another in essence and not only in degree, the common priesthood of the faithful and the ministerial or hierarchical priesthood are nonetheless interrelated. Each of them in its own special way is a participation in the one priesthood of Christ . . ." (No. 10).

"It is through the sacraments and the exercise of the virtues that the sacred nature and organic structure of the priestly community is brought into operation . . ." (No. 11). See Role of the Sacraments.)

Prophetic Office

"The holy People of God shares also in Christ's prophetic office. It spreads abroad a living witness to Him, especially by means of a life of faith and charity and by offering to God a sacrifice of praise. . . . The body of the faithful as a whole, anointed as they are by the Holy One (cf. Jn. 2:20, 27), cannot err in matters of belief. Thanks to a supernatural sense of faith which characterizes the People as a whole, it manifests this unerring quality when, 'from the bishops down to the last member of the laity,' it shows universal agreement in matters of faith and morals.

". . . God's People accepts not the word of men but the very Word of God (cf. 1 Thes. 2:13). It clings without fail to the faith once delivered to the saints (cf. Jude 3), penetrates it more deeply by accurate insights, and applies it more thoroughly to life. All this it does under the lead of a sacred teaching authority to which it loyally defers.

"It is not only through the sacraments and Church ministries that the same Holy Spirit sanctifies and leads the People of God. . . . He distributes special graces among the faithful of every rank. By these gifts He makes them fit and ready to undertake the various tasks or offices advantageous for the renewal and upbuilding of the Church. . . . These charismatic gifts . . . are to be received with thanksgiving and consolation, for they are exceedingly suitable and useful for the needs of the Church.

". . . Judgment as to their genuineness and proper use belongs to those who preside over the Church, and to whose special competence it belongs . . . to test all things and hold fast to that which is good (cf. 1 Thes. 5:12; 19-21)" (No. 12).

All Are Called

"All men are called to belong to the new People of God. Wherefore this People, while remaining one and unique, is to be spread throughout the whole world and must exist in all ages, so that the purpose of God's will may be fulfilled. In the beginning God made human nature one. After His children were scattered, He decreed that they should at length be united again (cf. Jn. 11:52). It was for this reason that God sent His Son . . . that He might be Teacher, King, and Priest of all, the Head of the New and universal people of the sons of God. For this God finally sent His Son's Spirit as Lord and Lifegiver. He it is who, on behalf of the whole Church and each and every one of those who believe, is the principle of their coming together and remaining together in the teaching of the apostles and in fellowship, in the breaking of bread and in prayers (cf. Acts 2:42)" (No. 13).

One People of God

"It follows that among all the nations of earth there is but one People of God, which takes its citizens from every race, making them citizens of a kingdom which is of a heavenly and not an earthly nature. For all the faithful scattered throughout the world are in communion with each other in the Holy Spirit . . . the Church or People of God . . . foster(s) and take(s) to herself, insofar as they are good, the ability, resources and customs of each people. Taking them to herself she purifies, strengthens, and enobles them. . . . This characteristic of universality which adorns the People of God is a gift from the Lord Himself. By reason of it, the Catholic Church strives energetically and constantly to bring all humanity with all its riches back to Christ its Head in the unity of His Spirit.

"In virtue of this catholicity each individual part of the Church contributes through its special gifts to the good of the other parts and of the whole Church. Thus through the common sharing of gifts . . . the whole and each of the parts receive increase. . . .

"All men are called to be part of this catholic unity of the People of God. . . . And there belong to it or are related to it in various ways, the Catholic faithful as well as all who believe in Christ, and indeed the whole of mankind. For all men are called to salvation by the grace of God" (No. 13).

The Catholic Church

"This sacred Synod turns its attention first to the Catholic faithful. Basing itself upon sacred Scripture and tradition, it teaches that the Church . . . is necessary for salvation. For Christ, made present to us in His Body, which is the Church, is the one Mediator and the unique Way of salvation. In explicit terms He Himself affirmed the necessity of faith and baptism (cf. Mk. 16:16; Jn. 3:5) and thereby affirmed also the necessity of the Church, for through baptism as through a door men enter the Church. Whosoever, therefore, knowing that the Catholic Church was made necessary by God through Jesus Christ, would refuse to enter her or to remain in her could not be saved.

"They are fully incorporated into the society of the Church who, possessing the Spirit of Christ, accept her entire system and all the means of salvation given to her, and through union with her visible structure are joined to Christ, who rules her through the Supreme Pontiff and the bishops. This joining is effected by the bonds of professed faith, of the sacraments, of ecclesiastical government, and of communion. He is not saved, however, who, though he is part of the body of the Church, does not persevere in charity. He remains indeed in the bosom of the Church, but . . . only in a 'bodily' manner and not 'in his heart.' . . .

"Catechumens who, moved by the Holy Spirit, seek with explicit intention to be incorporated into the Church are by that very intention joined to her. . . . Mother Church already embraces them as her own" (No. 14).

Other Christians, The Unbaptized

"The Church recognizes that in many ways she is linked with those who, being baptized, are honored with the name of Christian, though they do not profess the faith in its entirety or do not preserve unity of communion with the successor of Peter. . . .

" . . . We can say that in some real way they are joined with us in the Holy Spirit, for to them also He gives His gifts and graces, and is thereby operative among them with His sanctifying power . . ." (No. 15).

"Finally, those who have not yet received the gospel are related in various ways to the People of God. In the first place there is the people to whom the covenants and the promises were given and from whom Christ was born according to the flesh (cf. Rom. 9:4-5). On account of their fathers, this people remains most dear to God, for God does not repent of the gifts He makes nor of the calls He issues (cf. Rom. 11:28-29).

"But the plan of salvation also includes those who acknowledge the Creator. In the first place among these are the Moslems. . . . Nor is God Himself far distant from those who in shadows and images seek the unknown God. . . .

"Those also can attain to everlasting salvation who through no fault of their own do not know the gospel of Christ or His Church, yet sincerely seek God and, moved by grace, strive by their deeds to do His will as it is known to them through the dictates of conscience. Nor does divine Providence deny the help necessary for salvation to those who, without blame on their part, have not yet arrived at an explicit knowledge of God, but who strive to live a good life, thanks to His grace. Whatever goodness or truth is found among them is looked upon by the Church as a preparation for the Gospel. She regards such qualities as given by Him who enlightens all men so that they may finally have life . . ." (No. 16).

THE POPE, TEACHING AUTHORITY, COLLEGIALITY

The Roman Pontiff — the successor of St. Peter as the Vicar of Christ and head of the Church on earth — has full and supreme authority over the universal Church in matters pertaining to faith and morals (teaching authority), discipline and government (jurisdictional authority).

The primacy of the pope is real and supreme power. It is not merely a prerogative of honor — that is, of his being regarded as the first among equals. Neither does primacy imply that the pope is just the presiding officer of the collective body of bishops. The pope is the head of the Church.

Catholic belief in the primacy of the pope was stated in detail in the dogmatic constitution on the Church, *Pastor Aeternus,* approved in 1870 by the fourth session of the First Vatican Council. Some elaboration of the doctrine was made in the *Dogmatic Constitution on the Church* which was approved and promulgated by the Second Vatican Council Nov. 21, 1964. The entire body of teaching on the subject is based on Scripture and tradition and the centuries-long experience of the Church.

Infallibility

The essential points of doctrine concerning infallibility in the Church and the infallibility of the pope were stated by the Second Vatican Council in the *Dogmatic Constitution on the Church,* as follows:

"This infallibility with which the divine Redeemer willed his Church to be endowed in defining a doctrine of faith and morals extends as far as extends the deposit of divine revelation, which must be religiously guarded and faithfully expounded. This is the infallibility which the Roman Pontiff, the head of the college of bishops, enjoys in virtue of his office, when, as the supreme shepherd and teacher of all the faithful, who confirms his brethren in their faith (cf. Lk. 22:32), he proclaims by a definitive act some doctrine of faith or morals. Therefore his definitions, of themselves, and not from the consent of the Church, are justly styled irreformable, for they are pronounced with the assistance of the Holy Spirit, an assistance promised to him in blessed Peter. Therefore they need no approval of others, nor do they allow an appeal to any other judgment. For then the Roman Pontiff is not pronouncing judgment as a private person. Rather, as the supreme teacher of the universal Church, as one in whom the charism of the infallibility of the Church herself is individually present, he is expounding or defending a doctrine of Catholic faith.

"The infallibility promised to the Church resides also in the body of bishops when that body exercises supreme teaching authority with the successor of Peter. To the resultant definitions the assent of the Church can never be wanting, on account of the activity of that same Holy Spirit, whereby the whole flock of Christ is preserved and progresses in unity of faith.

"But when either the Roman Pontiff or the body of bishops together with him defines a judgment, they pronounce it in accord with revelation itself. All are obliged to maintain and be ruled by this revelation, which, as written or preserved by tradition, is transmitted in its entirety through the legitimate succession of bishops and especially through the care of the Roman Pontiff himself.

"Under the guiding light of the Spirit of truth, revelation is thus religiously preserved and faithfully expounded in the Church. The Roman Pontiff and the bishops, in view of their office and of the importance of the matter, strive painstakingly and by appropriate means to inquire properly into that revelation and to give apt expression to its contents. But they do not allow that there could be any new public revelation pertaining to the divine deposit of faith" (No. 25).

Authentic Teaching

The pope rarely speaks *ex cathedra* — that is, "from the chair" of St. Peter, for the purpose of making an infallible pronouncement. More often and in various ways he states authentic teaching in line with Scripture, tradition, the living experience of the Church, and the whole analogy of faith. Of such teaching, the Second Vatican Council said in its *Dogmatic Constitution on the Church* (No. 25):

". . . Religious submission of will and of mind must be shown in a special way to the authentic teaching authority of the Roman Pontiff, even when he is not speaking *ex cathedra*. That is, it must be shown in such a way that his supreme magisterium is acknowledged with reverence, the judgments made by him are sincerely adhered to, according to his manifest mind and will. His mind and will in the matter may be known chiefly either from the character of the documents, from his frequent repetition of the same doctrine, or from his manner of speaking."

With respect to bishops, the constitution said: "They are authentic teachers, that is, teachers endowed with the authority of Christ, who preach to the people committed to them the faith they must believe and put into practice. By the light of the Holy Spirit, they make that faith clear, bringing forth from the treasury of revelation new things and old (cf. Mt. 13:52), making faith bear fruit and vigilantly warding off any errors which threaten their flock (cf. Tm. 4:1-4).

"Bishops, teaching in communion with the Roman Pontiff, are to be respected by all as witnesses to divine and Catholic truth. In matters of faith and morals, the bishops speak in the name of Christ and the faithful are to accept their teaching and adhere to it with a religious assent of soul."

Magisterium—Teaching Authority

Responsibility for teaching doctrine and judging orthodoxy belongs to the official teaching authority of the Church.

This authority is personalized in the pope, the successor of St. Peter as head of the Church, and in the bishops together and in union with the pope, as it was originally committed to Peter and to the whole college of Apostles under his leadership. They are the official teachers of the Church.

Others have auxiliary relationships with the magisterium: theologians, in the study and clarification of doctrine; teachers — priests, religious, lay persons — who cooperate with the pope and bishops in spreading knowledge of religious truth; the faithful, who by their sense of faith and personal witness contribute to the development of doctrine and the establishment of its relevance to life in the Church and the world.

The magisterium, Pope Paul noted in an address at a general audience Jan. 11, 1967, "is a subordinate and faithful echo and secure interpreter of the divine word." It does not reveal new truths, "nor is it superior to Sacred Scripture." Its competence extends to the limits of divine revelation manifested in Scripture and tradition and the living experience of the Church, with respect to matters of faith and morals and related subjects.

Official teaching in these areas is infallible when it is formally defined, for belief and acceptance by all members of the Church, by the pope, acting in the capacity of supreme shepherd of the flock of Christg and when doctrine is proposed and taught with moral unanimity of bishops with the pope in a solemn collegial manner as in an ecumenical council, and/or in the ordinary course of events. Even when not infallibly defined, official teaching in the areas of faith and morals is authoritative and requires religious assent.

The teachings of the magisterium have been documented in creeds, formulas of faith, decrees and enactments of ecumenical and particular councils, various kinds of doctrinal statements, and other teaching instruments. They have also been incorporated into the liturgy, with the result that the law of prayer is said to be a law of belief.

Collegiality

The bishops of the Church, in union with the pope, have supreme teaching and pastoral authority over the whole Church in addition to the authority of office they have for their own dioceses.

This collegial authority is exercised in a solemn manner in an ecumenical council and can be exercised in other ways as well, "provided that the head of the college calls them to collegiate action, or at least so approves or freely accepts the united action of the dispersed bishops, that it is made a true collegiate act."

This doctrine is grounded on the fact that: "Just as, by the Lord's will, St. Peter and the other apostles constituted one apostolic college, so in a similar way the Roman Pontiff as the successor of Peter, and the bishops as the successors of the apostles are joined together."

Doctrine on collegiality was stated by the Second Vatican Council in the *Dogmatic Constitution on the Church* (Nos. 22 and 23).

REVELATION

Following are excerpts from the *Constitution on Revelation* promulgated by the Second Vatican Council. They describe the nature and process of divine revelation, inspiration and interpretation of Scripture, the Old and New Testaments, and the role of Scripture in the life of the Church.

I. Revelation Itself

". . . God chose to reveal Himself and to make known to us the hidden purpose of His will (cf. Eph. 1:9) by which through Christ, the Word made flesh, man has access to the Father in the Holy Spirit and comes to share in the divine nature (cf. Eph. 2:18; 2 Pt. 1:4). Through this revelation, therefore, the invisible God (cf. Col. 1:15; 1 Tm. 1:17) . . . speaks to men as friends (cf. Ex. 33:11; Jn. 15:14-15) and lives among them (cf. Bar. 3:38) so that He may invite and take them into fellowship with Himself. This plan of revelation is realized by deeds and words having an inner unity: the deeds wrought by God in the history of salvation manifest and confirm the teaching and realities signified by the words, while the words proclaim the deeds and clarify the mystery contained in them. By this revelation then, the deepest truth about God and the salvation of man is made clear to us in Christ, who is the Mediator and at the same time the fullness of all revelation" (No. 2).

"God . . . from the start manifested Himself to our first parents. Then after their fall His promise of redemption aroused in them the hope of being saved (cf. Gn. 3:15), and from that time on He ceaselessly kept the human race in His care, in order to give eternal life to those who perseveringly do good in search of salvation (cf. Rom. 2:6-7). . . . He called Abraham in order to make of him a great nation (cf. Gn. 12:2). Through the patriarchs, and after them through Moses and the prophets, He taught this nation to acknowledge Himself as the one living and true God . . . and to wait for the Savior promised by Him. In this manner He prepared the way for the gospel down through the centuries" (No. 3).

Revelation in Christ

"Then, after speaking in many places and varied ways through the prophets, God 'last of all in these days has spoken to us by His Son' (Hb. 1:1-2). . . . Jesus perfected revelation by fulfilling it through His whole work of making Himself present and manifesting Himself: through His words and deeds, His signs and wonders, but especially through His death and glorious resurrection from the dead and final sending of the spirit of truth. Moreover, He confirmed with divine testimony what revelation proclaimed: that God is with us to free us from the darkness of sin and death, and to raise us up to life eternal.

"The Christian dispensation, therefore, as the new and definitive covenant, will never pass away, and we now await no further new public revelation before the glorious manifestation of our Lord Jesus Christ (cf. 1 Tm. 6:14; Ti. 2:13)" (No. 4).

II. Transmission of Revelation

". . . God has seen to it that what He had revealed for the salvation of all nations would abide perpetually in its full integrity and be handed on to all generations. Therefore Christ the Lord, in whom the full revelation of the supreme God is brought to completion (cf. 2 Cor. 1:20; 3:16; 4:6), commissioned the apostles to preach to all men that gospel which is the source of all saving truth and moral teaching, and thus to impart to them divine gifts. This gospel had been promised in former times through the prophets, and Christ Himself fulfilled it and promulgated it with His own lips. This commission was faithfully fulfilled by the apostles who, by their oral preaching, by example, and by ordinances, handed on what they had received from . . . Christ . . . or what they had learned through the prompting of the Holy Spirit. The commission was fulfilled, too, by those apostles and apostolic men who under the inspiration of the same Holy Spirit committed the message of salvation to writing" (No. 7).

Tradition

"But in order to keep the gospel forever whole and alive within the Church, the apostles left bishops as their successors, 'handing over their own teaching role' to them. This sacred tradition, therefore, and sacred Scripture of both the Old and the New Testament are like a mirror in which the pilgrim Church on earth looks at God . . ." (No. 7).

". . . The apostolic preaching, which is expressed in a special way in the inspired books, was to be preserved by a continuous succession of preachers until the end of time. Therefore the apostles, handing on what they themselves had received, warn the faithful to hold fast to the traditions which they have learned. . . . Now what was handed on by the apostles includes everything which contributes to the holiness of life, and the increase in faith of the People of God; and so the Church, in her teaching, life, and worship, perpetuates and hands on to all generations all that she herself is, all that she believes" (No. 8).

Development of Doctrine

"This tradition which comes from the apostles develops in the Church with the help of the Holy Spirit. For there is a growth in the understanding of the realities and the words which have been handed down. This happens through the contemplation and study made by believers . . . through the intimate understanding of spiritual things they experience, and through the preaching of those who have received through episcopal succession the sure gift of truth. For, as the centuries succeed one another, the Church constantly moves forward toward the fullness of divine truth until the words of God reach their complete fulfillment in her.

"The words of the holy Fathers witness to the living presence of this tradition, whose wealth is poured into the practice and life of the believing and praying Church. Through the same tradition the Church's full canon of the sacred books is known, and the sacred writings themselves are more profoundly understood and unceasingly made active in her; . . . and the Holy Spirit, through whom the living voice of the gospel resounds in the Church, and through her, in the world, leads unto all truth those who believe and makes the word of Christ dwell abundantly in them (cf. Col. 3:16)" (No. 8).

Tradition and Scripture

"Hence there exist a close connection and communication between sacred tradition and sacred Scripture. For both of them, flowing from the same divine wellspring, in a certain way merge into a unity and tend toward the same end. For sacred Scripture is the word of God inasmuch as it is consigned to writing under the inspiration of the divine Spirit. To the successors of the apostles, sacred tradition hands on in its full purity God's word, which was entrusted to the apostles by Christ the Lord and the Holy Spirit. Thus, led by the light of the Spirit of truth, these successors can in their preaching preserve this word of God faithfully, explain it, and make it more widely known. Consequently, it is not from sacred Scripture alone that the Church draws her certainty about everything which has been revealed. Therefore both sacred tradition and sacred Scripture are to be accepted and venerated with the same sense of devotion and reverence" (No. 9).

"Sacred tradition and sacred Scripture form one sacred deposit of the word of God, which is committed to the Church" (No. 10).

Teaching Authority of Church

"The task of authentically interpreting the word of God, whether written or handed on, has been entrusted exclusively to the living teaching office of the Church, whose authority is exercised in the name of Jesus Christ. This teaching office is not above the word of God, but serves it, teaching only what has been handed on . . . it draws from this one deposit of faith everything which it presents for belief as divinely revealed.

"It is clear, therefore, that sacred tradition, sacred Scripture, and the teaching authority of the Church . . . are so linked and joined together that one cannot stand without the others, and that all together and each in its own way under the action of the one Holy Spirit contribute effectively to the salvation of souls" (No. 10).

III. Inspiration, Interpretation

"Those . . . revealed realities . . . contained and presented in sacred Scripture have been committed to writing under the inspiration of the Holy Spirit. Holy Mother Church, relying on the belief of the apostles, holds that the books of both the Old and New Testament in their entirety, with all their parts, are sacred and canonical because, having been written under the inspiration of the Holy Spirit (cf. Jn. 20:31; 2 Tm. 3:16; 2 Pt. 1:19-21; 3:15-16) they have God as their author and have been handed on as such to the Church herself. In composing the sacred books, God chose men and while employed by Him they made use of their powers and abilities, so that with Him acting in them and through them, they, as true authors, consigned to writing everything and only those things which He wanted" (No. 11).

Inerrancy

"Therefore, since everything asserted by the inspired authors or sacred writers must be held to be asserted by the Holy Spirit, it follows that the books of Scripture must be acknowledged as teaching firmly, faithfully, and without error that truth which God wanted put into the sacred writings for the sake of our salvation. Therefore 'all Scripture is inspired by God and useful for teaching, for reproving, for correcting, for instruction in justice; that the man of God may be perfect, equipped for every good work' (2 Tm. 3:16-17)" (No. 11).

Literary Forms

"However, since God speaks in sacred Scripture through men in human fashion, the interpreter of sacred Scripture, in order to see clearly what God wanted to communicate to us, should carefully investigate what meaning the sacred writers really intended, and what God wanted to manifest by means of their words.

". . . The interpreter must investigate what meaning the sacred writer intended to express and actually expressed in particular circumstances as he used contemporary literary forms in accordance with the situation of his own time and culture. For the correct understanding of what the sacred author wanted to assert, due attention must be paid to the customary and characteristic styles of perceiving, speaking, and narrating which prevailed at the time of the sacred writer, and to the customs men normally followed at that period in their everyday dealings with one another" (No. 12).

Analogy of Faith

". . . No less serious attention must be given to the content and unity of the whole of Scripture, if the meaning of the sacred texts is to be correctly brought to light. The living tradition of the whole Church must be taken into account along with the harmony which exists between elements of the faith. . . . all of what has been said about the way of interpreting Scripture is subject finally to the judgment of the Church, which carries out the divine commission and ministry of guarding and interpreting the word of God" (No. 12).

IV. The Old Testament

"In carefully planning and preparing the salvation of the whole human race, the God of supreme love, by a special dispensation, chose for Himself a people to whom He might entrust His promises. First He entered into a covenant with Abraham (cf. Gn. 15:18) and, through Moses, with the people of Israel (cf. Ex. 24:8). To this people which He had acquired for Himself, He so manifested Himself through words and deeds as the one true and living God that Israel came to know by experience the ways of God with men. . . . The plan of salvation, foretold by the sacred authors, recounted and explained by them, is found as the true word of God in the books of the Old Testament: these books, therefore, written under divine inspiration, remain permanently valuable . . ." (No. 14).

Principal Purpose

"The principal purpose to which the plan of the Old Covenant was directed was to prepare for the coming both of Christ, the universal Redeemer, and of the messianic kingdom. . . . Now the books of the Old Testament, in accordance with the state of mankind before the time of salvation established by Christ, reveal to all men the knowledge of God and of man and the ways in which God . . . deals with men. These books . . . show us true divine pedagogy . . ." (No. 15).
". . . The books of the Old Testament with all their parts, caught up into the proclamation of the gospel, acquire and show forth their full meaning in the New Testament (cf. Mt. 5:17; Lk. 24:27; Rom. 16:25-26; 2 Cor. 3:14-16) and in turn shed light on it and explain it" (No. 16).

V. The New Testament

"The word of God . . . is set forth and shows its power in a most excellent way in the writings of the New Testament. For when the fullness of time arrived (cf. Gal. 4:4), the Word was made flesh and dwelt among us in the fullness of grace and truth (cf. Jn. 1:14). Christ established the Kingdom of God on earth, manifested His Father and Himself by deeds and words, and completed His work by His death, resurrection, and glorious ascension and by the sending of the Holy Spirit. Having been lifted up from the earth, He draws all men to Himself (cf. Jn. 12:32). . . . This mystery had not been manifested to other generations as it was now revealed to His holy apostles and prophets in the Holy Spirit (cf. Eph. 3:4-6), so that they might preach the Gospel, stir up faith in Jesus, Christ and Lord, and gather the Church together. To these realities, the writings of the New Testament stand as a perpetual and divine witness" (No. 17).

The Gospels and Other Writings

". . . The Gospels have a special pre-eminence . . . for they are the principal witness of the life and teaching of the incarnate Word, our Savior.

"The Church has always and everywhere held and continues to hold that the four Gospels are of apostolic origin. For what the apostles preached . . . afterwards they themselves and apostolic men, under the inspiration of the divine Spirit, handed on to us in writing: the foundation of faith, namely, the fourfold Gospel, according to Matthew, Mark, Luke, and John" (No. 18).

". . . The four Gospels, . . . whose historical character the Church unhesitatingly asserts, faithfully hand on what Jesus Christ, while living among men, really did and taught for their eternal salvation until the day He was taken up into heaven (see Acts 1:1-2). Indeed, after the ascension of the Lord the apostles handed on to their hearers what He had said and done. . . . The sacred authors wrote the four Gospels, selecting some things from the many which had been handed on by word of mouth or in writing, reducing some of them to a synthesis, explicating some things in view of the situation of their churches, and preserving the form of proclamation but always in such fashion that they told us the honest truth about Jesus. For their intention in writing was that . . . we might know 'the truth' concerning those matters about which we have been instructed (cf. Lk. 1:2-4)" (No. 19).

"Besides the four Gospels, the canon of the New Testament also contains the Epistles of St. Paul and other apostolic writings, composed under the inspiration of the Holy Spirit. In these writings ... those matters which concern Christ the Lord are confirmed, His true teaching is more and more fully stated, the saving power of the divine work of Christ is preached, the story is told of the beginnings of the Church and her marvelous growth, and her glorious fulfillment is foretold" (No. 20).

VI. Scripture in Church Life

"The Church has always venerated the divine Scriptures just as she venerates the body of the Lord. ... She has always regarded the Scriptures together with sacred tradition as the supreme rule of faith, and will ever do so. For, inspired by God and committed once and for all to writing, they impart the word of God Himself without change, and make the voice of the Holy Spirit resound in the words of the prophets and apostles. Therefore, like the Christian religion itself, all the preaching of the Church must be nourished and ruled by sacred Scripture ..." (No. 21).

"Easy access to sacred Scripture should be provided for all the Christian faithful. That is why the Church from the very beginning accepted as her own that very ancient Greek translation of the Old Testament which is named after seventy men (the Septuagint); and she has always given a place of honor to other translations, Eastern and Latin, especially the one known as the Vulgate. But since the word of God should be available at all times, the Church with maternal concern sees to it that suitable and correct translations are made into different languages, especially from the original texts of the sacred books. And if, given the opportunity and the approval of Church authority, these translations are produced in cooperation with the separated brethren as well, all Christians will be able to use them" (No. 22).

Biblical Studies, Theology

The constitution encouraged the development and progress of biblical studies "under the watchful care of the sacred teaching office of the Church." (Such studies have made great progress in recent years.)

It noted also: "Sacred theology rests on the written word of God, together with sacred tradition, as its primary and perpetual foundation," and that "the study of the sacred page is, as it were, the soul of sacred theology" (Nos. 23, 24).

LATIN-IN-LITURGY SURVEY

"The use of Latin (in the celebration of Mass) is neither frequent nor widespread," according to responses to a survey conducted by the Congregation for the Sacraments and Divine Worship in the summer and fall of 1980. Responses were received from 1,750 bishops, representing three-fourths of the Latin Rite dioceses of the Church. Bishops from 153 US. dioceses were among the respondents.

Findings of the survey, originally made public in *Notitiae,* the official journal of the congregation, were reported in the January, 1982, newsletter of the U.S. Bishops' Committee on the Liturgy. The source and most of the wording of this account are from the report which appeared in the Feb. 11, 1982, edition of the N.C. Documentary Service, Origins (Vol. 11, No. 35).

One of the main purposes of the survey was to determine the extent to which Latin was used in the celebration of Mass, in either authorized or unauthorized forms.

The great majority of responses, 83.82 per cent, said there was no demand for the use of Latin in the liturgy.

According to letters received, Latin, as a liturgical language of the Church, was tending more and more to disappear. As a matter of fact, the overwhelming majority of celebrations took place in the languages of the various countries.

Even in dioceses where Mass was celebrated in Latin according to the approved rite of 1969, "the use of Latin is neither frequent nor widespread."

Authorized Latin Masses were celebrated occasionally in 79 U.S. dioceses and with some frequency in seven others. Fifty-seven U.S. bishops said there were no authorized Latin Masses in their dioceses. Eight dioceses reported occasional use of Gregorian Chant at Mass.

With respect to requests for Latin Masses, 108 U.S. bishops said they received none, while 43 reported occasional requests for either Latin Masses or the use of Gregorian Chant.

Tridentine Masses (according to directives from the Council of Trent, now superseded by the New Order of Mass approved in 1969) were celebrated by followers of dissident Archbishop Marcel Lefebvre in about four per cent of the world's Latin-Rite dioceses. Another 16 per cent of the bishops responding to the survey said such Masses were also celebrated by individuals or groups not identified with the archbishop.

The principal countries facing problems of unauthorized celebrations of the Tridentine Mass were the United States, France, Germany, Austria, Switzerland, Great Britian and New Zealand. Such Masses were celebrated in more than 70 per cent of the dioceses reporting from each of these countries.

Forty U.S. bishops reported that no Tridentine Masses were celebrated in their dioceses; 23 said there were celebrations of Tridentine Masses for unorganized groups.

THE BIBLE

The Catholic canon of the Old Testament consists of:

• The Pentateuch, the first five books: Genesis (Gn.), Exodus (Ex.), Leviticus (Lv.), Numbers (Nm.), Deuteronomy (Dt.).

• Historical Books: Joshua (Jos.), Judges (Jgs.), Ruth (Ru.), 1 and 2 Samuel (Sm.), 1 and 2 Kings (Kgs.), 1 and 2 Chronicles (Chr.), Ezra (Ezr.), Nehemiah (Neh.), Tobit (Tb.), Judith (Jdt.), Esther (Est.), 1 and 2 Maccabees (Mc.).

• Wisdom Books: Job (Jb.), Psalms (Ps.), Proverbs (Prv.), Ecclesiastes (Eccl.), Song of Songs (Song), Wisdom (Wis.), Sirach (Sir.).

• The Prophets: Isaiah (Is.), Jeremiah (Jer.), Lamentations (Lam.), Baruch (Bar.), Ezechiel (Ez.), Daniel (Dn.), Hosea (Hos.), Joel (Jl.), Amos (Am.), Obadiah (Ob.), Jonah (Jon.), Micah (Mi.), Nahum (Na.), Habakkùk (Hb.), Zephaniah (Zep.), Haggai (Hg.), Zechariah (Zec.), Malachi (Mal.).

The Catholic canon of the New Testament consists of:

• The Gospels of Matthew (Mt.), Mark (Mk.), Luke (Lk.), John (Jn.)

• The Acts of the Apostles (Acts).

• The Pauline Letters — Romans (Rom.), 1 and 2 Corinthians (Cor.), Galatians (Gal.), Ephesians (Eph.), Philippians (Phil.), Colossians (Col.), 1 and 2 Thessalonians (Thes.), 1 and 2 Timothy (Tm.), Titus (Ti.), Philemon (Phlm.), Hebrews (Heb.); the Catholic Letters — James (Jas.), 1 and 2 Peter (Pt.), 1, 2 and 3 John (Jn.), Jude (Jude).

• Revelation (Rv.).

Catholic and Other Canons

The Catholic canon of the Old Testament was determined by the tradition of the Church. It was firm by the fifth century, despite some questioning by scholars, and was stated by the African councils of Hippo in 393 and Carthage in 397 and 419, by Innocent I in 405, and by the Council of Florence in 1441. It was defined by the Council of Trent in the dogmatic decree *De Canonicis Scripturis,* Apr. 8, 1546.

The Jews, although they generally accepted 22 or 24 books as sacred in the first century A.D., did not have a definite canon of sacred writings until late in the second or early in the third century. This canon was fixed by the consensus of rabbinical schools.

The canon of the Hebrew Masoretic Text, which is accepted by modern Jews, consists of 24 books, as follows:

• The Law: Genesis, Exodus, Leviticus, Numbers, Deuteronomy.

• The Prophets: earlier prophets — Joshua, Judges, Samuel, Kings; later prophets — Isaiah, Jeremiah, Ezekiel, and 12 others in one book (Hosea, Joel, Amos, Obadiah, Jonah, Micah, Nahum, Habakkuk, Zephaniah, Haggai, Zechariah, Malachi).

• The Writings: Psalms, Job, Proverbs, Ruth, Song of Songs, Ecclesiastes, Lamentations, Esther, Daniel, Ezra-Nehemiah, Chronicles.

This canon does not include a number of books in the Alexandrian collection of sacred writings — viz., 1 and 2 Maccabees, Tobit, Judith, Sirach, Wisdom, Baruch, and portions of Esther and Daniel (chapters 13 and 14). These additional books and passages, contained in the Septuagint version of the Old Testament and called deuterocanonical, are in the Catholic canon.

These books and passages, called deuterocanonical in terminology coined by Sixtus of Siena (1520-1569), were under discussion for some time until questions about their canonicity were settled. Books admitted into the canon with little or no debate were called protocanonical. The canonical status of both categories of books is the same in the Catholic Bible.

The Protestant canon, in an arrangement of 39 books, is the same as the Hebrew canon.

The Old Testament canon has not been definitely settled by the Orthodox. Since the time of the Reformation, however, they have given some preference to the Protestant canon.

The New Testament canon was firm by the end of the fourth century. By the end of the second century all of the New Testament books were generally known and most of them were acknowledged as inspired. The Muratorian Fragment, dating from about 200, listed most of the books recognized in later decrees as canonical. Prior to the end of the fourth century, however, there were controversies over the inspired character of several books — viz., the Letter to the Hebrews, James, Jude, 2 Peter, 2 and 3 John, and Revelation. Controversy over these books ended in the fourth century, and the canon stated by the councils of Hippo and Carthage and reaffirmed by Innocent I in 405 was solemnly defined by the Council of Trent (1545-63).

Although Martin Luther eliminated the aforementioned books from his New Testament canon, they were reinstated by his followers by the year 1700. Anglicans and Calvinists always retained them.

The Greek and Russian Orthodox have the same New Testament canon as the Catholic Church. Some variations exist among other separated Eastern churches.

Languages of the Bible

Hebrew, Aramaic and Greek were the original languages of the Bible. Most of the Old Testament books were written in Hebrew. Portions of Daniel, Ezra, Jeremiah, Esther, and probably the books of Tobit and Judith were written in Aramaic. The Book of Wisdom, 2 Maccabees and all the books of the New Testament were written in Greek.

Manuscripts and Versions

The original writings of the inspired authors have been lost. The Bible has been transmitted through ancient copies called manuscripts and through translations or versions.

Authoritative Greek manuscripts include the Sinaitic and Vatican manuscripts of the fourth century and the Alexandrine and Parisian of the fifth century A. D.

The Septuagint and Vulgate translations are in a class by themselves.

The Septuagint version, a Greek translation of the Old Testament, was begun about 250 and completed about 100 B. C. The work of several Jewish translators at Alexandria, it differed from the Hebrew Bible in the arrangement of books and included several, later called deuterocanonical, which were not acknowledged as sacred by the community at Jerusalem.

The Vulgate was a Latin version of the Old and New Testaments produced from the original languages by St. Jerome from about 383 to 404. It became the most widely used Latin text for centuries and was regarded as basic long before the Council of Trent designated it as authentic and suitable for use in public reading, controversy, preaching and teaching. Because of its authoritative character, it became the basis for many translations into other languages. A critical revision, in work since 1965, was completed by a pontifical commission in 1977.

Hebrew and Aramaic manuscripts of great antiquity and value have figured more significantly than before in recent scriptural work by Catholic scholars, especially since their use was strongly encouraged, if not mandated, in 1943 by Pius XII in the encyclical *Divino Afflante Spiritu.*

The English translation of the Bible in general use among Catholics until recent years was the *Douay-Rheims,* so called because of the places where it was prepared and published, the New Testament at Rheims in 1582 and the Old Testament at Douay in 1609. The translation was made from the Vulgate text. As revised and issued by Bishop Richard Challoner in 1749 and 1750, it became the standard Catholic English version for about 200 years.

A revision of the Challoner New Testament, made on the basis of the Vulgate text by scholars of the Catholic Biblical Association of America, was published in 1941 in the United States under the sponsorship of the Episcopal Committee of the Confraternity of Christian Doctrine.

New American Bible

A new translation of the entire Bible, the first ever made directly into English from the original languages under Catholic auspices, was projected in 1944 and completed in the fall of 1970 with publication of the *New American Bible.* The Episcopal Committee of the Confraternity of Christian Doctrine sponsored the NAB. The translators were members of the Catholic Biblical Association of America and several fellow scholars of other faiths. The typical edition was produced by St. Anthony Guild Press, Paterson, N. J.

Old Testament portions of the NAB were published in separate volumes before undergoing final revision and being bound in one cover. Genesis and Psalms were issued in 1948 and 1950; Genesis to Ruth, in 1952; Job to Sirach, in 1955; the Prophets, in 1961; Samuel to the Maccabees, in 1969. The new translation of the New Testament was issued for the first time in 1970.

Versions of the Bible approved for use in the Catholic liturgy are the *Douay-Rheims,* the *New American Bible, A New Translation from the Latin Vulgate* by Ronald A. Knox, the Catholic edition of the *Revised Standard Version,* and the *Jerusalem Bible.*

The *Jerusalem Bible* is an English translation of a French version based on the original languages. It was published by Doubleday & Co., Inc., which is also working toward completion of the *Anchor Bible.*

The Protestant counterpart of the *Douay-Rheims Bible* was the *King James Bible,* called the *Authorized Version* in England. Originally published in 1611, it was in general use for more than three centuries. Its modern revisions include the *English Revised Version,* published between 1881 and 1885; the *American Revised Version,* 1901, and revisions of the New Testament (1946) and the Old Testament (1952) published in 1957 in the United States as the *Revised Standard Version.*

The latest revision, a translation in the language of the present day made from Greek and Hebrew sources, is the *New English Bible,* published Mar. 16, 1970. Its New Testament portion was originally published in 1961.

Biblical Federation

The World Catholic Federation for the Biblical Apostolate, established in 1969, sponsors a program designed to create greater awareness among Catholics of the Bible and its use in everyday life. Mill Hill Father Arnold Jurgens is the general secretary.

The Bible as the source of spiritual development, especially for priests, students for the priesthood and religious, was the theme of the 1978 meeting of the federation held in April in Malta, with an attendance of persons from 45 nations.

The U. S. Center for the Catholic Biblical Apostolate, under the direction of Father Stephen Hartdegen, O.F.M., is related to the Department of Education, U.S. Catholic Conference. Address: 1312 Massachusetts Ave. N.W., Washington, D.C. 20005.

APOCRYPHA

Apocrypha are books which have some resemblance to the canonical books in subject matter and title but which have not been recognized as canonical by the Church. They are characterized by a false claim to divine authority; extravagant accounts of events and miracles alleged to be supplemental revelation; material favoring heresy (especially in "New Testament" apocrypha); minimal, if any, historical value.

Among examples of this type of literature itemized by J. McKenzie, S.J., in *Dictionary of the Bible* are: *the Books of Adam and Eve, Martyrdom of Isaiah, Testament of the Patriarchs, Assumption of Moses, Sibylline Oracles; Gospel of James, Gospel of Thomas, Arabic Gospel of the Infancy, History of Joseph the Carpenter; Acts of John, Acts of Paul, Acts of Peter, Acts of Andrew,* and numerous epistles.

Books of this type are called pseudepigrapha by Protestants. They regard the deuterocanonical books in the Catholic canon of Scripture as apocrypha.

DEAD SEA SCROLLS

The Qumran Scrolls, popularly called the Dead Sea Scrolls, are a collection of manuscripts, all but one of them in Hebrew, found between 1947 and 1956 in caves in the Desert of Juda west of the Dead Sea.

Among the findings were a complete text of Isaiah dating from the second century, B.C., more or less extensive fragments of other Old Testament texts (including the deuterocanonical Tobit), and a commentary on Habakkuk. Until the discovery of these materials, the oldest known Hebrew manuscripts were from the 10th century, A.D.

Also found were messianic and apocalyptic texts, and other writings describing the beliefs and practices of the Essenes, a rigoristic Jewish sect.

The scrolls, dating from about the first century before and after Christ, are important sources of information about Hebrew literature, Jewish history during the period between the Old and New Testaments, and the history of Old Testament texts. They established the fact that the Hebrew text of the Old Testament was fixed before the beginning of the Christian era and have had definite effects in recent critical studies and translations of the Old Testament. Together with other scrolls found at Masada, they are still the subject of intensive study.

A theory was proposed in 1972 by Father Jose O'Callaghan, a Spanish papyrologist, that a scrap of one of the scrolls might be a fragment of St. Mark's Gospel dating from about the year 50. Father Pierre Benoit, O.P., discounted the hypothesis, stating that it was based on an erroneous analysis of a photocopy of the scrap in question.

BOOKS OF THE BIBLE

Old Testament

(Dates are before Christ.)

Pentateuch

The Pentateuch is the collective title of the first five books of the Bible. Substantially, they identify the Israelites as Yahweh's Chosen People, cover their history from Egypt to the threshold of the Promised Land, contain the Mosaic Law and Covenant, and disclose the promise of salvation to come. Principal themes concern the divine promise of salvation, Yahweh's fidelity, and the Covenant. Work on the composition of the Pentateuch was completed in the sixth century.

Genesis: The book of origins, according to its title in the Septuagint. In two parts, covers: religious prehistory, including accounts of the origin of the world and man, the original state of innocence and the fall, the promise of salvation, patriarchs before and after the Deluge, the Tower of Babel narrative, genealogies (first 11 chapters); the covenant with Abraham and patriarchal history from Abraham to Joseph (balance of the 50 chapters). Significant are the themes of Yahweh's universal sovereignty and mercy.

Exodus: Named with the Greek word for departure, is a religious epic which describes the oppression of the 12 tribes in Egypt and their departure, liberation or passover therefrom under the leadership of Moses; Yahweh's establishment of the Covenant with them, making them his Chosen People, through the mediation of Moses at Mt. Sinai; instructions concerning the tabernacle, the sanctuary and Ark of the Covenant; the institution of the priesthood. The book is significant because of its theology of liberation and redemption. In Christian interpretation, the Exodus is a figure of baptism.

Leviticus: Mainly legislative in theme and purpose, contains laws regarding sacrifices, ceremonies of ordination and the priesthood of Aaron, legal purity, the holiness code, atonement, the redemption of offerings, and other subjects. Summarily, Levitical laws provided directives for all aspects of religious observance and for the manner in which the Israelites were to conduct themselves with respect to Yahweh and each other. Leviticus was the liturgical handbook of the priesthood.

Numbers: Taking its name from censuses recounted at the beginning and near the end, is a continuation of Exodus. It combines narrative of the Israelites' desert pilgrimage from Sinai to the border of Canaan with laws related to and expansive of those in Leviticus.

Deuteronomy: The concluding book of the Pentateuch, recapitulates, in the form of a testament of Moses, the Law and much of the desert history of the Israelites; enjoins fidelity to the Law as the key to good or bad fortune for the people; gives an account of the commissioning of Joshua as the successor of Moses. Notable themes concern the election of Israel by Yahweh, observance of the Law, prohibitions against the worship of foreign gods, worship of and confidence in Yahweh, the power of Yahweh in nature. The Deuteronomic Code or motif, embodying all of these elements, was the norm for interpreting Israelite history.

Joshua, Judges, Ruth

Joshua: Records the fulfillment of Yahweh's promise to the Israelites in their conquest, occupation and division of Canaan under the leadership of Joshua. It also contains an account of the return of Transjordanian Israelites and of a renewal of the Covenant. It was redacted in final form probably in the sixth century or later.

Judges: Records the actions of charismatic leaders, called judges, of the tribes of Israel between the death of Joshua and the time of Samuel, and a crisis of idolatry among the people. The basic themes are sin and punishment, repentance and deliverance; its purpose was in line with the Deuteronomic motif, that the fortunes of the Israelites were related to their observance or non-observance of the Law and the Covenant. It was redacted in final form probably in the sixth century.

Ruth: Named for the Gentile (Moabite) woman who, through marriage with Boaz, became an Israelite and an ancestress of David (her son, Obed, became his grandfather). Themes are filial piety, faith and trust in Yahweh, the universality of messianic salvation. Dates ranging from c. 950 to the seventh century have been assigned to the origin of the book, whose author is unknown.

Historical Books

These books, while they contain a great deal of factual material, are unique in their preoccupation with interpreting it, in the Deuteronomic manner, in primary relation to the Covenant on which the nation of Israel was founded and in accordance with which community and personal life were judged.

The books are: Samuel 1 and 2, from the end of Judges (c. 1020) to the end of David's reign (c. 961); Kings 1 and 2, from the last days of David to the start of the Babylonian Exile and the destruction of the Temple (587); Chronicles 1 and 2, from the reign of Saul (c. 1020-1000) to the return of the people from the Exile (538); Ezra and Nehemiah, covering the reorganization of the Jewish community after the Exile (458-397); Maccabees 1 and 2, recounting the struggle against attempted suppression of Judaism (168-142).

Three of the books listed below — Tobit, Judith and Esther — are categorized as religious novels.

Samuel 1 and 2: A single work in concept and contents, containing episodic history of the last two Judges, Eli and Samuel, the establishment and rule of the monarchy under Saul and David, and the political consequences of David's rule. The royal messianic dynasty of David was the subject of Nathan's Oracle in 2 Sm. 7. They were edited in final form probably late in the seventh century or during the Exile.

Kings 1 and 2: Cover the last days of David and the career of Solomon, including the building of the Temple and the history of the kingdom during his reign; stories of the prophets Elijah and Elisha; the history of the divided kingdom to the fall of Israel in the North (721) and the fall of Judah in the South (587), the destruction of Jerusalem and the Temple. They reflect the Deuteronomic motif in attributing the downfall of the people to corruption of belief and practice in public and private life. They were completed probably in the sixth century.

Chronicles 1 and 2: A collection of historical traditions interpreted in such a way as to present an ideal picture of one people governed by divine law and united in one Temple worship of the one true God. Contents include genealogical tables from Adam to David, the careers of David and Solomon, coverage of the kingdom of Judah to the Exile, and the decree of Cyrus permitting the return of the people and rebuilding of Jerusalem. Both are related to and were written about 400 by the same author, the Chronicler, who composed Ezra and Nehemiah.

Ezra and Nehemiah: A running account of the return of the people to their homeland after the Exile and of practical efforts, under the leadership of Ezra and Nehemiah, to restore and reorganize the religious and political community on the basis of Israelite traditions, divine worship and observance of the Law. Events of great significance were the building of the second Temple, the building of a wall around Jerusalem, and the proclamation of the Law by Ezra. This restored community was the start of Judaism. Both are related to and were written about 400 by the same author, the Chronicler, who composed Chronicles 1 and 2.

Tobit: Written in the literary form of a novel and having greater resemblance to wisdom than to historical literature, narrates the personal history of Tobit, a devout and charitable Jew in exile, and persons connected with him, viz., his son Tobiah, his kinsman Raguel, and Raguel's daughter Sarah. Its purpose was to teach people how to be good Jews. One of its principal themes is patience under trial, with trust in divine Providence which is symbolized by the presence and action of the angel Raphael. It was written about 200.

Judith: Recounts, in the literary form of a historical novel or romance, the preservation of the Israelites from conquest and ruin through the action of Judith. The essential themes are trust in God for deliverance from danger and emphasis on observance of the Law. It was written probably during the Maccabean period.

Esther: Relates, in the literary form of a historical novel or romance, the manner in which Jews in Persia were saved from annihilation through the central role played by Esther, the Jewish wife of Ahasuerus; a fact commemorated by the Jewish feast of Purim. Like Judith, it has trust in divine Providence as its theme and indicates that God's saving will is sometimes realized by persons acting in unlikely ways. Its origin and date are uncertain; it may have been written about 200 near the beginning of the period of strong Hellenistic influence on the Jews.

Maccabees 1 and 2: While related to some extent because of common subject matter, are quite different from each other.

The first book recounts the background and events of the 40-year (175-135) struggle for religious and political freedom led by Judas Maccabaeus and his brothers against the Hellenist Seleucid kings and some Hellenophiles among the Jews. Victory was symbolized by the rededication of the Temple. Against the background of opposition between Jews and Gentiles, the author equated the survival of belief in the one true God with survival of the Jewish people, thus identifying religion with patriotism. It was written probably by a Palestinian Jew after 104.

The second book supplements the first to some extent, covering and giving a theological interpretation to events from 180 to 162. It explains the feast of the Dedication of the Temple, a key event in the survival of Judaism which is commemorated in the feast of Hanukkah; stresses the primacy of God's action in the struggle for survival; and indicates belief in an afterlife and the resurrection of the body. It was written probably by a Jew of Alexandria after 120.

Wisdom Books

With the exceptions of Psalms and the Song of Songs, the titles listed under this heading are called wisdom books because their purpose was to formulate the fruits of human experience in the context of meditation on sacred Scripture and to present them as an aid toward understanding the problems of life. Hebrew wisdom literature was distinctive from pagan literature of the same type, but it had limitations; these were overcome in the New Testament, which added the dimensions of the New Covenant to those of the Old. Solomon was regarded as the archtype of the wise man.

Job: A dramatic, didactic poem consisting mainly of several dialogues between Job and his friends concerning the mystery involved in the coexistence of the just God, evil, and the suffering of the just. It describes an innocent man's experience of suffering and conveys the truth that faith in and submission to God rather than complete understanding, which is impossible, make the experience bearable; also, that the justice of God cannot be defended by affirming that it is realized in this world. Of uncertain authorship, it was written probably between the fifth and third centuries.

Psalms: A collection of 150 religious songs or lyrics reflecting Israelite belief and piety dating from the time of the monarchy to the post-Exilic period, a span of well over 500 years. The psalms, which are a compendium of Old Testament theology, were used in the temple liturgy and were of several types suitable for the king, hymns, lamentations, expressions of confidence and thanksgiving, prophecy, historical meditation and reflection, and the statement of wisdom. About one-half of them are attributed to David; many, by unknown authors, date from the early post-Exilic period.

Proverbs: The oldest book of the wisdom type in the Bible, consisting of collections of sayings attributed to Solomon and other persons regarding a wide variety of subjects including wisdom and its nature, rules of conduct, duties with respect to one's neighbor, the conduct of daily affairs. It reveals many details of Jewish life. Its nucleus dates from the period before the Exile, but no definite date can be assigned for its final compilation.

Ecclesiastes: A treatise about many subjects whose unifying theme is the vanity of strictly human efforts and accomplishments with respect to the achievement of lasting happiness; the only things which are not vain are fear of the Lord and observance of his commandments. The pessimistic tone of the book is due to the absence of a concept of afterlife. It was written by an unknown author about 250.

Song of Songs: A collection of erotic lyrics reflecting various themes, including the celebration of fidelity and love between man and woman. According to one interpretation, the book is a parable of the love of Yahweh for Israel. It was written by an unknown author after the Exile.

Wisdom: Deals with many subjects including the reward of justice; praise of wisdom, a gift of Yahweh proceeding from belief in him and the practice of his Law; the part played by him in the history of his people, especially in their liberation from Egypt; the folly and shame of idolatry. Its contents are taken from the whole sacred literature of the Jews and represent a distillation of its wisdom based on the law, beliefs and traditions of Israel. Contains the first Old Testament affirmation of an afterlife with God. The last book of the Old Testament to be written, it was probably composed about 50 years before Christ by an unknown author to confirm the faith of the Jewish community in Alexandria.

Sirach: Resembling Proverbs, is a collection of sayings handed on by a grandfather to his grandson. It contains a variety of moral instruction and eulogies of patriarchs and other figures in Israelite history. Its moral maxims apply to individuals, the family and community, relations with God, friendship, education, wealth, the Law, divine worship. Its theme is that true wisdom consists in the Law. (It was formerly called Ecclesiasticus, the Church Book, because of its extensive use by the Church for moral instruction.) It was written in Hebrew between 200 and 175, during a period of strong Hellenistic influence, and was translated into Greek after 132.

The Prophets

These books and the prophecies they contain "express judgments of the people's moral conduct, on the basis of the Mosaic alliance between God and Israel. They teach sublime truths and lofty morals. They contain exhortations, threats, announcements of punishment, promises of deliverance. . . . In the affairs of men, their prime concern is the interests of God, especially in what pertains to the Chosen People through whom the Messiah is to come; hence their denunciations of idolatry and of that externalism in worship which exclude the interior spirit of religion. They are concerned also with the universal nature of the moral law, with personal responsibility, with the person and office of the Messiah, and with the conduct of foreign nations" (*The Holy Bible,* Prophetic Books, CCD Edition, 1961; Preface). There are four major (Isaiah, Jeremiah, Ezekiel, Daniel) and 12 minor prophets (distinguished by the length of books), Lamentations and Baruch. Earlier prophets, mentioned in historical books, include Samuel, Gad, Nathan, Elijah and Elisha.

Before the Exile, prophets were the intermediaries through whom God communicated revelation to the people. Afterwards, prophecy lapsed and the written word of the Law served this purpose.

Isaiah: Named for the greatest of the prophets whose career spanned the reigns of three Hebrew kings from 742 to the beginning of the seventh century, in a period of moral breakdown in Judah and threats of invasion by foreign enemies. It is an anthology of poems and oracles credited to him and a number of followers deeply influenced by him. Of special importance are the prophecies concerning Immanuel (6 to 12), including the prophecy of the virgin birth (7:14). Chapters 40 to 55, called Deutero-Isaiah, are attributed to an anonymous poet toward the end of the Exile; this portion contains the Songs of the Servant. The concluding part of the book (56-66) contains oracles by later disciples. One of many themes in Isaiah concerned the saving mission of the remnant of Israel in the divine plan of salvation. It was edited in its present form by 180.

Jeremiah: Combines history, biography and prophecy in a setting of crisis caused by internal and external factors, viz., idolatry and general infidelity to the Law among the Israelites and external threats from the Assyrians, Egyptians and Babylonians. Jeremiah prophesied the promise of a new covenant as well as the destruction of Jerusalem and the Temple. His career began in 626 and ended some years after the beginning of the Exile. The book, the longest in the Bible, was edited in final form after the Exile.

Lamentations: A collection of five laments or elegies over the fall of Jerusalem and the fate of the people in Exile, written by an unknown eyewitness not long after 587. They convey the message that Yahweh struck the people because of their sins and reflect confidence in his love and power to restore his converted people.

Baruch: Against the background of the already begun Exile, it consists of an introduction and several parts: an exile's prayer of confession and petition for forgiveness and the restoration of Israel; a poem praising wisdom and the Law of Moses; a lament in which Jerusalem, personified, bewails the fate of her people and consoles them with the hope of blessings to come; and a polemic against idolatry. Although ascribed to Baruch, Jeremiah's secretary, it was written by several authors probably in the second century.

Ezekiel: Named for the priest-prophet who prophesied in Babylon from 593 to 571, during the first phase of the Exile. To prepare his fellow early exiles for the impending fall of Jerusalem, he reproached the Israelites for past sins and predicted woes to come upon them. After the destruction of the city, the burden of his message was hope and promise of restoration. Ezekiel had great influence on the religion of Israel after the Exile. The book, which contains the substance of his teaching, had a number of authors and editors.

Daniel: The protagonist is a fictional young Jew, taken early to Babylon where he lived until 537, who figured in a series of edifying stories. The stories, which originated from Israelite tradition, recount the trials and triumphs of Daniel and his three companions, and other episodes including those concerning Susannah, Bel, and the Dragon. The book is more apocalyptic than prophetic: it envisions Israel in glory to come and conveys the message that men of faith can resist temptation and overcome adversity. It states the prophetic themes of right conduct, divine control of men and events, and the final triumph of the kingdom. It was written by an unknown author in the 160's to give moral support to Jews during the persecutions of the Maccabean period.

Hosea: Consists of a prophetic parallel between Hosea's marriage and Yahweh's relations with his people. As the prophet was married to a faithless wife whom he would not give up, Yahweh was bound in Covenant with an idolatrous and unjust Israel whom he would not desert but would chastise for purification. Hosea belonged to the Northern Kingdom of Israel and began his career about the middle of the eighth century. He inaugurated the tradition of describing Yahweh's relation to Israel in terms of marriage.

Joel: Is apocalyptic and eschatological regarding divine judgment, the Day of the Lord, which is symbolized by a ravaging invasion of locusts, the judgment of the nations in the Valley of Josaphat, and the outpouring of the Spirit in the messianic era to come. Its message is that God will vindicate and save Israel, in view of the prayer and repentance of the people, and will punish their enemies. It was composed after the period of Nehemiah.

Amos: Consists of an indictment against foreign enemies of Israel; a strong denunciation of the people of Israel, whose infidelity, idolatry and injustice made them subject to divine judgment and punishment; and a messianic oracle regarding Israel's restoration. Amos prophesied in the Northern Kingdom of Israel, at Bethel, in the first half of the eighth century; chronologically, he was the first of the canonical prophets.

Obadiah: A 21-verse prophecy, the shortest and one of the sternest in the Bible, against the Edomites, invaders of southern Judah and enemies of those returning from the Exile to their homeland. It was redacted in final form no later than the end of the fourth century.

Jonah: A parable of divine mercy with the theme that Yahweh wills the salvation of all, not just a few, men who respond to his call. Its protagonist is a disobedient prophet; forced by circumstances beyond his control to preach penance among Gentiles, he is highly successful in his mission but baffled by the divine concern for those who do not belong to the Chosen People. It was written after the Exile.

Micah: Attacks the injustice and corruption of priests, false prophets, officials and people; announces judgment and punishment to come; foretells the restoration of Israel; refers to the saving remnant of Israel. Micah was a contemporary of Isaiah.

Nahum: Dating from about 613, concerns the destruction of Nineveh in 612 and the overthrow of the Assyrian Empire by the Babylonians.

Habakkuk: Dating from about 605-597, concerns sufferings to be inflicted by oppressors on the people of Judah because of their infidelity to the Lord. It also sounds a note of confidence in the Lord, the Savior, and declares that the just will not perish.

Zephaniah: Exercising his ministry in the second half of the seventh century, during a time of widespread idolatry, superstition and religious degradation, he prophesied impending judgment and punishment for Jerusalem and its people. He prophesied too that a holy remnant of the people (Anawim, mentioned also by Amos) would be spared. Zephaniah was a forerunner of Jeremiah.

Haggai: One of the first prophets after the Exile, Haggai in 520 encouraged the returning exiles to reestablish their community and to complete the second Temple (dedicated in 515), for which he envisioned greater glory, in a messianic sense, than that enjoyed by the original Temple of Solomon.

Zechariah: A contemporary of Haggai, he prophesied in the same vein. A second part of the book, called Deutero-Zechariah and composed by one or more unknown authors, relates a vision of the coming of the Prince of Peace, the Messiah of the Poor.

Malachi: Written by an anonymous author, presents a picture of life in the post-Exilic community between 516 and the initiation of reforms by Ezra and Nehemiah about 432. Blame for the troubles of the community is placed mainly on priests for failure to carry out ritual worship and to instruct the people in the proper manner; other factors were religious indifference and the influence of doubters who were scandalized at the prosperity of the wicked. The vision of a universal sacrifice to be offered to Yahweh (1:11) is interpreted in Christian theology as a prophecy of the sacrifice of the Mass. Malachi was the last of the minor prophets.

OLD TESTAMENT DATES

c. 1800 — c. 1600: Period of the patriarchs (Abraham, Isaac, Jacob).

c. 1600: Israelites in Egypt.

c. 1250: Exodus of Israelites from Egypt.

c. 1210: Entrance of Israelites into Canaan.

c. 1210 — c. 1020: Period of the Judges.

c. 1020 — c. 1000: Reign of Saul, first king.

c. 1000 — c. 961: Reign of David.

c. 961 — 922: Reign of Solomon. Temple built during his reign.

922: Division of the Kingdom into Israel (North) and Judah (South).

721: Conquest of Israel by Assyrians.

587-538: Conquest of Judah by Babylonians. Babylonian Captivity and Exile. Destruction of Jerusalem and the Temple, 587. Captivity ended with the return of exiles, following the decree of Cyrus permitting the rebuilding of Jerusalem.

515: Dedication of the Second Temple.

458-397: Restoration and reform of the Jewish religious and political community; building of the Jerusalem wall, 439. Leaders in the movement were Ezra and Nehemiah.

168-142: Period of the Maccabees; war against Syrians.

142: Independence granted to Jews by Demetrius II of Syria.

135-37: Period of the Hasmonean dynasty.

63: Beginning of Roman rule.

37-4: Period of Herod the Great.

New Testament Books

Gospels

The term Gospel is derived from the Anglo-Saxon *god-spell* and the Greek *euangelion,* meaning good news, good tidings. In Christian use, it means the good news of salvation proclaimed by Christ and the Church, and handed on in written form in the Gospels of Matthew, Mark, Luke and John.

The initial proclamation of the coming of the kingdom of God was made by Jesus in and through his Person, teachings and actions, and especially through his Passion, death and resurrection. This proclamation became the center of Christian faith and the core of the oral Gospel tradition with which the Church spread the good news by apostolic preaching for some 30 years before it was committed to writing by the Evangelists.

According to an Instruction issued by the Pontifical Commission for Biblical Studies Apr. 21, 1964:

• The sacred writers selected from the material at their disposal (the oral Gospel tradition, some written collections of sayings and deeds of Jesus, eyewitness accounts) those things which were particularly suitable to the various conditions (liturgical, catechetical, missionary) of the faithful and the aims they had in mind, and they narrated these things in such a way as to correspond with those circumstances and their aims.

• The life and teaching of Jesus were not simply reported in a biographical manner for the purpose of preserving their memory but were "preached" so as to offer the Church the basis of doctrine concerning faith and morals.

• In their works, the Evangelists presented the true sayings of Jesus and the events of his life in the light of the better understanding they had following their enlightenment by the Holy Spirit. They did not transform Christ into a "mythical" Person, nor did they distort his teaching.

Passion narratives are the core of all the Gospels, covering the suffering, death and resurrection of Jesus as central events in bringing about and establishing the New Covenant. Leading up to them are accounts of the mission of John the Baptizer and the ministry of Jesus, especially in Galilee and finally in Jerusalem before the Passion. The infancy of Jesus is covered by Luke and Matthew with narratives inspired by Old Testament citations appropriate to the birth of the Messiah.

Matthew, Mark and Luke, while different in various respects, have so many similarities that they are called Synoptic; their relationships are the subject of the Synoptic Problem.

Matthew: Written in the 70's or 80's for Jewish Christians, with clear reference to Jewish background and identification of Jesus as the divine Messiah, the fulfillment of the Old Testament. Distinctive are the use of Old Testament citations regarding the Person, activity and teaching of Jesus, and the presentation of doctrine in sermons and discourses. The canonical Matthew was written in Greek, with dependence on Mark.

Mark: The first of the Gospels, dating from about 65. Written for Gentile Christians, it is noted for the realism and wealth of concrete details with which it reveals Jesus as Son of God and Savior more by his actions and miracles than by his discourses. Theologically, it is less refined than the other Gospels.

Luke: Written in the 70's or 80's for Gentile Christians. It is noted for the universality of its address, the insight it provides into the Christian way of life, the place it gives to women, the manner in which it emphasizes Jesus' friendship with sinners and compassion for the suffering.

John: Written sometime in the 90's, is the most sublime and theological of the Gospels, and is different from the Synoptics in plan and treatment. Combining accounts of signs with longer discourses and reflections, it progressively reveals the Person and mission of Jesus — as Word, Way, Truth, Life, Light — in line with the purpose, "to help you believe that Jesus is the Messiah, the Son of God, so that through this faith you may have life in his name" (Jn. 20:31). There are questions about the authorship but no doubt about the Johannine tradition behind the Gospel.

Acts of the Apostles

Acts of the Apostles: Written by Luke in the 70's or 80's as a supplement to his Gospel. It describes the origin and spread of Christian communities through the action of the Holy Spirit from the resurrection of Christ to the time of Paul's first Roman imprisonment in the early 60's.

Letters (Epistles)

These letters, the first documents of the New Testament, were written in response to existential needs of the early Christian communities for doctrinal and moral instruction, disciplinary action, practical advice, and exhortation to true Christian living.

Pauline Letters

These letters, which comprise approximately one-fourth of the New Testament, are primary and monumental sources of the development of Christian theology. Several of them may not have had Paul as their actual author, but evidence of the Pauline tradition behind them is strong. The letters to the Colossians, Philippians, Ephesians and Philemon have been called the "Captivity Letters" because of a tradition that they were written while Paul was under house arrest in Rome from 61 to 63.

Romans: Written in the late 50's from

Corinth on the central significance of Christ and faith in him for salvation, and the relationship of Christianity to Judaism; the condition of mankind without Christ; justification and the Christian life; duties of Christians.

Corinthians 1: Written near the beginning of 57 from Ephesus to counteract factionalism and disorders, it covers community dissensions, moral irregularities, marriage and celibacy, conduct at religious gatherings, the Eucharist, spiritual gifts (charisms) and their function in the Church, charity, the resurrection of the body.

Corinthians 2: Written later in the same year as 1 Cor., concerning Paul's defense of his apostolic life and ministry, and an appeal for a collection to aid poor Christians in Jerusalem.

Galatians: Written probably between 54 and 57 (perhaps earlier, according to some scholars) to counteract Judaizing opinions and efforts to undermine his authority, it asserts the divine origin of Paul's authority and doctrine, states that justification is not through Mosaic Law but through faith in Christ, insists on the practice of evangelical virtues, especially charity.

Ephesians: Written probably between 61 and 63, or perhaps in the 70's, mainly on the Church as the Mystical Body of Christ.

Philippians: Written between 61 and 63 primarily to thank the Philippians for their kindness to him while he was under house arrest in Rome.

Colossians: Written while he was under house arrest in Rome from 61 to 63 to counteract the influence of self-appointed teachers who were watering down doctrine concerning Christ. It includes two highly important Christological passages, a warning against false teachers, and an instruction on the ideal Christian life.

Thessalonians 1 and 2: Written within a short time of each other probably in 51 from Corinth, mainly on doctrine concerning the Parousia, the second coming of Christ.

Timothy 1 and 2, Titus: Written between 65 and 67, or perhaps in the 70's, giving pastoral counsels to Timothy and Titus who were in charge of churches in Ephesus and Crete, respectively. 1 Tm. emphasizes pastoral responsibility for preserving unity of doctrine; 2 Tm. describes Paul's imprisonment in Rome.

Philemon: A private letter written between 61 and 63 to a wealthy Colossian concerning a slave, Onesimus, who had escaped from him; Paul appealed for kind treatment of the man.

Hebrews: Dating from some time between the mid-60's and the 80's, a complex theological treatise on Christology, the priesthood and sacrifice of Christ, the New Covenant, and the pattern for Christian living. Critical opinion is divided as to whether it was addressed to Judaeo or Gentile Christians.

Catholic Letters, Revelation

These seven letters have been called "catholic" because it was thought for some time, not altogether correctly, that they were not addressed to particular communities.

James: Written sometime between the mid-60's and the 80's (although datable before 62 according to some scholars) in the spirit of Hebrew wisdom literature and the moralism of Tobit. An exhortation to practical Christian living, it is also noteworthy for the doctrine it states on good works and its citation regarding anointing of the sick.

Peter 1 and 2: The first letter may have been written in the mid-60's; the second dates from 100 to 125. Addressed to Christians in Asia Minor, both are exhortations to perseverance in the life of faith despite trials and difficulties arising from pagan influences, isolation from other Christians, and false teaching.

John 1: Written sometime in the 90's and addressed to Asian churches, its message is that God is made known to us in the Son and that fellowship with the Father is attained by living in the light, justice and love of the Son.

John 2: Written sometime in the 90's and addressed to a church in Asia, it commends the people for standing firm in the faith and urges them to perseverance.

John 3: Written sometime in the 90's, it appears to represent an effort to settle a jurisdictional dispute in one of the churches.

Jude: Written sometime between the 70's and 90's, it is a brief treatise against erroneous teachings and practices opposed to law, authority and true Christian freedom.

Revelation: Written in the 90's along the lines of Johannine thought, it is a symbolic and apocalyptic treatment of things to come combined with warning but hope and assurance to the Church regarding the coming of the Lord in glory.

BIBLICAL AUTHORSHIP

Some books of the Bible were not written by the authors to whom they have been traditionally attributed; New Testament examples are the Gospels of Matthew and John, Hebrews, 1 and 2 Timothy, Titus, James, Jude.

This fact, which has never been the subject of dogmatic definition by the Church, does not militate against the canonicity of the books, since canonicity concerns the theological matter of inspiration rather than the historical question of human authorship.

Questions concerning authorship are explained in various ways: (1) according to an old custom whereby literary works of importance were sometimes attributed to famous persons so they would get a reading; (2) authorship, by a disciple or school of disciples, of works derived from the doctrine of a master; (3) authorship by persons writing in the spirit and tradition of a master.

INTERPRETATION OF THE BIBLE

According to the *Constitution on Revelation* issued by the Second Vatican Council, "the interpreter of Sacred Scripture, in order to see clearly what God wanted to communicate to us, should carefully investigate what meaning the sacred writers really intended, and what God wanted to manifest by means of their words" (No. 12).

Hermeneutics, Exegesis

This careful investigation proceeds in accordance with the rules of hermeneutics, the normative science of biblical interpretation and explanation. Hermeneutics in practice is called exegesis.

The principles of hermeneutics are derived from various disciplines and many factors which have to be considered in explaining the Bible and its parts. These include: the original languages and languages of translation of the sacred texts, through philology and linguistics; the quality of texts, through textual criticism; literary forms and genres, through literary and form criticism; cultural, historical, geographical and other conditions which influenced the writers, through related studies; facts and truths of salvation history; the truths and analogy of faith.

Distinctive to biblical hermeneutics, which differs in important respects from literary interpretation in general, is the premise that the Bible, though written by human authors, is the work of divine inspiration in which God reveals his plan for the salvation of men through historical events and persons, and especially through the Person and mission of Christ.

Textual, Form Criticism

Textual criticism is the study of biblical texts, which have been transmitted in copies several times removed from the original manuscripts, for the purpose of establishing the real state of the original texts. This purpose is served by comparison of existing copies; by application to the texts of the disciplines of philology and linguistics; by examination of related works of antiquity; by study of biblical citations in works of the Fathers of the Church and other authors; and by other means of literary study.

Since about 1920, the sayings of Christ have been a particular object of New Testament study, the purpose being to analyze the forms of expression used by the Evangelists in order to ascertain the words actually spoken by him.

Literary Criticism

Literary criticism aims to determine the origin and kinds of literary composition, called forms or genres, employed by the inspired authors. Such determinations are necessary for decision regarding the nature and purpose and, consequently, the meaning of biblical passages. Underlying these studies is the principle that the manner of writing was conditioned by the intention of the authors, the meaning they wanted to convey, and the then-contemporary literary style, mode or medium best adapted to carry their message — e.g., true history, quasi-historical narrative, poems, prayers, hymns, psalms, aphorisms, allegories, discourses. Understanding these media is necessary for the valid interpretation of their message.

Literal Sense

The key to all valid interpretation is the literal sense of biblical passages. Regarding this matter and the relevance to it of the studies and procedures described above, Pius XII wrote the following in the encyclical *Divino Afflante Spiritu*.

"What the literal sense of a passage is, is not always as obvious in the speeches and writings of ancient authors of the East as it is in the works of our own time. For what they wished to express is not to be determined by the rules of grammar and philology alone nor solely by the context; the interpreter must, as it were, go back wholly in spirit to those remote centuries of the East and with the aid of history, archeology, ethnology, and other sciences accurately determine what modes of writing, so to speak, the authors of that ancient period would be likely to use and in fact did use. . . . In explaining the Sacred Scripture and in demonstrating and proving its immunity from all error (the Catholic interpreter) should make a prudent use of this means, determine to what extent the manner of expression or literary mode adopted by the sacred writer may lead to a correct and genuine interpretation; and let him be convinced that this part of his office cannot be neglected without serious detriment to Catholic exegesis."

The literal sense of the Bible is the meaning in the mind of and intended by the inspired writer of a book or passage of the Bible. This is determined by the application to texts of the rules of hermeneutics. It is not to be confused with word-for-word literalism.

Typical Sense

The typical sense is the meaning which a passage has not only in itself but also in reference to something else of which it is a type or foreshadowing. A clear example is the account of the Exodus of the Israelites: in its literal sense, it narrates the liberation of the Israelites from death and oppression in Egypt; in its typical sense, it foreshadowed the liberation of men from sin through the redemptive death and resurrection of Christ. The typical sense of this and other passages emerged in the working out of God's plan of salvation history. It did not have to be in the mind of the author of the original passage.

Accommodated Senses

Accommodated, allegorical and consequent senses are figurative and adaptive meanings given to books and passages of the Bible for moral and other purposes. Such interpretations involve the danger of stretching the literal sense beyond proper proportions. Hermeneutical principles require that interpretations like these respect the integrity of the literal sense of the passages in question.

In the Catholic view, the final word on questions of biblical interpretation belongs to the teaching authority of the Church. In other views, generally derived from basic principles stated by Martin Luther, John Calvin and other Reformers, the primacy belongs to individual judgment acting in response to the inner testimony of the Holy Spirit, the edifying nature of biblical subject matter, the sublimity and simplicity of the message of salvation, the intensity with which Christ is proclaimed.

Biblical Studies

The first center for biblical studies, in some strict sense of the term, was the School of Alexandria, founded in the latter half of the second century. It was noted for allegorical exegesis. Literal interpretation was a hallmark of the School of Antioch.

St. Jerome, who produced the Vulgate, and St. Augustine, author of numerous commentaries, were the most important figures in biblical studies during the patristic period. By the time of the latter's death, the Old and New Testament canons had been stabilized. For some centuries afterwards, there was little or no progress in scriptural studies, although collections were made of scriptural excerpts from the writings of the Fathers of the Church, and the systematic reading of Scripture became established as a feature of monastic life.

Advances were made in the 12th and 13th centuries with the introduction of new principles and methods of scriptural analysis stemming from renewed interest in Hebraic studies and the application of dialectics.

By the time of the Reformation, the Bible had become the first book set in movable type, and more than 100 vernacular editions were in use throughout Europe.

The Council of Trent

In the wake of the Reformation, the Council of Trent formally defined the Canon of the Bible; it also reasserted the authoritative role of tradition and the teaching authority of the Church as well as Scripture with respect to the rule of faith. In the heated atmosphere of the 16th and 17th centuries, the Bible was turned into a polemical weapon; Protestants used it to defend their doctrines, and Catholics countered with citations in support of the dogmas of the Church. One result of this state of affairs was a lack of substantial progress in biblical studies during the period.

Toward the end of the 17th century, Louis Cappel, a Protestant, introduced a methodology for textual criticism, and Richard Simon, a Catholic, inaugurated modern literary and historical criticism. Their work was poorly regarded, however, and went into eclipse until about the beginning of the 19th century. It was then taken over by men whose work threatened to destroy the credibility of not only the Bible but Christianity itself.

Rationalists, and later Modernists, denied the reality of the supernatural and doctrine concerning inspiration of the Bible, which they generally regarded as a strictly human production expressive of the religious sense and experience of mankind. In their hands, the tools of positive critical research became weapons for biblical subversion. The defensive Catholic reaction to their work had the temporary effect of alienating scholars of the Church from solid advances in archeology, philology, history, textual and literary criticism.

Catholic Developments

Major influences in bringing about a change in Catholic attitude toward use of these disciplines in biblical studies were two papal encyclicals and two institutes of special study, the Ecole Biblique, founded in Jerusalem in 1890, and the Pontifical Biblical Institute established in Rome in 1909. The encyclical *Providentissimus Deus,* issued by Leo XIII in 1893, marked an important breakthrough; in addition to defending the concept of divine inspiration and the formal inspiration of the Scriptures, it encouraged the study of allied and ancillary sciences and techniques for a more fruitful understanding of the sacred writings. The encyclical *Divino Afflante Spiritu,* 50 years later, gave encouragement for the use of various forms of criticism as tools of biblical research. The documents encouraged the work of scholars and stimulated wide communication of the fruits of their study.

Great changes in the climate and direction of biblical studies have occurred in recent years. One of them has been an increase in cooperative effort among Catholic, Protestant, Orthodox and Jewish scholars. Their common investigation of the Dead Sea Scrolls is well known. More recently productive was the collaboration in England of Catholics and Protestants in turning out a Catholic edition of the Revised Standard Version of the Bible.

The development and results of biblical studies in this century have directly and significantly affected all phases of the contemporary renewal movement in the Church. Their influence on theology, liturgy, catechetics, and preaching indicate the importance of their function in the life of the Church.

APOSTLES AND EVANGELISTS

The Apostles were the men selected, trained and commissioned by Christ to preach the Gospel, to baptize, to establish, direct and care for his Church as servants of God and stewards of his mysteries. They were the first bishops of the Church.

St. Matthew's Gospel lists the Apostles in this order: Peter, Andrew, James the Greater, John, Philip, Bartholomew, Thomas, Matthew, James the Less, Jude, Simon and Judas Iscariot. Matthias was elected to fill the place of Judas. Paul became an Apostle by a special call from Christ. Barnabas was called an Apostle.

Two of the Evangelists, John and Matthew, were Apostles. The other two, Luke and Mark, were closely associated with the apostolic college.

Andrew: Born in Bethsaida, brother of Peter, disciple of John the Baptist, a fisherman, the first Apostle called; according to legend, preached the Gospel in Northern Greece, Epirus and Scythia, and was martyred at Patras about 70; in art, is represented with an x-shaped cross, called St. Andrew's Cross; feast, Nov. 30; is honored as the patron of Russia and Scotland.

Barnabas: Originally called Joseph but named Barnabas by the Apostles, among whom he is ranked because of his collaboration with Paul; a Jew of the Diaspora, born on Cyprus; a cousin of Mark and member of the Christian community at Jerusalem, influenced the Apostles to accept Paul, with whom he became a pioneer missionary outside Palestine and Syria, to Antioch, Cyprus and southern Asia Minor; legend says he was martyred on Cyprus during the Neronian persecution; feast, June 11.

Bartholomew (Nathaniel): A friend of Philip; according to various traditions, preached the Gospel in Ethiopia, India, Persia, and Armenia where he was martyred by being flayed and beheaded; in art, is depicted holding a knife, an instrument of his death; feast, Aug. 24 in the Roman Rite, Aug. 25 in the Byzantine Rite.

James the Greater: A Galilean, son of Zebedee, brother of John (with whom he was called a "son of thunder"), a fisherman; with Peter and John, witnessed the raising of Jairus' daughter to life, the transfiguration, the agony of Jesus in the Garden of Gethsemani; first of the Apostles to die, by the sword in 44 during the rule of Herod Agrippa; there is doubt about a journey legend says he made to Spain and also about the authenticity of relics said to be his at Santiago de Compostela; in art, is depicted carrying a pilgrim's bell; feast, July 25 in the Roman Rite, Apr. 30 in the Byzantine Rite.

James the Less: Son of Alphaeus, called "Less" because he was younger in age or shorter in stature than James the Greater; one

of the "catholic" epistles bears his name; was stoned to death in 62 or thrown from the top of the temple in Jerusalem and clubbed to death in 66; in art, is depicted with a club or heavy staff; feast, May 3 in the Roman Rite, Oct. 9 in the Byzantine Rite.

John: A Galilean, son of Zebedee, brother of James the Greater (with whom he was called a "son of thunder"), a fisherman, probably a disciple of John the Baptist, one of the Evangelists, called the "beloved disciple"; with Peter and James the Greater, witnessed the raising of Jairus' daughter to life, the transfiguration, the agony of Jesus in the Garden of Gethsemani; Mary was commended to his special care by Christ; the fourth Gospel, three "catholic" Epistles and Revelation bear his name; according to various accounts, lived at Ephesus in Asia Minor for some time and died a natural death about 100; in art, is represented by an eagle, symbolic of the sublimity of the contents of his Gospel; feast, Dec. 27 in the Roman Rite, May 8 in the Byzantine Rite.

Jude Thaddeus: One of the "catholic" epistles, the shortest, bears his name; various traditions say he preached the Gospel in Mesopotamia, Persia and elsewhere, and was martyred; in art, is depicted with a halberd, the instrument of his death; feast, Oct. 28 in the Roman Rite, June 19 in the Byzantine Rite.

Luke: A Greek convert to the Christian community, called "our most dear physician" by Paul, of whom he was a missionary companion; author of the third Gospel and Acts of the Apostles; the place — Achaia, Bithynia, Egypt — and circumstances of his death are not certain; in art, is depicted as a man, a writer, or an ox (because his Gospel starts at the scene of Temple sacrifice); feast, Oct. 18.

Mark: A cousin of Barnabas and member of the first Christian community at Jerusalem; a missionary companion of Paul and Barnabas, then of Peter; author of the Gospel which bears his name; according to legend, founded the Church at Alexandria, was bishop there and was martyred in the streets of the city; in art, is depicted with his Gospel and a winged lion, symbolic of the voice of John the Baptist crying in the wilderness, at the beginning of his Gospel; feast, Apr. 25.

Matthew: A Galilean, called Levi by Luke and John and the son of Alphaeus by Mark, a tax collector, one of the Evangelists; according to various accounts, preached the Gospel in Judea, Ethiopia, Persia and Parthia, and was martyred; in art, is depicted with a spear, the instrument of his death, and as a winged man in his role as Evangelist; feast, Sept. 21 in the Roman Rite, Nov. 16 in the Byzantine Rite.

Matthias: A disciple of Jesus whom the faithful 11 Apostles chose to replace Judas before the Resurrection; uncertain traditions report that he preached the Gospel in Palestine, Cappadocia or Ethiopia; in art, is represented with a cross and a halberd, the instruments of his death as a martyr; feast, May 14 in the Roman Rite, Aug. 9 in the Byzantine Rite.

Paul: Born at Tarsus, of the tribe of Benjamin, a Roman citizen; participated in the persecution of Christians until the time of his miraculous conversion on the way to Damascus; called by Christ, who revealed himself to him in a special way; became the Apostle of the Gentiles, among whom he did most of his preaching in the course of three major missionary journeys through areas north of Palestine, Cyprus, Asia Minor and Greece; 14 epistles bear his name; two years of imprisonment at Rome, following initial arrest in Jerusalem and confinement at Caesarea, ended with martyrdom, by beheading, outside the walls of the city in 64 or 67 during the Neronian persecution; in art, is depicted in various ways with St. Peter, with a sword, in the scene of his conversion; feasts, June 29, Jan. 25 (Roman Rite).

Peter: Simon, son of Jona, born in Bethsaida, brother of Andrew, a fisherman; called Cephas or Peter by Christ who made him the chief of the Apostles and head of the Church as his vicar; named first in the listings of Apostles in the Synoptic Gospels and the Acts of the Apostles; with James the Greater and John, witnessed the raising of Jairus' daughter to life, the transfiguration, the agony of Jesus in the Garden of Gethsemani; was the first to preach the Gospel in and around Jerusalem and was the leader of the first Christian community there; established a local Church in Antioch; presided over the Council of Jerusalem in 51; wrote two "catholic" epistles to the Christians in Asia Minor; established his see in Rome where he spent his last years and was martyred by crucifixion in 64 or 65 during the Neronian persecution; in art, is depicted carrying two keys, symbolic of his primacy in the Church; feasts, June 29, Feb. 22 (Roman Rite).

Philip: Born in Bethsaida; according to legend, preached the Gospel in Phrygia where he suffered martyrdom by crucifixion; feast, May 3 in the Roman Rite, Nov. 14 in the Byzantine Rite.

Simon: Called the Cánanean or the Zealot; according to legend, preached in various places in the Near East and suffered martyrdom by being sawed in two; in art, is depicted with a saw, the instrument of his death, or a book, symbolic of his zeal for the Law; feast, Oct. 28 in the Roman Rite, May 10 in the Byzantine Rite.

Thomas (Didymus): Notable for his initial incredulity regarding the Resurrection and his subsequent forthright confession of the divinity of Christ risen from the dead; according to legend, preached the Gospel in places from the Caspian Sea to the Persian Gulf and eventually reached India where he was martyred near Madras; Thomas Christians trace their origin to him; in art, is depicted kneeling before the risen Christ, or with a carpenter's rule and square; feast, July 3 in the Roman Rite, Oct. 6 in the Byzantine Rite.

JUDAS

The Gospels record only a few facts about Judas, the Apostle who betrayed Christ.

The only non-Galilean among the Apostles, he was from Carioth, a town in southern Juda. He was keeper of the purse in the apostolic band. He was called a petty thief by John. He voiced dismay at the waste of money, which he said might have been spent for the poor, in connection with the anointing incident at Bethany. He took the initiative in arranging the betrayal of Christ. Afterwards, he confessed that he had betrayed an innocent man and cast into the Temple the money he had received for that action. Of his death, Matthew says that he hanged himself; the Acts of the Apostles states that he swelled up and burst open; both reports deal more with the meaning than the manner of his death — the misery of the death of a sinner.

The consensus of speculation over the reason why Judas acted as he did in betraying Christ focuses on disillusionment and unwillingness to accept a suffering Messiah.

APOSTOLIC FATHERS, FATHERS, DOCTORS OF THE CHURCH

The writers listed below, were outstanding and authoritative witnesses to authentic Christian belief and practice, and played significant roles in giving them expression.

Apostolic Fathers

The Apostolic Fathers were Christian writers of the first and second centuries who are known or believed to have had personal relations with the Apostles, and whose writings echo genuine apostolic teaching.

Chief in importance are: St. Clement (d.c. 97), bishop of Rome and third successor of St. Peter in the papacy; St. Ignatius (50-c.

107), bishop of Antioch and second successor of St. Peter in that see, reputed to be a disciple of St. John; St. Polycarp (69-155), bishop of Smyrna and a disciple of St. John. The authors of the *Didache* and the *Epistle of Barnabas* are also numbered among the Apostolic Fathers.

Other early ecclesiastical writers included: St. Justin, martyr (100-165), of Asia Minor and Rome, a layman and apologist; St. Irenaeus (130-202), bishop of Lyons, who opposed Gnosticism; and St. Cyprian (210-258), bishop of Carthage, who opposed Novatianism.

Fathers and Doctors

The Fathers of the Church were theologians and writers of the first eight centuries who were outstanding for sanctity and learning. They were such authoritative witnesses to the belief and teaching of the Church that their unanimous acceptance of doctrines as divinely revealed has been regarded as evidence that such doctrines were so received by the Church in line with apostolic tradition and Sacred Scripture. Their unanimous rejection of doctrines branded them as heretical. Their writings, however, were not necessarily free of error in all respects.

The greatest of these Fathers were: Sts. Ambrose, Augustine, Jerome and Gregory the Great in the West; Sts. John Chrysostom, Basil the Great, Gregory of Nazianzen and Athanasius in the East.

The Doctors of the Church were ecclesiastical writers of eminent learning and sanctity who have been given this title because of the great advantage the Church has derived from their work. These writings, however, were not necessarily free of error in all respects.

Albert the Great, St. (c. 1200-1280): Born in Swabia, Germany; Dominican; bishop of Regensburg (1260-1262); wrote extensively on logic, natural sciences, ethics, metaphysics, Scripture, systematic theology; contributed to development of Scholasticism; teacher of St. Thomas Aquinas; canonized and proclaimed doctor, 1931; named patron of natural scientists, 1941; called Doctor Universalis, Doctor Expertus; feast, Nov. 15.

Alphonsus Liguori, St. (1696-1787): Born near Naples, Italy; bishop of Agatha of the Goths (1762-1775); founder of the Redemptorists; in addition to his principal work, *Theologiae Moralis,* wrote on prayer, the spiritual life, and doctrinal subjects in response to controversy; canonized, 1839; proclaimed doctor, 1871; named patron of confessors and moralists, 1950; feast, Aug. 1.

Ambrose, St. (c. 340-397): Born in Treves, Germany; bishop of Milan (374-397); one of the strongest opponents of Arianism in the West; his homilies and other writings — on faith, the Holy Spirit, the Incarnation, the sacraments and other subjects — were pastoral and practical; influenced the development of a liturgy at Milan which was named for him; Father and Doctor of the Church; feast, Dec. 7.

Anselm, St. (1033-1109): Born in Aosta, Piedmont, Italy; Benedictine; archbishop of Canterbury (1093-1109); in addition to his principal work, *Cur Deus Homo,* on the atonement and reconciliation of man with God through Christ, wrote about the existence and attributes of God and defended the *Filioque* explanation of the procession of the Holy Spirit from the Father and the Son; canonized, 1494; proclaimed doctor, 1720; called Father of Scholasticism; feast, Apr. 21.

Anthony of Padua, St. (1195-1231): Born in Lisbon, Portugal; first theologian of the Franciscan Order; preacher; canonized, 1232; proclaimed doctor, 1946; called Evangelical Doctor; feast, June 13.

Athanasius, St. (c. 297-373): Born in Alexandria, Egypt; bishop of Alexandria (328-373); participant in the Council of Nicaea I while still a deacon; dominant opponent of Arians whose errors regarding Christ he refuted in *Apology against the Arians, Discourses against the Arians,* and other works; Father and Doctor of the Church; called Father of Orthodoxy; feast, May 2.

Augustine, St. (354-430): Born in Tagaste, North Africa; bishop of Hippo (395-430) after conversion from Manichaeism; works include the autobiographical and mystical *Confessions, City of God,* treatises on the Trinity, grace, passages of the Bible, and doctrines called into question and denied by Manichaeans, Pelagians and Donatists; had strong and lasting influence on Christian theology and philosophy; Father and Doctor of the Church; Doctor of Grace; feast, Aug. 28.

Basil the Great, St. (c. 329-379): Born in Caesarea, Cappadocia, Asia Minor; bishop of Caesarea (370-379); wrote three books *Contra Eunomium* in refutation of Arian errors, a treatise on the Holy Spirit, many homilies, and several rules for monastic life, on which he had lasting influence; Father and Doctor of the Church; called Father of Monasticism in the East; feast, Jan. 2.

Bede the Venerable, St. (c. 673-735): Born in Northumberland, England; Benedictine; in addition to his principal work, *Ecclesiastical History of the English Nation* (covering the period 597-731), wrote scriptural commentaries; regarded as probably the most learned man in Western Europe of his time; called Father of English History; feast, May 25.

Bernard of Clairvaux, St. (c. 1090-1153): Born near Dijon, France; abbot; monastic reformer, called the second founder of the Cistercian Order; mystical theologian with great influence on devotional life; opponent of the rationalism brought forward by Abelard and others; canonized, 1174; proclaimed doctor, 1830; called Mellifluous Doctor because of his eloquence; feast, Aug. 20.

Bonaventure, St. (c. 1217-1274): Born near Viterbo, Italy; Franciscan; bishop of Albano (1273-1274); cardinal; wrote *Itinerarium Mentis in Deum, De Reductione Artium ad Theologiam, Breviloquium,* scriptural commentaries, additional mystical works affecting devotional life, and a life of St. Francis of Assisi; canonized, 1482; proclaimed doctor, 1588; called Seraphic Doctor; feast, July 15.

Catherine of Siena, St. (c. 1347-1380): Born in Siena, Italy; member of the Third Order of St. Dominic; mystic; authored a long series of letters, mainly concerning spiritual instruction and encouragement, to associates, and *Dialogue,* a spiritual testament in four treatises; was active in support of a crusade against the Turks and efforts to end war between papal forces and the Florentine allies; had great influence in inducing Gregory XI to return himself and the Curia to Rome in 1376, to end the Avignon period of the papacy; canonized, 1461; proclaimed the second women doctor, Oct. 4, 1970; feast, Apr. 29.

Cyril of Alexandria, St. (c. 376-444): Born in Egypt; bishop of Alexandria (412-444); wrote treatises on the Trinity, the Incarnation and other subjects, mostly in refutation of Nestorian errors; made key contributions to the development of Christology; presided at the Council of Ephesus, 431; proclaimed doctor, 1882; feast, June 27.

Cyril of Jerusalem, St. (c. 315-387): Bishop of Jerusalem (350-387); vigorous opponent of Arianism; principal work, *Catecheses,* a pre-baptismal explanation of the creed of Jerusalem; proclaimed doctor, 1882; feast, Mar. 18.

Ephraem, St. (c. 306-373): Born in Nisibis, Mesopotamia; counteracted the spread of Gnostic and Arian errors with poems and hymns of his own composition; wrote also on the Eucharist and Mary; proclaimed doctor, 1920; called Deacon of Edessa and Harp of the Holy Spirit; feast, June 9.

Francis de Sales, St. (1567-1622): Born in Savoy; bishop of Geneva (1602-1622); spiritual writer with strong influence on devotional life through treatises such as *Introduction to a Devout Life,* and *The Love of God;* canonized, 1665; proclaimed doctor, 1877; patron of Catholic writers and the Catholic press; feast, Jan. 24.

Gregory Nazianzen, St. (c. 330-c. 390): Born in Arianzus, Cappadocia, Asia Minor; bishop of Constantinople (381-390); vigorous opponent of Arianism; in addition to five theological discourses on the Nicene Creed and the Trinity for which he is best known, wrote letters and poetry; Father and Doctor of the Church; called the Christian Demosthenes because of his eloquence and, in the Eastern Church, The Theologian; feast, Jan. 2.

Gregory I, the Great, St. (c. 540-604): Born in Rome; pope (590-604): wrote many scriptural commentaries, a compendium of theology in the *Book of Morals* based on Job, *Dialogues* concerning the lives of saints, the immortality of the soul, death, purgatory, heaven and hell, and 14 books of letters; enforced papal supremacy and established the position of the pope vis-a-vis the emperor; worked for clerical and monastic reform and the observance of clerical celibacy; Father and Doctor of the Church; feast, Sept. 3.

Hilary of Poitiers, St. (c. 315-368): Born in Poitiers, France; bishop of Poitiers (c. 353-368); wrote *De Synodis,* with the Arian controversy in mind, and *De Trinitate,* the first lengthy study of the doctrine in Latin; introduced Eastern theology to the West; contributed to the development of hymnology; proclaimed doctor, 1851; called the Athanasius of the West because of his vigorous defense of the divinity of Christ against Arians; feast, Jan. 13.

Isidore of Seville, St. (c. 560-636): Born in Cartagena, Spain; bishop of Seville (c. 600-636); in addition to his principal work, *Etymologiae,* an encyclopedia of the knowledge of his day, wrote on theological and historical subjects; regarded as the most learned man of his time; proclaimed doctor, 1722; feast, Apr. 4.

Jerome, St. (c. 343-420): Born in Stridon, Dalmatia; translated the Old Testament from Hebrew into Latin and revised the existing Latin translation of the New Testament to produce the Vulgate version of the Bible; wrote scriptural commentaries and treatises on matters of controversy; regarded as Father and Doctor of the Church from the eighth century; called Father of Biblical Science; feast, Sept. 30.

John Chrysostom, St. (c. 347-407): Born in Antioch, Asia Minor; archbishop of Constantinople (398-407); wrote homilies, scriptural commentaries and letters of wide influence in addition to a classical treatise on the priesthood; proclaimed doctor by the Council of Chalcedon, 451; called the greatest of the Greek Fathers; named patron of preachers, 1909; called golden-mouthed because of his eloquence; feast, Sept. 13.

John Damascene, St. (c. 675-c. 749): Born in Damascus, Syria; monk; wrote *Fountain of Wisdom,* a three-part work including a history of heresies and an exposition of the Christian faith, three *Discourses against the Iconoclasts,* homilies on Mary, biblical commentaries and treatises on moral subjects; proclaimed doctor, 1890; called Golden Speaker because of his eloquence; feast, Dec. 4.

John of the Cross, St. (1542-1591): Born in Old Castile, Spain; Carmelite; founder of Discalced Carmelites; one of the greatest mystical theologians, wrote *The Ascent of Mt. Carmel — The Dark Night, The Spiritual Canticle, The Living Flame of Love;* canonized, 1726; proclaimed doctor, 1926; called Doctor of Mystical Theology; feast, Dec. 14.

Lawrence of Brindisi, St. (1559-1619): Born in Brindisi, Italy; Franciscan (Capuchin); vigorous preacher of strong influence in the post-Reformation period; 15 tomes of collected works include scriptural commentaries, sermons, homilies and doctrinal writings; canonized, 1881; proclaimed doctor, 1959; feast, July 21.

Leo I, the Great, St. (c. 400-461): Born in Tuscany, Italy; pope (440-461); wrote the *Tome of Leo,* to explain doctrine concerning the two natures and one Person of Christ, against the background of the Nestorian and Monophysite heresies; other works included sermons, letters, and writings against the errors of Manichaeism and Pelagianism; was instrumental in dissuading Attila from sacking Rome in 452; proclaimed doctor, 1574; feast, Nov. 10.

Peter Canisius, St. (1521-1597): Born in Nijmegen, Holland; Jesuit; wrote popular expositions of the Catholic faith in several catechisms which were widely circulated in 20 editions in his lifetime alone; was one of the moving figures in the Counter-Reformation period, especially in southern and western Germany; canonized and proclaimed doctor, 1925; feast, Dec. 21.

Peter Chrysologus, St. (c. 400-450): Born in Imola, Italy; served as archbishop of Ravenna (c. 433-450); his sermons and writings, many of which were designed to counteract Monophysitism, were pastoral and practical; proclaimed doctor, 1729; feast, July 30.

Peter Damian, St. (1007-1072): Born in Ravenna, Italy; Benedictine; cardinal; his writings and sermons, many of which concerned ecclesiastical and clerical reform, were pastoral and practical; proclaimed doctor, 1828; feast, Feb. 21.

Robert Bellarmine, St. (1542-1621): Born in Tuscany, Italy; Jesuit; archbishop of Capua (1602-1605); wrote *Controversies,* a three-volume exposition of doctrine under attack during and after the Reformation, two catechisms and the spiritual work, *The Art of Dying Well,* was an authority on ecclesiology and Church-state relations; canonized, 1930; proclaimed doctor, 1931; feast, Sept. 17.

Theresa of Avila, St. (1515-1582): Born in Avila, Spain; entered the Carmelite Order, 1535; in the early 1560's, initiated a primitive Carmelite, discalced-Alcantarine reform which greatly influenced men and women religious, especially in Spain; wrote extensively on spiritual and mystical subjects; principal works included her *Autobiography, Way of Perfection, The Interior Castle, Meditations on the Canticle, The Foundations, Visitation of the Discalced Nuns;* canonized, 1614; proclaimed doctor, Sept. 27, 1970; feast, Oct. 15.

Thomas Aquinas, St. (1225-1274): Born near Naples, Italy; Dominican; teacher and writer on virtually the whole range of philosophy and theology; principal works were *Summa contra Gentiles,* a manual and systematic defense of Christian doctrine, and *Summa Theologiae,* a new (at that time) exposition of theology on philosophical principles; canonized, 1323; proclaimed doctor, 1567; called Doctor Communis, Doctor Angelicus, the Great Synthesizer because of the way in which he related faith and reason, theology and philosophy (especially that of Aristotle), and systematized the presentation of Christian doctrine; named patron of Catholic schools and education, 1880; feast, Jan. 28.

CREEDS

Creeds are formal and official statements of Christian doctrine. As summaries of the principal truths of faith, they are standards of orthodoxy and are useful for instructional purposes, for actual profession of the faith, and for expression of the faith in the liturgy.

The classical creeds are the Apostles' Creed and the Creed of Nicaea-Constantinople. Two others are the Athanasian Creed and the Creed of Pius IV.

Apostles' Creed

Text: I believe in God, the Father almighty, Creator of heaven and earth.

And in Jesus Christ, his only Son, our Lord; who was conceived by the Holy Spirit, born of the Virgin Mary, suffered under Pontius Pilate, was crucified, died, and was buried. He descended into hell; the third day he arose again from the dead; he ascended into heaven, sits at the right hand of God, the Father almighty; from thence he shall come to judge the living and the dead.

I believe in the Holy Spirit, the holy Catholic Church, the communion of saints, the forgiveness of sins, the resurrection of the body, and life everlasting. Amen.

Background: The Apostles' Creed reflects the teaching of the Apostles but is not of apostolic origin. It probably originated in the second century as a rudimentary formula of faith professed by catechumens before the reception of baptism. Baptismal creeds in fourth-century use at Rome and elsewhere in the West closely resembled the present text, which was quoted in a handbook of Christian doctrine written between 710 and 724. This text was in wide use throughout the West by the ninth century. The Apostles' Creed is common to all Christian confessional churches in the West, but is not used in Eastern Churches.

Nicene Creed

The following translation of the Latin text of the creed was prepared by the International Committee on English in the Liturgy.

Text: We believe in one God, the Father, the Almighty, maker of heaven and earth, of all that is seen and unseen.

We believe in one Lord, Jesus Christ, the only Son of God, eternally begotten of the Father, God from God, Light from Light, true God from true God, begotten, not made, one in Being with the Father. Through him all things were made. For us men and for our salvation he came down from heaven: by the power of the Holy Spirit he was born cf the Virgin Mary, and became man. For our sake he was crucified under Pontius Pilate; he suffered, died, and was buried. On the third day he rose again in fulfillment of the Scriptures; he ascended into heaven and is seated at the right hand of the Father. He will come again in glory to judge the living and the dead, and his kingdom will have no end.

We believe in the Holy Spirit, the Lord, the giver of life, who proceeds from the Father and the Son. With the Father and the Son he is worshiped and glorified. He has spoken through the prophets.

We believe in one holy catholic and apostolic Church. We acknowledge one baptism for the forgiveness of sins. We look for the resurrection of the dead, and the life of the world to come. Amen.

Background: The Nicene Creed (Creed of Nicaea-Constantinople) consists of elements of doctrine contained in an early baptismal creed of Jerusalem and enactments of the Council of Nicaea (325) and the Council of Constantinople (381). Its strong trinitarian content reflects the doctrinal errors, especially of Arianism, it served to counteract. Theologically, it is much more sophisticated than the Apostles' Creed. Since late in the fifth century, the Nicene Creed has been the only creed in liturgical use in the Eastern Churches. The Western Church adopted it for liturgical use by the end of the eighth century.

The Athanasian Creed

The Athanasian Creed, which has a unique structure, is a two-part summary of doctrine concerning the Trinity and the Incarnation-Redemption bracketed at the beginning and end with the statement that belief in the cited truths is necessary for salvation; it also contains a number of anathemas or condemnatory clauses regarding doctrinal errors. Although attributed to St. Athanasius, it was probably written after his death, between 381 and 428, and may have been authored by St. Ambrose. It is not accepted in the East; in the West, it has place in the liturgy of some other Christian churches as well as in the Roman-Rite Liturgy of the Hours and for the Solemnity of the Holy Trinity.

Creed of Pius IV

The Creed of Pius IV, also called the Profession of Faith of the Council of Trent, was promulgated in the bull *Injunctum Nobis,* Nov. 13, 1564. It is a summary of doctrine defined by the council concerning: Scripture and tradition, original sin and justification, the Mass and sacraments, veneration of the saints, indulgences, the primacy of the See of Rome. It was slightly modified in 1887 to include doctrinal formulations of the First Vatican Council.

REDDITIO OF CREED

The "giving back," by profession, of a baptismal creed by candidates for baptism to a bishop or his representative was one of the immediate preliminaries to reception of the sacrament at the conclusion of the catechumenate in the early Church.

MORAL OBLIGATIONS

The basic norm of Christian morality is life in Christ. This involves, among other things, the observance of the Ten Commandments, their fulfillment in the twofold law of love of God and neighbor, the implications of the Sermon on the Mount and the whole New Testament, and membership in the Church established by Christ.

The Ten Commandments

The Ten Commandments, the Decalogue, were given by God through Moses to his Chosen People for the guidance of their moral conduct in accord with the demands of the Covenant he established with them as a divine gift. Their observance was essential to participation in the Covenant and the order of salvation based on it.

In the traditional Catholic enumeration and according to Dt. 5:6-21, the Commandments are:

1. "I, the Lord, am your God . . . You shall not have other gods besides me. You shall not carve idols. . . ."

2. "You shall not take the name of the Lord, your God, in vain. . . ."

3. "Take care to keep holy the Sabbath day. . . ."

4. "Honor your father and your mother. . . ."

5. "You shall not kill."

6. "You shall not commit adultery."

7. "You shall not steal."

8. "You shall not bear dishonest witness against your neighbor."

9. "You shall not covet your neighbor's wife."

10. "You shall not desire your neighbor's house or field, nor his male or female slave, nor his ox or ass, nor anything that belongs to him" (summarily, his goods).

Another version of the Commandments, substantially the same, is given in Ex. 20:1-17.

The traditional enumeration of the Commandments in Protestant usage differs from the above. Thus: two commandments are made of the first, as above; the third and fourth are equivalent to the second and third, as above, and so on; and the 10th includes the ninth and 10th, as above.

Love of God and Neighbor

The first three of the commandments deal directly with man's relations with God, viz.: acknowledgment of one true God and the rejection of false gods and idols; honor due to God and his name; observance of the Sabbath as the Lord's day.

The rest cover interpersonal relationships, viz.: the obedience due to parents and, logically, to other persons in authority, and the obligations of parents to children and of persons in authority to those under their care; respect for life and physical integrity; fidelity in marriage, and chastity; justice and rights; truth; internal respect for faithfulness in marriage, chastity, and the goods of others.

Perfection in Christian Life

The moral obligations of the Ten Commandments are complemented by others flowing from the twofold law of love, the whole substance and pattern of Christ's teaching, and everything implied in full and active membership and participation in the community of salvation formed by Christ in his Church. Some of these matters are covered in other sections of the Almanac under appropriate headings.

Precepts of the Church

The precepts of the Church of Roman Rite oblige Catholics to:

1. Assist at Mass on Sundays and holy days of obligation. (Also, to desist from unnecessary servile work on these days.)

2. Fast and abstain on the days appointed. (The fasting obligation binds persons from the 21st until the 59th birthday; the days of fast are Ash Wednesday and Good Friday. The abstinence obligation binds from the 14th birthday on these days, and is obligatory for all Fridays in Lent in the U.S.) These regulations, which have been modified in recent years, are penitential in purpose but do not exhaust obligations of penance. Other ways of doing penance are left to personal option.

3. Confess their sins at least once a year.

4. Receive Holy Communion during the Easter time. (In the U.S., the Easter time extends from the First Sunday of Lent to Trinity Sunday.)

5. Contribute to the support of the Church.

6. Observe the laws of the Church concerning marriage.

SOCIAL DOCTRINE

(For additional social doctrine, see entries pertaining to Pope John Paul II.)

Since the end of the last century, Catholic social doctrine has been formulated in a progressive manner in a number of authoritative documents. Outstanding examples are the encyclicals: *Rerum Novarum,* issued by Leo XIII in 1891; *Quadragesimo Anno,* by Pius XI in 1931; *Mater et Magistra* ("Christianity and Social Progress") and *Pacem in Terris* ("Peace on Earth"), by John XXIII in 1961 and 1963, respectively; and *Populorum Progressio* ("Development of Peoples"), by Paul VI in 1967. Pius XII, among other accomplishments of ideological importance in the social field, made a distinctive contribution with his formulation of a plan for world peace and order in Christmas messages from 1939 to 1941, and in other documents.

These documents represent the most serious attempts in modern times to systematize the social implications of the Gospel and the rest of divine revelation as well as the socially relevant writings of the Fathers and Doctors of the Church. Their contents are theological penetrations into social life, with particular reference to human rights, the needs of the poor and those in underdeveloped countries, and humane conditions of life, freedom, justice and peace. In some respects, they read like juridical documents; underneath, however, they are Gospel-oriented and pastoral in intention.

Pope John, writing in *Christianity and Social Progress,* made the following statement about the nature and scope of the doctrine stated in the encyclicals in particular and related writings in general.

"What the Catholic Church teaches and declares regarding the social life and relationships of men is beyond question for all time valid.

"The cardinal point of this teaching is that individual men are necessarily the foundation, cause, and end of all social institutions . . . insofar as they are social by nature, and raised to an order of existence that transcends and subdues nature.

"Beginning with this very basic principle whereby the dignity of the human person is affirmed and defended, Holy Church — especially during the last century and with the assistance of learned priests and laymen, specialists in the field — has arrived at clear social teachings whereby the mutual relationships of men are ordered. Taking general norms into account, these principles are in accord with the nature of things and the changed conditions of man's social life, or with the special genius of our day. Moreover, these norms can be approved by all."

The Church in the World

Even more Gospel-oriented and pastoral in a distinctive way is the *Pastoral Constitution on the Church in the Modern World* promulgated by the Second Vatican Council in 1965.

Its purpose was to search out the signs of God's presence and meaning in and through the events of this time in human history. Accordingly, it dealt with the situation of men in present circumstances of profound change, challenge and crisis on all levels of life.

The first part of the constitution developed the theme of the Church and man's calling, and focused attention on the dignity of the human person, the problem of atheism, the community of mankind, man's activity throughout the world, and the serving and saving role of the Church in the world. This portion of the document, it has been said, represents the first presentation by the Church in an official text of an organized Christian view of man and society.

The second part of the document considered several problems of special urgency: fostering the nobility of marriage and the family (see Marriage Doctrine), the proper development of culture, socio-economic life, the life of the political community, the fostering of peace (see Peace and War), and the promotion of a community of nations.

In conclusion, the constitution called for action to implement doctrine regarding the role and work of the Church for the total good of mankind.

Following are a number of key excerpts from the ideological heart of the constitution.

One Human Family and Community: "God, who has fatherly concern for everyone, has willed that all men should constitute one family and treat one another in a spirit of brotherhood. . . .

"For this reason, love for God and neighbor is the first and greatest commandment. Sacred Scripture . . . teaches us that the love of God cannot be separated from love of neighbor. . . . To men growing daily more dependent on one another, and to a world becoming more unified every day, this truth proves to be of paramount importance . . ." (No. 24).

Human Person Is Central: "Man's social nature makes it evident that the progress of the human person and the advance of society itself hinge on each other. For the beginning, the subject and the goal of all social institutions is and must be the human person, which for its part and by its very nature stands completely in need of social life. This social life is not something added on to man. Hence, through his dealings with others, through reciprocal aims, and through fraternal dialogue he develops all his gifts and is able to rise to his destiny."

Influence of Social Circumstances: "But if by this social life the human person is greatly aided in responding to his destiny, even in its religious dimensions, it cannot be denied that men are often diverted from doing good and spurred toward evil by the social circumstances in which they live and are immersed from their birth. To be sure the disturbances which so frequently occur in the social order result in part from the natural tensions of economic, political, and social forms. But at a deeper level they flow from man's pride and selfishness, which contaminate even the social sphere. When the structure of affairs is flawed by the consequences of sin, man, already born with a bent toward evil, finds there new inducements to sin, which cannot be overcome without strenuous efforts and the assistance of grace" (No. 25).

"Every social group must take account of the needs and legitimate aspirations of other groups, and even of the general welfare of the entire human family."

Human Necessities: "At the same time however, there is a growing awareness of the exalted dignity proper to the human person, since he stands above all things, and his rights and duties are universal and inviolable. Therefore, there must be made available to all men everything necessary for leading a life truly human, such as food, clothing, and shelter; the right to choose a state of life freely and to found a family, the right to education, to employment, to a good reputation, to respect, to appropriate information, to activity in accord with the upright norm of one's own conscience, to protection of privacy and to rightful freedom in matters religious too.

"Hence, the social order and its development must unceasingly work to the benefit of the human person if the disposition of affairs is to be subordinate to the personal realm and not contrariwise, as the Lord indicated when He said that the Sabbath was made for man, and not man for the Sabbath."

Improvement of Social Order: "This social order requires constant improvement. It must be founded on truth, built on justice, and animated by love; in freedom it should grow every day toward a more humane balance. An improvement in attitudes and widespread changes in society will have to take place if these objectives are to be gained.

"God's Spirit, who with a marvelous providence directs the unfolding of time and renews the face of the earth, is not absent from this development. The ferment of the gospel, too, has aroused and continues to arouse in man's heart the irresistible requirements of his dignity" (No. 26).

Regard for Neighbor as Another Self: "Coming down to practical and particularly urgent consequences, this Council lays stress on reverence for man; everyone must consider his every neighbor without exception as another self, taking into account first of all his life and the means necessary to living it with dignity. . . .

"In our times a special obligation binds us to make ourselves the neighbor of absolutely every person, and of actively helping him when he comes across our path. . . ."

Inhuman Evils: ". . . Whatever is opposed to life itself, such as any type of murder, genocide, abortion, euthanasia, or willful self-destruction, whatever violates the integrity of the human person, such as mutilation, torments inflicted on body or mind, attempts to coerce the will itself; whatever insults human dignity, such as subhuman living conditions, arbitrary imprisonment, deportation, slavery, prostitution, the selling of women and children; as well as disgraceful working conditions, where men are treated as mere tools for profit, rather than as free and responsible persons; all these things and others of their like are infamies indeed. They poison human society, but they do more harm to those who practice them than those who suffer from the injury. Moreover, they are a supreme dishonor to the Creator" (No. 27).

Respect for Those Who Are Different: "Respect and love ought to be extended also to those who think or act differently than we do in social, political, and religious matters. In fact, the more deeply we come to understand their ways of thinking through such courtesy and love, the more easily will we be able to enter into dialogue with them."

Distinction between Error and Person in Error: "This love and good will,, to be sure, must in no way render us indifferent to truth and goodness. Indeed love itself impels the disciples of Christ to speak the saving truth to all men. But it is necessary to distinguish between error, which always merits repudiation, and the person in error, who never loses the dignity of being a person, even when he is flawed by false or inadequate religious notions. God alone is the judge and searcher of hearts; for that reason He forbids us to make judgments about the internal guilt of anyone.

"The teaching of Christ even requires that we forgive injuries, and extends the law of love to include every enemy . . ." (No. 28).

Men Are Equal but Different: "Since all men possess a rational soul and are created in God's likeness, since they have the same nature and origin, have been redeemed by Christ, and enjoy the same divine calling and destiny, the basic equality of all must receive increasingly greater recognition.

"True, all men are not alike from the point of view of varying physical power and the diversity of intellectual and moral resources. Nevertheless, with respect to the fundamental rights of the person, every type of discrimination, whether social or cultural, whether based on sex, race, color, social condition, language, or religion, is to be overcome and eradicated as contrary to God's intent. . . ."

Humane Conditions for All: ". . . Although rightful differences exist between men, the equal dignity of persons demands that a more humane and just condition of life be brought about. For excessive economic and social differences between the members of the one human family and population groups cause scandal, and militate against social justice, equity, the dignity of the human person, as well as social and international peace.

"Human institutions, both private and public, must labor to minister to the dignity and purpose of man. At the same time let them put up a stubborn fight against any kind of slavery, whether social or political, and safeguard the basic rights of man under every political system. Indeed human institutions themselves must be accommodated by degrees to the highest of all realities, spiritual ones, even though, meanwhile, a long enough time will be required before they arrive at the desired goal" (No. 29).

"Profound and rapid changes make it particularly urgent that no one, ignoring the trend of events or drugged by laziness, content himself with a merely individualistic morality. It grows increasingly true that the obligations of justice and love are fulfilled only if each person, contributing to the common good, according to his own abilities and the needs of others, also promotes and assists the public and private institutions dedicated to bettering the conditions of human life."

Social Necessities Are Prime Duties: "Let everyone consider it his sacred obligation to count social necessities among the primary duties of modern man, and to pay heed to them. For the more unified the world becomes, the more plainly do the offices of men extend beyond particular groups and spread by degrees to the whole world. But this challenge cannot be met unless individual men and their associations cultivate in themselves the moral and social virtues, and promote them in society. Thus, with the needed help of divine grace, men who are truly new and artisans of a new humanity can be forthcoming" (No. 30).

"In order for individual men to discharge with greater exactness the obligations of their conscience toward themselves and the various groups to which they belong, they must be carefully educated to a higher degree of culture through the use of the immense resources available today to the human race. . . ."

Living Conditions and Freedom: ". . . A man can scarcely arrive at the needed sense of responsibility unless his living conditions allow him to become conscious of his dignity, and to rise to his destiny by spending himself for God and for others. But human freedom is often crippled when a man falls into extreme poverty, just as it withers when he indulges in too many of life's comforts and imprisons himself in a kind of splendid isolation. Freedom acquires new strength, by contrast, when a man consents to the unavoidable requirements of social life, takes on the manifold demands of human partnership, and commits himself to the service of the human community.

"Hence, the will to play one's role in common endeavors should be everywhere encouraged . . ." (No. 31).

Communitarian Character of Life: "God did not create man for life in isolation, but, for the formation of social unity. So also 'it has pleased God to make men holy and save them not merely as individuals, without any mutual bonds, but by making them into a single people, a people which acknowledges Him in truth and serves Him in holiness' (*Dogmatic Constitution on the Church,* No. 9). So from the beginning of salvation history He has chosen men not just as individuals but as members of a certain community. Revealing His mind to them, God called these chosen ones 'His people' (Ex. 3:7-12), and, furthermore, made a covenant with them on Sinai.

"This communitarian character is developed and consummated in the work of Jesus Christ. For the very Word made flesh willed to share in the human fellowship. He was present at the wedding of Cana, visited the house of Zacchaeus, ate with publicans and sinners. He revealed the love of the Father and the sublime vocation of man in terms of the most common of social realities and by making use of the speech and the imagery of plain everyday life. Willingly obeying the laws of His country, He sanctified those human ties, especially family ones, from which social relationships arise. He chose to lead the life proper to an artisan of His time and place.

"In His preaching He clearly taught the sons of God to treat one another as brothers. In His prayers He pleaded that all His disciples might be 'one.' Indeed, as the Redeemer of all, He offered Himself for all even to the point of death. . . . He commanded His apostles to preach to all peoples the gospel message so that the human race might become the Family of God, in which the fullness of the Law would be love."

The Community Founded by Christ: "As the first-born of many brethren and through the gift of His Spirit, He founded after His death and resurrection a new brotherly community composed of all those who receive Him in faith and in love. This he did through His Body, which is the Church. There everyone, as members one of the other, would render mutual service according to the different gifts bestowed on each" (No. 32).

PEACE AND WAR

The following excerpts, stating principles and objectives of social doctrine concerning peace and war, are from the *Pastoral Constitution on the Church in the Modern World* (Nos. 77 to 82) promulgated by the Second Vatican Council.

Call to Peace: ". . . This Council fervently desires to summon Christians to cooperate with all men in making secure among themselves a peace based on justice and love, and in setting up agencies of peace. This Christians should do with the help of Christ, the Author of peace" (No. 77).

Conditions for Peace: "Peace is not merely the absence of war. Nor can it be reduced solely to the maintenance of a balance of power between enemies. Nor is it brought about by dictatorship. Instead, it is rightly and appropriately called 'an enterprise of justice' (Is. 32:7). Peace results from that harmony built into human society by its divine Founder, and actualized by men as they thirst after ever greater justice.

"The common good of men is in its basic sense determined by the eternal law. Still the concrete demands of this common good are constantly changing as time goes on. Hence peace is never attained once and for all, but

must be built up ceaselessly. Moreover, since the human will is unsteady and wounded by sin, the achievement of peace requires that everyone constantly master his passions and that lawful authority keep vigilant.

"But such is not enough. This peace cannot be obtained on earth unless personal values are safeguarded and men freely and trustingly share with one another the riches of their inner spirits and their talents. A firm determination to respect other men and peoples and their dignity, as well as the studied practice of brotherhood, are absolutely necessary for the establishment of peace. Hence peace is likewise the fruit of love, which goes beyond what justice can provide."

Renunciation of Violence: ". . . We cannot fail to praise those who renounce the use of violence in the vindication of their rights and who resort to methods of defense which are otherwise available to weaker parties too, provided that this can be done without injury to the rights and duties of others or of the community itself . . ." (No. 78).

Mass Extermination: ". . . The Council wishes to recall first of all the permanent binding force of universal natural law and its all-embracing principles. Man's conscience itself gives ever more emphatic voice to these principles. Therefore, actions which deliberately conflict with these same principles, as well as orders commanding such actions, are criminal. Blind obedience cannot excuse those who yield to them. Among such must first be counted those actions designed for the methodical extermination of an entire people, nation, or ethnic minority. These actions must be vehemently condemned as horrendous crimes. The courage of those who openly and fearlessly resist men who issue such commands merits supreme commendation."

International Agreements: "On the subject of war, quite a large number of nations have subscribed to various international agreements aimed at making military activity and its consequences less inhuman. Such are conventions concerning the handling of wounded or captured soldiers, and various similar agreements. Agreements of this sort must be honored. They should be improved upon."

Conscientious Objectors: ". . . It seems right that laws make humane provisions for the case of those who for reasons of conscience refuse to bear arms, provided, however, that they accept some other form of service to the human community."

Legitimate Defense: "Certainly, war has not been rooted out of human affairs. As long as the danger of war remains and there is no competent and sufficiently powerful authority at the international level, governments cannot be denied the right to legitimate defense once every means of peaceful settlement has been exhausted. Therefore, government authorities and others who share public responsibility have the duty to protect the welfare of the people entrusted to their care and to conduct such grave matters soberly.

"But it is one thing to undertake military action for the just defense of the people, and something else again to seek the subjugation of other nations. Nor does the possession of war potential make every military or political use of it lawful. Neither does the mere fact that war has unhappily begun mean that all is fair between the warring parties."

Nature of Military Service: "Those who are pledged to the service of their country as members of its armed forces should regard themselves as agents of security and freedom on behalf of their people. As long as they fulfill this role properly, they are making a genuine contribution to the establishment of peace" (No. 79).

Total War Condemned: ". . . This most holy Synod makes its own the condemnations of total war already pronounced by recent Popes, and issues the following declaration:

"Any act of war aimed indiscriminately at the destruction of entire cities or of extensive areas along with their population is a crime against God and man himself. It merits unequivocal and unhesitating condemnation.

"The unique hazard of modern warfare consists in this: it provides those who possess modern scientific weapons with a kind of occasion for perpetrating just such abominations. Moreover, through a certain inexorable chain of events, it can urge men on to the most atrocious decisions. That such in fact may never happen in the future, the bishops of the whole world, in unity assembled, beg all men, especially government officials and military leaders, to give unremitting thought to the awesome responsibility which is theirs before God and the entire human race" (No. 80).

Retaliation and Deterrence: "Scientific weapons, to be sure, are not amassed solely for use in war. The defensive strength of any nation is considered to be dependent upon its capacity for immediate retaliation against an adversary. Hence this accumulation of arms, which increases each year, also serves, in a way heretofore unknown, as a deterrent to possible enemy attack. Many regard this state of affairs as the most effective way by which peace of a sort can be maintained between nations at the present time."

Arms Race: "Whatever be the case with this method of deterrence, men should be convinced that the arms race in which so many countries are engaged is not a safe way to preserve a steady peace. Nor is the so-called balance resulting from this race a sure and authentic peace. Rather than being eliminated thereby, the causes of war threaten to grow gradually stronger.

"While extravagant sums are being spent for the furnishing of ever new weapons, an adequate remedy cannot be provided for the multiple miseries afflicting the whole modern world. Disagreements between nations are not really and radically healed. On the contrary other parts of the world are infected with them. New approaches initiated by reformed attitudes must be adopted to remove this trap and to restore genuine peace by emancipating the world from its crushing anxiety.

"Therefore, it must be said again: the arms race is an utterly treacherous trap for humanity, and one which injures the poor to an intolerable degree. It is much to be feared that, if this race persists, it will eventually spawn all the lethal ruin whose path it is now making ready . . ." (No. 81).

Outlaw War: "It is our clear duty, then, to strain every muscle as we work for the time when all war can be completely outlawed by international consent. This goal undoubtedly requires the establishment of some universal public authority acknowledged as such by all, and endowed with effective power to safeguard, on the behalf of all, security, regard for justice, and respect for rights."

Multilateral and Controlled Disarmament: "But before this hoped-for authority can be set up, the highest existing international centers must devote themselves vigorously to the pursuit of better means for obtaining common security. Peace must be born of mutual trust between nations rather than imposed on them through fear of one another's weapons. Hence everyone must labor to put an end at last to the arms race, and to make a true beginning of disarmament, not indeed a unilateral disarmament, but one proceeding at an equal pace according to agreement, and backed up by authentic and workable safeguards.

"In the meantime, efforts which have already been made and are still under way to eliminate the danger of war are not to be underrated. On the contrary, support should be given to the good will of the very many leaders who work hard to do away with war, which they abominate. . . ."

Public Opinion: ". . . Men should take heed not to entrust themselves only to the efforts of others, while remaining careless about their own attitudes. For government officials, who must simultaneously guarantee the good of their own people and promote the universal good, depend on public opinion and feeling to the greatest possible extent. It does them no good to work at building peace so long as feelings of hostility, contempt, and distrust, as well as racial hatred and unbending ideologies, continue to divide men and place them in opposing camps.

"Hence arises a surpassing need for renewed education of attitudes and for new inspiration in the area of public opinion. Those who are dedicated to the work of education . . . should regard as their most weighty task the effort to instruct all in fresh sentiments of peace" (No. 82).

Liturgy

The nature and purpose of the liturgy, along with norms for its revision, were the subject matter of the *Constitution on the Sacred Liturgy* promulgated by the Second Vatican Council. The principles and guidelines stated in this document, the first issued by the Council, are summarized here and/or are incorporated in other Almanac entries on liturgical subjects.

Nature and Purpose of Liturgy

"It is through the liturgy, especially the divine Eucharistic Sacrifice, that 'the work of our redemption is exercised.' The liturgy is thus the outstanding means by which the faithful can express in their lives, and manifest to others, the mystery of Christ and the real nature of the true Church . . ." (No. 2).

"The liturgy is considered as an exercise of the priestly office of Jesus Christ. In the liturgy the sanctification of man is manifested by signs perceptible to the senses, and is effected in a way which is proper to each of these signs; in the liturgy full public worship is performed by the Mystical Body of Jesus Christ, that is, by the Head and His members.

"From this it follows that every liturgical celebration, because it is an action of Christ the priest and of His Body the Church, is a sacred action surpassing all others. No other action of the Church can match its claim to efficacy, nor equal the degree of it" (No. 7).

"The liturgy is the summit toward which the activity of the Church is directed; at the same time it is the fountain from which all her power flows. For the goal of apostolic works is that all who are made sons of God by faith and baptism should come together to praise God in the midst of His Church, to take part in her sacrifice, and to eat the Lord's Supper.

". . . From the liturgy, therefore, and especially from the Eucharist, as from a fountain, grace is channeled into us; and the sanctification of men in Christ and the glorification of God, to which all other activities of the Church are directed as toward their goal, are most powerfully achieved" (No. 10).

Full Participation

"Mother Church earnestly desires that all the faithful be led to that full, conscious, and active participation in liturgical celebrations which is demanded by the very nature of the liturgy. Such participation by the Christian people as 'a chosen race, a royal priesthood, a holy nation, a purchased people' (1 Pt. 2:9; cf. 2:4-5), is their right and duty by reason of their baptism.

"In the restoration and promotion of the sacred liturgy, this full and active participation by all the people is the aim to be considered before all else; for it is the primary and indispensable source from which the faithful are to derive the true Christian spirit . . ." (No. 14).

"In order that the Christian people may more securely derive an abundance of graces from the sacred liturgy, holy Mother Church desires to undertake with great care a general restoration of the liturgy itself. For the liturgy is made up of unchangeable elements divinely instituted, and elements subject to change. The latter not only may but ought to be changed with the passing of time if features have by chance crept in which are less harmonious with the intimate nature of the liturgy, or if existing elements have grown less functional.

"In this restoration, both texts and rites should be drawn up so that they express more clearly the holy things which they signify. Christian people, as far as possible, should be able to understand them with ease and to take part in them fully, actively, and as befits a community . . ." (No. 21).

Norms

Norms regarding the reforms concern the greater use of Scripture; emphasis on the importance of the sermon or homily on biblical and liturgical subjects; use of vernacular languages for prayers of the Mass and for administration of the sacraments; provision for adaptation of rites to cultural patterns.

Approval for reforms of various kinds — in liturgical texts, rites, etc. — depends on the Holy See, regional conferences of bishops and individual bishops, according to provisions of law. No priest has authority to initiate reforms on his own. Reforms may not be introduced just for the sake of innovation, and any that are introduced in the light of present-day circumstances should embody sound tradition.

To assure the desired effect of liturgical reforms, training and instruction are necessary for the clergy, religious and the laity. The functions of diocesan and regional commissions for liturgy, music and art are to set standards and provide leadership for instruction and practical programs in their respective fields.

Most of the constitution's provisions regarding liturgical reforms have to do with the Roman Rite. The document clearly respects the equal dignity of all rites, leaving to the Eastern Churches control over their ancient liturgies.

(For coverage of the **Mystery of the Eucharist,** see The Mass; **Other Sacraments,** see separate entries.)

Sacramentals

Sacramentals, instituted by the Church, "are sacred signs which bear a resemblance to

227

the sacraments: they signify effects, particularly of a spiritual kind, which are obtained through the Church's intercession. By them men are disposed to receive the chief effect of the sacraments, and various occasions in life are rendered holy" (No. 60).

"Thus, for well-disposed members of the faithful, the liturgy of the sacraments and sacramentals sanctifies almost every event in their lives; they are given access to the stream of divine grace which flows from the paschal mystery of the passion, death, and resurrection of Christ, the fountain from which all sacraments and sacramentals draw their power. There is hardly any proper use of material things which cannot thus be directed toward the sanctification of men and the praise of God" (No. 61). Some common sacramentals are priestly blessings, blessed palm, candles, holy water, medals, scapulars, prayers and ceremonies of the Roman Ritual.

Liturgy of the Hours

The Liturgy of the Hours (Divine Office) is the public prayer of the Church for praising God and sanctifying the day. Its daily celebration is required as a sacred obligation by men in holy orders and by men and women religious who have professed solemn vows. Its celebration by others is highly commended and is to be encouraged in the communuty of the faithful.

"By tradition going back to early Christian times, the Divine Office is arranged so that the whole course of the day and night is made holy by the praises of God. Therefore, when this wonderful song of praise is worthily rendered by priests and others who are deputed for this purpose by Church ordinance, or by the faithful praying together with the priest in an approved form, then it is truly the voice of the bride addressing her bridegroom; it is the very prayer which Christ Himself, together with His body, addresses to the Father" (No. 84).

"Hence all who perform this service are not only fulfilling a duty of the Church, but also are sharing in the greatest honor accorded to Christ's spouse, for by offering these praises to God they are standing before God's throne in the name of the Church their Mother" (No. 85).

The Latin text of the Liturgy of the Hours, under revision since 1965, was described by Pope Paul in the apostolic constitution *Canticum Laudis,* dated Nov. 1, 1970. Its four complete volumes in authorized English translation have been published since May, 1975.

One-volume, partial editions of the Liturgy of the Hours have been published in approved English translation. Entitled *Christian Prayer,* they contain the Morning and Evening Prayers and other elements. They are intended for use by religious and lay persons who are not bound by obligation to pray the Liturgy of the Hours.

The revised Liturgy of the Hours consists of:

• Office of Readings, for reflection on the word of God. The pruncipal parts are three psalms, biblical and non-biblical readings.

• Morning and Evening Prayer, called the "hinges" of the Liturgy of the Hours. The principal parts are a hymn, two psalms, an Old or New Testament canticle, a brief biblical reading, Zechariah's canticle (the *Benedictus,* morning) or Mary's canticle (the *Magnificat,* evening), responsories, intercessions and a concluding prayer.

• Daytime Prayer. The principal parts are a hymn, three psalms, a brief biblical reading and one of three concluding prayers corresponding to the time at which the prayer is offered (midmorning, midday, midafternoon).

• Night Prayer: The principal parts are one or two psalms, a brief biblical reading, Simeon's canticle *(Nunc Dimittis),* a concluding prayer and an antiphon in honor of Mary.

In the new Office, the hours are shorter than they had been, with greater textual variety, meditation aids, and provision for intervals of silence and meditation. The psalms are distributed over a four-week period instead of a week; some psalms, entirely or in part, are not included. Additional canticles from the Old and New Testaments are assigned for Morning and Evening Prayer. Additional scriptural texts have been added and variously arranged for greater internal unity, correspondence to readings at Mass, and relevance to events and themes of salvation history. Readings include some of the best material from the Fathers of the Church and other authors and improved selections on the lives of saints.

The book used for recitation of the Office is the **Breviary.**

For coverage of the **Liturgical Year,** see Church Calendar.

Sacred Music

"The musical tradition of the universal Church is a treasure of immeasurable value, greater even than that of any other art. The main reason for this pre-eminence is that, as sacred melody united to words, it forms a necessary or integral part of the solemn liturgy.

". . . Sacred music increases in holiness to the degree that it is intimately linked with liturgical action, winningly expresses prayerfulness, promotes solidarity, and enriches sacred rites with heightened solemnity. The Church indeed approves of all forms of true art, and admits them into divine worship when they show appropriate qualities" (No. 112).

The constitution decreed:

• Vernacular languages for the people's parts of the liturgy, as well as Latin, may be used.

• Participation in sacred song by the whole body of the faithful, and not just by choirs, is to be encouraged and brought about.

• Provisions should be made for proper musical training for clergy, religious and lay persons.

• While Gregorian Chant has a unique dignity and relationship to the Latin liturgy, other kinds of music are acceptable.

• Native musical traditions should be used, especially in mission areas.

• Various instruments compatible with the dignity of worship may be used.

Gregorian Chant: A form and style of chant called Gregorian was the basis and most highly regarded standard of liturgical music for centuries. It originated probably during the formative period of the Roman liturgy and developed in conjunction with Gallican and other forms of chant. Gregory the Great's connection with it is not clear, although it is known that he had great concern for and interest in church music. The earliest extant written versions of Gregorian chant date from the ninth century. A thousand years later, the Benedictines of Solesmes, France, initiated a revival of chant which gave impetus to the modern liturgical movement.

Sacred Art and Furnishings

"Very rightly the fine arts are considered to rank among the noblest expressions of human genius. This judgment applies especially to religious art and to its highest achievement, which is sacred art. By their very nature both of the latter are related to God's boundless beauty, for this is the reality which these human efforts are trying to express in some way. To the extent that these works aim exclusively at turning men's thoughts to God persuasively and devoutly, they are dedicated to God and to the cause of His greater honor and glory" (No. 122).

The objective of sacred art is "that all things set apart for use in divine worship should be truly worthy, becoming, and beautiful, signs and symbols of heavenly realities. . . . The Church has . . . always reserved to herself the right to pass judgment upon the arts, deciding which of the works of artists are in accordance with faith, piety, and cherished traditional laws, and thereby suited to sacred purposes.

". . . Sacred furnishings should worthily and beautifully serve the dignity of worship . . ." (No. 122).

According to the constitution:

• Contemporary art, as well as that of the past, shall "be given free scope in the Church, provided that it adorns the sacred buildings and holy rites with due honor and reverence . . ." (No. 123).

• Noble beauty, not sumptuous display, should be sought in art, sacred vestments and ornaments.

• "Let bishops carefully exclude from the house of God and from other sacred places those works of artists which are repugnant to faith, morals, and Christian piety, and which offend true religious sense either by their distortion of forms or by lack of artistic worth, by mediocrity or by pretense.

• "When churches are to be built, let great care be taken that they be suitable for the celebration of liturgical services and for the active participation of the faithful" (No. 124).

• "The practice of placing sacred images in churches so that they may be venerated by the faithful is to be firmly maintained. Nevertheless, their number should be moderate and their relative location should reflect right order. Otherwise they may create confusion among the Christian people and promote a faulty sense of devotion" (No. 125).

• Artists should be trained and inspired in the spirit and for the purposes of the liturgy.

• The norms of sacred art should be revised. "These laws refer especially to the worthy and well-planned construction of sacred buildings, the shape and construction of altars, the nobility, location, and security of the Eucharistic tabernacle, the suitability and dignity of the baptistery, the proper use of sacred images, embellishments, and vestments . . ." (No. 128).

RITES

A rite is the manner in which liturgical worship is carried out. It includes the forms and ceremonial observances of liturgical worship.

Different rites have evolved in the course of Church history, giving to liturgical worship forms and usages peculiar and proper to the nature of worship itself and to the culture of the faithful in various circumstances of time and place. Thus, there has been development since apostolic times in prayers and ceremonies of the Mass, the administration of the sacraments, requirements for celebration of the Divine Office. Practices within the patriarchates of Antioch, Rome, Alexandria and Constantinople were the principal sources of the rites in present use.

Eastern Rites, described elsewhere in the Almanac, are proper to Eastern Catholic Churches.

The **Roman** or **Latin Rite,** described in this section, prevails in the Western Church. It was derived from Roman practices and the use of Latin as an official language from the third century onward. Other rites in limited use in the Western Church have been the Ambrosian, the Mozarabic, the Lyonnais, the Braga, and rites peculiar to some religious orders like the Dominicans, Carmelites and Carthusians.

MASS, EUCHARISTIC SACRIFICE AND BANQUET

Declarations of Vatican II

The Second Vatican Council made the following declarations, among others, with respect to the Mass.

"At the Last Supper, on the night when He was betrayed, our Savior instituted the Eucharistic Sacrifice of His Body and Blood. He did this in order to perpetuate the sacrifice of the Cross throughout the centuries until He should come again, and so to entrust to His beloved spouse, the Church, a memorial of His death and resurrection: a sacrament of love, a sign of unity, a bond of charity, a paschal banquet in which Christ is consumed, the mind is filled with grace, and a pledge of future glory is given to us" (*Constitution on the Sacred Liturgy*, No. 47).

". . . As often as the sacrifice of the cross in which 'Christ, our passover, has been sacrificed' (1 Cor. 5:7) is celebrated on an altar, the work of our redemption is carried on. At the same time, in the sacrament of the Eucharistic bread the unity of all believers who form one body in Christ (cf. 1 Cor. 10:17) is both expressed and brought about. All men are called to this union with Christ . . ." (*Dogmatic Constitution on the Church*. No. 3).

". . . The ministerial priest, by the sacred power he enjoys, molds and rules the priestly people. Acting in the person of Christ, he brings about the Eucharistic Sacrifice, and offers it to God in the name of all the people. For their part, the faithful join in the offering of the Eucharist by virtue of their royal priesthood . . ." (*Ibid.*, No. 10).

Declarations of Trent

Among its decrees on the Holy Eucharist, the Council of Trent stated the following points of doctrine on the Mass.

1. There is in the Catholic Church a true Sacrifice, the Mass instituted by Jesus Christ. It is the Sacrifice of His Body and Blood, Soul and Divinity, Himself, under the appearances of bread and wine.

2. This Sacrifice is identical with the Sacrifice of the Cross, inasmuch as Christ is the Priest and Victim in both. A difference lies in the manner of offering, which was bloody upon the Cross and is bloodless on the altar.

3. The Mass is a propitiatory Sacrifice, atoning for sins of the living and dead for whom it is offered.

4. The efficacy of the Mass is derived from the Sacrifice of the Cross, whose super-abundant merits it applies to men.

5. Although the Mass is offered to God alone, it may be celebrated in honor and memory of the saints.

6. Christ instituted the Mass at the Last Supper.

7. Christ ordained the Apostles priests, giving them power and the command to consecrate His Body and Blood to perpetuate and renew the Sacrifice.

ORDER OF MASS

The Mass consists of two principal divisions called the **Liturgy of the Word**, which features the proclamation of the Word of God, and the **Eucharistic Liturgy**, which focuses on the central act of sacrifice in the Consecration and on the Eucharistic Banquet in Holy Communion. (Formerly, these divisions were called, respectively, the **Mass of the Catechumens** and the **Mass of the Faithful**.) In addition to these principal divisions, there are ancillary introductory and concluding rites.

The following description covers the Mass as celebrated with participation by the people. This Order of the Mass was approved by Pope Paul VI in the apostolic constitution *Missale Romanum* dated Apr. 3, 1969, and promulgated in a decree issued Apr. 6, 1969, by the Congregation for Divine Worship. The assigned effective date was Nov. 30, 1969.

Introductory Rites

Entrance: The introductory rites begin with the singing or recitation of an entrance song while the priest approaches the altar, kisses it, and goes to the place where he will be seated. The song consists of one or more scriptural verses stating the theme of the mystery, season or feast commemorated in the Mass.

Greeting: The priest and people make the Sign of the Cross together. The priest then greets them in one of several alternative ways and they reply in a corresponding manner.

Introductory Remarks: At this point, the priest or another of the ministers may introduce the theme of the Mass.

Penitential Rite: The priest and people together acknowledge their sins as a preliminary step toward worthy celebration of the sacred mysteries. This rite includes a brief examination of conscience, a general confession of sin and plea for divine mercy in one of several ways, and a prayer of absolution by the priest. The *Kyrie, eleison* ("Lord, have mercy") is then said if it was not included in one of the foregoing pleas for divine mercy.

Glory to God: A doxology, a hymn of praise to God, sung or said on festive occasions.

Opening Prayer: A prayer of petition offered by the priest on behalf of the worshipping community.

I. Liturgy of the Word

Readings: The featured elements of this liturgy are several readings of passages from the Bible. If three readings are in order, the first is usually from the Old Testament, the second from the New Testament (Epistles, Acts, Revelation), and the third from one of the Gospels; the final reading is always a selection from a Gospel. The first reading(s) is concluded with the formula, "This is the Word of the Lord," to which the people respond, "Thanks be to God." The Gospel reading is concluded with the formula, "This is the Gospel of the Lord," to which the people respond, "Praise to you, Lord Jesus Christ," Between the readings, psalm verses and a Gospel acclamation are sung or said.

Homily: Sermon on a scriptural or liturgical subject; ideally, it should be related to the liturgical service in progress.

Creed: The Nicene profession of faith, by priest and people, on certain occasions.

Prayer of the Faithful: Litany-type prayers of petition, with participation by the people. Called general intercessions, they concern needs of the Church, the salvation of the world, public authorities, persons in need, the local community.

II. Eucharistic Liturgy

Offertory Song: Scriptural verses related to the theme of the Mass, or a suitable hymn, sung or said while things are prepared at the altar for the Eucharistic Liturgy and while the offerings of bread and wine are brought to the altar.

Offertory Procession: Presentation to the priest of the gifts of bread and wine, principally, by participating members of the congregation.

Offering of the Gifts: Consists of the prayers and ceremonies with which the priest offers bread and wine as the elements of the sacrifice to take place during the Eucharistic Prayer and of the Lord's Supper to be shared in Holy Communion. If singing takes place during the offering, the priest can say the prayers and carry out the action silently; if there is no singing, he says the prayers aloud and the people, after each offering, respond with the words, "Blessed be God forever."

Washing of Hands: After offering the bread and wine, the priest cleanses his fingers with water in a brief ceremony of purification.

Pray, Brethren: Prayer that the sacrifice to take place will be acceptable to God. The first part of the prayer is said by the priest; the second, by the people.

Prayer over the Gifts: A prayer of petition offered by the priest on behalf of the worshipping community.

Eucharistic Prayer

Preface: A hymn of praise, introducing the Eucharistic Prayer or Canon, sung or said by the priest following responses by the people. The Order of the Mass contains a variety of prefaces, for use on different occasions.

Holy, Holy, Holy; Blessed Is He: Divine praises sung or said by the priest and people.

Canon: The Eucharistic Prayer of the Mass whose central portion is the Consecration, when the essential act of sacrificial offering

takes place with the changing of bread and wine into the Body and Blood of Christ. The prayers of the Canon, which are said by the celebrant only, commemorate principal mysteries of salvation history and include petitions for the Church, the living and dead, and remembrances of saints. There are four Eucharistic Prayers, for use on various occasions and at the option of the priest. (Additional Canons for Masses with children and for reconciliation were approved in 1975.)

Doxology: A formula of divine praise sung or said by the priest while he holds aloft the chalice containing the consecrated wine in one hand and the paten containing the consecrated host in the other.

Communion Rite

Lord's Prayer: Sung or said by the priest and people.

Prayer for Deliverance from evil: Called an **embolism** because it is a development of the final petition of the Lord's Prayer; said by the priest. It concludes with a memorial of the return of the Lord to which the people respond, "For the kingdom, the power, and the glory are yours, now and forever."

Prayer for Peace: Said by the priest, with corresponding responses by the people. The priest can, in accord with local custom, bid the people to exchange a greeting of peace with each other.

Lamb of God: A prayer for divine mercy sung or said while the priest breaks the consecrated host and places a piece of it into the consecrated wine in the chalice.

Communion: The priest, after saying a preparatory prayer, administers Holy Communion to himself and then to the people, thus completing the sacrifice-banquet of the Mass. (This completion is realized even if the celebrant alone receives the Eucharist.) On giving the Eucharist to the people, the priest says, "The Body of Christ," to each recipient; the customary response is "Amen." If the Eucharist is administered under the forms of bread and wine, the priest says, "The Body and Blood of Christ."

Communion Song: Scriptural verses or a suitable hymn sung or said during the distribution of Holy Communion. After Holy Communion is received, some moments may be spent in silent meditation or in the chanting of a psalm or hymn of praise.

Prayer after Communion: A prayer of petition offered by the priest on behalf of the worshipping community.

Concluding Rite

Announcements: Brief announcements to the people are in order at this time.

Dismissal: Consists of a final greeting by the priest, a blessing, and a formula of dismissal. This rite is omitted if another liturgical action immediately follows the Mass; e.g., a procession, the blessing of the body during a funeral rite.

Some parts of the Mass are changeable with the liturgical season or feast, and are called the **proper** of the Mass. Other parts are said to be **common** because they always remain the same.

Additional Mass Notes

Catholics are seriously obliged to attend Mass in a worthy manner on Sundays and holy days of obligation. Failure to do so without a proportionately serious reason is gravely wrong.

It is the custom for priests to celebrate Mass daily whenever possible. To satisfy the needs of the faithful on Sundays and holy days of obligation, they are authorized to say Mass twice (**bination**) or even three times (**trination**). Bination is also permissible on weekdays. On Christmas and All Souls' Day every priest may say three Masses. Mass may be celebrated in the morning, afternoon or evening.

The **fruits of the Mass,** which in itself is of infinite value, are: **general,** for all the faithful; **special (ministerial),** for the intentions or persons specifically intended by the celebrant; **most special (personal),** for the celebrant himself. On Sundays and certain other days pastors are obliged to offer Mass for their parishioners. If a priest accepts a stipend or offering for a Mass, he is obliged in justice to apply the Mass for the designated intention. Mass may be applied for the living and the dead, or for any good intention.

Mass can be celebrated in several ways: e.g., with people present, without their presence (privately), with two or more priests as co-celebrants (concelebration), with greater or less solemnity.

Some of the various types of Masses are: **for the dead** (Funeral Mass or Mass of Christian Burial, Mass for the Dead — formerly called Requiem Mass); **nuptial,** for married couples, with or after the wedding ceremony; **votive,** to honor a Person of the Trinity, a saint, or for some special intention. A **red Mass** is a Votive Mass of the Holy Spirit, celebrated for members of the legal profession that they might exercise prudence and equity in their official capacities. **Gregorian Masses** are a series of 30 Masses celebrated on 30 consecutive days for a deceased person.

The only day of the year on which Mass is not celebrated is Good Friday. In its place, there is a **Solemn Liturgical Action.**

Places, Altars for Mass

The ordinary place for celebrating the Eucharist is a church or other sacred place, at a permanent or movable altar.

Outside of a sacred place, Mass may be celebrated in an appropriate place at a suitable table covered with a linen cloth and corporal.

An **altar stone** containing the relics of saints, which was formerly prescribed, is not required by regulations in effect since the promulgation Apr. 6, 1969, of *Institutio Generalis Missalis Romani.*

A **permanent altar** should have a table of stone, be consecrated, and have enclosed within it relics of some saints.

A **movable altar** may be made of any solid and suitable material. If made of stone and consecrated, it should have enclosed within it relics of some saints; if blessed rather than consecrated, the enclosure of relics is not required.

LITURGICAL VESTMENTS

In the early years of the Church, vestments worn by the ministers at liturgical functions were the same as the garments in ordinary popular use. They became distinctive when their form was not altered to correspond with later variations in popular style. Liturgical vestments are symbolic of the sacred ministry and add appropriate decorum to divine worship.

Mass Vestments

Alb: A body-length tunic of white fabric; a vestment common to all ministers of divine worship.

Amice: A rectangular piece of white cloth worn about the neck, tucked into the collar and falling over the shoulders; worn under the alb.

Chasuble: Originally, a large mantle or cloak covering the body, it is the outer vestment of a priest celebrating Mass or carrying out other sacred actions connected with the Mass.

Cincture: A cord which serves the purpose of a belt, holding the alb close to the body.

Dalmatic: The outer vestment worn by a deacon in place of a chasuble.

Stole: A long, band-like vestment worn about the neck and falling to about the knees. (A stole is used for other functions also.)

The material, form and ornamentation of the aforementioned and other vestments are subject to variation and adaptation, according to norms and decisions of the Holy See and concerned conferences of bishops. The overriding norm is that they should be appropriate for use in divine worship. The customary ornamented vestments are the chasuble, dalmatic and stole.

The minimal vestments required for a priest celebrating Mass are the alb, stole and chasuble.

Chasuble-Alb: A vestment combining the features of the chasuble and alb; for use with a stole by concelebrants and, by way of exception, by celebrants in certain circumstances.

Liturgical Colors

The colors of outer vestments vary with liturgical seasons, feasts and other circumstances. The colors and their use are:

Green: For the season of the year; symbolic of hope and the vitality of the life of faith.

Purple: For Advent and Lent; may also be used in Masses for the dead; symbolic of penance.

Red: For the Sunday of the Passion, the Wednesday of Holy Week, Good Friday, Pentecost; feasts of the Passion of Our Lord, the Apostles and Evangelists, martyrs; symbolic of the supreme sacrifice of life for the love of God.

Rose: May be used in place of purple on the Third Sunday of Advent (Gaudete Sunday) and the Fourth Sunday of Lent (Laetare Sunday); symbolic of anticipatory joy during a time of penance.

White: For Christmastide and Eastertide; feasts and commemorations of Our Lord, except those of the Passion; feasts and commemorations of the Blessed Virgin Mary, angels, saints who are not martyrs, All Saints (Nov. 1), St. John the Baptist (June 24), St. John the Evangelist (Dec. 27), the Chair of St. Peter (Feb. 22), the Conversion of St. Paul (Jan. 25). White, symbolic of purity and integrity of the life of faith, may generally be substituted for other colors, and can be used for funeral and other Masses for the dead.

Options are provided regarding the color of vestments used in offices and Masses for the dead. The newsletter of the U.S. Bishops' Committee on the Liturgy, in line with No. 308 of the "General Instruction of the Roman Missal," announced in July, 1970: "In the dioceses of the United States, **white** vestments may be used, in addition to violet (**purple**) and **black**, in offices and Masses for the dead."

On more solemn occasions, better than ordinary vestments may be used, even though their color (e.g., gold) does not match the requirements of the day.

Considerable freedom is permitted in the choice of colors of vestments worn for votive Masses.

Other Vestments

Cappa Magna: Flowing vestment with a train, worn by bishops and cardinals.

Cassock: A full-length, close-fitting robe worn by priests and other clerics under liturgical vestments and in ordinary use; usually black for priests, purple for bishops and other prelates, red for cardinals, white for the pope. In place of a cassock, priests belonging to religious institutes wear the habit proper to their institute.

Cope: A mantle-like vestment open in front and fastened across the chest; worn by sacred ministers in processions and other ceremonies, as prescribed by appropriate directives.

Gremial: A rectangular veil of silk or linen placed over the knees of a bishop when he is seated during various episcopal ceremonies.

Habit: The ordinary garb of members of religious institutes, analogous to the cassock of diocesan priests; the form of habits varies from institute to institute.

Humeral Veil: A rectangular vestment worn about the shoulders by a deacon. or priest in Eucharistic processions and for other prescribed liturgical ceremonies.

Mitre: A headdress worn at some liturgical functions by bishops, abbots and, in certain cases, other ecclesiastics.

Pallium: A circular band of white wool about two inches wide, with front and back pendants, marked with six crosses, worn about the neck. It is a symbol of the fullness of the episcopal office. Pope Paul VI, in a document issued July 20, 1978, on his own initiative and entitled *Inter Eximia Episcopalis,* restricted its use to the pope and archbishops of metropolitan sees. The pallium is made from the wool of lambs blessed by the pope on the feast of St. Agnes (Jan. 21).

Rochet: A knee-length, white linen-lace garment of prelates worn under outer vestments.

Surplice: A loose, flowing vestment of white fabric with wide sleeves. For some functions, it is interchangeable with an alb.

Zucchetto: A skullcap worn by bishops and other prelates.

SACRED VESSELS, LINENS

Vessels

Chalice and Paten: The principal sacred vessels required for the celebration of Mass are the **chalice** (cup) and **paten** (plate) in which wine and bread, respectively, are offered, consecrated and consumed. Both should be made of solid and noble material which is not easily breakable or corruptible. Gold coating is required of the interior parts of sacred vessels subject to rust. The cup of a chalice should be made of non-absorbent material.

Vessels for containing consecrated hosts (see below) can be made of material other than solid and noble metal — e. g., ivory, more durable woods — provided the substitute material is locally regarded as noble or rather precious and is suitable for sacred use.

Sacred vessels should be blessed or consecrated, according to prescribed requirements.

Vessels, in addition to the paten, for containing consecrated hosts are:

Ciborium: Used to hold hosts for distribution to the faithful and for reservation in the tabernacle.

Luna, Lunula, Lunette: A small receptacle which holds the sacred host in an upright position in the monstrance.

Monstrance, Ostensorium: A portable receptable so made that the sacred host, when enclosed therein, may be clearly seen, as at

Benediction or during extended exposition of the Blessed Sacrament.

Pyx: A watch-shaped vessel used in carrying the Eucharist to the sick.

Linens

Altar Cloth: A white cloth, usually of linen, covering the table of an altar. One cloth is sufficient. Three were used according to former requirements.

Burse: A square, stiff flat case, open at one end, in which the folded corporal is placed; the outside is covered with material of the same kind and color as the outer vestments of the celebrant.

Corporal: A square piece of white linen spread on the altar cloth, on which rest the vessels holding the Sacred Species — the consecrated host(s) and wine — during the Eucharistic Liturgy. The corporal is similarly used whenever the Blessed Sacrament is removed from the tabernacle; e. g., during Benediction the vessel containing the Blessed Sacrament rests on a corporal.

Finger Towel: A white rectangular napkin used by the priest to dry his fingers after cleansing them following the offering of gifts at Mass.

Pall: A square piece of stiff material, usually covered with linen, used to cover the chalice at Mass.

Purificator: A white rectangular napkin used for cleansing sacred vessels after the reception of Communion at Mass.

Veil: The chalice intended for use at Mass is covered with a veil made of the same material as the outer vestments of the celebrant.

THE CHURCH BUILDING

A church is a building set aside and dedicated for purposes of divine worship, the place of assembly for a worshiping community.

A Catholic church is the ordinary place in which the faithful assemble for participation in the Eucharistic Liturgy and other forms of divine worship.

In the early years of Christianity, the first places of assembly for the Eucharistic Liturgy were private homes (Acts 2:46; Rom. 16:5; 1 Cor. 16:5; Col. 4:15) and, sometimes, catacombs. Church building began in the latter half of the second century during lulls in persecution and became widespread after enactment of the Edict of Milan in 313, when it finally became possible for the Church to emerge completely from the underground. The oldest and basic norms regarding church buildings date from about that time.

The essential principle underlying all norms for church building was reformulated by the Second Vatican Council, as follows: "When churches are to be built, let great care be taken that they be suitable for the celebration of liturgical services and for the active participation of the faithful" *(Constitution on the Sacred Liturgy*, No. 124).

This principle was subsequently elaborated in detail by the Congregation for Divine Worship in a document entitled *Institutio Generalis Missalis Romani,* which was approved by Paul VI Apr. 3 and promulgated by a decree of the congregation dated Apr. 6, 1969. Coverage of the following items reflects the norms stated in Chapter V of this document.

Sanctuary: The part of the church where the altar of sacrifice is located, the place where the ministers of the liturgy lead the people in prayer, proclaim the word of God and celebrate the Eucharist. It is set off from the body of the church by a distinctive structural feature — e. g., elevation above the main floor — or by ornamentation. (The traditional **communion rail,** which has been removed in recent years in many churches, served this purpose of demarcation.) The customary location of the sanctuary is at the front of the church; it may, however, be centrally located.

Altar: The main altar of sacrifice and table of the Lord is the focal feature of the sanctuary and entire church. It stands by itself, so that the ministers can move about it freely, and is so situated that they face the people during the liturgical action. In addition to this main altar, there may also be others; in new churches, these are situated in side chapels or alcoves removed to some degree from the body of the church.

Adornment of the Altar: The altar table is covered with a suitable linen cloth. Required candelabra and a cross are placed upon or near the altar in plain sight of the people and are so arranged that they do not obscure their view of the liturgical action.

Seats of the Ministers: The seat of the celebrant, corresponding with his role as the presiding minister of the assembly, is best located behind the altar and facing the people; it is raised a bit above the level of the altar but must not have the appearance of a throne. The seats of other ministers are also located in the sanctuary.

Ambo, Pulpit: The stand at which scriptural lessons and psalm responses are read, the word of God preached, and the prayer of the faithful offered. It is so placed that the ministers can be easily seen and heard by the people.

Places for the People: Seats and kneeling benches (**pews**) and other accommodations for the people are so arranged that they can participate in the most appropriate way in the liturgical action and have freedom of movement for the reception of Holy Communion. Reserved seats are out of order.

Place for the Choir: Where it is located depends on the most suitable arrangement for maintaining the unity of the choir with the congregation and for providing its members maximum opportunity for carrying out their proper function and participating fully in the Mass.

Tabernacle: The best place for reserving the Blessed Sacrament is in a chapel suitable for the private devotion of the people. If this is not possible, reservation should be at a side altar or other appropriately adorned place. In either case, the Blessed Sacrament should be kept in a tabernacle, i.e., a safe-like, secure receptacle.

Statues: Images of the Lord, the Blessed Virgin Mary and the saints are legitimately proposed for the veneration of the faithful in churches. Their number and arrangement, however, should be ordered in such a way that they do not distract the people from the central celebration of the Eucharistic Liturgy. There should be only one statue of one and the same saint in a church.

General Adornment and Arrangement of Churches: Churches should be so adorned and fitted out that they serve the direct requirements of divine worship and the needs and reasonable convenience of the people.

Other Items

Ambry: A box containing the holy oils, attached to the wall of the sanctuary in some churches.

Baptistery: The place for administering baptism. Some churches have baptisteries adjoining or near the entrance, a position symbolizing the fact that persons are initiated in the Church and incorporated in Christ through this sacrament. Contemporary liturgical practice favors placement of the baptistery near the sanctuary and altar, or the use of a portable font in the same position, to emphasize the relationship of baptism to the Eucharist, the celebration in sacrifice and banquet of the death and resurrection of Christ.

Candles: Used more for symbolical than illuminative purposes, they represent Christ, the light and life of grace, at liturgical functions. They are made of beeswax.

Confessional: A booth-like structure for the hearing of confessions, with separate compartments for the priest and penitents and a grating or screen between them. The use of confessionals became general in the Roman Rite after the Council of Trent.

Crucifix: A cross bearing the figure of the body of Christ, representative of the Sacrifice of the Cross.

Cruets: Vessels containing the wine and water used at Mass. They are placed on a credence table in the sanctuary.

Holy Water Fonts: Receptacles containing holy water, usually at church entrances, for the use of the faithful.

Sanctuary Lamp: A lamp which is kept burning continuously before a tabernacle in which the Blessed Sacrament is reserved, as a sign of the Real Presence of Christ.

LITURGICAL DEVELOPMENTS

The principal developments covered in this article are enactments of the Holy See and actions related to their implementation in the United States.

Modern Movement

Origins of the modern movement for renewal in the liturgy date back to the 19th century. The key contributing factor was a revival of liturgical and scriptural studies. Of special significance was the work of the Benedictine monks of Solesmes, France, who aroused great interest in the liturgy through the restoration of Gregorian Chant. St. Pius X approved their work in a motu proprio of 1903 and gave additional encouragement to liturgical study and development.

St. Pius X did more than any other single pope to promote early first Communion and the practice of frequent Communion, started the research behind a revised breviary, and appointed a group to investigate possible revisions in the Mass.

The movement attracted some attention in the 1920's and 30's but made little progress.

Significant pioneering developments in the US during the 20's, however, were the establishment of the Liturgical Press, the beginning of publication of *Orate Fratres* (now *Worship*), and the inauguration of the League of the Divine Office by the Benedictines at St. John's Abbey, Collegeville, Minn. Later events of influence were the establishment of the Pius X School of Liturgical Music at Manhattanville College of the Sacred Heart and the organization of a summer school of liturgical music at Mary Manse College by the Gregorian Institute of America. The turning point toward real renewal was reached during and after World War II.

Pius XII gave it impetus and direction, principally through the background teaching in his encyclicals on the *Mystical Body* (1943), *Sacred Liturgy* (1947), and the *Discipline of Sacred Music* (1955), and by means of specific measures affecting the liturgy itself. His work was continued during the pontificates of John XXIII and Paul VI. The Second Vatican Council, in virtue of its *Constitution on the Sacred Liturgy,* inaugurated changes of the greatest significance.

Before and After Vatican II

The most significant liturgical changes made in the years immediately preceding the Second Vatican Council were the following:

(1) Revision of the Rites of Holy Week, for universal observance from 1956.

(2) Modification of the Eucharistic fast and permission for afternoon and evening Mass, in effect from 1953 and extended in 1957.

(3) The Dialogue Mass, introduced in 1958.

(4) Use of popular languages in administration of the sacraments.

(5) Calendar-missal-breviary reform, in effect from Jan. 1, 1961.

(6) Seven-step administration of baptism for adults, approved in 1962.

The *Constitution on the Sacred Liturgy* approved (2,174 to 4) and promulgated by the Second Vatican Council Dec. 4, 1963, marked the beginning of a profound renewal in the Church's corporate worship. Implementation of some of its measures was ordered by Paul VI Jan. 25, 1964, in the motu proprio *Sacram Liturgiam*. On Feb. 29, a special commission, the Consilium for Implementing the Constitution on the Sacred Liturgy, was formed to supervise the execution of the entire program of liturgical reform. Implementation of the program on local and regional levels was left to bishops acting through their own liturgical commissions and in concert with their fellow bishops in national conferences.

Liturgical reform in the United States has been carried out under the direction of the Liturgy Committee, National Conference of Catholic Bishops. Its secretariat, established early in 1965, is located at 1312 Massachusetts Ave. N.W., Washington, D.C. 20005.

Stages of Development

Liturgical development after the Second Vatican Council proceeded in several stages. It started with the formulation of guidelines and directives, and with the translation into vernacular languages of virtually unchanged Latin ritual texts. Then came structural changes in the Mass, the sacraments, the calendar, the Divine Office and other phases of the liturgy. These revisions were just about completed with the publication of a new order for the sacrament of penance in February, 1974. A continuing phase of development, in progress from the beginning, involves efforts to deepen the liturgical sense of the faithful, to increase their participation in worship and to relate it to full Christian life.

Texts and Translations

The master texts of all documents on liturgical reform were in Latin. Effective dates of their implementation depended on the completion and approval of appropriate translations into vernacular languages. English translations were made by the International Committee for English in the Liturgy.

The principal features of liturgical changes and the effective dates of their introduction in the United States are covered below under topical headings. (For expanded coverage of various items, especially the sacraments, see additional entries.)

The Mass

A new Order of the Mass, supplanting the one authorized by the Council of Trent in the 16th century, was introduced in the U.S. Mar. 22, 1970. It had been approved by Paul VI in the apostolic constitution *Missale Romanum,* dated Apr. 3, 1969.

Preliminary and related to it were the following developments.

Mass in English: Introduced Nov. 29, 1964. In the same year, Psalm 42 was eliminated from the prayers at the foot of the altar.

Incidental Changes: The last Gospel (prologue of John) and vernacular prayers following Mass were eliminated Mar. 7, 1965. At the same time, provision was made for the celebrant to say aloud some prayers formerly said silently.

Rubrics: An instruction entitled *Tres Abhinc Annos,* dated May 4 and effective June 29, 1967, simplified directives for the celebration of Mass, approved the practice of saying the canon aloud, altered the Communion and dismissal rites, permitted purple instead of black vestments in Masses for the dead, discontinued wearing of the maniple, and approved in principle the use of vernacular languages for the canon, ordination rites, and lessons of the Divine Office when read in choir.

Canons or Eucharistic Prayers: Three additional Eucharistic prayers authorized May 23, 1968, were approved for use in vernacular translation the following Aug. 15. They have the same basic structure as the traditional Roman Canon, whose use in English was introduced Oct. 22, 1967.

The customary Roman Canon, which dates at least from the beginning of the fifth century and has remained substantially unchanged since the seventh century, is the first in the order of listing of the Eucharistic prayers. It can be used at any time, but is the one of choice for most Sundays, some special feasts like Easter and Pentecost, and for feasts of the Apostles and other saints who are commemorated in the canon. Any preface can be used with it.

The second Eucharistic prayer, the shortest and simplest of all, is best suited for use on weekdays and various special circumstances. It has a preface of its own, but others may be used with it. This canon bears a close resemblance to the one framed by St. Hippolytus about 215.

The third Eucharistic prayer is suitable for use on Sundays and feasts as an alternative to the Roman Canon. It can be used with any preface and has a special formula for remembrance of the dead.

The fourth Eucharistic prayer, the most sophisticated of them all, presents a broad synthesis of salvation history. Based on the Eastern tradition of Antioch, it is best suited for use at Masses attended by persons versed in Sacred Scripture. It has an unchangeable preface.

Five additional Eucharistic prayers — three for Masses with children and two for Masses of reconciliation — were approved in 1974 and 1975, respectively, by the Congregation for the Sacraments and Divine Worship. The original approval for a limited period of experimentation was extended indefinitely, until further notice, according to a letter issued by the congregation Dec. 15, 1980.

Lectionary: A new compilation of scriptural readings and psalm responsories for Mass was published in 1969. The *Lectionary* contains a three-year cycle of readings for Sundays and solemn feasts, a two-year weekday cycle, and a one-year cycle for the feasts of saints, in addition to readings for a great variety of Masses, ritual Masses and Masses for various needs. There are also responsorial psalms to follow the first readings, and gospel or alleluia versicles to follow the second readings.

A second edition of the *Lectionary*, substantially the same as the first, was published in 1981. New features included an expanded introduction, extensive scriptural references and additional readings for a number of solemnities and feasts.

Sacramentary (Missal): The Vatican Polyglot Press began distribution in June, 1970, of the Latin text of a new *Roman Missal*, the first revision published in 400 years. The English translation was authorized for optional use beginning July 1, 1974; the mandatory date for use was Dec. 1, 1974.

The missal is the celebrant's book of prayers and sacramental formulas and does not include the readings of the Mass, such as the Gospel and the Epistle. It contains the texts of entrance songs, prefaces and other prayers of the Mass. The number of prefaces is four times greater than it had been. There are 10 commons (or sets of Mass prayers) of martyrs, two of doctors of the Church, and a dozen for saints or groups of saints of various kinds, such as religious, educators and mothers of families. There are Masses during which certain sacraments are administered and others for religious profession, the Church, the pope, priests, Christian unity, the evangelization of nations, persecuted Christians, and other intentions.

Mass for Special Groups: Reasons and norms for the celebration of Mass at special gatherings of the faithful were the subject of an instruction issued May 15, 1969. Two years earlier, the U.S. Bishops' Liturgy Committee went on record in support of the celebration of Mass in private homes.

Sunday Mass on Saturday: The Congregation for the Clergy, under date of Jan. 10, 1970, granted the request that the faithful, where bishops consider it pastorally necessary or useful, may satisfy the precept of participating in Mass in the late afternoon or evening hours of Saturdays and the days before holy days of obligation.

Trination: The Congregation for the Sacraments, under date of Jan. 20, 1970, granted to all U.S. bishops the authority to permit priests to celebrate Mass three times on Saturdays and days preceding holy days of obligation, on condition that the first and second Masses are celebrated for weddings and/or funerals and the third Mass is celebrated in the evening so that the precept (of participating in Mass) will be satisfied by the faithful.

Mass in Latin: According to notices issued by the Congregation for Divine Worship June 1, 1971, and Oct. 28, 1974: (1) Bishops may permit the celebration of Mass in Latin for mixed-language groups. (2) Bishops may permit the celebration of one or two Masses in Latin on weekdays or Sundays in any church, irrespective of mixed-language groups involved (1971). (3) Priests may celebrate Mass in Latin when people are not present. (4) The approved revised Order of the Mass is to be used in Latin as well as vernacular languages . (5) By way of exception, bishops may permit older and handicapped priests to use the Council of Trent's Order of the Mass in private celebration of the holy Sacrifice.

Inter-Ritual Concelebration: The Apostolic Delegation in Washington, D.C., announced in June, 1971, that it had received authorization to permit priests of Roman and Eastern rites to celebrate Mass together in the rite of the host church. It was understood that the inter-ritual concelebrations would always be "a manifestation of the unity of the Church and of communion among particular churches."

Ordo of the Sung Mass: In a decree dated June 24 and made public Aug. 24, 1972, the Congregation for Divine Worship issued a new *Ordo of the Sung Mass* — containing Gregorian chants in Latin — to replace the *Graduale Romanum*.

Mass for Children: Late in 1973, the Congregation for Divine Worship issued special guidelines for children's Masses, providing accommodations to the mentality and spiritual growth of pre-adolescents while retaining the principal parts and structures of the Mass. The *Directory for Masses with Children* was approved by Paul VI Oct. 22 and was dated Nov. 1, 1973. Three Eucharistic prayers for Masses with children were approved by the congregation in 1974; English versions were approved June 5, 1975. Their use, authorized originally for a limited period of experimentation, was extended indefinitely Dec. 15, 1980.

Sacraments

The general use of English in administration of the sacraments was approved for the U.S. Sept. 14, 1964. Structural changes of the rites were subsequently made and introduced in the U.S. as follows.

Anointing of the Sick: Revised rites, covering also administration of the Eucharist to sick persons, were approved Nov. 30,. 1972, and published Jan. 18, 1973. The effective date for use of the provisional English prayer formula was Dec. 1, 1974.

Baptism: New rites for the baptism of infants, approved Mar. 19, 1969, were introduced June 1, 1970.

Christian Initiation of Adults: Revised rites were issued Jan. 6, 1972, for the Christian initiation of adults — affecting preparation for and reception of baptism, the Eucharist and confirmation; also, the reception of already baptized adults into the Church. These rites, which were introduced in the U.S. on the completion of English translation, nullified a seven-step baptismal process approved in 1962.

Confirmation: Revised rites, issued Aug. 15, 1971, became mandatory in the U.S. Jan. 1, 1973.

Eucharist: Several enactments concerning the Eucharist have been issued since 1966 when permission was given for the superiors of convents to administer Holy Communion in the absence of priests. Paul VI issued an instruction on *Worship of the Eucharistic Mystery* May 25, 1967, and another on the manner of administering Holy Communion May 20, 1969. Limited permission for lay persons to serve as special ministers of the Eucharist was given in 1971 and extended in 1972. Also in 1972, instructions were issued regarding administration of the Eucharist to other Christians, and in particular circumstances.

Holy Orders: Revised ordination rites for deacons, priests and bishops, validated by prior experimental use, were approved in 1970. The sacrament of holy orders underwent further revision in 1972 with the elimination of the Church-instituted orders of porter, reader, exorcist, acolyte and subdeacon, and of the tonsure ceremony symbolic of entrance into the clerical state. The former minor orders of reader and acolyte were changed from orders to ministries.

Matrimony: New rites, issued Mar. 19, 1969, were introduced June 1, 1970. Minor revisions had been made in 1964.

Penance: Ritual revision of the sacraments was completed with the approval by Paul VI Dec. 2, 1973, of new directives for the sacrament of penance or reconciliation. The U.S. Bishops' Committee on the Liturgy set Feb. 27, 1977, as the mandatory date for use of the new rite. The committee also declared that it could be used from Mar. 7, 1976, after adequate preparation of priests and people. Earlier, authorization was given by the Holy See in 1968 for the omission of any reference to excommunication or other censures in the formula of absolution unless there was some indication that a censure had actually been incurred by a penitent.

Calendar: A revised liturgical calendar, approved by Paul VI Feb. 14 and made public May 9, 1969, went into effect in the U.S. in 1972.

Additional Developments

Funeral Rites: Revised rites oriented to the resurrection theme went into effect Nov. 1, 1971.

Holy Week: The English version of revised Holy Week rites went into effect in 1971. They introduced concelebration of Mass, placed new emphasis on commemorating the institution of the priesthood on Holy Thursday, and modified Good Friday prayers for other Christians, Jews and other non-Christians.

Liturgy of the Hours: The background, contents, scope and purposes of the revised Divine Office, called the Liturgy of the Hours, were described by Paul VI in the apostolic constitution *Canticum Laudis,* dated Nov. 1, 1970. A provisional English version, incorporating basic features of the master Latin text, was published in 1971. The four complete volumes of the Hours in English have been published since May, 1975. One-volume, partial editions, intended for use by religious and lay persons not bound to pray the Liturgy of the Hours, have also been published in approved form. Nov. 27, 1977, was set by the Congregation for Divine Worship and the National Conference of Catholic Bishops as the effective date for exclusive use in liturgical worship of the translation of the Latin text of the Office approved by the International Committee on English in the Liturgy.

Music: An *Instruction on Music in the Liturgy,* dated Mar. 5 and effective May 14, 1967, encouraged congregational singing during liturgical celebrations and attempted to clarify the role of choirs and trained singers. More significantly, the instruction indicated that a major development under way in the liturgy was a gradual erasure of the distinctive lines traditionally drawn between the sung liturgy and the spoken liturgy.

In the same year, the U.S. Bishops' Liturgy Committee approved the use of contemporary music, as well as guitars and other suitable instruments, in the liturgy. The Holy See authorized in 1968 the use of musical instruments other than the organ in liturgical services, "provided they are played in a manner suitable to worship."

Oils: The Congregation for Divine Worship issued a directive in 1971 permitting the use of other oils — from plants, seeds or coconuts — instead of the traditional olive oil in administering some of the sacraments. The directive also provided that oils could be blessed at other times than at the usual Mass of Chrism on Holy Thursday, and authorized bishops' conferences to permit priests to bless oils in cases of necessity.

Environment and Art in Catholic Worship:

A booklet with this title was issued by the U.S. Bishops' Committee on the Liturgy in March, 1978.

Eucharistic Ministers: Approval by the Congregation for Divine Worship was reported in August, 1978, of a provisional translation of a "Rite of Commissioning Special Ministers of Holy Communion." Note was made of the fact that such ministers should be called "special" instead of "extra-ordinary."

Doxology: The bishops' committee called attention in August, 1978, to the directive that the Doxology concluding the Eucharistic Prayer is said or sung by the celebrant (concelebrants) alone, to which the people respond, "Amen."

Churches, Altars, Chalices: The *Newsletter* of the U.S. Bishops' Committee on the Liturgy reported in November, 1978, that the Congregation for Divine Worship had given provisional approval of a new English translation for the rite of dedicating churches and altars, and of a new form for the blessing of chalices.

Study of the Mass: The Bishops' Committee on the Liturgy, following approval of the project by the National Conference of Catholic Bishops in May, 1979, began a study of the function and position of some elements of the Mass, including the Gloria, the sign of peace, the penitential rite and the readings. Completion of the first phase of the study was reported in July, 1980; its product was a 175-page study document. The second phase of the project got under way in the spring of 1981 with publication of a work book entitled *The Mystery of Faith: A Study of the Structural Elements of the Order of Mass.*

Eucharistic Hosts: Father Thomas Krosnicki, secretary of the Bishops' Committee on the Liturgy, reported in July, 1979, that the committee was preparing new guidelines on the preparation of hosts, in compliance with a request from the Congregation for the Doctrine of the Faith. He said the congregation had "questioned the contents of some of the recipes" used in this country. Cardinal Franjo Seper, prefect of the congregation, stressed the importance of carefully observing traditional theological principles relating to the making of hosts — which should be of wheat, unleavened, with the appearance of food, and capable of being broken and distributed to communicants. In 1980, the congregation ruled definitely against changes in the preparation of hosts, and so informed the bishops' committee. The same prohibition was stated in the "Instruction on Certain Norms concerning Worship of the Eucharistic Mystery" approved by the Pope Apr. 17, 1980.

Eucharistic Worship: This was the subject of two documents issued in 1980. *Dominicae Coenae* was a letter addressed by Pope John Paul to bishops throughout the world in connection with the celebration of Holy Thursday; it was dated Feb. 24 and released Mar. 18. It was more doctrinal in content than the "Instruction on Certain Norms concerning Worship of the Eucharistic Mystery" (*Inaestimabile Donum,* "The Priceless Gift"), which was approved by the Pope Apr. 17 and published by the Congregation for the Sacraments and Divine Worship May 23. Its stated purpose was to reaffirm and clarify teaching on liturgical renewal contained in enactments of the Second Vatican Council and in several related implementing documents.

Marian Statues: A new rite (order) for the coronation of statues of the Blessed Virgin Mary was approved and published in 1981 by the Congregation for the Sacraments and Divine Worship.

Sunday Communion

More than two-thirds of the U.S. bishops voted (187 to 82) during the general meeting of their national conference in November, 1978, or afterwards for allowing the reception of Holy Communion under the forms of bread and wine on Sundays and holy days — subject to the options of bishops of dioceses, priests celebrating Mass and persons receiving the Eucharist. (Reception of Communion in this manner on certain occasions was already provided for in directives of the Congregation for Divine Worship, but Sundays and holy days were not mentioned.)

Report on Liturgical Books, Rites

The Bishops' Committee on the Liturgy published in August, 1981, a compendium of information on the status of liturgical books and rites revised since 1965.

The *BCL Report: Ritual Revisions — A Status Report,* covered *The Roman Ritual, The Roman Pontifical, The Roman Missal* and *The Liturgy of the Hours.* The contents also included a chronological review of the revisions of rites initiated by the Second Vatican Council, from decrees of promulgation through publication in Latin, translations into English and adaptations authorized for use in the U.S.

Dancing and Worship

Dancing and worship was the subject of an essay which appeared in a 1975 edition of Notitiae (11, pp. 202-205), the official journal of the Congregation for the Sacraments and Divine Worship. The article was called a "qualified and authoritative sketch," and should be considered "an authoritative point of reference for every discussion of the matter."

The principal points of the essay were:
• "The dance has never been made an integral part of the official worship of the Latin Church."
• "If the proposal of the religious dance in the West is really to be made welcome, care will have to be taken that in its regard a place

be found outside of the liturgy, in assembly areas which are not strictly liturgical. Moreover, the priests must always be excluded from the dance."

MASS FOR NON-CATHOLICS

The Congregation for the Doctrine of the Faith released a decree June 11, 1976, authorizing the celebration of public Masses for deceased non-Catholic Christians under certain conditions.

The decree noted requests for the celebration of "Mass for deceased persons baptized in other churches or ecclesial communities, particularly when the departed showed special devotion and honor for the Catholic religion or held public office at the service of the whole civil community."

It declared: "There is, of course, no difficulty about the celebration of private Masses for these deceased persons."

"However, the present discipline lays down that they shall not be celebrated (publicly) for those who have died outside of full communion with the Catholic Church."

"In view of the present change in the religious and social situation that gave rise to the above-mentioned discipline, the Sacred Congregation for the Doctrine of the Faith has received inquiries from various quarters to ask if, in certain cases, even public Masses can be said for these deceased persons."

In reply, the congregation decreed:

"I. The present discipline regarding the celebration of public Masses for other Christians who have died shall continue to be the general rule. One reason for this is the consideration due to the conscience of these deceased persons, who did not profess the Catholic faith to the full."

"II. Exceptions can be allowed to this general rule, until the new code (of canon law) is promulgated, whenever both the following conditions are verified:

• "1. The public celebration of the Masses must be explicitly requested by the relatives, friends or subjects of the deceased person for a genuine religious motive.

• "2. In the Ordinary's judgment, there must be no scandal for the faithful.

"III. In these cases public Mass may be celebrated, provided, however, that the name of the deceased is not mentioned in the Eucharistic Prayer, since that mention presupposes full communion with the Catholic Church."

The decree was approved by Pope Paul.

COMMUNION IN HAND

(Source: *Notitiae,* the official bulletin of the Congregation for Divine Worship.)

The Holy See has approved in recent years the practice of in-hand reception of Holy Communion in regions and countries where it had the approval of the appropriate bishops'

conferences. Areas with this practice and the dates of approval are as follows.

Europe

Belgium (May, 1969), France and Germany (June, 1969), The Netherlands (September, 1969), Luxembourg, Scandinavia and Monaco (October, 1969), Austria (February, 1970), Yugoslavia (January, 1971), Portugal (July, 1975), Spain (February, 1976), England and Wales (March, 1976), Ireland (September, 1976), Scotland (July, 1977), Gibraltar (August, 1977).

Africa

Chad (September, 1969), North Africa (October, 1969), South Africa (February, 1970), Djibouti (March, 1970), Upper Volta and Niger (February, 1971), Zimbabwe (October, 1971), Madagascar (May, 1972), Mozambique (October, 1972), Angola (September, 1973), Zambia (March, 1974), Mali (July, 1974), Zaire (July, 1979).

Asia and Oceania

Japan (June, 1970), Indonesia (March, 1971), Korea (January, 1974), New Zealand (April, 1974), Australia (September, 1975), Pacific Episcopal Conference area: New Caledonia, New Hebrides (now Vanuatu), Gilbert Islands (now Kiribati), Wallis and Futuna, Cook Islands and Fiji (December, 1975), Papua New Guinea (April, 1976), Pakistan (October, 1976), Malaysia-Singapore (October, 1977), Turkey (September, 1978).

Central and South America

Bolivia and Uruguay (October, 1969), Jamaica (March, 1970), Paraguay (September, 1971), Panama (May, 1973), Chile (June, 1973), Costa Rica (September, 1973), Peru and Brazil (March, 1975), Cuba (March, 1978).

North America

Canada (February, 1970), Mexico (September, 1976), United States (June, 1977).

EUCHARISTIC MINISTERS

The designation of lay men and women to serve as special ministers of the Eucharist was authorized by Pope Paul in an "Instruction on Facilitating Communion in Particular Circumstances" *(Immensae Caritatis),* dated Jan. 29, 1973, and published by the Congregation for Divine Worship the following Mar. 29.

Qualified lay persons may serve as special ministers for specific occasions or extended periods in the absence of a sufficient number of priests and deacons to provide reasonable and appropriate pastoral service in the distribution of Holy Communion, during Mass and outside of Mass (to the sick and shut-ins).

Appointments of special ministers are made by priests with the approval of the appropriate bishop.

Sacraments

The sacraments are actions of Christ and his Church which signify grace, cause it in the act of signifying it, and confer it upon persons properly disposed to receive it. They perpetuate the redemptive activity of Christ, making it present and effective. They infallibly communicate the fruit of that activity — namely grace — to responsive persons with faith. Sacramental actions consist of the union of sensible signs (matter of the sacraments) with the words of the minister (form of the sacraments).

Christ himself immediately instituted the seven sacraments of the New Law by determining their essence and the efficacy of their signs to produce the grace they signify.

Christ is the principal priest or minister of every sacrament; human agents — an ordained priest, baptized persons contracting marriage with each other, any person conferring emergency baptism in a proper manner — are secondary ministers. Sacraments have efficacy from Christ, not from the personal dispositions of their human ministers.

Each sacrament confers sanctifying grace for the special purpose of the sacrament; this is, accordingly, called sacramental grace. It involves a right to actual graces corresponding to the purposes of the respective sacraments.

While sacraments infallibly produce the grace they signify, recipients benefit from them in proportion to their personal dispositions. One of these is the intention to receive sacraments as sacred signs of God's saving and grace-giving action. The state of grace is also necessary for fruitful reception of the Holy Eucharist, confirmation, matrimony, holy orders and anointing of the sick. Baptism is the sacrament in which grace is given in the first instance and original sin is remitted. Penance is the secondary sacrament of reconciliation, in which persons guilty of serious sin after baptism are reconciled with God and the Church, and in which persons already in the state of grace are strengthened in that state.

Role of Sacraments

The Second Vatican Council prefaced a description of the role of the sacraments with the following statement concerning participation by all the faithful in the priesthood of Christ and the exercise of that priesthood by receiving the sacraments (*Dogmatic Constitution on the Church,* Nos. 10 and 11).

". . . The baptized by regeneration and the anointing of the Holy Spirit are consecrated into a spiritual house and a holy priesthood. Thus through all those works befitting Christian men they can offer spiritual sacrifice and proclaim the power of Him who has called them out of darkness into His marvelous light (cf. 1 Pt. 2:4-10). . . ."

"Though they differ from one another in essence and not only in degree, the common priesthood of the faithful and the ministerial or hierarchical priesthood (of those ordained to holy orders) are nonetheless interrelated. Each of them in its own special way is a participation in the one priesthood of Christ. The ministerial priest, by the sacred power he enjoys, molds and rules the priestly people. Acting in the person of Christ, he brings about the Eucharistic Sacrifice, and offers it to God in the name of all the people. For their part, the faithful join in the offering of the Eucharist by virtue of their royal priesthood. They likewise exercise that priesthood by receiving the sacraments, by prayer and thanksgiving, by the witness of a holy life, and by self-denial and active charity."

"It is through the sacraments and the exercise of the virtues that the sacred nature and organic structure of the priestly community is brought into operation."

Baptism: "Incorporated into the Church through baptism, the faithful are consecrated by the baptismal character to the exercise of the cult of the Christian religion. Reborn as sons of God, they must confess before men the faith which they have received from God through the Church."

Confirmation: "Bound more intimately to the Church by the sacrament of confirmation, they are endowed by the Holy Spirit with special strength. Hence they are more strictly obliged to spread and defend the faith both by word and by deed as true witnesses of Christ."

Eucharist: "Taking part in the Eucharistic Sacrifice, which is the fount and apex of the whole Christian life, they offer the divine Victim to God, and offer themselves along with It. Thus, both by the act of oblation and through holy Communion, all perform their proper part in this liturgical service, not, indeed, all in the same way but each in that way which is appropriate to himself. Strengthened anew at the holy table by the Body of Christ, they manifest in a practical way that unity of God's People which is suitably signified and wondrously brought about by this most awesome sacrament."

Penance: "Those who approach the sacrament of penance obtain pardon from the mercy of God for offenses committed against Him. They are at the same time reconciled with the Church, which they have wounded by their sins, and which by charity, example, and prayer seeks their conversion."

Anointing of the Sick: "By the sacred anointing of the sick and the prayer of her priests, the whole Church commends those who are ill to the suffering and glorified Lord, asking that He may lighten their suffering and save them (cf. Jas. 5:14-16). She exhorts them, moreover, to contribute to the welfare of the whole People of God by associating themselves freely with the passion and death of Christ (cf. Rom. 8:17; Col. 1:24; 2 Tm. 2:11-12: 1 Pt. 4:13)."

Holy Orders: "Those of the faithful who are consecrated by holy orders are appointed to feed the Church in Christ's name with the Word and the grace of God."

Matrimony: "Christian spouses, in virtue of the sacrament of matrimony, signify and partake of the mystery of that unity and fruitful love which exists between Christ and His Church (cf. Eph. 5:32). The spouses thereby help each other to attain to holiness in their married life and by the rearing and education of their children. And so, in their state and way of life, they have their own special gift among the People of God (cf. 1 Cor. 7:7).

"For from the wedlock of Christians there comes the family, in which new citizens of human society are born. By the grace of the Holy Spirit received in baptism these are made children of God, thus perpetuating the People of God through the centuries. The family is, so to speak, the domestic Church. In it parents should, by their word and example, be the first preachers of the faith to their children. They should encourage them in the vocation which is proper to each of them, fostering with special care any religious vocation.

"Fortified by so many and such powerful means of salvation, all the faithful, whatever their condition or state, are called by the Lord, each in his own way, to that perfect holiness whereby the Father Himself is perfect."

Baptism

Baptism is the sacrament of spiritual regeneration by which a person is incorporated in Christ and made a member of His Mystical Body, given grace, and cleansed of original sin. Actual sins and the punishment due for them are remitted also if the person baptized was guilty of such sins (e.g., in the case of a person baptized after reaching the age of reason). The theological virtues of faith, hope and charity are given with grace. The sacrament confers a character on the soul and can be received only once.

The matter is the pouring of water. The form is: "I baptize you in the name of the Father and of the Son and of the Holy Spirit."

The minister of solemn baptism is a priest or deacon, but in case of emergency anyone, including a non-Catholic, can validly baptize. The minister pours water on the forehead of the person being baptized and says the words of the form while the water is flowing. The water used in solemn baptism is blessed during the rite.

The Church recognizes as valid baptism by **immersion, aspersion** (sprinkling of the water), or **infusion** (pouring of the water). In the Western Church, i.e., Roman Rite, the method of infusion is prescribed. The Church recognizes as valid baptisms properly performed by non-Catholic ministers. The baptism of infants has always been considered valid and the general practice of infant baptism was well established by the fifth century. Baptism is conferred conditionally when there is doubt about the validity of a previous baptism or the dispositions of the person.

Baptism is necessary for salvation. If a person cannot receive the baptism of water described above, this can be supplied by baptism of blood (martyrdom suffered for the Catholic faith or some Christian virtue) or by baptism of desire (perfect contrition joined with at least the implicit intention of doing whatever God wills that men should do for salvation).

A sponsor is required for the person being baptized. (See Godparents, below).

A person must be validly baptized before he can receive any of the other sacraments.

Christian Initiation of Infants: Infants should be solemnly baptized as soon after birth as conveniently possible. In danger of death, anyone may baptize an infant. If the child survives, the ceremonies of solemn baptism should be supplied.

The sacrament is ordinarily conferred by a priest or deacon of the parents' parish.

Only Catholics, in their 14th year or older, may be **godparents** or sponsors. Only one is required. Two, one of each sex, are permitted. A non-Catholic Christian cannot be a godparent for a Catholic child, but may serve as a witness to the baptism. A Catholic may not be a godparent for a child baptized in a non-Catholic religion, but may be a witness.

The role of godparents in baptismal ceremonies is secondary to the role of the parents. They serve as representatives of the community of faith and with the parents request baptism for the child and perform other ritual functions. Their function after baptism is to serve as proxies for the parents if the parents should be unable or fail to provide for the religious training of the child.

At baptism every child should be given a name with Christian significance, usually the name of a saint, to symbolize newness of life in Christ.

Christian Initiation of Adults: According to the *Ordo Initiationis Christianae Adultorum* ("Rite of the Christian Initiation of Adults") issued by the Congregation for Divine Worship under date of Jan. 6, 1972, adults are prepared for baptism and reception into the Church in several stages:

• An initial period of inquiry, instruction and evangelization.

• The catechumenate, a period of formal instruction and progressive formation in and familiarity with Christian life. It starts with a statement of purpose and includes a rite in which the catechumen is signed with the cross, blessings, exorcisms, and introduction into church for celebration of the word of God.

• Immediate preparation, called a period of purification and enlightenment, from the beginning of Lent to reception of the sacraments of initiation — baptism, confirmation, Holy Eucharist — at Easter. The period is marked by scrutinies, formal giving of the creed and the Lord's Prayer, the choice of a Christian name, and a final statement of intention.

• A final phase whose objective is greater familiarity with Christian life in the Church through observances of the Easter season and association with the community of the faithful.

The priest who baptizes a catechumen can also administer the sacrament of confirmation.

A sponsor is required for the person being baptized.

The *Ordo* also provides a simple rite of initiation for adults in danger of death and for cases in which all stages of the initiation process are not necessary, and guidelines for: (1) the preparation of adults for the sacraments of confirmation and Holy Eucharist in cases where they have been baptized but have not received further formation in the Christian life; (2) for the formation and initiation of children of catechetical age.

The Church recognizes the right of anyone over the age of seven to request baptism and to receive the sacrament after completing a course of instruction and giving evidence of good will. Practically, in the case of minors in a non-Catholic family or environment, the Church accepts them when other circumstances favor their ability to practice the faith — e.g., well-disposed family situation, the presence of another or several Catholics in the family. Those who are not in such favorable circumstances are prudently advised to defer reception of the sacrament until they attain the maturity necessary for independent practice of the faith.

Reception of Baptized Christians: Procedure for the reception of already baptized Christians into full communion with the Catholic Church is distinguished from the catechumenate, since they have received some Christian formation. Instruction and formation are provided as necessary, however; and conditional baptism is administered if there is reasonable doubt about the validity of the person's previous baptism.

In the rite of reception, the person is invited to join the community of the Church in professing the Nicene Creed and is asked to state: "I believe and profess all that the holy Catholic Church believes, teaches, and proclaims as revealed by God." The priest places his hand on the head of the person, states the formula of admission to full communion, confirms (in the absence of a bishop), gives a sign of peace, and administers Holy Communion during a Eucharistic Liturgy.

Confirmation

Confirmation is the sacrament by which a baptized person, through anointing with chrism and the imposition of hands, is endowed with the gifts and special strength of the Holy Spirit for mature Christian living. The sacrament, which completes the Christian initiation begun wth baptism, confers a character on the soul and can be received only once.

According to the apostolic constitution *Divinae Consortium Naturae* dated Aug. 15, 1971, in conjunction with the *Ordo Confirmationis* ("Rite of Confirmation"): "The sacrament of confirmation is conferred through the anointing with chrism on the forehead, which is done by the imposition of the hand (matter of the sacrament), and through the words: 'N . . . . , receive the seal of the Holy Spirit, the Gift of the Father' " (form of the sacrament). On May 5, 1975, bishops' conferences in English-speaking countries were informed by the Congregation for Divine Worship that Pope Paul had approved this English version of the form of the sacrament: "Be sealed with the gift of the Holy Spirit."

The ordinary minister of confirmation in the Roman Rite is a bishop. Priests may be delegated for the purpose. A pastor can confirm a parishioner in danger of death, and a priest can confirm in ceremonies of Christian initiation.

Ideally, the sacrament is conferred during the Eucharistic Liturgy. Elements of the rite include renewal of the promises of baptism, which confirmation ratifies and completes, and the laying on of hands — by symbolic elevation over the heads of those being confirmed — by the confirming bishop and priests participating in the ceremony.

"The entire rite," according to the *Ordo:* "has a twofold meaning. The laying of hands upon the candidates, done by the bishop and the concelebrating priests, expresses the biblical gesture by which the gift of the Holy Spirit is invoked. . . . The anointing with chrism and the accompanying words clearly signify the effect of the Holy Spirit. Signed with the perfumed oil by the bishop's hand, the baptized person receives the indelible character, the seal of the Lord, together with the Spirit who is given and who conforms the person more perfectly to Christ and gives him the grace of spreading the Lord's presence among men."

A sponsor is required for the person being confirmed. This can be one of the baptismal sponsors or another person. Parents can serve as sponsors for their own children.

In the Roman Rite, it has been customary for children to receive confirmation within a reasonable time after first Communion and confession. There is a developing trend, however, to defer confirmation until later when its significance for mature Christian living becomes more evident. In the Eastern Rites, confirmation is administered at the same time as baptism.

The Holy Eucharist

The Holy Eucharist is a sacrifice (see The Mass) and the sacrament in which Christ is present and is received under the appearances of bread and wine.

The matter is bread of wheat, unleavened in the Roman Rite and leavened in the Eastern Rites, and wine of grape. The form consists of the words of consecration said by the priest at Mass: "This is my body. . . . This is the cup of my blood" (according to the traditional usage of the Roman Rite).

Only a priest can consecrate bread and wine so they become the body and blood of Christ. After consecration, however, the Eucharist can be administered by deacons and, for various reasons, by religious and lay persons.

Priests celebrating Mass receive the Eucharist under the appearances of bread and wine. In the Roman Rite, others usually receive under the appearances of bread only, i.e., the consecrated host; in some circumstances, however, they may receive under the appearances of both bread and wine. In Eastern-Rite practice, the faithful generally receive a piece of consecrated leavened bread which has been dipped into consecrated wine (i.e., by intinction).

Conditions for receiving the Eucharist, commonly called **Holy Communion,** are the state of grace, the right intention, and observance of the Eucharistic fast.

The faithful of Roman Rite are required by a precept of the Church to receive the Eucharist at least once a year, during the Easter time (in the U.S., from the First Sunday of Lent to Trinity Sunday, inclusive).

(See Eucharistic Fast, Mass, Transubstantiation, Viaticum.)

First Communion and Confession: Children are to be prepared for and given opportunity for receiving both sacraments on reaching the age of discretion, at which time they become subject to general norms concerning confession and Communion. This, together with a stated preference for first confession before first Communion, was the central theme of a document entitled *Sanctus Pontifex* and published May 24, 1973, by the Congregation for the Discipline of the Sacraments and the Congregation for the Clergy, with the approval of Pope Paul VI.

What the document prescribed was the observance of practices ordered by St. Pius X in the decree *Quam Singulari* of Aug. 8, 1910. Its purpose was to counteract pastoral and catechetical experiments virtually denying children the opportunity of receiving both sacraments at the same time. Termination of such experiments was ordered by the end of the 1972-73 school year.

At the time the document was issued, two- or three-year experiments of this kind — routinely deferring reception of the sacrament of penance until after the first reception of Holy Communion — were in effect in more than half of the dioceses of the U.S. They have remained in effect in many places, despite the advisory from the Vatican.

One reason stated in support of such experiments is the view that children are not capable of serious sin at the age of seven or eight, when Communion is generally received for the first time, and therefore prior reception of the sacrament of penance is not necessary. Another reason is the purpose of making the distinctive nature of the two sacraments clearer to children.

The Vatican view reflected convictions that the principle and practice of devotional reception of penance are as valid for children as they are for adults, and that sound catechetical programs can avoid misconceptions about the two sacraments.

A second letter on the same subject and in the same vein was released May 19, 1977, by the aforementioned congregations. It was issued in response to the question:

" 'Whether it is allowed after the declaration of May 24, 1973, to continue to have, as a general rule, the reception of first Communion precede the reception of the sacrament of penance in those parishes in which this practice developed in the past few years.'

"The Sacred Congregations for the Sacraments and Divine Worship and for the Clergy, with the approval of the Supreme Pontiff, reply: Negative, and according to the mind of the declaration.

"The mind of the declaration is that one year after the promulgation of the same declaration, all experiments of receiving first Communion without the sacrament of penance should cease so that the discipline of the Church might be restored, in the spirit of the decree, *Quam Singulari*."

The two letters from the Vatican congregations have not produced uniformity of practice in this country. Simultaneous preparation for both sacraments is provided in some dioceses where a child has the option of receiving either sacrament first, with the counsel of parents, priests and teachers. Programs in other dioceses are geared first to reception of Communion and later to reception of the sacrament of reconciliation.

Commentators on the letters note that: they are disciplinary rather than doctrinal in content; they are subject to pastoral interpretation by bishops; they cannot be interpreted to mean that a person who is not guilty of serious sin must be required to receive the sacrament of penance before (even first) Communion.

Holy Communion under the Forms of Bread and Wine (by separate taking of the consecrated bread and wine or by intinction, the reception of the host dipped in the wine): Such reception is permitted under conditions stated in instructions issued by the Congregation for Divine Worship (May 25, 1967; June 29, 1970), the *General Instruction on the Roman Missal* (No. 242), and directives of bishops' conferences and individual bishops.

Accordingly, Communion can be administered in this way to: persons being baptized, received into communion with the Church, confirmed, receiving anointing of the sick; couples at their wedding or jubilee; religious at profession or renewal of profession; lay persons receiving an ecclesiastical assignment (e.g., lay missionaries); participants at concelebrated Masses, retreats, pastoral commission meetings, daily Masses and on other occasions.

Holy Communion Twice a Day: The reception of Holy Communion at Mass a second time on the same day is permitted in accord with provisions of the "Instruction on Facilitating Communion in Particular Circumstances" *(Immensae Caritatis)* approved by Pope Paul VI Jan. 20 and published by the Congregation for Divine Worship Mar. 29, 1973.

The occasions are: Sunday Mass on Saturday evening or a holy day Mass the previous evening; a second Mass on Christmas or Easter, following reception at midnight Mass or the Mass of the Easter Vigil; the evening Mass of Holy Thursday, following reception at the earlier Mass of Chrism; Masses in which baptism, confirmation, holy orders, matrimony, anointing of the sick, first Communion, Viaticum are administered; some Masses for the dead (e.g., of Christian burial, first anniversary); special occasions — consecration of a church or altar, religious profession, conferring an ecclesiastical assignment (e.g., to lay missionaries), feast of Corpus Christi, parochial visitation, canonical visitation or special meetings of religious, Eucharistic and other congresses, pilgrimages, preaching missions; other occasions designated by the local bishop.

Holy Communion and Eucharistic Devotion outside of Mass: These were the subjects of an instruction *(De Sacra Communione et de Cultu Mysterii Eucharistici extra Missam)* dated June 21 and made public Oct. 18, 1973, by the Congregation for Divine Worship.

Holy Communion can be given outside of Mass to persons unable for a reasonable cause to receive it during Mass on a given day. The ceremonial rite is modeled on the structure of the Mass, consisting of a penitential act, a scriptural reading, the Lord's Prayer, a sign or gesture of peace, giving of the Eucharist, prayer and final blessing. Viaticum and Communion to the sick can be given by extraordinary ministers (authorized lay persons) with appropriate rites.

Forms of devotion outside of Mass are exposition of the Blessed Sacrament (by men or women religious, especially, or lay persons in the absence of a priest; but only a priest can give the blessing), processions and congresses with appropriate rites.

Intercommunion: Church policy on intercommunion was stated in an "Instruction on the Admission of Other Christians to the Eucharist," dated June 1 and made public July 8, 1972, against the background of the *Decree on Ecumenism* approved by the Second Vatican Council, and the *Directory on Ecumenism* issued by the Secretariat for Promoting Christian Unity in 1967.

Basic principles related to intercommunion are:

• "There is an indissoluble link between the mystery of the Church and the mystery of the Eucharist, or between ecclesial and Eucharistic communion; the celebration of the Eucharist of itself signifies the fullness of profession of faith and ecclesial communion" (1972 Instruction).

• "Eucharistic communion practiced by those who are not in full ecclesial communion with each other cannot be the expression of that full unity which the Eucharist of its nature signifies and which in this case does not exist; for this reason such communion cannot be regarded as a means to be used to lead to full ecclesial communion" (1972 Instruction).

• The question of reciprocity "arises only with those churches which have preserved the substance of the Eucharist, the sacrament of orders and apostolic succession" (1967 Directory).

• "A Catholic cannot ask for the Eucharist except from a minister who has been validly ordained" (1967 Directory).

The policy distinguishes between separated Eastern Christians and other Christians.

With Separated Eastern Christians (e.g., Orthodox): These may be given the Eucharist (as well as penance and anointing of the sick) at their request. Catholics may receive these same sacraments from priests of separated Eastern churches if they experience genuine spiritual necessity, seek spiritual benefit, and access to a Catholic priest is morally or physically impossible. This policy (of reciprocity) derives from the facts that the separated Eastern churches have apostolic succession through their bishops, valid priests, and sacramental beliefs and practices in accord with those of the Catholic Church.

With Other Christians (e.g., members of Reformation-related churches, others): Admission to the Eucharist in the Catholic Church, according to the *Directory on Ecumenism,* "is confined to particular cases of those Christians who have a faith in the sacrament in conformity with that of the Church, who experience a serious spiritual need for the Eucharistic sustenance, who for a prolonged period are unable to have recourse to a minister of their own community and who ask for the sacrament of their own accord; all this provided that they have proper dispositions and lead lives worthy of a Christian." The spiritual need is defined as "a need for an increase in spiritual life and a need for a deeper involvement in the mystery of the Church and of its unity."

Circumstances under which Communion may be given to other properly disposed Christians are danger of death, imprisonment, persecution, grave spiritual necessity coupled with no chance of recourse to a minister of their own community. Judgment regarding these and other special circumstances rests with the local bishop.

Catholics cannot ask for the Eucharist from ministers of other Christian churches who have not been validly ordained to the priesthood.

Penance

Penance is the sacrament by which sins committed after baptism are forgiven and a person is reconciled with God and the Church.

A revised ritual for the sacrament — *Ordo Paenitentiae,* published by the Congregation of Divine Worship Feb. 7, 1974 — reiterates standard doctrine concerning the sacrament; emphasizes the social (communal and ecclesial) aspects of sin and conversion, with due regard for personal aspects and individual reception of the sacrament; prescribes three forms for celebration of the sacrament; and presents models for community penitential services.

The U.S. Bishops' Committee on the Liturgy recommended that adequate preparation of priests and people should precede introduction in this country of the revised ritual in English. Recommended dates for its use, after due preparation, were the first Sunday of Lent, 1976 (optional), and the first Sunday of Lent, 1977 (mandatory).

The basic elements of the sacrament are sorrow for sin because of a supernatural motive, confession (of previously unconfessed mortal or grave sins, required; of venial sins also, but not of necessity), and reparation (by means of prayer or other act enjoined by the confessor), all of which comprise the matter of the sacrament; and absolution, which is the form of the sacrament.

The traditional words of absolution — "I absolve you from your sins in the name of the Father, and of the Son, and of the Holy Spirit" — remain unchanged at the conclusion of a petition in the new rite that God may grant pardon and peace through the ministry of the Church.

The minister of the sacrament is an authorized priest — i.e., one who, besides having the power of orders to forgive sins, also has faculties of jurisdiction granted by an ecclesiastical superior and/or by canon law.

The sacrament can be celebrated in three ways.

• For individuals: The traditional manner remains acceptable but is enriched with additional elements including: reception of the penitent and making of the Sign of the Cross; an exhortation by the confessor to trust in God; a possible reading from Scripture; confession of sins; manifestation of repentance; petition for God's forgiveness through the ministry of the Church and the absolution of the priest; praise of God's mercy, and dismissal in peace. Some of these elements are optional.

• For several penitents, in the course of a community celebration including a liturgy of the Word of God and prayers, individual confession and absolution, and an act of thanksgiving.

• For several penitents, in the course of a community celebration, with general confession and general absolution. This method is reserved for special circumstances in which it is morally or physically impossible for persons to confess and be absolved individually, and in view of their need for reconciliation and reception of the Eucharist. Penitents are required to confess at their next individual confession any grave sins absolved in such a general celebration of the sacrament. Judgment regarding circumstances that warrant general confession and absolution belongs principally to the bishop of the place.

Communal celebrations of the sacrament are not held in connection with Mass.

The place of individual confession, as determined by episcopal conferences in accordance with given norms, can be the traditional confessional or another appropriate setting.

The sacrament is necessary, by the institution of Christ, for the reconciliation of persons guilty of grave sins committed after baptism.

A precept of the Church obliges the faithful guilty of grave sin to confess at least once a year.

The Church favors more frequent reception of the sacrament not only for the reconciliation of persons guilty of serious sins but also for reasons of devotion. Devotional confession — in which venial sins or previously forgiven sins are confessed — serves the purpose of confirming persons in penance and conversion.

Penitential Celebrations: Communal penitential celebrations are designed to emphasize the social dimensions of Christian life — the community aspects and significance of penance and reconciliation.

Elements of such celebrations are community prayer, hymns and songs, scriptural and other readings, examination of conscience, general confession and expression of sorrow for sin, acts of penance and reconciliation, and a form of non-sacramental absolution resembling the one in the penitential rite of the Mass.

If the sacrament is celebrated during the service, there must be individual confession and absolution of sin.

(See Absolution, Confession, Confessional, Confessor, Contrition, Faculties, Forgiveness of Sin, Power of the Keys, Seal of Confession, Sin.)

Anointing of the Sick

This sacrament, promulgated by St. James the Apostle (Jas. 5:13-15), is administered to persons who are dangerously ill. By the anointing with blessed oil and the prayer of a priest, the sacrament confers on the person comforting grace; the remission of venial sins and inculpably unconfessed mortal sins, together with at least some of the temporal punishment due for sins; and, sometimes, results in an improved state of health.

The matter of this sacrament is the anointing with blessed oil (of the sick — olive oil, or vegetable oil if necessary) of the forehead and hands; in cases of necessity, a single anointing of another portion of the body suffices. The form is: "Through this holy anointing and his most loving mercy, may the Lord assist you by the grace of the Holy Spirit so that, when you have been freed from your sins, he may save you and in his goodness raise you up."

Anointing of the sick, formerly called extreme unction, may be received more than once, e.g., in new or continuing stages of serious illness. Ideally, the sacrament should be administered while the recipient is conscious and in conjunction with the sacraments of penance and the Eucharist. It may be administered conditionally even after apparent death.

The sacrament can be administered during a communal celebration in some circumstances, as in a home for the aged.

Pope Paul VI authorized a revision of the rite for administration of the sacrament in the apostolic constitution *Sacram Unctionem Infirmorum* ("Sacred Anointing of the Sick") which was approved Nov. 30, 1972, and made public Jan. 18, 1973. He ordered the new rite into effect as of Jan. 1, 1974. The Latin version of the new rite went into effect Jan. 1, 1974. The provisional English version became effective in the U.S. Dec. 1, 1974.

Matrimony

Coverage of the sacrament of matrimony is given in the articles, Marriage Doctrine, Humanae Vitae, Marriage Laws, Procedural Rules, Pastoral Ministry for Divorced and Remarried.

Holy Orders

Holy orders is the sacrament by which spiritual power and grace are given to enable an ordained minister to consecrate the Eucharist, forgive sins, perform other pastoral and ecclesiastical functions, and form the community of the People of God. Holy orders confers a character on the soul and can be received only once. The minister of the sacrament is a bishop.

Holy orders, like matrimony but in a different way, is a social sacrament. As the Second Vatican Council declared in the *Dogmatic Constitution on the Church:*

'For the nurturing and constant growth of the People of God, Christ the Lord instituted in His Church a variety of ministries, which work for the good of the whole body. For those ministers who are endowed with sacred power are servants of their brethren, so that all who are of the People of God, and therefore enjoy a true Christian dignity, can work toward a common goal freely and in an orderly way, and arrive at salvation" (No. 18).

"With their helpers, the priests and deacons, bishops have . . . taken up the service of the community, presiding in place of God over the flock whose shepherds they are, as teachers of doctrine, priests of sacred worship, and officers of good order" (No. 20).

The fullness of the priesthood belongs to those who have received the order of **bishop.** Bishops, in hierarchical union with the pope and their fellow bishops, are the successors of the apostles as pastors of the Church: they have individual responsibility for the care of the local churches they serve and collegial responsibility for the care of the universal Church (see Collegiality). In the ordination or consecration of bishops, the essential form is the imposition of hands by the consecrator(s) and the assigned prayer in the preface of the rite of ordination.

A priest is an ordained minister with the power to celebrate Mass, administer the sacraments, preach and teach the word of God, impart blessings, and perform additional pastoral functions, according to the mandate of his ecclesiastical superior.

Concerning priests, the Second Vatican Council stated in the *Dogmatic Constitution on the Church* (No. 28):

". . . The divinely established ecclesiastical ministry is exercised on different levels by those who from antiquity have been called bishops, priests, and deacons. Although priests do not possess the highest degree of the priesthood, and although they are dependent on the bishops in the exercise of their power, they are nevertheless united with the bishops in sacerdotal dignity. By the power of the sacrament of orders, and in the image of Christ the eternal High Priest (Hb. 5:1-10; 7:24; 9:11-28), they are consecrated to preach the gospel, shepherd the faithful, and celebrate divine worship as true priests of the New Testament. . . .

"Priests, prudent cooperators with the episcopal order as well as its aides and instruments, are called to serve the People of God. They constitute one priesthood with their bishop, although that priesthood is comprised of different functions. . . ."

In the ordination of a priest of Roman Rite, the essential matter is the imposition of hands on the heads of those being ordained by the ordaining bishop. The essential form is the accompanying prayer in the preface of the ordination ceremony. Other elements in the rite are the presentation of the implements of sacrifice — the chalice containing wine and the paten containing a host — with accompanying prayers.

Regarding the order of **deacon**, the *Dogmatic Constitution on the Church* (No. 29) stated:

"At a lower level of the hierarchy are deacons, upon whom hands are imposed 'not unto the priesthood, but unto a ministry of service.' For strengthened by sacramental grace, in communion with the bishop and his group of priests, they serve the People of God in the ministry of the liturgy, of the word, and of charity. It is the duty of the deacon, to the extent that he has been authorized by competent authority, to administer baptism solemnly, to be custodian and dispenser of the Eucharist, to assist at and bless marriages in the name of the Church, to bring Viaticum to the dying, to read the sacred Scripture to the faithful, to instruct and exhort the people, to preside at the worship and prayer of the faithful, to administer sacramentals, and to officiate at funeral and burial services. (Deacons are) dedicated to duties of charity and administration. . . ."

". . . The diaconate can in the future be restored as a proper and permanent rank of the hierarchy. It pertains to the competent territorial bodies of bishops, of one kind or another, to decide, with the approval of the Supreme Pontiff, whether and where it is opportune for such deacons to be appointed for the care of souls. With the consent of the Roman Pontiff, this diaconate will be able to be conferred upon men of more mature age, even upon those living in the married state. It may also be conferred upon suitable young men.

For them, however, the law of celibacy must remain intact" (No. 29).

The Apostles ordained the first seven deacons (Acts 6:1-6): Stephen, Philip, Prochorus, Nicanor, Timon, Parmenas, Nicholas.

Other Ministries: The Church later assigned ministerial duties to men in several other orders, as:

Subdeacon, with specific duties in liturgical worship, especially at Mass. The order, whose first extant mention dates from about the middle of the third century, was regarded as minor until the 13th century; afterwards, it was called a major order in the West but not in the East.

Acolyte, to serve in minor capacities in liturgical worship; a function now performed by Mass servers.

Exorcist, to perform services of exorcism for expelling evil spirits; a function which came to be reserved to specially delegated priests.

Lector, to read scriptural and other passages during liturgical worship; a function now generally performed by lay persons

Porter, to guard the entrance to an assembly of Christians and to ward off undesirables who tried to gain admittance; an order of early origin and utility but of present insignificance.

Long after it became evident that these positions and functions had fallen into general disuse or did not require clerical ordination, the Holy See started a revision of the orders in 1971. By an indult of Oct. 5, the bishops of the United States were permitted to omit ordaining porters and exorcists. Another indult, dated three days later, permitted the use of revised rites for ordaining acolytes and lectors, and authorized the use of a service celebrating admission to the clerical state in place of the ceremony of tonsure which had previously served this purpose.

To complete the revision, Pope Paul VI abolished Sept. 14, 1972, the orders of porter, exorcist and subdeacon; decreed that laymen, as well as candidates for the diaconate and priesthood, can be installed (rather than ordained) in the ministries (rather than orders) of acolyte and lector; reconfirmed the suppression of tonsure and its replacement with a service of dedication to God and the Church; and stated that a man enters the clerical state on ordination to the diaconate.

There were no doctrinal obstacles to the Pope's action, because the abolished orders had been instituted by the Church for functional purposes and were not considered to be parts of the sacrament of holy orders.

The Congregation for the Sacraments and Divine Worship expressed concern in 1981 over "authorization abusively given to deacons and even to women religious" to confer the sacrament of anointing of the sick.

PERMANENT DIACONATE

Authorization for restoration of the permanent diaconate in the Roman Rite — making it possible for men to become deacons permanently, without going on to the priesthood — was promulgated by Pope Paul VI June 18, 1967, in a document entitled *Sacrum Diaconatus Ordinem* ("Sacred Order of the Diaconate").

The Pope's action implemented the desire expressed by the Second Vatican Council for reestablishment of the diaconate as an independent order in its own right not only to supply ministers for carrying on the work of the Church but also to complete the hierarchical structure of the Church of Roman Rite.

Permanent deacons have been traditional in the Eastern Church. The Western Church, however, since the fourth or fifth century, generally followed the practice of conferring the diaconate only as a sacred order preliminary to the priesthood, and of restricting the ministry of deacons to liturgical functions.

The Pope's document, issued on his own initiative, provided:

• Qualified unmarried men 25 years of age or older may be ordained permanent deacons. They cannot marry after ordination.

• Qualified married men 35 years of age or older may be ordained permanent deacons. The consent of the wife of a prospective deacon is required. A married deacon cannot remarry after the death of his wife.

• Preparation for the diaconate includes a course of study and formation over a period of at least three years.

• Candidates who are not religious must be affiliated with a diocese. Reestablishment of the permanent diaconate among religious is reserved to the Holy See.

• Deacons will practice their ministry under the direction of a bishop and with the priests with whom they will be associated. (For functions, see the description of deacon, under Holy Orders.)

Restoration of the permanent diaconate in the United States was approved by the Holy See in October, 1968. Shortly afterwards the U.S. bishops established a committee of the same name, which is chaired by Bishop John J. Snyder of St. Augustine. The committee operates through a secretariat, of which Msgr. Ernest J. Fiedler is executive director. Its offices are located at 1312 Massachusetts Ave. N. W., Washington, D.C. 20005.

Present Status

The bishops' secretariat reported in October, 1981, that 5,175 permanent deacons had been ordained in the U.S.; that 142 dioceses either had approved programs of formation or were in the process of preparing formation programs; that a total of 2,352 candidates were in training.

Deacons have various functions, depending on the nature of their assignments. Liturgically, they can officiate at baptisms, weddings, wake services and funerals, can preach and distribute Holy Communion. Some are engaged in religious education work. All are intended to carry out works of charity and pastoral service of one kind or another.

The majority of permanent deacons, 93 per cent of whom are married, continue in their secular work. Their ministry of service is developing in three dimensions: of liturgy, of the word, and of charity. Depending on the individual deacon's abilities and preference, he is assigned by his bishop to either a parochial ministry or to one particular field of service. The latter is the most challenging ministry to develop. Deacons are now active in a variety of ministries including those to prison inmates and their families, the sick in hospitals, nursing homes and homes for the aged, alienated youth, the elderly and the poor, and in various areas of legal service to the indigent, of education and campus ministry. A few have been assigned as quasi-pastors of multi-county, rural parishes. The unlimited possibilities for diaconal ministry are under realistic assessment, diocese by diocese.

Training Programs

There were 136 training centers for deacons as of October, 1981. The first four were established in 1969. One center may serve two or more dioceses in the formation of diaconal candidates.

Continuing efforts are made to recruit Spanish-speaking, black and other minority candidates in training programs. Of the permanent deacons ordained up to October, 1981, five per cent were black, and 14 per cent were Hispanic.

Training programs of spiritual, doctrinal and pastoral formation are generally based on *Permanent Deacons in the United States: Guidelines on Their Formation and Ministry,* published by the Bishops' Committee on the Permanent Diaconate in September, 1971.

National Association of Permanent Diaconate Directors: Membership organization of directors, vicars and other staff personnel of permanent diaconate programs. Established in 1977 to promote effective communication and facilitate the exchange of information and resources of members; to develop professional expertise and promote research, training and self evaluation; to foster accountability and seek ways to promote means of implementing solutions to problems. NAPDD is governed by an executive board of elected officers. President for the 1982-83 term: Rev. Michael O'Connor, 2260 Summit Ave., St. Paul, Minn. 55105.

1982 Report

A report issued by the secretariat of the Bishops' Committee on the Permanent Diaconate in April, 1982, indicated that there were 519 more deacons than in 1980 and 162 fewer candidates. The first report, issued in 1971, counted 58 deacons and 529 candidates.

Msgr. Ernest J. Fiedler, director of the secretariat, said that the "phenomenal growth" of the permanent diaconate program in the United States "demonstrates the importance of the role of deacons in the life of the Church and their acceptance by the Church, particularly the laity."

While noting it was the second consecutive year in which the number of candidates declined, Msgr. Fiedler said that a number of programs were being evaluated, after which an increase "can be expected to resume."

The report, based on information provided by directors of more than 130 diaconal formation programs or by chancery offices, showed that 80 per cent of the deacons were white, 14 per cent were Hispanic and five per cent were black. The largest group, 37 per cent, were in the 41-to-50 age group; 33 per cent were in the 51-to-60 group.

Ninety-three per cent of the deacons were married, five per cent were celibate and two per cent were widowers.

MARRIAGE DOCTRINE

The following excerpts, stating key points of doctrine on marriage, are from the *Pastoral Constitution on the Church in the Modern World* (Nos. 48 to 51) promulgated by the Second Vatican Council.

Conjugal Covenant

"The intimate partnership of married life and love has been established by the Creator and qualified by His laws. It is rooted in the conjugal covenant of irrevocable personal consent. . . .

". . . God Himself is the author of matrimony, endowed as it is with various benefits and purposes. All of these have a very decisive bearing on the continuation of the human race, on the personal development and eternal destiny of the individual members of a family, and on the dignity, stability, peace, and prosperity of the family itself and of human society as a whole. By their very nature, the institution of matrimony itself and conjugal love are ordained for the procreation and education of children, and find in them their ultimate crown.

"Thus a man and a woman . . . render mutual help and service to each other through an intimate union of their persons and of their actions. Through this union they experience the meaning of their oneness and attain to it with growing perfection day by day. As a mutual gift of two persons, this intimate union, as well as the good of the children, imposes total fidelity on the spouses and argues for an unbreakable oneness between them" (No. 48).

Sacrament of Matrimony

"Christ the Lord abundantly blessed this many-faceted love. . . . The Savior of men and the Spouse of the Church comes into the lives of married Christians through the sacrament of matrimony. He abides with them thereafter so that, just as He loved the Church and handed Himself over on her behalf, the spouses may love each other with perpetual fidelity through mutual self-bestowal.

". . . Graced with the dignity and office of fatherhood and motherhood, parents will energetically acquit themselves of a duty which devolves primarily on them, namely education, and especially religious education.

". . . The Christian family, which springs from marriage as a reflection of the loving covenant uniting Christ with the Church, and as a participation in that covenant, will manifest to all men the Savior's living presence in the world, and the genuine nature of the Church . . ." (No. 48).

Conjugal Love

"The biblical Word of God several times urges the betrothed and the married to nourish and develop their wedlock by pure conjugal love and undivided affection. . . .

"This love is an eminently human one since it is directed from one person to another through an affection of the will. It involves the good of the whole person. Therefore it can enrich the expressions of body and mind with a unique dignity, ennobling these expressions as special ingredients and signs of the friendship distinctive of marriage. This love the Lord has judged worthy of special gifts, healing, perfecting, and exalting gifts of grace and of charity.

"Such love, merging the human with the divine, leads the spouses to a free and mutual gift of themselves, a gift proving itself by gentle affection and by deed. Such love pervades the whole of their lives. Indeed, by its generous activity it grows better and grows greater. Therefore it far excels mere erotic inclination, which, selfishly pursued, soon enough fades wretchedly away.

"This love is uniquely expressed and perfected through the marital act. The actions within marriage by which the couple are united intimately and chastely are noble and worthy ones. Expressed in a manner which is truly human, these actions signify and promote that mutual self-giving by which spouses enrich each other with a joyful and a thankful will.

"Sealed by mutual faithfulness and hallowed above all by Christ's sacrament, this love remains steadfastly true in body and in mind, in bright days or dark. It will never be profaned by adultery or divorce. Firmly established by the Lord, the unity of marriage will radiate from the equal personal dignity of wife and husband, a dignity acknowledged by mutual and total love.

"The steady fulfillment of the duties of this Christian vocation demands notable virtue. For this reason, strengthened by grace for holiness of life, the couple will painstakingly cultivate and pray for constancy of love, largeheartedness, and the spirit of sacrifice . . ." (No. 49).

Fruitfulness of Marriage

"Marriage and conjugal love are by their nature ordained toward the begetting and educating of children. Children are really the supreme gift of marriage and contribute very substantially to the welfare of their parents. . . . God Himself . . . wished to share with man a certain special participation in His own creative work. Thus He blessed male and female, saying: 'Increase and multiply' (Gn. 1:28).

"Hence, while not making the other purposes of matrimony of less account, the true practice of conjugal love, and the whole meaning of the family life which results from it, have this aim: that the couple be ready with stout hearts to cooperate with the love of the Creator and the Savior, who through them will enlarge and enrich His own family day by day.

"Parents should regard as their proper mission the task of transmitting human life and educating those to whom it has been transmitted. They should realize that they are thereby cooperators with the love of God the Creator, and are, so to speak, the interpreters of that love. Thus they will fulfill their task with human and Christian responsibility . . ." (No. 50).

Norms of Judgment

"They will thoughtfully take into account both their own welfare and that of their children, those already born and those which may be foreseen. For this accounting they will reckon with both the material and the spiritual conditions of the times as well as of their state in life. Finally, they will consult the interests of the family group, of temporal society, and of the Church herself.

"The parents themselves should ultimately make this judgment in the sight of God. But in their manner of acting, spouses should be aware that they cannot proceed arbitrarily. They must always be governed according to a conscience dutifully conformed to the divine law itself, and should be submissive toward the Church's teaching office, which authentically interprets that law in the light of the gospel. That divine law reveals and protects the integral meaning of conjugal love, and impels it toward a truly human fulfillment. . . .

"Marriage to be sure is not instituted solely for procreation. Rather, its very nature as an unbreakable compact between persons, and the welfare of the children, both demand that the mutual love of the spouses, too, be embodied in a rightly ordered manner, that it grow and ripen. Therefore, marriage persists as a whole manner and communion of life, and maintains its value and indissolubility, even when offspring are lacking — despite, rather often, the very intense desire of the couple" (No. 50).

Love and Life

"This Council realizes that certain modern conditions often keep couples from arranging their married lives harmoniously, and that they find themselves in circumstances where at least temporarily the size of their families should not be increased. As a result, the faithful exercise of love and the full intimacy of their lives are hard to maintain. But where the intimacy of married life is broken off, it is not rare for its faithfulness to be imperiled and its quality of fruitfulness ruined. For then the upbringing of the children and the courage to accept new ones are both endangered.

"To these problems there are those who presume to offer dishonorable solutions. Indeed, they do not recoil from the taking of life. But the Church issues the reminder that a true contradiction cannot exist between the divine laws pertaining to the transmission of life and those pertaining to the fostering of authentic conjugal love.

"For God, the Lord of Life, has conferred on men the surpassing ministry of safeguarding life — a ministry which must be fulfilled in a manner which is worthy of men. Therefore from the moment of its conception life must be guarded with the greatest care, while abortion and infanticide are unspeakable crimes. The sexual characteristics of man and the human faculty of reproduction wonderfully exceed the dispositions of lower forms of life. Hence the acts themselves which are proper to conjugal love and which are exercised in accord with genuine human dignity must be honored with great reverence" (No. 51).

Church Teaching

"Therefore when there is question of harmonizing conjugal love with the responsible transmission of life, the moral aspect of any procedure does not depend solely on the sincere intentions or on an evaluation of motives. It must be determined by objective standards. These, based on the nature of the human person and his acts, preserve the full sense of mutual self-giving and human procreation in the context of true love. Such a goal cannot be achieved unless the virtue of conjugal chastity is sincerely practiced. Relying on these principles, sons of the Church may not undertake methods of regulating procreation which are found blameworthy by the teaching authority of the Church in its unfolding of the divine law.

"Everyone should be persuaded that human life and the task of transmitting it are not realities bound up with this world alone. Hence they cannot be measured or perceived only in terms of it, but always have a bearing on the eternal destiny of men" (No. 51).

HUMANAE VITAE

Marriage doctrine and morality were the subjects of the encyclical *Humanae Vitae* ("Of Human Life") issued by Pope Paul July 29, 1968. Following are a number of key excerpts from the document, which was framed in the pattern of traditional teaching and statements by the Second Vatican Council.

". . . each and every marriage act ('quilibet matrimonii usus') must remain open to the transmission of life" (No. 11).

"Indeed, by its intimate structure, the conjugal act, while most closely uniting husband and wife, capacitates them for the generation of new lives, according to laws inscribed in the very being of man and of woman. By safeguarding both these essential aspects, the unitive and the procreative, the conjugal act preserves in its fullness the sense of true mutual love and its ordination toward man's most high calling to parenthood" (No. 12).

"It is, in fact, justly observed that a conjugal act imposed upon one's partner without regard for his or her condition and lawful desires is not a true act of love, and therefore denies an exigency of right moral order in the relationships between husband and wife. Hence, one who reflects well must also recognize that a reciprocal act of love which jeopardizes the responsibility to transmit life — which God the Creator, according to particular laws, inserted therein — is in contradiction with the design constitutive of marriage and with the will of the Author of life. To use this divine gift, destroying, even if only partially, its meaning and its purpose, is to contradict the nature both of man and of woman and of their most intimate relationship, and therefore it is to contradict also the plan of God and His will" (No. 13).

Forbidden Actions: ". . . the direct interruption of the generative process already begun, and, above all, directly willed and procured abortion, even if for therapeutic reasons, are to be absolutely excluded as licit means of regulating birth.

"Equally to be excluded . . . is direct sterilization, whether perpetual or temporary, whether of the man or of the woman. Similarly excluded is every action which, either in anticipation of the conjugal act, or in its accomplishment, or in the development of its natural consequences, proposes, whether as an end or as a means, to render procreation impossible.

Inadmissible Principles: "To justify conjugal acts made intentionally infecund, one cannot invoke as valid reasons the lesser evil, or the fact that such acts would constitute a whole together with the fecund acts already performed or to follow later and hence would share in one and the same moral goodness. In truth, if it is sometimes licit to tolerate a lesser evil in order to avoid a greater evil or to promote a greater good, it is not licit, even for the gravest reasons, to do evil so that good may follow therefrom; that is, to make into the object of a positive act of the will something which is intrinsically disorder, and hence unworthy of the human person, even when the intention is to safeguard or promote individual, family or social well-being.

"Consequently, it is an error to think that a conjugal act which is deliberately made infecund, and so is intrinsically dishonest, could be made honest and right by the ensemble of a fecund conjugal life" (No. 14).

Rhythm: "If, then, there are serious motives to space out births, which derive from the physical or psychological conditions of husband and wife, or from external conditions, the Church teaches that it is then licit to take into account the natural rhythms immanent in the generative functions, for the use of marriage in the infecund periods only, and in this way to regulate birth without offending" earlier stated principles (No. 16).

Authoritative Teaching: Pope Paul called the foregoing teaching authoritative, although not infallible. He left it open for further study. As a practical norm to be followed, however, he said it involved the binding force of religious assent.

With pastoral concern, the Pope said: "We do not at all intend to hide the sometimes serious difficulties inherent in the life of Christian married persons; for them, as for everyone else, 'the gate is narrow and the way is hard that leads to life.' But the hope of that life must illuminate their way, as with courage they strive to live with wisdom, justice and piety in this present time, knowing that the figure of this world passes away.

"Let married couples, then, face up to the efforts needed, supported by the faith and hope which 'do not disappoint . . . because God's love has been poured into our hearts through the Holy Spirit, who has been given to us.' Let them implore divine assistance by persevering prayer; above all, let them draw from the source of grace and charity in the Eucharist. And, if sin should still keep its hold over them, let them not be discouraged but rather have recourse with humble perseverance to the mercy of God, which is poured forth in the sacrament of penance" (No. 25).

Reactions: Exception was taken to the binding force of the encyclical — notably by the bishops of Belgium, Austria and France, and many theologians — for several reasons: rights of conscience; questions concerning the natural-law concept underlying the encyclical; the thesis of totality; the proposition that contraception may in some cases be the lesser of two evils. All agreed, however, that conscientious objection to the encyclical could not be taken without serious reasons and reflection.

Pope Paul, after publication of the encyclical, never made any move to alter its contents or to mitigate its binding force.

MARRIAGE LAWS

The Catholic Church, in line with the belief that it was established and commissioned by Christ to provide and administer the means of salvation to men, claims jurisdiction over its members in matters pertaining to marriage, which is a sacrament. The purpose of its laws in this area, consisting of 132 canons, is to safeguard the validity and lawfulness of marriage.

Catholics are bound by all marriage laws of the Church. Non-Catholics, whether baptized or not, are not considered bound by these ecclesiastical laws except in cases of marriage with a Catholic. Certain natural laws, in the Catholic view, bind all men and women, irrespective of their religious beliefs; accordingly, marriage is prohibited before the time of puberty, without knowledge and free mutual consent, in the case of an already existing valid marriage bond, in the case of antecedent and perpetual impotence.

Formalities

These include, in addition to arrangements for the time and place of the marriage ceremony, doctrinal and moral instruction concerning marriage and the recording of data which verifies in documentary form the eligibility and freedom of the persons to marry. Records of this kind, which are confidential, are preserved in the archives of the church where the marriage takes place.

Premarital instructions are the subject matter of Pre-Cana Conferences.

Mixed Marriages

"Mixed Marriages" (*Matrimonia Mixta*) was the subject of: (1) a letter issued under this title by Pope Paul VI Mar. 31, 1970, and (2) a statement, *Implementation of the Apostolic Letter on Mixed Marriages,* approved by the National Conference of Catholic Bishops Nov. 16, 1970.

One of the key points in the bishops' statement referred to the need for mutual pastoral care by ministers of different faiths for the sacredness of marriage and for appropriate preparation and continuing support of parties to a mixed marriage.

Pastoral experience, which the Catholic Church shares with other religious bodies, confirms the fact that marriages of persons of different beliefs involve special problems related to the continuing religious practice of the concerned persons and to the religious education and formation of their children.

Pastoral measures to minimize these problems include instruction of a non-Catholic party in essentials of the Catholic faith for purposes of understanding. Desirably, some instruction should also be given the Catholic party regarding his or her partner's beliefs.

The Catholic party to a mixed marriage is required to declare his (her) intention of continuing practice of the Catholic faith and to promise to do all in his power to share his faith with children born of the marriage by having them baptized and raised as Catholics. No declarations or promises are required of the non-Catholic party, but he (she) must be informed of the declaration and promise made by the Catholic.

Notice of the Catholic's declaration and promise is an essential part of the application made to a bishop for dispensation from the impediment of mixed religion or disparity of worship (see below).

A mixed marriage can take place with a Nuptial Mass. (The bishops' statement added this caution: "To the extent that Eucharistic sharing is not permitted by the general discipline of the Church, this is to be considered when plans are being made to have the mixed marriage at Mass or not.")

The ordinary minister at a mixed marriage is an authorized priest, and the ordinary place is the parish church of the Catholic party. A non-Catholic minister may not only attend the marriage ceremony but may also address, pray with and bless the couple.

For appropriate pastoral reasons, a bishop can grant a dispensation from the Catholic form of marriage and can permit the marriage to take place in a non-Catholic Church with a non-Catholic minister as the officiating minister. A priest may not only attend such a ceremony but may also address, pray with and bless the couple.

"It is not permitted," however, the bishops statement declared, "to have two religious services or to have a single service in which both the Catholic marriage ritual and a non-Catholic marriage ritual are celebrated jointly or successively."

Banns

The banns are public announcements made in their parish churches, usually on three successive Sundays, of the names of persons who intend to marry. Persons who know of reasons in church law why a proposed marriage should not take place, are obliged to make them known to the pastor.

Marital Consent

The exchange of consent to the marriage contract, which is essential for valid marriage, must be rational, free, true and mutual.

Matrimonial consent can be invalidated by an essential defect, substantial error, the strong influence of force and fear, the presence of a condition or intention against the nature of marriage.

Form of Marriage

A Catholic is required, for validity and lawfulness, to contract marriage — with another Catholic or with a non-Catholic — in the presence of a competent priest or deacon and two witnesses.

There are two exceptions to this law. A Roman Rite Catholic (since Mar. 25, 1967) or an Eastern Rite Catholic (since Nov. 21, 1964) can contract marriage validly in the presence of a priest of a separated Eastern Rite Church, provided other requirements of law are complied with. With permission of the competent Roman-Rite or Eastern-Rite bishop, this form of marriage is lawful, as well as valid. (See Eastern Rite Laws, below.)

With these two exceptions, and aside from cases covered by special permission, the Church does not regard as valid any marriages involving Catholics which take place before non-Catholic ministers of religion or civil officials. (See Mixed Marriage Guidelines.)

An excommunication formerly in force against Catholics who celebrated marriage before a non-Catholic minister was abrogated in a decree issued by the Sacred Congregation for the Doctrine of the Faith on Mar. 18, 1966.

The ordinary place of marriage is the parish of the bride, of the Catholic party in case of a mixed marriage, or of an Eastern Rite groom.

Church law regarding the form of marriage does not affect non-Catholics in marriages among themselves. The Church recognizes as valid the marriages of non-Catholics before ministers of religion and civil officials, unless they are rendered null and void on other grounds.

Impediments

Impediments to marriage are factors which render a marriage unlawful or invalid.

Prohibitory Impediments, which make a marriage unlawful but do not affect validity:

• simple vows of virginity, perpetual chastity, celibacy, to enter a religious order or to receive sacred orders;

• difference of religion, which obtains when one party is a Catholic and the other is a baptized non-Catholic.

The impediment of legal relationship is not in force in the US.

Diriment Impediments, which make a marriage invalid as well as unlawful:

• age, which obtains before completion of the 14th year for a woman and the 16th year for a man;

• impotency, if it is antecedent to the marriage and permanent (this differs from sterility, which is not an impediment);

• the bond of an existing valid marriage;

• disparity of worship, which obtains when one party is a Catholic and the other party is unbaptized;

• sacred orders;

• religious profession of the solemn vow of chastity;

• abduction, which impedes the freedom of the person abducted;

• crime, variously involving elements of adultery, promise or attempt to marry, conspiracy to murder a husband or wife;

• blood relationship in the direct line (father-daughter, mother-son, etc.) and within the third degree of the collateral line (brother-sister, first and second cousins);

• affinity, or relationship resulting from a valid marriage, in any degree of the direct line and within the second degree of the collateral line;

• spiritual relationship arising through baptism — between a godchild and godparent, between the person baptized and the one who performed the baptism;

• public honesty, arising from an invalid marriage or from public or notorious concubinage; it renders either party incapable of marrying relatives of the other in the first and second degrees of the direct line.

Dispensations from Impediments: Persons hindered by impediments either may not or cannot marry unless they are dispensed therefrom in view of reasons recognized in canon law. Local bishops can dispense from the impediments most often encountered (e.g., difference of religion, disparity of worship) as well as others.

Decision regarding some dispensations is reserved to the Holy See.

Separation

A valid and consummated marriage of baptized persons cannot be dissolved by any human authority or any cause other than the death of one of the persons.

In other circumstances:

• 1. A valid but unconsummated marriage of baptized persons, or of a baptized and an unbaptized person, can be dissolved:

a. by the solemn religious profession of one of the persons, made with permission of the pope. In such a case, the bond is dissolved at the time of profession, and the other person is free to marry again;

b. by dispensation from the pope, requested for a grave reason by one or both of the persons. If the dispensation is granted, both persons are free to marry again.

Dispensations in these cases are granted for reasons connected with the spiritual welfare of the concerned persons.

• 2. A legitimate marriage, even consummated, of unbaptized persons can be dissolved in favor of one of them who subsequently receives the sacrament of baptism. This is the Pauline Privilege, so called because it was promulgated by St. Paul (1 Cor. 7:12-15) as a means of protecting the faith of converts. Requisites for granting the privilege are:

a. marriage prior to the baptism of either person;

b. reception of baptism by one person;

c. refusal of the unbaptized person to live in peace with the baptized person and without interfering with his or her freedom to practice the Christian faith. The privilege does not apply if the unbaptized person agrees to these conditions.

• 3. A legitimate and consummated marriage of a baptized and an unbaptized person can be dissolved by the pope in virtue of the Privilege of Faith, also called the Petrine Privilege.

Civil Divorce: Because of the unity and the indissolubility of marriage, the Church denies that civil divorce can break the bond of a valid marriage, whether the marriage involves two Catholics, a Catholic and a non-Catholic, or non-Catholics with each other.

In view of serious circumstances of marital distress, the Church permits an innocent and aggrieved party, whether wife or husband, to seek and obtain a civil divorce for the purpose of acquiring title and right to the civil effects of divorce, such as separate habitation and maintenance, and the custody of children. Permission for this kind of action should be obtained from proper church authority. The divorce, if obtained, does not break the bond of a valid marriage.

Under other circumstances — as would obtain if a marriage was invalid (see Decree of Nullity, below) — civil divorce is permitted for civil effects and as a civil ratification of the fact that the marriage bond really does not exist.

Decree of Nullity, sometimes improperly called an annulment. This is a decision by a competent church authority — e.g., a bishop, a diocesan marriage tribunal, the Sacred Roman Rota — that an apparently valid marriage was actually invalid from the beginning because of the unknown or concealed existence, from the beginning, of a diriment impediment, an essential defect in consent, radical incapability for marriage, or a condition placed by one or both of the parties against the very nature of marriage.

Eastern Rite Laws

Marriage laws of the Eastern Church differ in several respects from the legislation of the Roman Rite. The regulations in effect since May 2, 1949, were contained in the motu proprio *Crebre Allatae* issued by Pius XII the previous February.

According to both the Roman Code of Canon Law and the Oriental Code, marriages between Roman Rite Catholics and Eastern Rite Catholics ordinarily take place in the rite of the groom and have canonical effects in that rite.

Regarding the form for the celebration of marriages between Eastern Catholics and baptized Eastern non-Catholics, the Second Vatican Council declared:

"By way of preventing invalid marriages between Eastern Catholics and baptized Eastern non-Catholics, and in the interests of the permanence and sanctity of marriage and of domestic harmony, this sacred Synod decrees that the canonical 'form' for the celebration of such marriages obliges only for lawfulness. For their validity, the presence of a sacred minister suffices, as long as the other requirements of law are honored" *(Decree on Eastern Catholic Churches,* No. 18).

Marriages taking place in this manner are lawful, as well as valid, with permission of a competent Eastern Rite bishop.

The Rota

The Sacred Roman Rota is the ordinary court of appeal for marriage, and some other cases, which are appealed to the Holy See from lower church courts. Appeals are made to the Rota if decisions by diocesan and archdiocesan courts fail to settle the matter in dispute.

PROCEDURAL RULES

Pope Paul VI promulgated, June 11, 1971, a set of 13 rules designed to speed up the handling of cases in which the validity of marriage is questioned. Norms given in the document, which was issued by the Pope on his own initiative and became effective Oct.31, concern "the constitution of ecclesiastical tribunals and . . . the judicial process which will expedite the matrimonial process itself."

The norms do not affect the reasons for the validity or invalidity of marriages, but only the way in which cases of this kind are handled in church courts.

Pope Paul told judges of the Roman Rota Jan. 30, 1975, that national conferences of bishops seemed "unanimously satisfied" with the procedures authorized in 1971. He also said: "We strongly hope that, with the promulgation of the new code of procedures, unnecessary differences among various ecclesiastical regions will be removed."

U.S. Norms

Twenty-three experimental norms — drawn up by the Canon Law Society of America, approved by the National Conference of Catholic Bishops and the Holy See, and in effect since July, 1970 — were broader in some respects than those decreed by Pope Paul. Among other things, they provided for: one-priest tribunals for specific periods of time instead of just for individual cases; dispensation by the NCCB from the need for review of first decisions regarding the validity or invalidity of a marriage; circumstances affecting the competence of tribunals. Continuing use of the experimental procedural norms was authorized by Paul VI in a letter dated May 22 and announced June 8, 1974 — "until the new order of matrimonial court procedure is promulgated for the Latin Church" in connection with the on-going revision of the Code of Canon Law. Termination of their use had been scheduled for June 30, 1974, following an original authorization for one year and an extension for three more years.

Cases of Non-Consummation

Pope Paul VI promulgated May 31, 1972, norms designed to speed up the handling of cases involving questions about the validity of marriages entered legally but never consummated sexually. The regulations which went into effect July 1, granted local bishops powers previously reserved to the Holy See.

Accordingly local bishops can initiate procedures in cases of this type; testimony and documents are acceptable in any modern language and on tape; physical proof of non-consummation can be omitted if the bishop is satisfied with the statements of the parties and/or witnesses; the number of witnesses is left to the discretion of the bishop.

PASTORAL MINISTRY FOR DIVORCED AND REMARRIED

Ministry to divorced and remarried Catholics is a difficult field of pastoral endeavor, situated as it is in circumstances tantamount to the horns of a dilemma.

At Issue

On the one side is firm church teaching on the permanence of marriage and norms against reception of the Eucharist and full participation in the life of the Church by Catholics in irregular unions.

On the other side are men and women with broken unions followed by second and perhaps happier attempts at marriage which the Church does not recognize as valid and which may not be capable of being validated because of the existence of an earlier marriage bond.

The forces at work in these circumstances are those of the Church, upholding its doctrine and practice regarding the permanence of marriage, and those of many men and women in irregular second marriages who desire full participation in the life of the Church.

Sacramental participation is not possible for those whose first marriage was valid, although there is no bar to their attendance at Mass, to sharing in other activities of the Church, or to their efforts to have children baptized and raised in the Catholic faith.

An exception to this rule is the condition of a divorced and remarried couple living in a brother-sister relationship.

There is no ban against sacramental participation by separated or divorced persons who have not attempted a second marriage.

Unverified estimates of the number of U.S. Catholics who are divorced and remarried vary between three and five million.

Tribunal Action

What can the Church do for them and with them in pastoral ministry, is an old question charged with new urgency because of the rising number of divorced and remarried Catholics.

One way to help is through the agency of marriage tribunals charged with responsibility for investigating and settling questions concerning the validity or invalidity of a prior marriage. There are reasons in canon law justifying the Church in declaring a particular marriage null and void from the beginning, despite the short- or long-term existence of an apparently valid union.

Decrees of nullity are not new in the history of the Church. If such a decree is issued, a man or woman is free to validate a second marriage and live in complete union with the Church.

Canonist L. Mason Knox, writing in the Oct. 16, 1976, edition of *America,* reported that 442 formal decisions, of which 338 were declarations of nullity, were issued by U.S. tribunals in 1968. Following adoption of the American Procedural Norms (see Procedural Rules) in 1970, the number of formal decisions rose in 1974 to 9,293, of which about 80 to 90 per cent were declarations of nullity. Similar decisions were rendered the same year in other canonical processes on grounds of: defect of form (15,722), papal dispensation for non-consummation (120), Pauline Privilege (691), Privilege of Faith (1,761), summary procedure (1,331).

U.S. tribunals handed down approximately 43,000 decisions in 1978.

The increase in the number of declarations of nullity is a result not just of new procedures but also, and more significantly, of tribunal judgments regarding the radical incapability of persons to contract valid marriage in the first place.

Reasons behind Decrees

Pastoral experience reveals that some married persons, a short or long time after contracting an apparently valid marriage, exhibit signs that point back to the existence, at the time of marriage, of latent and serious personal deficiencies which made them incapable of valid consent and sacramental commitment.

Such deficiencies might include gross immaturity and those affecting in a serious way the capacity to love, to have a true interpersonal and conjugal relationship, to fulfill marital obligations, to accept the faith aspect of marriage.

Psychological and behavioral factors like these have been given greater attention by tribunals in recent years and have provided grounds for numerous decrees of nullity.

Decisions of this type do not indicate any softening of the Church's attitude regarding the permanence of marriage. They affirm, rather, that some persons who have married were really not capable of doing so.

Serious deficiencies in the capacity for real interpersonal relationship in marriage were the reasons behind a landmark decree of nullity issued in 1973 by the Roman Rota, the Vatican high court of appeals in marriage cases.

Decree Not Always Possible

The tribunal way to a decree of nullity regarding a previous marriage is not open to many persons in second marriages — because grounds are either lacking or, if present, cannot be verified in tribunal process.

Many men and women in this second category are aligned and in sympathy with aims of the North American Conference of Separated and Divorced Catholics, which has several hundred support groups in various parts of the United States and Canada. Formed early in 1972, the conference seeks a special pastoral ministry for divorced Catholics in second irregular unions.

This purpose is shared by the Judeans (founded in 1952) and by official ministries in many U.S. dioceses, by other church agencies and by hosts of priests.

The principal problem involved in such ministry is the degree of sacramental participation open to persons in irregular unions.

Unacceptable Solution

The Congregation for the Doctrine of the Faith advised bishops throughout the world in August, 1973, against one solution of the problem called "good conscience procedure." This involves administration of the sacraments of penance and the Eucharist to divorced and remarried Catholics unable to obtain a decree of nullity for a first marriage who are living in a subsequent marriage "in good faith."

This procedure, despite the fact that it has no standing or recognition in church law, is being advocated and practiced by some priests and remarried Catholics.

MARRIAGE ENCOUNTER

Marriage Encounter originated in Spain through the efforts of Father Gabriel Calvo who worked out its principal features between the early 1950s and 1962 with the collaboration of Diego and Fina Bartoneo and other parties interested in ministry to married couples. Along with Charismatic Renewal, it has been called one of the fastest growing contemporary movements in the Church, with an estimated participation of one and one-half to two million couples in more than 50 countries.

The first encounter was held with 28 couples in 1962 in Barcelona. Five years later the first encounter in the U.S. was conducted in conjunction with a convention of the Christian Family Movement at Notre Dame University. Marriage Encounter caught on from this beginning and went nationwide in 1969.

The Encounter

Marriage Encounter brings couples together for a weekend program of events directed by a team of several couples and a priest, for the purpose of developing their abilities to communicate with each other in their life together as husband and wife. This purpose is served by direction in techniques given by the team and by private dialogue of each couple. Subjects of the dialogue extend to the whole range of personal and marital concerns. The anticipated result is the enrichment and revitalization of all personal-marital relationships.

This communication and sharing by husband and wife, spurred by the encounter and open to development by subsequent daily dialogue between them, is the positive substance of the movement.

The composition of Marriage Encounter groups for the encounter varies; some of them are exclusively Catholic while others have participants of different religious, professional or other special-interest affiliations.

Commentators insist that Marriage Encounter is not for troubled marriages and is not an exercise in group dynamics. Neither is it a retreat, although it has potential for spiritual development.

National

National Marriage Encounter of the U.S. follows the program initiated by Father Calvo. Deeply rooted in Roman Catholic tradition, it is open to members of other faiths in accordance with teachings of the Second Vatican Council. Its stated purpose is continuing development and growth in marital and family relationships in the context of God's activity as perceived by married partners.

An executive team (Noel and Jo McCracken, 7241 N. Whippoorwill, Peoria, Ill. 61614, and Father Robert White, O.F.M., St. Bonaventure, N.Y. 14778), elected to a three-year term in August, 1981, serves approximately 150 groups in the U.S. The national office is maintained at the aforementioned address in Peoria.

The identifying logo or emblem of National Marriage Encounter consists of two wedding bands intertwined with the Greek letters Chi-Rho; inside each wedding band is a burning candle standing in the waters of life.

Worldwide

Worldwide Marriage Encounter, with the stated purpose of renewal of the Church by means of renewal of the sacrament of matrimony, was developed by a priest and several couples who experienced a weekend conducted under the leadership of Father Calvo at a conference of the Christian Family Movement held at the University of Notre Dame.

The U.S. executive team consists of Father Desmond Colleran of the Diocese of Orange, Calif., and Al and Barbara Regnier, with an office at 3711 Long Beach Blvd., Long Beach, Calif. 90807. They are also members of the international council which coordinates outreach of the movement to 56 countries.

In addition to the Catholic-oriented encounter, there are others expressive of the faith and theology of other churches. Communication among the various groups is facilitated through regular meetings of an interfaith board.

The identifying logo or emblem of Worldwide Marriage Encounter consists of wedding bands intertwined with a cross and surmounted by a red heart.

ENGAGED ENCOUNTER

Catholic Engaged Encounter is designed to prepare couples for marriage by focusing attention on its sacramental aspects and by increasing their potential for communication with each other. With appropriate modifications, it follows the pattern of the Marriage Encounter weekend and subsequent practice of dialogue.

Since 1975, Catholic Engaged Encounter has given new direction to marriage preparation programs in many dioceses of the United States.

The director of the movement is Father Robert Harrington, located at 1 Summer Ave., Newark, N.J. 07104. Serving with him on the national executive team are William and Shelly Meehan (elected to serve Aug. 1, 1982, to 1984), 20 Cranberry Lane, South Easton, Mass. 02375.

HUMAN DEVELOPMENT

The Campaign for Human Development was inaugurated by the U.S. Catholic Conference in November, 1969, to combat injustice, oppression, alienation and poverty in this country in three significant ways:

• by making people in this country, especially Catholics, aware of the poverty, oppression and/or injustice afflicting some 35 million persons, through programs of education and public instruction;

• by funding self-help programs begun and carried out by the poor or by the poor and non-poor working together;

• by seeking a re-evaluation of the priorities of individuals, families, the Church and the civic community with respect to the stewardship of God-given goods.

The campaign got under way with a collection taken up in all parishes throughout the country on Nov. 22, 1970. Seventy-five per cent of the money contributed in this and subsequent annual collections was placed in a national fund principally for funding self-help projects and also for educational purposes; 25 per cent remained in the dioceses where it was collected, for similar use on the local levels.

More than $55 million in grants have been allocated by the national office since 1970; grants to 160 projects in 1981 totaled a bit more than $6 million. Diocesan allocations since 1970 have amounted to approximately $20 million.

Aid requests are reviewed by a broadly representative committee of 40 members which passes its recommendations for funding on to the 13-member Bishops' Committee for the Campaign for Human Development. Requests for aid from the national office are about 10 times greater than the some 125 programs funded each year. Local-level requests and funding are handled by diocesan offices for the Campaign for Human Development.

Gloria Pitt of Kinston, N.C., was elected 1982 chairperson of the 40-member national committee at an April meeting in Washington. New members appointed at the same time to three-year terms on the committee were: Sister Serena Branson, Juan Cadena, Judith Fairbanks, Tep Falcon, Doris Johnson, William Leighton, Antonio Lopez, John Lucas, Mary Marbry, Frank Negron, Reynaldo Pascua, Louise Reeves, Father Vincent Rocco, Michael Stone and Thomas Ulrich.

More than $9.3 million was contributed to the campaign in 1981.

Father Marvin Mottet is executive director of the campaign; his assistant is Timothy Collins. Bishop Joseph H. Hodges of Wheeling-Charleston is chairman of the bishops' committee.

The national office is located at 1312 Massachusetts Ave. N.W., Washington, D.C. 20005.

The calendar of the Roman Church consists of an arrangement throughout the year of a series of liturgical seasons and feasts of saints for purposes of divine worship.

The purposes of this calendar were outlined in the *Constitution on the Sacred Liturgy* (Nos. 102-105) promulgated by the Second Vatican Council.

"Within the cycle of a year . . . (the Church) unfolds the whole mystery of Christ, not only from His incarnation and birth until His ascension, but also as reflected in the day of Pentecost, and the expectation of a blessed, hoped-for return of the Lord.

"Recalling thus the mysteries of redemption, the Church opens to the faithful the riches of her Lord's powers and merits, so that these are in some way made present at all times, and the faithful are enabled to lay hold of them and become filled with saving grace" (No. 102).

"In celebrating this annual cycle of Christ's mysteries, holy Church honors with special love the Blessed Mary, Mother of God . . ." (No. 103).

"The Church has also included in the annual cycle days devoted to the memory of the martyrs and the other saints. . . . (who) sing God's perfect praise in heaven and offer prayers for us. By celebrating the passage of these saints from earth to heaven the Church proclaims the paschal mystery as achieved in the saints who have suffered and been glorified with Christ; she proposes them to the faithful as examples who draw all to the Father through Christ, and through their merits she pleads for God's favors" (No. 104).

". . . In the various seasons of the year and according to her traditional discipline, the Church completes the formation of the faithful by means of pious practices for soul and body, by instruction, prayer, and works of penance and mercy. . ." (No. 105).

THE NEW CALENDAR

Pope Paul VI announced May 9, 1969, his approval of a reorganization of the liturgical year and calendar for the Roman Rite, in implementation of a directive from the Second Vatican Council in 1964. He made the announcement in a document issued on his own initiative and entitled *Paschalis Mysterii*.

The purpose of the action, the Pope said, was "no other . . . than to permit the faithful to communicate in a more intense way, through faith, hope and love, in 'the whole mystery of Christ which . . . unfolds within the cycle of a year.' "

The *motu proprio* was dated Feb. 14, 1969. The new calendar was promulgated a month later by a decree of the Congregation for Divine Worship and went into effect Jan. 1, 1970, with provisional modifications. Full implementation of all its parts was delayed in 1970 and 1971, pending the completion of work on related liturgical texts. The U.S. bishops ordered the whole new calendar into effect for 1972.

The Seasons

Advent: The liturgical year begins with the First Sunday of Advent, which introduces a season of four weeks or slightly less duration with the theme of expectation of the coming of Christ. During the first two weeks, the final coming of Christ as Lord and Judge at the end of the world is the focus of attention. From Dec. 17 to 24, the emphasis shifts to anticipation of the celebration of his Nativity on the Solemnity of Christmas.

Advent has four Sundays. Since the 10th century, the first Sunday has marked the beginning of the liturgical year in the Western Church. In the Middle Ages, a kind of pre-Christmas fast was in vogue during the season.

Christmastide: Christmastide opens with the Solemnity of the Nativity, Dec. 25, and lasts until the Sunday after Epiphany. The Holy Family is commemorated on the Sunday within the Christmas octave. Jan. 1 — formerly called the Octave Day of the Nativity and, before that, the feast of the Circumcision of Jesus — has the title of Solemnity of Mary the Mother of God. The Epiphany, scheduled for Jan. 6 in the universal calendar, is celebrated in the U.S. on the Sunday between Jan. 2 and 8. The Baptism of the Lord, observed on the Sunday following Epiphany, marks the end of Christmastide.

The period between the end of Christmastide and the beginning of Lent belongs to the Ordinary Time of the year. Of variable length, the pre-Lenten phase of this season includes what were formerly called the Sundays after Epiphany and the suppressed Sundays of Septuagesima, Sexagesima and Quinquagesima.

Lent: The penitential season of Lent begins on Ash Wednesday, which occurs between Feb. 4 and Mar. 11, depending on the date of Easter, and lasts until Easter. It has six Sundays and 40 weekdays. The climactic last week is called Holy Week. The last three days (Holy Thursday, Good Friday and Holy Saturday) are called the Paschal Triduum.

The origin of Lenten observances dates back to the fourth century or earlier.

Eastertide: Eastertide, whose theme is resurrection from sin to the life of grace, lasts for 50 days, from Easter to Pentecost. Easter, the first Sunday following the vernal equinox, occurs between Mar. 22 and Apr. 25. The terminal phase of Eastertide, between the Solemnities of the Ascension of the Lord and Pentecost, stresses anticipation of the coming and action of the Holy Spirit.

Ordinary Time: The season of Ordinary Time of the year includes not only the period between the end of Christmastide and the beginning of Lent, as noted above, but also all Sundays after Pentecost to the last Sunday of the liturgical year, which is celebrated as the feast of Christ the King. The number of Sundays before Lent and after Pentecost varies, depending on the date of the key feast of Easter. The overall purpose of the season is to elaborate the themes of salvation history.

The various liturgical seasons are characterized in part by the scriptural readings and Mass prayers assigned to each of them. During Advent, for example, the readings are messianic; during Eastertide, from the Acts of the Apostles, chronicling the Resurrection and the original proclamation of Christ by the Apostles, and from the Gospel of John; during Lent, baptismal and penitential passages. Mass prayers reflect the meaning and purpose of the various seasons.

Feasts of Saints

The feasts of saints are celebrated concurrently with the liturgical seasons and feasts of our Lord. Their purpose is to illustrate the paschal mysteries as reflected in the lives of saints, to honor them as heroes of holiness, and to appeal for their intercession.

In line with revised regulations, some former feasts have been either abolished or relegated to observance in particular places by local option for one of two reasons: (1) lack of sufficient historical evidence for observance of the feasts; (2) lack of universal significance.

The feast of a saint, as a general rule, is observed on the day of his death (*dies natalis,* day of birth to glory with God in heaven). Exceptions to this rule include the feasts of St. John the Baptist, who is honored on the day of his birth; Sts. Basil the Great and Gregory Nazianzen, and the brother Saints, Cyril and Methodius, who are commemorated in joint feasts.

Application of this general rule in the revised calendar resulted in date changes of some feasts.

Sundays and Feast Days

Sunday is the original Christian feast day because of the unusually significant events of salvation history which took place and are commemorated on the first day of the week — viz., the Resurrection of Christ, the key event of his life and the fundamental fact of Christianity; and the descent of the Holy Spirit upon the Apostles on Pentecost, the birthday of the Church. The transfer of observance of the Lord's Day from the Sabbath to Sunday was made in apostolic times. The Mass and Liturgy of the Hours (Divine Office) of each Sunday reflect the themes and set the tones of the various liturgical seasons.

Categories of feasts according to dignity and manner of observance are: solemnity (highest, corresponding to former first-class feasts); feast (corresponding to former second-class feasts); memorial (corresponding to former third-class feasts); optional memorial (observable by local choice). Feasts of the first three categories are observed universally in the Roman Rite.

Fixed feasts are those which are regularly celebrated on the same calendar day each year.

Movable feasts are those which are not observed on the same calendar day each year. Examples of these are Easter (the first Sunday after the first full moon following the vernal equinox), Ascension (40 days after Easter), Pentecost (50 days after Easter), Trinity Sunday (first after Pentecost), Christ the King (last Sunday of the liturgical year).

Holy Days of Obligation

Holy days of obligation are special feasts on which Catholics who have reached the age of reason are seriously obliged, as on Sundays, to assist at Mass and to avoid unnecessary servile work. Serious reasons excuse from the observance of either or both of these obligations.

By enactment of the Third Plenary Council of Baltimore, and with the approval of the Holy See, the holy days of obligation observed in the United States are: Christmas, the Nativity of Jesus, Dec. 25; Solemnity of Mary the Mother of God, Jan. 1; Ascension of the Lord; Assumption of Blessed Mary the Virgin, Aug. 15; All Saints' Day, Nov. 1; Immaculate Conception of Blessed Mary the Virgin, Dec. 8.

In addition to these, there are four other holy days of obligation prescribed in the general law of the Church which are not so observed in the U.S.: Epiphany; St. Joseph, Mar. 19; Corpus Christi; Sts. Peter and Paul, June 29.

Weekdays, Days of Prayer

Weekdays are those on which no proper feast or vigil is celebrated in the Mass or Liturgy of the Hours (Divine Office). On such days, the Mass may be that of the preceding Sunday, which expresses the liturgical spirit of the season, an optional memorial, a votive Mass, or a Mass for the dead. Weekdays of Advent and Lent are in a special category of their own.

Days of prayer: Dioceses, at times to be designated by local bishops, should observe "days or periods of prayer for the fruits of the earth, prayer for human rights and equality, prayer for world justice and peace, and penitential observance outside of Lent." So states the *Instruction on Particular Calendars* (No. 331) issued by the Congregation for the Sacraments and Divine Worship June 24, 1970.

These days are contemporary equivalents of what were formerly called ember and rogation days.

Ember days originated at Rome about the fifth century, probably as Christian replacements for seasonal festivals of agrarian cults. They were observances of penance, thanksgiving, and petition for divine blessing on the various seasons; they also were occasions of special prayer for clergy to be ordained. These days were observed four times a year.

Rogation days originated in France about the fifth century. They were penitential in character and also occasions of prayer for a bountiful harvest and protection against evil.

Days of Abstinence and Fast

The apostolic constitution *Paenitemini*, in effect since Feb. 23, 1966, authorized the substitution of other works of penance for the customary and common observances of abstinence and fast on various days of the year.

In this country, in line with provisions of the constitution and a 1974 decision of the National Conference of Catholic Bishops, Ash Wednesday and Good Friday are days of fast and abstinence, and all Fridays of Lent are days of abstinence.

The obligation to abstain from meat binds Catholics 14 years of age and older. The obligation to fast, limiting oneself to one full meal and two lighter meals in the course of a day, binds Catholics from the ages of 21 to 59.

BYZANTINE CALENDAR

As in the Roman usage, the dating of feasts follows the Gregorian Calendar. Formerly, until well into this century, the Julian Calendar was used. (The Julian Calendar, which is now about 13 days late, is still used by some Eastern-Rite Churches.)

The year has several cycles, which include proper seasons, the feasts of saints, and series of New Testament readings. All of these elements of worship are contained in liturgical books of the rite.

The ecclesiastical calendar, called the **Menologion**, explains the nature of feasts, other observances and matters pertaining to the liturgy for each day of the year. In some cases, its contents include the lives of saints and the history and meaning of feasts.

The Divine Liturgy (Mass) and Divine Office for the proper of the saints, fixed feasts, and the Christmas season are contained in the **Menaion**. The **Triodion** covers the pre-Lenten season of preparation for Easter; Lent begins two days before the Ash Wednesday observance of the Roman Rite. The **Pentecostarion** contains the liturgical services from Easter to the Sunday of All Saints, the first after Pentecost. The **Evangelion** and **Apostolos** are books in which the Gospels, and Acts of the Apostles and the Epistles, respectively, are arranged according to the order of their reading in the Divine Liturgy and Divine Office throughout the year.

The cyclic progression of liturgical music throughout the year, in successive and repetitive periods of eight weeks, is governed by the **Oktoechos**, the Book of Eight Tones.

Sunday Names

Many Sundays are named after the subject of the Gospel read in the Mass of the day or after the name of a feast falling on the day — e.g., Sunday of the Publican and Pharisee, of the Prodigal Son, of the Samaritan Woman, of St. Thomas the Apostle, of the Fore-Fathers (Old Testament Patriarchs). Other Sundays are named in the same manner as in the Roman calendar — e.g., numbered Sundays of Lent and after Pentecost.

Holy Days, Abstinence, Fast

The calendar lists about 28 holy days. Many of the major holy days coincide with those of the Roman calendar, but the feast of the Immaculate Conception is observed on Dec. 9 instead of Dec. 8, and the feast of All Saints falls on the Sunday after Pentecost rather than on Nov. 1. Instead of a single All Souls' Day, there are five All Souls' Saturdays.

According to regulations in effect in the Byzantine-Rite (Ruthenian) Archeparchy of Pittsburgh and its suffragan sees of Passaic and Parma, holy days are obligatory, solemn and simple, and attendance at the Divine Liturgy is required on five obligatory days — the feasts of the Epiphany, the Ascension, Sts. Peter and Paul, the Assumption of the Blessed Virgin Mary, and Christmas. Although attendance at the liturgy is not obligatory on 15 solemn and seven simple holy days, it is recommended.

In the Byzantine-Rite (Ukrainian) Archeparchy of Philadelphia and its suffragan sees of St. Nicholas (Chicago) and Stamford, the obligatory feasts are the Circumcision, Epiphany, Annunciation, Easter, Ascension, Pentecost, Dormition (Assumption of Mary), Immaculate Conception and Christmas.

Lent

The first day of Lent — the Monday before Ash Wednesday of the Roman Rite — and Good Friday are days of strict abstinence for persons between the ages of 21 and 59. No meat, eggs, or dairy products may be eaten on these days.

All persons over the age of 14 must abstain from meat on Fridays during Lent, Holy Saturday, and the vigils of the feasts of Christmas and Epiphany; abstinence is urged, but is not obligatory, on Wednesdays of Lent. The abstinence obligation is not in force on certain "free" or "privileged" Fridays.

Synaxis

An observance without a counterpart in the Roman calendar is the synaxis. This is a commemoration, on the day following a feast, of persons involved with the occasion for the feast — e.g., Sept. 9, the day following the feast of the Nativity of the Blessed Virgin Mary, is the Synaxis of Joachim and Anna, her parents.

JANUARY 1983

1—**Sat. Solemnity of Mary, Mother of God. Holy day of obligation.** (Nm. 6:22-27; Gal. 4:4-7; Lk 2:16-21.)

2—**Sun. Epiphany of the Lord (in U.S.); solemnity.** (Is. 60:1-6; Eph. 3:2-3a, 5-6; Mt. 2:1-12.) [Sts. Basil the Great and Gregory Nazianzen, bishops-doctors; memorial.]

3—Mon. Weekday.

4—Tues. St. Elizabeth Ann Seton; memorial (in U.S.).

5—Wed. St. John Neumann, bishop; memorial (in U.S.).

6—Thurs. Weekday (in U.S.). Epiphany is celebrated on a Sunday between Jan. 2 and 8 in the U.S.-

7—Fri. Weekday. St. Raymond of Peñafort, priest; optional memorial.

8—Sat. Weekday.

9—**Sun. Baptism of the Lord; feast.** (Is. 42: 1-4, 6-7; Acts 10:34-38; Lk. 3:15-16, 21-22.)

10—Mon. Weekday. (First Week of the Year.)

11—Tues. Weekday.

12—Wed. Weekday.

13—Thurs. Weekday. St. Hilary, bishop-doctor; optional memorial.

14—Fri. Weekday.

15—Sat. Weekday.

16—**Second Sunday of the Year.** (Is. 62:1-5; 1 Cor. 12:4-11; Jn. 2:1-12.)

17—Mon. St. Anthony, abbot; memorial.

18—Tues. Weekday.

19—Wed. Weekday.

20—Thurs. Weekday. St. Fabian, pope-martyr, or St. Sebastian, martyr; optional memorials.

21—Fri. St. Agnes, virgin-martyr; memorial.

22—Sat. Weekday. St. Vincent, deacon-martyr; optional memorial.

23—**Third Sunday of the Year.** (Neh. 8:1-4a, 5-6, 8-10; 1 Cor. 12:12-30; Lk. 1:1-4 and 4:14-21.)

24—Mon. St. Francis de Sales, bishop-doctor; memorial.

25—Tues. Conversion of St. Paul, apostle; feast.

26—Wed. Sts. Timothy and Titus, bishops; memorial.

27—Thurs. Weekday. St. Angela Merici, virgin; optional memorial.

28—Fri. St. Thomas Aquinas, priest-doctor; memorial.

29—Sat. Weekday.

30—**Fourth Sunday of the Year.** (Jer. 1:4-5, 17-19; 1 Cor. 12:31 to 13:13; Lk. 4:21-30.)

31—Mon. St. John Bosco, priest; memorial.

PRAYER INTENTIONS: For the recognition of Jesus Christ as the "Life of the World." For general interfaith dialogue with members of all faiths.

FEBRUARY 1983

1—Tues. Weekday.

2—Wed. Presentation of the Lord; feast.

3—Thurs. Weekday. St. Blase, bishop-martyr, or St. Ansgar, bishop; optional memorials.

4—Fri. Weekday.

5—Sat. St. Agatha, virgin-martyr; memorial.

6—**Fifth Sunday of the Year.** (Is. 6:1-2a, 3-8; 1 Cor. 15:1-11; Lk. 5:1-11.) [Sts. Paul Miki and Companions, martyrs; memorial.]

7—Mon. Weekday.

8—Tues. Weekday. St. Jerome Emiliani; optional memorial.

9—Wed. Weekday.

10—Thurs. St. Scholastica, virgin; memorial.

11—Fri.. Weekday. Our Lady of Lourdes; optional memorial.

12—Sat. Weekday.

13—**Sixth Sunday of the Year.** (Jer. 17:5-8; 1 Cor. 15:12, 16-20; Lk. 6:17, 20-26.)

14—Mon. Sts. Cyril, monk, and Methodius, bishop; memorial.

15—Tues. Weekday.

16—Ash Wednesday. Beginning of Lent. *Fast and abstinence.* Ashes are blessed on this day and imposed on the forehead of the faithful to remind them of their obligation to do penance for sin and to seek spiritual renewal by means of prayer, fasting, good works, and by bearing with patience and for God's purposes the trials and difficulties of everyday life.

17—Thurs. Weekday of Lent. [Seven Holy Founders of the Servite Order; optional memorial.]

18—Fri. Weekday of Lent. *Abstinence.*

19—Sat. Weekday of Lent.

20—**First Sunday of Lent.** (Dt. 26:4-10; Rom. 10:8-13; Lk. 4:1-13.)

21—Mon. Weekday of Lent. [St. Peter Damian, bishop-doctor; optional memorial.]

22—Tues. Chair of St. Peter, apostle; feast. Weekday of Lent.

23—Wed. Weekday of Lent. St. Polycarp, bishop-martyr; memorial.

24—Thurs. Weekday of Lent.

25—Fri. Weekday of Lent. *Abstinence.*

26—Sat. Weekday of Lent.

27—**Second Sunday of Lent.** (Gn. 15:5-12, 17-18; Phil. 3:17 to 4:1; Lk. 9:28b-36.)

28—Mon. Weekday of Lent.

GENERAL PRAYER INTENTION: For a more extensive appreciation of the Christian view of work, against the background of social teaching in Pope John Paul's third encyclical, *Laborem Exercens* ("On Human Work").

MISSION PRAYER INTENTION: That older missionaries adapt to new ways of serving the Church.

MARCH 1983

1—Tues. Weekday of Lent.
2—Wed. Weekday of Lent.
3—Thurs. Weekday of Lent.
4—Fri. Weekday of Lent. *Abstinence.* [St. Casimir; optional memorial.]
5—Sat. Weekday of Lent.
6—**Third Sunday of Lent.** (Ex. 3:1-8a, 13-15; 1 Cor. 10:1-6, 10-12; Lk. 13:1-9.)
7—Mon. Weekday of Lent. [Sts. Perpetua and Felicity; martyrs; memorial.]
8—Tues. Weekday of Lent. [St. John of God, religious; optional memorial.]
9—Wed. Weekday of Lent. [St. Frances of Rome, religious; optional memorial.]
10—Thurs. Weekday of Lent.
11—Fri. Weekday of Lent. *Abstinence.*
12—Sat. Weekday of Lent.
13—**Fourth Sunday of Lent.** (Jos. 5:9a, 10-12; 2 Cor. 5:17-21; Lk. 15:1-3, 11-32.)
14—Mon. Weekday of Lent.
15—Tues. Weekday of Lent.
16—Wed. Weekday of Lent.
17—Thurs. Weekday of Lent. [St. Patrick, bishop; optional memorial.]
18—Fri. Weekday of Lent. *Abstinence.* [St. Cyril of Jerusalem, bishop-doctor; optional memorial.]
19—Sat. St. Joseph; solemnity. Weekday of Lent.
20—**Fifth Sunday of Lent.** (Is. 43:16-21; Phil. 3:8-14; Jn. 8:1-11.)
21—Mon. Weekday of Lent.
22—Tues. Weekday of Lent.
23—Wed. Weekday of Lent. [St. Turibius, bishop; optional memorial.]
24—Thurs. Weekday of Lent.
25—Fri. Annunciation; solemnity. Weekday of Lent. *Abstinence.*
26—Sat. Weekday of Lent.
27—**Sunday of the Passion (Palm Sunday).** (Procession — Lk. 19:28-40. Mass — Is. 50:4-7; Phil. 2:6-11; Lk. 22:14 to 23:56.)
28—Monday of Holy Week.
29—Tuesday of Holy Week.
30—Wednesday of Holy Week.
31—Thursday of Holy Week. Holy Thursday. The Paschal Triduum begins with the evening Mass of the Supper of the Lord.

GENERAL PRAYER INTENTION: That Christians might consider Lent as a "time of truth." It is useful to recall the teaching of the Holy Father in his lenten messages. One such memorable message — "Moment of Truth," delivered by Pope John Paul Mar. 4, 1981 — is the source of this quotation.

MISSION PRAYER INTENTION: For respect for religious and family values in China. March is the month of the Novena of Grace, recalling the work of St. Francis Xavier for the conversion of China.

APRIL 1983

1—Friday of the Passion of the Lord. Good Friday. *Fast and abstinence.*
2—Holy Saturday. The Easter Vigil. [St. Francis of Paolo, hermit; optional memorial.]
3—**Easter Sunday; solemnity.** (Acts 10:34a, 37-43; 2 Col. 3:1-4 or 1 Cor. 5:6b-8; Jn. 20:1-9 or Lk. 24:1-12, or (Evening) Lk. 24:13-35.)
4—Monday of Easter Octave. [St. Isidore of Seville, bishop-doctor; optional memorial.]
5—Tuesday of Easter Octave. [St. Vincent Ferrer, priest; optional memorial.]
6—Wednesday of Easter Octave.
7—Thursday of Easter Octave. [St. John Baptist de la Salle, priest; memorial.]
8—Friday of Easter Octave.
9—Saturday of Easter Octave.
10—**Second Sunday of Easter.** (Acts 5:12-16; Rv. 1:9-11a, 12-13, 17-19; Jn. 20:19-31.)
11—Mon. St. Stanislaus, bishop-martyr; memorial.
12—Tues. Weekday.
13—Wed. Weekday. St. Martin I, pope-martyr; optional memorial.
14—Thurs. Weekday.
15—Fri. Weekday.
16—Sat. Weekday.
17—**Third Sunday of Easter.** (Acts 5:27b-32, 40b-41; Rv. 5:11-14; Jn. 21:1-19.) [Bl. Kateri Tekakwitha, virgin; memorial (in U.S.)]
18—Mon. Weekday.
19—Tues. Weekday.
20—Wed. Weekday.
21—Thurs. Weekday. St. Anselm, bishop-doctor; optional memorial.
22—Fri. Weekday.
23—Sat. Weekday. St. George, martyr; optional memorial.
24—**Fourth Sunday of Easter.** (Acts 13:14, 43-52; Rv. 7:9, 4b-17; Jn. 10:27-30.) [St. Fidelis of Sigmaringen, priest-martyr; optional memorial.]
25—Mon. St. Mark, evangelist; feast.
26—Tues. Weekday.
27—Wed. Weekday.
28—Thurs. Weekday. St. Peter Chanel, priest-martyr; optional memorial.
29—Fri. St. Catherine of Siena, virgin-doctor; memorial.
30—Sat. Weekday. St. Pius V, pope; optional memorial.

GENERAL PRAYER INTENTION: For a more equitable distribution of wealth and labor, a subject mentioned by Pope John Paul in an address delivered in June, 1980, in Rio de Janeiro.

MISSION PRAYER INTENTION: For responsibility on the part of all believers for evangelism, especially in support of missionary works.

MAY 1983

1—**Fifth Sunday of Easter.** (Acts 14:21-27; Rv. 21:1-5a; Jn. 13:31-33a, 34-35.) [St. Joseph the Worker; optional memorial.]
2—Mon. St. Athanasius, bishop-doctor; memorial.
3—Tues. Sts. Philip and James, apostles; feast.
4—Wed. Weekday.
5—Thurs. Weekday.
6—Fri. Weekday.
7—Sat.. Weekday.
8—**Sixth Sunday of Easter.** (Acts 15:1-2, 22-29; Rv. 21:10-14, 22-23; Jn. 14:23-29.)
9—Mon. Weekday.
10—Tues. Weekday.
11—Wed. Weekday.
12—Thurs. Ascension of the Lord; solemnity. Holy day of obligation. (Acts 1:1-11; Eph. 1:17-23; Lk. 24:46-53.) [Sts. Nereus and Achilleus, martyrs, or St. Pancras, martyr; optional memorials.]
13—Fri. Weekday.
14—Sat. St. Mathias, apostle; feast.
15—**Seventh Sunday of Easter.** (Acts. 7:55-60; Rv. 22:12-14, 16-17, 20; Jn. 17:20-26.)
16—Mon. Weekday.
17—Tues. Weekday.
18—Wed. Weekday. St. John I, pope-martyr; optional memorial.
19—Thurs. Weekday.
20—Fri. Weekday. St. Bernardine of Siena, priest; optional memorial.
21—Sat. Weekday.
22—**Sun. Pentecost; solemnity.** (Acts 2:1-11; 1 Cor. 12:3b-7, 12-13; Jn. 20:19-23.)
23—Mon. Weekday. (Eighth Week of the Year.)
24—Tues. Weekday.
25—Wed. Weekday. St. Bede the Venerable, priest-doctor, or St. Gregory VII, pope, or St. Mary Magdalene de Pazzi, virgin; optional memorials.
26—Thurs. St. Philip Neri, priest; memorial.
27—Fri. Weekday. St. Augustine of Canterbury, bishop; optional memorial.
28—Sat. Weekday.
29—**Trinity Sunday; solemnity.** (Prv. 8:22-31; Rom. 5:1-5; Jn. 16:12-15.)
30—Mon. Weekday. (Ninth Week of the Year.)
31—Tues. Visitation of Blessed Mary the Virgin; feast.
GENERAL PRAYER INTENTION: For the Christian family as "a believing and evangelizing community," in line with teaching contained in the apostolic exhortation, *Familiaris Consortio* ("Community of the Family").
MISSION PRAYER INTENTION: For the suitable formation of seminarians and novices of Asia, with respect to their spiritual, intellectual and apostolic development for sacred ministry.

JUNE 1983

1—Wed. St. Justin, martyr; memorial.
2—Thurs. Weekday. Sts. Marcellinus and Peter, martyrs; optional memorial.
3—Fri. Sts. Charles Lwanga and Companions, martyrs; memorial.
4—Sat. Weekday.
5—**Sun. Corpus Christi (in U.S.); solemnity.** (Gn. 14:18-20; 1 Cor. 11:23-26; Lk. 9:11b-17.) [St. Boniface, bishop-martyr; memorial.]
6—Mon. Weekday. St. Norbert, bishop; optional memorial. (Tenth Week of the Year.)
7—Tues. Weekday.
8—Wed. Weekday.
9—Thurs. Weekday. St. Ephraem, deacon-doctor; optional memorial.
10—Fri. Sacred Heart of Jesus; solemnity.
11—Sat. St. Barnabas, apostle; memorial. [Immaculate Heart of Mary; optional memorial.]
12—**Eleventh Sunday of the Year.** (2 Sm. 12:7-10, 13; Gal. 2:16, 19-21; Lk. 7:36 to 8:3.)
13—Mon. St. Anthony of Padua, priest-doctor; memorial.
14—Tues. Weekday.
15—Wed. Weekday.
16—Thurs. Weekday.
17—Fri. Weekday.
18—Sat. Weekday.
19—**Twelfth Sunday of the Year.** (Zec. 12:10-11; Gal. 3:26-29; Lk. 9:18-24.) [St. Romuald, abbot; optional memorial.]
20—Mon. Weekday.
21—Tues. St. Aloysius Gonzaga, religious; memorial.
22—Wed. Weekday. St. Paulinus of Nola, bishop, or Sts. John Fisher, bishop-martyr, and Thomas More, martyr; optional memorials.
23—Thurs. Weekday.
24—Fri. Birth of St. John the Baptist; solemnity.
25—Sat. Weekday.
26—**Thirteenth Sunday of the Year.** (1 Kgs. 19:16b, 19-21; Gal. 5:1, 13-18; Lk. 9:51-62.)
27—Mon. Weekday. St. Cyril of Alexandria, bishop-doctor; optional memorial.
28—Tues. St. Irenaeus, bishop-martyr; memorial.
29—Wed. Sts. Peter and Paul, apostles; solemnity.
30—Thurs. Weekday. First Martyrs of the Roman Church; optional memorial.
GENERAL PRAYER INTENTION: That priests might manifest the love of the heart of Christ.
MISSION PRAYER INTENTION: For application of the teaching in *Familiaris Consortio* in mission countries, where special difficulties affect families.

JULY 1983

1—Fri. Weekday.
2—Sat. Weekday.
3—**Fourteenth Sunday of the Year.** (Is. 66:10-14c; Gal. 6:14-18; Lk. 10:1-12, 17-20.) [St. Thomas, apostle; feast.]
4—Mon. Weekday. St. Elizabeth of Portugal; optional memorial. Independence Day Votive Mass (in U.S.).
5—Tues. Weekday. St. Anthony Zaccaria, priest; optional memorial.
6—Wed. Weekday. St. Maria Goretti, virgin-martyr; optional memorial.
7—Thurs. Weekday.
8—Fri.. Weekday.
9—Sat. Weekday.
10—**Fifteenth Sunday of the Year.** (Dt. 30:10-14; Col. 1:15-20; Lk. 10:25-37.)
11—Mon. St. Benedict, abbot; memorial.]
12—Tues. Weekday.
13—Wed. Weekday. St. Henry; optional memorial.
14—Thurs. Weekday. St. Camillus de Lellis, priest; optional memorial.
15—Fri. St. Bonaventure, bishop-doctor; memorial.
16—Sat. Weekday. Our Lady of Mt. Carmel; optional memorial.
17—**Sixteenth Sunday of the Year.** (Gn. 18:1-10a; Col. 1:24-28; Lk. 10:38-42.)
18—Mon. Weekday.
19—Tues. Weekday.
20—Wed. Weekday.
21—Thurs. St. Lawrence of Brindisi, priest-doctor; optional memorial.
22—Fri. St. Mary Magdalene; memorial.
23—Sat. Weekday. St. Bridget, religious; optional memorial.
24—**Seventeenth Sunday of the Year.** (Gn. 18:20-32; Col. 2:12-14; Lk. 11:1-13.)
25—Mon. St. James, apostle; feast.
26—Tues. Sts. Joachim and Anne, parents of Blessed Mary the Virgin; memorial.
27—Wed. Weekday.
28—Thurs. Weekday.
29—Fri. St. Martha; memorial.
30—Sat. Weekday. St. Peter Chrysologus, bishop-doctor; optional memorial.
31—**Eighteenth Sunday of the Year** (Eccl. 1:2 and 2:21-23; Col. 3:1-5, 9-11; Lk. 12:13-21.) [St. Ignatius of Loyola, priest; memorial.]
GENERAL PRAYER INTENTION: For the promotion of peace by the leaders of Central American nations, where violence is a daily threat to life and people of the Church are harassed for working for justice and peace.
MISSION PRAYER INTENTION: For religious institutes in Latin America, Asia and Africa, founded to serve foreign missions, Missionary co-responsibility needs the support of prayer and recognition by the entire Church.

AUGUST 1983

1—Mon. St. Alphonsus Liguori, bishop-doctor; memorial.
2—Tues. Weekday. St. Eusebius of Vercelli, bishop; optional memorial.
3—Wed. Weekday.
4—Thurs. St. John Vianney, priest; memorial.
5—Fri. Weekday. Dedication of St. Mary Major Basilica; optional memorial.
6—Sat. Transfiguration of the Lord; feast.
7—**Nineteenth Sunday of the Year.** (Wis. 18:6-9; Heb. 11:1-2, 8-19; Lk. 12:32-48.) [Sts. Sixtus II, pope, and Companions, martyrs, or St. Cajetan, priest; optional memorials.]
8—Mon. St. Dominic, priest; memorial.
9—Tues. Weekday.
10—Wed. St. Lawrence, deacon-martyr; feast.
11—Thurs. St. Clare, virgin; memorial.
12—Fri. Weekday.
13—Sat. Weekday. Sts. Pontian, pope, and Hippolytus, priest, martyrs; optional memorial.
14—**Twentieth Sunday of the Year.** (Jer. 38:4-6, 8-10; Heb. 12:1-4; Lk. 12:49-53.)
15—**Mon. Assumption of Blessed Mary the Virgin; solemnity. Holy day of obligation.** (Rv. 11:19a and 12:1-6a, 10ab; 1 Cor. 15:20-26; Lk. 1:39-56.)
16—Tues. Weekday. St. Stephen of Hungary; optional memorial.
17—Wed. Weekday.
18—Thurs. Weekday.
19—Fri. Weekday. St. John Eudes, priest; optional memorial.
20—Sat. St. Bernard of Clairvaux, abbot-doctor; memorial.
21—**Twenty-First Sunday of the Year.** (Is. 66:18-21; Heb. 12: 5-7, 11-13; Lk. 13:22-30.) [St. Pius X, pope; memorial.]
22—Mon. Queenship of Mary; memorial.
23—Tues. Weekday. St. Rose of Lima, virgin; optional memorial.
24—Wed. St. Bartholomew, apostle; feast.
25—Thurs. Weekday. St. Louis, or St. Joseph Calasanz, priest; optional memorials.
26—Fri. Weekday.
27—Sat. St. Monica; memorial.
28—**Twenty-Second Sunday of the Year.** (Sir. 3:17-18, 20, 28-29; Heb. 12:18-19, 22-24a; Lk. 14:1, 7-14.) [St. Augustine, bishop-doctor; memorial.]
29—Mon. Beheading of St. John the Baptist; memorial.
30—Tues. Weekday.
31—Wed. Weekday.
GENERAL PRAYER INTENTION: For the recitation and living of the "Our Father" by all Christians.
MISSION PRAYER INTENTION: For edifying example by Christian tourists visiting non-Christian countries.

SEPTEMBER 1983

1—Thurs. Weekday.
2—Fri.. Weekday.
3—Sat. St. Gregory the Great, pope-doctor; memorial.
4—**Twenty-Third Sunday of the Year.** (Wis. 9:13-18b; Phlm. 9b-10, 12-17; Lk. 14:25-33.)
5—Mon. Weekday.
6—Tues. Weekday.
7—Wed. Weekday.
8—Thurs. Birth of Mary; feast.
9—Fri. St. Peter Claver, priest; memorial (in U.S.). Weekday.
10—Sat. Weekday.
11—**Twenty-Fourth Sunday of the Year.** (Ex. 32:7-11, 13-14; 1 Tm. 1:12-17; Lk. 15:1-32.)
12—Mon. Weekday.
13—Tues. St. John Chrysostom, bishop-doctor; memorial.
14—Wed. Triumph of the Cross; feast.
15—Thurs. Our Lady of Sorrows; memorial.
16—Fri. Sts. Cornelius, pope, and Cyprian, bishop, martyrs; memorial.
17—Sat. Weekday. St. Robert Bellarmine, bishop-doctor; optional memorial.
18—**Twenty-Fifth Sunday of the Year.** (Am. 8:4-7; 1 Tm. 2:1-8; Lk. 16:1-13.)
19—Mon. Weekday. St. Januarius, bishop-martyr; optional memorial.
20—Tues. Weekday.
21—Wed. St. Matthew, apostle-evangelist; feast.
22—Thurs. Weekday.
23—Fri. Weekday.
24—Sat. Weekday.
25—**Twenty-Sixth Sunday of the Year.** (Am. 6:1a, 4-7; 1 Tm. 6:11-16; Lk. 16:19-31.)
26—Mon. Weekday. Sts. Cosmas and Damian, martyrs; optional memorial.
27—Tues. St. Vincent de Paul, priest; memorial.
28—Wed. Weekday. St. Wenceslaus, martyr; optional memorial.
29—Thurs. Sts. Michael, Gabriel and Raphael, archangels; feast.
30—Fri. St. Jerome, priest-doctor; memorial.
GENERAL PRAYER INTENTION: For a more extensive and efficacious adult catechesis. The development of such a program for instruction and formation in the faith is one of the central problems in the pastoral ministry of the Church. Guidelines for catechesis of this kind are provided in the apostolic exhortation, *Catechesi Tradendae* ("Catechetics in Our Times"), Oct. 16, 1979.
MISSION PRAYER INTENTION: For the Church in Malaysia, where Christians experience particular difficulties because of restrictions on the right to practice their religion. Malaysia ceased to be a missionary territory officially in 1973.

OCTOBER 1983

1—Sat. St. Therese of the Child Jesus, virgin; memorial.
2—**Twenty-Seventh Sunday of the Year.** (Hb. 1:2-3 and 2:2-4; 2 Tm. 1:6-8, 13-14; Lk. 17:5-10.) [Guardian Angels; memorial.]
3—Mon. Weekday.
4—Tues. St. Francis of Assisi; memorial.
5—Wed. Weekday.
6—Thurs. Weekday. St. Bruno, priest; optional memorial.
7—Fri. Our Lady of the Rosary; memorial.
8—Sat. Weekday.
9—**Twenty-Eighth Sunday of the Year.** (2 Kgs. 5:14-17; 2 Tm. 2:8-13; Lk. 17:11-19.) [Sts. Denis, bishop, and Companions, martyrs, or St. John Leonard, priest; optional memorials.]
10—Mon. Weekday.
11—Tues. Weekday.
12—Wed. Weekday.
13—Thurs. Weekday.
14—Fri. Weekday. St. Callistus I, pope-martyr; optional memorial.
15—Sat. St. Teresa of Avila, virgin-doctor; memorial.
16—**Twenty-Ninth Sunday of the Year.** (Ex. 17:8-13; 2 Tm. 3:14 to 4:2; Lk. 18:1-8.) [St. Hedwig, religious, or St. Margaret Mary Alacoque, virgin; optional memorials.]
17—Mon. St. Ignatius of Antioch, bishop-martyr; memorial.
18—Tues. St. Luke, evangelist; feast.
19—Wed. Sts. Isaac Jogues, John de Brebeuf, priests, and Companions, martyrs; memorial (in U.S.). Weekday. St. Paul of the Cross; optional memorial.
20—Thurs. Weekday.
21—Fri. Weekday.
22—Sat. Weekday.
23—**Thirtieth Sunday of the Year.** (Sir. 35:12-14, 16-18; 2 Tm. 4:6-8, 16-18; Lk. 18:9-14.) [St. John of Capistrano, priest; optional memorial.]
24—Mon. Weekday. St. Anthony Mary Claret, bishop; optional memorial.
25—Tues. Weekday.
26—Wed. Weekday.
27—Thurs. Weekday.
28—Fri. Sts. Simon and Jude, apostles; feast.
29—Sat. Weekday.
30—**Thirty-First Sunday of the Year.** (Wis. 11:23 to 12:2; 2 Thes. 1:11 to 2:2; Lk. 19:1-10.)
31—Mon. Weekday.
GENERAL PRAYER INTENTION: For the 1983 assembly of the Synod of Bishops and its success in deliberations and actions on the theme, "Reconciliation and Penance in the Ministry of the Church."
MISSION PRAYER INTENTION: For missionaries who suffer for the faith.

NOVEMBER 1983

1—**Tues. All Saints; solemnity. Holy day of obligation.** (Rv. 7:2-4, 9-14; 1 Jn. 3:1-3; Mt. 5:1-12a.)

2—Wed. Commemoration of All the Faithful Departed (All Souls' Day). Three Masses proper.

3—Thurs. Weekday. St. Martin de Porres, religious; optional memorial.

4—Fri. St. Charles Borromeo, bishop; memorial.

5—Sat. Weekday.

6—**Thirty-Second Sunday of the Year.** (2 Mc. 7:1-2, 9-14; 2 Thes. 2:16 to 3:5; Lk. 20:27-38.)

7—Mon. Weekday.

8—Tues. Weekday.

9—Wed. Dedication of St. John Lateran (Archbasilica of Most Holy Savior); feast.

10—Thurs. St. Leo the Great, pope-doctor; memorial.

11—Fri. St. Martin of Tours, bishop; memorial.

12—Sat. St. Josaphat, bishop-martyr; memorial.

13—**Thirty-Third Sunday of the Year.** (Mal. 3:19-20a; 2 Thes. 3:7-12; Lk. 21:5-19.) [St. Frances Xavier Cabrini, virgin; memorial (in U.S.).]

14—Mon. Weekday.

15—Tues. Weekday. St. Albert the Great, bishop-doctor; optional memorial.

16—Wed. Weekday. St. Margaret of Scotland, or St. Gertrude, virgin; optional memorials.

17—Thurs. St. Elizabeth of Hungary, religious; memorial.

18—Fri. Weekday. Dedication of Basilicas of Sts. Peter and Paul, apostles; optional memorial.

19—Sat. Weekday.

20—**Sun. Christ the King; solemnity.** (2 Sm. 5:1-3; Col. 1:12-20; Lk. 23:35-43.)

21—Mon. Presentation of Blessed Mary the Virgin; memorial. (Thirty-Fourth (last) Week of the Year.)

22—Tues. St. Cecilia, virgin-martyr; memorial. (Thirty-Fourth (last) Week of the Year.)

23—Wed. Weekday. St. Clement I, pope-martyr, or St. Columban, abbot; optional memorials.

24—Thurs. Thanksgiving Day Votive Mass (in U.S.). Weekday.

25—Fri. Weekday.

26—Sat. Weekday.

27—**First Sunday of Advent.** (Is. 2:1-5; Rom. 13:11-14; Mt. 24:37-44.)

28—Mon. Weekday.

29—Tues. Weekday.

30—Wed. St. Andrew, apostle; feast.

PRAYER INTENTIONS: For victory over terrorism and freedom in Albania.

DECEMBER 1983

1—Thurs. Weekday of Advent.

2—Fri. Weekday of Advent.

3—Sat. St. Francis Xavier, priest; memorial.

4—**Second Sunday of Advent.** (Is. 11:1-10; Rom. 15:4-9; Mt. 3:1-12.) [St. John Damascene, priest-doctor; optional memorial.]

5—Mon. Weekday of Advent.

6—Tues. Weekday of Advent. St. Nicholas, bishop; optional memorial.

7—Wed. St. Ambrose, bishop-doctor; memorial.

8—**Thurs. Immaculate Conception of Blessed Mary the Virgin; solemnity. Holy day of obligation.** (Gn. 3:9-15, 20; Eph. 1:3-6, 11-12; Lk. 1:26-38.)

9—Fri. Weekday of Advent.

10—Sat. Weekday of Advent.

11—**Third Sunday of Advent.** (Is. 35:1-6a, 10; Jas. 5:7-10; Mt. 11:2-11.) [St. Damasus I, pope; optional memorial.]

12—Mon. Our Lady of Guadalupe; memorial (in U.S.). Weekday. St. Jane Frances de Chantal, religious; optional memorial.

13—Tues. St. Lucy, virgin-martyr; memorial.

14—Wed. St. John of the Cross, priest-doctor; memorial.

15—Thurs. Weekday of Advent.

16—Fri. Weekday of Advent.

17—Sat. Weekday of Advent.

18—**Fourth Sunday of Advent.** (Is. 7:10-14; Rom. 1:1-7; Mt. 1:18-24.)

19—Mon. Weekday of Advent.

20—Tues. Weekday of Advent.

21—Wed. Weekday of Advent. [St. Peter Canisius, priest-doctor; optional memorial.]

22—Thurs. Weekday of Advent.

23—Fri. Weekday of Advent. [St. John of Kanty, priest; optional memorial.]

24—Sat. Weekday of Advent.

25—**Sun. Christmas. Birth of the Lord; solemnity.** (Midnight — Is. 9:1-6; Ti. 2:11-14; Lk. 2:1-14. Dawn — Is. 62:11-12; Ti. 3:4-7; Lk. 2:15-20. During the Day — Is. 52:7-10; Heb. 1:1-6; Jn. 1:1-18.)

26—Mon. St. Stephen, first martyr; feast.

27—Tues. St. John, apostle-evangelist; feast.

28—Wed. Holy Innocents, martyrs; feast.

29—Thurs. Fifth Day of Christmas Octave. St. Thomas Becket, bishop-martyr; optional memorial.

30—Fri. Holy Family; feast.

31—Sat. Seventh Day of Christmas Octave. St. Sylvester I, pope; optional memorial.

GENERAL PRAYER INTENTION: For the elimination of atomic weapons in all nations. This intention has been a recurrent theme of talks and of formal addresses by the Pope to responsible leaders of government.

MISSION PRAYER INTENTION: For respect for workers in the Third World.

TABLE OF MOVABLE FEASTS

Year	Ash Wednesday	Easter	Ascension	Pentecost	Weeks of Ordinary Time				First Sunday of Advent
					Before Lent		After Pent.		
					Week	Ends	Week	Begins	
1983	Feb. 16	Apr. 3	May 12	May 22	6	Feb. 15	8	May 23	Nov. 27
1984	Mar. 7	Apr. 22	May 31	June 10	9	Mar. 6	10	June 11	Dec. 2
1985	Feb. 20	Apr. 7	May 16	May 26	6	Feb. 19	8	May 27	Dec. 1
1986	Feb. 12	Mar. 30	May 8	May 18	5	Feb. 11	7	May 19	Nov. 30
1987	Mar. 4	Apr. 19	May 28	June 7	9	Mar. 3	10	June 8	Nov. 29
1988	Feb. 17	Apr. 3	May 12	May 22	6	Feb. 16	8	May 23	Nov. 27
1989	Feb. 8	Mar. 26	May 4	May 14	5	Feb. 7	6	May 15	Dec. 3
1990	Feb. 28	Apr. 15	May 24	June 3	8	Feb. 27	9	June 4	Dec. 2
1991	Feb. 13	Mar. 31	May 9	May 19	5	Feb. 12	7	May 20	Dec. 1
1992	Mar. 4	Apr. 19	May 28	June 7	9	Mar. 3	10	June 8	Nov. 29
1993	Feb.24	Apr. 11	May 20	May 30	7	Feb. 23	9	May 31	Nov. 28
1994	Feb. 16	Apr. 3	May 12	May 22	6	Feb. 15	8	May 23	Nov. 27
1995	Mar. 1	Apr. 16	May 25	June 4	8	Feb. 28	9	June 5	Dec. 3
1996	Feb. 21	Apr. 7	May 16	May 26	7	Feb. 20	8	May 27	Dec. 1
1997	Feb. 12	Mar. 30	May 8	May 18	5	Feb. 11	7	May 19	Nov. 30
1998	Feb. 25	Apr. 12	May 21	May 31	7	Feb. 24	9	June 1	Nov. 29
1999	Feb. 17	Apr. 4	May 13	May 23	6	Feb. 16	8	May 24	Nov. 28
2000	Mar. 8	Apr. 23	June 1	June 11	9	Mar. 7	10	June 12	Dec. 3
2001	Feb. 28	Apr. 15	May 24	June 3	8	Feb. 27	9	June 4	Dec. 2
2002	Feb. 13	Mar. 31	May 9	May 19	5	Feb. 12	7	May 20	Dec. 1
2003	Mar. 5	Apr. 20	May 29	June 8	8	Mar. 4	10	June 9	Nov. 30
2004	Feb. 25	Apr. 11	May 20	May 30	7	Feb. 24	9	May 31	Nov. 28
2005	Feb. 9	Mar. 27	May 5	May 15	5	Feb. 8	7	May 16	Nov. 27
2006	Mar. 1	Apr. 16	May 25	June 4	8	Feb. 28	9	June 5	Dec. 3

Season of Ordinary Time

Weeks between the end of Christmastide and the beginning of Lent, and from the day after Pentecost to the last Sunday of the liturgical year, belong to the season of Ordinary Time. The table indicates the number and terminal date of the week ending the first part, and the number and starting date of the week beginning the second part, of this season. In some years, a week of this season is eliminated because of calendar conditions.

Holiday Masses

Liturgical experiments in recent years have led to the development of votive Masses for national holidays, like those introduced in the U.S. for Thanksgiving Day in 1969 and July 4 in 1972. This development is in line with a custom whereby "from the earliest times the Church has crowned many non-Christian feasts with Christian fulfillment by instituting its own liturgical festivals" to coincide with them.

Labor Day, in lieu of a special votive Mass, may be observed with celebration of the Mass of St. Joseph the Worker.

Readings at Mass

The texts of scriptural readings for Mass on Sundays, holy days and some other days are indicated under the respective dates. The third (C) cycle of readings in the Lectionary is prescribed for the 1983 liturgical year (Nov. 28, 1982, to Nov. 26, 1983); the first (A) cycle is prescribed for the 1984 liturgical year which begins with the first Sunday of Advent, Nov. 27, 1983.

Weekday cycles of readings are the first and second, respectively, for liturgical years 1983 and 1984.

Monthly Prayer Intentions

General and mission intentions chosen and recommended by Pope John Paul II to the prayers of the Apostles of Prayer are given under each month of the 1983 calendar. He has expressed his desire that all Catholics make these intentions their own "in the certainty of being united with the Holy Father and praying according to his intentions and desires." These intentions represent the worldwide needs of the Church and its missions as seen through the eyes of the Pope.

HOLY DAYS, OTHER FEASTS

The following list includes the six holy days of obligation observed in the United States and additional observances of devotional and historical significance. The dignity or rank of observances is indicated by the terms: **solemnity** (highest in rank, the equivalent of former first class feasts): **feast** (equivalent to former second class feasts); **memorial** (equivalent to former third class feasts, for universal observance); **optional memorial** (for celebration by choice).

All Saints, Nov. 1, holy day of obligation, solemnity. Commemorates all the blessed in heaven, and is intended particularly to honor the blessed who have no special feasts. The background of the feast dates to the fourth century when groups of martyrs, and later other saints, were honored on a common day in various places. In 609 or 610, the Pantheon, a pagan temple at Rome, was consecrated as a Christian church for the honor of Our Lady and the martyrs (later all saints). In 835, Gregory IV fixed Nov. 1 as the date of observance.

All Souls, Commemoration of the Faithful Departed, Nov. 2 (transferable to Nov. 3). The dead were prayed for from the earliest days of Christianity. By the sixth century it was customary in Benedictine monasteries to hold a commemoration of deceased members of the order at Pentecost. A common commemoration of all the faithful departed on the day after All Saints was instituted in 998 by St. Odilo, of the Abbey of Cluny, and an observance of this kind was generally adopted throughout the Church. In 1915, Benedict XV granted priests throughout the world permission to celebrate three Masses for this commemoration. He also granted a special indulgence for the occasion.

Annunciation of the Lord (formerly, Annunciation of the Blessed Virgin Mary), Mar. 25, solemnity. A feast of the Incarnation which commemorates the announcement by the Archangel Gabriel to the Virgin Mary that she was to become the Mother of Christ (Lk. 1:26-38), and the miraculous conception of Christ by her. The feast was instituted about 430 in the East. The Roman observance dates from the seventh century, when celebration was said to be universal.

Ascension of the Lord, movable observance held 40 days after Easter, holy day of obligation, solemnity. Commemorates the Ascension of Christ into heaven 40 days after his Resurrection from the dead (Mk. 16:19; Lk. 24:51; Acts 1:2). The feast recalls the completion of Christ's mission on earth for the salvation of men and his entry into heaven with glorified human nature. The Ascension is a pledge of the final glorification of all who achieve salvation. Documentary evidence of the feast dates from early in the fifth century, but it was observed long before that time in connection with Pentecost and Easter.

Ash Wednesday, movable observance, six and one-half weeks before Easter. It was set as the first day of Lent by St. Gregory the Great (590-604) with the extension of an earlier and shorter penitential season to a total period including 40 weekdays of fasting before Easter. Ashes, symbolic of penance, are blessed and distributed among the faithful during the day. They are used to mark the forehead with the Sign of the Cross, with the reminder: "Remember, man, that you are dust, and unto dust you shall return," or: "Repent, and believe the Good News."

Assumption Aug. 15, holy day of obligation, solemnity. Commemorates the taking into heaven of Mary, soul and body, at the end of her life on earth, a truth of faith that was proclaimed a dogma by Pius XII on Nov. 1, 1950. One of the oldest and most solemn feasts of Mary, it has a history dating back to at least the seventh century when its celebration was already established at Jerusalem and Rome.

Baptism of the Lord, movable, celebrated on the Sunday after Epiphany, feast. Recalls the baptism of Christ by John the Baptist (Mk. 1:9-11), an event associated with the liturgy of the Epiphany. This baptism was the occasion for Christ's manifestation of Himself at the beginning of his public life.

Birth of Mary, Sept. 8, feast. This is a very old feast which originated in the East and found place in the Roman liturgy in the seventh century.

Candlemas Day, Feb. 2. See Presentation of the Lord.

Chair of Peter, Feb. 22, feast. Commemorates establishment of the see of Antioch by Peter. The feast, which has been in the Roman calendar since 336, is a liturgical expression of belief in the episcopacy and hierarchy of the Church.

Christmas, Birth of Our Lord Jesus Christ, Dec. 25, holy day of obligation, solemnity. Commemorates the birth of Christ (Lk. 2:1-20). This event was originally commemorated in the East on the feast of Epiphany or Theophany. The Christmas feast itself originated in the West; by 354 it was certainly kept on Dec. 25. This date may have been set for the observance to offset pagan ceremonies held at about the same time to commemorate the birth of the sun at the winter solstice. Priests may celebrate three Masses on Christmas Day. Christmastide begins with this feast and continues until the Sunday after Epiphany.

Christ the King, movable, celebrated on the last Sunday of the liturgical year, solemnity. Commemorates the royal prerogatives of Christ and is equivalent to a declaration of his rights to the homage, service and fidelity of men in all phases of individual and social life. Pius XI instituted the feast Dec. 11, 1925.

Corpus Christi, movable observance held in

the US on the Sunday following Trinity Sunday, solemnity. Commemorates the institution of the Holy Eucharist (Mt. 26:26-28). The feast originated at Liege in 1246 and was extended throughout the Church in the West by Urban IV in 1264. St. Thomas Aquinas composed the Office for the feast.

Dedication of St. John Lateran, Nov. 9, feast. Commemorates the first public consecration of a church, that of the Basilica of the Most Holy Savior by Pope St. Sylvester Nov. 9, 324. The church, as well as the Lateran Palace, was the gift of Emperor Constantine. Since the 12th century it has been known as St. John Lateran, in honor of John the Baptist after whom the adjoining baptistery was named. It was rebuilt by Innocent X (1644-55), reconsecrated by Benedict XIII in 1726, and enlarged by Leo XIII (1878-1903). This basilica is regarded as the church of highest dignity in Rome and throughout the Roman Rite.

Dedication of St. Mary Major, Aug. 5, optional memorial. Commemorates the rebuilding and dedication by Sixtus III (432-40) of a church in honor of Blessed Mary the Virgin. This is the Basilica of St. Mary Major on the Esquiline Hill in Rome. An earlier building was erected during the pontificate of Liberius (352-66); according to legend, it was located on a site covered by a miraculous fall of snow seen by a nobleman favored with a vision of Mary.

Easter, movable celebration held on the first Sunday after the full moon following the vernal equinox (between Mar. 22 and Apr. 25), solemnity with an octave. Commemorates the Resurrection of Christ from the dead (Mk. 16:1-7). The observance of this mystery, kept since the first days of the Church, extends throughout the Easter season which lasts until the feast of Pentecost, a period of 50 days. Every Sunday in the year is regarded as a "little" Easter. The date of Easter determines the dates of other movable feasts, such as Ascension and Pentecost, and the number of Sundays after Epiphany and Pentecost.

Easter Vigil (Holy Saturday), day before Easter. Ceremonies are all related to the Resurrection and renewal-in-grace theme of Easter: blessing of the new fire and Paschal Candle, reading of prophecies, blessing of water and the baptismal font, the baptism of converts and renewal of baptismal vows by the faithful, the Litany of the Saints, and the celebration of Mass. The vigil ceremonies are held after sundown, preferably at a time that makes possible the celebration of Mass at midnight.

Epiphany of Our Lord, Jan. 6 or (in the US) a Sunday between Jan. 2 and 8, solemnity. Commemorates the manifestations of the divinity of Christ. It is one of the oldest Christian feasts, with an Eastern origin traceable to the beginning of the third century and antedating the Western feast of Christmas. Originally, it commemorated the manifestations of Christ's divinity — or Theophany — in his birth, the homage of the Magi, and baptism by John the Baptist. Later, the first two of these commemorations were transferred to Christmas when the Eastern Church adopted that feast between 380 and 430. The central feature of the Eastern observance now is the manifestation or declaration of Christ's divinity in his baptism and at the beginning of his public life. The Epiphany was adopted by the Western Church during the same period in which the Eastern Church accepted Christmas. In the Roman Rite, commemoration is made in the Mass of the homage of the wise men from the East (Mt. 2:1-12).

Good Friday, the Friday before Easter, privileged feria of Holy Week. Liturgical elements of the observance are commemoration of the Passion and Death of Christ in the reading of the Passion (according to John), special prayers for the Church and people of all ranks, the veneration of the Cross, and a Communion service. The Solemn Liturgical Action takes place between noon and 9 p.m. This is the only day in the year on which the Eucharistic Liturgy is not celebrated in the Roman Rite.

Guardian Angels, Oct. 2, memorial. Commemorates the angels who protect men from spiritual and physical dangers and assist them in doing good. A feast in their honor celebrated in Spain in the 16th century was extended to the whole Church by Paul V in 1608. In 1670, Clement X set Oct. 2 as the date of observance. Earlier, guardian angels were honored liturgically in conjunction with the feast of St. Michael.

Holy Family, movable observance on the Sunday after Christmas, feast. Commemorates the Holy Family of Jesus, Mary and Joseph as the model of domestic society, holiness and virtue. The devotional background of the feast was very strong in the 17th century. In the 18th century, in prayers composed for a special Mass, a Canadian bishop likened the Christian family to the Holy Family. Leo XIII consecrated families to the Holy Family. In 1921, Benedict XV extended the Divine Office and Mass of the feast to the whole Church.

Holy Innocents, Dec. 28, feast. Commemorates the infants who suffered death at the hands of Herod's soldiers seeking to kill the child Jesus (Mt. 2:13-18). A feast has been observed since the fifth century.

Holy Thursday, the Thursday before Easter, privileged feria of Holy Week. Commemorates the institution of the Holy Eucharist (which is later celebrated on the special feast of Corpus Christi) and other events of the Last Supper. Ceremonies include the celebration of a principal Mass between 4 and 9 p.m., the washing of feet in imitation of the act of Christ who washed the feet of the Apostles at the Last Supper, the stripping of the altar at the conclusion of Mass. There is also a procession of the Blessed Sacrament to a special place of reposition where It is reserved for veneration by the faithful until the Solemn Liturgical Action on Good Friday. At a special Mass of Chrism, bishops bless oils (of catechumens, chrism, of the sick) for use during the year.

Immaculate Conception, Dec. 8, holy day of obligation, solemnity. Commemorates the fact that Mary, in view of her calling to be the Mother of Christ and in virtue of his merits, was preserved from the first moment of her conception from original sin and was filled with grace from the very beginning of her life. She was the only person so preserved from original sin. The present form of the feast dates from Dec. 8, 1854, when Pius IX defined the dogma of the Immaculate Conception. An earlier feast of the Conception, which testified to long-existing belief in this truth, was observed in the East by the eighth century, in Ireland in the ninth, and subsequently in European countries. In 1846, Mary was proclaimed patroness of the US under this title.

Immaculate Heart of Mary, Saturday following the second Sunday after Pentecost, optional memorial. On May 4, 1944, Pius XII ordered this feast observed throughout the Church in order to obtain Mary's intercession for "peace among nations, freedom for the Church, the conversion of sinners, the love of purity and the practice of virtue." Two years earlier, he consecrated the entire human race to Mary under this title. Devotion to Mary under the title of her Most Pure Heart originated during the Middle Ages. It was given great impetus in the 17th century by the preaching of St. John Eudes, who was the first to celebrate a Mass and Divine Office of Mary under this title. A feast, celebrated in various places and on different dates, was authorized in 1799.

Joachim and Ann, July 26, memorial. Commemorates the parents of Mary. A joint feast, celebrated Sept. 9, originated in the East near the end of the sixth century. Devotion to Ann, introduced in the eighth century at Rome, became widespread in Europe in the 14th century; her feast was extended throughout the Latin Church in 1584. A feast of Joachim was introduced in the West in the 15th century.

John the Baptist, Birth, June 24, solemnity. The precursor of Christ, whose cousin he was, was commemorated universally in the liturgy by the fourth century. He is the only saint, except the Blessed Virgin Mary, whose birthday is observed as a feast. Another feast, on Aug. 29, commemorates his passion and death at the order of Herod (Mk. 6:14-29).

Joseph, Mar. 19, solemnity. Joseph is honored as the husband of the Blessed Virgin Mary, the patron and protector of the universal Church and workman. Devotion to him already existed in the eighth century in the East, and in the 11th in the West. Various feasts were celebrated before the 15th century when Mar. 19 was fixed for his commemoration; this feast was extended to the whole Church in 1621 by Gregory XV. In 1955, Pius XII instituted the feast of St. Joseph the Workman for observance May 1; this feast, which may be celebrated by local option, supplanted the Solemnity or Patronage of St. Joseph formerly observed on the third Wednesday after Easter. St. Joseph was proclaimed protector and patron of the universal Church in 1870 by Pius IX.

Michael, Gabriel and Raphael, Archangels, Sept. 29, feast. A feast bearing the title of Dedication of St. Michael the Archangel formerly commemorated on this date the consecration in 530 of a church near Rome in honor of Michael, the first angel given a liturgical feast. For a while, this feast was combined with a commemoration of the Guardian Angels. The separate feasts of Gabriel (Mar. 24) and Raphael (Oct. 24) were suppressed by the calendar reform of 1969 and this joint feast of the three archangels was instituted.

Octave of Christmas, Jan. 1. See Solemnity of Mary, Mother of God.

Our Lady of Sorrows, Sept. 15, memorial. Recalls the sorrows experienced by Mary in her association with Christ: the prophecy of Simeon (Lk. 2:34-35), the flight into Egypt (Mt. 2:13-21), the three-day separation from Jesus (Lk. 2:41-50), and four incidents connected with the Passion: her meeting with Christ on the way to Calvary, the crucifixion, the removal of Christ's body from the cross, and his burial (Mt. 27:31-61; Mk. 15:20-47; Lk. 23:26-56; Jn. 19:17-42). A Mass and Divine Office of the feast were celebrated by the Servites, especially, in the 17th century, and in 1817 Pius VII extended the observance to the whole Church.

Our Lady of the Rosary, Oct. 7, memorial. Commemorates the Virgin Mary through recall of the mysteries of the Rosary which recapitulate events in her life and the life of Christ. The feast was instituted to commemorate a Christian victory over invading Mohammedan forces at Lepanto on Oct. 7, 1571, and was extended throughout the Church by Clement XI in 1716.

Passion (Palm) Sunday, the Sunday before Easter. Recalls the triumphal entry of Christ into Jerusalem at the beginning of the last week of his life (Mt. 21:1-9). A procession and other ceremonies commemorating this event were held in Jerusalem from very early Christian times and were adopted in Rome by the ninth century, when the blessing of palm for the occasion was introduced. Full liturgical observance includes the blessing of palm and a procession before the principal Mass of the day. The Passion, by Matthew, Mark or Luke, is read during the Mass.

Pentecost, also called **Whitsunday,** movable celebration held 50 days after Easter, solemnity. Commemorates the descent of the Holy Spirit upon the Apostles, the preaching of Peter and the other Apostles to Jews in Jerusalem, the baptism and aggregation of some 3,000 persons to the Christian community (Acts 2:1-41). It is regarded as the birthday of the Catholic Church. The original observance of the feast antedated the earliest extant documentary evidence from the third century.

Peter and Paul, June 29, solemnity. Commemorates the dual martyrdom of Peter by crucifixion and Paul by beheading during the Neronian persecution. This joint commemoration of the two greatest Apostles dates at least from 258 at Rome.

Presentation of the Lord (formerly called Purification of the Blessed Virgin Mary, also Candlemas), Feb. 2, feast. Commemorates the presentation of Jesus in the Temple — according to prescriptions of Mosaic Law (Lv. 12:2-8; Ex. 13:2; Lk. 2:22-32) — and the purification of Mary 40 days after his birth. In the East, where the feast antedated fourth century testimony regarding its existence, it was observed primarily as a feast of Our Lord; in the West, where it was adopted later, it was regarded more as a feast of Mary until the calendar reform of 1969. Its date was set for Feb. 2 after the celebration of Christmas was fixed for Dec. 25, late in the fourth century. The blessing of candles, probably in commemoration of Christ who was the Light to enlighten the Gentiles, became common about the 11th century and gave the feast the secondary name of Candlemas.

Queenship of Mary, Aug. 22, memorial. Commemorates the high dignity of Mary as Queen of heaven, angels and men. Universal observance of the memorial was ordered by Pius XII in the encyclical *Ad Caeli Reginam* Oct. 11, 1954, near the close of a Marian Year observed in connection with the centenary of the proclamation of the dogma of the Immaculate Conception and four years after the proclamation of the dogma of the Assumption. The original date of the memorial was May 31.

Resurrection. See Easter.

Sacred Heart of Jesus, movable observance held on the Friday after Corpus Christi, solemnity. The object of the devotion is the divine Person of Christ, whose heart is the symbol of his love for men — for whom he accomplished the work of Redemption. The Mass and Office now used on the feast were prescribed by Pius XI in 1929. Devotion to the Sacred Heart was introduced into the liturgy in the 17th century through the efforts of St. John Eudes who composed an Office and Mass for the feast. It was furthered as the result of the revelations of St. Margaret Mary Alacoque after 1675 and by the work of Claude de la Colombiere, S.J. In 1765, Clement XIII approved a Mass and Office for the feast, and in 1856 Pius IX extended the observance throughout the Roman Rite.

Solemnity of Mary, Mother of God, Jan. 1, holy day of obligation, solemnity. The calendar reform of 1969, in accord with Eastern tradition, reinstated the Marian character of this commemoration on the octave day of Christmas. The former feast of the Circumcision, dating at least from the first half of the sixth century, marked the initiation of Jesus (Lk. 2:21) in Judaism and by analogy focused attention on the initiation of persons in the Christian religion and their incorporation in Christ through baptism. The feast of the Solemnity supplants the former feast of the Maternity of Mary observed on Oct. 11.

Transfiguration of the Lord, Aug. 6, feast. Commemorates the revelation of his divinity by Christ to Peter, James and John on Mt. Tabor (Mt. 17:1-9). The feast, which is very old, was extended throughout the universal Church in 1457 by Callistus III.

Trinity, Most Holy, movable observance held on the Sunday after Pentecost, solemnity. Commemorates the most sublime mystery of the Christian faith, i.e., that there are Three Divine Persons — Father, Son and Holy Spirit — in one God (Mt. 28:18-20). A votive Mass of the Most Holy Trinity dates from the seventh century; an Office was composed in the 10th century; in 1334, John XXII extended the feast to the universal Church.

Triumph of the Cross, Sept. 14, feast. Commemorates the finding of the cross on which Christ was crucified, in 326 through the efforts of St. Helena, mother of Constantine; the consecration of the Basilica of the Holy Sepulchre nearly 10 years later: and the recovery in 628 or 629 by Emperor Heraclius of a major portion of the cross which had been removed by the Persians from its place of veneration at Jerusalem. The feast originated in Jerusalem and spread through the East before being adopted in the West. General adoption followed the building at Rome of the Basilica of the Holy Cross "in Jerusalem," so called because it was the place of enshrinement of a major portion of the cross of crucifixion.

Visitation, May 31, feast. Commemorates Mary's visit to her cousin Elizabeth after the Annunciation and before the birth of John the Baptist, the precursor of Christ (Lk. 1:39-47). The feast had a medieval origin and was observed in the Franciscan Order before being extended throughout the Church by Urban VI in 1389. It is one of the feasts of the Incarnation and is notable for its recall of the Magnificat, one of the few New Testament canticles, which acknowledges the unique gifts of God to Mary because of her role in the redemptive work of Christ. The canticle is recited at Vespers in the Liturgy of the Hours.

SAINTS

Biographical sketches of additional saints are under other Almanac titles. See Index.

An asterisk with a feast date indicates that a memorial or feast is observed according to the revised Roman-Rite calendar.

Adjutor, St. (d. 1131): Norman knight; fought in First Crusade; monk-recluse after his return; legendary accounts of incidents on journey to Crusade probably account for his patronage of yachtsmen; Apr. 30.

Agatha, St. (d. c. 250): Sicilian virgin-martyr; her intercession credited in Sicily with stopping eruptions of Mt. Etna; patron of nurses; Feb. 5*.

Agnes, St. (d. c. 304): Roman virgin-martyr; martyred at age of 10 or 12; patron of young girls; Jan. 21*.

Aloysius Gonzaga, St. (1568-1591): Italian Jesuit; died while nursing plague-stricken; canonized 1726; patron of youth; June 21*.

Amand, St. (d. c. 676): Apostle of Belgium; b. France; established monasteries throughout Belgium; Feb. 6.

Andre Grasset de Saint Sauveur, Bl. (1758-1792): Canadian priest; martyred in France, Sept. 2, 1792, during the Revolution; one of a group called the Martyrs of Paris who were beatified in 1926; Sept. 2.

Andrew Corsini, St. (1302-1373): Italian Carmelite; bishop of Fiesoli; mediator between quarrelsome Italian states; canonized 1629; Feb. 4.

Andrew Fournet, St. (1752-1834): French priest; co-founder with St. Jeanne Elizabeth des Anges of the Congregation of Daughters of the Cross; canonized 1933; May 13.

Angela Merici, St. (1474-1540): Italian nun; foundress of Institute of St. Ursula, 1535, the first teaching order of nuns in the Church; canonized 1807; Jan. 27*.

Anne Mary Javouhey, Bl. (1779-1851): French virgin; foundress of Institute of St. Joseph of Cluny, 1812; beatified 1950; July 15.

Ansgar, St. (801-865): Bishop, Benedictine monk; b. near Amiens; missionary in Denmark, Sweden, Norway and Northern Germany; apostle of Denmark; Feb. 3*.

Anthony Abbot, St. (c. 251-c. 354): Egyptian hermit; patriarch of all monks; established communities for hermits which became models for monastic life, especially in the East; friend and supporter of St. Athanasius in the latter's struggle with the Arians; Jan. 17*.

Anthony Mary Claret, St. (1807-1870): Spanish priest; founder of Missionary Sons of the Immaculate Heart of Mary (Claretians), 1849; archbishop of Santiago, Cuba, 1851-57; canonized 1950; Oct. 24*.

Anthony Mary Zaccaria, St. (1502-1539): Italian priest; founder of Barnabites (Clerks Regular of St. Paul), 1530; canonized 1897; July 5*.

Apollonia, St. (d. 249): Deaconess of Alexandria; martyred during persecution of Decius; her patronage of dentists probably rests on tradition that her teeth were broken by pincers by her persecutors; Feb. 9.

Augustine of Canterbury, St. (d. 604 or 605): Italian missionary; apostle of the English; sent by Pope Gregory I with 40 monks to evangelize England; arrived there 597; first archbishop of Canterbury; May 27*.

Benedict of Nursia, St. (c. 480-547): Abbot; founder of monasticism in Western Europe; established monastery at Monte Cassino; proclaimed patron of Europe by Paul VI in 1964; July 11*.

Benedict the Black (il Moro), St. (1526-1589): Sicilian Franciscan; born a slave; joined Franciscans as lay brother; appointed guardian and novice master; canonized 1807; Apr. 4.

Bernadette Soubirous, St. (1844-1879): French peasant girl favored with series of visions of Blessed Virgin Mary at Lourdes (see Lourdes Apparitions); joined Institute of Sisters of Notre Dame at Nevers, 1866; canonized 1933; Apr. 16.

Bernard of Menthon, St. (d. 1081): Italian priest; founded Alpine hospices near the two passes named for him; patron of mountaineers; May 28.

Bernardine of Feltre, Bl. (1439-1494): Italian Franciscan preacher; a founder of montes pietatis; Sept. 28.

Bernardine of Siena, St. (1380-1444): Italian Franciscan; noted preacher and missioner; spread of devotion to Holy Name is attributed to him; represented in art holding to his breast the monogram IHS; canonized 1450; May 20*.

Blase, St. (d. c. 316): Armenian bishop; martyr; the blessing of throats on his feast day derives from tradition that he miraculously saved the life of a boy who had half-swallowed a fish bone; Feb. 3*.

Boniface (Winfrid), St. (d. 754): English Benedictine; bishop, martyr; apostle of Germany; established monastery at Fulda which became center of German missionary work; archbishop of Mainz; martyred near Dukkum in Holland; June 5*.

Brendan, St. (c. 489-583): Irish abbot; founded monasteries; his patronage of sailors probably rests on tradition that he made a seven-year voyage in search of a fabled paradise; called Brendan the Navigator; May 16.

Bridget (Brigid), St. (c. 450-525): Irish nun; founded nunnery at Kildare, the first erected on Irish soil; patron, with Sts. Patrick and Columba, of Ireland; Feb. 1.

Bridget (Birgitta), St. (c. 1303-1373): Swedish mystic; widow; foundress of Order of Our Savior (Brigittines); canonized 1391; wrote

Revelationes, accounts of her visions; patroness of Sweden; July 23*.

Bruno, St. (1030-1101): German monk; founded Carthusians, 1084, in France; Oct. 6*.

Cabrini, Mother: See Index.

Cajetan of Thiene, St. (1480-1547): Italian lawyer; religious reformer; a founder of Oratory of Divine Love, forerunner of the Theatines; canonized 1671; Aug. 7*.

Callistus I, St. (d. 222): Pope, 217-222; martyr; condemned Sabellianism and other heresies; advocated a policy of mercy toward repentant sinners; Oct. 14*.

Camillus de Lellis, St. (1550-1614): Italian priest; founder of Camillians (Ministers of the Sick); canonized 1746; patron of the sick and of nurses; July 14*.

Casimir, St. (1458-1484): Polish prince; grand duke of Lithuania; noted for his piety; buried at cathedral in Vilna, Lithuania; canonized 1521; patron of Poland and Lithuania; Mar. 4*.

Cassian, St. (d. 298): Roman martyr; an official court stenographer who declared himself a Christian; patron of stenographers; Dec. 3.

Catherine Laboure, St. (1806-1876): French nun; favored with series of visions; first Miraculous Medal (see Index) struck as the result of one of the visions; canonized 1947; Dec. 31.

Catherine of Bologna, St. (1413-1463): Italian Poor Clare; mystic, writer, artist; canonized 1712; patron of artists; Mar. 9.

Cecilia, St. (2nd-3rd century): Roman virgin-martyr; traditional patron of musicians; Nov. 22*.

Charles Borromeo, St. (1538-1584): Italian cardinal; nephew of Pope Pius IV; cardinal bishop of Milan; influential figure in Church reform in Italy; promoted education of clergy; canonized 1610; Nov. 4*.

Charles Lwanga and Companions, Sts. (d. 1886 and 1887): Martyrs of Uganda; pages of King Mwanga of Uganda; Charles Lwanga and 12 companions were martyred near Rubaga, June 3, 1886; the other nine were martyred between May 26, 1886, and Jan. 27, 1887; canonized 1964; first martyrs of black Africa; June 3*.

Christopher, St. (3rd cent.): Early Christian martyr inscribed in Roman calendar about 1550; feast relegated to particular calendars because of legendary nature of accounts of his life; traditional patron of travelers; July 25.

Clare, St. (1194-1253): Foundress of Poor Clares; b. at Assisi; later joined in religious life her sisters Agnes and Beatrice, and her mother Ortolana; canonized 1255; patroness of television; Aug. 11*.

Clement I, St. (d. c. 100): Pope, 88-97; third successor of St. Peter; wrote important letter to Church in Corinth settling disputes there; venerated as a martyr; Nov. 23*.

Columba, St. (521-597): Irish monk; founded monasteries in Ireland; missionary in Scotland; established monastery at Iona which became the center for conversion of Picts, Scots, and Northern English; Scotland's most famous saint; June 9.

Columban, St. (545-615): Irish monk; scholar; founded monasteries in England and Brittany (famous abbey of Luxeuil), forced into exile because of his criticism of Frankish court; spent last years in northern Italy where he founded abbey at Bobbio; Nov. 23*.

Contardo Ferrini, Bl. (1859-1902): Italian secular Franciscan; model of the Catholic professor; beatified 1947; patron of universities; Oct. 17.

Cornelius, St. (d. 253): Pope, 251-253; promoted a policy of mercy with respect to readmission of repentant Christians who had fallen away during the persecution of Decius *(lapsi);* banished from Rome during persecution of Gallus; regarded as a martyr; Sept. 16 (with Cyprian)*.

Cosmas and Damian, Sts. (d. c. 303): Arabian twin brothers; physicians who were martyred during Diocletian persecution; patrons of physicians; Sept. 26*.

Crispin and Crispinian, Sts. (3rd cent.): Early Christian martyrs; said to have met their deaths in Gaul; patrons of shoemakers, a trade they pursued; Oct. 25.

Cyprian, St. (d. 258): Early ecclesiastical writer; b. Africa; bishop of Carthage, 249-258; supported Pope St. Cornelius concerning the readmission of Christians who had apostasized in time of persecution; erred in his teaching that baptism administered by heretics and schismatics was invalid; wrote *De Unitate;* Sept. 16 (with St. Cornelius)*.

Cyril and Methodius, Sts.: Greek missionaries; brothers venerated as apostles of the Slavs; Cyril (d. 869) and Methodius (d. 885) began their missionary work in Moravia in 863; developed a Slavonic alphabet; eventually their use of the vernacular in the liturgy was approved; declared patrons of Europe with St. Benedict, Dec. 31, 1980; Feb. 14*.

Damasus I, St. (d. 384): Pope, 366-384; opposed Arians and Apollinarians; commissioned St. Jerome to work on Bible translation; developed Roman liturgy; Dec. 11*.

Damian, St.: See Cosmas and Damian, Sts.

David, St. (5th-6th cent.): Welsh monk; founded monastery at Menevia; patron saint of Wales; Mar. 1.

Denis and Companions, Sts. (d. 3rd cent.): Denis, bishop of Paris, and two companions identified by early writers as Rusticus, a priest, and Eleutherius, a deacon; martyred near Paris; Denis is popularly regarded as apostle of France; Oct. 9*.

Dismas, St. (1st cent.): Name given to repentant thief (Good Thief) to whom Jesus promised salvation; regarded as patron of prisoners; Mar. 25.

Dominic, St. (Dominic de Guzman) (1170-1221): Spanish priest; founder of Dominican Order (Friars Preachers), 1215; preached against the Albigensian heresy; a contemporary of St. Francis of Assisi; canonized 1234; Aug. 8*.

Dominic Savio, St. (1842-1857): Italian youth; pupil of St. John Bosco; died before his 15th birthday; canonized 1954; patron of choir boys; Mar. 9.

Dunstan, St. (c. 910-988): English monk; archbishop of Canterbury; initiated reforms in religious life; royal counselor to several kings; considered one of greatest Anglo-Saxon saints; patron of armorers, goldsmiths, locksmiths, jewelers; May 17.

Dymphna, St. (dates uncertain): Nothing certain known of her life; presumably she was an Irish maiden whose relics were discovered at Gheel near Antwerp, Belgium, in the 13th century; since that time many cases of mental illness and epilepsy have been cured at her shrine; patron of those suffering from mental illness; May 15.

Edmund Campion, St. (1540-1581): English Jesuit; convert 1573; martyred at Tyburn; canonized 1970, one of the Forty English and Welsh Martyrs; Dec. 1.

Elizabeth Bayley Seton, St. (1774-1821): American foundress; convert, 1805; founded Sisters of Charity in the U.S.; beatified 1963; canonized Sept. 14, 1975; the first American-born saint; Jan. 4 (U.S.)*.

Elizabeth of Hungary, St. (1207-1231): Queen; became secular Franciscan after death of her husband in 1227; devoted life to poor and destitute; a patron of the Secular Franciscan Order; Nov. 17*.

Elizabeth of Portugal, St. (1271-1336): Queen of Portugal; b. Spain; retired to Poor Clare convent as a secular Franciscan after the death of her husband; July 4*.

Erasmus, St. (d. 303): Life surrounded by legend; martyred during Diocletian persecution; patron of sailors; June 2.

Ethelbert, St. (552-676): King of Kent; baptized by St. Augustine 597; issued legal code; furthered spread of Christianity; Feb. 24.

Euphrasia Pelletier, St. (1796-1868): French nun; founded Sisters of the Good Shepherd at Angers, 1829; canonized 1940; Apr. 24.

Eusebius of Vercelli, St. (283-370): Italian bishop; exiled from his see for a time because of his opposition to Arianism; considered a martyr because of sufferings he endured; Aug. 2*.

Fabian, St. (d. 250): Pope, 236-250; martyred under Decius; Jan. 20*.

Felicity, St.: See Perpetua and Felicity, Sts.

Ferdinand III, St. (1198-1252): King of Castile and Leon; waged successful crusade against Mohammedans in Spain; founded university at Salamanca; canonized 1671; May 30.

Fiacre, St. (d. c. 670): Irish hermit; patron of gardeners; Aug. 30.

Fidelis of Sigmaringen, St. (Mark Rey) (1577-1622): German Capuchin; lawyer before he joined the Capuchins; missionary to Swiss Protestants; stabbed to death by peasants who were told he was agent of Austrian emperor; Apr. 24*.

Frances of Rome, St. (1384-1440): Italian model for housewives and widows; happily married for 40 years; after death of her husband in 1436 joined community of Benedictine Oblates she had founded; canonized 1608; patron of motorists; Mar. 9*.

Frances Xavier Cabrini, St. (Mother Cabrini) (1850-1917): American foundress; b. Italy; foundress of Missionary Sisters of the Sacred Heart, 1877; settled in the U.S. 1889; became an American citizen at Seattle 1909; worked among Italian immigrants; canonized 1946, the first American citizen so honored; Nov. 13 (U.S.)*.

Francis Borgia, St. (1510-1572): Spanish Jesuit; joined Jesuits after death of his wife in 1546; became general of the Order, 1565; Oct. 10.

Francis of Assisi, St. (Giovanni di Bernardone) (1182-1226): Founder of the Franciscans, 1209; received stigmata 1224; canonized 1228; one of best known and best loved saints; patron of Italy, Catholic Action and ecologists; Oct. 4*.

Francis of Paola, St. (1416-1507): Italian hermit: founder of Minim Friars; Apr. 2*.

Francis Xavier, St. (1506-1552): Spanish Jesuit; missionary to Far East; canonized 1602; patron of foreign missions; considered one of greatest Christian missionaries; Dec. 3*.

Gabriel of the Sorrowful Mother, St. (Francis Possenti) (1838-1862): Italian Passionist; died while a scholastic; canonized 1920; Feb. 27.

Genesius, St. (d. c. 300): Roman actor; according to legend, was converted while performing a burlesque of Christian baptism and was subsequently martyred; patron of actors.

Genevieve, St. (422-500): French nun; a patroness and protectress of Paris; events of her life not authenticated; Jan. 3.

George, St. (d. c. 300): Martyr, probably during Diocletian persecution in Palestine; all other incidents of his life, including story of the dragon, are legendary; patron of England; Apr. 23*.

Gerard Majella, St. (1725-1755): Italian Redemptorist lay brother; noted for supernatural occurrences in his life including bilocation and reading of consciences; canonized 1904; patron of mothers; Oct. 16.

Gertrude, St. (1256-1302): German mystic; writer; helped spread devotion to the Sacred Heart; Nov. 16*.

Gregory VII (Hildebrand), St. (1020?-1085): Pope, 1075-1085; Benedictine monk; adviser to several popes; as pope, strengthened interior life of Church and fought against lay investiture; driven from Rome by Henry IV; died in exile; May 25*.

Gregory the Illuminator, St. (257-332): Martyr; bishop; apostle and patron saint of Armenia; helped free Armenia from the Persians; Sept. 30.

Hedwig, St. (1174-1243): Moravian noblewoman; married duke of Silesia, head of Polish royal family; fostered religious life in country; canonized 1266; Oct. 16*.

Helena, St. (250-330): Empress; mother of Constantine the Great; associated with discovery of the True Cross; Aug. 18.

Henry, St. (972-1024): Bavarian emperor; cooperated with Benedictine abbeys in restoration of ecclesiastical and social discipline; canonized 1146; July 13*.

Hippolytus, St. (d. c. 236): Roman priest; opposed Pope St. Callistus I in his teaching about the readmission of Christians who had apostasized during time of persecution; elected antipope; reconciled before his martyrdom; important ecclesiastical writer; Aug. 13*.

Hubert, St. (d. 727): Bishop; his patronage of hunters is based on legend that he was converted while hunting; Nov. 3.

Hugh of Cluny (the Great), St. (1024-1109): Abbot of Benedictine foundation at Cluny; supported popes in efforts to reform ecclesiastical abuses; canonized 1120; Apr. 29.

Ignatius of Antioch, St. (d. c. 107): Early ecclesiastical writer; martyr; bishop of Antioch in Syria for 40 years; Oct. 17*.

Ignatius of Loyola, St. (1491-1556): Spanish soldier; renounced military career after recovering from wounds received at siege of Pampeluna (Pamplona) in 1521; founded Society of Jesus (Jesuits), 1534, at Paris; canonized 1622; author *The Book of Spiritual Exercises;* July 31*.

Irenaeus of Lyons, St. (130-202): Early ecclesiastical writer; opposed Gnosticism; bishop of Lyons; traditionally regarded as a martyr; June 28*.

Isidore the Farmer, St. (d. 1170): Spanish layman; farmer; canonized 1622; patron of farmers; May 15 (US)*.

Jane Frances de Chantal, St. (1572-1641): French widow; foundress, under guidance of St. Francis de Sales, of Order of the Visitation; canonized 1767; Dec. 12*.

Januarius (Gennaro), St. (d. 304): Bishop of Benevento; martyred during Diocletian persecution; fame rests on liquefaction of some of his blood preserved in a phial at Naples, an unexplained phenomenon which has occurred regularly several times each year for over 400 years; declared patron of Campania region around Naples, 1980; Sept. 19*.

Jerome Emiliani, St. (1481-1537): Venetian priest; founded Somascan Fathers, 1532, for care of orphans; canonized 1767; patron of orphans and abandoned children; Feb. 8*.

Joan of Arc, St. (1412-1431): French heroine, called The Maid of Orleans, La Pucelle; led French army against English invaders; captured by Burgundians, turned over to ecclesiastical court on charge of heresy, found guilty and burned at the stake; her innocence was declared in 1456; canonized 1920; patroness of France; May 30.

John I, St. (d. 526): Pope, 523-526; martyr; May 18*.

John Baptist de la Salle, St. (1651-1719): French priest; founder of Brothers of the Christian Schools, 1680; canonized 1900; Apr. 7*.

John Berchmans, St. (1599-1621): Belgian Jesuit scholastic; patron of Mass servers; canonized 1888; Aug. 13.

John Bosco, St. (1815-1888): Italian priest; founded Salesians, 1859, for education of boys and cofounded the Daughters of Mary Help of Christians for education of girls; canonized 1934; Jan. 31*.

John Capistran, St. (1386-1456): Italian Franciscan; preacher; papal diplomat; canonized 1690; Oct. 23*.

John Eudes, St. (1601-1680): French priest; founder of Sisters of Our Lady of Charity of Refuge, 1642, and Congregation of Jesus-Mary (Eudists), 1643; canonized 1925; Aug. 19*.

John Fisher, St. (1469-1535): English prelate; theologian; martyr; bishop of Rochester, cardinal; refused to recognize validity of Henry VIII's marriage to Anne Boleyn; upheld supremacy of the pope; beheaded for refusing to acknowledge Henry as head of the Church; canonized 1935; June 22 (with St. Thomas More)*.

John Kanty (Cantius), St. (1395-1473): Polish theologian; canonized 1767; Dec. 23*.

John Leonardi, St. (1550-1609): Italian priest; worked among prisoners and the sick; founded Clerics Regular of the Mother of God; canonized 1938; Oct. 9*.

John Nepomucene, St. (1345-1393): Bohemian priest; regarded as a martyr; canonized 1729; patron of Czechoslovakia; May 16.

John Nepomucene Neumann, St. (1811-1860): American prelate; b. Bohemia; ordained in New York 1836; missionary among Germans near Niagara Falls before joining Redemptorists, 1840; bishop of Philadelphia, 1852; first bishop in U.S. to prescribe Forty Hours devotion in his diocese; beatified 1963; canonized June 19, 1977; Jan. 5 (U.S.)*.

John of God, St. (1495-1550): Portuguese founder; his work among the sick poor led to foundation of Brothers Hospitallers of St. John of God, 1540, in Spain; canonized 1690; patron of sick, hospitals, nurses; Mar. 8*.

John Vianney (Cure of Ars), St. (1786-1859): French parish priest; noted confessor, spent 16 to 18 hours a day in confessional;

canonized 1925; patron of parish priests; Aug. 4*.

Josaphat Kuncevyc, St. (1584-1623): Basilian monk; b. Poland; archbishop of Polotsk, Lithuania; worked for reunion of separated Easterners; martyred by mob of schismatics; canonized 1867; Nov. 12*.

Joseph Benedict Cottolengo, St. (1786-1842): Italian priest; established Little Houses of Divine Providence (Piccolo Casa) for care of orphans and the sick; canonized 1934; Apr. 30.

Joseph Cafasso, St. (1811-1860): Italian priest; renowned confessor; promoted devotion to Blessed Sacrament; canonized 1947; June 22.

Joseph Calasanz, St. (1556-1648): Spanish priest; founder of Piarists (Order of Pious Schools); canonized 1767; Aug. 25*.

Joseph of Cupertino, St. (1603-1663): Italian Franciscan; noted for remarkable incidents of levitation; canonized 1767; Sept. 18.

Justin Martyr, St. (100-165): Early ecclesiastical writer; *Apologies for the Christian Religion, Dialog with the Jew Tryphon;* martyred at Rome; June 1*.

Kateri Tekakwitha, Bl. (1656-1680): "Lily of the Mohawks." Indian maiden born at Ossernenon (Auriesville), N.Y.; baptized Christian, Easter, 1676, by Jesuit missionary Father Jacques de Lambertville; lived life devoted to prayer, penitential practices and care of sick and aged in Christian village near Montreal; buried at Caughnawaga, Ont.; beatified June 22, 1980; Apr. 17* (in U.S.).

Ladislaus, Saint (1040-1095): King of Hungary; supported Pope Gregory VII against Henry IV; canonized 1192; June 27.

Lawrence, St. (d. 258): Widely venerated martyr who suffered death, according to a long-standing but unverifiable legend, by being roasted alive on a gridiron; Aug. 10*.

Leonard of Port Maurice, St. (1676-1751): Italian Franciscan; ascetical writer; preached missions throughout Italy; canonized 1867; patron of parish missions; Nov. 26.

Louis IX, St. (1215-1270): King of France, 1226-1270; participated in Sixth Crusade; patron of Secular Franciscan Order; canonized 1297; Aug. 25*.

Louis de Montfort, St. (1673-1716): French priest; founder of Sisters of Divine Wisdom, 1703, and Missionaries of Company of Mary, 1715; wrote *True Devotion to the Blessed Virgin;* canonized 1947; Apr. 28.

Louise de Marillac, St. (1591-1660): French foundress, with St. Vincent de Paul, of the Sisters of Charity; canonized 1934; Mar. 15.

Lucy, St. (d. 304): Sicilian maiden; martyred during Diocletian persecution; one of most widely venerated early virgin-martyrs; patron of Syracuse, Sicily; invoked by those suffering from eye diseases (based on legend that she offered her eyes to a suitor who admired them); Dec. 13*.

Marcellinus and Peter, Sts. (d.c. 304): Early Roman martyrs; June 2*.

Margaret Clitherow, St. (1556-1586): English martyr; convert shortly after her marriage; one of Forty Martyrs of England and Wales; canonized 1970; Mar. 25.

Margaret Mary Alacoque, St. (1647-1690): French nun; spread devotion to Sacred Heart in accordance with revelations made to her in 1675 (see Sacred Heart); canonized 1920; Oct. 16*.

Margaret of Scotland, St. (1050-1093): Queen of Scotland; noted for solicitude for the poor and promotion of justice; canonized 1251; Nov. 16*.

Maria Goretti, St. (1890-1902): Italian virgin-martyr; a model of purity; canonized 1950; July 6*.

Mariana Paredes of Jesus, St. (1618-1645): South American recluse; Lily of Quito; canonized, 1950; May 26.

Martha, St. (1st cent.): Sister of Lazarus and Mary of Bethany; Gospel accounts record her concern for homely details; patron of cooks; July 29*.

Martin I, St. (d. 655): Pope, 649; banished from Rome by emperor because of his condemnation of Monothelites; considered a martyr; Apr. 13*.

Martin of Tours, St. (316-397): Bishop of Tours; opposed Arianism and Priscillianism; pioneer of Western monasticism, before St. Benedict; Nov. 11*.

Mary Magdalene, St. (1st cent.): Gospels record her as devoted follower of Christ to whom he appeared after the Resurrection; her identification with Mary of Bethany (sister of Martha and Lazarus) and the woman sinner (Lk 7:36-50) has been questioned; July 22*.

Mary Magdalene de Pazzi, St. (1566-1607): Italian Carmelite nun; recipient of mystical experiences; canonized 1669; May 25*.

Maximilian Kolbe, St. (1894-1941): Polish Conventual Franciscan; prisoner at Auschwitz who heroically offered his life in place of a fellow prisoner; beatified 1971, canonized 1982; Aug. 14.

Methodius, St.: See Index.

Monica, St. (332-387): Mother of St. Augustine; model of a patient mother; her feast is observed in the Roman calendar the day before her son's; Aug. 27*.

Nereus and Achilleus, Sts. (d. c. 100): Early Christian martyrs; soldiers who, according to legend, were baptized by St. Peter; May 12*.

Nicholas of Myra, St. (4th cent.): Bishop of Myra in Asia Minor; one of most popular saints in both East and West; most of the incidents of his life are based on legend; patron of Russia; Dec. 6*.

Nicholas of Tolentino, St. (1245-1365): Italian hermit; famed preacher; canonized 1446; Sept. 10.

Norbert, St. (1080-1134): German bishop; founder of Norbertines or Premonstratensians, 1120; promoted reform of the clergy, devotion to Blessed Sacrament; canonized 1582; June 6*.

Odilia, St. (d. c. 720): Benedictine abbess; according to legend she was born blind, abandoned by her family and adopted by a convent where her sight was miraculously restored; patron of blind; Dec. 13.

Oliver Plunket, St. (1629-1681): Irish martyr; theologian; archbishop of Armagh and primate of Ireland; beatified 1920; canonized, 1975; July 1.

Pancras, St. (d. c. 304): Roman martyr; May 12*.

Paschal Baylon, St. (1540-1592): Spanish Franciscan lay brother; spent life as doorkeeper in various Franciscan friaries; defended doctrine of Real Presence in Blessed Sacrament; canonized 1690; patron of all Eucharistic confraternities and congresses, 1897; May 17.

Patrick, St. (389-461): Famous missionary of Ireland; began missionary work in Ireland about 432; organized the Church there and established it on a lasting foundation; patron of Ireland, with Sts. Bridget and Columba; Mar. 17*.

Paul Miki and Companions, Sts. (d. 1597): Martyrs of Japan; Paul Miki, Jesuit, and twenty-five other priests and laymen were martyred at Nagasaki; canonized 1862, the first canonized martyrs of the Far East; Feb. 6*.

Paul of the Cross, St. (1694-1775): Italian religious; founder of the Passionists; canonized 1867; Oct. 19*.

Paulinus of Nola, St. (d. 451): Bishop of Nola (Spain); writer; June 22*.

Peregrine, St. (1260-1347): Italian Servite; invoked against cancer (he was miraculously cured of cancer of the foot after a vision); canonized 1726; May 1.

Perpetua and Felicity, Sts. (d. 203): Martyrs; Mar. 7*.

Peter Chanel, St. (1803-1841): French Marist; missionary to Oceania, where he was martyred; canonized 1954; Apr. 28*.

Peter Gonzalez, St. (1190-1246): Spanish Dominican; worked among sailors; court chaplain and confessor of King St. Ferdinand of Castile; patron of sailors; Apr. 14.

Peter of Alcantara, St. (1499-1562): Spanish Franciscan; mystic; initiated Franciscan reform; confessor of St. Teresa of Avila; canonized 1669; Oct. 19.

Philip Neri, St. (1515-1595): Italian religious; founded Congregation of the Oratory; considered a second apostle of Rome because of his mission activities there; canonized 1622; May 26*.

Philip of Jesus, St. (1571-1597): Mexican Franciscan; martyred at Nagasaki, Japan; canonized 1862; patron of Mexico City; Feb. 6*.

Pius V, St. (1504-1572): Pope, 1566-1572; enforced decrees of Council of Trent; organized expedition against Turks resulting in victory at Lepanto; canonized 1712; Apr. 30*.

Polycarp, St. (2nd cent.): Bishop of Smyrna; ecclesiastical writer; martyr; Feb. 23*.

Pontian, St. (d. c. 235): Pope, 230-235; exiled to Sardinia by the emperor; regarded as a martyr; Aug. 13 (with Hippolytus)*.

Raymond Nonnatus, St. (d. 1240): Spanish Mercedarian; cardinal; devoted his life to ransoming captives from the Moors; Aug. 31.

Raymond of Penyafort, St. (1175-1275): Spanish Dominican; confessor of Gregory IX; systematized and codified canon law, in effect until 1917; master general of Dominicans, 1238; canonized 1601; Jan. 7*.

Rita of Cascia, St. (1381-1457): Widow; cloistered Augustinian religious of Umbria; invoked in impossible and desperate cases; May 22.

Robert Southwell, St. (1561-1595): English Jesuit; poet; martyred at Tyburn; canonized 1970, one of the Forty English and Welsh Martyrs; Feb. 21.

Roch, St. (1350-1379): French layman; pilgrim; devoted life to care of plague-stricken; widely venerated; invoked against pestilence; Aug. 17.

Romuald, St. (951-1027): Italian monk; founded Camaldolese Benedictines; June 19*.

Rose of Lima, St. (1586-1617): Peruvian Dominican tertiary; first native-born saint of the New World; canonized 1671; Aug. 23*.

Scholastica, St. (d. c. 559): Sister of St. Benedict; regarded as first nun of the Benedictine Order; Feb. 10*.

Sebastian, St. (3rd cent.): Roman martyr; traditionally pictured as a handsome youth with arrows; martyred; patron of athletes, archers; Jan. 20*.

Seven Holy Founders of the Servants of Mary (Buonfiglio Monaldo, Alexis Falconieri, Benedict dell'Antello, Bartholomew Amidei, Ricovero Uguccione, Gerardino Sostegni, John Buonagiunta Monetti): Florentine youths who founded Servites, 1233, in obedience to a vision; canonized 1888; Feb. 17*.

Sixtus II and Companions, Sts. (d. 258): Sixtus, pope 257-258, and four deacons, martyrs; Aug. 7*.

Stanislaus, St. (1030-1079): Polish bishop; martyr; canonized 1253; Apr. 11*.

Stephen, St. (d. c. 33): First Christian martyr; chosen by the Apostles as the first of the seven deacons; stoned to death; Dec. 26*.

Stephen, St. (975-1038): King; apostle of Hungary; welded Magyars into national unity; canonized 1087; Aug. 16*.

Sylvester I, St. (d. 335): Pope 314-335; first ecumenical council held at Nicaea during his pontificate; Dec. 31*.

Tarcisius, St. (d. 3rd cent.): Early martyr; according to tradition, was martyred while carrying the Blessed Sacrament to some

Christians in prison; patron of first communicants; Aug. 15.

Therese Couderc, St. (1805-1885): French religious; foundress of the Religious of Our Lady of the Retreat in the Cenacle, 1827; canonized 1970; Sept. 26.

Therese of Lisieux, St. (1873-1897): French Carmelite nun; b. Therese Martin; allowed to enter Carmel at 15, died nine years later of tuberculosis; her "little way" of spiritual perfection became widely known through her spiritual autobiography; despite her obscure life, became one of the most popular saints; canonized 1925; patron of foreign missions; Oct. 1*.

Thomas Becket, St. (1118-1170): English martyr; archbishop of Canterbury; chancellor under Henry II; murdered for upholding rights of the Church; canonized 1173; Dec. 29*.

Thomas More, St. (1478-1535): English martyr; statesman, chancellor under Henry VIII; author of *Utopia;* opposed Henry's divorce, refused to renounce authority of the papacy; beheaded; canonized 1935; June 22 (with St. John Fisher)*.

Timothy, St. (d. c. 97): Bishop of Ephesus; disciple and companion of St. Paul; martyr; Jan. 26*.

Titus, St. (d. c. 96): Bishop; companion of St. Paul; recipient of one of Paul's epistles; Jan. 26*.

Valentine, St. (d. 269): Priest, physician; martyred at Rome; legendary patron of lovers; Feb. 14.

Vincent, St. (d. 304): Spanish deacon; martyr; Jan. 22*.

Vincent de Paul, St. (1581?-1660): French priest; founder of Congregation of the Mission (Vincentians, Lazarists) and co-founder of Sisters of Charity; declared patron of all charitable organizations and works by Leo XIII; canonized 1737; Sept. 27*.

Vincent Ferrer, St. (1350-1418): Spanish Dominican; famed preacher; Apr. 5*.

Wenceslaus, St. (d. 935): Duke of Bohemia; martyr; patron of Bohemia; Sept. 28*.

Zita, St. (1218-1278): Italian maid; noted for charity to poor; patron of domestics.

SAINTS—PATRONS AND INTERCESSORS

A patron is a saint who is venerated as a special intercessor before God. Most patrons have been so designated as the result of popular devotion and long-standing custom. In many cases, the fact of existing patronal devotion is clear despite historical obscurity regarding its origin. The Church has made official designation of relatively few patrons; in such cases, the dates of designation are given in the list below. The theological background of the patronage of saints includes the dogmas of the Mystical Body of Christ and the Communion of Saints.

Listed below are patron saints of occupations and professions, and saints whose intercession is sought for special needs.

Accountants: St. Matthew.

Actors: St. Genesius.

Advertisers: St. Bernardine of Siena (May 20, 1960).

Alpinists: St. Bernard of Menthon (Aug. 20, 1923).

Altar boys: St. John Berchmans.

Anesthetists: St. Rene Goupil.

Archers: St. Sebastian.

Architects: St. Thomas, Apostle.

Armorers: St. Dunstan.

Art: St. Catherine of Bologna.

Artists: St. Luke, St. Catherine of Bologna.

Astronomers: St. Dominic.

Athletes: St. Sebastian.

Authors: St. Francis de Sales.

Aviators: Our Lady of Loreto (1920), St. Therese of Lisieux, St. Joseph of Cupertino.

Bakers: St. Elizabeth of Hungary, St. Nicholas.

Bankers: St. Matthew.

Barbers: Sts. Cosmas and Damian, St. Louis.

Barren women: St. Anthony of Padua, St. Felicity.

Basket-makers: St. Anthony, Abbot.

Blacksmiths: St. Dunstan.

Blind: St. Odilia, St. Raphael.

Blood banks: St. Januarius.

Bodily ills: Our Lady of Lourdes.

Bookbinders: St. Peter Celestine.

Bookkeepers: St. Matthew.

Booksellers: St. John of God.

Boy Scouts: St. George.

Brewers: St. Augustine of Hippo, St. Luke, St. Nicholas of Myra.

Bricklayers: St. Stephen.

Brides: St. Nicholas of Myra.

Brush makers: St. Anthony, Abbot.

Builders: St. Vincent Ferrer.

Butchers: St. Anthony, Abbot, St. Luke.

Cab drivers: St. Fiacre.

Cabinetmakers: St. Anne.

Cancer patients: St. Peregrine.

Canonists: St. Raymond of Penyafort.

Carpenters: St. Joseph.

Catechists: St. Viator, St. Charles Borromeo, St. Robert Bellarmine.

Catholic Action: St. Francis of Assisi (1916).

Chandlers: St. Ambrose, St. Bernard of Clairvaux.

Charitable societies: St. Vincent de Paul (May 12, 1885).

Children: St. Nicholas of Myra.

Children of Mary: St. Agnes, St. Maria Goretti.

Choir boys: St. Dominic Savio (June 8, 1956), Holy Innocents.

Church: St. Joseph (Dec. 8, 1870).
Clerics: St. Gabriel of the Sorrowful Mother.
Comedians: St. Vitus.
Communications personnel: St. Bernardine.
Confessors: St. Alphonsus Liguori (Apr. 26, 1950), St. John Nepomucene.
Convulsive children: St. Scholastica.
Cooks: St. Lawrence, St. Martha.
Coopers: St. Nicholas of Myra.
Coppersmiths: St. Maurus.
Dairy workers: St. Brigid.
Deaf: St. Francis de Sales.
Dentists: St. Apollonia.
Desperate situations: St. Gregory of Neocaesarea, St. Jude Thaddeus, St. Rita of Cascia.
Dietitians (in hospitals): St. Martha.
Dyers: Sts. Maurice and Lydia.
Dying: St. Joseph.
Ecologists: St. Francis of Assisi (Nov. 29, 1979).
Editors: St. John Bosco.
Emigrants: St. Frances Xavier Cabrini (Sept. 8, 1950).
Epilepsy: St. Vitus.
Engineers: St. Ferdinand III.
Eucharistic congresses and societies: St. Paschal Baylon (Nov. 28, 1897).
Expectant mothers: St. Raymund Nonnatus, St. Gerard Majella.
Eye diseases: St. Lucy.
Falsely accused: St. Raymund Nonnatus.
Farmers: St. George, St. Isidore.
Farriers: St. John Baptist.
Firemen: St. Florian.
Fire prevention: St. Catherine of Siena.
First communicants: St. Tarcisius.
Fishermen: St. Andrew.
Florists: St. Therese of Lisieux.
Forest workers: St. John Gualbert.
Foundlings: Holy Innocents.
Fullers: St. Anastasius the Fuller, St. James the Less.
Funeral directors: St. Joseph of Arimathea, St. Dismas.
Gardeners: St. Adelard, St. Tryphon, St. Fiacre, St. Phocas.
Glassworkers: St. Luke.
Goldsmiths: St. Dunstan, St. Anastasius.
Gravediggers: St. Anthony, Abbot.
Greetings: St. Valentine.
Grocers: St. Michael.
Hairdressers: St. Martin de Porres.
Happy meetings: St. Raphael.
Hatters: St. Severus of Ravenna, St. James the Less.
Haymakers: Sts. Gervase and Protase.
Headache sufferers: St. Teresa of Avila.
Heart patients: St. John of God.
Hospital administrators: St. Basil the Great, St. Frances X. Cabrini.
Hospitals: St. Camillus de Lellis and St. John of God (June 22, 1886), St. Jude Thaddeus.
Housewives: St. Anne.
Hunters: St. Hubert, St. Eustachius.

Infantrymen: St. Maurice.
Innkeepers: St. Amand, St. Martha.
Invalids: St. Roch.
Jewelers: St. Eligius, St. Dunstan.
Journalists: St. Francis de Sales (Apr. 26, 1923).
Jurists: St. John Capistran.
Laborers: St. Isidore, St. James, St. John Bosco.
Lawyers: St. Ivo, St. Genesius, St. Thomas More.
Learning: St. Ambrose.
Librarians: St. Jerome.
Lighthouse keepers: St. Venerius.
Locksmiths: St. Dunstan.
Maids: St. Zita.
Marble workers: St. Clement I.
Mariners: St. Michael, St. Nicholas of Tolentino.
Medical record librarians: St. Raymond of Penyafort.
Medical social workers: St. John Regis.
Medical technicians: St. Albert the Great.
Mentally ill: St. Dymphna.
Merchants: St. Francis of Assisi, St. Nicholas of Myra.
Messengers: St. Gabriel.
Metal workers: St. Eligius.
Millers: St. Arnulph, St. Victor.
Missions, Foreign: St. Francis Xavier (Mar. 25, 1904), St. Therese of Lisieux (Dec. 14, 1927).
Missions, Negro: St. Peter Claver (1896, Leo XIII), St. Benedict the Black.
Missions, Parish: St. Leonard of Port Maurice (Mar. 17, 1023).
Mothers: St. Monica.
Motorcyclists: Our Lady of Grace.
Motorists: St. Christopher, St. Frances of Rome.
Mountaineers: St. Bernard of Menthon.
Musicians: St. Gregory the Great, St. Cecilia, St. Dunstan.
Nail makers: St. Cloud.
Notaries: St. Luke, St. Mark.
Nurses: St. Camillus de Lellis and St. John of God (1930, Pius XI), St. Agatha, St. Raphael.
Nursing and nursing service: St. Elizabeth of Hungary, St. Catherine of Siena.
Orators: St. John Chrysostom (July 8, 1908).
Organ builders: St. Cecilia.
Orphans: St. Jerome Emiliani.
Painters: St. Luke.
Paratroopers: St. Michael.
Pawnbrokers: St. Nicholas.
Pharmacists: Sts. Cosmas and Damian, St. James the Greater.
Pharmacists (in hospitals): St. Gemma Galgani.
Philosophers: St. Justin.
Physicians: St. Pantaleon, Sts. Cosmas and Damian, St. Luke, St. Raphael.
Pilgrims: St. James.
Plasterers: St. Bartholomew.

Poets: St. David, St. Cecilia.
Poison sufferers: St. Benedict.
Policemen: St. Michael.
Poor: St. Lawrence, St. Anthony of Padua.
Poor souls: St. Nicholas of Tolentino.
Porters: St. Christopher.
Possessed: St. Bruno, St. Denis.
Postal employees: St. Gabriel.
Priests: St. Jean-Baptiste Vianney (Apr. 23, 1929).
Printers: St. John of God, St. Augustine of Hippo, St. Genesius.
Prisoners: St. Dismas, St. Joseph Cafasso.
Protector of crops: St. Ansovinus.
Public relations: St. Bernardine of Siena (May 20, 1960).
Public relations (of hospitals): St. Paul, Apostle.
Radiologists: St. Michael (Jan. 15, 1941).
Radio workers: St. Gabriel.
Retreats: St. Ignatius Loyola (July 25, 1922).
Rheumatism: St. James the Greater.

Saddlers: Sts. Crispin and Crispinian.
Sailors: St. Cuthbert, St. Brendan, St. Eulalia, St. Christopher, St. Peter Gonzales, St. Erasmus, St. Nicholas.
Scholars: St. Brigid.
Schools, Catholic: St. Thomas Aquinas (Aug. 4, 1880), St. Joseph Calasanz (Aug. 13, 1948).
Scientists: St. Albert (Aug. 13, 1948).
Sculptors: St. Claude.
Seamen: St. Francis of Paola.
Searchers for lost articles: St. Anthony of Padua.
Secretaries: St. Genesius.
Seminarians: St. Charles Borromeo.
Servants: St. Martha, St. Zita.
Shoemakers: Sts. Crispin and Crispinian.
Sick: St. Michael, St. John of God and St. Camillus de Lellis (June 22, 1886).
Silversmiths: St. Andronicus.
Singers: St. Gregory, St. Cecilia.
Skaters: St. Lidwina.
Skiers: St. Bernard.
Social workers: St. Louise de Marillac (Feb. 12, 1960).
Soldiers: St. Hadrian, St. George, St. Ignatius, St. Sebastian, St. Martin of Tours, St. Joan of Arc.
Speleologists: St. Benedict.
Stenographers: St. Genesius, St. Cassian.
Stonecutters: St. Clement.
Stonemasons: St. Stephen.
Students: St. Thomas Aquinas.
Surgeons: Sts. Cosmas and Damian, St. Luke.
Swordsmiths: St. Maurice.
Tailors: St. Homobonus.
Tanners: Sts. Crispin and Crispinian, St. Simon.
Tax collectors: St. Matthew.
Teachers: St. Gregory the Great, St. John Baptist de la Salle (May 15, 1950).

Telecommunications workers: St. Gabriel (Jan. 12, 1951).
Telegraph/telephone workers: St. Gabriel.
Television: St. Clare of Assisi (Feb. 14, 1958).
Television workers: St. Gabriel.
Tertiaries (Franciscan): St. Louis of France, St. Elizabeth of Hungary.
Theologians: St. Augustine, St. Alphonsus Liguori.
Throat sufferers: St. Blase.
Travelers: St. Anthony of Padua, St. Nicholas of Myra, St. Christopher, St. Raphael.
Travel hostesses: St. Bona (Mar. 2, 1962).
Universities: Blessed Contardo Ferrini.
Vocations: St. Alphonsus.
Watchmen: St. Peter of Alcantara.
Weavers: St. Paul the Hermit, St. Anastasius the Fuller, St. Anastasia.
Wine merchants: St. Amand.
Women in labor: St. Anne.
Women's Army Corps: St. Genevieve.
Workingmen: St. Joseph.
Writers: St. Francis de Sales (Apr. 26, 1923), St. Lucy.
Yachtsmen: St. Adjutor.
Young girls: St. Agnes.
Youth: St. Aloysius Gonzaga (1729, Benedict XIII; 1926, Pius XI), St. John Berchmans, St. Gabriel of the Sorrowful Mother.

Patrons of Places

Alsace: St. Odile.
Americas: Our Lady of Guadalupe; St. Rose of Lima.
Argentina: Our Lady of Lujan.
Armenia: St. Gregory Illuminator.
Asia Minor: St. John, Evangelist.
Australia: Our Lady Help of Christians.
Belgium: St. Joseph.
Bohemia: Sts. Wenceslaus, Ludmilla.
Borneo: St. Francis Xavier.
Brazil: Nossa Senhora de Aparecida, Immaculate Conception; St. Peter of Alcantara.
Canada: St. Joseph; St. Anne.
Ceylon (Sri Lanka): St. Lawrence.
Chile: St. James; Our Lady of Mt. Carmel.
China: St. Joseph.
Colombia: St. Peter Claver; St. Louis Bertran.
Corsica: Immaculate Conception.
Czechoslovakia: St. Wenceslaus; St. John Nepomucene; St. Procopius.
Denmark: St. Ansgar; St. Canute.
Dominican Republic: Our Lady of High Grace; St. Dominic.
East Indies: St. Thomas, Apostle.
Ecuador: Sacred Heart.
England: St. George.
Europe: St. Benedict (1964); Sts. Cyril and Methodius, co-patrons (Dec. 31, 1980).
Finland: St. Henry.
France: Our Lady of the Assumption; St. Joan of Arc; St. Therese.
Germany: Sts. Boniface, Michael.

Gibraltar: Blessed Virgin Mary under title "Our Lady of Europe" (May 31, 1979).

Greece: St. Nicholas; St. Andrew.

Holland: St. Willibrord.

Hungary: Blessed Virgin, "Great Lady of Hungary"; St. Stephen, King.

India: Our Lady of Assumption.

Ireland: Sts. Patrick, Brigid and Columba.

Italy: St. Francis of Assisi; St. Catherine of Siena.

Japan: St. Peter Baptist.

Lesotho: Immaculate Heart of Mary.

Lithuania: St. Casimir, Bl. Cunegunda.

Malta: St. Paul; Our Lady of the Assumption.

Mexico: Our Lady of Guadalupe.

Monaco: St. Devota.

Moravia: Sts. Cyril and Methodius.

New Zealand: Our Lady Help of Christians.

Norway: St. Olaf.

Papua New Guinea (including northern Solomon Islands): St. Michael the Archangel (May 31, 1979)

Paraguay: Our Lady of Assumption.

Peru: St. Joseph.

Philippines: Sacred Heart of Mary.

Poland: St. Casimir; Bl. Cunegunda; St. Stanislaus of Cracow; Our Lady of Czestochowa.

Portugal: Immaculate Conception; St. Francis Borgia; St. Anthony of Padua; St. Vincent; St. George.

Republic of South Africa: Our Lady of Assumption.

Russia: St. Andrew; St. Nicholas of Myra; St. Therese of Lisieux.

Scandinavia: St. Ansgar.

Scotland: St. Andrew; St. Columba.

Silesia: St. Hedwig.

Slovakia: Our Lady of Sorrows.

South America: St. Rose of Lima.

Spain: St. James; St. Teresa.

Sweden: St. Bridget; St. Eric.

United States: Immaculate Conception.

Uruguay: Our Lady of Lujan.

Wales: St. David.

West Indies: St. Gertrude.

Apostles of Places, Peoples

Alps: St. Bernard of Menthon.

Andalusia (Spain): St. John of Avila.

Antioch: St. Barnabas.

Armenia: St. Gregory the Illuminator; St. Bartholomew.

Austria: St. Severine.

Bavaria: St. Killian.

Brazil: Jose Anchieta.

California: Junipero Serra.

Carinthia (Yugoslavia): St. Virgil.

Colombia: St. Louis Bertran.

Corsica: St. Alexander Sauli.

Crete: St. Titus.

Cyprus: St. Barnabas.

Denmark: St. Ansgar.

England: St. Augustine of Canterbury; St. Gregory the Great.

Ethiopia: St. Frumentius.

Finland: St. Henry.

Florence: St. Andrew Corsini.

France: St. Remigius; St. Martin of Tours; St. Denis.

Friesland (Germany): St. Suitbert; St. Willibrord.

Gaul: St. Irenaeus.

Gentiles: St. Paul.

Georgia (Russia): St. Nino.

Germany: St. Boniface; St. Peter Canisius.

Gothland (Sweden): St. Sigfrid.

Guelderland (Holland): St. Plechelm.

Highlanders (Scotland): St. Columba.

Hungarians (Magyars): St. Stephen, King; St. Gerard; Bl. Astricus.

India: St. Thomas, Apostle.

Indies: St. Francis Xavier.

Ireland: St. Patrick.

Iroquois: Francois Picquit.

Italy: St. Bernardine of Siena.

Japan: St. Francis Xavier.

Malta: St. Paul.

Mexico: The twelve Apostles of Mexico (Franciscans), headed by Fra. Martin de Valencia.

Negro Slaves: St. Peter Claver.

Netherlands: St. Willibrord.

Northumbria (Britain): St. Aidan.

Norway: St. Olaf.

Ottawas (Indians): Fr. Claude Allouez.

Persia: St. Maruthas.

Poland: St. Hyacinth.

Portugal: St. Christian.

Prussia (Slavs): St. Adalbert; St. Bruno of Querfurt.

Rome: St. Philip Neri.

Rumania: St. Nicetas.

Ruthenia: St. Bruno.

Sardinia: St. Ephesus.

Saxony: St. Willihad.

Scandinavia (North): St. Ansgar.

Scotland: St. Palladius.

Slavs: Sts. Cyril and Methodius, St. Adalbert.

Spain: St. James; Sts. Euphrasius and Felix.

Sweden: St. Ansgar.

Switzerland: St. Andeol.

Tournai (Belgium): St. Eligius, St. Piaton.

Emblems of Saints

St. Agatha: Tongs, veil.

St. Agnes: Lamb.

St. Ambrose: Bees, dove, ox, pen.

St. Andrew: Transverse cross.

St. Anne, Mother of the Blessed Virgin: A door.

St. Anthony, Abbot: Bell, hog.

St. Anthony of Padua: Infant Jesus, bread, book, lily.

St. Augustine of Hippo: Dove, child, shell, pen.

St. Barnabas: Stones, ax, lance.

St. Bartholomew: Knife, flayed and holding his skin.

St. Benedict: Broken cup, raven, bell, crosier, bush.

St. Bernard of Clairvaux: Pen, bees, instruments of Passion.

St. Bernardine of Siena: Tablet or sun inscribed with IHS.

St. Blase: Wax, taper, iron comb.

St. Bonaventure: Communion, ciborium, cardinal's hat.

St. Boniface: Oak, ax, book, fox, scourge, fountain, raven, sword.

St. Bridget of Sweden: Book, pilgrim's staff.

St. Bridget of Kildare: Cross, flame over her head, candle.

St. Catherine of Ricci: Ring, crown, crucifix.

St. Catherine of Siena: Stigmata, cross, ring, lily.

St. Cecilia: Organ.

St. Charles Borromeo: Communion, coat of arms with word *Humilitas*.

St. Christopher: Giant, torrent, tree, Child Jesus on his shoulders.

St. Clare of Assisi: Monstrance.

Sts. Cosmas and Damian: A phial, box of ointment.

St. Cyril of Alexandria: Blessed Virgin holding the Child Jesus, pen.

St. Cyril of Jerusalem: Purse, book.

St. Dominic: Rosary, star.

St. Edmund the Martyr: Arrow, sword.

St. Elizabeth of Hungary: Alms, flowers, bread, the poor, a pitcher.

St. Francis of Assisi: Deer, wolf, birds, fish, skull, the Stigmata.

St. Francis Xavier: Crucifix, bell, vessel, Negro.

St. Genevieve: Bread, keys, herd, candle.

St. George: Dragon.

St. Gertrude: Crown, taper, lily.

Sts. Gervase and Protase: Scourge, club, sword.

St. Gregory I (the Great): Tiara, crosier, dove.

St. Helena: Cross.

St. Hilary: Stick, pen, child.

St. Ignatius Loyola: Communion, chasuble, book, apparition of Our Lord.

St. Isidore: Bees, pen.

St. James the Greater: Pilgrim's staff, shell, key, sword.

St. James the Less: Square rule, halberd, club.

St. Jerome: Lion.

St. John Berchmans: Rule of St. Ignatius, cross, rosary.

St. John Chrysostom: Bees, dove, pen.

St. John of God: Alms, a heart, crown of thorns.

St. John the Baptist: Lamb, head cut off on platter, skin of an animal.

St. John the Evangelist: Eagle, chalice, kettle, armor.

St. Josaphat Kuncevyc: Chalice, crown, winged deacon.

St. Joseph, Spouse of the Blessed Virgin: Infant Jesus, lily, rod, plane, carpenter's square.

St. Jude: Sword, square rule, club.

St. Justin Martyr: Ax, sword.

St. Lawrence: Cross, book of the Gospels, gridiron.

St. Leander of Seville: A pen.

St. Liborius: Pebbles, peacock.

St. Longinus: In arms at foot of the cross.

St. Louis IX of France: Crown of thorns, nails.

St. Lucy: Cord, eyes.

St. Luke: Ox, book, brush, palette.

St. Mark: Lion, book.

St. Martha: Holy water sprinkler, dragon.

St. Mary Magdalene: Alabaster box of ointment.

St. Matilda: Purse, alms.

St. Matthew: Winged man, purse, lance.

St. Matthias: Lance.

St. Maurus: Scales, spade, crutch.

St. Meinrad: Two ravens.

St. Michael: Scales, banner, sword, dragon.

St. Monica: Girdle, tears.

St. Nicholas: Three purses or balls, anchor or boat, child.

St. Patrick: Cross, harp, serpent, baptismal font, demons, shamrock.

St. Paul: Sword, book or scroll.

St. Peter: Keys, boat, cock.

St. Philip, Apostle: Column.

St. Philip Neri: Altar, chasuble, vial.

St. Rita of Cascia: Rose, crucifix, thorn.

St. Roch: Angel, dog, bread.

St. Rose of Lima: Crown of thorns, anchor, city.

St. Sebastian: Arrows, crown.

Sts. Sergius and Bacchus: Military garb, palm.

St. Simon: Saw, cross.

St. Simon Stock: Scapular.

St. Teresa of Avila: Heart, arrow, book.

St. Therese of Lisieux: Roses entwining a crucifix.

St. Thomas, Apostle: Lance, ax.

St. Thomas Aquinas: Chalice, monstrance, dove, ox, person trampled under foot.

St. Vincent: Gridiron, boat.

St. Vincent de Paul: Children.

St. Vincent Ferrer: Pulpit, cardinal's hat, trumpet, captives.

U.N. Declaration

After 19 years of work on the document, the U.N. General Assembly approved Nov. 25, 1981, a Declaration on the Elimination of Religious Intolerance, providing:

• Everyone should have the right to freedom of thought, conscience and religion, including atheism.

• "No one shall be subject to coercion which would impair that freedom."

• "No one shall be subject to discrimination on the grounds of religion or other beliefs."

THE MOTHER OF JESUS IN CATHOLIC UNDERSTANDING

This article was written by the Rev. Eamon R. Carroll, O. Carm., member of the theological faculty of Loyola University, Chicago; author of "Understanding the Mother of Jesus" (published by M. Glazier, Wilmington, Del.; 1979).

Documents of the Second Vatican Council have provided the charter for current Catholic understanding of the Virgin Mary, Mother of Jesus. This conciliar teaching was expanded and applied in the pastoral letter, "Behold Your Mother: Woman of Faith," issued by the U.S. bishops Nov. 21, 1973. Pope Paul VI added guidelines for devotion, in the revised liturgy and with respect to the Rosary, in the letter *Marialis Cultus* ("To Honor Mary"), dated Feb. 2, 1974.

Conciliar Documents

The first conciliar document, the *Constitution on the Sacred Liturgy*, linked Mary with the life, death and exaltation of Jesus, stating: "In celebrating this annual cycle of Christ's mysteries, holy Church honors with special love blessed Mary, Mother of God, who is joined by an inseparable bond to the saving work of her Son. In her the Church holds up and admires the most excellent fruit of the redemption, and joyfully contemplates, as in a faultless manner, that which she herself wholly desires and hopes to be" (No. 103).

The eighth and final chapter of the *Dogmatic Constitution on the Church* is entitled "The Blessed Virgin Mary, Mother of God, in the Mystery of Christ and the Church." The seventh chapter deals with the communion of saints, the bond between the pilgrim Church on earth and the blessed joined to the risen Christ — what John deSatgé, an English Anglican, describes as the "mutual sharing and caring in Christ for one another." At the Eucharist, above all, "in union with the whole Church we honor Mary, the ever-Virgin Mother of Jesus Christ our Lord and God" (First Eucharistic Prayer; cf. *Constitution on the Church*, No. 50).

What Catholics believe about the Mother of Jesus is the basis for her place in their prayer life, both in the liturgy and particularly the Eucharist, and in other forms of piety, especially the Rosary. The Church's growth in insight about the Blessed Virgin comes about as Christians ponder the meaning of Mary in prayer as well as in study. The Church has come to know Mary's role by experience and by contemplation of her hidden holiness (*Constitution on the Church*, No. 64). The tradition about Mary has been transmitted by doctrinal teaching and also by life and worship, even as in her own life Mary treasured in her heart God's words and deeds (*Dogmatic Constitution on Divine Revelation*, No. 8).

Mary in the Bible

The possibility of consensus on the Virgin Mary in the Bible was the theme of a book published in 1978, entitled *Mary in the New Testament* (edited by R. E. Brown, J. A. Fitzmyer, J. Reumann and K. P. Donfried). Limiting their study to the New Testament and using critical techniques of interpretation, a team of 12 authors — Catholics, Lutherans, Anglicans and others — agreed on a biblical portrait of Mary the Virgin as the great gospel model of faith commitment.

One valuable insight centers on the "true kinsmen" incident (Mk. 3:31-35; Mt. 12:46-50; Lk. 8:19-21). One day while Jesus was preaching, word was sent to him that his "mother and brethren" wished to see him. In St. Mark, the oldest account, there is a sharp distinction between the circle of the hearers of Jesus, who were "inside" and counted as his "true family," and the relatives "outside," who failed to understand him. St. Mark does not clearly place Mary among the outsiders, but neither does he carefully distinguish her from the other relatives who did not esteem Jesus. St. Luke shifts the focus completely, placing the relatives, especially the Mother of Jesus, among the true followers, as he does also in the Acts of the Apostles by mentioning them in the Upper Room before Pentecost.

St. Luke is fond of speaking of the "word of God." At the Annunciation, Mary consented with the statement, "Be it done to me according to your word" (Lk. 1:26-38), and "the Word was made flesh" (Jn. 1:14). Jesus said in reply to the message about his visitors, "My mother and my brothers are those who hear the word of God and do it" (Lk. 8:21). St. Luke relates this event just after the parables of the sower and the seed and the lamp on the lampstand. Consistent with his high praise of the Virgin Mary in the infancy chapters, he regards Mary as the rich soil — she heard the word and brought forth fruit in abundance, the Holy One who is the Son of God. She is the pure light, rekindled by the coming of the Redeemer; she is the "woman clothed with the sun" (Rv. 12:1), for Jesus is the "sun of justice."

St. Luke alone saved one other mention of Mary during the public ministry of Jesus, in the story of the "enthusiastic woman" (Lk. 11:27-28). One day while Jesus was preaching, a woman cried out, "Blessed is the womb that bore you and the breasts that nursed you." He replied, "Still more blessed are those who hear the word of God and keep it." The obedient Mary, handmaid of the Lord, brought together opposed beatitudes — the anonymous woman's praise of her motherhood and Jesus' tribute to her faith.

In the opening chapter of St. Luke, Elizabeth did the same when, filled with the Holy Spirit, she returned Mary's greeting with the loud cry, "Of all women you are the most blessed, and blessed is the fruit of your womb." Continuing in praise of her young cousin's faith, she added: "Yes, blessed is she who has believed, for the things promised her by the Lord will be fulfilled" (Lk. 1:39-45).

Mary the Virgin

Both St. Luke and St. Matthew, whose infancy narratives differ so much otherwise, agree that Mary conceived Jesus virginally, that her Son had no human father. The Creed affirms that Jesus was "conceived of the Virgin Mary by the power of the Holy Spirit."

St. Luke writes of the virginal conception of Jesus from the standpoint of Mary. To her question, "How can this be since I know not man?" the angel replied by appealing to God's power.

St. Matthew's viewpoint is that of Joseph, who was informed in a dream-vision that Mary's child was of no human father. God accomplishes his saving purposes without dependence on the will of the flesh and the will of man (Jn. 1:13). God shows his favor where he chooses — whether for the barren Sara, wife of Abraham, or aged Elizabeth, the wife of Zechariah, or the Virgin Mary. In the words of the promise to Abraham, repeated by Gabriel to Mary, "Nothing is impossible to God" (Lk. 1:37; Gn. 18:14).

Mary and Joseph accepted as God's will the virginal conception, an unprecedented event, the sign of God sending his Son to be the Savior. Their lives were henceforth totally dedicated to the service of Jesus.

As various forms of Christian witness developed in the Church, the conviction that Mary remains always a virgin came to be held as Catholic doctrine. The Gospels leave undecided the identity of the "brethren" of Jesus. From lived experience, by the fourth century the Church had come to see Mary's life-long virginity as part of her commitment to her Son and his mission. Such "development of doctrine" remains a point of difference between Catholics and Protestants, although the great Reformers — Luther, Calvin and later John Wesley — all held that Mary was ever-Virgin.

St. Luke and St. John on Mary

Along with the role of Mary in the childhood of Jesus, St. Luke sees her as part of the fulfillment of messianic prophecy. The Second Vatican Council spoke of "the exalted daughter of Zion in whom the times are fulfilled after the long waiting for the promise, and the new economy inaugurated when the Son of God takes on human nature from her in order to free men from sin by the mysteries of his flesh." The expectations of Israel

for the Messiah reach their peak in Mary of Nazareth: "She stands out among the Lord's lowly and poor who confidently look for salvation from him" (*Constitution on the Church*, No. 55).

The Gospel of St. John introduces Mary at the opening and closing of her Son's ministry, which began with the first of his signs at Cana (Jn. 2:1-11) and ended on Calvary (Jn. 19). Both scenes deal with a "third day," both turn on the "hour," not yet come at Cana but achieved in the decisive event of Calvary. In both, Jesus addresses his Mother with the unaccustomed title, "woman." The request of Mary at Cana is for more than wine to save the wedding feast. She stands for Israel of old, symbolized by the water pots required for religious purifications; Mary stands also for the new Israel, the Church, the bride of Christ, symbolized by the abundant choice wine of the messianic banquet. The marriage feast looks forward to the hour when Christ, the bridegroom, will lay down his life in love for his bride, the Church.

When Jesus spoke from the cross to his Mother and the beloved disciple, "Woman, behold your son," and "Behold your Mother," more was meant than that the disciple should provide for Mary's care (Jn. 19:26-27). In his farewell discourse at the Last Supper, Jesus spoke of the woman in agony because her hour had come. "But when she has borne her child, she no longer remembers her pain for joy that a man has been born into the world" (Jn. 16:21). The longing of Israel for the coming of the Messiah was sometimes compared to labor pains. The "daughter of Zion" had been promised she would become the mother of all races and all nations. The words of Jesus on Calvary announced the fulfillment of that promise; Mary stands for the "woman" who is mother Church, new Israel, new People of God.

In St. John's Gospel, it is only after his words to his Mother and the disciple that Jesus, knowing "that everything was now finished," said, "I am thirsty," and then, "Now it is finished." "Then he bowed his head and delivered over his spirit" (Jn. 19:28-29).

The giving up of the spirit means both the expiring of Jesus and the giving of the Holy Spirit to the Church. The wine Mary requested at Cana was the wine of the Spirit, to be poured out at the messianic banquet. The prayer for the wine of the Spirit is answered through the self-surrender of Jesus on the cross. The triumphant Christ "gives up his spirit," and the Church comes into being. The Acts of the Apostles describe the effects of the outpouring of the Spirit at Pentecost and afterwards. What Mary requested at Cana, what she prayed for in agony at the cross of Jesus, what she sought before Pentecost in union with the Apostles and relatives and the women — all "with one accord devoted to prayer" — is the gift of the Spirit. At Nazareth Mary conceived her Son, and God became man by the power of the Holy Spirit; in the Upper Room she prayed for the Spirit that Jesus be born again in the members of his Church (*Constitution on the Church,* No. 59).

The New Eve

To the titles of Mary already familiar from the Gospels — "the Virgin," "Favored One," "Mother of Jesus," "Mother of my Lord" (Elizabeth's greeting, meaning "Mother of the Messianic King") — the early Church added other descriptions. By the mid-second century Mary was being compared to Eve. Eve was deceived by the word of the evil angel and by disobedience brought death; Mary, the obedient Virgin, heeded the message of the good angel and by her consent brought Life to the world. The title of "New Eve" became common for Mary. By the time of St. Jerome (d. 419), it was proverbial to say, "Death through Eve, life through Mary."

Immaculate Conception

Reflecting on the Blessed Virgin, Christians pondered various aspects of her holiness. The question arose of her freedom from original sin, God's gift of grace that came to be called her Immaculate Conception (not to be confused with the virginal conception of Jesus, for Mary was the child of the father and mother recalled as Joachim and Anne). It took centuries of development before the Immaculate Conception was held to be revealed by God and defined as dogma by Pius IX in 1854. The absence of clear scriptural evidence was one delaying factor, another was lack of clarity about the meaning of original sin, and most cogent was the requirement that Mary be beneficiary of the saving work of Christ. As the English Anglican John deSatgé expresses it, "Mary, who rejoiced in her Savior, was the last person to have no need of one." The Franciscan John Duns Scotus (d. 1308) suggested that Mary was kept free of original sin by a "preservative redemption" — in anticipation of the foreseen merits of Jesus Christ — the explanation eventually recognized as revealed truth.

The Assumption

The final facet of Mary's holiness is the Assumption, her union body and soul with the risen Christ in the glory of heaven, defined as dogma by Pope Pius XII in 1950. By the sixth century the feast of the Assumption was being celebrated in the East, a development from a still earlier August 15 feast that had been known as the Memory of Mary (like the birthdays into heaven of the martyrs), as the Passing of Mary, and as the Dormition or Falling Asleep of the Mother of God. There is no compelling biblical testimony; the appeal is to the concordant faith of the Church, convinced that the promise of the resurrection of the flesh in union with the risen Savior has already been fulfilled for the Mother of the Lord, who gave him human birth in her pure body and was his loyal disciple unto the end.

Model of the Church

All beliefs about the Blessed Virgin lead to Christ. God kept her free from original sin for the sake of Jesus, that she might give herself wholeheartedly to his life and work (*Constitution on the Church,* No. 56), and in consideration of his redemptive mission. Mary's Assumption is her reunion with her Son in the power of his resurrection. The Marian privileges of the Immaculate Conception and the Assumption enrich also the self-understanding of the Church, for she is the "most excellent fruit of the redemption, the spotless model of the Church," the one in whom Christians admire God's plan for his Church. "In the most holy Virgin the Church has already reached that perfection whereby she exists without spot or wrinkle (Eph. 5:27)" (*Constitution on the Church,* No. 65).

Mary Immaculate is a sign of the love of Christ for his bride, the Church; the bridegroom purifies her by his blood to make her all-holy. The preface for the Solemnity of the Immaculate Conception (December 8) addresses the Father: "You allowed no stain of sin to touch the Virgin Mary. Full of grace, she was to be a worthy Mother of your Son, your sign of favor to the Church at its beginning, and the promise of its perfection as the bride of Christ, radiantly beautiful."

Faithful to his promise, Christ has prepared a place for his bride, the Church. In Mary, daughter of the Church, now joined to Christ body and soul in glory, the pilgrim Church sees the successful completion of its own journey. The resurrection of Jesus is the central truth; the Assumption of Mary is the living sign of the Church's call to glory, to loving union with the victorious Redeemer. The preface at Mass for August 15 reads: "Today the Virgin Mother of God was taken up into heaven to be the beginning and the pattern of the Church in its perfection, and a sign of sure hope and comfort for your pilgrim people. You would not allow decay to touch her body, for she had given birth in the glory of the Incarnation to your Son, the Lord of all life." (Cf. also *Constitution on the Church,* No. 68.)

Mother of God

In 325 the first ecumenical council, at Nicaea, proclaimed that Jesus is truly Son of God. Defenders of the faith there were the first to call Mary "Mother of God." At the third ecumenical council, Ephesus, in 431, it was solemnly established that the Virgin Mary is indeed "Mother of God," for the Son to whom she gave birth is the pre-existent Second Person of the Blessed Trinity. "Mother of God" had already been used as a popular title in some parts of the Church, and after Ephesus it was adopted in the prayers of the Mass, as is still the practice in the Catholic Church and all Eastern Churches. For example, the current third Eucharistic Prayer reads: "May he (the Holy Spirit) make us an everlasting gift to you (the Father) and enable us to share in the inheritance of your saints, with Mary, the Virgin Mother of God."

Mother of the Church

When the Church began to celebrate the Assumption of Mary, it did so in the conviction Mary did not leave the members of the Church orphans when her days on earth were ended. She continues her interest for them in union with her Son, the supreme intercessor. By the time of the Council of Ephesus in 431, authors of both the East and West — like St. Ephrem of Syria (d. 373) and St. Ambrose of Italy (d. 397) — proposed Mary as the model of Christian life, and the practice of asking her to pray for her clients on earth began to appear. The feasts of the Nativity of Mary (September 8), the Annunciation (March 25) and the Presentation of Jesus (February 2, also known as the Purification of Mary or Candlemas) have been kept from the sixth and seventh centuries.

When the words of Gabriel and Elizabeth from St. Luke's infancy narrative became part of prayer, the first part of the Hail Mary, their use led to deeper awareness of Mary's holiness as well as to counting on her heavenly help — well expressed in the second part of the Hail Mary — "Holy Mary, Mother of God, pray for us sinners now and at the hour of our death," which reached its fixed form only in the fifteenth century. Mary's place in liturgical prayer and in private prayer reflected and strengthened the sense of her continuing role as loving friend in heaven of the Church on earth. People asked Mary's prayers on their behalf, recalling Mary's own "pilgrimage of faith" and trusting in her abiding maternal care.

Greek homilists like St. John of Damascus (d. ca. 749), St. Andrew of Crete (d. 740) and St. Germanus of Constantinople (d. ca. 733) sang Mary's praises and urged confidence in her loving intercession with Christ. In the West, after the upsurge of the Carolingian times (about 800), remembered for the origin of the Saturday observance in honor of Mary, came the flowering of medieval piety, as evidenced in the writings of St. Anselm (d. 1109), St. Bernard (d. 1153) and his fellow Cistercians, and the great scholastic doctors like St. Thomas Aquinas (d. 1274) and St. Bonaventure (d. 1274). The medieval authors described Mary as Mediatrix of grace, Dispensatrix of grace, spiritual Mother. Blessed Guerric, the Cistercian abbot of Igny (France, d. 1157), emphasized the maternal role of Mary in the formation of Christ in the faithful: "Like the Church of which she is a figure, Mary is Mother of all who are born to life."

Christian Unity and Mary

At the Reformation, in reaction to abuses, the invocation of the saints was rejected as harmful to confidence in Christ the unique Mediator. Since the sixteenth century Western Christians have been sharply divided in their understanding of the communion of saints and the legitimacy of "praying to Mary." Recent events, however, hold out hope for a meeting of minds and hearts even in this sensitive area. The Second Vatican Council offered a biblical portrait of Mary without neglecting later developments in doctrine and devotion. The council described the place of Mary in words designed to meet Protestant difficulties; e.g., the much misunderstood word, Mediatrix, was used once only and was explained as completely dependent on the unique mediatorship of Christ (*Constitution on the Church*, Nos. 67, 69).

The conciliar Decree on Ecumenism, issued Nov. 21, 1964, spoke of the "order" or "hierarchy of truths" among Catholic doctrines, which differ in their relationship to the foundation of the faith (No. 11). The foundation is Jesus Christ, and here all Christians share a common profession of faith. The document mentioned realistically some differences that still divide Catholics and other Christians, in this "order of truths": the meaning of the Incarnation and Redemption, the mystery and ministry of the Church, and the role of Mary in the work of salvation (No. 20). The decree also said in this context: "We rejoice to see our separated brethren looking to Christ as the source and center of ecclesiastical communion. Inspired by longing for union with Christ, they feel compelled to search for unity ever more ardently, and to bear witness to their faith among all the peoples of the earth."

The formation of the Ecumenical Society of the Blessed Virgin Mary in England in 1967, and of the American branch in 1976, is an encouraging sign. The American bishops' pastoral, *"Behold Your Mother,"* appealed to the "basic reverence" of all Christians for Mary, "a veneration deeper than doctrinal differences and theological disputes" (Nos. 101-112). Pope Paul VI's major document, *Marialis Cultus*, contains an appeal to other Christians (Nos. 32 and 33). With Christians of the East, said Pope Paul, Catholics honor the Mother of God as "hope of Christians." Catholics join with Anglicans and Protestants in common praise of God, using the Virgin's own words (Lk. 1:46-55).

It may well be that the growing interest in

the bonds between the Blessed Virgin and the Holy Spirit will help bring Christians together. The Spirit of unity inspired Mary's proph-

ecy: "All generations will call me blessed, because he who is mighty has done great things for me" (Lk. 1:48-49).

APPARITIONS OF THE BLESSED VIRGIN MARY

Only eight of the best known apparitions of the Blessed Virgin Mary are described briefly below.

The sites of the following apparitions have become shrines and centers of pilgrimage. Miracles of the moral and physical orders have been reported as occurring at these places and/or in connection with related practices of prayer and penance.

Banneux, near Liege, Belgium: Mary appeared eight times between Jan. 15 and Mar. 2, 1933, to an 11-year-old peasant girl, Mariette Beco, in a garden behind the family cottage in Banneux, near Liege. She called herself the Virgin of the Poor, and has since been venerated as Our Lady of the Poor, the Sick, and the Indifferent. A small chapel was built by a spring near the site of the apparitions and was blessed Aug. 15, 1933. Approval of devotion to Our Lady of Banneux was given in 1949 by Bishop Louis J. Kerkhofs of Liege, and a statue of that title was solemnly crowned in 1956.

Over 100 sanctuaries throughout the world are dedicated to the honor of Our Lady of Banneux.

The **International Union of Prayer,** for devotion to the Virgin of the Poor, has approximately two million members.

Beauraing, Belgium: Mary appeared 33 times between Nov. 29, 1932, and Jan. 3, 1933, to five children in the garden of a convent school in Beauraing. A chapel, which became a pilgrimage center, was erected on the spot. Reserved approval of devotion to Our Lady of Beauraing was given Feb. 2, 1943, and final approbation July 2, 1949, by Bishop Charue of Namur.

The **Marian Union of Beauraing,** a prayer association for the conversion of sinners, has thousands of members throughout the world (see Pro Maria Committee).

Fatima, Portugal: Mary appeared six times between May 13 and Oct. 13, 1917, to three children in a field called Cova da Iria near Fatima, north of Lisbon. She recommended frequent recitation of the Rosary; urged works of mortification for the conversion of sinners; called for devotion to herself under the title of her Immaculate Heart; asked that the people of Russia be consecrated to her under this title, and that the faithful make a Communion of reparation on the first Saturday of each month.

The apparitions were declared worthy of belief in October, 1930, after a seven-year canonical investigation, and devotion to Our Lady of Fatima was authorized under the title of Our Lady of the Rosary. In October, 1942,

Pius XII consecrated the world to Mary under the title of her Immaculate Heart. Ten years later, in the first apostolic letter addressed directly to the peoples of Russia, he consecrated them in a special manner to Mary.

Fatima, with its sanctuary and basilica, ranks with Lourdes as the greatest of modern Marian shrines.

(See First Saturday Devotion.)

Guadalupe, Mexico: Mary appeared four times in 1531 to an Indian, Juan Diego, on Tepeyac hill outside of Mexico City, and instructed him to tell Bishop Zumarraga of her wish that a church be built there. The bishop complied with the request about two years later after being convinced of the genuineness of the apparition by the evidence of a miraculously painted life-size figure of the Virgin on the mantle of the Indian. The mantle bearing the picture has been preserved and is enshrined in the Basilica of Our Lady of Guadalupe, which has a long history as a center of devotion and pilgrimage in Mexico. The shrine church, originally dedicated in 1709 and subsequently enlarged, has the title of basilica.

Benedict XIV, in a decree issued in 1754, authorized a Mass and Office under the title of Our Lady of Guadalupe for celebration on Dec. 12, and named Mary the patroness of New Spain. Our Lady of Guadalupe was designated patroness of Latin America by St. Pius X in 1910 and patroness of the Americas by Pius XII in 1945.

Knock, Ireland: An apparition of Mary, along with the figures of St. Joseph and St. John the Apostle, was witnessed by at least 15 persons in the evening of Aug. 21, 1879, near the parish church of Knock, County Mayo. A commission appointed by the Bishop of Tuam to investigate the matter reported that testimony confirming the apparition was "trustworthy and satisfactory."

La Salette, France: Mary appeared as a sorrowing and weeping figure Sept. 19, 1846, to two peasant children, Melanie Matthieu, 15, and Maximin Giraud, 11, at La Salette in southern France. The message she confided to them, regarding the necessity of penance, was communicated to Pius IX in 1851 and has since been known at the "secret" of La Salette. Bishop de Bruillard of Grenoble declared in 1851 that the apparition was credible, and devotion to Mary under the title of Our Lady of La Salette was authorized. The devotion has been confirmed by popes since the time of Pius IX, and a Mass and Office with this title were authorized in 1942.

The shrine church was given the title of minor basilica in 1879.

Lourdes, France: Mary, identifying herself as the Immaculate Conception, appeared 18 times between Feb. 11 and July 16, 1858, to 14-year-old Bernadette Soubirous at the grotto of Massabielle near Lourdes in southern France. Her message concerned the necessity of prayer and penance for the conversion of men. Mary's request that a chapel be built at the grotto and spring was fulfilled in 1862 after four years of rigid examination established the credibility of the apparitions. Devotion under the title of Our Lady of Lourdes was authorized later, and a Feb. 11 feast commemorating the apparitions was instituted by Leo XIII. St. Pius X extended this feast throughout the Church in 1907.

The Church of Notre Dame was made a basilica in 1870, and the Church of the Rosary was built later. The underground Church of St. Pius X, consecrated Mar. 25, 1958, is the second largest church in the world, with a capacity of 20,000 persons.

Our Lady of the Miraculous Medal, France: Mary appeared three times in 1830 to Catherine Laboure in the chapel of the motherhouse of the Daughters of Charity of St. Vincent de Paul, Rue de Bac, Paris. She commissioned Catherine to have made the medal of the Immaculate Conception, now known as the Miraculous Medal, and to spread devotion to her under this title. In 1832, the medal was struck according to the model revealed to Catherine.

Secret of Fatima

Sister Lucy, a Carmelite nun and one of the trio of shepherd children to whom Mary appeared, wrote a three-part account of an apparition which occurred July 13, 1917. The first part concerned a vision of hell. The second dealt with the conversion of the peoples of Russia through devotion to Mary under the title of her Immaculate Heart. The third part was the so-called "secret" which, it was said, was not to be opened until 1960 or the death of Sister Lucy, whichever came first. Presumably, the "secret" was a prophecy of dire events. To date, it has not been disclosed. Church officials have decried morbid concern about it.

THREE CANONIZATIONS

Three of the four saints canonized in 1982 were Crispin of Viterbo, June 20, and Marguerite Bourgeoys and Jeanne Delanoue, both on Oct. 31. (Maximilian Kolbe was canonized Oct. 10.)

St. Crispin of Viterbo

The canonization of Crispin of Viterbo, a Franciscan lay brother for 57 years, was a first for Pope John Paul. It was, he said "the first time during my service in the See of Peter that I have had the joyous destiny to carry out a canonization."

The newly declared saint was born Pietro Fioretti Nov. 13, 1668, in Viterbo, Italy. A shoemaker by trade, he joined the Friars Minor Capuchin in 1693. He served as an alms collector for his community and the poor for nearly 40 years in Orvieto, as a cook in houses of his order in Albano and Tolfa, as a nurse in Rome and as a gardener in Monterotondo. He died after two years of illness May 19, 1750, in Rome. He was beatified by Pope Pius VII in 1806.

The Pope called him an "authentic son of Francis of Assisi (who) offers a lesson of humble and faithful adhesion to God, to love, to poverty, to obedience to the Church, to commitment to Mary." He said his life was marked by joy and by an "heroic openness toward his fellow brothers and to the poor and needy of every category."

St. Marguerite Bourgeoys

Marguerite Bourgeoys was born Apr. 17, 1620, in Troyes, France.

Self-supporting but unsuccessful in attempts to join the Carmelites and Poor Clares, she was associated with a small community before going to Canada in 1653, where she began teaching, established the first school in Montreal and, in 1676, a school for Iroquois Indians. In 1658, she began the formation of a community that was approved as the Congregation of Notre Dame de Montreal by Bishop Laval of Quebec in 1676. She and other sisters of the institute were not permitted to profess vows, however, until 1698 because of controversy over their uncloistered way of life. She died Jan. 12, 1700, in Montreal.

Marguerite, one of the courageous women missionaries in Canada, was declared Blessed by Pope Pius XII in 1950.

St. Jeanne Delanoue

Jeanne Delanoue, foundress of the Sisters of St. Anne of Providence, was born in 1666 in Saumur, France.

Following a remarkable conversion from a self-seeking life-style to one of penance and austerity, she was inspired by grace to devote her resources of self and possessions to the service of the poor. She turned her own home into a "House of Providence," a haven for the unfortunate and hungry, and established similar houses in Breze and Puy-Notre-Dame, for the feeding and housing of homeless persons. Her own home was erected as a religious house in 1704. She died in poverty Aug. 17, 1736, in Saumur.

Jeanne was declared Blessed by Pope Pius XII Nov. 9, 1947.

Eastern Catholic Churches

The Second Vatican Council, in its *Decree on Eastern Catholic Churches,* stated the following points.

"The Catholic Church holds in high esteem the institutions of the Eastern Churches, their liturgical rites, ecclesiastical traditions, and Christian way of life. For, distinguished as they are by their venerable antiquity, they are bright with that tradition which was handed down from the apostles through the Fathers, and which forms part of the divinely revealed and undivided heritage of the universal Church" (No. 1).

"That Church, Holy and Catholic, which is the Mystical Body of Christ, is made up of the faithful who are organically united in the Holy Spirit through the same faith, the same sacraments, and the same government and who, combining into various groups held together by a hierarchy, form separate Churches or rites. ... It is the mind of the Catholic Church that each individual Church or rite retain its traditions whole and entire, while adjusting its way of life to the various needs of time and place" (No. 2).

"Such individual Churches, whether of the East or of the West, although they differ somewhat among themselves in what are called rites (that is, in liturgy, ecclesiastical discipline, and spiritual heritage) are, nevertheless, equally entrusted to the pastoral guidance of the Roman Pontiff, the divinely appointed successor of St. Peter in supreme government over the universal Church. They are consequently of equal dignity, so that none of them is superior to the others by reason of rite" (No. 3).

Eastern Heritage: "Each and every Catholic, as also the baptized ... of every non-Catholic Church or community who enters into the fullness of Catholic communion, should everywhere retain his proper rite, cherish it, and observe it to the best of his ability ..." (No. 4).

"... The Churches of the East, as much as those of the West, fully enjoy the right, and are in duty bound, to rule themselves. Each should do so according to its proper and individual procedures ..." (No. 5).

"All Eastern rite members should know and be convinced that they can and should always preserve their lawful liturgical rites and their established way of life, and that these should not be altered except by way of an appropriate and organic development ..." (No. 6)

Patriarchs: "The institution of the patriarchate has existed in the Church from the earliest times and was recognized by the first ecumenical Synods.

"By the name Eastern Patriarch is meant the bishop who has jurisdiction over all bishops (including metropolitans), clergy, and people of his own territory or rite, in accordance with the norms of law and without prejudice to the primacy of the Roman Pontiff ..." (No. 7).

"Though some of the patriarchates of the Eastern Churches are of later origin than others, all are equal in patriarchal dignity. Still the honorary and lawfully established order of precedence among them is to be preserved" (No. 8).

"In keeping with the most ancient tradition of the Church, the Patriarchs of the Eastern Churches are to be accorded exceptional respect, since each presides over his patriarchate as father and head.

"This sacred Synod, therefore, decrees that their rights and privileges should be re-established in accord with the ancient traditions of each Church and the decrees of the ecumenical Synods.

"The rights and privileges in question are those which flourished when East and West were in union, though they should be somewhat adapted to modern conditions.

"The Patriarchs with their synods constitute the superior authority for all affairs of the patriarchate, including the right to establish new eparchies and to nominate bishops of their rite within the territorial bounds of the patriarchate, without prejudice to the inalienable right of the Roman Pontiff to intervene in individual cases" (No. 9).

"What has been said of Patriarchs applies as well, under the norm of law, to major archbishops, who preside over the whole of some individual Church or rite" (No. 10).

Sacraments: "This sacred Ecumenical Synod endorses and lauds the ancient discipline of the sacraments existing in the Eastern Churches, as also the practices connected with their celebration and administration ..." (No. 12).

"With respect to the minister of holy chrism (confirmation), let that practice be fully restored which existed among Easterners in most ancient times. Priests, therefore, can validly confer this sacrament, provided they use chrism blessed by a Patriarch or bishop" (No. 13).

"In conjunction with baptism or otherwise, all Eastern-Rite priests can confer this sacrament validly on all the faithful of any rite, including the Latin; licitly, however, only if the regulations of both common and particular law are observed. Priests of the Latin rite, to the extent of the faculties they enjoy for administering this sacrament, can confer it also on the faithful of Eastern Churches, without prejudice to rite. They do so licitly if the regulations of both common and particular law are observed" (No. 14).

"The faithful are bound on Sundays and feast days to attend the divine liturgy or, according to the regulations or custom of their own rite, the celebration of the Divine Praises. That the faithful may be able to satisfy their obligation more easily, it is decreed that this obligation can be fulfilled from the Vespers of the vigil to the end of the Sunday or the feast day . . ." (No. 15).

"Because of the everyday intermingling of the communicants of diverse Eastern Churches in the same Eastern region or territory, the faculty for hearing confession, duly and unrestrictedly granted by his proper bishop to a priest of any rite, is applicable to the entire territory of the grantor, also to the places and the faithful belonging to any other rite in the same territory, unless an Ordinary of the place explicitly decides otherwise with respect to the places pertaining to his rite" (No. 16).

". . . This sacred Synod ardently desires that where it has fallen into disuse the office of the permanent diaconate be restored. The legislative authority of each individual church should decide about the subdiaconate and the minor orders . . ." (No. 17).

"By way of preventing invalid marriages between Eastern Catholics and baptized Eastern non-Catholics, and in the interests of the permanence and sanctity of marriage and of domestic harmony, this sacred Synod decrees that the canonical 'form' for the celebration of such marriages obliges only for lawfulness. For their validity, the presence of a sacred minister suffices, as long as the other requirements of law are honored" (No. 18).

Worship: "Henceforth, it will be the exclusive right of an ecumenical Synod or the Apostolic See to establish, transfer, or suppress feast days common to all the Eastern Churches. To establish, transfer, or suppress feast days for any of the individual Churches is within the competence not only of the Apostolic See but also of a patriarchal or archiepiscopal synod, provided due consideration is given to the entire region and to other individual Churches" (No. 19).

"Until such time as all Christians desirably concur on a fixed day for the celebration of Easter, and with a view meantime to promoting unity among the Christians of a given area or nation, it is left to the Patriarchs or supreme authorities of a place to reach a unanimous agreement, after ascertaining the views of all concerned, on a single Sunday for the observance of Easter" (No. 20).

"With respect to rules concerning sacred seasons, individual faithful dwelling outside the area or territory of their own rite may conform completely to the established custom of the place where they live. When members of a family belong to different rites, they are all permitted to observe sacred seasons according to the rules of any one of these rites" (No. 21).

"From ancient times the Divine Praises have been held in high esteem among all Eastern Churches. Eastern clerics and religious should celebrate these Praises as the laws and customs of their own traditions require. To the extent they can, the faithful too should follow the example of their forbears by assisting devoutly at the Divine Praises" (No. 22).

Origin

The Church had its beginnings in Palestine, whence it spread to other regions of the world. As it spread, certain cities or jurisdictions became key centers of Christian life and missionary endeavor — notably, Jerusalem, Alexandria, Antioch and Constantinople in the East, and Rome in the West — with the result that their practices became diffused throughout their spheres of influence. Various rites originated from these practices which, although rooted in the essentials of Christian faith, were different in significant respects because of their relationships to particular cultural patterns.

Patriarchal Jurisdictions

The main lines of Eastern Church organization and liturgy were drawn before the Roman Empire was separated into Eastern and Western divisions in 292. It was originally coextensive with the boundaries of the Eastern Empire. Its jurisdictions were those of the patriarchates of Alexandria and Antioch (recognized as such by the Council of Nicaea in 325), and of Jerusalem and Constantinople (given similar recognition by the Council of Chalcedon in 451). These were the major parent bodies of the Eastern Rite Churches which for centuries were identifiable only with limited numbers of nationality and language groups in Eastern Europe, the Middle East and parts of Asia and Africa. Their members are now scattered throughout the world.

NORTH AMERICAN COLLEGE

The North American College was founded by the bishops of the United States in 1859 as a residence and house of formation for U.S. seminarians and graduate students in Rome. The first ordination of an alumnus took place June 14, 1862. Pontifical status was granted the college by Leo XIII Oct. 25, 1884.

Students living at the college study theology and related subjects in the various pontifical universities and institutes in Rome, principally at the Pontifical Gregorian University.

The college is directed by an American rector and staff, and operates under the auspices of a U.S. bishops' committee which was set up in 1924.

RITES AND FAITHFUL OF EASTERN CHURCHES

(Principal source of statistics: *Annuario Pontificio*. The statistics are for Eastern-Rite jurisdictions only, and do not include Eastern-Rite Catholics under the jurisdiction of Roman-Rite bishops. Some of the figures reported are only approximate. Some of the jurisdictions listed may be inactive because of government suppression.)

The Byzantine, Alexandrian, Antiochene, Armenian and Chaldean are the five principal rites used in their entirety or in modified form by the various Eastern churches. The number of Eastern Catholics throughout the world is more than 12 million.

Alexandrian Rite

Called the Liturgy of St. Mark, the Alexandrian Rite was modified by the Copts and Melkites, and contains elements of the Byzantine Rite of St. Basil and the liturgies of Sts. Mark, Cyril and Gregory of Nazianzen. The liturgy is substantially that of the Coptic Church, which is divided into two branches — the Coptic or Egyptian, and the Ethiopian or Abyssinian.

The faithful of this rite are:

COPTS: Returned to Catholic unity about 1741; situated in Egypt, the Near East; liturgical languages are Coptic, Arabic. Jurisdictions (located in Egypt): patriarchate of Alexandria, three dioceses; 134,130.

ETHIOPIANS: Returned to Catholic unity in 1846: situated in Ethiopia, Eritrea, Jerusalem, Somalia; liturgical language is Geez. Jurisdictions (located in Ethiopia): one archdiocese, two dioceses; 101,246.

Antiochene Rite

This is the source of more derived rites than any of the other parent rites. Its origin can be traced to the Eighth Book of the *Apostolic Constitutions* and to the Liturgy of St. James of Jerusalem, which ultimately spread throughout the whole patriarchate and displaced older forms based on the *Apostolic Constitutions.*

The faithful of this rite are:

MALANKARESE: Returned to Catholic unity in 1930; situated in India; liturgical languages are Syriac, Malayalam. Jurisdictions (located in India): one archdiocese, two dioceses; 246,980.

MARONITES: United to the Holy See since the time of their founder, St. Maron; have no counterparts among the separated Eastern Christians: situated throughout the world: liturgical languages are Syriac, Arabic. Jurisdictions (located in Lebanon, Cyprus, Egypt, Syria, U.S., Brazil, Australia): patriarchate of Antioch, 16 archdioceses and dioceses, one patriarchal vicariate; 1,727,040. Where no special jurisdictions exist, they are under jurisdiction of local Roman-Rite bishops.

SYRIANS: Returned to Catholic unity in 1781; situated in Asia, Africa, the Americas, Australia; liturgical languages are Syriac, Arabic. Jurisdictions (located in Lebanon, Iraq, Egypt, Syria and Turkey): patriarchate of Antioch, seven archdioceses and dioceses, three patriarchal vicariates; 87,954.

Armenian Rite

Substantially, although using a different language, this is the Greek Liturgy of St. Basil; it is considered an older form of the Byzantine Rite, and incorporates some modifications from the Antiochene Rite.

The faithful of this rite are:

ARMENIANS, exclusively: Returned to Catholic unity during the time of the Crusades; situated in the Near East, Europe, Africa, the Americas, Australasia: liturgical language is Classical Armenian. Jurisdictions (located in Lebanon, Iran, Iraq, Egypt, Syria, Turkey, Poland, France, Greece, Rumania, Argentina — for Latin America, and the United States — for Canada and the U.S.): patriarchate of Cilicia, eight archdioceses and dioceses, two patriarchal vicariates, three exarchates, two ordinariates; 84,560.

Byzantine Rite

Based on the Rite of St. James of Jerusalem and the churches of Antioch, and reformed by Sts. Basil and John Chrysostom, the Byzantine Rite is proper to the Church of Constantinople. (The city was called Byzantium before Constantine changed its name; the modern name is Istanbul.) It is now used by the majority of Eastern Catholics and by the Eastern Orthodox Church (which is not in union with Rome). It is, after the Roman, the most widely used rite.

The faithful of this rite are:

ALBANIANS: Returned to Catholic unity about 1628; situated in Albania; liturgical language is Albanian. Jurisdiction (located in Albania): one apostolic administration.

BULGARIANS: Returned to Catholic unity about 1861; situated in Bulgaria; liturgical language is Old Slavonic. Jurisdiction (located in Bulgaria): one apostolic exarchate.

BYELORUSSIANS, also known as WHITE RUSSIANS: Returned to Catholic unity in the 17th century; situated in Europe, the Americas, Australia; liturgical language is Old Slavonic. They have an apostolic visitor residing at Rome.

GEORGIANS: Returned to Catholic unity in 1861; situated in Georgia (Southern Russia), France; liturgical language is Georgian. They have an apostolic administrator.

GREEKS: Returned to Catholic unity in 1829; situated in Greece, Asia Minor, Europe; liturgical language is Greek. Jurisdictions (located in Greece and Turkey): two exarchates; 2,560.

HUNGARIANS: Descendants of Ruthenians who returned to Catholic unity in 1646; situated in Hungary, the rest of Europe, the Americas; liturgical languages are Greek, Hungarian, English. Jurisdictions (located in Hungary): one diocese and one exarchate: 322,800.

ITALO-ALBANIANS: Have never been separated from Rome; situated in Italy, Sicily, the Americas; liturgical languages are Greek, Italo-Albanian. Jurisdictions (located in Italy): two dioceses, one abbacy; 70,054.

MELKITES (GREEK CATHOLICS-MELKITES): Returned to Catholic unity during the time of the Crusades, but definitive reunion did not take place until early in the 18th century; situated in the Middle East, Asia, Africa, Europe, the Americas, Australia; liturgical languages are Greek, Arabic, English, Portuguese, Spanish. Jurisdictions (located in Syria, Lebanon, Jordan, Israel, U.S., Brazil, Canada): patriarchate of Antioch (with patriarchal vicariates in Egypt, Sudan, Jerusalem, Iraq and Kuwait), 16 archdioceses and one exarchate; 584,156, (*Annuario Pontificio* figures. Some sources estimate 1,000,000.)

ROMANIANS: Returned to Catholic unity in 1697; situated in Rumania, the rest of Europe, the Americas; liturgical language is Modern Romanian. Jurisdictions (located in Rumania): one archdiocese, four dioceses. There were 1.5 million members in 1948 when they were forcibly incorporated into the Romanian Orthodox Church. They have an apostolic visitor in the U.S. where they number approximately 5,000.

RUSSIANS: Returned to Catholic unity about 1905; situated in Europe, the Americas, Australia, China; liturgical language is Old Slavonic. Jurisdictions (located in Russia and China): two exarchates.

RUTHENIANS, or CARPATHO-RUSSIANS (Rusins): Returned to Catholic unity in the Union of Brest-Litovek, 1596, and the Union of Uzhorod, Apr. 24, 1646; situated in Hungary, Czechoslovakia, elsewhere in Europe, the Americas, Australia; liturgical languages are Old Slavonic, English. Jurisdictions (located in Russia and the U.S.): one archdiocese, four dioceses.

SLOVAKS: Jurisdictions (located in Czechoslovakia and Canada): two dioceses.

UKRAINIANS, or GALICIAN RUTHENIANS: Returned to Catholic unity about 1595; situated in Europe, the Americas, Australasia; liturgical languages are Old Slavonic and Ukrainian. Jurisdictions (located in Russian Galicia, Poland, the U.S., Canada, England, Australia, Germany, France, Brazil, Argentina): three archdioceses, 10 dioceses, five apostolic exarchates: 4,373,112. This total in-

cludes the 1943 figure of 3.5 million Ukrainian Catholics in jurisdictions subsequently forced into the Russian Orthodox Church.

YUGOSLAVS, SERBS and CROATIANS: Returned to Catholic unity in 1611; situated in Yugoslavia, the Americas; liturgical language is Old Slavonic. Jurisdiction (located in Yugoslavia): one diocese (which also has jurisdiction over all Byzantine-Rite faithful in Yugoslavia); 48,875. They are under the jurisdiction of Ruthenian bishops elsewhere.

Chaldean Rite

This rite, listed as separate and distinct by the Sacred Congregation for the Oriental Churches, was derived from the Antiochene Rite.

The faithful of this rite are:

CHALDEANS: Descendants of the Nestorians, returned to Catholic unity in 1692; situated throughout the Middle East, in Europe, Africa, the Americas; liturgical languages are Syriac, Arabic. Jurisdictions (located in Egypt, Iraq, Iran, Lebanon, Syria, Turkey, U.S.); patriarchate of Babylonia, 20 archdioceses and dioceses, one apostolic exarchate; 368,798. There are patriarchal vicars for Jordan and Egypt.

SYRO-MALABARESE: Descended from the St. Thomas Christians of India; situated mostly in the Malabar region of India; they use a Westernized and Latinized form of the Chaldean Rite in Syriac and Malayalam. Jurisdictions (located in India): two archdioceses, 16 dioceses; 2,379,856.

EASTERN JURISDICTIONS

For centuries Eastern-Rite Catholics were identifiable with a limited number of nationality and language groups in certain countries of the Middle East, Eastern Europe, Asia and Africa. The persecution of religion in the Soviet Union since 1917 and in communist-controlled countries since World War II, however — in addition to decimating and destroying the Church in those places — has resulted in the emigration of many Eastern-Rite Catholics from their homelands. This forced emigration, together with voluntary emigration, has led to the spread of Eastern Rites and their faithful to many other countries.

Europe

(Archbishop Miroslav Marusyn is apostolic visitor for Byzantine Rite Catholics in western Europe who have no bishop of their own.)

ALBANIA: Byzantine Rite, apostolic administration.

AUSTRIA: Byzantine Rite, ordinariate.

BULGARIA: Byzantine Rite (Bulgarians), apostolic exarchate.

CZECHOSLOVAKIA: Byzantine Rite (Slovakians and other Byzantine-Rite Catholics), eparchy.

FRANCE: Byzantine Rite (Ukrainians), apostolic exarchate.
Armenian Rite, apostolic exarchate.
Ordinariate for all other Eastern-Rite Catholics.
GERMANY: Byzantine Rite (Ukrainians), apostolic exarchate.
GREAT BRITAIN: Byzantine Rite (Ukrainians), apostolic exarchate.
GREECE: Byzantine Rite, apostolic exarchate.
Armenian Rite, ordinariate.
HUNGARY: Byzantine Rite (Hungarians), eparchy, apostolic exarchate.
ITALY: Byzantine Rite (Italo-Albanians), two eparchies, one abbacy.
POLAND: Byzantine Rite (Ukrainian), apostolic exarchate.
Armenian Rite, archeparchy.
RUMANIA: Byzantine Rite (Romanians), metropolitan, four eparchies.
Armenian Rite, ordinariate.
RUSSIA: Byzantine Rite (Russians), apostolic exarchate; (Ruthenians), eparchy; (Ukrainians), major archeparchy, two eparchies.
YUGOSLAVIA: Byzantine Rite (Yugoslav and other Byzantine-Rite Catholics), eparchy.

Asia

CHINA: Byzantine Rite (Russians), apostolic exarchate.
CYPRUS: Antiochene Rite (Maronites), archeparchy.
INDIA: Antiochene Rite (Malankarese), metropolitan see, two eparchies.
Chaldean Rite (Syro-Malabarese), two metropolitan sees, 16 eparchies.
IRAN: Chaldean Rite (Chaldeans), two metropolitan sees, one archeparchy, one eparchy.
Armenian Rite, eparchy.
IRAQ: Antiochene Rite (Syrians), two archeparchies.
Byzantine Rite (Greek-Melkites), patriarchal vicariate.
Chaldean Rite (Chaldeans), patriarchate, two metropolitan sees, eight archeparchies and eparchies.
Armenian Rite, archeparchy.
ISRAEL (includes Jerusalem): Antiochene Rite (Syrians), patriarchal vicariate; (Maronites), patriarchal vicariate.
Byzantine Rite (Greek-Melkites), archeparchy, patriarchal vicariate.
Chaldean Rite (Chaldeans), patriarchal vicariate.
Armenian Rite, patriarchal vicariate.
JORDAN: Byzantine Rite (Greek-Melkites), archeparchy.
KUWAIT: Byzantine Rite (Greek-Melkites), patriarchal vicariate.
LEBANON: Antiochene Rite (Maronites), patriarchate, eight archeparchies and eparchies; (Syrians), patriarchate.
Byzantine Rite (Greek-Melkites), seven metropolitan and archeparchal sees.
Chaldean Rite (Chaldeans), eparchy.
Armenian Rite, patriarchate, eparchy.
SYRIAN ARAB REPUBLIC: Antiochene Rite (Maronites), two archeparchies, one eparchy; (Syrians), four archeparchies.
Byzantine Rite (Greek-Melkites), patriarchate, four metropolitan sees, one archeparchy.
Chaldean Rite (Chaldeans), eparchy.
Armenian Rite, archeparchy, eparchy, patriarchal vicariate.
TURKEY (Europe and Asia): Antiochene Rite (Syrians), patriarchal vicariate.
Byzantine Rite (Greeks), apostolic exarchate.
Chaldean Rite (Chaldeans), one archeparchy, two eparchies.
Armenian Rite, archeparchy.

Oceania

AUSTRALIA: Byzantine Rite (Ukrainians), apostolic exarchate.
Antiochene Rite (Maronites), eparchy.

Africa

EGYPT, ARAB REPUBLIC OF: Alexandrian Rite (Copts), patriarchate, three eparchies.
Antiochene Rite (Maronites), eparchy; (Syrians), eparchy.
Byzantine Rite (Greek-Melkites), patriarchal vicariate.
Chaldean Rite (Chaldeans), eparchy.
Armenian Rite, eparchy.
ETHIOPIA: Alexandrian Rite (Ethiopians), metropolitan see, two eparchies.
SUDAN: Byzantine Rite (Greek-Melkites), patriarchal vicariate.

North America

CANADA: Byzantine Rite (Ukrainians), one metropolitan, four eparchies; (Slovaks), eparchy; (Greek-Melkites), apostolic exarchate.
Armenian Rite, apostolic exarchate for Canada and the U.S. (New York is see city).
UNITED STATES: Antiochene Rite (Maronites), eparchy.
Byzantine Rite (Ukrainians), one metropolitan see, two eparchies; (Ruthenians), one metropolitan see, three eparchies; (Greek-Melkites), eparchy; (Romanians), apostolic visitor.
Armenian Rite, apostolic exarchate for Canada and U.S. (New York is see city).
Chaldean Rite, apostolic exarchate.
Other Eastern-Rite Catholics are under the jurisdiction of local Roman-Rite bishops. (See Eastern-Rite Catholics in the United States.)

South America

ARGENTINA: Byzantine Rite (Ukrainians), eparchy.

Armenian Rite, apostolic exarchate (for Latin America)

Ordinariate for all other Eastern-Rite Catholics.

BRAZIL: Antiochene Rite (Maronites), eparchy.

Byzantine Rite (Greek-Melkites), eparchy; (Ukrainians), eparchy.

Ordinariate for all other Eastern-Rite Catholics.

SYNODS, ASSEMBLIES

These assemblies are collegial bodies which have pastoral authority over members of the Eastern Rite Churches.

Patriarchal Synods: Maronites: Antoine Khoraiche, patriarch of Antioch of the Maronites.

Melkites: Maximos V Hakim, patriarch of Antioch of the Greek Catholics-Melkites.

Chaldeans: Paul II Cheikho, patriarch of Babylonia of the Chaldeans.

Copts: Cardinal Stephanos I Sidarouss, C.M., patriarch of Alexandria of the Copts.

Syrians: Ignace Antoine II Hayek, patriarch of Antioch of the Syrians.

Armenians: Jean Pierre XVIII Kasparian, patriarch of Cilicia of the Armenians.

Non-Patriarchal Synod: The Synod of the Ukrainian Catholic Hierarchy is an extraterritorial synod convoked with the assent of the Pope. Cardinal Josyf Slipyi, major archbishop of Lwow of the Ukrainians, is president.

Assemblies: Assembly of Ordinaries of the Arab Republic of Egypt: Cardinal Stephanos I Sidarouss, C.M., patriarch of Alexandria of the Copts, president.

Assembly of Catholic Patriarchs and Bishops of Lebanon: Antoine Khoraiche, patriarch of Antioch of the Maronites, president.

Assembly of Ordinaries of the Syrian Arab Republic: Maximos V Hakim, patriarch of Antioch of the Greek Catholics-Melkites, president.

Interritual Union of the Bishops of Iraq: Paul II Cheikho, patriarch of Babylonia of the Chaldeans, president.

Malabarese Episcopal Conference (June 4, 1970): Cardinal Joseph Parecattil, Ernakulam, president.

Iranian Episcopal Conference (Aug. 11, 1977): Most Rev. Youhannan Semaan Issayi, metropolitan of Teheran of the Chaldeans, president.

Of the collegial bodies listed above, the patriarchal synods have the most authority. In addition to other prerogatives, they have the right to elect bishops and regulate discipline for their respective rites.

EASTERN RITES IN U.S.

(Statistics, from the *Official Catholic Directory,* are membership figures reported by Eastern-Rite jurisdictions. Additional Eastern-Rite Catholics are included in statistics for Roman-Rite dioceses.)

Byzantine Rite

Ukrainians: There are 244,728 in three jurisdictions in the U.S.: the metropolitan see of Philadelphia (1924, metropolitan 1958) and the suffragan sees of Stamford, Conn. (1956), and St. Nicholas of Chicago (1961).

Ruthenians: There are 284,338 in four jurisdictions in the U.S.: the metropolitan see of Pittsburgh (est. 1924 at Pittsburgh; metropolitan and transferred to Munhall, 1969; transferred to Pittsburgh, 1977) and the suffragan sees of Passaic, N.J. (1963), Parma, Ohio (1969) and Van Nuys, Calif. (1981). Hungarian and Croatian Byzantine Catholics in the U.S. are also under the jurisdiction of Ruthenian-Rite bishops.

Melkites (Greek Catholics-Melkites): In 1982, 22,727 (of approximately 55,000) were reported under the jurisdiction of the Melkite eparchy of Newton, Mass. (established as an exarchate, 1965; eparchy, 1976).

Romanians: There are approximately 5,000 in 16 Romanian Catholic Byzantine Rite parishes in the U.S., each under the jurisdiction of the Roman-Rite bishop of the territory in which it is located: Cleveland diocese (3 parishes), Detroit (2), Erie (1), Gary (2), Pittsburgh (1), Rockford (2), Trenton (2), and Youngstown (3). No separate statistics are available.

Byelorussians: Have one parish in the U.S. — Christ the Redeemer, Chicago, Ill.

Russians: Have parishes in California (St. Andrew, El Segundo, and Our Lady of Fatima Center, San Francisco); Massachusetts (Our Lady of Kazan, Boston); New York (St. Michael's Chapel of St. Patrick's Old Cathedral, Pope John XXIII Reunion Center).

Antiochene Rite

In 1982, 34,226 (of approximately 153,000) Maronites were reported under the jurisdiction of the eparchy of St. Maron, Brooklyn (established at Detroit as an exarchate, 1966; eparchy, 1972; transferred to Brooklyn, 1977).

Armenian Rite

An apostolic exarchate for Canada and the United States (see city, New York) was established July 17, 1981.

Chaldean Rite

An apostolic exarchate for the United States (see city, Detroit) was established Jan. 26, 1982.

BYZANTINE DIVINE LITURGY

The Divine Liturgy in all rites is based on the consecration of bread and wine by the narration-reactualization of the actions of Christ at the Last Supper. Aside from this fundamental usage, there are differences between the Roman (Latin) Rite and Eastern Rites, and among the Eastern Rites themselves. Following is a general description of the Byzantine Divine Liturgy which is in widest use in the Eastern-Rite Churches.

In the Byzantine, as in all Eastern Rites, the bread and wine are prepared at the start of the Liturgy. The priest does this in a little niche or at a table in the sanctuary. Taking a round loaf of leavened bread stamped with religious symbols, he cuts out a square host and other particles while reciting verses expressing the symbolism of the action. When the bread and wine are ready, he says a prayer of offering and incenses the oblations, the altar, the icons and the people.

At the altar a litany for all classes of people is sung by the priest. The congregation answers, "Lord, have mercy."

The Little Entrance comes next. In procession, the priest leaves the sanctuary carrying the Book of the Gospels, and then returns. He sings prayers especially selected for the day and the feast. These are followed by the solemn singing of the prayer, "Holy God, Holy Mighty One, Holy Immortal One."

The Epistle follows. The Gospel is sung or read by the priest facing the people at the middle door of the sanctuary.

An interruption after the Liturgy of the Catechumens, formerly an instructional period for those learning the faith, is clearly marked. Catechumens, if present, are dismissed with a prayer. Following this are a prayer and litany for the faithful.

The Great Entrance or solemn Offertory Procession then takes place. The priest first says a long silent prayer for himself, in preparation for the great act to come. Again he incenses the oblations, the altar, the icons and people. He goes to the table on the gospel side for the veil-covered paten and chalice. When he arrives back at the sanctuary door, he announces the intention of the Mass in the prayer: "May the Lord God remember all of you in his kingdom, now and forever."

After another litany, the congregation recites the Nicene Creed.

Consecration

The most solemn portion of the sacrifice is introduced by the preface, which is very much like the preface of the Roman Rite. At the beginning of the last phrase, the priest raises his voice to introduce the singing of the Sanctus. During the singing he reads the introduction to the words of consecration.

The words of consecration are sung aloud, and the people sing "Amen" to both consecrations. As the priest raises the Sacred Species in solemn offering, he sings: "Thine of Thine Own we offer unto Thee in behalf of all and for all."

A prayer to the Holy Spirit is followed by the commemorations, in which special mention is made of the all-holy, most blessed and glorious Lady, the Mother of God and ever-Virgin Mary. The dead are remembered and then the living.

A final litany for spiritual gifts precedes the Our Father. The Sacred Body and Blood are elevated with the words, "Holy Things for the Holy." The Host is then broken and commingled with the Precious Blood. The priest recites preparatory prayers for Holy Communion, consumes the Sacred Species, and distributes Holy Communion to the people under the forms of both bread and wine. During this time a communion verse is sung by the choir or congregation.

The Liturgy closes quickly after this. The consecrated Species of bread and wine are removed to the side table to be consumed later by the priest. A prayer of thanksgiving is recited, a prayer for all the people is said in front of the icon of Christ, a blessing is invoked upon all, and the people are dismissed.

BYZANTINE FEATURES

Art: Named for the empire in which it developed, Byzantine art is a unique blend of imperial Roman and classic Hellenic culture with Christian inspiration. The art of the Greek Middle Ages, it reached a peak of development in the 10th or 11th century. Characteristic of its products, particularly in mosaic and painting, are majesty, dignity, refinement and grace. Its sacred paintings, called icons, are reverenced highly in all Eastern Rites.

Church Building: The classical model of Byzantine church architecture is the Church of the Holy Wisdom (Hagia Sophia), built in Constantinople in the first half of the sixth century and still standing. The square structure, extended in some cases in the form of a cross, is topped by a distinctive onion-shaped dome and surmounted by a triple-bar cross. The altar is at the eastern end of building, where the wall bellies out to form an apse. The altar and sanctuary are separated from the body of the church by a fixed or movable screen, the iconostas, to which icons or sacred pictures are attached (see below).

Clergy: The Byzantine Rite has married as well as celibate priests. In places other than the US, where married candidates have not been accepted for ordination since about 1929, men already married can be ordained to the diaconate and priesthood and can continue in marriage after ordination. Celibate deacons and priests cannot marry after ordination; neither can a married priest remarry after the death of his wife. Bishops must be unmarried.

Iconostas: A large screen decorated with sacred pictures or icons which separates the sanctuary from the nave of a church.

An iconostas has three doors through which the sacred ministers enter the sanctuary during the Divine Liturgy: smaller (north and south) Deacons' Doors and a large central Royal Door.

The Deacons' Doors usually feature the icons of Sts. Gabriel and Michael; the Royal Door, the icons of the Evangelists — Matthew, Mark, Luke and John. To the right and left of the Royal Door are the icons of Christ the Teacher and of the Blessed Virgin Mary with the Infant Jesus. To the extreme right and left are the icons of the patron of the church and St. John the Baptist (or St. Nicholas of Myra).

Immediately above the Royal Door is a picture of the Last Supper. To the right are six icons depicting the major feasts of Christ, and to the left are six icons portraying the major feasts of the Blessed Virgin Mary. Above the picture of the Last Supper is a large icon of Christ the King.

Some icon screens also have pictures of the 12 Apostles and the major Old Testament prophets surmounted by a crucifixion scene.

Liturgical Language: In line with Eastern tradition, Byzantine practice has favored the use of the language of the people in the liturgy. Two great advocates of the practice were Sts. Cyril and Methodius, apostles of the Slavs, who devised the Cyrillic alphabet and pioneered the adoption of Slavonic in the liturgy.

Sacraments: Baptism is administered by immersion, and confirmation is conferred at the same time. The Eucharist is administered by intinction, i.e., by giving the communicant a piece of consecrated leavened bread which has been dipped into the consecrated wine. When giving absolution in the sacrament of penance, the priest holds his stole over the head of the penitent. Distinctive marriage ceremonies include the crowning of the bride and groom. Ceremonies for anointing the sick closely resemble those of the Roman Rite. Holy orders are conferred by a bishop.

Sign of the Cross: Eastern-Rite Catholics have a distinctive way of making it (see entry in the Glossary). The sign of the cross in conjunction with a deep bow, instead of a genuflection, expresses reverence for the presence of Christ in the Blessed Sacrament.

VESTMENTS, APPURTENANCES

Sticharion: A long white garment of linen or silk with wide sleeves and decorated with embroidery; formerly the vestment for clerics in minor orders, acolytes, lectors, chanters, and subdeacons; symbolic of purity.

Epitrachelion: A stole with ends sewn together, having a loop through which the head is passed; its several crosses symbolize priestly duties.

Zone: A narrow clasped belt made of the same material as the epitrachelion; symbolic of the wisdom of the priest, his strength against enemies of the Church and his willingness to perform holy duties.

Epimanikia: Ornamental cuffs; the right cuff symbolizing strength, the left, patience and good will.

Phelonion: An ample cape, long in the back and sides and cut away in front; symbolic of the higher gifts of the Holy Spirit.

Antimension: A silk or linen cloth laid on the altar for the Liturgy; it may be decorated with a picture of the burial of Christ and the instruments of his passion; the relics of martyrs are sewn into the front border.

Eileton: A linen cloth which corresponds to the Roman-Rite corporal.

Poterion: A chalice or cup which holds the wine and Precious Blood.

Diskos: A shallow plate, which may be elevated on a small stand, corresponding to the Roman-Rite paten.

Asteriskos: Made of two curved bands of gold or silver which cross each other to form a double arch; a star depends from the junction, which forms a cross; it is placed over the diskos holding the consecrated bread and is covered with a veil.

Veils: Three are used, one to cover the poterion, the second to cover the diskos, and the third to cover both.

Spoon: Used in administering Holy Communion by intinction; consecrated leavened bread is dipped into consecrated wine and spooned onto the tongue of the communicant.

Lance: A metal knife used for cutting up the bread to be consecrated during the Liturgy.

JOHN XXIII CENTER

The John XXIII Ecumenical Center was established in 1951 by Father Feodor Wilcock, S.J., in cooperation with Fordham University. It is sponsored by the Jesuit Conference of the United States as a center for study as well as for apostolic and ecumenical activity with Eastern Christians, Catholics and Orthodox, in America. It publishes the periodical *Diakonia,* conducts special seminars and conferences, and sponsors the John XXIII Summer Institute which offers an academic degree for studies in the Eastern traditions of Christianity.

Programs are under routine study for expansion and development of services.

Father John F. Long, S.J., is superior and director of the center, located at 2502 Belmont Ave., Bronx, N.Y 10458.

SEPARATED EASTERN CHURCHES

Orthodox

Orthodox Churches, the largest and most widespread of the separated Eastern Churches, have much in common with their Eastern Catholic counterparts, including many matters of faith and morals, general discipline, valid orders and sacraments, and liturgy. One important difference is their acceptance of only the first seven ecumenical councils. Another is their rejection of any single supreme head of the Church. They do not acknowledge and hold communion with the pope.

Like their Catholic counterparts, Orthodox Churches are organized in jurisdictions under patriarchs. The patriarchs are the heads of approximately 15 autocephalic and several other autonomous jurisdictions organized along lines of nationality and/or language.

The Ecumenical Patriarch of Constantinople, Dimitrios I, has the primacy of honor among his equal patriarchs but his actual jurisdiction is limited to his own patriarchate. As the spiritual head of worldwide Orthodoxy, he keeps the book of the Holy Canons of the Autocephalous Churches, in which recognized Orthodox Churches are registered, and has the right to call Pan-Orthodox assemblies.

The definitive Orthodox break with Rome dates from 1054.

Top-level relations between the Churches have improved in recent years through the efforts of former Ecumenical Patriarch Athenagoras I, John XXIII, Paul VI and Patriarch Dimitrios I. Pope Paul met with Athenagoras three times before the latter's death in 1972. The most significant action of both spiritual leaders was their mutual nullification of excommunications imposed by the two Churches on each other in 1054.

The largest Orthodox body in the western hemisphere is the Greek Orthodox Archdiocese of North and South America consisting of the Archdiocese of New York, nine dioceses in the U.S., and one diocese each in Canada and South America; it is headed by Archbishop Iakovos and has an estimated membership of 1.9 million. The second largest is the Orthodox Church in America, with approximately one million members; it was given independent status by the Patriarchate of Moscow May 18, 1970, against the will of Athenagoras I who refused to register it in the book of the Holy Canons of Autocephalous Churches. An additional 650,000 or more Orthodox belong to smaller national and language jurisdictions.

Heads of Orthodox jurisdictions in this hemisphere hold membership in the Standing Conference of Canonical Orthodox Bishops in the Americas.

Jurisdictions

The principal jurisdictions of the Greek, Russian and other Orthodox Churches are as follows.

Greek: Patriarchate of Constantinople, with jurisdiction in Turkey, Crete, the Dodecanese, Western Europe, the Americas, Australia; Dimitrios I is Ecumenical Patriarch.

Patriarchate of Alexandria, with jurisdiction in Egypt and the rest of Africa; there is also a native African Orthodox Church in Kenya and Uganda.

Patriarchate of Antioch (Melkites or Syrian Orthodox), with jurisdiction in Syria, Lebanon, Iraq, Australasia, the Americas; Syrian or Arabic, in place of Greek, is the liturgical language.

Patriarchate of Jerusalem, with jurisdiction in Israel and Jordan.

Churches of Greece, Cyprus and Sinai are autocephalic but maintain relations with their fellow Orthodox.

Russian: Patriarchate of Moscow with jurisdiction centered in the Soviet Union.

Other: Patriarchate of Serbia, with jurisdiction in Yugoslavia, Western Europe, the Americas, Australasia.

Patriarchates of Rumania and Bulgaria.

Katholikate of Georgia, the Soviet Union.

Byelorussians and Ukrainian Byzantines.

Churches of Albania, China, Czechoslovakia, Estonia, Finland, Hungary, Japan, Latvia, Lithuania, Poland.

Other minor communities in various places; e.g., Korea, the US, Carpatho-Russia.

The Division of Archives and Statistics of the Eastern Orthodox World Foundation reported a 1970 estimate of more than 200 million Orthodox Church members throughout the world. Other sources estimate the total to be approximately 125 million.

Nestorians, Monophysites

Unlike the majority of Eastern Christian Churches, several bodies do not acknowledge all of the first seven ecumenical councils. Nestorians acknowledge only the first two councils; they do not accept the doctrinal definition of the Council of Ephesus concerning Mary as the Mother of God. Monophysite Armenians, Syrians, Copts, Ethiopians and Jacobites acknowledge only the first three councils; they do not accept the doctrinal definition of the Council of Chalcedon concerning the two natures in Christ.

The Armenian Church has communicants in the Soviet Union, the Middle and Far East, the Americas.

The Coptic Church has communicants in Egypt and elsewhere.

The Ethiopian or Abyssinian Church has

communicants in Africa, the Middle East, the Americas, India.

The Jacobite Church (West Syrians) has communicants in the Middle East, the Americas, India.

Nestorians (Assyrians) are scattered throughout the world.

It is estimated that there are approximately 10 million or more members of these other Eastern Churches throughout the world. For various reasons, a more accurate determination is not possible.

Conference of Orthodox Bishops

The Standing Conference of Canonical Orthodox Bishops in the Americas was established in 1960 to achieve cooperation among the various ethnic churches Office: 8-10 East 79th St., New York, N.Y. 10021.

Member churches of the conference are the: Albanian Orthodox Diocese of America (Ecumenical Patriarchate), American Carpatho-Russian Greek Catholic Church, Antiochian Orthodox Christian Archdiocese of North America, Bulgarian Eastern Orthodox Church, Greek Orthodox Archdiocese of North and South America, Orthodox Church in America, Romanian Orthodox Missionary Episcopate in America, Serbian Orthodox Church in the United States of America and Canada, Ukrainian Orthodox Church in America (Ecumenical Patriarchate), Holy Ukrainian Autocephalic Orthodox Church in Exile.

EASTERN ECUMENISM

The Second Vatican Council, in the *Decree on Eastern Catholic Churches,* pointed out the special role they have to play "in promoting the unity of all Christians, particularly Easterners." The document also stated in part:

"The Eastern Churches in communion with the Apostolic See of Rome have a special role to play in promoting the unity of all Christians, particularly Easterners, according to the principles of this sacred Synod's *Decree on Ecumenism* first of all by prayer, then by the example of their lives, by religious fidelity to ancient Eastern traditions, by greater mutual knowledge, by collaboration, and by a brotherly regard for objects and attitudes" (No. 24).

"If any separated Eastern Christian should, under the guidance of grace of the Holy Spirit, join himself to Catholic unity, no more should be required of him than what a simple profession of the Catholic faith demands. A valid priesthood is preserved among Eastern clerics. Hence, upon joining themselves to the unity of the Catholic Church, Eastern clerics are permitted to exercise the orders they possess, in accordance with the regulations established by the competent authority" (No. 25).

"Divine Law forbids any common worship (*communicatio in sacris*) which would damage the unity of the Church, or involve formal acceptance of falsehood or the danger of deviation in the faith, of scandal, or of indifferentism. At the same time, pastoral experience clearly shows that with respect to our Eastern brethren there should and can be taken into consideration various circumstances affecting individuals, wherein the unity of the Church is not jeopardized nor are intolerable risks involved, but in which salvation itself and the spiritual profit of souls are urgently at issue.

"Hence, in view of special circumstances of time, place, and personage, the Catholic Church has often adopted and now adopts a milder policy, offering to all the means of salvation and an example of charity among Christians through participation in the sacraments and in other sacred functions and objects. With these considerations in mind, and 'lest because of the harshness of our judgment we prove an obstacle to those seeking salvation,' and in order to promote closer union with the Eastern Churches separated from us, this sacred Synod lays down the following policy:

"In view of the principles recalled above, Eastern Christians who are separated in good faith from the Catholic Church, if they ask of their own accord and have the right dispositions, may be granted the sacraments of penance, the Eucharist, and the anointing of the sick. Furthermore, Catholics may ask for these same sacraments from those non-Catholic ministers whose Churches possess valid sacraments, as often as necessity or a genuine spiritual benefit recommends such a course of action, and when access to a Catholic priest is physically or morally impossible" (Nos. 26, 27).

"Again, in view of these very same principles, Catholics may for a just cause join with their separated Eastern brethren in sacred functions, things, and places" (No. 28).

"This more lenient policy with regard to common worship involving Catholics and their brethren of the separated Eastern Churches is entrusted to the care and execution of the local Ordinaries so that, by taking counsel among themselves and, if circumstances warrant, after consultation also with the Ordinaries of the separated Churches, they may govern relations between Christians by timely and effective rules and regulations" (No. 29).

EASTERN ECUMENICAL BRIEFS
Statement on the Church

Catholic and Orthodox theologians, meeting for their 10th consultation since 1966, issued an "Agreed Statement on the Church" Dec. 10, 1974. One of the central points in the statement was the difference of views regarding the position and status of the Pope and the Patriarch of Constantinople in the hierarchy of their churches.

"The Catholic Church recognizes that the position of Peter in the college of the Apostles finds visible expression in the Bishop of Rome who exercises those prerogatives defined by Vatican Council I within the whole church of Christ in virtue of this primacy.

"The Orthodox Church finds this teaching at variance with its understanding of primacy within the whole church. It appears to destroy the tension between independence and collegiality (in the universal and particular churches). For independence, a basic condition for collegiality, appears to be removed as a consequence of the jurisdictional teaching role attributed to the Patriarch of the West by Vatican Council I. The Orthodox believe that a necessary primacy in the church depends on the consent of the church and is at present exercised by the Patriarch of Constantinople.

"Our two traditions are not easily harmonized. Yet we believe that the Spirit is ever active to show us the way by which we can live together as one and many. We have the hope that we will be open to his promptings wherever they may lead."

The theological consultation was under the joint sponsorship of the U.S. Bishops' Committee for Ecumenical and Interreligious Affairs and the Standing Conference of Canonical Orthodox Bishops in America.

Orthodox Guidelines: A 66-page document entitled "Guidelines for Orthodox Churches in Ecumenical Relations" was published in February, 1974, by the Standing Conference of Canonical Orthodox Bishops in the Americas. Among the subjects of guidelines were:

• Marriage: Normally marriage in the Orthodox Church "takes place only between members of that Church." There are, however, occasions in which an Orthodox priest may perform a "mixed marriage," under certain conditions. Clergy of other churches may give a blessing or exhort a couple, but do not actually "assist" or "participate" in the marriage service.

• Baptism: Orthodox Churches accept baptism in the name of the Trinity in another church if "proof of the fact of baptism" can be authenticated.

• Eucharist: "Holy Communion will not be sought by Orthodox Christians outside the Church, nor will it be offered to those who do not confess the Orthodox Church as their mother."

• Reciprocity: The "principle of reciprocity" governs preaching in ecumenical situations, meaning that Orthodox priests may preach in non-Orthodox churches and non-Orthodox may speak in Orthodox churches.

Bishops and Presbyters

A document published in July, 1976, by the Orthodox-Roman Catholic Consultation in the U.S. Signatories indicated the following points of common understanding: (1) Ordina-

tion in apostolic succession is required for pastoral office in the Church. (2) Presiding at the Eucharistic celebration is a task belonging to those ordained to pastoral service. (3) The offices of bishop and presbyter are different realizations of the sacrament of order. (4) Those ordained are claimed permanently for the service of the Church. The statement noted that questions requiring serious study were the possible ordination of women, clerical celibacy, and the compatibility of certain occupations with pastoral office.

Principle of Economy

A statement issued by the same body at the same time, concerning God's plan and activity in human history for salvation. The concept of "economy" was not completely defined. It appeared that Orthodox understanding precludes recognition of the validity of the sacraments of other Christian churches.

Ministry

Ministry, especially that of bishop, was the principal subject under discussion at a meeting of an international group of Catholic and Orthodox theologians held in December, 1977, in Chambesy, Switzerland. In the context of a joint statement on the relationship between the incarnational and spiritual aspects of church life, they said: "There is no church of Christ without ministries of the Spirit, but there are no ministries without the church; hence, (there are) no ministries apart from or above the community" of the church.

Marriage

A statement entitled "The Sanctity of Marriage," issued in December, 1978, by the Eastern Orthodox-Roman Catholic Consultation in the U.S., acknowledged agreement about the sacramental nature and permanence of marriage while noting Orthodox positions regarding divorce (permitted in some circumstances) and validity (the marriage of Orthodox communicants must be blessed by an Orthodox priest).

Another statement related to marriage, regarding the religious faith and training of children of Catholic-Orthodox parents, was approved at a meeting of the consultation Oct. 10 and 11, 1980.

Russian Orthodox Dialogue

Catholic and Orthodox delegates met for the fifth time, Mar. 13 to 17, 1980, in Odessa for discussions related to the theme, "The Local Church and the Universal Church." In a communique issued at the end of the meeting, they said they "found themselves fully in accord on the following points:

• "The local church, in the ambit of the diocese, represents the people of God united around the bishop, legitimately ordained in the uninterrupted apostolic succession. The bishop, with whom the other members of the clergy collaborate and to whom they are subordinate, is the teacher of the faith, the minister of the sacraments — first of all, of the Eucharist — and the one in charge of the Christian life of this flock."

• "The concept of catholicity, understood as organic wholeness of the Church, as the fullness of the possession of the truth revealed by God and of the means of grace given for men's salvation, was deepened. The presence of the episcopate in the local churches guarantees the fullness of their Eucharistic life in grace."

• Despite their state of separation, the Catholic and Orthodox churches recognize one another as sister churches."

Catholic-Orthodox Commission

The Coordinating Committee of the Joint Commission for Dialogue between the Roman Catholic Church and the Orthodox Church reported signs of progress at a meeting May 25 to 30, 1981, in Venice. Reviewed at the meeting were Catholic and Orthodox views of the relationship between the mysteries of the Church, the Eucharist and the Holy Trinity.

The 60-member commission, meeting for the second time June 30 to July 6, 1982, in Vienna, focused discussion and study on the central significance of the Eucharist for an understanding of unity within the local church and unity among local churches and the universal Church. A press release issued at the end of the meeting said "large areas of agreement were outlined and foundations were laid for further consideration of questions about which there remain differences." Topics assigned for the next plenary session were baptism, confirmation and the Eucharist, as sacraments related to the unity of the Church.

The commission, the highest ranking and largest of its kind, was established after the meeting of Pope John Paul and Ecumenical Orthodox Patriarch Dimitrios I Nov. 29 and 30, 1979, in Istanbul.

HEALING

The basic premise of the Church's view of spiritual and physical healing is the power of God brought to bear directly and/or indirectly for the curing of human ills.

Miracles are examples of direct divine intervention for healing, beyond or against the ways of nature. The Bible contains accounts of many miracles of different kinds, especially those performed by Christ as well as those worked through the mediation of prophets, Apostles and others. The Church also acknowledges the fact of miracles accredited to the intercession of saints.

Direct divine intervention for healing takes place in and through the sacraments, especially those of reconciliation and anointing of the sick. The power (grace) of God is made present through the joining of sacramental sign with the prayer of the Church — for spiritual healing through the forgiveness of sins in the one case, and in the other case for spiritual strength to bear with suffering and, possibly also, to experience physical healing as well.

The power of God works indirectly, through the mediation of secondary causes and agents, in response to personal faith, official prayers of the Church and the prayers of individuals and groups, and through the reverent use of sacramentals and blessings.

The power of God works through people helping other people in need of healing; for example, through the means of medical and other forms of assistance, which are enjoined for use in the recovery and maintenance of health.

The Church has never had an ordinary ministry of healing, although the charism of healing has always been recognized as a free gift of the Holy Spirit for the good of the community.

A kind of healing ministry has developed in recent years, however, with good — but sometimes rather bizarre — results. Ultimate judgment about the validity of such ministry belongs to the teaching authority of the Church.

Underlying all aspects of healing are faith in the power and providence of God and a readiness to accept his permissive will, cure or no cure.

PROPHECY

Prophecy, according to one of its contemporary definitions, means giving witness by word, symbolic stance and corresponding action to a set of beliefs and values having a bearing on any one of a wide variety of causes, like peace, disarmament, justice, reconciliation, rights of minorities, human rights in any number of dimensions.

Conditions in the Church have also been taken under the umbrella of critical prophets.

It is a matter of Catholic doctrine that all baptized persons share in the prophetic mission of Christ, as his witnesses to the world.

The manner in which baptized persons carry out this mission depends on a number of factors, including personal opportunity and personal competence. They should always be guided by the teachings of the Church and have authentic concern for the good of the Church and the human community, especially the one they call their own.

Discernment of the validity of prophecy depends on rational norms of criticism and ultimately on the judgment of the teaching authority of the Church, according to a declaration by the Second Vatican Council.

(See separate entry for coverage of Prophecy in the Glossary.)

MEN, DOCTRINES, CHURCHES OF THE REFORMATION

Some of the leading figures, doctrines and churches of the Reformation are covered below. A companion article covers Major Protestant Churches in the United States.

John Wycliff (c. 1320-1384): English priest and scholar who advanced one of the leading Reformation ideas nearly 200 years before Martin Luther — that the Bible alone is the sufficient rule of faith — but had only an indirect influence on the 16th century Reformers. Supporting belief in an inward and practical religion, he denied the divinely commissioned authority of the pope and bishops of the Church; he also denied the Real Presence of Christ in the Holy Eucharist, and wrote against the sacrament of penance and the doctrine of indulgences. Nearly 20 of his propositions were condemned by Gregory XI in 1377; his writings were proscribed more extensively by the Council of Constance in 1415. His influence was strongest in Bohemia and Central Europe.

John Hus (c. 1369-1415): A Bohemian priest and preacher of reform who authored 30 propositions condemned by the Council of Constance. Excommunicated in 1411 or 1412, he was burned at the stake in 1415. His principal errors concerned the nature of the Church and the origin of papal authority. He spread some of the ideas of Wycliff but did not subscribe to his views regarding faith alone as the condition for justification and salvation, the sole sufficiency of Scripture as the rule of faith, the Real Presence of Christ in the Eucharist, and the sacramental system. In 1457 some of his followers founded the Church of the Brotherhood which later became known as the United Brethren or Moravian Church and is considered the earliest independent Protestant body.

Martin Luther (1483-1546): An Augustinian friar, the key figure in the Reformation. In 1517, as a special indulgence was being preached in Germany, and in view of needed reforms within the Church, he published at Wittenberg 95 theses concerning matters of Catholic belief and practice. Leo X condemned 41 statements from Luther's writings in 1520. Luther, refusing to recant, was excommunicated the following year. His teachings strongly influenced subsequent Lutheran theology; its statements of faith are found in the Book of Concord (1580).

Luther's doctrine included the following:

The sin of Adam, which corrupted human nature radically (but not substantially), has affected every aspect of man's being. Justification, understood as the forgiveness of sins and the state of righteousness, is by grace for Christ's sake through faith. Faith involves not merely intellectual assent but an act of confidence by the will. Good works are indispensably necessary concomitants of faith, but do not merit salvation. Of the sacraments, Luther retained baptism, penance and the Holy Communion as effective vehicles of the grace of the Holy Spirit; he held that in the Holy Communion the consecrated bread and wine are the Body and Blood of Christ. The rule of faith is the divine revelation in the Sacred Scriptures. He rejected purgatory, indulgences and the invocation of the saints, and held that prayers for the dead have no efficacy.

Lutheran tenets not in agreement with Catholic doctrine were condemned by the Council of Trent.

Anabaptism: Originated in Saxony in the first quarter of the 16th century and spread rapidly through southern Germany. Its doctrine included several key Lutheran tenets but was not regarded with favor by Luther, Calvin or Zwingli. Anabaptists believed that baptism is for adults only and that infant baptism is invalid. Their doctrine of the Inner Light, concerning the direct influence of the Holy Spirit on the believer, implied rejection of Catholic doctrine concerning the sacraments and the nature of the Church. Eighteen articles of faith were formulated in 1632 in Holland. Mennonites are Anabaptists.

Ulrich Zwingli (1484-1531): A priest who triggered the Reformation in Switzerland with a series of New Testament lectures in 1519, later disputations and by other actions. He held the Gospel to be the only basis of truth; rejected the Mass (which he suppressed in 1525 at Zurich), penance and other sacraments; denied papal primacy and doctrine concerning purgatory and the invocation of saints; rejected celibacy, monasticism and many traditional practices of piety. His symbolic view of the Eucharist, which was at odds with Catholic doctrine, caused an irreconcilable controversy with Luther and his followers. Zwingli was killed in a battle between the forces of Protestant and Catholic cantons in Switzerland.

John Calvin (1509-1564): French leader of the Reformation in Switzerland, whose key tenet was absolute predestination of some persons to heaven and others to hell. He rejected Catholic doctrine in 1533 after becoming convinced of a personal mission to reform the Church. In 1536 he published the first edition of *Institutes of the Christian Religion,* a systematic exposition of his doctrine which became the classic textbook of Reformed — as distinguished from Lutheran — theology. To Luther's principal theses — regarding

Scripture as the sole rule of faith, the radical corruption of human nature, and justification by faith alone — he added absolute predestination, certitude of salvation for the elect, and the incapability of the elect to lose grace. His Eucharistic theory, which failed to mediate the Zwingli-Luther controversy, was at odds with Catholic doctrine. From 1555 until his death Calvin was the virtual dictator of Geneva, the capital of the non-Lutheran Reformation in Europe.

Arminianism: A modification of the rigid predestinationism of Calvin, set forth by Jacob Arminius (1560-1609) and formally stated in the *Remonstrance* of 1610. Arminianism influenced some Calvinist bodies.

Unitarianism: A 16th century doctrine which rejected the Trinity and the divinity of Christ in favor of a uni-personal God. It claimed scriptural support for a long time but became generally rationalistic with respect to "revealed" doctrine as well as in ethics and its world-view. One of its principal early proponents was Faustus Socinus (1539-1604), a leader of the Polish Brethren.

A variety of communions developed in England in the Reformation and post-Reformation periods.

Anglican Communion: This communion, which regards itself as the same apostolic Church as that which was established by early Christians in England, derived not from Reformation influences but from the renunciation of papal jurisdiction by Henry VIII (1491-1547). His Act of Supremacy in 1534 called Christ's Church an assembly of local churches subject to the prince, who was vested with fullness of authority and jurisdiction. In spite of Henry's denial of papal authority, this Act did not reject substantially other principal articles of faith. Notable changes, proposed and adopted for the reformation of the church, took place in the subsequent reigns of James VI and Elizabeth, with respect to such matters as Scripture as the rule of faith, the sacraments, the nature of the Mass, and the constitution of the hierarchy.

The Anglican Communion is called Episcopal because its prelates have the title and function of bishops. (See Anglican Orders.)

Puritans: Extremists who sought church reform along Calvinist lines in severe simplicity. (Use of the term was generally discontinued after 1660.)

Presbyterians: Basically Calvinistic, called Presbyterian because church polity centers around assemblies of presbyters or elders. John Knox (c. 1513-1572) established the church in Scotland.

Congregationalists: Evangelical in spirit and seeking a return to forms of the primitive church, they uphold individual freedom in religious matters, do not require the acceptance of a creed as a condition for communion, and regard each congregation as autonomous. Robert Browne influenced the beginnings of Congregationalism.

Quakers: Their key belief is in internal divine illumination, the inner light of the living Christ, as the only source of truth and inspiration. George Fox (1624-1691) was one of their leaders in England. Called the Society of Friends, the Quakers are noted for their pacificism.

Baptists: So called because of their doctrine concerning baptism. They reject infant baptism and consider only baptism by immersion as valid. Leaders in the formation of the church were John Smyth (d. 1612) in England and Roger Williams (d. 1683) in America.

Methodists: A group who broke away from the Anglican Communion under the leadership of John Wesley (1703-1791), although some Anglican beliefs were retained. Doctrines include the witness of the Spirit to the individual and personal assurance of salvation. Wesleyan Methodists do not subscribe to some of the more rigid Calvinistic tenets held by other Methodists.

Universalism: A product of 18th-century liberal Protestantism in England. The doctrine is not Trinitarian and includes a tenet that all men will ultimately be saved.

MAJOR PROTESTANT CHURCHES IN THE UNITED STATES

There are more than 250 Protestant church bodies in the United States.

The majority of U.S. Protestants belong to the following denominations: Baptist, Methodist, Lutheran, Presbyterian, Protestant Episcopal, the United Church of Christ, the Christian Church (Disciples of Christ), Holiness Sects.

See Ecumenical Dialogues, Briefs and related entries for coverage of relations between the Catholic Church and other Christian churches.

Baptist Churches

(Courtesy of the Division of Communication, American Baptist Churches in the U.S.A.)

Baptist churches, comprising the largest of all American Protestant denominations, were first established by John Smyth near the beginning of the 17th century in England. The first Baptist church in America was founded at Providence by Roger Williams in 1639.

Largest of the nearly 30 Baptist bodies in the U.S. are:

The Southern Baptist Convention, 460 James Robertson Parkway, Nashville, Tenn. 37219, with 13.6 million members;

The National Baptist Convention, U.S.A., Inc., 915 Spain St., Baton Rouge, La. 70802, with 6.5 million members;

The National Baptist Convention of America, 954 Kings Rd., Jacksonville, Fla. 32204, with 2.6 million members.

The American Baptist Churches in the U.S.A., Valley Forge, Pa. 19481, with 1.5 million members.

The total number of U.S. Baptists is more than 29 million. The world total is 33 million.

Proper to Baptists is their doctrine on baptism. Called an "ordinance" rather than a sacrament, baptism by immersion is a sign that one has experienced and decided in favor of the salvation offered by Christ. It is administered only to persons who are capable of the experience of faith, which is the sole criterion of salvation and which involves the obligation to a life of virtue. Baptism is not administered to infants.

Baptists do not have a formal creed but generally subscribe to two professions of faith formulated in 1689 and 1832 and are in general agreement with classical Protestant theology regarding Scripture as the sole rule of faith, original sin, justification through faith in Christ, and the nature of the Church. Their local churches are autonomous.

Worship services differ in form from one congregation to another. Usual elements are the reading of Scripture, a sermon, hymns, vocal and silent prayer. The Lord's Supper, called an "ordinance," is celebrated at various intervals.

Methodist Churches

(Courtesy of Joe Hale, General Secretary of the World Methodist Council.)

John Wesley (1703-1791), an Anglican clergyman, was the founder of Methodism. In 1738, following a period of missionary work in America and strongly influenced by the Moravians, he experienced a new conversion to Christ and shortly thereafter became a leader in a religious awakening in England. By the end of the 18th century, Methodism was strongly rooted also in America.

The United Methodist Church, formed in 1968 by a merger of the Methodist Church and the Evangelical United Brethren Church, is the second largest Protestant denomination in the U.S., with nine million members; its principal agencies are located in New York, Evanston, Ill., Nashville, Tenn., Washington, D.C., Dayton, O., and Lake Junaluska, N.C. (World Methodist Council, P.O. Box 518. 28745). The second largest body, with more than two million communicants, is the African Methodist Episcopal Church. Four other major churches in the U.S. are the African Methodist Episcopal Zion, Christian Methodist Episcopal, Free Methodist Church and the Wesleyan Church. The total Methodist membership in the U.S. is about 14 million.

Worldwide, there are more than 63 autonomous Methodist/Wesleyan churches in 90 countries, with a membership of more than 21 million. All of them participate in the World Methodist Council, which gives global unity to the witness of Methodist communicants.

Methodism, although it has a base in Calvinistic theology, rejects absolute predestination and maintains that Christ offers grace freely to all men, not just to a select elite. Wesley's distinctive doctrine was the "witness of the Spirit" to the individual soul and personal assurance of salvation. He also emphasized the central themes of conversion and holiness. Methodists are in general agreement with classical Protestant theology regarding Scripture as the sole rule of faith, original sin, justification through faith in Christ, the nature of the Church, and the sacraments of baptism and the Lord's Supper. Church polity is structured along episcopal lines in America, with ministers being appointed to local churches by a bishop; churches stemming from British Methodism do not have bishops but vest appointive powers within an appropriate conference. Congregations are free to choose various forms of worship services; typical elements are readings from Scripture, sermons, hymns and prayers.

Lutheran Churches

(Courtesy of Thomas Hartley Dorris, editor of Ecumenical Press Service, Box 66, CH-1211 Geneva 20, Switzerland.)

The origin of Lutheranism is generally traced to Oct. 31, 1517, when Martin Luther tacked "95 Theses" to the door of the castle church in Wittenberg, Germany. This call to debate on the subject of indulgences and related concerns has come to symbolize the beginning of the Reformation. Luther and his supporters intended to reform the Church they knew. Though Lutheranism has come to be visible in separate denominations and national churches, at its heart it professes itself to be a confessional movement within the one, holy, catholic and apostolic Church.

The world's 70 million Lutherans form the third largest grouping of Christians, following Roman Catholics and Eastern Orthodox. About 54 million belong to churches which make up the Lutheran World Federation, headquartered in Geneva; its president, Josiah Kibira, is bishop of the Northwest Diocese of the Evangelical Lutheran Church in Tanzania. Eight countries count more than one million Lutherans each: West Germany (22.5 million), United States (8.5 million), Sweden (7.5 million), East Germany (8.7 million), Denmark (4.7 million), Finland (4.6 million), Norway (3.8 million), Indonesia (2.1 million).

Numbering about 9 million, Lutherans are the fourth largest grouping of North American Christians, exceeded by Roman Catholics, Baptists and Methodists. About 95 per cent of them belong to one of three denominations: Lutheran Church in America, three million members, 231 Madison Avenue, New York, N.Y. 10016; Lutheran Church-Missouri Synod, 2.6 million, 500 N. Broadway, St. Louis, Mo. 63102; American Lutheran Church, 2.3 million, 422 S. Fifth St., Minneapolis, Minn. 55415.

In addition, there are about a dozen other smaller Lutheran denominations in North America. The three largest are: Wisconsin Evangelical Lutheran Synod, 400,000 members, 3512 W. North Ave., Milwaukee, Wis. 53208; the Association of Evangelical Lutheran Churches, 110,000, 12015 Manchester Rd., St. Louis, Mo. 63131; Evangelical Lutheran Church of Canada, 82,000, 247 First Ave. North, Saskatoon, Saskatchewan S7K 4H5. (This is the only independent Canadian denomination; most other Canadian Lutherans belong to the Lutheran Church in America or the Missouri Synod.)

A union of the American Lutheran Church, the Lutheran Church in America and the Association of Evangelical Lutheran Churches is projected for 1988. Their Canadian counterparts are moving toward a merger in 1985. The new denominations would account for about two-thirds of the Lutherans in each country.

The three large bodies and the Association of Evangelical Lutheran Churches form the Lutheran Council in the U.S.A., a cooperative agency for work in theological studies; communication; research and planning; institutional, military and campus ministry; governmental affairs; higher education; immigration and refugee services; youth agency relations; American Indian concerns; domestic disaster relief and other social ministries. The council's main offices are at 360 Park Ave. South, New York, N.Y. 10010. A similar organization, the Lutheran Council in Canada, is headquartered at 500-365 Hargrave St., Winnipeg, Manitoba R3B 2K3.

The Lutheran Church in America, the American Lutheran Church and the Association of Evangelical Lutheran Churches also form Lutheran World Ministries, the U.S. agency of the Lutheran World Federation, headquartered at 360 Park Ave. South, New York, N.Y. 10010. Its Canadian counterpart is the Canadian National Committee of the Lutheran World Federation, headquartered at 500-365 Hargrave St., Winnipeg, Manitoba R3B 2K3.

The statements of faith which have shaped the confessional life of Lutheranism are found in the *Book of Concord.* This 1580 collection includes the three ancient ecumenical creeds (Apostles', Nicene and Athanasian), Luther's *Large and Small Catechisms* (1529), the *Augsburg Confession* (1530) and the *Apology* in defense of it (1531), the *Smalcald Articles* (including the "Treatise on the Power and Primacy of the Pope") (1537), and the *Formula of Concord* (1577).

The central Lutheran doctrinal proposition is that Christians "receive forgiveness of sins and become righteous before God by grace, for Christ's sake."

Baptism and the Lord's Supper (Holy Communion, the eucharist) are universally celebrated among Lutherans as sacramental means of grace in which the Word and promise of God are made visible by being bound to earthly elements — water, bread and wine. In baptism, a person is reborn and by God's gracious action is made a member of the Church catholic. Likewise, the eucharist celebrates and re-presents God's gracious action. With the body and blood of Christ — "in, with, and under" the bread and wine — come the gifts of life, salvation, forgiveness.

Lutherans also treasure the Word proclaimed in the reading of the Scriptures, preaching from the pulpit, and pronouncement of absolution. The Word read and preached is always part of the celebration of the sacrament of the altar. Absolution is usually imparted generally, but it may also be given individually in connection with private confession.

Although it was not the wish of the early Lutherans to deny the bishop's place as the ordinary minister of ordination, the general unwillingness of 16th century bishops to ordain Lutheran pastors led to the usual Lutheran system of presbyteral rather than episcopal ordination. Lutherans are concerned to preserve apostolic succession in life and doctrine, and generally concede the value, though not the necessity, of ordination by bishops.

Marriage and confirmation continue among Lutherans. Confirmation has been generally connected with first communion, though recent years have seen a tendency to separate the two. In the U.S., the tendency is to have first communion around grade-five age, though infant communion is not unknown. Confirmation, sometimes called affirmation of the baptismal covenant, generally occurs during the junior high school years, slightly younger than in European practice.

Lutheran jurisdictions corresponding to dioceses are called districts or synods in North America. There are more than 100 of them on the continent. Because they relate to different national denominations, more than one of these jurisdictions includes the same geographic area. The head of a district or synod, chosen by lay and clergy delegates to a convention, is known as a bishop or a president, depending on the denomination and jurisdiction. The terms "diocese" and "bishop" are common among European Lutherans and Asian, African and Latin American Lutherans whose roots derive from European missionary efforts.

A visitor to a North American Lutheran parish would generally find adornments, vestments, church calendars and an order of service similar to that of many Episcopal or Roman Catholic congregations. Though the Reformers continued to celebrate the eucharist every Sunday and on other special days, Lutherans strayed from their confessional norm under various historical and philosophic influences. The North American practice has until recent years been monthly celebration. Weekly celebration is increasingly common and is generally stressed as the desired practice by Lutheran liturgical and sacramental theologians. Lutherans generally like to sing in worship, and successive generations have built up a rich tradition of church music and hymnody. A new North American *Lutheran Book of Worship* was introduced in 1978. The Missouri Synod issued its own revision of the book in 1982.

Presbyterian Churches

(Courtesy of Gerald W. Gillette, United Presbyterian Church in the U.S.A.; and Office of the General Assembly, Presbyterian Church in the United States.)

Presbyterians are so called because of their tradition of governing the church through a system of representative bodies composed of elders (presbyters).

Presbyterianism is a part of the Reformed Family of Churches that grew out of the theological work of John Calvin following the Lutheran Reformation, to which it is heavily indebted. Countries in which it acquired early strength and influence were Switzerland, France, Holland, Scotland and England.

Presbyterianism spread widely in this country in the latter part of the 18th century and afterwards. Presently, it has approximately 4.5 million communicants in nine bodies. The largest of these are:

The United Presbyterian Church in the U.S.A., 475 Riverside Drive, New York, N.Y. 10027, with 2.5 million members. This body was formed May 28, 1958, by a merger of the Presbyterian Church in the U.S.A and the United Presbyterian Church of North America.

The Presbyterian Church in the United States, 341 Ponce de Leon Avenue N.E., Atlanta, Ga. 30308, with about 860,000 members.

These churches are closely allied with the Reformed Church in America and the United Church of Christ.

In Presbyterian doctrine, baptism and the Lord's Supper, viewed as seals of the covenant of grace, are regarded as sacraments. Baptism, which is not necessary for salvation, is conferred on infants and adults The Lord's Supper is celebrated as a covenant of the Sacrifice of Christ. In both sacraments, a doctrine of the real presence of Christ is considered the central theological principle.

The Church is twofold, being invisible and also visible; it consists of all of the elect and all those Christians who are united in Christ as their immediate head.

Presbyterians are in general agreement with classical Protestant theology regarding Scripture as the sole rule of faith and practice, salvation by grace, and justification through faith in Christ.

Presbyterian congregations are governed by a session composed of elders (presbyters) elected by the communicant membership. On higher levels there are presbyteries, synods and a general assembly with various degrees of authority over local bodies; all such representative bodies are composed of elected elders and ministers in approximately equal numbers.

Worship services, simple and dignified, include sermons, prayer, reading of the Scriptures and hymns. The Lord's Supper is celebrated at intervals.

Doctrinal developments of the past several years included approval in May, 1967, by the General Assembly of the United Presbyterian Church of a contemporary confession of faith to supplement the historic Westminster Confession. The new confession emphasizes the commitment of the Church and its members to reconciliatory and apostolic works in society.

Protestant Episcopal Church

The Protestant Episcopal Church in the U.S.A., also officially known as the Episcopal Church, regards itself as the same apostolic church as that which was established by early Christians in England. It was established in this country during the Revolutionary period. Its constitution and Prayer Book were adopted at a general convention held in 1789. It has approximately 3 million members.

Offices of the U.S. executive council are located at 815 Second Ave., New York, N.Y. 10017.

This church, which belongs to the Anglican Communion, subscribes to the branch theory of the Church of Christ, holding that it consists of the Church of Rome, the Eastern Orthodox Church, and the Anglican Communion. It accepts the pope as the "first among equals."

Worldwide, the Anglican Communion has 65 million members in 41 provinces. The chief prelate is the Archbishop of Canterbury.

There is considerable variety in Episcopalian beliefs and practices. Official statements of belief and practice are found in the Apostles' Creed, the Nicene Creed and the Book of Common Prayer, but interpretation is not uniform. Scripture has primary importance with respect to the rule of faith, and some authority is attached to tradition.

All seven sacraments, veneration of the saints, and a great many other Catholic teachings are accepted by Episcopalians but are not used by all.

An episcopal system of church government prevails, but clergymen of lower rank and lay persons also have an active voice in ecclesiastical affairs. The levels of government are the general convention, the executive council, territorial provinces and dioceses, and local parishes. At the parish level, the congregation has the right to select its own rector or pastor, with the consent of the bishop.

Liturgical worship is according to the Book of Common Prayer as adopted in 1979, but ceremonial practices correspond with the doctrinal positions of the various congregations and range from a ceremony similar to the Roman Mass to services of a less elaborate character.

United Church of Christ

(Courtesy of Joseph H. Evans, secretary of the United Church of Christ.)

The 1,736,244-member United Church of Christ was formed in 1957 by a union of the Congregational Christian and the Evangelical and Reformed Churches. The former was originally established by the Pilgrims and the Puritans of the Massachusetts Bay Colony, while the latter was founded in Pennsylvania in the early 1700's by settlers from Central Europe. The denomination has 6,462 congregations throughout the United States.

It considers itself "a united and uniting church" and keeps itself open to all ecumenical options.

Its headquarters are located at 105 Madison Ave., New York, N.Y. 10016.

Its statement of faith recognizes Jesus Christ as "our crucified and risen Lord (who) shared our common lot, conquering sin and death and reconciling the world to himself." It believes in the life after death, and the fact that God "judges men and nations by his righteous will declared through prophets and apostles."

The United Church further believes that Christ calls its members to share in his baptism "and eat at his table, to join him in his passion and victory." Ideally, according to its Lord's Day Service, Communion is to be celebrated weekly. Like other Calvinistic bodies, it believes that Christ is spiritually present in the sacrament.

The United Church is governed along congregational lines, and each local church is autonomous. However, the actions of its biennial General Synod are taken with great seriousness by congregations. Between synods, a 43-member executive council oversees the work of the church.

Baptist churches were among a number of Protestant denominational bodies in strong support of efforts toward passage of a prayer-in-public-school amendment.

Christian Church (Disciples of Christ)

(Courtesy of Robert L. Friedly, Executive Director, Office of Communication.)

The Christian Church (Disciples of Christ) originated early in the 1800's from two movements against rigid denominationalism led by Presbyterians Thomas and Alexander Campbell in western Pennsylvania and Barton W. Stone in Kentucky. The two movements developed separately for about 25 years before being merged in 1832.

The church, which identifies itself with the Protestant mainstream, now has approximately 1.2 million members in the U.S. and Canada. The greatest concentration of members in the U.S. is located roughly along the old frontier line, in an arc sweeping from Ohio and Kentucky through the Midwest and down into Oklahoma and Texas.

The general offices of the church are located at 222 South Downey Ave., Box 1986, Indianapolis, Ind. 46206.

The church's persistent concern for Christian unity is based on a conviction expressed in a basic document, *Declaration and Address,* dating from its founding. The document states: "The church of Christ upon earth is essentially, intentionally and constitutionally one."

The Disciples have no official doctrine or dogma. Their worship practices vary widely from more common informal services to what could almost be described as "high church" services. Membership is granted after a simple statement of belief in Jesus Christ and baptism by immersion; most congregations admit un-immersed transfers from other denominations. The Lord's Supper, generally called Communion, is always open to Christians of all persuasions. Lay men and women routinely preside over the Lord's Supper, which is celebrated each Sunday; they often preach and perform other pastoral functions as well. Distinction between ordained and non-ordained members is blurred somewhat because of the Disciples' emphasis on all members of the church as ministers.

The Christian Church is oriented to congregational government, and has a unique structure in which three levels of polity (general, regional and congregational) operate as equals rather than in a pyramid of authority. At the national or international level, it is governed by a general assembly which has voting representation direct from congregations and regions as well as all ordained clergy.

Other Churches

The following conservative churches were among those reporting membership gains between 1979 and 1980, according to the 1982 edition of the *Yearbook of American and Canadian Churches:*

Christian and Missionary Alliance, with 15,724 new members, for a total of 189,710;

Church of God (Cleveland, Tenn.), with 23,627 new members, for a total of 435,012;

Church of the Nazarene, with 9,456 new members, for a total of 484,276;

Seventh-Day Adventists, with 18,052 new members, for a total of 571,141;

Assemblies of God, with 103,347 new members, for a total of 1.73 million;

Church of Jesus Christ of Latter Day Saints (Mormons), with 105,000 new members, for a total of 2.81 million.

Evangelicalism

Evangelicalism, dating from 1735 in England (the Evangelical Revival) and after 1740 in the United States (the Great Awakening), has had and continues to have widespread influence in Protestant churches. It has been estimated that at least 50 per cent of American Protestants — communicants of both large denominations and small bodies — are evangelicals.

The Bible is their rule of faith and religious practice. Being born again in a life-changing experience through faith in Christ is the promise of salvation. Missionary work for the spread of the Gospel is a normal and necessary activity. Additional matters of belief and practice are generally of a conservative character.

Fundamentalists comprise an extreme right-wing subculture of evangelicalism. They are distinguished mainly by militant biblicism, belief in the absolute inerrancy of the Bible and emphasis on the Second Coming of Christ. Fundamentalism developed in the first third of the 20th century in reaction against liberal theology and secularizing trends in mainstream and other Protestant denominations.

The Holiness or Perfectionist wing of evangelicalism evolved from Methodist efforts to preserve, against a contrary trend, the personal-piety and inner-religion concepts of John Wesley. There are at least 30 Holiness bodies in the U.S.

Pentecostals, probably the most demonstrative of evangelicals, are noted for speaking in tongues and the stress they place on healing, prophecy and personal testimony to the practice and power of evangelical faith.

ECUMENISM

The modern ecumenical movement, which started about 1910 among Protestants and led to formation of the World Council of Churches in 1948, developed outside the mainstream of Catholic interest for many years. It has now become for Catholics as well one of the great religious facts of our time.

The magna charta of ecumenism for Catholics is a complex of several documents which include, in the first place, the *Decree on Ecumenism* promulgated by the Second Vatican Council Nov. 21, 1964. Other enactments underlying and expanding this decree are the *Dogmatic Constitution on the Church,* the *Decree on Eastern Catholic Churches,* and the *Pastoral Constitution on the Church in the Modern World.*

VATICAN II DECREE

The following excerpts from the *Decree on Ecumenism* cover the broad theological background and principles and indicate the thrust of the Church's commitment to ecumenism.

". . . Men who believe in Christ and have been properly baptized are brought into a certain, though imperfect, communion with the Catholic Church. Undoubtedly, the differences that exist in varying degrees between them and the Catholic Church — whether in doctrine and sometimes in discipline, or concerning the structure of the Church — do indeed create many and sometimes serious obstacles to full ecclesiastical communion. These the ecumenical movement is striving to overcome . . ." (No. 3).

Elements Common to Christians

"Moreover some, even very many, of the most significant elements or endowments which together go to build up and give life to the Church herself can exist outside the visible boundaries of the Catholic Church: the written word of God; the life of grace; faith, hope, and charity, along with other interior gifts of the Holy Spirit and visible elements. All of these, which come from Christ and lead back to Him, belong by right to the one Church of Christ" (No. 3).

[In a later passage, the decree singled out a number of elements which the Catholic Church and other churches have in common but not in complete agreement: confession of Christ as Lord and God and as mediator between God and man; belief in the Trinity; reverence for Scripture as the revealed word of God; baptism and the Lord's Supper; Christian life and worship; faith in action; concern with moral questions.]

"The brethren divided from us also carry out many of the sacred actions of the Christian religion. Undoubtedly, in ways that vary according to the condition of each Church or Community, these actions can truly engender a life of grace, and can be rightly described as capable of providing access to the community of salvation.

"It follows that these separated Churches and Communities, though we believe they suffer from defects already mentioned, have by no means been deprived of significance and importance in the mystery of salvation.

For the Spirit of Christ has not refrained from using them as means of salvation which derive their efficacy from the very fullness of grace and truth entrusted to the Catholic Church" (No. 3).

Unity Lacking

"Nevertheless, our separated brethren, whether considered as individuals or as Communities and Churches, are not blessed with that unity which Jesus Christ wished to bestow on all those whom He has regenerated and vivified into one body and newness of life — that unity which the holy Scriptures and the revered tradition of the Church proclaim. For it is through Christ's Catholic Church alone, which is the all-embracing means of salvation, that the fullness of the means of salvation can be obtained. It was to the apostolic college alone, of which Peter is the head, that we believe our Lord entrusted all the blessings of the New Covenant, in order to establish on earth the one Body of Christ into which all those should be fully incorporated who already belong in any way to God's People . . ." (No. 3).

What the Movement Involves

"Today, in many parts of the world, under the inspiring grace of the Holy Spirit, multiple efforts are being expended through prayer, word, and action to attain that fullness of unity which Jesus Christ desires. This sacred Synod, therefore, exhorts all the Catholic faithful to recognize the signs of the times and to participate skillfully in the work of ecumenism.

"The 'ecumenical movement' means those activities and enterprises which, according to various needs of the Church and opportune occasions, are started and organized for the fostering of unity among Christians. These are:

• "First, every effort to eliminate words, judgments, and actions which do not respond to the condition of separated brethren with truth and fairness and so make mutual relations between them more difficult.

• "Then, 'dialogue' between competent experts from different Churches and Communities (scholarly ecumenism). . . .

• "In addition, these Communions cooperate more closely in whatever projects a Christian conscience demands for the common good (social ecumenism).

• "They also come together for common prayer, where this is permitted (spiritual ecumenism).

• "Finally, all are led to examine their own faithfulness to Christ's will for the Church and, wherever necessary, undertake with vigor the task of renewal and reform.

". . . It is evident that the work of preparing and reconciling those individuals who wish for full Catholic communion is of its nature distinct from ecumenical action. But there is no opposition between the two, since both proceed from the wondrous providence of God" (No. 4).

Primary Duty of Catholics

"In ecumenical work, Catholics must assuredly be concerned for their separated brethren, praying for them, keeping them informed about the Church, making the first approaches towards them. But their primary duty is to make an honest and careful appraisal of whatever needs to be renewed and achieved in the Catholic household itself, in order that its life may bear witness more loyally and luminously to the teachings and ordinances which have been handed down from Christ through the apostles.

". . . Every Catholic must . . . aim at Christian perfection (cf. Jas. 1:4; Rom. 12:1-2) and, each according to his station, play his part so that the Church . . . may daily be more purified and renewed, against the day when Christ will present her to Himself in all her glory, without spot or wrinkle (cf. Eph. 5:27).

". . . Catholics must joyfully acknowledge and esteem the truly Christian endowments from our common heritage which are to be found among our separated brethren. . . .

"Nor should we forget that whatever is wrought by the grace of the Holy Spirit in the hearts of our separated brethren can contribute to our own edification. Whatever is truly Christian never conflicts with the genuine interests of the faith; indeed, it can always result in a more ample realization of the very mystery of Christ and the Church . . ." (No. 4).

Participation in Worship

Norms concerning participation by Catholics in the worship of other Christian Churches were sketched in this conciliar decree and elaborated in a number of other documents such as: the *Decree on Eastern Catholic Churches*, promulgated by the Second Vatican Council in 1964; *Interim Guidelines for Prayer in Common*, issued June 18, 1965, by the US Bishops' Committee for Ecumenical and Inter-Religious Affairs; a *Directory on Ecumenism*, published in 1967 by the Vatican Secretariat for Promoting Christian Unity; additional communications from the US Bishops' Committee, and numerous sets of guidelines issued locally by and for dioceses throughout the US.

The norms encourage common prayer services for Christian unity and other intentions. Beyond that, they draw a distinction between separated churches of the Reformation tradition and separated Eastern churches, in view of doctrine and practice the Catholic Church has in common with the latter concerning the apostolic succession of bishops, holy orders, liturgy, and other credal matters.

Full participation by Catholics in official Protestant liturgies is prohibited, because it implies profession of the faith expressed in the liturgy. Intercommunion by Catholics at Protestant liturgies is prohibited. Under certain conditions, Protestants may be given Holy Communion in the Catholic Church (see Intercommunion). A Catholic may stand as a witness, but not as a sponsor, in baptism, and as a witness in the marriage of separated Christians. Similarly, a Protestant may stand as a witness, but not as a sponsor, in a Catholic baptism, and as a witness in the marriage of Catholics.

Separated Eastern Churches

The principal norms regarding liturgical participation with separated Eastern Christians are included under Eastern Ecumenism.

ECUMENICAL AGENCIES

Vatican Secretariat

The top-level agency for Catholic ecumenical efforts is the Vatican Secretariat for Promoting Christian Unity, which originated in 1960 as a preparatory commission for the Second Vatican Council. Its purposes are to provide guidance and, where necessary, coordination for ecumenical endeavor by Catholics, and to establish and maintain relations with representatives of other Christian Churches for ecumenical dialogue and action.

The secretariat, first under the direction of Cardinal Augustin Bea, S. J., and now of Cardinal Johannes Willebrands, has established firm working relations with representative agencies of other churches and the World Council of Churches. It has joined in dialogue with Orthodox Churches, the Anglican Communion, the Lutheran World Federation, the World Alliance of Reformed Churches, the World Methodist Council and other religious bodies. In the past several years, staff members and representatives of the secretariat have been involved in one way or another in nearly every significant ecumenical enterprise and meeting held throughout the world, including the Fifth General Assembly of the World Council of Churches.

While the secretariat and its counterparts in other churches have focused primary attention on theological and other related problems of Christian unity, they have also begun, and in increasing measure, to emphasize the responsibilities of the churches for greater unity of witness and effort in areas of humanitarian need.

Bishops' Committee

The U.S. Bishops' Committee for Ecumenical and Interreligious Affairs was established by the American hierarchy in 1964. Its purposes are to maintain relationships with other Christian churches and other religious communities at the national level, to advise and assist dioceses in developing and applying ecumenical policies, and to maintain liaison with corresponding Vatican offices — the Secretariats for Christian Unity and Non-Christian Religions.

This standing committee of the National Conference of Catholic Bishops is chaired by Ernest L. Unterkoefler of Charleston, S.C. Operationally, the committee is assisted by the Rev. John F. Hotchkin, director; the Rev. Joseph W. Witmer, associate director; Dr. Eugene J. Fisher, executive secretary of the Secretariat for Catholic-Jewish Relations; the Rev. John B. Sheerin, consultant for Catholic-Jewish Relations.

The committee co-sponsors several national consultations with other churches and confessional families. These bring together on a regular basis Catholic representatives and their counterparts from the American Baptist Convention, the Christian Church (Disciples of Christ), the Episcopal Church, the Lutheran World Federation (U.S. Committee), the United Methodist Church, the Orthodox Churches, the Oriental Orthodox Churches, the Alliance of Reformed Churches (North American area), the Interfaith Witness Department of the Home Mission Board of the Southern Baptist Convention. Reports of consultations conducted under committee auspices are published periodically and are available through the Publications Office of the U.S. Catholic Conference. (See Ecumenical Dialogues.)

The committee relates with the National Council of Churches of Christ, through membership in the Faith and Order Commission and through observer relationship with the Commission on Regional and Local Ecumenism, and has sponsored a joint study committee investigating the possibility of Roman Catholic membership in that body.

Advisory and other services are provided by the committee to ecumenical commissions and agencies in dioceses throughout the country.

Through the Secretariat for Catholic-Jewish Relations, the committee is in contact with several national Jewish agencies and bodies. Issues of mutual interest and shared concern are reviewed for the purpose of furthering deeper understanding between the Catholic and Jewish communities.

Through the Secretariat for Non-Christians, the committee promotes activity in wider areas of dialogue. The Rev. John F. Hotchkin serves as executive secretary for this secretariat.

Offices of the committee are located at 1312 Massachusetts Ave. N.W., Washington, D.C. 20005.

In the past 20 years, there has been a great increase in the volume of ecumenical literature of all kinds.

World Council

The World Council of Churches is a fellowship of churches which acknowledge "Jesus Christ as Lord and Savior." It is a permanent organization providing constituent members — nearly 301 churches with some 450 million communicants in 100 countries — with opportunities for meeting, consultation and cooperative action with respect to doctrine, worship, practice, social mission, evangelism and missionary work, and other matters of mutual concern.

The WCC was formally established Aug. 23, 1948, in Amsterdam with ratification of a constitution by 147 communions. This action merged two previously existing movements — Life and Work (social mission), Faith and Order (doctrine) — which had initiated practical steps toward founding a fellowship of Christian churches at meetings held in Oxford, Edinburgh and Utrecht in 1937 and 1938. A third movement for cooperative missionary work, which originated about 1910 and, remotely, led to formation of the WCC, was incorporated into the council in 1971 under the title of the International Missionary Council (World Mission and Evangelism).

Four additional general assemblies of the council have been held since the charter meeting of 1948: in Evanston, Ill. (1954), New Delhi, India (1961), Uppsala, Sweden (1968) and Nairobi, Kenya (1975). The next assembly will convene July 24 to Aug. 10, 1983, in Vancouver, British Columbia, Canada.

Between assemblies, the council operates through a central committee which meets every 12 or 18 months, and an executive committee which meets every six months.

The council continues the work of the International Missionary Council, the Commission on Faith and Order, and the Commission on Church and Society. The structure of the council has three program units: Faith and Witness, Justice and Service, Education and Communication.

Liaison between the council and the Vatican has been maintained since 1966 through a joint working group. Roman Catholic membership in the WCC is a question officially on the agenda of this body. The Joint Commission on Society, Development and Peace (SODEPAX) was an agency of the council and the Pontifical Commission for Justice and Peace from 1968 to Dec. 31, 1980. Roman Catholics serve individually as full members of the Commission on Faith and Order and in various capacities on other program committees of the council.

WCC headquarters are located in Geneva, Switzerland. The United States Conference for the World Council of Churches at 475 Riverside Drive, New York, N.Y. 10115, provides liaison between the U.S. churches and Geneva. The WCC also maintains fraternal relations with regional, national and local councils of churches throughout the world.

The Rev. Philip A. Potter, a Methodist from the Island of Dominica, West Indies, was elected secretary general of the WCC in August, 1972.

WCC presidents are: Ms. Annie Jiagge, Ghana; the Rev. J. Miguez-Bonino, Argentina; General T. B. Simatupang, Indonesia; Archbishop O. Sundby, Sweden; Dr. Cynthia Wedel, U.S.A.; His Holiness Ilia, patriarch of the Gregorian Orthodox Church, S.S.R.

National Council

The National Council of the Churches of Christ in the U.S.A., the largest ecumenical body in the United States, is a cooperative organization of 32 Protestant, Orthodox and Anglican church bodies having about 40 million members.

The NCCC, established by the churches in 1950, was structured through the merger of 12 separate cooperative agencies. Presently, through three main program divisions and five commissions, the NCCC crries on work in behalf of member churches in home and overseas missions, Christian education, communications, disaster relief and rehabilitation, family life, stewardship, regional and local ecumenism, and other areas.

Policies of the NCCC are determined by a governing board of approximately 250 members appointed by the constituent churches. The governing board meets twice a year.

The NCCC's annual budget approximates $35 million, about 80 per cent of which is devoted to compassionate ministries of aid and relief to victims of disasters and endemic poverty in lands overseas.

The president and general secretary, respectively, are Bishop James Armstrong and Dr. Claire Randall.

NCCC headquarters are located at 475 Riverside Drive, New York, N.Y. 10115.

Consultation on Church Union

The Consultation on Church Union, officially begun in 1962, is a venture of American churches seeking a united church "truly catholic, truly evangelical, and truly reformed." The churches engaged in this process, representing 25 million Christians, are the African Methodist Episcopal Church, the African Methodist Episcopal Zion Church, the Christian Church (Disciples of Christ), the Christian Methodist Episcopal Church, the Episcopal Church, the Presbyterian Church in the United States, the United Church of Christ, the United Methodist Church, and the United Presbyterian Church in the U.S.A. The National Council of Community Churches is also a member of COCU.

From 1970 to 1973 the member churches studied the first draft of a plan of union for the proposed Church of Christ Uniting. The responses to this plan, on the one hand, gave evidence of an historic consensus on faith, worship, and ministry; on the other hand, they revealed the need for mature involvement in order to discover the structures of a united church. The 11th plenary at Memphis, April, 1973, called for a future agenda involving the congregations more intimately, explored divisive factors such as racism, and affirmed the doctrinal and liturgical rapprochement already achieved. An affirmation of mutual recognition of membership was accepted and sent to the churches at the 12th plenary held at Cincinnati Nov. 4 to 8, 1974. At the 1976 plenary meeting, six chapters of "an emerging consensus" as a "theological basis for union" were approved for study by COCU members.

A series of Eucharistic texts was published in 1978. The 1979 plenary accepted a series of questions to be posed to each church arising out of the mutual recognition of members, and moved ahead on a draft agreement on the ordained ministry. The 1980 plenary accepted a seventh chapter on ministry.

The 1982 plenary celebrated the 20th anniversary of the Consultation. During the meeting, two commissions — Interim Eucharistic Fellowship and Generating Communities, and the Task Force of Persons with Disabilities — made their final reports and were discharged. The 10 denominations were called upon to "covenant" together until the Uniting Church becomes a reality.

COCU publications include: three experimental liturgies — "An Order of Worship for the Proclamation of the Word of God and the Celebration of the Lord's Supper with Commentary" (1968), "An Order for Holy Baptism" (1973), "The Sacrament of the Lord's Supper: a New Text" (1982); an ecumenical lectionary; "An Order for and Affirmation of the Baptismal Covenant" (1980); "An Order of Thanksgiving for the Birth or Adoption of a Child" (1980); "God's Power and Our Weakness" (1982); "Oneness in Christ: The Quest and the Questions" (1981), by Gerald F. Moede, general secretary of the Consultation.

Bishop Arthur Marshall, Jr., of the A.M.E. Zion Church, was elected COCU president in March, 1981. Dr. William D. Watley was appointed associate general secretary in 1982.

Offices are located at 228 Alexander St., Princeton, N.J. 08540.

ECUMENICAL DIALOGUES

(Source: Bishops' Committee for Ecumenical and Interreligious Affairs, National Conference of Catholic Bishops.)

Following is a list of principal consultations, from Mar. 16, 1965, involving representatives of the U.S. Catholic Bishops' Committee for Ecumenical and Interreligious Affairs and representatives of other Christian Churches, with names of the churches, places and dates of meetings, and the subject matter of discussions.

Baptist Convention, American (Division of Cooperative Christianity): (1) De Witt, Mich., Apr. 3, 1967 — American Baptist and Roman Catholic dialogue; a Baptist view of areas of theological agreement. (2) Green Lake, Wis., Apr. 29, 1968 — Baptism and confirmation; Christian freedom and ecclesiastical authority. (3) Schiller Park, Ill., Apr. 28, 1969 — Nature and communication of grace; Christian freedom and ecclesiastical authority; baptism and confirmation. (4) Atchison, Kan., Apr. 17, 1970 — Role of the Church, resume of years past and the future; Roman Catholic-American Baptist dialogues; observations concerning bilateral ecumenical conversations and the future course of American Baptist-Roman Catholic conversations. (5) Detroit, Mich., Apr. 23 to 24, 1971 — Theological perspective on clergy and lay issues and relations; theology of the local church; growth in understanding. (6) Liberty, Mo., Apr. 14 to 15, 1972 — Relationships between Church and State.

Baptists, Southern (Ecumenical Institute, Wake Forest University): (1) Winston-Salem, N.C., May 8, 1969 — Impact of biblical criticism on Roman Catholicism and contemporary Christianity in general; holy use of the world; creeds and the Faith; liturgy and spontaneity in worship; retreat, revival and monasticism; world view of ecumenism.

(2) St. Benedict, La., Feb. 4, 1970 — Liturgy and spontaneity in worship; perspectives on Baptist views on Scripture and tradition; the priesthood of all Christians; authority of the Old Testament; Baptist concepts of the Church; retreat, revival and monasticism. (3) Louisville, Ky., May 13, 1970 — The priesthood of all Christians; the ecumenical tide — a pastoral perspective; the enduring meaning of the Old Testament; retreat, revival and monasticism.

(4) Daytona Beach, Fla., Feb. 1 to 3, 1971 — Issues and answers, prepared by the Interfaith Witness Department of the Home Mission Board, Southern Baptist Convention. (5) Houston, Tex., Oct. 16 to 18, 1972 — Second regional conference planned in conjunction with the Interfaith Witness Department.

(6) Marriottsville, Md., Feb. 4 to 6, 1974 — Third regional conference, planned in conjunction with the Interfaith and Witness Department, concerning different types of reform and their appropriateness at different levels of church life. (7) Menlo Park, Calif., Oct. 27 to 29, 1975 — Fourth regional conference. The theme: "Conversion to Christ and Life-Long Growth in the Spirit."

(8) Winston-Salem, N.C., Nov. 10-12, 1975

— Fraternal dialogue, planned in conjunction with the Ecumenical Institute of Wake Forest University and Belmont Abbey College, on the abortion issue in Christian perspective, with publication of a statement and proceedings.

(9) Winston-Salem, N.C., Nov. 3-5, 1976 — Dialogue, planned as above, on Church-state issues, with publication of a statement and proceedings.

(10) Kansas City, Mo., Nov. 28 to 30, 1977 — Fifth regional conference on the theme, "The Theology and Experience of Worship." (11) Cincinnati, O., Apr. 28 to 30, 1978 — Inauguration of a scholars' dialogue, with presentation of papers on the Church in the New Testament and the experience of God in the Church.

(12) Cincinnati, O., Nov. 3 to 5, 1978 — Roman Catholicism in the U.S.A., an historical perspective; Southern Baptist experience in America; overviews of each tradition by the other; the local congregation or church. (13) St. Louis, Mo., Apr. 20 to 22, 1979 — Salvation as understood and taught in both traditions.

(14) Cincinnati, O., Nov. 9 to 11, 1979 — The authority of Scripture from Southern Baptist and Roman Catholic viewpoints. (15) Conyers, Ga., Apr. 11 to 13, 1980 — Spirituality as understood in each tradition, including sacraments, saints and social justice; Roman Catholic teaching on ministry from the Scriptures and the Fathers of the Church.

(16) Kerrville, Tex., Nov. 21 to 23, 1980 — Mission and social action in Southern Baptist life; eschatology; review of previous papers toward publication. (17) Cincinnati, O., Apr. 16 to 18, 1982 — Initial meeting of second round of dialogue, on the theme, "The Life of Grace within Us."

Christian Church, Disciples of Christ (Council on Christian Unity): (1) Indianapolis, Ind., Mar. 16, 1967 — A look at Disciples for Catholics. (2) Kansas City, Mo., Sept. 25, 1967 — Roman Catholic view of the nature of unity being sought; opportunities in the contemporary ecumenical movement. (3) St. Louis, Mo., Apr. 29, 1968 — Eucharistic sharing.

(4) Washington, D.C., Oct. 16, 1968 — Disciple of Christ inquiry regarding the sacramentality of marriage; pastoral reflections on mixed marriage. (5) New York, N.Y., Apr. 25, 1969 — Recognition and reconciliation of ministries; theological presuppositions concerning ministry among the Disciples; role of the priest in the Catholic community.

(6) Columbus, O., Nov. 3 to 5, 1970 — The parish concept in a plan of union (Consultation on Church Union); directions emerging in Catholic parish life. (7) New York, N.Y., June 8 to 10, 1971 — Disciples' theology of baptism; meaning of baptism as liberation, incorporation, empowerment.

(8) Indianapolis, Ind., Mar. 8 to 10, 1972 — Ministry of healing and reconciliation as practiced in the two communities. (9) Madison, Wis., June 26 to 28, 1972 — Review and summary of five years of dialogue; planning for future themes.

(10) Pleasant Hill, Shaker Town, Ky., May 22 to 24, 1973 — The Church in the New Testament.

(11) Indianapolis, Ind., Jan. 5-6, 1977 — Planning session, with the Council on Christian Unity of the Christian Church and the International Disciples Ecumenical Consultative Council, for a five-year consultation on the topic, "Apostolicity and Catholicity in the Visible Unity of the Church."

(12) Indianapolis, Ind., Sept. 22 to 27, 1977 — First session of a new and international consultation on the nature of the Church and elements of unity relating to it from New Testament and historical perspectives.

(13) Rome, Italy, Dec. 9 to 14, 1978 — Baptism, gift and call in the search for unity; study of various modes of baptism.

(14) Annapolis, Md., Sept. 7 to 12, 1979 — The faith of the individual and the faith of the Church; tradition and the faith of the Church; an agreed account on both subjects.

(15) New Orleans, La., Dec. 5 to 10, 1980 — Unity as gift and call; dynamics of division of the church. (16) Ardfert, Kerry, Ireland, Sept. 10 to 17, 1981 — Completion of final report of this round, "Apostolicity and Catholicity in the Visible Unity of the Church," published June 1, 1982.

Episcopal (The Anglican-Roman Catholic Consultation, Joint Commission on Ecumenical Relations): (1) Washington, D.C., June 22, 1965 — Preliminary discussions. (2) Kansas City, Mo., Feb. 2, 1966 — Eucharist as source or expression of community; Eucharist as sign and cause of unity, and the Church as a Eucharistic fellowship.

(3) Providence, R.I., Oct. 10, 1966 — Function of the minister in Eucharistic celebration; minister of the Eucharist. (4) Milwaukee, Wis., May 2, 1967 — Eucharist. (5) Jackson, Miss., Jan. 5, 1968 — Various aspects of the ministerial priesthood and the priesthood of the faithful in Eucharistic celebration; the priest's place and function in the Church's mission of service; the laity in Episcopal Church government.

(6) Liberty, Mo., Dec. 2, 1968 — Directions of the ecumenical movement; episcopal symbol of unity in the Christian community; collegiality; Citizens for Educational Freedom; a layman's view of jurisdictional and cultural factors in division; Church and society in contemporary America.

(7) Boynton Beach, Fla., Dec. 8, 1969 — All in each place; toward the reconciliation of the Roman Catholic Church and Churches of the Anglican Communion; an approach to designing a Roman Catholic-Episcopal par-

ish; preparation of joint statement on the meeting. (8) Green Bay, Wis., June 17, 1970 — Is the (COCU — Consultation on Church Union) plan of union truly Catholic, with special reference to the priest and the episcopacy?; Anglican-Roman Catholic dialogue — achievement and prognostication.

(9) St. Benedict, La., Jan. 26 to 29, 1971 — The primacy of jurisdiction of the Roman Pontiff according to the First Vatican Council; the teaching of the Second Vatican Council concerning the hierarchy of truths; analysis of the ground of "Church Elements: An Ecclesiological Investigation."

(10) Liberty, Mo., June 20 to 23, 1971 — Gift of infallibility; sharing in the teaching authority of the Church; official view of episcopacy in the Episcopal Church in the USA; symposium on Hans Kung's *Infallibility? An Inquiry*; dogma as an ecumenical problem; Revelation and statement in Anglicanism; revised working paper on theological truth, propositions and Christian unity; reflections on the teaching ministry of the Church.

(11) New York, N.Y., Jan 20 to 24, 1972 — Theological truth, propositions and Christian unity; the Protestant Episcopal Church's view of authority, tradition and the Bible; a comment on the Windsor "Statement of Eucharistic Agreement" issued by the International Anglican-Roman Catholic Consultation.

(12) Cincinnati, O., June 12 to 15, 1972 — The notion of *typos* and *typoi* as applied to the forms of the Christian Church; correspondences and differences in the Anglican and Roman Catholic understanding and exercise of teaching authority.

(13) Cincinnati, O., Mar. 18 to 22, 1973 — Formulation of a preliminary draft on the purpose of the Church. (14) Vicksburg, Miss., Jan. 6 to 10, 1974 — Formulation of a response to the "Canterbury Statement" of the International Anglican-Roman Catholic Consultation on ministry and ordination; discussion and amendment of a draft on the purpose of the Church; other subjects in dialogue on the mission of the Church.

(15) Cincinnati, O., Nov. 10 to 13, 1974 — Discussion on the nature of authority in Anglicanism and Roman Catholicism. Report prepared on the purpose of the Church. (16) Cincinnati, O., June 22 to 25, 1975 — Special ad hoc consultation on women and orders.

(17) Erlanger, Ky., Oct. 21-24, 1975 — Continuation of discussion on women and orders, with release of joint statement on the ordination of women. (18) Overland Park, Kan., Mar. 10-13, 1976 — Continuation of discussion on authority in the Church.

(19) New Orleans, La., Jan. 19-22, 1977 — Presentation and discussion of a paper entitled "Some Implications of a 'Communio Ecclesiology' for the Authority Question";

formulation of an initial response to the "Venice Statement" (see separate entry); near completion of a 12-year report on the consultation.

(20) Cincinnati, O., Aug. 9 to 12, 1977 — Preparation of a second response to the Venice Statement, "Authority in the Church," and of a 12-year report, "Where We are: A Challenge for the Future" (planned for publication). (21) Savannah, Ga., Mar. 7 to 10, 1978 — Christian anthropology and discussion of issues raised by the topic of the 12-year report in dialogue.

(22) Cincinnati, O., Jan. 3 to 6, 1979 — Christian anthropology in the patristic period and documents of the Second Vatican Council on the subject; New Testament arguments for and against the ordination of women.

(23) Cincinnati, O., Oct. 29 to Nov. 1, 1979 — Christian anthropology from the viewpoints of biotechnology/bodiliness, and Mariology. (24) Cincinnati, O., June 17 to 20, 1980 — Maleness and femaleness in Christian anthropology.

(25) Cincinnati, O., Mar. 10 to 13, 1981 — Human sexuality in relation to Christology; ordination of women; homosexuality.

(26) Cincinnati, O., Dec. 8 to 11, 1981 — Work on the first draft of a document on Christian anthropology. (27) Savannah, Ga., June 7 to 10, 1982 — additional work on the aforementioned document.

Lutheran, U.S.A. (National Committee of the Lutheran World Federation): (1) Baltimore, Md., Mar. 16, 1965 — Exploratory discussion. (2) Baltimore, Md., July 6, 1965 — Nicene Creed as dogma of the Church. (3) Chicago, Ill., Feb. 10, 1966 — Baptism, in the context of the New Testament; Lutheran understanding; teaching of the Council of Trent.

(4) Washington, D.C., Sept. 22, 1966 — Eucharist as sacrifice, in traditional and contemporary Catholic and Lutheran contexts. (5) New York, N.Y., Apr 7, 1967 — Propitiation and five presentations on various aspects of the Eucharist. (6) St. Louis, Mo.. Sept. 29, 1967 — Eucharist. (7) New York, Mar. 8, 1968 — Intercommunion, with respect to Catholic discipline, Lutheran practice, and theological reflections.

(8) Williamsburg, Va., Sept. 27, 1968 — Ministry; the competent minister of the Eucharist; scriptural foundations of diakonia (ministry of service). (9) San Francisco, Calif., Feb. 21, 1969 — Apostolic succession in the patristic era and in a contemporary view; Lutheran view of the validity of Lutheran orders; Christian priesthood in the light of documents of the Second Vatican Council.

(10) Baltimore, Md., Sept. 26, 1969 — The minister of the Eucharist, according to the Council of Trent; the use of "Church" as applied to Protestant denominations in the documents of Vatican II; Lutheran doctrine of the ministry — Catholic and Reformed;

the ordained minister and layman in Lutheranism. (11) St. George, Bermuda, Feb. 19, 1970 — Preparation of joint statement on the ministry.

(12) New York, N.Y., May, 1970. (13) Chicago, Ill., Oct. 30 to Nov. 1, 1970. (14) Miami, Fla., Feb. 19 to 22, 1971 — Peter and the New Testament; the papacy in the late patristic era, Middle Ages, Renaissance; text of the *Dogmatic Constitution on the Church* (Vatican, II) with respect to the papacy and infallibility.

(15) Seabury, Conn., Sept. 24 to 27, 1971 — An investigation of the concept of divine right *(jus divinum);* teaching of the First Vatican Council on primacy and infallibility; a Lutheran understanding of what papal primacy in the Church might mean.

(16) New Orleans, La., Feb. 18 to 21, 1972 — Further discussion of the concept of divine right; ecumenical projections concerning the Petrine office; teaching authority in the Lutheran Church. (17) Minneapolis, Minn., Sept. 22 to 25, 1972 — Further investigation of the Petrine function; councils and conciliarism.

(18) San Antonio, Tex., Feb. 16 to 19, 1973 — Discussion of work and papers of the Petrine panel concerning ministry and the Church universal, Catholic and Lutheran interpretive statements; work on papal primacy papers. (19) Allentown, Pa., Sept. 21 to 24, 1973 — Work on a joint statement concerning ministry and the Church universal, the concluding session on this topic; selection of infallibility as the next topic for consideration. (20) Marriottsville, Md., Feb. 15 to 17, 1974 — Start of discussion on infallibility; commissioning of 16 future research papers.

(21) Princeton, N.J., Sept. 19 to 22, 1974 — Scriptural studies re infallibility, inquiries into the teachings of early Lutheranism. (22) St. Louis, Mo., Jan. 30 to Feb. 2, 1975 — Historical and systematic studies of the teaching of infallibility. (23) Washington, D.C., Apr. 2 to 3, 1975 — Special meeting of several Lutheran presidents and Catholic bishops to review the work of the scholars' consultation and propose future directions.

(24) Washington, D.C. Sept. 17 to 21, 1975 — Further historical and case studies re infallibility: ecumenical councils and marian definitions. (25) Scottsdale, Ariz., Feb. 19 to 22, 1976 — Infallibility discussion continued.

(26) Washington, D.C., Apr. 2-3, 1975 — Meeting of Lutheran presidents and Catholic bishops to evaluate the direction and progress of Lutheran-Catholic dialogue in the U.S., with release of a joint statement. (27) Washington, D.C., Feb. 4-5, 1976 — Continuation of discussion concerning the direction and progress of dialogue.

(28) Gettysburg, Pa., Sept. 15-18, 1976 — Presentation of papers entitled: "Draft I — Authority and Doctrine," "The Roman View of the Petrine Office in the Church 366-461,"

"The Status of the Nicene Creed as Dogma in the Church," "Ecumenical Methodology — Report of Task Force."

(29) Washington, D.C., Feb. 16-20, 1977 — Discussion of the second draft of a common statement; presentation of a "Note on the Papacy as an Object of Faith."

(30) Columbia, S.C., Sept. 14 to 18, 1977 — Continued discussion of the common statement, "Infallibility and Teaching Authority in the Church." (31) Lantana, Fla., Feb. 15 to 19, 1978 — Discussion on the fourth draft of a comon statement reporting the findings of dialogue on infallibility.

(32) Minneapolis, Minn., Sept. 13 to 17, 1978 — Statement on infallibility produced. (33) Cincinnati, O., Feb. 14 to 18, 1979 — Beginning of study of justification. (34) Princeton, N.J., Sept. 13 to 16, 1979 — Further study of justification.

(35) Atlanta, Ga., Mar. 5 to 9, 1980 — Justification by faith, in the Bible and the teaching of the Council of Trent.

(36) Gettysburg, Pa., Sept. 18 to 21, 1980 — Justification by faith, patristic and medieval views. (37) Cincinnati, O., Feb. 19 to 22, 1981 — Merit and reward language; additional biblical material on justification by faith.

(38) Paoli, Pa., Sept. 23 to 27, 1981 — Drafting session on document on justification by faith. (39) Biloxi, Miss., Feb. 18 to 21, 1982 — Drafting session. (40) New York, N.Y., Sept. 23 to 26, 1982 — Drafting session.

Methodist (United Methodist Church): (1) Chicago, Ill., June 28, 1966 — Methodists and Roman Catholics: comments for Catholic-Methodist conversation. (2) Chicago, Ill., Dec. 18, 1966 — Salvation, faith and good works; Catholic Church and faith. (3) Lake Junaluska, N.C., June 28, 1967 — Roman Catholic position regarding the Spirit in the Church; mission of the Holy Spirit, in the light of the Second Vatican Council's *Dogmatic Constitution on the Church* and the writings of John Wesley.

(4) New York, N.Y., Dec. 17, 1967 — Three generations of Church-State argumentation. (5) San Antonio, Tex., Sept. 30, 1968 — Shared convictions about education. (6) Delaware, O., Oct. 9, 1969 — Major Methodist ecumenical documents; an appraisal of some documents of Vatican II; racial confrontation in Roman Catholicism, Methodism and the National Council of Churches. (7) Chicago, Ill., Jan. 30, 1970 — Review and planning.

(8) Washington, D.C., Dec. 16, 1970 — Completion of a statement of shared convictions about education. Task force meetings during 1971. (9) Cincinnati, O., Feb. 25 to 26, 1972 — Ministry in the United Methodist Church and the spirituality of the ordained ministry; problems of ministry. (10) Dayton,

O., Oct. 13 to 14, 1972 — Dialogue on the holiness of the Church and Christian holiness.

(11) Washington, D.C., Mar. 9 to 10, 1973 — Spirituality of the ministry. (12) Washington, D.C., Nov. 1 to 2, 1973 — Start of preparatory work on a consensus statement on spirituality of the ministry.

(13) Washington, D.C., Jan. 30 to Feb. 2, 1975 — Report prepared on Catholic and United Methodist understandings of holiness and spirituality in the ordained ministry; statement on holiness and spirituality of the ordained ministry released in January, 1976.

(14) Washington, D.C., May 16, 1977 — Planning session for the next round of dialogue.

(15) Washington, D.C., Dec. 4 to 6, 1977 — New phase of dialogue on the Eucharist in both traditions. (16) Marriottsville, Md., Apr. 16 to 18, 1978 — Continuing research on Eucharistic theology as developed in the two churches.

(17) Washington, D.C., Oct. 12 to 14, 1978 — Eucharistic practice in both traditions. (18) Marriottsville, Md., May 17 to 19, 1979 — The Eucharist; contemporary eucharistic devotional practices of both traditions.

(19) Washington, D.C., Nov. 4 to 6, 1979 — The presence of Christ in the word, related to Eucharistic presence; the notion of sacrifice in the Eucharist. (20) Washington, D.C., May 4 to 6, 1980 — Comparison of liturgical texts of Methodists and Catholics; further exploration of the relationship of word and sacrament.

(21) Erlanger, Ky., Dec. 6 to 8, 1981 — Completion of statement, "Eucharistic Celebration: Converging Theology — Divergent Practice."

Orthodox (Standing Conference of Canonical Orthodox Bishops of America): Sept. 9, 1965 — Preliminary discussions. (1) New York, N.Y., Sept. 29, 1966 — Consultation led to appointment of task forces to investigate differences in theological methods, questions of sacramental sharing, possible cooperation in theological education and the formation of seminarians. (2) Worcester, Mass., May 5, 1967 — Theological diversity and unity; intercommunion; common witness in theological education. (3) Maryknoll, N.Y., Dec. 7, 1968 — Eucharist and Church; indissolubility of marriage; cooperation in theological education.

(4) Worcester, Mass., Dec. 12, 1969 — Orthodox and Catholic views of the Eucharist and membership in the Church; an agreed statement on the Eucharist. (5) New York, N.Y., May 19, 1970 — New Order of the Mass; membership of schismatics and heretics in the ancient Church; current legislation of the Catholic Church and current practices of the Greek Orthodox Church concerning common worship; current legislation of the Catholic Church concerning mixed marriages; Orthodox view of mixed marriages; an agreed statement on mixed marriages.

(6) Brookline, Mass., Dec. 4, 1970 — Ministers, doctrine and practice of matrimony in Eastern and Western traditions. (7) Barlin Acres, Mass., Nov. 3 to 4, 1971 — Ethical issues relating to marriage; revision of an agreed statement on mixed marriages; the primacy of Rome as seen by the Eastern Church.

(8) New York, N.Y., Dec. 6, 1973 — Study of a draft statement on the sanctity of marriage. (9) Washington, D.C., May 23 to 24, 1974 — Dialogical process; witness of the Church on the American scene; approval of an agreed statement on respect for life; Orthodox and Catholic views of contemporary Orthodoxy and Catholicism.

(10) New York, N.Y., Dec. 9 to 10, 1974 — Prepared and issued an agreed statement on the Church. (11) Washington, D.C., May 19 to 20, 1975 — Dialogue on the local church and on the theology of priesthood. (12) New York, N.Y., Jan. 23 to 24, 1976 — Further dialogue on the theology of priesthood, et al.

(13) Washington, D.C., May 18-19, 1976 — Additional discussion of theology of the priesthood, and ecumenical councils; release of joint statements entitled "The Principle of Economy" and "The Pastoral Office."

(14) Brookline, Mass., Jan. 13-14, 1977 — Presentations on "Orthodox/Roman Catholic Marriages Revisited" and of two reports on the first pre-synodal Pan-Orthodox Conference in preparation for the coming Great and Holy Council.

(15) Washington, D.C., Sept. 28 to 29, 1977 — Presentation and discussion of papers concerning the agenda of the forthcoming Great and Holy Council of the Orthodox Church, the theology of marriage and Orthodox-Roman Catholic marriages.

(16) New York, N.Y., Jan. 24 to 25, 1978 — Preparation of a common statement on the sanctity of marriage, authorization for writing a history of the Orthodox-Roman Catholic Consultation.

(17) Washington, D.C., May 15 to 16, 1978 — Additional work on a common statement on the sanctity of marriage, and initial discussion concerning the religious upbringing of children in Orthodox-Catholic marriages.

(18) New York, N.Y., Dec. 7 to 8, 1978 — Study of the religious formation of children of marriages between Eastern Orthodox and Roman Catholics; release of "An Agreed Statement on the Sanctity of Marriage."

(19) Washington, D.C., Mar. 15 to 16, 1979 — Continued study of a draft entitled "Joint Recommendations on the Spiritual Formation of Children of Marriages between Orthodox and Roman Catholics."

(20) Pittsburgh, Pa., Nov. 2 to 3, 1979 — Additional work on a document, "Spiritual

Formation of Children"; study of early Christian commissioning rites.

(21) New York, N.Y., Oct. 10 to 11, 1980 — Study of the theology of ordained ministry; approval of "Joint Recommendations on the Spiritual Formation of Children of Marriages between Orthodox and Roman Catholics."

(22) New York, N.Y., Oct. 1 to 3, 1981 — Papers on "The Priest as Icon of Christ" and "The Sacramental Life of the Church in Light of Trinitarian Ecclesiology." (23) Milwaukee, Wis., May 27 to 29, 1982 — Papers on "Aspects of the Theme: Spirit and Sacrament," and "The Theological and Canonical Traditions of Marriage in the Orthodox and Roman Catholic Traditions."

Orthodox, Oriental (Armenian, Coptic, Ethiopian, Indian Malabar and Syrian Orthodox Churches): (1) New York N.Y., Jan. 27, 1978 — Start of a new consultation, with initial consideration of a historical study of Oriental Orthodoxy.

(2) New York, N.Y., May 26 to 27, 1978 — Purpose and method of dialogue; histories of Oriental Orthodox Churches. (3) Washington, D.C., Dec. 1 to 2, 1978 — Presentation of papers on the Council of Chalcedon, Christology and the Church today, concluding that ancient controversy over Christology does not seem to apply at the present time.

(4) New York, N.Y., May 25 to 26, 1979 — Roman Catholic Christology; Eucharistic Liturgy of the Syrian Orthodox Church.

(5) New York, N.Y., Dec. 27 to 28, 1979 — Paper on Byzantine liturgical commentary; reflection on joint statements of Paul VI with Vasken I, Ignatius Jacoub III and Amba Shenouda III. (6) New York, N.Y., Apr. 18 to 19, 1980 — Paper on Coptic Orthodox Divine Liturgy followed by that Eucharistic Liturgy.

(7) Jamaica, N.Y., Nov. 14 to 15, 1980 — Adoption of a statement on the purpose, scope and method of the dialogue between the Oriental Orthodox and Roman Catholic Churches, and a paper on celebration of the Eucharistic liturgy of the Roman Catholic Church.

(8) New York, N.Y., Dec. 3 and 4, 1981 — Papers on the role of Christ and the Spirit in the Divine Liturgies of each tradition, and on the development of the Public Office in the Armenian Church.

Presbyterian and Reformed (The Roman Catholic-Presbyterian Consultation Group, North American Council of the World Alliance of Reformed Churches): (1) Washington, D.C., July 27, 1965 — Exploratory discussions. (2) Philadelphia, Pa., Nov. 26, 1965 — Role of the Holy Spirit in renewal and reform of the Church. (3) New York, May 12, 1966 — Roman Catholic view of Scripture and tradition; apostolic and ecclesiastical tradition.

(4) Chicago, Ill., Oct. 27, 1966 — Development of doctrine; dialogue, a program of peace, prayer and study for Roman Catholics and Protestants. (5) Collegeville, Minn., Apr. 26, 1967 — Order and ministry in the Reformed tradition; validity of orders; changes in mixed marriage. (6) Lancaster, Pa., Oct. 26, 1967 — Work was begun on a joint statement on ministry. (7) Bristow, Va., May 9, 1968 — Structures and ministries. (8) Allen Park, Mich., Oct. 24, 1968 — Marriage. (9) Charleston, S.C., May 21, 1969 — Validation of ministries and ministry; theological view of marriage.

(10) Macatawa, Mich., Oct. 30, 1969 — Apostles and apostolic succession in the patristic era; report concerning office; divorce and remarriage as understood in the United Presbyterian Church in the USA; the Church and second marriage; recommendations for changes regarding inter-Christian marriages. (11) Morristown, N.J., May 13, 1970 — Joint statements on ministry in the Church and women in Church and society.

(12) Princeton, N.J., Oct. 29 to 30, 1970 — Episcopal presbyteral polity; episcopacy. (13) Columbus, O., May 13 to 15, 1971 — Ministry in the Church; man-woman relationships; the future of the Church. (14) Richmond, Va., Oct. 28 to 30, 1971 — Reports finalized on women in the Church and ministry in the Church. (15) Oct. 26 to 29, 1972 — The shape of the unity we seek.

(16) Columbus, O., May 30 to June 2, 1973 — Theological and sociological views of the shape of unity we seek. (17) Columbus, O., Oct. 24 to 27, 1973 — Renewed discussion of the previous topic. (18) Columbus, O., May 8 to 11, 1974 — Further discussion of the previous topic in the light of Scripture, tradition, theology and reflection on the total Christian experience; worship and belief; discussion of plans for publication of a book on progress of the dialogue.

(17) Cincinnati, O., Oct. 24 to 26, 1974 — Dialogue on the unity we seek in worship and in structures. (18) Washington, D.C., May 22 to 24, 1975 — Report prepared on the mission and nature of the one Church of Christ, with attention to the unity sought in worship, in structure and in common faith.

(19) Princeton, N.J., Oct. 20-23, 1976 — Presentation of: an overview of the history of the consultation; a paper covering a Roman Catholic summary of the diversity and unity of current Christian responses to moral issues facing the Church; a paper on ethics and ethos in the Reformed/Presbyterian tradition.

(20) Washington, D.C., May 25 to 27, 1977 — Human rights, distributive justice and the abortion issue as faced by the churches. (21) Princeton, N.J., Oct. 6 to 7, 1977 — Discus-

sion of racism in South Africa and continuation of a study on human rights.

(22) Washington, D.C., May 30 to June 1, 1978 — Study of the problem of unwanted pregnancies; preparation of statements on abortion and human rights. (23) Washington, D.C., Mar. 4 to 6, 1979 — Re-drafting of proposed statements on abortion and human rights.

(24) Washington, D.C., Sept. 27 to 29, 1979 — Statements on abortion and human rights approved along with commentaries, and an interpretative report. (25) Princeton, N.J., May 19 to 21, 1982 — Beginning of the fourth round of dialogue, on the theme, "Church, Society and Kingdom of God."

INTERFAITH STATEMENTS

The ecumenical statements listed below, and others like them, reflect the views of participants in the dialogues which produced them. They have not been formally accepted by the respective churches as formulations of doctrine or points of departure for practical changes in discipline.

• The "Windsor Statement" on Eucharistic doctrine, published Dec. 31, 1971, by the Anglican-Roman Catholic International Commission of theologians. (For text, see pages 132-33 of the 1973 *Catholic Almanac.*)

• The "Canterbury Statement" on ministry and ordination, published Dec. 13, 1973, by the same commission (For excerpts, see pages 127-30 of the 1975 *Catholic Almanac.*)

• "Papal Primacy / Converging Viewpoints," published Mar. 4, 1974, by the dialogue group sanctioned by the U.S.A. National Convention of the World Lutheran Federation and the U.S. Bishops' Committee for Ecumenical and Interreligious Affairs. (For excerpts, see pages 130-31 of the 1975 *Catholic Almanac.*)

• An "Agreed Statement on the Purpose of the Church," published Oct. 31, 1975, by the Anglican-Roman Catholic Consultation in the U.S., in which the signatories agreed on the purpose and mission of the Church "insofar as it faithfully preaches the Gospel of salvation and manifests the love of God in service." It noted that "Roman Catholics and Episcopalians believe that there is but one Church of Christ," and endorsed social action for human liberation.

• "Christian Unity and Women's Ordination," published Nov. 7, 1975, by the same consultation, in which it was said that the ordination of women (approved in principle by the Anglican Communion but not by the Catholic Church) would "introduce a new element" in dialogue but would not mean the end of consultation nor the abandonment of its declared goal of full communion and organic unity. (A similar view was expressed in an exchange of letters between Pope Paul and Anglican Archbishop Donald Coggan of Canterbury, between July 8, 1975, and Mar. 23, 1976.)

• "Holiness and Spirituality of the Ordained Ministry," issued early in 1976 by theologians of the Catholic Church and the United Methodist Church.

• "Mixed Marriages," published in the spring of 1976 by the Anglican-Roman Catholic Consultation in the U.S. It was similar in some respects to the statement, "Implementation of the Apostolic Letter on Mixed Marriages," approved by the National Conference of Catholic Bishops Nov. 16, 1970. It differed in softening the statement of a Catholic party's responsibility to do everything possible to raise children in the Catholic faith and favored greater freedom for having the marriage ceremony according to the rite of another Christian church.

• "Bishops and Presbyters," see under Eastern Ecumenical Briefs.

• "The Principle of Economy," see under Eastern Ecumenical Briefs.

• "Venice Statement" on authority in the Church, published Jan. 20, 1977, by the Anglican-Roman Catholic International Commission of theologians. Its major headings were Christian authority, authority of the ordained ministry and of the community, authority in the community of churches, the primacy of the bishop of Rome, authority in matters of faith, conciliar and primatial authority. Differences were cited in Catholic and Anglican views with respect to scriptural passages related to claims of the Roman See to primacy of authority, the divine right of the successors of St. Peter, papal infallibility and universal jurisdiction over the Church. (For text, see pages 145-50 of the *1978 Catholic Almanac.*)

• "Response to the Venice Statement," issued Jan. 4, 1978, by the Anglican-Roman Catholic Consultation in the U.S.A., citing additional questions regarding the sharing of authority in the Church, the nature of the primacy of Rome, and the relation of indefectibility to infallibility.

• "The Presence of Christ in Church and World," published early in 1978 by representatives of the Vatican Secretariat for Promoting Christian Unity and the World Alliance of Reformed Churches. The wide-ranging statement noted considerable degrees of mutual understanding and some agreement, along with substantial differences of view on several subjects — especially papal infallibility.

• "An Ecumenical Approach to Marriage," published in January, 1978, in the form of a report on five or more years of dialogue among representatives of the Catholic Church, the Lutheran World Federation and the World Alliance of Reformed Churches. Significant agreement was reported on doctrinal and pastoral aspects of marriage. Objections continued from the Lutheran and Reformed sides, however, with respect to the sacramental nature of marriage, and to Catholic requirements in cases of mixed marriages: (1) that the marriage normally take place with a priest as the officiating minister, and (2) that the Catholic party promise to do everything possible to raise children in the Catholic faith.

• "Teaching Authority and Infallibility in the Church," released in October, 1978, by the Catholic-Lutheran dialogue group in the U.S., noting similarities and differences between Lutheran understanding of the indefectibility of the Church and the Catholic doctrine of papal infallibility.

• "The Eucharist," reported early in 1979, in which the Roman Catholic-Lutheran Commission indicated developing convergence of views concerning the nature and sacrificial aspect of the Mass, and the significance of believing, active participation in the Eucharist.

• "The Holy Spirit," issued Feb. 12, 1979, by the International Catholic-Methodist Commission, citing points of common faith in the Holy Spirit.

• The Final Report of the Anglican-Roman Catholic International Commission, released late in March, 1982, on the results of 12 years of dialogue. (See separate entry, Anglican-Catholic Final Report.)

• A report released June 9, 1982, by the Catholic Church-Disciples of Christ international commission concluded after five years of dialogue that the two churches already have a "unity of grace" which is "bearing fruit and which is disposing us for visible unity and urging us to move ahead to it." The report noted, however, that the two churches differ in their views of the relationship between the New Testament and later Catholic treaching embodied in liturgical texts, creeds and conciliar and papal statements.

CATHOLIC-JEWISH RELATIONS

The Second Vatican Council, in addition to the *Decree on Ecumenism* concerning the movement for unity among Christians, stated the mind of the Church on a similar matter in a *Declaration on the Relationship of the Church to Non-Christian Religions*. This document, as the following excerpts indicate, backgrounds the reasons and directions of the Church's regard for the Jews. (Other portions of the document, not cited here, refer to Hindus, Buddhists and Moslems.)

Spiritual Bond

"As this sacred Synod searches into the mystery of the Church, it recalls the spiritual bond linking the people of the New Covenant with Abraham's stock.

"For the Church of Christ acknowledges that, according to the mystery of God's saving design, the beginnings of her faith and her election are already found among the patriarchs, Moses, and the prophets. She professes that all who believe in Christ, Abraham's sons according to faith (cf. Gal. 3:7), are included in the same patriarch's call, and likewise that the salvation of the Church was mystically foreshadowed by the Chosen People's exodus from the land of bondage.

"The Church, therefore, cannot forget that she received the revelation of the Old Testament through the people with whom God in His inexpressible mercy deigned to establish the Ancient Covenant. Nor can she forget that she draws sustenance from the root of that good olive tree onto which have been grafted the wild olive branches of the Gentiles (cf. Rom.11:17-24). Indeed, the Church believes that by His cross Christ, our Peace, reconciled Jew and Gentile, making them both one in Himself (cf. Eph. 2:14-16).

". . . The Jews still remain most dear to God because of their fathers, for He does not repent of the gifts He makes nor of the calls He issues (cf. Rom. 11:28-29). In company with the prophets and the same Apostle (Paul), the Church awaits that day, known to God alone, on which all peoples will address the Lord in a single voice and 'serve him with one accord' (Zeph. 3:9; Cf. Is. 66:23; Ps. 65:4; Rom. 11:11-32).

"Since the spiritual patrimony common to Christians and Jews is thus so great, this sacred Synod wishes to foster and recommend that mutual understanding and respect which is the fruit above all of biblical and theological studies, and of brotherly dialogues.

No Anti-Semitism

"True, authorities of the Jews and those who followed their lead pressed for the death of Christ (cf. Jn. 19:6); still, what happened in His passion cannot be blamed upon all the Jews then living, without distinction, nor upon the Jews of today. Although the Church is the new People of God, the Jews should not be presented as repudiated or cursed by God, as if such views followed from the holy Scriptures. All should take pains, then, lest in catechetical instruction and in the preaching of God's Word they teach anything out of harmony with the truth of the gospel and the spirit of Christ.

"The Church repudiates all persecutions against any man. Moreover, mindful of her common patrimony with the Jews, and motivated by the gospel's spiritual love and by no political considerations, she deplores the hatred, persecutions, and displays of anti-Semitism directed against the Jews at any time and from any source. . . ." (4).

". . . The Church rejects, as foreign to the mind of Christ, any discrimination against men or harassment of them because of their race, color, condition of life, or religion. . . ." (No. 5).

Bishops' Secretariat

The American hierarchy's first move toward implementation of the Vatican II *Declaration on the Relationship of the Church to Non-Christian Religions* was to establish, in 1965, a Subcommission for Catholic-Jewish Relations in the framework of its Commission for Ecumenical and Interreligious Affairs. This subcommission was reconstituted and given the title of secretariat in September, 1967. Its moderator is Bishop Francis J. Mugavero of Brooklyn. The Secretariat for Catholic-Jewish Relations is located at 1312 Massachusetts Ave. N.W., Washington, D.C. 20005. The executive director is Dr. Eugene J. Fisher.

According to the key norm of a set of guidelines issued by the secretariat Mar. 16, 1967: "The general aim of all Catholic-Jewish meetings (and relations) is to increase our understanding both of Judaism and the Catholic faith, to eliminate sources of tension and misunderstanding, to initiate dialogue or conversations on different levels, to multiply intergroup meetings between Catholics and Jews, and to promote cooperative social action."

Vatican Guidelines

In a document issued Jan. 3, 1975, the Vatican Commission for Religious Relations with the Jews offered a number of suggestions and guidelines for implementing the Christian-Jewish portion of the Second Vatican Council's *Declaration on Relations with Non-Christian Religions.*

Among "suggestions from experience" were those concerning dialogue, liturgical links between Christian and Jewish worship, the interpretation of biblical texts, teaching and education for the purpose of increasing mutual understanding, and joint social action.

The document concluded with the statement:

"On Oct. 22, 1974, the Holy Father instituted for the universal Church this Commission for Religious Relations with the Jews, joined to the Secretariat for Promoting Christian Unity. This special commission, created to encourage and foster religious relations between Jews and Catholics — and to do so in collaboration with other Christians — will be, within the limits of its competence, at the service of all interested organizations, providing information for them and helping them to pursue their task in conformity with the instructions of the Holy See.

"The commission wishes to develop this collaboration in order to implement, correctly and effectively, the express intentions of the (Second Vatican) Council."

NCCB Statement

In a statement issued Nov. 20, 1975, in commemoration of the 10th anniversary of the Second Vatican Council's declaration on non-Christian religions, the National Conference of Catholic Bishops welcomed the Vatican guidelines and hailed the "new era in Catholic-Jewish affairs" which "ended a centuries-long silence between Church and Synagogue."

Lamenting the "de-Judaizing process" that set in early in the Church's history — and which "dulled our awareness of our Jewish beginnings," the bishops affirmed that "most essential concepts in the Christian creed grew at first in Judaic soil. Uprooted from that soil, these basic concepts cannot be perfectly understood."

The bishops called on theologians to reconsider the "long-neglected passages" of the Letter to the Romans (Chapters 9 to 11) as a base for "exploring the continuing relationship of the Jewish people with God and their spiritual bonds with the New Covenant" in a positive manner.

Noting also that "an overwhelming majority of Jews see themselves bound in one way or another to the land of Israel," the bishops stated that, "whatever difficulties Christians may experience in sharing this view, they should strive to understand this link between land and people which Jews have expressed in their writings and worship throughout two millenia as a longing for the homeland, holy Zion."

Papal Statements, Developments

(Courtesy of Dr. Eugene Fisher, Executive Director of the Secretariat for Catholic-Jewish Relations, National Conference of Catholic Bishops, and Consultor, since April, 1981, to the Vatican Commission for Religious Relations with the Jews.)

Pope John Paul, in a remarkable series of addresses beginning in 1979, has sought to promote and give shape to the development of dialogue between Catholics and Jews.

In a homily delivered June 7, 1979, at Auschwitz, which he called the "Golgatha of the Modern World," he prayed movingly for "the memory of the people whose sons and daughters were intended for total extermination."

In a key address delivered Nov. 17, 1980, to the Jewish community in Mainz during his visit to West Germany, the Pope articulated his vision of the three "dimensions" of the dialogue. The first — "that is, the meeting between the people of God of the Old Covenant never retracted by God (Rm. 11:29) on the one hand and the people of the New Covenant on the other" — he said, "is at the same time a dialogue within our own Church, so to speak, a dialogue between the first and second part of its Bible." The second dimension is the encounter of "mutual esteem" between today's Christian churches and today's people of the Covenant concluded with Moses." The third is the "holy duty" of witnessing to the one God in the world and "jointly to work for peace and justice."

In addressing representatives of episcopal conferences gathered in Rome by the Vatican Commission from around the world, the Pope again stressed Mar. 6, 1982, the continuing validity of God's covenant with the Jewish people, noting that "our two religious communities are linked at the very level of their identities," forging links between the two that "are grounded in the design of the God of the Covenant." In his 1982 address, the Pope called especially for a renewal of catechesis that "will not only present Jews and Judaism in an honest and objective manner, but will also do so with a lively awareness" of "our common spiritual heritage . . . taking into account the faith and religious life of the Jewish people as professed and lived now as well." The delegates to the meeting began the process of considering the biblical, theological, and contemporary dynamics of such a catechesis.

International Liaison Committee

The International Catholic-Jewish Liaison Committee, meeting for the ninth time in March, 1981, in London, held discussions on "The Challenge of Secularism to Our Religious Commitments." Speakers warned against "pernicious revisions of the history of the Holocaust," referring pointedly to recent pseudo-scholarly attempts to deny the reality of the Nazi genocide policy against the Jews.

"The Sanctity and Meaning of Human Life in the Present Situation of Violence" was the topic of the 10th meeting, held in September, 1982, in Milan.

Previous meetings discussed such topics as mission and witness (Venice, 1977), religious education (Madrid, 1978), and religious liberty and pluralism (Regensburg, 1979).

U.S. Dialogue

National Workshops on Christian-Jewish Relations have become an increasingly important forum for dialogue. they have been held in Dayton (1975), Memphis (1976), Detroit (1977), Los Angeles (1978), Dallas (1980), Milwaukee (1981), and Boston (April 25-28, 1982).

More than 650 persons took part in the Milwaukee workshop, at which Archbishop Rembert Weakland gave the keynote address, "In the Image of God: The Challenge of Diversity." The theme of the Boston meeting was "Toward a New Generation of Christian-Jewish Dialogue."

A continuing dialogue on religious tradition and social policy — sponsored by the Synagogue Council of America and the NCCB Secretariat for Catholic-Jewish Relations — has been held annually since 1979. The papers from the first two meetings, edited by Dr. Eugene Fisher and D. Polish, have been published by the University of Notre Dame Press under the titles, *Formation of Social Policy in the Catholic and Jewish Traditions* (1980) and *Liturgical Foundations of Social Policy in the Catholic and Jewish Traditions* (1982).

Ongoing relationships are also maintained by the NCCB Secretariat with other Jewish agencies, such as the American Jewish Committee and the Anti-Defamation League of B'nai B'rith. With the latter, a new program to develop model "parish-synagogue" dialogues in five dioceses, featuring lay participation, has been announced. One example of local initiative is the "Priest/Rabbi" committee of the Archdiocese of Los Angeles, which has produced joint statements on abortion, death and dying, covenant and the Kingdom of God.

JUDAISM

Judaism is the religion of the Old Testament and of contemporary Jews. Divinely revealed and with a patriarchal background (Abraham, Isaac, Jacob), it originated with the Mosaic Covenant, was identified with the Israelites, and achieved distinctive form and character as the religion of The Law from this Covenant and reforms initiated by Ezra and Nehemiah after the Babylonian Exile.

Judaism does not have a formal creed but its principal points of belief are clear. Basic is belief in one transcendent God who reveals himself through The Law, the prophets, the life of his people and events of history. The fatherhood of God involves the brotherhood of men. Religious faith and practice are equated with just living according to The Law. Moral conviction and practice are regarded as more important than precise doctrinal formulation and profession. Formal worship, whose principal act was sacrifice from Canaanite times to 70 A.D., is by prayer, reading and meditating upon the sacred writings, and observance of the Sabbath and festivals.

Judaism has messianic expectations of the complete fulfillment of the Covenant, the coming of God's kingdom, the ingathering of his people, final judgment and retribution for all men. Views differ regarding the manner in which these expectations will be realized — through a person, the community of God's people, an evolution of historical events, an eschatological act of God himself. Individual salvation expectations also differ, depending on views about the nature of immortality, punishment and reward, and related matters.

The sacred books are the 24 books of the Masoretic Hebrew Text of The Law, the Prophets and the Writings (see The Bible). Together, they contain the basic instruction or norms for just living. In some contexts, the term Law or Torah refers only to the Pentateuch (Genesis, Exodus, Leviticus, Numbers, Deuteronomy); in others, it denotes all the sacred books and/or the whole complex of written and oral tradition.

Also of great authority are two Talmuds which were composed in Palestine and Babylon in the fourth and fifth centuries A.D., respectively. They consist of the Mishna, a compilation of oral laws, and the Gemara, a collection of rabbinical commentary on the Mishna. Midrash are collections of scriptural comments and moral counsels.

Priests were the principal official ministers during the period of sacrificial and temple worship. Rabbis were, and continue to be, teachers and leaders of prayer. The synagogue is the place of community worship. The family and home are focal points of many aspects of Jewish worship and practice.

Of the various categories of Jews, Orthodox are the most conservative in adherence to strict religious traditions. Others — Reformed, Conservative, Reconstructionist — are liberal in comparison with the Orthodox. They favor greater or less modification of religious practices in accommodation to contemporary culture and living conditions.

Principal events in Jewish life include the circumcision of males, according to prescriptions of the Covenant; the bar mitzvah which marks the coming-of-age of boys in Judaism at the age of 13; marriage; and observance of the Sabbath and festivals.

Sabbath and Festivals

Observances of the Sabbath and festivals begin at sundown of the previous calendar day and continue until the following sundown.

Sabbath: Saturday, the weekly day of rest prescribed in the Decalogue.

Booths (Tabernacles): A seven-to-nine-day festival in the month of Tishri (Sept.-Oct.), marked by some Jews with Covenant-renewal and reading of The Law. It originated as an agricultural feast at the end of the harvest and got its name from the temporary shelters used by workers in the fields.

Hanukkah (The Festival of Lights, the Feast of Consecration and of the Maccabees): Commemorates the dedication of the new altar in the Temple at Jerusalem by Judas Maccabeus in 165 B.C. The eight-day festival, during which candles in an eight-branch candelabra are lighted in succession, one each day, occurs near the winter solstice, close to Christmas time.

Passover: A seven-day festival commemorating the liberation of the Israelites from Egypt. The narrative of the Exodus, the Haggadah, is read at ceremonial Seder meals on the first and second days of the festival, which begins on the 14th day of Nisan (Mar.-Apr.).

Pentecost (Feast of Weeks): Observed 50 days after Passover. Some Jews regard it as commemorative of the anniversary of the revelation of The Law to Moses.

Purim: A joyous festival observed on the 14th day of Adar (Feb.-Mar.), commemorating the rescue of the Israelites from massacre by the Persians through the intervention of Esther. The festival is preceded by a day of fasting. A gift- and alms-giving custom became associated with it in medieval times.

Rosh Hashana (Feast of the Trumpets, New Year): Observed on the first day of Tishri (Sept.-Oct.), the festival focuses attention on the day of judgment and is marked with meditation on the ways of life and the ways of death. It is second in importance only to the most solemn observance of Yom Kippur, which is celebrated 10 days later.

Yom Kippur (Day of Atonement): The highest holy day, observed with strict fasting. It occurs 10 days after Rosh Hashana.

ISLAM

Islam is the religion of Mohammed and his followers, called Moslems, or Muslims. Islam, meaning submission to God, originated with Mohammed (570-632), an Arabian, who taught that he had received divine revelation and was the last and greatest of the prophets.

Moslems believe in one God. There were six great prophets—Adam, Noah, Abraham, Moses, Jesus and Mohammed—and Mohammed was the greatest. The creed states: "There is no God but Allah and Mohammed is the prophet of Allah."

The principal duties of Moslems are to: profess the faith by daily recitation of the creed; pray five times a day facing in the direction of the holy city of Mecca; give alms; fast daily from dawn to dusk during the month of Ramadan; make a pilgrimage to Mecca once if possible.

Moslems believe in a final judgment, heaven and hell. Polygamy is practiced. Some dietary regulations are in effect. The weekly day of worship is Friday, and the principal service is at noon in a mosque. Moslems do not have an ordained ministry. The general themes of their prayer are adoration and thanksgiving.

The basis of Islamic belief is the Koran, the created word of God revealed to Mohammed by the angel Gabriel over a period of 20 years. The contents of this sacred book are complemented by the Sunna, a collection of sacred traditions, and reinforced by Ijma, the consensus of Moslems which guarantees them against error in matters of belief and practice.

There are several sects of Moslems.

The Second Vatican Council called for good relations between Christians and Moslems: "Although in the course of the centuries many quarrels and hostilities have arisen, . . . this most sacred Synod urges all to forget the past and to strive sincerely for mutual understanding."

NON-REVEALED RELIGIONS

Hinduism: The traditional religion of India with origins dating to about 5,000 B.C. Its history is complex, including original Vedic Hinduism, with a sacred literature (Veda) of hymns, incantations and other elements, and with numerous nature gods; Brahmanism, with emphasis on ceremonialism and its power over the gods; philosophical speculation, reflected in the Upanishads, with development of ideas concerning Karma, reincarnation, Brahman, and the manner of achieving salvation; the cults of Vishnu, Shiva and other deities; reforms in Hinduism and in relation to Islam and Christianity.

The principal tenets of Hinduism are open to various interpretations. Karma is the law of the deed, of sowing and reaping, of retribution. It determines the progress of a person toward liberation from the cycle of rebirths necessary for salvation. Liberation is accomplished in stages, through successive reincarnations which indicate the previous as well as the existing state of a person. The means of liberation are the practice of ceremonialism and asceticism; faith in, devotion to and worship of the gods Vishnu and Shiva in their several incarnations; and/or knowledge attained through disciplined meditation called Yoga. Salvation, according to philosophical Hinduism, consists in absorption in Brahman, the neuter world-soul. Vishnu, the sun-god, and Shiva, the destroyer or generative force of the universe, are the principal popular deities. Ancient belief in nature gods (pantheism) is reflected in sacred respect for some animals. The concept of reincarnation underlies the caste system in Indian society.

There are many sects in Hinduism, which does not have a definite creed. It lends itself easily to syncretism or amalgamation with other beliefs, as evidenced in the 15th century Sikh movement which adopted the monotheism and militancy of Islam. Hindu rituals are various and elaborate, with respect to foods, festivals, pilgrimages, marriage and other life-events.

Buddhism: Originated in the sixth century B.C. in reaction to formalism, pantheism and other trends in Hinduism. The Buddha, the Enlightened One, was Sidartha Gautama, an Indian prince, who sought to explain human suffering and evil and to find a middle way between the extremes of austerity and sensuality.

The four noble truths of Buddhism are: (1) existence involves suffering or pain; (2) suffering comes from craving: (3) craving can be overcome; (4) the way to overcome craving is to follow the "noble eightfold path" of right views, right intention, right speech, right action, right livelihood, right effort, right mindfulness and right concentration.

Karma, the deed-principle of judgment and retribution, and reincarnation are elements of Buddhism. The ultimate objective of life is Nirvana — the absorption of a person in the absolute — which ends the cycles of rebirth.

Buddhism is essentially atheistic and more of a moral philosophy and ethical system than a religion. It has a cultic element in veneration for Buddha. Monasteries, temples and shrines are places of contemplation and ritualistic observance. There are several categories of Buddhist monks and nuns.

Buddhism has many sects. Mahayana Buddhism, with an elaborate ideology, is strong in China, Korea and Japan. Hinayana Buddhism is common in Southeast Asia. Zen Buddhism is highly contemplative. Lamaism in Tibet is a combination of Buddhism and local demonolatry.

Confucianism: An ethical system based on the teachings of Confucius (c. 551-479 B.C.). It is oriented toward the moral perfection of individuals and society, the attainment of the harmony of individual and social life with the harmony of the universe, through conduct governed by the relationships of humanity, justice, ritual and courtesy, wisdom, and fidelity. Originally and basically humanistic, Confucianism was eventually mingled with elements of Chinese religion. It exerted a strong influence on national life in China from 125 to the beginning of the 20th century, despite some periods of decline.

Taoism: Originated in China several centuries before the Christian era and became a fully developed religious system by the fifth century A.D. As a religion of mystery, it developed extreme polytheism, with the Jade Emperor as the highest deity; sought blessings and long life by means of alchemy; fostered superstition and witchcraft; took on organizational and other aspects of Buddhism, with several categories of priests and nuns; exerted strong ethical influence on the lower classes; split into many sects; adopted features from other religions; became the starting point of many secret societies. One of its key tenets — that the way of nature is the guide to human conduct — resulted in a form of quietism opposed to the social concern of Confucianism.

Shinto: The way of the gods, the sum total of the cultic beliefs and practices of the ancestral religion of Japan which originated from nature and ancestor worship. Shinto is pantheistic and has many objects of devotion, the highest being the Ruler of Heaven; is practiced with detailed rituals in public shrines, which are cultic centers; has strong social influence. Sectarian Shinto has about 13 recognized sects and many offshoots. Shinto, with principal concern for this-worldly blessing, has ben affected by Buddhist and Confucian influences.

Eastern cults — with their mysticism and associated disciplines and practices — have recurrent periods of vogue in the West.

Glossary

A

Abbess: The female superior of a monastic community of nuns; e.g., Benedictines, Poor Clares, some others. Elected by members of the community, an abbess has general authority over her community but no sacramental jurisdiction. Earliest evidence of the use of the title, a feminine derivative of the Aramaic *abba* (father), dates from early in the sixth century.

Abbey: See Abbot, Monastery.

Abbot: The male superior of a monastic community of men religious; e.g., Benedictines, Cistercians, some others. Elected by members of the community, an abbot has ordinary jurisdiction and general authority over his community. He has some episcopal privileges. The title derives from the Aramaic *abba* (father); first given to the spiritual fathers and guides of hermits in Egypt in the fourth century, it was appropriated in the Rule of St. Benedict to the heads of abbeys and monasteries. Eastern-Rite equivalents of an abbot are a *hegumen* and an *archimandrite*.

A regular abbot is the head of an abbey or monastery. An abbot general or archabbot is the head of a congregation consisting of several monasteries. An abbot primate is the head of the modern Benedictine Confederation.

A few regular abbots have had jurisdiction, similar in some respects to that of a bishop in his diocese, over the residents and institutions of districts (*abbacies nullius*) not belonging to a diocese. Pope Paul stated in a document issued on his own initiative Dec. 29, 1976, that no more such abbacies would be established, except in cases of extraordinary necessity; also, that such abbacies, with the possible exception of ones of historical significance (like Monte Cassino, the cradle of the Benedictine Order) would be phased out of existence. The only *abbacy nullius* ever in the U.S. was Belmont Abbey, N.C.

Abjuration: Renunciation of apostasy, heresy or schism by a solemn oath.

Ablution: A term derived from Latin, meaning washing or cleansing, and referring to the cleansing of the hands of a priest celebrating Mass, after the offering of gifts; and to the cleansing of the chalice with water and wine after Communion.

Abortion: The expulsion of a nonviable human fetus from the womb of the mother, with moral implications stemming from the humanity of the fetus from the moment of conception and its consequent right to life.

Accidental expulsion, as in cases of miscarriage, is without moral fault.

Direct abortion, in which a fetus is intentionally removed from the womb, constitutes a direct attack on an innocent human being, a violation of the Fifth Commandment. It is punished in church law by the penalty of excommunication, which is automatically incurred by all baptized persons involved; i.e., the consenting mother and necessary physical and/or moral cooperators. Direct abortion is not justifiable for any reason, e.g.: therapeutic, for the physical and/or psychological welfare of the mother; preventive, to avoid the birth of a defective or unwanted child; social, in the interests of family and/or community.

Indirect abortion, which occurs when a fetus is expelled during medical or other treatment of the mother for a reason other than procuring expulsion, is permissible under the principle of double effect for a proportionately serious reason; e.g., when a medical or surgical procedure is necessary to save the life of the mother.

Absolution: The act by which an authorized priest, acting as the agent of Christ and minister of the Church, grants forgiveness of sins in the sacrament of penance. The essential formula of absolution is: "I absolve you from your sins; in the name of the Father, and of the Son, and of the Holy Spirit. Amen.

Priests receive the power to absolve in virtue of their ordination and the right to exercise this power in virtue of faculties of jurisdiction given them by their bishop, their religious superior, or by canon law. The faculties of jurisdiction can be limited or restricted regarding certain sins and penalties or censures.

In cases of necessity, and also in cases of the absence of their own confessors, Eastern and Roman Rite Catholics may ask for and receive sacramental absolution from a priest of a separated Eastern Church. Separated Eastern Christians may similarly ask for and receive sacramental absolution from an Eastern or Roman Rite priest.

Any priest can absolve a person in danger of death; in the absence of a priest with the usual faculties, this includes a laicized priest or a priest under censure.

(See additional entry under Sacraments.)

Absolution, General: (1) Sacramental absolution given without confession of sin, when confession is impossible. Persons so absolved are required to confess, in their next confession, the mortal sins from which they were so absolved.

(2) A blessing of the Church to which a plenary indulgence is attached, given at the hour of death, and at stated times to members of religious institutes and third orders.

Accessory to Another's Sin: One who culpably assists another in the performance of an evil action. This may be done by counsel, command, provocation, consent, praise, flattery, concealment, participation, silence, defense of the evil done.

Adoration: The highest act and purpose of religious worship, which is directed in love and reverence to God alone in acknowledgment of his infinite perfection and goodness, and of his total dominion over creatures. Adoration, which is also called *latria*, consists of internal and external elements, private and social prayer, liturgical acts and ceremonies, and especially sacrifice.

Adultery: (1) Sexual intercourse between a married person and another to whom one is not married; a violation of the obligations of chastity and justice. The Sixth Commandment prohibition against adultery is also regarded as a prohibition against all external sins of a sexual nature.

(2) Any sin of impurity (thought, desire, word, action) involving a married person who is not one's husband or wife has the nature of adultery.

Adventists: Members of several Christian sects whose doctrines are dominated by belief in a more or less imminent second advent or coming of Christ upon earth for a glorious 1,000-year reign of righteousness. This reign, following victory by the forces of good over evil in a final Battle of Armageddon, will begin with the resurrection of the chosen and will end with the resurrection of all other men and the annihilation of the wicked. Thereafter, the just will live forever in a renewed heaven and earth. A sleep of the soul takes place between the time of death and the day of judgment. There is no hell. The Bible, in fundamentalist interpretation, is regarded as the only rule of faith and practice.

About six sects have developed in the course of the Adventist movement which originated with William Miller (1782-1849) in the United States. Miller, on the basis of calculations made from the Book of Daniel, predicted that the second advent of Christ would occur between 1843 and 1844. After the prophecy went unfulfilled, divisions occurred in the movement and the Seventh Day Adventists, whose actual formation dates from 1860, emerged as the largest single body. The observance of Saturday instead of Sunday as the Lord's Day dates from 1844.

Advent Wreath: A wreath of laurel, spruce, or similar foliage with four candles which are lighted successively in the weeks of Advent to symbolize the approaching celebration of the birth of Christ, the Light of the World, at Christmas. The wreath originated among German Protestants.

Agape: A Greek word, meaning love, love feast, designating the meal of fellowship eaten at some gatherings of early Christians. Although held in some places in connection with the Mass, the agape was not part of the Mass, nor was it of universal institution and observance. Legislation against it was passed by the Council of Carthage (397) and other councils because of abuses. It was infrequently observed by the fifth century and disappeared altogether between the sixth and eighth centuries. In recent years, a limited revival has taken place in the course of the liturgical and ecumenical movements.

Age of Reason: (1) The time of life when one begins to distinguish between right and wrong, to understand an obligation and take on moral responsibility; seven years of age is the presumption in church law.

(2) Historically, the 18th century period of Enlightenment in England and France, the age of the Encyclopedists and Deists. According to a basic thesis of the Enlightenment, human experience and reason are the only sources of certain knowledge of truth; consequently, faith and revelation are discounted as valid sources of knowledge, and the reality of supernatural truth is called into doubt and/or denied.

Aggiornamento: An Italian word having the general meaning of bringing up to date, renewal, revitalization, descriptive of the processes of spiritual renewal and institutional reform and change in the Church; fostered by the Second Vatican Council.

Agnosticism: A theory which holds that man cannot have certain knowledge of immaterial reality, especially the existence of God and things pertaining to him. Immanuel Kant, one of the philosophical fathers of agnosticism, stood for the position that God, as well as the human soul, is unknowable on speculative grounds; nevertheless, he found practical imperatives for acknowledging God's existence, a view shared by many agnostics. The First Vatican Council declared that the existence of God and some of his attributes can be known with certainty by human reason, even without divine revelation. The word agnosticism was first used, in the sense given here, by T. H. Huxley in 1869.

Agnus Dei: A Latin phrase, meaning Lamb of God.

(1) A title given to Christ, the Lamb (victim) of the Sacrifice of the New Law (on Calvary and in Mass).

(2) A prayer said at Mass before the reception of Holy Communion.

(3) A sacramental. It is a round paschal-candle fragment blessed by the pope. On one side it bears the impression of a lamb, symbolic of Christ. On the reverse side, there may be any one of a number of impressions; e.g., the figure of a saint, the name and coat of arms of the reigning pope. The *agnus dei* may have originated at Rome in the fifth century. The first definite mention of it dates from about 820.

Alleluia: An exclamation of joy derived from Hebrew, All hail to him who is, praise God. It is used in the liturgy and other prayer on joyful occasions during the church year.

Allocution: A formal type of papal address,

as distinguished from an ordinary sermon or statement of views.

Alms: An act, gift or service of compassion, motivated by love of God and neighbor, for the help of persons in need; an obligation of charity, which is measurable by the ability of one person to give assistance and by the degree of another's need. Almsgiving, along with prayer and fasting, is regarded as a work of penance as well as an exercise of charity. (See Corporal and Spiritual Works of Mercy.)

Alpha and Omega: The first and last letters of the Greek alphabet, used to symbolize the eternity of God (Rv. 1:8) and the divinity and eternity of Christ, the beginning and end of all things (Rv. 21:6; 22:13). Use of the letters as a monogram of Christ originated in the fourth century or earlier.

Amen: A Hebrew word meaning truly, it is true. In the Gospels, Christ used the word to add a note of authority to his statements. In other New Testament writings, as in Hebrew usage, it was the concluding word to doxologies. As the concluding word of prayers, it expresses assent to and acceptance of God's will.

Anathema: A Greek word with the root meaning of cursed or separated and the adapted meaning of excommunication, used in church documents, especially the canons of ecumenical councils, for the condemnation of heretical doctrines and of practices opposed to proper discipline.

Anchorite: A kind of hermit living in complete isolation and devoting himself exclusively to exercises of religion and severe penance according to a rule and way of life of his own devising. In early Christian times, anchorites were the forerunners of the monastic life. The closest contemporary approach to the life of an anchorite is that of Carthusian and Camaldolese hermits.

Angels: Purely spiritual beings with intelligence and free will, whose name indicates their mission as ministers of God and ministering spirits to men. They were created before the creation of the visible universe; the devil and bad angels, who were created good, fell from glory through their own fault. In addition to these essentials of defined doctrine, it is held that angels are personal beings; they can intercede for men; fallen angels were banished from God's glory in heaven to hell; bad angels can tempt men to commit sin. The doctrine of guardian angels, although not explicitly defined as a matter of faith, is rooted in long-standing tradition. No authoritative declaration has ever been issued regarding choirs or various categories of angels: according to theorists, there are nine choirs, consisting of seraphim, cherubim, thrones, dominations, principalities, powers, virtues, archangels and angels. In line with scriptural usage, only three angels can be named—Michael, Raphael and Gabriel.

Angelus: A devotion which commemorates the Incarnation of Christ. It consists of three versicles, three Hail Marys and a special prayer, and recalls the announcement to Mary by the Archangel Gabriel that she was chosen to be the Mother of Christ, her acceptance of the divine will, and the Incarnation (Lk. 1:26-38). The Angelus is recited at 6 a.m., noon and 6 p.m. The practice of reciting the Hail Mary in honor of the Incarnation was introduced by the Franciscans in 1263. The *Regina Caeli*, commemorating the joy of Mary at Christ s Resurrection, replaces the Angelus during the Easter season.

Anger: Passionate displeasure arising from some kind of offense suffered at the hands of another person, frustration or other cause, combined with a tendency to strike back at the cause of the displeasure; a violation of the Fifth Commandment and one of the capital sins if the displeasure is out of proportion to the cause and/or if the retaliation is unjust.

Anglican Orders: Holy orders conferred according to the rite of the Anglican (Episcopal) Church, which Leo XIII declared null and void in the bull *Apostolicae Curae*, Sept. 13, 1896. The orders were declared null because they were conferred according to a rite that was considered substantially defective in form and intent, and because of a break in apostolic succession that occurred when Matthew Parker became head of the Anglican hierarchy in 1559.

In making his declaration, Pope Leo cited earlier arguments against validity made by Julius III in 1553 and 1554 and by Paul IV in 1555. He also noted related directives requiring absolute ordination, according to the Catholic ritual, of convert ministers who had been ordained according to the Anglican Ordinal.

Antichrist: The man of sin, the lawless and wicked antagonist of Christ and the work of God; a mysterious figure of prophecy mentioned in the New Testament. Supported by Satan, submitting to no moral restraints, and armed with tremendous power, Antichrist will set himself up in opposition to God, work false miracles, persecute the People of God, and employ unimaginable means to lead men into error and evil during a period of widespread defection from the Christian faith before the end of time; he will be overcome by Christ. Catholic thinkers have regarded Antichrist as a person, a caricature of Christ, who will lead a final violent struggle against God and His people; they have also applied the title to personal and impersonal forces in history hostile to God and the Church. Official teaching has said little about Antichrist. In 1318, it labeled as partly heretical, senseless, and fanciful the assertions made by the Fraticelli about his coming; in 1415, the Council of Constance condemned the Wycliff thesis that excommunications made by the pope and other prelates were the actions of Antichrist.

Antiphon: (1) A short verse or text, generally from Scripture, recited in the Liturgy of the Hours before and after psalms and canticles.

(2) Any verse sung or recited by one part of a choir or congregation in response to the other part, as in antiphonal or alternate chanting.

Apologetics: The science and art of building and presenting the case for, accounting for, explaining, defending, justifying the reasonableness of the Christian faith, by a wide variety of means including facts of experience, history, science, philosophy. The constant objective of apologetics, as well as of the total process of pre-evangelization, is preparation for response to God in faith; its ways and means, however, are subject to change in accordance with the various needs of people and different sets of circumstances.

Apostasy: (1) The total and obstinate rejection or abandonment of the Christian faith by a baptized person who continues to call himself a Christian. External manifestation of this rejection constitutes the crime of apostasy, and the person, called an *apostate,* automatically incurs a penalty of excommunication.

(2) Apostasy from orders is the unlawful withdrawal from or rejection of the obligations of the clerical state by a man who has received major orders. The canonical penalty for such apostasy is excommunication.

(3) Apostasy from the religious life occurs when a religious with perpetual vows unlawfully leaves the community with the intention of not returning, or actually remains outside the community for 30 days without permission. The canonical penalty for such apostasy is excommunication.

Apostolate: The ministry or work of an apostle. In Catholic usage, the word is an umbrella-like term covering all kinds and areas of work and endeavor for the service of God and the Church and the good of people. Thus, the apostolate of bishops is to carry on the mission of the Apostles as pastors of the People of God: of priests, to carry out the sacramental and pastoral ministry for which they are ordained; of religious, to follow and do the work of Christ in conformity with the evangelical counsels and their rule of life; of lay persons, as individuals and/or in groups, to give witness to Christ and build up the kingdom of God through practice of their faith, professional competence and the performance of good works in the concrete circumstances of daily life. Apostolic works are not limited to those done within the Church or by specifically Catholic groups, although some apostolates are officially assigned to certain persons or groups and are under the direction of church authorities. Apostolate derives from the commitment and obligation of baptism, confirmation, holy orders, matrimony, the duties of one's state in life, etc.

Apostolic Succession: Bishops of the Church, who form a collective body or college, are successors to the Apostles by ordination and divine right; as such they carry on the mission entrusted by Christ to the Apostles as guardians and teachers of the deposit of faith, principal pastors and spiritual authorities of the faithful. The doctrine of apostolic succession is based on New Testament evidence and the constant teaching of the Church, reflected as early as the end of the first century in a letter of Pope St. Clement to the Corinthians. A significant facet of the doctrine is the role of the pope as the successor of St. Peter, the vicar of Christ and head of the college of bishops. The doctrine of apostolic succession means more than continuity of apostolic faith and doctrine; its basic requisite is ordination by the laying on of hands in apostolic succession.

Archangel: An angel who carries out special missions for God in his dealings with men. Three of them are named in the Bible: Michael, leader of the angelic host and protector of the synagogue; Raphael, guide of Tobiah and healer of his father, who is regarded as the patron of travelers; Gabriel, called the angel of the Incarnation because of his announcement to Mary that she was to be the Mother of Christ.

Archdiocese: An ecclesiastical jurisdiction headed by an archbishop. An archdiocese is usually a metropolitan see, i.e., the principal one of a group of dioceses comprising a province; the other dioceses in the province are suffragan sees.

Archives: Documentary records, and the place where they are kept, of the spiritual and temporal government and affairs of the Church, a diocese, church agencies like the departments of the Roman Curia, bodies like religious institutes, and individual parishes. The collection, cataloguing, preserving, and use of these records are governed by norms stated in canon law and particular regulations. The strictest secrecy is always in effect for confidential records concerning matters of conscience, and documents of this kind are destroyed as soon as circumstances permit.

Archpriest: For some time, before and during the Middle Ages, a priest who took the place of a bishop at liturgical worship. In Europe, the term is sometimes used as an honorary title. It is also an honorary title in Eastern-Rite Churches.

Asceticism: The practice of self-discipline. In the spiritual life, asceticism — by personal prayer, meditation, self-denial, works of mortification, and outgoing interpersonal works — is motivated by love of God and contributes to growth in holiness.

Ashes: Religious significance has been associated with their use as symbolic of penance since Old Testament times. Thus, ashes of palm blessed on the previous Sunday of the Passion are placed on the foreheads of the faithful on Ash Wednesday to remind them to do works of penance, especially during the season of Lent, and that they are dust and unto dust will return. Ashes are a sacramental.

Aspergillum: A vessel or device used for sprinkling holy water. The ordinary type is a metallic rod with a bulbous tip which absorbs the water and discharges it at the motion of the user's hand.

Aspersory: A portable metallic vessel, similar to a pail, for carrying holy water.

Aspiration: Short exclamatory prayer; e.g., My Jesus, mercy.

Atheism: Denial of the existence of God, finding expression in a system of thought (speculative atheism) or a manner of acting (practical atheism) as though there were no God.

The Second Vatican Council, in its *Pastoral Constitution on the Church in the Modern World* (Nos. 19 to 21), noted that a profession of atheism may represent an explicit denial of God. the rejection of a wrong notion of God, an affirmation of man rather than of God, an extreme protest against evil. It said that such a profession might result from acceptance of such propositions as: there is no absolute truth; man can assert nothing, absolutely nothing, about God; everything can be explained by scientific reasoning alone; the whole question of God is devoid of meaning.

The constitution also cited two opinions of influence in atheistic thought. One of them regards recognition of dependence on God as incompatible with human freedom and independence. The other views belief in God and religion as a kind of opiate which sedates man on earth, reconciling him to the acceptance of suffering, injustice, shortcomings, etc., because of hope for greater things after death, and thereby hindering him from seeking and working for improvement and change for the better here and now.

All of these views, in one way or another, have been involved in the No-God and Death-of-God schools of thought in recent and remote history.

Atonement: The redemptive activity of Christ, who reconciled man with God through his Incarnation and entire life, and especially by his suffering and Resurrection. The word also applies to prayer and good works by which men join themselves with and take part in Christ's work of reconciliation and reparation for sin.

Attributes of God: Perfections of God. God possesses—and is—all the perfections of being, without limitation. Because he is infinite, all of these perfections are one, perfectly united in him. Man, however, because of the limited power of understanding, views these perfections separately, as distinct characteristics—even though they are not actually distinct in God. God is: almighty, eternal, holy, immortal, immense, immutable, incomprehensible, ineffable, infinite, invisible, just, loving, merciful, most high, most wise, omnipotent, omniscient, omnipresent, patient, perfect, provident, supreme, true.

Avarice (Covetousness): A disorderly and unreasonable attachment to and desire for material things; called a capital sin because it involves preoccupation with material things to the neglect of spiritual goods and obligations of justice and charity.

Ave Maria: See Hail Mary.

B

Baldachino: A canopy over an altar.

Beatification: A preliminary step toward canonization of a saint. It begins with an investigation of the candidate's life, writings and heroic practice of virtue, and the certification of at least two miracles worked by God through his intercession. If the findings of the investigation so indicate, the pope decrees that the Servant of God may be called *Blessed* and may be honored locally or in a limited way in the liturgy. Additional procedures lead to canonization (see separate entry).

Beatific Vision: The intuitive, immediate and direct vision and experience of God enjoyed in the light of glory by all the blessed in heaven. The vision is a supernatural mystery.

Beatitude: A literary form of the Old and New Testaments in which blessings are promised to persons for various reasons. Beatitudes are mentioned 26 times in the Psalms, and in other books of the Old Testament. The best known beatitudes — identifying blessedness with participation in the kingdom of God and his righteousness, and descriptive of the qualities of Christian perfection — are those recounted in Mt. 5:3-11 and Lk. 6:20-22.

In Matthew's account, the beatitudes are:

"How blest are the poor in spirit: the reign of God is theirs.

"Blest too are the sorrowing; they shall be consoled.

"(Blest are the lowly; they shall inherit the land.)

"Blest are they who hunger and thirst for holiness; they shall have their fill.

"Blest are they who show mercy; mercy shall be theirs.

"Blest are the single-hearted for they shall see God.

"Blest too are the peacemakers; they shall be called sons of God.

"Blest are those persecuted for holiness' sake; the reign of God is theirs.

"Blest are you when they insult you and persecute you and utter every kind of slander against you because of me."

In Luke's account, the beatitudes are:

"Blest are you poor; the reign of God is yours.

"Blest are you who hunger; you shall be filled.

"Blest are you who are weeping; you shall laugh.

"Blest shall you be when men hate you, when they ostracize you and insult you and proscribe your name as evil because of the Son of Man."

Benediction of the Blessed Sacrament: A short exposition of the Eucharist for adoration by and blessing of the faithful. Devotional practices include the singing of Eucharistic and other hymns, and recitation of the Divine Praises. Benediction, in its present form, dates from about the 15th century and is a form of liturgical worship.

Benedictus: The canticle or hymn of Zechariah at the circumcision of St. John the Baptist (Lk. 1:68-79). It is an expression of praise and thanks to God for sending John as a precursor of the Messiah. The *Benedictus* is recited in the Liturgy of the Hours as part of the Morning Prayer.

Bible Service: A devotion consisting essentially of common prayer of a biblical or liturgical character, several readings from Scripture, and a homily on the texts.

Biglietto: A papal document of notification of appointment to the cardinalate.

Biretta: A stiff, square hat with three ridges on top worn by clerics in church and on other occasions.

Blasphemy: Any expression of insult or contempt with respect to God, principally, and to holy persons and things, secondarily; a violation of the honor due to God in the context of the First and Second Commandments.

Blasphemy of the Spirit: Deliberate resistance to the Holy Spirit, called the unforgivable sin (Mt. 12:31) because it makes his saving action impossible. Thus, the only unforgivable sin is the one for which a person will not seek pardon from God.

Blessing: Invocation of God's favor, by official ministers of the Church or by private individuals. Blessings are recounted in the Old and New Testaments, and are common in the Christian tradition. The Church, through its ordained ministers (bishops and priests, especially), invokes divine favor in liturgical blessings; e.g., of the people at Mass, of the gifts to be consecrated at Mass, of persons and things on various occasions. Sacramentals — such as crucifixes, crosses, rosaries, scapulars, medals — are blessed by ministers of the Church for the invocation of God's favor on those who use them in the proper manner. Many types of blessings are listed in the *Roman Ritual*. Private blessings, as well as those of an official kind, are efficacious. Blessings are imparted with the Sign of the Cross and appropriate prayer.

Boat: A small vessel used to hold incense which is to be placed in the censer.

Brief, Apostolic: A papal letter, less formal than a bull, signed for the pope by a secretary and impressed with the seal of the Fisherman's Ring. Simple apostolic letters of this kind are issued for beatifications and with respect to other matters.

Bull, Apostolic: The most solemn form of papal document, beginning with the name and title of the pope (e.g., Paul VI, Servant of the Servants of God), dealing with an important subject, and having attached to it either a leaden seal called a bulla or a red ink imprint of the device on the seal. Bulls are known as apostolic letters with the seal. The seal, on one side, has representations of the heads of Sts. Peter and Paul; on the other side, the name of the reigning pope. Bulls are issued to confer the titles of bishops and cardinals, to promulgate canonizations, and for other purposes. A collection of bulls is called a *bullarium*.

Burial, Ecclesiastical: Interment with church rites and in consecrated ground. Catechumens as well as baptized Catholics have a right to ecclesiastical burial. A non-Catholic partner in a mixed marriage may be buried in a Catholic cemetery with the Catholic partner.

C

Calumny: Harming the name and good reputation of a person by lies; a violation of obligations of justice and truth. Restitution is due for calumny.

Calvary: A knoll about 15 feet high just outside the western wall of Jerusalem where Christ was crucified, so called from the Latin *calvaria* (skull) which described its shape.

Canon: A Greek word meaning rule, norm, standard, measure.

(1) The word designates the Canon of Sacred Scripture, which is the list of books recognized by the Church as inspired by the Holy Spirit.

(2) In the sense of regulating norms, the word designates the body or corpus of Canon Law enacted and promulgated by ecclesiastical authority for the orderly administration and government of the Church. The Code of Canon Law now in force in the Roman Church has been in effect since 1918. It consists of 2,414 canons which are divided into five books covering general rules, ecclesiastical persons, sacred things, trials, crimes and punishments. The code is now under review for the purpose of revision. Eastern-Rite Churches have their own canon law.

(3) The term also designates the four canons, (Eucharistic prayers, anaphoras) of the Mass, the core of the liturgy.

(4) Certain dignitaries of the Church have the title of Canon, and some religious are known as Canons.

Canonization: An infallible declaration by the pope that a person, who died as a martyr and/or practiced Christian virtue to a heroic degree, is now in heaven and is worthy of honor and imitation by all the faithful. Such a declaration is preceded by the process of beatification and another detailed investigation concerning the person's reputation for holiness, his writings, and (except in the case of martyrs) miracles ascribed to his intercession after his death. Miracles are not required for martyrs. The pope can dispense from some of the formalities ordinarily required in canonization procedures (equivalent canonization), as Pope John XXIII did in the canonization of St. Gregory Barbarigo on May 26, 1960. A saint is worthy of honor in liturgical worship throughout the universal Church.

From its earliest years the Church has venerated saints. Public official honor always required the approval of the bishop of the place. Martyrs were the first to be honored. St. Martin of Tours, who died in 397, was an early non-martyr venerated as a saint. The first official canonization by a pope for the universal Church was that of St. Ulrich by John XV in 993. Alexander III reserved the process of canonization to the Holy See in 1171. In 1588 Sixtus V established the Sacred Congregation of Rites for the principal purpose of handling causes for beatification and canonization: this function is now the work of the Congregation for the Causes of Saints. The present procedure is outlined in canons 1999-2141 of the Code of Canon Law and in a 1969 enactment by Paul VI.

The essential portion of a canonization decree states:

"For the honor of the holy and undivided Trinity; for the exaltation of the Catholic faith and the increase of Christian life; with the authority of our Lord Jesus Christ, of the blessed Apostles Peter and Paul, and with our own authority; after mature deliberation and with the divine assistance, often implored; with the counsel of many of our brothers.

"We decree and define that (name) is a saint and we inscribe him (her) in the Catalogue of Saints, stating that he (she) shall be venerated in the universal Church with pious devotion.

"In the name of the Father and of the Son and of the Holy Spirit. Amen."

The official listing of saints and blessed is contained in the *Roman Martyrology* and related decrees issued after its last publication. Butler's unofficial *Lives of the Saints* (1956) contains 2,565 entries.

The Church regards all persons in heaven as saints, not just those who have been officially canonized.

(See Beatification, Saints, Canonizations by Leo XIII and His Successors.)

Canticle: A scriptural chant or prayer differing from the psalms. Three of the canticles prescribed for use in the Liturgy of the Hours are: The *Magnificat* (Lk. 1:46-55), the *Benedictus* (Lk. 1:68-79), and the *Nunc Dimittis* (Lk. 2:29-32).

Capital Punishment: Punishment for crime by means of the death penalty. The political community, which has authority to provide for the common good, has the right to defend itself and its members against unjust aggression and may in extreme cases punish with the death penalty persons found guilty before the law of serious crimes against individuals and a just social order. Such punishment is essentially vindictive. Its value as a crime deterrent is a matter of perennial debate. The prudential judgment as to whether or not there should be capital punishment belongs to the civic community. The U.S. Supreme Court, in a series of decisions dating from June 29, 1972, ruled against the constitutionality of statutes on capital punishment except in specific cases and with appropriate consideration, with respect to sentence, of mitigating circumstances of the crime.

Capital punishment was the subject of a statement issued Mar. 1, 1978, by the Committee on Social Development and World Peace, U.S. Catholic Conference. The statement said, in part: "The use of the death penalty involves deep moral and religious questions as well as political and legal issues. In 1974, out of a commitment to the value and dignity of human life, the Catholic bishops of the United States declared their opposition to capital punishment. We continue to support this position, in the belief that a return to the use of the death penalty can only lead to the further erosion of respect for life in our society. Violent crime in our society is a serious matter which should not be ignored. We do not challenge society's right to punish the serious and violent offender, nor do we wish to debate the merits of the arguments concerning this right. Past history, however, shows that the death penalty in its present application has been discriminatory with respect to the disadvantaged, the indigent and the socially impoverished. Furthermore, recent data from correction sources definitely question the effectiveness of the death penalty as a deterrent to crime."

Additional statements against capital punishment have been issued by numerous bishops and other sources.

Capital Sins: Moral faults which, if habitual, give rise to many more sins. They are pride, covetousness, lust, anger, gluttony, envy, sloth.

The opposite virtues are: humility, liberality, chastity, meekness, temperance, brotherly love, diligence.

Cardinal Virtues: The four principal moral virtues are prudence, justice, temperance and fortitude.

Catacombs: Underground Christian cemeteries in various cities of the Roman Empire and Italy, especially in the vicinity of Rome; the burial sites of many martyrs and other Christians. Developed from aboveground cemeteries, their passageways, burial niches and assembly rooms were dug out of tuffa, a soft clay which hardened into rock-like consistency on drying. The earliest ones date from the third century; in the fourth, they became the scene of memorial services as the veneration of martyrs increased in popularity; in the seventh and eighth centuries, they were plundered by the Lombards and other invaders. The relics of many martyrs were removed to safer places in the ninth century; afterwards, the catacombs fell into neglect and oblivion until interest in them revived in the 16th century. The catacombs have been excavated extensively, yielding considerable information about early Christian symbolism and art, dating from the third century on, and other aspects of Christian life and practice.

Catafalque: A small structure like a bier, used at services for the dead in the absence of the corpse.

Catechism: A summary of Christian doctrine in question and answer form, used for purposes of instruction.

Catechumen: A person preparing, in a program of instruction and spiritual formation for baptism and reception into the Church.

Cathedra: A Greek word for chair, designating the chair or seat of a bishop in the principal church of his diocese, which is therefore called a cathedral (see separate entry).

Cathedraticum: The tax paid to a bishop by all churches and benefices subject to him for the support of episcopal administration and for works of charity.

Catholic: A Greek word, meaning universal, first used in the title Catholic Church in a letter written by St. Ignatius of Antioch about 107 to the Christians of Smyrna.

Celebret: A Latin word, meaning Let him celebrate, the name of a document issued by a bishop or other superior stating that a priest is in good standing and therefore should be given opportunity to celebrate Mass or perform other priestly functions.

Celibacy: The unmarried state of life, required in the Roman or Latin Church of candidates for holy orders and of men already ordained to holy orders, for the practice of perfect chastity and total dedication to the service of people in the ministry of the Church. Celibacy is enjoined as a condition for ordination by church discipline and law, not by dogmatic necessity.

In the Roman Church, a consensus in favor of celibacy developed in the early centuries while the clergy included both celibates and men who had been married once. The first local legislation on the subject was enacted by a local council held in Elvira, Spain, about 306; it forbade bishops, priests, deacons and other ministers to have wives. Similar enactments were passed by other local councils from that time on, and by the 12th century

particular laws regarded marriage by clerics in major orders to be not only unlawful but also null and void. The latter view was translated by the Second Lateran Council in 1139 into what seems to be the first written universal law making holy orders an invalidating impediment to marriage. In 1563 the Council of Trent ruled definitely on the matter and established the discipline still in force in the Roman Church.

Some exceptions to this discipline have been made in recent years. Several married Protestant ministers who became converts and were subsequently ordained to the priesthood have been permitted to continue in marriage. Married men over the age of 35 can be ordained to the permanent diaconate.

Recent agitation for optional rather than mandatory celibacy for priests has diminished, without change in church law.

Eastern Church discipline on celibacy differs from that of the Roman Church. In line with legislation enacted by the Synod of Trullo in 692 and still in force, candidates for holy orders may marry before becoming deacons and may continue in marriage thereafter, but marriage after ordination is forbidden. Eastern-Rite bishops in the US, however, do not ordain married candidates for the priesthood. Eastern-Rite bishops are unmarried.

Cenacle: The room in Jerusalem where Christ ate the Last Supper with his Apostles.

Censer: A metal vessel with a perforated cover and suspended by chains, in which incense is burned. It is used at some Masses, Benediction of the Blessed Sacrament and other liturgical functions.

Censorship of Books: An exercise of vigilance by the Church for safeguarding authentic religious teaching.

According to a decree issued by the Congregation for the Doctrine of the Faith Apr. 9, 1975, the following regulations are in effect.

(1) Pre-publication clearance is required for: editions of Sacred Scripture, liturgical texts and books of private devotion, catechisms and other writings relating to catechetical instruction. Books dealing with Scripture, theology, canon law, church history and religious or moral disciplines may not be used as basic texts in educational institutions (from elementary to university levels) unless they have been published with the approval of competent church authority.

(2) Pre-publication clearance is recommended for all books on the aforementioned subjects, even though they are not used as basic texts in teaching.

(3) Books or other writings dealing with religion or morals may not be displayed, sold or given out in churches or oratories unless published with the approval of competent ecclesiastical authority.

(4) Except for a just and reasonable cause,

Catholics should not write for newspapers, magazines or periodicals which regularly and openly prove to be inimical to the Catholic religion and good morals. The approval of the local bishop is required before clerics or members of religious institutes (who also need the approval of their superior) may write for such publications.

Permission to publish works of a religious character, together with the apparatus of reviewing them beforehand, falls under the authority of the bishop of the place where the writer lives or where the works are published.

Clearance for publication is usually indicated by the terms *Nihil obstat* (Nothing stands in the way) issued by the censor and *Imprimatur* (Let it be printed) authorized by the bishop. The clearing of works for publication does not necessarily imply approval of an author's viewpoint or his manner of handling a subject.

Censures: Spiritual penalties inflicted by the Church on baptized persons for committing certain serious sins, which are classified as crimes in canon law, and for being or remaining obstinate therein. Excommunication, suspension and interdict have been the censures in force since the time of Innocent III (1214). Their intended purposes are to deter persons from committing sins which, more seriously and openly than others, threaten the common good of the Church and its members; to punish and correct offenders; and to provide for the making of reparation for harm done to the community of the Church. Censures may be incurred automatically (*ipso facto*) on the commission of certain offenses for which fixed penalties have been laid down in church law (*latae sententiae*); or they may be inflicted by sentence of a judge (*ferendae sententiae*). Obstinacy in crime— also called contumacy, disregard of a penalty, defiance of church authority — is presumed by law in the commission of crimes for which automatic censures are decreed. The presence and degree of contumacy in other cases, for which judicial sentence is required, is subject to determination by a judge. Absolution can be obtained from any censure, provided the person repents and desists from obstinacy. Absolution may be reserved to the pope, the bishop of a place, or the major superior of an exempt clerical religious institute. In danger of death, any priest can absolve from all censures; in other cases, faculties to absolve from reserved censures can be exercised by competent authorities or given to other priests.

Ceremonies, Master of: One who directs the proceedings of a rite or ceremony during the function.

Chamberlain: (1) The Chamberlain of the Holy Roman Church is a cardinal who administers the property and revenues of the Holy See. On the death of the pope he becomes head of the College of Cardinals and summons and directs the conclave until a new pope is elected.

(2) The Chamberlain of the Sacred College of Cardinals has charge of the property and revenues of the College and keeps the record of business transacted in consistories.

(3) The Chamberlain of the Roman Clergy is the president of the secular clergy of Rome.

Chancellor: Notary of a diocese, who draws up written documents in the government of the diocese; takes care of, arranges and indexes diocesan archives, records of dispensations and ecclesiastical trials.

Chancery (1) A branch of church administration that handles written documents used in the government of a diocese.

(2) The administrative office of a diocese, a bishop's office.

Chapel: A building or part of another building used for divine worship; a portion of a church set aside for the celebration of Mass or for some special devotion.

Chaplain: A priest appointed for the pastoral service of any division of the armed forces, religious communities, institutions, various groups of the faithful.

Chaplet: A term, meaning little crown, applied to a rosary or, more commonly, to a small string of beads used for devotional purposes; e.g., the Infant of Prague chaplet.

Chapter: A general meeting of delegates of religious orders for elections and the handling of other important affairs of their communities.

Charisms: Gifts or graces given by God to men for the good of others and the Church. Examples are special gifts for apostolic work, prophecy, healing, discernment of spirits, the life of evangelical poverty, here-and-now witness to faith in various circumstances of life.

The Second Vatican Council made the following statement about charisms in the *Dogmatic Constitution on the Church* (No. 12):

"It is not only through the sacraments and Church ministries that the same Holy Spirit sanctifies and leads the People of God and enriches it with virtues. Allotting His gifts 'to everyone according as he will' (1 Cor. 12:11), He distributes special graces among the faithful of every rank. By these gifts He makes them fit and ready to undertake the various tasks or offices advantageous for the renewal and upbuilding of the Church, according to the words of the Apostle: 'The manifestation of the Spirit is given to everyone for profit' (1 Cor. 12:7). These charismatic gifts, whether they be the most outstanding or the more simple and widely diffused, are to be received with thanksgiving and consolation, for they are exceedingly suitable and useful for the needs of the Church.

"Still, extraordinary gifts are not to be rashly sought after, nor are the fruits of apostolic labor to be presumptuously expected from them. In any case, judgment as to their genuineness and proper use belongs to those who preside over the Church, and to whose special competence it belongs, not indeed to extinguish the Spirit, but to test all things and hold fast to that which is good" (cf. 1 Thes. 5:12; 19-21).

Charity: Love of God above all things for his own sake, and love of one's neighbor as oneself because and as an expression of one's love for God; the greatest of the three theological virtues. The term is sometimes also used to designate sanctifying grace.

Chastity: Properly ordered behavior with respect to sex. In marriage, the exercise of the procreative power is integrated with the norms and purposes of marriage. Outside of marriage, the rule is self-denial of the voluntary exercise and enjoyment of the procreative faculty in thought, word or action.

The vow of chastity, which reinforces the virtue of chastity with the virtue of religion, is an evangelical counsel and one of the three vows professed by religious.

Chirograph or Autograph Letter: A letter written by a pope himself, in his own handwriting.

Christ: The title of Jesus, derived from the Greek translation *Christos* of the Hebrew term *Messiah,* meaning the Anointed of God, the Savior and Deliverer of his people. Christian use of the title is a confession of belief that Jesus is the Savior.

Christianity: The sum total of things related to belief in Christ — the Christian religion, Christian churches, Christians themselves, society based on and expressive of Christian beliefs, culture reflecting Christian values.

Christians: The name first applied about the year 43 to followers of Christ at Antioch, the capital of Syria. It was used by the pagans as a contemptuous term. The word applies to persons who profess belief in the divinity and teachings of Christ and who give witness to him in life.

Christian Science: A religious doctrine consisting of Mary Baker Eddy's interpretation and formulation of the actions and teachings of Christ. Its basic tenets reflect Mrs. Eddy's ideas regarding the reality of spirit and its control and domination of what is not spirit. The basic statement of the doctrine is contained in *Science and Health, with Key to the Scriptures,* which she first published in 1875, nine years after being saved from death and healed on reading the New Testament.

Mary Baker Eddy (1821-1910) established the church in 1879, and in 1892 founded at Boston the First Church of Christ, Scientist, of which all other Christian Science churches are branches. The individual churches are self-governing and self-supporting under the general supervision of a board of directors. Services consist of readings of portions of Scripture and *Science and Health.* One of the church's publications, *The Christian Science Monitor,* has a worldwide reputation as a journal of news and opinion.

Church: (1) See several entries under Church, Catholic. The universal Church is the Church spread throughout the world. The local Church is the Church in a particular locality; e.g., a diocese. Inasmuch as the members of the Church are on earth, in purgatory, or in glory in heaven, the Church is called militant, suffering, or triumphant.

(2) In general, any religious body.

(3) Place of divine worship.

Churching: A rite of thanksgiving in which a blessing is given to women after childbirth. The rite is reminiscent of the Old Testament ceremony of purification (Lv. 12:2-8).

Circumcision: A ceremonial practice symbolic of initiation and participation in the covenant between God and Abraham.

Circumincession: The indwelling of each divine Person of the Holy Trinity in the others.

Clergy: Men ordained to holy orders and assigned to pastoral and other ministries for the service of the people and the Church.

(1) Diocesan or secular clergy are committed to pastoral ministry in parishes and in other capacities in a local church (diocese) under the direction of their bishop, to whom they are bound by a promise of obedience.

(2) Regular clergy belong to religious institutes (orders, congregations, societies) and are so called because they observe the rule (*regula,* in Latin) of their respective institutes. They are committed to the ways of life and apostolates of their institutes. In ordinary pastoral ministry, they are under the direction of local bishops as well as their own superiors.

Clericalism: A term generally used in a derogatory sense to mean action, influence and interference by the Church and the clergy in matters with which they allegedly should not be concerned. Anticlericalism is a reaction of antipathy, hostility, distrust and opposition to the Church and clergy arising from real and/or alleged faults of the clergy, overextension of the role of the laity, or for other reasons.

Cloister: The enclosure of a convent or monastery, which members of the community may not leave or outsiders enter without due permission. Enclosure is of two kinds: papal, in monasteries of religious with solemn vows; episcopal, in the houses of other religious.

Code: A digest of rules or regulations, such as the Code of Canon Law.

Collegiality: The bishops of the Church, in union with and subordinate to the pope — who has full, supreme and universal power over the Church which he can always exercise independently — have supreme teaching and pastoral authority over the whole Church. In addition to their proper authority of office for the good of the faithful in their respective dioceses or other jurisdictions, the bishops have authority to act for the good of the universal Church. This collegial authority is exercised in a solemn manner in an ecumenical council and can also be exercised in other ways sanctioned by the pope. Doctrine on collegiality was set forth by the Second Vatican Council in the *Dogmatic Constitution on the Church.* (See separate entry.)

By extension, the concept of collegiality is applied to other forms of participation and co-responsibility by members of a community.

Commissariat of the Holy Land: A special jurisdiction within the Order of Friars Minor, whose main purposes are the collecting of alms for support of the Holy Places in Palestine and staffing of the Holy Places and missions in the Middle East with priests and brothers. There are 69 such commissariats in 33 countries. One of them has headquarters at Mt. St. Sepulchre, Washington, D.C. Franciscans have had custody of the Holy Places since 1342.

Communion of Faithful, Saints: The communion of all the People of God — on earth, in heavenly glory, in purgatory — with Christ and each other in faith, grace, prayer and good works.

Concelebration: The liturgical act in which several priests, led by one member of the group, offer Mass together, all consecrating the bread and wine. Concelebration has always been common in churches of Eastern Rite. In the Roman Rite, it was long restricted, taking place only at the ordination of bishops and the ordination of priests. The *Constitution on the Sacred Liturgy* issued by the Second Vatican Council set new norms for concelebration.

Concordance, Biblical: An alphabetical verbal index enabling a user knowing one or more words of a scriptural passage to locate the entire text.

Concordat: A Church-state treaty with the force of law concerning matters of mutual concern — e.g., rights of the Church, appointment of bishops, arrangement of ecclesiastical jurisdictions, marriage laws, education. Approximately 150 agreements of this kind have been negotiated since the Concordat of Worms in 1122.

Concupiscence: Any tendency of the sensitive appetite. The term is most frequently used in reference to desires and tendencies for sinful sense pleasure.

Confession: Sacramental confession is the act by which a person tells or confesses his sins to a priest who is authorized to give absolution in the sacrament of penance.

Confessor: (1) A male saint who lived a life of eminent sanctity and heroic virtue, but who did not suffer martyrdom for his faith.

(2) A priest who administers the sacrament of penance.

Confraternity: An association whose members practice a particular form of religious devotion and/or are engaged in some kind of apostolic work. When a confraternity reaches the stage where affiliations similar to itself are formed and adopt its rules, it takes the name of archconfraternity.

Conscience: Practical judgment concerning the moral goodness or sinfulness of an action. In the Catholic view, this judgment is made by reference of the action, its attendant circumstances and the intentions of the person to the requirements of divine law as expressed in the Ten Commandments, the summary law of love for God and neighbor, the life and teaching of Christ, and the authoritative teaching and practice of the Church with respect to the total demands of divine Revelation.

A person is obliged: (1) to obey a certain and correct conscience; (2) to obey a certain conscience even if it is inculpably erroneous; (3) not to obey, but to correct, a conscience known to be erroneous or lax; (4) to rectify a scrupulous conscience by following the advice of a confessor and by other measures; (5) to resolve doubts of conscience before acting.

It is legitimate to act for solid and probable reasons when a question of moral responsibility admits of argument (see Probabilism). It is also legitimate to resolve doubts in difficult cases by having recourse to a reflex principle (e.g., by following the manner of acting of a well-informed and well-intentioned group of persons in similar circumstances).

Conscience, Examination of: Self-examination to determine one's spiritual state before God, especially regarding one's sins and faults. It is recommended as a regular practice and is practically necessary in preparing for the sacrament of penance. The *particular examen* is a regular examination to assist in overcoming specific faults and imperfections.

Consecration of a Church: See Dedication of a Church.

Consistory: An assembly of cardinals presided over by the pope. Consistories are secret (pope and cardinals only), semi-public (plus other prelates), and public (plus other attendants).

Constitution: (1) An apostolic or papal constitution is a document in which a pope enacts and promulgates law.

(2) A formal and solemn document issued by an ecumenical council on a doctrinal or pastoral subject, with binding force in the whole Church; e.g., the four constitutions issued by the Second Vatican Council on the Church, liturgy, Revelation, and the Church in the modern world.

(3) The constitutions of religious orders spell out details of and norms drawn from the various rules for the guidance and direction of the life and work of members of each institute.

Consubstantiation: A theory which holds that the Body and Blood of Christ coexist with the substance of bread and wine in the Holy Eucharist. This theory, also called *impanation,* is incompatible with the doctrine of transubstantiation.

Contraception: Anything done by positive interference to prevent sexual intercourse from resulting in conception. Direct contraception is against the order of nature. Indirect contraception — as a secondary effect of medical treatment or other action having a necessary, good, non-contraceptive purpose — is permissible under the principle of the double effect. The practice of rhythm is not contraception because it does not involve positive interference with the order of nature.

Contrition: Sorrow for sin coupled with a purpose of amendment. Contrition arising from a supernatural motive is necessary for the forgiveness of sin.

(1) Perfect contrition is total sorrow for and renunciation of attachment to sin, arising from the motive of pure love of God. Perfect contrition, which implies the intention of doing all God wants done for the forgiveness of sin, is sufficient for the forgiveness of serious sin and the remission of all temporal punishment due for sin. Confession is required before the reception of another sacrament. (The intention to receive the sacrament of penance is implicit — even if unrealized, as in the case of some persons — in perfect contrition.)

(2) Imperfect contrition or attrition is sorrow arising from a quasi-selfish supernatural motive; e.g., the fear of losing heaven, suffering the pains of hell, etc. Imperfect contrition is sufficient for the forgiveness of serious sin when joined with absolution in confession, and sufficient for the forgiveness of venial sin even outside of confession.

Contumely: Personal insult, reviling a person in his presence by accusation of moral faults, by refusal of recognition or due respect; a violation of obligations of justice and charity.

Corporal Works of Mercy: Feeding the hungry, giving drink to the thirsty, clothing the naked, visiting the imprisoned, sheltering the homeless, visiting the sick, burying the dead.

Councils: Bodies representative of various categories of members of the Church which participate with bishops and other church authorities in making decisions and carrying out action programs for the good of the Church and the accomplishment of its mission to its own members and society in general. Examples are priests' senates or councils, councils of religious and lay persons, parish councils, diocesan pastoral councils.

Councils, Plenary: National councils or councils of the bishops of several ecclesiastical provinces, assembled under the presidency of a papal legate to take action related to the life and mission of the Church in the area under their jurisdiction. The membership of such councils is fixed by canon law; their decrees, when approved by the Holy See, are binding in the territory (see Index, Plenary Councils of Baltimore).

Councils, Provincial: Meetings of the bishops of a province. The metropolitan, or ranking archbishop, of an ecclesiastical province convenes and presides over such councils in a manner prescribed by canon law to take action related to the life and mission of the Church in the province. Acts and decrees must be approved by the Holy See before being promulgated. Provincial councils should be held at least once every 20 years.

Counsels, Evangelical: Gospel counsels of perfection, especially voluntary poverty, perfect chastity and obedience, which were recommended by Christ to those who would devote themselves exclusively and completely to the immediate service of God. Religious bind themselves by public vows to observe these counsels in a life of total consecration to God and service to people through various kinds of apostolic works.

Counter-Reformation: The period of approximately 100 years following the Council of Trent, which witnessed a reform within the Church to stimulate genuine Catholic life and to counteract effects of the Reformation.

Covenant: A bond of relationship between parties pledged to each other. God-initiated covenants in the Old Testament included those with Abraham, Noah, Moses, Levi, David. The Mosaic (Sinai) covenant made Israel God's Chosen People on terms of fidelity to true faith, true worship, and righteous conduct according to the Decalogue. The New Testament covenant, prefigured in the Old Testament, is the bond men have with God through Christ. All men are called to be parties to this perfect and everlasting covenant, which was mediated and ratified by Christ.

Creation: The production by God of something out of nothing. The biblical account of creation is contained in the first two chapters of Genesis.

Creator: God, the supreme, self-existing Being, the absolute and infinite First Cause of all things.

Creature: Everything in the realm of being is a creature, except God.

Cremation: The reduction of a human corpse to ashes by means of fire. Cremation is not in line with Catholic tradition and practice, even though it is not opposed to any article of faith. It can be permitted for serious reasons. The general practice, however, was forbidden in a decree issued May 19, 1886, by the Sacred Congregation of the Holy Office.

This ruling was incorporated in the Code of Canon Law (Canons 1203, 1240), which generally banned the practice of cremation, forbade following orders for cremation, and deprived of the last rites and ecclesiastical burial those who directed that their bodies be cremated and did not retract the directions.

The principal reason behind the prohibition against cremation was the fact that, historically, the practice had represented an attempt to deny the doctrine of the resurrection of the body. It also appeared to be a form of violence against the body which, as the temple of the Holy Spirit during life, should be treated with reverence.

The Congregation for the Doctrine of the Faith, under date of May 8, 1963, circulated among bishops an instruction which upheld the traditional practices of Christian burial but modified anti-cremation legislation. Cremation may be permitted for serious reasons, of a private as well as public nature, provided it does not involve any contempt of the Church or of religion, or any attempt to deny, question, or belittle the doctrine of the resurrection of the body. The person may receive the last rites and be given ecclesiastical burial. A priest may say prayers for the deceased at the crematorium, but full liturgical ceremonies may not take place there.

Crib: A devotional representation of the birth of Jesus. The custom of erecting cribs is generally attributed to St. Francis of Assisi who in 1223 obtained from Pope Honorius III permission to use a crib and figures of the Christ Child, Mary, St. Joseph, and others, to represent the mystery of the Nativity.

Crosier: The bishop's staff, symbolic of his pastoral office, responsibility and authority.

Crypt: An underground or partly underground chamber; e.g., the lower part of a church used for worship and/or burial.

Cura Animarum: A Latin phrase, meaning care of souls, designating the pastoral ministry and responsibility of bishops and priests.

Curia: The personnel and offices through which (1) the pope administers the affairs of the universal Church, the *Roman Curia* (see separate entry), or (2) a bishop the affairs of a diocese, *diocesan curia*. The principal officials of a diocesan curia are the vicar general of the diocese, the chancellor, officials of the diocesan tribunal or court, examiners, consultors, auditors, notaries.

Custos: A religious superior who presides over a number of convents collectively called a custody. In some religious institutes, a custos may be the deputy of a higher superior.

D

Deaconess — A woman officially appointed and charged by the Church to carry out service-like functions. Phoebe apparently was one (Rom. 16:1-2); a second probable reference to the office is in Tm. 3:11.

The office — for assistance at the baptism of women, for pastoral service to women and for works of charity — had considerable development in the third and also in the fourth century when the actual term came into use (in place of such designations as *diacona, vidua, virgo canonica*). Its importance declined subsequently with the substitution of infusion in place of immersion as the common method of baptism in the West, and with the increase of the practice of infant baptism. There is no record of the ministry of deaconess in the West after the beginning of the 11th century.

Several Christian churches have had revivals of the office of deaconess since the 1830s. There is a contemporary movement in support of such a revival among some Catholics.

The Vatican's Theological Commission, in a paper prepared in 1971, noted that there had been in the past a form of diaconal ordination for women. With a rite and purpose distinctive to women, it differed essentially from the ordination of deacons, which had sacramental effects.

Dean: (1) A priest with supervisory responsibility over a section of a diocese known as a deanery. The post-Vatican II counterpart of a dean is an episcopal vicar.

(2) The senior or ranking member of a group.

Dean of the Sacred College: The president of the College of Cardinals (the ranking cardinal bishop). He is elected by the cardinals holding title to the suburban sees of Rome.

Decision: A judgment or pronouncement on a cause or suit, given by a church tribunal or official with judicial authority. A decision has the force of law for concerned parties.

Declaration: (1) An ecclesiastical document which presents an interpretation of an existing law.

(2) A position paper on a specific subject; e.g., the three declarations issued by the Second Vatican Council on religious freedom, non-Christian religions, and Christian education.

Decree: An edict or ordinance issued by a pope and/or by an ecumenical council, with binding force in the whole Church; by a department of the Roman Curia, with binding force for concerned parties; by a territorial body of bishops, with binding force for persons in the area; by individual bishops, with binding force for concerned parties until revocation or the death of the bishop.

The nine decrees issued by the Second Vatican Council were combinations of doctrinal and pastoral statements with executive orders for action and movement toward renewal and reform in the Church.

Dedication of a Church: The ceremony whereby a church is solemnly set apart for the worship of God. The custom of dedicating churches had an antecedent in Old Testament ceremonies for the dedication of the Temple, as in the times of Solomon and the Maccabees. The earliest extant record of the dedication of a Christian church dates from early in the fourth century, when it was done simply by the celebration of Mass. Other ceremonies developed later. A church can be dedicated by a simple blessing or a solemn consecration. The rite of consecration is performed by a bishop.

Definitors: Members of the governing council of a religious order, each one having a decisive vote equal to the vote of the general or provincial superior.

Deism: A system of natural religion which acknowledges the existence of God but regards him as so transcendent and remote from man and the universe that divine revelation and the supernatural order of things are irrelevant and unacceptable. It developed from rationalistic principles in England in the 17th and 18th centuries, and had Voltaire, Rousseau and the Encyclopedists among its advocates in France.

Despair: Abandonment of hope for salvation arising from the conviction that God will not provide the necessary means for attaining it, that following God's way of life for salvation is impossible, or that one's sins are unforgivable; a serious sin against the Holy Spirit and the theological virtues of hope and faith, involving distrust in the mercy and goodness of God and a denial of the truths that God wills the salvation of all men and provides sufficient grace for it. Real despair is distinguished from unreasonable fear with respect to the difficulties of attaining salvation, from morbid anxiety over the demands of divine justice, and from feelings of despair.

Detachment: Control of affection for creatures by two principles: (1) supreme love and devotion belong to God; (2) love and service of creatures should be an expression of love for God.

Detraction: Revelation of true but hidden faults of a person without sufficient and justifying reason; a violation of requirements of justice and charity, involving the obligation to make restitution when this is possible without doing more harm to the good name of the offended party. In some cases, e.g., to prevent evil, secret faults may and should be disclosed.

Devil: (1) Lucifer, Satan, chief of the fallen angels who sinned and were banished from heaven. Still possessing angelic powers, he can cause such diabolical phenomena as possession and obsession, and can tempt men to sin.

(2) Any fallen angel.

Devil's Advocate: See Promoter of the Faith.

Devotion: (1) Religious fervor, piety; dedication.

(2) The consolation experienced at times during prayer; a reverent manner of praying.

Devotions: Pious practices of members of the Church include not only participation in various acts of the liturgy but also in other acts of worship generally called popular or private devotions. Concerning these, the Second Vatican Council said in the *Constitution on the Sacred Liturgy* (No. 13): "Popular devotions of the Christian people are warmly commended, provided they accord with the laws and norms of the Church. Such is especially the case with devotions called for by the Apostolic See. Devotions proper to the individual churches also have a special dignity. . . . These devotions should be so drawn up that they harmonize with the liturgical seasons, accord with the sacred liturgy, are in some fashion derived from it, and lead the people to it, since the liturgy by its very nature far surpasses any of them."

Devotions of a liturgical type are Benediction of the Blessed Sacrament, recitation of the Little Office of the Blessed Virgin Mary or of Vespers and Compline. Examples of paraliturgical devotion are a Bible Service or Vigil, and the Angelus, Rosary and Stations of the Cross, which have a strong scriptural basis.

Dies Irae: The opening Latin words, Day of Wrath, of a hymn for requiem Masses, written in the 13th century by the Franciscan Thomas of Celano.

Diocese: A fully organized ecclesiastical jurisdiction under the pastoral direction of a bishop as local ordinary.

Discalced: Of Latin derivation and meaning without shoes, the word is applied to religious orders or congregations whose members go barefoot or wear sandals.

Disciple: A term used sometimes in reference to the Apostles but more often to a larger number of followers (70 or 72) of Christ mentioned in Lk. 10:1.

Disciplina Arcani: A Latin phrase, meaning discipline of the secret and referring to a practice of the early Church, especially during the Roman persecutions, to: (1) conceal Christian truths from those who, it was feared, would misinterpret, ridicule and profane the teachings, and persecute Christians for believing them; (2) instruct catechumens in a gradual manner, withholding the teaching of certain doctrines until the catechumens proved themselves of good faith and sufficient understanding.

Dispensation: The relaxation of a law in a particular case. Laws made for the common good sometimes work undue hardship in particular cases. In such cases, where sufficient reasons are present, dispensations may be granted by proper authorities. Bishops, religious superiors and others may dispense from certain laws; the pope can dispense from all ecclesiastical laws. No one has authority to dispense from obligations of the divine law.

Divination: Attempting to foretell future or hidden things by means of things like dreams,

338	*Glossary*

necromancy, spiritism, examination of entrails, astrology, augury, omens, palmistry, drawing straws, dice, cards, etc. Practices like these attribute to creatural things a power which belongs to God alone and are violations of the First Commandment.

Divine Praises: Fourteen praises recited or sung at Benediction of the Blessed Sacrament in reparation for sins of sacrilege, blasphemy and profanity. Some of these praises date from the end of the 18th century.

Blessed be God.

Blessed be his holy Name.

Blessed be Jesus Christ, true God and true Man.

Blessed be the Name of Jesus.

Blessed be his most Sacred Heart.

Blessed be his most Precious Blood.

Blessed be Jesus in the most holy Sacrament of the Altar.

Blessed be the Holy Spirit, the Paraclete.

Blessed be the great Mother of God, Mary most holy.

Blessed be her holy and Immaculate Conception.

Blessed be her glorious Assumption.

Blessed be the name of Mary, Virgin and Mother.

Blessed be St. Joseph, her most chaste Spouse.

Blessed be God in his Angels and in his Saints.

Double Effect Principle: Actions sometimes have two effects closely related to each other, one good and the other bad, and a difficult moral question can arise: Is it permissible to place an action from which two such results follow? It is permissible to place the action, if: the action is good in itself and is directly productive of the good effect; the circumstances are good; the intention of the person is good; the reason for placing the action is proportionately serious to the seriousness of the indirect bad effect. For example: Is it morally permissible for a pregnant woman to undergo medical or surgical treatment for a pathological condition if the indirect and secondary effect of the treatment will be the loss of the child? The reply is affirmative, for these reasons: The action, i.e., the treatment, is good in itself, cannot be deferred until a later time without very serious consequences, and is ordered directly to the cure of critically grave pathology. By means of the treatment, the woman intends to save her life, which she has a right to do. The loss of the child is not directly sought as a means for the cure of the mother but results indirectly and in a secondary manner from the placing of the action, i.e., the treatment, which is good in itself.

The double effect principle does not support the principle that the end justifies the means.

Doxology: (1) The lesser doxology, or ascription of glory to the Trinity, is the Glory be to the Father. The first part dates back to the third or fourth century, and came from the form of baptism. The concluding words, As it was in the beginning, etc., are of later origin.

(2) The greater doxology, Glory to God in the highest, begins with the words of angelic praise at the birth of Christ recounted in the Infancy Narrative (Lk. 2:14). It is often recited at Mass. Of early Eastern origin, it is found in the *Apostolic Constitutions* in a form much like the present.

Dulia: A Greek term meaning the veneration or homage, different in nature and degree from that given to God, paid to the saints. It includes honoring the saints and seeking their intercession with God.

Duty: A moral obligation deriving from the binding force of law, the exigencies of one's state in life, and other sources.

E

Easter Controversy: A three-phase controversy over the time for the celebration of Easter.

Some early Christians in the Near East, called Quartodecimans, favored the observance of Easter on the 14th day of Nisan, the spring month of the Hebrew calendar, whenever it occurred. Against this practice, Pope St. Victor I, about 190, ordered a Sunday observance of the feast.

The Council of Nicaea, in line with usages of the Church at Rome and Alexandria, decreed in 325 that Easter should be observed on the first Sunday following the first full moon of spring.

Uniformity of practice in the West was not achieved until several centuries later, when the British Isles, in delayed compliance with measures enacted by the Synod of Whitby in 664, accepted the Roman date of observance.

Unrelated to the controversy is the fact that some Eastern Christians, in accordance with traditional calendar practices, celebrate Easter at a different time than the Roman and Eastern-Rite churches.

Easter Duty: The serious obligation binding Catholics of Roman Rite, by a precept of the Church, to receive Holy Communion during the Easter time; in the US, from the first Sunday of Lent to Trinity Sunday.

Easter Water: Holy water blessed with special ceremonies and distributed on the Easter Vigil; used during Easter Week for blessing the faithful and homes.

Ecclesiology: Study of the nature, constitution, members, mission, functions, etc., of the Church.

Ecstasy: An extraordinary state of mystical experience in which a person is so absorbed in God that the activity of the exterior senses is suspended.

Ecumenism: The movement of Christians and their churches toward the unity willed by

Christ. The Second Vatican Council called the movement "those activities and enterprises which, according to various needs of the Church and opportune occasions, are started and organized for the fostering of unity among Christians" (*Decree on Ecumenism,* No. 4). Spiritual ecumenism, i.e., mutual prayer for unity, is the heart of the movement. The movement also involves scholarly and pew-level efforts for the development of mutual understanding and better interfaith relations in general, and collaboration by the churches and their members in the social area.

Elevation: The raising of the host after consecration at Mass for adoration by the faithful. The custom was introduced in the Diocese of Paris about the close of the 12th century to offset an erroneous teaching of the time which held that transubstantiation of the bread did not take place until after the consecration of the wine in the chalice. The elevation of the chalice following the consecration of the wine was introduced in the 15th century.

End Justifies the Means: An unacceptable ethical principle which states that evil means may be used to produce good effects.

Envy: Sadness over another's good fortune because it is considered a loss to oneself or a detraction from one's own excellence; one of the seven capital sins, a violation of the obligations of charity.

Epikeia: A Greek word meaning reasonableness and designating a moral theory and practice, a mild interpretation of the mind of a legislator who is prudently considered not to wish positive law to bind in certain circumstances. Use of the principle is justified in practice when the lawgiver himself cannot be appealed to and when it can be prudently assumed that in particular cases, e.g., because of special hardship, he would not wish the law to be applied in a strict manner. Epikeia may not be applied with respect to acts that are intrinsically wrong or those covered by laws which automatically make them invalid.

Episcopate: (1) The office, dignity and sacramental powers bestowed upon a bishop at his ordination.

(2) The body of bishops collectively.

Equivocation: (1) The use of words, phrases, or gestures having more than one meaning in order to conceal information which a questioner has no strict right to know. It is permissible to equivocate (have a broad mental reservation) in some circumstances.

(2) A lie, i.e., a statement of untruth. Lying is intrinsically wrong. A lie told in joking, evident as such, is not wrong.

Eschatology: Doctrine concerning the last things: death, judgment, heaven and hell, and the final state of perfection of the People and Kingdom of God at the end of time.

Eternity: The interminable, perfect possession of life in its totality without beginning or end; an attribute of God, who has no past or future but always is. Man's existence has a beginning but no end and is, accordingly, called immortal.

Ethics: Moral philosophy, the science of the morality of human acts deriving from natural law, the natural end of man, and the powers of human reason. It includes all the spheres of human activity — personal, social, economic, political, etc. Ethics is distinct from but can be related to moral theology, whose primary principles are drawn from divine Revelation.

Eucharistic Congresses: Public demonstrations of faith in the Holy Eucharist. Combining liturgical services, other public ceremonies, subsidiary meetings, different kinds of instructional and inspirational elements, they are unified by central themes and serve to increase understanding of and devotion to Christ in the Eucharist, and to relate this liturgy of worship and witness to life.

The first international congress developed from a proposal by Marie Marthe Tamisier of Touraine, organizing efforts of Msgr. Louis Gaston de Segur, and backing by industrialist Philibert Vrau. It was held with the approval of Pope Leo XIII at the University of Lille, France, and was attended by some 800 persons from France, Belgium, Holland, England, Spain and Switzerland.

International congresses are planned and held under the auspices of a permanent committee for international Eucharistic congresses. Participants include clergy, religious and lay persons from many countries, and representatives of national and international Catholic organizations. Popes have usually been represented by legates, but Paul VI attended two congresses personally, the 38th at Bombay and the 39th at Bogota.

Forty-one international congresses were held from 1881 to 1976:

Lille (1881), Avignon (1882), Liege (1883), Freiburg (1885), Toulouse (1886), Paris (1888), Antwerp (1890), Jerusalem (1893), Rheims (1894), Paray-le-Monial (1897), Brussels (1898), Lourdes (1899), Angers (1901), Namur (1902), Angouleme (1904), Rome (1905), Tournai (1906), Metz (1907), London (1908), Cologne (1909), Montreal (1910), Madrid (1911), Vienna (1912), Malta (1913), Lourdes (1914), Rome (1922), Amsterdam (1924), Chicago (1926), Sydney (1928), Carthage (1930), Dublin (1932), Buenos Aires (1934), Manila (1937), Budapest (1938), Barcelona (1952), Rio de Janeiro (1955), Munich, Germany (1960), Bombay, India (1964), Bogota, Colombia (1968), Melbourne, Australia (1973), Philadelphia (1976).

The 42nd International Eucharistic Congress was held July 16 to 23, 1981, at Lourdes.

Eugenics: The science of heredity and environment for the physical and mental improvement of offspring. Extreme eugenics is untenable in practice because it advocates immoral means, such as compulsory breeding of the select, sterilization of persons said to be unfit, abortion, and unacceptable methods of birth regulation.

Euthanasia: Mercy killing, the direct causing of death by painless means for the purpose of ending human suffering. Euthanasia is murder and is totally illicit, for the natural law forbids the direct taking of one's own life or that of an innocent person.

The use of drugs to relieve suffering in serious cases, even when this results in a shortening of life as an indirect and secondary effect, is permissible under conditions of the double effect principle. It is also permissible for a seriously ill person to refuse to follow — or for other responsible persons to refuse to permit — extraordinary medical procedures even though the refusal might entail shortening of life.

Evolution: Scientific theory concerning the development of the physical universe from unorganized matter (inorganic evolution) and, especially, the development of existing forms of vegetable, animal and human life from earlier and more primitive organisms (organic evolution). Various ideas about evolution were advanced for some centuries before scientific evidence in support of the main-line theory of organic evolution, which has several formulations, was discovered and verified in the second half of the 19th century and afterwards. This evidence — from the findings of comparative anatomy and other sciences — confirmed evolution within species and cleared the way to further investigation of questions regarding the processes of its accomplishment. While a number of such questions remain open with respect to human evolution, a point of doctrine not open to question is the immediate creation of the human soul by God.

For some time, theologians regarded the theory with hostility, considering it to be in opposition to the account of creation in the early chapters of Genesis and subversive of belief in such doctrines as creation, the early state of man in grace, and the fall of man from grace. This state of affairs and the tension it generated led to considerable controversy regarding an alleged conflict between religion and science. Gradually, however, the tension was diminished with the development of biblical studies from the latter part of the 19th century onwards, with clarification of the distinctive features of religious truth and scientific truth, and with the refinement of evolutionary concepts.

So far as the Genesis account of creation is concerned, the Catholic view is that the writer(s) did not write as a scientist but as the communicator of religious truth in a manner adapted to the understanding of the people of his time. He used anthropomorphic language, the figure of days and other literary devices to state the salvation truths of creation, the fall of man from grace, and the promise of redemption. It was beyond the competency and purpose of the writer(s) to describe creation and related events in a scientific manner.

Excommunication: A penalty or censure by which a baptized person is excluded from the communion of the faithful, for committing and remaining obstinate in certain sins specified in canon law and technically called crimes. As by baptism a person is made a member of the Church in which there is a communication of spiritual goods, so by excommunication he is deprived of the same spiritual goods until he repents and receives absolution. Even though excommunicated, a person is still responsible for the normal obligations of a Catholic.

Existentialism: A philosophy with radical concern for the problems of individual existence and identity viewed in particular here-and-now patterns of thought which presuppose irrationality and absurdity in human life and the whole universe. It is preoccupied with questions about freedom, moral decision and responsibility against a background of denial of objective truth and universal norms of conduct; is characterized by prevailing anguish, dread, fear, pessimism, despair; is generally atheistic, although its modern originator, Soren Kierkegaard (d. 1855), and Gabriel Marcel attempted to give it a Christian orientation. Pius XII called it "the new erroneous philosophy which, opposing itself to idealism, immanentism and pragmatism, has assumed the name of existentialism, since it concerns itself only with the existence of individual things and neglects all consideration of their immutable essences" (Encyclical *Humani Generis,* Aug. 12, 1950).

Exorcism: (1) Driving out evil spirits; a rite in which evil spirits are charged and commanded on the authority of God and with the prayer of the Church to depart from a person or to cease causing harm to a person suffering from diabolical possession or obsession. The sacramental is officially administered by a priest delegated for the purpose by the bishop of the place. Elements of the rite include the Litany of Saints; recitation of the Our Father, one or more creeds, and other prayers; specific prayers of exorcism; the reading of Gospel passages, and use of the Sign of the Cross. Private exorcism for the liberation of a person from the strong influence of evil spirits, through prayer and the use of sacramentals like holy water, can be done by anyone.

(2) Exorcisms which do not imply the conditions of either diabolical possession or obsession form part of the ceremony of baptism, and are also included in other formulas.

F

Faculties: Grants of jurisdiction, or authority, granted by the law of the Church or superiors (pope, bishop, religious superior) for exercise of the powers of holy orders; e.g., priests are given faculties to hear confessions, officiate at weddings; bishops are given faculties to grant dispensations, etc.

Faith: In religion, faith has several aspects. Catholic doctrine calls faith the assent of the mind to truths revealed by God, the assent being made with the help of grace and by command of the will on account of the authority and trustworthiness of God revealing. The term faith also refers to the truths that are believed (content of faith) and to the way in which a person, in response to Christ, gives witness to and expresses his belief in daily life (living faith).

All of these elements, and more, are included in the following statement:

" 'The obedience of faith' (Rom. 16:26; cf. 1:5; 2 Cor. 10:5-6) must be given to God who reveals, an obedience by which man entrusts his whole self freely to God, offering 'the full submission of intellect and will to God who reveals' (First Vatican Council, *Dogmatic Constitution on the Catholic Faith,* Chap. 3), and freely assenting to the truth revealed by Him. If this faith is to be shown, the grace of God and the interior help of the Holy Spirit must precede and assist, moving the heart and turning it to God, opening the eyes of the mind, and giving 'joy and ease to everyone in assenting to the truth and believing it' " (Second Council of Orange, Canon 7) (Second Vatican Council, *Constitution on Revelation,* No. 5). Faith is necessary for salvation.

Faith, Rule of: The norm or standard of religious belief. The Catholic doctrine is that belief must be professed in the divinely revealed truths in the Bible and tradition as interpreted and proposed by the infallible teaching authority of the Church.

Fast, Eucharistie: Eating and the drinking of any liquids except water are prohibited for one hour before the reception of Holy Communion. Water never breaks the Eucharistic fast, which is prescribed for reasons of reverence and preparation. By way of exception, the period of fasting is 15 minutes for the sick and aged, even though not confined to bed or a home, and those caring for them who wish to receive Communion with them but cannot fast for an hour without inconvenience (Instruction, *Immensae Caritatis,* Congregation for the Discipline of the Sacraments, Jan. 29, 1973).

Those who are ill, even though not confined to bed, may take nonalcoholic beverages and liquid or solid medicine before Holy Communion without any time limit.

Father: A title of priests, who are regarded as spiritual fathers because they are the ordinary ministers of baptism, by which persons are born to supernatural life, and because of their pastoral service to people.

Fear: A mental state caused by the apprehension of present or future danger. Grave fear does not necessarily remove moral responsibility for an act, but may lessen it.

First Friday: A devotion consisting of the reception of Holy Communion on the first Friday of nine consecutive months in honor of the Sacred Heart of Jesus and in reparation for sin. (See Sacred Heart, Promises.)

First Saturday: A devotion tracing its origin to the apparitions of the Blessed Virgin Mary at Fatima in 1917. Those practicing the devotion go to confession and, on the first Saturday of five consecutive months, receive Holy Communion, recite five decades of the Rosary, and meditate on the mysteries for 15 minutes.

Fisherman's Ring: A signet ring engraved with the image of St. Peter fishing from a boat, and encircled with the name of the reigning pope. It is not worn by the pope. It is used to seal briefs, and is destroyed after each pope's death.

Forgiveness of Sin: Catholics believe that sins are forgiven by God through the mediation of Christ in view of the repentance of the sinner and by means of the sacrament of penance. (See Penance.)

Fortitude: Courage to face dangers or hardships for the sake of what is good; one of the four cardinal virtues and one of the seven gifts of the Holy Spirit.

Fortune Telling: Attempting to predict the future or the occult by means of cards, palm reading, etc.; a form of divination, prohibited by the First Commandment.

Forty Hours Devotion: A Eucharistic observance consisting of solemn exposition of the Blessed Sacrament in commemoration of the time Christ's body lay in the tomb, coupled with special Masses and forms of prayer, for the purposes of making reparation for sin and praying for God's blessings of grace and peace. The devotion was instituted in 1534 in Milan. St. John Neumann of Philadelphia was the first bishop in the U.S. to prescribe its observance in his diocese. For many years in this country, the observance was held annually on a rotating basis in all parishes of a diocese. Simplified and abbreviated Eucharistic observances have taken the place of the devotion in some places.

Forum: The sphere in which ecclesiastical authority or jurisdiction is exercised.

(1) External: Authority is exercised in the external forum to deal with matters affecting the public welfare of the Church and its members. Those who have such authority because of their office (e.g., diocesan bishops) are called ordinaries.

(2) Internal: Authority is exercised in the internal forum to deal with matters affecting the private spiritual good of individuals. The

sacramental forum is the sphere in which the sacrament of penance is administered; other exercises of jurisdiction in the internal forum take place in the non-sacramental forum.

Franciscan Crown: A seven-decade rosary used to commemorate the seven Joys of the Blessed Virgin: the Annunciation, the Visitation, the Nativity of Our Lord, the Adoration of the Magi, the Finding of the Child Jesus in the Temple, the Apparition of the Risen Christ to his Mother, the Assumption and Coronation of the Blessed Virgin. Introduced in 1422, the Crown originally consisted only of seven Our Fathers and 70 Hail Marys. Two Hail Marys were added to complete the number 72 (thought to be the number of years of Mary's life), and one Our Father, Hail Mary and Glory be to the Father are said for the intention of the pope.

Freedom, Religious: The Second Vatican Council declared that the right to religious freedom in civil society "means that all men are to be immune from coercion on the part of individuals or of social groups and of any human power, in such wise that in matters religious no one is to be forced to act in a manner contrary to his own beliefs. Nor is anyone to be restrained from acting in accordance with his own beliefs, whether privately or publicly, whether alone or in association with others, within due limits" of requirements for the common good. The foundation of this right in civil society is the "very dignity of the human person" (*Declaration on Religious Freedom,* No. 2).

The conciliar statement did not deal with the subject of freedom within the Church. It noted the responsibility of the faithful "carefully to attend to the sacred and certain doctrine of the Church" (No. 14).

Freemasons: A fraternal order which originated in London in 1717 with the formation of the first Grand Lodge of Freemasons. From England, the order spread to Europe and elsewhere. Its original deistic and nondenominational ideology was transformed in Latin countries into a compound of atheism, anticlericalism and irreligion. Since 1877, Grand Orient Freemasonry has been denied recognition by the Scottish and York Rites because of its failure to require belief in God and the immortality of the soul as a condition of membership. In some places, Freemasonry has been regarded as subversive of the state; in Catholic quarters, it has been considered hostile to the Church and its doctrine. In the United States, Freemasonry is generally known as a fraternal and philanthropic order.

Catholics have been forbidden to join the Freemasons, under penalty of excommunication, for serious pastoral reasons. Eight different popes in 17 different pronouncements, and at least six different local councils, condemned Freemasonry. The first condemnation was made by Clement XII in 1738. Eastern Orthodox and many Protestant bodies have also opposed the order.

The existing prohibition against membership in the Freemasons by Catholics was modified by the contents of a letter written in 1974 by Cardinal Franjo Seper, prefect of the Congregation for the Doctrine of the Faith. The letter said that Catholic laymen may join Masonic lodges which do not plot against the Church. The letter also said: "Clerics, religious and members of secular institutes are still forbidden in every case to join any Masonic association."

Free Will: The faculty or capability of making a reasonable choice among several alternatives. Freedom of will underlies the possibility and fact of moral responsibility.

Friar: Term applied to members of mendicant orders to distinguish them from members of monastic orders. (See Mendicants.)

Fruits of the Holy Spirit: Charity, joy, peace, patience, benignity, goodness, longanimity, mildness, faith, modesty, continence, chastity.

G

Gambling: The backing of an issue with a sum of money or other valuables, which is permissible if the object is honest, if the two parties have the free disposal of their stakes without prejudice to the rights of others, if the terms are thoroughly understood by both parties, and if the outcome is not known beforehand. Gambling often falls into disrepute and may be forbidden by civil law, as well as by divine law, because of cheating, fraud and other accompanying evils.

Gehenna: Greek form of a Jewish name, *Gehinnom,* for a valley near Jerusalem, the site of Moloch worship; used as a synonym for hell.

Genuflection: Bending of the knee, a natural sign of adoration or reverence, as when persons genuflect with the right knee in passing before the tabernacle to acknowledge the Eucharistic presence of Christ.

Gethsemani: A Hebrew word meaning oil press, designating the place on the Mount of Olives where Christ prayed and suffered in agony the night before he died.

Gifts of the Holy Spirit: Supernatural habits disposing a person to respond promptly to the inspiration of grace; promised by Christ and communicated through the Holy Spirit, especially in the sacrament of confirmation. They are: wisdom, understanding, counsel, fortitude, knowledge, piety, fear of the Lord.

Gluttony: An unreasonable appetite for food and drink; one of the seven capital sins.

God: The infinitely perfect Supreme Being, uncaused and absolutely self-sufficient, eternal, the Creator and final end of all things.

The one God subsists in three equal Persons, the Father and the Son and the Holy Spirit. God, although transcendent and distinct from the universe, is present and active in the world in realization of his plan for the salvation of men, principally through Revelation, the operations of the Holy Spirit, the life and ministry of Christ, and the continuation of Christ's ministry in the Church.

The existence of God is an article of faith, clearly communicated in divine Revelation. Even without this Revelation, however, the Church teaches, in a declaration by the First Vatican Council, that men can acquire certain knowledge of the existence of God and some of his attributes. This can be done on the bases of principles of reason and reflection on human experience.

Non-revealed arguments or demonstrations for the existence of God have been developed from the principle of causality; the contingency of man and the universe; the existence of design, change and movement in the universe; human awareness of moral responsibility; widespread human testimony to the existence of God.

Grace: A free gift of God to men (and angels), grace is a created sharing or participation in the life of God. It is given to men through the merits of Christ and is communicated by the Holy Spirit. It is necessary for salvation. The principal means of grace are the sacraments (especially the Eucharist), prayer and good works.

Sanctifying or habitual grace makes men holy and pleasing to God, adopted children of God, members of Christ, temples of the Holy Spirit, heirs of heaven capable of supernaturally meritorious acts. With grace, God gives men the supernatural virtues and gifts of the Holy Spirit. The sacraments of baptism and penance were instituted to give grace to those who do not have it; the other sacraments, to increase it in those already in the state of grace. The means for growth in holiness, or the increase of grace, are prayer, the sacraments, and good works. Sanctifying grace is lost by the commission of serious sin.

Each sacrament confers sanctifying grace for the special purpose of the sacrament; in this context, grace is called sacramental grace.

Actual grace is a supernatural help of God which enlightens and strengthens a person to do good and to avoid evil. It is not a permanent quality, like sanctifying grace. It is necessary for the performance of supernatural acts. It can be resisted and refused. Persons in the state of serious sin are given actual grace to lead them to repentance.

Grace at Meals: Prayers said before meals, asking a blessing of God, and after meals, giving thanks to God. In addition to traditional prayers for these purposes, many variations suitable for different occasions are possible, at personal option.

H

Habit: (1) A disposition to do things easily, given with grace (and therefore supernatural) and/or acquired by repetition of similar acts.

(2) The garb worn by religious.

Hagiography: Writings or documents about saints and other holy persons.

Hail Mary: A prayer addressed to the Blessed Virgin Mary; also called the *Ave Maria* (Latin equivalent of Hail Mary) and the Angelic Salutation. In three parts, it consists of the words addressed to Mary by the Archangel Gabriel on the occasion of the Annunciation, in the Infancy Narrative (Hail full of grace, the Lord is with you, blessed are you among women.); the words addressed to Mary by her cousin Elizabeth on the occasion of the Visitation (Blessed is the fruit of your womb.); a concluding petition (Holy Mary, Mother of God, pray for us sinners now and at the hour of our death. Amen.). The first two salutations were joined in Eastern Rite formulas by the sixth century, and were similarly used at Rome in the seventh century. Insertion of the name of Jesus at the conclusion of the salutations was probably made by Urban IV about 1262. The present form of the petition was incorporated into the breviary in 1514.

Heaven: The state of those who, having achieved salvation, are in glory with God and enjoy the beatific vision.

The phrase, kingdom of heaven, refers to the order or kingdom of God, grace, salvation.

Hell: The state of punishment of the damned — i.e., those who die in mortal sin, in a condition of self-alienation from God and of opposition to the divine plan of salvation. The punishment of hell begins immediately after death and lasts forever.

Hermit: See Anchorite.

Heroic Act of Charity: The completely unselfish offering to God of one's good works and merits for the benefit of the souls in purgatory rather than for oneself. Thus a person may offer to God for the souls in purgatory all the good works he performs during life, all the indulgences he gains, and all the prayers and indulgences that will be offered for him after his death. The act is revocable at will, and is not a vow. Its actual ratification depends on the will of God.

Heterodoxy: False doctrine, teaching or belief; a departure from truth.

Holy See: (1) The diocese of the pope, Rome.

(2) The pope himself and/or the various officials and bodies of the Church's central administration at Vatican City — the Roman Curia — which act in the name and by authority of the pope.

Holy Spirit: God the Holy Spirit, third Person of the Holy Trinity, who proceeds from the Father and the Son and with whom he is equal in every respect; inspirer of the prophets and writers of sacred Scripture; promised by Christ to the Apostles as their advocate and strengthener; appeared in the form of a dove at the baptism of Christ and as tongues of fire at his descent upon the Apostles; soul of the Church and guarantor, by his abiding presence and action, of truth in doctrine; communicator of grace to men, for which reason he is called the sanctifier.

Holy Water: Water blessed by the Church and used as a sacramental, a practice which originated in apostolic times.

Holy Year: A year during which the pope grants the plenary Jubilee Indulgence to the faithful who fulfill certain conditions. For those who make a pilgrimage to Rome during the year, the conditions are reception of the sacraments of penance and the Eucharist, visits and prayer for the intention of the pope in the basilicas of St. Peter, St. John Lateran, St. Paul and St. Mary Major. For those who do not make a pilgrimage to Rome, the conditions are reception of the sacraments and prayer for the pope during a visit or community celebration in a church designated by the bishop of the locality.

Holy Year observances have biblical counterparts in the Years of Jubilee observed at 50-year intervals by the pre-exilic Israelites — when debts were pardoned and slaves freed (Lv. 25:25-54) — and in sabbatical years observed from the end of the Exile to 70 A.D. — in which debts to fellow Jews were remitted.

The practice of Christians from early times to go on pilgrimage to the Holy Land, the shrines of martyrs and the tombs of the Apostles in Rome influenced the institution of Holy Years. There was also a prevailing belief among the people that every 100th year was a year of "Great Pardon." Accordingly, even before Boniface VIII formally proclaimed the first Holy Year Feb. 22, 1300, scores of thousands of pilgrims were already on the way to or in Rome.

Medieval popes embodied in the observance of Holy Years the practice of good works (reception of the sacraments of penance and the Eucharist, pilgrimages and/or visits to the tombs of the Apostles, and related actions) and spiritual benefits (particularly, special indulgences for the souls in purgatory). These and related practices, with suitable changes for celebrations in local churches, remain staple features of Holy Year observances.

The first three Holy Years were observed in 1300, 1350 and 1390. Subsequent ones were celebrated at 25-year intervals except in 1800 and 1850 when, respectively, the French invasion of Italy and political turmoil made observance impossible. Pope Paul II (1464-1471) set the 25-year timetable. In 1500, Pope Alexander VI prescribed the start and finish ceremonies — the opening and closing of the Holy Doors in the major basilicas on successive Christmas Eves. All but a few of the earlier Holy Years were classified as ordinary. Several, like the one held in 1933 to commemorate the 19th centenary of the death and resurrection of Christ, were in the extraordinary category.

Holy Year 1975 coincided with the 10th anniversary of the closing of the Second Vatican Council. Its themes also coincided with the renewal emphasis which dominated the council, and were related to the main topic — the evangelization of the modern world — on the 1974 agenda of the Synod of Bishops.

Homosexuality: The condition of a person whose sexual orientation is toward persons of the same rather than the opposite sex. Some psychologists regard it as an arrested state of emotional development. The condition, usually discovered during adolescence rather than deliberately caused, is not normal but is not sinful in itself. Homosexual acts against nature are objectively wrong; subjective responsibility for such acts, however, may be conditioned and diminished by compulsion and related factors.

Hope: One of the three theological virtues, by which one firmly trusts that God wills his salvation and will give him the means to attain it.

Hosanna: A Hebrew word, meaning O Lord, save, we pray.

Host, The Sacred: The bread under whose appearances Christ is and remains present in a unique manner after the consecration which takes place during Mass. (See Transubstantiation.)

Humility: A virtue which induces a person to evaluate himself at his true worth, to recognize his dependence on God, and to give glory to God for the good he has and can do.

Hyperdulia: The special veneration accorded the Blessed Virgin Mary because of her unique role in the mystery of Redemption, her exceptional gifts of grace from God, and her pre-eminence among the saints. Hyperdulia is not adoration; only God is adored.

Hypnosis: A mental state resembling sleep, induced by suggestion, in which the subject does the bidding of the hypnotist. Hypnotism is permissible under certain conditions: the existence of a serious reason, e.g., for anesthetic or therapeutic purposes, and the competence and integrity of the hypnotist. Hypnotism may not be practiced for the sake of amusement. Experiments indicate that, contrary to popular opinion, hypnotized subjects may be induced to perform immoral acts which, normally, they would not do.

Hypostatic Union: The union of the human and divine natures in the one divine Person of Christ.

I

Icons: Byzantine-style paintings or representations of Christ, the Blessed Virgin and other saints, venerated in the Eastern Churches where they take the place of statues.

Idolatry: Worship of any but the true God; a violation of the First Commandment.

IHS: In Greek, the first three letters of the name of Jesus — Iota, Eta, Sigma.

Immortality: The survival and continuing existence of the human soul after death.

Immunity of the Clergy: Exemption of clerics from military duty and civil service.

Impurity: Unlawful indulgence in sexual pleasure. (See Chastity.)

Incardination: The affiliation of a priest to his diocese. Every secular priest must belong to a certain diocese. Similarly, every priest of a religious community must belong to some jurisdiction of his community; this affiliation, however, is not called incardination.

Incarnation: (1) The coming-into-flesh or taking of human nature by the Second Person of the Trinity. He became human as the Son of Mary, being miraculously conceived by the power of the Holy Spirit, without ceasing to be divine. His divine Person hypostatically unites his divine and human natures.

(2) The supernatural mystery coextensive with Christ from the moment of his human conception and continuing through his life on earth; his sufferings and death; his resurrection from the dead and ascension to glory with the Father; his sending, with the Father, of the Holy Spirit upon the Apostles and the Church; and his unending mediation with the Father for the salvation of men.

Incense: A granulated substance which, when burnt, emits an aromatic smoke. It symbolizes the zeal with which the faithful should be consumed, the good odor of Christian virtue, the ascent of prayer to God.

Incest: Sexual intercourse with relatives by blood or marriage; a sin of impurity and also a grave violation of the natural reverence due to relatives. Other sins of impurity (desire, etc.) concerning relatives have the nature of incest.

Index of Prohibited Books: A list of books which Catholics were formerly forbidden to read, possess or sell, under penalty of excommunication. The books were banned by the Holy See after publication because their treatment of matters of faith and morals and related subjects were judged to be erroneous or serious occasions of doctrinal error. Some books were listed in the Index by name; others were covered under general norms. The Congregation for the Doctrine of the Faith declared June 14, 1966, that the Index and its related penalties of excommunication no longer had the force of law in the Church. Persons are still obliged, however, to take normal precautions against occasions of doctrinal error.

The first *Roman Index of Prohibited Books*, which served the same purposes as earlier lists, was published in 1559 by the Holy Office at the order of Paul IV. The Council of Trent, with the approval of the same pope, authorized another Index in 1564. Seven years later, St. Pius V set up a special Congregation for the Reform of the Index and Correction of Books, and gave it universal jurisdiction. In the course of time, many additions and modifications affecting the Index were made. In 1897, Leo XIII issued complete legislation on the subject, and in 1917 Benedict XV turned over to the Congregation of the Holy Office the function of censoring publications in accordance with the provisions of canon law.

Indifferentism: A theory that any one religion is as true and good — or false — as any other religion, and that it makes no difference, objectively, what religion one professes, if any. The theory is completely subjective, finding its justification entirely in personal choice without reference to or respect for objective validity. It is also self-contradictory, since it regards as equally acceptable — or unacceptable — the beliefs of all religions, which in fact are not only not all the same but are in some cases opposed to each other.

Indulgence: According to *The Doctrine and Practice of Indulgences,* an apostolic constitution issued by Paul VI Jan. 1, 1967, an indulgence is the remission before God of the temporal punishment due for sins already forgiven as far as their guilt is concerned, which a follower of Christ — with the proper dispositions and under certain determined conditions — acquires through the intervention of the Church. The Church grants indulgences in accordance with doctrine concerning the superabundant merits of Christ and the saints, the Power of the Keys, and the sharing of spiritual goods in the Communion of Saints.

An indulgence is partial or plenary, depending on whether it does away with either part or all of the temporal punishment due for sin. Both types of indulgences can always be applied to the dead by way of suffrage; the actual disposition of indulgences applied to the dead rests with God.

(1) Partial indulgence: Properly disposed faithful who perform an action to which a partial indulgence is attached obtain, in addition to the remission of temporal punishment acquired by the action itself, an equal remission of punishment through the intervention of the Church. (This grant was formerly designated in terms of days and years.) The proper dispositions for gaining a partial indulgence are sorrow for sin and freedom from serious sin, performance of the required good work, and the intention (which can be general or immediate) to gain the indulgence.

In addition to customary prayers and other good works to which partial indulgences are attached, the *Enchiridion Indulgentiarum* published in 1968 included general grants of partial indulgences to the faithful who: (a) with some kind of prayer, raise their minds to God with humble confidence while carrying out their duties and bearing the difficulties of everyday life; (b) motivated by the spirit of faith and compassion, give of themselves or their goods for the service of persons in need; (c) in a spirit of penance, spontaneously refrain from the enjoyment of things which are lawful and pleasing to them.

(2) Plenary indulgence: To gain a plenary indulgence, it is necessary for a person to be free of all attachment to sin, to perform the work to which the indulgence is attached, and to fulfill the three conditions of sacramental confession, Eucharistic Communion, and prayer for the intention of the pope. The three conditions may be fulfilled several days before or after the performance of the prescribed work, but it is fitting that Communion be received and prayers for the intentions of the pope be offered on the same day the work is performed. The condition of praying for the pope's intention is fully satisfied by praying one Our Father and one Hail Mary, and sometimes the Creed, but persons are free to choose other prayers.

Four of the several devotional practices for which a plenary indulgence is granted are: (a) adoration of the Blessed Sacrament for at least one-half hour; (b) devout reading of sacred Scripture for at least one-half hour; (c) the Way of the Cross; (d) recitation of the Marian Rosary in a church or public oratory or in a family group, a religious community or pious association. Only one plenary indulgence can be gained in a single day.

Indult: A favor or privilege granted by competent ecclesiastical authority, giving permission to do something not allowed by the common law of the Church.

Infant Jesus of Prague: An 18-inch-high wooden statue of the Child Jesus which has figured in a form of devotion to the Holy Childhood and Kingship of Christ since the 17th century. Of uncertain origin, the statue was presented by Princess Polixena to the Carmelites of Our Lady of Victory Church, Prague, in 1628.

Infused Virtues: The theological virtues of faith, hope, and charity; principles or capabilities of supernatural action, they are given with sanctifying grace by God rather than acquired by repeated acts of a person. They can be increased by practice; they are lost by contrary acts. Natural-acquired moral virtues, like the cardinal virtues of prudence, justice, temperance, and fortitude, can be considered infused in a person whose state of grace gives them supernatural orientation.

Inquisition: A tribunal for dealing with heretics, authorized by Gregory IX in 1231 to search them out, hear and judge them, sentence them to various forms of punishment, and in some cases to hand them over to civil authorities for punishment. The Inquisition was a creature of its time when crimes against

faith, which threatened the good of the Christian community, were regarded also as crimes against the state, and when heretical doctrines of such extremists as the Cathari and Albigensians threatened the very fabric of society. The institution, which was responsible for many excesses, was most active in the second half of the 13th century.

Inquisition, Spanish: An institution peculiar to Spain and the colonies in Spanish America. In 1478, at the urging of King Ferdinand, Pope Sixtus IV approved the establishment of the Inquisition for trying charges of heresy brought against Jewish (Marranos) and Moorish (Moriscos) converts. It acquired jurisdiction over other cases as well, however, and fell into disrepute because of irregularities in its functions, cruelty in its sentences, and the manner in which it served the interests of the Spanish crown more than the accused persons and the good of the Church. Protests by the Holy See failed to curb excesses of the Inquisition, which lingered in Spanish history until early in the 19th century.

I N R I: The first letters of words in the Latin inscription atop the cross on which Christ was crucified: (I)esus (N)azaraenus, (R)ex (J)udaeorum — Jesus of Nazareth, King of the Jews.

Insemination, Artificial: The implanting of human semen by some means other than consummation of natural marital intercourse. In view of the principle that procreation should result only from marital intercourse, donor insemination is not permissible. The use of legitimate artificial means to further the fruitfulness of marital intercourse is permissible.

In Sin: The condition of a person called spiritually dead because he does not possess sanctifying grace, the principle of supernatural life, action and merit. Such grace can be regained through repentance.

Instruction: A document containing doctrinal explanations, directive norms, rules, recommendations, admonitions, issued by the pope, a department of the Roman Curia or other competent authority in the Church. To the extent that they so prescribe, instructions have the force of law.

Intercommunion: The common celebration and reception of the Eucharist by members of different Christian churches; a pivotal issue in ecumenical theory and practice. Catholic participation and intercommunion in the Eucharistic liturgy of another church without a valid priesthood and with a variant Eucharistic belief is out of order. Under certain conditions, other Christians may receive the Eucharist in the Catholic Church (see additional Intercommunion entry). Intercommunion is acceptable to some Protestant churches and unacceptable to others.

Interdict: An ecclesiastical penalty imposed on persons and places for certain violations of church law. If the interdict is personal, the interdicted persons may not take part in certain liturgical services, administer or receive certain sacraments. If the interdict is local, persons may not take part in certain liturgical services, administer or receive certain sacraments in the interdicted places.

Interdict is different from excommunication, and does not involve exclusion of a person from the community of the faithful.

Interregnum: The period of time between the death of a pope and the election of his successor. Another term applied to the period is *Sede vacante,* meaning the See (of Rome) being vacant.

The main concerns during an interregnum are matters connected with the death and burial of the pope, the election of his successor, and the maintenance of ordinary routine for the proper functioning of the Roman Curia and the Diocese of Rome.

Interregnum procedures follow norms contained in the apostolic constitution *Romano Pontifici Eligendo* (concerning the vacancy of the Apostolic See and the election of the Roman Pontiff) issued by Paul VI Oct. 1, 1975. This constitution superseded two others previously in force: *Vacantis Apostolicae Sedis,* issued by Pius XII Dec. 8, 1945, and *Summi Pontificis Electione,* issued by John XXIII Sept. 5, 1962.

"During the vacancy of the Apostolic See," the constitution states, "the government of the Church is entrusted to the Sacred College of Cardinals for the sole dispatch of ordinary business and of matters which cannot be postponed, and for the preparation of everything necessary for the election of the new pope."

The general congregation of the whole college, presided over by the dean, sub-dean or senior cardinal, has responsibility for major decisions during an interregnum. Other decisions of a routine nature are left to a particular congregation consisting of the chamberlain of the Holy Roman Church and three assistant cardinals.

The chamberlain of the Holy Roman Church and the dean of the college are the key officials, with directive responsibilities before and during the electoral conclave. The chamberlain is in general charge of ordinary administration. He — or the dean prior to a chamberlain's election by the cardinals — certifies the death of the pope; orders the destruction of the Fisherman's Ring and personal seals of the pope; and sets in motion procedures, carried out in collaboration with the dean, for informing the world about the pope's death, for funeral preparations, and for summoning and supervising the conclave for the election of a new pope.

Cardinals in charge of departments of the Roman Curia relinquish their offices at the death of the pope. Remaining in office, however, are the vicar of Rome, for ordinary jurisdiction over the diocese, and the major penitentiary. The substitute secretary of state or papal secretariat maintains the secretariat in a status quo. Papal representatives, such as nuncios and apostolic delegates, remain in office.

The congregations, offices and tribunals of the Curia retain ordinary jurisdiction for routine affairs but may not initiate new business during an interregnum.

If the pope should die during sessions of an ecumenical council or the Synod of Bishops, they would automatically be suspended.

The deceased pope is buried in St. Peter's Basilica, following prescribed ceremonies and traditional customs during a mourning period of nine days.

The conclave for the election of a new pope begins no sooner than 15 and no later than 20 days after the death of his predecessor. On the election of the new pope, the interregnum comes to an end. (See Papal Election.)

Intinction: A method of administering Holy Communion under the dual appearances of bread and wine, in which the consecrated host is dipped in the consecrated wine before being given to the communicant. The administering of Holy Communion in this manner, which has been traditional in Eastern-Rite liturgies, was authorized in the Roman Rite for various occasions by the *Constitution on the Sacred Liturgy* promulgated by the Second Vatican Council.

Irenicism: Peace-seeking, conciliation, as opposed to polemics; an important element in ecumenism, provided it furthers pursuit of the Christian unity willed by Christ without degenerating into a peace-at-any-price disregard for religious truth.

Irregularity: An impediment to the lawful reception or exercise of holy orders. The Church instituted irregularities — which include apostasy, heresy, homicide, attempted suicide — out of reverence for the dignity of the sacraments.

Itinerarium: Prayers for a spiritually profitable journey.

J

Jansenism: Opinions developed and proposed by Cornelius Jansenius (1585-1638). He held that: human nature was radically and intrinsically corrupted by original sin; some men are predestined to heaven and others to hell; Christ died only for those predestined to heaven; for those who are predestined, the operations of grace are irresistible. Jansenism also advocated an extremely rigorous code of morals and asceticism. The errors were proscribed by Urban VIII in 1642, by Innocent X in 1653, by Clement XI in 1713, and by other popes. Despite these condemnations, the rigoristic spirit of Jansenism lingered for a long time afterwards, particularly in France.

Jehovah's Witnesses: The Witnesses, together with the Watchtower and Bible Tract Society, trace their beginnings to a Bible class organized by Charles Taze Russell in 1872 at Allegheny, Pa. They take their name from a passage in Isaiah (43:12): " 'You are my witnesses,' says Jehovah." They are generally fundamentalist and revivalist with respect to the Bible, and believe that Christ is God's Son but is inferior to God. They place great emphasis on the Battle of Armageddon (as a decisive confrontation of good and evil) that is depicted vividly in Revelation, believing that God will then destroy the existing system of things and that, with the establishment of Jehovah's Kingdom, a small band of 144,000 spiritual sons of God will go to heaven, rule with Christ, and share in some way their happiness with some others.

Each Witness is considered by the society to be an ordained minister charged with the duty of spreading the message of Jehovah, which is accomplished through publications, house-to-house visitations, and other methods. The Witnesses refuse to salute the flag of any nation, regarding this as a form of idolatry, or to sanction blood transfusions even for the saving of life. There are approximately one million Witnesses in more than 22,000 congregations in some 80 countries. The freedom and activities of Witnesses are restricted in some places.

Jesus: The name of Jesus, meaning Savior in Christian usage, derived from the Aramaic and Hebrew *Yeshua* and *Joshua,* meaning *Yahweh* is salvation.

Jesus Prayer: A form of prayer dating back to the fifth century, "Lord Jesus Christ, Son of God, have mercy on me (a sinner)."

Joys of the Blessed Virgin Mary, Seven: (See Franciscan Crown.)

Judgment: (1) Last or final judgment: Final judgment by Christ, at the end of the world and the general resurrection.

(2) Particular judgment: The judgment that takes place immediately after a person's death, followed by entrance into heaven, hell or purgatory.

Jurisdiction: Right, power, authority to rule. Jurisdiction in the Church is of divine institution; has pastoral service for its purpose; includes legislative, judicial and executive authority; can be exercised only by persons with the power of orders.

(1) Ordinary jurisdiction is attached to ecclesiastical offices by law; the officeholders, called ordinaries, have authority over those who are subject to them.

(2) Delegated jurisdiction is that which is granted to persons rather than attached to offices. Its extent depends on the terms of the delegation.

Justice: One of the four cardinal virtues by which a person gives to others what is due to them as a matter of right. (See Cardinal Virtues.)

Justification: The act by which God makes a person just, and the consequent change in the spiritual status of a person, from sin to grace; the remission of sin and the infusion of sanctifying grace through the merits of Christ and the action of the Holy Spirit.

K

Kerygma: Proclaiming the word of God, in the manner of the Apostles, as here and now effective for salvation. This method of preaching or instruction, centered on Christ and geared to the facts and themes of salvation history, is designed to dispose people to faith in Christ and/or to intensify the experience and practice of that faith in those who have it.

Keys, Power of the: Spiritual authority and jurisdiction in the Church, symbolized by the keys of the kingdom of heaven. Christ promised the keys to St. Peter, as head-to-be of the Church (Mt. 16:19), and commissioned him with full pastoral responsibility to feed his lambs and sheep (Jn. 21:15-17), The pope, as the successor of St. Peter, has this power in a primary and supreme manner. The bishops of the Church also have the power, in union with and subordinate to the pope. Priests share in it through holy orders and the delegation of authority.

Examples of the application of the Power of the Keys are the exercise of teaching and pastoral authority by the pope and bishops, the absolving of sins in the sacrament of penance, the granting of indulgences, the imposing of spiritual penalties on persons who commit certain serious sins.

L

Laicization: (1) The process by which a man ordained to holy orders is relieved of the obligations of orders and the ministry and is returned to the status of a lay person. Applications by diocesan clergy are filed with their bishop and forwarded for processing to the congregation of the Roman Curia authorized to grant the indult of laicization.

(2) The process by which a religious is relieved of the obligations of vows and membership in his or her institute. Applications are filed with the proper religious superior and forwarded for processing to the Congregation for Religious which is authorized to grant the appropriate indult.

Languages of the Church: The first language in church use, for divine worship and the conduct of ecclesiastical affairs, was Aramaic, the language of the first Christians in and around Jerusalem. As the Church spread westward, Greek was adopted and prevailed until the third century when it was supplanted by Latin for official use in the West.

According to traditions established very early in churches of the Eastern Rites, many different languages were adopted for use in divine worship and for the conduct of ecclesiastical affairs. The practice was, and still is, to use the vernacular or a language closely related to the common tongue of the people.

In the Western Church, Latin prevailed as the general official language until the promulgation on Dec. 4, 1963, of the *Constitution on the Sacred Liturgy* by the second session of the Second Vatican Council. Since that time, vernacular languages have come into use in the Mass, administration of the sacraments, and the Liturgy of the Hours. The change was introduced in order to make the prayers and ceremonies of divine worship more informative and meaningful to all. Latin, however, remains the official language for administrative and procedural matters.

Law: An ordinance or rule governing the activity of things.

(1) Natural law: Moral norms corresponding to man's nature by which he orders his conduct toward God, neighbor, society and himself. This law, which is rooted in human nature, is of divine origin, can be known by the use of reason, and binds all men having the use of reason. The Ten Commandments are declarations and amplifications of natural law. The primary precepts of natural law, to do good and to avoid evil, are universally recognized, despite differences with respect to understanding and application resulting from different philosophies of good and evil.

(2) Divine positive law: That which has been revealed by God. Among its essentials are the twin precepts of love of God and love of neighbor, and the Ten Commandments.

(3) Ecclesiastical law: That which is established by the Church for the spiritual welfare of the faithful and the orderly conduct of ecclesiastical affairs. (See Canon Law.)

(4) Civil law: That which is established by a socio-political community for the common good.

Lector: A reader of scriptural passages and other selections at Mass and other services of worship.

Legitimation: Removal of the status of illegitimacy; e.g., by marriage of the parents.

Liberalism: A multiphased trend of thought and movement favoring liberty, independence and progress in moral, intellectual, religious, social, economic and political life. Traceable to the Renaissance, it developed through the Enlightenment, the rationalism of the 19th century, and modernist- and existentialist-related theories of the 20th century. Evaluations of various kinds of liberalism depend on the validity of their underlying principles. Extremist positions — regarding subjectivism, libertinarianism, naturalist denials of the supernatural, and the alienation of individuals and society from God and the Church were condemned by Gregory XVI in the 1830's, Pius IX in 1864, Leo XIII in 1899, and St. Pius X in 1907. There is, however, nothing objectionable about forms of liberalism patterned according to sound principles of Christian doctrine.

Life in Outer Space: Whether rational life exists on other bodies in the universe besides earth, is a question for scientific investigation to settle. The possibility can be granted, without prejudice to the body of revealed truth.

Limbo: The limbo of the fathers was the state of rest and natural happiness after death enjoyed by the just of pre-Christian times until they were admitted to heaven following the Ascension of Christ. Belief in this matter is stated in the Apostles' Creed. The existence of a limbo for unbaptized persons of infant status — a state of rest and natural happiness — has never been formally defined.

Litany: A prayer in the form of responsive petition; e.g., St. Joseph, pray for us, etc. There are seven litanies approved for liturgical use: Litanies of Loreto (Litany of the Blessed Mother), the Holy Name, All Saints, the Sacred Heart, the Precious Blood, St. Joseph, Litany for the Dying. Others may be used privately.

Little Office of the Blessed Virgin Mary: A shortened version of a Liturgy of the Hours honoring the Blessed Virgin. It dates from about the middle of the eighth century.

Liturgical Languages: (See Languages of the Church.)

Loreto, House of: A Marian shrine in Loreto, Italy, consisting of the home of the Holy Family which, according to an old tradition, was transported in a miraculous manner from Nazareth to Dalmatia and finally to Loreto between 1291 and 1294. Investigations conducted shortly after the appearance of the structure in Loreto revealed that its dimensions matched those of the house of the Holy Family missing from its place of enshrinement in a basilica at Nazareth. Among the many popes who regarded it with high honor was John XXIII, who went there on pilgrimage Oct. 4, 1962. The house of the Holy Family is enshrined in the Basilica of Our Lady.

Lust: A disorderly desire for sexual pleasure; one of the seven capital sins.

M

Magi: In the Infancy Narrative of St. Matthew's Gospel (2:1-12), three wise men from the East whose visit and homage to the Child Jesus at Bethlehem indicated Christ's manifestation of himself to non-Jewish people. The narrative teaches the universality of salvation. The traditional names of the Magi are Caspar, Melchior and Balthasar.

Magnificat: The canticle or hymn of the Virgin Mary on the occasion of her visitation to her cousin Elizabeth (Lk. 1:46-55). It is an expression of praise, thanksgiving and acknowledgment of the great blessings given by God to Mary, the Mother of the Second Person of the Blessed Trinity made Man. The Magnificat is recited in the Liturgy of the

Hours as part of the Evening Prayer.

Martyr: A Greek word, meaning witness, denoting one who voluntarily suffered death for the faith or some Christian virtue.

Martyrology: A catalogue of martyrs and other saints, arranged according to the calendar. The *Roman Martyrology* contains the official list of saints venerated by the Church. Additions to the list are made in beatification and canonization decrees of the Congregation for the Causes of Saints. The Martyrology is being revised to conform with other liturgical books.

Mass for the People: On Sundays and certain feasts throughout the year pastors are required to offer Mass for the faithful committed to their care. If they cannot offer the Mass on these days, they must do so at a later date or provide that another priest offer the Mass.

Master of Novices: The person in charge of the training and formation of candidates for a religious institute during novitiate.

Materialism: Theory which holds that matter is the only reality, and everything in existence is merely a manifestation of matter; there is no such thing as spirit, and the supernatural does not exist. Materialism is incompatible with Christian doctrine.

Meditation: Mental, as distinguished from vocal, prayer, in which thought, affections, and resolutions of the will predominate. There is a meditative element to all forms of prayer, which always involves the raising of the heart and mind to God.

Mendicants: A term derived from Latin and meaning beggars, applied to members of religious orders without property rights; the members, accordingly, worked or begged for their support. The original mendicants were Franciscans and Dominicans in the early 13th century; later, the Carmelites, Augustinians, Servites and others were given the mendicant title and privileges, with respect to exemption from episcopal jurisdiction and wide faculties for preaching and administering the sacrament of penance. The practice of begging is limited at the present time, although it is still allowed with the permission of competent superiors and bishops. Mendicants are supported by free will offerings and income received for spiritual services and other work.

Mercy, Divine: The love and goodness of God, manifested particularly in a time of need.

Merit: In religion, the right to a supernatural reward for good works freely done for a supernatural motive by a person in the state of and with the assistance of grace. The right to such reward is from God, who binds himself to give it. Accordingly, good works, as described above, are meritorious for salvation.

Metempsychosis: Theory of the passage or migration of the human soul after death from one body to another for the purpose of purification from guilt. The theory denies the unity of the soul and human personality, and the doctrine of individual moral responsibility.

Millennium: A thousand-year reign of Christ and the just upon earth before the end of the world. This belief of the Millenarians, Chiliasts, and some sects of modern times is based on an erroneous interpretation of Rv. 20.

Miracles: Observable events or effects in the physical or moral order of things, with reference to salvation, which cannot be explained by the ordinary operation of laws of nature and which, therefore, are attributed to the direct action of God. They make known, in an unusual way, the concern and intervention of God in human affairs for the salvation of men. The most striking examples are the miracles worked by Christ. Numbering about 35, they included his own Resurrection; the raising of three persons to life (Lazarus, the daughter of Jairus, the son of the widow of Naim); the healing of blind, leprous and other persons; nature miracles; and prophecies, or miracles of the intellectual order.

The foregoing notion of miracles, which is based on the concept of a fixed order of nature, was not known by the writers of Sacred Scripture. In the Old Testament, particularly, they called some things miraculous which, according to the definition in contemporary use, may or may not have been miracles. Essentially, however, the occurrences so designated were regarded as exceptional manifestations of God's care and concern for the salvation of his people. The miracles of Christ were miracles in the full sense of the term.

The Church believes it is reasonable to accept miracles as manifestations of divine power for purposes of salvation. God, who created the laws of nature, is their master; hence, without disturbing the ordinary course of things, he can — and has in the course of history before and after Christ — occasionally set aside these laws and has also produced effects beyond their power of operation. The Church does not call miraculous anything which does not admit of easy explanation; on the contrary, miracles are admitted only when the events have a bearing on the order of grace and every possible natural explanation has been tried and found wanting.

(The transubstantiation — i.e., the conversion of the whole substance of bread and wine, their sensible appearances alone remaining, into the Body and Blood of Christ in the act of Consecration at Mass — is not an observable event. Traditionally, however, it has been called a miracle.)

Missal: A liturgical book of Roman Rite also called the *Sacramentary*, containing the celebrant's prayers of the Mass, along with general instructions and ceremonial directives. The Latin text of the new *Roman Missal*, replacing the one authorized by the Council of Trent in the 16th century, was published by the Vatican Polyglot Press in 1970. Its use in English was made mandatory in the U.S. from Dec. 1, 1974. Readings and scriptural responsories formerly in the missal are contained in the *Lectionary*.

Missiology: Study of the missionary nature, constitution and activity of the Church in all aspects: theological reasons for missionary activity, laws and instructions of the Holy See, history of the missions, social and cultural background, methods, norms for carrying on missionary work.

Mission: (1) Strictly, it means being sent to perform a certain work, such as the mission of Christ to redeem mankind, the mission of the Apostles and the Church and its members to perpetuate the prophetic, priestly and royal mission of Christ.

(2) A place where: the Gospel has not been proclaimed; the Church has not been firmly established; the Church, although established, is weak.

(3) An ecclesiastical territory with the simplest kind of canonical organization, under the jurisdiction of the Congregation for the Evangelization of Peoples.

(4) A church or chapel without a resident priest.

(5) A special course of sermons and spiritual exercises conducted in parishes for the purpose of renewing and deepening the spiritual life of the faithful and for the conversion of lapsed Catholics.

Modernism: The "synthesis of all heresies," which appeared near the beginning of the 20th century. It undermines the objective validity of religious beliefs and practices which, it contends, are products of the subconscious developed by mankind under the stimulus of a religious sense. It holds that the existence of a personal God cannot be demonstrated, the Bible is not inspired, Christ is not divine, nor did he establish the Church or institute the sacraments. A special danger lies in modernism, which is still influential, because it uses Catholic terms with perverted meanings. St. Pius X condemned 65 propositions of modernism in 1907 in the decree *Lamentabili* and issued the encyclical *Pascendi* to explain and analyze its errors.

Monastery: The dwelling place, as well as the community thereof, of monks belonging to the Benedictine and Benedictine-related orders like the Cistercians and Carthusians; also, the Augustinians and Canons Regular. Distinctive of monasteries are: their separation from the world; the papal enclosure or strict cloister; the permanence or stability of attachment characteristic of their members; autonomous government in accordance with a monastic rule, like that of St. Benedict in the West or of St. Basil in the East; the special dedication of its members to the community celebration of the liturgy as well as to work that is suitable to the surrounding area and the needs of its people. Monastic superiors of men have such titles as abbot and prior; of women, abbess and prioress. In most essentials, an abbey is the same as a monastery.

Monk: A member of a monastic order — e.g., the Benedictines, the Benedictine-related Cistercians and Carthusians, and the Basilians, who bind themselves by religious profession to stable attachment to a monastery, the contemplative life and the work of their community. In popular use, the title is wrongly applied to many men religious who really are not monks.

Monotheism: Belief in and worship of one God.

Morality: Conformity or difformity of behavior to standards of right conduct. (See Commandments of God, Precepts of the Church, Conscience, Law.)

Mormons: Members of the Church of Jesus Christ of Latter-Day Saints. The church was established by Joseph Smith (1805-1844) at Fayette, N.Y., three years after he said he had received from an angel golden tablets containing the *Book of the Prophet Mormon*. This book, the Bible, *Doctrine and Covenants,* and *The Pearl of Great Price,* are the basic doctrinal texts of the church. Characteristic of the Mormons are strong belief in the revelations of their leaders, among whom was Brigham Young; a strong community of religious-secular concern; a dual secular and spiritual priesthood; and vigorous missionary activity. The headquarters of the church are located at Salt Lake City, Utah, where the Mormons first settled in 1847.

Mortification: Acts of self-discipline, including prayer, hardship, austerities and penances undertaken for the sake of progress in virtue.

Motu Proprio: A Latin phrase designating a document issued by a pope on his own initiative. Documents of this kind often concern administrative matters.

Mysteries of Faith: Supernatural truths whose existence cannot be known without revelation by God and whose intrinsic truth, while not contrary to reason, can never be wholly understood even after revelation. These mysteries are above reason, not against reason. Among them are the divine mysteries of the Trinity, Incarnation and Eucharist.

Some mysteries — e.g., concerning God's attributes — can be known by reason without revelation, although they cannot be fully understood.

N

Necromancy: Supposed communication with the dead; a form of divination.

Non-Expedit: A Latin expression. It is not expedient (fitting, proper), used to state a prohibition or refusal of permission.

Novena: A term designating public or private devotional practices over a period of nine consecutive days; or, by extension, over a period of nine weeks, in which one day a week is set aside for the devotions.

Novice: A person preparing, in a formal period of trial and formation called the *novitiate,* for membership in a religious institute. The novitiate lasts more than a year and ends with the profession of temporary vows or other temporary commitment to the religious life. Current norms require a total 12-month period of seclusion for novices; to this is added other periods of time spent in apostolic work for the sake of experience. A novice, while acquiring experience of the religious life, is not bound by the obligations of professed members of the institute, is free to leave at any time, and may be discharged at the discretion of competent superiors. The immediate superior of a novice is a master or mistress of novices.

Nun (1) Strictly, a member of a religious order of women with solemn vows (moniales).

(2) In general, all women religious, even those in simple vows who are more properly called sisters.

Nunc Dimittis: The canticle or hymn of Simeon at the sight of Jesus at the Temple on the occasion of his presentation (Lk. 2:29-32). It is an expression of joy and thanksgiving for the blessing of having lived to see the Messiah. It is one of the canticles prescribed in the Liturgy of the Hours.

O

Oath: Calling upon God to witness the truth of a statement. Violating an oath, e.g., by perjury in court, or taking an oath without sufficient reason, is a violation of the honor due to God.

Obedience: Submission to one in authority. General obligations of obedience fall under the Fourth Commandment. The vow of obedience professed by religious is one of the evangelical counsels.

Obsession, Diabolical: The extraordinary state of one who is seriously molested by evil spirits in an external manner. Obsession is more than just temptation.

Occultism: Practices involving ceremonies, rituals, chants, incantations, other cult-related activities intended to affect the course of nature, the lives of practitioners and others, through esoteric powers of magic, diabolical or other forces; one of many forms of superstition.

Octave: A period of eight days given over to the celebration of a major feast such as Easter.

Oils, Holy: The oils consecrated by bishops on Holy Thursday or another suitable day, and by priests under certain conditions for use in certain sacraments and consecrations.

(1) The oil of catechumens (olive or vegetable oil), used at baptism; also, poured with chrism into the baptismal water blessed in Easter Vigil ceremonies.

(2) Chrism (olive or vegetable oil mixed with balm), used at baptism, in confirmation, at the ordination of a priest and bishop, in the dedication of churches and altars.

(3) Oil of the sick (olive or vegetable oil) used in anointing the sick.

Old Catholics — Several sects, including: (1) the Church of Utrecht, which severed relations with Rome in 1724; (2) the National Polish Church in the U.S., which had its origin near the end of the 19th century; (3) German, Austrian and Swiss Old Catholics, who broke away from union with Rome following the First Vatican Council in 1870 because they objected to the dogma of papal infallibility.

The formation of the Old Catholic communion of Germans, Austrians and Swiss began in 1870 at a public meeting held in Nuremberg under the leadership of A. Dollinger. Four years later episcopal succession was established with the ordination of an Old Catholic German bishop by a prelate of the Church of Utrecht. In line with the "Declaration of Utrecht" of 1889, they accept the first seven ecumenical councils and doctrine formulated before 1054, but reject communion with the pope and a number of other Catholic doctrines and practices. They have a valid priesthood and valid sacraments. *The Oxford Dictionary of the Christian Church* notes that they have recognized Anglican ordinations since 1925, that they have had full communion with the Church of England since 1932, and that their bishops, using their own formula, have taken part in the ordination of Anglican bishops.

This communion does not recognize the "Old Catholic" status of several smaller sects calling themselves such. In turn, connection with it is disavowed by the Old Roman Catholic Church headquartered in Chicago, which contends that it has abandoned the traditions of the Church of Utrecht.

The United States is the only English-speaking country with Old Catholic communities.

Oratory: A chapel.

Ordinariate: An ecclesiastical jurisdiction for special purposes and people. Examples are the military ordinariate of the US, for service personnel, and Eastern-Rite ordinariates in places where Eastern-Rite dioceses do not exist.

Ordinary: One who has the jurisdiction of an office: the pope, diocesan bishops, vicars general, prelates of missionary territories, vicars apostolic, prefects apostolic, vicars capitular during the vacancy of a see, superiors general, abbots primate and other major superiors of men religious.

Ordination: The consecration of sacred ministers for divine worship and the service of men in things pertaining to God. The power of ordination comes from Christ and the Church, and must be conferred by a minister capable of communicating it.

Organ Transplants: The transplanting of organs from one person to another is permissible for serious reasons provided it is done with the consent of the concerned parties and does not result in the death or essential mutilation of the donor. Advances in methods and technology have increased the range of transplant possibilities in recent years. Despite such progress, unresolved problems have slowed the pace of some transplant practice, especially with respect to the heart. The first successful heart transplant was performed Dec. 3, 1967, on Louis Washkansky, 56, by a team headed by Dr. Christian Barnard in Cape Town, South Africa.

Original Sin: The sin of Adam (Gn. 2:8—3:24), personal to him and passed on to all men as a state of privation of grace. Despite this privation and the related wounding of human nature and weakening of natural powers, original sin leaves unchanged all that man himself is by nature. The scriptural basis of the doctrine was stated especially by St. Paul in 1 Cor. 15:21, ff., and Romans 5:12-21. Original sin is remitted by baptism and incorporation in Christ, through whom grace is given to persons.

O Salutaris Hostia: The first three Latin words, O Saving Victim, of a Benediction hymn.

Ostpolitik: Policy adopted by Pope Paul VI in an attempt to improve the situation of Eastern European Catholics through diplomatic negotiations with their governments.

Oxford Movement: A movement in the Church of England from 1833 to about 1845 which had for its objective a threefold defense of the church as a divine institution, the apostolic succession of its bishops, and the Book of Common Prayer as the rule of faith. The movement took its name from Oxford University and involved a number of intellectuals who authored a series of influential *Tracts for Our Times*. Some of its leading figures — e.g., F. W. Faber, John Henry Newman and Henry Edward Manning — became converts to the Catholic Church. In the Church of England, the movement affected the liturgy, historical and theological scholarship, the status of the ministry, and other areas of ecclesiastical life.

P

Paganism: A term referring to non-revealed religions, i.e., religions other than Christianity, Judaism and Mohammedanism.

Palms: Blessed palms are a sacramental. They are blessed and distributed on the Sunday of the Passion in commemoration of the triumphant entrance of Christ into Jerusalem. Ashes of the burnt palms are used on Ash Wednesday.

Pange Lingua: First Latin words, Sing, my tongue, of a hymn in honor of the Holy Eucharist, used particularly on Holy Thursday and in Eucharistic processions.

Pantheism: Theory that all things are part of God, divine, in the sense that God realizes himself as the ultimate reality of matter or spirit through being and/or becoming all things that have been, are, and will be. The theory leads to hopeless confusion of the Creator and the created realm of being, identifies evil with good, and involves many inherent contradictions.

Papal Election: The pope is elected by members of the College of Cardinals in a secret conclave or meeting convened ordinarily in secluded quarters of the Vatican Palace between 15 and 20 days after the death of his predecessor. Cardinals under the age of 80, totaling no more than 120, are eligible to participate in a papal election.

Following are some of the principal regulations decreed by Paul VI Oct. 1, 1975, in the apostolic constitution *Romano Pontifici Eligendo* (concerning the vacancy of the Apostolic See and the election of the Roman Pontiff).

The ordinary manner of election is by scrutiny, with two votes each morning and afternoon in the Sistine Chapel until one of the candidates receives a two-thirds plus one vote majority.

Alternative methods, which can be adopted by unanimous agreement of the cardinals in difficult cases, are provided for: (1) by delegation, in which the cardinals designate a limited number (nine to 15) to make the choice; (2) by changing the majority rule from two-thirds plus one vote to an absolute majority plus one; (3) by limiting final choice, if the procedure in force becomes protracted, to one between the two candidates who received the largest numbers of votes, but not a required majority, in the most recent balloting.

An unusual manner of election is by acclamation or inspiration — that is, by spontaneous, unanimous choice without any need for normal voting procedure.

The elected candidate is asked by the dean of the college if he accepts the election. If he does so and is already a bishop, he immediately becomes the bishop of Rome and pope, and signifies the name by which he will be called. The cardinals then pledge their obedience to him before the senior cardinal deacon proclaims his election to the world from the main balcony of the Vatican and the new pope imparts his blessing *Urbi et Orbi*. If the candidate is not a bishop, he is so ordained before receiving the pledge of obedience and being proclaimed pope. The subsequent coronation of the pope is a ceremonial recognition of the fact of his election.

The pope is elected for life. If one should resign, a new pope would be elected in accordance with the foregoing regulations.

Rigid rules govern the conclave — its personnel, freedom from internal and external influence and interference, absolute secrecy (with a ban on recording devices and a prohibition against any disclosures).

Ordinarily, the first indication that a new pope has been elected is a plume of white smoke rising from the Vatican on burning of the last ballots.

(See College of Cardinals, Interregnum.)

Early methods of electing a pope — with various degrees of participation by the clergy and people of Rome and others — were set aside by Pope Nicholas II, who decreed in 1059 that cardinal bishops would be the electors. Further modification of the process was decreed by the Lateran Council in 1179 (that election would take place by a two-thirds majority vote of the cardinals) and by Pope Gregory X in 1274 (regarding a secluded conclave arrangement for elections).

Paraclete: A title of the Holy Spirit meaning, in Greek, Advocate, Consoler.

Parental Duties: All duties related to the obligation of parents to provide for the welfare of their children. These obligations fall under the Fourth Commandment.

Parish: A community of the faithful served by a pastor charged with responsibility for providing them with full pastoral service. Most parishes are territorial, embracing all of the faithful in a certain area of a diocese; some are personal or national, for certain classes of people, without strict regard for their places of residence.

Parousia: The coming, or saving presence, of Christ which will mark the completion of salvation history and the coming to perfection of God's kingdom at the end of the world.

Paschal Candle: A large candle, symbolic of the risen Christ, blessed and lighted on the Easter Vigil and placed at the Gospel side of the altar until Ascension Day. It is ornamented with five large grains of incense, representing the wounds of Christ, inserted in the form of a cross; the Greek letters Alpha and Omega, symbolizing Christ the beginning and end of all things, at the top and bottom of the shaft of the cross; and the figures of the current year of salvation in the quadrants formed by the cross.

Paschal Precept: The church law requiring the faithful to receive Holy Communion during the Easter time.

Passion of Christ: Sufferings of Christ, recorded in the four Gospels.

Pastor: An ordained minister charged with responsibility for the doctrinal, sacramental and related service of people committed to his care; e.g., a bishop for the people in his diocese, a priest for the people of his parish.

Pater Noster: The initial Latin words, Our Father, of the Lord's Prayer.

Peace, Sign of: A gesture of greeting — e.g., a handshake — exchanged by the ministers and participants at Mass.

Pectoral Cross: A cross worn on a chain about the neck and over the breast by bishops and abbots as a mark of their office.

Penance or Penitence: (1) The spiritual change or conversion of mind and heart by which a person turns away from sin, and all that it implies, toward God, through a personal renewal under the influence of the Holy Spirit. In the apostolic constitution *Paenitemini,* Pope Paul VI called it "a religious, personal act which has as its aim love and surrender to God." Penance involves sorrow and contrition for sin, together with other internal and external acts of atonement. It serves the purposes of reestablishing in one's life the order of God's love and commandments, and of making satisfaction to God for sin. A divine precept states the necessity of penance for salvation: "Unless you do penance, you shall all likewise perish" (Lk. 13:3) . . . "Be converted and believe in the Gospel" (Mk. 1:15).

In the penitential discipline of the Church, the various works of penance have been classified under the headings of prayer (interior), fasting and almsgiving (exterior). The Church has established minimum requirements for the common and social observance of the divine precept by Catholics — e.g., by requiring them to fast and/or abstain on certain days of the year. These observances, however, do not exhaust all the demands of the divine precept, whose fulfillment is a matter of personal responsibility; nor do they have any real value unless they proceed from the internal spirit and purpose of penance.

Related to works of penance for sins actually committed are works of mortification. The purpose of the latter is to develop — through prayer, fasting, renunciations and similar actions — self-control and detachment from things which could otherwise become occasions of sin.

(2) Penance is a virtue disposing a person to turn to God in sorrow for sin and to carry out works of amendment and atonement.

(3) The sacrament of penance and sacramental penance.

Perjury: Taking a false oath, lying under oath, a violation of the honor due to God.

Persecution, Religious: A campaign waged against a church or other religious body by persons and governments intent on its destruction. The best known campaigns of this type against the Christian Church were the Roman persecutions which occurred intermittently from about 54 to the promulgation of the Edict of Milan in 313, The most extensive persecutions took place during the reigns of Nero, the first major Roman persecutor, Domitian, Trajan, Marcus Aurelius, and Diocletian. Besides the Roman persecutions, the Catholic Church has been subject to many others, including those of the 20th century in Communist-controlled countries.

Peter's Pence: A collection made each year among Catholics for the maintenance of the pope and his works of charity. It was originally a tax of a penny on each house, and was collected on St. Peter's day, whence the name. It originated in England in the eighth century.

Petition: One of the four purposes of prayer. In prayers of petition, persons ask of God the blessings they and others need.

Pharisees: Influential class among the Jews, referred to in the Gospels, noted for their self-righteousness, legalism, strict interpretation of the Law, acceptance of the traditions of the elders as well as the Law of Moses, and beliefs regarding angels and spirits, the resurrection of the dead and judgment. Most of them were laymen, and they were closely allied with the Scribes; their opposite numbers were the Sadducees. The Pharisaic and rabbinical traditions had a lasting influence on Judaism following the destruction of Jerusalem in 70 A.D.

Pious Fund: Property and money originally accumulated by the Jesuits to finance their missionary work in Lower California. When the Jesuits were expelled from the territory in 1767, the fund was appropriated by the Spanish Crown and used to support Dominican and Franciscan missionary work in Upper and Lower California. In 1842 the Mexican government took over administration of the fund, incorporated most of the revenue into the national treasury, and agreed to pay the Church interest of six per cent a year on the capital so incorporated. From 1848 to 1967 the fund was the subject of lengthy negotiations between the US and Mexican governments because of the latter's failure to make payments as agreed. A lump-sum settlement was made in 1967 with payment by Mexico to the US government of more than $700,000, to be turned over to the Archdiocese of San Francisco.

Polytheism: Belief in and worship of many gods or divinities, especially prevalent in pre-Christian religions.

Poor Box: Alms-box; found in churches from the earliest days of Christianity.

Pope Joan: Alleged name of a woman falsely said to have been pope from 855-858, the years of the reign of Benedict III. The myth was not heard of before the 13th century.

Portiuncula: (1) Meaning little portion (of land), the Portiuncula was the chapel of Our Lady of the Angels near Assisi, Italy, which the Benedictines gave to St. Francis early in the 13th century. He repaired the chapel and made it the first church of the Franciscan Order. It is now enshrined in the Basilica of St. Mary of the Angels in Assisi.

(2) The Portiuncula Indulgence, or Pardon of Assisi, was authorized by Honorius III. Originally, it could be gained for the souls in purgatory only in the chapel of Our Lady of the Angels; by later concessions, it could be gained also in other Franciscan and parish churches. According to legislation now in force, the Portiuncula Indulgence can be gained once on the day of Aug. 2, or on the following Sunday with permission of the bishop of the place. The conditions are, in addition to freedom from attachment to sin: reception of the sacraments of penance and the Eucharist on or near the day; a visit to a parish church on the day, during which the Our Father and Creed are offered for the intentions of the pope.

Possession, Diabolical: The extraordinary state of a person who is tormented from within by evil spirits who exercise strong influence over his powers of mind and body.

Postulant: One of several names used to designate a candidate for membership in a religious institute during the period before novitiate.

Poverty: (1) The quality or state of being poor, in actual destitution and need, or being poor in spirit. In the latter sense, poverty means the state of mind and disposition of persons who regard material things in proper perspective as gifts of God for the support of life and its reasonable enrichment, and for the service of others in need. It means freedom from unreasonable attachment to material things as ends in themselves, even though they may be possessed in small or large measure.

(2) One of the evangelical counsels professed by religious as a vow. It involves the voluntary renunciation of rights of ownership and of independent use and disposal of material goods (solemn vow); or, the right of independent use and disposal, but not of the radical right of ownership (simple vow). Religious institutes provide their members with necessary and useful goods and services from common resources. The manner in which goods are received and/or handled by religious is determined by poverty of spirit and the rule and constitutions of their institute. Practice of the vow of poverty is undergoing some change in the contemporary renewal in religious life.

Pragmatism: Theory that the truth of ideas, concepts and values depends on their utility or capacity to serve a useful purpose rather than on their conformity with objective standards; also called utilitarianism.

Prayer: The raising of the mind and heart to God in adoration, thanksgiving, reparation and petition. Prayer, which is always mental because it involves thought and love of God, may be vocal, meditative, private and personal, social, and official. The official prayer of the Church as a worshipping community is called the liturgy.

Precepts: Commands or orders given to individuals or communities in particular cases; they establish law for concerned parties. Preceptive documents are issued by the pope, departments of the Roman Curia and other competent authority in the Church.

Presence of God: A devotional practice of increasing one's awareness of the presence and action of God in daily life.

Presumption: A violation of the theological virtue of hope, by which a person striving for salvation either relies too much on his own capabilities or expects God to do things which he cannot do, in keeping with his divine attributes, or does not will to do, according to his divine plan. Presumption is the opposite of despair.

Preternatural Gifts: Exceptional gifts, beyond the exigencies and powers of human nature, enjoyed by Adam in the state of original justice: immunity from suffering and death, superior knowledge, integrity or perfect control of the passions. These gifts were lost as the result of original sin; their loss, however, implied no impairment of the integrity of human nature.

Pride: Unreasonable self-esteem; one of the seven capital sins.

Prie-Dieu: A French phrase, meaning pray God, designating a kneeler or bench suitable for kneeling while at prayer.

Priesthood of the Laity: Lay persons share in the priesthood of Christ in virtue of the sacraments of baptism and confirmation. They are not only joined with Christ for a life of union with him but are also deputed by him for participation in his mission, now carried on by the Church, of worship, teaching, witness and apostolic works. St. Peter called Christians "a royal priesthood" (1 Pt. 2:9) in this connection. St. Thomas Aquinas declared: "The sacramental characters (of baptism and confirmation) are nothing else than certain sharings of the priesthood of Christ, derived from Christ himself."

The priesthood of the laity differs from the official ministerial priesthood of ordained priests and bishops — who have the power of holy orders for celebrating the Eucharist, administering the other sacraments, and providing pastoral care. The ministerial priesthood, by divine commission, serves the universal priesthood. (See Role of Sacraments.)

Primary Option: The life-choice of a person for or against God which shapes the basic orientation of moral conduct.

Prior: A superior or an assistant to an abbot in a monastery.

Privilege: A favor, an exemption from the obligation of a law. Privileges of various kinds, with respect to ecclesiastical laws, are granted by the pope, departments of the Roman Curia and other competent authority in the Church.

Probabilism: A moral system for use in cases of conscience which involve the obligation of doubtful laws. There is a general principle that a doubtful law does not bind. Probabilism, therefore, teaches that it is permissible to follow an opinion favoring liberty, provided the opinion is certainly and solidly probable. Probabilism may not be invoked when there is question of: a certain law or the certain obligation of a law; the certain right of another party; the validity of an action; something which is necessary for salvation.

Pro-Cathedral: A church used as a cathedral.

Promoter of the Faith: An official of the Congregation for the Causes of Saints, whose role in beatification and canonization procedures is to establish beyond reasonable doubt the validity of evidence regarding the holiness of prospective saints and miracles attributed to their intercession.

Prophecies of St. Malachy: These so-called prophecies, listing the designations of 102 popes and 10 antipopes, bear the name they have because they have been falsely attributed to St. Malachy, bishop of Armagh, who died in 1148. Actually, they are forgeries by an unknown author and came to light only in the last decade of the 16th century.

The first 75 prophecies cover the 65 popes and 10 antipopes from Celestine II (1143-1144) to Gregory XIV (1590-91), and are exact with respect to names, coats of arms, birthplaces, and other identifying characteristics. This portion of the work, far from being prophetic, is the result of historical knowledge or hindsight. The 37 designations following that of Gregory are vague, fanciful, and subject to wide interpretation. According to the prophecies, John Paul II, from the Labor of the Sun, will have only two successors before the end of the world.

Prophecy: (1) The communication of divine revelation by inspired intermediaries, called prophets, between God and his people. Old Testament prophecy was unique in its origin and because of its ethical and religious content, which included disclosure of the saving will of Yahweh for the people, moral censures of sin and violations of the Law and Covenant, in the form of promises, admonitions, reproaches and threats. Although Moses and other earlier figures are called prophets, the period of prophecy is generally dated from the early years of the monarchy to about 100 years after the Babylonian Exile. From that time on the written Law and its interpreters supplanted the prophets as guides of the people. Old Testament prophets are cited in the New Testament, with awareness that God spoke through them and that some of their oracles were fulfilled in Christ. John the Baptist is the outstanding prophetic figure in the New Testament. Christ never claimed the title of prophet for himself, although some people thought he was one. There were prophets in the early Church, and St. Paul mentioned the charism of prophecy in 1 Cor. 14:1-5. Prophecy disappeared after New Testament times. Revelation is classified as the prophetic book of the New Testament.

(2) In contemporary non-scriptural usage, the term is applied to the witness given by persons to the relevance of their beliefs in everyday life and action.

Province: (1) A territory comprising one archdiocese called the metropolitan see and one or more dioceses called suffragan sees. The head of the archdiocese, an archbishop, has metropolitan rights and responsibilities over the province.

(2) A division of a religious order under the jurisdiction of a provincial superior.

Prudence: Practical wisdom and judgment regarding the choice and use of the best ways and means of doing good; one of the four cardinal virtues.

Punishment Due for Sin: The punishment which is a consequence of sin. It is of two kinds:

(1) Eternal punishment is the punishment of hell, to which one becomes subject by the commission of mortal sin. Such punishment is remitted when mortal sin is forgiven.

(2) Temporal punishment is a consequence of venial sin and/or forgiven mortal sin; it is not everlasting and may be remitted in this life by means of penance. Temporal punishment unremitted during this life is remitted by suffering in purgatory.

Purgatory: The state or condition in which those who have died in the state of grace, but with some attachment to sin, suffer for a time before they are admitted to the glory and happiness of heaven. In this state and period of passive suffering, they are purified of unrepented venial sins, satisfy the demands of divine justice for temporal punishment due for sins, and are thus converted to a state of worthiness of the beatific vision.

R

Racism: A theory which holds that any one or several of the different races of the human family are inherently superior or inferior to any one or several of the others. The teaching denies the essential unity of the human race, the equality and dignity of all men because of their common possession of the same human nature, and the participation of all men in the divine plan of redemption. It is radically opposed to the virtue of justice and the precept of love of neighbor. Differences of superiority and inferiority which do exist are the result of accidental factors operating in a wide variety of circumstances, and are in no way due to essential defects in any one or several of the branches of the one human race. The theory

of racism, together with practices related to it, is incompatible with Christian doctrine.

Rash Judgment: Attributing faults to another without sufficient reason; a violation of the obligations of justice and charity.

Rationalism: A theory which makes the mind the measure and arbiter of all things, including religious truth. A product of the Enlightenment, it rejects the supernatural, divine revelation, and authoritative teaching by any church.

Recollection: Meditation, attitude of concentration or awareness of spiritual matters and things pertaining to salvation and the accomplishment of God's will.

Relativism: Theory which holds that all truth, including religious truth, is relative, i.e., not absolute, certain or unchanging; a product of agnosticism, indifferentism, and an unwarranted extension of the notion of truth in positive science. Relativism is based on the tenet that certain knowledge of any and all truth is impossible. Therefore, no religion, philosophy or science can be said to possess the real truth; consequently, all religions, philosophies and sciences may be considered to have as much or as little of truth as any of the others.

Relics: The physical remains and effects of saints, which are considered worthy of veneration inasmuch as they are representative of persons in glory with God. First class relics are parts of the bodies of saints, and instruments of their penance and death; second class relics are objects which had some contact with their persons. Catholic doctrine proscribes the view that relics are not worthy of veneration. In line with norms laid down by the Council of Trent and subsequent enactments, discipline concerning relics is subject to control by the Congregation for the Causes of Saints.

Religion: The adoration and service of God as expressed in divine worship and in daily life. Religion is concerned with all of the relations existing between God and man, and between man and man because of the central significance of God. Objectively considered, religion consists of a body of truth which is believed, a code of morality for the guidance of conduct, and a form of divine worship. Subjectively, it is man's total response, theoretically and practically, to the demands of faith; it is living faith, personal engagement, self-commitment to God. Thus, by creed, code and cult, a person orders and directs his life in reference to God and, through what the love and service of God implies, to his fellow men and all things.

Reliquary: A vessel for the preservation and exposition of a relic; sometimes made like a small monstrance.

Reparation: The making of amends to God for sin committed; one of the four ends of prayer and the purpose of penance.

Rescript: A written reply by an ecclesiastical superior regarding a question or request; its provisions bind concerned parties only. Papal dispensations are issued in the form of rescripts.

Reserved Case: A sin or censure, absolution from which is reserved to religious superiors, bishops, the pope, or confessors having special faculties. Reservations are made because of the serious nature and social effects of certain sins and censures.

Restitution: An act of reparation for an injury done to another. The injury may be caused by taking and/or retaining what belongs to another or by damaging either the property or reputation of another. The intention of making restitution, usually in kind, is required as a condition for the forgiveness of sins of injustice, even though actual restitution is not possible.

Ring: In the Church a ring is worn as part of the insignia of bishops, abbots, et al.; by sisters to denote their consecration to God and the Church. The wedding ring symbolizes the love and union of husband and wife.

Ritual: A book of prayers and ceremonies used in the administration of the sacraments and other ceremonial functions. In the Roman Rite, the standard book of this kind is the Roman Ritual. Revisions have been made — e.g., in the rites of baptism — since the Second Vatican Council.

Rogito: The official notarial act or document testifying to the burial of a pope.

Rosary: A form of mental and vocal prayer centered on mysteries or events in the lives of Jesus and Mary. Its essential elements are meditation on the mysteries and the recitation of a number of decades of Hail Marys, each beginning with the Lord's Prayer. Introductory prayers may include the Apostles' Creed, an initial Our Father, three Hail Marys and a Glory be to the Father; each decade is customarily concluded with a Glory be to the Father; at the end, it is customary to say the Hail, Holy Queen and a prayer from the liturgy for the feast of the Blessed Virgin Mary of the Rosary.

The **Mysteries of the Rosary,** which are the subject of meditation, are: (1) Joyful — the Annunciation to Mary that she was to be the Mother of Christ, her visit to Elizabeth, the birth of Jesus, the presentation of Jesus in the Temple, the finding of Jesus in the Temple. (2) Sorrowful — Christ's agony in the Garden of Gethsemani, scourging at the pillar, crowning with thorns, carrying of the Cross to Calvary, and crucifixion. (3) Glorious — the Resurrection and Ascension of Christ, the descent of the Holy Spirit upon the Apostles, Mary's Assumption into heaven and her crowning as Queen of angels and men.

The complete Rosary, called the Dominican Rosary, consists of 15 decades. In customary practice, only five decades are usually said at one time. Rosary beads are used to aid in counting the prayers without distraction.

The Rosary originated through the coalescence of popular devotions to Jesus and Mary from the 12th century onward. Its present form dates from about the 15th century. Carthusians contributed greatly toward its development; Dominicans have been its greatest promoters.

S

Sabbath: The seventh day of the week, observed by Jews and Sabbatarians as the day for rest and religious observance.

Sacramentary: One of the first liturgical books, containing the celebrant's part of the Mass and rites for administration of the sacraments. The earliest book of this kind, the Leonine Sacramentary, dates from the middle or end of the sixth century.

The sacramentary, incorporating most of the contents of the *Roman Missal,* was reintroduced in the Roman Rite following the promulgation of the *Constitution on the Sacred Liturgy* by the Second Vatican Council.

Sacrarium: A basin with a drain leading directly into the ground; standard equipment of a sacristy.

Sacred Heart, Enthronement: An acknowledgment of the sovereignty of Jesus Christ over the Christian family, expressed by the installation of an image or picture of the Sacred Heart in a place of honor in the home, accompanied by an act of consecration.

Sacred Heart, Promises: Twelve promises to persons having devotion to the Sacred Heart of Jesus, which were communicated by Christ to St. Margaret Mary Alacoque in a private revelation in 1675: (1) I will give them all the graces necessary in their state in life. (2) I will establish peace in their homes. (3) I will comfort them in all their afflictions. (4) I will be their secure refuge during life and, above all, in death. (5) I will bestow abundant blessing upon all their undertakings. (6) Sinners shall find in my Heart the source and the infinite ocean of mercy. (7) By devotion to my Heart tepid souls shall grow fervent. (8) Fervent souls shall quickly mount to high perfection. (9) I will bless every place where a picture of my Heart shall be set up and honored. (10) I will give to priests the gift of touching the most hardened hearts. (11) Those who promote this devotion shall have their names written in my Heart, never to be blotted out. (12) I will grant the grace of final penitence to those who communicate (receive Holy Communion) on the first Friday of nine consecutive months.

Sacrilege: Violation of and irreverence toward a person, place or thing that is sacred because of public dedication to God; a sin against the virtue of religion. Personal sacrilege is violence of some kind against a cleric or religious, or a violation of chastity with a cleric or religious. Local sacrilege is the desecration of sacred places. Real sacrilege is irreverence with respect to sacred things, such as the sacraments and sacred vessels.

Sacristy: A utility room where vestments, church furnishings and sacred vessels are kept and where the clergy vest for sacred functions.

Sadducees: The predominantly priestly party among the Jews in the time of Christ, noted for extreme conservatism, acceptance only of the Law of Moses, and rejection of the traditions of the elders. Their opposite numbers were the Pharisees.

Saints, Cult of: The veneration, called dulia, of holy persons who have died and are in glory with God in heaven; it includes honoring them and petitioning them for their intercession with God. Liturgical veneration is given only to saints officially recognized by the Church; private veneration may be given to anyone thought to be in heaven. The veneration of saints is essentially different from the adoration given to God alone; by its very nature, however, it terminates in the worship of God.

According to the Second Vatican Council's *Dogmatic Constitution on the Church* (No. 50): "It is supremely fitting . . . that we love those friends and fellow heirs of Jesus Christ, who are also our brothers and extraordinary benefactors, that we render due thanks to God for them and 'suppliantly invoke them and have recourse to their prayers, their power and help in obtaining benefits from God through His Son, Jesus Christ, our Lord, who is our sole Redeemer and Savior.' For by its very nature every genuine testimony of love which we show to those in heaven tends toward and terminates in Christ, who is the 'crown of all saints.' Through Him it tends toward and terminates in God, who is wonderful in His saints and is magnified in them."

Salvation: The liberation of men from sin and its effects, reconciliation with God in and through Christ, the attainment of union with God forever in the glory of heaven as the supreme purpose of life and as the God-given reward for fulfillment of his will on earth. Salvation-in-process begins and continues in this life through union with Christ in faith professed and in action; its final term is union with God and the whole community of the saved in the ultimate perfection of God's kingdom. The Church teaches that: God wills the salvation of all men; men are saved in and through Christ; membership in the Church established by Christ, known and understood as the community of salvation, is necessary for salvation; men with this knowledge and understanding who deliberately reject this Church, cannot be saved. In the context of Catholic belief, the Catholic Church is the Church founded by Christ. (See below, Salvation outside the Church.)

Salvation History: The facts and the record

of God's relations with men, in the past, present and future, for the purpose of leading them to live in accordance with his will for the eventual attainment after death of salvation, or everlasting happiness with him in heaven.

The essentials of salvation history are: God's love for all men and will for their salvation; his intervention and action in the world to express this love and bring about their salvation; the revelation he made of himself and the covenant he established with the Israelites in the Old Testament; the perfecting of this revelation and the new covenant of grace through Christ in the New Testament; the continuing action-for-salvation carried on in and through the Mystical Body of Christ, the Church; the communication of saving grace to men through the merits of Christ and the operations of the Holy Spirit in the here-and-now circumstances of daily life and with the cooperation of men themselves.

Salvation outside the Church: The Second Vatican Council covered this subject summarily in the following manner: "Those also can attain to everlasting salvation who through no fault of their own do not know the gospel of Christ or His Church, yet sincerely seek God and, moved by grace, strive by their deeds to do His will as it is known to them through the dictates of conscience. Nor does divine Providence deny the help necessary for salvation to those who, without blame on their part, have not yet arrived at an explicit knowledge of God, but who strive to live a good life, thanks to His grace. Whatever good or truth is found among them is looked upon by the Church as a preparation for the gospel. She regards such qualities as given by Him who enlightens all men so that they may finally have life" *(Dogmatic Constitution on the Church,* No. 16).

Satanism: Worship of the devil, a blasphemous inversion of the order of worship which is due to God alone.

Scandal: Conduct which is the occasion of sin to another person.

Scapular: (1) A part of the habit of some religious orders like the Benedictines and Dominicans; a nearly shoulder-wide strip of cloth worn over the tunic and reaching almost to the feet in front and behind. Originally a kind of apron, it came to symbolize the cross and yoke of Christ.

(2) Scapulars worn by lay persons as a sign of association with religious orders and for devotional purposes are an adaptation of monastic scapulars. Approved by the Church as sacramentals, they consist of two small squares of woolen cloth joined by strings and are worn about the neck. They are given for wearing in a ceremony of investiture or enrollment. There are nearly 20 scapulars for devotional use: the five principal ones are generally understood to include those of Our Lady of Mt. Carmel (the brown Carmelite Scapular), the Holy Trinity, Our Lady of the

Seven Dolors, the Passion, the Immaculate Conception.

Scapular Medal: A medallion with a representation of the Sacred Heart on one side and of the Blessed Virgin Mary on the other. Authorized by St. Pius X in 1910, it may be worn or carried in place of a scapular by persons already invested with a scapular.

Scapular Promise: According to a legend of the Carmelite Order, the Blessed Virgin Mary appeared to St. Simon Stock in 1251 at Cambridge and declared that wearers of the brown Carmelite Scapular would be saved from hell and taken to heaven by her on the first Saturday after death. The validity of the legend has never been the subject of official decision by the Church. Essentially, it expresses belief in the intercession of Mary and the efficacy of sacramentals in the context of truly Christian life.

Schism: Derived from a Greek word meaning separation, the term designates formal and obstinate refusal by a baptized person, called a *schismatic,* to be in communion with the pope and the Church. The canonical penalty is excommunication. One of the most disastrous schisms in history resulted in the definitive separation of the Church in the East from union with Rome about 1054.

Scholasticism: The term usually applied to the Catholic theology and philosophy which developed in the Middle Ages.

Scribes: Hebrew intellectuals noted for their knowledge of the Law of Moses, influential from the time of the Exile to about 70 A.D. Many of them were Pharisees. They were the antecedents of rabbis and their traditions, as well as those of the Pharisees, had a lasting influence on Judaism following the destruction of Jerusalem in 70 A.D.

Scruple: A morbid, unreasonable fear and anxiety that one's actions are sinful when they are not, or more seriously sinful than they actually are. Compulsive scrupulosity is quite different from the transient scrupulosity of persons of tender or highly sensitive conscience, or of persons with faulty moral judgment.

Seal of Confession: The obligation of secrecy which must be observed regarding knowledge of things learned in connection with the confession of sin in the sacrament of penance. The seal covers matters whose revelation would make the sacrament burdensome. Confessors are prohibited, under penalty of excommunication, from making any direct revelation of confessional matter; this prohibition holds, outside of confession, even with respect to the person who made the confession unless the person releases the priest from the obligation. Persons other than confessors are obliged to maintain secrecy, but not under penalty of excommunication. General, non-specific discussion of confessional matter does not violate the seal.

Secularism: A school of thought, a spirit and manner of action which ignores and/or repudiates the validity or influence of supernatural religion with respect to individual and social life. In describing secularism in their annual statement in 1947, the bishops of the United States said in part: ". . . There are many men — and their number is daily increasing — who in practice live their lives without recognizing that this is God's world. For the most part they do not deny God. On formal occasions they may even mention his name. Not all of them would subscribe to the statement that all moral values derive from merely human conventions. But they fail to bring an awareness of their responsibility to God into their thought and action as individuals and members of society. This, in essence, is what we mean by secularism."

See: Another name for diocese or archdiocese.

Seminary: A house of study and formation for men, called seminarians, preparing for the priesthood. Traditional seminaries date from the Council of Trent in the middle of the 16th century; before that time, candidates for the priesthood were variously trained in monastic schools, universities under church auspices, and in less formal ways. At the present time, seminaries are undergoing considerable change for the improvement of academic and formation programs and procedures.

Sermon on the Mount: A compilation of sayings of Our Lord in the form of an extended discourse in Matthew's Gospel (5:1 to 7:27) and, in a shorter discourse, in Luke (6:17-49). The passage in Matthew, called the "Constitution of the New Law," summarizes the living spirit of believers in Christ and members of the kingdom of God. Beginning with the Beatitudes and including the Lord's Prayer, it covers the perfect justice of the New Law, the fulfillment of the Old Law in the New Law of Christ, and the integrity of internal attitude and external conduct with respect to love of God and neighbor, justice, chastity, truth, trust and confidence in God.

Servile Work: Work that is mainly physical and done for the sake of material purposes, in distinction from so-called liberal and artistic work which, although involving physical effort, is of a mental and intellectual nature. Commonly classified as servile are such works as farming, manufacturing, commercial operations, mining, etc. Liberal works are those like studying, teaching, designing, writing, typing, etc. The classification of work as servile or otherwise depends in part on custom and cultural interpretation. The reception of pay for work has nothing to do with its classification. Servile work is prohibited on Sundays and holy days of obligation unless there is sound reason for it.

Seven Last Words of Christ: Words of Christ on the Cross. (1) "Father, forgive them; for they do not know what they are doing." (2) To the penitent thief: "I assure you: today you will be with me in Paradise." (3) To Mary and his Apostle John: "Woman, there is your son . . . There is your mother." (4) "My God, my God, why have you forsaken me?" (5) "I am thirsty." (6) "Now it is finished." (7) "Father, into your hands I commend my spirit."

Shrine, Crowned: A shrine approved by the Holy See as a place of pilgrimage. The approval permits public devotion at the shrine and implies that at least one miracle has resulted from devotion at the shrine. Among the best known crowned shrines are those of the Virgin Mary at Lourdes and Fatima.

Shroud of Turin: A strip of brownish linen cloth, 14 feet, three inches in length and three feet, seven inches in width, bearing the front and back imprint of a human body. A tradition dating from the seventh century, which has not been verified beyond doubt, claims that the shroud is the fine linen in which the body of Christ was wrapped for burial. The early history of the shroud is obscure. It was enshrined at Lirey, France, in 1354 and was transferred in 1578 to Turin, Italy, where it has been kept in the cathedral down to the present time. Scientific investigation, which began in 1898, seems to indicate that the markings on the shroud are those of a human body. The shroud, for the first time since 1933, was placed on public view from Aug. 27 to Oct. 8, 1978, and was seen by an estimated 3.3 million people. Scientists conducted intensive studies of it for several days after the end of public viewing.

Sick Calls: When a person is confined at home by illness or other cause and is unable to go to church for reception of the sacraments, a parish priest should be informed and arrangements made for him to visit the person at home. Such visitations are common in pastoral practice, both for special needs and for providing persons with regular opportunities for receiving the sacraments.

Prepared for the visit should be: a conveniently placed table covered with a white cloth; on it should be a crucifix, two lighted candles, a glass with water, a spoon and napkin.

The priest, carrying the Blessed Sacrament, should be escorted to and from the sick person by someone carrying a lighted candle. Members of the household should be present when the sick person receives Holy Communion and/or anointing of the sick.

Sign of the Cross: A sign, ceremonial gesture or movement in the form of a cross by which a person confesses faith in the Holy Trinity and Christ, and intercedes for the blessing of himself, other persons, and things. In Roman-Rite practice, a person making the sign touches the fingers of the right hand to his forehead, below the breast, left shoulder and right shoulder while saying: "In the name of the Father, and of the Son, and of the Holy Spirit." The sign is also made with the thumb on the forehead, the lips, and the breast. For the blessing of persons and objects, a large sign of the cross is made by movement of the right hand. In Eastern-Rite practice, the sign is made with the thumb and first two fingers of the right hand joined together and touching the forehead, below the breast, the right shoulder and the left shoulder; the formula generally used is the doxology, "O Holy God, O Holy Strong One, O Immortal One." The Eastern manner of making the sign was general until the first half of the 13th century; by the 17th century, Western practice involved the whole right hand and the reversal of direction from shoulder to shoulder.

Signs of the Times: Contemporary events, trends and features in culture and society, the needs and aspirations of people, all the factors that form the context in and through which the Church has to carry on its saving mission. The Second Vatican Council spoke on numerous occasions about these signs and the relationship between them and a kind of manifestation of God's will, positive or negative, and about subjecting them to judgment and action corresponding to the demands of divine revelation through Scripture, Christ, and the experience, tradition and teaching authority of the Church.

Simony: The deliberate intention and act of selling and/or buying spiritual goods or material things so connected with the spiritual that they cannot be separated therefrom; a violation of the virtue of religion, and a sacrilege, because it wrongfully puts a material price on spiritual things, which cannot be either sold or bought. In church law, actual sale or purchase is subject to censure in some cases. The term is derived from the name of Simon Magus, who attempted to buy from Sts. Peter and John the power to confirm people in the Holy Spirit (Acts 8:4-24).

Sin: (1) Actual sin is rejection of God manifested by free and deliberate violation of his law by thought, word or action. (a) Mortal sin — involving serious matter, sufficient reflection and full consent — results in total alienation from God, making a person dead to sanctifying grace, incapable of performing meritorious supernatural acts and subject to everlasting punishment. (b) Venial sin — involving less serious matter, reflection and consent — does not have such serious consequences.

(2) Original sin (See separate entry).

Sins against the Holy Spirit: Despair of salvation, presumption of God's mercy, impugning the known truths of faith, envy at another's spiritual good, obstinacy in sin, final impenitence. Those guilty of such sins stubbornly resist the influence of grace and, as long as they do so, cannot be forgiven.

Sins, Occasions of: Circumstances (persons, places, things, etc.) which easily lead to sin. There is an obligation to avoid voluntary proximate occasions of sin, and to take precautions against the dangers of unavoidable occasions.

Sins That Cry to Heaven for Vengeance: Willful murder, sins against nature, oppression of the poor, widows and orphans, defrauding laborers of their wages.

Sister: Any woman religious, in popular speech; strictly, the title applies only to women religious belonging to institutes whose members never professed solemn vows. Most of the institutes whose members are properly called sisters were established during and since the 19th century. Women religious with solemn vows, or belonging to institutes whose members formerly professed solemn vows, are properly called nuns.

Sisterhood: A generic term referring to the whole institution of the life of women religious in the Church, or to a particular institute of women religious.

Situation Ethics: A subjective, individualistic ethical theory which denies the binding force of ethical principles as universal laws and preceptive norms of moral conduct, and proposes that morality is determined only by situational conditions and considerations and the intention of the person. In an instruction issued on the subject in May, 1956, the Congregation for the Holy Office said:

"It ignores the principles of objective ethics. This 'New Morality,' it is claimed, is not only the equal of objective morality, but is superior to it.

"The authors who follow this system state that the ultimate determining norm for activity is not the objective order as determined by the natural law and known with certainty from this law. It is instead some internal judgment and illumination of the mind of every individual by which the mind comes to know what is to be done in a concrete situation.

"This ultimate decision of man is, therefore, not the application of the objective law to a particular case after the particular circumstances of a 'situation' have been considered and weighed according to the rules of prudence, as the more important authors of objective ethics teach; but it is, according to them, immediate, internal illumination and judgment.

"With regard to its objective truth and correctness, this judgment, at least in many things, is not ultimately measured, is not to be measured or is not measurable by any objective norm found outside man and independent of his subjective persuasion, but it is fully sufficient in itself. . . .

"Much that is stated in this system of 'Situation Ethics' is contrary to the truth of reality and to the dictate of sound reason. It gives evidence of relativism and modernism, and deviates far from the Catholic teaching handed down through the ages."

Slander: Attributing to a person faults which he does not have; a violation of the obligations of justice and charity, for which restitution is due.

Sloth: One of the seven capital sins; spiritual laziness, involving distaste and disgust for spiritual things; spiritual boredom, which saps the vigor of spiritual life. Physical laziness is a counterpart of spiritual sloth.

Sorcery: A kind of black magic in which evil is invoked by means of diabolical intervention; a violation of the virtue of religion.

Soteriology: The division of theology which treats of the mission and work of Christ as Redeemer.

Species, Sacred: The appearances of bread and wine (color, taste, smell, etc.) which remain after the substance has been changed at the Consecration of the Mass into the Body and Blood of Christ. (See Transubstantiation.)

Spiritism: Attempts to communicate with spirits and departed souls by means of seances, table tapping, ouija boards, and other methods; a violation of the virtue of religion. Spiritualistic practices are noted for fakery.

Spiritual Works of Mercy: Works of spiritual assistance, motivated by love of God and neighbor, to persons in need: counseling the doubtful, instructing the ignorant, admonishing sinners, comforting the afflicted, forgiving offenses, bearing wrongs patiently, praying for the living and the dead.

Stational Churches, Days: Churches, especially in Rome, where the clergy and lay people were accustomed to gather with their bishop on certain days for the celebration of the liturgy. The 25 early titular or parish churches of Rome, plus other churches, each had their turn as the site of divine worship in practices which may have started in the third century. The observances were rather well developed toward the latter part of the fourth century, and by the fifth they included a Mass concelebrated by the pope and attendant priests. On some occasions, the stational liturgy was preceded by a procession from another church called a collecta. There were 42 Roman stational churches in the eighth century, and 89 stational services were scheduled annually in connection with the liturgical seasons. Stational observances fell into disuse toward the end of the Middle Ages. Some revival was begun by John XXIII in 1959 and continued by Paul VI.

Stations of the Cross: A series of meditations on the sufferings of Christ: his condemnation to death and taking up of the Cross; the first fall on the way to Calvary; meeting his Mother; being assisted by Simon of Cyrene, and by Veronica who wiped his face; the second fall; meeting the women of Jerusalem; the third fall; being stripped and nailed to the Cross; his death; the removal of his body from the Cross and his burial. Depictions of these scenes are mounted in most churches, chapels and in some other places, beneath small crosses.

A person making the Way of the Cross passes before these Stations, or stopping points, pausing at each for meditation. If the Stations are made by a group of people, only the leader has to pass from Station to Station. Prayer for the intentions of the pope is required for gaining the indulgence.

Those unable to make the Stations in the ordinary manner, because they are impeded from visiting a church or other place where the Stations are, can still practice the devotion by meditating on the sufferings of Christ; praying the Our Father, Hail Mary and Glory for each Station and five times in commemoration of the wounds of Christ; and praying for the intentions of the pope. This practice has involved the use of a Stations Crucifix.

A recent development in this devotion is toward greater awareness of the relation of the Passion to the Resurrection-Ascension; this trend, in some circles, has led to the erection of a 15th — unofficial — station. The concept amounts to an extension of the whole customary thrust of the devotion.

The Stations originated, remotely, from the practice of Holy Land pilgrims who visited the actual scenes of incidents in the Passion of Christ. Representations elsewhere of at least some of these scenes were known as early as the fifth century. Later, the Stations evolved in connection with and as a consequence of strong devotion to the Passion in the 12th and 13th centuries. Franciscans, who were given custody of the Holy Places in 1342, promoted the devotion widely; one of them, St. Leonard of Port Maurice, became known as the greatest preacher of the Way of the Cross in the 18th century. The general features of the devotion were fixed by Clement XII in 1731.

Statutes: Virtually the same as decrees (see separate entry), they almost always designate laws of a particular council or synod rather than pontifical laws.

Stigmata: Marks of the wounds suffered by Christ in his crucifixion, in hands and feet by nails, and side by the piercing of a lance. Some persons, called stigmatists, have been reported as recipients or sufferers of marks like these. The Church, however, has never issued any infallible declaration about their possession by anyone, even in the case of St. Francis of Assisi whose stigmata seem to be the best substantiated and may be commemorated in the Roman-Rite liturgy. Ninety percent of some 300 reputed stigmatists have been women. Judgment regarding the presence, significance, and manner of causation of stigmata would depend, among other things, on irrefutable experimental evidence.

Stipend, Mass: An offering given to a priest for applying the fruits of the Mass according to the intention of the donor. The offering is a contribution to the support of the priest. The disposition of the fruits of the sacrifice, in line with doctrine concerning the Mass in particular and prayer in general, is subject to the will of God. In the early Christian centuries, when Mass was not offered for the intentions of particular persons, the participants made offerings of bread and wine for the sacrifice and their own Holy Communion, and of other things useful for the support of the clergy and the poor. Some offerings may have been made as early as the fourth century for the celebration of Mass for particular intentions, and there are indications of the existence of this practice from the sixth century when private Masses began to be offered. The earliest certain proof of stipend practice, however, dates from the eighth century. By the 11th century, along with private Mass, it was established custom.

Stole Fee: An offering given on certain occasions; e.g., at a baptism, wedding, funeral, for the support of the clergy who administer the sacraments and perform other sacred rites.

Stoup: A vessel used to contain holy water.

Suffragan See: Any diocese, except the archdiocese, within a province.

Suicide: The taking of one's own life; a violation of God's dominion over human life. Ecclesiastical burial is denied to persons who deliberately commit suicide while in full possession of their faculties; it is permitted in cases of doubt.

Supererogation: Good and virtuous actions which go beyond the obligations of duty and the requirements enjoined by God's law as necessary for salvation. Examples of these works are the profession and observance of the evangelical counsels of poverty, chastity, and obedience, and efforts to practice charity to the highest degree.

Supernatural: Above the natural; that which exceeds and is not due or owed to the essence, exigencies, requirements, powers and merits of created nature. While man has no claim on supernatural things and does not need them in order to exist and act on a natural level, he does need them in order to exist and act in the higher order or economy of grace established by God for his salvation.

God has freely given to man certain things which are beyond the powers and rights of his human nature. Examples of the supernatural are: grace, a kind of participation by man in the divine life, by which man becomes capable of performing acts meritorious for salvation; divine revelation by which God manifests himself to man and makes known truth that is inaccessible to human reason alone; faith, by which man believes divine truth because of the authority of God who reveals it through Sacred Scripture and tradition and the teaching of his Church.

Superstition: A violation of the virtue of religion, by which God is worshipped in an unworthy manner or creatures are given honor which belongs to God alone. False, vain, or futile worship involves elements which are incompatible with the honor and respect due to God, such as error, deception, and bizarre practices. Examples are: false and exaggerated devotions, chain prayers and allegedly unfailing prayers, the mixing of unbecoming practices in worship. The second kind of superstition attributes to persons and things powers and honor which belong to God alone. Examples are: idolatry, divination, magic, spiritism, necromancy.

Suspension: A penalty by which a cleric is forbidden to exercise some or all of his powers of orders and jurisdiction, or to accept the financial support of his benefices.

Swearing: Taking an oath; calling upon God to witness the truth of a statement; a legitimate thing to do for serious reasons and under proper circumstances, as in a court of law. To swear without sufficient reason is to dishonor God's name; to swear falsely in a court of law is perjury.

Swedenborgianism: A doctrine developed in and from the writings of Emmanuel Swedenborg (1688-1772), who claimed that during a number of visions he had in 1745 Christ taught him the spiritual sense of Sacred Scripture and commissioned him to communicate it to others. He held that, just as Christianity succeeded Judaism, so his teaching supplemented Christianity. He rejected belief in the Trinity, original sin, the Resurrection, and all the sacraments except baptism and the Eucharist. His followers are members of the Church of the New Jerusalem or of the New Church.

Syllabus, The: (1) When not qualified, the term refers to the list of 80 errors accompanying Pope Pius IX's encyclical *Quanta Cura*, issued in 1864.

(2) The *Syllabus* of St. Pius X in the decree *Lamentabili*, issued by the Holy Office July 4, 1907, condemning 65 heretical propositions of modernism. This schedule of errors was followed shortly by that pope's encyclical *Pascendi*, the principal ecclesiastical document against modernism, issued Sept. 8, 1907.

Synod, Diocesan: Meeting of representative persons of a diocese — priests, religious, lay persons — with the bishop, called by him for the purpose of considering and taking action on matters affecting the life and mission of the Church in the diocese. Persons taking part in a synod have consultative status; the bishop alone is the legislator, with power to authorize synodal decrees. According to canon law, every diocese should have a synod every 10 years.

T

Te Deum: The opening Latin words, Thee, God, of a hymn of praise and thanksgiving prescribed for use in the Office of Readings (Matins of the Liturgy of the Hours) on many Sundays, solemnities and feasts.

Temperance: Moderation, one of the four cardinal virtues.

Temptation: Any enticement to sin, from any source: the strivings of one's own faculties, the action of the devil, other persons, circumstances of life, etc. Temptation itself is not sin. Temptation can be avoided and overcome with the use of prudence and the help of grace.

Thanksgiving: An expression of gratitude to God for his goodness and the blessings he grants; one of the four ends of prayer.

Theism: A philosophy which admits the existence of God and the possibility of divine revelation; it is generally monotheistic and acknowledges God as transcendent and also active in the world. Because it is a philosophy rather than a system of theology derived from revelation, it does not include specifically Christian doctrines, like those concerning the Trinity, the Incarnation and Redemption.

Theological Virtues: The virtues which have God for their direct object: faith, or belief in God's infallible teaching; hope, or confidence in divine assistance; charity, or love of God. They are given to a person with grace in the first instance, through baptism and incorporation in Christ.

Theology: Knowledge of God and religion, deriving from and based on the data of divine Revelation, organized and systematized according to some kind of scientific method. It involves systematic study and presentation of the truths of divine Revelation in Sacred Scripture, tradition, and the teaching of the Church.

The Second Vatican Council made the following declaration about theology and its relation to divine Revelation: "Sacred theology rests on the written word of God, together with sacred tradition, as its primary and perpetual foundation. By scrutinizing in the light of faith all truth stored up in the mystery of Christ, theology is most powerfully strengthened and constantly rejuvenated by that word. For the sacred Scriptures contain the word of God and, since they are inspired, really are the word of God; and so the study of the sacred page is, as it were, the soul of sacred theology" *(Constitution on Revelation.* No. 24).

Theology has been divided under various subject headings. Some of the major fields have been: dogma, moral, pastoral, ascetics (the practice of virtue and means of attaining holiness and perfection), mysticism (higher states of religious experience). Other subject headings include ecumenism (Christian unity, interfaith relations), ecclesiology (the nature and constitution of the Church), Mariology (doctrine concerning the Blessed Virgin Mary), the sacraments, etc.

Tithing: Contribution of a portion of one's income, originally one-tenth, for purposes of religion and charity. The practice is mentioned 46 times in the Bible. In early Christian times, tithing was adopted in continuance of Old Testament practices of the Jewish people, and the earliest positive church legislation on the subject was enacted in 567. Catholics are bound in conscience to contribute to the support of their church, but the manner in which they do so is not fixed by law. Tithing, which amounts to a pledged contribution of a portion of one's income, has aroused new attention in recent years in the United States.

Titular Sees: Dioceses where the Church once flourished but which later were overrun by pagans or Moslems and now exist only in name or title. Bishops without a territorial or residential diocese of their own; e.g., auxiliary bishops, are given titular sees.

Transfinalization, Transignification: Terms coined to express the sign value of consecrated bread and wine with respect to the presence and action of Christ in the Eucharistic sacrifice and the spiritually vivifying purpose of the Eucharistic banquet in Holy Communion. The theory behind the terms has strong undertones of existential and "sign" philosophy, and has been criticized for its openness to interpretations at variance with the doctrine of transubstantiation and the abiding presence of Christ under the appearances of bread and wine after the sacrifice of the Mass and Communion have been completed. The terms, if used as substitutes for transubstantiation, are unacceptable; if they presuppose transubstantiation, they are acceptable as clarifications of its meaning.

Transubstantiation; "The way Christ is made present in this sacrament (Holy Eucharist) is none other than by the change of the whole substance of the bread into his Body, and of the whole substance of the wine into his Blood (in the Consecration at Mass) . . . this ˙ unique and wonderful change the Catholic Church rightly calls transubstantiation" (encyclical *Mysterium Fidei* of Paul VI, Sept. 3, 1965). The first official use of the term was made by the Fourth Council of the Lateran in 1215. Authoritative teaching on the subject was issued by the Council of Trent.

Treasury of the Church: The superabundant merits of Christ and the saints from which the Church draws to confer spiritual benefits, such as indulgences.

Triduum: A three-day series of public or private devotions.

U-Z

Usury: Excessive interest charged for the loan and use of money; a violation of justice.

Veronica: A word resulting from the combination of a Latin word for true, *vera*, and a Greek word for image, *eikon*, designating a likeness of the face of Christ or the name of a woman said to have given him a cloth on which he caused an imprint of his face to appear. The veneration at Rome of a likeness depicted on cloth dates from about the end of the 10th century; it figured in a popular devotion during the Middle Ages, and in the Holy Face devotion practiced since the 19th century. A faint, undiscernible likeness said to be of this kind is preserved in St. Peter's Basilica. The origin of the likeness is uncertain, and the identity of the woman is unknown. Before the 14th century, there were no known artistic representations of an incident concerning a woman who wiped the face of Christ with a piece of cloth while He was carrying the Cross to Calvary.

Viaticum: Holy Communion given to those in danger of death. The word, derived from Latin, means provision for a journey through death to life hereafter.

Vicar General: A prelate appointed by a bishop to help him, as a deputy, in the administration of his diocese. Because of his office, he has the same jurisdictional authority as the bishop except in cases reserved to the bishop by himself or by church law.

Virginity: Observance of perpetual sexual abstinence. The state of virginity, which is embraced for the love of God by religious with a public vow or by others with a private vow, was singled out for high praise by Christ (Mt. 19:10-12) and has always been so regarded by the Church. In the encyclical *Sacra Virginitas,* Pius XII stated: "Holy virginity and that perfect chastity which is consecrated to the service of God is without doubt among the most perfect treasures which the founder of the Church has left in heritage to the society which he established."

Paul VI approved in 1970 a rite in which women can consecrate their virginity "to Christ and their brethren" without becoming members of a religious institute. The *Ordo Consecrationis Virginum,* a revision of a rite promulgated by Clement VII in 1596, is traceable to the Roman liturgy of about 500.

Virtue: A habit or established capability for performing good actions. Virtues are *natural* (acquired and increased by repeating good acts) and/or *supernatural* (given with grace by God).

Vocation: A call to a way of life. Generally, the term applies to the common call of all men, from God, to holiness and salvation. Specifically, it refers to particular states of life, each called a vocation, in which response is made to this universal call; viz., marriage, the religious life and/or priesthood, the single state freely chosen or accepted for the accomplishment of God's will. The term also applies to the various occupations in which persons make a living. The Church supports the freedom of each individual in choosing a particular vocation, and reserves the right to pass on the acceptability of candidates for the priesthood and religious life. Signs or indicators of particular vocations are many, including a person's talents and interests, circumstances and obligations, invitations of grace and willingness to respond thereto.

Vow: A promise made to God with sufficient knowledge and freedom, which has as its object a moral good that is possible and better than its voluntary omission. A person who professes a vow binds himself by the virtue of religion to fulfill his promise. The best known examples of vows are those of poverty, chastity and obedience professed by religious (see Evangelical Counsels, individual entries).

Public vows are made before a competent person, acting as an agent of the Church, who accepts the profession in the name of the Church, thereby giving public recognition to the person's dedication and consecration to God and divine worship. Vows of this kind are either solemn, rendering all contrary acts invalid as well as unlawful; or simple, rendering contrary acts unlawful. Solemn vows are for life; simple vows are for a definite period of time or for life. Vows professed without public recognition by the Church are called private vows. The Church, which has authority to accept and give public recognition to vows, also has authority to dispense persons from their obligations for serious reasons.

Week of Prayer for Christian Unity: Eight days of prayer, from Jan. 18 to 25, for the union of all men in the Church established by Christ. On the initiative of Father Paul James Francis, S.A., of Graymoor, N.Y., it originated in 1908 as the Chair of Unity Octave. In recent years, its observance on an interfaith basis has increased greatly.

Witness, Christian: Practical testimony or evidence given by Christians of their faith in all circumstances of life — by prayer and general conduct, through good example and good works, etc.; being and acting in accordance with Christian belief; actual practice of the Christian faith.

Zucchetto: A skullcap worn by bishops and other prelates.

OUR LADY OF CZESTOCHOWA

The Black Madonna, the icon of Our Lady of Czestochowa, is enshrined on the "Hill of Light," Jasna Gora, above the city of Czestochowa in south central Poland. Long the center and focus of Marian devotion since it was brought there in 1382, it is the primary symbol of Polish religious faith and freedom.

The icon is a portrayal of Mary holding the Child Jesus. Their faces and hands are dark, as though they had been burned or stained by smoke. Three cuts are on one of Mary's cheeks, put there by robbers who desecrated the icon in 1430.

The origin of the icon is not clear. Elements of the legend say it was painted by St. Luke on a panel made by St. Joseph for the home of the Holy Family in Nazareth; that it was transported from the Holy Land to Constantinople; that it was given in 988 to a Ukrainian princess, Anna, the wife of Vladimir of Kiev; and that it eventually was brought to Czestochowa in 1382. The *Catholic Encyclopedia* notes another possibility, that the icon was of Greek-Italian origin in the ninth century.

The location of the icon on the hill above Czestochowa was related to the establishment of a priory of Pauline monks there, also in 1382. A shrine was built some time after 1386. A church was erected in 1644, and a 344-foot tower was raised in 1702.

Our Lady of Czestochowa was declared the Queen of Poland in 1656, and the icon was solemnly crowned in 1717 during the pontificate of Pope Clement XI.

The shrine has a long history as the greatest pilgrimage and religious center in Central Europe.

The shrine has undergone changes, some of them violent, in the years since 1382. Even in this century it has been a target of search and harassment by officials of the Communist government in control of the country since the end of World War II.

One thing has not changed, however; that is the significance of the icon and Czestochowa in the religious and patriotic life of the Polish people.

There are those who claim that Czestochowa is a more important capital of the nation than Warsaw.

600th Anniversary

More than 200,000 persons converged on the Marian shrine at Jasna Gora Aug. 26, 1982, for a climactic celebration marking the 600th anniversary of the arrival of the icon of Our Lady of Czestochowa in Poland.

The celebration capped six years of preparation by Catholics throughout the country. During that time, the bishops said in a letter read in churches Aug. 6:

"The thread of Mary of Jasna Gora was woven incessantly through the program of the last six years. This was by way of commemoration of the religious-national events linked with the name of Mary over those 600 years, encouragement of gratitude, union between daily religious living and the vows of the millennium (the thousand years of Catholic faith in the country), and encouragement in a particular way to assist the Church."

Pope John Paul was prevented by government authorities from attending the celebration. This was one of the reasons for an extension of the jubilee year until September, 1983. It was expected that he would visit Poland and the shrine by that time.

The Church in Countries Throughout the World

(Principal sources for statistics: *Statistical Yearbook of the Church, 1980* (the latest edition available); *Annuario Pontificio, 1982*. Figures are as of Dec. 31, 1980, or Dec. 31 of the year indicated. See Index under names of countries for additional entries on 1982 events.)

Abbreviation code: archd. — archdiocese; dioc. — diocese; ap. ex. — apostolic exarchate; prel. — prelature; abb. — abbacy; v.a. — vicariate apostolic; p.a. — prefecture apostolic; a.a. — apostolic administration; card. — cardinal; abp. — archbishops (residential and auxiliary); nat. — native; bp. — bishops (residential and auxiliary); priests (dioc. — diocesan or secular priests; rel. — those belonging to religious orders); sem. — major seminarians, diocesan and religious; p.d. — permanent deacons; bros. — brothers; srs. — sisters; bap. — baptisms; Caths. — Catholic population; tot. pop. — total population.

Afghanistan: Republic in south-central Asia; capital, Kabul. Christianity antedated Moslem conquest in the seventh century but was overcome by it. All inhabitants are subject to the law of Islam. Christian missionaries are prohibited. Population (est.), 15,540,000.

Albania: Communist people's republic in the Balkans, bordering the Adriatic Sea; capital, Tirana. Christianity was introduced before the middle of the fourth century. The Byzantine-Rite Church broke from unity with Rome following the schism of 1054; it has been suppressed. The Latin (Roman) Church, which prevailed in the north, has been wiped out by persecution since 1945, with the expulsion of Italian missionaries; a number of death and prison sentences and other repressive measures against bishops, priests, religious and lay persons; the closing of Catholic schools and a seminary; the cutting of lines of communication with the Holy See. In 1967, the government proclaimed itself the first atheist state in the world.

Archd., 2; dioc., 3; abb., 1; a.a. 1; bp., 3 (impeded). No statistics are available. The Catholic population was estimated at 10% of the population in 1969. Tot. pop. (1980 est.), 2,730,000.

Algeria: Republic in northwest Africa: capital, Algiers. Christianity, introduced at an early date, succumbed to Vandal devastation in the fifth century and Moslem conquest in 709, but survived for centuries in small communities into the 12th century. Missionary work was unsuccessful except in service to traders, military personnel and captives along the coast. Church organization was established after the French gained control of the territory in the 1830's. A large number of Catholics were among the estimated million Europeans who left the country after it secured independence from France July 5, 1962. Islam is the state religion. Algeria maintains diplomatic relations with Vatican City.

Archd., 1; dioc., 3; card., 1; abp., 1; bp., 3 (2 nat.); parishes, 82; priests, 204 (86 dioc., 118 rel.); sem. 3; p.d., 2; bros., 21; srs., 516; bap., 67; Caths., 58,000 (.3%); tot. pop., 19,700,000.

Andorra: Autonomous principality in the Pyrenees, under the rule of co-princes — the French head of state and the bishop of Urgel, Spain; capital, Andorra la Vella. Christianity was introduced at an early date. Catholicism is the state religion. The principality is under the ecclesiastical jurisdiction of the Spanish diocese of Urgel.

Parishes, 7; priests, 17 (11 dioc., 6 rel.); srs., 22; sch., 4; bap., 412; Caths., 29,000 (95%); tot. pop., 31,000.

Angola: Independent (Nov. 11, 1975) republic in west Africa; capital, Luanda. Evangelization by Catholic missionaries, dating from about 1570, reached high points in the 17th and 18th centuries. Independence from Portugal in 1975 left the Church with a heavy loss of personnel when about half of the foreign missionaries fled the country. In 1977, two ecclesiastical provinces were established. All but one of the hierarchy are from the native clergy. Angola has an apostolic delegate.

Archd., 3; dioc., 9; abp., 3 (nat.); bp., 8 (7 nat.); parishes, 234; priests, 271 (93 dioc., 178 rel.); sem., 86; bros., 50; srs., 607; bap., 63,083; Caths., 3,153,000 (44.5%); tot. pop., 7,080,000.

Anguilla: Self-governing British island territory in the Caribbean; capital, The Valley. Under ecclesiastical jurisdiction of St. John's-Basseterre diocese, Antigua. Statistics included in St. Christopher (Kitts)-Nevis.

Antigua and Barbuda: Independent (Oct. 31, 1981) Caribbean island nation in the British Commonwealth; capital, St. John's, Antigua.

Dioc., 1; bp., 1; parishes, 2; priests, 3 (rel.); sem., 4; bros., 7; srs., 6; sch., 4; bap., 117; Caths., 7,000 (9.2%); tot. pop., 76,000.

Arabian Peninsula: Christianity, introduced in various parts of the peninsula in early Christian centuries, succumbed to Islam in the seventh century. The native population is entirely Moslem. The only Christians are foreigners. Most of the peninsula is under the ecclesiastical jurisdiction of the Vicariate Apostolic of Arabia located in Abu Dhabi, United Arab Emirates. The area has an apostolic delegate (to the Red Sea Region). See individual countries: Bahrain, Oman, Qatar, Saudi Arabia, United Arab Emirates, Yemen, and Peoples Democratic Republic of Yemen.

Argentina: Republic in southeast South America, bordering on the Atlantic; capital, Buenos Aires. Priests were with the Magellan exploration party and the first Mass in the country was celebrated Apr. 1, 1519. Missionary work began in the 1530's, diocesan organization in the late 1540's, and effective evangelization about 1570. Independence from Spain was proclaimed in 1816. Since its establishment in the country, the Church has been influenced by Spanish cultural and institutional forces, antagonistic liberalism, government interference and opposition; the latter reached a climax during the last five years of the first presidency of Juan Peron (1946-1955). Political chaos in recent years has resulted in widespread violations of human rights and increased terrorist violence. Catholicism is the state religion. Argentina maintains diplomatic relations with Vatican City. (See Index for papal visit to Argentina and other 1982 events.)

Archd., 12; dioc., 45; prel., 3; ap. ex., 1 (for Armenians of Latin America); ord., 1; card., 3; abp., 10; bp., 66; parishes, 2,158; priests, 5,450 (2,464 dioc., 2,986 rel.); sem., 1,373; p.d., 36; bros., 1,179; srs., 12,446; bap., 625,229; Caths., 25,168,000 (92.1%); tot. pop., 27,300,000.

Australia: Commonwealth, member of the British Commonwealth, island continent southeast of Asia; capital, Canberra. The first Catholics in the country were Irish under penal sentence, 1795-1804; the first public Mass was celebrated May 15, 1803. Official organization of the Church dates from 1820. The country was officially removed from mission status in March, 1976. Established diplomatic relations with Vatican City, 1973.

Archd., 7; dioc., 20; abb., 1; ap. ex., 1; card., 2; abp., 7; bp., 34; parishes, 1,408; priests, 3,854 (2,305 dioc., 1,549 rel.); sem., 500; p.d., 4; bros., 2,291; srs., 11,768; bap., 69,666; Caths., 3,861,000 (26.3%); tot. pop. 14,626,000.

Austria: Republic in central Europe; capital, Vienna. Christianity was introduced by the end of the third century, strengthened considerably by conversion of the Bavarians from about 600, and firmly established in the second half of the eighth century. Catholicism survived and grew stronger as the principal religion in the country in the post-Reformation period, but suffered from Josephinism in the 18th century. Although liberated from much government harassment in the aftermath of the Revolution of 1848, it came under pressure again some 20 years later in the Kulturkampf. During this time the Church became involved with a developing social movement. The Church faced strong opposition from Socialists after World War I and suffered persecution from 1938 to 1945 during the Nazi regime. Some Church-state matters are regulated by a concordat originally concluded in 1934. Austria maintains diplomatic relations with Vatican City.

Archd., 2; dioc., 7; abb., 1; ord., 1; card., 1; abp., 2; bp., 13; parishes, 3,061; priests, 6,151 (3,581 dioc., 2,570 rel.); sem., 548; p.d., 109; bros., 700; srs., 11,195; bap., 79,959; Caths., 6,603,000 (87.9%); tot. pop., 7,507,000.

Azores: North Atlantic island group 750 miles west of Portugal, of which it is part. Christianity was introduced in the second quarter of the 15th century.

Bahamas: Independent (July 10, 1973) island group in the British Commonwealth, consisting of some 700 (30 inhabited) small islands southeast of Florida and north of Cuba; capital, Nassau. On Oct. 12, 1492, Columbus landed on one of these islands, where the first Mass was celebrated in the New World. Organization of the Catholic Church in the Bahamas dates from about the middle of the 19th century. Established diplomatic relations with Vatican City in 1979.

Dioc., 1; bp., 1; parishes, 29; priests, 36 (6 dioc., 30 rel.); sem., 1; p.d., 4; bros., 6; srs., 58; bap., 1,588; Caths., 34,000 (14.1%); tot. pop., 240,000.

Bahrain: Island state in Persian Gulf; capital, Manama. Under ecclesiastical jurisdiction of Arabia vicariate apostolic.

Priests, 2 (rel); srs., 11; bap., 165; Caths., 6,000 (1.6%); tot. pop., 364,000

Balearic Islands: Spanish province consisting of an island group in the western Mediterranean. Statistics are included in those for Spain.

Bangladesh: Formerly the eastern portion of Pakistan. Officially constituted as a separate nation Dec. 16, 1971; capital, Dacca. Islam is the principal religion; freedom of religion is granted. There were Jesuit, Dominican and Augustinian missionaries in the area in the 16th century. A vicariate apostolic (of Bengali) was established in 1834; the hierarchy was erected in 1950. Established diplomatic relations with Vatican City, 1972.

Archd., 1; dioc., 3; abp., 1 (nat.); bp., 3 (nat.); parishes, 55; priests, 176 (46 dioc., 130 rel.); sem., 114; p.d., 1; bros., 60; srs., 449; bap., 5,494; Caths., 161,000 (.18%); tot. pop. 87,660,000.

Barbados: Parliamentary democracy in the British Commonwealth (independent since 1966), easternmost of the Caribbean islands; capital, Bridgetown. About 70 per cent of the people are Anglicans. Established diplomatic relations with Vatican City in 1979.

Dioc., 1; bp., 1; parishes, 5; priests, 11 (4 dioc., 7 rel.); sem., 4; bros., 7; srs., 32; bap., 219; Caths., 10,000 (3.8%); tot. pop., 260,000.

Belgium: Constitutional monarchy in northwestern Europe; capital, Brussels. Christianity was introduced about the first quarter of the fourth century and major evangelization was completed about 730. During the rest of the medieval period the Church had firm diocesan and parochial organization, generally vigorous monastic life, and influential monastic and cathedral schools. Lutherans and Calvinists made some gains during the Reformation period but there was a strong Catholic restoration in the first half of the 17th century, when the country was under Spanish rule. Jansenism disturbed the Church from about 1640 into the 18th century. Josephinism, imposed by an Austrian regime, hampered the Church late in the same century. Repressive and persecutory measures were enforced during the Napoleonic conquest. Freedom came with separation of Church and state in the wake of the Revolution of 1830, which ended the reign of William I. Thereafter, the Church encountered serious problems with philosophical liberalism and political socialism. Catholics have long been engaged in strong educational, social and political movements. Except for one five-year period (1880-1884), Belgium has maintained diplomatic relations with Vatican City since 1835.

Archd., 1; dioc., 7; card., 1; abp., 1; bp., 14; parishes, 3,974; priests, 12,915 (7,896 dioc., 5,019 rel.); sem., 321; p.d., 212; bros., 2,376; srs., 31,721; bap., 107,958; Caths., 9,009,000 (90.8%); tot. pop., 9,920,000.

Belize (formerly British Honduras): Independent (Sept. 21, 1981) republic on east coast of Central America; capital, Belmopan. Its history has points in common with Guatemala, where evangelization began in the 16th century.

Dioc., 1; bp., 2; parishes, 12; priests, 35 (10 dioc., 25 rel.); sem., 1; p.d., 1; bros., 8; srs., 80; bap., 2,945; Caths., 87,000 (54%); tot. pop., 160,000.

Benin (formerly Dahomey): Republic in west Africa, bordering on the Atlantic; capitals, Cotonou, Porto Novo. Missionary work was very limited from the 16th to the 18th centuries. Effective evangelization dates from 1861. The hierarchy was established in 1955. The majority of Christians are Catholics. Benin maintains diplomatic relations with Vatican City. (See Index for papal visit to Benin.)

Archd., 1; dioc., 5; card., 1 (nat.); abp., 2 (nat.); bp., 5 (4 nat.); parishes, 109; priests, 191 (85 dioc., 106 rel.); sem., 61 (dioc.); bros., 16; srs., 320; bap., 10,191; Caths., 571,000 (16%); tot. pop., 3,570,000.

Bermuda: British dependency, consisting of 360 islands (20 of them inhabited) nearly 600 miles east of Cape Hatteras; capital, Hamilton. Catholics were not permitted until about 1800. Occasional pastoral care was provided the few Catholics there by visiting priests during the 19th century. Early in the 1900's priests from Halifax began serving the area. A prefecture apostolic was set up in 1953. The first bishop assumed jurisdiction in 1956. The only Catholic school in Bermuda was the first to admit black students, in 1961.

Dioc., 1; bp., 1; parishes, 7; priests, 9 (1 dioc., 8 rel.); p.d., 1; bros., 7; srs., 9; bap., 132; Caths., 9,000 (14.4%); tot. pop., 62,100.

Bhutan: Constitutional monarchy in the Himalayas, northeast of India; capital, Thimphu. Most of the population are Buddhists. Jesuits (1963) and Salesians (1965) were invited to country to direct schools. Salesians were expelled in February, 1982, on disputed charges of proselytism. Six Jesuits and some Sisters remained *(Fides)*. Ecclesiastical jurisdiction is under the Darjeeling diocese, India.

Caths., 300; tot. pop., 1,298,000.

Bolivia: Republic in central South America; capital, Sucre; seat of government, La Paz. Catholicism, the official religion, was introduced in the 1530's and the first bishopric was established in 1552. Effective evangelization among the Indians, slow to start, reached high points in the middle of the 18th and the beginning of the 19th centuries and was resumed about 1840. Independence from Spain was proclaimed in 1825, at the end of a campaign that started in 1809. The republic inherited the Spanish right of nominating candidates for bishoprics. Church-state relations are regulated by a 1951 concordat with the Holy See. In recent years, human rights violations in conditions of political, economic and social turmoil have occasioned strong protests by members of the hierarchy and other people of the Church. Bolivia maintains diplomatic relations with Vatican City.

Archd., 4; dioc., 3; prel., 3; v.a., 6; card., 1; abp., 4; bp., 19; parishes, 435; priests, 929 (255 dioc., 674 rel.); sem., 167; p.d., 23; bros., 233; srs., 1,682; bap., 163,281; Caths., 5,250,000 (93.7%); tot. pop., 5,600,000.

Botswana: Republic (independent since 1966) in southern Africa, member of the British Commonwealth; capital, Gaborone. Botswana has an apostolic delegate (to Southern Africa).

Dioc., 1; bp., 1; priests, 24 (3 dioc., 21 rel.); sem., 2 (dioc.); bros., 2; srs., 54; bap., 995; Caths., 29,000 (3.5%); tot. pop., 819,000

Brazil: Republic in northeast South America; capital, Brasilia. One of several priests with the discovery party celebrated the first Mass in the country Apr. 26, 1500. Evangelization began some years later and the first diocese was erected in 1551. During the colonial period, which lasted until 1822, evangelization made some notable progress — especially in the Amazon region between 16 80 and 1750 — but was seriously hindered by government policy and the attitude of colonists regarding Amazon Indians the missionaries tried to protect from exploitation and slavery. The Jesuits were suppressed in 1782 and other missionaries expelled as well. Liberal anti-Church influence grew in strength. The government gave minimal support but exercised maximum control over the Church. After the proclamation of independence from Portugal in 1822 and throughout the regency, government control was tightened and the Church suffered greatly from dissident actions of ecclesiastical brotherhoods, Masonic anti-clericalism and general decline in religious life. Church and state were separated by the constitution of 1891, proclaimed two years after the end of the empire. The Church carried into the 20th century a load of inherited liabilities and problems amid increasingly difficult political, economic and social conditions affecting the majority of the population. A number of bishops, priests, religious and lay persons have been active in movements for social and religious reform. Brazil maintains diplomatic relations with Vatican City.

Archd., 35; dioc., 172; prel., 26; abb., 2; ord., 1; card., 7; abp., 37; bp., 239; parishes, 6,557; priests, 13,169 (5,112 dioc., 8,057 rel.); sem., 4,283; p.d., 308; bros., 2,701; srs., 37,024; bap., 2,784,580; Caths., 110,870,000 (90.1%); tot. pop., 123,030,000.

Brunei: State under British protection, on the northern coast of Borneo; scheduled for independence by end of 1983; capital, Bandar Seri Begawan. Under ecclesiastical jurisdiction of Miri diocese, Malaysia.

Parishes, 3; priests, 5 (2 dioc., 3 rel.); bros., 4; srs., 2; bap., 102; Caths., 5,000; tot. pop., 213,000.

Bulgaria: People's republic in southeastern Europe on the eastern part of the Balkan peninsula; capital, Sofia. Christianity was introduced before 343 but disappeared with the migration of Slavs into the territory. The baptism of Boris I about 865 ushered in a new period of Christianity which soon became involved in switches of loyalty between Constantinople and Rome. Through it all the Byzantine, and later Orthodox, element remained stronger and survived under the rule of Ottoman Turks into the 19th century. The few modern Latin Catholics in the country are traceable to 17th century converts from heresy. The Byzantines are products of a reunion movement of the 19th century. In 1947 the constitution of the new republic decreed the separation of Church and state. Catholic schools and institutions were abolished and foreign religious banished in 1948. A year later the apostolic delegate was expelled. Ivan Romanoff, vicar general of Plovdiv, died in prison in 1952. Bishop Eugene Bossilkoff, imprisoned in 1948, was sentenced to death in 1952; his fate remained unknown until 1975 when the Bulgarian government informed the Vatican that he had died in prison shortly after being sentenced. Roman and Bulgarian Rite vicars apostolic were permitted to attend the Second Vatican Council from 1962 to 1965. All church activity is under surveillance and/or control by the government, which professes to be atheistic. Pastoral and related activities are strictly limited. Most of the population is Orthodox. There was some improvement in Bulgarian-Vatican relations in 1975, following a visit of Bulgarian President Todor Zhivkov to Pope Paul VI June 19 and talks between Vatican and Bulgarian representatives at the Helsinki Conference in late July. The needs of the church in Bulgaria were outlined by Pope John Paul II in a private audience with the Bulgarian foreign minister in December, 1978. In 1979, the Sofia-Plovdiv vicariate apostolic was raised to a diocese and a bishop was appointed for the vacant see of Nicopoli.

Dioc., 2; ap. ex., 1; bp., 3; Caths. (est.), 65,000 (.7%); tot. pop., 8,860,000.

Burma: Union of Burma, a republic in southeast Asia, on the Bay of Bengal; capital, Rangoon. Christianity was introduced about 1500. Small-scale evangelization had limited results from the middle of the 16th century until the 1850's when effective organization of the Church began. The hierarchy was established in 1955. Buddhism was declared the state religion in 1961, but the state is now officially secular. In 1965, church schools and hospitals were nationalized. In 1966, all foreign missionaries who had entered the country after 1948 for the first time were forced to leave when the government refused to renew their work permits. Despite these setbacks, the Church has shown some progress in recent years. Burma has an apostolic delegate (pro-nuncio to Bangladesh).

Archd., 2; dioc., 6; p.a., 1; abp., 2 (nat.); bp., 6 (5 nat.); parishes, 141; priests, 212 (179 dioc., 33 rel.); sem., 186; bros., 60 srs., 702; bap., 17,874; Caths., 402,000 (1.2%); tot. pop., 33,625,000.

Burundi: Republic since 1966, near the equator in east-central Africa; capital, Bujumbura. The first permanent Catholic mission station was established late in the 19th century. Large numbers of persons were received into the Church following the ordination of the first Burundi priests in 1925. The first native bishop was appointed in 1959. Most education takes place in schools under Catholic auspices. In 1972-73, the country was torn by tribal warfare between the Tutsis, the ruling minority, and the Hutus. Since 1979, approximately 100 Catholic missionaries have been expelled. Burundi maintains diplomatic relations with Vatican City.

Archd., 1; dioc., 6; abp., 2 (nat.); bp., 6 (nat.); parishes, 194; priests, 338 (163 dioc., 175 rel.); sem., 73; bros., 169; srs., 768; bap., 71,246; Caths., 2,340,000 (51.9%); tot. pop., 4,510,000.

Cambodia (Peoples Republic of Kampuchea, Democratic Kampuchea): Republic (Oct. 9, 1970) in southeast Asia, bordering on the Gulf of Siam, Thailand, Laos and Vietnam; capital Phnom Penh. Evangelization dating from the second half of the 16th century had limited results, more among Vietnamese than Khmers. Thousands of Catholics of Vietnamese origin were forced to flee in 1970 because of Khmer hostility. The status of the Church remained uncertain following the Khmer Rouge take-over in April, 1975. Foreign missionaries were expelled immediately. Local clergy and religious were sent to work the land; whether they would be able to minister to the faithful was not known. Buddhism is the state religion.

V.a., 1; p.a., 2. No statistics available. Catholics numbered 13,835 (2% of the total population) in 1973. Tot. pop. (est.), 8,870,000.

Cameroon: Republic in west Africa, bordering on the Gulf of Guinea; capital, Yaounde. Effective evangelization began in the 1890's, although Catholics had been in the country long before that time. In the 40-year period from 1920 to 1960, the number of Catholics increased from 60,000 to 700,000. The first native priests were ordained in 1935. Twenty years later the first native bishops were ordained and the hierarchy established. In 1982, three new ecclesiastical provinces and one diocese were established. Cameroon maintains diplomatic relations with Vatican City.

Archd., 4; dioc., 10; abp., 4 (3 nat.); bp., 10 (8 nat.); parishes, 367; priests, 846 (314 dioc., 532 rel.); sem., 218; p.d., 24; bros., 244; srs., 1,245; bap., 75,622; Caths., 2,276,000 (26.8%); tot. pop., 8,500,000.

Canada: Independent federation in the British Commonwealth, comprising the northern half of North America; capital, Ottawa. Canada maintains diplomatic relations with Vatican City. (See The Church in Canada.)

Archd., 18; dioc., 52; abb., 1; ap. ex., 1; card., 4; (1 is a residential archbishop; 3 are retired); abp., 28 (17 residential, 1 titular, 10 retired); bp., 98 (50 residential, 26 auxiliary, 22 retired); parishes 5,787; priests, 12,626 (7,340 dioc., 5,286 rel.); sem., 1,055; p.d., 277; bros., 4,195; srs., 37,982; bap., 174,096; Caths., 10,425,087 (43.3%); tot. pop., 24,088,500. (Principal source: 1982 Directory of Canadian Conference of Catholic Bishops.)

Canary Islands: Two Spanish provinces, consisting of seven islands, off the northwest coast of Africa. Evangelization began about 1400. Almost all of the one million inhabitants are Catholics. Statistics are included in those for Spain.

Cape Verde: Independent (July 5, 1975) island group in the Atlantic 300 miles west of Senegal; formerly a Portuguese overseas province; capital, Praia, San Tiago Island. Evangelization began some years before the establishment of the first diocese in 1532. Cape Verde established diplomatic relations with Vatican City in 1976.

Dioc., 1; bp., 1; parishes, 30; priests, 51 (12 dioc., 39 rel.); sem., 4 (dioc.); bros., 5; srs., 43; bap., 6,259; Caths., 308,000 (95%); tot. pop., 324,000.

Carolines and Marshalls, The: U.S. trust territory in the southwest Pacific; scheduled for independence. Effective evangelization began in the late 1880's.

Dioc., 1; bp., 1; parishes, 26; priests, 34 (3 dioc., 31 rel.); sem., 6; p.d., 20; bros., 6; srs., 41; bap., 1,935; Caths., 51,000 (42%); tot. pop., 119,000.

Cayman Islands: British colony in Caribbean; capital, George Town on Grand Cayman. Under ecclesiastical jurisdiction of Kingston diocese, Jamaica.

Srs., 2; sch., 1 (elementary); bap., 16; Caths., 300; tot. pop., 17,000.

Central African Republic: Former French colony (independent since 1960) in central Africa; capital, Bangui. Effective evangelization dates from 1894. The region was organized as a mission territory in 1909. The first native priest was ordained in 1938. The hierarchy was organized in 1955. The Central African Republic established diplomatic relations with Vatican City in 1975.

Archd., 1; dioc., 5; abp., 1 (nat.); bp., 4; parishes, 85; priests, 214 (36 dioc., 178 rel.); sem., 68; bros., 67; srs., 278; bap., 14,409; Caths., 360,000 (15.4%); tot. pop., 2,338,000.

Ceuta: Spanish possession (city) on the northern tip of Africa, south of Gibraltar. Statistics are included in those for Spain.

Chad: Republic (independent since 1960) in north-central Africa; former French possession; capital, N'Djamena (Fort Lamy). Evangelization began in 1929, leading to firm organization in 1947 and establishment of the hierarchy in 1955. Chad has an apostolic delegate (pro-nuncio, Central African Republic).

Archd., 1; dioc., 3; abp., 1; bp., 3; parishes, 61; priests, 169 (14 dioc., 155 rel.); sem., 20; bros., 41; srs., 185; bap., 9,932; Caths., 246,000 (5.4%); tot. pop., 4,520,000.

Chile: Republic on the southwestern coast of South America; capital, Santiago. Priests were with the Spanish conquistadores on their entrance into the territory early in the 16th century. The first parish was established in 1547 and the first bishopric in 1561. Overall organization of the Church took place later in the century. By 1650 most of the peaceful Indians in the central and northern areas were evangelized. Missionary work was more difficult in the southern region. Church activity was hampered during the campaign for independence, 1810 to 1818, and through the first years of the new government, to 1830. Later gains were made, into this century, but hindering factors were shortages of native clergy and religious and attempts by the government to control church administration through the patronage system in force while the country was under Spanish control.

Separation of Church and state were decreed in the constitution of 1925. Church-state relations were strained during the regime of Marxist president Salvator Allende Gossens (1970-73). He was overthrown in a bloody coup and was reported to have committed suicide Sept. 11, 1973. Conditions remained unsettled under the military government which assumed control after the coup. Since 1974, the Chilean bishops have issued several statements criticizing government policies violating human rights and urging release of political prisoners. The Church-backed Vicariate of Solidarity was established in 1976 to give legal aid to political prisoners and aid their families. Human rights record worsened in 1980. In 1981, five members of the hierarchy issued a statement decreeing automatic excommunication for anyone involved in torture. Chile maintains diplomatic relations with Vatican City.

Archd., 5; dioc., 14; prel., 3; v.a., 2; card., 1; abp., 4; bp., 24; parishes, 813; priests, 2,020 (777 dioc., 1,243 rel.); sem., 663; p.d., 200; bros., 467; srs., 5,088; bap., 184,326; Caths., 9,490,000 (85.5%); tot. pop., 11,100,000.

China *(This article concerns mainland China which has been under Communist control since 1949):* People's Republic in eastern part of Asia; capital, Peking (Beijing), Christianity was introduced by Nestorians who had some influence on part of the area from 635 to 845 and again from the 11th century until 1368. John of Monte Corvino started a Franciscan mission in 1294; he was ordained an archbishop about 1307. Missionary activity involving more priests increased for a while thereafter but the Franciscan mission ended in 1368. The Jesuit Matteo Ricci initiated a remarkable period of activity in the 1580's. By 1700 the number of Catholics was reported to be 300,000. The Chinese Rites controversy, concerning the adaptation of rituals and other matters to Chinese traditions and practices, ran throughout the 17th century, ending in a negative decision by mission authorities in Rome. Bl. Francis de Capillas, the protomartyr of China, was killed in 1648. Persecution, a feature of Chinese history as recurrent as changes in dynasties, occurred several times in the 18th century and resulted in the departure of most missionaries from the country. The Chinese door swung open again in the 1840's and progress in evangelization increased with an extension of legal and social tolerance. At the turn of the 20th century, however, the Boxer Rebellion took one or the other kind of toll among an estimated 30,000 victims. Missionary work in the 1900's reached a new high in every respect before the disaster of persecution initiated by Communists before and especially since they established the republic in 1949. The Reds began a savage persecution as soon as they came into power. Among its results were the expulsion of over 5,000 foreign missionaries, 510 of whom were American priests, brothers and nuns; the arrest, imprisonment and harassment of all members of the native religious, clergy and hierarchy; the forced closing of 3,932 schools, 216 hospitals, 781 dispensaries, 254 orphanages, 29 printing presses and 55 periodicals; denial of the free exercise of religion to all the faithful; the detention of hundreds of priests, religious and lay persons in jail and their employment in slave labor; the proscription of the Legion of Mary and other Catholic Action groups for "counter-revolutionary activities" and "crimes against the new China"; complete outlawing of missionary work and pastoral activity. The government formally established a Patriotic Association of Chinese Catholics in July, 1957. Relatively few priests and lay persons joined the organization, which was condemned by Pius XII in 1958. The government formed the nucleus of what it hoped might become the hierarchy of a schismatic Chinese church by "electing" 26 bishops and having them consecrated validly but illicitly between Apr. 13, 1958, and Nov. 15, 1959, without the permission or approval of the Holy See. By Jan. 21, 1962, a total of 42 bishops were consecrated in this manner. In March, 1960, Bishop James E. Walsh, M.M., the last American missionary in China, was sentenced and placed in custody for a period of 20 years. He was released in the summer of 1970. (He died in 1981.) There seemed to be an opening to the West by China in 1979. What this, along with renewed activity of the Patriotic Association in 1980, might mean for the Church in that country is open to question.

Archd., 20; dioc., 92; p.a., 29. No Catholic statistics are available. In 1949 there were between 3,500,000-4,000,000 Catholics, about .7 per cent of the total population; the 1969 "CSMC World Mission Map" estimated 3,200,000 Catholics, .5 per cent of the population. The latter figure is only an estimate; there is no way of knowing the actual situation. Tot. pop. (1979 est.), 958,230,000.

Colombia: Republic in northwest South America, with Atlantic and Pacific borders; capital, Bogota. Evangelization began in 1508. The first two dioceses were established in 1534. Vigorous development of the Church was reported by the middle of the 17th century despite obstacles posed by the multiplicity of Indian languages, government interference through patronage rights and otherwise, rivalry among religious orders and the small number of native priests among the predominantly Spanish clergy. Some persecution, including the confiscation of property, followed in the wake of the proclamation of independence from Spain in 1819. The Church was affected in many ways by the political and civil unrest of the nation through the 19th century and into the 20th. Various aspects of Church-state relations are regulated by a concordat with the Vatican signed July 12, 1973, and ratified July 2, 1975. The new concordat replaced one which had been in effect with some modifications since 1887. In late 1976, the bishops released a statement reaffirming their concern for social justice but rejecting actions of radical Catholic groups such as Priests for Latin America and Christians for Socialism as Marxist-oriented and destructive of Church unity. Colombia maintains diplomatic relations with Vatican City.

Archd., 11; dioc., 30; prel., 2; v.a., 9; p.a., 7; card., 1; abp., 11; bp., 49; parishes, 2,250; priests, 5,254 (3,146 dioc., 2,108 rel.); sem., 1,857; p.d., 31; bros., 1,025; srs., 17,654; bap., 718,162; Caths., 25,890,000 (95.5%); tot. pop., 27,090,000.

Comoros: Consists of main islands of Grande Comore, Anjouan, Moheli and Mayotte in Indian Ocean off southeast coast of Africa; capital, Moroni, Grande Comore Island. Former French territory; independent (July 6, 1975) except Mayotte which voted to remain part of France. The majority of the population is Moslem. An apostolic administration for Catholics (formerly under administration of the Ambanja diocese, Madagascar) was established June 20, 1975.

A.a., 1; priests, 4 (1 dioc., 3 rel.); srs., 7; bap., 24; Caths., 1,350 (.4%); tot. pop., 351,000.

Congo Republic: Republic (independent since 1960) in west central Africa; former French possession; capital, Brazzaville. Small-scale missionary work with little effect preceded modern evangelization dating from the 1880's. The work of the Church has been affected by political instability, Communist influence, tribalism and hostility to foreigners. The hierarchy was established in 1955. Congo established diplomatic relations with the Vatican in 1977.

Archd., 1; dioc.; 2; abp., 1; bp., 2 (nat); parishes, 91; priests, 157 (38 dioc., 119 rel.); sem., 45; p.d., 2; bros., 35; srs., 195; bap., 13,795; Caths., 674,000 (43.8%); tot. pop., 1,540,000.

Cook Islands: Self-governing territory of New Zealand, an archipelago of small islands in Oceania. Evangelization by Protestant missionaries started in 1821, resulting in a predominantly Protestant population. The first Catholic missionary work began in 1894. The hierarchy was established in 1966.

Dioc., 1; bp., 1; parishes, 11; priests, 12 (4 dioc., 8 rel.); sem., 2; bros., 3; srs., 14; bap., 96; Caths., 3,000; tot. pop., 18,000.

Costa Rica: Republic in Central America; capital, San Jose. Evangelization began about 1520 and proceeded by degrees to real development and organization of the Church in the 17th and 18th centuries. The republic became independent in 1838. Twelve years later church jurisdiction also became independent

with the establishment of a bishopric in the present capital. Costa Rica maintains diplomatic relations with Vatican City.

Archd., 1; dioc., 3; v.a., 1; abp., 1; bp., 5; parishes, 166; priests, 434 (254 dioc., 180 rel.); sem., 189; bros., 31; srs., 867; bap., 53,966; Caths., 2,095,000 (93.5%); tot. pop., 2,240,000.

Cuba: Republic under Communist dictatorship, south of Florida; capital, Havana. Effective evangelization began about 1514, leading eventually to the predominance of Catholicism on the island. Native vocations to the priesthood and religious life were unusually numerous in the 18th century but declined in the 19th. The island became independent of Spain in 1902 following the Spanish-American War. Fidel Castro took control of the government Jan. 1, 1959. In 1961, after Cuba was officially declared a socialist state, the University of Villanueva was closed, 350 Catholic schools were nationalized and 136 priests expelled. A greater number of foreign priests and religious had already left the country. Freedom of worship and religious instruction are limited to church premises and no social action is permitted the Church, which survives under surveillance. A new constitution approved in 1976 guaranteed freedom of conscience but restricted its exercise. Cuba maintains diplomatic relations with Vatican City.

Archd., 2; dioc., 5; abp., 2; bp., 5; parishes, 237; priests, 200 (110 dioc., 90 rel.); sem., 50; bros., 22; srs., 214; bap., 19,711; Caths. 4,048,000 (41.2%); tot. pop., 9,830,000.

Cyprus: Republic in the eastern Mediterranean; capital, Nicosia. Christianity was preached on the island in apostolic times and has a continuous history from the fourth century. Latin and Eastern rites were established but the latter prevailed and became Orthodox after the schism of 1054. Roman and Orthodox Christians have suffered under many governments, particularly during the period of Turkish dominion from late in the 16th to late in the 19th centuries, and from differences between the 80 per cent Greek majority and the Turkish minority. About 80 per cent of the population are Orthodox. Cyprus established diplomatic relations with Vatican City in 1973. Maronite Rite Catholics are under the jurisdiction of the archdiocese of Cyprus (of the Maronites), whose archbishop resides in Lebanon. Roman Rite Catholics are under the jurisdiction of the Roman Rite patriarchate of Jerusalem.

Archd., 1 (Maronite); abp., 1 (resides in Lebanon); parishes, 10; priests, 22 (6 dioc., 16 rel.); bros.,2; srs., 101; bap., 48; Caths., 8,000 (1.9%); tot. pop., 630,000.

Czechoslovakia: Federal socialist republic (since 1969) in Central Europe, consisting of the Czech Socialist Republic, capital Prague; and the Slovak Socialist Republic, capital

Bratislava. The republics have local autonomy but are subordinate to the Federal Assembly at Prague made up of representatives from both regions. The Czech and Slovak regions of the country have separate religious and cultural backgrounds. Christianity was introduced in Slovakia in the 8th century by Irish and German missionaries and the area was under the jurisdiction of German bishops. In 863, at the invitation of the Slovak ruler Rastislav who wanted to preserve the cultural and liturgical heritage of the people, Sts. Cyril and Methodius began pastoral and missionary work in the region, ministering to the people in their own language. The saints introduced Old Slovak (Old Church Slavonic) into the liturgy and did so much to evangelize the territory that they are venerated as the apostles of Slovakia. A diocese established at Nitra in 880 had a continuous history except for a century ending in 1024. The Church in Slovakia was severely tested by the Reformation and political upheavals. After World War I, when it became part of the Republic of Czechoslovakia, it was 75 per cent Catholic. In the Czech lands, the martyrdom of Prince Wenceslaus in 929 triggered the spread of Christianity. Prague has had a continuous history as a diocese since 973. A parish system was organized about the 13th century in Bohemia and Moravia, the land of the Czechs. Mendicant orders strengthened relations with the Latin Rite in the 13th century. In the next century the teachings of John Hus in Bohemia brought trouble to the Church in the forms of schism and heresy, and initiated a series of religious wars which continued for decades following his death at the stake in 1415. Church property was confiscated, monastic communities were scattered and even murdered, ecclesiastical organization was shattered, and so many of the faithful joined the Bohemian Brethren that Catholics became a minority. The Reformation, with the way prepared by the Hussites and cleared by other factors, affected the Church seriously. A Counter Reformation got underway in the 1560's and led to a gradual restoration through the thickets of Josephinism, the Enlightenment, liberalism and troubled politics. In 1920, two years after the establishment of the Republic of Czechoslovakia, the schismatic Czechoslovak Church was proclaimed at Prague, resulting in numerous defections from the Catholic Church in the Czech region. In Ruthenia, 112,000 became Russian Orthodox between 1918 and 1930. Vigorous persecution of the church began in Slovakia before the end of World War II when Communists mounted a 1944 offensive against bishops, priests and religious. In 1945, church schools were nationalized, youth organizations were disbanded, the Catholic press was curtailed, the training of students for the priesthood was seriously impeded.

Msgr. Josef Tiso, president of the Slovak Republic, was tried for "treason" in December, 1947, and was executed the following April. Between 1945 and 1949 approximately 10 per cent of the Slovak population spent some time in jail or a concentration camp. Persecution began later in the Czech part of the country, following the accession of the Gottwald regime to power early in 1948. Hospitals, schools and property were nationalized and Catholic organizations were liquidated. A puppet organization was formed in 1949 to infiltrate the Church and implement an unsuccessful plan for establishing a schismatic church. In the same year Archbishop Josef Beran of Prague was placed under house arrest. (He left the country in 1965, was made a cardinal, and died in 1969 in Rome.) A number of theatrical trials of bishops and priests were staged in 1950. All houses of religious were taken over between March, 1950, and the end of 1951. Pressure was applied on the clergy and faithful of the Eastern Rite in Slovakia to join the Orthodox Church. Diplomatic relations with Vatican City were terminated in 1950. About 3,000 priests were deprived of liberty in 1951 and attempts were made to force "peace priests" on the people. In 1958 it was reported that 450 to 500 priests were in jail; an undisclosed number of religious and Byzantine Rite priests had been deported; two bishops released from prison in 1956 were under house arrest; one bishop was imprisoned at Leopoldov and two at the Mirov reformatory. In Bohemia, Moravia and Silesia, five of six dioceses were without ruling bishops; one archbishop and two bishops were active but subject to "supervision"; most of the clergy refused to join the "peace priests." In 1962 only three bishops were permitted to attend the first session of the Second Vatican Council. From January to October, 1968, Church-state relations improved to some extent under the Dubcek regime: a number of bishops were reinstated; some 3,000 priests were engaged in the pastoral ministry, although 1,500 were still barred from priestly work; the "peace priests" organization was disbanded; the Eastern Rite Church, with 147 parishes, was reestablished. In 1969, an end was ordered to rehabilitation trials for priests and religious, but no wholesale restoration of priests and religious to their proper ways of life and work was in prospect. In 1972 the government ordered the removal of nuns from visible but limited apostolates to farms and mental hospitals where they would be out of sight. In 1973, the government allowed the ordination of four bishops — one in the Czech region and three in the Slovak region. Reports from Slovakia late in the same year stated that authorities there had placed severe restrictions on the education of seminarians and the functioning of priests. Government restrictions continued to hamper the work of priests and nuns in recent years. Signatories of the human rights declaration called Charter 77 have been particular objects of government repression and retribution.

Archd., 3; dioc., 10; card., 1; bp., 6 (1 impeded); parishes, 4,189; priests, 3,848 (3,393 dioc., 455 rel.); sem., 284; bros., 39; srs., 4,721; bap., 111,371; Caths. (est.), 10,530,000 (68.7%); tot. pop., 15,320,000.

Denmark, including the Faroe Islands and Greenland: Constitutional monarchy in northwestern Europe, north of West Germany; capital, Copenhagen. Christianity was introduced in the ninth century and the first diocese for the area was established in 831. Intensive evangelization and full-scale organization of the Church occurred from the second half of the 10th century and ushered in a period of great development and influence in the 12th and 13th centuries. Decline followed, resulting in almost total loss to the Church during the Reformation when Lutheranism became the national religion. Catholics were considered foreigners until religious freedom was legally assured in 1849. Modern development of the Church dates from the second half of the 19th century. About 95 per cent of the population are Evangelical Lutherans. Established diplomatic relations with Vatican City in 1982.

Dioc., 1; bp., 1; parishes, 60; priests, 109 (36 dioc., 73 rel.); sem., 8; bros., 4; srs., 453; bap., 374; Caths., 28,000 (.5%); tot. pop., 5,123,000.

Djibouti (formerly French Territory of Afars and Issas): Independent (1977) republic in east Africa, on the Gulf of Aden; capital, Djibouti. Christianity in the area, formerly part of Ethiopia, antedated but was overcome by the Arab invasion of 1200. Modern evangelization, begun in the latter part of the 19th century, had meager results. The hierarchy was established in 1955. The territory has an apostolic delegate (to the Red Sea Region).

Dioc., 1; bp., 1; parishes, 7; priests, 7 (1 dioc., 6 rel.); p.d., 1; bros., 9; srs., 27; bap., 42; Caths., 12,000; tot. pop., 250,000.

Dominica: Independent (Nov. 3, 1978) state in Caribbean; capital, Roseau. Evangelization began in 1642. Established diplomatic relations with Vatican City in 1981.

Dioc., 1; bp., 1; parishes, 16; priests, 26 (2 dioc., 24 rel.); sem., 5; p.d., 1; bros., 5; srs., 35; bap., 1,380; Caths., 65,000 (81.2%); tot. pop., 80,000.

Dominican Republic: Caribbean republic on the eastern two-thirds of the island of Hispaniola, bordering on Haiti; capital, Santo Domingo. Evangelization began shortly after discovery by Columbus in 1492 and church organization, the first in America, was established by 1510. Catholicism is the state religion. The Dominican Republic maintains diplomatic relations with Vatican City.

Archd., 1; dioc., 7; card., 1; abp., 2; bp., 8;

parishes, 202; priests, 505 (124 dioc., 381 rel.); sem., 286; p.d., 30; bros., 90; srs., 1,496; bap., 94,442; Caths., 5,150,000 (94.8%); tot. pop., 5,430,000.

Ecuador: Republic on the west coast of South America; capital, Quito. Evangelization began in the 1530's. The first diocese was established in 1545. A synod, one of the first in the Americas, was held in 1570 or 1594. Multiphased missionary work, spreading from the coastal and mountain regions into the Amazon, made the Church highly influential during the colonial period. The Church was practically enslaved by the constitution enacted in 1824, two years after Ecuador, as part of Colombia, gained independence from Spain. Some change for the better took place later in the century, but from 1891 until the 1930's the Church labored under serious liabilities imposed by liberal governments. The concordat of 1866 was violated; foreign missionaries were barred from the country for some time; the property of religious orders was confiscated; education was taken over by the state; traditional state support was refused; legal standing was denied; attempts to control church offices were made through insistence on rights of patronage. A period of harmony and independence for the Church began after agreement was reached on Church-state relations in 1937. Ecuador maintains diplomatic relations with Vatican City.

Archd., 3; dioc., 10; prel., 1; v.a., 5; p.a., 3; card., 1; abp., 3; bp., 19; parishes, 715; priests, 1,513 (649 dioc., 864 rel.); sem., 185; p.d., 6; bros., 367; srs., 4,151; bap., 205,604; Caths., 7,530,000 (90.2%); tot. pop., 8,350,000.

Egypt, Arab Republic of: Republic in northeastern Africa, bordering on the Mediterranean; capital, Cairo. Alexandria was the influential hub of a Christian community established by the end of the second century; it became a patriarchate and the center of the Coptic Church, and had great influence on the spread of Christianity in various parts of Africa; Monasticism developed from desert communities of hermits in the third and fourth centuries. Arianism was first preached in Egypt in the 320's. In the fifth century, the Coptic church went Monophysite through failure to accept doctrine formulated by the Council of Chalcedon in 451 with respect to the two natures of Christ. The country was thoroughly Arabized after 640 and was under the rule of Ottoman Turks from 1517 to 1798. English influence was strong during the 19th century. A monarchy established in 1922 lasted about 30 years, ending with the proclamation of a republic in 1953-54. By that time Egypt had become the leader of pan-Arabism against Israel. It waged two unsuccessful wars against Israel in 1948-49 and 1967. Between 1958 and 1961 it was allied with Syria and Yemen, in the United Arab Republic. Islam, the religion of some 90 percent of the population, is the state religion. Egypt maintains diplomatic relations with Vatican City.

Patriarchate, 2 (Alexandria for the Copts and for the Melkites); dioc., 7; v.a., 3; card., 1; abp., 1; bp., 13; parishes, 199; priests, 353 (179 dioc., 174 rel.); sem., 69; p.d., 1; bros., 66; srs., 1,642; bap., 2,177; Caths., 158,000 (.37%); tot. pop., 41,990,000.

El Salvador: Republic in Central America; capital, San Salvador. Evangelization affecting the whole territory followed Spanish occupation in the 1520's. The country was administered by the captaincy general of Guatemala until 1821 when independence from Spain was declared and it was annexed to Mexico. El Salvador joined the Central American Federation in 1825, decreed its own independence in 1841 and became a republic formally in 1856. In recent years, Church efforts to achieve social justice has resulted in persecution of the Church. Archbishop Oscar Romero of San Salvador, peace advocate and outspoken champion of human rights, was murdered Mar. 24, 1980, while celebrating Mass. (See Index for coverage of events in late 1981 and 1982.) El Salvador maintains diplomatic relations with Vatican City.

Archd. , 1; dioc., 4; bp., 5; parishes, 237; priests, 361 (154 dioc., 207 rel.); sem., 105; bros., 88; srs., 836; bap., 109,108; Caths., 4,348,000 (90.4%); tot. pop., 4,810,000.

England: Center of the United Kingdom of Great Britain (England, Scotland, Wales) and Northern Ireland, off the northwestern coast of Europe; capital, London. The arrival of St. Augustine of Canterbury and a band of monks in 597 marked the beginning of evangelization. Real organization of the Church took place some years after the Synod of Whitby, held in 663. Heavy losses were sustained in the wake of the Danish invasion in the 780's, but recovery starting from the time of Alfred the Great and dating especially from the middle of the 10th century led to Christianization of the whole country and close Church-state relations. The Norman Conquest of 1066 opened the Church in England to European influence. The 13th century was climactic, but decline had already set in by 1300 when the country had an all-time high of 17,000 religious. In the 14th century, John Wycliff presaged the Protestant Reformation. Henry VIII, failing in 1529 to gain annulment of his marriage to Catherine of Aragon, refused to acknowledge papal authority over the Church in England, had himself proclaimed its head, suppressed all houses of religious, and persecuted persons — Sts. Thomas More and John Fisher, among others — for not subscribing to the Oath of Supremacy and Act of Succession. He held the line on other-than-papal doctrine, however, until his death in 1547. Doctrinal aberrations were introduced during the reign of Edward VI (1547-53), through the Order of Communion, two books of Common Prayer, and the Articles of the Established Church. Mary Tudor's attempted Catholic restoration (1553-58) was a disaster, resulting in the deaths of more than 300 Protestants. Elizabeth (1558-1603) firmed up the Established Church with formation of a hierarchy, legal enactments and multi-phased persecution. One hundred and 11 priests and 62 lay persons were among the casualties of persecution during the underground Catholic revival which followed the return to England of missionary priests from France and The Lowlands. Several periods of comparative toleration ensued after Elizabeth's death. The first of several apostolic vicariates was established in 1685; this form of church government was maintained until the restoration of the hierarchy and diocesan organization in 1850. The revolution of 1688 and subsequent developments to about 1781 subjected Catholics to a wide variety of penal laws and disabilities in religious, civic and social life. The situation began to improve in 1791, and from 1801 Parliament frequently considered proposals for the repeal of penal laws against Catholics. The Act of Emancipation restored citizenship rights to Catholics in 1829. Restrictions remained in force for some time afterwards, however, on public religious worship and activity. The hierarchy was restored in 1850. Since then the Catholic Church, existing side by side with the Established Churches of England and Scotland, has followed a general pattern of growth and development. Great Britain established diplomatic relations with Vatican City in 1982. (See Index for papal visit to Great Britain.)

Archd., 4; dioc., 15; ap. ex., 1; card., 1; abp., 3; bp., 34; parishes, 2,421; priests, 5,988 (3,940 dioc., 2,048 rel.); sem., 475; p.d., 54; bros., 706; srs., 11,074; bap., 73,976; Caths., 4,129,000 (8.6%); tot. pop., 48,100,000.

Equatorial Guinea: Republic on the west coast of Africa, consisting of Rio Muni on the mainland and the islands of Fernando Po and Annobon in the Gulf of Guinea: capital, Malabo (Santa Isabel). Evangelization began in 1841. The country became independent of Spain in 1968. The Church was severely repressed during the 11-year rule of Pres. Macias (Masie) Nguema. Developments since his overthrow (August 1979) indicated some measure of improvement. Established diplomatic relations with Vatican City in 1981. (See Index for papal visit to Equatorial Guinea.)

Dioc., 2; bp., 1 (nat., restored to his see of Bata, August, 1980); parishes, 37; priests, 39 (14 dioc., 25 rel.); sem., 17; bros., 19; srs., 138; bap., 5,402; Caths., 310,000; tot. pop., 363,000.

Estonia: Baltic republic forcibly absorbed by the U.S.S.R. in 1941; capital Tallinn. Catholicism was introduced in the 11th and 12th centuries. Jurisdiction over the area was made directly subject to the Holy See in 1215. Lutheran penetration was general in the Reformation period and Russian Orthodox influence was strong from early in the 18th century until 1917 when independence was attained. The first of several apostolic administrators was appointed in 1924. The small Catholic community was hard hit during and since Russian occupation in 1941. The Russian takeover of Estonia has not been recognized by the Holy See or the United States.

Ethiopia (Abyssinia): Constitutional monarchy in northeast Africa; capital, Addis Ababa. The country was evangelized by missionaries from Egypt in the fourth century and had a bishop by about 340. Following the lead of its parent body, the Egyptian (Coptic) Church, the Church in the area succumbed to the Monophysite heresy in the sixth century. Catholic influence was negligible for centuries. An ordinariate for the Ethiopian Rite was established in Eritrea in 1930. An apostolic delegation was set up in Addis Ababa in 1937 and several jurisdictions were organized, some under the Congregation for the Oriental Churches and others under the Congregation for the Evangelization of Peoples. Most of the Catholics in the country are in the former Italian colony of Eritrea. Ethiopia maintains diplomatic relations with Vatican City.

Archd., 1; dioc., 2; v.a., 4; p.a., 2; abp., 1; bp., 6; parishes, 202; priests, 535 (166 dioc., 369 rel.); sem. 158; p.d., 1; bros., 132; srs., 862; bap., 13,955; Caths., 210,000 (.7%); tot. pop., 31,070,000.

Falkland Islands: British colony off the southern tip of South America; capital, Stanley. The islands are called Islas Malvinas by Argentina which also claims sovereignty.

P.a., 1; parish, 1; priests, 2 (rel.); bap., 3; Caths., 200; tot. pop., 1,900.

Faroe Islands: Self-governing island group in North Atlantic; Danish possession. Under ecclesiastical jurisdiction of Copenhagen diocese. Catholics number about 100. Total pop., 44,000.

Fiji: Independent member of the British Commonwealth, 100 inhabited islands in the southwest Pacific; capital, Suva. Marist missionaries began work in 1844 after Methodism had been firmly established. A prefecture apostolic was organized in 1863. The hierarchy was established in 1966. Established diplomatic relations with Vatican City, 1978.

Archd., 1; abp., 1; parishes, 33; priests, 85 (16 dioc., 69 rel.); sem., 42; bros., 52; srs., 257; bap., 1,950; Caths., 54,000 (8.5%); tot. pop., 631,000.

Finland: Republic in northern Europe; capital, Helsinki. Swedes evangelized the country in the 12th century. The Reformation swept the country, resulting in the prohibition of Catholicism in 1595, general reorganization of ecclesiastical life and affairs, and dominance of the Evangelical Lutheran Church. Catholics were given religious liberty in 1781 but missionaries and conversions were forbidden by law. The first Finnish priest since the Reformation was ordained in 1903 in Paris. A vicariate apostolic for Finland was erected in 1920. A law on religious liberty, enacted in 1923, banned the foundation of monasteries. Finland maintains diplomatic relations with Vatican City.

Dioc., 1; bp., 1; parishes, 5; priests, 17 (1 dioc., 16 rel.); bros., 2; srs., 31; bap., 77; Caths., 3,221 (.06%); tot. pop., 4,780,000.

France: Republic in western Europe; capital, Paris. Christianity was known around Lyons by the middle of the second century. By 250 there were 30 bishoprics. The hierarchy reached a fair degree of organization by the end of the fourth century. Vandals and Franks subsequently invaded the territory and caused barbarian turmoil and doctrinal problems because of their Arianism. The Frankish nation was converted following the baptism of Clovis about 496. Christianization was complete by some time in the seventh century. From then on the Church, its leaders and people, figured in virtually every important development — religious, cultural, political and social — through the periods of the Carolingians, feudalism, the Middle Ages and monarchies to the end of the 18th century. The great University of Paris became one of the intellectual centers of the 13th century. Churchmen and secular rulers were involved with developments surrounding the Avignon residence of the popes and curia from 1309 until near the end of the 14th century and with the disastrous Western Schism that followed. Strong currents of Gallicanism and conciliarism ran through ecclesiastical and secular circles in France; the former was an ideology and movement to restrict papal control of the Church in the country, the latter sought to make the pope subservient to a general council. Calvinism invaded the country about the middle of the 16th century and won a strong body of converts. Jansenism with its rigorous spirit and other aberrations appeared in the next century, to be followed by the highly influential Enlightenment. The Revolution which started in 1789 and was succeeded by the Napoleonic period completely changed the status of the Church, taking a toll of numbers by persecution and defection and disenfranchising the Church in practically every way. Throughout the 19th century the Church was caught up in the whirl of imperial and republican developments and made the victim of official hostility, popular indifference and liberal opposition. In this century, the Church has struggled with problems involving the heritage of the Revolution and its aftermath, the alienation of intellectuals, liberalism, the estrangement of the working classes because of the Church's former identification with the ruling class, and the massive needs of contemporary society. France maintains diplomatic relations with Vatican City.

Archd., 18; dioc., 75; prel., 1; ap. ex., 2; ord., 1; card., 7; abp., 16; bp., 102; parishes, 38,391; priests, 38,876 (31,481 dioc., 7,395 rel.); sem., 1,278; p.d., 108; bros., 5,333; srs., 87,044; bap., 513,501; Caths., 45,503,000 (84.7%); tot. pop., 53,710,000.

Gabon: Republic on the west coast of Equatorial Africa; capital, Libreville. Sporadic missionary effort took place before 1881 when effective evangelization began. The hierarchy was established in 1955. Gabon maintains diplomatic relations with Vatican City. (See Index for papal visit to Gabon.)

Archd., 1; dioc., 3; abp., 1 (nat.); bp., 4 (nat.); parishes, 60; priests, 117 (30 dioc., 87 rel.); sem., 17; p.d., 1; bros., 39; srs., 149; bap., 7,911; Caths., 435,000 (57.9%); tot. pop., 750,300.

Gambia, The: Republic (1970) on the northwestern coast of Africa, smallest state in Africa, member of the British Commonwealth; capital, Banjui. The country was under the jurisdiction of a vicariate apostolic until 1931. The hierarchy was established in 1957. Established diplomatic relations with Vatican City, 1978.

Dioc., 1; bp., 1; parishes, 3; priests, 18 (rel.); sem. 7 (dioc.); bros., 3; srs., 22; bap., 622; Caths., 13,000 (2.2%); tot. pop., 600,000.

Germany: Country in northern Europe partitioned in 1949 into the Communist German Democratic Republic in the East (capital, East Berlin) and the German Federal Republic in the West (capital, Bonn). Christianity was introduced in the third century, if not earlier. Trier, which became a center for missionary activity, had a bishop by 400. Visigoth invaders introduced Arianism in the fifth century but were converted in the seventh century by the East Franks, Celtic and other missionaries. St. Boniface, the apostle of Germany, established real ecclesiastical organization in the eighth century. The Church had great influence during the Carolingian period. Bishops from that time onward began to act in dual roles as pastors and rulers, a state of affairs which led inevitably to confusion and conflict in Church-state relations and perplexing problems of investiture. The Church developed strength and vitality through the Middle Ages but succumbed to abuses which antedated and prepared the ground for the Reformation. Luther's actions from 1517 made Germany a confessional battleground. Religious strife continued until conclusion of the Peace of Westphalia at the end of the Thirty Years' War in 1648. Nearly a century earlier the Peace of Augsburg (1555) had been designed, without success, to assure a degree of tranquillity by recognizing the legitimacy of different religious confessions in different states, depending on the decisions of princes. The implicit principle that princes should control the churches emerged in practice into the absolutism and Josephinism of subsequent years. St. Peter Canisius and his fellow Jesuits spearheaded a Counter Reformation in the second half of the 16th century. Before the end of the century, however, 70 per cent of the population of north and central Germany were Lutheran. Calvinism also had established a strong presence. The Church gained internal strength in a defensive position. Through much of the 19th century, however, its influence was eclipsed by Protestant intellectuals and other influences. It suffered some impoverishment also as a result of shifting boundaries and the secularization of property shortly after 1800. It came under direct attack in the Kulturkampf of the 1870's but helped to generate the opposition which resulted in a dampening of the campaign of Bismarck against it. Despite action by Catholics on the social front and other developments, discrimination against the Church spilled over into the 20th century and lasted beyond World War I. Catholics in politics struggled with others to pull the country through numerous postwar crises. The dissolution of the Center Party, agreed to by the bishops in 1933 without awareness of the ultimate consequences, contributed negatively to the rise of Hitler to supreme power. Church officials protested the Nazi anti-Church and anti-Semitic actions, but to no avail. After World War II Christian leadership had much to do with the recovery of Western Germany. East Germany, gone Communist under Russian auspices, initiated a program of control and repression of the Church in 1948 and 1949. With no prospect of success for measures designed to split bishops, priests, religious and lay persons, the regime has concentrated most of its attention on mind control, especially of the younger generation, by the elimination of religious schools, curtailment of freedom for religious instruction and formation, severe restriction of the religious press, and the substitution since the mid-50's of youth initiation and Communist ceremonies for the rites of baptism, confirmation, marriage, and funerals. Bishops are generally forbidden to travel outside the Republic. The number of priests is decreasing, partly because of reduced seminary enrollments ordered by the government since 1958. In 1973, the Vatican appointed three apostolic administrators and one auxiliary (all titular bishops) for the areas of three West German dioceses located in East Germany. West Germany maintains diplomatic relations with Vatican City.

West Germany: Archd., 5; dioc., 16 (also part of the Berlin diocese); ap., ex., 1; card., 4; abp., 5; bp., 58; parishes, 11,851; priests,

23,547 (17,353 dioc., 6,194 rel.); sem., 2,550; p.d., 721; bros., 3,247; srs., 62,730; bap., 253,756; Caths., 28,564,000 (46.4%); tot. pop., 61,561,000.

East Germany: Dioc., 2 (Dresden-Meissen and Berlin, since most of its territory ies in East Germany); a.a., 1 (Gorlitz; there are also 3 territories with apostolic administrators); bp., 10 (includes Berlin bishop who resides in eastern portion of diocese); parishes, 920; priests, 1,516 (1,278 dioc., 238 rel.); sem., 145; p.d., 37; bros., 50; srs., 2,986; bap., 7,379; Caths., 1,268,000 (7.5%); tot. pop., 16,737,000.

Ghana: Republic on the western coast of Africa, bordering on the Gulf of Guinea, member of the British Commonwealth; capital, Accra. Priests visited the country in 1482, 11 years after discovery by the Portuguese, but missionary effort — hindered by the slave trade and other factors — was slight until 1880 when systematic evangelization began. A prefecture apostolic was set up in 1879. The hierarchy was established in 1950. Ghana maintains diplomatic relations with Vatican City.

Archd., 2; dioc., 7; abp., 2 (nat.); bp., 7 (nat.); parishes, 202; priests, 455 (194 dioc., 261 rel.); sem., 243; bros., 137; srs., 456; bap., 39,523; Caths., 1,365,000 (11.9%); tot. pop., 11,450,000.

Gibraltar: British colony on the tip of the Spanish Peninsula on the Mediterranean. Evangelization took place after the Moors were driven out near the end of the 15th century. The Church was hindered by the British who acquired the colony in 1713. Most of the Catholics were, and are, Spanish and Italian immigrants and their descendants. A vicariate apostolic was organized in 1817. The diocese was erected in 1910.

Dioc., 1; bp., 1; parishes, 5; priests, 12 (dioc.); sem., 3; srs., 23; bap., 328; Caths., 22,000 (66.6%); tot. pop., 33,000.

Greece, including Crete: Kingdom in southeastern Europe on the Balkan Peninsula; capital, Athens. St. Paul preached the Gospel at Athens and Corinth on his second missionary journey and visited the country again on his third tour. Other Apostles may have passed through also. Two bishops from Greece attended the First Council of Nicaea. After the division of the Roman Empire, the Church remained Eastern in rite and later broke ties with Rome as a result of the schism of 1054. A Latin-Rite jurisdiction was set up during the period of the Latin Empire of Constantinople, 1204-1261, but crumbled afterwards. Unity efforts of the Council of Florence had poor results. The country now has Greek Catholic and Latin jurisdictions. The Greek Orthodox Church is predominant. Established diplomatic relations with Vatican City in 1980.

Archd., 4; dioc., 4; v.a., 1; ap. ex., 1; ord., 1;

abp., 3; bp., 1; parishes, 72; priests, 113 (60 dioc., 53 rel.); sem., 6; bros., 42; srs., 156; bap., 363; Caths., 48,000 (.5%); tot. pop., 9,506,000.

Greenland (Kalaalit Nunaat): Danish island province northeast of North America; granted self rule in 1979; capital, Nuuk (Godthaab). Catholicism was introduced about 1000. The first diocese was established in 1124 and a line of bishops dated from then until 1537. The first known churches in the western hemisphere, dating from about the 11th century, were on Greenland; the remains of 19 have been unearthed. The departure of Scandinavians and spread of the Reformation reduced the Church to nothing. The Moravian Brethren evangelized the Eskimos from the 1720's to 1901. By 1930 the Danish Church — Evangelical Lutheran — was in full possession. Since 1930 priests have been in Greenland, which is part of the Copenhagen diocese. There are about 60 Catholics in the area.

Grenada: Independent island state in the West Indies; capital, St. George's. Established diplomatic relations with Vatican City in 1979.

Dioc., 1; bp., 1; parishes, 20; priests, 22 (7 dioc., 15 rel.); sem., 8; p.d., 1; bros., 8; srs., 22; bap., 1,219; Caths., 71,000 (62.2%); tot. pop., 114,000.

Guadeloupe: French overseas department in the Leeward Islands of the West Indies; capital, Basse-Terre. Catholicism was introduced in the islands in the 16th century.

Dioc., 1; bp., 1; parishes, 46; priests, 77 (41 dioc., 36 rel.); sem., 5; bros., 5; srs., 198; bap., 5,073; Caths., 299,000 tot. pop., 330,000.

Guam: Outlying area of U.S. in the southwest Pacific; capital, Agana. The first Mass was offered in the Mariana Islands in 1521. The islands were evangelized by the Jesuits, from 1668, and other missionaries. The first native Micronesian bishop was ordained in 1970.

Dioc., 1; bp., 1 (nat.); parishes, 27; priests, 47 (17 dioc., 30 rel.); sem., 15 (includes Marianas and Wake Island); p.d., 7; bros., 7; srs., 125; bap., 1,874; Caths., 112,000; (93%); tot. pop., 120,000. (Figures are for Island of Guam, except where indicated. See Marianas.)

Guatemala: Republic in Central America; capital, Guatemala City. Evangelization dates from the beginning of Spanish occupation in 1524. The first diocese, for all Central American territories administered by the captaincy general of Guatemala, was established in 1534. The country became independent in 1839, following annexation to Mexico in 1821, secession in 1823 and membership in the Central American Federation from 1825. In 1870, a government installed by a liberal revolution repudiated the concordat of 1853 and took active measures against the Church. Separation of Church and state was decreed; religious orders were suppressed and their property seized; priests and religious were exiled; schools were secularized. Full freedom was subsequently granted. The country has been in a virtual state of civil war in recent years, with violence and repression directed at all segments of the population. Since 1976, at least nine priests were reported missing or killed. Guatemala maintains diplomatic relations with Vatican City.

Archd., 1; dioc., 8; prel., 2; a.a., 2; card., 1; bp., 14; parishes, 339; priests, 699 (206 dioc., 493 rel.); sem., 244; p.d., 3; bros., 136; srs., 1,191; bap., 179,703; Caths. 6,070,000 (83.6%); tot. pop. 7,260,000.

Guiana, French (Cayenne): French overseas department on the northeast coast of South America; capital, Cayenne. Catholicism was introduced in the 17th century. The Cayenne diocese was established in 1956.

Dioc., 1; bp., 1; parishes, 28; priests, 31 (9 dioc., 22 rel.); bros., 2; srs., 104; bap., 1,355; Caths., 52,000; tot. pop., 66,000.

Guinea: Republic on the west coast of Africa; capital, Conakry. Occasional missionary work followed exploration by the Portuguese about the middle of the 15th century; organized effort dates from 1877. The hierarchy was established in 1955. Following independence from France in 1958, Catholic schools were nationalized, youth organizations banned and missionaries restricted. Foreign missionaries were expelled in 1967. Archbishop Tchidimbo of Conakry, sentenced to life imprisonment in 1971 on a charge of conspiring to overthrow the government, was released in August, 1979; he resigned his see. Guinea has an apostolic delegate.

Archd., 1; dioc., 1; p.a., 1; abp., 1 (nat.); bp., 1 (nat.); parishes, 28; priests, 20 (18 dioc., 2 rel.); sem., 14 (dioc.); bros., 1; srs., 22; bap., 914; Caths., 49,000 (.9%); tot. pop., 5,010,000.

Guinea-Bissau (formerly Portuguese Guinea): Independent state on the west coast of Africa; capital, Bissau. Catholicism was introduced in the second half of the 15th century but limited missionary work, hampered by the slave trade, had meager results. Missionary work in this century dates from 1933. A prefecture apostolic was established in 1955 (made a diocese in 1977). Guinea-Bissau has an apostolic delegate.

Dioc., 1; bp., 1; parishes, 15; priests, 40 (rel); sem., 4; bros., 11; srs., 29; bap., 612; Caths., 47,000; tot. pop., 638,000.

Guyana: Republic on the northern coast of South America; capital, Georgetown. In 1899 the Catholic Church and other churches were given equal status with the Church of England and the Church of Scotland, which had sole rights up to that time. Most of the Catholics are Portuguese. The Georgetown diocese was established in 1956, 10 years before Guyana became independent of England. The first native bishop was appointed in 1971. Schools were nationalized in 1976. Increased

government interference was reported in 1980-81. The Catholic newspaper was forced to close and missionaries were denied access to certain areas.

Dioc., 1; bp., 1; parishes, 23; priests, 59 (6 dioc., 53 rel.); sem., 5; bros., 5; srs., 53; bap., 1,929; Caths., 101,000 (11.4%); tot. pop., 880,000.

Haiti: Caribbean republic on the western third of Hispaniola adjacent to the Dominican Republic; capital, Port-au-Prince. Evangelization followed discovery by Columbus in 1492. Capuchins and Jesuits did most of the missionary work in the 18th century. From 1804, when independence was declared, until 1860, the country was in schism. Relations were regularized by a concordat concluded in 1860, when an archdiocese and four dioceses were established. Factors hindering the development of the Church have been a shortage of native clergy, inadequate religious instruction and the prevalence of voodoo. Political upheavals in the 1960's had serious effects on the Church. Haiti maintains diplomatic relations with Vatican City.

Archd., 1; dioc., 6; abp., 1; bp., 6; parishes, 186; priests, 405 (195 dioc., 210 rel.); sem., 139; bros., 239; srs., 900; bap., 104,472; Caths., 4,969,000 (83.4%); tot. pop. 5,955,230.

Honduras: Republic in Central America; capital, Tegucigalpa. Evangelization preceded establishment of the first diocese in the 16th century. Under Spanish rule and after independence from 1823, the Church held a favored position until 1880 when equal legal status was given to all religions. Harassment of priests and nuns working among peasants and Salvadorean refugees was reported in recent years. Honduras maintains diplomatic relations with Vatican City.

Archd., 1; dioc., 4; prel., 1; abp., 1; bp., 6; parishes, 125; priests, 236 (65 dioc., 171 rel.); sem., 26; bros., 22; srs., 359; bap., 108,410; Caths., 3,536,000 (95.8%); tot. pop., 3,690,000.

Hong Kong: British crown colony at the mouth of the Canton River, adjacent to the southeast Chinese province of Kwangtung. A prefecture apostolic was established in 1841. Members of the Pontifical Institute for Foreign Missions began work there in 1858. The Hong Kong diocese was erected in 1946.

Dioc., 1; bp., 1; parishes, 54; priests, 367 (74 dioc., 293 rel.); sem., 14; bros., 93; srs., 833; bap., 4,967; Caths., 260,000 (5.1%); tot. pop., 5,070,000.

Hungary: People's republic in east central Europe; capital, Budapest. The early origins of Christianity in the country, whose territory was subject to a great deal of change, is not known. Magyars accepted Christianity about the end of the 10th century. St. Stephen I (d. 1038) promoted its spread and helped to organize some of its historical dioceses. Bishops early became influential in politics as well as in the Church. For centuries the country served as a buffer for the Christian West against barbarians from the East, notably the Mongols in the 13th century. Religious orders, whose foundations started from the 1130's, provided the most effective missionaries, pastors and teachers. Outstanding for years were the Franciscans and Dominicans; the Jesuits were noted for their work in the Counter-Reformation from the second half of the 16th century onwards. Hussites and Waldensians prepared the way for the Reformation which struck at almost the same time as the Turks. The Reformation made considerable progress after 1526, resulting in the conversion of large numbers to Lutheranism and Calvinism by the end of the century. Most of them or their descendants returned to the Church later, but many Magyars remained staunch Calvinists. Turks repressed the churches, Protestant as well as Catholic, during a reign of 150 years but they managed to survive. Domination of the Church was one of the objectives of government policy during the reigns of Maria Theresa and Joseph II in the second half of the 18th century; their Josephinism affected Church-state relations until the first World War. More than 100,000 Eastern Rite schismatics were reunited with Rome about the turn of the 18th century. Secularization increased in the second half of the 19th century, which also witnessed the birth of many new Catholic organizations and movements to influence life in the nation and the Church. Catholics were involved in the social chaos and anti-religious atmosphere of the years following World War I, struggling with their compatriots for religious as well as political survival. After World War II Communist strength, which had manifested itself with less intensity earlier in the century, was great long before it forced the legally elected president out of office in 1947 and imposed a Soviet type of constitution on the country in 1949. The campaign against the Church started with the disbanding of Catholic organizations in 1946. In 1948, "Caritas," the Catholic charitable organization, was taken over and all Catholic schools, colleges and institutions were suppressed. Interference in church administration and attempts to split the bishops preceded the arrest of Cardinal Mindszenty on Dec. 26, 1948, and his sentence to life imprisonment in 1949. (He was free for a few days during the unsuccessful uprising of 1956. He then took up residence at the U.S. Embassy in Budapest where he remained until September, 1971, when he was permitted to leave the country. He died in 1975 in Vienna.) In 1950, religious orders and congregations were suppressed and 10,000 religious were interned. At least 30 priests and monks were assassinated, jailed or deported. About 4,000 priests and religious were confined in jail or concentration camps. The government sponsored a national "Progressive Catholic" church and captive organizations for priests and "Catholic Action," which attracted only a small minority. Signs were clear in 1965 and 1966 that a 1964 agreement with the Holy See regarding episcopal appointments had settled nothing. Six bishops were appointed by the Holy See and some other posts were filled, but none of the prelates were free from government surveillance and harassment. Four new bishops were appointed by the Holy See in January and ordained in Budapest in February, 1969; three elderly prelates resigned their sees. Shortly thereafter, peace priests complained that the "too Roman" new bishops would not deal with them. Talks between Vatican and Hungarian representatives during the past several years have resulted in the appointment of bishops to fill all of Hungary's 11 residential sees.

Archd., 3; dioc., 8; abb., 1; ap. ex., 1; card, 1; abp., 4; bp., 13; parishes, 2,266; priests, 3,203 (3,126 dioc., 77 rel.); sem., 270; srs., 52; bap., 83,830; Caths., 6,573,000 (61.3%); tot. pop., 10,710,000.

Iceland: Island republic between Norway and Greenland; capital, Reykjavik. Irish hermits were there in the eighth century. Missionaries subsequently evangelized the island and Christianity was officially accepted about 1000. The first bishop was ordained in 1056. The Black Death had dire effects and spiritual decline set in during the 15th century. Lutheranism was introduced from Denmark between 1537 and 1552 and made the official religion. Some Catholic missionary work was done in the 19th century. Religious freedom was granted to the few Catholics in 1874. A vicariate was erected in 1929 (made a diocese in 1968). Iceland maintains diplomatic relations with Vatican City.

Dioc., 1; bp., 1; parishes, 2; priests, 7 (2 dioc., 5 rel.); sem., 6; srs., 38; bap., 18; Caths., 2,000; tot. pop., 229,000.

India: Republic on the subcontinent of south central Asia, member of the British Commonwealth; capital, New Delhi. Long-standing tradition credits the Apostle Thomas with the introduction of Christianity in the Kerala area. Evangelization followed the establishment of Portuguese posts and the conquest of Goa in 1510. Jesuits, Franciscans, Dominicans, Augustinians and members of other religious orders figured in the early missionary history. An archdiocese for Goa, with two suffragan sees, was set up in 1558. Five provincial councils were held between 1567 and 1606. The number of Catholics in 1572 was estimated to be 280,000. This figure rose to 800,000 in 1700 and declined to 500,000 in 1800. Missionaries had some difficulties with the British East India Co. which exercised virtual government control from 1757 to 1858. They also had trouble because of a conflict that developed between policies of the Portuguese government, which pressed its rights of patronage in episcopal and clerical appointments, and the Congregation for the Propagation of the Faith, which sought greater freedom of action in the same appointments. This struggle eventuated in the schism of Goa between 1838 and 1857. In 1886, when the number of Catholics was estimated to be one million, the hierarchy for India and Ceylon was restored. Jesuits contributed greatly to the development of Catholic education in the second half of the 19th century. A large percentage of the Catholic population is located around Goa and Kerala and farther south. The country is predominantly Hindu. India maintains diplomatic relations with Vatican City. So-called anti-conversion laws in effect in several states have had a restrictive effect on pastoral ministry and social service.

Patriarchate, 1 (titular of East Indies); archd., 19; dioc., 88; p.a., 2; card., 2; abp., 17; bp., 94; parishes, 5,037; priests, 11,733 (6,828 dioc., 4,905 rel.); sem., 4,995; p.d., 26; bros., 2,994; srs., 50,936; bap., 297,603; Caths., 10,528,000 (1.5%); tot. pop., 683,810,000. (Catholic and total population figures are from 1981 Bulletin of Indian Episcopal Conference as reported in Fides.)

Indonesia: Republic southeast of Asia, consisting of some 3,000 islands including Kalimantan (most of Borneo), Sulawesi (Celebes), Java, the Lesser Sundas, Moluccas, Sumatra, Timor and West Irian (Irian Jaya, western part of New Guinea); capital, Jakarta. Evangelization by the Portuguese began about 1511. St. Francis Xavier, greatest of the modern missionaries, spent some 14 months in the area. Christianity was strongly rooted in some parts of the islands by 1600. Islam's rise to dominance began at this time. The Dutch East Indies Co., which gained effective control in the 17th century, banned evangelization by Catholic missionaries for some time but Dutch secular and religious priests managed to resume the work. A vicariate of Batavia for all the Dutch East Indies was set up in 1841. About 90 per cent of the population is Moslem. The hierarchy was established in 1961. Indonesia maintains diplomatic relations with Vatican City.

Archd., 7; dioc., 26; card., 1; abp., 5; bp., 28; parishes, 417; priests, 1,715 (218 dioc., 1,497 rel.); sem., 1,037; p.d., 8; bros., 766; srs., 4,118; bap., 161,713; Caths., 3,390,000 (2.2%); tot. pop., 151,890,000. (Statistics for former Portuguese Timor which was annexed by Indonesia in 1976 are listed separately; see Timor, Eastern.)

Iran: Constitutional monarchy in southwestern Asia, between the Caspian Sea and the Persian Gulf; capital, Teheran. Some of the earliest Christian communities were established in this area outside the (then) Roman Empire. They suffered persecution in the fourth century and were then cut off from the outside world. Nestorianism was generally professed in the late fifth century. Islam became dominant after 640. Some later missionary work was attempted but without success. Religious liberty was granted in 1834, but Catholics were the victims of a massacre in 1918. Islam is the religion of perhaps 98 per cent of the population. In 1964 the country had 100,000 Monophysites, the largest group of Christians, and some 20,000 Nestorians. Catholics belong to the Latin, Armenian and Chaldean rites. Iran (Persia until 1935) maintains diplomatic relations with Vatican City.

Archd., 4; dioc., 2; abp., 3; bp., 1; parishes, 26; priests, 32 (13 dioc., 19 rel.); sem., 3; p.d., 10; bros., 2; srs., 45, bap., 242; Caths., 19,000 (.05%); tot. pop., 37,450,000.

Iraq: Republic in southwestern Asia, between Iran and Saudi Arabia; capital, Baghdad. Some of the earliest Christian communities were established in the area, whose history resembles that of Iran. Catholics belong to the Armenian, Chaldean, Latin and Syrian rites; Chaldeans are most numerous. Islam is the religion of some 90 per cent of the population. Iraq maintains diplomatic relations with Vatican City.

Patriarchate, 1; archd., 9; dioc., 5; patriarch, 1; abp., 9; bp., 4; parishes, 107; priests, 152 (122 dioc., 30 rel.); sem., 15; p.d., 4; bros., 26; srs., 224; bap., 5,609; Caths., 378,000; tot. pop., 13,080,000.

Ireland: Republic in the British Isles; capital, Dublin. St. Patrick, who is venerated as the apostle of Ireland, evangelized parts of the island for some years after the middle of the fifth century. Conversion of the island was not accomplished, however, until the seventh century or later. Celtic monks were the principal missionaries. The Church was organized along monastic lines at first, but a movement developed in the 11th century for the establishment of jurisdiction along episcopal lines. By that time many Roman usages had been adopted. The Church gathered strength during the period from the Norman Conquest of England to the reign of Henry VIII despite a wide variety of rivalries, wars, and other disturbances. Henry introduced an age of repression of the faith which continued for many years under several of his successors. The Irish suffered from proscription of the Catholic faith, economic and social disabilities, subjection to absentee landlords and a plantation system designed to keep them from owning property, and actual persecution which took an uncertain toll of lives up until about 1714. Most of those living in the northern part of Ireland became Anglican and Presbyterian in the 1600's but the south remained strong in faith. Some penal laws remained in force until emancipation in 1829. Nearly 100 years later Ireland was divided by two enactments which made Northern Ireland, consisting of six counties, part of the United Kindgom (1920) and gave dominion status to the Irish Free State, made up of the other 26 counties (1922). This state (Eire, in Gaelic) was proclaimed the Republic of Ireland in 1949. The Catholic Church predominates but religious freedom is guaranteed for all. Ireland maintains diplomatic relations with Vatican City.

Archd., 4; dioc., 22; card., 1; abp., 3; bp., 28; parishes, 1,301; priests, 6,156 (3,740 dioc., 2,416 rel.); sem., 1,149; bros., 1,941; srs., 12,637; bap., 85,148 (preceding figures include Northern Ireland); Caths., 3,135,000 (93%); tot. pop., 3,367,000.

Ireland, Northern: Part of the United Kingdom, it consists of six of the nine counties of Ulster in the northeast corner of Ireland; capital, Belfast. History is given under Ireland, above. For recent developments, see Index.

Caths. (approx.), 505,000 (32%); tot. pop., 1,540,000 (other statistics are included in Ireland).

Israel: Parliamentary democracy in the Middle East, at the eastern end of the Mediterranean; capitals, Jerusalem and Tel Aviv (diplomatic). Israel was the birthplace of Christianity, the site of the first Christian communities. Some persecution was suffered in the early Christian era and again during the several hundred years of Roman control. Moslems conquered the territory in the seventh century and, except for the period of the Kingdom of Jerusalem established by Crusaders, remained in control most of the time up until World War I. The Church survived in the area, sometimes just barely, but it did not prosper greatly or show any notable increase in numbers. The British took over the protectorate of the area after World War I. Partition into Israel for the Jews and Palestine for the Arabs was approved by the United Nations in 1947. War broke out a year later with the proclamation of the Republic of Israel. The Israelis won the war and 50 percent more territory than they had originally been ceded. War broke out again for six days in June, 1967, and in October, 1973, resulting in a Middle East crisis which persists to the present time. Caught in the middle of the conflict are hundreds of thousands of dispossessed Palestinian refugees. Judaism is the faith professed by about 85 percent of the inhabitants; approximately one-third of them are considered observants. Most of the Arab minority are Moslems. The Acre archdiocese for Melkites is situated in Israel. Maronites are subject to the bishop of Tyr, Lebanon. Latins are under the jurisdiction of the Roman patriarchate of Jerusalem. Israel has an apostolic delegate. The *1980 Statistical Yearbook of the Church* reported a Catholic population of 147,000 in a total population of 3,870,000.

Italy: Republic in southern Europe; capital, Rome. A Christian community was formed early at Rome, probably by the middle of the first century. St. Peter established his see there. He and St. Paul suffered death for the faith there in the 60s. The early Christians were persecuted at various times there, as in other parts of the empire, but the Church developed in numbers and influence, gradually spreading out from towns and cities in the center and south to rural areas and the north. Organization, in the process of formation in the second century, developed greatly between the fifth and eighth centuries. By the latter date the Church had already come to grips with serious problems, including doctrinal and disciplinary disputes that threatened the unity of faith, barbarian invasions, and the need for the pope and bishops to take over civil responsibilities because of imperial default. The Church has been at the center of life on the peninsula throughout the centuries. It emerged from underground in 313, with the Edict of Milan, and rose to a position of prestige and lasting influence. It educated and converted the barbarians, preserved culture through the early Middle Ages and passed it on to later times, suffered periods of decline and gained strength through recurring reforms, engaged in military combat for political reasons and intellectual combat for the preservation and development of doctrine, saw and patronized the development of the arts, experienced all human strengths and weaknesses in its members, knew triumph and the humiliation of failure. For long centuries, from the fourth to the 19th, the Church was a temporal as well as spiritual power. This temporal aspect complicated its history in Italy. Since the 1870's, however, when the Papal States were annexed by the Kingdom of Italy, the history became simpler — but remained complicated — as the Church, shorn of temporal power, began to find new freedom for the fulfillment of its spiritual mission. Italy maintains diplomatic relations with Vatican City.

Patriarchate, 1; archd., 57; dioc., 210; prel., 4; abb., 9; card., 33; abp., 47; bp. (approx.), 200; parishes, 28,618; priests, 63,729 (40,649 dioc., 23,080 rel.); sem., 5,076; p.d., 210; bros., 6,626; srs., 146,182; bap., 691,558; Caths., 55,620,000 (97.5%); tot. pop., 57,040,000.

Ivory Coast: Republic in western Africa; capital, Abidjan. The Holy Ghost Fathers began systematic evangelization in 1895. The first native priests from the area were ordained in 1934. The hierarchy was set up in 1955. Ivory Coast maintains diplomatic relations with Vatican City.

Archd., 1; dioc., 9 (2 new ones established in 1982); abp., 1 (nat.); bp., 10 (nat.); parishes, 155; priests, 427 (135 dioc., 292 rel.); sem., 71; p.d., 1; bros., 104; srs., 504; bap., 18,913; Caths., 766,000 (9.6%); tot. pop., 7,970,000.

Jamaica: Parliamentary democracy in the West Indies, member of the British Commonwealth; capital, Kingston. Franciscans and Dominicans evangelized the island from about 1512 until 1655. Missionary work was interrupted after the English took possession but was resumed by Jesuits about the turn of the 19th century. A vicariate apostolic was organized in 1837. The hierarchy was established in 1967. Established diplomatic relations with Vatican City in 1979.

Archd., 1; dioc., 1; abp., 1; bp., 1; parishes, 30; priests, 109 (19 dioc., 90 rel.); sem., 4; p.d., 2; bros., 7; srs., 215; bap., 2,750; Caths., 198,000 (9%); tot. pop., 2,190,000.

Japan: Constitutional monarchy in the northwest Pacific; capital, Tokyo. Jesuits began evangelization in the middle of the 16th century and about 300,000 converts, most of them in Kyushu, were reported at the end of the century. The Nagasaki Martyrs were victims of persecution in 1597. Another persecution took some 4,000 lives between 1614 and 1651. Missionaries, banned for two centuries, returned about the middle of the 19th century and found Christian communities still surviving in Nagasaki and other places in Kyushu. A vicariate was organized in 1866. Religious freedom was guaranteed in 1889. The hierarchy was established in 1891. Japan maintains diplomatic relations with Vatican City.

Archd., 3; dioc., 13; p.a., 1; card., 1; abp., 2; bp., 14; parishes, 758; priests, 1,973 (503 dioc., 1,470 rel.); sem., 200; p.d., 3; bros., 476; srs., 7,258; bap., 9,962; Caths., 398,000 (.3%); tot. pop., 116,780,000.

Jerusalem: The entire city, site of the first Christian community, has been under Israeli control since the Israeli-Arab war of June, 1967. There are two patriarchates in the city, Melkite and Latin. Jerusalem has an apostolic delegate.

Jordan: Constitutional monarchy in the Middle East; capital, Amman. Christianity there dates from apostolic times. Survival of the faith was threatened many times under the rule of Moslems from 636 and Ottoman Turks from 1517 to 1918, and in the Islamic Emirate of Trans-Jordan from 1918 to 1949. Since the creation of Israel, some 500,000 Palestinian refugees, some of them Christians, have been in Jordan. Islam is the state religion but religious freedom is guaranteed for all. Jordan has an apostolic delegate.

The Greek Melkite-Rite Archdiocese of Petra and Philadelphia is located in Jordan. Latin (Roman)-Rite Catholics are under the jurisdiction of the Latin patriarchate of Jerusalem.

Archd., 1; abp., 1; parishes, 61; priests, 66 (52 dioc., 14 rel.); sem. 4; bros., 5; srs., 221; bap., 1,066; Caths., 76,000; tot. pop., 3,190,000.

Kashmir and Jammu: Statistics included in India.

Kenya: Republic in eastern Africa bordering on the Indian Ocean, member of the British Commonwealth; capital, Nairobi. Systematic evangelization by the Holy Ghost Fathers began in 1892, nearly 40 years after the start of work by Protestant missionaries. The hierarchy was established in 1953. Kenya maintains diplomatic relations with Vatican City.

Archd., 1; dioc., 13; p.a., 1; card., 1 (nat.); bp., 13 (9 nat.); parishes, 341; priests, 879 (230 dioc., 649 rel.); sem., 501; p.d., 2; bros., 222; srs., 1,954; bap., 184,512; Caths., 3,101,000 (18%); tot. pop., 16,400,000.

Kiribati (Gilbert Islands): Former British colony in Oceania; became independent July 12, 1979; capital Bairiki on Tarawa. French Missionaries of the Sacred Heart began work in the islands in 1888. A vicariate for the islands was organized in 1897. The hierarchy was established in 1966.

Dioc., 1; bp., 1; parishes, 21; priests, 18 (2 dioc., 16 rel.); sem., 5; bros., 2; srs., 45; bap., 470; Caths., 28,000; tot. pop., 57,000. (Statistics include Tuvalu.)

Korea: Peninsula in eastern Asia, east of China, divided into the (Communist) Democratic People's Republic in the North, formed May 1, 1948, with Pyongyang as its capital; and the Republic of Korea in the South, with Seoul as the capital. Some Catholics may have been in Korea before it became a "hermit kingdom" toward the end of the 16th century and closed its borders to foreigners. The real introduction to Catholicism came through lay converts in the last quarter of the 18th century. A priest arriving in the country in 1794 found 4,000 Catholics there who had never seen a priest. A vicariate was erected in 1831 but was not manned for several years thereafter. There were 15,000 Catholics by 1857. Four persecutions in the 19th century took a terrible toll; several thousands died in the last one, 1866-69. Freedom of religion was granted in 1883 when Korea opened its borders. Progress was made thereafter. The hierarchy was established in 1962. Since the war of 1950-1953, there have been no signs of Catholic life in the North, which has been blanketed by a news blackout. In July, 1972, both Koreas agreed to seek peaceful means of reunification. The South maintains diplomatic relations with Vatican City. Bishop Tji of Won Ju, South Korea, convicted and sentenced to 15 years' imprisonment in 1974 on a charge of inciting to rebellion, was released in February, 1975.

North Korea: Dioc., 2; abb., 1; bp., 1 (exiled); tot. pop., 17,900,000. No recent Catholic statistics available; there were an estimated 100,000 Catholics reported in 1969.

South Korea: Archd., 3; dioc., 11; card., 1; abp., 2; bp., 13; parishes, 595; priests, 1,107 (797 dioc., 310 rel.); sem., 658; bros., 201; srs., 3,165; bap., 112,974; Caths. 1,268,000 (3.3%); tot. pop., 38,200,000.

Kuwait: Constitutional monarchy (sultanate or sheikdom) in southwest Asia bordering on the Persian Gulf. Remote Christian origins probably date to apostolic times. Islam is the predominant and official religion. Kuwait maintains diplomatic relations with Vatican City.

V.a., 1; bp., 1; parishes, 4; priests, 9 (4 dioc., 5 rel.); srs., 31; bap., 581; Caths., 49,000; tot. pop., 1,360,000.

Laos: Constitutional monarchy in southeast Asia, surrounded by China, Vietnam, Kampuchea, Thailand and Burma; capital, Vientiane. Systematic evangelization by French missionaries started about 1881; earlier efforts ended in 1688. A vicariate apostolic was organized in 1899 when there were 8,000 Catholics and 2,000 catechumens in the country. Most of the foreign missionaries were expelled following the communist takeover in 1975. Buddhism is the state religion. Laos has an apostolic delegate.

V.a., 4; bp., 3 (nat.). No statistics available. Catholics numbered 35,000 (1% of the total population) in 1974. Tot. pop. (1980), 3,720,000.

Latvia: Baltic republic forcibly absorbed by the U.S.S.R. in the early 1940s; capital, Riga. Catholicism was introduced late in the 12th century. Lutheranism became the dominant religion after 1530. Catholics were free to practice their faith during the long period of Russian control and during independence from 1918 to 1940. The relatively small Catholic community has been repressed since the start of Soviet occupation. The Russian takeover of Latvia has not been recognized by the Holy See or the United States.

Archd., 1; dioc., 1; bp., 3 (none residential); parishes, 178; priests, 128 (119 dioc., 9 rel.); bap., 4,226; Caths., 248,000; tot. pop. 2,521,000.

Lebanon: Republic in the Middle East, north of Israel; capital, Beirut. Christianity, introduced in apostolic times, was firmly established by the end of the fourth century and has remained so despite heavy Moslem influence since early in the seventh century. The country is the center of the Maronite Rite. Lebanon maintains diplomatic relations with Vatican City.

There are 18 ecclesiastical jurisdictions in Lebanon serving the following rites: Armenian (1 diocese); Chaldean (1 diocese); Roman (1 vicariate apostolic); Maronite (3 archdioceses and 5 dioceses); Greek Melkite (1 metropolitan see, 6 archdioceses); the Syrians are served by a patriarchal vicar. The patriarchs of Antioch of the Syrians, Antioch of the Maronites and Cilicia of the Armenians reside in Lebanon. Catholics, 1,215,000; tot. pop., 3,160,000.

Lesotho: Constitutional monarchy, an enclave in the southeastern part of the Republic of South Africa; capital, Maseru. Oblates of Mary Immaculate, the first Catholic missionaries in the area, started evangelization in 1862. A prefecture apostolic was organized in 1894. The hierarchy was established in 1951. Lesotho maintains diplomatic relations with Vatican City.

Archd., 1; dioc., 3; abp., 1 (nat.); bp., 3 (nat.); parishes, 72; priests, 142 (22 dioc., 120 rel.); sem., 61; bros., 59; srs., 705; bap., 24,481; Caths., 571,000 (42.6%); tot. pop., 1,340,000.

Liberia: Republic in western Africa, bordering on the Atlantic; capital, Monrovia. Missionary work and influence, dating interruptedly from the 16th century, were slight before the Society of African Missions undertook evangelization in 1906. The hierarchy was established in 1982. Liberia maintains diplomatic relations with Vatican City.

Archd., 1; dioc., 1; abp., 1 (nat.); bp., 1 (nat.); parishes, 45; priests, 48 (8 dioc., 40 rel.); sem., 21; p.d., 3; bros., 29; srs., 89; bap. 2,034; Caths., 36,000 (1.9%); tot. pop., 1,870,000.

Libya: Arab republic in northern Africa, on the Mediterranean between Egypt and Tunisia; capitals are Tripoli and Benghasi. Christianity was probably preached in the area at an early date but was overcome by the spread of Islam from the 630's. Islamization was complete by 1067 and there has been no Christian influence since then. The Catholics in the country belong to the foreign colony. Islam is the state religion. Libya has an apostolic delegate.

V.a., 3; p.a., 1; bp., 2; parishes, 3; priests, 14 (3 dioc., 11 rel.); srs., 147; bap., 61; Caths., 35,000 (1.1%); tot. pop., 2,980,000.

Liechtenstein: Constitutional monarchy in central Europe, in the Alps and on the Rhine between Switzerland and Austria; capital, Vaduz. Christianity in the country dates from the fourth century; the area has been under the jurisdiction of Chur, Switzerland, since about that time. The Reformation had hardly any influence in the country. Catholicism is the state religion but religious freedom for all is guaranteed by law.

Parishes, 10; priests, 32 (20 dioc., 12 rel); bros., 11; srs., 102; bap., 350; Caths., 24,000 (92%); tot. pop., 26,000.

Lithuania: Baltic republic forcibly absorbed and under Soviet domination since 1945; captial, Vilna (Vilnius). Catholicism was introduced in 1251 and two dioceses were established by 1260. Effective evangelization took place between 1385 and 1417, when Catholicism became the state religion. Losses to Lutheranism in the 16th century were overcome. Efforts of czars to "russify" the Church between 1795 and 1918 were strongly resisted. Concordat relations with the Vatican were established in 1927, nine years after independence from Russia and 13 years before the start of another kind of Russian control with the following results, among others: all convents closed since 1940; four seminaries shut down; appointment to one seminary (Kaunas) only with government approval; priests restricted in pastoral ministry and subject to appointment by government officials; no religious services outside churches; no religious press; religious instruction banned; parish installations and activities controlled by directives enacted in 1976; two bishops — Msgr. Vincentas Sladkevicius and Msgr. Julijonas Steponavicius — forbidden to act as bishops and relegated to remote parishes since 1957 and 1961, respectively; arrest, imprisonment or detention in Siberia for four bishops, 185 priests, 275 lay persons between 1945 and 1955. Despite such developments and conditions, there remains a strong and vigorous underground Church in Lithuania, where the Soviet government finds its repressive potential limited by the solidarity of popular resistance. In July, 1982, two episcopal appointments were made: Rev. Antanas Vaicius was named titular bishop of Cubda and apostolic administrator of the Telsiai diocese and Klaipeda prelature; Bishop Vincentas Sladkevicius, titular bishop of Abora and auxiliary bishop of Kaisiadorys, was named apostolic administrator of that diocese. The Soviet takeover of Lithuania is not recognized by the Holy See or the United States.

Archd., 2 (Kaunas and Vilna, which includes territory in political confines of Poland); dioc., 4; prel., 1; bp., 5 (one residential); parishes 630; priests, 705 (696 dioc., 9 rel.); sem., 89; Caths., 2,522,000; tot. pop., 3,153,000.

Luxembourg: Constitutional monarchy in western Europe, between Belgium, Germany and France; capital, Luxembourg. Christianity, introduced in the fifth and sixth centuries, was firmly established by the end of the eighth century. A full-scale parish system was in existence in the ninth century. Monastic influence was strong until the Reformation, which had minimal influence in the country. The Church experienced some adverse influence from the currents of the French Revolution. Luxembourg maintains diplomatic relations with Vatican City.

Dioc., 1; bp., 1; parishes, 274; priests, 442 (348 dioc., 94 rel.); sem., 21; bros., 30; srs., 1,263; bap., 3,391; Caths. 346,000 (95%); tot. pop., 364,000.

Macao: Portuguese province in southeast Asia across the Pearl River estuary from Hong Kong. Christianity was introduced by the Jesuits in 1557. Diocese was established in 1576. Macao served as a base for missionary work in Japan and China.

Dioc., 1; bp., 1; parishes, 8; priests, 82 (46 dioc., 36 rel.); sem., 3; bros., 16; srs., 194; bap., 671; Caths., 39,000; tot. pop., 282,000.

Madagascar (Malagasy Republic): Republic off the eastern coast of Africa; capital, Antananarivo. Missionary efforts were generally fruitless from early in the 16th century

until the Jesuits were permitted to start open evangelization about 1845. A prefecture apostolic was set up in 1850 and a vicariate apostolic in the north was placed in charge of the Holy Ghost Fathers in 1898. There were 100,000 Catholics by 1900. The first native bishop was ordained in 1936. The hierarchy was established in 1955. Madagascar maintains diplomatic relations with Vatican City.

Archd., 3; dioc., 14; card., 1 (nat.); abp., 2 (nat.); bp., 15 (14 nat.); parishes, 222; priests, 674 (149 dioc., 525 rel.); sem., 140; bros., 369; srs., 1,785; bap., 72,847; Caths., 1,994,000 (22.2%); tot. pop. 8,740,000.

Madeira Islands: Portuguese province, an archipelago 340 miles west of the northwestern coast of Africa; capital, Funchal. Catholicism has had a continuous history since the first half of the 15th century. Statistics are included in those for Portugal.

Malawi: Republic in the interior of eastern Africa, member of the British Commonwealth; capital, Lilongwe. Missionary work, begun by Jesuits in the late 16th and early 17th centuries, was generally ineffective until the end of the 19th century. The White Fathers arrived in 1889 and later were joined by others. A vicariate was set up in 1897. The hierarchy was established in 1959. Malawi maintains diplomatic relations with Vatican City.

Archd., 1; dioc., 6; abp., 1 (nat.); bp., 6 (5 nat.); parishes, 129; priests, 326 (108 dioc., 218 rel.); sem., 146; bros., 95; srs., 606; bap., 47,443; Caths., 1,194,000 (20%); tot. pop., 5,970,000.

Malaysia: Parliamentary democracy in southeastern Asia, member of the British Commonwealth, federation of former states of Malaya, Sabah (former Br. North Borneo), and Sarawak; capital, Kuala Lumpur. Christianity, introduced by Portuguese colonists about 1511, was confined almost exclusively to Malacca until late in the 18th century. The effectiveness of evangelization increased from then on because of the recruitment and training of native clergy. Singapore (see separate entry), founded in 1819, became a center for missionary work. Seventeen thousand Catholics were in the Malacca diocese in 1888. Effective evangelization in Sabah and Sarawak began in the second half of the 19th century. The hierarchy was established in 1973. Malaysia has an apostolic delegate.

Archd., 2; dioc., 4; abp., 2; bp., 5 (nat.); parishes, 156; priests, 260 (166 dioc., 94 rel.); sem., 35; p.d., 1; bros., 117; srs., 587; bap., 14,133; Caths., 410,000 (3%); tot. pop., 13,440,000.

Maldives: Republic, an archipelago 400 miles southwest of India and Ceylon; capital, Male. No serious attempt was ever made to evangelize the area, which is completely Moslem.

Tot. pop., 150,000.

Mali: Republic, inland in western Africa; capital, Bamako. Catholicism was introduced late in the second half of the 19th century. Missionary work made little progress in the midst of the predominantly Moslem population. A vicariate was set up in 1921. The hierarchy was established in 1955. Established diplomatic relations with Vatican City in 1979.

Archd., 1; dioc., 5; abp., 1 (nat.); bp., 5 (3 nat.); parishes, 38; priests, 139 (23 dioc., 116 rel.); sem., 19; bros., 30; srs., 160; bap., 2,339; Caths., 68,000 (1%); tot. pop., 6,910,000.

Malta: Parliamentary democracy, member of the British Commonwealth, 58 miles south of Sicily; capital, Valletta. Early catacombs and inscriptions are evidence of the early introduction of Christianity. St. Paul was shipwrecked on Malta in 60. Saracens controlled the island(s) from 870 to 1090, a period of difficulty for the Church. The line of bishops extends from 1090 to the present. Malta maintains diplomatic relations with Vatican City.

Archd., 1; dioc., 1; abp., 1; bp., 1; parishes, 79; priests, 1,120 (662 dioc., 458 rel.); sem., 139; bros., 135; srs., 1,665; bap., 5,684; Caths., 328,000 (91%); tot. pop., 360,000.

Marianas, The: U.S. Trust territory in Pacific (scheduled to become a U.S. commonwealth). Under ecclesiastical jurisdiction of Agana diocese, Guam.

Parishes, 8; priests, 9 (6 dioc., 3 rel.); p.d., 3; srs., 20; bap., 614; Caths., 22,000; tot. pop., 24,000.

Martinique: French overseas department in the West Indies, about 130 miles south of Guadeloupe; capital, Fort-de-France. Catholicism was introduced in the 16th century. The hierarchy was established in 1967.

Archd., 1; abp., 1; parishes, 47; priests, 101 (44 dioc., 57 rel.); sem., 10; bros., 14; srs., 226; bap., 4,032; Caths., 299,000; tot. pop., 330,000.

Mauritania: Islamic republic on the northwest coast of Africa; capital, Nouakchott. With few exceptions, the Catholics in the country are members of the foreign colony. Mauritania has an apostolic delegate.

Dioc., 1; bp., 1; parishes, 6; priests, 11 (2 dioc., 9 rel.); bros., 1; srs., 26; bap., 65; Caths., 5,000 (.3%); tot. pop., 1,630,000.

Mauritius: Self-governing island state, member of the British Commonwealth, 500 miles east of Madagascar; capital, Port Louis. Catholicism was introduced by Vincentians in 1722. Port Louis, made a vicariate in 1819, was a jumping-off point for missionaries to Australia, Madagascar and South Africa. Mauritius maintains diplomatic relations with Vatican City.

Dioc., 1; bp., 1; parishes, 45; priests, 162 (84 dioc., 78 rel.); sem., 5; bros., 48; srs., 320; bap., 6,376; Caths., 345,000 (35.9%); tot. pop., 960,000.

Melilla: Spanish possession in northern Africa. Statistics are included in those for Spain.

Mexico (United States of Mexico): Republic in Middle America. Christianity was introduced early in the 16th century. Mexico City, made a diocese in 1530, became the missionary and cultural center of the whole country. Missionary work, started in 1524 and forwarded principally by Franciscans, Dominicans, Augustinians and Jesuits, resulted in the baptism of all persons in the central plateau by the end of the century. Progress there and in the rest of the country continued in the following century but tapered off and went into decline in the 18th century, for a variety of reasons ranging from diminishing government support to relaxations of Church discipline. The wars of independence, 1810-21, in which some Catholics participated, created serious problems of adjustment for the Church. Social problems, political unrest and government opposition climaxed in the constitution of 1917 which practically outlawed the Church. Persecution took serious tolls of life and kept the Church underground, under Calles, 1924-1928, again in 1931, and under Cardenas in 1934. President Camacho, 1940-1946, ended persecution and instituted a more lenient policy. The Church, however, still labors under legal and practical disabilities. Mexico has an apostolic delegate; the Mexican president has a personal envoy to the Vatican.

Archd., 11; dioc., 53; prel., 7; v.a., 2; card., 3; abp., 10; bp., 74; parishes, 3,972; priests, 10,087 (7,030 dioc., 3,057 rel.); sem., 2,947; p.d., 41; bros., 1,127; srs., 25,598; bap., 2,029,449; Caths., 66,756,000 (92.8%); tot. pop., 71,910,000.

Monaco: Constitutional monarchy, an enclave on the Mediterranean coast of France near the Italian border; capital, Monaco-Ville. Christianity was introduced before 1000. Catholicism is the official religion but freedom is guaranteed for all. Monaco has a minister at Vatican City.

Archd., 1; abp., 1; parishes, 5; priests, 25 (5 dioc., 20 rel.); sem., 4; p.d., 1; bros., 35; srs., 63; bap., 204; Caths., 25,000 (96%); tot. pop., 26,000.

Mongolian Peoples' Republic: Republic in north central Asia; capital Ulaanbaatar. Christianity was introduced by Nestorians. Some Franciscans were in the country in the 13th and 14th centuries, en route to China. Limited evangelization efforts from the 18th century had little success among the Mongols in Outer Mongolia, where Buddhism has predominated for hundreds of years. No Christians were known to be there in 1953. There may be a few Catholics in Inner Mongolia. No foreign missionaries have been in the country since 1953.

Pop., 1,670,000.

Montserrat: British island possession in

Caribbean; capital, Plymouth. Under ecclesiastical jurisdiction of St. John's-Basseterre diocese, Antigua.

Parish, 1; priests, 3 (1 dioc., 2 rel.); p.d.; 1; srs., 5; bap., 41; Caths., 1,000; tot. pop., 13,000.

Morocco: Constitutional monarchy in northwest Africa with Atlantic and Mediterranean coastlines; capital, Rabat. Christianity was known in the area by the end of the third century. Bishops from Morocco attended a council at Carthage in 484. Catholic life survived under Visigoth and, from 700, Arab rule; later it became subject to influence from the Spanish, Portuguese and French. Islam is the state religion. The hierarchy was established in 1955. Morocco maintains diplomatic relations with Vatican City.

Archd., 2; abp., 1; parishes, 63; priests, 104 (26 dioc., 78 rel.); bros., 16; srs., 434; bap., 110; Caths., 77,000 (.38%); tot. pop., 20,240,000.

Mozambique: Independent (June 25, 1975) republic in southeast Africa, bordering on the Indian Ocean; former Portuguese territory; capital, Maputo (formerly Lourenco Marques). Christianity was introduced by Portuguese Jesuits about the middle of the 16th century. Evangelization continued from then until the 18th century when it went into decline largely because of the Portuguese government's expulsion of the Jesuits. Conditions worsened in the 1830's, improved after 1881, but deteriorated again during the anticlerical period from 1910 to 1925. Conditions improved in 1940, the year Portugal concluded a new concordat with the Holy See and the hierarchy was established. Outspoken criticism by missionaries of Portuguese policies in Mozambique resulted in Church-state tensions in the years immediately preceding independence. Tension continues to be a factor, although to a smaller degree, in relations between the Church and the Marxist-oriented government in power since 1975. The first two native bishops were ordained March 9, 1975. Mozambique has an apostolic delegate.

Archd., 1; dioc., 8; abp., 1 (nat.); bp., 8 (6 nat.); parishes, 242; priests, 270 (23 dioc., 247 rel.); sem., 17; bros., 77; srs., 492; bap., 21,798; Caths., 1,638,000 (15.6%); tot. pop., 10,470,000.

Namibia (South West Africa): Territory in South Africa in dispute between the Republic of South Africa and the United Nations; capital, Windhoek. The area shares the history of the Republic of South Africa. Namibia has an apostolic delegate (to South Africa).

V.a., 2; bp., 2 (1 nat); parishes, 63; priests, 72 (2 dioc., 70 rel.); sem., 5; p.d., 14; bros., 54; srs., 290; bap., 7,220; Caths., 162,000 (15.8%); tot. pop., 1,022,000.

Nauru: Independent republic in western Pacific; capital, Yaren. Under ecclesiastical jurisdiction of Tarawa, Nauru and Funafuti diocese (seat in Tarawa).

Parish, 1; priest, 1 (rel.); srs., 4; bap., 70; Caths., 2,000; tot. pop., 7,000.

Nepal: Constitutional monarchy, the only Hindu kingdom in the world, in central Asia south of the Himalayas between India and Tibet; capital, Kathmandu. Little is known of the country before the 15th century. Some Jesuits passed through from 1628 and some sections were evangelized in the 18th century, with minimal results, before the country was closed to foreigners. Conversions from Hinduism, the state religion, are not recognized in law. Christian missionary work is not allowed. Catholics in the country have been under the jurisdiction of the Patna diocese, India, since 1919.

Priests, 28 (rel); bros., 3; srs., 20; bap., 7; Caths., 300; tot. pop., 14,010,000.

Netherlands: Kingdom in northwestern Europe; capital, Amsterdam (seat of the government, The Hague). Evangelization, begun about the turn of the sixth century by Irish, Anglo-Saxon and Frankish missionaries, resulted in Christianization of the country by 800 and subsequent strong influence on The Lowlands. Invasion by French Calvinists in 1572 brought serious losses to the Catholic Church and made the Reformed Church dominant. Catholics suffered a practical persecution of official repression and social handicap in the 17th century. The schism of Utrecht occurred in 1724. Only one-third of the population was Catholic in 1726. The Church had only a skeleton organization from 1702 to 1853, when the hierarchy was re-established. Despite this upturn, cultural isolation was the experience of Catholics until about 1914. From then on new vigor came into the life of the Church, and a whole new climate of interfaith relations began to develop. Before and for some years following the Second Vatican Council, the thrust and variety of thought and practice in the Dutch Church moved it to the vanguard position of "progressive" renewal. A particular synod of Dutch bishops held at the Vatican in January, 1980, and aimed at internal improvement of the Church in the Netherlands, had disappointing results, according to reports in 1981. The Netherlands maintains diplomatic relations with Vatican City.

Archd., 1; dioc., 6; card., 3; bp., 10; parishes, 1,796; priests 6,962 (2,718 dioc., 4,244 rel.); sem., 293; p.d., 15; bros., 3,561; srs., 22,231; bap., 56,730; Caths., 5,639,000 (39.9%); tot. pop., 14,144,000.

Netherlands Antilles (Curacao): Autonomous part of the Kingdom of The Netherlands. Consists of two groups of islands in the Caribbean: Curacao, Aruba and Bonaire, off the northern coast of Venezuela; and St. Eustatius, Saba and the southern part of St. Martaan, southeast of Puerto Rico; capital,

Willemstad on Curacao. Christianity was introduced in the 16th century. Apostolic delegation was established in 1975.

Dioc., 1; bp., 1; parishes, 47; priests, 65 (9 dioc., 56 rel.); sem., 1; bros., 64; srs., 168; bap., 3,713; Caths., 223,000 (83.8%); tot. pop., 266,000.

New Caledonia: French territory consisting of several islands in Oceania east of Queensland, Australia; capital, Noumea. Catholicism was introduced in 1843, nine years after Protestant missionaries began evangelization. A vicariate was organized in 1847. The hierarchy was established in 1966.

Archd., 1; abp., 1; parishes, 36; priests, 60 (10 dioc., 50 rel.); sem., 5; bros., 75; srs., 204; bap., 1,808; Caths., 92,000 (65.2%); tot. pop., 141,000.

New Zealand: Dominion in the British Commonwealth, a group of islands in Oceania 1,200 miles southeast of Australia: capital, Wellington. Protestant missionaries were the first evangelizers. On North Island, Catholic missionaries started work before the establishment of two dioceses in 1848; their work among the Maoris was not organized until about 1881. On South Island, whose first resident priest arrived in 1840, a diocese was established in 1869. These three jurisdictions were joined in a province in 1896. The Marists were the outstanding Catholic missionaries in the area. Established diplomatic relations with Vatican City, 1973.

Archd., 1; dioc., 5; abp., 1; bp., 6; parishes, 284; priests, 829 (446 dioc., 383 rel.); sem., 114; bros., 366; srs., 2,152; bap., 7,901; Caths. 494,000 (15.7%); tot. pop., 3,129,000.

Nicaragua: Republic in Central America: capital, Managua. Evangelization began shortly after the Spanish conquest about 1524 and eight years later the first bishop took over jurisdiction of the Church in the country. Jesuits were leaders in missionary work during the colonial period, which lasted until the 1820's. Evangelization endeavor increased after establishment of the republic in 1838. In this century it was extended to the Atlantic coastal area where Protestant missionaries had begun work about the middle of the 1900's. Many church leaders, clerical and lay, supported the aims but not necessarily all the methods of the revolution which forced the resignation and flight July 17, 1979, of Anastasio Somoza Debayle, whose family had controlled the government since the early 1930s. (See News Events for 1982 developments.) Nicaragua maintains diplomatic relations with Vatican City.

Archd., 1; dioc., 4; prel., 2; v.a., 1; abp., 1; bp., 7; parishes, 182; priests, 340 (119 dioc., 221 rel.); sem., 49; p.d., 18; bros., 100; srs., 692; bap., 68,059; Caths., 2,474,000 (91.6%); 2,700,000.

Niger: Republic in west central Africa; capital, Niamey. The first mission was set up in

1831. A prefecture apostolic was organized in 1942 and the first diocese was established in 1961. The country is predominantly Moslem. Niger maintains diplomatic relations with Vatican City.

Dioc., 1; bp., 1; parishes, 11; priests, 29 (6 dioc., 23 rel.); sem., 1; bros., 14; srs., 78; bap., 163; Caths., 14,000 (.26%); tot. pop., 5,310,000.

Nigeria: Republic in western Africa; capital, Lagos. The Portuguese introduced Catholicism in the coastal region in the 15th century. Capuchins did some evangelization in the 17th century but systematic missionary work did not get under way along the coast until about 1840. A vicariate for this area was organized in 1870. A prefecture was set up in 1911 for missions in the northern part of the country where Islam was strongly entrenched. From 1967, when Biafra seceded, until early in 1970 the country was torn by civil war. The hierarchy was established in 1950. Nigeria maintains diplomatic relations with Vatican City. (See Index for papal visit to Nigeria.)

Archd., 3; dioc., 28; card., 1 (nat.); abp., 3 (nat.); bp., 27 (21 nat.); parishes, 433; priests, 1,235 (679 dioc., 556 rel.); sem., 1,077; p.d., 9; bros., 168; srs., 1,234; bap., 269,108; Caths., 5,316,000 (6.9%); tot. pop., 77,080,000.

Niue: New Zealand self-governing territory in South Pacific. Under ecclesiastical jurisdiction of Rarotonga diocese, Cook Islands.

Parish, 1; priest, 1 (rel.); Caths., 200; tot. pop., 3,000.

Norway: Constitutional monarchy in northern Europe, the western part of the Scandinavian peninsula; capital, Oslo. Evangelization begun in the ninth century by missionaries from England and Ireland put the Church on a firm footing about the turn of the 11th century. The first diocese was set up in 1153 and development of the Church progressed until the Black Death in 1349 inflicted losses from which it never recovered. Lutheranism, introduced from outside in 1537 and furthered cautiously, gained general acceptance by about 1600 and was made the state religion. Legal and other measures crippled the Church, forcing priests to flee the country and completely disrupting normal activity. Changes for the better came in the 19th century, with the granting of religious liberty in 1845 and the repeal of many legal disabilities in 1897. Norway was administered as a single apostolic vicariate from 1892 to 1932, when it was divided into three jurisdictions under the supervision of the Congregation for the Propagation of the Faith. Established diplomatic relations with Vatican City in 1982.

Dioc., 1; prel., 2; bp., 4; parishes, 27; priests, 68 (22 dioc., 46 rel.); sem., 3; bro., 1; srs., 362; bap., 257; Caths., 15,000; tot. pop., 4,090,000.

Oman: Independent monarchy in eastern corner of Arabian Peninsula; capital, Muscat.

Under ecclesiastical jurisdiction of Arabia vicariate apostolic.

Parish, 1; priests, 2 (1 dioc., 1 rel.); bap., 45; Caths., 4,000; tot. pop., 890,000.

Pakistan: Islamic republic in southwestern Asia, member of the British Commonwealth; capital, Islamabad. (Formerly included East Pakistan which became the independent nation of Bangladesh in 1971.) Islam, firmly established in the eighth century, is the state religion. Christian evangelization of the native population began about the middle of the 19th century, years after earlier scattered attempts. The hierarchy was established in 1950. Pakistan maintains diplomatic relations with Vatican City.

Archd., 1; dioc., 5; card., 1 (nat.); bp., 7 (5 nat.); parishes, 51; priests, 239 (89 dioc., 150 rel.); sem., 39; p.d., 1; bros., 56; srs., 661; bap., 25,985; Caths., 452,000 (.5%); tot. pop., 82,440,000.

Panama: Republic in Central America; capital, Panama City. Catholicism was introduced by Franciscan missionaries and evangelization started in 1514. The Panama diocese, oldest in the Americas, was set up at the same time. The Catholic Church has favored status and state aid for missions, charities and parochial schools, but religious freedom is guaranteed to all religions. Panama maintains diplomatic relations with Vatican City.

Archd., 1; dioc., 3; prel., 1; v.a., 1; abp., 1; bp., 6; parishes, 130; priests, 290 (76 dioc., 214 rel.); sem., 52; p.d., 7; bros., 46; srs., 457; bap., 35,333; Caths., 1,705,000 (88.8%); tot. pop., 1,919,000.

Papua New Guinea: Independent (Sept. 16, 1975) republic (formerly under Australian administration) in southwest Pacific; member of British Commonwealth. Consists of the eastern half of the southwestern Pacific island of New Guinea and the Northern Solomon Islands; capital, Port Moresby. (For statistics on the Indonesian portion of New Guinea, see Indonesia.) Marists began evangelization about 1844 but were handicapped by many factors, including "spheres of influence" laid out for Catholic and Protestant missionaries. A prefecture apostolic was set up in 1896 and placed in charge of the Divine Word Missionaries. The territory suffered greatly during World War II. Hierarchy was established for New Guinea and adjacent islands in 1966. Papua New Guinea established diplomatic relations with the Vatican in 1977.

Archd., 4; dioc., 13; abp., 4; bp., 14; parishes, 292; priests, 529 (55 dioc., 474 rel.); sem., 169; p.d., 12; bros., 340; srs., 962; bap., 32,551; Caths., 913,000 (29.6%); tot. pop., 3,082,000.

Paraguay: Republic in central South America; capital, Asuncion. Catholicism was introduced in 1542, evangelization began almost immediately. A diocese erected in 1547 was occupied for the first time in 1556. On many occasions thereafter dioceses in the country were left unoccupied because of political and other reasons. Jesuits who came into the country after 1609 devised the reductions system for evangelizing the Indians, teaching them agriculture, husbandry, trades and other useful arts, and giving them experience in property use and community life. The reductions were communes of Indians only, under the direction of the missionaries. About 50 of them were established in southern Brazil, Uruguay and northeastern Argentina as well as in Paraguay. They had an average population of three to four thousand. At their peak, some 30 reductions had a population of 100,000. Political officials regarded the reductions with disfavor because they did not control them and feared that the Indians trained in them might foment revolt and upset the established colonial system under Spanish control. The reductions lasted until about 1768 when their Jesuit founders and directors were expelled from Latin America. Church-state relations following independence from Spain in 1811 were tense as often as not because of government efforts to control the Church through continued exercise of Spanish patronage rights and by other means. The Church as well as the whole country suffered a great deal during the War of the Triple Alliance from 1865-70. After that time, the Church had the same kind of experience in Paraguay as in the rest of Latin America with forces of liberalism, anticlericalism, massive educational needs, poverty, a shortage of priests and other personnel. Most recently church leaders have been challenging the government to initiate long-needed economic and social reforms. Paraguay maintains diplomatic relations with Vatican City.

Archd., 1; dioc., 8; prel., 2; v.a., 2; abp., 1; bp., 15; parishes, 264; priests, 543 (196 dioc., 347 rel.); sem., 151; p.d., 16; bros., 106; srs., 932; bap., 89,919; Caths., 2,798,000 (91.2%); tot. pop., 3,067,000.

Peru: Republic on the western coast of South America; capital, Lima. An effective diocese became operational in 1537, five years after the Spanish conquest. Evangelization, already underway, developed for some time after 1570 but deteriorated before the end of the colonial period in the 1820's. The first native-born saint of the new world was a Peruvian, Rose of Lima, a Dominican tertiary who died in 1617 and was canonized in 1671. In the new republic founded after the wars of independence the Church experienced problems of adjustment and many of the difficulties that cropped up in other South American countries: government efforts to control it through continuation of the patronage rights of the Spanish crown; suppression of houses of religious and expropriation of church property; religious indifference and outright hostility. The Church was given special status but was not made the established religion. Repressive measures by the government against labor protests have been condemned by Church leaders in the past several years. Peru maintains diplomatic relations with Vatican City.

Archd., 7; dioc., 12; prel., 14; v.a., 8; card., 1; abp., 6; bp., 42; parishes, 1,184; priests, 2,233 (913 dioc., 1,320 rel.); sem., 693; p.d., 38; bros., 443; srs., 4,732; bap., 422,782; Caths., 16,390,000 (92.1%); tot. pop., 17,780,000.

Philippine Islands: Republic, an archipelago of 7,000 islands off the southeast coast of Asia; capital, Quezon City. Systematic evangelization was begun in 1564 and resulted in firm establishment of the Church by the 19th century. During the period of Spanish rule, which lasted from the discovery of the islands by Magellan in 1521 to 1898, the Church experienced difficulties with the patronage system under which the Spanish crown tried to control ecclesiastical affairs through episcopal and other appointments. This system ended in 1898 when the United States gained possession of the islands and instituted a policy of separation of Church and state. Anticlericalism flared late in the 19th century. The Aglipayan schism, an attempt to set up a nationalist church, occurred a few years later, in 1902. The government of Ferdinand Marcos has been under attack by people of the church for the past several years for violations of human rights. The republic maintains diplomatic relations with Vatican City.

Archd., 14; dioc., 34; prel., 13; v.a., 4; card., 2; abp., 14; bp., 68; parishes, 1,994; priests, 4,964 (2,763 dioc., 2,201 rel.); sem., 3,970; p.d., 9; bros., 349; srs., 8,069; bap., 1,341,863; Caths., 40,450,000 (83.5%); tot. pop., 48.400.000.

Poland: People's republic in eastern Europe; capital, Warsaw. The first traces of Christianity date from the second half of the ninth century. Its spread was accelerated by the union of the Slavs in the 10th century. The first bishopric was set up in 968. The Gniezno archdiocese, with suffragan sees and a mandate to evangelize the borderlands as well as Poland, was established in 1000. Steady growth continued thereafter, with religious orders and their schools playing a major role. Some tensions with the Orthodox were experienced. The Reformation, supported mainly by city dwellers and the upper classes, peaked from about the middle of the 16th century, resulting in numerous conversions to Lutheranism, the Reformed Church and the Bohemian Brethren. A successful Counter-Reformation, with the Jesuits in a position of leadership, was completed by about 1632. The movement served a nationalist as well as religious purpose; in restoring religious unity to a large degree, it united the country against potential invaders, the Swedes, Russians and Turks. The Counter-Reformation had bad side effects, leading to the repression of Protestants long after it was over and to prejudice against Orthodox who returned to allegiance with Rome in 1596 and later. The Church, in the same manner as the entire country, was adversely affected by the partitions of the 18th and 19th centuries. Russification hurt the Orthodox who had reunited with Rome and the Latins who were in the majority. Germans extended their Kulturkampf to the area they controlled. The Austrians exhibited some degree of tolerance. In the republic established after World War I the Church reorganized itself, continued to serve as a vital force in national life, and enjoyed generally harmonious relations with the state. Progressive growth was strong until 1939 when disaster struck in the form of invasion by German and Russian forces and six years of war. In 1945, seven years before the adoption of a Soviet-type of constitution, the Communist-controlled government initiated a policy that included a constant program of atheistic propaganda; a strong campaign against the hierarchy and clergy; the imprisonment in 1948 of 700 priests and even more religious; rigid limitation of the activities of religious; censorship and curtailment of the Catholic press and Catholic Action; interference with church administration and appointments of the clergy; the "deposition" of Cardinal Wyszynski in 1953 and the imprisonment of other members of the hierarchy; the suppression of "Caritas," the Catholic charitable organization; promotion of "Progressive Catholic" activities and a small minority of "patriotic priests." Establishment of the Gomulka regime, the freeing of Cardinal Wyszynski in October, 1956, and the signing of an agreement two months later by bishops and state officials, led to some improvement of conditions. The underlying fact, however, was that the regime conceded to Catholics only so much as was necessary to secure support of the government as a more tolerable evil than the harsh and real threat of a Russian-imposed puppet government like that in Hungary. This has been the controlling principle in Church-state relations. Auxiliary Bishop Ladislaw Rubin of Gniezno sketched the general state of affairs in March, 1968. He said that there was no sign that the government had any intention of releasing its oppressive grip on the Church. As evidence of the "climate of asphyxiation" in the country he cited: persistent questioning of priests by officials concerning their activities; the prohibition against Catholic schools, hospitals and charitable works; the financial burden of a 60 per cent tax on church income. Cardinal Wyszynski denounced "enforced atheism" in a Lenten pastoral in the same year. In May, 1969, the bishops drafted a list of grievances against the government which, they said, were "only some examples of difficulties which demonstrated the situation of the Church in our homeland." The grievances were: refusal of permits to build new churches and establish new parishes; refusal of permission "for the organization of new religion classes"; pressure on Catholics who attend religious ceremonies; censorship and the lack of an independent Catholic daily newspaper; lack of representation in public life; restriction of "freedom to conduct normal pastoral work" in the western portion of the country. There was a move toward improvement in Church-state relations in 1971-72. In 1973, the Polish bishops issued a pastoral letter urging Catholics to resist the official atheism imposed by the government. In 1974 the Polish bishops expressed approval of renewed Vatican efforts at regularizing Church-state relations but insisted that they (the bishops) be consulted on every step of the negotiations. The bishops have continued their sharp criticism of anti-religious policies and programs of the government. Regular contacts on a working level were established by the Vatican and Poland in 1974. (See Index for 1982 events.)

Archd., 7; dioc., 21; card., 2; abp., 2; bp., 77; parishes, 7,504; priests, 19,515 (15,157 dioc., 4,358 rel.); sem., 6,101; bros., 1,420; srs., 24,537; bap., 685,037; Caths., 33,350,000 (93.7%); tot. pop., 35,580,000.

Polynesia, French: French possession in the southern Pacific, including Tahiti and the Marquesas Islands; capital, Papeete. The first phase of evangelization in the Marquesas Islands, begun in 1838, resulted in 216 baptisms in 10 years. A vicariate was organized in 1848 but real progress was not made until after the baptism of native rulers in 1853. Persecution caused missionaries to leave the islands several times. By the 1960's, more than 95 per cent of the population was Catholic. Isolated attempts to evangelize Tahiti were made in the 17th and 18th centuries. Two Picpus Fathers began missionary work in 1831. A vicariate was organized in 1848. By 1908, despite the hindrances of Protestant opposition, disease and other factors, the Church had firm roots.

Archd., 1; dioc., 1; abp., 1 (nat.); bp., 1; parishes, 77; priests, 37 (8 dioc., 29 rel.); sem., 4; p.d., 4; bros., 30; srs., 65; bap., 1,254; Caths., 51,000; tot. pop., 155,000.

Portugal: Republic in the western part of the Iberian peninsula; capital, Lisbon. Christianity was introduced before the fourth century. From the fifth century to early in the eighth century the Church experienced difficulties from the physical invasion of barbarians and the intellectual invasion of doctrinal errors in the forms of Arianism, Priscillianism and Pelagianism. The Church survived under the rule of Arabs from about 711 and of the Moors until 1249. Ecclesiastical life was fairly vigorous from 1080

to 1185, and monastic influence became strong. A decline set in about 1450. Several decades later Portugal became the jumping-off place for many missionaries to newly discovered colonies. The Reformation had little effect in the country. Beginning about 1750, Pombal, minister of foreign affairs and prime minister, mounted a frontal attack on the Jesuits whom he succeeded in expelling from Portugal and the colonies. His anti-Jesuit campaign successful Pombal also attempted, and succeeded to some extent, in controlling the Church in Portugal until his fall from power about 1777. Liberal revolutionaries with anti-Church policies made the 19th century a difficult one for the Church. Similar policies prevailed in Church-state relations in this century until the accession of Salazar to power in 1928. In 1940 he concluded a concordat with the Holy See which regularized Church-state relations but still left the Church in a subservient condition. The prevailing spirit of church authorities in Portugal has been conservative. In 1971 several priests were tried for subversion for speaking out against colonialism and for taking part in guerrilla activities in Angola. A military coup of Apr. 25, 1974, triggered a succession of chaotic political developments which led to an attempt by Communists, after receiving only 18 per cent of the votes cast in a national election, to take over the government in the summer of 1975. Portugal maintains diplomatic relations with Vatican City. (See Index for papal visit to Portugal.)

Patriarchate, 1; archd., 2; dioc., 17; card., 1; abp., 2; bp., 23; parishes, 4,263; priests, 4,964 (3,801 dioc., 1,163 rel.); sem., 600; p.d., 5; bros., 598; srs., 7,791; bap., 160,338; Caths., 9,350,000 (94%); tot. pop., 9,930,000.

Puerto Rico: A U.S. commonwealth, the smallest of the Greater Antilles, 885 miles southeast of the southern coast of Florida; capital, San Juan. Following its discovery by Columbus in 1493, the island was evangelized by Spanish missionaries and remained under Spanish ecclesiastical as well as political control until 1898 when it became a possession of the United States. The original diocese, San Juan, was erected in 1511. The present hierarchy was established in 1960. Puerto Rico has an apostolic delegate (nuncio to Dominican Republic).

Archd., 1; dioc., 4; card., 1; bp., 8; parishes, 256; priests, 726 (253 dioc., 473 rel.); sem., 190; p.d., 73; bros., 108; srs., 1,425; bap., 50,369; Caths., 2,802,080 (81.4%); tot. pop., 3,440,000.

Qatar: Independent state in the Persian Gulf; capital, Doha. Under ecclesiastical jurisdiction of Arabia vicariate apostolic.

Priest, 1 (rel.); bap., 59; Caths., 5,000; tot. pop., 220,000.

Reunion: French overseas department, 450 miles east of Madagascar; capital, Saint-Denis. Catholicism was introduced in 1667 and some intermittent missionary work was done through the rest of the century. A prefecture apostolic was organized in 1712. Vincentians began work there in 1817 and were joined later by Holy Ghost Fathers. Reunion has an apostolic delegate.

Dioc., 1; bp., 1; parishes, 68; priests, 112 (57 dioc., 55 rel.); sem., 6; bros., 48; srs., 457; bap., 11,500; Caths., 449,000; tot. pop., 503,000.

Rhodes: Greek island in the Aegean Sea, 112 miles from the southwestern coast of Asia Minor. A diocese was established about the end of the third century. A bishop from Rhodes attended the Council of Nicaea in 325. Most of the Christians followed the Eastern Churches into schism in the 11th century and became Orthodox. Turks controlled the island from 1522 to 1912. The small Catholic population, for whom a diocese existed from 1328 to 1546, lived in crossfire between Turks and Orthodox. After 1719 Franciscans provided pastoral care for the Catholics, for whom an archdiocese was erected in 1928. Statistics are included in Greece.

Romania: Socialist republic in southeastern Europe; capital, Bucharest. Latin Christianity, introduced in the third century, all but disappeared during the barbarian invasions. The Byzantine Rite was introduced by the Bulgars about the beginning of the eighth century and established firm roots. It eventually became Orthodox, but a large number of its adherents returned later to union with Rome. Attempts to reintroduce the Latin Rite on any large scale have been unsuccessful. Communists took over the government following World War II, forced the abdication of Michael I in 1947, and enacted a Soviet type of constitution in 1952. By that time a campaign against religion was already in progress. In 1948 the government denounced a concordat concluded in 1929, nationalized all schools and passed a law on religions which resulted in the disorganization of Church administration. The 1.5 million-member Romanian Byzantine Rite Church, by government decree, was incorporated into the Romanian Orthodox Church, and the Orthodox bishops then seized the cathedrals of Roman Catholic bishops. Five of the six Latin Rite bishops were immediately disposed of by the government, and the last was sentenced to 18 years' imprisonment in 1951, when a great many arrests of priests and laymen were made. Religious orders were suppressed in 1949. Since 1948 more than 50 priests have been executed and 200 have died in prison. One hundred priests were reported in prison at the end of 1958. Some change for the better in Church-state relations was reported after the middle of the summer of 1964, although restrictions were still in effect.

About 1,200 priests were engaged in parish work in August, 1965.

Archd., 2; dioc., 8; ord., 1; bp., 2. No recent statistics are available on the number of Catholics. There were an estimated 1,140,000 Catholics (5.9% of the population) in 1969. Tot. pop., 22,270,000.

Rwanda: Republic in east central Africa; capital, Kigali. Catholicism was introduced about the turn of the 20th century. The hierarchy was established in 1959. Intertribal warfare between the ruling Hutus (90 per cent of the population) and the Tutsis (formerly the ruling aristocracy) has plagued the country for several years. Rwanda maintains diplomatic relations with Vatican City.

Archd., 1; dioc., 7; abp., 1 (nat.); bp., 7 (6 nat.); parishes, 110; priests, 443 (253 dioc., 190 rel.); sem., 150; bros., 194; srs., 740; bap., 90,813; Caths., 2,099,000 (41.6%); tot. pop., 5,046,000.

Ryukyu Islands: Consists of Okinawa and 72 other islands in western Pacific. Statistics included in Japan.

St. Christopher (Kitts)-Nevis: British Associated State in West Indies; capital, Basseterre, on St. Christopher. Under ecclesiastical jurisdiction of St. John's-Basseterre diocese, Antigua.

Parishes, 7; priests, 4 (rel.); bap., 70; Caths., 4,000; tot. pop., 67,000. Statistics include Anguilla.

St. Lucia: Independent (Feb. 22, 1979) island state in West Indies; capital, Castries.

Archd., 1; abp., 1; parishes, 19; priests, 32 (5 dioc., 27 rel.); sem., 4; p.d., 1; bros., 1; srs., 33; bap., 3,135; Caths., 109,000; tot. pop., 120,000.

St. Pierre and Miquelon: French overseas department, islands near the southwest coast of Newfoundland. Catholicism was introduced about 1689.

V.a., 1; bp., 1; parishes, 3; priests, 4 (rel.); srs., 14; bap., 100; Caths., 6,290; tot. pop., 6,350.

St. Vincent and the Grenadines: Independent State in West Indies; capital, Kingstown. Under ecclesiastical jurisdiction of Bridgetown-Kingstown diocese, Barbados.

Parishes, 5; priests, 4 (rel.); bros., 6; srs., 11; bap., 232; Caths., 16,000; tot. pop., 122,000.

Samoa, American: Unincorporated U.S. territory in southwestern Pacific, consisting of six small islands; capital, Fagotogo on the Island of Tutuila. Under ecclesiastical jurisdiction of Samoa and Tokelau diocese, Samoa.

Parishes, 5; priests, 4 (1 dioc., 3 rel.); bros., 8; srs., 14; bap., 277; Caths., 6,000; tot. pop., 32,000.

Samoa, Western: Independent state in the southwestern Pacific; capital, Apia. Catholic missionary work began in 1845. Most of the missions now in operation were established by 1870 when the Catholic population numbered about 5,000. Additional progress was made in missionary work from 1896. The first Samoan priest was ordained in 1892. The hierarchy was established in 1966.

Dioc., 1; card., 1; parishes, 18; priests, 39 (9 dioc., 30 rel.); sem., 36; bros., 33; srs., 109; bap., 1,478; Caths., 32,000; tot. pop., 156,000.

San Marino: Republic, a 24-square-mile enclave in northeastern Italy; capital, San Marino. The date of initial evangelization is not known, but a diocese was established by the end of the third century. Ecclesiastically, it forms part of the diocese of San Marino-Montefeltro in Italy. San Marino is represented by a minister at Vatican City.

Parishes, 12; priests, 26 (13 dioc., 13 rel.); bro., 1; srs., 33; bap., 219; Caths., 20,000 (95%); tot. pop., 21,000.

Sao Tome and Principe: Independent republic (July 12, 1975), consisting of two islands off the western coast of Africa in the Gulf of Guinea; former Portuguese territory; capital Sao Tome. Evangelization was begun by the Portuguese who discovered the islands in 1471-72. The Sao Tome diocese was established in 1534.

Dioc., 1; parishes, 12; priests, 8 (rel.); bro., 1; srs., 14; bap., 2,332; Caths., 70,000 (82%); tot. pop., 85,000.

Saudi Arabia: Monarchy occupying four-fifths of Arabian peninsula; capital, Riyadh (Taif, summer capital). Under ecclesiastical jurisdiction of Arabia vicariate apostolic.

Priests, 7 (rel.); srs., 2; bap., 87; Caths., 10,000; tot. pop., 9,522,000 (1979).

Scotland: Part of the United Kingdom, in the northern British Isles; capital, Edinburgh. Christianity was introduced by the early years of the fifth century. The arrival of St. Columba and his monks in 563 inaugurated a new era of evangelization which reached into remote areas by the end of the sixth century. He was extremely influential in determining the character of the Celtic Church, which was tribal, monastic, and in union with Rome. Considerable disruption of church activity resulted from Scandinavian invasions in the late eighth and ninth centuries. By 1153 the Scottish Church took a turn away from its insularity and was drawn into closer contact with the European community. Anglo-Saxon religious and political relations, complicated by rivalries between princes and ecclesiastical superiors, were not always the happiest. Religious orders expanded greatly in the 12th century. From shortly after the Norman Conquest of England to 1560 the Church suffered adverse effects from the Hundred Years' War, the Black Death, the Western Schism and other developments. In 1560 parliament abrogated papal supremacy over the Church in Scotland and committed the country to Protestantism in 1567. The Catholic Church was proscribed, to remain that way for more than 200 years, and the hierarchy was disbanded. Defections made the Church a minority religion from that time on. Presbyterian church government was ratified in 1690. Priests launched the Scottish Mission in 1653, incorporating themselves as a mission body under a prefect apostolic and working underground to serve the faithful in much the same way their confreres did in England. About 100 heather priests, trained in clandestine places in the heather country, were ordained by the early 19th century. Catholics got some relief from legal disabilities in 1793 and more later. Many left the country about that time. Some of their numbers were filled subsequently by immigrants from Ireland. The hierarchy was restored in 1878. Scotland, though predominantly Protestant, has a better record for tolerance than Northern Ireland. (See Index for papal visit to Scotland.)

Archd., 2; dioc., 6; card., 1; abp., 1; bp., 9; parishes, 475; priests, 1,169 (913 dioc., 256 rel.); sem., 137; p.d., 1; bros., 137; srs., 1,244; bap., 14,277 Caths., 827,568 (16%); tot. pop., 5,143,700 (1982 Annuario Pontificio).

Senegal: Republic in western Africa; capital, Dakar. The country had its first contact with Catholicism through the Portuguese some time after 1460. Some incidental missionary work was done by Jesuits and Capuchins in the 16th and 17th centuries. A vicariate for the area was placed in charge of the Holy Ghost Fathers in 1779. More effective evangelization efforts were accomplished after the Senegambia vicariate was organized in 1863. The hierarchy was established in 1955. Senegal maintains diplomatic relations with Vatican City.

Archd., 1; dioc., 4; p.a., 1; card., 1 (nat.); bp., 4 (nat.); parishes, 50; priests, 216 (57 dioc., 159 rel.); sem., 60; bros., 136; srs., 649; bap., 8,224; Caths., 227,000 (4%); tot. pop., 5,660,000.

Seychelles: Independent (1976) group of 92 islands in the Indian Ocean 970 miles east of Kenya; capital, Victoria on Mahe. Catholicism was introduced in the 18th century. A vicariate apostolic was organized in 1852. All education in the islands was conducted under Catholic auspices until 1954. Seychelles has an apostolic delegate (pro-nuncio to Kenya).

Dioc., 1; bp., 1 (nat.); parishes, 17; priests, 24 (7 dioc., 17 rel.); bros., 11; srs., 56; bap., 1,602; Caths., 62,000; tot. pop., 65,000.

Sierra Leone: Republic, member of the British Commonwealth, on the western coast of Africa; capital, Freetown. Catholicism was introduced in 1858. Members of the African Missions Society, the first Catholic missionaries in the area, were joined by Holy Ghost Fathers in 1864. Protestant missionaries were active in the area before their Catholic counterparts. Educational work had a major part in Catholic endeavor. The hierarchy was established in 1950. Sierra Leone has an apostolic delegate.

Archd., 1; dioc., 2; abp., 1; bp., 1; parishes, 26; priests, 122 (13 dioc., 109 rel.); sem., 23; bros., 14; srs., 89; bap., 2,413; Caths., 61,000 (1.7%); tot. pop., 3,470,000.

Singapore: Independent island republic off the southern tip of the Malay Peninsula; member of the British Commonwealth; capital, Singapore. Christianity was introduced in the area by Portuguese colonists about 1511. Singapore was founded in 1819; the first parish church was built in 1846. Established diplomatic relations with Vatican City, 1981.

Archd., 1; abp., 1 (nat.); parishes, 25; priests, 91 (59 dioc., 32 rel.); sem., 12; bros., 44; srs., 248; bap., 2,637; Caths., 92,820 (3.8%); tot. pop., 2,400,000.

Solomon Islands: Independent (July 7, 1978) island group in Oceania; capital, Honiara, on Guadalcanal. Evangelization of the Southern Solomons, begun earlier but interrupted because of violence against them, was resumed by the Marists in 1898. A vicariate apostolic was organized in 1912. A similar jurisdiction was set up for the Western Solomons in 1959. World War II caused a great deal of damage to mission installations. Catholic statistics for the Northern Solomons, where Catholic missionary work started in 1899 and a vicariate was set up in 1930, are included in those reported for Papua New Guinea. The area has an apostolic delegate.

Archd., 1; dioc., 1; abp., 1; bp., 1; parishes, 24; priests, 40 (10 dioc., 30 rel.); sem., 2; bros., 32; srs., 129; bap., 1,849; Caths., 40,000; tot. pop., 221,000.

Somalia: Republic on the eastern coast of Africa; capital, Mogadishu. The country has been Moslem for centuries. Pastoral activity has been confined to immigrants. Schools and hospitals were nationalized in 1972, resulting in the departure of some foreign missionaries. Somalia has an apostolic delegate (to the Red Sea Region).

Dioc., 1; bp., 1; parishes, 2; priests, 8 (rel.); bros., 2; srs., 72; bap., 14; Caths., 2,100 (.1%); tot. pop., 3,540,000.

South Africa: Republic in the southern part of Africa; capitals, Cape Town (legislative) and Pretoria (administrative). Christianity was introduced by the Portuguese who discovered the Cape of Good Hope in 1488. Boers, who founded Cape Town in 1652, expelled Catholics from the region. There was no Catholic missionary activity from that time until the 19th century. After a period of British opposition, a bishop established residence in 1837 and evangelization got underway thereafter among the Bantus and white immigrants. In recent years church authorities have strongly protested the white supremacy policy of apartheid which seriously infringes the human rights of the native blacks and impedes the Church from carrying out its pastoral, educational and social service functions. The hierarchy was established in 1951. South Africa has an apostolic delegate.

Archd., 4; dioc., 18; abb., 1; p.a., 3; card., 1; abp., 3; bp., 20; parishes, 628; priests, 1,210 (301 dioc., 909 rel.); sem., 156; p.d., 53; bros., 371; srs., 3,866; bap., 65,450; Caths., 2,020,000 (6.9%); tot. pop., 29,290,000. Statistics include autonomous homelands of Transkei, Bophuthatswana, Venda and Ciskei.

Spain: Nominal monarchy on the Iberian peninsula in southwestern Europe; capital, Madrid. Christians were on the peninsula by 200; some of them suffered martyrdom during persecutions of the third century. A council held in Elvira about 304/6 enacted the first legislation on clerical celibacy in the West. Vandals invaded the peninsula in the fifth century, bringing with them an Arian brand of Christianity which they retained until their conversion following the baptism of their king Reccared, in 589. One of the significant developments of the seventh century was the establishment of Toledo as the primatial see. The Visigoth kingdom lasted to the time of the Arab invasion, 711-14. The Church survived under Moslem rule but experienced some doctrinal and disciplinary irregularities as well as harassment. Reconquest of most of the peninsula was accomplished by 1248; unification was achieved during the reign of Ferdinand and Isabella. The discoveries of Columbus and other explorers ushered in an era of colonial expansion in which Spain became one of the greatest mission-sending countries in history. In 1492, in repetition of anti-Semitic actions of 694, the expulsion of unbaptized Jews was decreed, leading to mass baptisms but a questionable number of real conversions in 1502. (The Jewish minority numbered about 165,000.) Activity by the Inquisition followed. Spain was not seriously affected by the Reformation. Ecclesiastical decline set in about 1650. Anti-Church actions authorized by a constitution enacted in 1812 resulted in the suppression of religious and other encroachments on the leaders, people and goods of the Church. Political, religious and cultural turmoil recurred during the 19th century and into the 20th. A revolutionary republic was proclaimed in 1931, triggering a series of developments which led to civil war from 1936 to 1939. During the conflict, which pitted leftist Loyalists against the forces of Francisco Franco, 6,632 priests and religious and an unknown number of lay persons perished in addition to thousands of victims of combat. One-man, one-party rule, established after the civil war and with rigid control policies with respect to personal liberties and social and economic issues, continued for more than 35 years before giving way after the death of Franco to democratic reforms. The Catholic Church, long the established religion, was disestablished under a new constitution providing guarantees of freedom for other religions as well. Disestablishment was ratified with modifications of a 1976 revision of the earlier concordat of 1953. Spain maintains diplomatic relations with Vatican City.

Archd., 13; dioc., 52; card., 4; abp., 10; bp., 61; parishes, 21,434; priests, 32,776 (22,234 dioc., 10,542 rel.); sem., 3,010; p.d., 9; bros., 7,757; srs., 79,885; bap., 585,344; Caths., 36,884,000 (98.5%); tot. pop., 37,430,000.

Sri Lanka (formerly Ceylon): Independent socialist republic, island southeast of India; capital, Colombo. Effective evangelization began in 1543 and made great progress by the middle of the 17th century. The Church was seriously hampered during the Dutch period from about 1650 to 1795. Anti-Catholic laws were repealed by the British in 1806. The hierarchy was established in 1886. Leftist governments and other factors have worked against the Church since the country became independent in 1948. The high percentage of indigenous clergy and religious has been of great advantage to the Church. Sri Lanka maintains diplomatic relations with Vatican City.

Archd., 1; dioc., 8; card., 1 (nat.); abp., 1 (nat.); bp., 9 (nat.); parishes, 296; priests, 522 (358 dioc., 164 rel.); sem., 188; p.d., 2; bros., 272; srs., 2,245; bap., 29,033; Caths., 1,046,000 (7%); tot. pop., 14,740,000.

Sudan: Republic in northeastern Africa, the largest country on the continent; capital, Khartoum. Christianity was introduced from Egypt and gained acceptance in the sixth century. Under Arab rule, it was eliminated in the northern region. No Christians were in the country in 1600. Evangelization attempts begun in the 19th century in the south yielded hard-won results. By 1931 there were nearly 40,000 Catholics there, and considerable progress was made by missionaries after that time. In 1957, a year after the republic was established, Catholic schools were nationalized. An act restrictive of religious freedom went into effect in 1962, resulting in the harassment and expulsion of foreign missionaries. By 1964 all but a few Sudanese missionaries had been forced out of the southern region. The northern area, where Islam predominates, is impervious to Christian influence. Late in 1971 some missionaries were allowed to return to work in the South. Southern Sudan was granted regional autonomy within a unified country in March, 1972, thus ending often bitter fighting between the North and South dating back to 1955. The hierarchy was established in 1974. Sudan maintains diplomatic relations with Vatican City.

Archd., 2; dioc., 5; abp., 1 (nat.); bp., 6 (nat.); parishes, 88; priests, 145 (46 dioc., 99 rel.); sem., 36; p.d., 1; bros., 40; srs., 202; bap.,

16,830; Caths., 908,000 (4.8%); tot. pop., 18,690,000.

Suriname (formerly Dutch Guiana): Independent (Nov. 25, 1975) state in northern South America; capital, Paramaribo, Catholicism was introduced in 1683. Evangelization began in 1817.

Dioc., 1; bp., 1; parishes, 22; priests, 32 (2 dioc., 30 rel.); sem., 2; p.d., 1; bros., 27; srs., 104; bap., 1,985; Caths., 82,000 (21%); tot. pop., 389,000.

Swaziland: Constitutional monarchy in southern Africa; almost totally surrounded by the Republic of South Africa; capital, Mbabane. Missionary work was entrusted to the Servites in 1913. A prefecture apostolic was organized in 1923. The hierarchy was established in 1951. Swaziland has an apostolic delegate (to Southern Africa).

Dioc., 1; priests, 39 (4 dioc., 35 rel.); sem., 7; bros., 9; srs., 129; bap., 988; Caths., 38,000 (6.9%); tot. pop., 550,000.

Sweden: Kingdom in northwestern Europe; capital, Stockholm. Christianity was introduced by St. Ansgar, a Frankish monk, in 829/30. The Church became well established in the 12th century and was a major influence at the end of the Middle Ages. Political and other factors favored the introduction and spread of the Lutheran Church which became the state religion in 1560. The Augsburg Confession of 1530 was accepted by the government; all relations with Rome, in the country since the 12th century, were severed; monasteries were suppressed; the very presence of Catholics in the country was forbidden in 1617. A decree of tolerance for foreign Catholics was issued about 1781. Two years later a vicariate apostolic was organized for the country. In 1873 Swedes were given the legal right to leave the Lutheran Church and join another Christian church. (Membership in the Lutheran Church is presumed by law unless notice is given of membership in another church.) In 1923 there were only 11 priests and five churches in the country. Since 1952 Catholics have enjoyed almost complete religious freedom. The hierarchy was established in 1953. Hindrances to growth of the Church are the strongly entrenched established church, limited resources, a clergy shortage and the size of the country. Established diplomatic relations with Vatican City in 1982.

Dioc., 1; bp., 1; parishes, 31; priests, 105 (32 dioc., 73 rel.); sem., 2; bros., 6; srs., 246; bap., 767; Caths., 103,000; (1.2%); tot. pop., 8,311,000.

Switzerland: Republic in central Europe; capital, Bern. Christianity was introduced in the fourth century or earlier and was established on a firm footing before the barbarian invasions of the sixth century. Constance, established as a diocese in the seventh century, was a stronghold of the faith against the pagan Alamanni, in particular, who were not converted until some time in the ninth century. During this period of struggle with the barbarians, a number of monasteries of great influence were established. The Reformation in Switzerland was triggered by Zwingli in 1519 and furthered by him at Zurich until his death in battle against the Catholic cantons in 1531. Calvin set in motion the forces that made Geneva the international capital of the Reformation and transformed it into a theocracy. Catholics mobilized a Counter-Reformation in 1570, six years after Calvin's death. Struggle between Protestant and Catholic cantons was a fact of Swiss life for several hundred years. The Helvetic Constitution enacted at the turn of the 19th century embodied anti-Catholic measures and consequences, among them the dissolution of 130 monasteries. The Church was reorganized later in the century to meet the threats of liberalism, radicalism and the Kulturkampf. In the process, the Church, even though on the defensive, gained the strength and cohesion that characterizes it to the present time. The six dioceses in the country are immediately subject to the Holy See. In 1973, constitutional articles banning Jesuits from the country and prohibiting the establishment of convents and monasteries were repealed. There is a papal nuncio to Switzerland, but Switzerland does not have a diplomatic officer accredited to Vatican City (See Index for papal visit to Switzerland.)

Dioc., 6; abb., 2; bp., 7; parishes, 1,694; priests, 4,274 (2,561 dioc., 1,713 rel.); sem., 276; p.d., 11; bros., 413; srs., 9,705; bap., 35,805; Caths., 3,116,000 (48.8%); tot. pop., 6,373,000.

Syria: Arab republic in southwest Asia; capital, Damascus. Christian communities were formed in apostolic times. It is believed that St. Peter established a see at Antioch before going to Rome. Damascus became a center of influence. The area was the place of great men and great events in the early history of the Church. Monasticism developed there in the fourth century. So did the Monophysite and Monothelite heresies to which portions of the Church succumbed. Byzantine Syrians who remained in communion with Rome were given the name Melkites. Christians of various persuasions — Jacobites, Orthodox and Melkites — were subject to various degrees of harassment from the Arabs who took over in 638 and from the Ottoman Turks who isolated the country and remained in control from 1516 to the end of World War II. Syria maintains diplomatic relations with Vatican City.

There are 19 ecclesiastical jurisdictions in Syria serving the following rites: Armenian (1 archdiocese, 1 diocese); Chaldean (1 diocese); Roman (1 vicariate apostolic); Maronite (1 patriarchate, whose patriarch resides in Lebanon,

2 archdioceses and 1 diocese); Greek Melkite (1 patriarchate, 5 archdioceses); Syrian (1 patriarchate, whose patriarch resides in Lebanon, 4 archdioceses). Catholics, 227,000 (2.5%); tot. pop., 8,980,000.

Taiwan (Formosa): Location of the Nationalist Government of the Republic of China, an island 100 miles off the southern coast of mainland China; capital, Taipei. Attempts to introduce Christianity in the 17th century were unsuccessful. Evangelization in the 19th century resulted in some 1,300 converts in 1895. Missionary endeavor was hampered by the Japanese who occupied the island following the Sino-Japanese war of 1894-95. Nine thousand Catholics were reported in 1938. Great progress was made in missionary endeavor among the Chinese who emigrated to the island following the Communist take-over of the mainland in 1949. The hierarchy was established in 1952. Nationalist China maintains diplomatic relations with Vatican City.

Archd., 1; dioc., 6; abp., 1; bp., 8; parishes, 456; priests, 764 (204 dioc., 560 rel.); sem., 93; bros., 101; srs., 1,240; bap., 4,584; Caths., 286,000 (1.6%); tot. pop., 17,805,000.

Tanzania: Republic (consisting of former Tanganyika on the eastern coast of Africa and former Zanzibar, an island group off the eastern coast); capital, Dar es Salaam (future capital, Dodoma). The first Catholic mission in the former Tanganyikan portion of the republic was manned by Holy Ghost Fathers in 1868. The hierarchy was established there in 1953. Zanzibar was the landing place of Augustinians with the Portuguese in 1499. Some evangelization was attempted between then and 1698 when the Arabs expelled all priests from the territory. There was no Catholic missionary activity from then until the 1860's. The Holy Ghost Fathers arrived in 1863 and were entrusted with the mission in 1872. Zanzibar was important as a point of departure for missionaries to Tanganyika, Kenya and other places in East Africa. A vicariate for Zanzibar was set up in 1906. Tanzania maintains diplomatic relations with Vatican City.

Archd., 2; dioc., 23; card., 1 (nat.); abp., 1 (nat.); bp., 23 (21 nat.); parishes, 613; priests, 1,536 (733 dioc., 803 rel.); sem., 349; p.d., 1; bros., 372; srs., 3,813; bap., 138,087; Caths., 3,595,000 (19.4%); tot. pop., 18,519,000.

Thailand (Siam): Constitutional monarchy in southeastern Asia; capital, Bangkok. The first Christians in the region were Portuguese traders who arrived early in the 16th century. A number of missionaries began arriving in 1554 but pastoral care was confined mostly to the Portuguese until the 1660's. Evangelization of the natives got underway from about that time. A seminary was organized in 1665, a vicariate was set up four years later, and a point of departure was established for missionaries to Tonkin, Cochin China and China. Persecution and death for some of the missionaries ended evangelization efforts in 1688. It was resumed, however, and made progress from 1824 onwards. In 1881 missionaries were sent from Siam to neighboring Laos. The hierarchy was established in 1965. Thailand maintains diplomatic relations with Vatican City.

Archd., 2; dioc., 8; abp., 2 (nat.); bp., 8 (7 nat.); parishes, 222; priests, 393 (170 dioc., 223 rel.); sem., 263; bros., 160; srs., 1,239; bap., 6,186; Caths., 196,000 (.4%); tot. pop., 47,170,000.

Tibet: Autonomous region of China in eastern Asia, north of the Himalayas; capital, Lhasa. Christian contact and evangelization attempts have been almost fruitless. Some 1,200 Catholics were reported in Tibet about 1950. Syrians visited the area in the seventh century and evangelization attempts were made by Jesuits, 1624-35 and later, Capuchins, 1707-45, and others afterwards. They all met resistance and some met death. Missionaries do not have access to the country.

Tot. pop., 2,000,000.

Timor, Eastern: Former Portuguese overseas province in the Malay archipelago; annexed by Indonesia in 1976.

Dioc., 1; parishes, 19; priests, 22 (21 dioc., 1 rel.); bros., 4; srs., 41; bap., 19,260; Caths., 235,000; tot. pop., 760,000.

Togo: Republic on the western coast of Africa; capital, Lome. The first Catholic missionaries in the area, where slave raiders operated for nearly 200 years, were members of the African Missions Society who arrived in 1563. They were followed by Divine Word Missionaries in 1914, when a prefecture apostolic was organized. At that time the Catholic population numbered about 19,000. The African Missionaries returned after their German predecessors were deported following World War I. The first native priest was ordained in 1922. The hierarchy was established in 1955. Established diplomatic relations with Vatican City, 1981.

Archd., 1; dioc., 3; abp., 1 (nat.); bp., 3 (2 nat.); parishes, 70; priests, 176 (74 dioc., 102 rel.); sem., 55; bap., 18,191; Caths., 568,000 (21%); tot. pop., 2,699,000.

Tokelau Islands: Pacific islands administered by New Zealand. Under ecclesiastical jurisdiction of Samoa and Tokelau diocese, Western Samoa.

Parish, 1; priest, 1 (dioc.); srs., 2; bap., 16; Caths., 1,000; tot. pop., 2,000.

Tonga: Polynesian monarchy in the southwestern Pacific, consisting of about 150 islands, member of the British Commonwealth; capital Nuku'alofa. Marists started missionary work in 1842, some years after Protestants had begun evangelization. By 1880 the Catholic population numbered about 1,700. A vicariate was organized in 1937. The hierarchy was established in 1966.

Dioc., 1; bp., 1 (nat); parishes, 13; priests, 25 (9 dioc., 16 rel.); sem., 21; bros., 5; srs., 42; bap., 614; Caths., 17,000 (17.5%); tot. pop., 97,000.

Trinidad and Tobago: Independent nation, consisting of two islands in the Caribbean, member of the British Commonwealth; capital, Port-of-Spain. The first Catholic church in Trinidad was built in 1591, years after several missionary ventures had been launched and a number of missionaries killed. Capuchins were there from 1618 until about 1802. Missionary work continued after the British gained control early in the 19th century. Cordial relations have existed between the Church and state, both of which have manifested their desire for the development of native clergy. Established diplomatic relations with Vatican City in 1978.

Archd., 1; abp., 1; parishes, 59; priests, 135 (23 dioc., 112 rel.); sem., 14; p.d., 1; bros., 26; srs., 200; bap., 9,460; Caths., 383,000 (33.6%); tot. pop., 1,139,000.

Tunisia: Republic on the northern coast of Africa; capital, Tunis. There were few Christians in the territory until the 19th century. A prefecture apostolic was organized in 1843 and the Carthage archdiocese was established in 1884. The Catholic population in 1892 consisted of most of the approximately 50,000 Europeans in the country. When Tunis became a republic in 1956, most of the Europeans left the country. The Holy See and the Tunisian government concluded an agreement in 1964 which changed the Carthage archdiocese into a prelacy and handed over some ecclesiastical property to the republic. A considerable number of Moslem students are in Catholic schools, but the number of Moslem converts to the Church has been small. Tunisia maintains diplomatic relations with Vatican City.

Prel., 1; abp., 1; parishes, 24; priests, 61 (26 dioc., 35 rel.); p.d., 1; bros., 19; srs., 250; bap., 58; Caths., 18,000 (.28%); tot. pop., 6,363,000.

Turkey: Republic in Asia Minor and southeastern Europe, capital, Ankara. Christian communities were established in apostolic times, as attested in the Acts of the Apostles, some of the Epistles of St. Paul, and Revelation. The territory was the scene of heresies and ecumenical councils, the place of residence of Fathers of the Church, the area in which ecclesiastical organization reached the dimensions of more than 450 sees in the middle of the seventh century. The region remained generally Byzantine except for the period of the Latin occupation of Constantinople from 1204 to 1261, but was conquered by the Ottoman Turks in 1453 and remained under their domination until establishment of the republic in 1923. Christians, always a minority, numbered more Orthodox than Latins; they were all under some restriction during the Ottoman period. They suffered persecution in the 19th and 20th centuries, the Armenians being the most numerous victims. Turkey is overwhelmingly Moslem. Catholics are tolerated to a degree. Turkey maintains diplomatic relations with Vatican City.

Patriarchate, 1 (Cilicia for the Armenians, the patriarch resides in Lebanon); archd., 2; dioc., 2; v.a., 2; mission "sui juris," 1; ap. ex., 1; Caths., 17,000; tot. pop., 44,920,000.

Turks and Caicos Islands: British possession in West Indies; capital, Grand Turk. Under ecclesiastical jurisdiction of Nassau diocese, Bahamas.

Caths., 100; tot. pop., 8,000.

Tuvalu (Ellice Islands): Independent island nation in Oceania. Statistics included in Kiribati.

Uganda: Republic in eastern Africa, member of the British Commonwealth; capital, Kampala. The White Fathers were the first Catholic missionaries, starting in 1879. Persecution broke out from 1885 to 1887, taking a toll of 22 Catholic martyrs, who were canonized in 1964, and a number of Anglican victims. (Pope Paul honored all those who died for the faith during a visit to Kampala in 1969.) By 1888, there were more than 8,000 Catholics. Evangelization was resumed in 1894, after being interrupted by war, and proceeded thereafter. The first native African bishop was ordained in 1939. The hierarchy was established in 1953. The Church was suppressed during the erratic regime of Pres. Idi-Amin, who was deposed in the spring of 1979. Uganda maintains diplomatic relations with Vatican City.

Archd., 1; dioc., 13; card., 1 (nat.); bp., 13 (11 nat.); parishes, 303; priests, 902 (529 dioc., 373 rel.); sem., 685; p.d., 1; bros., 300; srs., 2,048; bap., 209,862; Caths., 5,306,000 (38.8%); tot. pop., 13,675,000.

Union of Soviet Socialist Republics: Union of 15 Soviet Socialist Republics in northern Eurasia, from the Baltic Sea to the Pacific; Russian capital, Moscow. The Orthodox Church has been predominant in Russian history. It developed from the Byzantine Church before 1064. Some of its members subsequently established communion with Rome as the result of reunion movements but most of them remained Orthodox. The government has always retained some kind of general or particular control of this church. Latins, always a minority, had a little more freedom. From the beginning of the Communist government in 1917, all churches of whatever kind — including Jews and Moslems — became the targets of official campaigns designed to negate their influence on society and/or to eliminate them entirely. An accurate assessment of the situation of the Catholic Church in Russia is difficult to make. Its dimensions, however, can be gauged from the findings of a team of research specialists made public by the Judi-

ciary Committee of the U.S. House of Representatives in 1964. It was reported: "The fate of the Catholic Church in the USSR and countries occupied by the Russians from 1917 to 1959 shows the following: (a) the number killed: 55 bishops; 12,800 priests and monks; 2.5 million Catholic believers; (b) imprisoned or deported: 199 bishops; 32,000 priests and 10 million believers; (c) 15,700 priests were forced to abandon their priesthood and accept other jobs; and (d) a large number of seminaries and religious communities were dissolved; 1,600 monasteries were nationalized, 31,779 churches were closed. 400 newspapers were prohibited, and all Catholic organizations were dissolved." Several Latin Rite churches are open; e.g., in Moscow, Leningrad, Odessa and Tiflis. An American chaplain is stationed in Moscow to serve Catholics at the U.S. embassy there. Recent reports indicate that, despite repression and attempts at Sovietization, the strongholds of Catholicism in the USSR are Lithuania (incorporated in the USSR in 1940, together with Estonia and Latvia) and the Ukraine. No Catholic statistics are available for the USSR. See separate entries for Estonia, Latvia, Lithuania.

Tot. pop., 262,400,000.

United Arab Emirates: Independent state along Persian Gulf; capital, Abu Dhabi.

V.a., 1; bp., 1; parishes, 3; priests, 8 (2 dioc., 6 rel.); srs., 33; bap., 580; Caths., 25,000; tot. pop., 800,000.

United States: See Catholic History in the United States, Statistics of the Church in the United States.

Upper Volta: Republic inland in western Africa; capital, Ouagadougou. White Fathers started the first missions in 1900 and 1901. White Sisters began work in 1911. A minor and a major seminary were established in 1926 and 1942, respectively. The first native bishop in modern times from West Africa was ordained in 1956 and the first cardinal created in 1965. The hierarchy was established in 1955. Upper Volta established diplomatic relations with Vatican City in 1973.

Archd., 1; dioc., 8; card., 1 (nat.); bp., 9 (nat.); parishes, 99; priests, 379 (162 dioc., 217 rel.); sem., 90; bros., 141; srs., 626; bap., 22,588; Caths., 500,000 (7.2%); tot. pop., 6,910,000.

Uruguay: Republic (called the Eastern Republic of Uruguay) on the southeast coast of South America; capital, Montevideo. The Spanish established a settlement in 1624 and evangelization followed. Missionaries followed the reduction pattern to reach the Indians, form them in the faith and train them in agriculture, husbandry, other useful arts, and the experience of managing property and living in community. Montevideo was made a diocese in 1878. The constitution of 1830 made Catholicism the religion of the state and subsidized some of its activities, principally the missions to the Indians. Separation of Church and state was provided for in the constitution of 1917. Uruguay maintains diplomatic relations with Vatican City.

Archd., 1; dioc., 9; abp., 1; bp., 10; parishes, 224; priests, 587 (198 dioc., 389 rel.); sem., 67; p.d., 16; bros., 149; srs., 1,621; bap., 41,673; Caths., 2,280,000 (78.6%); tot. pop., 2,900,000.

Vanuatu (New Hebrides): Independent (July 29, 1980) island group in the southwest Pacific, about 500 miles west of Fiji; formerly under joint British-French administration; capital, Vila. Effective, though slow, evangelization by Catholic missionaries began about 1887. A vicariate apostolic was set up in 1904. The hierarchy was established in 1966.

Dioc., 1; bp., 1; parishes, 17; priests, 26 (2 dioc., 24 rel.); sem., 14; bros., 9; srs., 65; bap., 615; Caths., 16,143; tot. pop., 112,596.

Vatican City: See separate entry.

Venezuela: Republic in northern South America; capital, Caracas. Evangelization began in 1513-14 and involved members of a number of religious orders who worked in assigned territories, developing missions into pueblos or towns and villages of Indian converts. Nearly 350 towns originated as missions. Fifty-four missionaries met death by violence from the start of missionary work until 1817. Missionary work was seriously hindered during the wars of independence in the second decade of the 19th century and continued in decline through the rest of the century as dictator followed dictator in a period of political turbulence. Restoration of the missions got underway in 1922. The first diocese was established in 1531. Most of the bishops have been native Venezuelans. The first diocesan synod was held in 1574. Church-state relations are regulated by an agreement concluded with the Holy See in 1964. Venezuela maintains diplomatic relations with Vatican City.

Archd., 6; dioc., 18; v.a., 4; card., 1; abp., 6; bp., 29; parishes, 989; priests, 1,995 (796 dioc., 1,199 rel.); sem., 371; p.d., 21; bros., 326; srs., 4,345; bap., 349,463; Caths., 12,834,000 (92.2%); tot. pop., 13,910,000.

Vietnam: Country in southeastern Asia, reunited officially July 2, 1976, as the Socialist Republic of Vietnam; capital, Hanoi. Previously, from 1954, partitioned into the Democratic Peoples' Republic of Vietnam in the North (capital, Hanoi) and the Republic of Vietnam in the South (capital, Saigon). Catholicism was introduced in 1533 but missionary work was intermittent until 1615 when Jesuits arrived to stay. One hundred thousand Catholics were reported in 1639. Two vicariates were organized in 1659. A seminary was set up in 1666 and two native priests were ordained two years later. A congregation of native women religious formed in 1670 is still active. Severe persecution broke out in 1698, three times in the 18th century, and again in the 19th. Between 100,000 and 300,000 persons suffered in some way from persecution during the 50 years before 1883 when the French moved in to secure religious liberty for the Catholics. Most of the 117 beatified Martyrs of Vietnam were killed during this 50-year period. After the French were forced out of Vietnam in 1954, the country was partitioned at the 17th parallel. The North went Communist and the Viet Cong, joined by North Vietnamese regular army troops in 1964, fought to gain control of the South. In 1954 there were approximately 1,114,000 Catholics in the North and 480,000 in the South. More than 650,000 fled to the South to avoid the government repression that silenced the Church in the North. In South Vietnam, the Church continued to develop during the war years. Fragmentary reports about the status of the Church since the end of the war in 1975 have been ominous. Freedom of religious belief and practice was promised by the Revolutionary Government in May, 1975, shortly after its capture of Saigon (Ho Chi Min City). The hierarchy was established in 1960. The apostolic delegation, formerly in Saigon, was transferred to Hanoi in 1976; it is presently vacant.

Archd., 3; dioc., 22; card., 1; abp., 5; bp., 38. No statistics are available. There were 2,749,475 Catholics (6.4% of the total population) in 1974. Pop., 52,300,000.

Virgin Islands: Organized unincorporated U.S. territory, about 34 miles east of Puerto Rico; capital, Charlotte Amalie on St. Thomas (one of the three principal islands). The islands were discovered by Columbus in 1493 and named for St. Ursula and her virgin companions. Missionaries began evangelization in the 16th century. A church on St. Croix dates from about 1660; another, on St. Thomas, from 1774. The Baltimore archdiocese had jurisdiction over the islands from 1804 to 1820 when it was passed on to the first of several places in the Caribbean area. Some trouble arose over a pastoral appointment in the 19th century, resulting in a small schism. The Redemptorists took over pastoral care in 1858; normal conditions have prevailed since.

Dioc., 1; bp., 1; parishes, 6; priests, 14 (1 dioc., 13 rel.); bro., 1; srs., 18; bap., 726; Caths., 27,000; tot. pop., 100,000.

Wales: Part of the United Kingdom, on the western part of the island of Great Britain. Celtic missionaries completed evangelization by the end of the sixth century, the climax of what has been called the age of saints. Welsh Christianity received its distinctive Celtic character at this time. Some conflict developed when attempts were made — and proved successful later — to place the Welsh Church under the jurisdiction of Canterbury; the Welsh opted for direct contact with

Rome. The Church made progress despite the depredations of Norsemen in the eighth and ninth centuries. Norman infiltration occurred near the middle of the 12th century, resulting in a century-long effort to establish territorial dioceses and parishes to replace the Celtic organizational plan of monastic centers and satellite churches. The Western Schism produced split views and allegiances. Actions of Henry VIII in breaking away from Rome had serious repercussions. Proscription and penal laws crippled the Church, resulted in heavy defections and touched off a 150-year period of repression in which more than 91 persons died for the faith. Methodism prevailed by 1750. Modern Catholicism came to Wales with Irish immigrants in the 19th century, when the number of Welsh Catholics was negligible. Catholic emancipation was granted in 1829. The hierarchy was restored in 1850. (See Index for papal visit to Wales.)

Archd., 1; dioc., 1; abp., 1; bp., 2; parishes, 169; priests, 324 (179 dioc., 145 rel.); sem., 24; p.d., 1; bros., 29; srs., 657; bap., 3,252; Caths., 146,163 (5.1%); tot. pop., 2,859,000.

Wallis and Futuna Islands: French overseas territory in the southwestern Pacific. Marists, who began evangelizing the islands in 1836-7, were the first Catholic missionaries. The entire populations of the two islands were baptized by the end of 1842 (Wallis) and 1843 (Futuna). The first missionary to the latter island was killed in 1841; he was the first martyr of the Pacific. Most of the priests on the islands are native Polynesians. The hierarchy was established in 1966.

Dioc., 1; bp., 1 (nat.); parishes, 6; priests, 16 (8 dioc., 8 rel.); sem., 2; bros., 7; srs., 51; bap., 359; Caths., 10,000; tot. pop., 10,412.

Western Sahara: Former Spanish overseas province (Spanish Sahara) on the northwestern coast of Africa. Territory is under control of Morocco. Islam is the religion of non-Europeans. A prefecture apostolic was established in 1954 for the European Catholics there.

P.a., 1; parishes, 2; priests, 3 (rel.); Caths., 365.

Yemen: Arab republic in southwestern Arabia; capital, Sanaa. Christians perished in the first quarter of the sixth century. Moslems have been in control since the seventh century. The state religion is Islam. In 1973, for the first time in 1,400 years, Catholic personnel — priests, religious, lay persons — were invited to work in the country as staff of a government hospital; they were not to engage in proselytizing. Under ecclesiastical jurisdiction of Arabia vicariate apostolic.

Tot. pop., 7,080,000.

Yemen, Peoples Democratic Republic of: Republic in the southern part of the Arabian peninsula; capitals, Aden and Medina as-Shaab. No Christian community has existed there since the Moslem conquest of the seventh century. Under ecclesiastical jurisdiction of Arabia vicariate apostolic.

Tot. pop., 1,853,000.

Yugoslavia: Socialist republic in southeastern Europe; capital, Belgrade. Christianity was introduced from the seventh to ninth centuries in the regions which were combined to form the nation after World War I. Since these regions straddled the original line of demarcation for the Western and Eastern Empires (and churches), and since the Reformation had little lasting effect, the Christians are nearly all either Roman Catholics or Byzantines (some in communion with Rome, the majority Orthodox). Yugoslavia was proclaimed a Socialist republic in 1945. Repression of religion became government policy. Between May, 1945, and December, 1950, persecution took the following toll: almost two-thirds of 22 dioceses lost their bishops; about 348 priests were killed; 200 priests were under arrest and in prison; 12 of 18 seminaries were closed; the Catholic press was confiscated; religious instruction was suppressed in all schools; 300 religious houses and institutions were confiscated, and nuns and other religious driven out; all Church property was expropriated; the ministry of priests was severely restricted and subject to government interference; many thousands of the faithful shared the fate of priests and religious in death, imprisonment and slave labor. Cardinal Stepinac, arrested in 1946 and the symbol of the Church under persecution in Yugoslavia, died Feb. 10, 1960. In an agreement signed June 25, 1966, the government recognized the Holy See's spiritual jurisdiction over the Church in the country and guaranteed to bishops the possibility of maintaining contact with Rome in ecclesiastical and religious matters. The Holy See confirmed the principle that the activity of ecclesiastics, in the exercise of priestly functions, must take place within the religious and ecclesiastical sphere, and that abuse of these functions for political ends would be illegal. Less than two months after the agreement was signed, a group of exiled Croatian priests issued a statement in which they accused the Yugoslav government of failing to abide by it. According to others, an improvement was noticeable. Yugoslavia maintains diplomatic relations with Vatican City.

Archd., 8; dioc., 14; a.a., 1, abp., 8; bp., 22; parishes, 2,761; priests, 4,251 (2,797 dioc., 1,454 rel.); sem., 710; p.d., 3; bros., 271; srs., 6,387; bap., 81,355; Caths., 7,090,000 (31.7%); tot. pop., 22,340,000.

Zaire (formerly the Congo): Republic in south central Africa; capital, Kinshasa. Christianity was introduced in 1484 and evangelization began about 1490. The first native bishop in black Africa was ordained in 1518. Subsequent missionary work was hindered by faulty methods of instruction and formation, inroads of the slave trade, wars among the tribes, and Portuguese policy based on the patronage system and having all the trappings of anti-clericalism in the 18th and 19th centuries. Modern evangelization started in the second half of the 19th century. The hierarchy was established in 1959. In the civil disorders which followed independence in 1960, some missions and other church installations were abandoned, thousands of people reverted to tribal religions and many priests and religious were killed. Church-state tensions have developed in recent years because of the Church's criticism of the anti-Christian thrust of Pres. Mobutu's "Africanization" policies. Zaire maintains diplomatic relations with Vatican City.

Archd., 6; dioc., 41; card., 1 (nat.); abp., 5 (nat.); bp., 45 (40 nat.); parishes, 961; priests, 2,543 (696 dioc., 1,847 rel.); sem., 1,579; p.d., 1; bros., 1,007; srs., 4,337; bap., 358,977; Caths., 12,617,000 (44.5%); tot. pop., 28,290,000.

Zambia: Republic in central Africa; capital, Lusaka. Portuguese priests did some evangelizing in the 16th and 17th centuries but no results of their work remained in the 19th century. Jesuits began work in the south in the 1880's and White Fathers in the north and east in 1895. Evangelization of the western region began for the first time in 1831. The number of Catholics doubled in the 20 years following World War II. Zambia maintains diplomatic relations with Vatican City.

Archd., 2; dioc., 7; abp., 2 (nat.); bp., 7 (5 nat.); parishes, 206; priests, 498 (92 dioc., 406 rel.); sem., 111; p.d., 1; bros., 171; srs., 684; bap., 46,262; Caths., 1,638,000 (28%); tot. pop., 5,830,000.

Zimbabwe (formerly Rhodesia): Independent republic (Apr. 18, 1980) in south central Africa; capital, Harare (Salisbury). Earlier unsuccessful missionary ventures preceded the introduction of Catholicism in 1879. Missionaries began to make progress after 1893. The hierarchy was established in 1955; the first black bishop was ordained in 1973. In 1969, four years after the government of Ian Smith made a unilateral declaration of independence from England, a new constitution was enacted for the purpose of assuring continued white supremacy over the black majority. Catholic and Protestant prelates in the country protested rigorously against the constitution and related enactments as opposed to human rights of the blacks and restrictive of the Church's freedom to carry out its pastoral, educational and social service functions. The Smith regime was ousted in 1979 after seven years of civil war in which at least 25,000 people were killed. Diplomatic relations with the Vatican were established in 1980.

Archd., 1; dioc., 4; p.a., 1; abp., 1 (nat.); bp., 5 (3 nat.); priests, 336 (55 dioc., 281 rel.); sem., 69; p.d., 11 bros., 122; srs., 922; bap., 12,660; Caths., 676,000 (9.2%); tot. pop., 7,360,000.

CATHOLIC WORLD STATISTICS

(Principal sources: Statistical Yearbook of the Church, 1980, the latest edition available; Annuario Pontificio, 1982. Figures are from Dec. 31, 1980, except for jurisdictions and hierarchy which have been updated to June, 1982, in most cases.)

Patriarchates: 13. Eastern Rites, 8 (Africa, 2; Asia, 6). Roman Rite, 5 (Asia, 2; Europe, 2; West Indies, 1). The West Indies patriarchate has been vacant since 1963.

Archdioceses: 501 (Africa, 56; North and Middle America, 77; South America, 86; Asia, 122; Europe, 144; Oceania, 16).

Dioceses: 1,873 (Africa, 300; North and Middle America, 304; South America, 336; Asia, 350; Europe, 535; Oceania, 48).

Prelatures: 80 (Africa, 1; North and Middle America, 12; South America, 45; Asia, 14; Europe, 8).

Abbacies: 20 (Africa, 1; North and Middle America, 1; South America, 2; Asia, 1; Europe, 14; Oceania, 1).

Vicariates Apostolic: 71 (Africa, 12; North and Middle America, 6; South America, 36; Asia, 16; Europe, 1).

Prefectures Apostolic: 58 (Africa, 11; South America, 11; Asia, 36).

Apostolic Administrations: 8 (Africa, 1; North and Middle America, 2; Asia, 1; Europe, 4).

Missions "Sui Juris": 3 (Africa, 1; Asia, 2).

Apostolic Exarchates, Ordinariates: 21 (North and Middle America, 2; South America, 3; Asia, 2; Europe, 13; Oceania, 1).

Military Vicariates: 27 (Africa, 3; North and Middle America, 4; South America, 7; Asia, 2; Europe, 9; Oceania, 2).

Cardinals (as of Sept. 9, 1982): 122 (Africa, 12; North and Middle America, 19; South America, 16; Asia, 10; Europe, 62; Oceania, 3).

Archbishops: 424 (Africa, 49; North and Middle America, 75; South America, 91; Asia, 110; Europe, 110; Oceania, 16). Figures for archbishops and bishops (below) include residential and auxiliary prelates only. Titular archbishops and bishops engaged in other apostolates and retired members of the hierarchy are not included. The total number of archbishops and bishops was 680 amd 2,985, respectively, according to the *1980 Statistical Yearbook of the Church.*

Bishops: 2,420 (Africa, 314; North and Middle America, 482; South America, 516; Asia, 325; Europe, 719; Oceania, 64). See note under archbishops, above.

Priests, Total: 413,600 (Africa, 17,346; North

and Middle America, 86,315; South America, 33,817; Asia, 27,136; Europe, 243,319; Oceania, 5,667).

Priests, Diocesan: 257,409 (Africa, 6,052; North and Middle America, 51,459; South America, 14,523; Asia, 13,555; Europe, 168,908; Oceania, 2,912).

Priests, Religious: 156,191 (Africa, 11,294; North and Middle America, 34,856; South America, 19,294; Asia, 13,581; Europe, 74,411; Oceania, 2,755).

Permanent Deacons: 7,654 (Africa, 131; North and Middle America, 5,207; South America, 696; Asia, 70; Europe, 1,500; Oceania, 50).

Brothers: 73,090 (Africa, 5,364; North and Middle America, 15,908; South America, 7,030; Asia, 6,117; Europe, 35,445; Oceania, 3,226).

Sisters: 960,991 (Africa, 35,586; North and Middle America, 203,801; South America, 89,936; Asia, 87,889; Europe, 527,707; Oceania, 16,072).

Seminarians: 66,042 (Africa, 6,549; North and Middle America, 12,883; South America, 9,817; Asia, 12,190; Europe, 23,666; Oceania, 937). Figures are for diocesan (44,143) and religious order (21,899) major seminarians.

Baptisms: 17,541,164 (Africa, 2,001,104; North and Middle America, 4,092,196; South America, 5,590,295; Asia, 2,083,389; Europe, 3,648,783; Oceania, 125,397). Includes 16,410,161 baptisms up to the age of seven and 1,131,003 over the age of seven.

Marriages: 4,156,264 (Africa, 177,685; North and Middle America, 892,730; South America, 1,119,673; Asia, 381,697; Europe, 1,551,099; Oceania, 33,380). Includes 3,820,462 marriages between Catholics and 335,802 between Catholics and non-Catholics.

Parishes: 206,503 (Africa, 7,162; North and Middle America, 30,688; South America, 15,663; Asia, 11,854; Europe, 138,828; Oceania, 2,308).

Elementary or Primary Schools: 75,454 (Africa, 18,654; North and Middle America, 12,740; South America, 9,172; Asia, 11,108; Europe, 21,373; Oceania, 2,407).

Elementary or Primary School Students: 20,661,202 (Africa, 5,610,700; North and Middle America, 3,735,889; South America, 3,102,729; Asia, 3,752,622; Europe, 3,978,952; Oceania, 480,310).

Secondary Schools: 29,637 (Africa, 3,244; North and Middle America, 3,755; South America, 4,905; Asia, 6,207; Europe, 10,844; Oceania, 682).

Secondary School Students: 11,014,951 (Africa, 806,533; North and Middle America, 1,492,922; South America, 1,871,037; Asia, 3,150,892; Europe, 3,435,984; Oceania, 257,583).

Students in Higher Institutes and Universities:

2,093,589 (Africa, 7,368; North and Middle America, 793,154; South America, 460,154; Asia, 615,229; Europe, 214,449; Oceania, 3,235).

Hospitals: 6,700 (Africa, 978; North and Middle America, 1,094; South America, 1,326; Asia, 1,089; Europe, 2,030; Oceania, 183).

Dispensaries: 11,789 (Africa, 3,115; North and Middle America, 1,145; South America, 2,656; Asia, 2,241; Europe, 2,418; Oceania, 214).

Leprosaria: 630 (Africa, 283; North and Middle America, 18; South America, 51; Asia, 266; Europe, 7; Oceania, 5).

Homes for Aged, Chronically Ill, Handicapped: 9,642 (Africa, 281; North and Middle America, 962; South America, 1,227; Asia, 519; Europe, 6,485; Oceania, 168).

Orphanages: 6,185 (Africa, 358, North and Middle America, 408; South America, 1,023; Asia, 1,629; Europe, 2,709; Oceania, 58).

Nurseries: 4,860 (Africa, 360; North and Middle America, 189; South America, 850; Asia, 872; Europe, 2,561; Oceania, 28).

Catholic Population: 783,660,000 (17.9 per cent of the total world population of 4,371,266,000). Africa, 58,676,000 (12.5 per cent; total population, 469,543,000). North and Middle America, 166,081,000 (44.2 per cent; total population, 375,583,000). South America, 218,735,000 (90.7 per cent; total population 241,224,000). Asia, 62,713,000 (2.4 per cent; total population, 2,581,687,000). Europe, 271,649,000 (39.9 per cent; total population, 680,490,000). Oceania, 5,806,000 (25.5 per cent; total population, 22,739,000).

COMMUNISM

The substantive principles of modern Communism, a theory and system of economics and social organization, were stated about the middle of the 19th century by Karl Marx, author of *The Communist Manifesto* and, with Friedrich Engels, *Das Kapital.*

The elements of Communist ideology include: radical materialism; dialectical determinism; the inevitability of class struggle, tablishment of a worldwide classless society; common ownership of productive and other goods; the subordination of all persons and institutions to the dictatorship of the collectivity; denial of the rights, dignity and liberty of persons; militant atheism and hostility to religion; utilitarian morality.

Communism in theory and practice has been the subject of many papal documents and statements. Pius IX condemned it in 1846. Leo XIII dealt with it at length in the encyclicals *Quod Apostolici Muneris* in 1878 and *Rerum Novarum* in 1891. Pius XI wrote the encyclicals *Quadragesimo Anno* in 1931 and *Divini Redemptoris* in 1937.

EPISCOPAL CONFERENCES

(Principal source: *Annuario Pontificio*.)

Episcopal conferences, organized and operating under general norms and particular statutes approved by the Holy See, are official bodies in and through which the bishops of a given country or territory act together as pastors of the Church.

Listed below according to countries or regions are titles and addresses of conferences and names and sees of presidents (archbishops unless otherwise noted).

Africa, North: Conference Episcopale d'Afrique du Nord, 13 rue Khelifa Boukhalfa, Algiers, Algeria. Card. Leon-Etienne Duval (Algiers).

Africa, South: Southern African Catholic Bishops' Conference (SACBC), P.O. Box 941, Pretoria 0001, S. Africa. Denis Eugene Hurley, O.M.I. (Durban).

Angola and Sao Tome: Conferencia Episcopal de Angola e Sao Tome (CEAST), C.P. 1230, Luanda, Angola. Manuel F. da Costa (Huambo).

Antilles: Antilles Episcopal Conference, 27 Maraval Rd., Port of Spain, Trinidad. Gordon Anthony Pantin (Port of Spain).

Arab Countries: Conference des Eveques Latins dans les Regions Arabes (CELRA), Latin Patriarchate, P.O. Box 14152, Jerusalem (Old City). Patriarch Giacomo Beltritti (Jerusalem).

Argentina: Conferencia Episcopal Argentina (CEA), Calle Paraguay 1867, Buenos Aires. Card. Raul Francisco Primatesta (Cordoba).

Australia: Australian Episcopal Conference, P.O. Box 297, Kingston, A.C.T., 2604. Card. James Darcy Freeman (Sydney).

Austria: Osterreichische Bischofskonferenz, Rotenturmstrasse 2, A1010 Vienna. Card. Franz Koenig (Vienna).

Bangladesh: Catholic Bishops' Conference (CBCB), P.O. Box 3, Ramna, Dacca-2. Michael Rozario (Dacca).

Belgium: Bisschoppenconferentie van Belgie — Conference Episcopale de Belgique, Wollemarkt 15, B-2800 Mechelen. Godfried Danneels (Mechelen-Brussel).

Benin: Conference Episcopale du Benin, B.P. 491, Cotonou. Christophe Adimou (Cotonou).

Bolivia: Conferencia Episcopal de Bolivia (CEB), Casilla 2309, La Paz. Luis Rodriguez Pardo (Santa Cruz de la Sierra).

Brazil: Conferencia Nacional dos Bispos do Brasil (CNBB), C.P. 13-2067, 70000 Brasilia, D.F. Bp. Jose Ivo Lorscheiter (Santa Maria).

Bulgaria: Ulitza Pashovi 10-B, Sofia VI. Bp. Metodio Dimitrow Stratiew (Apostolic Exarch, Sofia).

Burma: Burma Catholic Bishops' Conference (BCBC), 292 Prome Rd., Sanchaung P.O., Rangoon. Alphonse U Than Aung (Mandalay).

Burundi: Conference Episcopale du Burundi, B. P. 1390, Bujumbura. Coad. Abp. Joachim Ruhuna (Gitega).

Cameroon: Conference Episcopale Nationale du Cameroun, P.O. Box 82, Mankon-Bamenda. Bp. Paul Verdzekov (Bamenda).

Canada: See Canadian Conference of Catholic Bishops.

Central African Republic: Conference Episcopale Centrafricaine (CECA), B.P. 798, Bangui. Joachim N'Dayen (Bangui).

Chad: Conference Episcopale du Tchad, B.P., 87, Sarh. Bp. Henri Veniat, S.J. (Sarh).

Chile: Conferencia Episcopal de Chile (CECH), Casilla 13191, Correo 21, Santiago de Chile. Bp. Jose Manuel Santos Ascarza (Valdivia).

China (Republic of China, Taiwan): Regional Episcopal Conference of China, Lane 32, Kuangfu Rd., Taipeh 34, Taiwan. Matthew Kia Yen-Wen (Taipeh).

Colombia: Conferencia Episcopal de Colombia, Apartado 7448, Bogota D.E. Mario Revollo Bravo (Nueva Pamplona).

Congo: Conference Episcopale du Congo, B.P. 2301, Brazzaville. Bp. Georges Singha (Owanda).

Costa Rica: Conferencia Episcopal de Costa Rica (CECOR), Apartado 497, San Jose. Roman Arrieta Villalobos (San Jose de Costa Rica).

Cuba: Conferencia Episcopal de Cuba (CEC), Apartado 26, Santiago de Cuba. Pedro Meurice Estiu (Santiago de Cuba).

Dominican Republic: Conferencia del Episcopado Dominicano (CED), Apartado 1313, Abp-Bp. Higuey Hugo Eduardo Polanco Brito (Nuestra Senora de la Altagracia en Higuey).

Ecuador: Conferencia Episcopal Ecuatoriana, Apartado 1081, Quito. Card. Pablo Munoz Vega, S.J. (Quito).

El Salvador: Conferencia Episcopal de El Salvador (CEDES). Apartado Postal 43, San Miguel. Bp. Jose Alvarez Ramirez, C.M. (San Miguel).

Ethiopia: Conferenza Episcopale di Etiopia, P.O. Box 21903, Addis Ababa. Paulos Tzadua (Addis Ababa).

France: Conference Episcopale Francaise, 106 rue du Bac, 75341 Paris CEDEX 07. Bp. Jean Vilnet (Saint-Die).

Gabon: Conference Episcopale du Gabon, B.P. 230, Franceville. Felicien-Patrice Makouaka (Franceville).

Gambia, Liberia and Sierra Leone: Inter-Territorial Episcopal Conference, P.O. Box 893, Freetown, Sierra Leone. Joseph Ganda (Freetown and Bo.).

Germany: Deutsche Bischofskonferenz, Kaiserstrasse 163, D-5300 Bonn. Card. Joseph Hoeffner (Cologne). Berliner Bischofskonferenz, Franzosische Strasse 34,

DDR-108 Berlin. Bp. Gerhard Schaffran (Dresden-Meissen).

Ghana: Ghana Bishops' Conference, P.O. Box 247, Accra. Bp. Dominic Kodwo Andoh (Accra).

Great Britain: Bishops' Conference of England and Wales, Archbishop's House, Westminster, London, S.W. 1. Card. George Basil Hume, O.S.B. (Westminster). Bishops' Conference of Scotland, 42 Greenhill Gardens, Edinburgh 10. Card. Gordon J. Gray (Saint Andrews and Edinburgh).

Greece: Conferenza Episcopale di Grecia, Archeveche Catholique, Corfu. Antonio Varthalitis (Corfu, Zante and Cefalonia.)

Guatemala: Conferencia Episcopal de Guatemala (CEG), 4 Calle 9-45, zona 1, Ciudad de Guatemala. Bp. Juan Gerardi Conedera (Santa Cruz del Quiche).

Guinea: Conference Episcopale de la Guinee, B.P. 1006 Bis, Conakry.

Haiti: Conference Episcopale de Haiti (CEH). Archbishopric, Port-au-Prince. Francois-Wolff Ligonde (Port-au-Prince).

Honduras: Conferencia Episcopal de Honduras (CEH), Arzobispado, Tegucigalpa. Hector Enrique Santos Hernandez, S.D.B. (Tegucigalpa).

Hungary: Magyar Puspoki Kar, Berenyi Zsigmond u. 2, Pf. 25, H-2501 Esztergom. Card. Laszlo Lekai (Esztergom).

India: Catholic Bishops' Conference of India (CBCI), CBCI Centre, Goldakkana, New Delhi-110001. Card. Lawrence Trevor Picachy (Calcutta).

Indonesia: General Conference of the Ordinaries of Indonesia (Majelis Agung Waligerija Indonesia — MAWI), Pusat Jalan Cut Mutiah 10, Jakarta II/14. Bp. Francis Xavier Sudartanto Hadisumarta, O. Carm. (Malang).

Ireland: Episcopal Meetings, "Ara Coeli," Armagh. Card. Tomas O'Fiaich (Armagh).

Italy: Conferenza Episcopale Italiana (CEI), Circonvallazione Aurelia, 50, 00165 Roma. Card. Anastasio Alberto Ballestrero, O.C.D. (Turin).

Ivory Coast: Conference Episcopale de la Cote d'Ivoire, B.P. 1287, Abidjan. Bernard Yago (Abidjan).

Japan: Japan Catholic Bishops' Conference, Catholic Center, 10-34 Uenomachi, Nagasaki-shi. Card. Joseph Asajiro Satowaki (Nagasaki).

Kenya: Kenya Episcopal Conference (KEC), P.O. Box 842, Eldoret. Bp. John Njenga (Eldoret).

Korea: Catholic Conference of Korea, Box 16, Seoul. Card. Stephen Sou Hwan Kim (Seoul).

Laos and Cambodia: Conference Episcopale du Laos et du Cambodge, Centre Catholique, Vientiane, Laos. Bp. Thomas Nantha (vic, ap. Vientiane).

Latvia: Pils Jela, 2, Riga. Bp. Giuliano Vaivods (Ap. Admin., Riga and Liepaja).

Lesotho: Lesotho Catholic Bishops' Conference, P.O. Box 267, Maseru. Alfonso Liguori Morapeli, O.M.I. (Maseru).

Liberia: See Gambia, Liberia and Sierra Leone.

Lithuania: Vilniaus gatve 4, 233000 Kaunas. Bp. Liudas Povilonis (Ap. Admin., Kaunas and Vilkaviskis).

Madagascar: Conference Episcopale du Madagascar, 102 bis, Av. Marechal Joffre Antanimena, B. P 667, Tananarive. Card. Victor Razafimahatratra, S.J. (Tananarive).

Malawi: Episcopal Conference of Malawi, Catholic Secretariat of Malawi, P.O. Box 30384, Lilongwe 3. Bp. Felix Mkhori (Chikwawa).

Malaysia-Singapore-Brunei: Catholic Bishops' Conference of Malaysia-Singapore-Brunei, (BCMSB), Archbishop's House, 31 Victoria St., Singapore 0718. Gregory Yong Sooi Nghean (Singapore).

Mali: Conference Episcopale du Mali, B.P. 298, Bamako. Luc Auguste Sangare (Bamako).

Malta: Conferenza Episcopale Maltese, Archbishop's Curia, Valletta. Joseph Mercieca (Malta).

Mexico: Conferencia del Episcopado Mexicano (CEM), Apartado Postal 22-119, Victoria 21, Tlalpan 22, D.F. Card. Ernesto Corripio Ahumada (Mexico).

Mozambique: Conferencia Episcopal de Mocambique (CEM), C.P. 286, Maputo. Bp. Jaime Pedro Goncalves (Beira).

Netherlands: Nederlandse Bisschoppen Konferentie, Postbus 13049, Biltstraat 121, Utrecht. Card. Johannes Willebrands (Utrecht).

New Zealand: New Zealand Episcopal Conference, P.O. Box 198, Wellington. Thomas Stafford Williams (Wellington).

Nicaragua: Conferencia Episcopal de Nicaragua, Arzobispado, Managua. Miguel Obando Bravo, S.D.B. (Managua).

Niger: See Upper Volta.

Nigeria: National Episcopal Conference of Nigeria, P.O. Box 951, Lagos. Francis Arinze (Onitsha).

Pacific: Conference des Eveques du Pacifique (CEPAC), P.O. Box 1200, Suva, Fiji. Bp. Patelisio Punou-Ki-Hihifo Finau, S.M. (Tonga).

Pakistan: Pakistan Episcopal Conference, St. Patrick's Cathedral, Karachi 3. Card. Joseph Cordeiro (Karachi).

Panama: Conferencia Episcopal de Panama (CEP), Apartado 386, Panama 1. Marcos Gregorio McGrath, C.S.C. (Panama).

Papua New Guinea and Solomon Islands: Bishops' Conference of Papua New Guinea and Solomon Islands, Southern Highlands, P.O. Box 69, Mendi, Papua New Guinea. Bp. Firmin Schmidt, O.F.M. Cap. (Mendi).

Paraguay: Conferencia Episcopal Paraguaya (CEP), Calle Alberdi 782, Casilla Correo 1436, Asuncion. Bp. Felipe Santiago Benitez Avalos (Villarrica).

Peru: Conferencia Episcopal Peruana, Apartado 310, Lima 1. Card. Juan Landazuri Ricketts, O.F.M. (Lima).

Philippine Islands: Catholic Bishops' Conference of the Philippines (CBCP), P.O. Box 1160, Manila. Antonio Mabutas y Lloren (Davao).

Poland: Konferencja Episkopatu Polski, Ul. Miodowa 17, 00-246 Warsaw.

Portugal: Conferencia Episcopal Portuguesa, Campo dos martires de Patria, 43-1 Esq., 1198 Lisbon Bp. Manuel D'Almeida Trindade (Aveiro).

Puerto Rico: Conferencia Episcopal Puertorriquena (CEP), Apartado 1967, San Juan de Puerto Rico 00903. Card. Luis Aponte Martinez (San Juan).

Rhodesia: See Zimbabwe.

Rumania: Vacant.

Rwanda: Conference Episcopale du Rwanda (C.Ep.R.), B.P. 715, Kigali. Vincent Nsengiyumva (Kigali).

Scandinavia: Conferentia Episcopalis Scandiae, Bredgade 69 A, DK 1260 Copenhagen K, Denmark. Bp. John W. Gran, O.C.S.O. (Oslo, Norway).

Senegal-Mauritania: Conference Episcopale du Senegal-Mauritania, B.P. 5082, Dakar, Fann. Senegal. Card. Hyacinthe Thiandoum (Dakar).

Sierra Leone: See Gambia, Liberia and Sierra Leone.

Spain: Conferencia Episcopal Espanola, Alfonso XI, 4, 1⁰, Madrid 14. Gabino Diaz Merchan (Oviedo).

Sri Lanka: Catholic Bishops' Conference of Sri Lanka, Archbishop's House, Borella, Colombo 8. Bp. Frank Marcus Fernando (Chilaw).

Sudan: Sudan Episcopal Conference (SEC), P.O. Box 49, Khartoum. Gabriel Zubeir Wako (Khartoum).

Switzerland: Conference des Eveques Suisses, Secretariat, av. Moleson 30, CH-1700 Fribourg 1. Bp. Otmar Mader (Sankt Gallen).

Tanzania: Tanzania Episcopal Conference (TEC), P.O. Box 2133, Dar-es-Salaam. Bp. Mario Epifanio Abdallah Mgulunde (Iringa).

Thailand: Conference des Eveques de Thailand, Assumption Cathedral, Bangrak, Bangkok 5. Michael Michai Kitbunchu (Bangkok).

Togo: Conference Episcopale du Togo, B.P. 348, Lome. Robert Dosseh Anyron (Lome).

Turkey: Conferenza Episcopale di Turchia, Olcek Sokak 83, Harbiya, Istanbul. Bp. Gauthier Pierre Dubois, O.F.M. Cap. (V.A., Istanbul).

Uganda: Uganda Episcopal Conference, P.O. Box 2886, Kampala. Bp. Hadrian Ddungu (Masaka).

United States: See National Conference of Catholic Bishops.

Upper Volta and Niger: Conference des Eveques de la Haute-Volta et du Niger, B.P. 90, Ouagadougou, Upper Volta. Bp. Dieudonne Yougbare (Koupela, Upper Volta).

Uruguay: Conferencia Episcopal Uruguaya (CEU), Avenida Uruguay 1319, Montevideo. Bp. Jose Gottardi Cristelli, S.D.B. (Aux., Montevideo).

Venezuela: Conferencia Episcopal de Venezuela (CEV), Apartado Postal 954, Caracas 101. Domingo Roa Perez (Maracaibo).

Vietnam: Conference Episcopale du Vietnam, 40 Pho Nha Chung, Hanoi. Card. Joseph-Marie Trinh van-Can (Hanoi).

Yugoslavia: Biskupska Konferencija Jugoslavije, Kaptol 31, P.B. 02-406, Zagreb. Franjo Kuharic (Zagreb).

Zaire: Conference Pleniere des Ordinaires du Zaire (CEZ), B.P. 3258, Kinshasa-Gombe. Bp. Kaseba (Kalemie-Kirungu).

Zambia: Zambia Episcopal Conference, P.O. Box 31965, Lusaka. Bp. Dennis Harold De Jong (Ndola).

Zimbabwe: Zimbabwe Catholic Bishops' Conference (ZCBC), P.O. Box 8135, Causeway, Harare. Patrick Chakaipa (Harare).

Territorial Conferences

Territorial as well as national episcopal conferences have been established in some places. Some conferences of this kind are still in the planning stage.

Africa: Association of Member Episcopal Conferences in Eastern Africa (AMECEA): Represents Uganda, Kenya, Tanzania, Zambia and Malawi; Ethiopia was accepted as associate member in 1977. Bishop Medard Joseph Mazombwe, Chipata, Zambia, president. Address: P.O. Box 21191, Nairobi, Kenya.

Symposium of Episcopal Conferences of Africa and Madagascar (SECAM) (Symposium des Conferences Episcopales d'Afrique et de Madagascar, SCEAM): Cardinal Paul Zoungrano, P.A., Ouagadougou, Upper Volta, president. Address: Secretariat, P.O. Box 7530, Accra-North, Ghana.

Regional Episcopal Conference of French-Speaking West Africa (Conference Episcopale Regionale de l'Afrique de l'Ouest Francophone, CERAO): Card. Paul Zoungrana, Ouagadougou, president. Address: B.P. 1471, Ouagadougou, Upper Volta.

Association of Episcopal Conferences of Anglo-Speaking West Africa (AECAWA): Card. Dominic Ignatius Ekandem, Ikot Ekpene, Nigeria, president. Address: P.O. Box 297, Monrovia, Liberia.

Association of Episcopal Conferences of Congo, Central African Republic and Chad (ACECCT): Abp. Joachim N'Dayen, Bangui, Central African Republic, president. Address: Secretariat, B.P. 1518, Bangui, Central African Republic.

Inter-Regional Meeting of Bishops of Southern Africa (IMBISA): Abp. Joseph R. Fitzgerald, O.M.I., bishop of Johannesburg, S. Africa, president. Address: P.O. Box 17054, Hillbrow 2038, Johannesburg, S. Africa.

Asia: Federation of Asian Bishops' Conferences (FABC): Represents 14 Asian episcopal conferences (excluding the Middle East). Headquarters, P.O. Box 2948, Hong Kong. Established in 1970; statutes approved experimentally Dec. 6, 1972. Bishop Mariano Gaviola, Garces, Military Vicar, Philippines, secretary general.

Europe: Council of European Bishops' Conferences (Consilium Conferentiarum Episcopalium Europae, CCEE): Card. George Basil Hume, O.S.B., Westminster, England, president. Address of secretariat: Klosterhof 6b, CH-9000 St. Gallen, Switzerland.

Central and South America: Latin American Bishops' Conference (Consejo Episcopal LatinoAmericano, CELAM): Established in 1956; statutes approved Nov. 9, 1974. Represents 22 Latin American national bishops' conferences. Abp. Alfonso Lopez Trujillo, Medellin, Colombia, president. Address of the secretariat: Calle 78, no. 11-17, Apartado Aereo 5278, Bogota, D.E., Colombia.

Episcopal Secretariat of Central America and Panama (Secretariado Episcopal de America Central y Panama, SEDAC): Statutes approved experimentally Sept. 26, 1970. Archbishop Miguel Obando Bravo, Managua, Nicaragua, president.

INTERNATIONAL CATHOLIC ORGANIZATIONS

(Principal sources: Conference of International Catholic Organizations; Pontifical Council for the Laity; Almanac survey.)

Guidelines

International organizations wanting to call themselves "Catholic" are required to meet standards set by the Vatican's Council for the Laity and to register with and get the approval of the Papal Secretariat of State, according to guidelines dated Dec. 3 and published in *Acta Apostolicae Sedis* under date of Dec. 23, 1971.

Among conditions for the right of organizations to "bear the name Catholic" are:

• leaders "will always be Catholics," and candidates for office will be approved by the Secretariat of State;

• adherence by the organization to the Catholic Church, its teaching authority and teachings of the Gospel;

• evidence that the organization is really international with a universal outlook and that it fulfills its mission through its own management, meetings and accomplishments.

The guidelines also stated that leaders of the organizations "will take care to maintain necessary reserve as regards taking a stand or engaging in public activity in the field of politics or trade unionism. Abstention in these fields will normally be the best attitude for them to adopt during their term of office."

The guidelines were in line with a provision stated by the Second Vatican Council in the *Decree on the Apostolate of the Laity*: "No project may claim the name 'Catholic' unless it has obtained the consent of the lawful church authority."

They made it clear that all organizations are not obliged to apply for recognition, but that the Church "reserves the right to recognize as linked with her mission and her aims those organizations or movements which see fit to ask for such recognition."

Conference

Conference of International Catholic Organizations: A permanent body for collaboration among various organizations which seek to promote the development of international life along the lines of Christian principles. Eleven international Catholic organizations participated in its foundation and first meeting in 1927 at Fribourg, Switzerland. In 1951, the conference established its general secretariat and adopted governing statutes which were approved by the Vatican Secretariat of State in 1953.

The permanent secretariat is located at 37-39 rue de Vermont, CH-1202 Geneva, Switzerland. Other office addresses are: 1 rue de Varembe, C.P. 43, CH-1211 Geneva 20, Switzerland (Information Center); 9, rue Cler, F-75007 Paris, France (International Catholic Center for UNESCO); ICO Information Center, 323 East 47th St., New York, N.Y. 10017.

International Organizations

International Catholic organizations are listed below. Information includes name, date and place of establishment (when available), address of general secretariat. An asterisk indicates that the organization is a member of the Conference of International Catholic Organizations. Approximately 24 of the organizations have consultative status with other international or regional non-governmental agencies.

Apostleship of Prayer (1849): Borgo Santo Spirito 5, I-00193 Rome, Italy. National secretariat in most countries. (See Index.)

Apostolatus Maris (Apostleship of the Sea) (1922, Glasgow, Scotland): Pontifical Commission for Migration and Tourism, Piazza San Calisto 16, I-00153 Rome, Italy. (See Index.)

Associationes Juventutis Salesianae (Associations of Salesian Youth) (1847): Via della Pisana, 1111, 00163 Rome, Italy.

Blue Army of Our Lady of Fatima: (See Index.)

Caritas Internationalis* (1951, Rome, Italy): Piazza San Calisto 16, I-00153, Rome, Italy. Coordinates relief aid on an international level.

Catholic International Education Office* (1952): 60, rue des Eburons, B-1040 Brussels, Belgium.

Catholic International Federation for Physical and Sports Education* (1911; present name, 1957): 5, rue Cernuschi, F-75017 Paris, France.

Catholic International Union for Social Service* (1925, Milan, Italy): rue de la Poste 111, B-1030 Brussels, Belgium (general secretariat).

Christian Fraternity of the Sick and Handicapped: 9, Avenue de la Gare, CH-1630, Bulle, Switzerland.

"Focolari" (1943, Trent, Italy): Via di Frascati, 302, I-00040 Rocca di Papa (Rome), Italy. (See Index: Focolare Movement.)

International Association of Charities of St. Vincent de Paul* (1617, Chatillon les Dombes, France): 38, rue d'Alsace-Lorraine, B-1050 Brussels, Belgium. (See Index: St. Vincent de Paul Society.)

International Association of Children of Mary (1847): 67 rue de Sèvres, F-75006 Paris, France.

International Catholic Association for Service to Young Women and Girls* (1897): 37-39 rue de Vermont, Case Postale n 22, CH-1211 Geneva 20 CIC, Switzerland. Welfare of Catholic girls living away from home.

International Catholic Auxiliaries (1937, Belgium): 91, rue de la Servette, CH-1202 Geneva, Switzerland.

International Catholic Child Bureau* (1947): 65, rue de Lausanne, CH-1202 Geneva, Switzerland.

International Catholic Conference of Guiding* (1965): Rue Paul-Emile Janson, 35, B-1050 Brussels, Belgium. Founded by member bodies of interdenominational World Association of Guides and Girl Scouts.

International Catholic Conference of Scouting* (1948): 21, rue de Dublin, B-1050 Brussels, Belgium.

International Catholic Film Organization* (1928, The Hague, The Netherlands): 8, rue de l'Orme, B-1040 Brussels, Belgium (general secretariat). Federation of national Catholic film offices.

International Catholic Migration Commission* (1951): 65, rue de Lausanne, CH-1202 Geneva, Switzerland. Coordinates Catholic activities to help migrants.

International Catholic Rural Association (1962, Rome): Piazza San Calisto 16, I-00153 Rome, Italy. International body for agricultural and rural organizations.

International Catholic Union of the Press*: 37-39 rue de Vermont, Case Postale 197 CH-1211 Geneva 20 CIC, Switzerland. Coordinates and represents at the international level the activities of Catholics and Catholic federations or associations in the field of press and information. Has five specialized branches: International Federation of Catholic Dailies and Periodicals (1928); International Federation of Catholic Journalists (1927); International Federation of Catholic Press Agencies (1950); International Catholic Association of Teachers and Scientific or Technical Research Workers on Information (1968); Federation of Church Press Associations (1974).

International Centre for Studies in Religious Education* (1934-35, Louvain, Belgium, under name Catechetical Documentary Centre; present name, 1956): 184, rue Washington, B-1050 Brussels, Belgium. Also referred to as Lumen Vitae Centre; concerned with all aspects of religious formation.

International Committee of Catholic Nurses* (1933): Piazza San Calisto, 16, 00153 Rome, Italy.

International Cooperation for Socio-Economic Development (1965, Rome, Italy): 104, Avenue Princess Elisabeth, B-1030 Brussels, Belgium.

International Council of Catholic Men* (Unum Omnes) (1948): Piazza San Calisto 16, I-00153 Rome, Italy.

International Crusade for the Blind (1957): 88, Avenue Denfert-Rochereau, F-75014 Paris, France, Coordinates action of Catholic groups and associations for the blind and develops their apostolate.

International Federation of Catholic Medical Associations (1954)): D'Monte Park Rd., 64, Bandra, Bombay, 400.050, India.

International Federation of Catholic Parochial Youth Communities* (1962, Rome, Italy): Kipdorp 30, B-2000 Antwerp, Belgium.

International Federation of Catholic Pharmacists* (1954): 59, Bergstrasse, B-4700 Eupen, Belgium.

International Federation of Catholic Rural Movements* (1964, Lisbon, Portugal): 92, rue Africaine, B-1050 Brussels, Belgium.

International Federation of Catholic Universities* (1949): 78A, rue de Sevres, F-75341 Paris Codex 7, France.

International Federation of Institutes for Social and Socio-Religious Research (1952): Vlamingenstraat, 116, B-3000 Leuven, Belgium.

International Military Apostolate (1967): 20, rue Notre-Dame des Champs, F-75006 Paris, France. Comprised of organizations of military men.

International Movement of Apostolate of Children* (1929, France): 8, rue Duguay-Trouin, F-75006 Paris, France.

International Movement of Apostolate in Middle and Upper Classes* (1963): Piazza San Calisto 16, I-00153 Rome, Italy. Evangelization of adults of the independent milieus (that part of population known as old or recent middle class, aristocracy, bourgeoisie or "white collar").

International Movement of Catholic Agricultural and Rural Youth (1954, Annevoie, Belgium): Tiensevest 68, B-3000 Leuven, Belgium (permanent secretariat).

International Young Catholic Students* (1946, Fribourg, Switzerland; present name, 1954): 171 rue de Rennes, F-75006 Paris, France.

International Young Christian Workers* (1925, Belgium): 11, rue Plantin, B-1070 Brussels, Belgium.

Laity and Christian Community (1966, Algiers, Algeria): 80, rue de Tourbillon, CH-1950 Sion, Switzerland. Universal brotherhood.

Legion of Mary* (1921, Dublin, Ireland): De Montfort House, North Brunswick St., Dublin, Ireland. (See Index.)

Medicus Mundi: P.O. Box 1547, 6501 BN Nijmegen, Netherlands. Place medicine at service of poor.

Movement for a Better World (1952): Viva Vinovo, 58, 00166, Rome, Italy. (See Index.)

Our Lady's Teams (Equipes Notre-Dame) (1937, France): 49, rue de la Glacière, F-75013 Paris, France. Movement for spiritual formation of couples.

Pax Christi (1950): Kerkstraat, 150, B-2000 Antwerp, Belgium. (See Index.)

Pax Romana* (1921, Fribourg, Switzerland, divided into two movements, 1947):

    International Movement of Catholic Students* (1921): 171, rue de Rennes, F-75006, Paris, France. For undergraduates.

    International Catholic Movement for Intellectual and Cultural Affairs* (1947): 37-39 rue de Vermont, Case Postale n 85, CH-1211 Geneva 20 CIC, Switzerland. For university graduates. Has professional secretariats at: Stradhouderskade 86, Amsterdam, The Netherlands (artists); Biesselsebaan, 40, Nijmegen, The Netherlands (teachers); 18 rue de Varenne, F-75007 Paris, France (engineers); via della Conciliazione 4d, I-00193 Rome, Italy (lawyers).

St. Joan's International Alliance (1911 in England; present title, 1931): 48, chemin des Coudriers, CH-1209 Geneva, Switzerland.

Salesian Cooperators (1876): Don Bosco College, Newton, N.J. 07860. Third Salesian family founded by St. John Bosco. Members commit themselves to an apostolate at the service of the Church, giving particular atten-tion to youth in the Salesian spirit and style.

Secular Franciscan Order (1221, first Rule approved): Via Piemonte, 70, 00187, Rome, Italy. (See Index.)

Serra International (1953, in U.S.): (See Index.)

Society of St. Vincent de Paul* (1933): 5, rue Pré-aux-Clercs, F-75007 Paris, France.

The Grail (1921, Nijmegen, The Netherlands): Duisburgerstrasse 470, D-4330, Mulheim, West Germany. (See Index.)

Third Order of St. Dominic (1285): Convento Santa Sabina, Piazza Pietro d'Illiria, Aventino, I-00153 Rome, Italy. (See Index.)

Unda: International Catholic Association for Radio and Television* (1928, Cologne, Germany): rue de l'Orme, 12, B-1040 Brussels, Belgium. (See Index.)

Unio Internationalis Laicorum in Servitio Ecclesiae (1965, Aachen, Germany): Postfach 990125, Am Kielshof 2, 5000 Cologne, Germany 91. Consists of national and diocesan associations of persons who give professional services to the Church.

Union of Adorers of the Blessed Sacrament (1937): Largo dei Monti Parioli 3, I-00197, Rome, Italy.

World Catholic Federation for the Biblical Apostolate (1969, Rome): Mittelstrasse, 12, D 7000, Stuttgart 1, Germany.

World Federation of Christian Life Communities* (1953): 8, Borgo Santo Spirito, I-00193, Rome, Italy. First Sodality of Our Lady founded in 1563.

World Movement of Christian Workers* (1961): 90, rue des Palais, B-1030 Brussels, Belgium.

World Organization of Former Students of Catholic Schools (1967, Rome): Largo Nazareno 25, I-00167 Rome, Italy.

World Union of Catholic Philosophical Societies (1948, Amsterdam, The Netherlands): The Catholic University of America, Washington, D.C. 20064.

World Union of Catholic Teachers* (1951): Piazza San Calisto 16, I-00153, Rome, Italy.

World Union of Catholic Women's Organizations* (1910): 20, rue Notre Dame des Champs, F-75006 Paris, France.

Regional Organizations

European Federation for Catholic Adult Education (1963, Lucerne, Switzerland): Bildunghaus Turnseestrasse 24, D-7800, Freiburg 1. B2, Germany.

European Forum of National Committees of the Laity (1968): 12, Brookwood Lawn Artane, Dublin 5, Ireland.

Movimiento Familiar Cristiano (1949-50, Montevideo and Buenos Aires): Carrera 17 n. 4671, Bogota, D.E., Colombia. Christian Family Movement of Latin America.

A 1982 report said that Catholic Charismatic Renewal might seek the status of an International Catholic Organization.

The first date in the remote background of the Catholic history of Canada was July 7, 1534, when a priest in the exploration company of Jacques Cartier celebrated Mass on the Gaspe Peninsula.

Successful colonization and the significant beginnings of the Catholic history of the country date from the foundation of Quebec in 1608 by Samuel Champlain and French settlers. Montreal was established in 1642.

The earliest missionaries were Franciscan Recollects and Jesuits who arrived in 1615 and 1625, respectively. They provided some pastoral care for the settlers but worked mainly among the 100,000 Indians — Algonquins and Huron-Iroquois — in the interior and in the Lake Ontario region. Five Jesuits of the group of eight North American Martyrs were killed in the 1640s; Isaac Jogues and two lay missionaries were martyred at Ossernenon (Auriesville, N.Y.). Sulpician Fathers, who arrived in Canada late in the 1640's, played a part in the great missionary period which ended about 1700.

Kateri Tekakwitha, "Lily of the Mohawks," who was baptized in 1676 and died in 1680, was declared "Blessed" June 22, 1980.

The communities of women religious with the longest histories in Canada are the Canonesses of St. Augustine, since 1637; the Ursulines, since 1639; and the Hospitallers of St. Joseph, since 1642. Communities of Canadian origin are the Congregation of Notre Dame, founded by St. Marguerite Bourgeoys in 1658, and the Grey Nuns, formed by Bl. Marie Marguerite d'Youville in 1738.

Mother Marie (Guyard) of the Incarnation, an Ursuline nun, was one of the first three women missionaries to New France; called "Mother of the Church in Canada," she was declared "Blessed" June 22, 1980.

Start of Church Organization

Ecclesiastical organization began with the appointment in 1658 of Francois De Montmorency-Laval, "Father of the Church in Canada," as vicar apostolic of New France. He was the first bishop of Quebec from 1674 to 1688, with jurisdiction over all French-claimed territory in North America. He was declared "Blessed" June 22, 1980.

In 1713, the French Canadian population numbered 18,000. In the same year, the Treaty of Utrecht ceded Acadia, Newfoundland and the Hudson Bay Territory to England. The Acadians were scattered among the American Colonies in 1755.

The English acquired possession of Canada and its 70,000 French-speaking inhabitants in virtue of the Treaty of Paris in 1763. Anglo-French and Anglican-Catholic differences and tensions developed. The pro-British government at first refused to recognize the titles of church officials, hindered the clergy in their work and tried to install a non-Catholic educational system. Laws were passed which guaranteed religious liberties to Catholics (Quebec Act of 1774, Constitutional Act of 1791, legislation approved by Queen Victoria in 1851), but it took some time before actual respect for these liberties matched the legal enactments. The initial moderation of government antipathy toward the Church was caused partly by the loyalty of Catholics to the Crown during the American Revolution and the War of 1812.

Growth

The 15 years following the passage in 1840 of the Act of Union, which joined Upper and Lower Canada, were significant. New communities of men and women religious joined those already in the country. The Oblates of Mary Immaculate, missionaries par excellence in Canada, advanced the penetration of the West which had been started in 1818 by Abbe Provencher. New jurisdictions were established, and Quebec became a metropolitan see in 1844. The first Council of Quebec was held in 1851. The established Catholic school system enjoyed a period of growth.

Laval University was inaugurated in 1854 and canonically established in 1876.

Archbishop Elzear-Alexandre Taschereau of Quebec was named Canada's first cardinal in 1886.

The apostolic delegation to Canada was set up in 1899. It became a nunciature October 16, 1969, with the establishment of diplomatic relations with the Vatican.

Early in this century, Canada had eight ecclesiastical provinces, 23 dioceses, three vicariates apostolic, 3,500 priests, 2.4 million Catholics, about 30 communities of men religious, and 70 or more communities of women religious. The Church in Canada was phased out of mission status and removed from the jurisdiction of the Congregation for the Propagation of the Faith in 1908.

The greatest concentration of Catholics is in the eastern portion of the country. In the northern and western portions, outside metropolitan centers, there are some of the most difficult parish and mission areas in the world. Bilingual (English-French) differences in the general population are reflected in the Church; for example, in the parallel structures of the Canadian Conference of Catholic Bishops, which was established in 1943. Quebec is the center of French cultural influence. Many language groups are represented among Catholics, who include about 211,265 members of Eastern Rite in a metropolitan see, five.eparchies and an apostolic exarchate.

Education, a past source of friction between the Church and the government, is administered by the civil provinces in a variety of arrangements authorized by the Canadian Constitution. Denominational schools have tax support in one way in Quebec and Newfoundland, and in another way in Alberta, Ontario and Saskatchewan. Several provinces provide tax support only for public schools, making private financing necessary for separate church-related schools.

ECCLESIASTICAL JURISDICTIONS OF CANADA

PROVINCES

Names of ecclesiastical provinces and metropolitan sees in bold face: suffragan sees in parentheses.

Edmonton (Calgary, St. Paul).

Grouard-McLennan (Mackenzie-Ft. Smith, Prince George, Whitehorse).

Halifax (Antigonish, Charlottetown, Yarmouth).

Keewatin-LePas (Churchill-Hudson Bay, Labrador-Schefferville, Moosonee).

Kingston (Alexandria-Cornwall, Peterborough, Sault Ste. Marie).

Moncton (Bathurst, Edmundston, St. John).

Montreal (Joliette, St. Jean-de-Quebec, St. Jerome, Valleyfield).

Ottawa (Hearst, Hull, Mont-Laurier, Pembroke, Rouyn-Noranda, Timmins).

Quebec (Amos, Chicoutimi, Ste.-Anne-de-la-Pocatiere, Trois Rivieres).

Regina (Gravelbourg, Prince Albert, Saskatoon, Abbey of St. Peter).

Rimouski (Gaspe, Hauterive).

St. Boniface (no suffragans).

St. John's (Grand Falls, St. George).

Sherbrooke (Nicolet, St. Hyacinthe).

Toronto (Hamilton, London, St. Catharines, Thunder Bay).

Vancouver (Kamloops, Nelson, Victoria).

Winnipeg — Ukrainian (Edmonton, New Westminster, Saskatoon, Toronto).

Jurisdictions immediately subject to the Holy See: Roman-Rite Archdiocese of Winnipeg, Byzantine-Rite Eparchy of Sts. Cyril and Methodius for Slovaks, Byzantine-Rite Apostolic Exarchate for Greek Melkites.

ARCHDIOCESES, ARCHBISHOPS

Edmonton, Alta. (St. Albert, 1871; archdiocese, transferred Edmonton, 1912): Joseph N. MacNeil, archbishop, 1973.

Grouard-McLennan, Alta. (v.a. Athabaska-Mackenzie, 1862; Grouard, 1927; archdiocese Grouard-McLennan, 1967); Henri Legare, O.M.I., archbishop, 1972.

Halifax, N.S. (1842; archdiocese, 1852): James M. Hayes, archbishop, 1967.

Keewatin-Le Pas, Man. (v.a., 1910; archdiocese, 1967): Paul Dumouchel, O.M.I., archbishop, 1967.

Kingston, Ont. (1826; archdiocese, 1889): Francis J. Spence, archbishop, 1982.

Moncton, N.B. (1936): Donat Chiasson, archbishop, 1972.

Montreal, Que. (1836; archdiocese, 1886): Paul Gregoire, archbishop, 1968. Valerien Belanger, Andre Cimichella, O.S.M., Leonard Crowley, Gerard Tremblay, Jude Saint-Antoine, Jean-Claude Turcotte, auxiliaries.

Ottawa, Ont. (Bytown, 1847, name changed, 1854; archdiocese, 1886): Joseph Aurele Plourde, archbishop, 1967. John Beahen, Gilles Belisle, auxiliaries.

Quebec, Que. (v.a., 1658; diocese, 1674; archdiocese, 1819; metropolitan, 1844; primatial see, 1956): Louis-Albert Vachon, archbishop, 1981. Lionel Audet, Jean-Paul Labrie, Maurice Couture, Marc Leclerc, auxiliaries.

Regina, Sask. (1910; archdiocese, 1915): Charles A. Halpin, archbishop, 1973.

Rimouski, Que. (1867; archdiocese, 1946): Gilles Ouellet, P.M.E., archbishop, 1973.

St. Boniface, Man. (1847; archdiocese, 1871): Antoine Hacault, archbishop, 1974.

St. John's, Nfld. (p.a., 1784; v.a., 1796; diocese, 1847; archdiocese, 1904): Alphonsus Penney, archbishop, 1979.

Sherbrooke, Que. (1874; archdiocese, 1951); J.-M. Fortier, archbishop, 1968.

Toronto, Ont. (1841; archdiocese, 1870): Cardinal G. Emmett Carter, archbishop, 1978. Aloysius M. Ambrozic, Michael Pearse Lacey, Robert B. Clune, Leonard J. Wall, auxiliaries.

Vancouver, B. C. (v.a. British Columbia, 1863; diocese New Westminster, 1890; archdiocese Vancouver, 1908): James F. Carney, archbishop, 1969. Lawrence Sabatini, C.S., auxiliary.

Winnipeg, Man. (1915): Adam Exner, O.M.I, archbishop, 1982.

Winnipeg, Man. (Ukrainian Byzantine Rite) (Ordinariate of Canada, 1912; ap. ex. Central Canada, 1948; ap. ex. Manitoba, 1951; archdiocese Winnipeg, 1956): Maxim Hermaniuk, C.SS.R., archbishop, 1956. Myron Daciuk, O.S.B.M., auxiliary.

DIOCESES, BISHOPS

Alexandria-Cornwall, Ont. (1890): Eugene Philippe LaRocque, bishop, 1974.

Amos, Que. (1938): Gerard Drainville, bishop, 1978.

Antigonish, N.S. (Arichat, 1844; transferred, 1886): William E. Power, bishop, 1960.

Bathurst, N.B. (Chatham, 1860; transferred, 1938): Edgar Godin, bishop, 1969.

Calgary, Alta. (1912): Paul J. O'Byrne, bishop, 1968.

Charlottetown, P.E.I. (1829): James H. MacDonald, C.S.C., bishop, 1982.

Chicoutimi, Que. (1878): Jean-Guy Couture, bishop, 1979. Roch Pedneault, auxiliary.

Churchill-Hudson Bay, Man. (p.a., 1925; v.a. Hudson Bay, 1931; diocese Churchill, 1967; Churchill-Hudson Bay, 1968): Omer Robidoux, O.M.I., bishop, 1970.

Edmonton, Alta. (Ukrainian Byzantine Rite) (ap. ex., 1948; diocese, 1956): Nile Nicholas Savaryn, O.S.B.M., bishop, 1948. Martin Greschuk, auxiliary.

Edmundston, N.B. (1944): Fernand Lacroix, C.J.M., bishop, 1970.

Gaspe, Que. (1922): Bertrand Blanchet, bishop, 1973.

Grand Falls, Nfld. (Harbour Grace, 1856; present title, 1964): Joseph Faber MacDonald, bishop, 1980.

Gravelbourg, Sask. (1930): Noel Delaquis, bishop, 1974.

Hamilton, Ont. (1856): Paul F. Reding, bishop, 1973.

Hauterive, Que. (p.a., 1882; v.a., 1905; diocese Gulf of St. Lawrence, 1945; name changed, 1960): Roger Ebacher, bishop, 1979.

Hearst, Ont. (p.a., 1918; v.a., 1920; diocese, 1938): Roger Despatie, bishop, 1973.

Hull, Que. (1963): Adolphe Proulx, bishop, 1974. (Title of see changed to Gatineau-Hull, 1982.)

Joliette, Que. (1904): Rene Audet, bishop, 1968.

Kamloops, B.C. (1945): Vacant as of Aug. 1, 1982.

Labrador (Nfld.)-Schefferville, Que. (v.a. Labrador, 1945; diocese, 1967): Peter A. Sutton, O.M.I., bishop, 1974.

London, Ont. (1855; transferred Sandwich, 1859; London, 1869): John Sherlock, bishop, 1978. Marcel Gervais, auxiliary.

Mackenzie-Fort Smith, N.W.T. (v.a. Mackenzie, 1901; diocese Mackenzie-Fort Smith, 1967): Paul Piché, O.M.I., bishop, 1967.

Mont-Laurier, Que. (1913): Jean Gratton, bishop, 1978.

Moosonee, Ont. (v.a. James Bay, 1938; diocese Moosonee, 1967): Jules Leguerrier, O.M.I., bishop, 1967.

Nelson, B.C. (1936): Wilfred Emmett Doyle, bishop, 1958.

New Westminster, B.C. (Ukrainian Byzantine Rite) (1974): Jerome Chimy, O.S.B.M., bishop, 1974.

Nicolet, Que. (1885): Albertus Martin, bishop, 1950.

Pembroke, Ont. (v.a. 1882; diocese, 1898): Joseph R. Windle, bishop, 1971.

Peterborough, Ont. (1882): James L. Doyle, bishop, 1976.

Prince Albert, Sask. (v.a., 1890; diocese, 1907): Laurent Morin, bishop, 1959. Blaise Morand, coadjutor.

Prince George, B.C. (p.a., 1908; v.a. Yukon and Prince Rupert, 1944; diocese Prince George, 1967): J. Fergus O'Grady, O.M.I., bishop, 1967.

Rouyn-Noranda, Que. (1973): Jean-Guy Hamelin, bishop, 1974.

St. Catharines, Ont. (1958): Thomas B. Fulton, bishop, 1978.

St. George's, Nfld. (p.a., 1870; v.a., 1890; diocese, 1904): Richard T. McGrath, bishop, 1970.

St. Hyacinthe, Que. (1852): Louis-de-Gonzague Langevin, bishop, 1979.

Saint-Jean-de-Quebec (1933): Bernard Hubert, bishop, 1978. (Title of see changed to St. Jean-Longueuil, 1982.)

St. Jerome, Que. (1951): Charles Valois, bishop, 1977. Raymond Saint-Gelais, auxiliary.

Saint John, N.B. (1842): Arthur J. Gilbert, bishop, 1974.

St. Paul in Alberta (1948): Raymond Roy, bishop, 1972.

Sts. Cyril and Methodius, Toronto, Ont. (Slovakian Byzantine Rite) (1981): Michael Rusnak, C.Ss.R., bishop, 1981.

Sainte-Anne-de-la-Pocatiere, Que. (1951): C.-H. Levesque, bishop, 1968.

Saskatoon, Sask. (1933): James P. Mahoney, bishop, 1967.

Saskatoon, Sask. (Ukrainian Byzantine Rite) (ap. ex., 1951; diocese, 1956): Andrew J. Roborecki, bishop, 1951.

Sault Ste. Marie, Ont. (1904): Alexander Carter, bishop, 1958. Bernard F. Pappin, Gerard Dionne, auxiliaries.

Thunder Bay, Ont. (Ft. William, 1952; transferred, 1970): John A. O'Mara, bishop, 1976.

Timmins, Ont. (v.a. Temiskaming, 1908; diocese Haileybury, 1915; present title, 1938): Jacques Landriault, bishop, 1971.

Toronto, Ont. (Ukrainian Byzantine Rite) (ap. ex., 1948; diocese, 1956): Isidore Borecky, bishop, 1948.

Trois-Rivieres, Que. (1852): Laurent Noel, bishop, 1975.

Valleyfield, Que. (1892): Robert Lebel, bishop, 1976.

Victoria, B.C. (diocese Vancouver Is., 1846; archdiocese, 1903; diocese Victoria, 1908): Remi J. De Roo, bishop, 1962.

Whitehorse, Y.T. (v.a., 1944; diocese 1967): Hubert P. O'Connor, O.M.I., bishop, 1971.

Yarmouth, N.S. (1953): Augustin-Emile Burke, bishop, 1968.

Apostolic Exarchate for Greek Melkites (Montreal, Que.) (1980): Archbishop Michel Hakim, B.S., exarch, 1980.

Military Vicariate of Canada (1951): Archbishop Francis J. Spence, military vicar.

Abbacy of St. Peter, Muenster, Sask. (1921): Jerome Weber, O.S.B. (blessed, 1960).

STATISTICS OF CATHOLIC CHURCH IN CANADA

(Principal source: *1982 Directory of the Canadian Conference of Catholic Bishops.* Permanent deacon statistics are from the *1982 Annuario Pontificio.* Archdioceses are indicated by an asterisk. For dioceses marked +, see Canadian Dioceses with Interprovincial Lines.)

Canada's 10 civil provinces and two territories are divided into 17 ecclesiastical provinces consisting of 17 metropolitan sees (archdioceses) and 52 suffragan sees (51 dioceses and one abbacy); there are also one archdiocese, one eparchy and one exarchate immediately subject to the Holy See. (See listing of Ecclesiastical Provinces elsewhere in this section.)

This table presents a regional breakdown of Catholic statistics. In some cases, the totals are approximate because diocesan boundaries fall within several civil provinces.

Civil Province Diocese	Cath. Pop.	Dioc. Priests	Rel. Priests	Total Priests	Perm. Deacs.	Bros.	Srs.	Par- ishes
Newfoundland	216,108	121	39	160	—	96	513	218
*St. John's	123,276	60	18	78	—	63	337	86
Grand Falls	33,691	29	3	32	—	15	68	45
Labrador- Schefferville+	19,727	1	17	18	—	9	29	26
St. George's	39,414	31	1	32	—	9	79	61
Prince Edward Island								
Charlottetown	50,597	75	1	76	1	—	235	57
Nova Scotia	261,965	285	57	342	11	9	1,151	219
*Halifax	97,500	75	30	105	11	1	550	51
Antigonish	127,625	187	9	196	—	7	536	127
Yarmouth	36,840	23	18	41	—	1	65	41
New Brunswick	347,460	310	102	412	1	54	1,254	259
*Moncton	76,340	78	49	127	—	24	402	64
Bathurst	110,667	87	28	115	—	17	382	57
Edmundston	55,453	58	13	71	—	11	235	37
St. John	105,000	87	12	99	1	2	235	101
Quebec	5,585,513	4,284	2,918	7,202	84	3,280	26,151	1,915
*Montreal	1,533,777	715	1,166	1,881	—	906	8,336	282
*Quebec	954,903	836	640	1,476	37	666	6,223	274
*Rimouski	162,593	234	63	297	2	47	981	117
*Sherbrooke	247,484	319	143	462	4	134	1,462	150
Amos	105,855	93	23	116	—	23	328	81
Chicoutimi	271,540	292	86	378	4	128	982	106
Gaspe	104,655	108	21	129	1	11	274	63
Hauterive	111,315	63	31	94	—	29	266	52
Hull	186,000	95	73	168	2	23	368	65
Joliette	157,342	149	58	207	1	140	635	58
Mont Laurier	70,526	71	49	120	—	47	235	59
Nicolet	166,649	230	39	269	8	148	1,132	85
Rouyn-Noranda	54,333	33	25	58	—	18	178	41
Ste.-Anne-de-la Pocatiere	92,392	190	9	199	—	16	428	54
St. Hyacinthe	299,737	244	123	367	19	344	1,699	112
St. Jean de Quebec	421,921	168	98	266	—	149	755	88
St. Jerome	238,403	111	111	222	2	152	306	66
Trois Rivieres	238,088	210	102	312	3	214	1,183	97
Valleyfield	168,000	123	58	181	1	85	380	65
Ontario	2,556,642	1,317	1,244	2,561	137	531	5,112	1,146
*Kingston	62,651	73	5	78	—	—	258	68
*Ottawa	285,303	158	244	402	10	106	1,179	112
*Toronto	1,000,000	234	501	735	88	305	995	187
Alexandria-Cornwall	47,344	46	9	55	1	10	128	34
Hamilton	298,441	144	154	298	1	28	554	120
Hearst	34,512	36	5	41	—	4	60	43

Civil Province Diocese	Cath. Pop.	Dioc. Priests	Rel. Priests	Total Priests	Perm. Deacs.	Bros.	Srs.	Par- ishes
Ontario								
London	333,405	244	119	363	—	21	772	177
Moosonee+	3,000	—	13	13	1	12	11	8
Pembroke+	55,495	62	16	78	—	4	302	72
Peterborough	51,791	67	6	73	—	2	175	77
St. Catharines	100,000	57	38	95	—	3	83	47
Sault Ste. Marie	170,000	134	72	206	35	13	425	115
Thunder Bay	55,000	26	43	69	—	2	70	54
Timmins	59,700	36	19	55	1	21	100	32
Manitoba	**205,700**	**147**	**214**	**361**	**21**	**63**	**1,018**	**231**
*Keewatin-LePas+	23,000	1	35	36	2	12	49	32
*St. Boniface	80,000	98	79	177	6	38	605	108
*Winnipeg	97,500	48	83	131	13	10	355	68
Churchill-Hudson Bay+	5,200	—	17	17	—	3	9	23
Saskatchewan	**214,005**	**189**	**154**	**343**	**—**	**30**	**803**	**397**
*Regina	92,300	87	44	131	—	5	243	183
Gravelbourg	13,784	30	6	36	—	3	95	49
Prince Albert	47,421	38	32	70	—	5	193	88
Saskatoon	48,000	34	44	78	—	4	176	53
St. Peter Muenster (Abb.)	12,500	—	28	28	—	13	96	24
Alberta	**365,000**	**226**	**231**	**457**	**1**	**37**	**937**	**446**
*Edmonton	165,000	104	117	221	—	21	604	179
*Grouard-McLennan	30,000	5	40	45	—	4	69	77
Calgary	130,000	93	59	152	1	10	189	123
St. Paul	40,000	24	15	39	—	2	75	67
British Columbia	**312,586**	**167**	**185**	**352**	**—**	**53**	**611**	**309**
*Vancouver	175,000	87	109	196	—	31	326	70
Kamloops	28,000	17	14	31	—	6	48	76
Nelson	39,586	29	16	45	—	—	59	56
Prince George	26,000	6	24	30	—	8	49	48
Victoria	44,000	28	22	50	—	8	129	59
Yukon Territory								
Whitehorse+	**7,770**	**—**	**16**	**16**	**—**	**2**	**12**	**15**
Northwest Territories								
MacKenzie-Ft. Smith+	**18,390**	**1**	**35**	**36**	**—**	**22**	**41**	**50**
Eastern Rites	**211,265**	**167**	**70**	**237**	**21**	**18**	**138**	**465**
*Winnipeg	55,000	38	18	56	5	1	30	124
Edmonton	41,065	31	15	46	5	9	35	98
New Westminster	7,000	10	4	14	1	1	6	20
Saskatoon	25,000	15	17	32	2	5	42	136
Toronto	83,200	73	16	89	8	2	25	87
Sts. Cyril and Methodius (Slovaks)	No separate statistics available							
Greek Melkites (Ap. Ex.)	No separate statistics available							
Military Vicariate	**72,086**	**51**	**20**	**71**	**—**	**—**	**6**	**60**
TOTALS 1982	**10,425,087**	**7,340**	**5,286**	**12,626**	**277**	**4,195**	**37,982**	**5,787**
Totals 1981	10,344,046	7,413	5,218	12,631	245	4,445	38,112	5,797

Canadian Constitution

Four months after approval by the Canadian Parliament and a few weeks after ratification in Great Britain, the Constitution Act was signed by Queen Elizabeth II in April, 1982, and became the nation's first truly Canadian Constitution, replacing the British North America Act of 1867 and ending Britain's nominal role in the government.

PERCENTAGE OF CATHOLICS

Catholic population statistics are from the 1982 Directory of the Canadian Conference of Catholic Bishops; total population figures are 1981 estimates.

The table presents a regional breakdown of Catholic percentage in total population. In some cases, the Catholic totals are approximate because diocesan boundaries fall within several civil provinces. See Index: Canadian Dioceses with Interprovincial Lines.

Civil Province Territory	Cath. Pop.	Total Pop.	Cath. Pct.
Alberta	365,000	2,135,900	17.1
British Columbia	312,586	2,687,000	11.6
Manitoba	205,700	1,027,000	20.0
New Brunswick	347,460	709,100	49.0
Newfoundland	216,108	583,600	37.0
Nova Scotia	261,965	856,100	30.6
Ontario	2,556,642	8,600,500	29.7
Prince Edward Is.	50,597	124,100	40.8
Quebec	5,585,513	6,325,200	88.3
Saskatchewan	214,005	975,700	21.9
Northwest Territories	18,390	42,800	42.9
Yukon	7,770	21,500	36.1
Eastern Rites	211,265	—	—
Military Vicariate	72,086	—	—
TOTALS 1982	10,425,087	24,088,500	43.3
Totals 1981	10,344,046	23,809,900	43.4

Dioceses with Interprovincial Lines

The following dioceses, indicated by + in the table, have interprovincial lines.

Churchill-Hudson Bay includes part of Northwest Territories.

Keewatin-Le Pas includes part of Manitoba and Saskatchewan provinces.

Labrador-Schefferville includes the Labrador region of Newfoundland and the northern part of Quebec province.

MacKenzie-Fort Smith, Northwest Territories, includes part of Alberta and Saskatchewan provinces.

Moosonee, Ont., includes part of Quebec province.

Pembroke, Ont., includes one county of Quebec province.

Whitehorse, Y.T., includes part of British Columbia.

ORGANIZATIONS

The Catholic Church Extension Society of Canada supports home missions. Address: 67 Bond St., Toronto, Ontario M5B 1X6.

The Oblate Indian-Eskimo Council of Canada, 238 Argyle St., Ottawa.

The Canadian Catholic Women's League, with a membership of more than 100,000. Address: 3081 Ness Ave., Winnipeg, Man. R2J 2G3.

G. K. Chesterton Society, 1437 College Dr., Saskatoon, Sask. S7N OW8.

CONFERENCE OF BISHOPS

The Canadian Conference of Catholic Bishops was established Oct. 12, 1943, as a permanent voluntary association of the bishops of Canada, was given official approval by the Holy See in 1948, and acquired the status of an episcopal conference after the Second Vatican Council.

The CCCB acts in two ways: (1) as a strictly ecclesiastical body through which the bishops act together with pastoral authority and responsibility for the Church throughout the country; (2) as an operational secretariat through which the bishops act on a wider scale for the good of the Church and society.

At the top of the CCCB organizational table are the president, an executive committee, an administrative board and a plenary assembly. The membership consists of all the bishops of Canada.

Departments and Offices

The CCCB's work is planned and co-ordinated by a Pastoral Team of 14 members — six bishops and six staff members (lay and clergy) and the two general secretaries.

The CCCB has six departments and four offices all of which work in both French and English: (I) Department for Theology and Canon Law; (II) Department for Christian Education and Migration and Tourism; (III) Department for Social Affairs and Laity; (IV) Department for Missions, Ecumenism and Non-Believers; (V) Department for Clergy and Religious; (VI) Department for Liturgy and Social Communications. Offices for (1) Christian Education (2) Liturgy (3) Missions (4) Social Affairs.

The general secretariat consists of a French and an English general secretary and their assistants and directors of public relations.

Administrative services for purchasing, archives and library, accounting, personnel, publications, printing and distribution are supervised by directors who relate to the general secretaries.

Various advisory councils and committees with mixed memberships of lay persons, religious, priests and bishops also serve the CCCB on a variety of topics.

Operations

Meetings for the transaction of business are held at least once a year by the plenary assembly, eight times a year by the executive committee, and four times a year by the administrative board.

Archbishop Henri Legare, O.M.I., of Grouard-McLennan, Alta., is president of the CCCB; Bishop Paul Reding of Hamilton, Ont., is vice-president.

Headquarters are located at 90 Parent Ave., Ottawa, K1N 7B1, Canada.

BIOGRAPHIES OF CANADIAN BISHOPS

(Sources: Almanac survey; *1982 Directory of Canadian Conference of Catholic Bishops; Annuario Pontificio.* Data as of July 10, 1982.)

Ambrozic, Aloysius M.: b. Jan. 27, 1930; ord. priest June 4, 1955; ord. titular bishop of Valabria and auxiliary bishop of Toronto, May 27, 1976.

Audet, Lionel: b. May 22, 1908, Ste. Marie de Beauce, Que.; ord. priest July 8, 1934; ord. titular bishop of Tibari and auxiliary bishop of Quebec, May 1, 1952.

Audet, Rene: b. Jan. 18, 1920, Montreal, Que.; ord. priest May 30, 1948; ord. titular bishop of Chonochora and auxiliary bishop of Ottawa, July 31, 1963; bishop of Joliette, Jan. 3, 1968.

Baudoux, Maurice: b. July 10, 1902, Louviere, Belgium; ord. priest July 17, 1929; ord. bishop of St. Paul in Alberta, Oct. 28, 1948; titular archbishop of Preslavus and coadjutor archbishop of St. Boniface, Mar. 4, 1952; archbishop of St. Boniface, Sept. 14, 1955; retired Sept. 7, 1974.

Beahen, John: b. Feb. 14, 1922, Ottawa, Ont.; ord. priest June 15, 1946; ord. titular bishop of Ploaghe and auxiliary bishop of Ottawa, June 21, 1977.

Belanger, Valerien: b. Apr. 6, 1902, Valleyfield, Que.; ord. priest May 29, 1926; ord titular bishop of Cyrene and auxiliary bishop of Montreal, May 11, 1956.

Belisle, Gilles: b. Oct. 7, 1923, Clarence Creek, Ont.; ord. priest Feb. 2, 1950; ord. titular bishop of Uccula and auxiliary bishop of Ottawa, June 21, 1977.

Blais, Leo: b. Apr. 28, 1904, Dollar Bay, Mich.; ord. priest June 14, 1930; ord. bishop of Prince Albert, Aug. 28, 1952; titular bishop of Geron and auxiliary bishop of Montreal, 1959-64. Retired.

Blanchet, Bertrand: b. Sept. 19, 1932, Saint Thomas de Montmagny, Que.; ord. priest May 20, 1956; ord. bishop of Gaspe, Dec. 8, 1973.

Borecky, Isidore: b. Oct. 1, 1911, Ostrovec, Ukraine; ord. priest July 17, 1938; ord. titular bishop of Amathus in Cypro and exarch of Toronto, May 27, 1948; bishop of Toronto (Ukrainians), Nov. 3, 1956.

Brodeur, Rosario L.: b. Oct. 30, 1889, Acton Vale, Que.; ord. priest June 17, 1916; ord. titular bishop of Mideo and coadjutor bishop of Alexandria, June 30, 1941; bishop of Alexandria, July 27, 1941; retired Oct. 15, 1966.

Burke, Augustin-Emile: b. Jan. 22, 1922, Sluice Point, N.S.; ord. priest Mar. 25, 1950; ord. bishop of Yarmouth, May 14, 1968.

Cabana, Georges: b. Oct. 23, 1894, Notre Dame de Granby, Que; ord. priest July 28, 1918; ord. titular archbishop of Anchialo and coadjutor archbishop of St. Boniface, June 30, 1941; coadjutor archbishop of Sherbrooke, Jan. 20, 1952; archbishop of Sherbrooke, May 28, 1952; retired Feb. 7, 1968.

Carew, William A.: b. Oct. 23, 1922, St. John's, Nfld., ord. priest June 15, 1947; ord. titular archbishop of Telde, Jan. 4, 1970; nuncio to Rwanda and Burundi, 1970-74; apostolic delegate to Jerusalem and Palestine and pro-nuncio to Cyprus, 1974.

Carney, James F.: b. June 28, 1915, Vancouver, B.C.; ord. priest Mar. 21, 1942; ord. titular bishop of Obori and auxiliary bishop of Vancouver, Feb. 11, 1966; archbishop of Vancouver, Jan. 8, 1969.

Carter, Alexander: b. Apr. 16, 1909, Montreal, Que.; ord. priest June 6, 1936; ord. titular bishop of Sita and coadjutor bishop of Sault Ste. Marie, Feb. 2, 1957; bishop of Sault Ste. Marie, Nov. 22, 1958.

Carter, G. Emmett: (See Cardinals, Biographies.)

Charbonneau, Paul E.: b. May 4, 1922, Ste. Therese de Blainville, Que.; ord. priest May 31, 1947; ord. titular bishop of Thapsus and auxiliary bishop of Ottawa, Jan. 18, 1961; first bishop of Hull, May 21, 1963; retired Apr. 12, 1973, because of ill health.

Chiasson, Donat: b. Jan. 2, 1930, Paquetville, N.B.; ord. priest May 6, 1956; ord. archbishop of Moncton, June 1, 1972.

Chimy, Jerome I., O.S.B.M.: b. Mar. 12, 1919, Radway, Alta.; ord. priest, June 29, 1944; ord. first bishop of New Westminster, B.C., for the Ukrainians, Sept. 5, 1974.

Cimichella, Andre, O.S.M.: b. Feb. 21, 1921, Grotte Santo Stefano, Italy; ord. priest May 26, 1945; ord. titular bishop of Quiza and auxiliary of Montreal, July 16, 1964.

Clune, Robert B.: b. Sept. 18, 1920, Toronto, Ont.; ord. priest May 26, 1945; ord. titular bishop of Lacubaza and auxiliary bishop of Toronto, June 21, 1979.

Coderre, Gerard Marie: b. Dec. 19, 1904, St. Jacques de Montcalm, Que.; ord. priest May 30, 1931; ord. titular bishop of Aegae and coadjutor bishop of St.-Jean-de-Quebec, Sept. 12, 1951; bishop of St.-Jean-de-Quebec, Feb. 3, 1955. Retired May 3, 1978.

Couture, Jean-Guy: b. May 6, 1929, St.-Jean-Baptiste de Quebec, Que.; ord. priest May 30, 1953; ord. bishop of Hauterive, Que., Aug. 15, 1975; bishop of Chicoutimi, Apr. 5, 1979.

Couture, Maurice, R.S.V.: b. 1927, Saint-Pierre-de-Broughton, Que.; ord. priest June 17, 1951; app. titular bishop of Talaptula and auxiliary bishop of Quebec, July 24, 1982.

Couturier, Gerard: b. Jan. 12, 1913, St. Louis du Ha Ha, Que; ord. priest Mar. 25, 1938; ord. bishop of Hauterive, Feb. 28, 1957; resigned see Sept. 7, 1974.

Crowley, Leonard: b. Dec. 28, 1921, Montreal, Que.; ord. priest May 31, 1947; ord. titular bishop of Mons and auxiliary bishop of Montreal, Mar. 24, 1971.

Daciuk, Myron, O.S.B.M.: Appointed titular bishop of Thyatira and auxiliary bishop of Winnipeg (Ukrainians), July 7, 1982

Decosse, Aime: b. June 21, 1903, Somerset, Man.; ord. priest July 4, 1926; ord. bishop of Gravelbourg, Jan. 20, 1954; retired May 12, 1973.

Delaquis, Noel: b. Dec. 25, 1934, Notre-Dame-de-Lourdes, Man.; ord. priest June 5, 1958; ord. bishop of Gravelbourg, Feb. 19, 1974.

De Roo, Remi J.: b. Feb. 24, 1924, Swan Lake, Man.; ord. priest June 8, 1950; ord. bishop of Victoria, Dec. 14, 1962.

Despatie, Roger: b. Apr. 12, 1927, Sudbury, Ont.; ord. priest Apr. 12, 1952; ord. titular bishop of Usinaza and auxiliary bishop of Sault Ste. Marie, June 28, 1968; bishop of Hearst, Feb. 8, 1973.

Dionne, Gerard: b. June 19, 1919, Saint-Basile, N.B.; ord. priest May 1, 1948; ord. titular bishop of Garba and auxiliary bishop of Sault Ste. Marie, Apr. 8, 1975.

Douville, Arthur: b. July 22, 1894, St. Casimir de Portneuf, Que.; ord. priest May 25, 1919; ord. titular bishop of Vita and auxiliary bishop of St. Hyacinthe, Jan. 29, 1940; coadjutor bishop of St. Hyacinthe, Mar. 21, 1942; bishop of St. Hyacinthe, Nov. 27, 1942; retired June 13, 1967.

Doyle, James L.: b. June 20, 1929, Chatham, Ont.; ord. priest June 12, 1954; ord. bishop of Peterborough June 28, 1976.

Doyle, W. Emmett: b. Feb. 18, 1913, Calgary, Alta.: ord. priest June 5, 1938; ord. bishop of Nelson, Dec. 3, 1958.

Drainville, Gerard: b. May 20, 1930, L'Isle-du-Pas, Que.; ord. priest May 30, 1953; ord. bishop of Amos, June 12, 1978.

Dumouchel, Paul, O.M.I.: b. Sept. 19, 1911, St. Boniface, Man.; ord. priest June 24, 1936; ord. titular bishop of Sufes and vicar apostolic of Keewatin, May 24, 1955; archbishop of Keewatin-Le Pas, July 13, 1967.

Ebacher, Roger: b. Oct. 6, 1936, Amos, Que.; ord. priest May 27, 1961; ord. bishop of Hauterive, July 31, 1979.

Exner, Adam, O.M.I.: b. Dec. 24, 1928, Killaly, Sask.; ord. priest July 7, 1957; ord. bishop of Kamloops, B.C., Mar. 12, 1974; archbishop of Winnipeg, April, 1982.

Flahiff, George F.: (See Cardinals Biographies.)

Fortier, Jean-Marie: b. July 1, 1920, Quebec, Que.; ord. priest June 16, 1944; ord. titular bishop of Pomaria and auxiliary bishop of Ste. Anne-de-la-Pocatiere, Jan. 23, 1961; bishop of Gaspe, Jan. 19, 1965; archbishop of Sherbrooke, Apr. 20, 1968.

Frenette, Emilien: b. May 6, 1905, Montreal, Que.; ord. priest May 30, 1931; ord. bishop of St. Jerome, Sept. 12, 1951; retired June 11, 1971.

Fulton, Thomas B.: b. Jan. 13, 1918, St. Catharines, Ont.; ord. priest June 7, 1941;

ord. titular bishop of Cursola and auxiliary bishop of Toronto, Jan. 6, 1969; bishop of St. Catharines, July 7, 1978.

Gagnon, Edouard, P.S.S.: b. Jan. 15, 1918, Port Daniel, Que.; ord. priest Aug. 15, 1940; ord. bishop Mar. 25, 1969; bishop of St. Paul in Alberta 1969-72; rector of Canadian College in Rome, 1972-77; vice-president and secretary of Vatican Committee for the Family, 1973-80; special assignment in Family Life Apostolate.

Gervais, Marcel A.: b. Sept. 21, 1931, Elie, Man.; ord. priest May 31, 1958; ord. titular bishop of Rosmarkaeum and auxiliary bishop of London, Ont., June 11, 1980.

Gilbert, Arthur J.: b. Oct. 26, 1915, Oromocto, N.B.; ord. priest June 3, 1943; ord. bishop of St. John, N.B., June 19, 1974.

Godin, Edgar: b. May 31, 1911, Neguac, N.B.; ord. priest June 15, 1941; ord. bishop of Bathurst, July 25, 1969.

Gratton, Jean: b. Dec. 4, 1924, Wendover, Ont.; ord. priest Apr. 27, 1952; ord. bishop of Mont Laurier, June 29, 1978.

Gregoire, Paul: b. Oct. 24, 1911, Verdun, Que.; ord. priest May 22, 1937; ord. titular bishop of Curubis and auxiliary bishop of Montreal, Dec. 27, 1961; archbishop of Montreal, Apr. 20, 1968.

Greschuk, Martin: b. Nov. 7, 1923, Innisfree, Alta.; ord. priest June 11, 1950; ord. titular bishop of Nazianus and auxiliary bishop of Edmonton of the Ukrainians, Oct. 3, 1974.

Hacault, Antoine: b. Jan. 17, 1926, Bruxelles, Man.; ord. priest May 20, 1951; ord. titular bishop of Media and coadjutor of St. Boniface, Sept. 8, 1964; archbishop of St. Boniface, Sept. 7, 1974.

Hains, Gaston: b. Sept. 10, 1921, Drummondville, Que.; ord. priest June 15, 1946; ord. titular bishop of Belesana and auxiliary bishop of St. Hyacinthe, Oct. 10, 1964; coadjutor bishop of Amos, 1967; bishop of Amos, Oct. 31, 1968; retired 1978.

Hakim, Michel: b. Apr. 21, 1921, Magdouche, South Lebanon; ord. priest Nov. 10, 1947; ord. archbishop of Saida of Greek Melkites, Sept. 10, 1977; app. titular archbishop of Caesarea in Cappadocia and apostolic exarch of Greek Melkite Catholics in Canada, Oct. 13, 1980.

Halpin, Charles A.: b. Aug. 30, 1930, St. Eustache, Man.; ord. priest May 27, 1956; ord. archbishop of Regina, Nov. 26, 1973.

Hamelin, Jean-Guy: b. Oct. 8, 1925, St. Severin-de-Proulxville, Que.; ord. priest June 11, 1949; ord. first bishop of Rouyn-Noranda, Que., Feb. 9, 1974.

Hayes, James M.: b. May 27, 1924, Halifax, N.S.; ord. priest June 15, 1947; ord. titular bishop of Reperi and apostolic administrator of Halifax, Apr. 20, 1965; archbishop of Halifax, June 22, 1967.

Hermaniuk, Maxim, C.Ss.R.: b. Oct. 30,

1911, Nove Selo, Ukraine; ord. priest Sept. 4, 1938; ord. titular bishop of Sinna and exarch of Manitoba (Ukrainians), June 29, 1951; archbishop of Winnipeg (Ukrainians), Nov. 3, 1956.

Hubert, Bernard: b. June 1, 1929, Beloeil, Que.; ord. priest May 30, 1953; ord. bishop of St. Jerome, Sept. 12, 1971; coadjutor bishop of Saint-Jean-de-Quebec, 1977; succeeded as bishop of Saint-Jean-de-Quebec, May 3, 1978.

Jette, Edouard: b. Aug. 9, 1898, St. Jacques, Que.; ord. priest May 31, 1923; ord. titular bishop of Tabe and auxiliary of Joliette, Apr. 14, 1948; retired 1968.

Labrie, Jean-Paul: b. Nov. 4, 1922, Laurieville, Que.; ord. priest May 20, 1951; ord. titular bishop of Urci and auxiliary bishop of Quebec, May 14, 1977.

Lacey, Michael Pearse: b. Nov. 26, 1916, Toronto, Ont.; ord. priest May 23, 1943; ord. titular bishop of Diana and auxiliary bishop of Toronto, June 21, 1979.

Lacroix, Fernand, C.J.M.: b. Oct. 16, 1919, Quebec; ord. priest Feb. 10, 1946; ord. bishop of Edmundston, Oct. 20, 1970.

Landriault, Jacques: b. Sept. 23, 1921, Alfred, Ont.; ord. priest Feb. 9, 1947; ord. titular bishop of Cadi and auxiliary bishop of Alexandria, July 25, 1962; bishop of Hearst, May 27, 1964; app. bishop of Timmins, Mar. 24, 1971.

Langevin, Louis-de-Gonzague, P.B.: b. Oct. 31, 1921, Oka, Que.; ord. priest Feb. 2, 1950; ord. titular bishop of Rosemarkie and auxiliary of St. Hyacinthe Sept. 23, 1974; bishop of St. Hyacinthe, July 18, 1979.

LaRocque, Eugene Philippe: b. Mar. 27, 1927, Windsor, Ont.; ord. priest June 7, 1952; ord. bishop of Alexandria, Ont., Sept. 3, 1974; title of see changed to Alexandria-Cornwall, 1976.

Lebel, Robert: b. Nov. 8, 1924, Trois-Pistoles, Que.; ord. priest June 18, 1950; ord. titular bishop of Alinda and auxiliary of St. Jean de Quebec, May 12, 1974; bishop of Valleyfield, May 12, 1976.

Le Blanc, Camille A.: b. Aug. 25, 1898, Barachois, N.B.; ord. priest Apr. 5, 1924; ord. bishop of Bathurst, Sept. 8, 1942; retired Jan. 8, 1969.

Leclerc, Marc: b. 1933, Saint-Gregoire Montmorency, Que; ord. priest, May, 1958; app. titular bishop of Eguga and auxiliary bishop of Quebec, July, 1982.

Legare, Henri, O.M.I.: b. Feb. 20, 1918, Willow Bunch, Sask.; ord. priest June 29, 1943; ord. first bishop of Labrador-Schefferville, Sept. 9, 1967; archbishop of Grouard-McLennan, Nov. 21, 1972. President of Canadian Conference of Catholic Bishops, 1979.

Leger, Paul-Emile: (See Cardinals, Biographies).

Leguerrier, Jules, O.M.I.: b. Feb. 18, 1915,

Clarence Creek, Ont.; ord. priest June 19, 1943; ord. titular bishop of Bavagaliana and vicar apostolic of James Bay, June 29, 1964; first bishop of Moosonee, July 13, 1967.

Lemieux, Marie Joseph, O.P.: b. May 10, 1902, Quebec, Que.; ord. priest Apr. 15, 1928; ord. bishop of Sendai, Japan, June 29, 1936; titular bishop of Calydon, 1941; apostolic administrator of Gravelbourg, 1942; bishop of Gravelbourg, Apr. 15, 1944; archbishop of Ottawa, June 20, 1953; retired Sept. 16, 1966 (titular archbishop of Salde).

Levesque, Charles Henri: b. Dec. 29, 1921, St. Andre de Kamouraska, Que.; ord. priest June 13, 1948; ord. titular bishop of Guzabeta and auxiliary bishop of Ste.-Anne-de-la-Pocatiere, Dec. 27, 1965; bishop of Ste.-Anne-de-la-Pocatiere, Aug. 17, 1968.

Levesque, Louis: b. May 27, 1908, Amqui, Que.; ord. priest June 26, 1932; ord. bishop of Hearst, Aug. 15, 1952; titular archbishop of Egnatia and coadjutor of Rimouski, Apr. 13, 1964; archbishop of Rimouski, Feb. 25, 1967; retired May 14, 1973.

Lussier, Philippe, C.Ss.R.: b. Oct. 3, 1911, Weedon, Que.; ord. priest Sept. 18, 1937; ord. bishop of St. Paul in Alberta, Aug. 17, 1952; retired Aug. 17, 1968.

McCarthy, Thomas J.: b. Oct. 4, 1905, Goderich, Ont.; ord. priest May 25, 1929; ord. bishop of Nelson, Aug. 1, 1955; bishop of St. Catharines, Nov. 9, 1958. Retired 1978.

MacDonald, James H., C.S.C.: b. Apr. 28, 1925, Wycogama, N.S.; ord. priest June 28, 1953; ord. titular bishop of Gibba and auxiliary bishop of Hamilton April 17, 1978; app. bishop of Charlottetown, August, 1982.

MacDonald, Joseph Faber: b. Jan. 20, 1932, Little Pond, P.E.I.; ord. priest Mar. 8, 1963; ord. bishop of Grand Falls, Mar. 25, 1980.

McGrath, Richard T.: b. June 17, 1912, Oderin, Placentia Bay, Nfld.; ord. priest June 24, 1936; ord. bishop of St. George's, Nfld., July 22, 1970.

MacNeil, Joseph N.: b. Apr. 15, 1924, Sydney, N.S.; ord. priest May 23, 1948; ord. bishop of St. John, N.B., June 24, 1969; archbishop of Edmonton, July 6, 1973. President Canadian Conference of Catholic Bishops, 1979-81.

Mahoney, James P.: b. Dec. 7, 1927, Saskatoon, Sask.; ord. priest June 7, 1952; ord. bishop of Saskatoon, Dec. 13, 1967.

Martin, Albertus: b. Oct. 4, 1913, Southbridge, Mass.; ord. priest May 18, 1939; ord. titular bishop of Bassiana and coadjutor bishop of Nicolet, Oct. 7, 1950; bishop of Nicolet, Nov. 8, 1950.

Melancon, Georges: b. Apr. 7, 1886, Saint-Guillaume d'Upton, Que.; ord. priest Sept. 12, 1909; ord. bishop of Chicoutimi, July 23, 1940; retired Feb. 18,1961.

Morand, Blaise E.: b. Sept. 12, 1932, Tecumseh, Ont.; ord. priest Mar. 22, 1958;

ord. coadjutor bishop of Prince Albert, June 29, 1981.

Morin, Laurent: b. Feb. 14, 1908, Montreal, Que.; ord. priest May 27, 1934; ord. titular bishop of Arsamosata and auxiliary bishop of Montreal, Oct. 30, 1955; bishop of Prince Albert, Feb. 28, 1959.

Noel, Laurent: b. Mar. 19, 1920, Saint-Just-de-Bretenieres, Que.; ord. priest June 16, 1944; ord. titular bishop of Agathopolis and auxiliary bishop of Quebec, Aug. 29, 1963; bishop of Trois Rivieres, Nov. 5, 1975.

O'Byrne, Paul J.: b. Dec. 21, 1922, Calgary, Alta.; ord. priest Feb. 21, 1948; ord. bishop of Calgary, Aug. 22, 1968.

O'Connor, Hubert P., O.M.I.: b. Feb. 17, 1928, Huntingdon, Que.; ord. priest June 5, 1955; ord. bishop of Whitehorse, Dec. 8, 1971.

O'Grady, John Fergus, O.M.I.: b. July 27, 1908, Macton, Ont.; ord. priest June 29, 1934; ord. titular bishop of Aspendus and vicar apostolic of Prince Rupert, Mar. 7, 1956; first bishop of Prince George, July 13, 1967.

O'Mara, John A.: b. Nov. 17, 1924, Buffalo, N.Y.; ord. priest June 1, 1951; ord. bishop of Thunder Bay, June 29, 1976.

O'Neill, Michael C.: b. Feb. 15, 1898, Kemptville, Ont.; ord. priest Dec. 21, 1927; ord. archbishop of Regina, Apr. 14, 1948; retired Sept. 26, 1973.

Ouellet, Gilles, P.M.E.: b. Aug. 14, 1922, Bromptonville, Que.; ord. priest June 30, 1946; ord. bishop of Gaspe, Nov. 23, 1968; app. archbishop of Rimouski, Apr. 27, 1973. President Canadian Conference of Catholic Bishops, 1977-79.

Ouellette, Andre: b. Feb. 4, 1913, Salem, Mass.; ord. priest June 11, 1938; ord. titular bishop of Carre and auxiliary bishop of Mont-Laurier, Feb. 25, 1957; bishop of Mont-Laurier, Mar. 27, 1965; retired Feb. 1978.

Pappin, Bernard F.: b. July 10, 1928, Westmeath, Ont.; ord. priest May 27, 1954; ord. titular bishop of Aradi and auxiliary bishop of Sault Ste. Marie, Apr. 11, 1975.

Pare, Marius: b. May 22, 1903, Montmagny, Que.; ord. priest July 3, 1927; ord. titular bishop of Aegae and auxiliary bishop of Chicoutimi, May 1, 1956; bishop of Chicoutimi, Feb. 18, 1961. Retired Apr. 5, 1979.

Pedneault, Roch: b. Apr. 10, 1927, Saint Joseph d'Alma, Que.; ord. priest Feb. 8, 1953; ord. titular bishop of Aggersel and auxiliary of Chicoutimi, Que., June 29, 1974.

Pelletier, Georges Leon: b. Aug. 19, 1904, Saint-Epiphane, Que.; ord. priest June 24, 1931; ord. titular bishop of Hephaestus and auxiliary bishop of Quebec, Feb. 24, 1943; bishop of Trois Rivieres, July 26, 1947; retired Oct. 31, 1975.

Penney, Alphonsus L.: b. Sept. 17, 1924, St. John's, Nfld.; ord. priest June 29, 1949; ord.

bishop of Grand Falls, Jan. 18, 1973; archbishop of St. John's, Nfld., Apr. 5, 1979.

Piche, Paul, O.M.I.: b. Sept. 14, 1909, Gravelbourg, Sask.; ord. priest Dec. 23, 1934; ord. titular bishop of Orcistus and vicar apostolic of Mackenzie, June 11, 1959; first bishop of Mackenzie-Fort Smith, July 13, 1967.

Plourde, Joseph Aurele: b. Jan. 12, 1915, St. Francois de Madawaska, N.B.; ord. priest May 7, 1944; ord. titular bishop of Lapda and auxiliary bishop of Alexandria, Aug. 26, 1964; archbishop of Ottawa, Jan. 2, 1967.

Pocock, Philip: b. July 2, 1906, St. Thomas, Ont.; ord. priest June 14, 1930; ord. bishop of Saskatoon, June 29, 1944; titular archbishop of Aprus and coadjutor archbishop of Winnipeg, Aug. 6, 1951; archbishop of Winnipeg, Jan. 14, 1952; titular archbishop of Isauropolis and coadjutor archbishop of Toronto, Feb. 18, 1961; archbishop of Toronto, Mar. 30, 1971; retired Apr. 29, 1978.

Power, William E.: b. Sept. 27, 1915; Montreal, Que.; ord. priest June 7, 1941; ord. bishop of Antigonish, July 20, 1960; president Canadian Conference of Catholic Bishops, 1971-73.

Proulx, Adolphe J.: b. Dec. 12, 1927, Hanmer, Ont., Canada; ord. priest Apr. 17, 1954; ord. titular bishop of Missua and auxiliary bishop of Sault Ste. Marie, Feb. 24, 1965; bishop of Alexandria, Apr. 28, 1967; bishop of Hull, Feb. 13, 1974.

Reding, Paul F.: b. Feb. 14, 1925, Hamilton, Ont.; ord. priest June 3, 1950; ord. titular bishop of Liberalia and auxiliary bishop of Hamilton, Sept. 14, 1966; bishop of Hamilton, Sept. 14, 1973.

Robidoux, Omer, O.M.I.: b. Nov. 19, 1913 Saint-Pierre-Jolys, Man.; ord. priest June 29, 1939; ord. bishop of Churchill-Hudson Bay, May 20, 1970.

Roborecki, Andrew: b. Dec. 12, 1910, in western Ukraine; arrived Winnipeg, Man., 1912; ord. priest July 18, 1934; ord. titular bishop of Tanais and auxiliary bishop of Ukrainian Catholic Diocese of Central Canada, May 27, 1948; exarch of Saskatchewan, 1951; bishop of Saskatoon (Ukrainians), Nov. 3, 1956.

Routhier, Henri, O.M.I.: b. Feb. 28, 1900, Pincher Creek, Alta.; ord. priest Sept. 7, 1924; ord. titular bishop of Naissus and coadjutor vicar apostolic of Grouard, Sept. 8, 1945; vicar apostolic of Grouard, 1953; archbishop of Grouard-McLennan, July 13, 1967; retired Nov. 2 1, 1972.

Roy, Maurice: (Cardinals, Biographies.)

Roy, Raymond: b. May 3, 1919, St. Boniface, Man.; ord. priest May 31, 1947; ord. bishop of St. Paul in Alberta, July 18, 1972.

Rusnak, Michael, C.Ss.R.: b. Aug. 21, 1921, Beaverdale, Pa.; ord. priest July 3, 1949; ord. titular bishop of Tzernicus and auxiliary bishop of Toronto eparchy and apostolic visitator to Slovak Catholics of Byzantine rite in Canada, Jan. 2, 1965; first bishop of Sts Cyril and Methoduis Eparchy for Slovaks of Byzantine Rite, Feb. 28, 1981.

Ryan, Joseph F.: b. Mar. 1, 1897, Dundas, Ont.; ord. priest May 21, 1921; ord. bishop of Hamilton, Oct. 19, 1937; retired Mar. 27, 1973.

Sabatini, Lawrence, C.S.: b. May 15, 1930, Chicago, Ill.; ord. priest Mar. 19, 1957; ord. titular bishop of Nasai and auxiliary bishop of Vancouver, Sept. 21, 1978.

Saint-Antoine, Jude: b. Oct. 29, 1930, Montreal, Que.; ord. priest May 31, 1956; ord. titular bishop of Scardona and auxiliary bishop of Montreal, May 22, 1981. Episcopal vicar of west central region.

Saint-Gelais, Raymond: b. Mar. 23, 1936, Baie St. Paul, Que.; ord. priest June 12, 1960; ord. titular bishop of Diana and auxiliary bishop of St. Jerome, July 31, 1980.

Sanschagrin, Albert, O.M.I.: b. Aug. 5, 1911, Saint-Tite, Que.; ord. priest May 24, 1936; ord. titular bishop of Bagi and coadjutor bishop of Amos Sept. 14, 1957; bishop of Saint-Hyacinthe, June 13, 1967. Retired July 18, 1979.

Savaryn, Nile Nicholas, O.S.B.M.: b. May 19, 1905, Stary Sambir, Ukraine; ord. priest Aug. 23, 1931; ord. titular bishop of Jos and auxiliary bishop of the Catholic Ukrainian diocese in Canada, July 1, 1943; bishop of apostolic exarchate for western Canada, 1948; bishop of Edmonton (Ukrainians), Nov. 3, 1956.

Sherlock, John M.: b. Jan. 20, 1926, Regina, Sask.; ord. priest June 3, 1950; ord. titular bishop of Macriana and auxiliary of London, Ont., Aug. 28, 1974; bishop of London, July 7, 1978.

Skinner, Patrick J., C.J.M.: b. Mar. 9, 1904, St. John's, Nfld.; ord. priest May 30, 1929; ord. titular bishop of Zenobia and auxiliary bishop of St. John's, Mar. 17, 1950; archbishop of St. John's, Mar. 23, 1951. Retired Apr. 5, 1979.

Smith, William J.: b. Jan. 2, 1897, Greenfield, Ont.; ord. priest June 16, 1927; ord. bishop of Pembroke, July 25, 1945; retired Feb. 8, 1971.

Spence, Francis J.: b. June 3, 1926, Perth, Ont.; ord. priest Apr. 16, 1950; ord. titular bishop of Nova and auxiliary bishop of the military vicariate, June 15, 1967; bishop of Charlottetown, Aug. 15, 1970; military vicar of Canada, March 1982; archbishop of Kingston, May, 1982.

Sutton, Peter A., O.M.I.: b. Oct. 18, 1934, Chandler, Que.; ord. priest Oct. 22, 1960; ord. bishop of Labrador-Schefferville, July 18, 1974.

Tessier, Maxime: b. Oct. 9, 1906, St. Sebastien, Que.; ord. priest June 14, 1930; ord. titular bishop of Christopolis and auxiliary bishop of Ottawa, Aug. 2, 1951; coadjutor

bishop of Timmins, 1953; bishop of Timmins, May 8, 1955; retired Mar. 24, 1971.

Tremblay, Gerard, P.S.S.: b. Oct. 27, 1918, Montreal, Que.; ord. priest June 16, 1946; ord. titular bishop of Trisipa and auxiliary bishop of Montreal, May 22, 1981.

Turcotte, Jean-Claude: Appointed titular bishop of Suas and auxiliary bishop of Montreal, April, 1982.

Vachon, Louis-Albert: b. Feb. 4, 1912, Saint-Frederic, Que.; ord. priest June 11, 1938; ord. titular bishop of Mesarfelta and auxiliary bishop of Quebec, May 14, 1977; archbishop of Quebec, Apr. 4, 1981.

Valois, Charles: b. Apr. 24, 1924, Montreal, Que.; ord. priest June 3, 1950; ord. bishop of St. Jerome, June 29, 1977.

Wall, Leonard J.: b. Sept. 27, 1924, Windsor, Ont.; ord. priest June 11, 1949; ord. titular bishop of Leptiminus and auxiliary bishop of Toronto, June 21, 1979.

Wilhelm, Joseph L.: b. Nov. 16, 1909, Walkerton, Ont.; ord. priest June 9, 1934; ord. titular bishop of Saccaea and auxiliary bishop of Calgary, Aug. 22, 1963; archbishop of Kingston, Dec. 14, 1966; retired March, 1982.

Windle, Joseph R.: b. Aug. 28, 1917, Ashdad, Ont.; ord. priest May 16, 1943; ord. titular bishop of Uzita and auxiliary bishop of Ottawa, Jan. 18, 1961; coadjutor bishop of Pembroke, 1969; bishop of Pembroke, Feb. 15, 1971.

CANADIAN SHRINES

Our Lady of the Cape (Cap de la Madeleine), Queen of the Most Holy Rosary: The Three Rivers, Quebec, parish church, built of fieldstone in 1714 and considered the oldest stone church on the North American continent preserved in its original state, was rededicated June 22, 1888, as a shrine of the Queen of the Most Holy Rosary. Thereafter, the site increased in importance as a pilgrimage and devotional center, and in 1904 St. Pius X decreed the crowning of a statue of the Blessed Virgin which had been donated 50 years earlier to commemorate the dogma of the Immaculate Conception. In 1909, the First Plenary Council of Quebec declared the church a shrine of national pilgrimage. In 1964, the church at the shrine was given the status and title of minor basilica.

St. Anne de Beaupre: The devotional history of this shrine in Quebec, began with the reported cure of a cripple, Louis Guimont, on Mar. 16, 1658, the starting date of construction work on a small chapel of St. Anne. The original building was successively enlarged and replaced by a stone church which was given the rank of minor basilica in 1888. The present structure, a Romanesque-Gothic basilica, houses the shrine proper in its north transept. The centers of attraction are an eight-foot-high oaken statue and the great relic of St. Anne, a portion of her forearm.

St. Joseph's Oratory: The massive oratory basilica standing on the western side of Mount Royal and overlooking the city of Montreal had its origin in a primitive chapel erected there by Blessed Andre Bessette, C.S.C., in 1904. Eleven years later, a large crypt was built to accommodate an increasing number of pilgrims, and in 1924 construction work was begun on the large church. A belfry, housing a 60-bell carillon and standing on the site of the original chapel, was dedicated May 15, 1955, as the first major event of the jubilee year observed after the oratory was given the rank of minor basilica.

Martyrs' Shrine: A shrine commemorating several of the Jesuit Martyrs of North America who were killed between 1642 and 1649 in the Ontario and northern New York area is located on the former site of old Forte Sainte Marie. Before its location was fixed near Midland, Ont., in 1925, a small chapel had been erected in 1907 at old Mission St. Ignace to mark the martyrdom of Fathers Jean de Brebeuf and Gabriel Lalemant. This sanctuary has a US counterpart in the Shrine of the North American Martyrs near Auriesville, N.Y., under the care of the Jesuits.

Others

Other shrines and historic churches in Canada include the following.

In Quebec City: the Basilica of Notre Dame, dating from 1650, once the cathedral of a diocese stretching from Canada to Mexico; Notre Dame des Victoires, on the waterfront, dedicated in 1690; the Ursuline Convent, uilt in 1720, on du Parloir St.

In Montreal: Notre Dame Church, patterned after the famous basilica of the same name in Paris, constructed in 1829; the Shrine of Mary, Queen of All Hearts.

Near Montreal: the Chapel of Mother d'Youville, foundress of the Grey Nuns; Notre Dame de Lourdes, at Rigaud.

CONFERENCE OF RELIGIOUS

The Canadian Religious Conference, founded in 1954, is a union of major superiors of men and women in Canada. Offices are located at 324 Laurier Ave. E., Ottawa, Ont. KIN 6P6.

CANADIAN PUBLICATIONS

(Sources: *Catholic Press Directory,* Canadian Conference of Catholic Bishops.)

Newspapers

British Columbia Catholic, The, w; 150 Robson St., Vancouver, B.C. V6B 2A7.

Catholic New Times (national), biweekly; 80 Sackville St., Toronto, Ont. M5A 3E5.

Catholic Register, The (national), w; 67 Bond St., Toronto, Ont. M5B 1X6.

Catholic Times, The, 10 times a year; 190 Bolton Ave., St. Lambert, Que. J4R 1W1.

Diocesan News, m; P.O. Box 1689, Charlottetown, P.E.I. CIA 7N4.

Monitor, The, m; P.O. Box 986, St. John's, Nfld. A1C 5M3.

New Freeman, The, w; Box 6609, Sta. A, St. John, N.B. E2L 4S1.

Pastoral Reporter, The, 4 times a year; 1916 Second St. S.W., Calgary. Alta. T25 153.

Prairie Messenger, w; Box 10, Muenster, Sask. SOK 2Y0.

Presence, m; 256 King Edward Ave., Ottawa, Ont. K1N 7M1.

Teviskes, Ziburiai (Lithuanian), w; 2185 Stavebank Rd., Mississauga, Ont. L5C 1T3.

Western Catholic Reporter, w; 10562 109th St., Edmonton, Alta. T5H 3B2.

Magazines

Annals of St. Anne de Beaupre, m; Box 1000, St. Anne de Beaupre, Que. GOA 3CO; Basilica of St. Anne.

Apostolat, bm; 460, Primiere Rue, Richelieu, Que. J3L 4B5, Oblates of Mary Immaculate.

Bulletin (French-English), m; 324 E. Laurier St., Ottawa, Ont. K1N 6P6. Canadian Religious Conference.

Canadian League, The, 4 times a year; 3081 Ness Ave., Winnipeg, Man. R2J 2G3. Catholic Women's League of Canada.

Chesterton Review, q; 1437 College Dr., Saskatoon, Sask. S7N 0W8.

Companion of St. Francis and St. Anthony, m; P.O. Box 535, Sta. F., Toronto, Ont. M4Y 2L8; Conventual Franciscan Fathers.

Global Village Voice, The, 5 times a year; 3028 Danforth Ave., Toronto, Ont. M4C IN2. Canadian Catholic Organization for Development and Peace.

Indian Record, 4 times a year; 1301 Wellington Crescent, Winnipeg, Man. R3N 0A9.

Kateri (English-French), q; P.O. Box 70, Caughnawaga, Que. JOL 1BO.

Logos (Ukrainian, English and French), q; 165 Catherine St., P.O. Box 220, Yorkton, Sask. S3N 2V7.

Martyrs' Shrine Message, q; Midland, Ont. L4R 4K3.

Messager de Saint Antoine, 10 times a year; Lac-Bouchette, Que. GOW 1VO.

Messenger of the Sacred Heart, m; 833 Broadview Ave., Toronto, Ont. M4K 2P9.

Missions Etrangeres, 6 times a year; 59 Rue Desnoyers, Laval, Que. H7G 1A4.

Oblate Missions, q; 17 Graham Ave., Ottawa, Ont. K1S 0B6.

Oratory, 5 times a year; 3800 Ch. Reine-Marie, Montreal, Que. H3V 1H6.

Our Family, m; P.O. Box 249, Battleford, Sask.; S0M 0E0; Oblates of Mary Immaculate.

Prete et Pasteur, m; 4450 St. Hubert St., Montreal, Que. H2J 2W9.

Redeemer's Voice, m; 165 Catherine St., P.O. Box 220, Yorkton, Sask. S3N 2V7.

Regard de Foi, 6 times a year; 5875 Est. rue Sherbrooke, Montreal, Que. H1N 1B6.

Relations, m; 8100 Blvd., Saint-Laurent, Montreal Que. H2P 2L9; Jesuit Fathers.

Restoration, m; Madonna House, Combermere, Ont., KOJ 1LO.

Sainte Anne de Beaupre, m; Basilica of St. Anne, Que. GOA 3CO.

Scarboro Missions, m; 2685 Kingston Rd., Scarboro, Ont. M1M 1M4.

Spiritan News, 4 times a year; 2475 Queen St., Toronto, Ont. M4E 1H8.

Unity, bm; 308 Young St., Montreal, Que. H3C 2G2.

MISSIONARIES TO THE AMERICAS

Allouez, Claude Jean (1622-1689): French Jesuit; missionary in Canada and midwestern US; preached to 20 different tribes of Indians and baptized over 10,000; vicar general of Northwest.

Altham, John (1589-1640): English Jesuit; missionary among Indians in Maryland.

Anchieta, Jose de, Bl. (1534-1597): Portuguese Jesuit, b. Canary Islands; missionary in Brazil; writer; beatified June 22, 1980.

Andreis, Felix de (1778-1820): Italian Vincentian; missionary and educator in western US.

Aparicio, Sebastian, Bl. (1502-1600): Franciscan brother, born Spain; settled in Mexico, c. 1533; worked as road builder and farmer before becoming Franciscan at about the age of 70; beatified, 1787; feast, Feb. 25.

Badin, Stephen T. (1768-1853): French missioner; came to US, 1792, when Sulpician seminary in Paris was closed; ordained, 1793, Baltimore, the first priest ordained in US; missionary in Kentucky, Ohio and Michigan; bought land on which Notre Dame University now stands; buried on its campus.

Baraga, Frederic (1797-1868): Slovenian missionary bishop in US; studied at Ljubljana and Vienna, ordained, 1823; came to US, 1830; missionary to Indians of Upper Michigan; first bishop of Marquette, 1857-1868; wrote Chippewa grammar, dictionary, prayer book and other works.

Bertran, Louis, St. (1526-1581): Spanish Dominican; missionary in Colombia and Caribbean, 1562-69; canonized, 1671; feast, Oct. 9.

Bourgeoys, Marguerite, St. (1620-1700): French foundress, missionary; settled in Canada, 1653; founded Congregation of Notre Dame de Montreal, 1658; beatified, 1950; canonized 1982; feast, Jan. 19.

Brebeuf, John de, St. (1593-1649): French Jesuit; missionary among Huron Indians in Canada; martyred by Iroquois, Mar. 16, 1649; canonized, 1930; one of Jesuit North American martyrs; feast, Oct. 19.

Cancer de Barbastro, Louis (1500-1549): Spanish Dominican; began missionary work in Middle America, 1533; killed at Tampa Bay, Fla.

Castillo, John de, Bl. (1596-1628): Spanish Jesuit; worked in Paraguay Indian mission settlements (reductions); martyred; beatified, 1934; feast, Nov. 17.

Catala, Magin (1761-1830): Spanish Franciscan; worked in California mission of Santa Clara for 36 years.

Chabanel, Noel, St. (1613-1649): French Jesuit; missionary among Huron Indians in Canada; murdered by renegade Huron, Dec. 8, 1649; canonized, 1930; one of Jesuit North American martyrs; feast, Oct. 19.

Chaumonot, Pierre Joseph (1611-1693): French Jesuit; missionary among Indians in Canada.

Claver, Peter, St. (1581-1654): Spanish Jesuit; missionary among Negroes of South America and West Indies; canonized, 1888; patron of Catholic missions among Negroes; feast, Sept. 9.

Daniel, Anthony, St. (1601-1648): French Jesuit; missionary among Huron Indians in Canada; martyred by Iroquois, July 4, 1648; canonized, 1930; one of Jesuit North American martyrs; feast, Oct. 19.

De Smet, Pierre Jean (1801-1873): Belgian-born Jesuit; missionary among Indians of northwestern US; served as intermediary between Indians and US government; wrote on Indian culture.

Duchesne, Rose Philippine, Bl. (1769-1852): French nun; educator and missionary in the US; established first convent of the Society of the Sacred Heart in the US, at St. Charles, Mo. (later Florissant); founded schools for girls; did missionary work among Indians; beatified, 1940; feast, Nov. 17.

Farmer, Ferdinand (family name, Steinmeyer) (1720-1786): German Jesuit; missionary in Philadelphia, where he died; one of the first missionaries in New Jersey.

Flaget, Benedict J. (1763-1850): French Sulpician bishop; came to US, 1792; missionary and educator in US; first bishop of Bardstown, Ky. (now Louisville), 1810-32; 1833-50.

Gallitzin, Demetrius (1770-1840): Russian prince, born The Hague; convert, 1787; ordained priest at Baltimore, 1795; frontier missionary, known as Father Smith; Gallitzin, Pa., named for him.

Garnier, Charles, St. (c. 1606-1649): French Jesuit; missionary among Hurons in Canada; martyred by Iroquois, Dec. 7, 1649; canonized, 1930; one of Jesuit North American martyrs; feast, Oct. 19.

Gibault, Pierre (1737-1804): Canadian missionary in Illinois and Indiana; aided in securing states of Ohio, Indiana, Illinois, Michigan and Wisconsin for the Americans during Revolution.

Gonzalez, Roch, Bl. (1576-1628): Paraguayan Jesuit; worked in Paraguay Indian mission settlements (reductions); martyred; beatified, 1934; feast, Nov. 17.

Goupil, Rene, St. (1607-1642): French Jesuit brother; missionary companion of St. Isaac Jogues among the Hurons; martyred, Sept. 29, 1642; canonized, 1930; one of Jesuit North American martyrs; feast, Oct. 19.

Gravier, Jacques (1651-1708): French Jesuit; missionary among Indians of Canada and midwestern US.

Jesuit North American Martyrs: Isaac Jogues, Anthony Daniel, John de Brebeuf, Gabriel Lalemant, Charles Garnier, Noel Chabanel (Jesuit priests), and Rene Goupil and John Lalande (lay missionaries) who were martyred between Sept. 29, 1642, and Dec. 9, 1649, in the missions of New France; canonized June 29, 1930; feast, Oct. 19. See separate entries.

Jogues, Isaac, St. (1607-1646): French Jesuit; missionary among Indians in Canada; martyred near present site of Auriesville, N.Y., by Mohawks, Oct. 18, 1646; canonized, 1930; one of Jesuit North American martyrs; feast, Oct. 19.

Kino, Eusebio (1645-1711): Italian Jesuit; missionary and explorer in US; arrived Southwest, 1681; established 25 Indian missions, took part in 14 exploring expeditions in northern Mexico, Arizona and southern California; helped develop livestock raising and farming in the area. He was selected in 1965 to represent Arizona in Statuary Hall.

Lalande, John, St. (d. 1646): French lay missionary, companion of Isaac Jogues; martyred by Mohawks at Auriesville, N.Y., Oct. 19, 1646; canonized, 1930; one of Jesuit North American martyrs; feast, Oct. 19.

Lalemant, Gabriel, St. (1610-1649): French Jesuit; missionary among the Hurons in Canada; martyred by the Iroquois, Mar. 17, 1649; canonized, 1930; one of Jesuit North American martyrs; feast, Oct. 19.

Lamy, Jean Baptiste (1814-1888): French prelate; came to US, 1839; missionary in Ohio and Kentucky; bishop in Southwest from 1850; first bishop (later archbishop) of Santa Fe, 1850-1885. He was nominated in 1951 to represent New Mexico in Statuary Hall.

Las Casas, Bartolome (1474-1566): Spanish Dominican; missionary in Haiti, Jamaica and Venezuela; reformer of abuses against Indians and Negroes; bishop of Chalapas, Mexico, 1544-47; historian.

Manogue, Patrick (1831-1895): Missionary bishop in US, b. Ireland; migrated to US; miner in California; studied for priesthood at St. Mary's of the Lake, Chicago, and St. Sulpice, Paris; ordained, 1861; missionary among Indians of California and Nevada; coadjutor bishop, 1881-84, and bishop,

1884-86, of Grass Valley; first bishop of Sacramento, 1886-1895, when see was transferred there.

Margil, Antonio (1657-1726): Spanish Franciscan; missionary in Middle America; apostle of Guatemala; established missions in Texas.

Marie of the Incarnation, Bl. (Marie Guyard) (1599-1672): French Ursuline nun; arrived in Canada, 1639; first superior of Ursulines in Quebec; missionary to Indians; writer; beatified June 22, 1980.

Marquette, Jacques (1637-1675): French Jesuit; missionary and explorer in America; sent to New France, 1666; began missionary work among Ottawa Indians on Lake Superior, 1668; accompanied Joliet down the Mississippi to mouth of the Arkansas, 1673, and returned to Lake Michigan by way of Illinois River; made a second trip over the same route; his diary and map are of historical significance. He was selected in 1895 to represent Wisconsin in Statuary Hall.

Massias, John de, St. (1585-1645); Dominican brother, a native of Spain; entered Dominican Friary at Lima, Peru, 1622; served as doorkeeper until his death; beatified, 1837; canonized 1975; feast, Sept. 18.

Mazzuchelli, Samuel C. (1806-1864): Italian Dominican; missionary in midwestern US; called Builder of the West; writer.

Membre, Zenobius (1645-1687): French Franciscan; missionary among Indians of Illinois; accompanied LaSalle expedition down the Mississippi (1681-1682) and Louisiana colonizing expedition (1684) which landed in Texas; murdered by Indians.

Nerinckx, Charles (1761-1824): Belgian priest; missionary in Kentucky; founded Sisters of Loretto at the Foot of the Cross.

Nobrega, Manoel (1517-1570): Portuguese Jesuit; leader of first Jesuit missionaries to Brazil, 1549.

Padilla, Juan de (d. 1542): Spanish Franciscan; missionary among Indians of Mexico and southwestern US; killed by Indians in Kansas; protomartyr of the U.S.

Palou, Francisco (c. 1722-1789): Spanish Franciscan; accompanied Junipero Serra to Mexico, 1749; founded Mission Dolores in San Francisco; wrote history of the Franciscans in California.

Pariseau, Mother Mary Joseph (1833-1902): Canadian Sister of Charity of Providence; missionary in state of Washington from 1856; founded first hospitals in northwest territory; artisan and architect. Represents Washington in National Statuary Hall.

Peter of Ghent (d. 1572): Belgian Franciscan brother; missionary in Mexico for 49 years.

Porres, Martin de, St. (1579-1639): Peruvian Dominican oblate; his father was a Spanish soldier and his mother a Negro freedwoman from Panama; called wonder worker of Peru; beatified, 1837; canonized, 1962; feast, Nov. 3.

Quiroga, Vasco de (1470-1565): Spanish missionary in Mexico; founded hospitals; bishop of Michoacan, 1537.

Ravalli, Antonio (1811-1884): Italian Jesuit; missionary in far-western United States, mostly Montana, for 40 years.

Raymbaut, Charles (1602-1643): French Jesuit; missionary among Indians of Canada and northern US.

Richard, Gabriel (1767-1832): French Sulpician; missionary in Illinois and Michigan; a founder of University of Michigan; elected delegate to Congress from Michigan, 1823; first priest to hold seat in the House of Representatives.

Rodriguez, Alonso, Bl. (1598-1628): Spanish Jesuit; missionary in Paraguay; martyred; beatified, 1934; feast, Nov. 17.

Rosati, Joseph (1789-1843): Italian Vincentian; missionary bishop in US (vicar apostolic of Mississippi and Alabama, 1822; coadjutor of Louisiana and the Two Floridas, 1823-26; administrator of New Orleans, 1826-29; first bishop of St. Louis, 1826-1843).

Sahagun, Bernardino de (c. 1500-1590): Spanish Franciscan; missionary in Mexico for over 60 years; expert on Aztec archaeology.

Seelos, Francis X. (1819-1867): Redemptorist missionary, born Bavaria; ordained, 1844, at Baltimore; missionary in Pittsburgh and New Orleans.

Serra, Junipero (1713-1784): Spanish Franciscan, b. Majorca; missionary in America; arrived Mexico, 1749, where he did missionary work for 20 years; began work in Upper California in 1769 and established nine of the 21 Franciscan missions along the Pacific coast; baptized some 6,000 Indians and confirmed almost 5,000; a cultural pioneer of California. Represents California in Statuary Hall.

Seghers, Charles J. (1839-1886): Belgian missionary bishop in North America; Apostle of Alaska; archbishop of Oregon City (now Portland), 1880-1884; murdered by berserk companion while on missionary journey.

Solanus, St. Francis (1549-1610): Spanish Franciscan; missionary in Paraguay, Argentina and Peru; Wonder Worker of the New World; canonized, 1726.

Sorin, Edward F. (1814-1893): French priest; member of Congregation of Holy Cross; sent to US in 1841; founder and first president of the University of Notre Dame; missionary in Indiana and Michigan.

Todadilla, Anthony de (1704-1746): Spanish Capuchin; missionary to Indians of Venezuela; killed by Motilones.

Turibius de Mogrovejo, St. (1538-1606): Spanish archbishop of Lima, Peru, c. 1580-1606; canonized 1726; feast, Apr. 27.

Twelve Apostles of Mexico (early 16th century): Franciscan priests; arrived in Mexico, 1524: Fathers Martin de Valencia (leader), Francisco de Soto, Martin de la Coruna, Juan Suares, Antonio de Ciudad Rodrigo, Toribio de Benevente, Garcia de Cisneros, Luis de Fuensalida, Juan de Ribas, Francisco Ximenes; Brothers Andres de Coroboda, Juan de Palos.

Valdivia, Luis de (1561-1641): Spanish Jesuit; defender of Indians in Peru and Chile.

Vasques de Espinosa, Antonio (early 17th century): Spanish Carmelite; missionary and explorer in Mexico, Panama and western coast of South America.

Vieira, Antonio (1608-1687): Portuguese Jesuit; preacher; missionary in Peru and Chile; protector of Indians against exploitation by slave owners and traders; considered foremost prose writer of 17th-century Portugal.

White, Andrew (1579-1656): English Jesuit; missionary among Indians in Maryland.

Wimmer, Boniface (1809-1887): German Benedictine; missionary among German immigrants in the US.

Youville, Marie Marguerite d', Bl. (1701-1771): Canadian widow; foundress of Sisters of Charity (Grey Nuns), 1738, at Montreal: beatified, 1959.

Zumarraga, Juan de (1468-1548): Spanish Franciscan; missionary; first bishop of Mexico; introduced first printing press in New World, published first book in America, a catechism for Aztec Indians; extended missions in Mexico and Central America; vigorous opponent of exploitation of Indians; approved of devotions at Guadalupe; leading figure in early church history in Mexico.

FRANCISCAN MISSIONS

The 21 Franciscan missions of Upper California were established during the 54-year period from 1769 to 1822. Located along the old El Camino Real, or King's Highway, they extended from San Diego to San Francisco and were the centers of Indian civilization, Christianity and industry in the early history of the state.

Fray Junipero Serra was the great pioneer of the missions of Upper California. He and his successor as superior of the work, Fray Fermin Lasuen, each directed the establishment of nine missions. One hundred and 46 priests of the Order of Friars Minor, most of them Spaniards, labored in the region from 1769 to 1845; 67 of them died at their posts, two as martyrs. The regular time of mission service was 10 years.

The missions were secularized by the Mexican government in the 1830's but were subsequently restored to the Church by the US government. They are now variously used as the sites of parish churches, a university, houses of study and museums.

The Catholic Church in the United States

The starting point of the mainstream of Catholic history in the United States was Baltimore at the end of the Revolutionary War, although before that time Catholic explorers had traversed much of the country and missionaries had done considerable work among the Indians in the Southeast, Northeast and Southwest.

Beginning of Organization

Father John Carroll's appointment as superior of the American missions on June 9, 1784, was the first step toward organization of the Church in this country.

At that time, according to a report he made to Rome in 1785, there were approximately 25,000 Catholics in the general population of four million. Many of them had been in the Colonies for several generations. Among them were such outstanding figures as Charles Carroll, a member of the Continental Congress and signer of the Declaration of Independence; Thomas FitzSimons of Philadelphia and Oliver Pollock, the Virginia agent, who raised funds for the militia; Commander John Barry, father of the American Navy, and numerous high-ranking army officers. For the most part, however, Catholics were an unknown minority laboring under legal and social handicaps.

Father Carroll, the brother of Charles Carroll, was named the first American bishop in 1789 and placed in charge of the Diocese of Baltimore, whose boundaries were coextensive with those of the United States. He was consecrated in England Aug. 15, 1790, and installed in his see the following Dec. 12.

Ten years later, Father Leonard Neale became his coadjutor and the first bishop ordained in the United States. Bishop Carroll became an archbishop in 1808 when Baltimore was designated a metropolitan see and the new dioceses of Boston, New York, Philadelphia and Bardstown were established. These jurisdictions were later subdivided, and by 1840 there were, in addition to Baltimore, 15 dioceses, 500 priests and 663,000 Catholics in the general population of 17 million.

Priests and First Seminaries

The number of the 24 original priests was gradually augmented with the arrival of others from France, after the Civil Constitution on the Clergy went into effect there, and other countries. Among the earliest arrivals were several Sulpicians who established the first seminary in the US, St. Mary's, Baltimore, in 1791. By 1815, 30 alumni of the school had been ordained to the priesthood. By that time, two additional seminaries were in operation: Mt. St. Mary's, established in 1809 at Emmitsburg, Md., and St. Thomas, founded two years later, at Bardstown, Ky.

These and similar institutions founded later played key roles in the development and growth of the American clergy.

Early Schools

Early educational enterprises included the establishment in 1791 of a school at Georgetown which later became the first Catholic university in the US; the opening of a secondary school for girls, conducted by Visitation Nuns, in 1792 at Georgetown; and the start of a similar school in the first decade of the 19th century at Emmitsburg, Md., by Saint Elizabeth Ann Seton and the Sisters of Charity of St. Joseph, the first religious community of American foundation.

By the 1840's, which saw the beginnings of the present public school system, more than 200 Catholic elementary schools, half of them west of the Alleghenies, were in operation. From this start, the Church subsequently built the greatest private system of education in the world.

Trusteeism

The initial lack of organization in ecclesiastical affairs, nationalistic feeling among Catholics and the independent action of some priests were factors involved in several early crises.

In Philadelphia, some German Catholics withdrew from one parish in 1789 and founded one of their own, Holy Trinity, which they maintained until 1802. Controversy over the affair reached the point of schism in 1796. Philadelphia was also the scene of the Hogan Schism, which developed in the 1820's when Father William Hogan, with the aid of lay trustees, seized control of St. Mary's Cathedral. His movement, for churches and parishes controlled by other than canonical procedures and run in extra-legal ways, was nullified by a decision of the Pennsylvania Supreme Court in 1822.

Similar troubles seriously disturbed the peace of the Church in other places, principally New York, Baltimore, Buffalo, Charleston and New Orleans.

Dangers arising from the exploitation of lay control were gradually diminished with the extension and enforcement of canonical procedures and with changes in civil law about the middle of the century.

Bigotry

Bigotry against Catholics waxed and waned during the 19th century and into the 20th. The first major campaign of this kind, which developed in the wake of the panic of 1819 and lasted for about 25 years, was mounted in 1830 when the number of Catholic immigrants began to increase to a noticeable degree. Nativist anti-Catholicism generated a great deal of violence, represented by climaxes in loss of life and property in Charlestown, Mass., in 1834, and in Philadelphia 10 years later. Later bigotry was fomented by the Know-Nothings, in the 1850's; the Ku Klux Klan, from 1866; the American Protective Association, from 1887; and the Guardians of Liberty. Perhaps the last eruption of overt anti-Catholicism occurred during the campaign of Alfred E. Smith for the presidency in 1928. Observers feel the issue was laid to rest in the political area with the election of John F. Kennedy to the presidency in 1960.

Growth and Immigration

Between 1830 and 1900, the combined factors of natural increase, immigration and conversion raised the Catholic population to 12 million. A large percentage of the growth figure represented immigrants: some 2.7 million, largely from Ireland, Germany and France, between 1830 and 1880; and another 1.25 million during the 80's when eastern and southern Europeans came in increasing numbers. By the 1860's the Catholic Church, with most of its members concentrated in urban areas, was one of the largest religious bodies in the country.

The efforts of progressive bishops to hasten the acculturation of Catholic immigrants occasioned a number of controversies, which generally centered around questions concerning national or foreign-language parishes. One of them, called Cahenslyism, arose from complaints that German Catholic immigrants were not being given adequate pastoral care.

Immigration continued after the turn of the century, but its impact was more easily cushioned through the application of lessons learned earlier in dealing with problems of nationality and language.

Councils of Baltimore

The bishops of the growing US dioceses met at Baltimore for seven provincial councils between 1829 and 1849.

In 1846, they proclaimed the Blessed Virgin Mary patroness of the United States under the title of the Immaculate Conception, eight years before the dogma was proclaimed.

After the establishment of the Archdiocese of Oregon City in 1846 and the elevation to metropolitan status of St. Louis, New Orleans, Cincinnati and New York, the first of the three plenary councils of Baltimore was held.

The first plenary assembly was convoked on May 9, 1852, with Archbishop Francis P. Kenrick of Baltimore as papal legate. The bishops drew up regulations concerning parochial life, matters of church ritual and ceremonies, the administration of church funds and the teaching of Christian doctrine.

The second plenary council, meeting from Oct. 7 to 21, 1866, under the presidency of Archbishop Martin J. Spalding, formulated a condemnation of several current doctrinal errors and established norms affecting the organization of dioceses, the education and conduct of the clergy, the management of ecclesiastical property, parochial duties and general education.

Archbishop (later Cardinal) James Gibbons called into session the third plenary council which lasted from Nov. 9 to Dec. 7, 1884. Among highly significant results of actions taken by this assembly were the preparation of the line of Baltimore catechisms which became a basic means of religious instruction in this country; legislation which fixed the pattern of Catholic education by requiring the building of elementary schools in all parishes; the establishment of the Catholic University of America in Washington, D.C., in 1889; and the determination of six holy days of obligation for observance in this country.

The enactments of the three plenary councils have had the force of particular law for the Church in the United States.

The Holy See established the Apostolic Delegation at Washington, D.C., on Jan. 24, 1893.

Slavery and Negroes

In the Civil War period, as before, Catholics reflected attitudes of the general population with respect to the issue of slavery. Some supported it, some opposed it, but none were prominent in the Abolition Movement. Gregory XVI had condemned the slave trade in 1839, but no contemporary pope or American bishop published an official document on slavery itself. The issue did not split Catholics in schism as it did Baptists, Methodists and Presbyterians.

Catholics fought on both sides in the Civil War. Five hundred members of 20 or more sisterhoods served the wounded of both sides.

One hundred thousand of the four million slaves emancipated in 1863 were Catholics; the highest concentrations were in Louisiana, about 60,000, and Maryland, 16,000. Three years later, their pastoral care was one of the subjects covered in nine decrees issued by the Second Plenary Council of Baltimore. The measures had little practical effect with respect to integration of the total Catholic community, predicated as they were on the proposition that individual bishops should handle questions regarding segregation in churches and related matters as best they could in the pattern of local customs.

Long entrenched segregation practices continued in force through the rest of the 19th century and well into the 20th. The first effective efforts to alter them were initiated by Cardinal Joseph Ritter of St. Louis in 1947, Cardinal (then Archbishop) Patrick O'Boyle of Washington in 1948, and Bishop Vincent Waters of Raleigh in 1953.

Friend of Labor

The Church became known during the 19th century as a friend and ally of labor in seeking justice for the working man. Cardinal Gibbons journeyed to Rome in 1887, for example, to defend and prevent a condemnation of the Knights of Labor by Leo XIII. The encyclical *Rerum Novarum* was hailed by many American bishops as a confirmation, if not vindication, of their own theories. Catholics have always formed a large percentage of union membership, and some have served unions in positions of leadership.

The American Heresy

Near the end of the century some controversy developed over what was characterized as Americanism or the phantom heresy. It was alleged that Americans were discounting the importance of contemplative virtues, exalting the practical virtues, and watering down the purity of Catholic doctrine for the sake of facilitating convert work.

The French translation of Father Walter Elliott's *Life of Isaac Hecker,* which fired the controversy, was one of many factors that led to the issuance of Leo XIII's *Testem Benevolentiae* in January, 1899, in an attempt to end the matter. It was the first time the orthodoxy of the Church in the US was called into question.

Schism

In the 1890's, serious friction developed between Poles and Irish in Scranton, Buffalo and Chicago, resulting in schism and the establishment of the Polish National Church. A central figure in the affair was Father Francis Hodur, who was excommunicated by Bishop William O'Hara of Scranton in 1898. Nine years later, his ordination by the Old Catholic Archbishop of Utrecht gave the new church its first bishop.

Another schism of the period led to formation of the American Carpatho-Russian Orthodox Greek Catholic Church.

Coming of Age

In 1900, there were 12 million Catholics in the total US population of 76 million, 82 dioceses in 14 provinces, and 12,000 priests and members of about 40 communities of men religious. Many sisterhoods, most of them of European origin and some of American foundation, were engaged in Catholic educational and hospital work, of which they have always been the main support.

The Church in the United States was removed from mission status with promulgation of the apostolic constitution *Sapienti Consilio* by Pope St. Pius X on June 29, 1908.

Before that time, and even into the early 20's, the Church in this country received financial assistance from mission-aid societies in France, Bavaria and Austria. Already, however, it was making increasing contributions of its own. At the present time, it is the heaviest national contributor to the worldwide Society for the Propagation of the Faith.

American foreign missionary personnel increased from 14 or less in 1906 to 7,148 by 1975 (197 diocesan priests, 3,692 religious priests and brothers, 2,850 sisters, 65 seminarians, 344 lay persons). The first missionary seminary in the US was in operation at Techny, Ill., in 1909, under the auspices of the Society of the Divine Word. Maryknoll, the first American missionary society, was established in 1911 and sent its first priests to China in 1918. Despite these contributions, the Church in the US has not matched the missionary commitment of some other nations.

Bishops' Conference

A highly important apparatus for mobilizing the Church's resources was established in 1917 under the title of the National Catholic War Council. Its name was changed to National Catholic Welfare Conference several years later, but its objectives remained the same: to serve as an advisory and coordinating agency of the American bishops for advancing works of the Church in fields of social significance and impact — education, communications, immigration, social action, legislation, youth and lay organizations.

The forward thrust of the bishops' social thinking was evidenced in a program of social reconstruction they recommended in 1919. By 1945, all but one of their twelve points had been enacted into legislation.

The NCWC was renamed the United States Catholic Conference (USCC) in November, 1966, when the hierarchy also organized itself as a territorial conference with pastoral-juridical authority under the title, National Conference of Catholic Bishops. The USCC is carrying on the functions of the former NCWC.

Pastoral Concerns

The potential for growth of the Church in this country by immigration was sharply reduced but not entirely curtailed after 1921 with the passage of restrictive federal legislation. As a result, the Catholic population became more stabilized and, to a certain extent and for many reasons, began to acquire an identity of its own.

Some increase-from-outside has taken place in the past 50 years, however; from Canada, from central and eastern European countries, and from Puerto Rico and Latin American countries since World War II. This influx, while not as great as that of the 19th century and early 20th, has enriched the Church here with a sizable body of Eastern-Rite Catholics for whom eight ecclesiastical jurisdictions were established between 1924 and 1969. It has also created a challenge for pastoral care of the Spanish-speaking.

The Church continues to grapple with serious pastoral problems in rural areas, where about 600 counties are no-priest land. The National Catholic Rural Life Conference was established in 1922 in an attempt to make the Catholic presence felt on the land, and the Glenmary Society since its foundation in 1939 has devoted itself to this single apostolate. Religious communities and diocesan priests are similarly engaged.

Other challenges lie in the cities and suburbs where 75 percent of the Catholic population lives. Conditions peculiar to each segment of the metropolitan area have developed in recent years as the flight to the suburbs has not only altered some traditional aspects of parish life but has also, in combination with many other factors, left behind a complex of special problems in the inner city.

Phenomena of Change

The Church in the US is presently in a stage of transition from a relatively stable and long established order of life and action to a new order of things. Some of the phenomena of this period are:
  • differences in trends and emphasis in theology, and in interpretation and implementation of directives of the Second Vatican Council, resulting in situations of conflict;
  • the changing spiritual formation, professional education, style of life and ministry of priests and religious (men and women), which are altering influential patterns of pastoral and specialized service;
  • vocations to the priesthood and religious life, which are generally in decline;
  • departures from the priesthood and religious life which, while small percentage-wise, are numerous enough to be a matter of serious concern;
  • decline of traditional devotional practices;
  • exercise of authority along the lines of collegiality and subsidiarity;
  • structure and administration, marked by a trend toward greater participation in the life and work of the Church by its members on all levels, from the parish on up;
  • alienation from the Church, leading some persons into the catacombs of an underground church, "anonymous Christianity" and religious indifferentism;
  • education, undergoing crisis and change in Catholic schools and seeking new ways of reaching out to the young not in Catholic schools and to adults;
  • social witness in ministry to the world, which is being shaped by the form of contemporary needs — e.g., race relations, poverty, the peace movement, the Third World;
  • ecumenism, involving the Church in interfaith relations on a wider scale than before.

BACKGROUND DATES IN U.S. CATHOLIC CHRONOLOGY

Dates in this section refer mostly to earlier "firsts" and developments in the background of Catholic history in the United States. For other dates, see various sections of the Almanac.

Alabama

1540: Priests crossed the territory with De Soto's expedition.

1560: Five Dominicans in charge of mission at Santa Cruz des Nanipacna.

1682: La Salle claimed territory for France.

1704: First parish church established at Fort Louis de la Mobile under the care of diocesan priests.

1829: Mobile diocese established (redesignated Mobile-Birmingham, 1954-69).

1830: Spring Hill College, Mobile, established.

1834: Visitation Nuns established an academy at Summerville.

1969: Birmingham diocese established.

1980: Mobile made metropolitan see.

Alaska

1779: Mass celebrated for first time on shore of Port Santa Cruz on lower Bucareli Bay on May 13 by Franciscan Juan Riobo.

1868: Alaska placed under jurisdiction of Vancouver Island.

1879: Father John Althoff became first resident missionary.

1886: Archbishop Charles J. Seghers, "Apostle of Alaska," murdered by a guide; had surveyed southern and northwest Alaska in 1873 and 1877, respectively.

Sisters of St. Ann first nuns in Alaska.

1887: Jesuits enter Alaska territory.

1894: Alaska made prefecture apostolic.

1902: Sisters of Providence opened hospital at Nome.

1916: Alaska made vicariate apostolic.

1917: In first ordination in territory, Rev. G. Edgar Gallant raised to priesthood.

1951: Juneau diocese established.

1962: Fairbanks diocese established.

1966: Anchorage archdiocese established.

Arizona

1539: Franciscan Marcos de Niza explored the state.

1540: Franciscans Juan de Padilla and Marcos de Niza accompanied Coronado expedition through the territory.

1629: Spanish Franciscans began work among Moqui Indians.

1632: Franciscan Martin de Arvide killed by Indians.

1680: Franciscans Jose de Espeleta, Augustin de Santa Maria, Jose de Figueroa and Jose de Trujillo killed in Pueblo Revolt.

1700: Jesuit Eusebio Kino established mission at San Xavier del Bac, near Tucson.

1767: Jesuits expelled; Franciscans took over 10 missions.

1828: Spanish missionaries expelled by Mexican government.

1863: Jesuits returned to San Xavier del Bac briefly.

1869: Sisters of Loretto arrived to conduct schools at Bisbee and Douglas.

1897: Tucson diocese established.

1969: Phoenix diocese established.

Arkansas

1541: Priests accompanied De Soto expedition through the territory.

1673: Marquette visited Indians in east.

1686: Henri de Tonti established trading post, first white settlement in territory.

1700-1702: Fr. Nicholas Foucault working among Indians.

1805: Bishop Carroll of Baltimore appointed Administrator Apostolic of Arkansas.

1838: Sisters of Loretto opened first Catholic school.

1843: Little Rock diocese established. There were about 700 Catholics in state, two churches, one priest.

1851: Sisters of Mercy founded St. Mary's Convent in Little Rock.

California

1542: Cabrillo discovered Upper (Alta) California; name of priest accompanying expedition unknown.

1602: On Nov. 12 Carmelite Andres de la Ascencion offered first recorded Mass in California on shore of San Diego Bay.

1697: Missionary work in Lower and Upper Californias entrusted to Jesuits.

1767: Jesuits expelled from territory. Spanish Crown confiscated their property, including the Pious Fund for Missions. Upper California missions entrusted to Franciscans.

1769: Franciscan Junipero Serra began establishment of Franciscan missions in California, in present San Diego. (See Franciscan Missions of Upper California.)

1775: Franciscan Luis Jayme killed by Indians at San Diego Mission.

1779: Diocese of Sonora, Mexico, which included Upper California, established.

1781: On Sept. 4 an expedition from San Gabriel Mission founded present city of Los Angeles — Pueblo "de Nuestra Senora de los Angeles."

Franciscans Francisco Hermenegildo Garces, Juan Antonio Barreneche, Juan Marcello Diaz and Jose Matias Moreno killed by Indians.

1812: Franciscan Andres Quintana killed at Santa Cruz Mission.

1822: Dedication on Dec. 8 of Old Plaza Church, "Assistant Mission of Our Lady of the Angels."

1833: Missions secularized, finally confiscated.

1840: Pope Gregory XVI established Diocese of Both Californias.

1846: Peter H. Burnett, who became first governor of California in 1849, received into Catholic Church.

1848: Mexico ceded California to the United States.

1850: Monterey diocese erected; title changed to Monterey-Los Angeles, 1859; and to Los Angeles-San Diego, 1922.

1851: University of Santa Clara chartered. Sisters of Notre Dame de Namur opened women's College of Notre Dame at San Jose; chartered in 1868; moved to Belmont, 1923.

1852: Baja California detached from Monterey diocese.

1853: San Francisco archdiocese established.

1855: Negotiations inaugurated to restore confiscated California missions to Church.

1868: Grass Valley diocese established; transferred to Sacramento in 1886.

1922: Monterey-Fresno diocese established; became separate dioceses, 1967.

1934: Sesquicentennial of Serra's death observed; Serra Year officially declared by Legislature and Aug. 24 observed as Serra Day.

1936: Los Angeles made archdiocese. San Diego diocese established.

1952: Law exempting non-profit, religious-sponsored elementary and secondary schools from taxation upheld in referendum, Nov. 4.

1953: Archbishop James Francis McIntyre of Los Angeles made cardinal by Pius XII.

1962: Oakland, Santa Rosa and Stockton dioceses established.

1973: Archbishop Timothy Manning of Los Angeles made cardinal by Pope Paul VI.

1976: Orange diocese established.

1978: San Bernardino diocese established.

1981: San Jose diocese established. Byzantine-Rite eparchy of Van Nuys established.

Colorado

1858: First parish in Colorado established.

1864: Sisters of Loretto at the Foot of the Cross, first nuns in the state, established academy at Denver.

1868: Vicariate Apostolic of Colorado and Utah established.

1887: Denver diocese established.

1888: Regis College founded.

1941: Denver made archdiocese. Pueblo diocese established.

Connecticut

1651: Probably first priest to enter state was Jesuit Gabriel Druillettes; ambassador of Governor of Canada, he participated in a New England Colonial Council at New Haven.

1756: Catholic Acadians, expelled from Nova Scotia, settled in the state.

1791: Rev. John Thayer, first native New England priest, offered Mass at the Hartford home of Noah Webster, his Yale classmate.

1808: Connecticut became part of Boston diocese.

1818: Religious freedom established by new constitution, although the Congregational Church remained, in practice, the state church.

1829: Father Bernard O'Cavanaugh became first resident priest in state.

Catholic Press of Hartford established.

1830: First Catholic church in state dedicated at Hartford.

1843: Hartford diocese established.

1882: Knights of Columbus founded by Father Michael J. McGivney.

1942: Fairfield University founded.

1953: Norwich and Bridgeport dioceses established. Hartford made archdiocese.

1956: Byzantine Rite Exarchate of Stamford established; made eparchy, 1958.

Delaware

1730: Mount Cuba, New Castle County, the scene of Catholic services.

1750: Jesuit mission at Apoquiniminck administered from Maryland.

1772: First permanent parish established at Coffee Run.

1792: French Catholics from Santo Domingo settled near Wilmington.

1816: St. Peter's Church, later the cathedral of the diocese, erected at Wilmington.

1830: Daughters of Charity opened school and orphanage at Wilmington.

1868: Wilmington diocese established.

1869: Visitation Nuns established residence in Wilmington.

District of Columbia

1641: Jesuit Andrew White evangelized Anacosta Indians.

1774: Father John Carroll ministered to Catholics.

1789: Georgetown, first Catholic college in US, established.

1791: Pierre Charles L'Enfant designed the Federal City of Washington. His plans were not fully implemented until the early 1900's.

1792: James Hoban designed the White House.

1794: Father Anthony Caffrey began St. Patrick's Church, first parish church in the new Federal City.

1801: Poor Clares opened school for girls in Georgetown; first school established by nuns in US.

1802: First mayor of Washington, appointed by President Jefferson, was Judge Robert Brent.

1889: Catholic University of America founded.

1893: Apostolic Delegation established with Archbishop Francesco Satolli as the first delegate.

1919: National Catholic Welfare Conference (now the United States Catholic Conference) organized by American hierarchy to succeed National Catholic War Council.

1920: Cornerstone of National Shrine of Immaculate Conception laid.

1939: Washington made archdiocese of equal rank with Baltimore, under direction of same archbishop.

1947: Washington archdiocese received its own archbishop, was separated from Baltimore; became a metropolitan see in 1965.

1967: Archbishop Patrick A. O'Boyle of Washington made cardinal by Pope Paul VI.

1976: Archbishop William Baum of Washington made a cardinal by Pope Paul VI; transferred to Roman Curia in 1980 as prefect of Sacred Congregation for Catholic Education.

Florida

1513: Ponce de Leon discovered Florida.

1521: Missionaries accompanying Ponce de Leon and other explorers probably said first Masses within present limits of US.

1528: Franciscans landed on western shore.

1539: Twelve missionaries landed with De Soto at Tampa Bay.

1549: Dominican Luis Cancer de Barbastro and two companions slain by Indians near Tampa Bay.

1565: City of St. Augustine, oldest in US, founded by Pedro Menendez de Aviles, who was accompanied by four secular priests.

America's oldest mission, Nombre de Dios, was established.

Father Martin Francisco Lopez de Mendoza Grajales became the first parish priest of St. Augustine, where the first parish in the US was established.

1572: St. Francis Borgia, general of the Society, withdrew Jesuits from Florida.

1606: Bishop Juan de las Cabeyas de Altamirano, O.P., conducted the first episcopal visitation in the US.

1620: The chapel of Nombre de Dios was dedicated to Nuestra Senora de la Leche y Buen Parto (Our Nursing Mother of the Happy Delivery); oldest shrine to the Blessed Mother in the US.

1704: Destruction of Florida's northern missions by English and Indian troops led by Governor James Moore of South Carolina. Franciscans Juan de Parga, Dominic Criodo, Tiburcio de Osorio, Augustine Ponze de Leon, Marcos Delgado and two Indians, Anthony Enixa and Amador Cuipa Feliciano, were slain by the invaders.

1735: Bishop Francis Martinez de Tejadu Diaz de Velasco, auxiliary of Santiago, was the first bishop to take up residence in US, at St. Augustine.

1793: Florida and Louisiana were included in Diocese of New Orleans.

1857: Eastern Florida made a vicariate apostolic.

1870: St. Augustine diocese established.

1917: Convent Inspection Bill passed; repealed 1935.

1958: Miami diocese established.

1968: Miami made metropolitan see; Orlando and St. Petersburg dioceses established.

1976: Pensacola-Tallahassee diocese established.

Georgia

1540: First priests to enter were chaplains with De Soto. They celebrated first Mass within territory of 13 original colonies.

1566: Pedro Martinez, first Jesuit martyr of the New World, was slain by Indians on Cumberland Island.

1569: Jesuit mission was opened at Guale Island by Father Antonio Sedeno.

1572: Jesuits withdrawn from area.

1595: Five Franciscans assigned to Province of Guale.

1597: Five Franciscan missionaries (Fathers Pedro de Corpa, Blas de Rodriguez, Miguel de Anon, Francisco de Berascolo and Brother Antonio de Badajoz) killed in coastal missions.

1606: Bishop Altamirano, O.P., conducted visitation of the Georgia area.

1612: First Franciscan province in US erected under title of Santa Elena; it included Georgia, South Carolina and Florida.

1655: Franciscans had nine flourishing missions among Indians.

1742: Spanish missions ended as result of English conquest at Battle of Bloody Marsh.

1796: Augustinian Father Le Mercier was first post-colonial missionary to Georgia.

1798: Catholics granted right of refuge.

1800: First church erected in Savannah on lot given by city council.

1810: First church erected in Augusta on lot given by State Legislature.

1850: Savannah diocese established; became Savannah-Atlanta, 1937; divided into two separate sees, 1956.

1962: Atlanta made metropolitan see.

Hawaii

1825: Pope Leo XII entrusted missionary efforts in Islands to Sacred Hearts Fathers.

1827: The first Catholic missionaries arrived — Fathers Alexis Bachelot, Abraham Armand and Patrick Short, along with three lay brothers. After three years of persecution, the priests were forcibly exiled.

1836: Father Arsenius Walsh, SS. CC., a British subject, was allowed to remain in Islands but was not permitted to proselytize or conduct missions.

1839: Hawaiian government signed treaty with France granting Catholics freedom of worship and same privileges as Protestants.

1844: Vicariate Apostolic of Sandwich Islands (Hawaii) erected.

1873: Father Damien de Veuster of the Sacred Hearts Fathers arrived in Molokai and spent the remainder of his life working among lepers.

1941: Honolulu diocese established, made a suffragan of San Francisco.

Idaho

1840: Jesuit Pierre de Smet preached to the Flathead and Pend d'Oreille Indians; probably offered first Mass in state.

1842: Jesuit Nicholas Point opened a mission among Coeur d'Alene Indians near St. Maries.

1863: Secular priests sent from Oregon City to administer to incoming miners.

1867: Sisters of Holy Names of Jesus and Mary opened first Catholic school at Idaho City.

1868: Idaho made a vicariate apostolic.

1870: First church in Boise established.

Church lost most of missions among Indians of Northwest Territory when Commission on Indian Affairs appointed Protestant missionaries to take over.

1893: Boise diocese established.

Illinois

1673: Jesuit Jacques Marquette, accompanying Joliet, preached to Indians.

1674: Pere Marquette set up a cabin for saying Mass in what later became City of Chicago.

1675: Pere Marquette established Mission of the Immaculate Conception among Kaskaskia Indians.

1679: La Salle brought with him Franciscans Louis Hennepin, Gabriel de la Ribourde, and Zenobius Membre.

1680: Father Ribourde was killed by Kickapoo Indians.

1689: Jesuit Claude Allouez died after 32 years of missionary activity among Indians of Midwest; he had evangelized 100,000 Indians of 20 different tribes and baptized 10,000. Jesuit Jacques Gravier succeeded Allouez as vicar general of Illinois.

1730: Father Gaston, a diocesan priest, was killed at the Cahokia Mission.

1763: Jesuits were banished from the territory.

1778: Father Pierre Gibault championed Colonial cause in the Revolution and aided greatly in securing states of Ohio, Indiana, Illinois, Michigan and Wisconsin for Americans.

1827: The present St. Patrick's Parish at Ruma, oldest English-speaking Catholic congregation in state, was founded.

1833: Visitation Nuns established residence in Kaskaskia.

1843: Chicago diocese established.

1853: Quincy diocese established; transferred to Alton, 1857; Springfield, 1923.

1860: Quincy College founded.

1877: Peoria diocese established.

1880: Chicago made archdiocese.

1887: Belleville diocese established.

1908: Rockford diocese established.

First American Missionary Congress held in Chicago.

1924: Archbishop Mundelein of Chicago made cardinal by Pope Pius XI.

1926: The 28th International Eucharistic Congress, first held in US, convened in Chicago.

1946: Blessed Frances Xavier Cabrini, former resident of Chicago, was canonized; first US citizen raised to dignity of altar.

Archbishop Samuel A. Stritch of Chicago made cardinal by Pope Pius XII.

1948: Joliet diocese established.

1958: Cardinal Stritch appointed Pro-Prefect of the Sacred Congregation for the Propagation of the Faith — the first US-born prelate to be named to the Roman Curia.

1959: Archbishop Albert G. Meyer of Chicago made cardinal by Pope John XXIII.

1961: Eparchy of St. Nicholas of the Ukrainians established at Chicago.

1967: Archbishop John P. Cody of Chicago made cardinal by Pope Paul VI.

Indiana

1679: Recollects Louis Hennepin and Gabriel de la Ribourde passed through state.

1686: Land near present Notre Dame University at South Bend given by French government to Jesuits for mission.

1749: Beginning of the records of St. Francis Xavier Church. These records continue with minor interruptions to the present.

1778: Father Gibault aided George Rogers Clark in campaign against British in conquest of Northwest Territory.

1834: Vincennes diocese, later Indianapolis, established.

1840: Sisters of Providence founded St. Mary-of-the-Woods College for women.

1842: University of Notre Dame founded by Holy Cross Father Edward Sorin and Brothers of St. Joseph on land given the diocese of Vincennes by Father Stephen Badin.

1843: Immigration of German farmers to Indiana swelled Catholic population.

1853: First Benedictine community established in state at St. Meinrad. It became an abbey in 1870 and an archabbey in 1954.

1857: Fort Wayne diocese established; changed to Fort Wayne-South Bend, 1960.

1944: Indianapolis made archdiocese. Lafayette and Evansville dioceses established.

1957: Gary diocese established.

Iowa

1673: A Peoria village on Mississippi was visited by Pere Marquette.

1679: Fathers Louis Hennepin and Gabriel de la Ribourde visited Indian villages.

1836: First permanent church, St. Raphael's, founded at Dubuque by Dominican Samuel Mazzuchelli.

1837: Dubuque diocese established.

1838: St. Joseph's Mission founded at Council Bluffs by Jesuit Father De Smet.

1843: Sisters of Charity of the Blessed Virgin Mary were first sisterhood in state.

Sisters of Charity opened Clarke College, Dubuque.

1850: First Trappist Monastery in state, Our Lady of New Melleray, was begun.

1881: Davenport diocese established.

1882: St. Ambrose College, Davenport, established.

1893: Dubuque made archdiocese.

1902: Sioux City diocese established.

1911: Des Moines diocese established.

Kansas

1542: Franciscan Juan de Padilla, first martyr of the United States, was killed in central Kansas.

1858: St. Benedict's College founded.

1863: Sisters of Charity opened orphanage at Leavenworth, and St. John's Hospital in following year.

1877: Leavenworth diocese established; transferred to Kansas City in 1947.

1887: Dioceses of Concordia (transferred to Salina in 1944) and Wichita established.

1888: Oblate Sisters of Providence opened an orphanage for Negro boys at Leavenworth, first west of Mississippi.

1951: Dodge City diocese established.

1952: Kansas City made archdiocese.

Kentucky

1775: First Catholic settlers came to Kentucky.

1787: Father Charles Maurice Whelan, first resident priest, ministered to settlers in the Bardstown district.

1793: Father Stephen T. Badin began missionary work in Kentucky.

1806: Dominican Fathers built Priory at St. Rose of Lima.

1808: Bardstown diocese established with Benedict Flaget as its first bishop; transferred to Louisville, 1841.

1811: Rev. Guy I. Chabrat first priest ordained west of the Allegheny Mountains.

St. Thomas Seminary founded.

1812: Sisters of Loretto founded by Rev. Charles Nerinckx; first religious community in the United States without foreign affiliation.

Sisters of Charity of Nazareth founded, the second native community of women founded in the West.

1814: Nazareth College for women established.

1816: Cornerstone of St. Joseph's Cathedral, Bardstown, laid.

1836: Hon. Benedict J. Webb founded *Catholic Advocate* first Catholic weekly newspaper in Kentucky.

1848: Trappist monks took up residence in Gethsemani.

1849: Cornerstone of Cathedral of the Assumption laid at Louisville.

1852: Know-Nothing troubles in state.

1853: Covington diocese established.

1937: Louisville made archdiocese. Owensboro diocese established.

Louisiana

1682: La Salle's expedition, accompanied by two priests, completed discoveries of De Soto at mouth of Mississippi. LaSalle named territory Louisiana.

1699: French Catholics founded colony of Louisiana.

First recorded Mass offered Mar. 3, by Franciscan Father Anastase Douay.

1706: Father John Francis Buisson de St. Cosme was killed near Donaldsonville.

1717: Franciscan Anthony Margil established first Indian mission school of San Miguel de Linares.

1718: City of New Orleans founded by Jean Baptiste Le Moyne de Bienville.

1720: First resident priest in New Orleans was the French Recollect Prothais Boyer.

1725: Capuchin Fathers opened school for boys.

1727: Ursuline Nuns founded convent in New Orleans, oldest convent in what is now US; they conducted a school, hospital and orphan asylum.

1793: New Orleans diocese established.

1850: New Orleans made archdiocese.

1853: Natchitoches diocese established; transferred to Alexandria in 1910; became Alexandria-Shreveport in 1977.

1892: Sisters of Holy Family, a Negro congregation, established at New Orleans.

1912: Loyola University of South established.

1918: Lafayette diocese established.

1925: Xavier University established in New Orleans.

1961: Baton Rouge diocese established.

1962: Catholic schools on all levels desegregated in New Orleans archdiocese.

1977: Houma-Thibodaux diocese established.

1980: Lake Charles diocese established.

Maine

1604: First Mass in territory celebrated by Father Nicholas Aubry, accompanying De Monts' expedition which was authorized by King of France to begin colonizing region.

1605: Colony founded on St. Croix Island; two secular priests served as chaplains.

1613: Four Jesuits attempted to establish permanent French settlement near mouth of Kennebec River.

1619: French Franciscans began work among settlers and Indians; driven out by English in 1628.

1630: New England made a prefecture apostolic in charge of French Capuchins.

1633: Capuchin Fathers founded missions on Penobscot River.

1646: Jesuits established Assumption Mission on Kennebec River.

1688: Church of St. Anne, oldest in New England, built at Oldtown.

1704: English soldiers destroyed French missions.

1724: English forces again attacked French settlements, killed Jesuit Sebastian Rale.

1853: Portland diocese established.

1854: Know-Nothing uprising resulted in burning of church in Bath.

1856: Anti-Catholic feeling continued; church at Ellsworth burned.

1864: Sisters of Congregation of Notre Dame from Montreal opened academy at Portland.

1875: James A. Healy, first bishop of Negro blood consecrated in US, became second Bishop of Portland.

Maryland

1634: Maryland established by Lord Calvert. Two Jesuits among first colonists.

First Mass offered on Island of St. Clement in Lower Potomac by Jesuit Father Andrew White.

St. Mary's founded by English and Irish Catholics.

1641: St. Ignatius Parish founded by English Jesuits at Chapel Point, near Port Tobacco.

1649: Religious Toleration Act passed by Maryland Assembly. It was repealed in 1654 by Puritan-controlled government.

1651: Cecil Calvert, second Lord Baltimore, gave Jesuits 10,000 acres for use as Indian mission.

1658: Lord Baltimore restored Toleration Act.

1672: Franciscans came to Maryland under leadership of Father Massius Massey.

1688: Maryland became royal colony as a result of the Revolution in England; Anglican Church became the official religion (1692); Toleration Act repealed; Catholics disenfranchised and persecuted until 1776.

1784: Father John Carroll appointed prefect apostolic for the territory embraced by new Republic.

1789: Baltimore became first diocese established in US, with John Carroll as first bishop.

1790: Carmelite Nuns founded convent at Port Tobacco, the first in the English-speaking Colonies.

1791: First Synod of Baltimore held.

St. Mary's Seminary, first seminary in US, established.

1793: Rev. Stephen T. Badin first priest ordained by Bishop Carroll.

1800: Jesuit Leonard Neale became first bishop consecrated in present limits of US.

1806: Cornerstone of Assumption Cathedral, Baltimore, was laid.

1808: Baltimore made archdiocese.

1809: St. Joseph's College, first women's college in US, founded.

Sisters of Charity of St. Joseph founded by St. Elizabeth Ann Seton; first native American sisterhood.

1821: Assumption Cathedral, Baltimore, formally opened.

1829: Oblate Sisters of Providence, a Negro congregation, established at Baltimore.

First Provincial Council of Baltimore held; six others followed, in 1833, 1837, 1840, 1843, 1846 and 1849.

1836: Roger B. Taney appointed Chief Justice of Supreme Court by President Jackson.

1852: First of the three Plenary Councils of Baltimore convened. Subsequent councils were held in 1866 and 1884.

1855: German Catholic Central Verein founded.

1886: Archbishop Gibbons of Baltimore made cardinal by Pope Leo XIII.

1965: Archbishop Shehan of Baltimore made cardinal by Pope Paul VI.

Massachusetts

1630: New England made a prefecture apostolic in charge of French Capuchins.

1647: Massachusetts Bay Company enacted an anti-priest law.

1732: Although Catholics were not legally admitted to colony, a few Irish families were in Boston; a priest was reported working among them.

1755-56: Acadians landing in Boston were denied services of a Catholic priest.

1775: General Washington discouraged Guy Fawkes Day procession in which pope was carried in effigy, and expressed surprise that there were men in his army "so void of common sense as to insult the religious feelings of the Canadians with whom friendship and an alliance are being sought."

1780: The Massachusetts State Constitution granted religious liberty, but required a religious test to hold public office and provided for tax to support Protestant teachers of piety, religion and morality.

1788: First public Mass said in Boston on Nov. 2 by Abbe de la Poterie, first resident priest.

1803: Church of Holy Cross erected in Boston with financial aid given by Protestants headed by John Adams.

1808: Boston diocese established.

1831: Irish Catholic immigration increased.

1832: St. Vincent's Orphan Asylum, oldest charitable institution in Boston, opened by Sisters of Mercy.

1834: Ursuline Convent in Charlestown burned by a Nativist mob.

1843: Holy Cross College founded.

1855: Catholic militia companies disbanded; nunneries' inspection bill passed.

1859: St. Mary's, first parochial school in Boston, opened.

1860: Portuguese Catholics from Azores settled in New Bedford.

1870: Springfield diocese established.

1875: Boston made archdiocese.

1904: Fall River diocese established.

1911: Archbishop O'Connell of Boston made cardinal by Pope Pius X.

1950: Worcester diocese established.

1958: Archbishop Richard J. Cushing of Boston made cardinal by Pope John XXIII.

1966: Apostolic Exarchate for Melkites in the US established, with headquarters in Boston; made an eparchy in 1976.

1973: Archbishop Humberto S. Medeiros of Boston made cardinal by Pope Paul VI.

Michigan

1641: Jesuits Isaac Jogues and Charles Raymbaut preached to Chippewas; named the rapids Sault Sainte Marie.

1660: Jesuit Rene Menard opened first regular mission in Lake Superior region.

1668: Pere Marquette founded Sainte Marie Mission at Sault Sainte Marie.

1671: Pere Marquette founded St. Ignace Mission at Michilimackinac.

1701: Fort Pontchartrain founded on present site of Detroit and placed in command of Antoine de la Mothe Cadillac. The Chapel of Sainte-Anne-de-Detroit founded.

1706: Franciscan Father Delhalle killed by Indians at Detroit.

1823: Father Gabriel Richard elected delegate to Congress from Michigan territory; he was the first priest chosen for the House of Representatives.

1833: Father Frederic Baraga celebrated first Mass in present Grand Rapids.

Detroit diocese established, embracing whole Northwest Territory.

1843: *Western Catholic Register* founded at Detroit.

1845: St. Vincent's Hospital, Detroit, opened by Sisters of Charity.

1848: Cathedral of Sts. Peter and Paul, Detroit, consecrated.

1853: Vicariate Apostolic of Upper Michigan established.

1857: Sault Ste. Marie diocese established; later transferred to Marquette.

1877: University of Detroit founded.

1882: Grand Rapids diocese established.

1897: Nazareth College for women founded.

1937: Detroit made archdiocese. Lansing diocese established.

1938: Saginaw diocese established.

1946: Archbishop Edward Mooney of Detroit created cardinal by Pope Pius XII.

1949: Opening of St. John's Theological (major) Seminary at Plymouth; this was first seminary in US serving an entire ecclesiastical province (Detroit).

1966: Apostolic Exarchate for Maronites in the United States established, with headquarters in Detroit; made an eparchy in 1972; transferred to Brooklyn, 1977.

1969: Archbishop John Dearden of Detroit made cardinal by Pope Paul VI.

1971: Gaylord and Kalamazoo dioceses established.

1982: Apostolic Exarchate for Armenian-Rite Catholics in United States established. Detroit designated see city.

Minnesota

1680: Falls of St. Anthony discovered by Franciscan Louis Hennepin.

1727: First chapel, St. Michael the Archangel, erected near town of Frontenac and placed in charge of French Jesuits.

1732: Fort Charles built; Jesuits ministered to settlers.

1736: Jesuit Jean Pierre Aulneau killed by Indians.

1839: Swiss Catholics from Canada settled near Fort Snelling; Bishop Loras of Dubuque, accompanied by Father Pellamourgues, visited the Fort and administered sacraments.

1841: Father Lucian Galtier built Church of St. Paul, thus forming nucleus of modern city of same name.

1850: St. Paul diocese established.

1851: Sisters of St. Joseph arrived in state.

1857: St. John's University founded.

1888: St. Paul made archdiocese; name changed to St. Paul and Minneapolis in 1966.

1889: Duluth, St. Cloud and Winona dioceses established.

1909: Crookston diocese established.

1957: New Ulm diocese established.

Mississippi

1540: Chaplains with De Soto expedition entered territory.

1682: Franciscans Zenobius Membre and Anastase Douay preached to Taensa and Natchez Indians. Father Membre offered first recorded Mass in the state on Mar. 29, Easter Sunday.

1698: Priests of Quebec Seminary founded missions near Natchez and Fort Adams.

1702: Father Nicholas Foucault murdered by Indians near Fort Adams.

1721: Missions practically abandoned, with only Father Juif working among Yazoos.

1725: Jesuit Mathurin de Petit carried on mission work in northern Mississippi.

1729: Indians tomahawked Jesuit Paul du Poisson near Fort Rosalie; Father Jean Souel shot by Yazoos.

1736: Jesuit Antoine Senat burned at stake by Chickasaws.

1822: Vicariate Apostolic of Mississippi and Alabama established.

1825: Mississippi made a separate vicariate apostolic.

1837: Natchez diocese established; became Natchez-Jackson in 1956; transferred to Jackson in 1977.

1848: Sisters of Charity opened orphan asylum and school in Natchez.

1977: Biloxi diocese established.

Missouri

1700: Jesuit Gabriel Marest established a mission among Kaskaskia Indians near St. Louis.

1734: French Catholic miners and traders settled Old Mines and Sainte Genevieve.

1750: Jesuits visited French settlers.

1762: Mission established at St. Charles.

1767: Carondelet mission established.

1770: First church founded at St. Louis.

1811: Jesuits established Indian mission school at Florissant.

1818: Bishop Dubourg arrrrived at St. Louis, with Vincentians Joseph Rosati and Felix de Andreis. St. Louis University, the diocesan (Kenrick) seminary and the Vincentian Seminary in Perryville trace their origins to them.

1826: St. Louis diocese established.

1828: Sisters of Charity opened first hospital west of the Mississippi, at St. Louis.

1832: *The Shepherd of the Valley,* first Catholic paper west of the Mississippi.

1845: First conference of Society of St. Vincent de Paul in US founded at St. Louis.

1847: St. Louis made archdiocese.

1865: A Test Oath Law passed by State Legislature (called Drake Convention) to crush Catholicism in Missouri. Law declared unconstitutional by Supreme Court in 1866.

1867: College of St. Teresa for women founded at Kansas City.

1868: St. Joseph diocese established.

1880: Kansas City diocese established.

1946: Archbishop John J. Glennon of St. Louis made cardinal by Pope Pius XII.

1956: Kansas City and St. Joseph dioceses combined into one see. Jefferson City and Springfield-Cape Girardeau dioceses established.

1961: Archbishop Joseph E. Ritter of St. Louis made cardinal by Pope John XXIII.

1969: Archbishop John J. Carberry of St. Louis made cardinal by Pope Paul VI.

Montana

1743: Pierre and Francois Verendrye, accompanied by Jesuit Father Coquart, may have explored territory.

1833: Indian missions handed over to care of Jesuits by Second Provincial Council of Baltimore.

1840: Jesuit Pierre De Smet began missionary work among Flathead and Pend d'Oreille Indians.

1841: St. Mary's Mission established by Father De Smet and two companions on the Bitter Root River in present Stevensville.

1845: Jesuit Antonio Ravalli arrived at St. Mary's Mission; Ravalli County named in his honor.

1859: Fathers Point and Hoecken established St. Peter's Mission near the Great Falls.

1869: Sisters of Charity founded a hospital and school in Helena.

1884: Helena diocese established.

1904: Great Falls diocese established; redesignated Great Falls-Billings in 1980.

1910: Carroll College founded.

1935: Rev. Joseph M. Gilmore became first Montana priest elevated to hierarchy.

Nebraska

1541: Coronado expedition, accompanied by Franciscan Juan de Padilla, reached the Platte River.

1673: Pere Marquette visited Nebraska Indians.

1720: Franciscan Juan Miguel killed by Indians near Columbus.

1855: Father J. F. Tracy administered to Catholic settlement of St. Patrick and to Catholics in Omaha.

1856: Land was donated by Governor Alfred Cumming for a church in Omaha.

1857: Nebraska vicariate apostolic established.

1878: Creighton University established.

1881: Poor Clares, first contemplative group in state, arrived in Omaha.

Duchesne College established.

1885: Omaha diocese established.

1887: Lincoln diocese established.

1912: Kearney diocese established; name changed to Grand Island, 1917.

1917: Father Flanagan founded Boy's Town for homeless boys, an institution which gained national and international recognition in subsequent years.

1945: Omaha made archdiocese.

Nevada

1774: Franciscan missionaries passed through Nevada on way to California missions.

1860: First parish, serving Genoa, Carson City and Virginia City, established.

1862: Rev. Patrick Manogue appointed pastor of Virginia City. He established a school for boys and girls, an orphanage and hospital.

1871: Church erected at Reno.

1931: Reno diocese established; name changed to Reno-Las Vegas, 1977.

New Hampshire

1630: Territory made part of a prefecture apostolic embracing all of New England.

1784: State Constitution included a religious test which barred Catholics from public office; local support was provided for public Protestant teachers of religion.

1818: The Barber family of Claremont was visited by their son Virgil (converted to Catholicism in 1816) accompanied by Father Charles Ffrench, O.P. The visit led to the conversion of the entire Barber family.

1823: Father Virgil Barber, minister who became a Jesuit priest, built first Catholic church and school at Claremont.

1830: Church of St. Aloysius dedicated at Dover.

1853: New Hampshire made part of the Portland diocese.

1858: Sisters of Mercy began to teach school at St. Anne's, Manchester.

1877: Catholics obtained full civil liberty and rights.

1884: Manchester diocese established.

1893: St. Anselm's College opened; St. Anselm's Abbey canonically erected.

1937: Francis P. Murphy became first Catholic governor of New Hampshire.

New Jersey

1668: William Douglass of Bergen was refused a seat in General Assembly because he was a Catholic.

1672: Fathers Harvey and Gage visited Catholics in Woodbridge and Elizabethtown.

1701: Tolerance granted to all but "papists."

1744: Jesuit Theodore Schneider of Pennsylvania visited German Catholics of New Jersey.

1762: Fathers Ferdinand Farmer and Robert Harding working among Catholics in state.

1765: First Catholic community organized in New Jersey at Macopin in Passaic County.

1776: State Constitution tacitly excluded Catholics from office.

1799: Foundation of first Catholic school in state, St. John's at Trenton.

1814: First church in Trenton erected.

1844: Catholics obtained full civil liberty and rights.

1853: Newark diocese established.

1856: Seton Hall University established.

1881: Trenton diocese established.

1937: Newark made archdiocese. Paterson and Camden dioceses established.

1947: US Supreme Court ruled on N.J. bus case, permitting children attending non-public schools to ride on buses and be given other health services provided for those in public schools.

1957: Seton Hall College of Medicine and Dentistry established: the first medical school in state; it was run by Seton Hall until 1965.

1963: Byzantine Éparchy of Passaic established.

New Mexico

1539: Territory explored by Franciscan Marcos de Niza.

1581: Franciscans Agustin Rodriguez, Juan de Santa Maria and Francisco Lopez named the region "New Mexico"; they later died at hands of Indians.

1598: Juan de Onate founded a colony at Chamita, where first chapel in state was built.

1609-10: Santa Fe founded.

1631: Franciscan Pedro de Miranda was killed by Indians.

1632: Franciscan Francisco Letrado was killed by Indians.

1672: Franciscan Pedro de Avila y Ayala was killed by Indians.

1675: Franciscan Alonso Gil de Avila was killed by Indians.

1680: Pueblo Indian revolt; 21 Franciscan missionaries massacred; missions destroyed.

1692: Franciscan missions refounded and expanded.

1696: Indians rebelled, five more Franciscan missionaries killed.

1850: Jean Baptiste Lamy appointed head of newly established Vicariate Apostolic of New Mexico.

1852: Sisters of Loretto arrived in Santa Fe.

1853: Santa Fe diocese established.

1859: Christian Brothers arrived, established first school for boys in New Mexico (later St. Michael's College).

1865: Sisters of Charity started first orphanage and hospital in Santa Fe. It was closed in 1966.

1875: Santa Fe made archdiocese.

1939: Gallup diocese established.

New York

1524: Giovanni da Verrazano was first white man to enter New York Bay.

1642: Jesuits Isaac Jogues and Rene Goupil were mutilated by Mohawks; Rene Goupil was killed by them shortly afterwards. Dutch Calvinists rescued Father Jogues.

1646: Jesuit Isaac Jogues and John Lalande were martyred by Iroquois at Ossernenon, now Auriesville.

1654: The Onondagas were visited by Jesuits from Canada.

1655: First permanent mission established near Syracuse.

1656: Church of St. Mary erected on Onondaga Lake, in first French settlement within state.

Kateri Tekakwitha, "Lily of the Mohawks," was born at Ossernenon, now Auriesville (d. in Canada, 1680). She was beatified in 1980.

1658: Indian uprisings destroyed missions among Cayugas, Senecas and Oneidas.

1664: English took New Amsterdam. Freedom of conscience allowed by the Duke of York, the new Lord Proprietor.

1667: Missions were restored under protection of Garaconthie, Onondaga chief.

1678: Franciscan Louis Hennepin, first white man to describe Niagara Falls, celebrated Mass there.

1682: Thomas Dongan appointed governor by Duke of York.

1683: English Jesuits came to New York, later opened a school.

1700: Although Assembly enacted a bill calling for religious toleration of all Christians in 1683, other penal laws were now enforced against Catholics; all priests were ordered out of the province.

1709: French Jesuit missionaries obliged to give up their central New York missions.

1741: Because of an alleged popish plot to burn city of New York, four whites were hanged and 11 Negroes burned at stake.

1777: State Constitution gave religious liberty, but the naturalization law required an oath to renounce allegiance to any foreign ruler, ecclesiastical as well as civil.

1785: Cornerstone was laid for St. Peter's Church, New York City, first permanent structure of Catholic worship in state.

Trusteeism began to cause trouble at New York.

1806: Anti-Catholic 1777 Test Oath for naturalization repealed.

1808: New York diocese established.

1828: New York State Legislature enacted a law upholding sanctity of seal of confession.

1834: First native New Yorker to become a secular priest, Rev. John McCloskey, was ordained.

1841: Fordham University and Manhattanville College established.

1847: Albany and Buffalo dioceses established.

1850: New York made archdiocese.

1853: Brooklyn diocese established.

1856: Present St. Bonaventure University and Christ the King Seminary founded at Allegany.

1858: Cornerstone was laid of second (present) St. Patrick's Cathedral, New York City. The cathedral was completed in 1879.

1868: Rochester diocese established.

1872: Ogdensburg diocese established.

1875: Archbishop John McCloskey of New York made first American cardinal by Pope Pius IX.

1878: Franciscan Sisters of Allegany were first native American community to send members to foreign missions.

1880: William R. Grace was first Catholic mayor of New York City.

1886: Syracuse diocese established.

1911: Archbishop John M. Farley of New York made cardinal by Pope Pius X.

Catholic Foreign Mission Society of America (Maryknoll) opened a seminary for foreign missions, the first of its kind in US. The Maryknollers were also unique as the first US-established foreign mission society.

1917: Military Ordinariate established with headquarters at New York.

1919: Alfred E. Smith became first elected Catholic governor.

1924: Archbishop Patrick Hayes of New York made cardinal by Pope Pius XI.

1930: Jesuit Martyrs of New York and Canada were canonized on June 29.

1946: Archbishop Francis J. Spellman of New York made cardinal by Pope Pius XII.

1957: Rockville Centre diocese established.

1969: Archbishop Terence Cooke of New York made cardinal by Pope Paul VI.

1981: Apostolic Exarchate for Armenian-Rite Catholics in the United States and Canada established. New York designated see city.

North Carolina

1526: The Ayllon expedition attempted to establish a settlement on Carolina coast.

1540: De Soto expedition, accompanied by chaplains, entered state. .

1776: State Constitution denied office to "those who denied the truths of the Protestant religion."

1805: The few Catholics in state were served by visiting missionaries.

1821: Bishop John England celebrated Mass in the ballroom of the home of William Gaston at New Bern, marking the start of organization of the first parish, St. Paul's, in the state.

1835: William Gaston, State Supreme Court Justice, succeeded in having repealed the article denying religious freedom.

1852: First Catholic church erected in Charlotte.

1868: North Carolina vicariate apostolic established.

Catholics obtained full civil liberty and rights.

1874: Sisters of Mercy arrived, opened an academy, several schools, hospitals and an orphanage.

1876: Benedictine priory and school (later Belmont Abbey College) founded at Belmont; priory designated an abbey in 1884.

1910: Belmont Abbey established as an abbacy nullius; nullius status suppressed in 1977.

1924: Raleigh diocese established.

1971: Charlotte diocese established.

North Dakota

1742: Pierre and Francois Verendrye, accompanied by Jesuit Father Coquart, explored territory.

1818: Canadian priests ministered to Catholics in area.

1840: Jesuit Father De Smet made first of five trips among Mandan and Gros Ventre Indians.

1848: Father George Belcourt, first American resident priest in territory, reestablished Pembina Mission.

1874: Grey Nuns arrived at Fort Totten to conduct a school.

1889: Jamestown diocese established; transferred to Fargo in 1897.

1893: Benedictines founded St. Gall Monastery at Devil's Lake. (It was moved to Richardton in 1899 and became an abbey in 1903.)

1909: Bismarck diocese established.

1959: Archbishop Aloysius J. Muench, bishop of Fargo, made cardinal by Pope John XXIII.

Ohio

1749: Jesuits in expedition of Céleron de Blainville preached to Indians.

First religious services were held within present limits of Ohio. Jesuit Joseph de Bonnecamps celebrated Mass at mouth of Little Miami River and in other places.

1751: First Catholic settlement founded among Huron Indians near Sandusky by Jesuit Father de la Richardie.

1790: Benedictine Pierre Didier ministered to French immigrants.

1812: Bishop Flaget of Bardstown visited and baptized Catholics of Lancaster and Somerset Counties.

1818: Dominican Father Edward Fenwick (later first bishop of Cincinnati) built St. Joseph's Church and established first Dominican convent in Ohio.

1821: Cincinnati diocese established.

1831: Xavier University founded.

1843: Members of Congregation of Most Precious Blood arrived in Cincinnati from Switzerland.

1845: Cornerstone laid for St. Peter's Cathedral, Cincinnati.

1847: Cleveland diocese established.

1850: Cincinnati made archdiocese.

Marianists opened St. Mary's Institute, now University of Dayton.

1865: Sisters of Charity opened hospital in Cleveland, first institution of its kind in city.

1868: Columbus diocese established.

1871: Ursuline College for women opened at Cleveland.

1910: Toledo diocese established.

1935: Archbishop John T. McNicholas, O.P., founded the Institutum Divi Thomae in Cincinnati for fundamental research in natural sciences.

1943: Youngstown diocese established.

1944: Steubenville diocese established.

1969: Byzantine Rite Eparchy of Parma established.

Oklahoma

1540: De Soto expedition, accompanied by chaplains, explored territory.

1541: Coronado expedition, accompanied by Franciscan Juan de Padilla, explored state.

1630: Spanish Franciscan Juan de Salas labored among Indians.

1700: Scattered Catholic families were visited by priests from Kansas and Arkansas.

1874: First Catholic church built by Father Smyth at Atoka.

1876: Prefecture Apostolic of Indian Territory established with Benedictine Isidore Robot as its head.

1886: First Catholic day school for Choctaw and white children opened by Sisters of Mercy at Krebs.

1891: Vicariate Apostolic of Oklahoma and Indian Territory established.

1905: Oklahoma diocese established; title changed to Oklahoma City and Tulsa, 1930.

1917: Benedictine Heights College for women founded.

Carmelite Sisters of St. Theresa of the Infant Jesus founded at Oklahoma City.

1972: Oklahoma City made archdiocese. Tulsa diocese established.

Oregon

1603: Vizcaino explored northern Oregon coast.

1774: Franciscan missionaries accompanied Juan Perez on his expedition to coast, and Heceta a year later.

1811: Catholic Canadian trappers and traders with John J. Astor expedition founded first American settlement — Astoria.

1834: Indian missions in Northwest entrusted to Jesuits by Holy See.

1838: Abbe Blanchet appointed vicar general to Bishop of Quebec with jurisdiction over area which included Oregon Territory.

1839: First Mass celebrated at present site of St. Paul.

1843: Oregon vicariate apostolic established.

St. Joseph's College for boys opened.

1844: Jesuit Pierre de Smet established Mission of St. Francis Xavier near St. Paul.

Sisters of Notre Dame de Namur, first to enter Oregon, opened an academy for girls.

1846: Vicariate made an ecclesiastical province with Bishop Blanchet as first Archbishop of Oregon City (now Portland).

Walla Walla diocese established; suppressed in 1853.

1847: First priest was ordained in Oregon.

1848: First Provincial Council of Oregon.

1857: Death of Dr. John McLoughlin, "Father of Oregon."

1865: Rev. H. H. Spalding, a Protestant missionary, published the Whitman Myth to hinder work of Catholic missionaries.

1874: Catholic Indian Mission Bureau established.

1875: St. Vincent's Hospital, first in state, opened at Portland.

1903: Baker diocese established.

1922: Anti-private school bill sponsored by Scottish Rite Masons was passed by popular vote, 115,506 to 103,685.

1925: US Supreme Court declared Oregon anti-private school bill unconstitutional.

1953: First Trappist monastery on West Coast established in Willamette Valley north of Lafayette.

Pennsylvania

1673: Priests from Maryland ministered to Catholics in the Colony.

1682: Religious toleration was extended to members of all faiths.

1720: Jesuit Joseph Greaton became first resident missionary of Philadelphia.

1734: St. Joseph's Church, first Catholic church in Philadelphia, was opened.

1741: Jesuit Fathers Schneider and Wappeler ministered to German immigrants.

Conewego Chapel, a combination chapel and dwelling, was built by Father William Wappeler, S.J., a priest sent to minister to the German Catholic immigrants who settled in the area in the 1730's.

1782: St. Mary's Parochial School opened at Philadelphia.

1788: Holy Trinity Church, Philadelphia, was incorporated; first exclusively national church organized in US.

1797: Augustinian Matthew Carr founded St. Augustine parish, Philadelphia.

1799: Prince Demetrius Gallitzin (Father Augustine Smith) built church in western Pennsylvania, at Loretto.

1808: Philadelphia diocese established.

1814: St. Joseph's Orphanage was opened at Philadelphia; first Catholic institution for children in US.

1842: University of Villanova founded by Augustinians.

1843: Pittsburgh diocese established.

1844: Thirteen persons killed, two churches and a school burned in Know-Nothing riots at Philadelphia.

1846: First Benedictine Abbey in New World founded near Latrobe by Father Boniface Wimmer.

1852: Redemptorist John Nepomucene Neumann became fourth bishop of Philadelphia. He was beatified in 1963 and canonized in 1977.

1853: Erie diocese established.

1868: Scranton and Harrisburg dioceses established.

1871: Chestnut Hill College, first for women in state, founded.

1875: Philadelphia made archdiocese.

1901: Altoona-Johnstown diocese established.

1913: Byzantine Rite Apostolic Exarchate of Philadelphia established; became metropolitan see, 1958.

1921: Archbishop Dennis Dougherty made cardinal by Pope Benedict XV.

1924: Byzantine Rite Apostolic Exarchate of Pittsburgh established; made an eparchy in 1963; raised to metropolitan status and transferred to Munhall, 1969; transferred back to Pittsburgh in 1977.

1951: Greensburg diocese established.

1958: Archbishop John O'Hara, C.S.C., of Philadelphia made cardinal by Pope John.

1961: Allentown diocese established.

1967: Archbishop John J. Krol of Philadelphia made cardinal by Pope Paul VI.

1969: Bishop John J. Wright of Pittsburgh made cardinal by Pope Paul VI and transferred to Curia post.

1976: The 41st International Eucharistic Congress, the second held in the U.S. convened in Philadelphia, August 1-8.

Rhode Island

1663: Colonial Charter granted freedom of conscience.

1719: Laws denied Catholics the right to hold public office.

1829: St. Mary's Church, Pawtucket, was first Catholic church in state.

1837: Parochial schools inaugurated in state.

First Catholic church in Providence was built.

1851: Sisters of Mercy began work in Rhode Island.

1872: Providence diocese established.

1900: Trappists took up residence in state.

1917: Providence College founded.

South Carolina

1569: Jesuit Juan Rogel was the first resident priest in the territory.

1573: First Franciscans arrived in southeastern section.

1606: Bishop Altamirano conducted visitation of area.

1655: Franciscans had two missions among Indians; later destroyed by English.

1697: Religious liberty granted to all except "papists."

1790: Catholics given right to vote.

1820: Charleston diocese established.

1822: Bishop England founded *U.S. Catholic Miscellany*, first Catholic paper of a strictly religious nature in US.

1830: Sisters of Our Lady of Mercy, first in state, took up residence at Charleston.

1847: Cornerstone of Cathedral of St. John the Baptist, Charleston, was laid.

1861: Cathedral and many institutions destroyed in Charleston fire.

South Dakota

1842: Father Augustine Ravoux began ministrations to French and Indians at Fort Pierre, Vermilion and Prairie du Chien; printed devotional book in Sioux language the following year.

1867: Parish organized among the French at Jefferson.

1878: Benedictines opened school for Sioux children at Fort Yates.

1889: Sioux Falls diocese established.

1902: Lead diocese established; transferred to Rapid City, 1930.

1950: Mount Marty College for women founded.

1952: Blue Cloud Abbey, first Benedictine foundation in state, was dedicated.

Tennessee

1541: Cross planted on shore of Mississippi by De Soto; accompanying the expedition were Fathers John de Gallegos and Louis De Soto.

1682: Franciscan Fathers Membre and Douay accompanied La Salle to present site of Memphis; may have offered the first Masses in the territory.

1800: Catholics were served by priests from Bardstown, Ky.

1822: Non-Catholics assisted in building church in Nashville.

1837: Nashville diocese established.

1843: Sisters of Charity opened a school for girls in Nashville.

1921: Sisters of St. Dominic opened Siena College for women at Memphis; closed in 1971.

1940: Christian Brothers College founded at Memphis.

1970: Memphis diocese established.

Texas

1541: Missionaries with De Soto and Coronado entered territory.

1553: Dominicans Diego de la Cruz, Hernando Mendez, Juan Ferrer, Brother Juan de Mina killed by Indians.

1675: Bosque-Larios missionary expedition entered region; Father Juan Larios offered first recorded Mass.

1682: Mission Corpus Christi de Isleta (Ysleta) founded by Franciscans near El Paso, first mission in present-day Texas.

1690: Mission San Francisco de los Tejas founded in east Texas.

1703: Mission San Francisco de Solano founded on Rio Grande; rebuilt in 1718 as San Antonio de Valero or the Alamo.

1717: Franciscan Antonio Margil founded six missions in northeast.

1720: San Jose y San Miguel de Aguayo Mission founded by Fray Antonio Margil de Jesus.

1721: Franciscan Brother Jose Pita killed by Indians at Carnezeria.

1728: Site of San Antonio settled.

1738: Construction of San Fernando Cathedral at San Antonio.

1744: Mission church of the Alamo built.

1750: Franciscan Francisco Xavier was killed by Indians; so were Jose Ganzabal in

1752, and Alonzo Ferrares and Jose San Esteban in 1758.

1793: Mexico secularized missions.

1825: Governments of Cohuila and Texas secularized all Indian missions.

1838-39: Irish priests ministered to settlements of Refugio and San Patricio.

1841: Vicariate of Texas established.

1847: Ursuline Sisters established their first academy in territory at Galveston.

Galveston diocese established.

1852: Oblate Fathers and Franciscans arrived in Galveston to care for new influx of German Catholics.

St. Mary's College founded at San Antonio.

1854: Know-Nothing Party began to stir up hatred against Catholics.

1858: Texas Legislature passed law entitling all schools granting free scholarships and meeting state requirements to share in school fund.

1874: San Antonio diocese established.

Vicariate of Brownsville established.

1881: St. Edward's College founded: became first chartered college in state in 1889.

Sisters of Charity founded Incarnate Word College at San Antonio.

1890: Dallas diocese established; changed to Dallas-Ft. Worth, 1953; made two separate dioceses, 1969.

1912: Corpus Christi diocese established.

1914: El Paso diocese established.

1926: San Antonio made archdiocese. Amarillo diocese established.

1947: Austin diocese established.

1959: Galveston diocese redesignated Galveston-Houston.

1961: San Angelo diocese established.

1965: Brownsville diocese established.

1966: Beaumont diocese established.

1982: Victoria diocese established.

Utah

1776: Franciscans Silvestre de Escalante and Atanasio Dominguez reached Utah (Salt) Lake; first white men known to enter the territory.

1858: Jesuit Father De Smet accompanied General Harney as chaplain on expedition sent to settle troubles between Mormons and US Government.

1866: On June 29 Father Edward Kelly offered first Mass in Salt Lake City in Mormon Assembly Hall.

1886: Utah vicariate apostolic established.

1891: Salt Lake City diocese established.

1926: College of St. Mary-of-the-Wasatch for women was founded.

Vermont

1609: Champlain expedition passed through territory.

1666: Captain La Motte built fort and shrine of St. Anne on Isle La Motte; Sulpician Father Dollier de Casson celebrated first Mass.

1668: Bishop Laval of Quebec (beatified in 1980), administered confirmation in region; this was the first area in northeastern US to receive an episcopal visit.

1710: Jesuits ministered to Indians near Lake Champlain.

1793: Discriminatory measures against Catholics were repealed.

1830: Father Jeremiah O'Callaghan became first resident priest in state.

1853: Burlington diocese established.

1854: Sisters of Charity of Providence arrived to conduct St. Joseph's Orphanage at Burlington.

1904: St. Michael's College founded.

1951: First Carthusian foundation in America established at Whitingham.

Virginia

1526: Dominican Antonio de Montesinos offered first Mass on Virginia soil.

1561: Dominicans visited the coast.

1571: Father John Baptist de Segura and seven Jesuit companions killed by Indians.

1642: Priests outlawed and Catholics denied right to vote.

1689: Capuchin Christopher Plunket was captured and exiled to a coastal island where he died in 1697.

1776: Religious freedom granted.

1791: Father Jean Dubois arrived at Richmond with letters from Lafayette. The House of Delegates was placed at his disposal for celebration of Mass.

1796: A church was built at Alexandria.

1820: Richmond diocese established.

1822: Trusteeism created serious problems in diocese; Bishop Kelly resigned the see.

1848: Sisters of Charity opened an orphan asylum at Norfolk.

1866: School Sisters of Notre Dame and Sisters of Charity opened academies for girls at Richmond.

1974: Arlington diocese established.

Washington

1774: Spaniards explored the region.

1838: Fathers Blanchet and Demers, "Apostles of the Northwest," were sent to territory by archbishop of Quebec.

1840: Cross erected on Whidby Island, Puget Sound.

1843: Vicariate Apostolic of Oregon, including Washington, was established.

1844: Mission of St. Paul founded at Colville.

Six Sisters of Notre Dame de Namur began work in area.

1850: Nesqually diocese established; transferred to Seattle, 1907.

1856: Providence Academy, the first permanent Catholic school in the Northwest, was built at Fort Vancouver by Mother

Joseph Pariseau of the Sisters of Charity of Providence.

1887: Gonzaga University founded.
1913: Spokane diocese established.
1951: Seattle made archdiocese. Yakima diocese established.

West Virginia

1749: Father Joseph de Bonnecamps, accompanying the Bienville expedition, may have offered first Mass in the territory.
1821: First Catholic church in Wheeling.
1838: Sisters of Charity founded school at Martinsburg.
1848: Visitation Nuns established academy for girls in Wheeling.
1850: Wheeling diocese established; name changed to Wheeling-Charleston, 1974.
Wheeling Hospital incorporated, the oldest Catholic charitable institution in territory.
1955: Wheeling College established.

Wisconsin

1661: Jesuit Rene Menard, first known missionary in the territory, was killed or lost in the Black River district.
1665: Jesuit Claude Allouez founded Mission of the Holy Ghost at La Pointe Chegoimegon, now Bayfield; was the first permanent mission in region.
1673: Father Marquette and Louis Joliet traveled from Green Bay down the Wisconsin and Mississippi rivers.
1762: Suppression of Jesuits in French Colonies closed many missions for 30 years.
1843: Milwaukee diocese established.
1853: St. John's Cathedral, Milwaukee, was built.
1864: State charter granted for establishment of Marquette University. First students admitted, 1881.
1868: Green Bay and La Crosse dioceses established.
1875: Milwaukee made archdiocese.
1905: Superior diocese established.
1946: Madison diocese established.

Wyoming

1840: Jesuit Pierre de Smet offered first Mass near Green River.
1851: Father De Smet held peace conference with Indians near Fort Laramie.
1867: Father William Kelly, first resident priest, arrived in Cheyenne and built first church a year later.
1873: Father Eugene Cusson became first resident pastor in Laramie.
1875: Sisters of Charity of Leavenworth opened school and orphanage at Laramie.
1884: Jesuits took over pastoral care of Shoshone and Arapaho Indians.
1887: Cheyenne diocese established.
1949: Weston Memorial Hospital opened near Newcastle.

Puerto Rico

1493: Island discovered by Columbus on his second voyage; he named it San Juan de Borinquen (the Indian name for Puerto Rico).
1509: Juan Ponce de Leon, searching for gold, colonized the island and became its first governor; present population descended mainly from early Spanish settlers.
1511: Diocese of Puerto Rico established as suffragan of Seville, Spain; Bishop Alonso, Manso, sailing from Spain in 1512, became first bishop to take up residence in New World.
1645: Synod held in Puerto Rico to regulate frequency of Masses according to distances people had to walk.
1898: Puerto Rico ceded to U.S. (became self-governing Commonwealth in 1952); inhabitants granted U.S. citizenship in 1917.
1924: Diocese of Puerto Rico renamed San Juan de Puerto Rico and made immediately subject to the Holy See; Ponce diocese established.
1948: Catholic University of Puerto Rico founded at Ponce through efforts of Bishop James E. McManus, C.SS.R., 1947-63.
1960: San Juan made metropolitan see. Arecibo diocese established.
1964: Caguas diocese established.
1973: Archbishop Luis Aponte Martinez of San Juan made first native Puerto Rican cardinal by Pope Paul VI.
1976: Mayaguez diocese established.
Virgin of Providence officially approved as Patroness of Puerto Rico by Pope Paul VI.

Catholics Represented in National Statuary Hall

Statues of 13 Catholics deemed worthy of national commemoration by the donating states are among 93 enshrined in National Statuary Hall and other places in the US Capitol. The Hall, formerly the chamber of the House of Representatives, was erected by Act of Congress July 2, 1864.

Donating states, names and years of placement are listed. An asterisk indicates placement of a statue in the Hall itself.

Arizona: Rev. Eusebio Kino, S. J., missionary, 1965.
California: Rev. Junipero Serra, O. F. M.* missionary, 1931.
Hawaii: Father Damien, missionary, 1969.
Illinois: Gen. James Shields, statesman, 1893.
Louisiana: Edward D. White, Justice of the US Supreme Court (1894-1921), 1955.
Maryland: Charles Carroll,* statesman, 1901.
Nevada: Patrick A. McCarran,* statesman, 1960.
New Mexico: Dennis Chavez, statesman, 1966. (Archbishop Jean B. Lamy, pioneer

prelate of Santa Fe, was nominated for Hall honor in 1951.)

North Dakota: John Burke,* US treasurer, 1963.

Oregon: Dr. John McLoughlin, pioneer, 1953.

Washington: Mother Mary Joseph Pariseau, pioneer missionary and humanitarian.

West Virginia: John E. Kenna, statesman, 1901.

Wisconsin: Rev. Jacques Marquette, S.J., missionary, explorer, 1895.

Catholics in Presidents' Cabinets

Roger B. Taney, Attorney General 1831-33, Secretary of Treasury 1833-34; app. by Andrew Jackson.

James Campbell, Postmaster General 1853-57; app. by Franklin Pierce.

John B. Floyd, Secretary of War 1857-61; app. by James Buchanan.

Joseph McKenna, Attorney General 1897-98; app. by William McKinley.

Robert J. Wynne, Postmaster General 1904-05; app. by Theodore Roosevelt.

Charles Bonaparte, Secretary of Navy 1905-06, Attorney General 1906-09; app. by Theodore Roosevelt.

James A. Farley, Postmaster General 1933-40; app. by Franklin D. Roosevelt.

Frank Murphy, Attorney General 1939-40; app. by Franklin D. Roosevelt.

Frank C. Walker, Postmaster General 1940-45; app. by Franklin D. Roosevelt.

Robert E. Hannegan, Postmaster General 1945-47; app. by Harry S. Truman.

J. Howard McGrath, Attorney General 1949-52; app. by Harry S. Truman.

Maurice J. Tobin, Secretary of Labor; 1949-53; app. by Harry S. Truman.

James P. McGranery, Attorney General 1952-53; app. by Harry S. Truman.

Martin P. Durkin, Secretary of Labor 1953; app. by Dwight D. Eisenhower.

James P. Mitchell, Secretary of Labor 1953-61; app. by Dwight D. Eisenhower.

Robert F. Kennedy, Attorney General 1961-65; app. by John F. Kennedy, reapp. by Lyndon B. Johnson.

Anthony Celebrezze, Secretary of Health, Education and Welfare 1962-65; app. by John F. Kennedy, reapp. by Lyndon B. Johnson.

John S. Gronouski, Postmaster General 1963-65; app. by John F. Kennedy, reapp. by Lyndon B. Johnson.

John T. Connor, Secretary of Commerce 1965-67; app. by Lyndon B. Johnson.

Lawrence O'Brien, Postmaster General 1965-68; app. by Lyndon B. Johnson.

Walter J. Hickel, Secretary of Interior 1969-71; app. by Richard M. Nixon.

John A. Volpe, Secretary of Transportation 1969-72; app. by Richard M. Nixon.

Maurice H. Stans, Secretary of Commerce, 1969-72; app. by Richard M. Nixon.

Peter J. Brennan, Secretary of Labor, 1973-75; app. by Richard M. Nixon, reapp. by Gerald R. Ford.

William E. Simon, Secretary of Treasury, 1974-76; app. by Richard M. Nixon, reapp. by Gerald R. Ford.

Joseph A. Califano, Jr., Secretary of Health, Education and Welfare, 1977-79; app. by Jimmy Carter.

Benjamin Civiletti, Attorney General, 1979-81; app. by Jimmy Carter.

Moon Landrieu, Secretary of Housing and Urban Development, 1979-81; app. by Jimmy Carter.

Edmund S. Muskie, Secretary of State, 1980-81; app. by Jimmy Carter.

Alexander M. Haig, Secretary of State, 1981-82; app. by Ronald Reagan.

Raymond J. Donovan, Secretary of Labor, 1981- ; app. by Ronald Reagan.

Men who became Catholics after leaving Cabinet posts: Thomas Ewing, Secretary of Treasury under William A. Harrison, and Secretary of Interior under Zachary Taylor; Luke E. Wright, Secretary of War under Theodore Roosevelt; Albert B. Fall, Secretary of Interior under Warren G. Harding.

Catholic Justices of the Supreme Court

Roger B. Taney, Chief Justice 1836-64; app. by Andrew Jackson.

Edward D. White, Associate Justice 1894-1910, app. by Grover Cleveland; Chief Justice 1910-21, app. by William H. Taft.

Joseph McKenna, Associate Justice 1898-1925; app. by William McKinley.

Pierce Butler, Associate Justice 1923-39; app. by Warren G. Harding.

Frank Murphy, Associate Justice 1940-49; app. by Franklin D. Roosevelt.

William Brennan, Associate Justice 1956-; app. by Dwight D. Eisenhower.

Sherman Minton, Associate Justice from 1949 to 1956, became a Catholic several years before his death in 1965.

AGRIMISSIO

Agrimissio is a service office established for the purpose of assisting missionaries in rural development work. Founded in 1970 by Msgr. Luigi Ligutti, its honorary president, it is sponsored by the Union of Superiors General (of male religious), the International Union of Superiors General (of female religious), and the National Catholic Rural Life Conference in the U.S. It promotes cooperation among missionaries, the Rome headquarters of religious orders, governmental and nongovernmental organizations, especially the international Food and Agriculture Organization.

Msgr. John F. McDonald is executive secretary. Headquarters are located at the Palazzo S. Calisto, 00120, Vatican City.

CHURCH-STATE DECISIONS OF THE SUPREME COURT

(Among sources of this listing of U.S. Supreme Court decisions was *The Supreme Court on Church and State*, Joseph Tussman, editor; Oxford University Press, New York, 1962.)

Terrett v. Taylor, 9 Cranch 43 (1815): The Court declared unconstitutional an act of the Virginia Legislature which denied property rights to Protestant Episcopal churches in the state. Religious corporations, like other corporations, have rights to their property.

Vidal v. Girard's Executors, 2 Howard 205 (1844): The Court upheld the will of Stephen Girard, which barred ministers of any religion from serving as faculty members or visitors in a school he established for orphans.

Watson v. Jones, 13 Wallace 679 (1872): The Court declared that a member of a religious organization may not appeal to secular courts against a decision made by a church tribunal within the area of its competence.

Reynolds v. United States, 98 US 145 (1879): The Court declared, in reference to the Mormon practice of polygamy, that one may not knowingly violate by external practices the law of the land on religious grounds, since such conduct would make the professed doctrines of belief superior to federal or state law. One must keep the external practice of religion within the framework of laws enacted for the common welfare. This was the first decision rendered on the Free Exercise Clause of the First Amendment.

Davis v. Beason, 133 US 333 (1890): The Court upheld the denial of the right of Mormons to vote in Idaho if they refused to sign a registration oath stating that they were not bigamists or polygamists and would not encourage or preach bigamy or polygamy.

Church of Latter-Day Saints v. United States, 136 US 1 (1890): The Court upheld an Act of Congress which annulled the charter of the Corporation of the Church of Jesus Christ of Latter-Day Saints, and declared "forfeited to the government all its real estate except a small portion used exclusively for public worship" (Tussman, *op. cit.,* p. 33). The Court held that the Corporation continually used its power to violate US laws prohibiting polygamy.

Church of the Holy Trinity v. United States, 143 US 457 (1892): The Court declared it is not "a misdemeanor for a church of this country to contract for the services of a Christian minister residing in another nation" (from the text of the decision).

Bradfield v. Roberts, 175 US 291 (1899): The Court denied that an appropriation of government funds for an institution (Providence Hospital, Washington, D.C.) run by Roman Catholic sisters violated the No Establishment Clause of the First Amendment.

Pierce v. Society of Sisters, 268 US 510 (1925): The Court denied that a state can require children to attend public schools only. The Court held that the liberty of the Constitution forbids standardization by such compulsion, and that the parochial schools involved had claims to protection under the Fourteenth Amendment.

Cochran v. Board of Education, 281 US 370 (1930): The Court upheld a Louisiana statute providing textbooks at public expense for children attending public or parochial schools. The Court held that the children and state were beneficiaries of the appropriations, with incidental secondary benefit going to the schools.

United States v. MacIntosh, 283 US 605 (1931): The Court denied that anyone can place allegiance to the will of God above his allegiance to the government, since such a person could make his own interpretation of God's will the decisive test as to whether he would or would not obey the nation's law. The Court stated that the nation, which has a duty to survive, can require citizens to bear arms in its defense.

Hamilton v. Regents of University of California, 293 US 245 (1934): The Court rejected a "claim to exemption from R.O.T.C. based on conscientious objection to war" (Tussman *op. cit.,* p. 64). If such an exemption were allowed, the liberties of the objector might be extended to the point of refusal to pay taxes in furtherance of a war or any other end condemned by his conscience. This would be an undue exaltation of the right of private judgment.

Cantwell v. Connecticut, 310 US 296 (1940): The Court declared that the right to religious freedom is violated by a statute requiring a person to secure a permit from a government official before soliciting money for alleged religious purposes from someone not of his or her sect. Such a practice would constitute censorship of religion.

Minersville School District v. Gobitis, 310 US 586 (1940): The Court upheld the right of a state to require the salute to the national flag from school children, even from those who refused to do so for sincere religious reasons.

Jones v. City of Opelika, 316 US 584 (1942): The court upheld licensing ordinances in three municipalities against "the claim by Jehovah's Witnesses that they interfere with the free exercise of religion" (Tussman, *op. cit.,* p. 91).

Murdock v. Commonwealth of Pennsylvania, 319 US 105 (1943): In a reversal of the decision handed down in Jones v. City of Opelika, the Court declared the licensing unconstitutional since it violated a freedom guaranteed under the First Amendment. The selling of religious literature by traveling preachers does not make evangelism the equivalent of a commercial enterprise taxable by the State.

Jones v. City of Opelika, 316 US 584 105 (1943): The Court declared that the Constitution denies a city the right to control the expression of men's minds and denies also the right of men to win others to their views through a program of taxes levied against such activity.

Douglas v. City of Jeannette, 319 US 157 (1943): The Court again upheld the proselytizing rights of Jehovah's Witnesses, ruling unconstitutional the action of any public authority in regulating or taxing such activity.

West Virginia State Board of Education v. Barnette, 319 US 624 (1943): In a reversal of the decision handed down in Minersville School District v. Gobitis, the Court declared unconstitutional a state statute requiring of all children a salute to the national flag and a pledge of allegiance which a child may consider contrary to sincere religious beliefs.

Prince v. Commonwealth of Massachusetts, 321 US 158 (1944): The Court upheld a "child-labor regulation against the claim that it prevents a child from performing her religious duty" (Tussman, *op. cit.,* p. 170). The Court asserted a general principle that the state has a wide range of power for limiting parental freedom and authority in things affecting the child's welfare.

United States v. Ballard, 322 US 78 (1944): The Court upheld the general principle that "the truth of religious claims is not for secular authority to determine" (Tussman, *op. cit.,* p. 181).

In Re Summers, 325 US 561 (1945): The Court upheld "the denial, to an otherwise qualified applicant, of admission to the bar on the basis of the applicant's religiously motivated 'conscientious scruples against participation in war' " (Tussman, *op. cit.,* p. 192). The petitioner was barred because he could not in good faith take the prescribed oath to support the Constitution of Illinois which required service in the state militia in times of necessity.

Girouard v. United States, 328 US 61 (1946): In a ruling related to that handed down in United States v. MacIntosh, the Court affirmed the opinion that the refusal of an alien to bear arms does not deny him citizenship.

Everson v. Board of Education, 330 US 1 (1947): The Court upheld the constitutionality of a New Jersey statute authorizing free school bus transportation for parochial as well as public school students. The Court expressed the opinion that the benefits of public welfare legislation, included under such bus transportation, do not run contrary to the concept of separation of Church and State.

McCollum v. Board of Education, 333 US 203 (1948): The Court declared unconstitutional a program for releasing children, with parental consent, from public school classes so they could receive religious instruction on public school premises from representatives of their own faiths.

Zorach v. Clauson, 343 US 306 (1952): The Court upheld the constitutionality of a New York statute permitting, on a voluntary basis, the release during school time of students from public school classes for religious instruction given off public school premises.

Kedroff v. St. Nicholas Cathedral, 344 US 94 (1952): The Court ruled against an action of New York in taking "control of St. Nicholas Cathedral away from the Moscow hierarchy" (Tussman, *op. cit.,* p. 292), on the ground that the controversy involved a matter of church government.

Fowler v. Rhode Island, 345 US 67 (1953): The Court upheld the right of a Jehovah's Witness to preach in a public park against a city ordinance which forbade such preaching. The Court held that the ordinance, as construed and applied, discriminated against the Witness and therefore amounted to preferment by the state of other religious groups.

Torcaso v. Watkins, 367 US 488 (1961): The Court declared unconstitutional a Maryland requirement that one must make a declaration of belief in the existence of God as part of the oath of office for notaries public.

McGowan v. Maryland, 81 Sp Ct 1101; **Two Guys from Harrison v. McGinley,** 81 Sp Ct 1135; **Gallagher v. Crown Kosher Super Market,** 81 Sp Ct 1128; **Braunfield v. Brown,** 81 Sp Ct 1144 (1961): The Court ruled that Sunday closing laws do not violate the No Establishment of Religion Clause of the First Amendment, even though the laws were religious in their inception and still have some religious overtones. The Court held that, "as presently written and administered, most of them, at least, are of a secular rather than of a religious character, and that presently they bear no relationship to establishment of religion as those words are used in the Constitution of the United States."

Engel v. Vitale, 370 US 42 (1962): The Court declared that the voluntary recitation in public schools of a prayer composed by the New York State Board of Regents is unconstitutional on the ground that it violates the No Establishment of Religion Clause of the First Amendment.

Abington Township School District v. Schempp and **Murray v. Curlett,** 83 Sp Ct 1560 (1963): The Court ruled that Bible reading and recitation of the Lord's Prayer in public schools, with voluntary participation by students, are unconstitutional on the ground that they violate the No Establishment of Religion Clause of the First Amendment.

Sherbert v. Verner, 83 A Sp Ct 1790 (1963): The Court ruled that individuals of any religious faith may not, because of their faith or lack of it, be deprived of the benefits of public welfare legislation.

Chamberlin v. Dade County, 83 Sp Ct 1864 (1964): The Court reversed a decision of the Florida Supreme Court concerning the constitutionality of prayer and devotional Bible reading in public schools during the school day, as sanctioned by a state statute which specifically related the practices to a sound public purpose.

Board of Education v. Allen, No. 660 (1968): The Court declared constitutional the New York school book loan law which requires local school boards to purchase books with state funds and lend them to parochial and private school students.

Flast v. Cohen, No. 416 (1968): The Court held that individual taxpayers can bring suits to challenge federal expenditures on grounds that they violate the principle of separation of Church and State even though generally taxpayers cannot challenge federal expenditures in court.

Walz v. Tax Commission of New York (1970): The Court upheld the constitutionality of a New York statute exempting church-owned property from taxation.

Earle v. DiCenso, Robinson v. DiCenso, Lemon v. Kurtzman, Tilton v. Richardson (1971): In Earle v. DiCenso and Robinson v. DiCenso, the Court ruled unconstitutional a 1969 Rhode Island statute which provided salary supplements to teachers of secular subjects in parochial schools; in Lemon v. Kurtzman, the Court ruled unconstitutional a 1968 Pennsylvania statute which authorized the state to purchase services for the teaching of secular subjects in nonpublic schools. The principal argument against constitutionality in these cases was that the statutes and programs at issue entailed excessive entanglement of government with religion. In Tilton v. Richardson, the Court held that this argument did not apply to a prohibitive degree with respect to federal grants, under the Higher Education Facilities Act of 1963, for the construction of facilities for nonreligious purposes by four church-related institutions of higher learning, three of which were Catholic, in Connecticut.

Amish Decision (1972): In a case appealed on behalf of Yoder, Miller and Yutzy, the Court ruled that Amish parents were exempt from a Wisconsin statute requiring them to send their children to school until the age of 16. The Court said in its decision that secondary schooling exposed Amish children to attitudes, goals and values contrary to their beliefs, and substantially hindered "the religious development of the Amish child and his integration into the way of life of the Amish faith-community at the crucial adolescent state of development."

Committee for Public Education and Religious Liberty, et al., v. Nyquist, et al., No.

72-694 (1973): The Court ruled that provisions of a 1972 New York statute were unconstitutional on the grounds that they were violative of the No Establishment Clause of the First Amendment and had the "impermissible effect" of advancing the sectarian activities of church-affiliated schools. The programs ruled unconstitutional concerned: (1) maintenance and repair grants, for facilities and equipment, to ensure the health, welfare and safety of students in nonpublic, nonprofit elementary and secondary schools serving a high concentration of students from low income families; (2) tuition reimbursement ($50 per grade school child, $100 per high school student) for parents (with income less than $5,000) of children attending nonpublic elementary or secondary schools; tax deduction from adjusted gross income for parents failing to qualify under the above reimbursement plan, for each child attending a nonpublic school.

Sloan, Treasurer of Pennsylvania, et al., v. Lemon, et al., No. 72-459 (1973): The Court ruled unconstitutional a Pennsylvania Parent Reimbursement Act for Nonpublic Education which provided funds to reimburse parents (to a maximum of $150) for a portion of tuition expenses incurred in sending their children to nonpublic schools. The Court held that there was no significant difference between this and the New York tuition reimbursement program (above), and declared that the Equal Protection Clause of the Fourteenth Amendment cannot be relied upon to sustain a program held to be violative of the No Establishment Clause.

Levitt, et al., v. Committee for Public Education and Religious Liberty, et al., No. 72-269 (1973): The Court ruled unconstitutional the Mandated Services Act of 1970 under which New York provided $28 million ($27 per pupil from first to seventh grade, $45 per pupil from seventh to 12th grade) to reimburse nonpublic schools for testing, recording and reporting services required by the state. The Court declared that the act provided "impermissible aid" to religion in contravention of the No Establishment Clause.

In related decisions handed down June 25, 1973, the Court: (1) affirmed a lower court decision against the constitutionality of an Ohio tax credit law benefiting parents with children in nonpublic schools; (2) reinstated an injunction against a parent reimbursement program in New Jersey; (3) affirmed South Carolina's right to grant construction loans to church-affiliated colleges, and dismissed an appeal contesting its right to provide loans to students attending church-affiliated colleges (**Hunt v. McNair, Durham v. McLeod**).

Wheeler v. Barrera (1974): The Court ruled that nonpublic school students in Missouri must share in federal funds for educationally deprived students on a comparable basis with public school students under Title I of the Elementary and Secondary Education Act of 1965.

Norwood v. Harrison (93 S. Ct. 2804): The Court ruled that public assistance which avoids the prohibitions of the "effect" and "entanglement" tests (and which therefore does not substantially promote the religious mission of sectarian schools) may be confined to the secular functions of such schools.

Wiest v. Mt. Lebanon School District (1974): The Court upheld a lower court ruling that invocation and benediction prayers at public high school commencement ceremonies do not violate the principle of separation of Church and state.

Meek v. Pittenger (1975): The Court ruled unconstitutional portions of a Pennsylvania law providing auxiliary services for students of nonpublic schools; at the same time, it ruled in favor of provisions of the law permitting textbook loans to students of such schools. In denying the constitutionality of auxiliary services, the Court held that they had the "primary effect of establishing religion" and involved "excessive entanglement" of Church and state officials with respect to supervision; objection was also made against providing such services only on the premises of non-public schools and only at the request of such schools.

Roemer v. Board of Public Works of Maryland, 96 S. Ct. 2337 (1976): The Court ruled that a Maryland statute which authorized state funds to any private institution meeting certain minimal criteria was constitutional. The Court said the statute met the test previously outlined in Lemon v. Kurtzman because the colleges were not pervasively sectarian and the aid was in fact intended only for secular purposes.

Serbian Eastern Orthodox Diocese v. Milivojevich, 96 S. Ct. 2372 (1976): The Court held unconstitutional the decision of the Illinois Supreme Court that the Serbian Orthodox Church had arbitrarily removed one of its bishops and that its reorganization of the diocese was beyond the power of the church. The Court declared that the First Amendment does not permit civil courts to make ecclesiastical decisions.

TWA, Inc., v. Hardison, 75-1126; **International Association of Machinists and Aero Space Workers v. Hardison**, 75-1385 (1977): The Court ruled that federal civil rights legislation does not require employers to make more than minimal efforts to accommodate employees who want a particular working day off as their religion's Sabbath Day, and that an employer cannot accommodate such an employee by violating seniority systems determined by a union collective bargaining agreement. The Court noted that its ruling was not a constitutional judgment but an interpretation of existing law.

Wolman v. Walter (1977): The Court ruled constitutional portions of an Ohio statute providing tax-paid textbook loans and some auxiliary services (standardized and diagnostic testing, therapeutic and remedial services, off school premises) for nonpublic school students. It decided that other portions of the law, providing state funds for nonpublic school field trips and instructional materials (audio-visual equipment, maps, tape recorders), were unconstitutional.

Decisions since 1977

Clergymen (1978): The Court struck down the last state ban against the holding of public office by clergymen, nullifying the 182-year-old provision of the Tennessee constitution which held that involvement in politics might affect the clergy's "dedication to God and the care of souls."

Lay Teachers (1979): The Court ruled that lay teachers in church-related schools are not covered by the National Labor Relations Act. The decision was based, not on church-state grounds, but on the lack of any affirmative decision of the Congress to include such teachers in coverage of the law.

Church Property (1979): The Court ruled, in Jones v. Wolf, that civil courts are not always bound to yield to decisions of church courts in settling local church property disputes.

Parochiaid (1979): The Court decided, in Byrne v. Public Funds for Public Schools, against the constitutionality of a 1976 New Jersey law providing state income tax deductions for tuition paid by parents of students attending parochial and other private schools.

Religious Belief v. Union (1979): The Court supported the claim of a San Diego man that his right to religious freedom was violated when he was fired from his job because his Seventh Day Adventist beliefs prevented him from belonging to a union.

Student Bus Transportation (1979): The Court upheld a Pennsylvania law providing bus transportation at public expense for students to non-public schools up to 10 miles away from the boundaries of the public school districts in which they lived.

Reimbursement (1980): The Court upheld the constitutionality of a 1974 New York law providing direct cash payment to non-public schools for the costs of state-mandated testing and record-keeping.

Solicitation of Funds (1980): The Court struck down a Schaumburg, Ill., ordinance permitting the solicitation of funds only by groups spending a specific percentage of their funds for charitable purposes.

Remedial Teaching (1980): The Court refused to hear an appeal from a lower court ruling in support of a New York law permitting the use of federal funds to pay for remedial teaching in non-public schools.

Ten Commandments (1980): The Court struck down a 1978 Kentucky law requiring the posting of the Ten Commandments in public school classrooms in the state.

Christmas Carols (1980): The Court refused to hear an appeal from a lower court ruling permitting the singing of Christmas carols in public school holiday programs in Sioux City, S.D.

Highway Prayer (1981): The Court ruled that North Carolina could not publish a prayer for highway safety on official state maps.

Unemployment Benefits (1981): The Court decided, in Thomas v. Review Board, that a worker who, for religious reasons, quits his job rather than help to produce armaments cannot be denied state unemployment benefits.

Unemployment Taxes (1981): The Court ruled, in St. Martin Evangelical Lutheran Church v. South Dakota, that church-run schools do not have to pay state unemployment compensation taxes for their employees, because the relevant 1976 law did not "reveal any clear intent to repeal" their tax-exempt status.

Campus Worship (1981): The Court ruled, in Widmar v. Vincent, that the University of Missouri at Kansas City could not deny student religious groups the use of campus facilities for worship services. The Court also, in 'Brandon v. Board of Education of Guilderland Schools, declined without comment to hear an appeal for reversal of lower court decisions denying a group of New York high school students the right to meet for prayer on public school property before the beginning of the school day.

Americans United (1982): The Court ruled that Americans United for the Separation of Church and State did not have legal standing to challenge in court the transfer of government property to a Protestant college in Pennsylvania.

Social Security Taxes (1982): The Court ruled that Amish businessmen must pay Social Security taxes for their employees even if such payments violate their religious beliefs.

Unification Church (1982): The Court struck down a Minnesota law, aimed at the Unification Church, which required detailed financial reports from religious groups which raise more than half of their funds from nonmembers.

THE WALL OF SEPARATION

Thomas Jefferson, in a letter written to the Danbury (Conn.) Baptist Association Jan. 1, 1802, coined the metaphor, "a wall of separation between Church and State," to express a theory concerning interpretation of the religion clauses of the First Amendment: "Congress shall make no law respecting an establishment of religion or prohibiting the free exercise thereof."

The metaphor was cited for the first time in judicial proceedings in 1879, in the opinion by Chief Justice Waite in Reynolds v. United States. It did not, however, figure substantially in the decision.

Accepted as Rule

In 1947 the wall of separation gained acceptance as a constitutional rule, in the decision handed down in Everson v. Board of Education. Associate Justice Black, in describing the principles involved in the No Establishment Clause, wrote:

"Neither a state nor the Federal Government can set up a church. Neither can pass laws which aid one religion, aid all religions, or prefer one religion over another. Neither can force nor influence a person to go to or to remain away from church against his will or force him to profess a belief or disbelief in any religion. No person can be punished for entertaining or professing religious beliefs or disbeliefs, for church attendance or non-attendance. No tax in any amount, large or small, can be levied to support any religious

activities or institutions, whatever they may be called, or whatever form they may adopt to teach or practice religion. Neither a state nor the Federal Government can, openly or secretly, participate in the affairs of any religious organizations or groups and vice versa. In the words of Jefferson, the clause against establishment of religion by law was intended to erect 'a wall of separation between Church and State.' "

Mr. Black's associates agreed with his statement of principles, which were framed without reference to the Freedom of Exercise Clause. They disagreed, however, with respect to application of the principles, as the split decision in the case indicated. Five members of the Court held that the benefits of public welfare legislation — in this case, free bus transportation to school for parochial as well as public school students — did not run contrary to the concept of separation of Church and State embodied in the First Amendment.

Different Opinions

Inside and outside the legal profession, opinion is divided concerning the wall of separation and the balance of the religion clauses of the First Amendment.

The view of absolute separationists, carried to the extreme, would make government the adversary of religion. The bishops of the United States, following the McCollum decision in 1948, said that the wall metaphor had become for some persons the "shibboleth of doctrinaire secularism."

Proponents of governmental neutrality toward religion are of the opinion that such neutrality should not be so interpreted as to prohibit incidental aid to religious institutions providing secular services.

In the realm of practice, federal and state legislatures have enacted measures involving incidental benefits to religious bodies. Examples of such measures are the tax exemption of church property; provision of bus rides, book loans and lunch programs to students in church-related as well as public schools; military chaplaincies; loans to church-related hospitals; the financing of studies by military veterans at church-related colleges under GI bills of rights.

CHURCH TAX EXEMPTION

The exemption of church-owned property was ruled constitutional by the US Supreme Court May 4, 1970, in the case of Walz v. The Tax Commission of New York.

Suit in the case was brought by Frederick Walz, who purchased in June, 1967, a 22-by-29-foot plot of ground in Staten Island valued at $100 and taxable at $5.24 a year. Shortly after making the purchase, Walz instituted a suit in New York State, contending that the exemption of church property from taxation authorized by state law increased his own tax rate and forced him indirectly to support churches in violation of his constitutional right to freedom of religion under the First Amendment. Three New York courts dismissed the suit, which had been instituted by mail. The Supreme Court, judging that it had probable jurisdiction, then took the case.

In a 7-1 decision affecting Church-state relations in every state in the nation, the Court upheld the New York law under challenge.

For and Against

Chief Justice Warren E. Burger, who wrote the majority opinion, said that Congress from its earliest days had viewed the religion clauses of the Constitution as authorizing statutory real estate tax exemption to religious bodies. He declared: "Nothing in this national attitude toward religious tolerance and two centuries of uninterrupted freedom from taxation has given the remotest sign of leading to an established church or religion, and on the contrary it has operated affirmatively to help guarantee the free exercise of all forms of religious beliefs."

Justice William O. Douglas wrote in dissent that the involvement of government in religion as typified in tax exemption may seem inconsequential but: "It is, I fear, a long step down the establishment path. . . . Perhaps I have been misinformed. But, as I read the Constitution and the philosophy, I gathered that independence was the price of liberty."

Burger rejected Douglas' "establishment" fears. If tax exemption is the first step toward establishment, he said, "the second step has been long in coming."

The basic issue centered on the following question: Is there a contradiction between federal constitutional provisions against the establishment of religion, or the use of public funds for religious purposes, and state statutes exempting church property from taxation?

In the Walz' decision, the Supreme Court ruled that there is no contradiction.

Legal Background

The U.S. Constitution makes no reference to tax exemption.

There was no discussion of the issue in the Constitutional Convention nor in debates on the Bill of Rights.

In the Colonial and post-Revolutionary years, some churches had established status and were state-supported. This state of affairs changed with enactment of the First Amendment, which laid down no-establishment as the federal norm. This norm was adopted by the states which, however, exempted churches from tax liabilities.

No establishment, no hindrance, was the early American view of Church-state relationships.

This view, reflected in custom law, was not generally formulated in statute law until the second half of the 19th century, although specific tax exemption was provided for churches in Maryland in 1798, in Virginia in 1800, and in North Carolina in 1806.

The first major challenge to church property exemption was initiated by the Liberal League in the 1870's. It reached the point that President Grant included the recommendation in a State of the Union address in 1875, stating that church property should bear its own proportion of taxes. The plea fell on deaf ears in Congress, but there was some support for the idea at state levels. The exemption, however, continued to survive various challenges.

About 36 state constitutions contain either mandatory or permissive provisions for exemption. Statutes provide for exemption in all other states.

There has been considerable litigation challenging this special exemption, but most of it focused on whether a particular property satisfied statutory requirements. Few cases before Walz focused on the strictly constitutional question, whether directly under the First Amendment or indirectly under the Fourteenth Amendment.

Objectors to the tax exempt status of churches feel that churches should share, through taxation, in the cost of the ordinary benefits of public services they enjoy, and/or that the amount of "aid" enjoyed through exemption should be proportionate to the amount of social good they do.

According to one opinion, exemption is said to weaken the independence of churches from the political system which benefits them by exemption.

In another view, exemption is said to involve the government in decisions regarding what is and what is not religion.

Unrelated Income

Taxation of the unrelated business income of churches is a different matter. In a joint statement on this subject issued in May, 1969, the U.S. Catholic Conference and the National Council of Churches said they favored "elimination of the specific exemption of churches from taxation on income from regularly conducted commercial business activi-

ties which are unrelated to their exempt functions."

The two groups prefaced the statement with the observation:

"Under existing law many types of organizations are granted exemption from the income tax. Certain exempt organizations, including charitable, educational and some religious organizations, labor unions, business leagues, etc., are nevertheless subjected to tax upon their incomes from any unrelated business; and rents derived from debt-financed property (under leases for periods in excess of five years) are included in unrelated business taxable income.

"The tax upon unrelated business taxable income does not apply to churches, or conventions or associations of churches.

"Such exemption makes available to churches a potential advantage over taxpaying organizations engaged in commercial business activities."

CHARISMATIC RENEWAL

(Written with the assistance of the staff of the Service Committee of the Catholic Charismatic Renewal of the U.S.)

The movement originated with a handful of Duquesne University students and faculty members in the 1966-67 academic year and spread from there to Notre Dame, Michigan State University, the University of Michigan and to other campuses and cities throughout the country.

According to a Gallup poll reported in the Feb. 22, 1980, issue of *Christianity Today,* 18 per cent of adult Catholics in the U.S. — nearly 6 million — considered themselves charismatic. More than 4,660 U.S. groups are listed in the latest issue of the *International Directory of Catholic Charismatic Prayer Groups.* Findings of a survey conducted by Father Kenneth Metz of the Archdiocese of Milwaukee and reported in August, 1981, estimated that there were 6,364 Catholic charismatic prayer groups in the U.S. Some 13,000 persons attended the 1982 annual national conference at the University of Notre Dame.

The movement is strong in Canada and some 110 other countries, probably involving more than a million participants. Many Catholics participated in a major ecumenical charismatic conference in May, 1982, in Strasbourg, France. The Catholic charismatic renewal is growing rapidly in South America, with some countries having more than 1,000 prayer groups. A large number of Latin American bishops are active in the renewal.

Keys to the Movement

Scriptural keys to the renewal are:
• Christ's promise to send the Holy Spirit upon the Apostles;
• the description, in the Acts of the Apostles, of the effects of the coming of the

Holy Spirit upon the Apostles on Pentecost;
• St. Paul's explanation, in the Letter to the Romans, of the charismatic gifts (for the good of the Church and persons) the Holy Spirit would bestow on Christians;
• New Testament evidence concerning the effects of charismatic gifts in and through the early Church.

The personal key to the renewal is baptism of the Holy Spirit. This is not a new sacrament but the personally experienced actualization of grace already sacramentally received.

The experience of baptism of the Holy Spirit is often accompanied by the reception of one or more charismatic gifts.

Among the movement's strongest points of emphasis are prayer, openness to the Holy Spirit, community experience and the sharing of spiritual gifts.

The characteristic form of the renewal is the weekly prayer meeting, a gathering which includes periods of spontaneous prayer, singing, sharing of experience and testimony, fellowship and teaching.

Father Fio Mascarenhas, S.J., is director of the movement's International Communication Office, Via Feruccio, 19, 00185 Rome, Italy. Kevin M. Ranaghan is executive director of the National Service Committee, 237 N. Michigan St., South Bend, Ind. 46601. Auxiliary Bishop Joseph McKinney of Grand Rapids is episcopal consultant to the National Service Committee.

Cardinal Leo Suenens resigned early in 1982 as episcopal advisor to the movement's international office and council.

It was estimated during the summer of 1982 that only about 20 per cent of the charismatic renewal communities in the world had members of different faiths.

The organizational structure of the Catholic Church in the United States consists of 33 provinces with as many archdioceses (metropolitan sees), 140 suffragan sees (dioceses), two jurisdictions immediately subject to the Holy See (the Eparchy of St. Maron for the Maronites and the Melkite Eparchy of Newton), an apostolic exarchate for Chaldean-Rite Catholics and the Military Ordinariate. An Armenian-Rite apostolic exarchate for the United States and Canada has its seat in New York. Each of these jurisdictions is under the direction of an archbishop or bishop, called an ordinary, who has apostolic responsibility and authority for the pastoral service of the people in his care.

The structure includes the territorial episcopal conference known as the National Conference of Catholic Bishops. In and through this body, which is strictly ecclesiastical and has defined juridical authority, the bishops exercise their collegiate pastorate over the Church in the entire country (see Index).

Related to the NCCB is the United States Catholic Conference, a civil corporation and operational secretariat through which the bishops, in cooperation with other members of the Church, act on a wider-than-ecclesiastical scale for the good of the Church and society in the United States (see Index).

The representative of the Holy See to the Church in this country is an Apostolic Delegate.

ECCLESIASTICAL PROVINCES

(Sources: *The Official Catholic Directory,* NC News Service.)

The 33 ecclesiastical provinces bear the names of archdioceses, i.e., of metropolitan sees.

Anchorage: Archdiocese of Anchorage and suffragan sees of Fairbanks, Juneau. Geographical area: Alaska.

Atlanta: Archdiocese of Atlanta (Ga.) and suffragan sees of Savannah (Ga.), Charlotte and Raleigh (N.C.), Charleston (S.C.). Geographical area: Georgia, North Carolina, South Carolina.

Baltimore: Archdiocese of Baltimore (Md.) and suffragan sees of Wilmington (Del.), Arlington and Richmond (Va.), Wheeling-Charleston (W. Va.). Geographical area: Maryland (except five counties), Delaware, Virginia, West Virginia.

Boston: Archdiocese of Boston (Mass.) and suffragan sees of Fall River, Springfield and Worcester (Mass.), Portland (Me.), Manchester (N.H.), Burlington (Vt.). Geographical area: Massachusetts, Maine, New Hampshire, Vermont.

Chicago: Archdiocese of Chicago and suffragan sees of Belleville, Joliet, Peoria, Rockford, Springfield. Geographical area: Illinois.

Cincinnati: Archdiocese of Cincinnati and suffragan sees of Cleveland, Columbus, Steubenville, Toledo, Youngstown. Geographical area: Ohio.

Denver: Archdiocese of Denver (Colo.) and suffragan sees of Pueblo (Colo.), Cheyenne (Wyo.). Geographical area: Colorado, Wyoming.

Detroit: Archdiocese of Detroit and suffragan sees of Gaylord, Grand Rapids, Kalamazoo, Lansing, Marquette, Saginaw. Geographical area: Michigan.

Dubuque: Archdiocese of Dubuque and suffragan sees of Davenport, Des Moines, Sioux City. Geographical area: Iowa.

Hartford: Archdiocese of Hartford (Conn.) and suffragan sees of Bridgeport and Norwich (Conn.), Providence (R.I.). Geographical area: Connecticut, Rhode Island.

Indianapolis: Archdiocese of Indianapolis and suffragan sees of Evansville, Fort Wayne-South Bend, Gary, Lafayette. Geographical area: Indiana.

Kansas City (Kans.): Archdiocese of Kansas City and suffragan sees of Dodge City, Salina, Wichita. Geographical area: Kansas.

Los Angeles: Archdiocese of Los Angeles and suffragan sees of Fresno, Monterey, Orange, San Bernardino, San Diego. Geographical area: Southern and Central California.

Louisville: Archdiocese of Louisville (Ky.) and suffragan sees of Covington and Owensboro (Ky.), Memphis and Nashville (Tenn.). Geographical area: Kentucky, Tennessee.

Miami: Archdiocese of Miami and suffragan sees of Orlando, Pensacola-Tallahassee, St. Augustine, St. Petersburg. Geographical area: Florida.

Milwaukee: Archdiocese of Milwaukee and suffragan sees of Green Bay, La Crosse, Madison, Superior. Geographical area: Wisconsin.

Mobile: Archdiocese of Mobile, Ala., and suffragan sees of Birmingham (Ala.) and Biloxi and Jackson (Miss.). Geographical area: Alabama, Mississippi.

Newark: Archdiocese of Newark and suffragan sees of Camden, Metuchen, Paterson, Trenton. Geographical area: New Jersey.

New Orleans: Archdiocese of New Orleans and suffragan sees of Alexandria-Shreveport, Baton Rouge, Houma-Thibodaux, Lafayette and Lake Charles. Geographical area: Louisiana.

New York: Archdiocese of New York and suffragan sees of Albany, Brooklyn, Buffalo, Ogdensburg, Rochester, Rockville Centre, Syracuse. Geographical area: New York.

Oklahoma City: Archdiocese of Oklahoma City (Okla.) and suffragan sees of Tulsa

(Okla.) and Little Rock (Ark.). Geographical area: Oklahoma, Arkansas.

Omaha: Archdiocese of Omaha and suffragan sees of Grand Island, Lincoln. Geographical area: Nebraska.

Philadelphia: Archdiocese of Philadelphia and suffragan sees of Allentown, Altoona-Johnstown, Erie, Greensburg, Harrisburg, Pittsburgh, Scranton. Geographical area: Pennsylvania.

Philadelphia (Byzantine Rite): Metropolitan See of Philadelphia (Byzantine Rite) and Eparchies of St. Nicholas of the Ukrainians in Chicago and Stamford, Conn. The jurisdiction extends to all Ukrainian Catholics in the U.S. from the ecclesiastical province of Galicia in the Ukraine.

Pittsburgh (Byzantine Rite): Metropolitan See of Pittsburgh, Pa. and Eparchies of Passaic (N.J.), Parma (Ohio), Van Nuys (Calif.).

Portland: Archdiocese of Portland (Ore.) and suffragan sees of Baker (Ore.), Boise (Ida.), Great Falls-Billings and Helena (Mont.). Geographical area: Oregon, Idaho, Montana.

St. Louis: Archdiocese of St. Louis and suffragan sees of Jefferson City, Kansas City-St. Joseph, Springfield-Cape Girardeau. Geographical area: Missouri.

St. Paul and Minneapolis: Archdiocese of St. Paul and Minneapolis (Minn.) and suf-fragan sees of Crookston, Duluth, New Ulm, St. Cloud and Winona (Minn.), Bismarck and Fargo (N.D.), Rapid City and Sioux Falls (S.D.). Geographical area: Minnesota, North Dakota, South Dakota.

San Antonio: Archdiocese of San Antonio (Tex.) and suffragan sees of Amarillo, Austin, Beaumont, Brownsville, Corpus Christi, Dallas, Fort Worth, Galveston-Houston, San Angelo and Victoria (Tex.). Geographical area: Texas (except the Diocese of El Paso).

San Francisco: Archdiocese of San Francisco (Calif.) and suffragan sees of Oakland, Sacramento, San Jose, Santa Rosa and Stockton (Calif.), Agaña (Guam), Honolulu (Hawaii), Reno-Las Vegas (Nev.), Salt Lake City (Utah). Geographical area: Northern California, Nevada, Utah, Hawaii, Guam, the Marianas Islands and Ryukyus Islands.

Santa Fe: Archdiocese of Santa Fe (N.M.) and suffragan sees of Gallup (N.M.), Phoenix and Tucson (Ariz.), El Paso (Tex.). Geographical area: New Mexico, Arizona, Diocese of El Paso (Tex.).

Seattle: Archdiocese of Seattle and suffragan sees of Spokane, Yakima. Geographical area: Washington.

Washington: Archdiocese of Washington, D.C., and suffragan see of St. Thomas (Virgin Islands). Geographical area: District of Columbia, five counties of Maryland, Virgin Islands.

ARCHDIOCESES, DIOCESES, ARCHBISHOPS, BISHOPS

(Sources: *The Official Catholic Directory;* NC News Service. As of Aug. 1, 1982.)

Information includes name of diocese, year of foundation (as it appears on the official document erecting the see), present ordinaries and auxiliaries (for biographies, see Index), former ordinaries.

Archdioceses are indicated by an asterisk.

Albany, N.Y. (1847): Howard J. Hubbard, bishop, 1977.

Former bishops: John McCloskey, 1847-64; John J. Conroy, 1865-77; Francis McNeirny, 1877-94; Thomas M. Burke, 1894-1915; Thomas F. Cusack, 1915-18; Edmund F. Gibbons, 1919-54; William A. Scully, 1954-69; Edwin B. Broderick, 1969-76.

Alexandria-Shreveport, La. (1853): Vacant as of Aug. 1, 1982. William B. Friend, auxiliary.

Established at Natchitoches, transferred to Alexandria 1910; present title 1977.

Former bishops: Augustus M. Martin, 1853-75; Francis X. Leray, 1877-79, administrator, 1879-83; Anthony Durier, 1885-1904; Cornelius Van de Ven, 1904-32; D. F. Desmond, 1933-45; Charles P. Greco, 1946-73; Lawrence P. Graves, 1973-82.

Allentown, Pa. (1961): Joseph M. McShea, bishop, 1961.

Altoona-Johnstown, Pa. (1901): James J. Hogan, bishop, 1966.

Established as Altoona, name changed, 1957.

Former bishops: Eugene A. Garvey, 1901-20; John J. McCort, 1920-36; Richard T. Guilfoyle, 1936-57; Howard J. Carroll, 1958-60; J. Carroll McCormick, 1960-66.

Amarillo, Tex. (1926): Leroy T. Matthiesen, bishop, 1980.

Former bishops; Rudolph A. Gerken, 1927-33; Robert E. Lucey, 1934-41; Laurence J. Fitzsimon, 1941-58; John L. Morkovsky, 1958-63; Lawrence M. De Falco, 1963-79.

Anchorage,* Alaska (1966): Francis T. Hurley, archbishop, 1976.

Former archbishop: Joseph T. Ryan, 1966-75.

Arlington, Va. (1974): Thomas J. Welsh, bishop, 1974.

Atlanta,* Ga. (1956; archdiocese, 1962): Thomas A. Donnellan, archbishop, 1968.

Former ordinaries: Francis E. Hyland, 1956-61; Paul J. Hallinan, first archbishop, 1962-68.

Austin, Tex. (1947): Vincent M. Harris, bishop, 1971.

Former bishop: Louis J. Reicher, 1947-71.

Baker, Ore. (1903): Thomas J. Connolly, bishop, 1971.

Established as Baker City, name changed, 1952.

Former bishops: Charles J. O'Reilly, 1903-

18; Joseph F. McGrath, 1919-50; Francis P. Leipzig, 1950-71.

Baltimore,* Md. (1789; archdiocese, 1808): William D. Borders, archbishop, 1974. T. Austin Murphy, P. Francis Murphy, J. Francis Stafford, auxiliaries.

Former ordinaries: John Carroll, 1789-1815, first archbishop; Leonard Neale, 1815-17; Ambrose Marechal, S.S., 1817-28; James Whitfield, 1828-34; Samuel Eccleston, S.S., 1834-51; Francis P. Kenrick, 1851-63; Martin J. Spalding, 1864-72; James R. Bayley, 1872-77; Cardinal James Gibbons, 1877-1921; Michael J. Curley, 1921-47; Francis P. Keough, 1947-61, Cardinal Lawrence J. Shehan, 1961-74.

Baton Rouge, La. (1961): Joseph V. Sullivan, bishop, 1974.

Former bishop: Robert E. Tracy, 1961-74.

Beaumont, Tex. (1966): Bernard J. Ganter, bishop, 1977.

Former bishops: Vincent M. Harris, 1966-71; Warren L. Boudreaux, 1971-77.

Belleville, Ill. (1887): John N. Wurm, bishop, 1981. Stanley G. Schlarman, auxiliary.

Former bishops: John Janssen, 1888-1913; Henry Althoff, 1914-47; Albert R. Zuroweste, 1948-76; William M. Cosgrove, 1976-81.

Biloxi, Miss. (1977): (Joseph) Lawson E. Howze, bishop, 1977.

Birmingham, Ala. (1969): Joseph G. Vath, bishop, 1969.

Bismarck, N. Dak. (1909): John F. Kinney, bishop, 1982.

Former bishops: Vincent Wehrle, O.S.B., 1910-39; Vincent J. Ryan, 1940-51; Lambert A. Hoch, 1952-56; Hilary B. Hacker, 1957-82.

Boise, Ida. (1893): Sylvester Treinen, bishop, 1962.

Former bishops: Alphonse J. Glorieux, 1893-1917; Daniel M. Gorman, 1918-27; Edward J. Kelly, 1928-56; James J. Byrne, 1956-62.

Boston,* Mass. (1808; archdiocese, 1875): Cardinal Humberto S. Medeiros, archbishop, 1970. Lawrence J. Riley, Thomas V. Dailey, John M. D'Arcy, John J. Mulcahy, Daniel A. Hart, Alfred C. Hughes, auxiliaries.

Former ordinaries: John L. de Cheverus, 1810-23; Benedict J. Fenwick, S.J., 1825-46; John B. Fitzpatrick, 1846-66; John J. Williams, 1866-1907, first archbishop; Cardinal William O'Connell, 1907-44; Cardinal Richard Cushing, 1944-70.

Bridgeport, Conn. (1953): Walter W. Curtis, bishop, 1961.

Former bishop: Lawrence J. Shehan, 1953-61.

Brooklyn, N.Y. (1853): Francis J. Mugavero, bishop, 1968. Anthony Bevilacqua, Joseph M. Sullivan, Rene Valero, auxiliaries.

Former bishops: John Loughlin, 1853-91; Charles E. McDonnell, 1892-1921; Thomas

E. Molloy, 1921-56; Bryan J. McEntegart, 1957-68.

Brownsville, Tex. (1965): John J. Fitzpatrick, bishop, 1971.

Former bishops: Adolph Marx, 1965; Humberto S. Medeiros, 1966-70.

Buffalo, N.Y. (1847): Edward D. Head, bishop, 1973. Pius A. Benincasa, Bernard J. McLaughlin, auxiliaries.

Former bishops: John Timon, C.M., 1847-67; Stephen V. Ryan, C.M., 1868-96; James E. Quigley, 1897-1903; Charles H. Colton, 1903-15; Dennis J. Dougherty, 1915-18; William Turner, 1919-36; John A. Duffy, 1937-44; John F. O'Hara, C.S.C., 1945-51; Joseph A. Burke, 1952-62; James McNulty, 1963-72.

Burlington, Vt. (1853): John A. Marshall, bishop, 1972.

Former bishops: Louis De Goesbriand, 1853-99; John S. Michaud, 1899-1908; Joseph J. Rice, 1910-38; Matthew F. Brady, 1938-44; Edward F. Ryan, 1945-56; Robert F. Joyce, 1957-71.

Camden, N.J. (1937): George H. Guilfoyle, bishop, 1968. James L. Schad, auxiliary.

Former bishops: Bartholomew J. Eustace, 1938-56; Justin J. McCarthy, 1957-59; Celestine J. Damiano, 1960-67.

Charleston, S.C. (1820): Ernest L. Unterkoefler, bishop, 1964.

Former bishops: John England, 1820-42; Ignatius W. Reynolds, 1844-55; Patrick N. Lynch, 1858-82; Henry P. Northrop, 1883-1916; William T. Russell, 1917-27; Emmet M. Walsh, 1927-49; John J. Russell, 1950-58; Paul J. Hallinan, 1958-62; Francis F. Reh, 1962-64.

Charlotte, N.C. (1971): Michael J. Begley, bishop, 1972.

Cheyenne, Wyo. (1887): Joseph Hart, bishop, 1978.

Former bishops: Maurice F. Burke, 1887-93; Thomas M. Lenihan, 1897-1901; James J. Keane, 1902-11; Patrick A. McGovern, 1912-51; Hubert M. Newell, 1951-78.

Chicago,* Ill. (1843; archdiocese, 1880): Joseph L. Bernardin, archbishop, 1982. Alfred L. Abramowicz, Nevin W. Hayes, O. Carm., auxiliaries.

Former ordinaries: William Quarter, 1844-48; James O. Van de Velde, S.J., 1849-53; Anthony O'Regan, 1854-58; James Duggan, 1859-70; Thomas P. Foley, administrator, 1870-79; Patrick A. Feehan, 1880-1902, first archbishop; James E. Quigley, 1903-15; Cardinal George Mundelein, 1915-39; Cardinal Samuel Stritch, 1939-58; Cardinal Albert Meyer, 1958-65; Cardinal John Cody, 1965-82.

Cincinnati,* Ohio (1821; archdiocese, 1850): Vacant as of Aug. 1, 1982. Nicholas Elko (titular archbishop), Daniel E. Pilarczyk, auxiliaries.

Former ordinaries: Edward D. Fenwick,

O.P., 1822-32; John B. Purcell, 1833-83, first archbishop; William H. Elder, 1883-1904; Henry Moeller, 1904-1925; John T. McNicholas, O.P., 1925-50; Karl J. Alter, 1950-69; Paul F. Leibold, 1969-72; Joseph L. Bernardin, 1972-82.

Cleveland, Ohio (1847): Anthony M. Pilla, bishop, 1980. Gilbert I. Sheldon, James P. Lyke, O.F.M., James A. Griffin, A. Edward Pevec, auxiliaries.

Former bishops: L. Amadeus Rappe, 1847-70; Richard Gilmour, 1872-91; Ignatius F. Horstmann, 1892-1908; John P. Farrelly, 1909-21; Joseph Schrembs, 1921-45; Edward F. Hoban, 1945-66; Clarence G. Issenmann, 1966-74; James A. Hickey, 1974-80.

Columbus, Ohio (1868): Edward J. Herrmann, bishop, 1973. George A. Fulcher, auxiliary.

Former bishops: Sylvester H. Rosecrans, 1868-78; John A. Watterson, 1880-99; Henry Moeller, 1900-03; James J. Hartley, 1904-44; Michael J. Ready, 1944-57; Clarence Issenmann, 1957-64; John J. Carberry, 1965-68; Clarence E. Elwell, 1968-73.

Corpus Christi, Tex. (1912): Thomas J. Drury, bishop, 1965.

Former bishops: Paul J. Nussbaum, C.P., 1913-20; Emmanuel B. Ledvina, 1921-49; Mariano S. Garriga, 1949-65.

Covington, Ky. (1853): William A. Hughes, bishop, 1979.

Former bishops: George A. Carrell, S.J., 1853-68; Augustus M. Toebbe, 1870-84; Camillus P. Maes, 1885-1914; Ferdinand Brossart, 1916-23; Francis W. Howard, 1923-44; William T. Mulloy, 1945-59; Richard Ackerman, C.S.Sp., 1960-78.

Crookston, Minn. (1909): Victor Balke, bishop, 1976.

Former bishops: Timothy Corbett, 1910-38; John H. Peschges, 1938-44; Francis J. Schenk, 1945-60; Laurence A. Glenn, 1960-70; Kenneth J. Povish, 1970-75.

Dallas, Tex. (1890): Thomas Tschoepe, bishop, 1969.

Established 1890, as Dallas, title changed to Dallas-Ft. Worth 1953; redesignated Dallas, 1969, when Ft. Worth was made diocese.

Former bishops: Thomas F. Brennan, 1891-92; Edward J. Dunne, 1893-1910; Joseph P. Lynch, 1911-54; Thomas K. Gorman, 1954-69.

Davenport, Ia. (1881): Gerald F. O'Keefe, bishop, 1966.

Former bishops: John McMullen, 1881-83; Henry Cosgrove, 1884-1906; James Davis, 1906-26; Henry P. Rohlman, 1927-44; Ralph L. Hayes, 1944-66.

Denver,* Colo. (1887; archdiocese, 1941): James V. Casey, archbishop, 1967. George R. Evans, Richard C. Hanifen, auxiliaries.

Former ordinaries: Joseph P. Machebeuf, 1887-89; Nicholas C. Matz, 1889-1917; J.

Henry Tihen, 1917-31; Urban J. Vehr, 1931-67, first archbishop.

Des Moines, Ia. (1911): Maurice J. Dingman, bishop, 1968.

Former bishops: Austin Dowling, 1912-19; Thomas W. Drumm, 1919-33; Gerald T. Bergan, 1934-48; Edward C. Daly, O.P., 1948-64; George J. Biskup, 1965-67.

Detroit,* Mich. (1833; archdiocese, 1937): Edmund C. Szoka, archbishop, 1981. Thomas J. Gumbleton, Walter J. Schoenherr, auxiliaries.

Former ordinaries: Frederic Rese, 1833-71; Peter P. Lefevere, administrator, 1841-69; Caspar H. Borgess, 1871-88; John S. Foley, 1888-1918; Michael J. Gallagher, 1918-37; Cardinal Edward Mooney, 1937-58, first archbishop; Cardinal John F. Dearden, 1958-80.

Dodge City, Kans. (1951): Eugene J. Gerber, bishop, 1976.

Former bishops: John B. Franz, 1951-59; Marion F. Forst, 1960-76.

Dubuque,* Iowa (1837; archdiocese, 1893): James J. Byrne, archbishop, 1962. Francis J. Dunn, auxiliary.

Former ordinaries: Mathias Loras, 1837-58; Clement Smyth, O.C.S.O., 1858-65; John Hennessy, 1866-1900, first archbishop; John J. Keane, 1900-11; James J. Keane, 1911-29; Francis J. Beckman, 1930-46; Henry P. Rohlman, 1946-54; Leo Binz, 1954-61.

Duluth, Minn. (1889): Vacant as of Aug. 30, 1982.

Former bishops: James McGolrick, 1889-1918; John T. McNicholas, O.P., 1918-25; Thomas A. Welch, 1926-59; Francis J. Schenk, 1960-69; Paul F. Anderson, 1969-82.

El Paso, Tex. (1914): Raymond J. Pena, bishop, 1980.

Former bishops: Anthony J. Schuler, S.J., 1915-42; Sidney M. Metzger, 1942-78. Patrick F. Flores, 1978-79.

Erie, Pa. (1853): Michael J. Murphy, bishop, 1982.

Former bishops: Michael O'Connor, 1853-54; Josue M. Young, 1854-66; Tobias Mullen, 1868-99; John E. Fitzmaurice, 1899-1920; John M. Gannon, 1920-66; John F. Whealon, 1966-69; Alfred M. Watson, 1969-82.

Evansville, Ind. (1944): Francis Raymond Shea, bishop, 1970.

Former bishops: Henry J. Grimmelsman, 1944-65; Paul F. Leibold, 1966-69.

Fairbanks, Alaska (1962): Robert L. Whelan, S.J., bishop, 1968.

Former bishop: Francis D. Gleeson, S.J., 1962-68.

Fall River, Mass. (1904): Daniel A. Cronin, bishop, 1970.

Former bishops: William Stang, 1904-07; Daniel F. Feehan, 1907-34; James E. Cassidy, 1934-51; James L. Connolly, 1951-70.

Fargo, N. Dak. (1889): Justin A. Driscoll, bishop, 1970.

Established at Jamestown, transferred, 1897.

Former bishops: John Shanley, 1889-1909; James O'Reilly, 1910-34; Aloysius J. Muench, 1935-59; Leo F. Dworschak, 1960-70.

Fort Wayne-South Bend, Ind. (1857): William E. McManus, bishop, 1976. Joseph R. Crowley, auxiliary.

Established as Fort Wayne, name changed, 1960.

Former bishops: John H. Luers, 1858-71; Joseph Dwenger, C.Pp. S., 1872-93; Joseph Rademacher, 1893-1900; Herman J. Alerding, 1900-24; John F. Noll, 1925-56; Leo A. Pursley, 1957-76.

Fort Worth, Tex. (1969): Joseph P. Delaney, bishop, 1981.

Former bishop: John J. Cassata, 1969-80.

Fresno, Calif. (1967): Joseph J. Madera, M.Sp.S., bishop, 1980.

Formerly Monterey-Fresno, 1922.

Former bishops (Monterey-Fresno): John J. Cantwell, administrator, 1922-24; John B. MacGinley, first bishop, 1924-32; Philip G. Sher, 1933-53; Aloysius J. Willinger, 1953-67.

Former bishops (Fresno): Timothy Manning, 1967-69; Hugh A. Donohoe, 1969-80.

Gallup, N. Mex. (1939): Jerome J. Hastrich, bishop, 1969.

Former bishop: Bernard T. Espelage, O.F.M., 1940-69.

Galveston-Houston, Tex. (1847): John L. Morkovsky, bishop, 1975. John E. McCarthy, auxiliary.

Established as Galveston, name changed, 1959.

Former bishops: John M. Odin, C.M., 1847-61; Claude M. Dubuis, 1862-92; Nicholas A. Gallagher, 1892-1918; Christopher E. Byrne, 1918-50; Wendelin J. Nold, 1950-75.

Gary, Ind. (1956): Andrew G. Grutka, bishop, 1957.

Gaylord, Mich. (1971): Robert J. Rose, bishop, 1981.

Former bishop: Edmund C. Szoka, 1971-81.

Grand Island, Neb. (1912): Lawrence McNamara, bishop, 1978.

Established at Kearney, transferred, 1917.

Former bishops: James A. Duffy, 1913-31; Stanislaus V. Bona, 1932-44; Edward J. Hunkeler, 1945-51; John L. Paschang, 1951-72; John J. Sullivan, 1972-77.

Grand Rapids, Mich. (1882): Joseph M. Breitenbeck, bishop, 1969. Joseph C. McKinney, auxiliary.

Former bishops: Henry J. Richter, 1883-1916; Michael J. Gallagher, 1916-18; Edward D. Kelly, 1919-26; Joseph G. Pinten, 1926-40; Joseph C. Plagens, 1941-43; Francis J. Haas, 1943-53; Allen J. Babcock, 1954-69.

Great Falls-Billings, Mont. (1904): Thomas J. Murphy, bishop, 1978.

Established as Great Falls; name changed, 1980.

Former bishops: Mathias C. Lenihan, 1904-30; Edwin V. O'Hara, 1930-39; William J. Condon, 1939-67; Eldon B. Schuster, 1968-77.

Green Bay, Wis. (1868): Aloysius J. Wycislo, bishop, 1968. Robert F. Morneau, auxiliary.

Former bishops: Joseph Melcher, 1868-73; Francis X. Krautbauer, 1875-85; Frederick X. Katzer, 1886-91; Sebastian G. Messmer, 1892-1903; Joseph J. Fox, 1904-14; Paul P. Rhode, 1915-45; Stanislaus V. Bona, 1945-67.

Greensburg, Pa. (1951): William G. Connare, bishop, 1960. Norbert F. Gaughan, auxiliary.

Former bishop: Hugh L. Lamb, 1951-59.

Harrisburg, Pa. (1868): Joseph T. Daley, bishop, 1971. William H. Keeler, auxiliary.

Former bishops: Jeremiah F. Shanahan, 1868-86; Thomas McGovern, 1888-98; John W. Shanahan,1899-1916; Philip R. McDevitt, 1916-35; George L. Leech, 1935-71.

Hartford,* Conn. (1843; archdiocese, 1953): John F. Whealon, archbishop, 1969. John F. Hackett, Peter A. Rosazza, auxiliaries.

Former ordinaries: William Tyler, 1844-49; Bernard O'Reilly, 1850-56; F. P. MacFarland, 1858-74; Thomas Galberry, O.S.A., 1876-78; Lawrence S. McMahon, 1879-93; Michael Tierney, 1894-1908; John J. Nilan, 1910-34; Maurice F. McAuliffe, 1934-44; Henry J. O'Brien, 1945-68, first archbishop.

Helena, Mont. (1884): Elden F. Curtiss, bishop, 1976.

Former bishops: John B. Brondel, 1884-1903; John P. Carroll, 1904-25; George J. Finnigan, C.S.C., 1927-32; Ralph L. Hayes, 1933-35; Joseph M. Gilmore, 1936-62; Raymond Hunthausen, 1962-75.

Honolulu, Hawaii (1941): Joseph A. Ferrario, bishop, 1982.

Former bishops: James J. Sweeney, 1941-68; John J. Scanlan, 1968-81.

Houma-Thibodaux, La. (1977): Warren L. Boudreaux, bishop, 1977.

Indianapolis,* Ind. (1834; archdiocese, 1944): Edward T. O'Meara, archbishop, 1980.

Established at Vincennes, transferred, 1898.

Former ordinaries: Simon G. Bruté, 1834-39; Celestine de la Hailandiere, 1839-47; John S. Bazin, 1847-48; Maurice de St. Palais, 1849-77; Francis S. Chatard, 1878-1918; Joseph Chartrand, 1918-33; Joseph E. Ritter, 1934-46, first archbishop; Paul C. Schulte, 1946-70; George J. Biskup, 1970-79.

Jackson, Miss. (1837): Joseph B. Brunini, bishop, 1968. William R. Houck, auxiliary.

Established at Natchez; title changed to Natchez-Jackson, 1956; transferred to Jackson, 1977 (Natchez made titular see).

Former bishops: John J. Chanche, S.S., 1841-52; James Van de Velde, S.J., 1853-55;

William H. Elder, 1857-80; Francis A. Jansens, 1881-88; Thomas Heslin, 1889-1911; John E. Gunn, S.M., 1911-24; Richard O. Gerow, 1924-67.

Jefferson City, Mo. (1956): Michael F. McAuliffe, bishop, 1969.

Former bishop: Joseph Marling, C.Pp.S., 1956-69.

Joliet, Ill. (1948): Joseph I. Imesch, bishop, 1979. Raymond J. Vonesh, Daniel L. Ryan, auxiliaries.

Former bishop: Martin D. McNamara, 1949-66. Romeo Blanchette, 1966-79.

Juneau, Alaska (1951): Michael H. Kenny, bishop, 1979.

Former bishops: Dermot O'Flanagan, 1951-68; Joseph T. Ryan, administrator, 1968-71; Francis T. Hurley, 1971-76, administrator, 1976-79.

Kalamazoo, Mich. (1971): Paul V. Donovan, bishop, 1971.

Kansas City,* Kans. (1877; archdiocese, 1952): Ignatius J. Strecker, archbishop, 1969. Marion F. Forst, auxiliary.

Established as vicariate apostolic, 1850, became Diocese of Leavenworth, 1877, transferred to Kansas City 1947.

Former ordinaries: J. B. Miege, vicar apostolic, 1851-74; Louis M. Fink, O.S.B., vicar apostolic, 1874-77, first bishop, 1877-1904; Thomas F. Lillis, 1904-10; John Ward, 1910-29; Francis Johannes, 1929-37; Paul C. Schulte, 1937-46; George J. Donnelly, 1946-50; Edward Hunkeler, 1951-69, first archbishop.

Kansas City-St. Joseph, Mo. (Kansas City, 1880; St. Joseph, 1868; united 1956): John J. Sullivan, bishop, 1977. George K. Fitzsimons, auxiliary.

Former bishops: John J. Hogan, 1880-1913; Thomas F. Lillis, 1913-38; Edwin V. O'Hara, 1939-56; John P. Cody, 1956-61; Charles H. Helmsing, 1962-77.

Former bishops (St. Joseph): John J. Hogan, 1868-80, administrator, 1880-93; Maurice F. Burke, 1893-1923; Francis Gilfillan, 1923-33; Charles H. Le Blond, 1933-56.

La Crosse, Wis. (1868): Frederick W. Freking, bishop, 1965. John J. Paul, auxiliary.

Former bishops: Michael Heiss, 1868-80; Kilian C. Flasch, 1881-91; James Schwebach, 1892-1921; Alexander J. McGavick, 1921-48; John P. Treacy, 1948-64.

Lafayette, Ind. (1944): Raymond J. Gallagher, bishop, 1965.

Former bishops: John G. Bennett, 1944-57; John J. Carberry, 1957-65.

Lafayette, La. (1918): Gerard L. Frey, bishop, 1973.

Former bishops: Jules B. Jeanmard, 1918-56; Maurice Schexnayder, 1956-72.

Lake Charles, La. (1980): Jude Speyrer, bishop, 1980.

Lansing, Mich. (1937): Kenneth J. Povish, bishop, 1975. James Sullivan, auxiliary.

Former bishops: Joseph H. Albers, 1937-65; Alexander Zaleski, 1965-75.

Lincoln, Neb. (1887): Glennon P. Flavin, bishop, 1967.

Former bishops: Thomas Bonacum, 1887-1911; J. Henry Tihen, 1911-17; Charles J. O'Reilly, 1918-23; Francis J. Beckman, 1924-30; Louis B. Kucera, 1930-57; James V. Casey, 1957-67.

Little Rock, Ark. (1843): Andrew J. McDonald, bishop, 1972.

Former bishops: Andrew Byrne, 1844-62; Edward Fitzgerald, 1867-1907; John Morris, 1907-46; Albert L. Fletcher, 1946-72.

Los Angeles,* Calif. (1840; archdiocese, 1936): Cardinal Timothy Manning, archbishop, 1970. John J. Ward, Juan A. Arzube, auxiliaries.

Former ordinaries: Francisco Garcia Diego y Moreno, O.F.M., 1840-46; Joseph S. Alemany, O.P., 1850-53; Thaddeus Amat, C.M., 1854-78; Francis Mora, 1878-96; George T. Montgomery, 1896-1903; Thomas J. Conaty, 1903-15; John J. Cantwell, 1917-47, first archbishop; Cardinal James McIntyre, 1948-70.

Louisville,* Ky. (1808; archdiocese, 1937): Thomas C Kelly, O.P., archbishop, 1982. Charles G. Maloney, auxiliary.

Established at Bardstown, transferred, 1841.

Former ordinaries: Benedict J. Flaget, S.S. 1810-32; John B. David, S.S., 1832-33; Benedict J. Flaget, S.S., 1833-50; Martin J. Spalding, 1850-64; Peter J. Lavialle, 1865-67; William G. McCloskey, 1868-1909; Denis O'Donaghue, 1910-24; John A. Floersh, 1924-67, first archbishop; Thomas J. McDonough, 1967-81.

Madison, Wis. (1946): Cletus F. O'Donnell, bishop, 1967. George O. Wirz, auxiliary.

Former bishop: William P. O'Connor, 1946-67.

Manchester, N.H. (1884): Odore J. Gendron, bishop, 1974. Robert Mulvee, auxiliary.

Former bishops: Denis M. Bradley, 1884-1903; John B. Delany, 1904-06; George A. Guertin, 1907-32; John B. Peterson, 1932-44; Matthew F. Brady, 1944-59; Ernest J. Primeau, 1960-74.

Marquette, Mich. (1857): Mark F. Schmitt, bishop, 1978.

Former bishops: Frederic Baraga, 1857-68; Ignatius Mrak, 1869-78; John Vertin, 1879-99; Frederick Eis, 1899-1922; Paul J. Nussbaum, C.P., 1922-35; Joseph C. Plagens, 1935-40; Francis Magner, 1941-47; Thomas L. Noa, 1947-68; Charles A. Salatka, 1968-77.

Memphis, Tenn. (1970): Vacant as of Aug. 1, 1982.

Former bishop: Carroll T. Dozier, 1971-82.

Metuchen, N.J. (1981): Theodore E. McCarrick, bishop, 1981.

Miami,* Fla. (1958; archdiocese, 1968): Edward A. McCarthy, archbishop, 1977. John J. Nevins, Agustin A. Roman, auxiliaries.

Former ordinary: Coleman F. Carroll, 1958-77, first archbishop.

Milwaukee,* Wis. (1843; archdiocese, 1875): Rembert G. Weakland, O.S.B., archbishop, 1977. Leo J. Brust, Richard J. Sklba, auxiliaries.

Former ordinaries: John M. Henni, 1844-81, first archbishop; Michael Heiss, 1881-90; Frederick X. Katzer, 1891-1903; Sebastian G. Messmer, 1903-30; Samuel A. Stritch, 1930-39; Moses E. Kiley, 1940-53; Albert G. Meyer, 1953-58; William E. Cousins, 1959-77.

Mobile,* Ala. (1829; archdiocese, 1980): Oscar H. Lipscomb, first archbishop, 1980.

Former bishops: Michael Portier, 1829-59; John Quinlan, 1859-83; Dominic Manucy, 1884; Jeremiah O'Sullivan, 1885-96; Edward P. Allen, 1897-1926; Thomas J. Toolen, 1927-69; John L. May, 1969-80.

Monterey in California (1967): Thaddeus A. Shubsda, bishop, 1982.

Formerly Monterey-Fresno, 1922.

Former bishops (Monterey-Fresno): John J. Cantwell, administrator, 1922-24; John B. MacGinley, first bishop, 1924-32; Philip G. Sher, 1933-53; Aloysius J. Willinger, 1953-67.

Former bishop (Monterey): Harry A. Clinch, 1967-82.

Nashville, Tenn. (1837): James D. Niedergeses, bishop, 1975.

Former bishops: Richard P. Miles, O.P., 1838-60; James Whelan, O.P., 1860-64; Patrick A. Feehan, 1865-80; Joseph Rademacher, 1883-93; Thomas S. Byrne, 1894-1923; Alphonse J. Smith, 1924-35; William L. Adrian, 1936-69; Joseph A. Durick, 1969-75.

Newark,* N.J. (1853; archdiocese, 1937): Peter L. Gerety, archbishop, 1974. John J. Dougherty, Jerome Pechillo, T.O.R., Robert F. Garner, Joseph A. Francis, S.V.D., Dominic A. Marconi, auxiliaries.

Former ordinaries: James R. Bayley, 1853-72; Michael A. Corrigan, 1873-80; Winand M. Wigger, 1881-1901; John J. O'Connor, 1901-27; Thomas J. Walsh, 1928-52, first archbishop; Thomas A. Boland, 1953-74.

New Orleans,* La. (1793; archdiocese, 1850): Philip M. Hannan, archbishop, 1965. Harold R. Perry, S. V. D., Stanley J. Ott, auxiliaries.

Former ordinaries: Luis Penalver y Cardenas, 1793-1801; John Carroll, administrator, 1809-15; W. Louis Dubourg, S.S., 1815-25; Joseph Rosati, C.M., administrator, 1826-29; Leo De Neckere, C.M., 1829-33; Anthony Blanc, 1835-60, first archbishop; Jean Marie Odin, C.M., 1861-70; Napoleon J. Perche, 1870-83; Francis X. Leray, 1883-87; Francis A. Janssens, 1888-97; Placide L. Chapelle, 1897-1905; James H. Blenk, S.M., 1906-17; John W. Shaw, 1918-34; Joseph F. Rummel, 1935-64; John P. Cody, 1964-65.

Newton, Mass. (Melkite Rite) (1966; eparchy, 1976): Archbishop Joseph Tawil, exarch, 1969, first eparch, 1976.

Former ordinary: Justin Najmy, 1966-68.

New Ulm, Minn. (1957): Raymond A. Lucker, bishop, 1975.

Former bishop: Alphonse J. Schladweiler, 1958-75.

New York,* N.Y. (1808; archdiocese, 1850): Cardinal Terence J. Cooke, archbishop, 1968. Patrick V. Ahern, James P. Mahoney, Anthony F. Mestice, Austin Vaughan, Francisco Garmendia, Joseph T. O'Keefe, Emerson Moore, auxiliaries.

Former ordinaries: Richard L. Concanen, O.P., 1808-10; John Connolly, O.P., 1814-25; John Dubois, S.S., 1826-42; John J. Hughes, 1842-64, first archbishop; Cardinal John McCloskey, 1864-85; Michael A. Corrigan, 1885-1902; Cardinal John Farley, 1902-18; Cardinal Patrick Hayes, 1919-38; Cardinal Francis Spellman, 1939-67.

Norwich, Conn. (1953): Daniel P. Reilly, bishop, 1975.

Former bishops: Bernard J. Flanagan, 1953-59; Vincent J. Hines, 1960-75.

Oakland, Calif. (1962): John S. Cummins, bishop, 1977.

Former bishop: Floyd L. Begin, 1962-77.

Ogdensburg, N.Y. (1872): Stanislaus J. Brzana, bishop, 1968.

Former bishops: Edgar P. Wadhams, 1872-91; Henry Gabriels, 1892-1921; Joseph H. Conroy, 1921-39; Francis J. Monaghan, 1939-42; Bryan J. McEntegart, 1943-53; Walter P. Kellenberg, 1954-57; James J. Navagh, 1957-63; Leo R. Smith, 1963; Thomas A. Donnellan, 1964-68.

Oklahoma City,* Okla. (1905; archdiocese, 1972): Charles A. Salatka, archbishop, 1977.

Former ordinaries: Theophile Meerschaert, 1905-24; Francis C. Kelley, 1924-48; Eugene J. McGuinness, 1948-57; Victor J. Reed, 1958-71; John R. Quinn, 1971-77, first archbishop.

Omaha,* Nebr. (1885; archdiocese, 1945): Daniel E. Sheehan, archbishop, 1969. Anthony Milone, auxiliary.

Former ordinaries: James O'Gorman, O.C.S.O., 1859-74, vicar apostolic; James O'Connor, vicar apostolic, 1876-85, first bishop, 1885-90; Richard Scannell, 1891-1916; Jeremiah J. Harty, 1916-27; Francis Beckman, administrator, 1926-28; Joseph F. Rummel, 1928-35; James H. Ryan, 1935-47, first archbishop; Gerald T. Bergan, 1948-69.

Orange, Calif. (1976): William R. Johnson, bishop, 1976.

Orlando, Fla. (1968): Thomas J. Grady, bishop, 1974.

Former bishop: William Borders, 1968-74.

Owensboro, Ky. (1937): Vacant as of Aug. 1, 1982.

Former bishops: Francis R. Cotton, 1938-60, Henry J. Soenneker, 1961-82.

Parma, Ohio (Byzantine Rite) (1969): Emil Mihalik, eparch, 1969.

Passaic, N.J. (Byzantine Rite) (1963): Michael J. Dudick, eparch, 1968.

Former bishop: Stephen Kocisko, 1963-68.

Paterson, N.J. (1937): Frank J. Rodimer, bishop, 1978.

Former bishops: Thomas H. McLaughlin, 1937-47; Thomas A. Boland, 1947-52; James A. McNulty, 1953-63; James J. Navagh, 1963-65; Lawrence B. Casey, 1966-77.

Pensacola-Tallahassee, Fla. (1975): Rene H. Gracida, bishop, 1975.

Peoria, Ill. (1877): Edward W. O'Rourke, bishop, 1971.

Former bishops: John L. Spalding, 1877-1908; Edmund M. Dunne, 1909-29; Joseph H. Schlarman, 1930-51; William E. Cousins, 1952-58; John B. Franz, 1959-71.

Philadelphia,* Pa. (1808; archdiocese, 1875): Cardinal John Krol, archbishop, 1961. John J. Graham, Martin J. Lohmuller, Edward T. Hughes, Francis B. Schulte, Louis A. De Simone, auxiliaries.

Former ordinaries: Michael Egan, O.F.M., 1810-14; Henry Conwell, 1820-42; Francis P. Kenrick, 1842-51; John N. Neumann, C.SS.R., 1852-60; James F. Wood, 1860-83, first archbishop; Patrick J. Ryan, 1884-1911; Edmond F. Prendergast, 1911-18; Cardinal Dennis Dougherty, 1918-51; Cardinal John O'Hara, C.S.C., 1951-60.

Philadelphia,* Pa. (Byzantine Rite) (1924; metropolitan, 1958): Stephen Sulyk, archbishop, 1981. Robert Moskal, auxiliary.

Former ordinaries: Stephen Ortynsky, O.S.B.M., 1907-16; Constantine Bohachevsky, 1924-61; Ambrose Senyshyn, O.S.B.M., 1961-76; Joseph Schmondiuk, 1977-78; Myroslav J. Lubachivsky, 1979-80, apostolic administrator, 1980-81.

Phoenix, Ariz. (1969): Thomas J. O'Brien, bishop, 1982.

Former bishops: Edward A. McCarthy, 1969-76; James S. Rausch, 1977-81.

Pittsburgh,* Pa. (Byzantine Rite) (1924; metropolitan, 1969): Stephen J. Kocisko, eparch, 1968, first metropolitan, 1969. John M. Bilock, auxiliary.

Former ordinaries: Basil Takach 1924-48; Daniel Ivancho, 1948-54; Nicholas T. Elko, 1955-67.

Pittsburgh, Pa. (1843): Vincent M. Leonard, bishop, 1969. John B. McDowell, Anthony G. Bosco, auxiliaries.

Former bishops: Michael O'Connor, 1843-53, 1854-60; Michael Domenec, C.M., 1860-76; J. Tuigg, 1876-89; Richard Phelan, 1889-1904; J.F. Regis Canevin, 1904-20; Hugh C. Boyle, 1921-55; John F. Dearden, 1950-58; John J. Wright, 1959-69.

Portland, Me. (1853): Edward C. O'Leary, bishop, 1974. Amedee W. Proulx, auxiliary.

Former bishops: David W. Bacon, 1855-74; James A. Healy, 1875-1900; William H.

O'Connell, 1901-06; Louis S. Walsh, 1906-24; John G. Murray, 1925-31; Joseph E. McCarthy, 1932-55; Daniel J. Feeney, 1955-69; Peter L. Gerety, 1969-74.

Portland,* Ore. (1846): Cornelius M. Power, archbishop, 1974. Paul E. Waldschmidt, C.S.C., Kenneth D. Steiner, auxiliaries.

Established as Oregon City, name changed, 1928.

Former ordinaries: Francis N. Blanchet, 1846-80 vicar apostolic, first archbishop; Charles J. Seghers, 1880-84; William H. Gross, C.SS.R., 1885-98; Alexander Christie, 1899-1925; Edward D. Howard, 1926-66; Robert J. Dwyer, 1966-74.

Providence, R.I. (1872): Louis E. Gelineau, bishop, 1972. Kenneth A. Angell, auxiliary.

Former bishops: Thomas F. Hendricken, 1872-86; Matthew Harkins, 1887-1921; William A. Hickey, 1921-33; Francis P. Keough, 1934-47; Russell J. McVinney, 1948-71.

Pueblo, Colo. (1941): Arthur N. Tafoya, bishop, 1980.

Former bishops: Joseph C. Willging, 1942-59; Charles A. Buswell, 1959-79.

Raleigh, N.C. (1924): F. Joseph Gossman, bishop, 1975. George E. Lynch, auxiliary.

Former bishops: William J. Hafey, 1925-37; Eugene J. McGuinness, 1937-44; Vincent S. Waters, 1945-75.

Rapid City, S. Dak. (1902): Harold J. Dimmerling, bishop, 1969.

Established at Lead, transferred, 1930.

Former bishops: John Stariha, 1902-09; Joseph F. Busch, 1910-15; John J. Lawler, 1916-48; William T. McCarty, C.SS.R., 1948-69.

Reno-Las Vegas, Nev. (1931): Norman F. McFarland, bishop, 1976.

Established at Reno; title changed to Reno-Las Vegas, 1976.

Former bishops: Thomas K. Gorman, 1931-52; Robert J. Dwyer, 1952-66; Joseph Green, 1967-74.

Richmond, Va. (1820): Walter F. Sullivan, bishop, 1974.

Former bishops: Patrick Kelly, 1820-22; Richard V. Whelan, 1841-50; John McGill, 1850-72; James Gibbons, 1872-77; John J. Keane, 1878-88; Augustine Van de Vyver, 1889-1911; Denis J. O'Connell, 1912-26; Andrew J. Brennan, 1926-45; Peter L. Ireton, 1945-58; John J. Russell, 1958-73.

Rochester, N.Y. (1868): Matthew H. Clark, bishop, 1979. Dennis W. Hickey, auxiliary.

Former bishops: Bernard J. McQuaid, 1868-1909; Thomas F. Hickey, 1909-28; John F. O'Hern, 1929-33; Edward F. Mooney, 1933-37; James E. Kearney, 1937-66; Fulton J. Sheen, 1966-69; Joseph L. Hogan, 1969-78.

Rockford, Ill. (1908): Arthur J. O'Neill, bishop, 1968.

Former bishops: Peter J. Muldoon, 1908-27; Edward F. Hoban, 1928-42; John J.

Boylan, 1943-53; Raymond P. Hillinger, 1953-56; Loras T. Lane, 1956-68.

Rockville Centre, N.Y. (1957): John R. McGann, bishop, 1976. Gerald Ryan, James Daly, auxiliaries.

Former bishop: Walter P. Kellenberg, 1957-76.

Sacramento, Calif. (1886): Francis A. Quinn, bishop, 1979. Alphonse Gallegos, O.A.R., auxiliary.

Former bishops: Patrick Manogue, 1886-95; Thomas Grace, 1896-1921; Patrick J. Keane, 1922-28; Robert J. Armstrong, 1929-57; Joseph T. McGucken, 1957-62; Alden J. Bell, 1962-79.

Saginaw, Mich. (1938): Kenneth E. Untener, bishop, 1980.

Former bishops: William F. Murphy, 1938-50; Stephen S. Woznicki, 1950-68; Francis F. Reh, 1969-80.

St. Augustine, Fla. (1870): John J. Snyder, bishop, 1979.

Former bishops: Augustin Verot, S.S., 1870-76; John Moore, 1877-1901; William J. Kenny, 1902-13; Michael J. Curley, 1914-21; Patrick J. Barry, 1922-40; Joseph P. Hurley, 1940-67; Paul F. Tanner, 1968-79.

St. Cloud, Minn. (1889): George H. Speltz, bishop, 1968.

Former bishops: Otto Zardetti, 1889-94; Martin Marty, O.S.B., 1895-96; James Trobec, 1897-1914; Joseph F. Busch, 1915-53; Peter Bartholome, 1953-68.

St. Louis,* Mo. (1826; archdiocese, 1847): John L. May, archbishop, 1980. George J. Gottwald, Charles R. Koester, auxiliaries.

Former ordinaries: Joseph Rosati, C.M., 1827-43; Peter R. Kenrick, 1843-95, first archbishop; John J. Kain, 1895-1903; Cardinal John Glennon, 1903-46; Cardinal Joseph Ritter, 1946-67; Cardinal John J. Carberry, 1968-79.

St. Maron, Brooklyn, N.Y. (Maronite Rite) (1966; diocese, 1971): Francis Zayek, exarch, 1966, first eparch, 1972. John Chedid, auxiliary.

Established at Detroit; transferred to Brooklyn, 1977.

St. Nicholas in Chicago (Byzantine Rite Eparchy of St. Nicholas of the Ukrainians) (1961): Innocent H. Lotocky, O.S.B.M., bishop, 1981.

Former bishop: Jaroslav Gabro, 1961-80.

St. Paul and Minneapolis,* Minn. (1850; archdiocese, 1888): John R. Roach, archbishop, 1975. William H. Bullock, J. Richard Ham, M.M., auxiliaries.

Former ordinaries: Joseph Cretin, 1851-57; Thomas L. Grace, O.P., 1859-84; John Ireland, 1884-1918, first archbishop; Austin Dowling, 1919-30; John G. Murray, 1931-56; William O. Brady, 1956-61; Leo Binz, 1962-75.

St. Petersburg, Fla. (1968): W. Thomas

Larkin, bishop, 1979. J. Keith Symons, auxiliary.

Former bishop: Charles McLaughlin, 1968-78.

Salina, Kans. (1887): Daniel W. Kucera, O.S.B., bishop, 1980.

Established at Concordia, transferred, 1944.

Former bishops: Richard Scannell, 1887-91; John J. Hennessy, administrator, 1891-98; John F. Cunningham, 1898-1919; Francis J. Tief, 1921-38; Frank A. Thill, 1938-57; Frederick W. Freking, 1957-64; Cyril J. Vogel, 1965-79.

Salt Lake City, Utah (1891): William K. Weigand, bishop, 1980.

Former bishops: Lawrence Scanlan, 1891-1915; Joseph S. Glass, C.M., 1915-26; John J. Mitty, 1926-32; James E. Kearney, 1932-37; Duane G. Hunt, 1937-60; J. Lennox Federal, 1960-80.

San Angelo, Tex. (1961): Joseph A. Fiorenza, bishop, 1979.

Former bishops: Thomas J. Drury, 1962-65; Thomas Tschoepe, 1966-69; Stephen A. Leven, 1969-79.

San Antonio,* Tex. (1874; archdiocese, 1926): Patrick F. Flores, archbishop, 1979. Ricardo Ramerez, C.S.B., auxiliary.

Former ordinaries: Anthony D. Pellicer, 1874-80; John C. Neraz, 1881-94; John A. Forest, 1895-1911; John W. Shaw, 1911-18; Arthur Jerome Drossaerts, 1918-40, first archbishop; Robert E. Lucey, 1941-69; Francis Furey, 1969-79.

San Bernardino, Calif. (1978): Phillip F. Straling, bishop, 1978.

San Diego, Calif. (1936): Leo T. Maher, bishop, 1969. Gilbert Espinoza Chavez, auxiliary.

Former bishops: Charles F. Buddy, 1936-66; Francis J. Furey, 1966-69.

San Francisco,* Calif. (1853): John R. Quinn, archbishop, 1977. Daniel F. Walsh, auxiliary.

Former ordinaries: Joseph S. Alemany, O.P., 1853-84; Patrick W. Riordan, 1884-1914; Edward J. Hanna, 1915-35; John Mitty, 1935-61; Joseph T. McGucken, 1962-77.

San Jose, Calif. (1981): R. Pierre DuMaine, first bishop, 1981.

Santa Fe,* N. Mex. (1850; archdiocese, 1875): Robert Sanchez, archbishop, 1974.

Former ordinaries: John B. Lamy, 1850-85, first archbishop; John B. Salpointe, 1885-94; Placide L. Chapelle, 1894-97; Peter Bourgade, 1899-1908; John B. Pitaval, 1909-18; Albert T. Daeger, O.F.M., 1919-32; Rudolph A. Gerken, 1933-43; Edwin V. Byrne, 1943-63; James P. Davis, 1964-74.

Santa Rosa, Calif. (1962): Mark J. Hurley, bishop, 1969.

Former bishop: Leo T. Maher, 1962-69.

Savannah, Ga. (1850): Raymond W. Lessard, bishop, 1973.

Former bishops: Francis X. Gartland, 1850-54; John Barry, 1857-59; Augustin Verot, S.S., 1861-70; Ignatius Persico, O.F.M. Cap., 1870-72; William H. Gross, C.SS.R., 1873-85; Thomas A. Becker, 1886-99; Benjamin J. Keiley, 1900-22; Michael Keyes, S.M., 1922-35; Gerald P. O'Hara, 1935-59; Thomas J. McDonough, 1960-67; Gerard L. Frey, 1967-72.

Scranton, Pa. (1868): J. Carroll McCormick, bishop, 1966. James C. Timlin, auxiliary.

Former bishops: William O'Hara, 1868-99; Michael J. Hoban, 1899-1926; Thomas C. O'Reilly, 1928-38; William J. Hafey, 1938-54; Jerome D. Hannan, 1954-65.

Seattle,* Wash. (1850; archdiocese, 1951): Raymond G. Hunthausen, archbishop, 1975. Nicholas E. Walsh, auxiliary.

Established as Nesqually, name changed, 1907.

Former ordinaries; Augustin M. Blanchet, 1850-79; Aegidius Junger, 1879-95; Edward J. O'Dea, 1896-1932; Gerald Shaughnessy, S.M., 1933-50; Thomas A. Connolly, first archbishop, 1950-75.

Sioux City, Ia. (1902): Frank H. Greteman, bishop, 1970.

Former bishops: Philip J. Garrigan, 1902-19; Edmond Heelan, 1919-48; Joseph M. Mueller, 1948-70.

Sioux Falls, S. Dak. (1889): Paul V. Dudley, bishop, 1978. Paul F. Anderson, auxiliary.

Former bishops: Martin Marty, O.S.B., 1889-94; Thomas O'Gorman, 1896-1921; Bernard J. Mahoney, 1922-39; William O. Brady, 1939-56; Lambert A. Hoch, 1956-78.

Spokane, Wash. (1913): Lawrence H. Welsh, bishop, 1978.

Former bishops: Augustine F. Schinner, 1914-25; Charles D. White, 1927-55; Bernard J. Topel, 1955-78.

Springfield, Ill. (1853): Joseph A. McNicholas, bishop, 1975.

Established at Quincy, transferred to Alton 1857; transferred to Springfield 1923.

Former bishops: Henry D. Juncker, 1857-68; Peter J. Baltes, 1870-86; James Ryan, 1888-1923; James A. Griffin, 1924-48; William A. O'Connor, 1949-75.

Springfield, Mass. (1870): Joseph F. Maguire, bishop, 1977. Leo E. O'Neil, auxiliary.

Former bishops: Patrick T. O'Reilly, 1870-92; Thomas D. Beaven, 1892-1920; Thomas M. O'Leary, 1921-49; Christopher J. Weldon, 1950-77.

Springfield-Cape Girardeau, Mo. (1956): Bernard F. Law, bishop, 1973.

Former bishops: Charles Helmsing, 1956-62; Ignatius J. Strecker, 1962-69; William Baum, 1970-73.

Stamford, Conn. (Byzantine Rite) (1956); Basil Losten, eparch, 1977.

Former eparchs: Ambrose Senyshyn, O.S.B.M., 1956-61; Joseph Schmondiuk, 1961-77.

Steubenville, Ohio (1944): Albert H. Ottenweller, bishop, 1977.

Former bishop: John K. Mussio, 1945-77.

Stockton, Calif. (1962): Roger M. Mahony, bishop, 1980.

Former bishops: Hugh A. Donohoe, 1962-69; Merlin J. Guilfoyle, 1969-79.

Superior, Wis. (1905): George A. Hammes, bishop, 1960. Raphael M. Fliss, coadjutor.

Former bishops: Augustine F. Schinner, 1905-13; Joseph M. Koudelka, 1913-21; Joseph G. Pinten, 1922-26; Theodore M. Reverman, 1926-41; William P. O'Connor, 1942-46; Albert G. Meyer, 1946-53; Joseph Annabring, 1954-59.

Syracuse, N.Y. (1886): Francis J. Harrison, bishop, 1976. Thomas J. Costello, auxiliary.

Former bishops: Patrick A. Ludden, 1887-1912; John Grimes, 1912-22; Daniel J. Curley, 1923-32; John A. Duffy, 1933-37; Walter A. Foery, 1937-70; David F. Cunningham, 1970-76.

Toledo, Ohio (1910): James R. Hoffman, bishop, 1980.

Former bishops: Joseph Schrembs, 1911-21; Samuel A. Stritch, 1921-30; Karl J. Alter, 1931-50; George J. Rehring, 1950-67; John A. Donovan, 1967-80.

Trenton, N.J. (1881): John C. Reiss, bishop, 1980. Edward U. Kmiec, auxiliary.

Former bishops: Michael J. O'Farrell, 1881-94; James A. McFaul, 1894-1917; Thomas J. Walsh, 1918-28; John J. McMahon, 1928-32; Moses E. Kiley, 1934-40; William A. Griffin, 1940-50; George W. Ahr, 1950-79.

Tucson, Ariz. (1897): Manuel D. Moreno, bishop, 1982.

Former bishops: Peter Bourgade, 1897-99; Henry Granjon, 1900-22; Daniel J. Gercke, 1923-60; Francis J. Green, 1960-81.

Tulsa, Okla. (1972): Eusebius J. Beltran, bishop, 1978.

Former bishop: Bernard J. Ganter, 1973-77.

Van Nuys, Calif. (Byzantine Rite) (1981): Thomas Dolinay, bishop, 1982.

Victoria, Tex. (1982): Charles Grahmann, bishop, 1982.

Washington,* D.C. (1939): James A. Hickey, archbishop, 1980. Thomas W. Lyons, Eugene A. Marino, S.S.J., Thomas Kelly, O.P., auxiliaries.

Former ordinaries: Michael J. Curley, 1939-47; Cardinal Patrick O'Boyle, 1948-73; Cardinal William Baum, 1973-80.

Wheeling-Charleston, W. Va. (1850): Joseph H. Hodges, bishop, 1962. James E. Michaels, S.S.C., auxiliary.

Established as Wheeling; name changed, 1974.

Former bishops: Richard V. Whelan, 1850-74; John J. Kain, 1875-93; Patrick J. Donahue, 1894-1922; John J. Swint, 1922-62.

Wichita, Kans. (1887): Vacant as of Aug. 1, 1982.

Former bishops: John J. Hennessy, 1888-1920; Augustus J. Schwertner, 1921-39; Christian H. Winkelmann, 1940-46; Mark K. Carroll, 1947-67; David M. Maloney, 1967-82.

Wilmington, Del. (1868): Thomas J. Mardaga, bishop, 1968.

Former bishops: Thomas A. Becker, 1868-86; Alfred A. Curtis, 1886-96; John J. Monaghan, 1897-1925; Edmond Fitzmaurice, 1925-60; Michael Hyle, 1960-67.

Winona, Minn. (1889): Loras J. Watters, bishop, 1969.

Former bishops: Joseph B. Cotter, 1889-1909; Patrick R. Heffron, 1910-27; Francis M. Kelly, 1928-49; Edward A. Fitzgerald, 1949-69.

Worcester, Mass. (1950): Bernard J. Flanagan, bishop, 1959. Timothy J. Harrington, auxiliary.

Former bishop: John J. Wright, 1950-59.

Yakima, Wash. (1951): William Skylstad, bishop, 1977.

Former bishops: Joseph P. Dougherty, 1951-69; Cornelius M. Power, 1969-74; Nicholas E. Walsh, 1974-76.

Youngstown, Ohio (1943): James W. Malone, bishop, 1968. Benedict C. Franzetta, auxiliary.

Former bishops: James A. McFadden, 1943-52; Emmet M. Walsh, 1952-68.

Apostolic Exarchate for the United States and Canada, New York, N.Y. (Armenian Rite) (1981); Nerses Mikail Setian, exarch, 1981.

Apostolic Exarchate for Chaldean-Rite Catholics in the United States, Detroit, Mich. (1982): Ibrahim Ibrahim, exarch, 1982.

Military Ordinariate (1917): Cardinal Terence J. Cooke, military vicar, 1968. Joseph T. Ryan, coadjutor archbishop, 1975. John J. O'Connor, military delegate.

Former military vicars: Cardinal Patrick Hayes, 1917-38; Cardinal Francis Spellman, 1939-67.

Military Ordinariate

The Military Ordinariate or Vicariate, is the diocese which serves members of the armed forces of the United States wherever they are. It has jurisdiction over: military and Veterans Administration hospital chaplains; personnel of the armed forces and members of their families and dependents habitually living with them; members of the Coast Guard, National Guard, Air National Guard and Civil Air Patrol when on active duty; persons living on military installations and/or attached to military offices or VA facilities.

The ordinariate was canonically established on a permanent basis by a decree of the Sacred Consistorial Congregation dated Sept. 8, 1957. Cardinal Terence J. Cooke, Archbishop of New York, is Military Vicar. Offices of the ordinariate are located at 1011 First Ave., New York, N.Y. 10022.

MISSIONARY BISHOPS

Africa

Namibia (South West Africa): Keetmanshoop (vicariate apostolic), Edward F. Schlotterback, O.S.F.S.

Nigeria: Sokoto (diocese), Michael J. Dempsey, O.P.

South Africa: De Aar (diocese), Joseph A. De Palma, S.C.J.

Keimos (diocese), John Minder, O.S.F.S.

Tanzania: Arusha (diocese), Dennis V. Durning, C.S.Sp.

Nachingwea (diocese), Arnold R. Cotey, S.D.S.

Asia

China: Chowtsun (diocese), Henry A. Pinger, O.F.M. Expelled.

Wuchow (diocese), Frederick A. Donaghy, M.M. Expelled.

India: Bhagalpur (diocese), Urban McGarry, T.O.R.

Indonesia: Agats (diocese), Alphonse A. Sowada, O.S.C.

Iraq: Mossul (Chaldean-rite archdiocese), George Garmo.

Korea: Inchon (diocese), William J. McNaughton, M.M.

Pakistan: Multan (diocese), Ernest B. Boland, O.P.

Philippine Islands: Cotabato (archdiocese), Philip F. Smith, O.M.I.

Jolo (vicariate apostolic), Georges Dion, O.M.I.

Taiwan: Taichung (diocese), William F. Kupfer, M.M.

Central America, West Indies

Belize: Belize (diocese), Robert L. Hodapp, S.J.

Dominican Republic: San Juan de la Maguana (diocese), Ronald G. Connors, C.SS.R.,

Honduras: Comayagua (diocese), Gerald Scarpone, O.F.M.

Nicaragua: Bluefields (vicariate apostolic), Salvator Schlaefer, O.F.M.Cap.

Virgin Islands: St. Thomas (diocese), Edward Harper, C.SS.R.

North America

Mexico: Mexico City (archdiocese), Ricardo Watty Urquidi, M.Sp.S., auxiliary.

Oceania

Caroline and Marshall Islands (diocese), Martin J. Neylon, S.J.
Papua New Guinea: Goroko (diocese), Raymond R. Caesar, S.V.D.
    Madang (archdiocese), Leo Arkfeld, S.V.D.
    Mendi (diocese), Firmin Schmidt, O.F.M.Cap.
    Mount Hagen (archdiocese), George Bernarding, S.V.D.
    Wewak (diocese), Raymond P. Kalisz, S.V.D.
Vanuatu (New Hebrides): Port Vila (diocese), Francis Lambert, S.M.

South America

Bolivia: Coroico (prelacy), Thomas R. Manning, O.F.M.
    La Paz (archdiocese), Andrew B. Schierhoff, auxiliary.
    Santa Cruz (archdiocese), Charles A. Brown, M.M., auxiliary.

Brazil: Abaetetuba (diocese), Angelo Frosi, S.X.
    Belem do Para (archdiocese), Jude Prost, O.F.M., auxiliary.
    Borba (prelacy), Adrian J. M. Veigle, T.O.R.
    Cristalandia (prelacy), James A. Schuck, O.F.M.
    Jatai (diocese), Benedict D. Coscia, O.F.M. Michael P. Mundo, auxiliary.
    Paranagua (diocese), Bernard Nolker, C.SS.R.
    Rui Barbosa (diocese), Mathias Schmidt, O.S.B.
    Santarem (diocese), James C. Ryan, O.F.M.
    Sao Paulo (archdiocese), Alfred Novak, C.SS.R., auxiliary.
    Sao Salvador da Bahia (archdiocese), Thomas W. Murphy, C.SS.R., auxiliary.
Peru: Chulucanas (prelacy), John McNabb, O.S.A.

CATHOLIC POPULATION OF THE UNITED STATES

(Source: *The Official Catholic Directory, 1982;* figures as of Jan. 1, 1982. Archdioceses are indicated by an asterisk; for dioceses marked +, see Dioceses with Interstate Lines.)

Section, State Diocese	Catholics	Dioc. Priests	Rel. Priests	Total Priests	Perm. Deacons	Bros.	Sisters	Parishes
NEW ENGLAND	5,606,800	4,155	2,543	6,698	511	761	13,185	1,701
Maine, Portland	272,306	223	119	342	—	43	821	144
New Hampshire, Manchester	291,081	287	103	390	1	60	1,141	128
Vermont, Burlington	158,118	163	64	227	12	23	369	100
Massachusetts	2,942,673	2,161	1,722	3,883	182	369	7,087	785
*Boston	1,913,827	1,319	1,188	2,507	125	211	4,634	408
Fall River	340,000	232	206	438	13	38	738	113
Springfield	351,520	260	126	386	—	21	935	136
Worcester	337,326	350	202	552	44	99	780	128
Rhode Island, Providence	618,860	390	204	594	60	170	1,251	159
Connecticut	1,323,762	931	331	1,262	256	96	2,516	385
*Hartford	793,908	541	151	692	198	64	1,492	222
Bridgeport	331,350	244	101	345	31	7	687	87
Norwich+	198,504	146	79	225	27	25	337	76
MIDDLE ATLANTIC	13,068,212	9,494	5,411	14,905	1,082	1,860	33,741	3,898
New York	6,404,479	4,417	2,942	7,359	487	1,168	15,485	1,713
*New York	1,839,000	1,034	1,578	2,612	170	453	5,401	412
Albany	408,648	399	222	621	35	93	1,250	201
Brooklyn	1,372,402	936	388	1,324	85	289	2,318	221
Buffalo	825,991	589	314	903	48	92	2,227	296
Ogdensburg	168,896	193	39	232	20	34	355	122
Rochester	376,124	379	145	524	—	55	934	161
Rockville Centre	1,042,280	495	138	633	91	134	2,025	129
Syracuse	371,138	392	118	510	38	18	975	171
New Jersey	2,912,451	1,901	923	2,824	510	320	5,386	692
*Newark	1,374,484	825	443	1,268	222	167	2,521	248
Camden	351,603	374	43	417	69	25	551	127
Metuchen	411,010	148	69	217	49	24	548	93
Paterson	327,439	294	253	547	70	51	1,103	104
Trenton	447,915	260	115	375	100	53	663	120
Pennsylvania	3,751,282	3,176	1,546	4,722	85	372	12,870	1,493
*Philadelphia	1,386,247	963	646	1,609	17	227	5,563	305
Allentown	263,365	300	113	413	—	28	904	152
Altoona-Johnstown	153,209	183	91	274	1	21	170	120

Section, State Diocese	Catholics	Dioc. Priests	Rel. Priests	Total Priests	Perm. Deacons	Bros.	Sisters	Par- ishes
Pennsylvania								
Erie	225,773	276	53	329	—	8	721	128
Greensburg	224,926	194	116	310	1	10	425	117
Harrisburg	205,951	175	85	260	39	12	846	110
Pittsburgh	926,635	622	318	940	27	59	3,088	321
Scranton	365,176	463	124	587	—	7	1,153	240
SOUTH ATLANTIC	**3,183,504**	**2,230**	**2,080**	**4,310**	**427**	**562**	**6,712**	**1,292**
Delaware, Wilmington+	**121,262**	**122**	**110**	**232**	**21**	**37**	**431**	**55**
Maryland, *Baltimore	**425,998**	**333**	**394**	**727**	**102**	**92**	**1,795**	**152**
District of Columbia								
*Washington+	**396,741**	**338**	**659**	**997**	**105**	**174**	**959**	**130**
Virginia	**294,276**	**224**	**150**	**374**	**47**	**17**	**658**	**162**
Arlington	179,025	79	98	177	44	10	316	56
Richmond	115,251	145	52	197	3	7	342	106
West Virginia								
Wheeling-Charleston	**106,420**	**131**	**83**	**214**	**15**	**25**	**444**	**126**
North Carolina	**100,828**	**127**	**89**	**216**	**2**	**16**	**323**	**122**
Charlotte	51,792	61	65	126	—	10	210	64
Raleigh	49,036	66	24	90	2	6	113	58
South Carolina, Charleston	**65,871**	**82**	**51**	**133**	**21**	**26**	**253**	**77**
Georgia	**164,604**	**160**	**137**	**297**	**26**	**41**	**394**	**100**
*Atlanta	109,651	93	96	189	9	32	175	55
Savannah	54,953	67	41	108	17	9	219	45
Florida	**1,507,504**	**713**	**407**	**1,120**	**88**	**134**	**1,455**	**368**
*Miami	896,702	351	207	558	34	68	651	134
Orlando	183,000	121	52	173	3	2	180	66
Pensacola-Tallahassee	44,430	56	17	73	36	—	78	38
St. Augustine	72,046	64	26	90	3	8	125	44
St. Petersburg	311,326	121	105	226	12	56	421	86
EAST NORTH CENTRAL	**10,299,843**	**7,836**	**4,715**	**12,551**	**1,236**	**1,894**	**28,977**	**4,168**
Ohio	**2,336,103**	**2,050**	**977**	**3,027**	**239**	**501**	**7,147**	**952**
*Cincinnati	506,000	460	422	882	52	242	1,951	256
Cleveland	942,300	648	281	929	41	168	2,439	246
Columbus	195,333	224	69	293	22	12	640	107
Steubenville	53,650	166	17	183	1	8	126	74
Toledo	347,608	277	126	403	107	26	1,512	152
Youngstown	291,212	275	62	337	16	45	479	117
Indiana	**723,547**	**724**	**586**	**1,310**	**53**	**303**	**2,640**	**447**
*Indianapolis	201,846	220	189	409	—	95	1,152	142
Evansville	89,917	131	25	156	16	4	434	68
Ft. Wayne-South Bend	151,725	125	231	356	17	171	602	89
Gary	193,600	145	77	222	15	25	302	85
Lafayette	86,459	103	64	167	5	8	150	63
Illinois	**3,576,130**	**2,248**	**1,736**	**3,984**	**587**	**665**	**8,626**	**1,103**
*Chicago	2,374,138	1,248	1,220	2,468	418	310	4,955	444
Belleville	122,408	165	55	220	25	12	476	130
Joliet	411,000	212	163	375	49	261	1,105	113
Peoria	245,663	260	111	371	35	17	633	170
Rockford	236,428	179	82	261	60	20	525	102
Springfield	186,493	184	105	289	—	45	932	144
Michigan	**2,068,088**	**1,298**	**638**	**1,936**	**199**	**142**	**4,576**	**810**
*Detroit	1,259,807	594	418	1,012	113	103	2,516	337
Gaylord	86,718	59	23	82	2	4	156	59
Grand Rapids	152,835	165	43	208	17	5	633	91
Kalamazoo	96,461	61	32	93	19	6	289	47
Lansing	209,019	151	67	218	20	18	575	84
Marquette	90,353	126	25	151	1	3	157	88
Saginaw	172,895	142	30	172	27	3	250	104
Wisconsin	**1,595,975**	**1,516**	**778**	**2,294**	**158**	**283**	**5,988**	**856**
*Milwaukee	707,110	638	485	1,123	107	159	3,563	268
Green Bay	344,306	293	188	481	51	95	860	194

Section, States Diocese	Catholics	Dioc. Priests	Rel. Priests	Total Priests	Perm. Deacons	Bros.	Sisters	Par- ishes
Wisconsin								
La Crosse	230,774	268	40	308	—	15	626	169
Madison	220,639	212	45	257	—	13	641	138
Superior	93,146	105	20	125	—	1	298	87
EAST SOUTH CENTRAL	**698,333**	**966**	**419**	**1,385**	**185**	**321**	**3,659**	**638**
Kentucky	**365,626**	**527**	**150**	**677**	**66**	**147**	**2,513**	**287**
*Louisville	211,550	259	110	369	66	126	1,441	126
Covington	104,000	189	23	212	—	8	782	85
Owensboro	50,076	79	17	96	—	13	290	76
Tennessee	**120,417**	**151**	**63**	**214**	**73**	**72**	**344**	**104**
Memphis	48,140	66	27	93	34	52	169	43
Nashville	72,277	85	36	121	39	20	175	61
Alabama	**115,368**	**148**	**132**	**280**	**32**	**31**	**442**	**131**
*Mobile	59,713	87	70	157	13	26	264	76
Birmingham	55,655	61	62	123	19	5	178	55
Mississippi	**96,922**	**140**	**74**	**214**	**14**	**71**	**360**	**116**
Biloxi	53,300	64	30	94	6	53	88	44
Jackson	43,622	76	44	120	8	18	272	72
WEST NORTH CENTRAL	**3,434,732**	**4,007**	**2,058**	**6,065**	**396**	**724**	**14,709**	**18,903**
Minnesota	**1,069,326**	**987**	**470**	**1,457**	**80**	**182**	**4,028**	**698**
*St. Paul and Minneapolis	573,425	399	219	618	65	72	1,659	219
Crookston	43,886	51	23	74	—	1	314	47
Duluth	96,464	94	36	130	6	—	328	78
New Ulm	73,510	113	5	118	2	—	161	94
St. Cloud	154,721	158	171	329	7	72	856	136
Winona	127,320	172	16	188	—	37	710	124
Iowa	**544,579**	**872**	**123**	**995**	**75**	**55**	**2,295**	**534**
*Dubuque	237,596	356	87	443	26	36	1,452	191
Davenport	110,917	192	21	213	16	18	423	119
Des Moines	83,313	117	8	125	18	1	203	84
Sioux City	112,753	207	7	214	15	—	217	140
Missouri	**824,757**	**937**	**812**	**1,749**	**134**	**331**	**4,353**	**506**
*St. Louis	543,021	570	536	1,106	43	202	3,345	249
Jefferson City	85,574	122	18	140	33	12	150	94
Kansas City-St. Joseph	144,038	162	185	347	57	57	641	100
Springfield- Cape Girardeau	52,124	83	73	156	1	60	217	63
North Dakota	**177,698**	**211**	**97**	**308**	**24**	**24**	**602**	**185**
Bismarck	78,852	71	60	131	8	18	271	74
Fargo	98,846	140	37	177	16	6	331	111
South Dakota	**140,129**	**184**	**115**	**299**	**14**	**40**	**488**	**177**
Rapid City	40,138	39	47	86	11	13	23	55
Sioux Falls	99,991	145	68	213	3	27	465	122
Nebraska	**331,662**	**423**	**229**	**652**	**68**	**60**	**834**	**273**
*Omaha	208,007	218	203	421	68	42	655	137
Grand Island	54,945	87	1	88	—	—	32	51
Lincoln	68,710	118	25	143	—	18	147	85
Kansas	**346,581**	**393**	**212**	**605**	**1**	**32**	**2,109**	**360**
*Kansas City	147,059	121	130	251	—	25	1,075	121
Dodge City	38,747	57	12	69	1	—	180	46
Salina	61,627	80	41	121	—	4	340	98
Wichita	99,148	135	29	164	—	3	514	95
WEST SOUTH CENTRAL	**4,236,601**	**2,104**	**1,705**	**3,809**	**802**	**604**	**7,009**	**1,624**
Arkansas, Little Rock	**61,298**	**108**	**66**	**174**	**27**	**58**	**519**	**88**
Louisiana	**1,330,713**	**728**	**562**	**1,290**	**177**	**275**	**1,990**	**482**
*New Orleans	525,029	244	323	567	79	198	1,150	137
Alexandria-Shreveport	83,283	115	41	156	2	12	219	84
Baton Rouge	180,795	92	72	164	14	12	185	70
Houma-Thibodaux	132,733	52	9	61	26	10	65	36
Lafayette	320,191	185	83	268	39	39	320	120
Lake Charles	88,682	40	34	74	17	4	51	35

Section, States Diocese	Catholics	Dioc. Priests	Rel. Priests	Total Priests	Perm. Deacons	Bros.	Sisters	Par- ishes
Oklahoma	128,848	168	68	236	38	26	485	130
*Oklahoma City	79,609	104	31	135	18	14	266	75
Tulsa	49,239	64	37	101	20	12	219	55
Texas	2,715,742	1,100	1,009	2,109	560	245	4,015	924
*San Antonio	589,373	207	230	437	102	100	1,450	171
Amarillo	80,744	66	24	90	53	6	160	66
Austin	128,099	98	56	154	6	36	177	82
Beaumont	94,497	54	29	83	6	—	117	45
Brownsville	402,000	52	78	130	23	9	174	61
Corpus Christi	310,750	82	90	172	13	25	419	77
Dallas	178,047	110	93	203	94	5	309	64
El Paso+	244,958	104	78	182	45	14	345	82
Fort Worth	99,349	68	48	116	17	13	157	81
Galveston-Houston	514,490	207	245	452	134	37	654	145
San Angelo	73,435	52	38	90	67	—	53	50
Victoria	No separate statistics available.							
MOUNTAIN	1,769,451	1,188	820	2,008	363	267	3,167	804
Montana	130,817	213	57	270	11	11	251	137
Great Falls-Billings	65,792	89	37	126	4	4	179	74
Helena	65,025	124	20	144	7	7	72	63
Idaho, Boise	77,386	93	30	123	16	4	204	71
Wyoming, Cheyenne+	67,500	57	8	65	3	3	73	39
Colorado	418,450	310	260	570	76	65	1,146	191
*Denver	309,284	210	211	421	72	48	933	132
Pueblo	109,166	100	49	149	4	17	213	59
New Mexico	381,664	195	166	361	74	113	645	150
*Santa Fe	323,319	142	111	253	66	86	465	93
Gallup+	58,345	53	55	108	8	27	180	57
Arizona	488,027	213	191	404	151	42	607	134
Phoenix	263,027	116	118	234	75	31	265	77
Tucson	225,000	97	73	170	76	11	342	57
Utah, Salt Lake City	61,607	53	55	108	31	20	119	41
Nevada, Reno-Las Vegas	144,000	54	53	107	1	9	122	41
PACIFIC	6,186,084	2,991	2,713	5,704	443	856	9,739	1,543
Washington	402,676	381	333	714	75	46	1,348	228
*Seattle	270,251	224	235	459	49	37	825	130
Spokane	74,525	99	87	186	25	8	464	58
Yakima	57,900	58	11	69	1	1	59	40
Oregon	327,230	229	256	485	4	90	914	156
*Portland	301,369	183	246	429	4	90	828	127
Baker	25,861	46	10	56	—	—	86	29
California	5,206,275	2,289	1,960	4,249	315	649	7,011	1,040
*Los Angeles	2,303,560	618	677	1,295	124	135	2,643	281
*San Francisco	351,424	308	395	703	16	89	1,100	104
Fresno	310,500	122	55	177	2	10	191	86
Monterey	129,922	84	33	117	—	16	202	43
Oakland	401,800	156	233	389	32	189	680	87
Orange	365,004	127	84	211	30	20	446	51
Sacramento	256,833	184	77	261	15	47	294	93
San Bernardino	248,881	181	84	265	29	19	192	87
San Diego	330,043	248	91	339	35	25	517	89
San Jose	301,000	131	175	306	20	45	538	47
Santa Rosa	89,989	81	25	106	2	47	129	40
Stockton	117,319	49	31	80	10	7	79	32
Alaska	40,903	41	58	99	40	12	105	55
*Anchorage	20,933	19	16	35	5	4	43	18
Fairbanks	14,500	7	40	47	27	8	45	27
Juneau	5,470	15	2	17	8	—	17	10
Hawaii, Honolulu	209,000	51	106	157	9	59	361	64

Section, States Diocese	Catholics	Dioc. Priests	Rel. Priests	Total Priests	Perm. Deacons	Bros.	Sisters	Par- ishes
EASTERN RITES	586,019	542	108	650	26	31	472	502
*Philadelphia	167,506	116	12	128	1	—	209	111
St. Nicholas	30,222	33	11	44	3	—	19	36
Stamford	47,000	58	20	78	—	17	49	49
*Pittsburgh	151,886	81	10	91	—	5	138	84
Parma	35,904	53	4	57	3	—	24	56
Passaic	96,548	96	22	118	4	1	22	87
Van Nuys	No separate statistics available.							
St. Maron	34,226	66	1	67	4	5	8	48
Newton	22,727	39	28	67	11	3	3	31
Armenians (Ap. Ex.)	No separate statistics available.							
Chaldeans (Ap. Ex.)	No separate statistics available.							
MILITARY VICARIATE	2,138,000	—	—	—	—	—	—	—
TOTALS 1982	51,207,579	35,513	22,572	58,085	5,471	7,880	121,370	18,903
Totals 1981	50,449,842	35,627	22,771	53,398	4,725	7,966	122,653	18,829
Totals 1972	48,390,990	36,727	20,694	57,421	—	9,740	146,914	18,259

Dioceses with Interstate Lines

Diocesan lines usually fall within a single state and in some cases include a whole state.

The following dioceses, with their statistics as reported in tables throughout the Almanac, are exceptions.

Norwich, Conn., includes Fisher's Island, N.Y.

Wilmington, Del., includes all of Delaware and nine counties of Maryland.

Baltimore, includes all of Maryland except

nine counties under the jurisdiction of Wilmington and five under Washington.

Washington, D.C., includes five counties of Maryland.

El Paso, Tex., includes seven counties of New Mexico.

Gallup, N.M., has jurisdiction over several counties of Arizona.

Cheyenne, Wyo., includes all of Yellowstone National Park.

PERCENTAGE OF CATHOLICS IN U.S. POPULATION

(Source: *The Official Catholic Directory, 1982;* figures are as of Jan. 1, 1982. Total general population figures at the end of the table are U.S. Census Bureau estimates for Jan. 1 of the respective years. Archdioceses are indicated by an asterisk; for dioceses marked +, see Dioceses with Interstate Lines.)

Section, State Diocese	Catholic Pop.	Total Pop.	Cath. Pct.
NEW ENGLAND	**5,606,800**	**12,142,402**	**46.17**
Maine, Portland	272,306	1,028,000	26.49
New Hampshire			
Manchester	291,081	919,114	31.67
Vermont, Burlington	158,118	511,456	30.91
Massachusetts	2,942,673	5,627,525	52.30
*Boston	1,913,827	3,662,832	52.25
Fall River	340,000	530,000	64.15
Springfield	351,520	790,725	44.33
Worcester	337,326	643,968	52.38
Rhode Island, Providence	618,860	947,154	65.34
Connecticut	1,323,762	3,109,153	42.58
*Hartford	793,908	1,725,892	45.99
Bridgeport	331,350	808,700	40.97
Norwich+	198,504	574,561	34.55
MIDDLE ATLANTIC	**13,068,212**	**37,519,577**	**34.83**
New York	6,404,479	17,930,758	35.72
*New York	1,839,000	5,044,800	36.45
Albany	408,648	1,472,684	27.75
Brooklyn	1,372,402	4,122,261	33.29

Section, State Diocese	Catholic Pop.	Total Pop.	Cath. Pct.
New York			
Buffalo	825,991	1,664,728	49.62
Ogdensburg	168,896	395,563	42.70
Rochester	376,124	1,419,843	26.49
Rockville Centre	1,042,280	2,603,226	40.04
Syracuse	371,138	1,207,653	30.73
New Jersey	2,912,451	7,370,605	39.51
*Newark	1,374,484	2,756,902	49.86
Camden	351,603	1,145,494	30.69
Metuchen	411,010	977,223	42.06
Paterson	327,439	971,370	33.71
Trenton	447,915	1,519,616	29.48
Pennsylvania	3,751,282	12,218,214	30.70
*Philadelphia	1,386,247	3,662,506	37.85
Allentown	263,365	1,025,424	25.68
Altoona-Johnstown	153,209	654,338	23.41
Erie	225,773	911,529	24.77
Greensburg	224,926	722,738	31.12
Harrisburg	205,951	2,029,478	10.15
Pittsburgh	926,635	2,241,430	41.34
Scranton	365,176	970,771	37.62
SOUTH ATLANTIC	**3,183,504**	**36,933,835**	**8.62**
Delaware, Wilmington+	121,262	890,608	13.62
Maryland, *Baltimore	425,998	2,508,418	16.98

Section, State Diocese	Catholic Pop.	Total Pop.	Cath. Pct.
District of Columbia			
*Washington+	396,741	2,098,200	18.91
Virginia	294,276	5,405,861	5.44
Arlington	179,025	1,472,678	12.16
Richmond	115,251	3,933,183	2.93
West Virginia			
Wheeling-Charleston	106,420	1,949,644	5.46
North Carolina	100,828	5,862,912	1.76
Charlotte	51,792	3,101,207	1.67
Raleigh	49,036	2,761,705	1.78
South Carolina			
Charleston	65,871	3,121,820	2.11
Georgia	164,604	5,269,950	3.12
*Atlanta	109,651	3,345,400	3.28
Savannah	54,953	1,924,550	2.86
Florida	1,507,504	9,826,422	15.34
*Miami	896,702	3,450,641	25.99
Orlando	183,000	2,107,000	8.69
Pensacola-Tallahassee	44,430	862,237	5.15
St. Augustine	72,046	1,084,388	6.64
St. Petersburg	311,326	2,322,156	13.41
EAST NORTH CENTRAL	**10,299,843**	**41,419,725**	**24.87**
Ohio	2,336,103	10,791,426	21.65
*Cincinnati	506,000	2,716,193	18.63
Cleveland	942,300	2,843,377	33.14
Columbus	195,333	1,940,333	10.07
Steubenville	53,650	541,093	9.92
Toledo	347,608	1,486,614	23.38
Youngstown	291,212	1,263,816	23.04
Indiana	723,547	5,389,231	13.43
*Indianapolis	201,846	2,127,915	9.49
Evansville	89,917	441,854	20.35
Ft. Wayne-S. Bend	151,725	980,952	15.47
Gary	193,600	773,410	25.03
Lafayette	86,459	1,065,100	8.12
Illinois	3,576,130	11,413,344	31.33
*Chicago	2,374,138	5,693,562	41.70
Belleville	122,408	856,845	14.29
Joliet	411,000	1,200,000	34.25
Peoria	245,663	1,501,917	16.36
Rockford	236,428	1,027,342	23.01
Springfield	186,493	1,133,678	16.45
Michigan	2,068,088	9,117,621	22.68
*Detroit	1,259,807	4,387,783	28.71
Gaylord	86,718	384,189	22.57
Grand Rapids	152,835	906,483	16.86
Kalamazoo	96,461	863,911	11.17
Lansing	209,019	1,541,807	13.56
Marquette	90,353	320,028	28.23
Saginaw	172,895	713,420	24.23
Wisconsin	1,595,975	4,708,103	33.90
*Milwaukee	707,110	2,029,553	34.84
Green Bay	344,306	736,053	46.78
La Crosse	230,774	751,203	30.72
Madison	220,639	882,556	24.94
Superior	93,146	308,738	30.17
EAST SOUTH CENTRAL	**698,333**	**14,224,969**	**4.91**
Kentucky	365,626	3,616,669	10.11
*Louisville	211,550	1,301,024	16.26
Kentucky			
Covington	104,000	1,550,000	6.71
Owensboro	50,076	765,645	6.54
Tennessee	120,417	4,312,098	2.79
Memphis	48,140	1,500,000	3.21
Nashville	72,277	2,812,098	2.57
Alabama	115,368	3,865,048	2.98
*Mobile	59,713	1,415,213	4.22
Birmingham	55,655	2,449,835	2.27
Mississippi	96,922	2,431,154	3.99
Biloxi	53,300	631,154	8.44
Jackson	43,622	1,800,000	2.42
WEST NORTH CENTRAL	**3,434,732**	**17,146,012**	**20.03**
Minnesota	1,069,326	4,060,348	26.34
*St. Paul and Minneapolis	573,425	2,173,572	26.38
Crookston	43,886	239,045	18.36
Duluth	96,464	425,924	22.65
New Ulm	73,510	279,054	26.34
St. Cloud	154,721	409,791	37.76
Winona	127,320	532,962	23.89
Iowa	544,579	2,898,457	18.79
*Dubuque	237,596	995,648	23.86
Davenport	110,917	733,591	15.12
Des Moines	83,313	667,726	12.48
Sioux City	112,753	501,492	22.48
Missouri	824,757	4,907,409	16.81
*St. Louis	543,021	1,919,042	28.30
Jefferson City	85,574	730,592	11.71
Kansas City-St. Joseph	144,038	1,260,051	11.43
Springfield-Cape Girardeau	52,124	997,724	5.22
North Dakota	177,698	642,270	27.67
Bismarck	78,852	269,310	29.28
Fargo	98,846	372,960	26.50
South Dakota	140,129	660,556	21.21
Rapid City	40,138	178,208	22.52
Sioux Falls	99,991	482,348	20.73
Nebraska	331,662	1,566,351	21.17
*Omaha	208,007	750,582	27.71
Grand Island	54,945	306,000	17.96
Lincoln	68,710	509,769	13.48
Kansas	346,581	2,410,621	14.38
*Kansas City	147,059	952,000	15.45
Dodge City	38,747	220,972	17.53
Salina	61,627	348,387	17.69
Wichita	99,148	889,262	11.15
WEST SOUTH CENTRAL	**4,236,601**	**23,684,141**	**17.89**
Arkansas, Little Rock	61,298	2,284,037	2.68
Louisiana	1,330,713	3,990,347	33.35
*New Orleans	525,029	1,263,200	41.56
Alexandria-Shreveport	83,283	1,083,132	7.69
Baton Rouge	180,795	717,855	25.19
Houma-Thibodaux	132,733	201,222	65.96
Lafayette	320,191	498,093	64.28
Lake Charles	88,682	226,845	39.09
Oklahoma	128,848	2,920,496	4.41
*Oklahoma City	79,609	1,663,896	4.78
Tulsa	49,239	1,256,600	3.92

Section, State Diocese	Catholic Pop.	Total Pop.	Cath. Pct.	Section, State Diocese	Catholic Pop.	Total Pop.	Cath. Pct.
Texas	2,715,742	14,489,261	18.74	PACIFIC	6,186,084	31,894,741	19.40
*San Antonio	589,373	1,552,611	37.96	Washington	402,676	4,061,104	9.92
Amarillo	80,744	733,400	11.01	*Seattle	270,251	3,091,138	8.74
Austin	128,099	1,289,794	9.93	Spokane	74,525	574,966	12.96
Beaumont	94,497	675,600	13.99	Yakima	57,900	395,000	14.66
Brownsville	402,000	537,607	74.78	Oregon	327,230	2,634,317	12.42
Corpus Christi	310,750	601,193	51.69	*Portland	301,369	2,280,217	13.22
Dallas	178,047	2,788,800	6.38	Baker	25,861	354,100	7.30
El Paso+	244,958	900,000	27.22	California	5,206,275	23,779,335	21.90
Fort Worth	99,349	1,544,855	6.43	*Los Angeles	2,303,560	8,306,216	27.73
Galveston-Houston	514,490	3,253,961	15.81	*San Francisco	351,424	1,490,090	23.58
San Angelo	73,435	611,440	12.01	Fresno	310,500	1,463,878	21.21
Victoria	No separate statistics available.			Monterey	129,922	649,614	19.20
				Oakland	401,800	1,778,852	22.59
MOUNTAIN	1,769,451	11,028,543	16.04	Orange	365,004	1,931,570	18.90
				Sacramento	256,833	2,027,480	12.67
Montana	130,817	720,126	18.17	San Bernardino	248,881	1,522,491	16.35
Great Falls-Billings	65,792	351,858	18.70	San Diego	330,043	1,992,010	16.57
Helena	65,025	368,268	17.66	San Jose	301,000	1,295,071	23.24
Idaho, Boise	77,386	944,038	8.20	Santa Rosa	89,989	628,813	14.31
Wyoming, Cheyenne+	67,500	460,000	14.67	Stockton	117,319	693,250	16.92
Colorado	418,450	2,887,151	14.49	Alaska	40,903	430,985	9.49
*Denver	309,284	2,414,825	12.81	*Anchorage	20,933	250,000	8.37
Pueblo	109,166	472,326	23.11	Fairbanks	14,500	125,000	11.60
New Mexico	381,664	1,116,428	34.19	Juneau	5,470	55,985	9.77
*Santa Fe	323,319	780,000	41.45	Hawaii, Honolulu	209,000	989,000	21.13
Gallup+	58,345	336,428	17.34	EASTERN RITES	586,019	—	—
Arizona	488,027	2,610,800	17.16	MILITARY			
Phoenix	263,027	1,719,800	15.29	VICARIATE	2,138,000	—	—
Tucson	225,000	891,000	25.25	TOTALS 1982	51,207,579	231,009,000	22.17
Utah, Salt Lake City	61,607	1,490,000	4.13	Totals 1981	50,449,842	228,811,000	22.05
Nevada, Reno-Las Vegas	144,000	800,000	18.00	Totals 1972	48,390,990	208,056,000	23.26

INFANT BAPTISMS AND CONVERTS IN THE UNITED STATES

(Source: *The Official Catholic Directory, 1982;* figures as of Jan. 1, 1982. Archdioceses are indicated by an asterisk; for dioceses marked +, see Dioceses with Interstate Lines.)

Section, State Diocese	Infant Baptisms	Converts	TOTAL	Section, State Diocese	Infant Baptisms	Converts	TOTAL
NEW ENGLAND	82,023	3,384	85,407	New York			
				Brooklyn	24,874	655	25,529
Maine, Portland	4,298	526	4,824	Buffalo	10,039	488	10,527
New Hampshire, Manchester	5,002	282	5,284	Ogdensburg	3,037	250	3,287
Vermont, Burlington	2,447	236	2,683	Rochester	6,999	587	7,586
Massachusetts	43,416	1,311	44,727	Rockville Centre	19,284	287	19,571
*Boston	27,217	722	27,939	Syracuse	7,249	569	7,818
Fall River	5,669	166	5,835	New Jersey	45,006	1,859	46,865
Springfield	5,495	236	5,731	*Newark	17,713	423	18,136
Worcester	5,035	187	5,222	Camden	7,134	569	7,703
Rhode Island, Providence	7,644	284	7,928	Metuchen	5,613	200	5,813
Connecticut	19,216	745	19,961	Paterson	6,709	224	6,933
*Hartford	11,615	379	11,994	Trenton	7,837	443	8,280
Bridgeport	4,511	193	4,704	Pennsylvania	69,793	6,433	76,226
Norwich+	3,090	173	3,263	*Philadelphia	33,972	2,829	36,801
				Allentown	4,133	198	4,331
MIDDLE ATLANTIC	227,304	12,503	239,807	Altoona-Johnstown	2,627	339	2,966
				Erie	4,123	570	4,693
New York	112,505	4,211	116,716	Greensburg	3,258	416	3,674
*New York	34,360	1,375	35,735	Harrisburg	4,263	830	5,093
Albany	6,663	—	6,663	Pittsburgh	11,913	906	12,819
				Scranton	5,504	345	5,849

Section, State Diocese	Infant Baptisms	Converts	TOTAL
SOUTH ATLANTIC	**57,483**	**9,036**	**66,519**
Delaware, Wilmington+	2,621	278	2,899
Maryland, *Baltimore	8,462	1,300	9,762
District of Columbia			
*Washington+	6,248	1,060	7,308
Virginia	6,334	1,220	7,554
Arlington	3,765	501	4,266
Richmond	2,569	719	3,288
West Virginia			
Wheeling-Charleston	1,962	662	2,624
North Carolina	2,333	647	2,980
Charlotte	1,205	358	1,563
Raleigh	1,128	289	1,417
South Carolina, Charleston	1,655	500	2,155
Georgia	3,143	993	4,136
*Atlanta	2,086	534	2,620
Savannah	1,057	459	1,516
Florida	24,725	2,376	27,101
*Miami	13,301	716	14,017
Orlando	3,732	542	4,274
Pensacola-Tallahassee	983	262	1,245
St. Augustine	1,578	401	1,979
St. Petersburg	5,131	455	5,586
EAST NORTH CENTRAL	**179,046**	**25,020**	**204,066**
Ohio	38,864	5,968	44,832
*Cincinnati	9,613	1,409	11,022
Cleveland	13,379	1,525	14,904
Columbus	3,916	1,139	5,055
Steubenville	1,053	264	1,317
Toledo	6,291	957	7,248
Youngstown	4,612	674	5,286
Indiana	14,408	3,344	17,752
*Indianapolis	4,697	1,315	6,012
Evansville	1,901	428	2,329
Ft. Wayne-South Bend	2,950	615	3,565
Gary	3,233	415	3,648
Lafayette	1,627	571	2,198
Illinois	60,635	7,940	68,575
*Chicago	36,024	4,281	40,305
Belleville	2,580	644	3,224
Joliet	8,188	543	8,731
Peoria	4,831	1,060	5,891
Rockford	5,206	568	5,774
Springfield	3,806	844	4,650
Michigan	35,848	5,351	41,199
*Detroit	19,372	2,195	21,567
Gaylord	1,701	284	1,985
Grand Rapids	3,315	750	4,065
Kalamazoo	1,797	381	2,178
Lansing	4,814	1,073	5,887
Marquette	1,821	223	2,044
Saginaw	3,028	445	3,473
Wisconsin	29,291	2,417	31,708
*Milwaukee	12,656	962	13,618
Green Bay	6,201	385	6,586
La Crosse	4,525	479	5,004
Madison	3,780	368	4,148
Superior	2,129	223	2,352

Section, State Diocese	Infant Baptisms	Converts	TOTAL
EAST SOUTH CENTRAL	**14,419**	**3,881**	**18,300**
Kentucky	7,491	1,557	9,048
*Louisville	4,020	769	4,789
Covington	2,222	484	2,706
Owensboro	1,249	304	1,553
Tennessee	2,486	850	3,336
Memphis	1,031	321	1,352
Nashville	1,455	529	1,984
Alabama	2,242	971	3,213
*Mobile	1,256	454	1,710
Birmingham	986	517	1,503
Mississippi	2,200	503	2,703
Biloxi	1,310	256	1,566
Jackson	890	247	1,137
WEST NORTH CENTRAL	**75,828**	**11,466**	**87,294**
Minnesota	23,840	2,032	25,872
*St. Paul and Minneapolis	12,344	1,052	13,396
Crookston	1,051	125	1,176
Duluth	2,124	222	2,346
New Ulm	1,761	177	1,938
St. Cloud	3,700	234	3,934
Winona	2,860	222	3,082
Iowa	12,235	2,148	14,383
*Dubuque	4,923	758	5,681
Davenport	2,620	545	3,165
Des Moines	1,956	475	2,431
Sioux City	2,736	370	3,106
Missouri	15,593	3,345	18,938
*St. Louis	10,080	1,758	11,838
Jefferson City	1,744	359	2,103
Kansas City-St. Joseph	2,748	801	3,549
Springfield-Cape Girardeau	1,021	427	1,448
North Dakota	4,325	313	4,638
Bismarck	2,001	182	2,183
Fargo	2,324	131	2,455
South Dakota	3,405	548	3,953
Rapid City	1,107	149	1,256
Sioux Falls	2,298	399	2,697
Nebraska	7,967	1,279	9,246
*Omaha	4,822	611	5,433
Grand Island	1,339	290	1,629
Lincoln	1,806	378	2,184
Kansas	8,463	1,801	10,264
*Kansas City	3,273	678	3,951
Dodge City	983	150	1,133
Salina	1,507	324	1,831
Wichita	2,700	649	3,349
WEST SOUTH CENTRAL	**113,473**	**8,810**	**122,283**
Arkansas, Little Rock	1,581	582	2,163
Louisiana	29,270	2,277	31,547
*New Orleans	9,913	685	10,598
Alexandria-Shreveport	2,070	456	2,526
Baton Rouge	5,013	525	5,538
Houma-Thibodaux	2,669	83	2,752
Lafayette	7,555	205	7,760
Lake Charles	2,050	323	2,373

Section, State Diocese	Infant Baptisms	Converts	TOTAL
Oklahoma	3,152	1,075	4,227
*Oklahoma City	2,085	653	2,738
Tulsa	1,067	422	1,489
Texas	79,470	4,876	84,346
*San Antonio	15,866	624	16,490
Amarillo	3,758	272	4,030
Austin	3,818	383	4,201
Beaumont	2,077	322	2,399
Brownsville	9,149	47	9,196
Corpus Christi	6,500	166	6,666
Dallas	6,393	965	7,358
El Paso+	10,434	191	10,625
Fort Worth	3,096	491	3,587
Galveston-Houston	15,134	1,260	16,394
San Angelo	3,245	155	3,400
Victoria	No separate statistics available.		
MOUNTAIN	**47,766**	**4,472**	**52,238**
Montana	3,079	456	3,535
Great Falls-Billings	1,767	311	2,078
Helena	1,312	145	1,457
Idaho, Boise	2,090	589	2,679
Wyoming, Cheyenne+	1,824	241	2,065
Colorado	12,336	1,099	13,435
*Denver	9,701	909	10,610
Pueblo	2,635	190	2,825
New Mexico	9,823	631	10,454
*Santa Fe	7,951	346	8,297
Gallup+	1,872	285	2,157
Arizona	14,288	863	15,151
Phoenix	7,943	558	8,501
Tucson	6,345	305	6,650
Utah, Salt Lake City	1,785	267	2,052
Nevada, Reno-Las Vegas	2,541	326	2,867
PACIFIC	**161,179**	**11,537**	**172,716**
Washington	9,433	1,943	11,376
*Seattle	6,288	1,355	7,643
Spokane	1,475	426	1,901
Yakima	1,670	162	1,832

Section, State Diocese	Infant Baptisms	Converts	TOTAL
Oregon	4,488	1,175	5,663
*Portland	3,716	954	4,670
Baker	772	221	993
California	141,295	7,839	149,134
*Los Angeles	66,071	2,381	68,452
*San Francisco	7,489	561	8,050
Fresno	11,936	477	12,413
Monterey	3,255	219	3,474
Oakland	7,322	647	7,969
Orange	9,569	687	10,256
Sacramento	6,342	678	7,020
San Bernardino	6,768	682	7,450
San Diego	9,490	652	10,142
San Jose	7,011	350	7,361
Santa Rosa	2,110	174	2,284
Stockton	3,932	331	4,263
Alaska	1,177	186	1,363
*Anchorage	625	117	742
Fairbanks	408	18	426
Juneau	144	51	195
Hawaii, Honolulu	4,786	394	5,180
EASTERN RITES	**4,300**	**386**	**4,686**
*Philadelphia	790	34	824
St. Nicholas	367	61	428
Stamford	326	14	340
*Pittsburgh	645	37	682
Parma	512	94	606
Passaic	589	39	628
Van Nuys	No separate statistics available.		
St. Maron	670	45	715
Newton	401	62	463
Armenians (Ap. Ex.)	No separate statistics available.		
Chaldeans (Ap. Ex.)	No separate statistics available.		
MILITARY VICARIATE	**19,765**	**2,366**	**22,131**
TOTALS 1982	**982,586**	**92,861**	**1,075,447**
Totals 1981	943,632	88,942	1,032,574
Totals 1972	1,054,933	79,012	1,133,945

STATISTICAL SUMMARY OF THE CHURCH IN THE U.S.

(Principal source: *The Official Catholic Directory, 1982.* Comparisons are with figures reported in the previous edition.)

Catholic Population: 51,207,579; increase, 757,737. Percent of total population: 1982 — 22.1; 1981 — 22.05.

Jurisdictions: 33 archdioceses, 142 dioceses (including Guam), 2 apostolic exarchates, the military vicariate.

Cardinals: 9 (4 head archiepiscopal sees, 1 is a Roman Curia official, 4 are retired). As of Aug. 1, 1982.

Archbishops: 54 (32 residential archbishops, including 4 cardinals; 2 titular archbishops; 17 retired, including 4 cardinals; 3 serving outside the U.S.). As of Aug. 1, 1982.

Bishops: 370 (137 residential bishops; 1 coadjutor bishop; 109 auxiliary bishops; 83 retired; 40 serving outside the U.S.) As of Aug. 1, 1982.

Abbots: 92.

Priests: 58,085; decrease, 313. Includes diocesan or secular priests, 35,513 (decrease, 114); religious order priests, 22,572 (decrease, 199).

Permanent Deacons: 5,471; increase, 746.

Brothers: 7,880; decrease, 86.

Sisters: 121,370; decrease, 1,283.

Seminarians: 11,645; decrease, 823. Includes: diocesan seminarians, 7,625 (decrease, 329); religious order seminarians, 4,020 (decrease, 494).

Infant Baptisms: 982,586; increase, 38,954.

Converts: 92,861; increase, 3,919.

Marriages: 353,375; increase, 2,630.

Deaths: 425,241; increase, 8,194.

Parishes: 18,903; increase, 74.

Seminaries, Diocesan: 86; decrease, 2.

Religious Seminaries, Novitiates, Scholasticates: 217; decrease, 23.

Colleges and Universities: 237; increase, 1. Students, 533,086; decrease, 3,592.

High Schools: 1,470; decrease, 34. Students, 833,902; decrease, 4,345.

Elementary Schools: 8,079; decrease, 38. Students, 2,333,469; increase, 37,089.

Teachers: 173,230; increase, 2,254. Includes: priests, 5,101 (decrease, 436); scholastics, 160 (decrease, 59); brothers, 2,889 (decrease, 128); sisters, 36,066 (decrease, 2,719); lay teachers, 129,014 (increase, 5,596).

Public School Students in Religious Instruction Programs: 4,300,496; decrease, 90,009. Includes: high school students, 977,098 (increase, 14,186); elementary school students, 3,323,398 (decrease, 104,195).

Catholic Hospitals: 710. decrease, 19. Patients treated, 37,168,573; increase, 175,471.

Nurses Schools: 121; decrease, 3. Student nurses, 20,027; decrease, 361.

Homes for Aged: 560; increase, 36. Residents, 70,861; increase, 4,334.

Orphanages: 190; children, 13,296. Children in Foster Homes, 15,317.

CATHEDRALS IN THE UNITED STATES

A cathedral is the principal church in a diocese, the one in which the bishop has his seat *(cathedra)*. He is the actual rector, although many functions of the church, which usually serves a parish, are the responsibility of a priest serving as the administrator. Because of the dignity of a cathedral, the dates of its dedication and its patronal feast are observed throughout a diocese.

The pope's cathedral, the Basilica of St. John Lateran, is the highest-ranking church in the world.

(Archdioceses are indicated by asterisk.)

Albany, N.Y.: Immaculate Conception.

Alexandria-Shreveport, La.: St. Francis Xavier. (Alexandria); St. John Berchmans (Shreveport Co-Cathedral).

Allentown, Pa.: St. Catherine of Siena.

Altoona-Johnstown, Pa.: Blessed Sacrament (Altoona); St. John Gualbert (Johnstown Co-Cathedral).

Amarillo, Tex.: St. Laurence.

Anchorage,* Alaska: Holy Family.

Arlington, Va: St. Thomas More.

Atlanta,* Ga.: Christ the King.

Austin, Tex.: St. Mary (Immaculate Conception).

Baker, Ore.: St. Francis de Sales.

Baltimore,* Md.: Mary Our Queen; Basilica of the Assumption of the Blessed Virgin Mary (Co-Cathedral).

Baton Rouge, La.: St. Joseph.

Beaumont, Tex.: St. Anthony (of Padua).

Belleville, Ill.: St. Peter.

Biloxi, Miss.: Nativity of the Blessed Virgin Mary.

Birmingham, Ala.: St. Paul.

Bismarck, N.D.: Holy Spirit.

Boise, Ida.: St. John the Evangelist.

Boston,* Mass.: Holy Cross.

Bridgeport, Conn.: St. Augustine.

Brooklyn, N.Y.: St. James (Minor Basilica).

Brownsville, Tex.: Immaculate Conception.

Buffalo, N.Y.: St. Joseph.

Burlington, Vt.: Immaculate Conception.

Camden, N.J.: Immaculate Conception.

Charleston, S.C.: St. John the Baptist.

Charlotte, N.C.: St. Patrick.

Cheyenne, Wyo.: St. Mary.

Chicago,* Ill.: Holy Name (of Jesus).

Cincinnati,* Ohio: St. Peter in Chains.

Cleveland, Ohio: St. John the Evangelist.

Columbus, Ohio: St. Joseph.

Corpus Christi, Tex.: Corpus Christi.

Covington, Ky.: Basilica of the Assumption.

Crookston, Minn.: Immaculate Conception.

Dallas, Tex.: Cathedral-Santuario de Guadalupe.

Davenport, Ia.: Sacred Heart.

Denver,* Colo.: Immaculate Conception (Minor Basilica).

Des Moines, Ia.: St. Ambrose.

Detroit,* Mich.: Blessed Sacrament.

Dodge City, Kans.: Sacred Heart.

Dubuque,* Ia.: St. Raphael.

Duluth, Minn.: Holy Rosary.

El Paso, Tex.: St. Patrick.

Erie, Pa.: St. Peter.

Evansville, Ind.: Most Holy Trinity (Pro-Cathedral).

Fairbanks, Alaska: Sacred Heart.

Fall River, Mass.: St. Mary of the Assumption.

Fargo, N.D.: St. Mary.

Fort Wayne-S. Bend, Ind.: Immaculate Conception (Fort Wayne); St. Matthew (South Bend Co-Cathedral).

Fort Worth, Tex.: St. Patrick.

Fresno, Calif.: St. John the Baptist.

Gallup, N.M.: Sacred Heart.

Galveston-Houston, Tex.: St. Mary (Minor Basilica, Galveston); Sacred Heart (Houston Co-Cathedral).

Gary, Ind.: Holy Angels.

Gaylord, Mich.: St. Mary, Our Lady of Mt. Carmel.

Grand Island, Nebr.: Nativity of Blessed Virgin Mary.

Grand Rapids, Mich.: St. Andrew.

Great Falls-Billings, Mont.: St. Ann (Great Falls); St. Patrick (Billings Co-Cathedral).

Green Bay, Wis.: St. Francis Xavier.

Greensburg, Pa.: Blessed Sacrament.

Harrisburg, Pa.: St. Patrick.

Hartford,* Conn.: St. Joseph.

Helena, Mont.: St. Helena.

Honolulu, Hawaii: Our Lady of Peace.

Houma-Thibodaux, La.: St. Francis de Sales (Houma); St. Joseph (Thibodaux Co-Cathedral).

Indianapolis,* Ind.: Sts. Peter and Paul.

Jackson, Miss.: St. Peter.
Jefferson City, Mo.: St. Joseph.
Joliet, Ill.: St. Raymond Nonnatus.
Juneau, Alaska: Nativity of the Blessed Virgin Mary.
Kalamazoo, Mich.: St. Augustine.
Kansas City,* Kans.: St. Peter the Apostle.
Kansas City-St. Joseph, Mo.: Immaculate Conception (Kansas City); St. Joseph (St. Joseph Co-Cathedral).
La Crosse, Wis.: St. Joseph.
Lafayette, Ind.: St. Mary.
Lafayette, La.: St. John the Evangelist.
Lake Charles, La.: Immaculate Conception.
Lansing, Mich.: St. Mary.
Lincoln, Nebr.: Cathedral of the Risen Christ.
Little Rock, Ark.: St. Andrew.
Los Angeles,* Calif.: St. Vibiana.
Louisville,* Ky.: Assumption.
Madison, Wis.: St. Raphael.
Manchester, N.H.: St. Joseph.
Marquette, Mich.: St. Peter.
Memphis, Tenn.: Immaculate Conception.
Metuchen, N.J.: St. Francis (of Assisi).
Miami,* Fla.: St. Mary (Immaculate Conception).
Milwaukee,* Wis.: St. John.
Mobile,* Ala.: Immaculate Conception (Minor Basilica).
Monterey, Calif.: San Carlos Borromeo.
Nashville, Tenn.: Incarnation.
Newark,* N.J.: Sacred Heart.
New Orleans,* La.: Cathedral (Basilica) of St. Louis.
Newton, Mass. (Melkite Rite): Our Lady of the Annunciation (Boston).
New Ulm, Minn.: Holy Trinity.
New York,* N.Y.: St. Patrick.
Norwich, Conn.: St. Patrick.
Oakland, Calif.: St. Francis de Sales.
Ogdensburg, N.Y.: St. Mary (Immaculate Conception).
Oklahoma City,* Okla.: Our Lady of Perpetual Help.
Omaha,* Nebr.: St. Cecilia.
Orange, Calif.: Holy Family.
Orlando, Fla.: St. James.
Owensboro, Ky.: St. Stephen.
Parma, Ohio (Byzantine Rite): St. John the Baptist.
Passaic, N.J. (Byzantine Rite): St. Michael.
Paterson, N.J.: St. John the Baptist.
Pensacola-Tallahassee, Fla.: Sacred Heart (Pensacola); St. Thomas More (Tallahassee Co-Cathedral).
Peoria, Ill.: St. Mary.
Philadelphia,* Pa.: Sts. Peter and Paul (Minor Basilica).
Philadelphia,* Pa. (Byzantine Rite): Immaculate Conception.
Phoenix, Ariz.: Sts. Simon and Jude.
Pittsburgh,* Pa. (Byzantine Rite): St. John the Baptist, Munhall.
Pittsburgh, Pa.: St. Paul.
Portland, Me.: Immaculate Conception.

Portland,* Ore.: Immaculate Conception.
Providence, R.I.: Sts. Peter and Paul.
Pueblo, Colo.: Sacred Heart.
Raleigh, N.C.: Sacred Heart.
Rapid City, S.D.: Our Lady of Perpetual Help.
Reno-Las Vegas, Nev.: St. Thomas Aquinas (Reno), Guardian Angel (Las Vegas Co-Cathedral).
Richmond, Va.: Sacred Heart.
Rochester, N.Y.: Sacred Heart.
Rockford, Ill.: St. Peter.
Rockville Centre, N.Y.: St. Agnes.
Sacramento, Calif.: Blessed Sacrament.
Saginaw, Mich.: St. Mary.
St. Augustine, Fla.: St. Augustine (Minor Basilica).
St. Cloud, Minn.: St. Mary.
St. Louis,* Mo.: St. Louis.
St. Maron, Brooklyn, N.Y. (Maronite Rite): Our Lady of Lebanon.
St. Nicholas in Chicago (Byzantine Rite): St. Nicholas.
St. Paul and Minneapolis,* Minn.: St. Paul (St. Paul); Basilica of St. Mary (Minneapolis Co-Cathedral).
St. Petersburg, Fla.: St. Jude the Apostle.
Salina, Kans.: Sacred Heart.
Salt Lake City, Utah: The Madeleine.
San Angelo, Tex.: Sacred Heart.
San Antonio,* Tex.: San Fernando.
San Bernardino, Calif: Our Lady of the Rosary.
San Diego, Calif.: St. Joseph.
San Francisco,* Calif.: St. Mary (Assumption).
San Jose, Calif.: St. Patrick.
Santa Fe,* N.M.: San Francisco de Asis.
Santa Rosa, Calif.: St. Eugene.
Savannah, Ga.: St. John the Baptist.
Scranton, Pa.: St. Peter.
Seattle,* Wash.: St. James.
Sioux City, Ia.: Epiphany.
Sioux Falls, S.D.: St. Joseph.
Spokane, Wash.: Our Lady of Lourdes.
Springfield, Ill.: Immaculate Conception.
Springfield, Mass.: St. Michael.
Springfield-Cape Girardeau, Mo.: St. Agnes (Springfield): St. Mary (Cape Girardeau Co-Cathedral).
Stamford, Conn. (Byzantine Rite): St. Vladimir.
Steubenville, Ohio: Holy Name.
Stockton, Calif: Annunciation.
Superior, Wis.: Christ the King.
Syracuse, N.Y.: Immaculate Conception.
Toledo, Ohio: Blessed Virgin Mary of the Holy Rosary.
Trenton, N.J.: St. Mary (Assumption).
Tucson, Ariz.: St. Augustine.
Tulsa, Okla.: Holy Family.
Van Nuys, Calif. (Byzantine Rite). St. Mary.
Victoria, Tex.: Our Lady of Victory.
Washington,* D.C.: St. Matthew.
Wheeling-Charleston, W. Va.: St. Joseph

(Wheeling); Sacred Heart (Charleston Co-Cathedral).
Wichita, Kans.: Immaculate Conception.
Wilmington, Del.: St. Peter.
Winona, Minn.: Sacred Heart.
Worcester, Mass.: St. Paul.

Yakima, Wash.: St. Paul:
Youngstown, Ohio: St. Columba.
Apostolic Exarhate for Chaldean-Rite Catholics in the United States: Our Lady of Chaldeans Cathedral (Mother of God Church), Southfield, Mich.

BASILICAS IN U.S., CANADA

Basilica is a title assigned to certain churches because of their antiquity, dignity, historical importance or significance as centers of worship. Major basilicas have the papal altar and holy door, which is opened at the beginning of a Jubilee Year; minor basilicas enjoy certain ceremonial privileges.

Among the major basilicas are the patriarchal basilicas of St. John Lateran, St. Peter, St. Paul Outside the Walls and St. Mary Major in Rome; St. Francis and St. Mary of the Angels in Assisi, Italy.

The patriarchal basilica of St. Lawrence, Rome, is a minor basilica.

The dates in the listings below indicate when the churches were designated as basilicas.

Minor Basilicas in U.S., Puerto Rico

Alabama: Mobile, Cathedral of the Immaculate Conception (Mar. 10, 1962).

California: San Francisco, Mission Dolores (Feb. 8, 1952); Carmel, Old Mission of San Carlos (Feb. 5, 1960); Alameda, St. Joseph (Jan. 21, 1972); San Diego, Mission San Diego de Alcala (Nov. 17, 1975).

Colorado: Denver, Cathedral of the Immaculate Conception (Nov. 3, 1979).

Florida: St. Augustine, Cathedral of St. Augustine (Dec. 4, 1976).

Illinois: Chicago, Our Lady of Sorrows (May 4, 1956), Queen of All Saints (Mar. 26, 1962).

Indiana: Vincennes, Old Cathedral (Mar. 14, 1970).

Iowa: Dyersville, St. Francis Xavier (May 11, 1956).

Kentucky: Trappist, Our Lady of Gethsemani (May 3, 1949); Covington, Cathedral of Assumption (Dec. 8, 1953).

Louisiana: New Orleans, St. Louis King of France (Dec. 9, 1964).

Maryland: Baltimore, Assumption of the Blessed Virgin Mary (Sept. 1, 1937).

Massachusetts: Roxbury, Perpetual Help ("Mission Church") (Sept. 8, 1954).

Michigan: Grand Rapids, St. Adalbert (Aug. 22, 1979).

Minnesota: Minneapolis. St. Mary (Feb. 1, 1926).

Missouri: Conception, Basilica of Immaculate Conception (Sept. 14, 1940); St. Louis, St. Louis King of France (Jan. 27, 1961).

New York: Brooklyn, Our Lady of Perpetual Help (Sept. 5, 1969), Cathedral-Basilica of St. James (June 22, 1982); Lackawanna, Our Lady of Victory (1926); Youngstown, Blessed Virgin Mary of the Rosary of Fatima (Oct. 7, 1975).

Ohio: Carey, Shrine of Our Lady of Consolation (Oct. 21, 1971).

Pennsylvania: Latrobe, St. Vincent Basilica, Benedictine Archabbey (Aug. 22, 1955); Conewago, Basilica of the Sacred Heart (June 30, 1962); Philadelphia, Sts. Peter and Paul (Sept. 27, 1976).

Texas: Galveston, St. Mary Cathedral (Aug. 11, 1979).

Wisconsin: Milwaukee, St. Josaphat (Mar. 10, 1929).

Puerto Rico: San Juan, Cathedral of San Juan (Jan. 25, 1978).

Minor Basilicas in Canada

Manitoba: St. Boniface, Cathedral Basilica of St. Boniface (June 10, 1949).

Newfoundland: St. John's, Cathedral Basilica of St. John the Baptist.

Nova Scotia: Halifax, St. Mary's Basilica (June 14, 1950).

Ontario: Ottawa, Basilica of Notre Dame; London, St. Peter's Cathedral (Dec. 13, 1961).

Prince Edward Island: Charlottetown, Basilica of St. Dunstan.

Quebec: Sherbrooke, Cathedral Basilica of St. Michael (July 31, 1959). Montreal, Cathedral Basilica of St. James the Greater; St. Joseph of Mount Royal. Cap-de-la-Madeleine, Basilica of Our Lady of the Cape (Aug. 15, 1964). Quebec, Basilica of Notre Dame; St. Anne de Beaupre, Basilica of St. Anne.

AMERICAN COLLEGE, LOUVAIN

The American College was founded by the bishops of the United States in 1857 as a residence and house of formation for U.S. seminarians and graduate students pursuing courses in theology and related subjects at the Catholic Universities of Leuven and Louvain-la-Neuve (dating from 1425) in Belgium.

The college is administered by an American rector and staff, and operates under the auspices of a special committee of the National Conference of Catholic Bishops. Archbishop Peter L. Gerety of Newark is chairman of the committee. The present rector, the 10th, is Father William J. Greytak of Helena, Mont.

The address is: American College, University of Louvain, Naamsestraat 10, B-3000 Leuven, Belgium.

The current enrollment of the American College includes students from more than 43 dioceses in the U.S., Canada and Europe.

CHANCERY OFFICES OF U.S. ARCHDIOCESES AND DIOCESES

A chancery office, under this or another title, is the central administrative office of an archdiocese or diocese.

(Archdioceses are indicated by asterisk.)

Albany, N.Y.: 465 State St., Box 6297, Quail Station. 12206.

Alexandria-Shreveport, La.: 2417 Texas Ave., P.O. Box 7417, Alexandria. 71306.

Allentown, Pa.: 202 N. 17th St., P.O. Box F. 18105.

Altoona-Johnstown, Pa.: Box 126, Logan Blvd., Hollidaysburg, Pa. 16648.

Amarillo, Tex.: 1800 N. Spring St., P.O. Box 5644. 79107.

Anchorage,* Alaska: P.O. Box 2239. 99510.

Arlington, Va.: 200 N. Glebe Rd. 22203.

Atlanta,* Ga.: Catholic Center, 680 W. Peachtree St. N.W. 30308.

Austin, Tex.: N. Congress and 16th, P.O. Box 13327. Capitol Sta. 78711.

Baker, Ore.: Baker and First Sts., P.O. Box 826, 97814.

Baltimore,* Md.: 320 Cathedral St. 21201.

Baton Rouge, La.: P.O. Box 2028. 70821.

Beaumont, Tex.: 703 Archie St., P.O. Box 3948. 77704.

Belleville, Ill.: The Catholic Center, 220 W. Lincoln St. 62221.

Biloxi, Miss.: P.O. Box 1189. 39533.

Birmingham, Ala.: P.O. Box 2086. 35201.

Bismarck, N.D.: 420 Raymond St., Box 1575. 58501.

Boise, Ida.: Box 769. 83701.

Boston,* Mass.: 2121 Commonwealth Ave., Brighton, Mass. 02135.

Bridgeport, Conn.: The Catholic Center, 238 Jewett Ave. 06606.

Brooklyn, N.Y.: 75 Greene Ave., P.O. Box C. 11202.

Brownsville, Tex.: P.O. Box 2279. 78520.

Buffalo, N.Y.: 35 Lincoln Parkway. 14222.

Burlington, Vt.: 351 North Ave. 05401.

Camden, N.J.: 1845 Haddon Ave., P.O. Box 709, 01801.

Charleston, S.C.: 119 Broad St., P.O. Box 818. 29402.

Charlotte, N.C.: P.O. Box 36776. 28236.

Cheyenne, Wyo.: Box 426. 82001.

Chicago,* Ill.: 155 E. Superior. 60611.

Cincinnati,* O.: 100 E. 8th St. 45202.

Cleveland, O.: Chancery Bldg., 1027 Superior Ave. 44114.

Columbus, O.: 198 E. Broad St. 43215.

Corpus Christi, Tex.: 620 Lipan St. 78401.

Covington, Ky.: 1140 Madison Ave., P.O. Box 192. 41012.

Crookston, Minn.: 1200 Memorial Dr., P.O. Box 610. 56716.

Dallas, Tex.: 3915 Lemmon Ave., P.O. Box 190507. 75219.

Davenport, Ia.: St. Vincent Center, 2706 Gaines St. 52804.

Denver,* Colo.: 200 Josephine St. 80206.

Des Moines, Ia.: 2910 Grand Ave., P.O. Box 1816. 50306.

Detroit,* Mich.: 1234 Washington Blvd. 48226.

Dodge City, Kans.: 910 Central Ave., P.O. Box 849. 67801.

Dubuque,* Ia.: 1229 Mt. Loretta Ave. 52001.

Duluth, Minn.: 215 W. 4th St. 55806.

El Paso, Tex.: 499 St. Matthews. 79907.

Erie, Pa.: 205 W. 9th St. 16501.

Evansville, Ind.: P.O. Box 4169. 47711.

Fairbanks, Alaska: 1316 Peger Rd. 99701.

Fall River, Mass.: 47 Underwood St., Box 2577. 02722.

Fargo, N.D.: 1310 Broadway, Box 1750. 58107.

Fort Wayne-South Bend, Ind.: P.O. Box 390, Fort Wayne. 46801.

Fort Worth, Tex.: 1206 Throckmorton St. 76102.

Fresno, Calif.: P.O. Box 1668, 1550 N. Fresno St. 93717.

Gallup, N. Mex.: 711 S. Puerco Dr., P.O. Box 1338. 87301.

Galveston-Houston, Tex.: 1700 San Jacinto St., Houston. 77002.

Gary, Ind.: 975 W. Sixth Ave., P.O. Box M-474. 46401.

Gaylord, Mich.: M-32 West, P.O. Box 700. 49735.

Grand Island, Nebr.: 311 W. 17th St., P.O. Box 996. 68801.

Grand Rapids, Mich.: 265 Sheldon Ave. S.E. 49503.

Great Falls-Billings, Mont.: P.O. Box 1399, Great Falls. 59403.

Green Bay, Wis.: Box 66. 54305.

Greensburg, Pa.: 723 E. Pittsburgh St. 15601.

Harrisburg, Pa.: P.O. Box 2153. 17105.

Hartford,* Conn.: 134 Farmington Ave. 06105.

Helena, Mont.: 515 North Ewing, P.O. Box 1729. 59624.

Honolulu, Hawaii: 1184 Bishop St. 96813.

Houma-Thibodaux, La.: 1220 Aycock St., P.O. Box 9077, Houma, La. 70361.

Indianapolis,* Ind.: 1350 N. Pennsylvania St. 46202.

Jackson, Miss.: 237 E. Amite St., P.O. Box 2248. 39205.

Jefferson City, Mo.: 605 Clark Ave. P.O. Box 417. 65101.

Joliet, Ill.: 425 Summit St. 60435.

Juneau, Alaska: 419 6th St. 99801.

Kalamazoo, Mich.: 215 N. Westnedge. Ave., P.O. Box 949, 49005.

Kansas City,* Kans.: 2220 Central Ave., P.O. Box 2328. 66110.

Kansas City-St. Joseph, Mo.: P.O. Box 1037, Kansas City. 64141.

La Crosse, Wis.: P.O. Box 69. 54601.

Lafayette in Indiana: P.O. Box 260, 47902.

Lafayette, La.: P.O. Drawer 3387. 70502.

Lake Charles, La.: P.O. Box 3223. 70602.

Lansing, Mich.: 300 W. Ottawa. 48933.

Lincoln, Nebr.: 3400 Sheridan Blvd., P.O. Box 80328. 68501.

Little Rock, Ark.: 2415 N. Tyler St. 72217.

Los Angeles,* Calif.: 1531 W. 9th St. 90015.

Louisville,* Ky.: 212 E. College St., P.O. Box 1073. 40201.

Madison, Wis.: 15 E. Wilson St. 53701.

Manchester, N. H.: 153 Ash St. 03105.

Marquette, Mich.: 444 S. Fourth St., P.O. Box 550. 49855.

Memphis, Tenn.: 1325 Jefferson Ave., 38104.

Metuchen, N.J.: 10 Library Pl., P.O. Box 191. 08840.

Miami,* Fla.: 6301 Biscayne Blvd. 33138.

Milwaukee,* Wis.: 345 N. 95th St., P.O. Box 2018. 53201.

Mobile,* Ala.: 400 Government St., P.O. Box 1966. 36633.

Monterey, Calif.: 580 Fremont Blvd. 93940.

Nashville, Tenn.: 2400 21st Ave. S. 37212.

Newark,* N.J.: 31 Mulberry St. 07102.

New Orleans,* La.: 7887 Walmsley Ave. 70125.

Newton, Mass. (Melkite Rite): 19 Dartmouth St., W. Newton, Mass. 02165.

New Ulm, Minn.: 1400 Chancery Drive. 56073.

New York,* N.Y.: 1011 First Ave. 10022.

Norwich, Conn.: 201 Broadway, P.O. Box 587. 06360.

Oakland, Calif.: 2900 Lakeshore Ave. 94610.

Ogdensburg, N.Y.: 622 Washington St. 13669.

Oklahoma City,* Okla.: P.O. Box 18838. 73154.

Omaha,* Nebr.: 100 N. 62nd St. 68132.

Orange, Calif.: 2811 E. Villa Real Dr. 92667.

Orlando, Fla.: P.O. Box 1800. 32802.

Owensboro, Ky.: 4003 Frederica St. 42301.

Parma, Ohio (Byzantine Rite): 1900 Carlton Rd. 44134.

Passaic, N.J. (Byzantine Rite): 101 Market St. 07055.

Paterson, N.J.: 777 Valley Rd., Clifton. 07013.

Pensacola-Tallahassee, Fla.: P.O. Drawer 17329, Pensacola. 32522.

Peoria, Ill.: 607 N.E. Madison Ave., P.O. Box 1406. 61655.

Philadelphia,* Pa.: 222 N. 17th St. 19103.

Philadelphia,* Pa. (Byzantine Rite): 815 N. Franklin St. 19123.

Phoenix, Ariz.: 400 E. Monroe St. 85004.

Pittsburgh,* Pa. (Byzantine Rite): 54 Riverview Ave. 15214.

Pittsburgh, Pa.: 111 Blvd. of the Allies. 15222.

Portland, Me.: 510 Ocean Ave., Woodfords P.O. Box H. 04103.

Portland in Oregon*: P.O. Box 351, 97207.

Providence, R.I.: One Cathedral Sq. 02903.

Pueblo, Colo.: 1426 Grand Ave. 81003.

Raleigh, N.C.: 300 Cardinal Gibbons Dr. 27606.

Rapid City, S.D.: 606 Cathedral Dr., P.O. Box 678. 57709.

Reno-Las Vegas, Nev.: 515 Court St., Reno 89509. (Mailing address: P.O. Box 1211, Reno. 89504.)

Richmond, Va.: 811 Cathedral Pl., Suite C. 23220.

Rochester, N.Y.: 1150 Buffalo Rd. 14624.

Rockford, Ill.: 1245 N. Court St. 61101.

Rockville Centre, N.Y.: 50 N. Park Ave. 11570.

Sacramento, Calif.: 1119 K St., P.O. Box 1706. 95808.

Saginaw, Mich.: 5800 Weiss St. 48603.

St. Augustine, Fla.: Suite 1648, Gulf Life Tower, Jacksonville, Fla. 32207.

St. Cloud, Minn.: P.O. Box 1248. 56302.

St. Louis,* Mo.: 4445 Lindell Blvd. 63108.

St. Maron (Maronite Rite), Brooklyn, N.Y.: 8120 15th Ave., Brooklyn. 11228.

St. Nicholas in Chicago (Byzantine Rite): 2245 W. Rice St. 60622.

St. Paul and Minneapolis,* Minn.: 226 Summit Ave., St. Paul. 55102.

St. Petersburg, Fla.: 6363 9th Ave. N. 33710. P.O. Box 402000. 33743.

Salina, Kans.: 421 Country Club Rd., P.O. Box 999. 67401.

Salt Lake City, Utah: 27 C St., 84103.

San Angelo, Tex.: 116 S. Oakes. Box 1829. 76902.

San Antonio,* Tex.: 9123 Lorene Lane, P.O. Box 32648. 78284.

San Bernardino, Calif.: 1450 North D St. 92405.

San Diego, Calif.: P.O. Box 80428. 92138.

San Francisco,* Calif.: 445 Church St. 94114.

San Jose, Calif.: 7600 St. Joseph Ave., Los Altos 94022.

Santa Fe,* N. Mex.: 202 Morningside Dr. S.E., Albuquerque. 87108.

Santa Rosa, Calif.: 547 "B" St., P.O. Box 1297. 95402.

Savannah, Ga.: 225 Abercorn St., P.O. Box 8789. 31412.

Scranton, Pa.: 300 Wyoming Ave. 18503.

Seattle,* Wash.: 907 Terry Ave. 98104.

Sioux City, Ia.: P.O. Box 1530. 51102.

Sioux Falls, S.D.: 423 N. Duluth Ave., Box 5033. 57117.

Spokane, Wash.: 1023 W. Riverside Ave. 99201.

Springfield, Illinois: 524 E. Lawrence Ave., P.O. Box 1667. 62705.

Springfield, Mass.: 76 Elliot St. 01105. P.O. Box 1730, 01101.

Springfield-Cape Girardeau, Mo.: 200 McDaniel Bldg., Springfield. 65806.

Stamford, Conn. (Byzantine Rite): 161 Glenbrook Rd. 06902.

Steubenville, Ohio: 422 Washington St., P.O. Box 969. 43952.

Stockton, Calif.: 1105 N. Lincoln St. 95203. P.O. Box 4237. 95204.

Superior, Wis.: 1201 Hughitt Ave. 54880.

Syracuse, N.Y.: 240 E. Onondaga St., 13202.
Toledo, Ohio: 2544 Parkwood Ave. 43610.
Trenton, N.J.: 701 Lawrenceville Rd. 08648.
Tucson, Ariz.: 192 S. Stone Ave., Box 31, 85702.
Tulsa, Okla.: P.O. Box 2009. 74101.
Van Nuys, Calif. (Byzantine Rite): 5335 Sepulveda Blvd. 91411.
Victoria, Tex.: P.O. Box 3687. 77903 (cathedral mailing address).
Washington,* D.C.: 5001 Eastern Ave., P.O. Box 29260. 20017..
Wheeling-Charleston, W. Va.: 1300 Byron St., Wheeling. 26003.

Wichita, Kans.: 424 N. Broadway. 67202.
Wilmington, Del.: P.O. Box 2030. 19899.
Winona, Minn.: P.O. Box 588. 55987.
Worcester, Mass.: 49 Elm St. 01609.
Yakima, Wash.: 222 Washington Mutual Bldg., P.O. Box 505. 98907.
Youngstown, Ohio: 144 W. Wood St. 44503.
Armenian-Rite Apostolic Exarchate for the United States and Canada: Sacred Heart Church, 44 Mary St., Paterson, N.J. 07503.
Chaldean-Rite Apostolic Exarchate for the United States: Our Lady of Chaldeans Cathedral, 25585 Berg Rd., Southfield, Mich. 48034.

NATIONAL CATHOLIC CONFERENCES

The two conferences described below are related in membership and directive control but distinct in nature, purpose and function.

The National Conference of Catholic Bishops (NCCB) is a strictly ecclesiastical body in and through which the bishops of the United States act together, officially and with authority as pastors of the Church. It is the sponsoring organization of the United States Catholic Conference.

The United States Catholic Conference (USCC) is a civil corporation and operational secretariat in and through which the bishops, together with other members of the Church, act on a wider scale for the good of the Church and society. It is sponsored by the National Conference of Catholic Bishops.

The principal officers of both conferences are: Archbishop John R. Roach, president; Bishop James W. Malone, vice president; Archbishop Edmund C. Szoka, treasurer; Archbishop Thomas C. Kelly, O.P., secretary.

The membership of the Administrative Committee of the NCCB and the Administrative Board of the USCC is identical.

Headquarters of both conferences are located at 1312 Massachusetts Ave. N.W., Washington, D.C. 20005.

NCCB

The National Conference of Catholic Bishops, established by action of the U.S. hierarchy Nov. 14, 1966, is a strictly ecclesiastical body with defined juridical authority over the Church in this country. It was set up with the approval of the Holy See and in line with directives from the Second Vatican Council. Its constitution was formally ratified during the November, 1967, meeting of the U.S. hierarchy.

The NCCB is a development from the Annual Meeting of the Bishops of the United States, whose pastoral character was originally approved by Pope Benedict XV Apr. 10, 1919.

The address of the Conference is 1312 Massachusetts Ave. N.W., Washington, D.C. 20005. Rev. Msgr. Daniel F. Hoye is general secretary.

Pastoral Council

The conference, one of many similar territorial conferences envisioned in the conciliar *Decree on the Pastoral Office of Bishops in the Church* (No. 38), is "a council in which the bishops of a given nation or territory (in this case, the United States) jointly exercise their pastoral office to promote the greater good which the Church offers mankind, especially through the forms and methods of the apostolate fittingly adapted to the circumstances of the age."

Its decisions, "provided they have been approved legitimately and by the votes of at least two-thirds of the prelates who have a deliberative vote in the conference, and have been recognized by the Apostolic See, are to have juridically binding force only in those cases prescribed by the common law or determined by a special mandate of the Apostolic See, given either spontaneously or in response to a petition of the conference itself."

All bishops who serve the Church in the U.S., its territories and possessions, have membership and voting rights in the NCCB.

Officers, Committees

The conference operates through a number of bishops' committees with functions in specific areas of work and concern. Their basic assignments are to prepare materials on the basis of which the bishops, assembled as a conference, make decisions, and to put suitable action plans into effect.

The principal officers are: Archbishop John R. Roach, president; Bishop James W. Malone, vice president; Archbishop Edmund C. Szoka, treasurer; Archbishop Thomas C. Kelly, O.P., secretary.

These officers, with several other bishops, hold positions on executive-level committees — Executive Committee, the Committee on Budget and Finance, the Committee on Personnel and Administrative Services, and the Committee on Research, Plans and Programs. They also, with other bishops, serve on the NCCB Administrative Board.

The standing committees and their chairmen

(Archbishops and Bishops) are as follows.

American Board of Catholic Missions, Robert F. Sanchez.

Boundaries of Dioceses and Provinces, John R. Roach.

Canonical Affairs, Anthony J. Bevilacqua.

Church in Latin America, Juan Arzube.

Conciliation and Arbitration, George H. Guilfoyle.

Doctrine, James A. Hickey.

Ecumenical and Interreligious Affairs, John F. Whealon.

Human Values, Howard J. Hubbard.

Laity, James R. Hoffman.

Liaison with Priests, Religious and Laity, John J. Nevins.

Liturgy, John S. Cummins.

Men Religious, Joseph A. Francis, S.V.D.

Missions, Edward T. O'Meara.

Nomination of Bishops, John R. Roach.

North American College, Louvain, Peter L. Gerety.

North American College, Rome, Andrew G. Grutka.

Pastoral Research and Practices, Raymond W. Lessard.

Permanent Diaconate, John J. Snyder.

Priestly Formation, Thomas J. Murphy.

Priestly Life and Ministry, Justin A. Driscoll.

Vocations, Anthony F. Mestice.

Welfare Emergency Relief, John R. Roach.

Women Religious, Frank J. Harrison.

Ad hoc committees and their chairmen are as follows.

Bicentennial of Establishment of U.S. Hierarchy, William D. Borders.

Call to Action Plan, Joseph A. Francis, S.V.D.

Campaign for Human Development, Joseph H. Hodges.

Capitalism and Christianity, Rembert Weakland, O.S.B.

Catholic Charismatic Renewal, Kenneth J. Povish.

Church-Government Issues, John L. May.

Economic Concerns of Holy See: Edward T. O'Meara.

Evangelization, Edward T. O'Meara.

Farm Labor, Roger M. Mahony.

Hispanic Affairs, Robert Sanchez.

Inter-Rite, William G. Connare.

Liaison with National Office for Black Catholics, Eugene A. Marino, S.S.J.

Migration and Tourism, Anthony J. Bevilacqua.

Mission Statement, Daniel Pilarczyk.

Nomination of Conference Offices, James V. Casey.

Parishes, Edward C. O'Leary.

Pro-Life Activities, Cardinal Terence J. Cooke.

War and Peace Issues, Joseph L Bernardin.

Women in Society and Church, Michael F. McAuliffe.

USCC

The United States Catholic Conference, Inc. (USCC), is the operational secretariat and service agency of the National Conference of Catholic Bishops for carrying out the civic-religious work of the Church in this country. It is a civil corporation related to the NCCB in membership and directive control but distinct from it in purpose and function.

The address of the Conference is 1312 Massachusetts Ave. N.W., Washington, D.C. 20005. Rev. Msgr. Daniel F. Hoye is general secretary.

Service Secretariat

The USCC, as of Jan. 1, 1967, took over the general organization and operations of the former National Catholic Welfare Conference, Inc., whose origins dated back to the National Catholic War Council of 1917. The council underwent some change after World War I and was established on a permanent basis Sept. 24, 1919, as the National Catholic Welfare Council to serve as a central agency for organizing and coordinating the efforts of U.S. Catholics in carrying out the social mission of the Church in this country. In 1923, its name was changed to National Catholic Welfare Conference, Inc., and clarification was made of its nature as a service agency of the bishops and the Church rather than as a conference of bishops with real juridical authority in ecclesiastical affairs.

The Official Catholic Directory states that the USCC assists "the bishops in their service to the Church in this country by uniting the people of God where voluntary collective action on a broad interdiocesan level is needed. The USCC provides an organizational structure and the resources needed to insure coordination, cooperation, and assistance in the public, educational and social concerns of the Church at the national or interdiocesan level."

Officers, Departments

The principal officers of the USCC are Archbishop John R. Roach, president; Bishop James W. Malone, vice president; Archbishop Edmund C. Szoka, treasurer; Archbishop Thomas C. Kelly, O.P., secretary. These officers, with several other bishops, hold positions on executive-level committees — the Executive Committee; the Committee on Research, Plans and Programs; the Committee on Budget and Finance; the Committee on Personnel and Administrative Services. They also serve on the Administrative Board.

The Executive Committee, organized in 1969, is authorized to handle matters of urgency between meetings of the Administrative Board and the general conference, to coordinate items for the agenda of general meetings, and to speak in the name of the USCC.

The major departments and their chairmen (Archbishops and Bishops) are: Communications, Norbert F. Gaughan; Education, Edward T. Hughes; Social Development and World Peace, Mark J. Hurley. Each department is supervised by a committee composed of an equal number of episcopal and non-episcopal members, including lay persons.

A national Advisory Council of bishops, priests, men and women religious, lay men and women advises the Administrative Board on overall plans and operations of the USCC.

The administrative general secretariat, in addition to other duties, supervises staff-service offices of Finance and Administration, General Counsel, Government Liaison, and Research, Plans and Programs.

Most of the organizations and associations affiliated with the USCC are covered in separate Almanac entries.

NCCB-USCC REGIONS

For meeting and other operational purposes, the members of the National Conference of Catholic Bishops and the U.S. Catholic Conference are grouped in the following geographical regions.

I. Maine, Vermont, New Hampshire, Massachusetts, Rhode Island, Connecticut.

II. New York.

III. New Jersey, Pennsylvania.

IV. Delaware, District of Columbia, Florida, Georgia, Maryland, North Carolina, South Carolina, Virgin Islands, Virginia, West Virginia.

V. Alabama, Kentucky, Louisiana, Mississippi, Tennessee.

VI. Michigan, Ohio.

VII. Illinois, Indiana, Wisconsin.

VIII. Minnesota, North Dakota, South Dakota.

IX. Iowa, Kansas, Missouri, Nebraska.

X. Arkansas, Oklahoma, Texas.

XI. California, Hawaii, Nevada, Guam.

XII. Idaho, Montana, Alaska, Washington, Oregon.

XIII. Utah, Arizona, New Mexico, Colorado, Wyoming.

1981 MEETING OF U.S. BISHOPS

More than 280 bishops attended the annual meeting of the National Conference of Catholic Bishops and the United States Catholic Conference Nov. 16 to 19, 1981, in Washington, D.C. The presiding officer was Archbishop John R. Roach, head of both conferences.

Presidential Address

Church-state relations, nuclear arms, abortion and the plight of the poor were key subjects in the opening address of Archbishop Roach.

• Church and State: "I agree fully with the principle of separation of Church and state. I do not agree that absence of dialogue about and between religion and politics serves either the Church or the state. . . . We should not accept or allow the separation of Church and state to be used to separate the Church from society."

Accordingly, the archbishop called for an "explicit, public, systematic dialogue about the relationship of religious communities and the political process in the United States. . . . Neither the rigor of reasonable argument nor the controversy which surrounds the role of religion and politics should make us timid about stating and defending public positions and key issues."

Three such issues, he said, were the nuclear arms race, abortion and the plight of the poor.

• Nuclear Arms: "On a global scale, the most dangerous moral issue in the public order today is the nuclear arms race."

Noting a "sense of moral urgency" about it, he said: "The Church needs to say 'no' clearly and decisively to the use of nuclear weapons. This is surely the direction of Vatican II teachings on the arms race and its condemnation of attacks on civilian centers. The 'no' we utter should shape our policy advice and our pastoral guidance of Catholics."

• Abortion: "The horror of legalized, permissive abortion is tragically real. The destruction of unborn life now occurs in the nation at the staggering rate of 1.5 million abortions annually."

"We remain committed to the proclamation of the Gospel message concerning the sanctity of human life and to the practical steps and programs required to eradicate the conditions which cause some to turn to abortion as a solution to personal and social problems. But we also recognize the need for a remedy in law in order to undo the harm done under the guise of law. Without this, 'the sanctity of human life' can only be a hollow phrase."

• Poor People: "We are called to this role of advocacy for the poor . . . by our social teachings. . . . We know from experience the impossible choices the poor face in our society: not between guns and butter, but between bread and rent, between money for heating oil and the need to pay for health care for children. We know also that private agencies of the nation cannot fill the gap created by recent (federal budget) cuts. We have neither the resources nor, I suppose, even the mandate to do this. We will do our part, but our own social teaching calls upon the state to do its part."

Items of Business

The bishops dealt with the following subjects during the meeting.

Abortion: Approved, with only one dissenting vote, support for the Hatch Amendment, providing: "A right to abortion is not secured by this Constitution (of the U.S.). The Congress and the several states shall have the concurrent power to restrict and prohibit abortions: Provided, that a law of a state which is more restrictive than a law of Congress shall govern."

Those favoring the measure did so because of the convictions: (1) that it might, under existing circumstances, have a better chance of adoption than a more sweeping (and more desirable) Human Life Amendment; (2) that its adoption might result in fewer abortions. (Approval of support for the Hatch Amendment was not intended to diminish pressure for eventual passage of a Human Life Amendment.)

Budget: Approved an NCCB-USCC 1982 budget of $20,139,385, the largest ever. Major allocations were for: Migration and Relief Services ($5.75 million), General Secretariat and Staff ($4.8 million), Publishing Services ($2.8 million), NCCB Committees ($1.7 million), Education ($1.1 million), Communications Secretariat ($653,000), Social Development and World Peace ($627,000), Chaplain Services ($75,000).

Not included in the budget were funds of special collections, the Campaign for Human Development, the Catholic Communications Campaign, and other projects.

Central America: Declared in a statement that the principal problems in the region were "internal conditions of poverty and the denial of basic human rights." The bishops rejected the view that subversion by outside forces was the major cause of trouble, declaring: "Any conception of the problems in Central America which is cast principally in terms of global security issues, military responses, arms transfers and preservation of a situation which fails to promote meaningful participation of the majority of the population in their societies, is, in our view, profoundly mistaken."

The statement urged a ban on military aid to the government of El Salvador, advocating instead efforts toward a political solution to chaotic problems there; it also contained an appeal for political asylum for thousands of refugees from the continuing civil war. Concern was expressed about preservation of the religious character of the people of Nicaragua, and criticism was sounded regarding U.S. attempts to isolate the country and block its access to resources needed for reconstruction. The statement cited "a pattern of violence (in Guatemala) designed to silence the voice of the Church" and called for U.S. diplomacy to be "directed toward enhancing the protection of human rights and assisting the meeting of basic human needs."

Health Care Pastoral: "Health and Healing, A Pastoral Letter of the American Catholic Bishops," addressed the rights of health care employees, a proposal for national health insurance and commitment to the ethical direction of Catholic health care facilities.

The letter called for "full recognition of the rights of employees to organize and bargain collectively with the institution (of their employment) through whatever association or organization they freely choose. . . . Justice also demands that employees realize the special responsibility they have to their employer and the responsibilities they have as workers who care for the sick in a Christian facility," in light of the Catholic identity of the institutions.

Regarding "the development of a national health insurance program," the letter said: "It is the responsibility of the federal government to establish a comprehensive health care system that will insure a basic level of health care for all Americans."

Portions of the letter covering ethical direction were keyed to firm rules on medical-moral issues like abortion, sterilization, care for the terminally ill and other subjects.

Liturgical Language: Received notice that Pope John Paul had granted their request to omit the word "men" from the formula of the Consecration at Mass. Accordingly and immediately, the authorized wording became ". . . for you and for all (instead of "for you and for all men") so that sins may be forgiven." Deletion of the word "men," despite its generic connotation in traditional usage, was requested in order to make the language of the formula less "exclusive," according to the Bishops' Committee on the Liturgy.

Marian Request: Submitted to Pope John Paul a request that he consecrate the world, and especially Russia, to Mary under the title of her Immaculate Heart. The action, which took place during an executive session of the annual meeting, was announced Nov. 30.

Officers: Elected were: Archbishop Edmund C. Szoka, treasurer of both conferences; chairman of eight NCCB committees and a chairman of one USCC committee (all listed in articles on the conferences).

Region: Established a new region, the 13th, for meeting and operational purposes, of the bishops of Utah, Colorado, Wyoming, Arizona and New Mexico.

Rules on Public Statements: Approved new rules governing public statements, regarding their nature and authority. (1) Public statements of committees of the U.S. Catholic Conference require pre-publication approval by a majority of the administrative board. (2) "An NCCB or USCC statement or publication will have a preface signed by the general secretary that will clearly distinguish the statement's origin and authority from the approval of its text. The preface will also explicitly identify the person or persons who officially approved the statement's text and are accountable for it." (3) "Committee statements ... do not commit the entire membership of the conference to a position, but they do offer important guidance for assessing the subjects they treat."

Seminaries: Received several recommendations of a national study group. (1) No new seminaries or schools of theology should be started. (2) Planning for future staff and faculty should be done on the assumption that the total enrollment of candidates for the priesthood will not increase. (3) National seminaries are needed, along with some amalgamation of existing institutions. (4) The number of non-ordination-bound persons studying theology in seminaries is increasing. (5) There is clear need for seminaries to retain their distinctive identity through control of their academic and formational programs.

Synod Delegates: Elected delegates to the 1983 assembly of the Synod of Bishops: Archbishops John R. Roach, Joseph L. Bernardin and Patrick F. Flores, and Auxiliary Bishop Austin B. Vaughan. Elected alternates were Archbishop Rembert G. Weakland and Auxiliary Bishop John M. D'Arcy.

War and Peace: Received a report from the Ad Hoc Committee on War and Peace on its efforts to draft a pastoral statement on the subject.

Archbishop Joseph L. Bernardin, chairman, said there is need for a positive theology of peace and that papal teaching on the use of force needs to be affirmed and extended. He noted that it "probably will be the moral problem of nuclear war which will present the committee its most challenging task."

Archbishop Bernardin also said:

"The very created order is threatened by nuclear war. We who believe that we are stewards of life and creation, not its masters, must use all the religious and moral vision we have to prevent a threat to what God has created, what we could destroy but never re-create."

"We need to be convinced that some actions can never be taken, even for survival; that there are limits to the argument that, because our adversaries are considering something, we must be prepared to do it also."

Our "goal must be not only to state the teaching of the Church on nuclear warfare clearly, but to find ways and means to bring this teaching to our parishes, pupils and schools."

The first draft of the proposed letter was completed and circulated among bishops and others by the spring of 1982, for comments and suggestions. It was then announced that writing of the letter would take longer than originally expected.

Reports and Other Items

Reports: Reports on a variety of subjects included those on: the revised Code of Canon Law, the family, the laity, the National Catholic Telecommunications Network, plans for the 1982 Bishops' Assembly for Prayer and Reflection on Episcopal Ministry in the United States, military chaplains.

Miscellaneous Items: Approved were: a statement on the mission of the conferences, a set of accounting principles and reporting procedures for church-related organizations, an appeal for a name change of the submarine Corpus Christi.

EASTERN BISHOPS' MEETING

Eight prelates attended the annual meeting of Eastern Catholic bishops of the United States Feb. 23, 1982, in Parma, Ohio.

Under discussion were:

• proposals and suggestions related to Eastern Canon Law, which was in the process of codification by a special commission of bishops and experts;

• an outline, approved and moved for completion to publication in book form, of a statement of faith for adult Eastern Catholics, under theological, moral, liturgical and other headings.

The meeting was attended by: Archbishops Stephen J. Kocisko of Pittsburgh (Ruthenian), Stephen Sulyk of Philadelphia (Ukrainian), Joseph Tawil of Newton (Melkite), and Bishops Michael J. Dudick of Passaic (Ruthenian), Basil H. Losten of Stamford (Ukrainian), Robert Moskal (auxiliary) of Philadelphia and Francis M. Zayek of St. Maron (Maronite). The host prelate of the meeting was Ruthenian Bishop Emil J. Mihalik of Parma.

BISHOPS' ASSEMBLY FOR PRAYER AND REFLECTION

The first-of-its-kind closed Assembly of U.S. Bishops for Prayer and Reflection on Episcopal Ministry was attended by 252 bishops June 13 to 23, 1982, on the campus of St. John's University, Collegeville, Minn.

Its purpose, according to Bishop James W. Malone of Youngstown, head of the planning committee, was to invite "Catholic bishops in the United States to come together in a prayerful and reflective atmosphere, and to consider various implications for pastoral ministry in the 1980s in the light of the Second Vatican Council."

Themes

Accordingly, the assembly provided the bishops with a retreat-like experience of prayer, reflection and discussion related to the following themes presented by several of their colleagues.

• "Universality and Collegiality," by Cardinal John F. Dearden;

• "The Bishop as Teacher," by Archbishop James A. Hickey of Washington;

• "The Bishop as Sanctifier," by Archbishop Rembert G. Weakland of Milwaukee;

• "The Bishop as Evangelizer," by Archbishop Robert Sanchez of Santa Fe;

• "The Bishop as Builder of Community," by Archbishop William D. Borders of Baltimore;

• "The Bishop in the American Political and Economic Context," by Auxiliary Bishop Thomas J. Gumbleton of Detroit.

British Cardinal George Basil Hume keynoted the assembly at the opening Mass on June 13.

The presiding officers at the gathering were Archbishop John R. Roach and Bishop Malone, president and vice president, respectively, of the National Conference of Catholic Bishops.

Preparations for the meeting included a series of bishops' meetings at regional and provincial levels in the fall of 1981, at which the themes for the assembly were identified and decided upon.

STATE CATHOLIC CONFERENCES

These conferences are agencies of bishops and dioceses in the various states. Their general purposes are to develop and sponsor cooperative programs designed to cope with pastoral and common-welfare needs, and to represent the dioceses before governmental bodies, the public, and in private sectors. Their membership consists of representatives from the dioceses in the states — bishops, clergy and lay persons in various capacities.

The **National Association of State Catholic Conference Directors** maintains liaison with the general secretariat of the United States Catholic Conference. Howard J. Fetterhoff, executive director of the Pennsylvania Catholic Conference, is president.

Arizona Catholic Conference, 400 E. Monroe St., Phoenix, Ariz. 85004; exec. dir., Thomas F. Allt.

California Catholic Conference, 926 J St., Suite 1100, Sacramento, Calif. 95814; exec. dir., Msgr. John A. Dickie.

Colorado Catholic Conference, 200 Josephine St., Denver, Colo. 80206; exec. dir., Sr. Loretto Anne Madden, S.L.

Connecticut Catholic Conference, 134 Farmington Ave., Hartford, Conn. 06105; exec. dir., William Wholean.

Florida Catholic Conference, P.O. Box 1571, Tallahassee, Fla. 32302; exec. dir., Thomas A. Horkan, Jr.

Georgia Catholic Conference, Office Building, Villa Marie Apts., 3200 Deans Bridge Rd., Augusta, Ga. 30906; exec. dir., Cheatham E. Hodges, Jr.

Hawaii Catholic Conference, 1184 Bishop St., Honolulu, H.I. 96813; exec. sec., Mrs. Maggie Bunson.

Illinois Catholic Conference, One East Superior St., Chicago, Ill. 60611; 300 E. Monroe St., Springfield, Ill. 62701; exec. dir., Rev. William J. Lion.

Indiana Catholic Conference, Suite 315, 5435 Emerson Way N., Indianapolis, Ind. 46226; exec. dir., Raymond R. Rufo.

Iowa Catholic Conference, 818 Insurance Exchange Building, Des Moines, Iowa 50309; exec. dir., Timothy McCarthy.

Kansas Catholic Conference, 702 Commercial National Bank Bldg., Kansas City, Kan. 66101; exec. dir., Robert Runnels, Jr.

Kentucky Catholic Conference, P.O. Box 1073, Louisville, Ky. 40201; chairman, Most Rev. Thomas C. Kelly, O.P., Archbishop of Louisville.

Louisiana Catholic Conference, P.O. Box 52948, New Orleans, La. 70152; exec. dir., Emile Comar.

Maryland Catholic Conference, 320 Cathedral St., Baltimore, Md. 21201; exec. dir., Francis X. McIntyre.

Massachusetts Catholic Conference, Parker House, Room 180, Boston, Mass. 02107; exec. dir., Gerald D. D'Avolio, Esq.

Michigan Catholic Conference, 505 N. Capitol Ave., Lansing, Mich. 48933; exec. dir., Msgr. Herman H. Zerfas.

Minnesota Catholic Conference, 296 Chester St., St. Paul, Minn. 55107; exec. dir., Rev. Msgr. James D. Habiger.

Missouri Catholic Conference, P.O. Box 1022, Jefferson City, Mo. 65102; exec. dir., Louis C. DeFeo, Jr.

Montana Catholic Conference, P.O. Box 1708, Helena, Mont. 59601; exec. dir., John Frankino.

Nebraska Catholic Conference, 521 S. 14th St., Lincoln, Nebr. 68508; exec. dir., James R. Cunningham.

New Jersey Catholic Conference, 211 N. Warren St., Trenton, N.J. 08618; exec. dir., Edward J. Leadem.

New York State Catholic Conference, 11 N. Pearl St., Albany, N.Y. 12207; exec. dir., J. Alan Davitt.

North Dakota Catholic Conference, 107 N. 4th St. — Room 25, Bismarck, N. Dak. 58501; exec. dir., Mrs. Corrine Engelstad.

Ohio, Catholic Conference of, 35 E. Gay St., Suite 502, Columbus, Ohio 43215; exec. dir., Nelson N. Harper.

Oregon Catholic Conference, 2838 E. Burnside, Portland, Ore. 97214; sec., Rev. Joseph Jacobberger.

Pennsylvania Catholic Conference, 222 North St., Harrisburg, Pa. 17105; exec. dir., Howard J. Fetterhoff.

Texas Catholic Conference, 3001 S. Congress Ave., Austin, Tex. 78704; exec. dir., Bro. Richard Daly, C.S.C.

Washington State Catholic Conference, 1402 3rd Ave., Suite 618, Seattle, Wash. 98101; exec. dir. Rev. D. Harvey McIntyre.

Wisconsin Catholic Conference, 30 W. Mifflin St., Suite 910, Madison, Wis. 53703; exec. dir., Charles M. Phillips.

Biographies of American Bishops

(Sources: Almanac survey, *The Official Catholic Directory,* NC News Service. As of Aug. 15, 1982.)

A

Abramowicz, Alfred L.: b. Jan. 27, 1919, Chicago, Ill.; educ. St. Mary of the Lake Seminary (Mundelein, Ill.), Gregorian Univ. (Rome); ord. priest May 1, 1943; ord. titular bishop of Paestum and auxiliary bishop of Chicago, June 13, 1968.

Ackerman, Richard Henry, C.S.Sp.: b. Aug. 30, 1903, Pittsburgh, Pa.; educ. Duquesne Univ. (Pittsburgh, Pa.), St. Mary's Scholasticate (Norwalk, Conn.), Univ. of Fribourg (Switzerland); ord. priest Aug. 28, 1926; ord. titular bishop of Lares and auxiliary bishop of San Diego, May 22, 1956; app. bishop of Covington, Apr. 4, 1960; resigned Nov. 28, 1978.

Ahern, Patrick V.: b. Mar. 8, 1919, New York, N.Y.; educ. Manhattan College and Cathedral College (New York City), St. Joseph's Seminary (Yonkers, N.Y.), St. Louis Univ. (St. Louis, Mo.), Notre Dame Univ. (Notre Dame, Ind.); ord. priest Jan. 27, 1945; ord. titular bishop of Naiera and auxiliary bishop of New York, Mar. 19, 1970.

Ahr, George William: b. June 23, 1904, Newark, N.J.; educ. St. Vincent College (Latrobe, Pa.), Seton Hall College (S. Orange, N.J.), North American College (Rome); ord. priest July 29, 1928; ord. bishop of Trenton, Mar. 20, 1950; resigned 1979.

Anderson, Paul F.: b. Apr. 20, 1917, Roslindale, Mass.; educ. Boston College (Chestnut Hill, Mass.), St. John's Seminary (Brighton, Mass.); ord. priest Jan. 6, 1943; ord. titular bishop of Polignando and coadjutor bishop of Duluth, Oct. 17, 1968; bishop of Duluth, Apr. 30, 1969; resigned August, 1982; app. auxiliary bishop of Sioux Falls.

Angell, Kenneth A.: b. Aug. 3, 1930, Providence, R.I.; educ. St. Mary's Seminary (Baltimore, Md.); ord. priest May 26, 1956; ord. titular bishop of Septimunicia and auxiliary bishop of Providence, R.I., Oct. 7, 1974.

Arkfeld, Leo, S.V.D.: b. Feb. 4, 1912, Butte, Nebr.; educ. Divine Word Seminary (Techny, Ill.), Sacred Heart College (Girard, Pa.); ord. priest Aug. 15, 1943; ord. titular bishop of Bucellus and vicar apostolic of Central New Guinea, Nov. 30, 1948; name of vicariate changed to Wewak, May 15, 1952; first bishop of Wewak, Nov. 15, 1966; app. archbishop of Madang, Papua New Guinea, Dec. 19, 1975.

Arliss, Reginald, C.P.: b. Sept. 8, 1906, East Orange, N.J.; educ. Immaculate Conception Seminary (Jamaica, N.Y.) and other Passionist houses of study; ord. priest Apr. 28, 1934; missionary in China for 16 years, expelled 1951; missionary in Philippines; rector of the Pontifical Philippine College Seminary in Rome, 1961-69; ord. titular bishop of Cerbali and prelate of Marbel, Philippines, Jan. 30, 1970; resigned Oct. 1, 1981.

Arzube, Juan: b. June 1, 1918, Guayaquil, Ecuador; educ. Rensselaer Polytechnic Institute (Troy, N.Y.), St. John's Seminary (Camarillo, Calif.); ord. priest May 5, 1954; ord. titular bishop of Civitate and auxiliary bishop of Los Angeles, Mar. 25, 1971.

B

Balke, Victor: b. Sept. 29, 1931, Meppen, Ill.; educ. St. Mary of the Lake Seminary (Mundelein, Ill.), St. Louis Univ. (St. Louis, Mo.); ord. priest May 24, 1958; ord. bishop of Crookston, Sept. 2, 1976.

Baum, William W.: (See Cardinals, Biographies.)

Begley, Michael J.: b. Mar. 12, 1909, Mattineague, Mass.; educ. Mt. St. Mary Seminary (Emmitsburg, Md.); ord. priest May 26, 1934; ord. first bishop of Charlotte, N.C., Jan. 12, 1972.

Beltran, Eusebius J.: b. Aug. 31, 1934, Ashley, Pa.; educ. St. Charles Seminary (Philadelphia, Pa.); ord. priest May 14, 1960; ord. bishop of Tulsa, Apr. 20, 1978.

Benincasa, Pius A.: b. July 8, 1913, Niagara Falls, N.Y.; educ. Propaganda Univ. and Lateran Univ. (Rome); ord. priest Mar. 27, 1937; served in Vatican Secretariat of State, 1954-64; ord. titular bishop of Buruni and auxiliary bishop of Buffalo, June 29, 1964.

Bernardin, Joseph L.: b. Apr. 2, 1928, Columbia, S.C.; educ. St. Mary's Seminary (Baltimore, Md.), Catholic Univ. (Washington, D.C.); ord. priest Apr. 26, 1952; ord. titular bishop of Lugura and auxiliary bishop of Atlanta, Apr. 26, 1966; general secretary of the USCC and NCCB, 1968-72; app. archbishop of Cincinnati, Nov. 21, 1972; installed Dec. 19, 1972; president NCCB/USCC, 1974-77; app. archbishop of Chicago, July 10, 1982; installed Aug. 25, 1982.

Bernarding, George, S.V.D.: b. Feb. 15, 1912, Carrick, Pa.; educ. Divine Word Seminary (Girard, Pa.); ord. priest Aug. 13, 1939; ord. titular bishop of Belabitene and first vicar apostolic of Mount Hagen, New Guinea, Apr. 21, 1960; first bishop of Mount Hagen, Nov. 15, 1966; app. first archbishop Mar. 29, 1982, when see was elevated to metropolitan rank.

Bevilacqua, Anthony J.: b. June 17, 1923, Brooklyn, N.Y.; educ. Cathedral College (Brooklyn, N.Y.), Immaculate Conception Seminary (Huntington, N.Y.), Gregorian Univ. (Rome), Columbia Univ. and St. John's Univ. (New York); ord. priest June 11, 1949; ord. titular bishop of Aquae Albae in

Byzacena and auxiliary bishop of Brooklyn, Nov. 24, 1980.

Bilock, John M.: b. June 20, 1916, McAdoo, Pa.; educ. St. Procopius College and Seminary (Lisle, Ill.); ord. priest Feb. 3, 1946; vicar general of Byzantine archdiocese of Munhall, 1969; ord. titular bishop of Pergamum and auxiliary bishop of Munhall, May 15, 1973; title of see changed to Pittsburgh, 1977.

Boccella, John H., T.O.R.: b. June 25, 1912, Castelfranci, Italy; came to US at the age of two; educ. St. Francis College and Seminary (Loretto, Pa.), Angelicum Univ. (Rome), Catholic Univ. (Washington, D.C.); ord. priest Mar. 29, 1941; minister general of Third Order Regular, 1947-65; ord. archbishop of Izmir, Turkey, Apr. 17, 1968; transferred to titular see of Ephesus, Dec. 7, 1978.

Boland, Ernest B., O.P.: b. July 10, 1925, Providence, R.I.; educ. Providence College (Rhode Island), Dominican Houses of Study (Somerset, Ohio; Washington, D.C.); ord. priest June 9, 1955; ord. bishop of Multan, Pakistan, July 25, 1966.

Borders, William D.: b. Oct. 9, 1913, Washington, Ind.; educ. St. Meinrad Seminary (St. Meinrad, Ind.), Notre Dame Seminary (New Orleans, La.), Notre Dame Univ. (Notre Dame, Ind.); ord. priest May 18, 1940; ord. first bishop of Orlando, June 14, 1968; app. archbishop of Baltimore, Apr. 2, 1974, installed June 26, 1974.

Bosco, Anthony G.: b. Aug. 1, 1927, New Castle, Pa.; educ. St. Vincent Seminary (Latrobe, Pa.), Lateran Univ. (Rome); ord. priest June 7, 1952; ord. titular bishop of Labicum and auxiliary of Pittsburgh, June 30, 1970.

Boudreaux, Warren L.: b. Jan. 25, 1918, Berwick, La.; educ. St. Joseph's Seminary (St. Benedict, La.), St. Sulpice Seminary (Paris, France), Notre Dame Seminary (New Orleans, La.), Catholic Univ. (Washington, D.C.); ord. priest May 30, 1942; ord. titular bishop of Calynda and auxiliary bishop of Lafayette, La., July 25, 1962; app. bishop of Beaumont, June 5, 1971; app. first bishop of Houma-Thibodaux, installed June 5, 1977.

Breitenbeck, Joseph M.: b. Aug. 3, 1914, Detroit, Mich.; educ. University of Detroit, Sacred Heart Seminary (Detroit, Mich.), North American College and Lateran Univ. (Rome), Catholic Univ. (Washington, D.C.); ord. priest May 30, 1942; ord. titular bishop of Tepelta and auxiliary bishop of Detroit, Dec. 20, 1965; app. bishop of Grand Rapids, Oct. 15, 1969, installed Dec. 2, 1969.

Brizgys, Vincas: b. Nov. 10, 1903, Plyniai, Lithuania; ord. priest June 5, 1927; ord. titular bishop of Bosano and auxiliary bishop of Kaunas, Lithuania, May 10, 1940; taken into custody and deported to Germany, 1944; liberated by Americans, 1945; U.S. citizen, 1958.

Broderick, Edwin B.: b. Jan. 16, 1917, New York, N.Y.; educ. Cathedral College (New York City), St. Joseph's Seminary (Yonkers, N.Y.), Fordham Univ. (New York City); ord. priest May 30, 1942; ord. titular bishop of Tizica and auxiliary of New York, Apr. 21, 1967; bishop of Albany, 1969-76; executive director of Catholic Relief Services, 1976.

Brown, Charles, A., M.M.: b. Aug. 20, 1919, New York, N.Y.; educ. Cathedral College (New York City), Maryknoll Seminary (Maryknoll, N.Y.); ord. priest June 9, 1946; ord. titular bishop of Vallis and auxiliary bishop of Santa Cruz, Bolivia, Mar. 27, 1957.

Brunini, Joseph B.: b. July 24, 1909, Vicksburg, Miss.; educ. Georgetown Univ. (Washington, D.C.), North American College (Rome), Catholic Univ. (Washington, D.C.); ord. priest Dec. 5, 1933; ord. titular bishop of Axomis and auxiliary bishop of Natchez-Jackson, Jan. 29, 1957; apostolic administrator of Natchez-Jackson, 1966; app. bishop of Natchez-Jackson, Dec. 2, 1967, installed Jan. 29, 1968; title of see changed to Jackson, 1977.

Brust, Leo J.: b. Jan. 7, 1916, St. Francis, Wis.; educ. St. Francis Seminary (Milwaukee, Wis.), Canisianum (Innsbruck, Austria), Catholic Univ. (Washington, D.C.); ord. priest May 30, 1942; ord. titular bishop of Suelli and auxiliary bishop of Milwaukee, Oct. 16, 1969.

Brzana, Stanislaus J.: b. July 1, 1917, Buffalo, N.Y.; educ. Christ the King Seminary (St. Bonaventure, N.Y.), Gregorian Univ. (Rome); ord. priest June 7, 1941; ord. titular bishop of Cufruta and auxiliary bishop of Buffalo, June 29, 1964; bishop of Ogdensburg, Oct. 22, 1968.

Bullock, William H.: b. Apr. 13, 1927, Maple Lake, Minn.; educ. St. Thomas College and St. Paul Seminary (St. Paul, Minn.), Notre Dame Univ. (Notre Dame, Ind.); ord. priest June 7, 1952; ord. titular bishop of Natchez and auxiliary bishop of St. Paul and Minneapolis, Aug. 12, 1980.

Burke, James C., O.P.: b. Nov. 30, 1926, Philadelphia, Pa.; educ. King's College (Wilkes-Barre, Pa.), Providence College (R.I.); ord. priest June 8, 1956; ord. titular bishop of Lamiggiga and prelate of Chimbote, Peru, May 25, 1967, resigned 1978. Vicar for urban affairs, Wilmington, Del., diocese.

Buswell, Charles A.: b. Oct. 15, 1913, Homestead, Okla.; educ. St. Louis Preparatory Seminary (St. Louis, Mo.), Kenrick Seminary (Webster Groves, Mo.), American College, Univ. of Louvain (Belgium); ord. priest July 9, 1939; ord. bishop of Pueblo, Sept. 30, 1959; resigned Sept. 18, 1979.

Byrne, James J.: b. July 28, 1908, St. Paul, Minn.; educ. Nazareth Hall Preparatory Seminary and St. Paul Seminary (St. Paul, Minn.), Univ. of Minnesota (Minneapolis,

Minn.); Louvain Univ. (Belgium); ord. priest June 3, 1933; ord. titular bishop of Etenna and auxiliary bishop of St. Paul, July 2, 1947; app. bishop of Boise, June 16, 1956; app. archbishop of Dubuque, Mar. 19, 1962, installed May 8, 1962.

C

Caesar, Raymond R., S.V.D.: b. Feb. 14, 1932, Eunice, La.; educ. Divine Word Seminary (Bay St. Louis, Miss.); Catholic Univ. (Washington, D.C.); ord. priest June 4, 1961; missionary in New Guinea from 1962; ord. coadjutor bishop of Goroka, Papua New Guinea, Oct. 25, 1978; bishop of Goroko, Aug. 30, 1980.

Caillouet, L. Abel.: b. Aug. 2, 1900, Thibodaux, La.; educ. St. Joseph's Preparatory Seminary (St. Benedict, La.), St. Mary's Seminary (Baltimore, Md.), North American College (Rome); ord. priest Mar. 7, 1925; ord. titular bishop of Setea and auxiliary bishop of New Orleans, Oct. 28, 1947; retired July 7, 1976.

Carberry, John J.: (See Cardinals, Biographies.)

Carroll, Mark K.: b. Nov. 19, 1896, St. Louis, Mo.; educ. St. Louis Preparatory Seminary and Kenrick Seminary (St. Louis, Mo.); ord. priest June 10, 1922; ord. bishop of Wichita, Apr. 23, 1947; retired, 1963, but retained title; resigned, 1967.

Casey, James V.: b. Sept. 22, 1914, Osage, Ia.; educ. Loras College (Dubuque, Ia.), North American College (Rome), Catholic Univ. (Washington, D.C.); ord. priest Dec. 8, 1939; ord. titular bishop of Citium and auxiliary bishop of Lincoln, Apr. 24, 1957; bishop of Lincoln, June 14, 1957; app. archbishop of Denver, Feb. 22, 1967, installed May 17, 1967.

Cassata, John J.: b. Nov. 8, 1908, Galveston, Tex.; educ. St. Mary's Seminary (La Porte, Tex.), North American College, Urban Univ. and Gregorian Univ. (Rome); ord. priest Dec. 8, 1932; ord. titular bishop of Bida and auxiliary bishop of Dallas-Fort Worth, June 5, 1968; app. bishop of Fort Worth, Aug. 27, 1969, installed Oct. 21, 1969; retired Sept. 16, 1980.

Chavez, Gilbert Espinoza: b. May 9, 1932, Ontario, Calif.; educ. St. Francis Seminary (El Cajon, Calif.), Immaculate Heart Seminary (San Diego), Univ. of California; ord. priest Mar. 19, 1960; ord. titular bishop of Magarmel and auxiliary of San Diego, June 21, 1974.

Chedid, John: b. July 4, 1923, Eddid, Lebanon; educ. seminaries in Lebanon and Pontifical Urban College (Rome); ord. priest Dec. 21, 1951, in Rome; ord. titular bishop of Callinico and auxiliary bishop of St. Maron of Brooklyn for the Maronites, Jan. 25, 1981.

Clark, Matthew H.: b. July 15, 1937, Troy, N.Y.; educ. St. Bernard's Seminary (Rochester, N.Y.), Gregorian Univ. (Rome); ord. priest Dec. 19, 1962; ord. bishop of Rochester, May 27, 1979; installed June 26, 1979.

Clinch, Harry A.: b. Oct. 27, 1908, San Anselmo, Calif.; educ. St. Joseph's College (Mountain View, Calif.), St. Patrick's Seminary (Menlo Park, Calif.); ord. priest June 6, 1936; ord. titular bishop of Badiae and auxiliary bishop of Monterey-Fresno, Feb. 27, 1957; app. first bishop of Monterey in California, installed Dec. 14, 1967; resigned Jan. 19, 1982.

Cohill, John Edward, S.V.D.: b. Dec. 13, 1907, Elizabeth, N.J.; educ. Divine Word Seminary (Techny, Ill.); ord. priest Mar. 20, 1936; ord. first bishop of Goroko, Papua New Guinea, Mar. 11, 1967; resigned Aug. 30, 1980.

Comber, John W., M.M.: b. Mar. 12, 1906, Lawrence, Mass.; educ. St. John's Preparatory College (Danvers, Mass.), Boston College (Boston, Mass.), Maryknoll Seminary (Maryknoll, N.Y.); ord. priest Feb. 1, 1931; superior general of Maryknoll, 1956-66; ord. titular bishop of Foratiana, Apr. 9, 1959.

Connare, William G.: b. Dec. 11, 1911, Pittsburgh, Pa.; educ. Duquesne Univ. (Pittsburgh, Pa.), St. Vincent Seminary (Latrobe, Pa.); ord. priest June 14, 1936; ord. bishop of Greensburg, May 4, 1960.

Connolly, James L.: b. Nov. 15, 1894, Fall River, Mass.; educ. St. Charles College (Catonsville, Md.), St. Mary's Seminary (Baltimore, Md.), Catholic Univ. (Washington, D.C.), Louvain Univ. (Belgium); ord. priest Dec. 21, 1923; rector of St. Paul (Minn.) minor seminary 1940-43, major seminary 1943-45; ord. titular bishop of Mylasa and coadjutor of Fall River, May 24, 1945; bishop of Fall River, May 17, 1951; resigned Oct. 30, 1970.

Connolly, Thomas Arthur: b. Oct. 5, 1899, San Francisco, Calif.; educ. St. Patrick's Seminary (Menlo Park, Calif.), Catholic Univ. (Washington, D.C.); ord. priest June 11, 1926; ord. titular bishop of Sila and auxiliary bishop of San Francisco, Aug. 24, 1939; app. coadjutor bishop of Seattle, Feb. 28, 1948; succeeded as bishop of Seattle, May 18, 1950; first archbishop of Seattle, June 23, 1951; retired Feb. 25, 1975.

Connolly, Thomas J.: b. July 18, 1922, Tonopah, Nev.; educ. St. Patrick's Seminary (Menlo Park, Calif.), Catholic Univ. (Washington, D.C.), Lateran Univ. (Rome); ord. priest Apr. 8, 1947; ord. bishop of Baker, June 30, 1971.

Connors, Ronald G., C.SS.R.: b. Nov. 1, 1915, Brooklyn, N.Y.; ord. priest June 22, 1941; ord. titular bishop of Equizetum and coadjutor bishop of San Juan de la Maguana, Dominican Republic, July 20, 1976; succeeded as bishop of San Juan de la Maguana, July 20, 1977.

Cooke, Terence J.: (See Cardinals, Biographies.)

Coscia, Benedict Dominic, O.F.M.: b. Aug. 10, 1922, Brooklyn, N.Y.; educ. St. Francis College (Brooklyn, N.Y.), Holy Name College (Washington, D.C.); ord. priest June 11, 1949; ord. bishop of Jatai, Brazil, Sept. 21, 1961.

Cosgrove, William M.: b. Nov. 26, 1916, Canton, Ohio; educ. John Carroll Univ. (Cleveland, O.); ord. priest Dec. 18, 1943; ord. titular bishop of Trisipa and auxiliary bishop of Cleveland, Sept. 3, 1968; app. bishop of Belleville, installed Oct. 28, 1976; retired May 19, 1981.

Costello, Thomas J.: b. Feb. 23, 1929, Camden, N.Y.; educ. Niagara Univ. (Niagara Falls, N.Y.), St. Bernard's Seminary (Rochester, N.Y.), Catholic Univ. (Washington, D.C.); ord. priest June 5, 1954; ord. titular bishop of Perdices and auxiliary bishop of Syracuse Mar. 13, 1978.

Cotey, Arnold R., S.D.S.: b. June 15, 1921, Milwaukee, Wis.; educ. Divine Savior Seminary (Lanham, Md.), Marquette Univ. (Milwaukee, Wis.); ord. priest June 7, 1949; ord. first bishop of Nachingwea, Tanzania, Oct. 20, 1963.

Cousins, William E.: b. Aug. 20, 1902, Chicago, Ill.; educ. Quigley Seminary (Chicago, Ill.), St. Mary of the Lake Seminary (Mundelein, Ill.); ord. priest Apr. 23, 1927; ord. titular bishop of Forma and auxiliary bishop of Chicago, Mar. 7, 1949; app. bishop of Peoria, May 21, 1952; archbishop of Milwaukee, Jan. 27, 1959; retired 1977.

Cronin, Daniel A.: b. Nov. 14, 1927, Newton, Mass.; educ. St. John's Seminary (Boston, Mass.), North American College and Gregorian Univ. (Rome); ord. priest Dec. 20, 1952; attaché apostolic nunciature (Addis Ababa), 1957-61; served in papal Secretariat of State, 1961-68; ord. titular bishop of Egnatia and auxiliary bishop of Boston, Sept. 12, 1968; bishop of Fall River, Dec. 16, 1970.

Crowley, Joseph R.: b. Jan. 12, 1915, Fort Wayne, Ind.; educ. St. Mary's College (St. Mary, Ky.), St. Meinrad Seminary (St. Meinrad, Ind.); served in US Air Force, 1942-46; ord. priest May 1, 1953; editor of *Our Sunday Visitor* 1958-67; ord. titular bishop of Maraguis and auxiliary bishop of Fort Wayne-South Bend, Aug. 24, 1971.

Cummins, John S.: b. Mar. 3, 1928, Oakland, Calif.; educ. St. Patrick's Seminary (Menlo Park, Calif.), Catholic Univ. (Washington, D.C.), Univ. of California; ord. priest Jan. 24, 1953; executive director of the California Catholic Conference 1971-76; ord. titular bishop of Lambaesis and auxiliary bishop of Sacramento, May 16, 1974; app. bishop of Oakland, installed June 30, 1977.

Curtis, Walter W.: b. May 3, 1913, Jersey City, N.J.; educ. Fordham Univ. (New York City), Seton Hall Univ. (South Orange, N.J.), Immaculate Conception Seminary (Darlington, N.J.), North American College and Gregorian Univ. (Rome), Catholic Univ. (Washington, D.C.); ord. priest Dec. 8, 1937; ord. titular bishop of Bisica and auxiliary bishop of Newark, Sept. 24, 1957; app. bishop of Bridgeport, 1961, installed Nov. 21, 1961.

Curtiss, Elden F.: b. June 16, 1932, Baker, Ore.; educ. St. Edward Seminary College and St. Thomas Seminary (Kenmore, Wash.); ord. priest May 24, 1958; ord. bishop of Helena, Mont., Apr. 28, 1976.

D

Daily, Thomas V.: b. Sept. 23, 1927, Belmont, Mass.; educ. Boston College, St. John's Seminary (Brighton, Mass.); ord. priest Jan. 10, 1952; missionary in Peru for five years as a member of the Society of St. James the Apostle; ord. titular bishop of Bladia and auxiliary bishop of Boston, Feb. 11, 1975.

Daley, Joseph T.: b. Dec. 21, 1915, Connerton, Pa.; educ. St. Charles Borromeo Seminary (Philadelphia, Pa.); ord. priest June 7, 1941; ord. titular bishop of Barca and auxiliary bishop of Harrisburg, Pa., Jan. 7, 1964; coadjutor bishop of Harrisburg, Aug. 2, 1967; bishop of Harrisburg, Oct. 19, 1971.

Daly, James: b. Aug. 14, 1921, New York, N.Y.; educ. Cathedral College (Brooklyn, N.Y.), Immaculate Conception Seminary (Huntington, L.I.); ord. priest May 22, 1948; ord. titular bishop of Castra Nova and auxiliary bishop of Rockville Centre, May 9, 1977.

Danglmayr, Augustine: b. Dec. 11, 1898, Muenster, Tex.; educ. Subiaco College (Arkansas), St. Mary's Seminary (La Porte, Tex.), Kenrick Seminary (St. Louis, Mo.); ord. priest June 10, 1922; ord. titular bishop of Olba, Oct. 7, 1942; auxiliary bishop of Dallas-Ft. Worth, 1942-69.

D'Antonio, Nicholas, O.F.M.: b. July 10, 1916, Rochester, N.Y.; educ. St. Anthony's Friary (Catskill, N.Y.); ord. priest June 7, 1942; ord. titular bishop of Giufi Salaria and prelate of Olancho, Honduras, July 25, 1966; resigned 1977; app. vicar general of New Orleans archdiocese and episcopal vicar for Spanish Speaking, August, 1977.

D'Arcy, John M.: b. Aug. 18, 1932, Brighton, Mass.; educ. St. John's Seminary (Brighton, Mass.), Angelicum Univ. (Rome); ord. priest Feb. 2, 1957; spiritual director of St. John's Seminary; ord. titular bishop of Mediana and auxiliary bishop of Boston, Feb. 11, 1975.

Davis, James Peter: b. June 9, 1904, Houghton, Mich.; educ. St. Joseph's College (Mountain View, Calif.), St. Patrick's Seminary (Menlo Park, Calif.); ord. priest May 19, 1929; ord. bishop of San Juan, Puerto Rico, Oct. 6, 1943; app. first archbishop of San Juan, July 30, 1960; app. archbishop of Santa

Fe, installed Feb. 25, 1964; resigned June 4, 1974.

Dearden, John Francis: (See Cardinals, Biographies.)

Deksnys, Antanas L.: b. May 9, 1906, Buteniskiai, Lithuania; educ. Metropolitan Seminary and Theological and Philosophical Faculty at Vytautas the Great Univ. (all at Kaunas, Lithuania), Univ. of Fribourg (Switzerland); ord. priest May 30, 1931; served in US parishes at Mt. Carmel, Pa., and East St. Louis, Ill.; ord. titular bishop of Lavellum, June 15, 1969; assigned to pastoral work among Lithuanians in Western Europe.

Delaney, Joseph P.: b. Aug. 29, 1934, Fall River, Mass.; educ. Cardinal O'Connell Seminary (Boston, Mass.), Theological College (Washington, D.C.), North American College (Rome), Rhode Island College (Providence, R.I.); ord. priest Dec. 18, 1960; ord. bishop of Fort Worth, Tex., Sept. 13, 1981.

Dempsey, Michael J., O.P.: b. Feb. 22, 1912, Providence, R.I.; entered Order of Preachers (Dominicans), Chicago province, 1935; ord. priest June 11, 1942; ord. bishop of Sokoto, Nigeria, Aug. 15, 1967.

Denning, Joseph P.: b. Jan. 4, 1907, Flushing, L.I.; educ. Cathedral College (Brooklyn, N.Y.), Immaculate Conception Seminary (Huntington, L.I.), St. Mary's Seminary (Baltimore, Md.); ord. priest May 21, 1932; ord. titular bishop of Mallus and auxiliary bishop of Brooklyn, Apr. 22, 1959; resigned Apr. 13, 1982.

De Palma, Joseph A., S.C.J.: b. Sept. 4, 1913, Walton, N.Y.; ord. priest May 20, 1944; superior general of Congregation of Priests of the Sacred Heart, 1959-67; ord. first bishop of De Aar, South Africa, July 19, 1967.

De Simone, Louis A.: b. Feb. 21, 1922, Philadelphia, Pa.; educ. Villanova Univ. (Villanova, Pa.), St. Charles Borromeo Seminary (Overbrook, Pa.); ord. priest May 10, 1952; ord. titular bishop of Cillium and auxiliary bishop of Philadelphia, Aug. 12, 1981.

Dimmerling, Harold J.: b. Sept. 23, 1914, Braddock, Pa.; educ. St. Fidelis Preparatory Seminary (Herman, Pa.), St. Charles Seminary (Columbus, O.), St. Francis Seminary (Loretto, Pa.); ord. priest May 2, 1940; ord. bishop of Rapid City, Oct. 30, 1969.

Dingman, Maurice J.: b. Jan. 20, 1914, St. Paul, Ia.; educ. St. Ambrose College (Davenport, Ia.), North American College and Gregorian Univ. (Rome), Catholic Univ. (Washington, D.C.); ord. priest Dec. 8, 1939; ord. bishop of Des Moines, June 19, 1968.

Dion, Georges E., O.M.I.: b. Sept. 25, 1911, Central Falls, R.I.; educ. Holy Cross College (Worcester, Mass.), Oblate Juniorate (Colebrook, N.H.), Oblate Scholasticates (Natick, Mass., and Ottawa, Ont.); ord. priest June 24, 1936; ord. titular bishop of Arpaia and vicar apostolic of Jolo, Philippine Islands, Apr. 23, 1980.

Dolinay, Thomas V.: b. July 24, 1923, Uniontown, Pa.; educ. St. Procopius College (Lisle, Ill.); ord. priest May 16, 1948; editor *Eastern Catholic Life,* 1966-82; ord. titular bishop of Tiatira and auxiliary bishop of Byzantine-Rite diocese of Passaic, Nov. 23, 1976; app. first bishop Byzantine-Rite diocese of Van Nuys, Calif., Dec. 3, 1981, installed Mar. 9, 1982.

Donaghy, Frederick Anthony, M.M.: b. Jan. 13, 1903, New Bedford, Mass.; educ. Holy Cross College (Worcester, Mass.), St. Mary's Seminary (Baltimore, Md.), Maryknoll Seminary (Maryknoll, N.Y.); ord. priest Jan. 29, 1929; ord. titular bishop of Setea and vicar apostolic of Wuchow, China, Sept. 21, 1939; title changed to bishop of Wuchow, Apr. 11, 1946; expelled by Communists.

Donnellan, Thomas A.: b. Jan. 24, 1914, New York, N.Y.; educ. Cathedral College and St. Joseph's Seminary (New York, N.Y.), Catholic Univ. (Washington, D.C.); ord. priest June 3, 1939; ord. bishop of Ogdensburg, Apr. 9, 1964; app. archbishop of Atlanta, installed July 16, 1968.

Donohoe, Hugh A.: b. June 28, 1905, San Francisco, Calif.; educ. St. Patrick's Preparatory and Major Seminaries (Menlo Park, Calif.), Catholic Univ. (Washington, D.C.); ord. priest June 14, 1930; ord. titular bishop of Taium and auxiliary bishop of San Francisco, Oct. 7, 1947; app. first bishop of Stockton, Jan. 27, 1962; app. bishop of Fresno, Aug. 27, 1969, installed Oct. 7, 1969; retired July 1, 1980.

Donovan, John A.: b. Aug. 5, 1911, Chatham, Ont., Canada; educ. Sacred Heart Seminary (Detroit, Mich.), North American College and Gregorian Univ. (Rome); ord. priest Dec. 8, 1935; ord. titular bishop of Rhasus and auxiliary bishop of Detroit, Oct. 26, 1954; app. bishop of Toledo, installed Apr. 18, 1967; retired July 29, 1980.

Donovan, Paul V.: b. Sept. 1, 1924, Bernard, Iowa; educ. St. Gregory's Seminary (Cincinnati, Ohio), Mt. St. Mary's Seminary (Norwood, Ohio), Lateran Univ. (Rome); ord. priest May 20, 1950; ord. first bishop of Kalamazoo, Mich., July 21, 1971.

Dougherty, John J.: b. Sept. 16, 1907, Jersey City, N.J.; educ. Seton Hall Univ. (S. Orange, N.J.), Immaculate Conception Seminary (Darlington, N.J.), North American College, Gregorian Univ., Pontifical Biblical Institute (Rome); ord. priest July 23, 1933; ord. titular bishop of Cotenna and auxiliary bishop of Newark, Jan. 24, 1963.

Dozier, Carroll T.: b. Aug. 18, 1911, Richmond, Va.; educ. Holy Cross College (Worcester, Mass.), Gregorian Univ. (Rome); ord. priest, Mar. 19, 1937, Rome; ord. first bishop of Memphis, Jan. 6, 1971; resigned July 27, 1982.

Driscoll, Justin A.: b. Sept. 30, 1920,

Bernard, Ia.; educ. Loras College (Dubuque, Ia.), Catholic Univ. (Washington, D.C.); ord. priest July 28, 1945; president of Loras College, 1967-70; ord. bishop of Fargo, Oct. 28, 1970.

Drury, Thomas J.: b. Jan. 4, 1908, Co. Sligo, Ireland; educ. St. Benedict's College (Atchison, Kans.), Kenrick Seminary (St. Louis, Mo.); ord. priest June 2, 1935; ord. first bishop of San Angelo, Tex., Jan. 24, 1962; app. bishop of Corpus Christi, installed Sept. 1, 1965.

Dudick, Michael J.: b. Feb. 24, 1916, St. Clair, Pa.; educ. St. Procopius College and Seminary (Lisle, Ill.); ord. priest Nov. 13, 1945; ord. bishop of Byzantine Rite Eparchy of Passaic, Oct. 24, 1968.

Dudley, Paul: b. Nov. 27, 1926, Northfield, Minn.; educ. Nazareth College and St. Paul Seminary (St. Paul, Minn.); ord. priest June 2, 1951; ord. titular bishop of Ursona and auxiliary bishop of St. Paul and Minneapolis, Jan. 25, 1977; app. bishop of Sioux Falls, installed Dec. 13, 1978.

Duhart, Clarence James, C.SS.R.: b. Mar. 23, 1912, New Orleans, La.; ord. priest June 29, 1937; ord. bishop of Udon Thani, Thailand, Apr. 21, 1966; resigned Oct. 2, 1975.

DuMaine, (Roland) Pierre: b. Aug. 2, 1931, Paducah, Ky.; educ. St. Joseph's College (Mountain View, Calif.), St. Patrick's College and Seminary (Menlo Park, Calif.), Univ. of California (Berkeley), Catholic Univ. (Washington, D.C.); ord. priest June 15, 1957; ord. titular bishop of Sarda and auxiliary bishop of San Francisco, June 29, 1978; app. first bishop of San Jose, Jan. 27, 1981; installed Mar. 18, 1981.

Dunn, Francis J.: b. Mar. 22, 1922, Elkader, Ia.; educ. Loras College (Dubuque, Ia.), Kenrick Seminary (St. Louis, Mo.), Angelicum (Rome, Italy); ord. priest Jan. 11, 1948; chancellor of Dubuque, Aug. 27, 1960; ord. titular bishop of Turris Tamallani and auxiliary bishop of Dubuque, Aug. 27, 1969, app. vicar general, Aug. 28, 1969.

Durick, Joseph Aloysius: b. Oct. 13, 1914, Dayton, Tenn.; educ. St. Bernard Minor Seminary (St. Bernard, Ala.), St. Mary's Seminary (Baltimore, Md.), Urban Univ. (Rome); ord. priest May 23, 1940; ord. titular bishop of Cerbal and auxiliary bishop of Mobile-Birmingham, Mar. 24, 1955; app. coadjutor bishop of Nashville, Tenn., installed Mar. 3, 1964; apostolicadministrator, 1966; bishop of Nashville, Sept. 10, 1969; resigned Apr. 4, 1975, to work with inmates of Federal correctional institutions and their families.

Durning, Dennis V., C.S.Sp.: b. May 18, 1923, Germantown, Pa.; educ. St. Mary's Seminary (Ferndale, Conn.); ord. priest June 3, 1949; ord. first bishop of Arusha, Tanzania, May 28, 1963.

E

Elko, Nicholas T.: b. Dec. 14, 1909, Donora, Pa.; educ. Duquesne Univ. (Pittsburgh, Pa.), Seminary of Uzhorod (Czechoslovakia) Louvain Univ. (Belgium); ord. priest Sept. 30, 1934; ord. titular bishop of Apollonias and apostolic administrator of Byzantine-Rite exarchy of Pittsburgh, Mar. 6, 1955; succeeded as exarch of Pittsburgh, Sept. 5, 1955; became eparch when Pittsburgh was raised to eparchy, July, 1963; app. titular archbishop of Dara, 1967, and ordaining prelate for Byzantine Rite in Rome; head of Oriental liturgical commission; app. auxiliary bishop of Cincinnati, Aug. 10, 1971.

Etteldorf, Raymond P.: b. Aug. 12, 1911, Ossian, Ia.; educ. Loras College (Dubuque, Ia.), Gregorian Univ. (Rome); ord. priest Dec. 8, 1937; secretary general of Supreme Council for direction of Pontifical Missionary Works, 1964-68; secretary of Pontifical Commission for Economic Affairs, 1968-69; ord. titular archbishop of Tindari, Jan. 6, 1969; papal representative to New Zealand and the Pacific Islands, 1968-74; pro-nuncio to Ethiopia, 1974.

Evans, George R.: b. Sept. 25, 1922, Denver, Colo.; educ. Notre Dame Univ. (Notre Dame, Ind.), St. Thomas Seminary (Denver, Colo.), Apollinare Univ. (Rome, Italy); ord. priest May 31, 1947; ord. titular bishop of Tubyza and auxiliary bishop of Denver, Apr. 23, 1969.

F

Federal, Joseph Lennox: b. Jan. 13, 1910, Greensboro, N.C.; educ. Belmont Abbey College (Belmont Abbey, N.C.), Niagara Univ. (Niagara Falls, N.Y.), Univ. of Fribourg (Switzerland), North American College and Gregorian Univ. (Rome); ord. priest Dec. 8, 1934; ord. titular bishop of Appiaria and auxiliary bishop of Salt Lake City, Apr. 11, 1951; app. coadjutor with right of succession, May, 1958; bishop of Salt Lake City, Mar. 31, 1960; retired Apr. 22, 1980.

Ferrario, Joseph A.: b. Mar. 3, 1926, Scranton, Pa.; educ. St. Charles College (Catonsville, Md.), St. Mary's Seminary (Baltimore, Md.), Catholic Univ. (Washington, D.C.); Univ. of Scranton; ord. priest May 19, 1951; ord. titular bishop of Cuse and auxiliary bishop of Honolulu Jan. 13, 1978; bishop of Honolulu, May 13, 1982.

Fiorenza, Joseph A.: b. Jan. 25, 1931, Beaumont, Tex.; educ. St. Mary's Seminary (LaPorte, Tex.); ord. priest May 29, 1954; ord. bishop of San Angelo, Oct. 25, 1979.

Fitzpatrick, John J.: b. Oct. 12, 1918, Trenton, Ont., Canada; educ. Urban Univ. (Rome), Our Lady of the Angels Seminary (Niagara Falls, N.Y.); ord. priest Dec. 13, 1942; ord. titular bishop of Cenae and auxiliary bishop of Miami, Aug. 28, 1968; bishop of Brownsville, Tex., May 28, 1971.

Fitzsimons, George K.: b. Sept. 4, 1928, Kansas City, Mo.; educ. Rockhurst College (Kansas City, Mo.), Immaculate Conception Seminary (Conception, Mo.); ord. priest Mar. 18, 1961; ord. titular bishop of Pertusa and auxiliary bishop of Kansas City-St. Joseph, July 3, 1975.

Flanagan, Bernard Joseph: b. Mar. 31, 1908, Proctor, Vt.; educ. Holy Cross College (Worcester, Mass.), North American College (Rome), Catholic Univ. (Washington, D.C.); ord. priest Dec. 8, 1931; ord. first bishop of Norwich, Nov. 30, 1953; app. bishop of Worcester, installed, Sept. 24, 1959.

Flavin, Glennon P.: b. Mar. 2, 1916, St. Louis, Mo.; educ. Kenrick Seminary (St. Louis, Mo.); ord. priest Dec. 20, 1941; ord. titular bishop of Joannina and auxiliary bishop of St. Louis, May 30, 1957; app. bishop of Lincoln, installed Aug. 17, 1967.

Fliss, Raphael M.: b. Oct. 25, 1930, Milwaukee, Wis.; educ. St. Francis Seminary (Milwaukee, Wis.), Catholic University (Washington, D.C.), Pontifical Lateran Univ. (Rome); ord. priest May 26, 1956; ord. coadjutor bishop of Superior with right of succession, Dec. 20, 1979.

Flores, Felixberto C.: b. Jan. 13, 1921, Agana, Guam; educ. St. John's Seminary (Brighton, Mass.), Fordham Univ. (New York); ord. priest Apr. 30, 1949; ord. titular bishop of Stonj, May 17, 1970, and apostolic administrator of the diocese of Agana, Guam; installed second residential bishop of Agana, July 12, 1972.

Flores, Patrick F.: b. July 26, 1929, Ganado, Tex.; educ. St. Mary's Seminary (Houston, Tex.); ord. priest May 26, 1956; ord. titular bishop of Itolica and auxiliary bishop of San Antonio, May 5, 1970 (first Mexican-American bishop); app. bishop of El Paso, Apr. 4, 1978, installed May 29, 1978; app. archbishop of San Antonio 1979.

Forst, Marion F.: b. Sept. 3, 1910, St. Louis, Mo.; educ. St. Louis Preparatory Seminary (St. Louis, Mo.), Kenrick Seminary (Webster Groves, Mo.); ord. priest June 10, 1934; ord. bishop of Dodge City, Mar. 24, 1960; app. titular bishop of Scala and auxiliary bishop of Kansas City, Kans. Oct. 16, 1976.

Francis Joseph A., S.V.D.: b. Sept. 30, 1923, Lafayette, La.; educ. St. Augustine Seminary (Bay St. Louis, Miss.), St. Mary Seminary (Techny, Ill.), Catholic Univ. (Washington, D.C.); ord. priest Oct. 7, 1950; president Conference of Major Superiors of Men, 1974-76, and the National Black Catholic Clergy Caucus; ord. titular bishop of Valliposita and auxiliary bishop of Newark, June 25, 1976.

Franz, John B.: b. Oct. 29, 1896, Springfield, Ill.; educ. Quincy College (Quincy, Ill.),

Kenrick Seminary (Webster Groves, Mo.), Catholic Univ. (Washington, D.C.); ord. priest June 13, 1920; ord. first bishop of Dodge City, Aug. 29, 1951; app. bishop of Peoria, installed Nov. 4, 1959; resigned May 24, 1971.

Franzetta, Benedict C.: b. Aug. 1, 1921, East Liverpool, O.; educ. St. Charles College (Catonsville, Md.), St. Mary Seminary (Cleveland, O.); ord. priest Apr. 29, 1950; ord. titular bishop of Oderzo and auxiliary bishop of Youngstown, Sept. 4, 1980.

Freking, Frederick W.: b. Aug. 11, 1913, Heron Lake, Minn.; educ. St. Mary's College (Winona, Minn.), North American College and Gregorian Univ. (Rome), Catholic Univ. (Washington, D.C.); ord. priest July 31, 1938; ord. bishop of Salina, Nov. 30, 1957; app. bishop of La Crosse, Dec. 30, 1964, installed Feb. 24, 1965.

Frey, Gerard L.: b. May 10, 1914, New Orleans, La.; educ. Notre Dame Seminary (New Orleans, La.); ord. priest Apr. 2, 1938; ord. bishop of Savannah, Aug. 8, 1967; app. bishop of Lafayette, La., Nov. 7, 1972, installed Jan, 7, 1973.

Friend, William B.: b. Oct. 22, 1931, Miami, Fla.; educ. St. Mary's College (St. Mary, Ky.), Mt. St. Mary Seminary (Emmitsburg, Md.), Catholic Univ. (Washington, D.C.), Notre Dame Univ. (Notre Dame, Ind.); ord. priest May 7, 1959; ord. titular bishop of Pomaria and auxiliary bishop of Alexandria-Shreveport, La., Oct. 30, 1979.

Frosi, Angelo, S. X.: b. Jan. 31, 1924, Baffano Cremona, Italy; ord. priest May 6, 1948; U.S. citizen; ord. titular bishop of Magneto, May 1, 1970, and prelate of Abaete do Tocantins, Brazil; app. first bishop of Abaetetuba, Brazil, Sept. 17, 1981.

Fulcher, George A.: b. Jan. 30, 1922, Columbus, Ohio; educ. St. Charles Borromeo Seminary (Columbus, O.), Mt. St. Mary of the West Seminary (Norwood, O.), North American College and Angelicum (Rome); ord. priest Feb. 28, 1948; ord. titular bishop of Morosbisdus and auxiliary bishop of Columbus, July 18, 1976.

Furlong, Philip J.: b. Dec. 8, 1892, New York, N.Y.; educ. Cathedral College (New York, N.Y.), St. Joseph's Seminary (Yonkers, N.Y.); ord. priest May 18, 1918; ord. titular bishop of Araxa and auxiliary to military vicar, Jan. 25, 1956. Retired 1971.

G

Gallagher, Raymond J.: b. Nov. 19, 1912, Cleveland, Ohio; educ. John Carroll Univ. and Our Lady of the Lake Seminary (Cleveland, O.); ord. priest Mar. 25, 1939; secretary of the National Conference of Catholic Charities 1961-65; ord. bishop of Lafayette in Indiana, Aug. 11, 1965.

Gallegos, Alphonse, O.A.R.: b. Feb. 20, 1931, Albuquerque, N. Mex., ord priest May

24, 1958; ord. titular bishop of Sasabe and auxiliary bishop of Sacramento, Nov. 4, 1981.

Ganter, Bernard J.: b. July 17,1928, Galveston, Tex.; educ. Texas A & M Univ. (College Sta., Tex.), St. Mary's Seminary (La Porte, Tex.), Catholic Univ. (Washington, D.C.); ord. priest May 22, 1952; chancellor of Galveston-Houston diocese, 1966-73; ord. first bishop of Tulsa, Feb. 7, 1973; app. bishop of Beaumont, Tex., Oct. 18, 1977, installed Dec. 13, 1977.

Garmendia, Francisco: b. Nov. 6, 1924, Lozcano, Spain; ord. priest June 29, 1947, in Spain; came to New York in 1964; became naturalized citizen; ord. titular bishop of Limisa and auxiliary bishop of New York, June 29, 1977. Vicar for Spanish pastoral development in New York archdiocese.

Garmo, George: b. Dec. 8, 1921, Telkaif, Iraq; educ. St. Peter Chaldean Patriarchal Seminary (Mossul, Iraq), Pontifical Urban Univ. (Rome); ord. priest Dec. 8, 1945; pastor of Chaldean parish in Detroit archdiocese, 1960-64, 1966-80; ord. archbishop of Chaldean-Rite archdiocese of Mossul, Iraq, Sept. 14, 1980.

Garner, Robert F.: b. Apr. 27, 1920, Jersey City, N.J.; educ. Seton Hall Univ. (S. Orange, N.J.), Immaculate Conception Seminary (Darlington, N.J.); ord. priest June 15, 1946; ord. titular bishop of Blera and auxiliary bishop of Newark, June 25, 1976.

Gaughan, Norbert F.: b. May 30, 1921, Pittsburgh, Pa.; educ. St. Vincent College (Latrobe, Pa.), Univ. of Pittsburgh; ord. priest Nov. 4, 1945; ord. titular bishop of Taraqua and auxiliary bishop of Greensburg, June 26, 1975.

Gelineau, Louis E.: b. May 3, 1928, Burlington, Vt.; educ. St. Michael's College (Winooski, Vt.), St. Paul's Univ. Seminary (Ottawa, Ont.), Catholic Univ. (Washington, D.C.); ord. priest June 5, 1954; ord. bishop of Providence, R.I., Jan. 26, 1972.

Gendron, Odore: b. Sept. 13, 1921, Manchester, N.H.; educ. St. Charles Borromeo Seminary (Sherbrooke, Que., Canada), Univ. of Ottawa, St. Paul Univ. Seminary (Ottawa, Ont., Canada); ord. priest May 31, 1947; ord. bishop of Manchester, Feb. 3, 1975.

Gerber, Eugene J.: b. Apr. 30, 1931, Kingman, Kans.; educ. St. Thomas Seminary (Denver, Colo.), Wichita State Univ.; Catholic Univ. (Washington, D.C.), Angelicum (Rome); ord. priest May 19, 1959; ord. bishop of Dodge City, Dec. 14, 1976.

Gerbermann, Hugo, M.M.: b. Sept. 11, 1913, Nada, Tex.; educ. St. John's Minor and Major Seminary (San Antonio, Tex.), Maryknoll Seminary (Maryknoll, N.Y.); ord. priest Feb. 7, 1943; missionary work in Ecuador and Guatemala; ord. titular bishop of Amathus and prelate of Huehuetenango, Guatemala, July 22, 1962; first bishop of Huehuetenango, Dec. 23, 1967; app. titular

bishop of Pinkel and auxiliary bishop of San Antonio, July 24, 1975; resigned June 30, 1982.

Gerety, Peter L.: b. July 19, 1912, Shelton, Conn.; educ. Sulpician Seminary (Paris, France); ord. priest June 29, 1939; ord. titular bishop of Crepedula and coadjutor bishop of Portland, Me., with right of succession, June 1, 1966; app. apostolic administrator of Portland, 1967; bishop of Portland, Me., Sept. 15, 1969; app. archbishop of Newark, Apr. 2, 1974; installed June 28, 1974.

Gerrard, James J.: b. June 9, 1897, New Bedford, Mass.; educ. St. Laurent College (Montreal, Que.), St. Bernard's Seminary (Rochester, N.Y.); ord. priest May 26, 1923; ord. titular bishop of Forma and auxiliary bishop of Fall River, Mar. 19, 1959. Retired January, 1976.

Gleeson, Francis D., S.J.: b. Jan. 17, 1895, Carrollton, Mo.: educ. Mount St. Michael's Scholasticate (Spokane, Wash.), St. Francis Xavier College (Ona, Spain); entered the Society of Jesus, 1912; ord. priest July 29, 1926; ord. titular bishop of Cotenna and vicar apostolic of Alaska, Apr. 5, 1948; first bishop of Fairbanks, Aug. 8, 1962; retired Nov. 15, 1968.

Glenn, Laurence A.: b. Aug. 25, 1900, Bellingham, Wash.; educ. St. John's Univ. (Collegeville, Minn.), Catholic Univ. (Washington, D.C.); ord. priest June 11, 1927; ord. titular bishop of Tuscamia and auxiliary bishop of Duluth, Sept. 12, 1956; app. bishop of Crookston, Jan. 27, 1960, installed Apr. 20, 1960; resigned 1970.

Glennie, Ignatius T., S.J.: b. Feb. 5, 1907, Mexico City; educ. Mt. St. Michael's Scholasticate (Spokane, Wash.), Pontifical Seminary (Kandy, Ceylon), St. Mary's College (Kurdeong, India); entered Society of Jesus, 1924; ord. priest Nov. 21, 1938; ord. bishop of Trincomalee, Ceylon, Sept. 21, 1947; title of see changed to Trincomalee-Batticaloa (Sri Lanka), 1967; resigned Feb. 15, 1974.

Gossman, F. Joseph: b. Apr. 1, 1930, Baltimore, Md.: educ. St. Charles College (Catonsville, Md.), St. Mary's Seminary (Baltimore, Md.), North American College (Rome), Catholic Univ. (Washington, D.C.); ord. priest Dec. 17, 1955; ord. titular bishop of Agunto and auxiliary bishop of Baltimore, Sept. 11, 1968; named urban vicar, June 13, 1970; app. bishop of Raleigh April 8, 1975.

Gottwald, George J.: b. May 12, 1914, St. Louis, Mo.; educ. Kenrick Seminary (Webster Groves, Mo.); ord. priest June 9, 1940; ord. titular bishop of Cedamusa and auxiliary bishop of St. Louis, Aug. 8, 1961.

Gracida, Rene H.: b. June 9, 1923, New Orleans, La.; educ. Rice Univ. and Univ. of Houston (Houston, Tex.), Univ. of Fribourg (Switzerland); ord. priest May 23, 1959; ord. titular bishop of Masuccaba and auxiliary bishop of Miami, Jan. 25, 1972; app. first bishop of Pensacola-Tallahassee, Oct. 1, 1975, installed Nov. 6, 1975.

Grady, Thomas J.: b. Oct. 9, 1914, Chicago, Ill.; educ. St. Mary of the Lake Seminary (Mundelein, Ill.), Gregorian Univ. (Rome), Loyola Univ. (Chicago, Ill.); ord. priest Apr. 23, 1938; ord. titular bishop of Vamalla and auxiliary bishop of Chicago, Aug. 24, 1967; app. bishop of Orlando, Fla., Nov. 11, 1974, installed Dec. 16, 1974.

Graham, John J.: b. Sept. 11, 1913, Philadelphia, Pa.; educ. St. Charles Borromeo Seminary (Philadelphia, Pa.), Pontifical Roman Seminary (Rome, Italy); ord. priest Feb. 26, 1938; ord. titular bishop of Sabrata and auxiliary bishop of Philadelphia, Jan. 7, 1964.

Grahmann, Charles V.: b. July 15, 1931, Halletsville, Tex.; educ. The Assumption-St. John's Seminary (San Antonio, Tex.); ord. priest Mar. 17, 1956; ord. titular bishop of Equilium and auxiliary bishop of San Antonio, Aug. 20, 1981; app. first bishop of Victoria, Tex., Apr. 13, 1982.

Graves, Lawrence P.: b. May 4, 1916, Texarkana, Ark.; educ. St. John's Seminary (Little Rock, Ark.), North American College (Rome), Catholic Univ. (Washington, D.C.); ord. priest June 11, 1942; ord. titular bishop of Vina and auxiliary bishop of Little Rock, Apr. 25, 1969; app. bishop of Alexandria, May 22, 1973, installed Sept. 18, 1973; title of see changed to Alexandria-Shreveport, Jan. 12, 1977; resigned July 20, 1982.

Graziano, Lawrence, O.F.M.: b. Apr. 5, 1921, Mt. Vernon, N.Y.; educ. Mt. Alvernia Seminary (Wappingers Falls, N.Y.); ord. priest Jan. 26, 1947; ord. titular bishop of Limata and auxiliary bishop of Santa Ana, El Salvador, Sept. 21, 1961; app. coadjutor bishop of San Miguel, El Salvador, with right of succession, 1965; bishop of San Miguel, Jan. 10, 1968; resigned June 27, 1969.

Greco, Charles Paschal: b. Oct. 29, 1894, Rodney, Miss.; educ. St. Joseph's Seminary (St. Benedict, La.), Louvain Univ. (Belgium), Dominican Univ. (Fribourg, Switzerland); ord. priest July 25, 1918; ord. bishop of Alexandria Feb. 25, 1946; retired May 22, 1973.

Green, Francis J.: b. July 7, 1906, Corning, N.Y.; educ. St. Patrick's Seminary (Menlo Park, Calif.); ord. priest May 15, 1932; ord. titular bishop of Serra and auxiliary bishop of Tucson, Sept. 17, 1953; named coadjutor of Tucson with right of succession, May 11, 1960; bishop of Tucson, Oct. 26, 1960; retired July 27, 1981.

Green, Joseph: b. Oct. 13, 1917, St. Joseph, Mich.; educ. St. Joseph Seminary (Grand Rapids, Mich.). St. Gregory Seminary (Cincinnati, O.), St. Mary's Seminary (Norwood, O.), Lateran Univ. (Rome); ord. priest July 14, 1946; ord. titular bishop of Trisipa and auxiliary bishop of Lansing, Aug. 28, 1962; app. bishop of Reno, installed May 25, 1967; resigned Dec. 6, 1974.

Grellinger, John B.: b. Nov. 5, 1899, Milwaukee, Wis.; educ. Marquette Univ. and St. Francis Seminary (Milwaukee, Wis.), Urban Univ. and Gregorian Univ. (Rome); ord. priest July 14, 1929; ord. titular bishop of Syene and auxiliary bishop of Green Bay, July 14, 1949; retired Sept. 22, 1974.

Greteman, Frank H.: b. Dec. 25, 1907, Willey, Ia.; educ. Loras Academy and Loras College (Dubuque, Ia.), North American College (Rome), Catholic Univ. (Washington, D.C.); ord. priest Dec. 8, 1932; ord. titular bishop of Vissalsa and auxiliary bishop of Sioux City, May 26, 1965; bishop of Sioux City, Dec. 9, 1970.

Griffin, James A.: b. June 13, 1934, Fairview Park, O.; educ. St. Charles College (Baltimore, Md.), Borromeo College (Wicklife, O.); St. Mary Seminary (Cleveland, O.); Lateran Univ. (Rome); Cleveland State Univ.; ord. priest May 28, 1960; ord. titular bishop of Holar and auxiliary bishop of Cleveland, Aug. 1, 1979.

Grutka, Andrew G.: b. Nov. 17, 1908, Joliet, Ill.; educ. St. Procopius College and Seminary (Lisle, Ill.), Urban Univ. and Gregorian Univ. (Rome); ord. priest Dec. 5, 1933; app. moderator of lay activities in Gary diocese, 1955; ord. first bishop of Gary, Feb. 25, 1957; app. member of Pontifical Marian Academy, Jan. 5, 1970.

Guilfoyle, George H.: b. Nov. 13, 1913, New York, N.Y.; educ. Georgetown Univ. (Washington, D.C.), Fordham Univ. (New York City), St. Joseph's Seminary (Dunwoodie, N.Y.), Columbia Univ. Law School (New York City); ord. priest Mar. 25, 1944; ord. titular bishop of Marazane and auxiliary bishop of New York, Nov. 30, 1964; app. bishop of Camden, installed Mar. 4, 1968.

Gumbleton, Thomas J.: b. Jan. 26, 1930, Detroit, Mich.; educ. St. John Provincial Seminary (Detroit, Mich.), Pontifical Lateran Univ. (Rome); ord. priest June 2, 1956; ord. titular bishop of Ululi and auxiliary bishop of Detroit, May 1, 1968.

H

Hacker, Hilary B.: b. Jan. 10, 1913, New Ulm, Minn.; educ. St. Paul Seminary (St. Paul, Minn.), Gregorian Univ. (Rome); ord. priest June 4, 1938; ord. bishop of Bismarck, N. Dak., Feb. 27, 1957; resigned June 30, 1982.

Hackett, John F.: b. Dec. 7, 1911, New Haven, Conn.; educ. St. Thomas Seminary (Bloomfield, Conn.), Seminaire Ste. Sulpice (Paris); ord. priest June 29, 1936; ord. titular bishop of Helenopolis in Palaestina and auxiliary bishop of Hartford, Mar. 19, 1953.

Hagarty, Paul Leonard, O.S.B.: b. Mar. 20, 1909, Greene, Ia.; educ. Loras College (Dubuque, Ia.), St. John's Seminary and St. John's Univ. (Collegeville, Minn.); entered Order of St. Benedict, 1931; ord. priest June

6, 1936; ord. titular bishop of Arba and vicar apostolic of the Bahamas, Oct. 19, 1950; first bishop of Nassau, July 5, 1960; retired 1981.

Ham, J. Richard, M.M.: b. July 11, 1921, Chicago, Ill.; educ. Maryknoll Seminary (New York); ord. priest June 12, 1948; missionary to Guatemala, 1958; ord. titular bishop of Puzia di Numidia and auxiliary bishop of Guatemala, Jan. 6, 1968; resigned see 1979; app. vicar for Hispanic ministry in St. Paul and Minneapolis archdiocese, January, 1980; auxiliary bishop of St. Paul and Minneapolis, October, 1980.

Hammes, George A.: b. Sept. 11, 1911, St. Joseph Ridge, Wis.; educ. St. Lawrence Seminary (Mt. Calvary. Wis.), St. Louis Preparatory Seminary (St. Louis, Mo.), Kenrick Seminary (Webster Groves, Mo.), Sulpician Seminary, Catholic Univ. (Washington, D.C.); ord. priest May 22, 1937; ord. bishop of Superior, May 24, 1960.

Hanifen, Richard C.: b. June 15, 1931, Denver, Colo,; educ. Regis College and St. Thomas Seminary (Denver, Colo.), Catholic Univ. (Washington, D.C.), Lateran Univ. (Rome); ord. priest June 6, 1959; ord. titular bishop of Abercorn and auxiliary bishop of Denver, Sept. 20, 1974.

Hannan, Philip M.: b. May 20, 1913, Washington, D.C.; educ. St. Charles College (Catonsville, Md.), Catholic Univ. (Washington, D.C.), North American College (Rome); ord. priest Dec. 8, 1939; ord. titular bishop of Hieropolis and auxiliary bishop of Washington, D.C., Aug. 28, 1956; app. archbishop of New Orleans, installed Oct. 13, 1965.

Harper, Edward, C.SS.R.: b. July 23, 1910, Brooklyn, N.Y.; educ. Redemptorist Houses of Study; ord. priest June 18, 1939; ord. titular bishop of Heraclea Pontica and first prelate of Virgin Islands, Oct. 6, 1960; became first bishop, 1977, when prelacy was made diocese of St. Thomas.

Harrington, Timothy J.: b. Dec. 19, 1918, Holyoke, Mass.; educ. Holy Cross College (Worcester, Mass.), Grand Seminary (Montreal, Que.), Boston College School of Social Work; ord. priest Jan. 19, 1946; ord. titular bishop of Rusuca and auxiliary bishop of Worcester, Mass., July 2, 1968.

Harris, Vincent M.: b. Oct. 14, 1913, Conroe, Tex.; educ. St. Mary's Seminary (La Porte, Tex.), North American College and Gregorian Univ. (Rome), Catholic Univ. (Washington, D.C.); ord. priest Mar. 19, 1938; ord. first bishop of Beaumont, Tex., Sept. 28, 1966; app. titular bishop of Rotaria and coadjutor bishop of Austin, Apr. 27, 1971; bishop of Austin, Nov. 16, 1971.

Harrison, Francis J.: b. Aug. 12, 1912; Syracuse, N.Y.; educ. Notre Dame Univ. (Notre Dame, Ind.), St. Bernard's Seminary (Rochester, N.Y.), ord. priest June 4, 1937; ord. titular bishop of Aquae in Numidia and auxiliary bishop of Syracuse, Apr. 22, 1971;

app. bishop of Syracuse, Nov. 9, 1976, installed Feb. 6, 1977.

Hart, Daniel A.: b. Aug. 24, 1927, Lawrence, Mass.; educ. St. John's Seminary (Brighton, Mass.); ord. priest Feb. 2, 1953; ord. titular bishop of Tepelta and auxiliary bishop of Boston, Oct. 18, 1976.

Hart, Joseph: b. Sept. 26, 1931, Kansas City, Missouri; educ. St. John Seminary (Kansas City, Mo.), St. Meinrad Seminary (Indianapolis, Ind.); ord. priest May 1, 1956; ord. titular bishop of Thimida Regia and auxiliary bishop of Cheyenne, Wyo., Aug. 31, 1976; app. bishop of Cheyenne, installed June 12, 1978.

Hastrich, Jerome J.: b. Nov. 13, 1914, Milwaukee, Wis.; educ. Marquette Univ., St. Francis Seminary (Milwaukee, Wis.); ord. priest Feb. 9, 1941; ord. titular bishop of Gurza and auxiliary bishop of Madison, Sept. 3, 1963; app. bishop of Gallup, N.Mex., Sept. 3, 1969.

Hayes, Nevin W., O.Carm: b. Feb. 17, 1922, Chicago, Ill.; entered Carmelite novitiate Aug. 15, 1939; educ. Mt. Carmel College (Niagara Falls, Canada), Whitefriars Hall and Catholic Univ. (Washington, D.C.); ord. priest June 8, 1946; prelate nullius of Sicuani, Peru, 1959; ord. titular bishop of Nova Sinna and prelate of Sicuani, Aug. 5, 1965; resigned November 1970; app. auxiliary bishop of Chicago, Feb. 2, 1971.

Head, Edward D.: b. Aug. 5, 1919, White Plains, N.Y.; educ. Cathedral College, St. Joseph's Seminary, Columbia Univ. (New York City); ord. priest Jan. 27, 1945; director of New York Catholic Charities; ord. titular bishop of Ardsratha and auxiliary bishop of New York, Mar. 19, 1970; app. bishop of Buffalo, Jan. 23, 1973, installed Mar. 19, 1973.

Helmsing, Charles H.: b. Mar. 23, 1908, Shrewsbury, Mo.; educ. St. Louis Preparatory Seminary (St. Louis, Mo.), Kenrick Seminary (Webster Groves, Mo.); ord. priest June 10, 1933; ord. titular bishop of Axomis and auxiliary bishop of St. Louis, Apr. 19, 1949; first bishop of Springfield-Cape Girardeau, Aug. 24, 1956; bishop of Kansas City-St. Joseph, 1962, installed Apr. 3, 1962; resigned June 25, 1977.

Herrmann, Edward J.: b. Nov. 6, 1913, Baltimore, Md.; educ. Mt. St. Mary's Seminary (Emmitsburg, Md.), Catholic Univ. (Washington, D.C.); ord. priest June 12, 1947; ord. titular bishop of Lamzella and auxiliary bishop of Washington, D.C., Apr. 26, 1966; app. bishop of Columbus, June 26, 1973.

Hettinger, Edward Gerhard: b. Oct. 14, 1902, Lancaster, O.; educ. St. Vincent's College (Beatty, Pa.); ord. priest June 2, 1928; ord. titular bishop of Teos and auxiliary bishop of Columbus, Feb. 24, 1942; retired October, 1977.

Hickey, Dennis W.: b. Oct. 28, 1914,

Dansville, N.Y.; educ. Colgate Univ. and St. Bernard's Seminary (Rochester, N.Y.); ord. priest June 7, 1941; ord. titular bishop of Rusuccuru and auxiliary bishop of Rochester, N.Y., Mar. 14, 1968.

Hickey, James A.: b. Oct. 11, 1920, Midland, Mich.; educ. Sacred Heart Seminary (Detroit, Mich.), Catholic Univ. (Washington, D.C.), Lateran Univ. and Angelicum (Rome), Michigan State Univ.; ord. priest June 15, 1946; ord. titular bishop of Taraqua and auxiliary bishop of Saginaw, Apr. 14, 1967; rector of North American College, Rome, 1969-74; app. bishop of Cleveland, June 5, 1974; installed July 16, 1974; app. archbishop of Washington, D.C., installed Aug. 5, 1980.

Hines, Vincent J.: b. Sept. 14, 1912, New Haven, Conn.; educ. St. Thomas Seminary (Bloomfield, Conn.), St. Sulpice Seminary (Paris), Lateran Univ. (Rome); ord. priest May 2, 1937; ord. bishop of Norwich, Conn., Mar. 17, 1960; retired June 17, 1975.

Hoch, Lambert A.: b. Feb. 6, 1903, Elkton, S.D.; educ. Creighton Univ. (Omaha, Nebr.), St. Paul Seminary (St. Paul, Minn.); ord. priest May 30, 1928; ord. bishop of Bismarck, Mar. 25, 1952; app. bishop of Sioux Falls Dec. 5, 1956; retired June 1978.

Hodapp, Robert L., S.J.: b. Oct. 1, 1910. Mankato, Minn.; educ. St. Stanislaus Seminary (Florissant, Mo.), St. Louis Univ. (St. Louis, Mo.); ord. priest June 18, 1941; ord. bishop of Belize, June 26, 1958.

Hodges, Joseph H.: b. Oct. 8, 1911, Harper's Ferry, W.Va.; educ. St. Charles College (Catonsville, Md.), North American College (Rome); ord. priest Dec. 8, 1935; ord. titular bishop of Rusadus and auxiliary bishop of Richmond, Oct. 15, 1952; named coadjutor bishop of Wheeling with right of succession, May 24, 1961; bishop of Wheeling, Nov. 23, 1962; title of see changed to Wheeling-Charleston 1974.

Hoffman, James R.: b. June 12, 1932, Fremont, O.; educ. Our Lady of the Lake Minor Seminary (Wawasee, Ind.), St. Meinrad College (St. Meinrad, Ind.); Mt. St. Mary Seminary (Norwood, O.); Catholic Univ. (Washington, D.C.); ord. priest July 28, 1957; ord. titular bishop of Italica and auxiliary bishop of Toledo, June 23, 1978; bishop of Toledo, Dec. 16, 1980.

Hogan, James J.: b. Oct. 17, 1911, Philadelphia, Pa.; educ. St. Charles College (Catonsville, Md.), St. Mary's Seminary (Baltimore), Gregorian Univ. (Rome), Catholic Univ. (Washington, D.C.); ord. priest Dec. 8, 1937; ord. titular bishop of Philomelium and auxiliary bishop of Trenton, Feb. 25, 1960; app. bishop of Altoona-Johnstown, installed July 6, 1966.

Hogan, Joseph L.: b. Mar. 11, 1916, Lima, N.Y.; educ. St. Bernard's Seminary (Rochester, N.Y.), Canisius College (Buffalo, N.Y.),

Angelicum (Rome); ord. priest June 6, 1942; ord. bishop of Rochester, Nov. 28, 1969; resigned Nov. 28, 1978.

Houck, William Russell: b. June 26, 1926, Mobile Ala.; educ. St. Bernard Junior College (Cullman, Ala.), St. Mary's Seminary College and St. Mary's Seminary (Baltimore, Md.), Catholic Univ. (Washington, D.C.); ord. priest May 19, 1951; ord. titular bishop of Alessano and auxiliary bishop of Jackson, Miss., May 27, 1979, by Pope John Paul II.

Howard, Edward Daniel: b. Nov. 5, 1877, Cresco, Ia.; educ. St. Joseph's College (Dubuque, Ia.), St. Mary's College (St. Mary's, Kans.), St. Paul Seminary (St. Paul, Minn.); ord. priest June 12, 1906; ord. titular bishop of Isauropolis and auxiliary bishop of Davenport, Apr. 8, 1924; app. archbishop of Oregon City, Apr. 30, 1926; title changed to archbishop of Portland, Sept. 26, 1928; resigned Dec. 14, 1966; assigned titular see of Albule.

Howze, (Joseph) Lawson E.: b. Aug. 30, 1923, Daphne, Ala.; convert to Catholicism, 1948; educ. St. Bonaventure Univ. (St. Bonaventure, N.Y.); ord. priest May 7, 1959; ord. titular bishop of Massita and auxiliary bishop of Natchez-Jackson, Jan. 28, 1973; app. first bishop of Biloxi, Miss., Mar. 8, 1977; installed June 6, 1977.

Hubbard, Howard J.: b. Oct. 31, 1938, Troy, N.Y.; educ. St. Joseph's Seminary (Dunwoodie, N.Y.); North American College and Gregorian Univ. (Rome), Catholic Univ. (Washington, D.C.); ord. priest Dec. 18, 1963; ord. bishop of Albany, Mar. 27, 1977.

Hughes, Alfred C.: b. Dec. 2, 1932, Boston, Mass.; educ. St. John Seminary (Brighton, Mass), Gregorian Univ. (Rome); ord. priest Dec. 15, 1957, in Rome; ord. titular bishop of Maximiana in Byzacena and auxiliary bishop of Boston, Sept. 14, 1981.

Hughes, Edward T.: b. Nov. 13, 1920, Landowne, Pa.; educ. St. Charles Seminary, Univ. of Pennsylvania (Philadelphia, Pa.); ord. priest May 31, 1947; ord. titular bishop of Segia and auxiliary bishop of Philadelphia, July 21, 1976.

Hughes, William A.: b. Sept. 23, 1921, Youngstown, O.; educ. St. Charles College (Catonsville, Md.), St. Mary's Seminary (Cleveland, O.) Notre Dame Univ. (Notre Dame, Ind.); ord. priest Apr. 6, 1946; ord. titular bishop of Inis Cathaig and auxiliary bishop of Youngstown, Sept. 12, 1974; app. bishop of Covington, installed May 8, 1979.

Hunthausen, Raymond G.: b. Aug. 21, 1921, Anaconda, Mont.; educ. Carroll College (Helena, Mont.), St. Edward's Seminary (Kenmore, Wash.), St. Louis Univ. (St. Louis, Mo.), Catholic Univ. (Washington, D.C.), Fordham Univ. (New York City), Notre Dame Univ. (Notre Dame, Ind.); ord. priest June 1, 1946; ord. bishop of Helena, Aug. 30, 1962; app. archbishop of Seattle, Feb. 25, 1975.

Hurley, Francis T.: b. Jan. 12, 1927, San Francisco, Calif.; educ. St. Patrick's Seminary (Menlo Park, Calif.), Catholic Univ. (Washington, D.C.); ord. priest June 16, 1951; assigned to NCWC in Washington, D.C., 1957; assistant (1958) and later (1968) associate secretary of NCCB and USCC; ord. titular bishop of Daimlaig and auxiliary bishop of Juneau, Alaska, Mar. 19, 1970; app. bishop of Juneau, July 20, 1971, installed Sept. 8, 1971; app. archbishop of Anchorage, May 4, 1976, installed July 8, 1976.

Hurley, Mark J.: b. Dec. 13, 1919, San Francisco, Calif.; educ. St. Patrick's Seminary (Menlo Park, Calif.), Univ. of California (Berkeley), Catholic Univ. (Washington, D.C.), Lateran Univ. (Rome), Univ. of Portland (Portland, Ore.); ord. priest Sept. 23, 1944; ord. titular bishop of Thunusuda and auxiliary bishop of San Francisco, Jan. 4, 1968; app. bishop of Santa Rosa, Nov. 19, 1969.

I-J

Ibrahim, Ibrahim N.: b. Oct. 1, 1937, Telkaif, Mosul, Iraq.; educ. Patriarchal Seminary (Mosul, Iraq), St. Sulpice Seminary (Paris, France); ord. priest Dec. 30, 1962, in Baghdad, Iraq; ord. titular bishop of Anbar and apostolic exarch for Chaldean-Rite Catholics in the United States, Mar. 8, 1982, in Baghdad; installed in Detroit, Apr. 18, 1982.

Imesch, Joseph L.: b. June 21, 1931, Detroit, Mich.; educ. Sacred Heart Seminary (Detroit, Mich.), North American College, Gregorian Univ. (Rome); ord. priest Dec. 16, 1956; ord. titular bishop of Pomaria and auxiliary bishop of Detroit, Apr. 3, 1973; app. bishop of Joliet, June 30, 1979.

Johnson, William R.: b. Nov. 19, 1918, Tonopah, Nev.; educ. Los Angeles College and St. John's Seminary (Camarillo, Calif.), National Catholic School of Social Service, Catholic Univ. (Washington, D.C.); ord. priest May 28, 1944; ord. titular bishop of Blera and auxiliary bishop of Los Angeles, Mar. 25, 1971; app. first bishop of Orange, Calif., Mar. 30, 1976, installed June 18, 1976.

Joyce, Robert F.: b. Oct. 7, 1896, Proctor, Vt.; educ. Univ. of Vermont (Burlington, Vt.), Grand Seminary (Montreal, Canada); ord. priest May 26, 1923; ord. titular bishop of Citium and auxiliary bishop of Burlington, Oct. 28, 1954; installed as bishop of Burlington, Feb. 26, 1957; resigned Dec. 14, 1971.

K

Kalisz, Raymond P., S.V.D.: b. Sept. 25, 1927, Melvindale, Mich.; educ. St. Mary's Seminary (Techny, Ill.); ord. priest Aug. 15, 1954; ord. bishop of Wewak, Papua New Guinea, August 15, 1980.

Keeler, William Henry: b. Mar. 4, 1931, San Antonio, Tex.; educ. St. Charles Seminary (Overbrook, Pa.), North American Col-

lege, Pontifical Gregorian Univ. (Rome); ord. priest July 17, 1955; ord. titular bishop of Ulcinium and auxiliary bishop of Harrisburg, Sept. 21, 1979.

Kellenberg, Walter P.: b. June 3, 1901, New York, N.Y.; educ. Cathedral College (New York, City), St. Joseph Seminary (Dunwoodie, N.Y.); ord. priest June 2, 1928; ord. titular bishop of Joannina and auxiliary bishop of New York, Oct. 5, 1953; app. bishop of Ogdensburg, Jan. 19, 1954; app. first bishop of Rockville Centre Apr. 16, 1957, installed May 27, 1957; retired May 4, 1976.

Kelly, Thomas C., O.P.: b. July 14, 1931, Rochester, N.Y.; educ. Providence College (Providence, R.I.), Immaculate Conception College (Washington, D.C.), Angelicum (Rome); professed in Dominicans, Aug. 26, 1952; secretary, apostolic delegation, Washington, D.C., 1965-71; associate general secretary, 1971-77, and general secretary, 1977-81, NCCB/USCC; ord. titular bishop of Tusurus and auxiliary bishop of Washington, D.C., Aug. 15, 1977; app. archbishop of Louisville, Dec. 28, 1981, installed Feb. 18, 1982.

Kenny, Michael H.: b. June 26, 1937, Hollywood, Calif.; educ. St. Joseph College (Mountain View, Calif.), St. Patrick's Seminary (Menlo Park, Calif.), Catholic Univ. (Washington, D.C.); ord. priest Mar. 30, 1963; ord. bishop of Juneau, May 27, 1979.

Kinney, John: b. June 11, 1937, Oelwein, Iowa; educ. Nazareth Hall and St. Paul Seminaries (St. Paul, Minn.); Pontifical Lateran University (Rome); ord. priest Feb. 2, 1963; ord. titular bishop of Caorle and auxiliary bishop of St. Paul and Minneapolis, Jan. 25, 1977; app. bishop of Bismarck June 30, 1982.

Kocisko, Stephen: b. June 11, 1915, Minneapolis, Minn.; educ. Nazareth Hall Minor Seminary (St. Paul, Minn.), Pontifical Ruthenian College, Urban Univ. (Rome); ord. priest Mar. 30, 1941; ord. titular bishop of Teveste and auxiliary bishop of apostolic exarchate of Pittsburgh, Oct. 23, 1956; installed as first eparch of the eparchy of Passaic, Sept. 10, 1963; app. eparch of Byzantine-Rite diocese of Pittsburgh, installed Mar. 5, 1968; app. first metropolitan of Munhall, installed June 11, 1969; title of see changed to Pittsburgh, 1977.

Koester, Charles R.: b. Sept. 16, 1915, Jefferson City, Mo.; educ. Conception Academy (Conception, Mo.), St. Louis Preparatory Seminary and Kenrick Seminary (St. Louis, Mo.), North American College (Rome); ord. priest Dec. 20, 1941; ord. titular bishop of Suacia and auxiliary bishop of St. Louis, Feb. 11, 1971.

Krawczak, Arthur H.: b. Feb. 2, 1913, Detroit, Mich.; educ. Sacred Heart Seminary, Sts. Cyril and Methodius Seminary (Orchard Lake, Mich.), Catholic Univ. (Washington, D.C.); ord. priest May 18, 1940; ord. titular bishop of Subbar and auxiliary bishop of Detroit, Apr. 3, 1973; retired 1982.

Krol, John J.: (See Cardinals, Biographies.)

Kucera, Daniel, O.S.B.: b. May 7, 1923, Chicago, Ill.; educ. St. Procopius College (Lisle, Ill.), Catholic Univ. (Washington, D.C.); professed in Order of St. Benedict, June 16, 1944; ord. priest May 26, 1949; abbot, St. Procopius Abbey, 1964-71; pres. Illinois Benedictine College, 1959-65 and 1971-76; ord. titular bishop of Natchez and auxiliary bishop of Joliet, July 21, 1977; app. bishop of Salina, Mar. 5, 1980.

Kupfer, William F., M.M.: b. Jan. 28, 1909, Brooklyn, N.Y.; educ. Cathedral College (Brooklyn, N.Y.), Maryknoll Seminary (Maryknoll, N.Y.); ord. priest June 11, 1933; missionary in China; app. prefect apostolic of Taichung, Formosa, 1951; ord. first bishop of Taichung, July 25, 1962.

L

Lambert, Francis, S.M.: b. Feb. 7, 1921, Lawrence, Mass.; educ. Marist Seminary (Framingham, Mass.); ord. priest, June 29, 1946; served in Marist missions in Oceania; provincial of Marist Oceania province, 1971; ord. bishop of Port Vila, Vanuatu (New Hebrides), Mar. 20, 1977.

Larkin, W. Thomas: b. Mar. 31, 1923, Mt. Morris, N.Y.; educ. St. Andrew Seminary and St. Bernard Seminary (Rochester, N.Y.); Angelicum Univ. (Rome); ord. priest May 15, 1947; ord. bishop of St. Petersburg, May 27, 1979.

Law, Bernard F.: b. Nov. 4, 1931, Torreon, Mexico; educ. Harvard Univ. (Cambridge, Mass.), St. Joseph Seminary (St. Benedict, La.), Pontifical College Josephinum (Worthington, O.); ord. priest May 21, 1961; editor of *Mississippi Register* (now *Mississippi Today*), 1963-68; director of NCCB Committee on Ecumenical and Interreligious Affairs, 1968-71; vicar general of Natchez-Jackson diocese, 1971-73; ord. bishop of Springfield-Cape Girardeau, Mo., Dec. 5, 1973.

Leech, George Leo: b. May 21, 1890, Ashley, Pa.; educ. St. Charles Borromeo Seminary (Overbrook, Pa.), Catholic Univ. (Washington, D.C.); ord. priest May 29, 1920; ord. titular bishop of Mela and auxiliary bishop of Harrisburg, Oct. 17, 1935; bishop of Harrisburg Dec. 19, 1935; resigned Oct. 19, 1971; app. titular bishop of Allegheny.

Lemay, Leo, S.M.: b. Sept. 23, 1909, Lawrence, Mass.; educ. Marist College (Washington, D.C.), Gregorian Univ. (Rome); ord. priest Apr. 15, 1933; ord. titular bishop of Agbia and vicar apostolic of North Solomon Islands, Sept. 21, 1960; first bishop of Bougainville, Nov. 15, 1966; resigned July 1, 1974.

Leonard, Vincent M.: b. Dec. 11, 1908, Pittsburgh, Pa.; educ. Duquesne Univ. (Pittsburgh, Pa.), St. Vincent Seminary (Latrobe, Pa.); ord. priest June 16, 1935; ord. titular bishop of Arsacal and auxiliary bishop of Pittsburgh, Apr. 21, 1964; app. bishop of Pittsburgh, installed July 2, 1969.

Lessard, Raymond W.: b. Dec. 21, 1930, Grafton, N.D.; educ. St. Paul Seminary (St. Paul, Minn.), North American College (Rome); ord. priest Dec. 16, 1956; served on staff of the Congregation for Bishops in the Roman Curia, 1964-73; ord. bishop of Savannah, Apr. 27, 1973.

Leven, Stephen A.: b. Apr. 30, 1905, Blackwell, Okla.; educ. St. Gregory's College (Shawnee, Okla.), St. Benedict's College (Atchison, Kans.), St. Mary's Seminary (La Porte, Tex.), American College (Louvain, Belgium); ord. priest June 10, 1928; ord. titular bishop of Bure and auxiliary bishop of San Antonio, Feb. 8, 1956; app. bishop of San Angelo, Tex., installed Nov. 25, 1969; resigned 1979.

Lipscomb, Oscar H.: b. Sept. 21, 1931, Mobile, Ala.; educ. McGill Institute, St. Bernard College (Cullman, Ala.), North American College and Gregorian Univ. (Rome), Catholic Univ. (Washington, D.C.); ord. priest July 15, 1956; ord. first archbishop of Mobile, Nov. 16, 1980.

Lohmuller, Martin J.: b. Aug. 21, 1919, Philadelphia, Pa.; educ. St. Charles Borromeo Seminary (Philadelphia, Pa.), Catholic Univ. (Washington, D.C.); ord. priest June 3, 1944; ord. titular bishop of Ramsbury and auxiliary bishop of Philadelphia, Apr. 2, 1970.

Losten, Basil: b. May 11, 1930, Chesapeake City, Md.; educ. St. Basil's College (Stamford, Conn.), Catholic University (Washington, D.C.); ord. priest June 10, 1957; ord. titular bishop of Arcadiopolis in Asia and auxiliary bishop of Ukrainian archeparchy of Philadelphia, May 25, 1971; app. apostolic administrator of archeparchy, 1976; app. bishop of Ukrainian eparchy of Stamford, 1977.

Lotocky, Innocent Hilarius, O.S.B.M.: b. Nov. 3, 1915, Petlykiwci, Ukraine; educ. seminaries in Ukraine, Czechoslovakia and Austria; ord. priest Nov. 24, 1940; ord. bishop of St. Nicholas of Chicago for the Ukrainians, Mar. 1, 1981.

Lubachivsky, Myroslav J.: b. June 24, 1914, Dolynian, Ukraine; educ. Innsbruck Univ. (Austria), Gregorian Univ. and Biblicum (Rome); began pastoral work in U.S. in 1947; ord. archbishop of Ukrainian-Rite archeparchy of Philadelphia, Nov. 12, 1979; app. coadjutor archbishop of Lwow of the Ukrainians, Mar. 27, 1980.

Lucker, Raymond A.: b. Feb. 24, 1927, St. Paul, Minn.; educ. St. Paul Seminary (St. Paul, Minn.); University of Minnesota (Minneapolis), Angelicum (Rome); ord. priest June 7, 1952; director of USCC department of education, 1968-71; ord. titular bishop of Meta and auxiliary bishop of St. Paul and Minneapolis, Sept. 8, 1971; app. bishop of New Ulm, Dec. 23, 1975, installed Feb. 19, 1976.

Lyke, James Patterson, O.F.M.: b. Feb. 18, 1939, Chicago, Ill.; educ. Quincy College (Quincy, Ill.), Antonianum (Rome), Union Graduate School (Cincinnati, O.); professed in Order of Friars Minor, June 21, 1963; ord. priest June 24, 1966; president of National Black Catholic Clergy Caucus; ord. titular bishop of Furnos Maior and auxiliary bishop of Cleveland, Aug. 1, 1979.

Lynch, George E.: b. Mar. 4, 1917, New York, N.Y.; educ. Fordham Univ. (New York), Mt. St. Mary's Seminary (Emmitsburg, Md.), Catholic Univ. (Washington, D.C.); ord. priest May 29, 1943; ord. titular bishop of Satafi and auxiliary bishop of Raleigh Jan. 6, 1970.

Lyons, Thomas W.: b. Sept. 26, 1923, Washington, D.C.; educ. St. Charles College (Catonsville, Md.), St. Mary's Seminary (Baltimore, Md.); ord. priest May 22, 1948; ord. titular bishop of Mortlach and auxiliary bishop of Washington, D.C., Sept. 12, 1974.

M

McAuliffe, Michael F.: b. Nov. 22, 1920, Kansas City, Mo.; educ. St. Louis Preparatory Seminary (St. Louis, Mo.), Catholic Univ. (Washington, D.C.): ord. priest May 31, 1945; ord. bishop of Jefferson City, Aug. 18, 1969.

McCarrick, Theodore E.: b. July 7, 1930, New York, N.Y.; educ. Fordham Univ. (Bronx, N.Y.), St. Joseph's Seminary (Dunwoodie, N.Y.), Catholic Univ. (Washington, D.C.); ord. priest May 31, 1958; dean of students Catholic Univ. of America, 1961-63; pres., Catholic Univ. of Puerto Rico, 1965-69; secretary to Cardinal Cooke, 1970; ord. titular bishop of Rusubisir and auxiliary bishop of New York, June 29, 1977; app. first bishop of Metuchen, N.J., Nov. 19, 1981, installed Jan. 31, 1982.

McCarthy, Edward A.: b. Apr. 10, 1918, Cincinnati, O.; educ. Mt. St. Mary Seminary (Norwood, O.), Catholic Univ. (Washington, D.C.), Lateran and Angelicum (Rome); ord. priest May 29, 1943; ord. titular bishop of Tamascani and auxiliary bishop of Cincinnati, June 15, 1965; first bishop of Phoenix, Ariz., Dec. 2, 1969; app. coadjutor archbishop of Miami, Fla., July 7, 1976; succeeded as archbishop of Miami, July 26, 1977.

McCarthy, John E., b. June 21, 1930, Houston, Tex.; educ. Univ. of St. Thomas (Houston, Tex.); ord. priest May 26, 1956; assistant director Social Action Dept. USCC, 1967-69; executive director Texas Catholic Conference; ord. titular bishop of Pedena and auxiliary bishop of Galveston-Houston, Mar. 14, 1979.

McCauley, Vincent, C.S.C.: b. Mar. 8, 1906, Council Bluffs, Ia.; educ. Notre Dame Univ. (Notre Dame, Ind.), Holy Cross Seminary (Washington, D.C.); ord. priest June 24, 1943; ord. first bishop of Fort Portal, Uganda, May 18, 1961; resigned to Africanize the diocese Dec. 1, 1972; general secretary of Association of Member Episcopal Conferences in Eastern Africa (AMECEA).

McCormick, J. Carroll: b. Dec. 15, 1907, Philadelphia, Pa.; educ. College Ste. Marie (Montreal), St. Charles Seminary (Overbrook, Pa.), Minor and Major Roman Seminary (Rome); ord. priest July 10, 1932; ord. titular bishop of Ruspae and auxiliary bishop of Philadelphia, Apr. 23, 1947; app. bishop of Altoona-Johnstown, installed Sept. 21, 1960; app. bishop of Scranton, installed May 25, 1966.

McDonald, Andrew J.: b. Oct. 24, 1923, Savannah, Ga.; educ. St. Mary's Seminary (Baltimore, Md.), Catholic Univ. (Washington, D.C.), Lateran Univ. (Rome); ord. priest May 8, 1948; ord. bishop of Little Rock, Sept. 5, 1972.

McDonald, William J.: b. June 17, 1904, Mooncoin, Ireland; educ. St. Kieran's College and Seminary (Kilkenny, Ireland), Catholic Univ. (Washington, D.C.); ord. priest June 10, 1928; rector of Catholic Univ. of America, 1957-67; ord. titular bishop of Aquae Regiae and auxiliary bishop of Washington, May 19, 1964; app. auxiliary bishop of San Francisco, July 26, 1967; retired 1979.

McDonough, Thomas J.: b. Dec. 5, 1911, Philadelphia, Pa.; educ. St. Charles Seminary (Overbrook, Pa.), Catholic Univ. (Washington, D.C.); ord. priest May 26, 1938; ord. titular bishop of Thenae and auxiliary bishop of St. Augustine, Apr. 30, 1947; app. auxiliary bishop of Savannah, Jan. 2, 1957; named bishop of Savannah, installed Apr. 27, 1960; app. archbishop of Louisville, installed May 2, 1967; resigned Sept. 29, 1981.

McDowell, John B.: b. July 17, 1921, New Castle, Pa.; educ. St. Vincent College, St. Vincent Theological Seminary (Latrobe, Pa.), Catholic Univ. (Washington, D.C.); ord. priest Nov. 4, 1945; superintendent of schools, Pittsburgh diocese, 1955-70; ord. titular bishop of Tamazuca, and auxiliary bishop of Pittsburgh, Sept. 8, 1966.

McEleney, John J., S.J.: b. Nov. 13, 1895, Woburn, Mass.; educ. Boston College (Boston, Mass.), Jesuit Scholasticate (New England Province); entered Society of Jesus, 1918; ord. priest June 18, 1930; app. provincial of New England Province, 1944; ord. titular bishop of Zeugma and vicar apostolic of Jamaica, Apr. 15, 1950; title changed to bishop of Kingston, Feb. 29, 1956; archbishop of Kingston, Sept. 14, 1967; retired Sept. 1, 1970.

McFarland, Norman F.: b. Feb. 21, 1922, Martinez, Calif.; educ. St. Patrick's Seminary

(Menlo Park, Calif.), Catholic Univ. (Washington, D.C.); ord. priest June 15, 1946; ord. titular bishop of Bida and auxiliary bishop of San Francisco, Sept. 8, 1970; apostolic adminstrator of Reno, 1974; app. bishop of Reno, Feb. 10, 1976, installed Mar. 31, 1976; title of see changed to Reno-Las Vegas.

McGann, John R.: b. Dec. 2, 1924, Brooklyn, N.Y.; educ. Cathedral College (Brooklyn, N.Y.), Immaculate Conception Seminary (Huntington, L.I.); ord. priest June 3, 1950; ord. titular bishop of Morosbisdus and auxiliary bishop of Rockville Centre, Jan. 7, 1971; vicar general and episcopal vicar; app. bishop of Rockville Centre May 3, 1976, installed June 24, 1976.

McGarry, Urban, T.O.R.: b. Nov. 11, 1911, Warren, Pa.; ord. priest Oct. 3, 1942, in India; prefect apostolic of Bhagalpur, Aug. 7, 1956; ord. first bishop of Bhagalpur, India, May 10, 1965.

McGucken, Joseph T.: b. Mar. 13, 1902, Los Angeles, Calif.; educ. St. Patrick's Seminary (Menlo Park, Calif.), North American College (Rome); ord. priest Jan. 15, 1928; ord. titular bishop of Sanavus and auxiliary bishop of Los Angeles, Mar. 19, 1941; app. coadjutor bishop of Sacramento with right of succession, Oct. 26, 1955; bishop of Sacramento, Jan. 14, 1957; archbishop of San Francisco, installed Apr. 3, 1962; resigned Feb. 22, 1977.

McGurkin, Edward A., M.M.: b. June 22, 1905, Hartford, Conn.; educ. Maryknoll Seminary (Maryknoll, N.Y.); ord. priest Sept. 14, 1930; ord. first bishop of Maswa, Tanganyika, Oct. 3, 1956; title of see changed to Shinyanga (Tanzania), 1957; resigned Jan. 30, 1975.

McKinney, Joseph C.: b. Sept. 10, 1928, Grand Rapids, Mich.: educ. St. Joseph's Seminary (Grand Rapids, Mich.), Seminaire de Philosophie (Montreal, Canada), Urban Univ. (Rome, Italy); ord. priest Dec. 20, 1953; ord. titular bishop of Lentini and auxiliary bishop of Grand Rapids, Sept. 26, 1968.

McLaughlin, Bernard J.: b. Nov. 19, 1912, Buffalo, N.Y.; educ. Urban Univ. (Rome, Italy); ord. priest Dec. 21, 1935, at Rome; ord. titular bishop of Mottola and auxiliary bishop of Buffalo, Jan. 6, 1969.

McManus, William E.: b. Jan. 27, 1914, Chicago, Ill.; educ. St. Mary of the Lake Seminary (Mundelein, Ill.), Catholic Univ. (Washington, D.C.); ord. priest Apr. 15, 1939; ord. titular bishop of Mesarfelta and auxiliary bishop of Chicago, Aug. 24, 1967; app. bishop of Fort Wayne-South Bend, Aug. 31, 1976, installed Oct. 19, 1976.

McNabb, John C., O.S.A.: b. Dec. 11, 1925, Beloit, Wis.; educ. Villanova Univ. (Villanova, Pa.), Augustinian College and Catholic Univ. (Washington, D.C.), De Paul Univ. (Chicago, Ill.); ord. priest May 24, 1952; ord.

titular bishop of Saia Maggiore and prelate of Chulucanas, Peru, June 17, 1967.

McNamara, Lawrence J.: b. Aug. 5, 1928, Chicago, Ill.; educ. St. Paul Seminary (St. Paul, Minn.), Catholic Univ. (Washington, D.C.); ord. priest May 30, 1953; executive director of Campaign for Human Development 1973-77; ord. bishop of Grand Island, Nebr., Mar. 28, 1978.

McNaughton, William J., M.M.: b. Dec. 7, 1926, Lawrence, Mass.; educ. Maryknoll Seminary (Maryknoll, N.Y.); ord. priest June 13, 1953; ord. titular bishop of Thuburbo Minus and vicar apostolic of Inchon, Korea, Aug. 24, 1961; title changed to bishop of Inchon, Mar. 10, 1962.

McNicholas, Joseph A.: b. Jan. 13, 1923, St. Louis, Mo.; educ. Cardinal Glennon College, Kenrick Seminary and St. Louis Univ. (all in St. Louis, Mo.); ord. priest June 7, 1949; ord. titular bishop of Scala and auxiliary bishop of St. Louis, Mar. 25, 1969; app. bishop of Springfield, Ill., July 22, 1975, installed Sept. 3, 1975.

McShea, Joseph M.: b. Feb. 22, 1907, Latimer, Pa.; educ. St. Charles Seminary (Philadelphia, Pa.), Major Pontifical Roman Seminary (Rome); ord. priest Dec. 6, 1931; ord. titular bishop of Mina and auxiliary bishop of Philadelphia, Mar. 19, 1952; app. first bishop of Allentown, installed Apr. 11, 1961.

Madera, Joseph J., M.Sp.S.: b. Nov. 27, 1927, San Francisco, Calif.; educ. Domus Studiorum of the Missionaries of the Holy Spirit (Coyoacan, D.F. Mexico); ord. priest June 15, 1957; ord. coadjutor bishop of Fresno, Mar. 4, 1980; bishop of Fresno, July 1, 1980.

Maginn, Edward J.: b. Jan. 4, 1897, Glasgow, Scotland; educ. Holy Cross College (Worcester, Mass.), St. Joseph's Seminary (Yonkers, N.Y.); ord. priest June 10, 1922; ord. titular bishop of Curium and auxiliary bishop of Albany, Sept. 12, 1957; apostolic administrator of Albany, 1966-69; retired July 8, 1972.

Maguire, John J.: b. Dec. 11, 1904, New York, N.Y.; educ. Cathedral College (New York City), St. Joseph's Seminary (Dunwoodie, N.Y.), North American College (Rome); ord. priest Dec. 22, 1928; ord. titular bishop of Antiphrae and auxiliary bishop of New York, June 29, 1959; app. titular archbishop of Tabalta and coadjutor archbishop of New York, Sept. 15, 1965; retired Jan. 8, 1980.

Maguire, Joseph F.: b. Sept. 4, 1919, Boston, Mass.; educ. Boston College, St. John's Seminary (Boston, Mass.); ord. priest June 29, 1945; ord. titular bishop of Macteris and auxiliary bishop of Boston, Feb. 2, 1972; app. coadjutor bishop of Springfield, Mass., Apr. 13, 1976; succeeded as bishop of Springfield, Mass., Oct. 15, 1977.

Maher, Leo T.: b. July 1, 1915, Mount Union, Ia.; educ. St. Joseph's College (Mountain View, Calif.); St. Patrick's Seminary (Menlo Park, Calif.); ord. priest Dec. 18, 1943; ord. first bishop of Santa Rosa, April 5, 1962; bishop of San Diego, Oct. 4, 1969.

Mahoney, James P.: b. Aug. 16, 1925, Kingston, N.Y.; educ. St. Joseph's Seminary (Dunwoodie, N.Y.); ord. priest May 19, 1951; ord. titular bishop of Ipagro and auxiliary bishop of New York, Sept. 15, 1972.

Mahony, Roger M.: b. Feb. 27, 1936, Hollywood, Calif.; educ. St. John's Seminary (Camarillo, Calif.), National Catholic School of Social Service (Catholic Univ., Washington, D.C.); ord. priest May 1, 1962; ord. titular bishop of Tamascani and auxiliary bishop of Fresno, Mar. 19, 1975; app. bishop of Stockton, installed Apr. 25, 1980.

Malone, James W.: b. Mar. 8, 1920, Youngstown, O.; educ. St. Charles Preparatory Seminary (Catonsville, Md.), St. Mary's Seminary (Cleveland, O.), Catholic Univ. (Washington, D.C.); ord. priest May 26, 1945; ord. titular bishop of Alabanda and auxiliary bishop of Youngstown, Mar. 24, 1960; apostolic administrator, 1966; bishop of Youngstown, installed June 20, 1968.

Maloney, Charles G.: b. Sept. 9, 1912, Louisville, Ky.; educ. St. Joseph's College (Rensselaer, Ind.), North American College (Rome); ord. priest Dec. 8, 1937; ord. titular bishop of Capsa and auxiliary bishop of Louisville, Feb. 2, 1955.

Maloney, David M.: b. Mar. 15, 1912, Littleton, Colo.; educ. St. Thomas Seminary (Denver, Colo.), Gregorian Univ. and Apollinare Univ. (Rome); ord. priest Dec. 8, 1936; ord. titular bishop of Ruspe and auxiliary bishop of Denver, Jan. 4, 1961; app. bishop of Wichita, Kans., Dec. 6, 1967; resigned July 16, 1982.

Manning, Thomas R., O.F.M.: b. Aug. 29, 1922, Baltimore, Md.; educ. Duns Scotus College (Southfield, Mich.), Holy Name College (Washington, D.C.); ord. priest June 5, 1948; ord. titular bishop of Arsamosata and prelate of Coroico, Bolivia, July 14, 1959.

Manning, Timothy: (See Cardinals, Biographies.)

Marcinkus, Paul C.: b. Jan. 15, 1922, Cicero, Ill.; ord. priest May 3, 1947; served in Vatican secretariat from 1952; ord. titular bishop of Orta, Jan. 6, 1969; secretary (1968-71) and president (1971-) of Institute for Works of Religion (Vatican Bank); titular archbishop, Sept. 26, 1981; pro-president of Pontifical Commission for the State of Vatican City.

Marconi, Dominic A.: b. Mar. 13, 1927, Newark, N.J.; educ. Seton Hall Univ. (S. Orange, N.J.), Immaculate Conception Seminary (Darlington, N.J.), Catholic Univ. (Washington, D.C.); ord. priest May 30, 1953; ord. titular bishop of Bure and auxiliary bishop of Newark, June 25, 1976.

Mardaga, Thomas J.: b. May 14, 1913, Baltimore, Md.; educ. St. Charles College (Catonsville, Md.), St. Mary's Seminary (Baltimore, Md.); ord. priest May 14, 1940; ord. titular bishop of Mutugenna and auxiliary bishop of Baltimore, Jan. 25, 1967; app. bishop of Wilmington, installed Apr. 6, 1968.

Marino, Eugene A., S.S.J.: b. May 29, 1934, Biloxi, Miss.; educ. Epiphany Apostolic College and Mary Immaculate Novitiate (Newburgh, N.Y.), St. Joseph's Seminary (Washington, D.C.), Catholic Univ. (Washington, D.C.), Loyola Univ. (New Orleans, La.), Fordham Univ. (New York City); ord. priest June 9, 1962; ord. titular bishop of Walla Walla and auxiliary bishop of Washington, D.C., Sept. 12, 1974.

Marshall, John A.: b. Apr. 26, 1928, Worcester, Mass.; educ. Holy Cross College (Worcester, Mass.), Sulpician Seminary (Montreal), North American College and Gregorian Univ. (Rome), Assumption College (Worcester); ord. priest Dec. 19, 1953; ord. bishop of Burlington, Jan. 25, 1972.

Matthiesen, Leroy Theodore: b. June 11, 1921, Olfen, Tex.; educ. Josephinum College (Columbus, O.), Catholic Univ. (Washington, D.C.), Register School of Journalism; ord. priest Mar. 10, 1946; ord. bishop of Amarillo, May 30, 1980.

May, John L.: b. Mar. 31, 1922, Evanston, Ill.; educ. St. Mary of the Lake Seminary (Mundelein, Ill.); ord. priest May 3, 1947; general secretary and vice-president of the Catholic Church Extension Society, 1959; ord. titular bishop of Tagarbala and auxiliary bishop of Chicago, Aug. 24, 1967; bishop of Mobile, Ala., Sept. 29, 1969; app. archbishop of St. Louis, installed Mar. 25, 1980.

Medeiros, Humberto S.: (See Cardinals, Biographies.)

Mendez, Alfred, C.S.C.: b. June 3, 1907, Chicago, Ill.; educ. Notre Dame Univ. (Notre Dame, Ind.), Institute of Holy Cross (Washington, D.C.); ord. priest June 24, 1935; ord. first bishop of Arecibo, Puerto Rico, Oct. 28, 1960; resigned Jan. 24, 1974.

Mestice, Anthony F.: b. Dec. 6, 1923, New York, N.Y.; educ. St. Joseph Seminary (Yonkers, N.Y.); ord. priest June 4, 1949; ord. titular bishop of Villa Nova and auxiliary bishop of New York Apr. 27, 1973.

Metzger, Sidney Matthew: b. July 11, 1902, Fredericksburg, Tex.; educ. St. John's Seminary (San Antonio, Tex.), North American College (Rome); ord. priest Apr. 3, 1926; ord. titular bishop of Birtha and auxiliary bishop of Santa Fe, Apr. 10, 1940; app. coadjutor bishop of El Paso, Dec. 26, 1941; bishop of El Paso, Dec. 1, 1942; retired May 29, 1978.

Michaels, James E., S.S.C.: b. May 30, 1926, Chicago, Ill.; educ. Columban Seminary (St. Columban, Neb.), Gregorian Univ.

(Rome); ord. priest Dec. 21, 1951; ord. titular bishop of Verbe and auxiliary bishop of Kwang Ju, Korea, Apr. 14, 1966; app. auxiliary bishop of Wheeling, Apr. 3, 1973; title of see changed to Wheeling-Charleston, 1974.

Mihalik, Emil J.: b. Feb. 6, 1920, Pittsburgh, Pa.; educ. St. Procopius Seminary (Lisle, Ill.), Duquesne Univ. (Pittsburgh, Pa.); ord. priest Sept. 21, 1945; ord. first bishop of Byzantine Rite diocese of Parma, O., June 12, 1969.

Milone, Anthony: b. Sept. 24, 1932, Omaha, Nebr.; educ. North American College (Rome); ord. priest Dec. 15, 1957, in Rome; ord. titular bishop of Plestia and auxiliary bishop of Omaha, Jan. 6, 1982.

Minder, John, O.S.F.S.: b. Nov. 1, 1923, Philadelphia, Pa.; ord. priest June 3, 1950; ord. bishop of Keimos, South Africa, Jan. 10, 1968.

Moore, Emerson John: b. May 16, 1938, New York, N.Y.; educ. Cathedral College (New York City), St. Joseph's Seminary (Yonkers, N.Y.); New York University, Columbia Univ. School of Social Work (New York City); ord. priest May 30, 1964; ord. auxiliary bishop of Curubi and auxiliary bishop of New York, Sept. 8, 1982.

Moran, William J.: b. Jan. 15, 1906, San Francisco, Calif.; educ. St. Patrick's Seminary (Menlo Park, Calif.); ord. priest June 20, 1931; Army chaplain, 1933; ord. titular bishop of Centuria and auxiliary to the military vicar, Dec. 13, 1965; retired 1981.

Moreno, Manuel D.: b. Nov. 27, 1930, Placentia, Calif.; educ. Univ. of California (Los Angeles), Our Lady Queen of Angels (San Fernando, Calif.), St. John's Seminary (Camarillo, Calif.); ord. priest Apr. 25, 1961; ord. titular bishop of Tanagra and auxiliary bishop of Los Angeles, Feb. 19, 1977; bishop of Tucson, Jan. 12, 1982, installed Mar. 11, 1982.

Morkovsky, John Louis: b. Aug. 16, 1909, Praha, Tex.; educ. St. John's Seminary (San Antonio, Tex.), North American College, Urban Univ. and Gregorian Univ. (Rome), Catholic Univ. (Washington, D.C.); ord. priest Dec. 5, 1933; ord titular bishop of Hieron and auxiliary bishop of Amarillo, Feb. 22, 1956; app. bishop of Amarillo, Aug. 27, 1958; titular bishop of Tigava and coadjutor bishop of Galveston-Houston with right of succession, June 11, 1963; apostolic administrator; president Texas Conference of Churches, 1970-72; bishop of Galveston-Houston, Apr. 22, 1975.

Morneau, Robert F.: b. Sept. 10, 1938, New London, Wis.; educ. St. Norbert's College (De Pere, Wis.), Sacred Heart Seminary (Oneida, Wis.), Catholic Univ. (Washington, D.C.); ord. priest May 28, 1966; ord. titular bishop of Massa Lubrense and auxiliary bishop of Green Bay, Feb. 22, 1979.

Morrow, Louis La Ravoire, S.D.B.: b. Dec.

24, 1892, Weatherford, Tex.; educ. Salesian School and Palafox (Puebla, Mexico); professed in Salesians of St. John Bosco, Sept. 29, 1912; ord. priest May 21, 1921; ord. bishop of Krishnagar, India, Oct. 29, 1939; resigned Oct. 31, 1969.

Moskal, Robert: b. Oct. 24, 1937, Carnegie, Pa.; educ. St. Basil Minor Seminary (Stamford, Conn.), St. Josaphat Seminary and Catholic Univ. (Washington, D.C.); ord. priest Mar. 25, 1963; ord. titular bishop of Agatopoli and auxiliary bishop of the Ukrainian-Rite archeparchy of Philadelphia, Oct. 13, 1981.

Mugavero, Francis John: b. June 8, 1914, Brooklyn, N.Y.; educ. Cathedral College (Brooklyn, N.Y.), Immaculate Conception Seminary (Huntington, N.Y.), Fordham Univ. (New York City); ord. priest May 18, 1940; ord. bishop of Brooklyn, Sept. 12, 1968.

Mulcahy, John J.: b. June 26, 1922, Dorchester, Mass.; educ. St. John's Seminary (Brighton, Mass.); ord. priest May 1, 1947; rector Pope John XXIII Seminary for Delayed Vocations, 1969-73; ord. titular bishop of Penafiel and auxiliary bishop of Boston, Feb. 11, 1975.

Mulrooney, Charles R.: b. Jan. 13, 1906, Brooklyn, N.Y.; educ. Cathedral College (Brooklyn, N.Y.), St. Mary's Seminary (Baltimore, Md.), Sulpician Seminary (Washington, D.C.); ord. priest June 10, 1930; ord. titular bishop of Valentiniana and auxiliary bishop of Brooklyn, Apr. 22, 1959; retired 1981.

Mulvee, Robert E.: b. Feb. 15, 1930, Boston, Mass.; educ. St. Thomas Seminary (Bloomfield, Conn.), University Seminary (Ottawa, Ont., Canada), American College (Louvain, Belgium), Lateran Univ. (Rome); ord. priest June 30, 1957; ord. titular bishop of Summa and auxiliary bishop of Manchester, N.H., Apr. 14, 1977.

Mundo, Michael P.: b. July 25, 1937, New York, N.Y.; educ. Fordham Univ. (Bronx, N.Y.), St. Jerome's College (Kitchener, Ont., Canada), St. Francis Seminary (Loretto, Pa.); ord. May 19, 1962; missionary in Brazil from 1963; ord. titular bishop of Blanda Julia and auxiliary bishop of Jatai, Brazil, June 2, 1978.

Murphy, Michael J.: b. July 1, 1915, Cleveland, O.; educ. Niagara Univ. (Niagara Falls, N.Y.); North American College (Rome), Catholic Univ. (Washington, D.C.); ord. priest Feb. 28, 1942; ord. titular bishop of Ariendela and auxiliary bishop of Cleveland, June 11, 1976; app. coadjutor bishop of Erie, Nov. 20, 1978; bishop of Erie, July 16, 1982.

Murphy, Philip Francis: b. Mar. 25, 1933, Cumberland, Md.; educ. St. Mary Seminary (Baltimore, Md.), North American College (Rome); ord. priest Dec. 20, 1958; ord. titular bishop of Tacarata and auxiliary bishop of Baltimore, Feb. 29, 1976.

Murphy, T. Austin: b. May 11, 1911, Baltimore, Md.; educ. St. Charles College (Catonsville, Md.), St. Mary's Seminary (Baltimore, Md.); ord priest June 10, 1937; ord. titular bishop of Appiaria and auxiliary bishop of Baltimore, July 3, 1962.

Murphy, Thomas J.: b. Oct. 3, 1932, Chicago, Ill.; educ. Quigley Preparatory Seminary (Chicago, Ill.), St. Mary of the Lake Seminary (Mundelein, Ill.); ord. priest Apr. 12, 1958; ord. bishop of Great Falls, Mont. Aug. 21, 1978; title of see changed to Great Falls-Billings, 1980.

Murphy, Thomas W., C.SS.R.: b. Dec. 17, 1917, Omaha, Nebr.; educ. St. Joseph's College (Kirkwood, Mo.); ord. priest June 29, 1943; ord. first bishop of Juazeiro, Brazil, Jan. 2, 1963; resigned Dec. 29, 1973; app. titular bishop of Sululos and auxiliary bishop of Sao Salvador da Bahia, Brazil, Jan. 31, 1974.

N

Nelson, Knute Ansgar, O.S.B.: b. Oct. 1, 1906, Copenhagen, Denmark; educ. Abbey of Maria Laach (Germany), Brown Univ. (Providence, R.I.); professed in the Order of St. Benedict, May 30, 1932; ord. priest May 22, 1937; became an American citizen, Mar. 4, 1941; ord. titular bishop of Bilta and coadjutor bishop of Stockholm, Sweden, Sept. 8, 1947; succeeded as bishop of Stockholm, Oct. 1, 1957; retired; titular bishop of Dura. 1962.

Nevins, John J.: b. Jan. 19, 1932, New Rochelle, N.Y.; educ. Iona College (New Rochelle, N.Y.), Catholic Univ. (Washington, D.C.); ord. priest June 6, 1959; ord. titular bishop of Rusticana and auxiliary bishop of Miami, Mar. 24, 1979.

Newell, Hubert M.: b. Feb. 16, 1904, Denver, Colo.; educ. Regis College and St. Thomas Seminary (Denver, Colo.), Catholic Univ. (Washington, D.C.); ord. priest June 15, 1930; ord. titular bishop of Zapara and coadjutor bishop of Cheyenne, Sept. 24, 1947; bishop of Cheyenne, Nov. 10, 1951; retired Jan. 3, 1978.

Neylon, Martin J., S.J.: b. Feb. 13, 1920, Buffalo, N.Y.; ord. priest June 18, 1950; ord. titular bishop of Libertina and coadjutor vicar apostolic of the Caroline and Marshall Islands, Feb. 2, 1970; vicar apostolic of Caroline and Marshall Is., Sept. 20, 1971; first bishop when vicarate apostolic was raised to diocese, 1979.

Niedergeses, James D.: b. Feb. 2, 1917, Lawrenceburg, Tenn.; educ. St. Bernard College (St. Bernard, Ala.), St. Ambrose College (Davenport, Ia.), Mt. St. Mary Seminary of the West and Athenaeum (Cincinnati, Ohio); ord. priest May 20, 1944; ord. bishop of Nashville May 20, 1975.

Nolker, Bernard, C.SS.R.: b. Sept. 25, 1912, Baltimore, Md.; educ. St. Mary's College (North East, Pa.), St. Mary's College (Ilchester, Md.), Mt. St. Alphonsus Seminary

(Esopus, N.Y.); ord. priest June 18, 1939; ord. first bishop of Paranagua, Brazil, Apr. 25, 1963.

Novak, Alfred, C.SS.R.: b. June 2, 1930, Dwight, Nebr.; educ. Immaculate Conception Seminary (Oconomowoc, Wis.); ord. priest July 2, 1956; ord. titular bishop of Vardimissa and auxiliary bishop of Sao Paulo, Brazil, May 25, 1979.

O

O'Boyle, Patrick A.: (See Cardinals, Biographies.)

O'Brien, Thomas Joseph: b. Nov. 29, 1935, Indianapolis, Ind.; educ. St. Meinrad High School Seminary, St. Meinrad College Seminary (St. Meinrad, Ind); ord. priest May 7, 1961; ord. bishop of Phoenix, Jan. 6, 1982.

O'Connor, John J.: b. Jan. 15, 1920, Philadelphia, Pa.; educ. St. Charles Borromeo Seminary (Philadelphia, Pa.), Catholic Univ., Georgetown Univ. (Washington, D.C.); ord. priest Dec. 15, 1945; U.S. Navy chief of chaplains, 1975; ord. titular bishop of Cursola and auxiliary to the military vicar, May 27, 1979.

O'Connor, Martin J.: b. May 18, 1900, Scranton, Pa.; educ. St. Thomas College (Scranton, Pa.), St. Mary's Seminary (Baltimore, Md.), North American College, Urban Univ. and Apollinaris (Rome); ord. priest Mar. 15, 1924; ord. titular bishop of Thespia and auxiliary bishop of Scranton, Jan. 27, 1943; rector of North American College 1946-1964; app. titular archbishop of Laodicea in Syria, Sept. 5, 1959; apostolic nuncio to Malta, 1965-69; president emeritus Pontifical Commission for Social Communication.

O'Connor, William A.: b. Dec. 27, 1903, Chicago, Ill.; educ. Quigley Seminary (Chicago, Ill.), St. Mary of the Lake Seminary (Mundelein, Ill.), Urban Univ. (Rome); ord. priest Sept. 24, 1927; ord. bishop of Springfield, Ill., Mar. 7, 1949; retired July 22, 1975.

O'Donnell, Cletus F.: b. Aug. 22, 1917, Waukon, Ia.; educ. St. Mary Seminary (Mundelein, Ill.), Catholic Univ. (Washington, D.C.); ord. priest May 3, 1941; ord. titular bishop of Abritto and auxiliary bishop of Chicago, Dec. 21, 1960; app. bishop of Madison, Feb. 22, 1967, installed Apr. 25, 1967.

O'Keefe, Gerald F.: b. Mar. 30, 1918, St. Paul, Minn.; educ. College of St. Thomas, St. Paul Seminary (St. Paul, Minn.); ord. priest Jan. 29, 1944; ord. titular bishop of Candyba and auxiliary bishop of St. Paul July 2, 1961; bishop of Davenport, Oct. 20, 1966, installed Jan. 4, 1967.

O'Keefe, Joseph Thomas: b. Mar. 12, 1919, New York, N.Y.; educ. Cathedral College (New York City), St. Joseph's Seminary (Yonkers, N.Y.), Catholic Univ. (Washington, D.C.); ord. priest Apr. 17, 1948; ord.

titular bishop of Tre Taverne and auxiliary bishop of New York, Sept. 8, 1982.

O'Leary, Edward C.: b. Aug. 21, 1920, Bangor, Me.; educ. Holy Cross College (Worcester, Mass.), St. Paul's Seminary (Ottawa, Canada); ord. priest June 15, 1946; ord. titular bishop of Moglena and auxiliary bishop of Portland, Me., Jan. 25, 1971; app. bishop of Portland, installed Dec. 18, 1974.

O'Meara, Edward T.: b. Aug. 3, 1921, St. Louis, Mo.; educ. Cardinal Glennon College and Kenrick Seminary (St. Louis, Mo.), Angelicum (Rome); ord. priest Dec. 21, 1946; app. national director of Society for the Propagation of the Faith, 1967; ord. titular bishop of Thisiduo and auxiliary bishop of St. Louis, Feb. 13, 1972; app. archbishop of Indianapolis, installed Jan. 10, 1980.

O'Neil, Leo E.: b. Jan. 31, 1928, Holyoke, Mass.; educ. Maryknoll Seminary (Maryknoll, N.Y.), St. Anselm's College (Manchester, N.H.), Grand Seminary (Montreal, Canada); ord. priest June 4, 1955; ord. titular bishop of Bencenna and auxiliary bishop of Springfield, Mass., Aug. 22, 1980.

O'Neill, Arthur J.: b. Dec. 14, 1917, East Dubuque, Ill.; educ. Loras College (Dubuque, Ia.), St. Mary's Seminary (Baltimore, Md.); ord. priest Mar. 27, 1943; ord. bishop of Rockford, Oct. 11, 1968.

O'Rourke, Edward W.: b. Oct. 31, 1917, Downs, Ill.; educ. St. Mary's Seminary (Mundelein, Ill.), Aquinas Institute of Philosophy and Theology (River Forest, Ill.); ord. priest May 28, 1944; exec. dir. National Catholic Rural Life Conference, 1960-71; ord. bishop of Peoria, July 15, 1971.

Ott, Stanley J.: b. June 29, 1927, Gretna, La.; educ. Notre Dame Seminary (New Orleans, La.), North American College and Gregorian Univ. (Rome); ord. priest Dec. 8, 1951; ord. titular bishop of Nicives and auxiliary bishop of New Orleans, June 29, 1976.

Ottenweller, Albert H.: b. Apr. 5, 1916, Stanford, Mont.; educ. St. Joseph's Seminary (Rensselaer, Ind.), Catholic Univ. (Washington, D.C.); ord. priest June 19, 1943; ord. titular bishop of Perdices and auxiliary bishop of Toledo, May 29, 1974; app. bishop of Steubenville, Oct. 11, 1977, installed Nov. 22, 1977.

P

Pardy, James V., M.M.: b. Mar. 9, 1898, Brooklyn, N. Y.; educ. St. Francis College (Brooklyn), Fordham Univ. (New York City), Catholic Univ. (Washington, D.C.); ord. priest. Jan. 26, 1930; ord. titular bishop of Irenopolis and first vicar apostolic of Cheong Ju, Korea, Sept. 16, 1958; title changed to bishop of Cheong Ju, Mar. 10, 1962; retired June 17, 1969.

Paschang, John L.: b. Oct. 5, 1895, Hemingford, Nebr.; educ. Conception College (Conception, Mo.), St. John Seminary (Col-

legeville, Minn.), Catholic Univ. (Washington, D.C.); ord. priest June 12, 1921; ord. bishop of Grand Island, Oct. 9, 1951; resigned July 25, 1972.

Paul, John J.: b. Aug. 17, 1918, La Crosse, Wis.; educ. Loras College (Dubuque, Iowa), St. Mary's Seminary (Baltimore, Md.), Marquette Univ. (Milwaukee, Wis.), ord. priest Jan. 24, 1943; ord. titular bishop of Lambaesis and auxiliary bishop of La Crosse, Aug. 4, 1977.

Pearce, George H., S.M.: b. Jan. 9, 1921, Brighton, Mass.; educ. Marist College and Seminary (Framington, Mass.); ord. priest Feb. 2, 1947; ord. titular bishop of Attalea in Pamphylia and vicar apostolic of the Samoa and Tokelau Islands, June 29, 1956; title changed to bishop of Apia, June 21, 1966; app. archbishop of Suva, Fiji Islands, June 22, 1967; resigned Apr. 10, 1976.

Pechillo, Jerome, T.O.R.: b. May 16, 1919, Brooklyn, N.Y.; educ. Catholic Univ. (Washington, D.C.); ord. priest June 10, 1947; ord. titular bishop of Novasparsa and prelate of Coronel Oviedo, Paraguay, Jan. 25, 1966; app. auxiliary bishop of Newark, N.J., Mar. 6, 1976.

Pena, Raymond J.: b. Feb. 19, 1934, Robstown, Tex.; educ. Assumption Seminary (San Antonio, Tex.); ord. priest May 25, 1957; ord. titular bishop of Trisipa and auxiliary bishop of San Antonio, Dec. 13, 1976; app. bishop of El Paso, Apr. 29, 1980.

Pernicone, Joseph M.: b. Nov. 4, 1903, Regalbuto, Sicily; educ. Cathedral College (New York City), St. Joseph's Seminary (Dunwoodie, N.Y.), Catholic Univ. (Washington, D.C.); ord. priest Dec. 18, 1926; ord. titular bishop of Hadrianapolis and auxiliary bishop of New York, May 5, 1954; app. episcopal vicar, 1966. Retired.

Perry, Harold R., S.V.D.: b. Oct. 9, 1916, Lake Charles, La.; educ. St. Augustine Seminary (Bay St. Louis, Miss.), St. Mary's Seminary (Techny, Ill.); ord. priest Jan. 6, 1944; app. provincial of southern province of Society of the Divine Word, 1964; ord. titular bishop of Mons in Mauretania and auxiliary bishop of New Orleans, Jan. 6, 1966.

Pevec, A. Edward: b. Apr. 16, 1925, Cleveland, O.; educ. St. Mary's Seminary, John Carroll Univ. (Cleveland, O.); ord. priest Apr. 29, 1950; ord. titular bishop of Mercia and auxiliary bishop of Cleveland, July 2, 1982.

Pilarczyk, Daniel E.: b. Aug. 12, 1934, Dayton, Ohio; educ. St. Gregory's Seminary (Cincinnati, O.), Urban Univ. (Rome), Xavier Univ. and Univ. of Cincinnati (Cincinnati, O.); ord. priest Dec. 20, 1959; ord. titular bishop of Hodelm and auxiliary bishop of Cincinnati, Dec. 20, 1974.

Pilla, Anthony M.: b. Nov. 12, 1932, Cleveland, O.; educ. St. Gregory College Seminary (Cincinnati, O.), Borromeo College Seminary

(Wickliffe, O.), St. Mary Seminary and John Carroll Univ. (Cleveland, O.); ord. priest May 23, 1959; ord. titular bishop of Scardona and auxiliary bishop of Cleveland, Aug. 1, 1979; app. apostolic administrator of Cleveland, 1980; bishop of Cleveland, Nov. 13, 1980.

Pinger, Henry A., O.F.M.: b. Aug. 16, 1897, Lindsay, Nebr.; educ. Our Lady of Angels Seminary (Cleveland, O.), St. Anthony's Seminary (St. Louis, Mo.); professed in the Order of Friars Minor, June 18, 1918; ord. priest June 27, 1924; ord. titular bishop of Capitolias and vicar apostolic of Chowtsun, China, Sept. 21, 1937; title changed to bishop of Chowtsun, Apr. 11, 1946; imprisoned by Reds in 1951, released in 1956; expelled.

Povish, Kenneth J.: b. Apr. 19, 1924, Alpena, Mich.; educ. St. Joseph's Seminary (Grand Rapids, Mich.), Sacred Heart Seminary (Detroit, Mich.), Catholic Univ. (Washington, D.C.); ord. priest June 3, 1950; ord. bishop of Crookston, Sept. 29, 1970; app. bishop of Lansing, Oct. 8, 1975, installed Dec. 11, 1975.

Power, Cornelius M.: b. Dec. 18, 1913, Seattle, Wash.; educ. St. Patrick's College (Menlo Park, Calif.), St. Edward's Seminary (Kenmore, Wash.), Catholic Univ. (Washington, D.C.); ord. priest June 3, 1939; ord. bishop of Yakima, May 1, 1969, installed May 20, 1969; app. archbishop of Portland, Ore., Jan. 22, 1974, installed Apr. 17, 1974.

Primeau, Ernest J.: b. Sept. 17, 1909, Chicago, Ill.; educ. Loyola Univ. (Chicago, Ill.), St. Mary of the Lake Seminary (Mundelein, Ill.), Lateran Univ. (Rome); ord. priest Apr. 7, 1934; ord. bishop of Manchester, Feb. 25, 1960; resigned Jan. 30, 1974; director of Villa Stritch, Rome, 1974-79.

Prost, Jude, O.F.M.: b. Dec. 6, 1915, Chicago, Ill.; educ. Our Lady of the Angels Seminary (Cleveland, O.), St. Joseph's Seminary (Teutopolis, Ill.); ord. priest June 24, 1942; ord. titular bishop of Fronta and auxiliary bishop of Belem do Para, Brazil, Nov. 1, 1962.

Proulx, Amedee W.: b. Aug. 31, 1932, Sanford, Me.; educ. St. Hyacinthe Seminary (Quebec), St. Paul Univ. Seminary (Ottawa), Catholic Univ. (Washington, D.C.); ord. priest May 31, 1958; ord. titular bishop of Clipia and auxiliary bishop of Portland, Me., Nov. 12, 1975.

Pursley, Leo A.: b. Mar. 12, 1902, Hartford City, Ind.; educ. Mt. St. Mary's Seminary (Cincinnati, O.); ord. priest June 11, 1927; ord. titular bishop of Hadrianopolis in Pisidia and auxiliary bishop of Fort Wayne, Sept. 19, 1950; app. apostolic administrator of Fort Wayne, Mar. 9, 1955; installed as bishop of Fort Wayne, Feb. 26, 1957; title of see changed to Fort Wayne-South Bend, 1960; resigned Aug. 31, 1976.

Q

Quinn, Francis A.: b. Sept. 11, 1921, Los Angeles, Calif.; educ. St. Joseph's College (Mountain View, Calif.), St. Patrick's Seminary (Menlo Park, Calif.), Catholic Univ. (Washington, D.C.); Univ. of California (Berkley); ord. priest June 15, 1946; ord. titular bishop of Numana and auxiliary bishop of San Francisco, June 29, 1978; app. bishop of Sacramento Dec. 18, 1979.

Quinn, John R.: b. Mar. 28, 1929, Riverside, Calif.; educ. St. Francis Seminary (El Cajon, Calif.), North American College (Rome); ord. priest July 19, 1953; ord. titular bishop of Thisiduo and auxiliary bishop of San Diego, Dec. 12, 1967; bishop of Oklahoma City and Tulsa, Nov. 30, 1971; first archbishop of Oklahoma City, Dec. 19, 1972; app. archbishop of San Francisco Feb. 22, 1977, installed Apr. 26, 1977; president NCCB, USCC, 1977-80.

R

Ramirez, Ricardo, C.S.B.: b. Sept. 12, 1936, Bay City, Tex.; educ. Univ. of St. Thomas (Houston, Tex.), Univ. of Detroit (Detroit, Mich.), St. Basil's Seminary (Toronto, Ont.); Seminario Concilium (Mexico City, Mexico), East Asian Pastoral Institute (Manila, Philippines); ord. priest Dec. 10, 1966; ord titular bishop of Vatarba and auxiliary of San Antonio, Dec. 6, 1981.

Raya, Joseph M.: b. July 20, 1917, Zahle, Lebanon; educ. St. Louis College (Paris, France), St. Anne's Seminary (Jerusalem); ord. priest July 20, 1941; came to U.S., 1949, became U.S. citizen; ord. archbishop of Acre, Israel, of the Melkites, Oct. 20, 1968; resigned Aug. 20, 1974; assigned titular metropolitan see of Scytopolis.

Regan, Joseph W., M.M.: b. Apr. 5, 1905, Boston, Mass.; educ. Boston College (Boston, Mass.), St. Bernard's Seminary (Rochester, N.Y.), Maryknoll Seminary (Maryknoll, N.Y.); ord. priest Jan. 27, 1929; missionary in China 15 years; in Philippines since 1952; ord. titular bishop of Isinda and prelate of Tagum, Philippine Islands, Apr. 25, 1962; resigned 1980.

Reh, Francis F.: b. Jan. 9, 1911, New York, N.Y.; educ. St. Joseph's Seminary (Dunwoodie, N.Y.), North American College and Gregorian Univ. (Rome); ord. priest Dec. 8, 1935; ord. bishop of Charleston, S.C., June 29, 1962; named titular bishop of Macriana in Mauretania, 1964; rector of North American College, 1964-68; bishop of Saginaw, installed Feb. 26, 1969; resigned Apr. 28, 1980.

Reicher, Louis J.: b. June 14, 1890, Piqua, O.; educ. St. Mary's Seminary (Cincinnati, O.), St. Mary's Seminary (La Porte, Tex.): ord. priest Dec. 6, 1918; ord. first bishop of Austin, Apr. 14, 1948; resigned Nov. 15, 1971.

Reilly, Daniel P.: b. May 12, 1928, Providence, R.I.; educ. Our Lady of Providence Seminary (Warwick, R.I.), St. Brieuc Major Seminary (Cotes du Nord, France); ord. priest May 30, 1953; ord. bishop of Norwich, Aug. 6, 1975.

Reilly, Thomas F., C.SS.R.: b. Dec. 20, 1908, Boston, Mass.; educ. Mt. St. Alphonsus Seminary (Esopus, N.Y.), Catholic Univ. (Washington, D.C.); ord. priest June 10, 1933; ord. titular bishop of Themisonium and prelate of San Juan de la Maguana, Dominican Republic, Nov. 30, 1956; first bishop of San Juan de la Maguana, Nov. 21, 1969; retired 1977.

Reiss, John C.: b. May 13, 1922, Red Bank, N.J.; educ. Catholic Univ. (Washington, D.C.), Immaculate Conception Seminary (Darlington, N.J.); ord. priest May 31, 1947; ord. titular bishop of Simidicca and auxiliary bishop of Trenton, Dec. 12, 1967; app. bishop of Trenton, Mar. 11, 1980.

Riley, Lawrence J.: b. Sept. 6, 1914; Boston, Mass.; educ. Boston College and St. John's Seminary (Boston, Mass.), North American College and Gregorian Univ. (Rome), Catholic Univ. (Washington, D.C.); ord. priest Sept. 21, 1940; ord. titular bishop of Daimlaig and auxiliary bishop of Boston, Feb. 2, 1972.

Roach, John R.: b. July 31, 1921, Prior Lake, Minn.; educ. St. Paul Seminary (St. Paul, Minn.), Univ. of Minnesota (Minneapolis); ord. priest June 18, 1946; ord. titular bishop of Cenae and auxiliary bishop of St. Paul and Minneapolis, Sept. 8, 1971; app. archbishop of St. Paul and Minneapolis, May 28, 1975; vice-president NCCB/USCC, 1977-80; president, 1980.

Rodimer, Frank J.: b. Oct. 25, 1927, Rockaway, N.J.; educ. Seton Hall Prep (South Orange, N.J.), St. Charles College (Catonsville, Md.), St. Mary's Seminary (Baltimore, Md.), Immaculate Conception Seminary (Darlington, N.J.), Catholic Univ. (Washington, D.C.); ord. priest May 19, 1951; ord. bishop of Paterson, Feb. 28, 1978.

Rodriguez, Migúel, C.SS.R.: b. Apr. 18, 1931, Mayaguez, P.R.; educ. St. Mary's Minor Seminary (North East, Pa.), Mt. St. Alphonsus Major Seminary (Esopus, N.Y.); ord. priest June 22, 1958; ord. bishop of Arecibo, P.R., Mar. 23, 1974.

Roman, Agustin: b. May 5, 1928, San Antonio de los Banos, Havana, Cuba; educ. San Alberto Magno Seminary (Matanzas, Cuba), Missions Etrangeres (Montreal, Canada), Barry College (Miami, Fla.); ord. priest July 5, 1959, Cuba; vicar for Spanish speaking in Miami archdiocese, 1976; ord. titular bishop of Sertei and auxiliary bishop of Miami, Mar. 24, 1979.

Rosazza, Peter Anthony: b. Feb. 13, 1935, New Haven, Conn.; educ. St. Thomas Seminary (Bloomfield, Conn.), Dartmouth College (Hanover, N.H.), St. Bernard's Seminary (Rochester, N.Y.), St. Sulpice (Issy, France); ord. priest June 29, 1961; ord. titular bishop of Oppido Nuovo and auxiliary bishop of Hartford, June 24, 1978.

Rose, Robert John: b. Feb. 28, 1930, Grand Rapids, Mich.; educ. St. Joseph's Seminary (Grand Rapids, Mich.), Seminaire de Philosophie (Montreal, Canada), Pontifical Urban University (Rome), Univ. of Michigan (Ann Arbor, Mich.); ord. priest Dec. 21, 1955; ord. bishop of Gaylord, Dec. 6, 1981.

Rudin, John J., M.M.: b. Nov. 27, 1916, Pittsfield, Mass.; educ. Maryknoll Seminary (Maryknoll, N.Y.), Gregorian Univ. (Rome); ord. priest June 11, 1944; ord. first bishop of Musoma, Tanzania, Oct. 3, 1957; retired 1979.

Russell, John J.: b. Dec. 1, 1897, Baltimore, Md.; educ. St. Charles College (Catonsville, Md.), St. Mary's Seminary (Baltimore, Md.), North American College (Rome); ord. priest July 8, 1923; ord. bishop of Charleston, Mar. 14, 1950; bishop of Richmond, July 3, 1958; retired Apr. 30, 1973.

Ryan, Daniel L.: b. Sept. 28, 1930, Mankato, Minn.; educ. St. Procopius Seminary (Lisle, Ill.), Lateran Univ. (Rome); ord. priest May 3, 1956; ord. titular bishop of Surista and auxiliary bishop of Joliet, Sept. 30, 1981.

Ryan, Gerald: b. Aug. 24, 1923, Brooklyn, N.Y.; educ. Cathedral College (Brooklyn, N.Y.), Immaculate Conception Seminary (Huntington, L.I.), Fordham Univ. Graduate School of Social Work (Bronx, N.Y.); ord. priest June 3, 1950; ord. titular bishop of Munatiana and auxiliary bishop of Rockville Centre, May 9, 1977.

Ryan, James C., O.F.M.: b. Nov. 17, 1912, Chicago, Ill.; educ. St. Joseph's Seraphic Seminary (Westmont, Ill.), Our Lady of the Angels Seminary (Cleveland, O.); ord. priest June 24, 1938; ord. titular bishop of Margo and prelate of Santarem, Brazil, April 9, 1958; first bishop of Santarem, 1979.

Ryan, Joseph T.: b. Nov. 1, 1913, Albany, N.Y.; educ. Manhattan College (New York City); ord. priest June 3, 1939; national secretary of Catholic Near East Welfare Assn. 1960-65; ord. first archbishop of Anchorage, Alaska, Mar. 25, 1966; app. titular archbishop of Gabi and coadjutor archbishop of the military ordinariate, Oct. 24, 1975, installed Dec. 13, 1975.

S

Salatka, Charles A.: b. Feb. 26, 1918, Grand Rapids, Mich.; educ. St. Joseph's Seminary (Grand Rapids, Mich.), Catholic Univ. (Washington, D.C.), Lateran Univ. (Rome); ord. priest Feb. 24, 1945; ord. titular bishop of Cariana and auxiliary bishop of Grand Rapids, Mich., Mar. 6, 1962; app. bishop of Marquette, installed Mar. 25, 1968; app.

archbishop of Oklahoma City, Sept. 27, 1977; installed Dec. 15, 1977.

Sanchez, Robert: b. Mar. 20, 1934, Socorro, N.M.; educ. Immaculate Heart Seminary (Santa Fe, N.M.), Gregorian Univ. (Rome), Catholic Univ. (Washington, D.C.); ord. priest Dec. 20, 1959; ord. archbishop of Santa Fe, N.M., July 25, 1974.

Scanlan, John J.: b. May 24, 1906, County Cork, Ireland; educ. National Univ. of Ireland (Dublin), All Hallows College (Dublin); ord. priest June 22, 1930; U.S. citizen 1938; ord. titular bishop of Cenae and auxiliary bishop of Honolulu, Sept. 21, 1954; bishop of Honolulu, installed May 1, 1968; retired 1981.

Scarpone, Gerald, O.F.M.: b. Oct. 1, 1928, Watertown, Mass.; ord. priest June 24, 1956; ord. coadjutor bishop of Comayagua, Honduras, Feb. 21, 1979; succeeded as bishop of Comayagua, May 30, 1979.

Schad, James L.: b. July 20, 1917, Philadelphia, Pa.; educ. St. Mary's Seminary (Baltimore, Md.); ord. priest Apr. 10, 1943; ord. titular bishop of Panatoria and auxiliary bishop of Camden, Dec. 8, 1966.

Schierhoff, Andrew B.: b. Feb. 10, 1922, St. Louis, Mo.; ord. priest Apr. 14, 1948; missionary in Bolivia from 1956; ord. titular bishop of Cerenza and auxiliary of La Paz, Bolivia, Jan. 6, 1969.

Schladweiler, Alphonse: b. July 18, 1902, Milwaukee, Wis.; educ. St. Joseph College (Teutopolis, Ill.), St. Paul's Seminary (St. Paul, Minn.), Univ. of Minnesota (Minneapolis, Minn.); ord. priest June 9, 1929; ord. first bishop of New Ulm, Jan. 29, 1958; retired Dec. 23, 1975.

Schlaefer, Salvator, O.F.M. Cap.: b. June 27, 1920, Campbellsport, Wis.; ord. priest June 5, 1946; missionary in Bluefields, Nicaragua from 1947; ord. titular bishop of Fiumepiscense and vicar apostolic of Bluefields, Nicaragua, Aug. 12, 1970.

Schlarman, Stanley Gerard: b. July 27, 1933, Belleville, Ill.; educ. St. Henry Prep Seminary (Belleville, Ill.), Gregorian Univ. (Rome), St. Louis Univ. (St. Louis, Mo.); ord. priest July 13, 1958, Rome; ord. titular bishop of Capri and auxiliary bishop of Belleville, May 14, 1979.

Schlotterback, Edward F., O.S.F.S.: b. Mar. 2, 1912, Philadelphia, Pa.; educ. Catholic Univ. (Washington, D.C.); ord. priest Dec. 17, 1938; ord. titular bishop of Balanea and vicar apostolic of Keetmanshoop, Namibia, June 11, 1956.

Schmidt, Firmin M., O.F.M.Cap.: b. Oct. 12, 1918, Catherine, Kans.; educ. Catholic Univ. (Washington, D.C.); ord. priest June 2, 1946; app. prefect apostolic of Mendi, Papua New Guinea, Apr. 3, 1959; ord. titular bishop of Conana and first vicar apostolic of Mendi, Dec. 15, 1965; became first bishop of Mendi when vicariate apostolic was raised to a diocese, Nov. 15, 1966.

Schmidt, Mathias, O.S.B.: b. Apr. 21, 1931, Wortonville, Kans.; ord. priest May 30, 1957; missionary in Brazil; ord, titular bishop of Mutugenna and auxiliary bishop of Jatai, Brazil, Sept. 10, 1972; bishop of Rui Barbosa, Brazil, May 14, 1976.

Schmitt, Mark: b. Feb. 14, 1923, Algoma, Wis., educ. Salvatorian Seminary (St. Nazianz, Wis.), St. John's Seminary (Collegeville, Minn.); ord. priest May 22, 1948; ord. titular bishop of Ceanannus Mor and auxiliary bishop of Green Bay, June 24, 1970; app. bishop of Marquette, Mar. 21, 1978, installed May 8, 1978.

Schoenherr, Walter J.: b. Feb. 28, 1920, Detroit, Mich.; educ. Sacred Heart Seminary (Detroit, Mich.), Mt. St. Mary Seminary (Norwood, O.); ord. priest Oct. 27, 1945; ord. titular bishop of Timidana and auxiliary bishop of Detroit, May 1, 1968.

Schuck, James A., O.F.M.: b. Jan. 17, 1913, Treverton, Pa.; educ. St. Joseph's Seminary (Callicoon, N.Y.), St. Bonaventure University (St. Bonaventure, N.Y.). Holy Name College (Washington, D.C.); ord. priest June 11, 1940; ord. titular bishop of Avissa and prelate of Cristalandia, Brazil, Feb. 24, 1959.

Schulte, Francis B.: b. Dec. 23, 1926, Philadelphia, Pa.; educ. St. Charles Borromeo Seminary (Overbrook, Pa.): ord. priest May 10, 1952; app. Titular bishop of Afufenia and auxiliary bishop of Philadelphia, June 30, 1981.

Schulte, Paul Clarence: b. Mar. 18, 1890, Fredericktown, Mo.; educ. St. Francis Solanus College (Quincy, Ill.), Kenrick Seminary (Webster Groves, Mo.); ord. priest June 11, 1915; ord. bishop of Leavenworth, Sept. 21, 1937; archbishop of Indianapolis, July 27, 1946; resigned Jan. 14, 1970; assigned titular see of Elicrora.

Schuster, Eldon B.: b. Mar. 10, 1911, Calio, N. Dak.; educ. Loras College (Dubuque, Ia.), Catholic Univ. (Washington, D.C.), Oxford Univ. (England), St. Louis Univ. (St. Louis, Mo.); ord. priest May 27, 1937; ord. titular bishop of Ambladaand auxiliary bishop of Great Falls, Mont., Dec. 21, 1961; app. bishop of Great Falls, Dec. 2, 1967, installed Jan. 23, 1968; resigned Dec. 28, 1977.

Setian, Nerses Mikail: b. Oct. 18,1918, Sebaste, Turkey; educ. Armenian Pontifical College and Gregorian Univ. (Rome); ord. priest Apr. 13, 1941, in Rome; ord. titular bishop of Ancira of the Armenians and first exarch of the apostolic exarchate for Armenian-Rite Catholics in Canada and the United States (see city New York), Dec. 5, 1981.

Shea, Francis R.: b. Dec. 4, 1913, Knoxville, Tenn.; educ. St. Mary's Seminary (Baltimore, Md.), North American College (Rome), Peabody College (Nashville, Tenn.);

ord. priest Mar. 19, 1939; ord. bishop of Evansville, Ind., Feb. 3, 1970.

Sheehan, Daniel E.: b. May 14, 1917, Emerson, Nebr.; educ. Creighton Univ. (Omaha, Nebr.), Kenrick Seminary (Webster Groves, Mo.), Catholic Univ. (Washington, D.C.): ord. priest May 23, 1942; ord. titular bishop of Capsus and auxiliary bishop of Omaha, Mar. 19, 1964; app. archbishop of Omaha, installed Aug. 11, 1969.

Shehan, Lawrence Joseph: (See Cardinals, Biographies.)

Sheldon, Gilbert I.: b. Sept. 20, 1926, Cleveland, O.; educ. John Carroll Univ. and St. Mary Seminary (Cleveland, O.); ord. priest Feb. 28, 1953; ord. titular bishop of Taparura and auxiliary bishop of Cleveland, June 11, 1976.

Shubsda, Thaddeus A.: b. Apr. 2, 1925, Los Angeles, Calif.; educ. St. John's Seminary (Camarillo, Calif.); ord. priest Apr. 26, 1950; ord. titular bishop of Trau and auxiliary bishop of Los Angeles, Feb. 19, 1977; app. bishop of Monterey, June 1, 1982.

Sklba, Richard J.: b. Sept. 11, 1935, Racine, Wis.; educ. Old St. Francis Minor Seminary (Milwaukee, Wis.), North American College, Gregorian Univ., Pontifical Biblical Institute, Angelicum (Rome); ord. priest Dec. 20, 1959; ord. titular bishop of Castra and auxiliary bishop of Milwaukee, Dec. 19, 1979.

Skylstad, William: b. Mar. 2, 1934, Omak, Wash.; educ. Pontifical College Josephinum (Worthington, Ohio), Washington State Univ. (Pullman, Wash.), Gonzaga Univ. (Spokane, Wash.); ord. priest May 21, 1960; ord. bishop of Yakima, May 12, 1977.

Smith, Philip F., O.M.I.: b. Oct. 16, 1924, Lowell, Mass.; ord. priest Oct. 29, 1950; ord. titular bishop of Lamfua and vicar apostolic of Jolo, Philippine Islands, Sept. 8, 1972; app. coadjutor archbishop of Cotabato, Philippines, April 11, 1979; archbishop of Cotabato. Mar. 14, 1980.

Snyder, John J.: b. Oct. 25, 1925, New York, N.Y.; educ. Cathedral College (Brooklyn, N.Y.), Immaculate Conception Seminary (Huntington, N.Y.); ord. priest June 9, 1951; ord. titular bishop of Forlimpopli and auxiliary bishop of Brooklyn, Feb. 2, 1973; app. bishop of St. Augustine, installed Dec. 5, 1979.

Soenneker, Henry J.: b. May 27, 1907, Melrose, Minn.; educ. Pontifical Josephinum College (Worthington, O.), Catholic Univ. (Washington, D.C.); ord. priest May 26, 1934; ord. bishop of Owensboro, Apr. 26, 1961; resigned June 30, 1982.

Sowada, Alphonse A., O.S.C.: b. June 23, 1933, Avon, Minn.; educ. Holy Cross Scholasticate (Fort Wayne, Ind.), Catholic Univ. (Washington, D.C.), ord. priest May 31, 1958; missionary in Indonesia from 1958; ord.

bishop of Agats, Indonesia, Nov. 23, 1969.

Speltz, George H.: b. May 29, 1912, Altura, Minn.; educ. St. Mary's College, St. Paul's Seminary (St. Paul, Minn.), Catholic Univ. (Washington, D.C.); ord. priest June 2, 1940; ord. titular bishop of Claneus and auxiliary bishop of Winona, Mar. 25, 1963; app. coadjutor bishop of St. Cloud, Apr. 4, 1966; bishop of St. Cloud, Jan. 31, 1968.

Speyrer, Jude: b. Apr. 14, 1929, Leonville, La.; educ. St. Joseph Seminary (Covington, La.), Notre Dame Seminary (New Orleans, La.), Gregorian Univ. (Rome), Univ. of Fribourg (Switzerland); ord. priest July 25, 1953; ord. first bishop of Lake Charles, La., Apr. 25, 1980.

Stafford, James Francis: b. July 26, 1932, Baltimore, Md.; educ. St. Mary's Seminary (Baltimore, Md.), North American College and Gregorian Univ. (Rome); ord. priest Dec. 15, 1957; ord. titular bishop of Respecta and auxiliary bishop of Baltimore, Feb. 29, 1976.

Steiner, Kenneth Donald: b. Nov. 25, 1936, David City, Nebr.; educ. Mt. Angel Seminary (St. Benedict, Ore.), St. Thomas Seminary (Seattle, Wash.); ord. priest, May 19, 1962; ord. titular bishop of Avensa and auxiliary bishop of Portland, Ore., Mar. 2, 1978.

Stemper, Alfred M., M.S.C.: b. Jan. 2, 1913, Black Hammer, Minn.; ord. priest June 26, 1940; ord. titular bishop of Eleutheropolis and vicar apostolic of Kavieng, New Guinea, Oct. 28, 1957; first bishop of Kavieng, Nov. 15, 1966; retired 1980.

Straling, Phillip F.: b. Apr. 25, 1933, San Bernardino, Calif.; educ. Immaculate Heart Seminary, St. Francis Seminary, Univ. of San Diego and San Diego State University (San Diego, Calif.), North American College (Rome); ord. priest Mar. 19, 1959; ord. first bishop of San Bernardino, Nov. 6, 1978.

Strecker, Ignatius J.: b. Nov. 23, 1917, Spearville, Kans.; educ. St. Benedict's College (Atchison, Kans.), Kenrick Seminary (Webster Groves, Mo.), Catholic Univ. (Washington, D.C.); ord. priest Dec. 19, 1942; ord. bishop of Springfield-Cape Girardeau, Mo., June 20, 1962; archbishop of Kansas City, Kans., Oct. 28, 1969.

Sullivan, James S.: b. July 23, 1929, Kalamazoo, Mich.; educ. Sacred Heart Seminary (Detroit, Mich.), St. John Provincial Seminary (Plymouth, Mich.); ord. priest June 4, 1955; ord. titular bishop of Siccessi and auxiliary bishop of Lansing, Sept. 21, 1972.

Sullivan, John J.: b. July 5, 1920, Horton, Kans.; educ. Kenrick Seminary (St. Louis, Mo.); ord. priest Sept. 23, 1944; vice-president of Catholic Church Extension Society and national director of Extension Lay Volunteers, 1961-68; ord. bishop of Grand Island, Sept. 19, 1972; app. bishop of Kansas City-St. Joseph, June 27, 1977, installed Aug. 17, 1977.

Sullivan, Joseph P.: b. Mar. 23, 1930, Brooklyn, N.Y.; educ. Immaculate Conception Seminary (Huntington, N.Y.), Fordham Univ. (New York); ord. priest June 2, 1956; ord. titular bishop of Suliana and auxiliary bishop of Brooklyn, Nov. 24, 1980.

Sullivan, Joseph V.: b. Aug. 15, 1919, Kansas City, Mo.; educ. Sulpician Seminary (Washington, D.C.), Catholic Univ. (Washington, D.C.); ord. priest June 1, 1946; ord. titular bishop of Tagamuta and auxiliary bishop of Kansas City-St. Joseph, Apr. 3, 1967; app. Bishop of Baton Rouge, Aug. 13, 1974.

Sullivan, Walter F.: b. June 10, 1928, Washington, D.C.; educ. St. Mary's Seminary (Baltimore, Md.), Catholic Univ. (Washington, D.C.); ord. priest May 9, 1953; ord. titular bishop of Selsea and auxiliary bishop of Richmond, Va., Dec. 1, 1970; app. bishop of Richmond, June 4, 1974.

Sulyk, Stephen: b. Oct. 2, 1924, Balnycia, Western Ukraine; migrated to U.S. 1948; educ. Ukrainian Catholic Seminary of the Holy Spirit (Hirschberg, Germany), St. Josaphat's Seminary and Catholic Univ. (Washington, D.C.); ord. priest June 14, 1952; ord. archbishop of the Ukrainian-Rite archeparcy of Philadelphia, Mar. 1, 1981.

Swanstrom, Edward E.: b. Mar. 20, 1903, New York, N.Y.; educ. Fordham Univ. (New York City), St. John's Seminary (Brooklyn, N.Y.), New York School of Social Work; ord. priest June 2, 1928; director of Catholic Relief Services 1947-76; ord. titular bishop of Arba and auxiliary bishop of New York, Oct. 28, 1960; retired Mar. 20, 1978.

Symons, J. Keith: b. Oct. 14, 1932, Champion, Mich.; educ. St. Thomas Seminary (Bloomfield, Conn.), St. Mary Seminary (Baltimore, Md.); ord. priest May 18, 1958; ord. titular bishop of Sigus and auxiliary bishop of St. Petersburg, Mar. 19, 1981.

Szoka, Edmund C.: b. Sept. 14, 1927, Grand Rapids, Mich.; educ. Sacred Heart Seminary (Detroit, Mich.), St. John's Provincial Seminary (Plymouth, Mich.), Lateran Univ. (Rome); ord. priest June 5, 1954; ord. first bishop of Gaylord, Mich., July 20, 1971; app. archbishop of Detroit, Mar. 28, 1981, installed May 17, 1981.

T

Tafoya, Arthur N.: b. Mar. 2, 1933, Alameda, N.M.; educ. St. Thomas Seminary (Denver, Colo.), Conception Seminary (Conception, Mo.); ord. priest May 12, 1962; ord. bishop of Pueblo, Sept. 10, 1980.

Tanner, Paul F.: b. Jan. 15, 1905, Peoria, Ill.; educ. Marquette Univ. (Milwaukee, Wis.), Kenrick Seminary (Webster Groves, Mo.), St. Francis Seminary (Milwaukee,. Wis.), Catholic Univ. (Washington, D.C.): ord. priest May 30, 1931; assistant director NCWC Youth Department 1940-45; assistant

general secretary of NCWC 1945-58; general secretary of NCWC (now USCC) 1958-68; ord. titular bishop of Lamasba, Dec. 21, 1965; bishop of St. Augustine, Mar. 27, 1968; resigned 1979.

Tawil, Joseph: b. Dec. 25, 1913, Damascus, Syria; ord. priest July 20, 1936; ord. titular archbishop of Mira and patriarchal vicar for eparchy of Damascus of the Patriarchate of Antioch for the Melkites, Jan. 1, 1960; apostolic exarch for faithful of the Melkite rite in the U.S., Oct. 31, 1969; app. first eparch when exarchate was raised to eparchy, July 15, 1976; title of see changed to Newton, 1977.

Timlin, James C.: b. Aug. 5, 1927, Scranton, Pa.; educ. St. Charles College (Catonsville, Md.), St. Mary's Seminary (Baltimore, Md.), North American College (Rome); ord. priest July 16, 1951; ord. titular bishop of Gunugo and auxiliary bishop of Scranton, Sept. 21, 1976.

Topel, Bernard J.: b. May 31, 1903, Bozeman, Mont.; educ. Carroll College (Helena, Mont.), Grand Seminary (Montreal), Catholic Univ. (Washington, D.C.), Harvard Univ. (Cambridge, Mass.), Notre Dame Univ. (Notre Dame, Ind.); ord. priest June 7, 1927; ord. titular bishop of Binda and coadjutor bishop of Spokane, Sept. 21, 1955; bishop of Spokane, Sept. 25, 1955; retired Apr. 11, 1978.

Treinen, Sylvester: b. Nov. 19, 1917, Donnelly, Minn.; educ. Crosier Seminary (Onamia, Minn.), St. Paul Seminary (St. Paul, Minn.); ord. priest June 11, 1946; ord. bishop of Boise, July 25, 1962.

Tschoepe, Thomas: b. Dec. 17, 1915, Pilot Point, Tex.; educ. Pontifical College Josephinum (Worthington, O.); ord. priest May 30, 1943; ord. bishop of San Angelo, Tex., Mar. 9, 1966; app. bishop of Dallas, Tex., Aug. 27, 1969.

U-V

Untener, Kenneth E.: b. Aug. 3, 1937, Detroit, Mich.; educ. Sacred Heart Seminary (Detroit, Mich.), St. John's Provincial Seminary (Plymouth, Mich.), Gregorian Univ. (Rome); ord. priest June 1, 1963; ord. bishop of Saginaw, Nov. 24, 1980.

Unterkoefler, Ernest L.: b. Aug. 17, 1917, Philadelphia, Pa.; educ. Catholic Univ. (Washington, D.C.); ord. priest May 18, 1944; ord. titular bishop of Latopolis and auxiliary bishop of Richmond, Va., Feb. 22, 1962; app. bishop of Charleston, Dec. 12, 1964, installed Feb. 22, 1965.

Valero, René A.: b. Aug. 15, 1930, New York, N.Y.; educ. Cathedral College, Immaculate Conception Seminary (Huntington, N.Y.), Fordham Univ. (New York); ord. priest June 2, 1956; ord. titular bishop of Turris Vicus and auxiliary bishop of Brooklyn, Nov. 24, 1980.

Vath, Joseph G.: b. Mar. 12, 1918, New Orleans, La.; educ. Notre Dame Seminary (New Orleans, La.), Catholic Univ. (Washington, D.C.); ord. priest June 7, 1941; ord. titular bishop of Novaliciana and auxiliary bishop of Mobile-Birmingham, May 26, 1966; app. first bishop of Birmingham, Oct. 8, 1969.

Vaughan, Austin B.: b. Sept. 27, 1927, New York, N.Y.; educ. North American College and Gregorian Univ. (Rome), ord. priest Dec. 8, 1951; pres. Catholic Theological Society of America, 1967; rector of St. Joseph's Seminary (Dunwoodie, N.Y.), 1973; ord. titular bishop of Cluain Iraird and auxiliary bishop of New York, June 29, 1977.

Veigle, Adrian J.M., T.O.R.: b. Sept. 15, 1912, Lilly, Pa.; educ. St. Francis College (Loretto, Pa.), Pennsylvania State College; ord. priest May 22, 1937; ord. titular bishop of Gigthi and prelate of Borba, Brazil, June 9, 1966.

Vonesh, Raymond J.: b. Jan. 25, 1916, Chicago, Ill.; educ. St. Mary of the Lake Seminary (Mundelein, Ill.). Gregorian Univ. (Rome); ord. priest May 3, 1941; ord. titular bishop of Vanariona and auxiliary bishop of Joliet, Ill., Apr. 3, 1968.

W

Waldschmidt, Paul E., C.S.C.: b. Jan. 7, 1920, Evansville, Ind.; educ. Notre Dame Univ. (Notre Dame, Ind.), Holy Cross College (Washington, D.C.), Laval Univ. (Quebec), Angelicum (Rome) Louvain (Belgium), Sorbonne (Paris), ord. priest June 24, 1946; president University of Portland, 1962-77; ord. titular bishop of Citium and auxiliary bishop of Portland, Ore., Mar. 2, 1978.

Walsh, Daniel Francis: b. Oct. 2, 1937, San Francisco, Calif.; educ. St. Joseph Seminary (Mountain View, Calif.), St. Patrick Seminary (Menlo Park, Calif.) Catholic Univ. (Washington, D.C.); ord. priest Mar. 30, 1963; ord.titular bishop of Tigia and auxiliary bishop of San Francisco, Sept. 24, 1981.

Walsh, Nicholas E.: b. Oct. 20, 1916, Burnsville, Minn.; educ. St. Paul Seminary (St. Paul, Minn.), Catholic Univ. (Washington, D.C.), Pontifical Palafoxianum Seminary (Puebla, Mexico), Register College of Journalism (Denver, Colo.); ord. priest June 6, 1942; first editor of *Idaho Register;* diocesan vicar for Mexican Americans; ord. bishop of Yakima, Oct. 28, 1974; app. titular bishop of Bolsena and auxiliary bishop of Seattle, Aug. 10, 1976.

Ward, John J.: b. Sept. 28, 1920, Los Angeles, Calif.; educ. St. John's Seminary (Camarillo, Calif.), Catholic Univ. (Washington, D.C.); ord. priest May 4, 1946; ord. titular bishop of Bria and auxiliary of Los Angeles, Dec. 12, 1963.

Watson, Alfred M.: b. July 11, 1907, Erie, Pa.; educ. St. Mary's Seminary (Baltimore, Md.), Catholic Univ. (Washington, D.C.); ord. priest May 10, 1934; ord. titular bishop of Nationa and auxiliary bishop of Erie, June 29, 1965; app. bishop of Erie, 1969, installed May 13, 1969; resigned July 16, 1982.

Watters, Loras J.: b. Oct. 14, 1915, Dubuque, Ia.; educ. Loras College (Dubuque, Ia.), Gregorian Univ. (Rome), Catholic Univ. (Washington, D.C.); ord. priest June 7, 1941; ord. titular bishop of Fidoloma and auxiliary bishop of Dubuque, Aug. 26, 1965; bishop of Winona, installed Mar. 13, 1969.

Watty Urquidi, Ricardo, M.Sp.S.: b. July 16, 1938, San Diego, Calif.; ord. priest June 8, 1968; ord. titular bishop of Macomedes and auxiliary bishop of Mexico City, July 19, 1980.

Weakland, Rembert G., O.S.B.: b. Apr. 2, 1927, Patton, Pa.; joined Benedictines, 1945; ord. priest June 24, 1951; abbot-primate of Benedictine Confederation, 1967-77; ord. archbishop of Milwaukee, Nov. 8, 1977.

Weigand, William K.: b. May 23, 1937, Bend, Ore.; educ. Mt. Angel Seminary (St. Benedict, Ore.), St. Edward's Seminary and St. Thomas Seminary (Kenmore, Wash.); ord. priest May 25, 1963; ord. bishop of Salt Lake City, Nov. 17, 1980.

Welsh, Lawrence H.: b. Feb. 1, 1935, Winton, Wyo.; educ. Univ. of Wyoming (Laramie, Wyo.), St. John's Seminary (Collegeville, Minn.), Catholic Univ. (Washington, D.C.); ord. priest May 26, 1962; ord. bishop of Spokane, Dec. 14, 1978.

Welsh, Thomas J.: b. Dec. 20, 1921, Weatherly, Pa.; educ. St. Charles Borromeo Seminary (Philadelphia, Pa.), Catholic Univ. (Washington, D.C.); ord. priest May 30, 1946; ord. titular bishop of Scattery Island and auxiliary bishop of Philadelphia, Apr. 2, 1970; app. first bishop of Arlington, Va., June 4, 1974, installed Aug. 13, 1974.

Whealon, John F.: b. Jan. 15, 1921, Barberton, O.; educ. St. Charles College (Catonsville, Md.), St. Mary's Seminary (Cleveland, O.); ord. priest May 26, 1945; ord. titular bishop of Andrapa and auxiliary bishop of Cleveland, July 6, 1961; app. bishop of Erie, Dec. 9, 1966, installed Mar. 7, 1967; archbishop of Hartford, installed Mar. 19, 1969.

Whelan, Robert L., S.J.: b. Apr. 16, 1912, Wallace, Ida.; educ. St. Michael's College (Spokane, Wash.), Alma College (Alma, Calif.); ord. priest June 17, 1944; ord. titular bishop of Sicilibba and coadjutor bishop of Fairbanks, Alaska, with right of succession, Feb. 22, 1968; bishop of Fairbanks, Nov. 30, 1968.

Wildermuth, Augustine F., S.J.: b. Feb. 20, 1904, St. Louis, Mo.; educ. St. Stanislaus Seminary (Florissant, Mo.), St. Michael's Scholasticate (Spokane, Wash.), Sacred Heart College (Shembaganur, S. India), St. Mary's College (Kurseong, India), Gregorian Univ. (Rome); entered Society of Jesus, 1922;

ord. priest July 25, 1935; ord. bishop of Patna, India, Oct. 28, 1947; retired 1980.

Wirz, George O.: b. Jan. 17, 1929, Monroe, Wis.; educ. St. Francis Seminary and Marquette Univ. (Milwaukee, Wis.); Cath. Univ. (Washington, D.C.); ord. priest May 31, 1952; ord. titular bishop of Municipa and auxilary bishop of Madison, Mar. 9, 1978.

Wurm, John N.: b. Dec. 6, 1927, Overland, Mo.; educ. Kenrick Seminary and St. Louis Univ. (St. Louis, Mo.); ord. priest Apr. 3, 1954; ord. titular bishop of Plestia and auxiliary bishop of St. Louis, Aug. 17, 1976; app. bishop of Belleville, Sept. 21, 1981, installed Nov. 4, 1981.

Wycislo, Aloysius John: b. June 17, 1908, Chicago, Ill.; educ. St. Mary's Seminary (Mundelein, Ill.), Catholic Univ. (Washington, D.C.); ord. priest Apr. 4, 1934; ord. titular bishop of Stadia and auxiliary bishop of Chicago, Dec. 21, 1960; app. bishop of Green Bay, installed Apr. 16, 1968.

Z

Zayek, Francis: b. Oct. 18, 1920, Manzanillo, Cuba; ord. priest Mar. 17, 1946; ord. titular bishop of Callinicum and auxiliary bishop for Maronites in Brazil, Aug. 5, 1962; named apostolic exarch for Maronites in U.S., with headquarters in Detroit; installed June 11, 1966; first eparch of St. Maron of Detroit, Mar. 25, 1972; see transferred to Brooklyn, June 27, 1977.

Zuroweste, Albert R.: b. Apr. 26, 1901, East St. Louis, Ill.; educ. St. Francis College (Quincy, Ill.), Kenrick Seminary (Webster Groves, Mo.), Catholic Univ. (Washington, D.C.); ord. priest June 8, 1924; ord. bishop of Belleville, Jan. 29, 1948; retired Oct. 29, 1976.

RETIRED U.S. PRELATES

Information, as of Aug. 15, 1982, includes name of the prelate and see held at the time of retirement or resignation; archbishops are indicated by an asterisk. Most of the prelates listed below resigned their sees because of age. See Index: Biographies of American Bishops.

The preferred form of address of retired prelates is *Former Archbishop* or *Bishop of* (last see held).

Richard H. Ackerman, C.S.Sp. (Covington), George W. Ahr (Trenton), Reginald Arliss, C.P. (Marbel, Philippines, prelate), Alden J. Bell (Sacramento), John H. Boccella, T.O.R.* (Izmir, Turkey), James C. Burke, O.P. (Chimbote, Peru, prelate), Charles A. Buswell (Pueblo), L. Abel Caillouet (New Orleans, auxiliary), Cardinal John Carberry* (St. Louis), Mark K. Carroll (Wichita), John J. Cassata (Fort Worth), Harry A. Clinch (Monterey), John E. Cohill, S.V.D. (Goroka, Papua New Guinea), James L. Connolly (Fall River), Thomas Connolly* (Seattle), William M. Cosgrove (Belleville), William E.

Cousins* (Milwaukee), Augustine Danglmayr (Ft. Worth, auxiliary), Nicholas D'Antonio, O.F.M. (Olancha, Honduras).

James P. Davis* (Santa Fê), Cardinal John F. Dearden* (Detroit), Joseph P. Denning (Brooklyn, auxiliary), Hugh A. Donohoe (Fresno), John A. Donovan (Toledo), Carroll T. Dozier (Memphis), Clarence J. Duhart, C.SS.R. (Udon Thani, Thailand), Joseph A. Durick (Nashville), J. Lennox Federal (Salt Lake City), John B. Franz (Peoria), Philip J. Furlong (Military Vicariate, delegate).

Hugo Gerbermann, M.M. (San Antonio, auxiliary), James J. Gerrard (Fall River, auxiliary), Francis D. Gleeson, S.J. (Fairbanks), Laurence A. Glenn (Crookston), Ignatius T. Glennie, S.J. (Trincomalee-Batticaloa, Sri Lanka), Lawrence Graziano, O.F.M. (San Miguel, El Salvador), Lawrence P. Graves (Alexandria-Shreveport), Charles P. Greco (Alexandria), Francis J. Green (Tucson), Joseph Green (Reno), John B. Grellinger, (Green Bay, auxiliary).

Hilary B. Hacker (Bismarck), Paul L. Hagarty (Nassau, Bahamas), Charles H. Helmsing (Kansas City-St. Joseph), Edward G. Hettinger (Columbus, auxiliary), Vincent J. Hines (Norwich), Lambert A. Hoch (Sioux Falls), Joseph L. Hogan (Rochester), Edward D. Howard* (Portland, Ore.), Robert F. Joyce (Burlington), Walter P. Kellenberg (Rockville Centre), Arthur H. Krawczak (Detroit, auxiliary), George L. Leech (Harrisburg), Leo Lemay, S.M. (Bougainville, Solomon Is.), Stephen A. Leven (San Angelo).

William McDonald (San Francisco, auxiliary), Thomas J. McDonough* (Louisville), John J. McEleney, S.J.* (Kingston, Jamaica), Joseph T. McGucken* (San Francisco), Edward A. McGurkin, M.M. (Shinyanga, Tanzania), Edward J. Maginn (Albany, auxiliary), John J. Maguire* (New York, coadjutor), David M. Maloney (Wichita), Alfred Mendez, C.S.C. (Arecibo, P.R.), Sidney M. Metzger (El Paso), William J. Moran (Military Vicariate, delegate).

Louis La Ravoire Morrow, S.D.B. (Krishnagar, India), Charles R. Mulrooney (Brooklyn, auxiliary), Knute Ansgar Nelson, O.S.B. (Stockholm, Sweden), Hubert M. Newell (Cheyenne), Cardinal Patrick O'Boyle* (Washington, D.C.).

Martin J. O'Connor* (Prefect Emeritus, Pontifical Commission for Social Communications), William A. O'Connor (Springfield, Ill.), James V. Pardy, M.M. (Cheong Ju, Korea), John L. Paschang (Grand Island), George H. Pearce, S.M.* (Suva, Fiji Islands), Joseph M. Pernicone (New York, auxiliary), Ernest J. Primeau (Manchester), Leo A. Pursley (Fort Wayne-South Bend), Joseph M. Raya* (Acre), Joseph W. Regan, M.M. (Tagum, P.I., Prelate), Francis F. Reh (Saginaw).

Louis J. Reicher (Austin), Thomas F. Reilly, C.SS.R. (San Juan de la Maguana, Dominican Republic), John J. Rudin, M.M. (Musoma, Tanzania), John J. Russell (Richmond), John J. Scanlan (Honolulu), Alphonse Schladweiler (New Ulm), Paul C. Schulte* (Indianapolis; titular archbishop of Elicora), Eldon B. Schuster (Great Falls).

Cardinal Lawrence J. Shehan* (Baltimore), Henry J. Soenneker (Owensboro), Alfred M. Stemper, M.S. C. (Kavieng, Papua New Guinea), Edward E. Swanstrom (New York, auxiliary), Paul F. Tanner (St. Augustine), Bernard J. Topel (Spokane), Alfred M. Watson (Erie), Augustine Wildermuth, S.J. (Patna, India), Albert R. Zuroweste (Belleville).

BISHOP-BROTHERS

(The asterisk indicates brothers who were bishops at the same time.)

There have been nine pairs of brother-bishops in the history of the U.S. hierarchy.

Living: Francis T. Hurley,* archbishop of Anchorage and Mark J. Hurley* of Santa Rosa.

Deceased: Francis Blanchet* of Oregon City (Portland) and Augustin Blanchet* of Walla Walla; John S. Foley of Detroit and

Thomas P. Foley of Chicago; Francis P. Kenrick,* apostolic administrator of Philadelphia, bishop of Philadelphia and Baltimore, and Peter R. Kenrick* of St. Louis; Matthias C. Lenihan of Great Falls and Thomas M. Lenihan of Cheyenne; James O'Connor, vicar apostolic of Nebraska and bishop of Omaha, and Michael O'Connor of Pittsburgh and Erie; Jeremiah F. and John W. Shanahan, both of Harrisburg; Sylvester J. Espelage, O.F.M.,* of Wuchang, China, who died 10 days after the ordination of his brother, Bernard T. Espelage,* O.F.M., of Gallup; Coleman F. Carroll* of Miami and Howard Carroll* of Altoona-Johnstown.

U.S. BISHOPS OVERSEAS

Cardinal William W. Baum, prefect of the Sacred Congregation for Catholic Education; Archbishop Raymond P. Etteldorf, pro-nuncio to Ethiopia; Bishop Anthony L. Deksnys, pastoral work among Lithuanians in Western Europe; Archbishop Paul C. Marcinkus, president of Institute for Works of Religion (Vatican Bank) and pro-president of Pontifical Commission for the State of Vatian City.

(See also Missionary Bishops.)

LIBERATION THEOLOGY

Liberation theology deals with the relevance of Christian faith and salvation — and, therefore, of the mission of the Church — to efforts for the promotion of human rights, social justice and human development.

It originated in the religious, social, political and economic environment of Latin America, with its contemporary need for a theory and corresponding action by the Church, in the pattern of its overall mission, for human rights and integral human development.

The pastoral and social doctrine of the Church provides the basic theoretical background of liberation theology worthy of the name. Of particular importance are the expressions of this teaching in: the papal encyclicals *Mater et Magistra* (1961), *Pacem in Terris* (1963) and *Populorum Progressio* (1967); *Gaudium et Spes,* issued by the Second Vatican Council (1965); documents which emanated from the meeting of the Latin American Bishops' Council at Medellin, Colombia, under the title, *The Church in the Present-Day Transformation of Latin America in the Light of the* (Second Vatican) *Council* (1968); statements of the Synod of Bishops (1971 and 1974); the apostolic exhortation of Pope Paul, "Evangelization in Today's World" (1975).

Some versions of liberation theology are at variance with this body of teaching because of their special concept of Christ as liberator, and also because they play down the primary spiritual nature and mission of the Church; they translate sociology — especially Marx-

ism — into theology; they advocate violence in social activism.

Risk in Sociological Commitment

The International Theological Commission said this about the subject in 1976:

"Theological treatments of liberation must deal simultaneously with theories that come from the social sciences, which study objectively what the 'outcry of the people' expresses.

"Theology, however, cannot deduce concrete political norms sheerly from theological principles; and so the theologian cannot settle profound sociological issues by theology's specific resources. Theological treatises which strive to build a more human society must take into account the risks that the use of sociological theories involves. In every instance these theories must be tested for their degree of certitude, inasmuch as they are often no more than conjectures and not infrequently harbor explicit or implicit ideological elements that rest on debatable philosophical assumptions or on an erroneous anthropology. This is true, for instance, of significant segments of analyses inspired by Marxism and Leninism. Anyone who employs such theories and analyses should be aware that these do not achieve a greater degree of truth simply because theology introduces them into its expositions. In fact, theology ought to recognize the pluralism that exists in scientific interpretations of society and realize that it cannot be fettered to any concrete sociological analysis."

Religious

Religious orders and congregations, collectively called **religious institutes,** are special societies in the Church. Their members, called **religious,** commit themselves to observance of the evangelical counsels of poverty, chastity and obedience in a community kind of life in accordance with rules and constitutions approved by church authority.

Religious Institutes

The particular goal of each institute and the means of realizing it in practice are stated in the rule and constitutions proper to the institute. Local bishops, with permission of the Holy See, can give approval for rules and constitutions of **institutes of diocesan rank. Pontifical rank** belongs to institutes approved by the Holy See. General jurisdiction over all religious is exercised by the Congregation for Religious and Secular Institutes. General legislation concerning religious is contained in Canons 487 to 681 of the Code of Canon Law and in subsequent enactments, especially since the Second Vatican Council.

All religious institutes are commonly called religious orders, despite the fact that there are differences between orders and congregations. The best known **orders** include the Benedictines, Trappists, Franciscans, Dominicans, Carmelites and Augustinians, for men; and the Carmelites, Poor Clares, Dominicans of the Second Order and Visitation Nuns, for women. Members of the orders have solemn vows; their communities have papal enclosure and exemption, and are bound to perform the Liturgy of the Hours (Divine Office) in choir as a common practice. Members of the **congregations** have simple vows. The orders are older than the congregations, which did not appear until the 16th century.

Contemplative institutes are oriented to divine worship and service within the confines of their communities, by prayer, penitential practices, other spiritual activities and self-supporting work; engagement in outside active ministry is subordinate to their contemplative pursuits. Examples are the Trappists and Carthusians, the Carmelite and Poor Clare nuns. **Active institutes** are geared primarily for the ministry and many kinds of apostolic work. **Mixed institutes** combine elements of the contemplative and active ways of life. While most institutes of men and women can be classified as active, all of them have some contemplative aspects.

Historical Development

The basis of the life of religious institutes was the invitation Christ extended to men (Mt. 19:16ff.) to follow him with special dedication in a life like his own, which was that of a poor and chaste man under obedience to the Father.

In the earliest years of Christianity, some men and women dedicated themselves to the service of God in a special manner. Among them were holy women, deaconesses and virgins mentioned in the Acts of the Apostles, and confessors and ascetics like St. Clement of Rome, St. Ignatius of Antioch and St. Polycarp.

In the third and fourth centuries, there were traces of a kind of religious profession, and the root idea of the life began to produce significant results in the solitary and community hermitages of Egypt and Syria under the inspiration of men like St. Paul of Thebes, St. Anthony the Abbot and St. Pachomius.

St. Basil, "Father of Monasticism in the East," exerted a deep and still continuing influence on the development of religious life among men and women. His opposite number in the West was St. Benedict, whose rule or counsels, dating from about 530, set the pattern of monastic life for men and women which prevailed for nearly six centuries and which still endures. Before his time, St. Augustine framed guidelines for community life which are still being followed by some men and women religious.

Mendicant orders, whose members were freer than the monks for works of the active ministry, made their appearance early in the 13th century and began to change some of the established aspects of religious life. Religious women, however, continued to live in the monastic manner.

A significant change in religious life developed in the 16th century when several communities of men with simple rather than solemn vows were approved; among them were **clerics regular** like the Jesuits and Barnabites. Some of these communities are considered to be orders, although they differ in some respects from the older orders.

The Sisters of Charity, in 1633, were the first community of women with simple vows to gain church approval. Since that time, the number and variety of female communities have greatly increased. Women religious, no longer restricted to the hidden life of prayer, became engaged in many kinds of work including education, health and social service, and missionary endeavor.

Clerical communities of men — i. e., those whose membership is predominantly composed of priests — are similarly active in many types of work. Their ditinctive fields are education, home and foreign missions, retreats, special assignments and the communications media, as well as the internal life and conduct of their own communities. They also engage in the ordinary pastoral ministry which is the principal work of diocesan or secular priests. They are generally called **regular clergy** because of the rule of life (*regula* in Latin) they follow.

Non-clerical or lay institutes of men are the various brotherhoods whose non-ordained members (called **lay brothers,** or simply **brothers**) are engaged in educational and hospital work, missionary endeavors, and other special fields.

Some of the institutes of men listed below have a special kind of status because their members, while living a common life like that which is characteristic of religious, do not profess the vows of religious. Examples are the Maryknoll Fathers, the Oratorians of St. Philip Neri, the Paulists and Sulpicians. They are called **societies of the common life without vows.**

RENEWAL OF RELIGIOUS LIFE

Following are key excerpts from the *Decree on the Appropriate Renewal of Religious Life* promulgated by the Second Vatican Council.

"A life consecrated by a profession of the counsels (of poverty, chastity and obedience) is of surpassing value. Such a life has a necessary role to play in the circumstances of the present age. That this kind of life and its contemporary role may achieve greater good for the Church, this sacred Synod issues the following decrees. They concern only the general principles which must underlie an appropriate renewal of the life and rules of religious communities. These principles apply also to societies living a community life without the exercise of vows, and to secular institutes, though the special character of both groups is to be maintained. After the Council, the competent authority will be obliged to enact particular laws opportunely spelling out and applying what is legislated here" (No. 1).

"The appropriate renewal of religious life involves two simultaneous processes: (1) a continuous return to the sources of all Christian life and to the original inspiration behind a given community and (2) an adjustment of the community to the changed conditions of the times. . . .

"(a) Since the fundamental norm of the religious life is a following of Christ as proposed by the gospel, such is to be regarded by all communities as their supreme law.

"(b) It serves the best interests of the Church for communities to have their own special character and purpose. Therefore loyal recognition and safekeeping should be accorded to the spirit of founders, as also to all the particular goals and wholesome traditions which constitute the heritage of each community.

"(c) All communities should participate in the life of the Church. According to its individual character, each should make its own and foster in every possible way the enterprises and objectives of the Church in such fields as these: the scriptural, liturgical, doctrinal, pastoral, ecumenical, missionary, and social.

"(d) Communities should promote among their members a suitable awareness of contemporary human conditions and of the needs of the Church. . . .

"(e) Since the religious life is intended above all else to lead those who embrace it to an imitation of Christ and to union with God through the profession of the evangelical counsels, the fact must be honestly faced that even the most desirable changes made on behalf of contemporary needs will fail of their purpose unless a renewal of spirit gives life to them. Indeed such an interior renewal must always be accorded the leading role even in the promotion of external works" (No. 2).

"The manner of living, praying, and working should be suitably adapted to the physical and psychological conditions of today's religious and also, to the extent required by the nature of each community, to the needs of the apostolate, the requirements of a given culture, the social and economic circumstances anywhere, but especially in missionary territories."

Allowance should be made for prudent experimentation in the direction of renewal and adaptation (No. 3).

". . . The hope of renewal must be lodged in a more diligent observance of rule and of constitution rather than in a multiplication of individual laws" (No. 4).

Various Communities

"The members of each community should recall above everything else that by their profession of the evangelical counsels they have given answer to a divine call to live for God alone not only by dying to sin (cf. Rom. 6:11) but also by renouncing the world. They have handed over their entire lives to God's service in an act of special consecration which is deeply rooted in their baptismal consecration and which provides an ampler manifestation of it.

"Inasmuch as their self-dedication has been accepted by the Church, they should realize that they are committed to her service as well.

". . . The members of each community should combine contemplation with apostolic love. By the former they adhere to God in mind and heart; by the latter they strive to associate themselves with the work of redemption and to spread the Kingdom of God" (No. 5).

"Members of those communities which are totally dedicated to contemplation give themselves to God alone in solitude and silence and through constant prayer and ready penance. No matter how urgent may be the needs of the active apostolate, such communities will always have a distinguished part to play in Christ's Mystical Body. . . . Their manner of living should be revised according to the aforementioned principles and standards of appropriate renewal, though their withdrawal from the world and the practices of their contemplative life should be maintained at their holiest" (No. 7).

Communities geared for apostolic action "should skillfully harmonize their observances and practices with the needs of the apostolate to which they are dedicated," with due regard for diversity (No. 8). This norm applies to monastic institutes, which should preserve their special character; to communities which "closely join the apostolic life with choral prayer and monastic observances"; and to "the lay religious life, for both men and women" (Nos. 9 and 10).

[See Secular Institutes for a quotation from the decree on the subject.]

The Vows, Authority

"That chastity which is practiced 'on behalf of the heavenly Kingdom' (Mt. 19:12), and which religious profess, deserves to be esteemed as a surpassing gift of grace. For it liberates the human heart in a unique way (cf. 1 Cor. 7:32-35) and causes it to burn with greater love for God and all mankind. It is therefore an outstanding token of heavenly riches, and also a most suitable way for religious to spend themselves readily in God's service and in works of the apostolate. . . .

"Since the observance of total continence intimately involves the deeper inclinations of human nature, candidates should not undertake the profession of chastity nor be admitted to its profession except after a truly adequate testing period and only if they have the needed degree of psychological and emotional maturity" (No. 12).

"Poverty voluntarily embraced in imitation of Christ provides a witness which is highly esteemed, especially today. Let religious painstakingly cultivate such poverty, and give it new expressions if need be. . . .

". . . Members of a community ought to be poor in both fact and spirit, and have their treasures in heaven (cf. Mt. 6:20).

". . . Communities as such should aim at giving a kind of corporate witness to their own poverty. . . .

"To the degree that their rules and constitutions permit, religious communities can rightly possess whatever is necessary for their temporal life and their mission. Still, let them avoid every appearance of luxury, of excessive wealth, and accumulation of possessions" (No. 13).

"Through the profession of obedience, religious offer to God a total dedication of their own wills as a sacrifice of themselves; they thereby unite themselves with greater steadiness and security to the saving will of God. . . . Under the influence of the Holy Spirit, religious submit themselves to their superiors, whom faith presents as God's repre-sentatives, and through whom they are guided into the service of all their brothers in Christ. . . . In this way . . . religious assume a firmer commitment to the ministry of the Church and labor to achieve the mature measure of the fullness of Christ (cf. Eph. 4:13).

"Therefore, in a spirit of faith and of love for God's will, let religious show humble obedience to their superiors in accord with the norms of the rule and constitution. . . . Let them bring to the execution of commands and to the discharge of assignments entrusted to them the resources of their minds and wills, and their gifts of nature and grace. Lived in this manner, religious obedience will not diminish the dignity of the human person but will rather lead it to maturity in consequence of that enlarged freedom which belongs to the sons of God.

". . . Each superior should himself be docile to God's will in the exercise of his office. Let him use his authority in a spirit of service for the brethren. . . . Governing his subjects as God's own sons, and with regard for their human personality, a superior will make it easier for them to obey gladly. Therefore he must make a special point of leaving them appropriately free with respect to the sacrament of penance and direction of conscience. Let him give the kind of leadership which will encourage religious to bring an active and responsible obedience to the offices they shoulder and the activities they undertake. Therefore a superior should listen willingly to his subjects and encourage them to make a personal contribution to the welfare of the community and of the Church. Not to be weakened, however, is the superior's authority to decide what must be done and to require the doing of it.

"Let chapters and councils faithfully acquit themselves of the governing role given to them; each should express in its own way the fact that all members of the community have a share in the welfare of the whole community and a responsibility for it" (No. 14).

NFPC

The National Federation of Priests' Councils was organized by 233 delegates from 127 priests' organizations at a charter meeting held in Chicago May 20 and 21, 1968.

Its stated purpose is to give priests' councils, official or unofficial, a representative voice in matters of presbyteral, pastoral and ministerial concern to the U.S. and the universal Church.

The NFPC has a membership of 110 senates (councils and associations), religious institutes, PADRES and the National Black Catholic Clergy Caucus.

Headquarters are located at 1307 S. Wabash Ave., Chicago, Ill. 60605.

RELIGIOUS INSTITUTES OF MEN IN THE UNITED STATES

(Sources: *Official Catholic Directory;* Catholic Almanac survey.)

African Missions, Society of, S.M.A.: Founded 1856, at Lyons, France, by Bishop Melchior de Marion Brésillac. Generalate, Rome, Italy; American provincialate, 23 Bliss Ave., Tenafly, N.J. 07670. Missionary work in West Africa, Bahama Islands and inner city parishes.

Assumptionists (Augustinians of the Assumption), AA.: Founded 1845, at Nimes, France, by Rev. Emmanuel d'Alzon; in U.S., 1946. General motherhouse, Rome, Italy; U.S. province, 329 W. 108th St., New York, N.Y. 10025. Educational, parochial, ecumenical, retreat, foreign mission work.

Atonement, Franciscan Friars of the, S.A.: Founded as an Anglican Franciscan community in 1898 at Garrison, N.Y., by Rev. Paul Wattson. Community corporately received into the Catholic Church in 1909. Motherhouse, St. Paul Friary, Graymoor, Garrison N.Y. 10524. Ecumenical, mission, retreat and charitable works.

Augustinian Recollects, O.A.R.: Founded 1588: in U.S., 1944. General motherhouse, Rome, Italy. Missionary, parochial, education work.

St. Augustine Province (1944), 29 Ridgeway Ave., W. Orange, N.J. 07052.

St. Nicholas Province (Madrid): U.S. Delegate, 2288 Light St., Bronx, N.Y. 10466.

Augustinians (Order of St. Augustine), O.S.A.: Established canonically in 1256 by Pope Alexander IV; in U.S., 1796. General motherhouse, Rome, Italy.

St. Thomas of Villanova Province (1796), Villanova, Pa. 19085.

Our Mother of Good Counsel Province (1941), Tolentine Center, 20300 Governors Hwy., Olympia Fields, Ill. 60461.

St. Augustine Province (1969), 2060 N. Vermont Ave., Los Angeles, Calif. 90027.

Good Counsel Vice-Province, St. Augustine Priory, Richland, N.J. 08350.

U.S. Vicariate of Castile, Spain, Province, P.O. Box 190, Waxahachie, Tex. 75165.

Barnabites (Clerics Regular of St. Paul), C.R.S.P.: Founded 1530, in Milan, Italy, by St. Anthony M. Zaccaria. Generalate, Rome, Italy; American headquarters, 1023 Swann Rd., Youngstown, N.Y. 14174. Parochial, educational, mission work.

Basil the Great, Order of St. (Ukrainian), O.S.B.M.: General motherhouse, Rome, Italy; U.S. province, 31-12 30th St., Long Island City, N.Y. 11106. Parochial work among Byzantine Ukrainian Rite Catholics.

Basilian Fathers (Congregation of the Priests of St. Basil), C.S.B.: Founded 1822, at Annonay, France. General motherhouse, 20 Humewood Dr., Toronto, Ont. M6C 2W2, Canada. Educational, parochial work.

Basilian Salvatorian Fathers: Founded 1684, at Saida, Lebanon, by Eftimios Saifi; in U.S., 1953. General motherhouse, Saida, Lebanon; American headquarters, 30 East St., Methuen, Mass. 01844. Educational, parochial work among Eastern Rite peoples.

Benedictines (Order of St. Benedict), O.S.B.: Founded 529, in Italy, by St. Benedict of Nursia; in U.S., 1846.

• American Cassinese Federation (1855). Rt. Rev. Martin Burne, O.S.B., pres., St. Mary's Abbey, Delbarton, Morristown, N.J. 07960. Abbeys and Priories belonging to the federation:

St. Vincent Archabbey, Latrobe, Pa. 15650; St. John's Abbey, Collegeville, Minn. 56321; St. Benedict's Abbey, Atchison, Kans. 66002; St. Mary's Abbey, Delbarton, Morristown, N.J. 07960; Belmont Abbey, Belmont, N.C. 28012; St. Bernard Abbey, St. Bernard, Ala. 35055; St. Procopius Abbey, Lisle, Ill. 60532; St. Gregory's Abbey, Shawnee, Okla. 74801; St. Leo Abbey, St. Leo, Fla. 33574; Assumption Abbey, Richardton, N. Dak. 58652;

St. Bede Abbey, Peru, Ill. 61354; St. Martin's Abbey, Lacey, Wash. 98503; Holy Cross Abbey, Canon City, Colo. 81212; St. Anselm's Abbey, Manchester, N.H. 03102; St. Andrew's Abbey, 2900 East Blvd., Cleveland, O. 44104; Holy Trinity Monastery, Butler, Pa. 16001; St. Maur Priory, 4545 Northwestern Ave., Indianapolis, Ind. 46208; Newark Abbey, 528 High St., Newark, N.J. 07102; St. Mark's Priory, South Union, Ky. 42283; Benedictine Priory, 6502 Seawright Dr., Savannah, Ga. 31406; Woodside Priory, 302 Portola Rd., Portola Valley, Calif. 94025.

• Swiss-American Federation (1870), Rt. Rev. Raphael De Salvo O.S.B., pres., New Subiaco Abbey, New Subiaco, Ark. 72865. Abbeys and priory belonging to the federation:

St. Meinrad Archabbey, St. Meinrad, Ind. 47577; Conception Abbey, Conception, Mo. 64433; Mt. Michael Abbey, Elkhorn, Nebr. 68022; New Subiaco Abbey, Subiaco, Ark. 72865; St. Joseph's Abbey, St. Benedict, La. 70457; Mt. Angel Abbey, St. Benedict, Ore. 97373; Marmion Abbey, Butterfield Rd., Aurora, Ill. 60504;

St. Benedict's Abbey, Benet Lake, Wis. 53102; Glastonbury Abbey, 16 Hull St., Hingham, Mass. 02043; Westminster Abbey, Mission, B.C., Canada; St. Pius X Abbey, Pevely, Mo. 63070; Blue Cloud Abbey, Marvin, S. Dak. 57251; Corpus Christi Abbey, Star Route, Box A-38-A, Sandia, Tex. 78383; Our Lady of Guadalupe Abbey, Pecos N. Mex. 87552; St. Charles Priory, Benet Hill, Oceanside, Calif. 92054.

• English Benedictine Congregation: St. Anselm's Abbey, 4501 S. Dakota Ave. N.E.,

Washington, D.C. 20017; Abbey of St. Gregory, Cory's Lane, Portsmouth, R.I. 02871; Priory of St. Mary and St. Louis, 500 S. Mason Rd., St. Louis, Mo. 63141.

• Congregation of St. Ottilien for Foreign Missions, St. Paul's Abbey, Newton, N.J. 07860; Benedictine Mission House, Schuyler, Neb. 68661.

• Congregation of the Annunciation, St. Andrew Priory, Valyermo, Calif. 93563.

• Houses not in Congregations: Mount Saviour Monastery, Pine City, N.Y. 14871; Conventual Priory of St. Gabriel the Archangel, Weston, Vt. 05161.

Benedictines, Olivetan, O.S.B.: General motherhouse, Siena, Italy. U.S. foundation, Our Lady of Mt. Olivet Monastery, 4029 Ave. G, Lake Charles, La. 70601.

Benedictines, Sylvestrine, O.S.B.: Founded 1231, in Italy by Sylvester Gozzolini. General motherhouse, Rome, Italy; U.S. foundations; 17320 Rosemont Rd., Detroit, Mich. 48219; 2711 E. Drahner Rd., Oxford, Mich. 48051; 1697 State Highway 3, Clifton, N.J. 07012.

Bethlehem Missionaries, Society of, S.M.B.: Founded 1921, at Immensee, Switzerland, by Rt. Rev. Canon Peter Bondolfi. General motherhouse, Immensee, Switzerland; U.S. headquarters, 5630 E. 17th Ave., Denver, Colo. 80220. Foreign mission work.

Blessed Sacrament, Congregation of the, S.S.S.: Founded 1856, at Paris, France, by St. Pierre Julien Eymard; in U.S., 1900. General motherhouse, Rome, Italy; U.S. province, 5384 Wilson Mills Rd., Cleveland, O. 44143. Eucharistic apostolate.

Brigittine Monks (Order of the Most Holy Savior), O.SS.T.: Monastery of the Most Holy Savior, 5539 Kanawha Turnpike, St. Albans, W. Va. 25177.

Camaldolese Congregation, Cam. O.S.B.: Founded 1012, at Camaldoli, near Arezzo, Italy, by St. Romuald; in U.S. 1958. General motherhouse, Arezzo, Italy; U.S. foundation, Immaculate Heart Hermitage, Big Sur, Calif. 93920.

Camaldolese Hermits of the Congregation of Monte Corona, Er. Cam.: Founded 1520, from Camaldoli, Italy, by Bl. Paul Giustiniani. General motherhouse, Frascati (Rome), Italy; U.S. foundation, Holy Family Hermitage, Rt. 2, Box 36, Bloomingdale, O. 43910.

Camillian Fathers and Brothers (Order of St. Camillus; Clerics Regular, Ministers of the Sick), O.S.Cam.: Founded 1582, at Rome, by St. Camillus de Lellis; in U.S., 1923. General motherhouse, Rome, Italy; North American province, 10213 W. Wisconsin Ave., Wauwatosa, Wis. 53226.

Carmelites (Order of Our Lady of Mt. Carmel), O. Carm.: General motherhouse, Rome, Italy. Educational, charitable work.

Most Pure Heart of Mary Province (1864), 45 E. Dundee Rd., Barrington, Ill. 60010.

St. Elias Province (1931), 69-34 52nd Ave., Maspeth, N.Y. 11378.

Mt. Carmel Hermitage, Pineland, R.D. 1, Box 36, New Florence, Pa. 15944 (immediately subject to Prior General.)

Carmelites, Order of Discalced, O.C.D.: Established 1562, a Reform Order of Our Lady of Mt. Carmel; in U.S., 1935. Generalate, Rome, Italy. Spiritual direction, retreat, parochial work.

St. Therese of Oklahoma Province (1935), 1125 S. Walker St., P.O. Box 26127, Oklahoma City, Okla. 73126.

Immaculate Heart of Mary Province (1947), P.O. Box 67, Hubertus, Wis. 53033.

Anglo-Irish Province (1924), 510 N. El Molino St., Alhambra, Calif. 91801.

Polish Province of the Holy Spirit, 1628 Ridge Rd., Munster, Ind. 46321.

Carthusians, Order of, O. Cart.: Founded 1084, in France, by St. Bruno; in U.S., 1951. General motherhouse, St. Pierre de Chartreuse, France; U.S. charterhouse, Arlington, Vt. 05250. Cloistered contemplatives; semi-eremitic.

Charity, Servants of, S.C.: Founded 1908, in Italy, by Bl. Luigi Guanella. General motherhouse, Rome, Italy; U.S. headquarters, Don Guanella School, Sproul Rd., Springfield, Pa. 19064.

Christ, Society of, S.Ch.: Founded 1932, General Motherhouse, Poznan, Poland; U.S. address, 3000 Eighteen Mile Rd., Sterling Heights, Mich. 48078.

Cistercians, Order of, O. Cist.: Founded 1098, by St. Robert. Headquarters, Rome, Italy.

Our Lady of Spring Bank Abbey, 34639 W. Fairview Rd., Oconomowoc, Wis. 53066.

Our Lady of Gerowval Monastery, Rose Hill, Miss. 39356.

Our Lady of Dallas Monastery, Rt. 2, Box 1, Irving, Tex. 75062.

Cistercian Monastery of Our Lady of Fatima, Hainesport-Mt. Laurel Rd., Mt. Laurel, N.J. 08054.

Cistercian Monastery of Saint Mary, R.D. 1, New Ringgold, Pa. 17960.

Cistercians of the Strict Observance, Order of (Trappists), O.C.S.O.: Founded 1098, in France, by St. Robert; in U.S., 1848. Generalate, Rome, Italy.

Our Lady of Gethsemani Abbey (1848), Trappist P.O., Ky. 40073.

Our Lady of New Melleray Abbey (1849), Dubuque, Iowa 52001.

St. Joseph's Abbey (1825), Spencer, Mass. 01562.

Holy Spirit Monastery (1944), Conyers, Ga. 30208.

Our Lady of Guadalupe Abbey (1947), Lafayette, Ore. 97127.

Our Lady of the Holy Trinity Abbey (1947), Huntsville, Utah 84317.

Abbey of the Genesee (1951), Piffard, N.Y. 14533.

Our Lady of Mepkin Abbey (1949), Route 3, Box 800, Moncks Corner, S. Car. 29461.

Our Lady of the Holy Cross Abbey (1950), Berryville, Va. 22611.

Our Lady of the Assumption Abbey (1950), Rt. 5, Box 193, Ava, Mo. 65608.

Abbey of New Clairvaux (1955), Vina, Calif. 96092.

St. Benedict's Monastery (1956), Snowmass, Colo. 81654.

Claretians (Missionary Sons of the Immaculate Heart of Mary), C.M.F.: Founded 1849, at Vich, Spain, by St. Anthony Mary Claret. General headquarters, Rome, Italy. Missionary, parochial, educational, retreat work.

Western Province, 1119 Westchester Pl., Los Angeles, Calif. 90019.

Eastern Province, 400 N. Euclid Ave. Oak Park, Ill. 60302.

Clerics Regular Minor (Adorno Fathers) C.R.M.: Founded 1588, at Naples, Italy, by Ven. Augustine Adorno and St. Francis Caracciolo. General motherhouse, Rome, Italy; U.S. address, 575 Darlington Ave., Ramsey, N.J. 07446.

Columban, Society of St. (St. Columban Foreign Mission Society, S.S.C.): Founded 1918. General headquarters, Dublin, Ireland. U.S. headquarters, St. Columbans, Nebr. 68056. Foreign mission work.

Comboni Missionaries of the Heart of Jesus (Verona Fathers), M.C.C.J.: Founded 1885, in Italy by Bp. Daniele Comboni. General motherhouse, Rome, Italy; North American headquarters, Comboni Mission Center, 8108 Beechmont Ave., Cincinnati, O. 45230. Mission work in Africa and the Americas.

Consolata Society for Foreign Missions, I.M.C.: Founded 1901, at Turin, Italy, by Father Joseph Allamano. General motherhouse, Rome, Italy; U.S. headquarters, P.O. Box C, Lincoln Hwy., Somerset, N.J. 08873.

Crosier Fathers (Canons Regular of the Order of the Holy Cross), O.S.C.: Founded 1210, in Belgium by Bl. Theodore De Celles. Generalate, Amersfoort, Netherlands; U.S. province, 711 Lincoln Ave., St. Paul, Minn. 55105. Mission, retreat, educational work.

Cross, Priests of the Congregation of Holy, C.S.C.: Founded 1837, in France; in U.S., 1841. Generalate, Rome, Italy. Educational and pastoral work; home missions and retreats; foreign missions; social services and apostolate of the press.

Indiana Province (1841), 1304 E. Jefferson Blvd., South Bend, Ind. 46617.

Eastern Province (1952), 835 Clinton Ave., Bridgeport, Conn. 06604.

Southern Province (1968), 1828 S. Carrollton Ave., New Orleans, La. 70118.

Divine Word, Society of the, S.V.D.: Founded 1875, in Holland, by Bl. Arnold Janssen. North American Province founded 1897 with headquarters in Techny, Ill. General motherhouse, Rome, Italy.

Province of the Blessed Virgin (Northern Province), (1964), Techny, Ill. 60082.

Sacred Heart Province (Eastern Province) (1940), 1025 Michigan Ave. N.E., Washington, D.C. 20017.

St. Augustine's Province (Southern Province) (1940), 201 Ruella Ave., Bay St. Louis, Miss. 39520.

St. Therese Province (Western Province) (1964), 2181 W. 25th St., Los Angeles, Calif. 90018.

Dominicans (Order of Friars Preachers), O.P.: Founded early 13th century by St. Dominic de Guzman. General headquarters, Santa Sabina, Rome, Italy. Preaching, teaching, missions, research, parishes.

St. Joseph Province (1806), 141 E. 65th St., New York, N.Y. 10021.

Holy Name of Jesus Province (1912), 5877 Birch Ct., Oakland, Calif. 94618.

St. Albert the Great Province (1939), 1909 S. Ashland Ave., Chicago, Ill. 60608.

Southern Dominican Province (1979), 3407 Napoleon Ave., New Orleans, La. 70125.

St. Dominic Province (1873), 5353 Notre Dame de Grace Ave., Montreal, Que. H4A 1L2, Canada.

Spanish Province, U.S. foundation (1933), P.O. Box 279, San Diego, Tex. 78384.

Edmund, Society of St., S.S.E.: Founded 1843, in France, by Fr. Jean Baptiste Muard. General motherhouse, Edmundite Generalate, Fairholt, S. Prospect St., Burlington, Vt. 05401. Educational, missionary work.

Eudists (Congregation of Jesus and Mary), C.J.M.: Founded 1643, in France, by St. John Eudes. General motherhouse, Rome, Italy; North American province, 6125 Première Ave., Charlesbourg, Quebec G1H 2V9, Canada. Parochial, educational, pastoral, missionary work.

Francis, Third Order Regular of St., T.O.R.: Founded 1221, in Italy; in U.S., 1910. General motherhouse, Rome, Italy. Educational, parochial, missionary work.

Most Sacred Heart of Jesus Province (1910), 601 Pitcairn Pl., Pittsburgh, Pa. 15232.

Immaculate Conception Province (1925), 2006 Edgewater Parkway, Silver Springs, Md. 20903.

Commissariat of the Spanish Province (1924), 301 Jefferson Ave., Waco, Tex. 76702.

Francis de Sales, Oblates of St., O.S.F.S.: Founded 1871, by Fr. Louis Brisson. General motherhouse, Rome, Italy. Educational, missionary, parochial work.

Wilmington-Philadelphia Province (1906), 2200 Kentmere Parkway, Box 1452, Wilmington, Del. 19899.

Toledo-Detroit Province (1966), Box 4683, Toledo, Ohio 43620.

Franciscans (Order of Friars Minor),

O.F.M.: A family of the First Order of St. Francis (of Assisi) founded in 1209 and established as a separate jurisdiction in 1517; in U.S., 1844. General headquarters, Rome, Italy. Preaching, missionary, educational, parochial, charitable work.

St. John the Baptist Province (1844), 1615 Vine St., Cincinnati, Ohio 45210.

Sacred Heart Province (1858), 3140 Meramec St., St. Louis, Mo. 63118.

Assumption of the Blessed Virgin Mary Province (1887), Pulaski, Wis. 54162.

Most Holy Name of Jesus Province (1901), 135 W. 31st St., New York, N.Y. 10001.

St. Barbara Province (1915), 1500 34th Ave., Oakland, Calif. 94601.

Immaculate Conception Province (1855), 147 Thompson St., New York, N.Y. 10012.

Holy Cross Custody (1912), 1400 Main St., P.O. Box 608, Lemont, Ill. 60439.

Most Holy Savior Custody, 232 S. Home Ave., Pittsburgh, Pa. 15202.

St. John Capistran Custody (1928), 1290 Hornberger Ave., Roebling, N.J. 08554.

St. Stephen Transylvanian Commissariat (1948), 517 S. Belle Vista Ave., Youngstown, Ohio 44509.

Holy Family Croatian Custody, (1927), 4848 S. Ellis Ave., Chicago, Ill. 60615.

St. Casimir Lithuanian Vicariate, Kennebunkport, Me. 04046.

Holy Gospel Province (Mexico), U.S. foundation, 2400 Marr St., El Paso, Tex. 79903.

Saints Francis and James Province (Jalisco, Mexico), U.S. foundation, 504 E. Santa Clara St., Hebbronville, Tex. 78361.

Commissariat of the Holy Land, Mt. St. Sepulchre, 14th and Quincy Sts. N.E., Washington, D.C. 20017.

St. Mary of the Angels Custody, Byzantine Slavonic Rite, P.O. Box 270, Sybertsville, Pa. 18251.

Academy of American Franciscan History, P.O. Box 34440, West Bethesda, Md. 20817.

Franciscans (Order of Friars Minor Capuchin), O.F.M. Cap.: A family of the First Order of St. Francis (of Assisi) founded in 1209 and established as a separate jurisdiction in 1528. General motherhouse, Rome, Italy. Missionary, parochial work, chaplaincies.

St. Joseph Province (1857), 1740 Mt. Elliott Ave., Detroit, Mich. 48207.

St. Augustine Province (1873), 220 37th St., Pittsburgh, Pa. 15201.

St. Mary Province (1952), 30 Gedney Park Dr., White Plains, N.Y. 10605.

Province of the Stigmata (1918), St. Francis Friary, Box G, Newton, N.J. 07860.

Western American Capuchin Province, Our Lady of the Angels, 1721 Hillside Dr., Burlingame, Calif. 94010.

Sts. Adalbert and Stanislaus Province (Warsaw, Poland), Manor Dr., Oak Ridge, N.J. 07438.

Province of Mid-America (1977), St. Conrad Friary, 2 E. 75th St., Kansas City, Mo. 64114.

Texas Capuchin Fraternity (Province of Navarre, Spain), 5605 Bernal Dr., Dallas, Tex. 75212.

Franciscans (Order of Friars Minor Conventual), O.F.M. Conv.: A family of the First Order of St. Francis (of Assisi) founded in 1209 and established as a separate jurisdiction in 1517; first U.S. foundation, 1852. General curia, Rome, Italy. Missionary, educational, parochial work.

Immaculate Conception Province (1872), P.O. Box 830, Union City, N.J. 07087.

St. Anthony of Padua Province (1905), 1300 Dundalk Ave., Baltimore, Md. 21222.

St. Bonaventure Province (1939), 6107 Kenmore Ave., Chicago, Ill.

Our Lady of Consolation Province (1926), Mt. St. Francis, Ind. 47146.

Our Lady of Guadalupe Custody (vice-province), St. Cecilia Friary, P.O. Box 430, Jal, N. Mex. 88252.

St. Joseph Cupertino Province (1981), P.O. Box 1113, Arroyo Grande, Calif. 93420.

Glenmary Missioners (The Home Missioners of America): Founded 1939, in U.S. General headquarters, Fairfield, Ohio; mailing address, P.O. Box 46404, Cincinnati, Ohio 45246. Home mission work.

Holy Family, Congregation of the Missionaries of the, M.S.F.: Founded 1895, in Holland, by Rev. John P. Berthier. General motherhouse, Rome, Italy; U.S. headquarters, 10415 Midland Blvd., St. Louis, Mo. 63114. Belated vocations for the missions.

Holy Family, Sons of the, S.F.: Founded 1864, at Barcelona, Spain, by Joseph Mananet y Vives; in U.S., 1920. General motherhouse, Barcelona, Spain; U.S. address, 401 Randolph Rd., Silver Spring, Md. 20904.

Holy Ghost Fathers, C.S.Sp.: Founded 1703, in Paris, by Claude Francois Poullart des Places; in U.S., 1872. Generalate, Rome, Italy. Missions, education.

Eastern Province (1872), 6230 Brush Run Rd., Bethel Park, Pa. 15102.

Western Province (1968), 919 Briarcliff, San Antonio, Tex. 78213.

Holy Ghost Fathers of Ireland (1971), U.S. delegate (East), 48-49 37th St., Long Island City, N.Y. 11101.

Holy Spirit, Missionaries of the, M.Sp.S.: Founded 1914, at Mexico City, Mexico, by Felix Rougier. General motherhouse, Mexico City; U.S. headquarters, 1005 Colonia Rd., Oxnard, Calif. 93030. Missionary work.

Jesuits (Society of Jesus), S.J.: Founded 1534, in France, by St. Ignatius of Loyola; received papal approval, 1540; first U.S. province, 1833. Generalate, Rome, Italy. Missionary, educational, literary work.

Maryland Province (1833), 5704 Roland Ave., Baltimore, Md. 21210.

New York Province (1943), 501 E. Fordham Rd., Bronx, N.Y. 10458.

Missouri Province (1823), 4511 W. Pine Blvd., St. Louis, Mo. 63108.

New Orleans Province (1907), 500 S. Jefferson Davis Pkwy., New Orleans, La. 70119.

California Province (1909), College at Prospect Aves., P.O. Box 519, Los Gatos, Calif. 95030.

New England Province (1926), 393 Commonwealth Ave., Boston, Mass. 02115.

Chicago Province, 2058 N. Clark St., Chicago, Ill. 60614.

Oregon Province (1932), 2222 N.W. Hoyt, Portland, Ore. 97210.

Detroit Province (1955), 7303 W. Seven Mile Rd., Detroit, Mich. 48221.

Wisconsin Province (1955), 2120 W. Clybourn St., Suite 200, Milwaukee, Wis. 53233.

Joseph, Congregation of St., C.S.J.: General motherhouse, Rome, Italy; U.S. vice province, 551 W. O'Farrell St., San Pedro, Calif. 90731. Parochial, missionary, educational work.

Joseph, Oblates of St., O.S.J.: Founded 1878, in Italy, by Bishop Joseph Marello. General motherhouse, Rome, Italy. Parochial, educational work.

Eastern Province, 62 W. Oak St., Pittston, Pa. 18640.

Western Province, 544 W. Cliff Dr., Santa Cruz, Calif. 95060.

Josephite Fathers, C.J.: General motherhouse, Ghent, Belgium; U.S. foundation, 989 Brookside Ave., Santa Maria, Calif. 93454.

Josephites (St. Joseph's Society of the Sacred Heart), S.S.J.: Founded 1866, in England, by Cardinal Vaughan; in U.S., 1871. General motherhouse, 1130 N. Calvert St., Baltimore, Md. 21202. Work in Negro missions.

LaSalette, Missionaries of Our Lady of, M.S.: Founded 1852, by Msgr. de Bruillard; in U.S., 1892. Motherhouse, Rome, Italy.

Our Lady of Seven Dolors Province (1933), P.O. Box 6127, Hartford, Conn. 06106.

Immaculate Heart of Mary Province (1945), P.O. Box 538, Attleboro, Mass. 02703.

Mary Queen Province (1958), 4650 S. Broadway, St. Louis, Mo. 63111.

Mary Queen of Peace Vice Province (1967), P.O. Box 95, Georgetown, Ill. 61846.

Legionaries of Christ, L.C.: Founded 1941, in Mexico, by Rev. Marcial Maciel. General headquarters, Rome, Italy; U.S. novitiate, 393 Derby Ave., Orange, Conn. 06477.

Marian Fathers and Brothers, M.I.C.: Founded 1673; U.S. foundation, 1913. General motherhouse, Rome, Italy. Educational, parochial, mission, publication work.

St. Casimir Province (1930), 6336 S. Kilbourn Ave., Chicago, Ill. 60629.

St. Stanislaus Kostka Province (1948), Eden Hill, Stockbridge, Mass. 01262.

Marianists (Society of Mary; Brothers of Mary), S.M.: Founded 1817, at Bordeaux, France, by Rev William-Joseph Chaminade; in U.S., 1849. General motherhouse, Rome, Italy. Educational work.

Cincinnati Province (1849), 4435 E. Patterson Rd., Dayton, Ohio 45430.

St. Louis Province (1908), 4538 Maryland Ave., St. Louis, Mo. 63156.

Pacific Province (1948), P.O. Box AC, Cupertino, Calif. 95015.

New York Province (1961), 4301 Roland Ave., Baltimore, Md. 21210.

Province of Meribah (1976), 240 Emory Rd., Mineola, N.Y. 11501.

Mariannhill, Congregation of the Missionaries of, C.M.M.: Trappist monastery, begun in 1882 by Abbot Francis Pfanner in Natal, South Africa, became an independent modern congregation in 1909; in U.S., 1920. Generalate, Rome, Italy; U.S.-Canadian province, St. Joseph Mission House, Route 1, Center Valley, Pa. 18034. Foreign mission work.

Marist Fathers (Society of Mary), S.M.: Founded 1816, at Lyons, France, by Jean Claude Colin; in U.S., 1863. General motherhouse, Rome, Italy. Educational, foreign mission, pastoral work.

Washington Province (1924), 4408 8th St. N.E., Washington D.C. 20017.

Northeast Province (1924), 72 Beacon St., Chestnut Hill, Mass. 02167.

San Francisco Western Province (1961), 625 Pine St., San Francisco, Calif. 94108.

Mary Immaculate, Missionary Oblates of, O.M.I.: Founded 1816, in France, by Bl. Charles Joseph Eugene de Mazenod; in U.S., 1849. General motherhouse, Rome, Italy. Parochial, foreign mission, educational work; ministry to marginal.

Southern U.S. Province (1904), 7711 Madonna Rd., San Antonio, Tex. 78216.

Our Lady of Hope, Eastern Province (1883), 350 Jamaicaway, Boston, Mass. 02130.

St. John the Baptist Province (1921), 45 Kenwood Ave., Worcester, Mass. 01605.

Central Province (1924), 104 N. Mississippi River Blvd., St. Paul, Minn. 55104.

Western Province (1953), 290 Lenox Ave., Oakland, Calif. 94610.

Italian Province, U.S. foundation, St. Nicholas Church, 442 Brinkerhoff Ave., Palisades Park, N.J. 07650.

Maryknoll (Catholic Foreign Mission Society of America), M.M.: Founded 1911, in U.S., by Frs. Thomas F. Price and James A. Walsh. General Center, Maryknoll, N.Y. 10545.

Mekhitarist Order of Vienna, C.M.Vd.: Established 1773. General headquarters, Vienna, Austria. U.S. addresses: Holy Cross Church, 100 Mt. Auburn St., Cambridge, Mass. 02138; Our Lady Queen of Martyrs Church, 1327 Pleasant Ave., Los Angeles, Calif. 90033. Work among Armenians in U.S..

Mercedarians (Order of Our Lady of Mercy), O. de M.: Founded 1218, in Spain, by St. Peter Nolasco. General motherhouse, Rome, Italy; U.S. headquarters, 8692 Lake St., LeRoy, N.Y. 14482.

Mercy, Congregation of Priests of (Fathers of Mercy), C.P.M.: Founded 1808, in France, by Rev. Jean Baptiste Rauzan; in U.S., 1839. General mission house, Cold Spring, N.Y. 10516. Mission work.

Mill Hill Missionaries (St. Joseph's Society for Foreign Missions), M.H.M.: Founded 1866, in England, by Cardinal Vaughan; in U.S., 1951. General motherhouse, London, England; American headquarters, Albany, N.Y. 12203.

Missionhurst — CICM (Congregation of the Immaculate Heart of Mary): Founded 1862, at Scheut, Brussels, Belgium, by Very Rev. Theophile Verbist. General motherhouse, Rome, Italy; U.S. province, 4651 N. 25th St., Arlington, Va. 22207. Home and foreign mission work.

Missionaries of St. Charles, Congregation of the, C.S.: Founded 1887, at Piacenza, Italy, by Bishop John Baptist Scalabrini. General motherhouse, Rome, Italy.

St. Charles Borromeo Province (1888), 27 Carmine St., New York, N.Y. 10014.

St. John Baptist Province (1903), 546 N. East Ave., Oak Park, Ill. 60302.

Missionaries of the Holy Apostles, M.Ss.A.: Founded 1962, Washington, D.C., by Eusebe M. Menard. North American headquarters, 33 Prospect Hill Rd., Cromwell, Conn. 06416.

Montfort Missionaries (Missionaries of the Company of Mary), S.M.M.: Founded 1715, by St. Louis Marié Grignon de Montfort; in U.S., 1948. General motherhouse, Rome, Italy; U.S. headquarters, 101-18 104th St., Ozone Park, N.Y. 11416. Mission work.

Mother Co-Redemptrix, Congregation of, C.M.C.: Founded 1953 at Lein-Thuy, Vietnam (North), by Fr. Dominic Mary Tran Dinh Thu; in U.S., 1975. General house, Hochiminhville, Vietnam; U.S. provincial house, 1900 Grand Ave., Carthage, Mo. 64836. Work among Vietnamese Catholics in U.S.

Oratorians (Congregation of the Oratory of St. Philip Neri), C.O.: Founded 1575, at Rome, by St. Philip Neri. A confederation of autonomous houses. U.S. addresses: P.O. Box 11586, Rock Hill, S.C. 29730; P.O. Box 1688, Monterey, Calif. 93940; 4040 Bigelow Blvd., Pittsburgh, Pa. 15213; P.O. Box 211, Yarnell, Ariz. 85362; P.O. Drawer II, Pharr, Tex. 78577.

Pallottines (Society of the Catholic Apostolate), S.A.C.: Founded 1835, at Rome, by St. Vincent Pallotti. Generalate, Rome, Italy. Charitable, educational, parochial, mission work.

Immaculate Conception Province (1953), P.O. Box 573, Pennsauken, N.J. 08810.

Mother of God Province (1946), 5424 W. Blue Mound Rd., Milwaukee, Wis. 53208.

Irish Province, U.S. address: 3352 4th St., Wyandotte, Mich. 48192.

Queen of Apostles Province (1909), 448 E. 116th St., New York, N.Y. 10029.

Christ the King Province, 3452 Niagara Falls, Blvd., N. Tonawanda, N.Y. 14120.

Paraclete, Servants of the, s.P.: Founded 1947, Santa Fe, N.M., archdiocese. General motherhouse, Rome, Italy; U.S. motherhouse, Via Coeli, Jemez Springs, N.M. 87025. Devoted to care of priests.

Paris Foreign Missions Society, M.E.P.: Founded 1662, at Paris, France. Headquarters, Paris, France; U.S. establishment, 930 Ashbury St., San Francisco, Calif. 94117. Mission work and training of native clergy.

Passionists (Congregation of the Passion), C.P.: Founded 1720, in Italy, by St. Paul of the Cross. General motherhouse, Rome, Italy.

St. Paul of the Cross Province (1852), 80 David St., South River, N.J. 08882.

Holy Cross Province (Western Province), 5700 N. Harlem Ave., Chicago, Ill. 60631.

Patrick's Missionary Society, St., S.P.S.: Founded 1932, at Wicklow, Ireland, by Msgr. Patrick Whitney; in U.S., 1953. International headquarters, Kiltegan Co., Wicklow, Ireland. U.S. foundations: 70 Edgewater Rd., Cliffside Park, N.J. 07010; 19536 Eric Dr., Saratoga, Calif. 95070; 1347 W. Granville Ave., Chicago, Ill. 60660.

Pauline Fathers (Order of St. Paul the First Hermit), O.S.P.: Founded 1215; established in U.S., 1955. General motherhouse, Czestochowa, Jasna Gora, Poland; U.S. headquarters, P.O. Box 151, Doylestown, Pa. 18901.

Pauline Fathers and Brothers (Society of St. Paul for the Apostolate of Communications), S.S.P.: Founded 1914, by Very Rev. James Alberione; in U.S., 1932. Motherhouse, Rome, Italy; American province, 6746 Lake Shore Rd., Derby, N.Y. 14047. Social communications work.

Paulists (Missionary Society of St. Paul the Apostle), C.S.P.: Founded 1858, in New York, by Fr. Isaac Thomas Hecker. General offices, 86 Dromore Rd., Scarsdale, N.Y. 10583. Missionary, ecumenical, pastoral work.

Penitents, Order of, of St. Francis of Assisi, O. Pent.: Holy Trinity Monastery, Dunhampton Rd., Palmer, Mass. 01069.

Piarists (Order of the Pious Schools), Sch.P.: Founded 1617, at Rome, Italy, by St.

Joseph Calasanctius. General motherhouse, Rome, Italy. American province, 1339 Monroe St. N.E., Washington, D.C. 20017; New York-Puerto Rico vice-province (Calasanzian Fathers), 88 Convent Ave., New York, N.Y. 10027. Educational work.

Pontifical Institute for Foreign Missions, P.I.M.E.: Founded 1850, in Italy, at request of Pope Pius IX. General motherhouse, Rome, Italy; U.S. headquarters,17330 Quincy Ave., Detroit, Mich. 48221. Foreign mission work.

Precious Blood, Society of, C.Pp.S.: Founded 1815, in Italy, by St. Gaspar del Bufalo. General motherhouse, Rome, Italy.

Cincinnati Province, 431 E. Second St., Dayton, O. 45402.

Kansas City Province, Ruth Ewing Rd., Liberty, Mo. 64068.

Pacific Province, 1427 Sixth St., Alameda, Calif. 94501.

Atlantic Vicariate, 381 Robbins Ave., Niles, O. 44446.

Premonstratensians (Order of the Canons Regular of Premontre; Norbertines), O. Praem.: Founded 1120, at Premontre, France, by St. Norbert. Generalate, Rome, Italy. Educational, parish work.

St. Norbert Abbey, 1016 N. Broadway, De-Pere, Wis. 54115.

Daylesford Abbey, 220 S. Valley Rd., Paoli, Pa. 19301.

St. Michael's Priory, 1042 Star Route, Orange, Calif. 92667.

Providence, Sons of Divine, F.D.P.: Founded 1893, at Tortona, Italy, by Bl. Luigi Orione; in U.S., 1933. General motherhouse, Tortona, Italy; U.S. address, 111 Orient Ave., E. Boston, Mass. 02128.

Redemptorists (Congregation of the Most Holy Redeemer), C.SS.R.: Founded 1732, in Italy, by St. Alphonsus Mary Liguori. Generalate, Rome, Italy. Mission work.

Baltimore Province (1850), 7509 Shore Rd., Brooklyn, N.Y. 11209.

St. Louis Province (1875), Box 6, Glenview, Ill. 60025.

Oakland Province (1952), 3696 Clay St., San Francisco, Calif. 94118.

New Orleans Vice-Province, 1527 3rd St., New Orleans, La., 70130.

Resurrectionists (Priests of the Congregation of the Resurrection), C.R.: Founded 1836, in France, under direction of Bogdan Janski. Motherhouse, Rome, Italy;

Chicago Province, 2250 N. Latrobe Ave., Chicago, Ill. 60639.

Ontario Kentucky Province, Resurrection College, Westmont Rd., N., Waterloo, Ont. N2L 3G7, Canada.

Rogationist Fathers, R.C.J.: Founded 1926. General motherhouse, Rome, Italy. U.S. addresses: P.O. Box 248, Mendota, Calif. 93640; P.O. Box 335, Sanger, Calif. 93657.

Rosminians (Institute of Charity), I.C.:

Founded 1828, in Italy, by Antonio Rosmini-Serbati. General motherhouse, Rome, Italy; U.S. address, 2327 W. Heading Ave., Peoria, Ill. 61604. Charitable work.

Sacerdotal Fraternity, Congregation of the, C.F.S.: Founded 1901, at Paris, France. General house, 500 Ave. Claremont, Montreal (Westmount), Que. H3Y 2N5 Canada. Care of priests.

Sacred Heart, Missionaries of the, M.S.C.: Founded 1854, by Rev. Jules Chevelier. General motherhouse, Rome, Italy; U.S. province, 305 S. Lake St., P.O. Box 270, Aurora, Ill. 60507.

Sacred Heart of Jesus, Congregation of the (Sacred Heart Fathers and Brothers), S.C.J.: Founded 1877, in France. General motherhouse, Rome, Italy; U.S. headquarters, Sacred Heart Monastery, Hales Corners, Wis. 53130. Educational, preaching, mission work.

Sacred Hearts, Fathers of the (Picpus Fathers), SS.CC.: Founded 1805, in France, by Fr. Coudrin. General motherhouse, Rome, Italy. Mission, educational work.

Eastern Province (1946), 3 Adams St. (Box 111), Fairhaven, Mass. 02719.

Western Province (1970), 32481 Sage Rd., Hemet, Calif. 92343.

Hawaiian Province, Box 797, Kaneohe, Oahu, Hawaii 96744.

Sacred Hearts of Jesus and Mary, Missionaries of the, M.SS.CC.: Founded at Naples, Italy, by Ven. Cajetan Errico. General motherhouse, Rome, Italy; U.S. headquarters, 2249 Shore Rd., Linwood, N.J. 08221.

Salesians of St. John Bosco (Society of St. Francis de Sales), S.D.B.: Founded 1859, by St. John (Don) Bosco. General motherhouse, Rome, Italy.

St. Philip the Apostle Province (1902), 148 Main St., New Rochelle, N.Y. 10802.

San Francisco Province (1926), 1100 Franklin St., San Francisco, Calif. 94109.

Salvatorians (Society of the Divine Savior), S.D.S.: Founded 1881, in Rome, by Fr. Francis Jordan; in U.S., 1896. General headquarters, Rome, Italy; U.S. province, 1735 Hi-Mount Blvd., Milwaukee, Wis. 53208. Educational, parochial, mission work; campus ministries, chaplaincies.

Scalabrinians: See Missionaries of St. Charles, Congregation of the.

Servites (Order of Friar Servants of Mary), O.S.M.: Founded 1233, at Florence, Italy, by Seven Holy Founders. Generalate, Rome, Italy. General apostolic ministry.

Eastern Province (1967) 3401 S. Home Ave., Berwyn, Ill. 60402.

Western Province (1967), 5210 Somerset St., Buena Park, Calif. 90621.

Somascan Fathers, C.R.S.: Founded 1534, at Somasca, Italy, by St. Jerome Emiliani. General motherhouse, Rome, Italy; U.S. addresses: 628 Hanover St., Manchester, N.H.

03104; Pine Haven Boys Center, River Rd., Allenstown, P.O. Suncook, N.H. 03275; Allenbrook Home for Boys, Allen Rd., S. Burlington, Vt. 05401.

Sons of Mary Missionary Society (Sons of Mary, Health of the Sick), F.M.S.I.: Founded 1952, in the Boston archdiocese, by Rev. Edward F. Garesche, S.J. Headquarters, 567 Salem End Rd., Framingham, Mass. 01701. Dedicated to health of the sick; medical, catechetical and social work in home and foreign missions.

Stigmatine Fathers and Brothers (Congregation of the Sacred Stigmata), C.S.S.: Founded 1816, by Bl. Gaspare Bertoni. General motherhouse, Rome, Italy; U.S. headquarters, 36 Fairmont Ave., Newton, Mass. 02158. Parish work.

Sulpicians (Society of Priests of St. Sulpice), S.S.: Founded 1641, at Paris, by Rev. Jean Jacques Olier. General motherhouse, Paris, France; U.S. province, 5408 Roland Ave., Baltimore, Md. 21210. Education of seminarians and priests.

Theatines (Congregation of Clerics Regular): C.R.: Founded 1524, at Rome, by St. Cajetan. General motherhouse, Rome, Italy; U.S. headquarters, 1050 S. Birch St., Denver, Colo. 80222.

Trappists: See Cistercians of the Strict Observance.

Trinitarians (Order of the Most Holy Trinity), O.SS.T.: Founded 1198, by St. John of Matha. General motherhouse, Rome, Italy; U.S. headquarters, P.O. Box 5719, Baltimore, Md. 21208.

Trinity, Missionary Servants of the Most Holy, S.T.: Founded 1929, by Fr. Thomas Augustine Judge. Generalate, 1215 N. Scott St., Arlington, Va. 22209. Home mission work.

Viatorian Fathers (Clerics of St. Viator), C.S.V.: Founded 1831, in France, by Fr. Louis Joseph Querbes. General motherhouse, Rome, Italy: U.S. headquarters, 1212 E. Euclid St., Arlington Hts., Ill. 60004. Educational work.

Vincentians (Congregation of the Mission; Lazarists), C.M.: Founded 1625, in Paris, by St. Vincent de Paul; in U.S., 1817. General motherhouse, Rome, Italy. Educational work.

Eastern Province (1867), 500 E. Chelten Ave., Philadelphia, Pa. 19144.

Midwest Province (1888), 1723 Pennsylvania Ave., St. Louis, Mo. 63104.

New England Province (1975), 1109 Prospect Ave., W. Hartford, Conn. 06105.

American Italian Branch, Our Lady of Pompei Church, 3600 Claremont St., Baltimore, Md. 21224.

American Spanish Branch (Barcelona, Spain), 134 Vernon Ave., Brooklyn, N.Y. 11206.

American Spanish Branch (Zaragoza, Spain), Holy Agony Church, 1834 3rd Ave., New York, N.Y. 10029.

Western Province (1975), 649 W. Adams Blvd., Los Angeles, Calif. 90007.

Southern Province (1975), 1302 Kipling St., Houston, Tex. 77006.

Vocationist Fathers (Society of Divine Vocations), S.D.V.: Founded 1920, in Italy; in U.S., 1962. General motherhouse, Naples, Italy; U.S. address, 170 Broad St., Newark, N.J. 07104.

White Fathers of Africa (Society of Missionaries of Africa), W.F.: Founded 1868, at Algiers, by Cardinal C.M.A. Lavigerie. Generalate, Rome, Italy; U.S. headquarters, 1624 21st St. N.W., Washington, D.C. 20009. Missionary work in Africa.

Xaverian Missionary Fathers, S.X.: Founded 1895, by Archbishop Conforti, at Parma, Italy. General motherhouse, Rome, Italy; U.S. province, 12 Helene Ct., Wayne, N.J. 07470. Foreign mission work.

INSTITUTES OF BROTHERS

Alexian Brothers, C.F.A.: Founded 14th century in western Germany and Belgium during the Black Plague. Motherhouse, Aachen, Germany; generalate, Signal Mountain, Tenn. 37377. Hospital and general health work.

Carmelite Brothers of the Holy Eucharist, C.F.S.E.: Founded 1975 by Bro. Aloysius Scafidi. Motherhouse, 2264 Marshall Ave., Elm Grove, Wheeling, W. Va. 26003. Educational, clerical, social, nursing work.

Charity, Brothers of, F.C.: Founded 1807, in Belgium, by Canon Peter J. Triest. General motherhouse, Rome, Italy: American District, 1008 N. 70th Ave., Philadelphia, Pa. 19126. Charitable, educational work.

Charity, Missionary Brothers of, M.C.: Founded 1963. U.S. address, 235 Winston St., Los Angeles, Calif. 90013. Work among poor and outcast.

Christian Brothers, Congregation of, C.F.C. (formerly Christian Brothers of Ireland): Founded 1802 at Waterford, Ireland, by Edmund Ignatius Rice. General motherhouse, Rome, Italy. Educational work.

American Province, Eastern U.S. (1916), 21 Pryer Terr., New Rochelle, N.Y. 10804. 354.

American Province, Western U.S. (1966), P.O. Box 85R, Romeoville, Ill. 60441.

Christian Instruction, Brothers of (La Mennais Brothers), F.I.C.: Founded 1817, at Ploermel, France, by Abbe Jean Marie de la Mennais and Abbe Gabriel Deshayes. General motherhouse, Rome, Italy; American province, Notre Dame Institute, Alfred, Me. 04002.

Christian Schools, Brothers of the (Christian Brothers), F.S.C.: Founded 1680, at Reims, France, by St. Jean Baptiste de la Salle. General motherhouse, Rome, Italy; U.S. Conference, 100 De La Salle Dr., Romeoville, Ill. 60441. Educational, charitable work.

Baltimore Province (1845), Box 29, Adamstown, Md. 21710.

Chicago Province (1966), 200 De La Salle Dr., Romeoville, Ill. 60441.

New York Province (1848), 820 Newman Springs Rd., Lincroft, N.J. 07738.

Long Island-New England Province (1957), Christian Brothers Center, 635 Ocean Ave., Narragansett, R.I. 02882.

St. Louis Province (1849), 1886 Rue de la Salle, Glencoe, Mo. 63038.

San Francisco Province (1868), P.O. Box A-D, Saint Mary's College, Moraga, Calif. 94575.

New Orleans-Santa Fe Province (1921), De La Salle Christian Brothers, 1522 Breaux Bridge Rd., Lafayette, La. 70501.

Winona Province (1963), 807 Summit Ave., St. Paul, Minn. 55105.

Cross, Congregation of Holy, C.S.C.: Founded 1837, in France, by Rev. Basil Moreau; U.S. province, 1841. Generalate, Rome, Italy. Educational, social work; missions.

Midwest Province (1841), Box 460, Notre Dame, Ind. 46556.

Southwest Province (1956), St. Edward's University, Austin, Tex. 78704.

Eastern Province (1956), 85 Overlook Circle, New Rochelle, N.Y. 10804.

Francis, Brothers of Poor of St., C.F.P.: Founded 1857. Motherhouse, Aachen, Germany; U.S. province, 6942 Windward St., Cincinnati, Ohio. 45227. Educational work, especially with poor and emotionally disturbed youth.

Francis Xavier, Brothers of St. (Xaverian Brothers), C.F.X.: Founded 1839, in Belgium, by Theodore J. Ryken. Generalate, Rome, Italy. Educational work.

Sacred Heart Province, 10516 Summit Ave., Kensington, Md. 20895.

St. Joseph Province, 704 Brush Hill Rd., Milton, Mass. 02186.

Franciscan Brothers of Brooklyn, O.S.F.: Founded in Ireland; established at Brooklyn, 1858. Generalate, 135 Remsen St., Brooklyn, N.Y. 11201. Educational work.

Franciscan Brothers of Christ the King, O.S.F.: Founded 1961. General motherhouse, 1310 W. Pleasant St., Davenport, Ia. 52808.

Franciscan Brothers of the Good News, O.S.F.: Founded 1970 in Archdiocese of New York. Central friary, Mount Road, Cummington, Mass. 01026. Combine volunteer works of mercy with contemplative life of prayer in hermitages.

Franciscan Brothers of the Holy Cross, F.F.S.C.: Founded 1862, in Germany. Generalate, Hausen, Linz Rhein, West Germany; U.S. region, R.R. 1, Springfield, Ill. 62707. Educational work.

Franciscan Missionary Brothers of the Sacred Heart of Jesus, O.S.F.: Founded 1927, in the St. Louis, Mo., archdiocese. Motherhouse, R.R. 3, Box 39, Eureka, Mo. 63025. Care of aged, infirm, homeless men and boys.

Good Shepherd, Society of Brothers of the, B.G.S.: Founded 1951, by Bro. Mathias Barrett. Motherhouse, P.O. Box 389, Albuquerque, N.M. 87102. Operate shelters and refuges for aged and homeless; homes for handicapped men and boys, alcoholic rehabilitation center.

Guadalupe, Brothers of Our Lady of, H.N.S.G.: Founded 1974 in Gallup, N. Mex., by Bishop Jerome Hastrich. Motherhouse, 500 S. Woodrow Dr., Gallup, N. Mex. 87301. Team ministry apostolate.

Holy Eucharist, Brothers of the, F.S.E.: Founded in U.S., 1957. Generalate, P.O. Box 25, Plaucheville, La. 71362. Teaching, social, clerical, nursing work.

Immaculate Heart of Mary, Brothers of the, F.I.C.M.: Founded 1948, at Steubenville, Ohio, by Bishop John K. Mussio. Motherhouse, Villa Maria, 609 N. 7th St., Steubenville, Ohio 43952. Educational, charitable work.

John of God, Brothers of the Hospitaller Order of St., O.H.: Founded 1537, in Spain. General motherhouse, Rome, Italy; American province, 2425 S. Western Ave., Los Angeles, Calif. 90018; Irish Province of Immaculate Conception, 532 Delsea Dr., Westville Grove, N.J. 08093. Nursing work and related fields.

Little Brothers of Jesus: Generalate, London, England; U.S. foundation, 2833 Cochrane, Detroit, Mich. 48216.

Little Brothers of St. Francis, O.S.F.: Founded 1970 in Archdiocese of Boston. General fraternity, 789 Parker St., Mission Hill (Boston), Mass. 02120. Combine contemplative life with evangelical street ministry

Marist Brothers, F.M.S.: Founded 1817, in France, by Bl. Marcellin Champagnat. General motherhouse, Rome, Italy; U.S. address, 1241 Kennedy Blvd., Bayonne, N.J. 07002. Educational, social, catechetical work.

Mercy, Brothers of, F.M.M.: Founded 1856, in Germany. General motherhouse, Montabaur, Germany. American headquarters, 4520 Ransom Rd., Clarence, N.Y. 14031. Hospital work.

Mercy, Brothers of Our Lady of, C.F.M.M.: Founded 1844, in The Netherlands by Abp. J. Zwijsen. Generalate, Tilburg, The Netherlands; U.S. region, 2336 South "C" St., Oxnard, Calif. 93030.

Patrician Brothers (Brothers of St. Patrick), F.S.P.: Founded 1808, in Ireland, by Bishop Daniel Delaney; U.S. novitiate, 7820 Bolsa Ave., Midway City, Calif. 92655. Educational work.

Pius X, Brothers of St.: Founded 1952, at La Crosse, Wis., by Bishop John P. Treacy.

Motherhouse, 208 S. 15th St., La Crosse, Wis. 54601. Education.

Presentation Brothers, F.P.M.: Founded 1802, at Waterford, Ireland, by Edmund Ignatius Rice. General motherhouse, Cork, Ireland. U.S. foundation (Canadian Province), 368 S. Ellsworth, Marshall, Mo. 65340.

Rosary, Brothers of the Holy, F.S.R.: Founded 1956, in US. Motherhouse and novitiate, 101 Boynton Lane, Reno, Nev. 89502.

Sacred Heart, Brothers of the, S.C.: Founded 1821, in France, by Rev. Andre Coindre. General motherhouse, Rome, Italy, Educational work.

New Orleans Province (1847), P.O. Box 89, Bay St. Louis, Miss. 39520.

New England Province (1945), Rt. 98, R.R. 1, Pascoag, R.I. 02859.

New York Province (1960), P.O. Box 68, Beividere, N.J. 07823.

MEMBERSHIP OF RELIGIOUS INSTITUTES OF MEN

(Principal source: *Annuario Pontificio*. Statistics as of Jan. 1, 1981, unless indicated otherwise.)

Listed below are world membership statistics of institutes of men of pontifical right with 500 or more members; the number of priests is in parentheses. Also listed are institutes with less than 500 members with houses in the United States.

Jesuits (19,845)	26,905
Franciscans (Friars Minor) (14,229)	20,337
Salesians (11,079)	16,915
Franciscans (Capuchins) (8,602)	11,944
Brothers of Christian Schools	10,238
Benedictines (6,063)	9,683
Dominicans (5,546)	7,164
Marist Brothers	6,843
Redemptorists (4,928)	6,593
Oblates of Mary Immaculate (4,600)	5,923
Society of the Divine Word (3,271)	5,290
Vincentians (3,612)	4,062
Franciscans (Conventuals) (2,707)	4,037
Holy Spirit, Congregation (3,049)	3,863
Augustinians (2,705)	3,533
Discalced Carmelties (2,365)	3,287
Passionists (2,343)	3,052
Trappists (1,477)	3,045
White Fathers (2,599)	2,992
Claretians (1,956)	2,905
Christian Brothers	2,801
Priests of the Sacred Heart (1,913)	2,713
Missionaries of the Sacred Heart of Jesus (1,855)	2,536
Pallottines (1,470)	2,197
Marianists (618)	2,084
Holy Cross, Congregation (939)	2,073
Brothers of the Sacred Heart (51)	2,042
Carmelites (Ancient Observance) (1,560)	1,993
Marists (1,548)	1,930
Combonian Missionaries of the Heart of Jesus (1,284)	1,835
Hospitallers of St. John of God (116)	1,721
Piarists (1,344)	1,683
Brothers of Christian Instruction	1,588
Congregation of the Immaculate Heart of Mary (1,304)	1,555
Sacred Hearts, Congregation (Picpus) (1,218)	1,468
Brothers of Christian Instruction of St. Gabriel *(1976)* (22)	1,434
Society of African Missions (1,226)	1,399

Cistercians (Common Observance) (891)	1,398
Montfort Missionaries (1,056)	1,392
Blessed Sacrament, Congr. of (813)	1,304
Augustinians (Recollects) (988)	1,264
Assumptionists (1,036)	1,245
Premonstratensians *(1980)* (1,011)	1,241
Servants of Mary (946)	1,238
Salvatorians (835)	1,231
Society of St. Paul (566)	1,197
Viatorians (452)	1,142
Little Workers of Divine Providence (756)	1,069
Missionaries of Holy Family (748)	1,057
Consolata Missionaries (849)	1,046
Ministers of Sick (670)	1,017
Mill Hill Missionaries (853)	968
Oblates of St. Francis de Sales (716)	933
Maryknollers (761)	927
Columbans (852)	912
Brothers of Charity	909
LaSalette Missionaries (644)	897
Xaverian-Missionaries (653)	858
Franciscans (Third Order Regular) (608)	853
Canons Regular of St. Augustine (702)	851
Legionaries of Christ (140)	794
Missionaries of the Most Precious Blood (589)	740
Scalabrinians (599)	736
Mercedarians (536)	731
Congregation of St. Joseph (565)	730
Brothers of the Immaculate Conception (5)	673
Pontifical Institute for Foreign Missions (605)	666
Brothers of Our Lady of Mercy	611
Paris Foreign Mission Society (597)	599
Trinitarians (390)	597
Crosier Fathers and Brothers (443)	583
Sulpicians (543)	543
Eudists (450)	519
Congr. of St. Basil (Canada) (416)	507
Missionaries of St. Francis de Sales of Annecy (322)	503
Servants of Charity (371)	497
Brothers of Our Lady of Lourdes	470
Barnabites (377)	468
Oratorians *(1979)* (351)	468
Xaverian Brothers	463
Mariannhill Missionaries (273)	458

RELIGIOUS INSTITUTES OF WOMEN IN THE UNITED STATES

(Sources: Catholic Almanac survey; *Official Catholic Directory.*)

Africa, Missionary Sisters of Our Lady of (Sisters of Africa), S.A.: Founded 1869, at Algiers, Algeria, by Cardinal Lavigerie; in US, 1929. General motherhouse, Frascati, Italy; US headquarters, 5335 16th St., N.W., Washington, D.C. 20011. Medical, educational, catechetical and social work in Africa.

Agnes, Sisters of St., C.S.A.: Founded 1858, in US, by Caspar Rehrl. General motherhouse, 475 Gillett St., Fond du Lac, Wis. 54935. Education, health care, social services.

Ann, Sisters of St., S.S.A.: Founded 1834, in Italy; in US, 1952. General motherhouse, Rome, Italy; US headquarters, Mount St. Ann, Ebensburg, Pa. 15931.

Anne, Sisters of St., S.S.A.: Founded 1850, at Vaudreuil, Que., Canada; in US, 1866. General motherhouse, Lachine, Que., Canada; US address, 720 Boston Post Rd., Marlboro, Mass. 01752. Retreat work, pastoral ministry, religious education.

Anthony, Missionary Servants of St., M.S.S.A.: Founded 1929, in US, by Rev. Peter Baque. General motherhouse, 100 Peter Baque Rd., San Antonio, Tex. 78209. Social work.

Apostolate, Sisters Auxiliaries of the, A.A.: Founded 1903, in Canada; in US, 1911. General motherhouse, 689 Maple Terr., Monongah, W. Va. 26554. Education, nursing.

Assumption, Little Sisters of the, L.S.A.: Founded 1865, in France; in US, 1891. General motherhouse, Paris, France; US provincialate, 1195 Lexington Ave., New York, N.Y. 10028. Social work, nursing, family life education.

Assumption, Religious of the, R.A.: Founded 1839, in France; in US, 1919. General motherhouse, Paris, France; US province, 227 N. Bowman Ave., Merion, Pa. 19066. Educational work.

Assumption of the Blessed Virgin, Sisters of the, S.A.S.V.: Founded 1853, in Canada; in US, 1891. General motherhouse, Nicolet, Que., Canada; American province, North Main St., Box 128, Petersham, Mass. 01366. Education, mission, pastoral ministry.

Basil the Great, Sisters of St. (Pittsburgh Byzantine Rite), O.S.B.M.: Founded fourth century, by St. Basil the Great. Motherhouse, Mount St. Macrina. 500 W. Main St., Uniontown, Pa. 15401. Education, health care.

Basil the Great, Sisters of the Order of St. (Ukrainian Byzantine Rite), O.S.B.M.: Founded fourth century, in Cappadocia, by St. Basil the Great; in US, 1911. Generalate, Rome, Italy; US motherhouse, 710 Fox Chase Rd., Philadelphia, Pa. 19111. Education.

Benedict, Sisters of the Order of St., O.S.B.: Our Lady of Mount Caritas Monastery (founded 1979, Ashford, Conn.), RR No. 2 Seckar Rd., West Willington, Conn. 06279. Contemplative.

Benedict, Sisters of the Order of St. (of the Congregation of Solesmes), O.S.B.: U.S. establishment, 1981, in Burlington diocese. Monastery of the Immaculate Heart of Mary, Westfield, Vt. 05874. Cloistered, papal enclosure.

Benedictine Nuns of the Primitive Observance, O.S.B.: Founded c. 529, in Italy; in US, 1948. Abbey of Regina Laudis, Flanders Rd., Bethlehem, Conn. 06751. Cloistered.

Benedictine Sisters, O.S.B.: Founded c. 529, in Italy; in US, 1852. General motherhouse, Eichstatt, Bavaria, Germany. US addresses: St. Vincent's Archabbey, Latrobe, Pa. 15650; St. Emma's Retreat House and

Convent, 1001 Harvey St., Greensburg, Pa. 15601; St. Walburga Convent, 6717 S. Boulder Rd., Boulder, Colo. 80302.

Benedictine Sisters (Bedford, N.H.), O.S.B.: Founded 1627, in Lithuania as cloistered community; reformed 1918 as active community; established in US 1957, by Mother M. Raphaela Simonis. Regina Pacis, 333 Wallace Rd., Bedford, N.H. 03102.

Benedictine Sisters, Missionary, O.S.B.: Founded 1885. Generalate, Rome, Italy; US motherhouse, 300 N. 18th St., Norfolk, Nebr. 68701.

Benedictine Sisters, Olivetan, O.S.B.: Founded 1887, in US. General motherhouse, Holy Angels Convent, Jonesboro, Ark. 72401. Educational, hospital work.

Benedictine Sisters of Perpetual Adoration of Pontifical Jurisdiction, Congregation of the, O.S.B.: Founded in US, 1874, from Maria Rickenbach, Switzerland. General motherhouse, 8300 Morganford Rd., St. Louis, Mo. 63123.

Benedictine Sisters of Pontifical Jurisdiction, O.S.B.: Founded c. 529, in Italy. No general motherhouse in US. Three federations.

• Federation of St. Scholastica (1922). Pres., Sister Johnette Putnam, O.S.B., St. Scholastica Priory, Box 1118, Covington, La. 70433. Motherhouses belonging to the federation:

Emmanuel Priory, 8080 New Cut Rd., Severn, Md. 21144; Mt. St. Scholastica, Atchison, Kans. 66002; Benedictine Sisters of Elk Co., St. Joseph's Convent, St. Mary's, Pa. 15857; Mt. St. Benedict Priory, 6101 E. Lake Rd., Erie, Pa. 16511; Benedictine Sisters of Chicago, St. Scholastica Priory, 7430 Ridge Blvd., Chicago, Ill. 60645; Benedictine Convent of the Sacred Heart, 1910 Maple Ave., Lisle, Ill. 60532; Our Lady of Sorrows Convent, 5900 W. 147th St., Oak Forest, Ill. 60452; St. Walburga Convent, 851 N. Broad St., Elizabeth, N.J. 07208; Benedictine Sisters, Mt. St. Mary Priory, 4530 Perrysville Ave., Pittsburgh, Pa. 15229;

Red Plains Priory, P.O. Box 60165, Oklahoma City, Okla. 73146; St. Joseph's Convent, 2200 S. Lewis, Tulsa, Okla. 74114; St. Gertrude's Priory, Ridgely P.O., Md. 21660; St. Walburga Convent, Villa Madonna, 2500 Amsterdam Rd., Covington, Ky. 41016; Sacred Heart Convent, Cullman, Ala. 35055; St. Scholastica Priory, Stafford Rd., Covington, La. 70433; Holy Family Convent, Benet Lake, Wis. 53102; St. Benedict's Convent, Bristow, Va. 22013; St. Scholastica Convent, P.O. Box 700, Boerne, Tex. 78006; St. Lucy's Priory, Glendora, Calif. 91740; Holy Name Priory, St. Leo, Fla. 33574; Benet Hill Priory, 25555 N. Chelton Rd., Colorado Springs, Colo. 80909; Queen of Heaven Convent (Byzantine Rite), 8640 Squires Lane N.E., Warren, O. 44484.

• Federation of St. Gertrude the Great (1937). Pres., Sister Anselm Hammerling, O.S.B., St. Benedict Priory, 225 Masters Ave., RR 1, Winnipeg, Man. R3C 4A3, Canada. Motherhouses belonging to the federation:

Mother of God Priory, Watertown, S. Dak. 57201; Sacred Heart Convent, Yankton, S. Dak. 57078; Mt. St. Benedict Convent, Crookston, Minn. 56716; Sacred Heart Priory, Richardton, N. Dak. 58652; St. Martin's Priory of the Black Hills, R.R. 4, Box 253, Rapid City, S. Dak. 57701; Convent of the Immaculate Conception, 802 E. 10th St., Ferdinand, Ind. 47532; Priory of St. Gertrude, Cottonwood, Ida. 83522;

St. Benedict Priory, Fox Bluff, Box 5070, Madison, Wis. 53705; Queen of Angels Priory, Mt. Angel, Ore. 97362; St. Scholastica's Convent, Albert Pike and Rogers Ave., Fort Smith, Ark. 72913; Our Lady of Peace Convent, 1511 Wilson, Columbia, Mo. 65201; Queen of Peace Priory, 701 Rolla, Belcourt, N. Dak. 58316. Convent of Our Lady of Grace, Beech Grove, Ind. 46107; Holy Spirit Convent, 9725 Pigeon Pass Rd., Sunnymead, Calif. 92388; St. Benedict's Priory, Winnipeg, Manitoba, R3C 4A3, Canada.

• Federation of St. Benedict (1947). Pres., Sister Margaret Michaud, O.S.B., St. Bede Priory, Eau Claire, Wis. 54702. Motherhouses belonging to the federation:

St. Benedict's Convent, St. Joseph, Minn. 56374; St. Scholastica Priory, Kenwood Ave., Duluth, Minn. 55811; St. Bede Priory, Priory Rd., Eau Claire, Wis. 54702; St. Mary Priory, Nauvoo, Ill. 62354; Annunciation, Priory, Apple Creek Rd., Bismarck, N. Dak. 58501; St. Paul's Priory, 2675 Larpenteur Ave. E., St. Paul, Minn. 55109; St. Placid Priory, 4600 Martin Way, Olympia, Wash. 98506.

Bethany, Sisters of, C.V.D.: Founded 1928, in El Salvador; in US 1949. General motherhouse, Santa Tecla, El Salvador. US address: 850 N. Hobart Blvd., Los Angeles, Calif. 90029.

Bethlemita Sisters, Daughters of the Sacred Heart of Jesus, S.C.I.F.: Founded 1861, in Guatemala. Motherhouse, Bogota, Colombia; US address, St. Joseph Residence, 330 W. Pembroke St., Dallas, Tex. 75208.

Blessed Virgin Mary, Institute of the (Loreto Sisters), I.B.V.M.: Founded 17th century in Belgium; in US, 1954. Motherhouse, Rathfarnham, Dublin, Ireland; US addresses: 6351 N. 27th Ave., Phoenix, Ariz. 85017; 810 Patrick Lane, Prescott, Ariz. 86301; 202 S. Kendrick, Flagstaff, Ariz. 86001.

Blessed Virgin Mary, Institute of the (Loretto Sisters), I.B.V.M.: Founded 1609, in Belgium; in US, 1880. US address, Loretto Convent, Box 508, Wheaton, Ill. 60187. Educational work.

Bon Secours, Sisters of, C.B.S.: Founded 1824, in France; in US, 1881. Generalate, Rome, Italy; US provincial house, Marriottsville Rd., Marriottsville, Md. 21104. Hospital work.

Brigid, Congregation of St., C.S.B.: Founded 1807, in Ireland; in US, 1953. US regional house, 5118 Loma Linda Dr., San Antonio, Tex. 78201.

Brigittine Sisters (Order of the Most Holy Savior), O.SS.S.: Founded 1344, at Vadstena, Sweden, by St. Bridget; in US, 1957. General motherhouse, Rome, Italy; US address,· Vikingsborg, Darien, Conn. 06820.

Carmel, Congregation of Our Lady of Mount, O. Carm.: Founded 1825, in France; in US, 1833. General motherhouse, P.O. Box 476, Lacombe, La. 70445. Education, social services, pastoral ministry, retreat work.

Carmel, Institute of Our Lady of Mount, O. Carm.: Founded 1854, in Italy; in US, 1947. General motherhouse, Rome, Italy; US novitiate, 5 Wheatland St., Peabody, Mass. 01960. Apostolic work.

Carmel Community, C.C.: Founded 1975, Columbus, O. Address, 2065 Barton Pl., Columbus, O. 43209. Contemplative.

Carmelite Missionaries of St. Theresa, C.M.S.T.: Founded 1903, in Mexico. General motherhouse, Mexico City, Mexico; US foundation, 9600 Deertrail Rd., Houston, Tex. 77003.

Carmelite Sisters (Corpus Christi), O. Carm.: Founded 1908, in England; in US, 1920. General motherhouse, Tunapuna, Trinidad, W.I. US addresses: Carmelite Retreat House, 21 Battery St., Newport, R.I. 02840; Mt. Carmel Home, 412 W. 18th St., Kearney, Nebr. 68847; Carmelite Sisters, 765 W. 18th St., Eugene, Ore. 97405. Home and foreign mission work.

Carmelite Sisters for the Aged and Infirm, O. Carm.: Founded 1929, at New York, by Mother M. Angeline Teresa, O. Carm. Motherhouse, Avila-on-Hudson, Germantown, N.Y. 12526. Social work, nursing and educating in the field of gerontology.

Carmelite Sisters of Charity, C.a.Ch.: Founded 1826 at Vich, Spain, by St. Joaquina de Vedruna. General motherhouse, Rome, Italy; US address, 4200 16th St. N.W., Washington, D.C. 20011.

Carmelite Sisters of St. Therese of the Infant Jesus, C.S.T.: Founded 1917, in US. General motherhouse, 1300 Classen Dr., Oklahoma City, Okla. 73103. Educational work.

Carmelite Sisters of the Divine Heart of Jesus, D.C.J.: Founded 1891, in Germany; in US, 1912. General motherhouse, Sittard, Netherlands. US provincial houses: 1230 Kavanaugh Pl., Milwaukee, Wis. 52313 (Northern Province); 10341 Manchester Rd., St. Louis, Mo. 63122 (Central Province); 8585 La Mesa Blvd., La Mesa, Calif. 92041 (South Western Province). Social services, mission work.

Carmelite Sisters of the Sacred Heart, O.C.D.: Founded 1904, in Mexico. General motherhouse, Guadalajara, Mexico; US provincialate and novitiate, 920 E. Alhambra Rd., Alhambra, Calif. 91801. Social services, retreat and educational work.

Carmelites, Calced (Carmelite Nuns of the Ancient Observance), O. Carm.: Founded 1452, in The Netherlands; in US, 1930, from Naples, Italy, convent. US monasteries: Carmel of the Little Flower, R.D. 3, Box 551, Coopersburg, Pa. 18036; Carmel of Mary, Wahpeton, N.D. 58075; Carmel of the Sacred Heart, 430 Laurel Ave., Hudson, Wis. 54016. Papal enclosure.

Carmelites, Discalced, O.C.D.: Founded 1562, Spain. First foundation in US in 1790, at Charles County, Md.; this monastery was moved to Baltimore. Monasteries in US are listed below, according to states.

Alabama: 716 Dauphin Island Pkwy., Mobile 36606. Arkansas: 7201 W. 32nd St., Little Rock 72204. California: 215 E. Alhambra Rd., Alhambra 91801; 27601 Highway 1, Carmel 93923; 68 Rincon Rd., Kensington 94707; 3361 E. Ocean Blvd., Long Beach 90803; 8300 King Rd., Loomis 95650, 5158 Hawley Blvd., San Diego 92116; 721 Parker Ave., San Francisco 94118; 530 Blackstone Dr., San Rafael 94903; 1000 Lincoln St., Santa Clara 95050.

Colorado: 6138 S. Gallup St., Littleton 80120. Georgia: Coffee Bluff, 11 W. Back St., Savannah 31406; Illinois: River Rd. and Central, Des Plaines 60016. Indiana: 2500 Cold Springs Rd., Indianapolis 46222; 63 Allendale Pl., Terre Haute 47802. Iowa: Carmelite Rd., Eldridge 52748; 2901 S. Cecilia St., Sioux City 51106. Kansas: 3535 Wood Ave., Kansas City, 66102. Kentucky: 1740 Newburg Rd., Louisville 40205. Louisiana: Carmel Ave., Lafayette 70507; 1611 Mirabeau Ave., New Orleans 70122.

Maryland: 1318 Dulaney Valley Rd., Towson, Baltimore 21204; R.R. 4, Box 4035A, LaPlata, Md. 20646. Massachusetts: 61 Mt. Pleasant Ave., Roxbury, Boston 02119; 15 Mt. Carmel Rd., Danvers 01923; Sol-E-Mar Rd., S. Dartmouth 02748. Michigan: 16630 Wyoming Ave., Detroit 48221; 1036 Valley Ave. N.W., Grand Rapids 49504; U.S. 2 Highway, P.O. Box 397, Iron Mountain 49801; 3501 Silver Lake Rd., Traverse City 49684. Minnesota: 8251 De Montreville Trail N., Lake Elmo 55042. Mississippi: 2155 Terry Rd., Jackson 39204.

Missouri: 2201 W. Main St., Jefferson City 65101; 9150 Clayton Rd., Ladue, St. Louis Co. 63124; 424 E. Republic Rd., Springfield 65807. Nevada: 1950 La Fond Dr., Reno 89509. New Hampshire: 275 Pleasant St., Concord, 03301. New Jersey: P.O. Box 785, Flemington 08822; 189 Madison Ave., Morristown 07960. New Mexico: Mt. Carmel Rd., Santa Fe 87501. New York: 745 St. John's Pl., Brooklyn 11216; 1381 University Ave., Bronx, 10452; 75 Carmel Rd., Buffalo 14214; 1931 W. Jefferson Rd., Pittsford 14534; 68 Franklin Ave., Saranac Lake 12983; 428 Duane Ave., Schenectady 12304.

Ohio: 3176 Fairmount Blvd., Cleveland Heights 44118. Oklahoma: 4200 N. Meridian Ave., Oklahoma City 73112. Oregon: 87609 Green Hill Rd., Eugene 97402. Pennsylvania: Thornbrow, Elysburg 17824; 510 E. Gore Rd., Erie 16509; R.D. 6, Box 28, Center Dr., Latrobe 15650; P.O. Box 57, Loretto 15940; 66th Ave. and Old York Rd. (Oak Lane), Philadelphia 19126. Rhode Island: Watson Ave. at Nayatt Rd., Barrington 02806.

Texas: 600 South Flowers Ave., Dallas 75211; 1600 Sunset Terr., Ft. Worth 76102; 1100 Parthenon Pl., Roman Forest, New Caney 77357. 1104 Kentucky Ave., San Antonio 78201. Utah: 5714 Holladay Blvd., Salt Lake City 84121. Vermont: Beckley Hill, Barre, 05641. Washington: 2215 N.E. 147th St., Seattle 98155. Wisconsin: W267 N2517 Meadowbrook Rd., Pewaukee 53072.

Casimir, Sisters of St., S.S.C.: Founded 1907, in US by Mother Maria Kaupas. General motherhouse, 2601 W. Marquette Rd., Chicago, Ill. 60629. Education, missions, social services.

Cenacle, Congregation of Our Lady of the Retreat in the, R.C.: Founded 1826, in France; in US, 1892. General motherhouse, Rome, Italy. US provinces: 154-27 Horace Harding Expressway, Flushing, N.Y. 11367; 284 Foster St., Brighton, Mass. 02135; 513 Fullerton Pkwy., Chicago, Ill. 60614.

Charity, Daughters of Divine, F.D.C.: Founded 1868, at Vienna, Austria; in US, 1913. General motherhouse, Rome, Italy. US provinces: 56 Meadowbrook Rd., White Plains, N.Y. 10605; 39 Portage Path, Akron, O. 44303; 1315 N. Woodward Ave., Bloomfield Hills, Mich'. 48013. Education, social services.

Charity, Little Missionary Sisters of, P.M.C.: Founded 1915, in Italy; in US, 1949. General motherhouse, Rome, Italy; US headquarters, 201 Washington St., S. Groveland, Mass. 01834.

Charity, Missionaries of, M.C.: Founded 1950, in Calcutta, India, by Mother Teresa. General motherhouse, 54A Acharya Jagadish C. Bose Road, Calcutta 16, India. U.S. address, 335 E. 145th St., Bronx, N.Y. 10451. Service of the poor.

Charity, Religious Sisters of, R.S.C.: Founded 1815, in Ireland; in US, 1953. Motherhouse, Dublin, Ireland; US headquarters, Marycrest Manor, 10664 St. James Dr., Culver City, Calif. 90230.

Charity, Sisters of (of Seton Hill), S.C.: Founded 1870, at Altoona, Pa., from Cincinnati foundation. Administrative Offices, De Paul Center, Mt. Thor Rd., Greensburg, Pa. 15601. Educational, hospital, social, foreign mission work.

Charity, Sisters of (Grey Nuns of Montreal), S.G.M.: Founded 1737, in Canada by Bl. Marie Marguerite d'Youville; in US, 1855. General administration, Montreal, Que. H2Y 2L7, Canada; US provincial house, 10 Pelham Rd., Lexington, Mass. 02173.

Charity, Sisters of (of Leavenworth), S.C.L.: Founded 1858, in US. Motherhouse, Leavenworth, Kans. 66048.

Charity, Sisters of (of Nazareth), S.C.N.: Founded 1812, in US. General motherhouse, Nazareth P. O., Nelson Co., Ky. 40048.

Charity, Sisters of (of St. Augustine), C.S.A.: Founded 1851, at Cleveland, O. Motherhouse, 5232 Broadview Rd., Richfield, O. 44286.

Charity, Sisters of Christian, S.C.C.: Founded 1849, in Paderborn, Germany; in US, 1873. General motherhouse, Rome, Italy. US provinces: Mallinckrodt Convent, Mendham, N.J. 07945; Maria Immaculata Convent, 1041 Ridge Rd., Wilmette, Ill. 60091, Education, health services, other apostolic work.

Charity, Vincentian Sisters of, V.S.C.: Founded 1835, in Austria; in US, 1902. General motherhouse, 8200 McKnight Rd., Pittsburgh, Pa. 15237.

Charity, Vincentian Sisters of, V.S.C.: Founded 1928, at Bedford, O. General motherhouse, 1160 Broadway, Bedford, O. 44146.

Charity of Cincinnati, Ohio, Sisters of, S.C.: Founded 1829. General motherhouse, Mt. St. Joseph, Ohio 45051. Educational, hospital, social work.

Charity of Ottawa, Sisters of (Grey Nuns of the Cross), S.C.O.: Founded 1845, at Ottawa, Canada; in US, 1857. General motherhouse, Ottawa, Canada; US provincial house, 975 Varnum Ave., Lowell, Mass. 01854. Educational, hospital work, extended health care.

Charity of Our Lady, Mother of Mercy, Sisters of, S.C.M.M.: Founded 1832, in Holland; in US, 1874. General motherhouse, Rome, Italy; US provincialate, 520 Thompson Ave., East Haven Conn. 06512.

Charity of Our Lady of Mercy, Sisters of, O.L.M.: Founded 1829, in US. Generalate and motherhouse, Charleston, S.C. 29412. Education, campus ministry, social services.

Charity of Quebec, Sisters of (Grey Nuns), S.C.Q.: Founded 1849, at Quebec; in US, 1890. General motherhouse, 2655 rue Le Pelletier, Beauport, Quebec GIC 3X7, Canada. Social work.

Charity of St. Elizabeth, Sisters of (Convent, N.J.), S.C.: Founded 1859, at Newark, N. J. Generalate, Convent, N. J. 07961. Education, pastoral ministry, social services.

Charity of St. Hyacinthe, Sisters of (Grey Nuns), S.C.S.H.: Founded 1840, at St. Hyacinthe, Canada; in US, 1878. General motherhouse, 665 Avenue Bourdages, SUD, St. Hyacinthe, Quebec J2T 4J8, Canada. Regional house, 98 Campus Ave., Lewiston Me. 04240.

Charity of St. Joan Antida, Sisters of, S.C.S.J.A.: Founded 1799, in France; in US, 1932. General motherhouse, Rome, Italy; US provincial house, 8560 N. 76th Pl., Milwaukee, Wis. 53223.

Charity of St. Louis, Sisters of, S.C.S.L.: Founded 1803, in France; in US, 1910. General motherhouse, Rome, Italy; US provincial house, 29 Casablanca Court, Clifton Park, N.Y. 12065.

Charity of St. Vincent de Paul, Daughters of, D.C.: Founded 1633, in France; in US 1809, at Emmitsburg, Md., by St. Elizabeth Ann Seton. General motherhouse, Paris, France. US provinces: Emmitsburg, Md. 21727; 7800 Natural Bridge Rd., St. Louis, Mo. 63121; 9400 New Harmony Rd., Evansville, Ind. 47712; 96 Menands Rd., Albany, N.Y. 12204; 26000 Altamont Rd., Los Altos Hills, Calif. 94022.

Charity of St. Vincent de Paul, Sisters of, S.V.Z.: Founded 1845, in Croatia; in U.S., 1955. General motherhouse, Zagreb, Yugoslavia; U.S. foundation, 171 Knox Ave., West Seneca, N.Y. 14224.

Charity of St. Vincent de Paul, Sisters of, Halifax, S.C.H.: Founded 1856, at Halifax, N. S., from Emmitsburg, Md., foundation. Generalate, Mt. St. Vincent, Halifax, N. S., Canada. U.S. addresses: Boston Province, 50 Aspen Ave., Auburndale, Mass. 02166; New York Province, 410 Grant Ave., Brooklyn, N.Y. 11208. Educational, hospital, social work.

Charity of St. Vincent de Paul, Sisters of, New York, S.C.: Founded 1817, from Emmitsburg, Md. General motherhouse, Mt. St. Vincent on Hudson, New York, N.Y. 10471. Educational, hospital work.

Charity of the Blessed Virgin Mary, Sisters of, B.V.M.: Founded 1833, in US. General motherhouse, Mt. Carmel, Dubuque, Ia. 52001. Education, pastoral ministry, social services.

Charity of the Immaculate Conception of Ivrea, Sisters of, S.C.I.C.: General motherhouse, Rome, Italy; US address, Immaculate Virgin of Miracles Convent, R.D. 2, Mt. Pleasant, Pa. 15666.

Charity of the Incarnate Word, Congregation of the Sisters of, C.C.V.I.: Founded 1869, at San Antonio, Tex., by Bishop C. M. Dubuis. General motherhouse, 4503 Broadway, San Antonio, Tex. 78209.

Charity of the Incarnate Word, Congregation of the Sisters of (Houston, Tex.), C.C.V.I.: Founded 1866, in US, by Bishop C. M. Dubuis. General motherhouse, 6510 Lawndale Ave., Houston, Tex. 77023. Educational, hospital, social work.

Charity of the Sacred Heart, Daughters of,

F.C.S.C.J.: Founded 1823, at La Salle de Vihiers, France; in US, 1905. General motherhouse, La Salle de Vihiers, France; U.S. address, Sacred Heart Province, P.O. Box 642, Littleton, N.H. 03561.

Charles Borromeo, Missionary Sisters of St. (Scalabrini Srs.): Founded 1895, in Italy; in US, 1941. American novitiate, 1414 N. 37th Ave., Melrose Park, Ill. 60601.

Child Jesus, Sisters of the Poor, P.C.J.: Founded 1844, at Aix-la-Chapelle, Germany; in US, 1924. General motherhouse, Simpelveld, Holland; American provincialate, 4567 Olentangy River Rd., Columbus, O. 43214.

Chretienne, Sisters of Ste., S.S.CH.: Founded 1807, in France; in US, 1903. General motherhouse, Metz, France; American provincial house, 297 Arnold St., Wrentham, Mass. 02093. Educational, hospital, mission work.

Christ, Adorers of the Blood of, A.S.C.: Founded 1834, in Italy; in US, 1870. General motherhouse, Rome, Italy. US provinces: Ruma Province, Rt. 1, Box 115, Red Bud, Ill. 62278; 1400 South Sheridan, Wichita, Kans. 67213; Columbia, Pa. 17512. Education, retreats, social services, pastoral ministry.

Christ the King, Sister Servants of, S.S.C.K.: Founded 1936, in US. General motherhouse, Loretto Convent, Mt. Calvary, Wis. 53057. Social services.

Christian Doctrine, Sisters of Our Lady of, R.C.D.: Founded 1910, at New York. Motherhouse, Marydell, Montebello Rd., Suffern, N.Y. 10901.

Christian Education, Religious of, R.C.E.: Founded 1817, in France; in US, 1905. General motherhouse, Paris, France; US provincial residence, 36 Hillcrest Rd., Belmont, Mass. 02178.

Cistercian Nuns of the Strict Observance, Order of, O.C.S.O.: Founded 1125, in France, by St. Stephen Harding; in US, 1949. US addresses: Mt. St. Mary's Abbey, Arnold St. (R.F.D. Box 500), Wrentham, Mass. 02093; Our Lady of the Santa Rita Abbey, Box 97, Sonoita, Ariz. 85637; Our Lady of the Redwoods Abbey, Whitethorn, Calif. 95489; Abbey of Our Lady of the Mississippi, R.R. 3, Dubuque, Ia. 52001.

Clergy, Congregation of Our Lady, Help of the, C.L.H.C.: Founded 1961, in US. Motherhouse, Maryvale Convent, Rt. 1, Box 164, Vale, N.C. 28168.

Clergy, Servants of Our Lady Queen of the, S.R.C.: Founded 1929, in Canada; in US, 1936. General motherhouse, Lac-au-Saumon, Que., GOJ 1MO, Canada.

Colettines: See Franciscan Poor Clare Nuns.

Columban, Missionary Sisters of St., S.S.C.: Founded 1922, in Ireland; in US, 1930. General motherhouse, Wicklow, Ireland; US region, 1250 W. Loyola Ave., Chicago, Ill. 60626.

Comboni Missionary Sisters (Missionary Sisters of Verona), C.M.S.: Founded 1872, in Italy; in U.S., 1950. U.S. address, 1307 S. Lakeside Ave., Richmond, Va. 23228.

Consolata Missionary Sisters, M.C.: Founded 1910, in Italy; in US, 1954. General motherhouse, Turin, Italy; US headquarters, 6801 Belmont Rd., Belmont, Mich. 49306.

Cross, Daughters of the, D.C.: Founded 1640, in France; in US, 1855. General motherhouse, 1000 Fairview St., Shreveport, La. 71104. Educational work.

Cross, Daughters of, of Liege, F.C.: Founded 1833, in Liege, Belgium; in US, 1958. US address, 165 W. Eaton Ave., Tracy, Calif. 95376.

Cross, Sisters, Lovers of the Holy (Phat Diem): Founded 1670, in Vietnam; in U.S. 1976. U.S. address, Mary Immaculate Seminary Convent, Northampton, Pa. 18067.

Cross, Sisters of the Holy, C.S.C.: Founded 1841, at Le Mans, France; in US, 1843. General motherhouse, Saint Mary's, Notre Dame, Ind. 46556. Education, health care, social services, pastoral ministry.

Cross, Sisters of the Holy (Sisters of the Holy Cross and Seven Dolors), C.S.C.: Founded 1841, at La Mans, France, established 1847, in Canada; in US, 1881. General motherhouse, St. Laurent, Montreal, Que., Canada; US provincial house, Fairview Rd., Pittsfield, N.H. 03263. Educational work.

Cross and Passion, Sisters of the (Passionist Sisters), C.P.: Founded 1852; in US, 1924. General motherhouse, Bolton, England; US address: Mt. St. Joseph, 670 Tower Hill Rd., Wakefield, R.I. 02880.

Cross and Passion of Our Lord Jesus Christ, Nuns of the (Passionist Nuns), C.P.: Founded 1771, in Italy, by St. Paul of the Cross; in US, 1910. US convents: 2715 Churchview Ave., Pittsburgh, Pa. 15227; 631 Griffin Pond Rd., Clarks Summit, Pa. 18411; 1420 Benita Ave., Owensboro, Ky. 42301; 751 Donaldson Hwy., Erlanger, Ky. 41018; 1032 Clayton Rd., Ellisville, Mo. 63011. Contemplatives.

Cyril and Methodius, Sisters of Sts., SS.C.M.: Founded 1909, in US, by Rev. Matthew Jankola. General motherhouse, Danville, Pa. 17821. Education, care of aged.

Disciples of the Divine Master, Sister, P.D.D.M.: Founded 1924; in US, 1948. General motherhouse, Rome, Italy; US headquarters, 12830 Warren Ave., Dearborn, Mich. 48126.

Divine Compassion, Sisters of, R.D.C.: Founded 1886, in US. General motherhouse, 52 N. Broadway, White Plains, N.Y. 10603. Education, other ministries.

Divine Love, Oblates to, Sisters, R.O.D.A.: Founded 1923, in Italy; in US, 1947. General motherhouse, Rome, Italy; US provincial

house, St. Clare's Convent, 1925 Hon Ave., Bronx, N.Y. 10461.

Divine Spirit, Congregation of the, C.D.S.: Founded 1956, in US, by Archbishop John M. Gannon. Motherhouse, 409 W. 6th St., Erie, Pa. 16507. Education, social services.

Dominicans

Nuns of the Order of Preachers (Dominican Nuns), O.P.: Founded 1206 by St. Dominic at Prouille, France. Cloistered, contemplative. Two branches in the United States:

• Dominican Nuns having perpetual adoration. First monastery established 1880, in Newark, N.J., from Oullins, France, foundation (1869). Seven autonomous monasteries.

St. Dominic, 13th Ave. and S. 10th St., Newark, N.J. 07103; Corpus Christi, 1230 Lafayette Ave., Bronx, N.Y. 10474; Blessed Sacrament, 29575 Middlebelt Rd., Farmington Hills, Mich. 48018; Holy Name, 3020 Erie Ave., Hyde Park, Cincinnati, O. 45208; Monastery of the Angels, 1977 Carmen Ave., Los Angeles, Calif. 90068; Corpus Christi, 215 Oak Grove Ave., Menlo Park, Calif. 94025; Infant Jesus, 1501 Lotus Lane, Lufkin, Tex. 75901.

• Dominican Nuns devoted to the perpetual Rosary. First monastery established 1891, in Union City, N.J., from Calais, France, foundation (1880). Thirteen autonomous monasteries (some also observe perpetual adoration).

Dominican Nuns of Perpetual Rosary, 14th and West Sts., Union City, N.J. 07087; Presentation Monastery, 217 N. 68th St., Milwaukee, Wis. 53213; Dominican Monastery, 720 Maiden Choice Lane, Catonsville, Md. 21228; Perpetual Rosary, 1500 Haddon Ave., Camden, N.J. 08103; Our Lady of the Rosary, 335 Doat St., Buffalo, N.Y. 14211; St. Dominic, 3000 South Ave., La Crosse, Wis. 54601; Our Lady of the Rosary, 543 Springfield Ave., Summit, N.J. 07901; Mother of God, 1430 Riverdale St., W. Springfield, Mass. 01089; Perpetual Rosary, 802 Court St., Syracuse, N.Y. 13208; Immaculate Heart of Mary, 1834 Lititz Pike, Lancaster, Pa. 17601; Mary the Queen, 1310 W. Church St., Elmira, N.Y. 14905; St. Jude, Marbury, Ala. 36051; Our Lady of Grace, North Guilford, Conn. 06437.

Dominican Rural Missionaries, O.P.: Founded 1932, in France; in US, 1951, at Abbeville, La. General motherhouse, Luzarches, France; US address, 1318 S. Henry St., Abbeville, La. 70510.

Dominican Sisters of Bethany, Congregation, O.P.: Founded 1866, in France. Motherhouse, France; US novitiate, 204 Ridge St., Millis, Mass. 02054.

Dominican Sisters of the Presentation, O.P.: Founded 1684, in France; in US, 1906. General motherhouse, Tours, France; US headquarters, 3012 Elm St., Dighton, Mass. 02715. Hospital work.

Dominican Sisters of the Roman Congregation of St. Dominic, O.P.: Founded 1621, in France; in US, 1904. General motherhouse, Rome, Italy; US province, 2624 Fillmore St., Davenport, Ia. 52804. Educational work.

Eucharistic Missionaries of St. Dominic, O.P.: Founded 1927, in Louisiana. General motherhouse, 1101 Aline St., New Orleans, La. 70115. Parish work, social services.

Maryknoll Sisters of St. Dominic, M.M.: Founded 1912, in New York. Center, Maryknoll, N.Y. 10545.

Religious Missionaries of St. Dominic, O.P.: General motherhouse, Rome, Italy. US foundations: 808 S. Wright St., Alice, Texas 78332; 47 E. Gramman St., Beeville, Tex. 78102; 432 N. Oak St., Santa Paula, Calif. 93060.

Sisters of St. Dominic, O.P.: Thirty congregations in the US. Educational, hospital work. Names of congregations are given below, followed by the date of foundation, and location of motherhouse.

St. Catharine of Siena, 1822. St. Catharine, Ky. 40061.

St. Mary of the Springs, 1830. Columbus Ohio 43219.

Most Holy Rosary, 1847. Sinsinawa, Wis. 53824.

Most Holy Name of Jesus, 1850. San Rafael, Calif. 94901.

Holy Cross, 1853. Albany Ave., Amityville, N.Y. 11701.

Most Holy Rosary, 1859. Mt. St. Mary on Hudson, Newburgh, N.Y. 12550.

St. Cecilia, 1860. Eighth Ave. N. and Clay St., Nashville, Tenn. 37208.

St. Mary, 1860. 580 Broadway, New Orleans, La. 70118.

St. Catherine of Siena, 1862. 5635 Erie St., Racine, Wis. 53402.

Our Lady of the Sacred Heart, 1873. 1237 W. Monroe St., Springfield, Ill. 62704.

Our Lady of the Rosary, 1876. Sparkill, N.Y. 10976.

Queen of the Holy Rosary, 1876. Mission San Jose, Calif. 94538.

Most Holy Rosary, 1892. Adrian, Mich. 49221.

Our Lady of the Sacred Heart, 1877. 2025 E. Fulton St., Grand Rapids, Mich. 49503.

St. Dominic, 1878. Blauvelt, N.Y. 10913.

Immaculate Conception (Dominican Sisters of the Sick Poor), 1879. P.O. Box 231, Ossining, N.Y. 10562. Social work.

St. Catherine de Ricci, 1880. 2850 N. Providence Rd., Media, Pa. 19063.

Sacred Heart of Jesus, 1881. Mt. St. Dominic, Caldwell, N.J. 07006.

Sacred Heart, 1882. 6501 Almeda Rd., Houston, Tex. 77021.

St. Thomas Aquinas, 1888. 423 E. 152nd St., Tacoma, Wash. 98445.

Holy Cross, 1890. P.O. Box 280, Edmonds, Wash. 98020.

St. Catherine of Siena, 1891. 37 Park St., Fall River, Mass. 02721.

St. Rose of Lima (Servants of Relief for Incurable Cancer), 1896. Hawthorne, N.Y. 10532.

Immaculate Conception, 1902. 3600 Broadway, Great Bend, Kans. 67530.

St. Catherine of Siena, 1911. 4600 93rd St., Kenosha, Wis. 53140.

St. Rose of Lima, 1923. 775 Drahner Rd., Oxford, Mich. 48051.

Immaculate Conception, 1929. 9000 W. 81st St., Justice, Ill. 60458.

Immaculate Heart of Mary, 1929. Akron, Ohio 44313.

Immaculate Heart of Mary Province (Dominican Sisters of Spokane). W. 3102 Fort George Wright Dr., Spokane, Wash. 99204.

Dominican Sisters of Oakford (St. Catherine of Siena), 1889. Motherhouse, Oakford, Natal, South Africa. US regional house, 1965. Villa Siena, 1855 Miramonte Ave., Mountain View, Calif. 94040.

(End, Listing of Dominicans)

Dorothy, Institute of the Sisters of St., S.S.D.: Founded 1834, in Italy; in US, 1911. General motherhouse, Rome, Italy; US provincialate, Villa Fatima, Taunton, Mass. 02780.

Eucharist, Religious of the, R.E.: Founded 1857, in Belgium; in US, 1900. General motherhouse, Belgium; US foundation, 2907 Ellicott Terr., N.W., Washington, D.C. 20008.

Eucharistic Missionary Sisters, E.M.S.: Founded 1943, in Mexico. Motherhouse, Our Lady of Loretto Convent, 267 N. Belmont Ave., Los Angeles, Calif. 90026.

Family, Congregation of the Sisters of the Holy, S.S.F.: Founded 1842, in US. General motherhouse, 6901 Chef Menteur Hway., New Orleans, La. 70126. Educational, hospital work.

Family, Little Sisters of the Holy, P.S.S.F.: Founded 1880, in Canada; in US, 1900. General motherhouse, Sherbrooke, Que., Canada. US novitiate, 285 Andover St., Lowell, Mass. 01852.

Family, Sisters of the Holy, S.H.F.: Founded 1872, in US. General motherhouse, P.O. Box 3248, Mission San Jose, Calif. 94538. Educational, social work.

Family of Nazareth, Sisters of the Holy, C.S.F.N.: Founded 1875, in Italy; in US, 1885. General motherhouse, Rome, Italy. US provinces: 353 N. River Rd., Des Plaines, Ill. 60016; 9701 Frankford Ave., Philadelphia, Pa. 19114; 285 Bellevue Rd., Pittsburgh, Pa. 15229; Marian Heights, 1428 Monroe Turnpike, Monroe, Conn. 06468; 1814 Egyptian Way, Box 757, Grand Prairie, Tex. 75050.

Filippini, Religious Teachers, M.P.F.: Founded 1692, in Italy; in US, 1910. General motherhouse, Rome, Italy; US provinces: St. Lucy Filippini Province, Villa Walsh, Morristown, N.J. 07960; Queen of Apostles Province, 474 East Rd., Bristol, Conn. 06010. Educational work.

Francis de Sales, Oblate Sisters of St., O.S.F.S.: Founded 1866, in France; in US, 1951. General motherhouse, Troyes, France; US headquarters, Villa Aviat Convent, Childs, Md. 21916. Educational, social work.

Franciscans

Bernardine Sisters of the Third Order of St. Francis, O.S.F.: Founded 1457, at Cracow, Poland; in US, 1894. Generalate, 647 Spring Mill Rd., Villanova, Pa. 19085. Educational, hospital, social work.

Capuchin Sisters of St. Clare (Madres Clarisas Capuchinas): U.S. establishment, 1981, Amarillo diocese. Convent of the Blessed Sacrament and Our Lady of Guadalupe, 4201 N.E. 18th St., Amarillo, Tex. 79107. Cloistered.

Congregation of the Servants of the Holy Infancy of Jesus, O.S.F.: Founded 1855, in Germany; in US, 1929. General motherhouse, Wuerzburg, Germany; American motherhouse, Villa Maria, P.O. Box 708, Plainfield, N.J. 07061.

Congregation of the Third Order of St. Francis of Mary Immaculate, O.S.F.: Founded 1865, in US, by Fr. Pamphilus da Magliano, O.F.M. General motherhouse, 520 Plainfield Ave., Joliet, Ill. 60435. Educational and pastoral work.

Daughters of St. Francis of Assisi, D.S.F.: Founded 1890, in Austria-Hungary; in US, 1946. Provincial motherhouse, 507 N. Prairie St., Lacon, Ill. 61540. Nursing, CCD work.

Felician Sisters (Congregation of the Sisters of St. Felix), C.S.S.F.: Founded 1855, in Poland; in US, 1874. General motherhouse, Rome, Italy. US provinces: 36800 Schoolcraft Rd., Livonia, Mich. 48150; 600 Doat St., Buffalo, N.Y. 14211; 3800 Peterson Ave., Chicago, Ill. 60659; 260 South Main St., Lodi, N.J. 07644; 1500 Woodcrest Ave., Coraopolis, Pa. 15108; 1315 Enfield St., Enfield, Conn. 06082; 4210 Meadowlark Lane, S.E., Rio Rancho, N. Mex. 87174.

Franciscan Handmaids of the Most Pure Heart of Mary, F.H.M.: Founded 1917, in US. General motherhouse, 15 W. 124th St., New York, N.Y. 10027. Educational, social work.

Franciscan Hospitaller Sisters of the Immaculate Conception, F.H.I.C.: Founded 1876, in Portugal; in US, 1960. General motherhouse, Oporto, Portugal; US novitiate, 300 S. 17th St., San Jose, Calif. 95112.

Franciscan Missionaries of Mary, F.M.M.: Founded 1877, in India; in US, 1904. General motherhouse, Rome, Italy; US provincialate, 225 E. 45th St., New York, N.Y. 10017. Mission work.

Franciscan Missionaries of Our Lady, O.S.F.: Founded 1854, at Calais, France; in US, 1913. General motherhouse, Desvres, France; US motherhouse, 4200 Essen Lane, Baton Rouge, La. 70809. Hospital work.

Franciscan Missionaries of St. Joseph (Mill Hill Sisters), F.M.S.J.: Founded 1883, at Rochdale, Lancashire, England; in US, 1952. General motherhouse, Eccleshall, Stafford, England; US headquarters, Franciscan House, 1006 Madison Ave., Albany, N.Y. 12208.

Franciscan Missionaries of the Divine Motherhood, F.M.D.M.: Founded 1935, in England; US foundation, Convent of the Holy Spirit, East Greenbush, N.Y. 12061.

Franciscan Missionaries of the Infant Jesus: Generalate, Rome, Italy. US novitiate, St. Margaret Convent, Third and Beech Sts., Woodbury Heights, N.J. 08097.

Franciscan Missionary Sisters for Africa, O.S.F.: American foundation, 1953. Generalate, Ireland; US headquarters, 172 Foster St., Brighton, Mass. 02135.

Franciscan Missionary Sisters of Assisi, F.M.S.A.: First foundation in US, 1961. General motherhouse, Assisi, Italy; US address, St. Francis Convent, 1039 Northampton St., Holyoke, Mass. 01040.

Franciscan Missionary Sisters of Our Lady of Sorrows, O.S.F.: Founded 1937, in China, by Bishop R. Palazzi, O.F.M.; in US, 1949. US address, 2385 Laurel Glen Rd., Santa Cruz, Calif. 95065. Educational, social, domestic, retreat and foreign mission work.

Franciscan Missionary Sisters of the Divine Child, F.M.D.C.: Founded 1927, at Buffalo, N.Y., by Bishop William Turner. General motherhouse, 6380 Main St., Williamsville, N.Y. 14221. Educational, social work.

Franciscan Missionary Sisters of the Immaculate Conception, O.S.F.: Founded 1874, in Mexico; in US, 1926. US provincial house, 11306 Laurel Canyon Blvd., San Fernando, Calif. 91340.

Franciscan Missionary Sisters of the Immaculate Heart of Mary, F.M.I.H.M.: Founded at Cairo, Egypt by Mother Catarino di S. Rosa (Costanzo Troiano). Generalate, Rome, Italy; U.S. address, Ave Maria House, 3501 Good Intent Rd., Deptford, N.J. 08096.

Franciscan Missionary Sisters of the Sacred Heart, F.M.S.C.: Founded 1860, in Italy; in US, 1865. Generalate, Rome, Italy; US provincialate, 250 South St., Peekskill, N.Y. 10566. Educational and social welfare apostolates and specialized services.

Franciscan Poor Clare Nuns (Poor Clares, Order of St. Clare, Poor Clares of St. Colette), P.C., O.S.C., P.C.C.: Founded 1212, at Assisi, Italy, by St. Francis of Assisi; in US, 1875. Proto-monastery, Assisi, Italy. Addresses of autonomous motherhouses in US are listed below.

3626 N. 65th Ave., Omaha, Nebr. 68104;

720 Henry Clay Ave., New Orleans, La. 70118; 509 S. Kentucky Ave., Evansville, Ind. 47714; 1310 Dellwood Ave., Memphis Tenn. 38127; 920 Centre St., Jamaica Plain, Mass. 02130; 201 Crosswicks St., Bordentown, N.J. 08505; 1271 Langhorne-Newton Rd., Langhorne, Pa. 19047; 4419 N. Hawthorne St., Spokane, Wash. 99205; 142 Hollywood Ave., Bronx, N.Y. 10465; 421 S. 4th St., Sauk Rapids, Minn. 56379; 8650 Russell Ave. S., Minneapolis, Minn. 55431; 3501 Rocky River Dr., Cleveland, O. 44111; 89th and Kean Ave., Hickory Hills, Ill. 60457; 280 State Park Dr., Aptos, Calif. 95003; 2111 S. Main St., Rockford, Ill. 61102; 215 E. Los Olivos St., Santa Barbara, Calif. 93105; P.O. Box 333, Lowell, Mass. 01853; 809 E. 19th St., Roswell, N. Mex. 88201; 28210 Natoma Rd., Los Altos Hills, Calif. 94022; 1916 N. Pleasantburg Dr., Greenville, S.C. 29609; 28 Harpersville Rd., Newport News, Va. 23601; 805 N. Malfalfa Rd., Kokoma, Ind. 46901; 4000 Sherwood Blvd., Delray Beach, Fla. 33445; 200 Marycrest Dr., St. Louis, Mo. 63129.

Franciscan Sisters, Daughters of the Sacred Hearts of Jesus and Mary, O.S.F.: Founded 1860, in Germany; in US, 1872. Generalate, Rome, Italy; US motherhouse, P.O. Box 667, Wheaton, Ill. 60187. Educational, hospital, foreign mission, social work.

Franciscan Sisters of Allegany, N.Y., O.S.F.: Founded 1859, at Allegany, N.Y., by Fr. Pamphilus da Magliano, O.F.M. General motherhouse Allegany, N.Y. 14706. Educational, hospital, foreign mission work.

Franciscan Sisters of Baltimore, O.S.F.: Founded 1868, in England; in US, 1881. General motherhouse, 3725 Ellerslie Ave., Baltimore, Md. 21218. Educational work; social services.

Franciscan Sisters of Chicago, O.S.F.: Founded 1894, in US. General motherhouse, 1220 Main St., Lemont, Ill. 60439. Educational work, social services.

Franciscan Sisters of Christian Charity, O.S.F.: Founded 1869, in US. Holy Family Convent, 2409 S. Alverno Rd., Manitowoc, Wis. 54220. Educational, hospital work.

Franciscan Sisters of Little Falls, Minn., O.S.F.: Founded 1891, in US. General motherhouse, Little Falls, Minn. 56345. Health, education, social services, pastoral ministry, mission work.

Franciscan Sisters of Mary Immaculate of the Third Order of St. Francis of Assisi, F.M.I.: Founded 16th century, in Switzerland; in US, 1932. General motherhouse, Bogota, Colombia; US provincial house, 4301 N.E. 18th Ave., Amarillo, Tex. 79107. Education.

Franciscan Sisters of Our Lady of Perpetual Help, O.S.F.: Founded 1901, in US, from Joliet, Ill., foundation. General motherhouse,

201 Brotherton Lane, St. Louis, Mo. 63135. Educational, hospital work.

Franciscan Sisters of Ringwood, F.S.R.: Founded 1927, at Passaic, N.J. General motherhouse, Mt. St. Francis, Ringwood, N.J. 07456. Educational work.

Franciscan Sisters of St. Elizabeth, F.S.S.E.: Founded 1866, at Naples, Italy; in US, 1919. General motherhouse, Rome; US novitiate, 449 Park Rd., Parsippany, N.J. 07054. Educational work, social services.

Franciscan Sisters of St. Joseph, F.S.S.J.: Founded 1897, in US. General motherhouse, 5286 S. Park Ave., Hamburg, N.Y. 14075. Educational, hospital work.

Franciscan Sisters of the Atonement, Third Order Regular of St. Francis (Graymoor Sisters), S.A.: Founded 1898, in US, as Anglican community; entered Church, 1909. General motherhouse, Graymoor, Garrison P.O., N.Y. 10524. Mission work.

Franciscan Sisters of the Blessed Virgin Mary of the Holy Angels, B.M.V.A.: Founded 1863, at Neuwied, Germany; in US, 1923. General motherhouse, Rhine, Germany; US motherhouse, 1388 Prior Ave. S., St. Paul, Minn. 55116. Educational, hospital, social work.

Franciscan Sisters of the Immaculate Conception, O.S.F.: Founded in Germany; in US, 1928. General motherhouse, Kloster, Bonlanden, Germany; US province, 291 W. North St., Buffalo, N.Y. 14201.

Franciscan Sisters of the Immaculate Conception, O.S.F.: Founded 1901, in US. General motherhouse, 1000 30th St., Rock Island, Ill. 61201. Health care.

Franciscan Sisters of the Immaculate Conception, Missionary, O.S.F.: Founded 1873, in US. General motherhouse, Rome, Italy; US address, 790 Centre St., Newton, Mass. 02158. Educational work.

Franciscan Sisters of the Immaculate Conception and St. Joseph for the Dying, O.S.F.: Founded 1919, in US. General motherhouse, 485 Church St., Monterey, Calif. 93940.

Franciscan Sisters of the Poor, S.F.P.: Founded 1845, at Aachen, Germany, by Bl. Frances Schervier; in US, 1858. Community service center, 23 Middagh St., Brooklyn, N.Y. 11201. Hospital, social work and foreign missions.

Franciscan Sisters of the Sacred Heart, O.S.F.: Founded 1866, in Germany; in U.S., 1876. General motherhouse, Mokena, Ill. 60448. Education, health care, other service ministries.

Hospital Sisters of the Third Order of St. Francis, O.S.F.: Founded 1844, in Germany; in US, 1875. General motherhouse, Muenster, Germany; US motherhouse, Box 42, Springfield, Ill. 62705. Hospital work.

Institute of the Franciscan Sisters of the Eucharist, F.S.E.: Founded 1973. Motherhouse, 405 Allen Ave., Meriden, Conn. 06450.

Little Franciscan Sisters of Mary, P.F.M.: Founded 1889, in US. General motherhouse, Baie St. Paul, Que., Canada. US province, 55 Moore Ave., Worcester, Mass. 01602. Educational, hospital, social work.

Little Sisters of St. Francis, O.S.F.: Founded 1979, in Boston archdiocese. Address, 785 Parker St., Mission Hill, Mass. 02120. Combine contemplative life with street ministry apostolate.

Missionaries of the Third Order of St. Francis of Our Lady of the Prairies, O.L.P.: Founded 1960, in US. General motherhouse, Powers Lake, N.D. 58773.

Missionary Sisters of the Immaculate Conception of the Mother of God, S.M.I.C.: Founded 1910, in Brazil; in US, 1922, Generalate, 779 Broadway, Paterson, N.J. 07514; provincialate, P.O. Box 3026, Paterson, N.J. 07509. Mission, educational, health work, social services.

Mothers of the Helpless, M.D.: Founded 1873, in Spain; in US, 1916. General motherhouse, Valencia, Spain; US address, San Jose Day Nursery, 432 W. 20th St., New York, N.Y. 10011.

Philip Neri Missionary Teachers, Sisters of St., R.F.: Founded 1858, in Spain; in US, 1956. Motherhouse, Madrid, Spain; US address: Sisters of St. Philip Neri, St. Albert's Convent, 1259 St. Alberts St., Reno, Nev. 89503.

Poor Clares of Perpetual Adoration, P.C.P.A.: Founded 1854, at Paris, France; in US, 1921, at Cleveland, Ohio. US monasteries: 4200 N. Market Ave., Canton, O. 44714; 2311 Timlin Rd., Portsmouth, O. 45662; 4108 Euclid Ave., Cleveland, O. 44103; 3900 13th St. N.E., Washington, D.C. 20017; 5817 Old Leeds Rd., Birmingham, Ala. 35210. Contemplative, cloistered, perpetual adoration.

School Sisters of St. Francis, O.S.F.: Founded 1874, in US. General motherhouse, 1501 Layton Blvd., Milwaukee, Wis. 53215.

School Sisters of St. Francis (Bethlehem, Pa.), O.S.F.: Founded in Austria, 1843; in U.S., 1913. General motherhouse, Rome, Italy; U.S. province, 395 Bridle Path Rd., Bethlehem, Pa. 18017. Educational, mission work.

School Sisters of St. Francis, (Pittsburgh, Pa.), O.S.F.: Established 1913, in US. Motherhouse, Mt. Assisi Convent, 934 Forest Ave., Pittsburgh, Pa. 15202. Education, health care services and related ministries.

School Sisters of the Third Order of St. Francis (Panhandle, Tex.), O.S.F.: Founded 1845, in Austria; in US, 1942. General motherhouse, Vienna, Austria; US center and novitiate, Sancta Maria Convent, Panhandle, Tex. 79068. Educational, social work.

Sisters of Charity of Our Lady, Mother of the Church, S.C.M.C.: Established 1970, in US. Motherhouse, Baltic, Conn. 06330. Teaching, nursing, care of aged, and dependent children.

Sisters of Our Lady of Mercy (Mercedarians), S.O.L.M.: General motherhouse, Rome, Italy; US addresses: 133 27th Ave., Brooklyn, N.Y. 11214; St. Edward School, Pine Hill, N.J. 08021.

Sisters of Mercy of the Holy Cross, S.C.S.C.: Founded 1856, in Switzerland; in US. 1912. General motherhouse, Ingenbohl, Switzerland; US provincial house, 1500 O'Day St., Merrill, Wis. 54452.

Sisters of St. Elizabeth, S.S.E.: Founded 1931, at Milwaukee, Wis. General motherhouse, 745 N. Brookfield Rd., Brookfield, Wis. 53005.

Sisters of St. Francis (Clinton, Iowa), O.S.F.: Founded 1868, in US. General motherhouse, Bluff Blvd. and Springdale Dr., Clinton, Ia. 57232. Educational, hospital, social work.

Sisters of St. Francis (Maryville, Mo.), O.S.F.: Founded 1894, in US. Motherhouse, Mt. Alverno Convent, R.R. 3, Box 64, Maryville, Mo. 64468. Hospital work.

Sisters of St. Francis (Millvale, Pa.), O.S.F.: Founded 1865, Pittsburgh, Pa. General motherhouse, 146 Hawthorne Rd., Millvale P.O., Pittsburgh, Pa. 15209. Educational, hospital work.

Sisters of St. Francis of Christ the King, O.S.F.: Founded 1869, in Austria. General motherhouse, Rome, Italy; US provincial house, 1600 Main St., Lemont, Ill. 60439. Educational work, home for aged.

Sisters of St. Francis of Penance and Christian Charity, O.S.F.: Founded 1835, in Holland; in US, 1874. General motherhouse, Rome, Italy. US provinces: 4421 Lower River Rd., Stella Niagara, N.Y. 14144; 2851 W. 52nd Ave., Denver, Colo. 80221; 3910 Bret Harte Dr., P.O. Box 1028, Redwood City, Calif. 94064.

Sisters of St. Francis of Philadelphia, O.S.F.: Founded 1855, at Philadelphia, by Mother Mary Francis Bachmann and St. John N. Neumann. General motherhouse, Convent of Our Lady of the Angels, Glen Riddle, Aston, Pa. 19014. Education, health care, social services.

Sisters of St. Francis of Savannah, Mo., O.S.F.: Founded 1850, in Austria; in U.S., 1922. Provincial house, La Verna Heights, Savannah, Mo. 64485. Educational, hospital work.

Sisters of St. Francis of the Congregation of Our Lady of Lourdes, O.S.F.: Founded 1916, in US. General motherhouse, 6832 Convent Blvd., Sylvania, O. 43560. Education, health care, social services, pastoral ministry.

Sisters of St. Francis of the Holy Cross, O.S.F.: Founded 1881, in US, by Rev. Edward Daems, O.S.C. General motherhouse, 3025 Bay Settlement Rd., Green Bay, Wis. 54301. Educational, nursing work, pastoral ministry, foreign missions.

Sisters of St. Francis of the Holy Eucharist,

O.S.F.: Founded 1424, in Switzerland; in US, 1893. General motherhouse, 2100 N. Noland Rd., Independence, Mo. 64050. Education, health care, social services, foreign missions.

Sisters of St. Francis of the Holy Family, O.S.F.: Founded 1875, in US. Motherhouse, Mt. St. Francis, Dubuque, Ia. 52001. Varied apostolates.

Sisters of St. Francis of the Immaculate Conception, O.S.F.: Founded 1890, in US. General motherhouse, 2408 W. Heading Ave., Peoria, Ill. 61604. Education, care of aging, pastoral ministry.

Sisters of St. Francis of the Immaculate Heart of Mary, O.S.F.: Founded 1241, in Bavaria; in US, 1913. General motherhouse, Rome, Italy; US motherhouse, Hankinson, N.D. 58041. Education, social services.

Sisters of St. Francis of the Martyr St. George, O.S.F.: Founded 1859, in Germany; in US, 1923. General motherhouse, Thuine, West Germany; US provincial house, Alton, Ill. 62002. Education, social services, foreign mission work.

Sisters of St. Francis of the Mission of the Immaculate Virgin, O.S.F.: Founded 1893, in New York. General motherhouse, Hastings-on-Hudson, N.Y. 10706. Education, parish ministry, social services.

Sisters of St. Francis of the Perpetual Adoration, O.S.F.: Founded 1863, in Germany; in US, 1875. General motherhouse, Olpe, Germany. US provinces: Box 766, Mishawaka, Ind. 46544; P.O. Box 1060, Colorado Springs, Colo. 80901. Educational, hospital work.

Sisters of St. Francis of the Providence of God, O.S.F.: Founded 1922, in US, by Msgr. M. L. Krusas. General motherhouse, Grove and McRoberts Rds., Pittsburgh, Pa. 15234. Education, varied apostolates.

Sisters of St. Joseph of the Third Order of St. Francis, S.S.J.: Founded 1901, in US. Novitiate, 12215 Granger Rd., Cleveland, Ohio 44125. Education, health care, social services.

Sisters of St. Mary of the Third Order of St. Francis, S.S.M.: Founded 1872, in St. Louis, Mo. General motherhouse, 1100 Bellevue Ave., St. Louis, Mo. 63117. Health care, social services.

Sisters of the Infant Jesus, I.J.: Founded 1662, at Rouen, France; in US, 1950. Motherhouse, Paris, France. Generalate, Rome, Italy. US addresses: 20 Reiner St., Colma, Calif. 94014; St. John the Baptist School, Healdsburg, Calif. 95448; 60 Bellevue Ave., Daly City, Calif. 94014.

Sisters of the Sorrowful Mother (Third Order of St. Francis), S.S.M.: Founded 1883, in Italy; in US, 1889. General motherhouse, Rome, Italy. US provinces: 6618 N. Teutonia Ave., Milwaukee, Wis. 53209; 9 Pocono Rd., Denville, N.J. 07834; Tulsa Provincialate,

17600 E. 51st St. S., Broken Arrow, Okla. 74012. Educational, hospital work.

Sisters of the Third Franciscan Order Minor Conventuals, O.S.F.: Founded 1860, at Syracuse, N.Y. Generalate offices, 100 Michaels Ave., Syracuse, N.Y. 13208. Educational, hospital work.

Sisters of the Third Order of St. Francis, O.S.F.: Founded 1877, in US, by Bishop John L. Spalding. Motherhouse, Edgewood Hills, E. Peoria, Ill. 61611. Hospital work.

Sisters of the Third Order of St. Francis, O.S.F.: Founded 1861, at Buffalo, N.Y., from Philadelphia foundation. General motherhouse, 400 Mill St., Williamsville, N.Y. 14221. Educational, hospital work.

Sisters of the Third Order of St. Francis (Oldenburg, Ind.), O.S.F.: Founded 1851, in US. General motherhouse, Convent of the Immaculate Conception, Oldenburg, Ind. 47036. Education, social services, pastoral ministry, foreign missions.

Sisters of the Third Order of St. Francis of Assisi, O.S.F.: Founded 1849, in US. General motherhouse, 3221 S. Lake Dr., Milwaukee, Wis. 53207. Education, other ministries.

Sisters of the Third Order of St. Francis of Penance and Charity, O.S.F.: Founded 1869, in US, by Rev. Joseph Bihn. Motherhouse, St. Francis Convent, St. Francis Ave., Tiffin, O. 44883. Education, social services.

Sisters of the Third Order of St. Francis of the Perpetual Adoration, F.S.P.A.: Founded 1849, in US. Generalate, 912 Market St., La Crosse, Wis. 54601. Education, health care.

Sisters of the Third Order Regular of St. Francis of the Congregation of Our Lady of Lourdes, O.S.F.: Founded 1877, in US. General motherhouse, Assisi Heights, Rochester, Minn. 55901. Education, health care, social services.

(End, Listing of Franciscans)

Good Shepherd Sisters (Servants of the Immaculate Heart of Mary), S.C.I.M.: Founded 1850, in Canada; in US, 1882. General motherhouse, Quebec, Canada; Provincial House, Bay View, Saco, Maine 04072. Educational, social work.

Good Shepherd, Sisters of Our Lady of Charity of the, R.G.S.: Founded 1641, in France; in US, 1843. Generalate, Rome, Italy. US provinces: 9517 Leebrook Dr., Cincinnati, O. 45231; 82-31 Doncaster Pl., Jamaica, N.Y. 11432; 504 Hexton Hill Rd., Silver Spring, Md. 20904; 7654 Natural Bridge Rd., St. Louis, Mo. 63121; 2041 Laurel Ave., St. Paul, Minn. 55104.

Graymoor Sisters: See Franciscan Sisters of the Atonement.

Grey Nuns of the Sacred Heart, G.N.S.H.: Founded 1921, in US. General motherhouse, Quarry Rd., Yardley, Pa. 19067.

Guadalupe, Sisters of, O.L.G.: Founded 1946, in Mexico City. General motherhouse,

Mexico City, Mexico; US address, St. Mary's College, Winona, Minn. 55987.

Guardian Angels, Sisters of the Holy, S.A.C.: Founded 1839, in France. General motherhouse, Madrid, Spain; US foundation, 1245 S. Van Ness, Los Angeles, Calif. 90019.

Handmaids of Mary Immaculate, A.M.I.: Founded 1952 in Helena, Mont. Address: Ave Maria Institute, Washington, N.J. 07882.

Handmaids of the Precious Blood, Congregation of, H.P.B.: Founded 1947, at Jemez Springs, N.M. Motherhouse and novitiate, Cor Jesu Monastery, Jemez Springs, N.M. 87025.

Helpers, Society of, H.H.S.: Founded 1856, in France; in US, 1892. General motherhouse, Paris, France; American province, 303 W. Barry Ave., Chicago, Ill. 60657.

Hermanas Catequistas Guadalupanas, H.C.G.: Founded 1923, in Mexico; in US, 1950. General motherhouse, Mexico; US foundation, 4110 S. Flores, San Antonio, Tex. 78214.

Holy Child Jesus, Society of the, S.H.C.J.: Founded 1846, in England; in US, 1862. General motherhouse, Rome, Italy. US province: 620 Edmonds Ave., Drexel Hill, Pa. 19026.

Holy Faith, Congregation of the Sisters of the, C.H.F.: Founded 1856, in Ireland; in US, 1953. General motherhouse, Dublin, Ireland; US regional superior, 13817 S. Pioneer Blvd., Norwalk, Calif. 90650.

Holy Ghost, Sisters of the, C.H.G.: Founded 1913, in US, by Most Rev. J. F. Regis Canevin. General motherhouse, 5246 Clarwin Ave., Ross Township, Pittsburgh, Pa. 15229. Educational, nursing work; care of aged.

Holy Ghost and Mary Immaculate, Sister Servants of, S.H.G.: Founded 1893, in US. Motherhouse, 301 Yucca St., San Antonio, Tex. 78203. Education, hospital work.

Holy Heart of Mary, Servants of the, S.S.C.M.: Founded 1860, in France; in US, 1889. General motherhouse, Montreal, Que., Canada; US province, 145 S. 4th St., Kankakee, Ill. 60901. Educational, hospital, social work.

Holy Names of Jesus and Mary, Sisters of the, S.N.J.M.: Founded 1843, in Canada; in US, 1859. General motherhouse, Pierrefonds H9K 1C6, P.Q., Canada. US addresses: Oregon Province, Marylhurst, Ore. 97036; California Province, P.O. Box 907, Los Gatos, Calif. 95031; New York Province, 1061 New Scotland Rd., Albany, N.Y. 12208; Washington Province, W. 2911 Ft. Wright Dr., Spokane, Wash. 99204.

Holy Spirit, Daughters of the, D.H.S.: Founded 1706, in France; in US, 1902. Generalate, Rennes, France; US motherhouse, 72 Church St., Putnam, Conn. 06260. Educational work, district nursing; pastoral ministry.

Holy Spirit, Mission Sisters of the, M.S.Sp.: Founded 1932, at Cleveland, O. Motherhouse, 1030 N. River Rd., Saginaw, Mich. 48603.

Holy Spirit, Missionary Sisters, Servants of the: Founded 1889, in Holland; in US, 1901. Generalate, Rome, Italy; US motherhouse, Convent of the Holy Spirit, Techny, Ill. 60082.

Holy Spirit, Sisters of the, C.S.Sp.: Founded 1890, in Rome, Italy; in US, 1929. General motherhouse, 10102 Granger Rd., Garfield Hts., Ohio 44125. Educational, social, nursing work.

Holy Spirit of Perpetual Adoration, Sister Servants of the: Founded 1896, in Holland; in US, 1915. General motherhouse, Steyl, Holland; US motherhouse, 2212 Green St., Philadelphia, Pa. 19130.

Home Mission Sisters of America (Glenmary Sisters): Founded 1952, in US. Motherhouse, Morning Star, P.O. Box 39188, Cincinnati, O. 45239.

Home Visitors of Mary, Sisters, H.V.M.: Founded 1949, in Detroit, Mich. Motherhouse, 356 Arden Park, Detroit, Mich. 48202.

Humility of Mary, Congregation of, C.H.M.: Founded 1854, in France; in US, 1864. US address, Convent of Humility of Mary, Ottumwa, Ia. 52501.

Humility of Mary, Sisters of the, H.M.: Founded 1854, in France; in US, 1864. US address, Villa Maria, Pa. 16155.

Immaculate Conception, Little Servant Sisters of the: Founded 1850, in Poland; in US, 1926. General motherhouse, Poland; US provincial house, 184 Amboy Ave., Woodbridge, N.J. 07095. Education, social services, African missions.

Immaculate Conception, Sisters of the, R.C.M.: Founded 1892, in Spain; in U.S., 1962. General motherhouse, Madrid, Spain; U.S. foundation, 867 Oxford, Clovis, Calif. 93612.

Immaculate Conception, Sisters of the, C.I.C.: Founded 1874, in US. General motherhouse, 4920 Kent St., Metairie, La. 70002.

Immaculate Conception of the Blessed Virgin Mary, Sisters of the (Lithuanian): Founded 1918, at Mariampole, Lithuania; in US, 1936. General motherhouse, Lithuania; US headquarters, Immaculate Conception Convent, Putnam, Conn. 06260.

Immaculate Heart of Mary, Missionary Sisters, I.C.M.: Founded 1897, in India; in US, 1919. Generalate, Rome, Italy; US address, 1710 N. Glebe Rd., Arlington, Va. 22207. Educational social, foreign mission work.

Immaculate Heart of Mary, Sisters of the: Founded 1848, in Spain; in US, 1878. General motherhouse, Rome, Italy. US province, 4100 Sabino Canyon Rd., Tucson, Ariz. 85715. Educational work.

Immaculate Heart of Mary, Sisters of the (California Institute of the Most Holy and Immaculate Heart of the B.V.M.), I.H.M.:

Founded 1848, in Spain; in US, 1871. Generalate, 3431 Waverly Dr., Los Angeles, Calif. 90027.

Immaculate Heart of Mary, Sisters, Servants of the, I.H.M.: Founded 1845, at Monroe, Mich., by Rev. Louis Florent Gillet. Three independent branches: Generalate, 610 W. Elm St., Monroe, Mich. 48161; Villa Maria, Immaculata, Pa. 19345; Immaculate Heart of Mary Generalate, Marywood, Scranton, Pa. 18509.

Incarnate Word and Blessed Sacrament, Congregation of, V.I.: Founded 1625, in France; in US, 1853. Incarnate Word Convent, 3400 Bradford Pl., Houston, Tex. 77028.

Incarnate Word and Blessed Sacrament, Congregation of the, of the Archdiocese of San Antonio, I.W.B.S.: Motherhouses: 1101 Northeast Water St., Victoria, Tex. 77901; 2930 S. Alameda, Corpus Christi, Tex. 78404.

Incarnate Word and Blessed Sacrament, Sisters of the, S.I.W.: Founded 1625, in France; in US 1853. Motherhouse, 6618 Pearl Rd., Parma Heights, Cleveland, O. 44130.

Infant Jesus, Congregation of the (Nursing Sisters of the Sick Poor), C.I.J.: Founded 1835, in France; in US, 1905. General motherhouse, 310 Prospect Park W., Brooklyn, N.Y. 11215.

Jeanne d'Arc, Sisters of Ste.: Founded 1914, in America, by Rev. Marie Clement Staub, A.A. General motherhouse, 1681 Chemin St. Louis, Quebec, G1S 1G4, Canada; US novitiate, 2121 Commonwealth Ave., Brighton, Mass. 02135. Spiritual and temporal service of priests.

Jesus, Daughters of, F.I.: Founded 1871, in Spain; in US, 1950. General motherhouse, Rome, Italy; US address, South Side Mission, 329 S. 4th St., Brooklyn, N.Y. 11211.

Jesus, Daughters of (Filles de Jesus), F.J.: Founded 1834, in France; in US, 1904. General motherhouse, Kermaria, Locmine, France; American provincial house, 9040 84th Ave., Edmonton, Alberta T6C 1E4, Canada. Educational, hospital, parish and social work.

Jesus, Little Sisters of: Founded 1939, in Sahara; in US, 1952. General motherhouse, Rome, Italy; US headquarters, 700 Irving St. N.E., Washington, D.C. 20017.

Jesus, Society of the Sisters, Faithful Companions of, F.C.J.: Founded 1820, in France; in US, 1896. General motherhouse, Kent, England. US convents: 46 Woodland St., Fitchburg, Mass. 01420; 20 Atkins St., Providence, R.I. 02908; St. Philomena Convent, Portsmouth, R.I. 02871.

Jesus Crucified, Congregation of: Founded 1930, in France; in US, 1955. General motherhouse, Brou, France; US foundations: Regina Mundi Priory, Devon, Pa. 19333; St. Paul's Priory, 61 Narragansett, Newport, R.I. 02840.

Jesus Crucified and the Sorrowful Mother, Poor Sisters of, C.J.C.: Founded 1924, in US, by Rev. Alphonsus Maria, C.P. Motherhouse, 261 Thatcher St., Brockton, Mass. 02402. Education, nursing homes, catechetical centers.

Jesus-Mary, Religious of, R.J.M.: Founded 1818, at Lyons, France; in US, 1877. General motherhouse, Rome, Italy; US province, 8908 Riggs Rd., Hyattsville, Md. 20783. Educational work.

Jesus, Mary and Joseph, Missionaries of, M.J.M.J.: Founded 1942, in Spain; in US, 1956. General motherhouse, Madrid, Spain; US regional house, 12940 Up River Rd., Corpus Christi, Tex. 78410.

John the Baptist, Sisters of St., C.S.J.B.: Founded 1878, in Italy; in US, 1906. General motherhouse, Rome, Italy; US provincialate, Anderson Hill Rd., Purchase, N.Y. 10577. Education, parish and retreat work; social services.

Joseph, Missionary Servants of St., M.S.S.J.: Founded 1874, in Spain; in US, 1957. General motherhouse, Salamanca, Spain; US address, 203 N. Spring St., Falls Church, Va. 22046.

Joseph, Poor Sisters of St.: Founded 1880, in Argentina. General motherhouse, Muniz, Argentina; US addresses, Casa Belen, 305 E. 4th St., Bethlehem, Pa. 78015; St. Gabriel Convent, 4319 Sano St., Alexandria, Va. 22312.

Joseph, Religious Daughters of St., F.S.J.: Founded 1875, in Spain. General motherhouse, Spain; US foundation, 319 N. Humphreys Ave., Los Angeles, Calif. 90022.

Joseph, Religious Hospitallers of St., R.H.S.J.: Founded 1636, in France; in US, 1894. Generalate, 5621 Canterbury Ave., Montreal, Que., H3T 15B, Canada. Hospital work.

Joseph, Sisters of St., C.S.J.: Founded 1650, in France; in US, 1836, at St. Louis. US independent motherhouses:

637 Cambridge St., Brighton, Mass. 02135; 1515 W. Ogden Ave., La Grange Park, Ill., 60525; 480 S. Batavia St., Orange, Calif. 92668; Mt. St. Joseph Convent, Chestnut Hill, Philadelphia, Pa. 19118.

St. Joseph Convent, Brentwood, N.Y. 11717; 23 Agassiz Circle, Buffalo, N.Y. 14214; Avila Hall, Clement Rd., Rutland, Vt. 05701; 3430 Rocky River Dr., Cleveland, O. 44111; Main St. and Division Rd., Tipton, Ind. 46072; Nazareth, Mich. 49074; 1425 Washington St., Watertown, N.Y. 13601; St. Joseph Motherhouse, Baden, Pa. 15005; 819 W. 8th St., Erie, Pa. 16502.

4095 East Ave., Rochester, N.Y. 14610; 215 Court St., Concordia, Kans. 66901; Holyoke, Mass. 01040; 1412 E. 2nd St., Superior, Wis. 54880; Pogue Run Rd., Wheeling, W. Va. 26003; 3700 E. Lincoln St., Wichita, Kans. 67218.

Joseph, Sisters of St. (Lyons, France), C.S.J.: Founded 1650, in France; in US, 1906. General motherhouse, Lyons, France; US provincialate, 93 Halifax St., Winslow, Me. 04901. Educational, hospital work.

Joseph, Sisters of St., of Peace, C.S.J.: Founded 1884, in England. Generalate, 1234 Massachusetts Ave. N.W., Washington, D.C. 20005. Educational, hospital, social service work.

Joseph of Carondelet, Sisters of St., C.S.J.: Founded 1650, in France; in US, 1836, at St. Louis, Mo. US headquarters, 2307 S. Lindbergh Blvd., St. Louis, Mo. 63131.

Joseph of Chambery, Sisters of St.: Founded 1650, in France; in US, 1885. Generalate, Rome, Italy; US provincial house, 27 Park Rd., West Hartford, Conn. 06119. Educational, hospital, social work.

Joseph of Cluny, Sisters of St., S.J.C.: Founded 1807, in France. Generalate, Paris, France; US provincial house, Brenton Rd., Newport, R.I. 02840.

Joseph of Medaille, Sisters of, C.S.J.: Founded 1823, in France; in US, 1855. Became an American congregation Nov. 30, 1977. Central office, 5108 Reading Rd., Cincinnati, Ohio 45237.

Joseph of St. Augustine, Fla., Sisters of St., S.S.J.: General motherhouse, 241 St. George St., St. Augustine, Fla. 32084. Educational, hospital, pastoral, social work.

Joseph of St. Mark, Sisters of St., S.S.J.S.M.: Founded 1845, in France; in US, 1937. General motherhouse, 21800 Chardon Rd., Euclid, Cleveland, O. 44117. Nursing homes.

Joseph the Worker, Sisters of St., S.J.W.: General motherhouse, St. Joseph Convent, 143 S. Main St., Walton, Ky. 41094.

Lamb of God, Sisters of the, A.D.: Founded 1945, in France; in US, 1958. General motherhouse, France; US foundation, 1516 Parrish Ave., Owensboro, Ky. 42301.

Living Word, Sisters of the, S.L.W.: Founded 1975, in US. Motherhouse, The Center, 7200 N. Osceola Ave., Chicago, Ill. 60648. Education, hospital, parish ministry work.

Loretto at the Foot of the Cross, Sisters of, S.L.: Founded 1812 in US, by Rev. Charles Nerinckx. General motherhouse, Nerinx, Ky. 40049. Educational work.

Louis, Congregation of Sisters of St., S.S.L.: Founded 1842, in France; in US, 1949. General motherhouse, Monaghan, Ireland; US novitiate, 22300 Mulholland Dr., Woodland Hills, Calif. 91364. Educational, medical, parish, foreign mission work.

Marian Sisters of the Diocese of Lincoln: Founded 1954. Motherhouse, Marycrest, Waverly, Nebr. 68462.

Marian Society of Dominican Catechists, O.P.: Founded 1954 in Louisiana. General

motherhouse, Boyce, La. 71409. Community of Alexandria-Shreveport, La., diocese.

Marianites of Holy Cross, Congregation of the Sisters, M.S.C.: Founded 1841, in France; in US, 1843. Motherhouse, Le Mans, Sarthe, France. US provinces: 4123 Woodland Dr., New Orleans, La. 70114; Great Rd. and Drakes Corner, Princeton, N.J. 08540; Cresci Blvd., Hazlet, N.J. 07730 (vice province).

Marist Sisters, Congregation of Mary, S.M.: Founded 1824, in France. General motherhouse, Rome, Italy; US convents: St. Albert the Great, Dearborn Hts., Mich. 48125; St. Barnabas, E. Detroit, Mich. 48021; Our Lady of Peace, Wheeling, W. Va. 26002.

Maronite Antonine Sisters: Established in US, 1966. US address, 2961 N. Lipkey Rd., R.D. 2, North Jackson, Ohio 44451.

Martha of Prince Edward Island, Sisters of St., C.S.M.: Founded 1916, in Canada; in US, 1961. General motherhouse, 141 Mt. Edward Rd., Charlottetown, P.E.I., CIA 7M8, Canada.

Marthe, Sisters of Sainte (of St. Hyacinthe), S.M.S.H.: Founded 1883, in Canada; in US, 1929. General motherhouse 675 ouest, rue St.-Pierre, Hyacinthe, Que., Canada J2T IN7.

Mary, Company of, O.D.N.: Founded 1607, in France; in US, 1926. General motherhouse, Rome, Italy; US motherhouse, 16791 E. Main St., Tustin, Calif. 92680.

Mary, Daughters of the Heart of, D.H.M.: Founded 1790, in France; in US, 1851. Generalate, Paris, France; US provincialate, 1339 Northampton St., Holyoke, Mass. 01040. Education retreat work.

Mary, Little Company of, Nursing Sisters, L.C.M.: Founded 1877, in England; in US, 1893. General motherhouse, Rome, Italy; US provincial house, 9350 S. California Ave., Evergreen Park, Ill. 60642.

Mary, Mantellate Sisters Servants of, O.S.M.: Founded 1861, in Italy; in US, 1916. Generalate, Rome, Italy; US motherhouse, 13811 S. Western Ave., Blue Island, Ill. 60406. Educational work.

Mary, Missionary Sisters of the Society of (Marist Sisters), S.M.S.M.: Founded 1845, at St. Brieuc, France; in US, 1922. General motherhouse, Rome, Italy; US regional house, 357 Grove St., Waltham, Mass. 02154. Foreign missions.

Mary, Servants of, O.S.M.: Founded 13th century, in Italy; in US, 1893. Generalate, Rome, Italy; US provincial motherhouse, 7400 Military Ave., Omaha, Nebr. 68134.

Mary, Servants of (Servite Sisters), O.S.M.: Founded 13th century, in Italy; in US, 1912. General motherhouse, Our Lady of Sorrows Convent, Ladysmith, Wis. 54848.

Mary, Sisters of St., of Oregon, S.S.M.O.: Founded 1886, in Oregon, by Bishop William H. Gross, C.Ss.R. General motherhouse,

4440 S.W. 148th Ave., Beaverton, Ore. 97007. Educational, nursing work.

Mary, Sisters Servants of (Trained Nurses), S.M.: Founded 1851, at Madrid, Spain; in US, 1914. General motherhouse, Rome, Italy; US motherhouse, 800 N. 18th St., Kansas City, Kans. 66102. Home nursing.

Mary and Joseph, Daughters of, D.M.J.: Founded 1817, in Belgium; in US, 1926. Generalate, Rome, Italy; American novitiate, 6037 W. 78th St., Los Angeles, Calif. 90045.

Mary Help of Christians, Daughters of (Salesian Sisters of St. John Bosco), F.M.A.: Founded 1872, in Italy, by St. John Bosco and St. Mary Dominic Mazzarello; in US, 1908. General motherhouse, Rome, Italy; US motherhouse, Haledon, N.J. 07508. Education, youth work.

Mary Immaculate, Daughters of (Marianist Sisters), F.M.I.: Founded 1816, in France, by Very Rev. William-Joseph Chaminade. General motherhouse, Rome, Italy; US foundation, 251 W. Ligustrum Dr., San Antonio, Tex. 78228. Educational work.

Mary Immaculate, Religious of, R.M.I.: Founded 1876, in Spain; in US, 1954. General motherhouse, Rome, Italy: US foundations, 719 Augusta St., San Antonio, Tex. 78215; 539 W. 54th St., New York, N.Y. 10019.

Mary Immaculate, Sisters Servants of, S.M.I: Founded 1892, in Ukraine; in US, 1935. General motherhouse, Rome, Italy; US province, 209 W. Chestnut Hill Ave., Philadelphia, Pa. 19118. Educational, hospital work.

Mary Immaculate of Mariowka, Sister Servants of, S.S.M.I.: Founded 1878 in Poland. General motherhouse, Poland; American provincialate, 1220 Tugwell Dr., Catonsville, Md. 21228.

Mary of Namur, Sisters of St., S.S.M.N.: Founded 1819, at Namur, Belgium; in US, 1863. General motherhouse, Namur, Belgium. US provinces: 3756 Delaware Ave., Kenmore, N.Y. 14217; 3300 Hemphill St., Ft. Worth, Tex. 76110.

Mary of Providence, Daughters of St., D.S.M.P.: Founded 1872, at Como, Italy; in US, 1913. General motherhouse, Rome, Italy; US provincial house, 4200 N. Austin Ave., Chicago, Ill. 60634. Special education for mentally handicapped.

Mary of the Immaculate Conception, Daughters of, D.M.: Founded 1904, in US, by Msgr. Lucian Bojnowski. General motherhouse, 314 Osgood Ave., New Britain, Conn. 06053. Educational, hospital work.

Mary Reparatrix, Society of, S.M.R.: Founded 1857, in France; in US, 1908. Generalate, Rome, Italy. US province, 14 E. 29th St., New York, N.Y. 10016.

Medical Mission Sisters (Society of Catholic Medical Missionaries, Inc.), S.C.M.M.: Founded 1925, in US, by Mother Anna Dengel. Generalate, Rome, Italy; US head-

quarters, 8400 Pine Rd., Philadelphia, Pa. 19111. Medical work, health education, especially in mission areas.

Medical Missionaries of Mary, M.M.M.: Founded 1937, in Ireland, by Mother Mary Martin; in US, 1950. General motherhouse, Drogheda, Ireland; US headquarters, 563 Minneford Ave., City Island, Bronx, N.Y. 10464. Medical aid in missions.

Mercedarian Missionaries of Berriz, M.M.B.: Founded 1930, in Spain; in US, 1946. General motherhouse, Berriz, Spain; US headquarters, 918 E. 9th St., Kansas City, Mo. 64106.

Mercy, Daughters of Our Lady of, D.M.: Founded 1837, in Italy, by St. Mary Joseph Rossello; in US, 1919. General motherhouse, Savona, Italy; US motherhouse, Villa Rossello, Catawba Ave., Newfield, N.J. 08344. Educational, hospital work.

Mercy, Missionary Sisters of Our Lady of, M.O.M.: Founded 1938, in Brazil; in US, 1955. General motherhouse, Brazil; US address, 388 Franklin St., Buffalo, N.Y. 14202.

Mercy, Sisters of, R.S.M.: Founded 1831, in Ireland, by Mother Mary Catherine McAuley. US motherhouses:

634 New Scotland Ave., Albany, N.Y. 12208; 273 Willoughby Ave., Brooklyn, N.Y. 11205; S. 5245 Murphy Rd., Orchard Park, N.Y. 14127; 100 Mansfield Ave., Burlington, Vt. 05401; 1125 Prairie Dr., N.E., Cedar Rapids, Ia. 52402; 444 E. Grandview Blvd., Erie, Pa. 16504; 249 Steele Rd., W. Hartford, Conn. 06117.

Windham, N.H. 03087; Merion, Pa. 10966; 3333 Fifth Ave., Pittsburgh, Pa. 15213; 605 Stevens Ave., Portland, Me. 04103; Belmont, N. Car. 28012; 1437 Blossom Rd., Rochester, N.Y. 14610; 535 Sacramento St., Auburn, Calif. 95603.

2300 Adeline Dr., Burlingame, Calif. 94010; US Route 22 at Terrill Rd., Plainfield, N.J. 07061; 101 Barry Rd., Worcester, Mass. 01609.

Mercy, Sisters of, of the Union in the United States of America, R.S.M.: Founded 1831 in Ireland, by Mother M. Catherine McAuley; union formed in 1929. U.S. provinces:

P.O. Box 10490, Baltimore, Md. 21209; 10024 S. Central Park Ave., Chicago, Ill. 60642; 2301 Grandview Ave., Cincinnati, Ohio 45206; 29000 Eleven Mile Rd., Farmington Hills, Mich. 48024; 541 Broadway, Dobbs Ferry, N.Y. 10522; 1801 S. 72nd St., Omaha, Nebr. 68124; R.D. 3, Cumberland, R.I. 02864; 2039 N. Geyer Rd., St. Louis, Mo. 63131; Dallas, Pa. 18612.

Mercy, Sisters of, Daughters of Christian Charity of St. Vincent de Paul, S.M.D.C.: Founded 1842, in Hungary; US foundation, Rt. 1, Box 353, Hewitt, N.J. 07421.

Mercy of the Blessed Sacrament, Sisters of: Founded 1910 in Mexico. U.S. foundation,

555 E. Mountain View, Barstow, Calif. 92311.

Mill Hill Sisters; See Franciscan Missionaries of St. Joseph.

Minim Sisters of Mary Immaculate, C.F.M.M.: Founded 1886, in Mexico; in U.S. 1926. General motherhouse, Leon, Guanajuato, Mexico; US address, St. Joseph Hospital Convent, Target Range Rd., Nogales, Ariz. 85621.

Misericordia Sisters, S.M.: Founded 1848, in Canada; in US, 1887. General motherhouse. 12435 Ave. Misericorde, Montreal H4J 2G3, Canada. Social work with unwed mothers and their children; hospital work.

Mission Helpers of the Sacred Heart, M.H.S.H.: Founded 1890, in US. General motherhouse, 1001 W. Joppa Rd., Baltimore, Md. 21204. Religious education, evangelization.

Missionary Catechists of the Sacred Hearts of Jesus and Mary (Violetas), M.C.: Founded 1918, in Mexico; in US, 1943. Motherhouse, Tlalpan, Mexico; US address, 209 W. Murray St., Victoria, Tex. 77901.

Missionary Sisters of the Catholic Apostolate (Pallottine Missionary Sisters), S.A.C.: Founded in Rome, 1843; in US, 1912. Generalate, Rome, Italy; US provincialate, Rt. 2, 15270 Old Halls Ferry Rd., Florissant, Mo. 63034.

Mother of God, Missionary Sisters of the, M.S.M.G.: Byzantine, Ukrainian Rite, Stamford. Motherhouse, 711-719 N. Franklin St., Philadelphia, Pa. 19123.

Mother of God, Sisters Poor Servants of the, S.M.G.: Founded 1869, at London, England; in US, 1947. General motherhouse, Maryfield, Roehampton, London. US addresses: Maryfield Nursing Home, Greensboro Rd., High Point, N.C. 27260; St. Mary's Hospital, 916 Virginia Ave., Norton, Va. 24273; Holy Spirit School, 1800 Geary St., Philadelphia, Pa. 19145. Hospital, educational work.

Nazareth, Poor Sisters of: Founded in England; U.S. foundation, 1924. General motherhouse, Hammersmith, London, England; US novitiate, 3333 Manning Ave., Los Angeles, Calif. 90064. Social services, education.

Notre Dame, School Sisters of, S.S.N.D.: Founded 1833, in Germany; in US, 1847. General motherhouse, Rome, Italy. US provinces: 700 W. Highland Rd., Mequon, Wis. 53092; 6401 N. Charles St., Baltimore, Md. 21212; 320 E. Ripa Ave., St. Louis, Mo. 63125; Good Counsel Hill, Mankato, Minn. 56001; 345 Belden Hill Rd., Wilton, Conn. 06897; Rt. 2, Box 4, Irving, Tex. 75062; 1431 Euclid Ave., Berwyn, Ill. 60402.

Notre Dame, Sisters of, S.N.D.: Founded 1850, at Coesfeld, Germany; in US, 1874. General motherhouse, Rome, Italy. US provinces: 13000 Auburn Rd., Chardon, O. 44024; 1601 Dixie Highway, Covington, Ky. 41011; 3837 Secor Rd., Toledo, O. 43623; 1776 Hendrix Ave., Thousand Oaks, Calif. 91360.

Notre Dame, Sisters of the Congregation of, C.N.D.: Founded 1653, in Canada; in US, 1860. General motherhouse, Montreal, Que., Canada; U.S. province, 223 West Mountain Rd., Ridgefield, Conn. 06877. Education.

Notre Dame de Namur, Sisters of, S.N.D.: Founded 1803, in France; in US, 1840. General motherhouse, Rome, Italy. US provinces: 328 Dartmouth St., Boston, Mass. 02116; Jeffrey's Neck Rd., Ipswich, Mass. 01938; 1561 N. Benson Rd., Fairfield, Conn. 06431; Landing Rd., Ilchester, Md. 21083; 701 E. Columbia Ave., Cincinnati, O. 45215; 14800 Bohlman Rd., Saratoga, Calif. 95070. Educational work.

Notre Dame de Sion, Congregation of, N.D.S.: Founded 1843, in France; in US, 1892. Generalate, Rome, Italy; US provincial house, 3823 Locust St., Kansas City, Mo. 64109. Creation of better understanding and relations between Christians and Jews.

Notre Dame des Anges, Missionary Sisters of, M.N.D.A.: Founded 1922, in Canada; in US, 1949. General motherhouse, Lennoxville, Canada; US address, St. Mary's Catechetical School, 320 N. Main St., Union City, Conn. 06770.

Notre Dame Sisters: Founded 1853, in Czechoslovakia; in US, 1910. General motherhouse, Javornik, Czechoslovakia; US motherhouse, 3501 State St., Omaha, Nebr. 68112. Educational work.

Our Lady of Charity, North American Union of Sisters of (Sisters of Our Lady of Charity of the Refuge), O.L.C.: Founded 1641, in Caen, France, by St. John Eudes; in U.S., 1855. Autonomous houses were federated in 1944 and in May, 1978, the North American Union of the Sisters of Our Lady of Charity was established. General motherhouse and administrative center, Box 327, Wisconsin Dells, Wis. 53965. Primarily devoted to reeducation and rehabilitation of women and girls in residential and non-residential settings.

Our Lady of Mercy, Sisters of: General motherhouse, Wexford, Ireland; US foundation, St. Peter's Convent, 445 W. New York Ave., Deland, Fla. 32720.

Our Lady of Sorrows, Sisters of, O.L.S.: Founded 1839, in Italy; in US, 1947. General motherhouse, Rome, Italy; US headquarters, 10450 Ellerbe Rd., Shreveport, La. 71106.

Our Lady of the Garden, Sisters of, O.L.G.: Founded 1829, in Italy, by St. Anthony Mary Gianelli. Motherhouse, Rome, Italy; U.S. address, St. Brendan School, 445½ Whalley Ave., New Haven, Conn. 06511.

Pallottine Sisters of the Catholic Apostolate, C.S.A.C.: Founded 1843, at Rome, Italy; in US, 1889. General motherhouse, Rome; US motherhouse, St. Patrick's Villa, Harriman Heights, Harriman, N.Y. 10926. Educational work.

Parish Visitors of Mary Immaculate, P.V.M.I.: Founded 1920, in New York. General motherhouse, Box 658, Monroe, N.Y. 10950. Mission work.

Passionist Sisters: See Cross and Passion, Sisters of the.

Paul, Angelic Sisters of St.: Founded 1535, in Milan, Italy; US address, Fatima Shrine, Swan Rd., Youngstown, N.Y. 14174.

Paul, Daughters of St. (Missionary Sisters of the Media of Communication), D.S.P.: Founded 1915, at Alba, Piedmont, Italy; in US, 1932. General motherhouse, Rome, Italy; US provincial house, 50 St. Paul's Ave., Jamaica Plain, Mass. 02130. Apostolate of the communications arts.

Paul of Chartres, Sisters of St., S.P.C.: Founded 1696, in France. General house, Rome, Italy; US address, County Road 492, Marquette, Mich. 49855.

Peter Claver, Missionary Sisters of St., S.S.P.C.: Founded 1894; in US, 1914. General motherhouse, Rome, Italy; US address, 667 Woods Mill Rd. S., Chesterfield, Mo. 63017.

Pious Schools, Sisters of, Sch. P.: Founded 1829 in Spain; in US, 1954. General motherhouse, Rome, Italy; US headquarters, 9925 Mason Ave., Chatsworth, Calif. 91311.

Poor, Little Sisters of the, L.S.P.: Founded 1839, in France; in US, 1868. General motherhouse, St. Pern, France. US provinces: 110-30 221st St., Queens Village, N.Y. 11429; 601 Maiden Choice Lane, Baltimore, Md. 21228; 80 W. Northwest Hwy., Palatine, Ill. 60067. Care of aged.

Poor Clare Missionary Sisters (Misioneras Clarisas), M.C.: Founded Mexico. General motherhouse, Rome, Italy; US novitiate, 1019 N. Newhope, Santa Ana, Calif. 92703.

Poor Clare Nuns: See Franciscan Poor Clare Nuns.

Poor Clares (Sisters of St. Clare), P.C.: General motherhouse, Dublin, Ireland; US foundation, 37 E. Emerson, Chula Vista, Calif. 92011.

Poor Handmaids of Jesus Christ (Ancilla Domini Sisters), P.H.J.C.: Founded 1851, in Germany; in US, 1868. General motherhouse, Dernbach, Westerwald, Germany; US motherhouse, Donaldson, Ind. 46513. Educational, hospital work, social services.

Precious Blood, Daughters of Charity of the Most: Founded 1872, at Pagani, Italy; in US, 1908. General motherhouse, Rome, Italy; US convent, 1482 North Ave., Bridgeport, Conn. 06604.

Precious Blood, Missionary Sisters of the, C.P.S.: Founded 1885, at Mariannhill, South Africa; in US, 1925. Generalate, Rome, Italy; US novitiate, New Holland Ave., P.O. Box 97, Shillington, Pa. 19607. Home and foreign mission work.

Precious Blood, Sisters Adorers of the, A.P.B.: Founded 1861, in Canada; in US,

1890. General motherhouses: 2520, rue Girouard, St. Hyacinthe, Que. J2S 7B8, Canada (French); 301 Ramsay Rd., London, Ont. N6G 1N7, Canada (English). Contemplatives.

Precious Blood, Sisters of the, C.Pp.S.: Founded 1834, in Switzerland; in US, 1844. Generalate, 4000 Denlinger Rd., Dayton, Ohio 45426. Education, health care, other ministries.

Precious Blood, Sisters of the Most, C.Pp.S.: Founded 1845, in Steinerberg, Switzerland; in US, 1870. General motherhouse, 204 N. Main St., O'Fallon, Mo. 63366. Education, other ministries.

Presentation, Sisters of St. Mary of the, S.M.P.: Founded 1829, in France; in US, 1903. General motherhouse, Broons, Cotes-du-Nord, France. US address, Maryvale Novitiate, Valley City, N. Dak. 58072. Educational, hospital work.

Presentation of Mary, Sisters of the, P.M.: Founded 1796, in France; in US, 1873. General motherhouse, Castel Gandolfo, Italy. US provincial houses: 495 Mammoth Rd., Manchester, N.H. 03104; 209 Lawrence St., Methuen, Mass. 01844.

Presentation of the B.V.M., Sisters of the, P.B.V.M.: Founded 1775, in Ireland; in US, 1854, in San Francisco. US motherhouses: 2360 Carter Rd., Dubuque, Ia. 52001; R.D. 2, Box 101, Newburgh, N.Y. 12550; 8931 Callaghan Rd., San Antonio, Tex. 78230; 2340 Turk Blvd., San Francisco, Calif. 94118; Watervliet, N.Y. 12189.

Route 1, Fargo, N. Dak. 58103; 250 S. Davis Dr., P.O. Box 1113, Warner Robbins, Ga. 31093; 1500 N. Main, Aberdeen, S. Dak. 57401; 1300 E. Cedar, Globe, Ariz. 85501; 1555 E. Dana, Mesa, Ariz. 85201; 366 South St., Fitchburg, Mass. 01420; 419 Woodrow Rd., Annadale, Staten Island, N.Y. 10312.

Providence, Daughters of Divine, F.D.P.: Founded 1832, Italy; in US, 1964. General motherhouse, Rome, Italy; US address, 1625 Missouri St., Chalmette, La. 70043.

Providence, Missionary Catechists of Divine, M.C.D.P.: Founded 1930, as a filial society; adjunct branch of Sisters of Divine Providence (Helotes, Tex.). Motherhouse, 2318 Castroville Rd., San Antonio, Tex. 78237.

Providence, Oblate Sisters of, O.S.P.: Founded 1829, in US. General motherhouse, 701 Gun Rd., Baltimore, Md. 21227. Educational work.

Providence, Sisters of, S.P.: Founded 1861, in Canada; in US, 1873. General motherhouse, Our Lady of Victory Convent, Brightside, Holyoke, Mass. 01040.

Providence, Sisters of, S.P.: Founded 1843, in Canada; in US, 1854. General motherhouse, Montreal, Canada. US provinces: 1511 Third Ave., Seattle, Wash. 98101; 9 E. 9th Ave., Spokane, Wash. 99202.

Providence, Sisters of (of St. Mary-of-the-Woods), S.P.: Founded 1806, in France; in US, 1840. Generalate, St. Mary-of-the-Woods, Ind. 47876.

Providence, Sisters of Divine, C.D.P.: Founded 1762, in France; in US, 1866. Generalate, Box 197, Helotes, Tex. 78023. Educational, hospital work.

Providence, Sisters of Divine, C.D.P.: Founded 1851, in Germany; in US, 1876. Generalate, Rome, Italy. US provinces: 9000 Babcock Blvd., Allison Park, Pa. 15101; 8351 Florissant Rd., Normandy, Mo. 63121; Box 2, Rte. 80, Kingston, Mass. 02364. Educational, hospital work.

Providence, Sisters of Divine (of Kentucky), C.D.P.: Founded 1762, in France; in US, 1889. General motherhouse, Moselle, France; US province, Melbourne, Ky. 41059. Education, social services, other ministries.

Redeemer, Oblates of the Most Holy, O.SS.R.: Founded 1864, in Spain. General motherhouse, Spain; US foundation, 60-80 Pond St., Jamaica Plain, Mass. 02130.

Redeemer, Order of the Most Holy, O.SS.R.: Founded 1731, by St. Alphonsus Liguori; in US, 1957. US addresses: Mother of Perpetual Help Monastery, Esopus, N.Y. 12429; St. Alphonsus Monastery, Liguori, Mo. 63057.

Redeemer, Sisters of the Divine, S.D.R.: Founded 1849, in Niederbronn, France; in US, 1912. General motherhouse, Rome, Italy; US province, 999 Rock Run Road, Elizabeth, Pa. 15037. Educational, hospital work; care of the aged.

Redeemer, Sisters of the Holy, S.H.R.: Founded 1849, in Alsace; in US, 1924. General motherhouse, Wuerzburg, Germany; US provincial house, Huntingdon Valley, Pa. 19006. Personalized medical care in hospitals, homes for aged, private homes; retreat work.

Reparation of the Congregation of Mary, Sisters of, S.R.C.M.: Founded 1903, in US. Motherhouse, St. Zita's Villa, Monsey, N.Y. 10952.

Resurrection, Sisters of the, C.R.: Founded 1891, in Italy; in US, 1900. General motherhouse, Rome, Italy. US provinces: 7432 Talcott Ave., Chicago, Ill. 60631; Mt. St. Joseph, Castleton-on-Hudson, N.Y. 12033. Education, nursing.

Rita, Sisters of St., O.S.A.: General motherhouse, Wurzburg, Germany. US foundation, St. Monica's Convent, 3920 Green Bay Rd., Racine, Wis. 53404.

Rosary, Congregation of Our Lady of the Holy, R.S.R.: Founded 1874, in Canada; in US, 1899. General motherhouse, C.P. 2020, Rimouski, Que., Canada. US regional house, 20 Thomas St., Portland, Me. 04102. Educational work.

Rosary, Missionary Sisters of Our Lady of the Holy, H.R.S.: Founded 1924, in Ireland; in US, 1954. Motherhouse, Dublin, Ireland.

US novitiate, 214 Ashwood Rd., Villanova, Pa. 19085. African missions.

Sacrament, Missionary Sisters of the Most Blessed, M.SS.S.: General motherhouse, Madrid, Spain; US foundation: 1111 Wordin Ave., Bridgeport, Conn. 06605.

Sacrament, Nuns of the Perpetual Adoration of the Blessed, A.P.: Founded 1807, in Rome, Italy; in US, 1925. US monasteries: 145 N. Cotton Ave., El Paso, Tex. 79901; 771 Ashbury St., San Francisco, Calif. 94117.

Sacrament, Oblate Sisters of the Blessed, O.S.B.S.: Founded 1935, in US; motherhouse, St. Sylvester Convent, Marty, S.D. 57361. Care of American Indians.

Sacrament, Religious Mercedarians of the Blessed, R.M.S.S.: Founded 1910, in Mexico; in US, 1926. General motherhouse, Mexico City, Mexico; US convent, 222 W. Cevallos St., San Antonio, Tex. 78204.

Sacrament, Servants of the Blessed, S.S.S.: Founded 1858, in France, by St. Pierre Julien Eymard; in US, 1947. General motherhouse, Rome, Italy; American vice-provincial house, 101 Silver St., Waterville, Me. 04901. Contemplative.

Sacrament, Sisters of the Blessed, for Indians and Colored People, S.B.S.: Founded 1891, in US. General motherhouse, Bensalem, Pa. 19020.

Sacrament, Sisters of the Most Holy, M.H.S.: Founded 1851, in France; in US, 1872. General motherhouse, 409 W. St. Mary Blvd. (P.O. Box 2429), Lafayette, La. 70502.

Sacrament, Sisters Servants of the Blessed, S.S.B.S.: Founded 1904, in Mexico. General motherhouse, Guadalajara, Mexico. US address, Our Lady of Guadalupe School, 536 Rockwood Ave., Calexico, Calif. 92231.

Sacramentine Nuns (Religious of the Order of the Blessed Sacrament and Our Lady), O.S.S.: Founded 1639, in France; in US, 1912. US monasteries: 23 Park Ave., Yonkers, N.Y. 10703; US 31, Conway, Mich. 49722. Perpetual adoration of the Holy Eucharist.

Sacred Heart, Daughters of Our Lady of the: Founded 1882, in France; in US, 1955. General motherhouse, Rome, Italy; US address, 424 E. Browning Rd., Bellmawr, N.J. 08031. Educational work.

Sacred Heart, Missionary Sisters of the (Cabrini Sisters), M.S.C.: Founded 1880, in Italy, by St. Frances Xavier Cabrini; in US, 1889. General motherhouse, Rome, Italy; US provinces: 223 E. 19th St., New York, N.Y. 10003 (Eastern); 467 W. Deming Pl., Chicago, Ill. 60614 (Western). Educational, health, social and catechetical work.

Sacred Heart, Religious of the Apostolate of the, R.A.: General motherhouse, Madrid, Spain; US address, 1120 6th St., Miami Beach, Fla., 33139.

Sacred Heart, Society Devoted to the, S.D.S.H.: Founded 1940, in Hungary; in US,

1956. US motherhouse, 2121 W. Olive Dr., Burbank, Calif. 91506. Educational work.

Sacred Heart, Society of the, R.S.C.J.: Founded 1800, in France; in US, 1818. General motherhouse, Rome, Italy. US provinces: 1177 King St., Greenwich, Conn. 06830; 2047 W. Fargo, Chicago, Ill. 60645; 541 S. Mason Rd., St. Louis, Mo. 63141; 453 Miller Ave., S. San Francisco, Calif. 94080; 842 Commonwealth Ave., Newton, Mass. 02159. Educational work.

Sacred Heart of Jesus, Apostles of, A.S.C.J.: Founded 1894, in Italy; in US, 1902. General motherhouse, Rome, Italy; US motherhouse, 265 Benham St., Hamden, Conn. 06514. Educational, social work.

Sacred Heart of Jesus, Handmaids of the, A.C.J.: Founded 1877, in Spain. General motherhouse, Rome, Italy; US province, 616 Coopertown Rd., Haverford, Pa. 19041. Educational, retreat work.

Sacred Heart of Jesus, Missionary Sisters of the Most (Hiltrup), M.S.C.: Founded 1899, in Germany; in US, 1908. General motherhouse, Rome, Italy; US province, Hyde Park, Reading, Pa. 19605. Education, health care, pastoral ministry.

Sacred Heart of Jesus, Oblate Sisters of the, O.S.H.J.: Founded 1894; in US, 1949. General motherhouse, Rome, Italy; US headquarters, 50 Warner Rd., Hubbard, Ohio 44425. Educational, social work.

Sacred Heart of Jesus, Servants of the Most: Founded 1894, in Poland; in US, 1959. General motherhouse, Cracow, Poland; US address, 231 Arch St., Cresson, Pa. 16630. Education, health care, social services.

Sacred Heart of Jesus, Sisters of the, S.S.C.J.: Founded 1816, in France; in US, 1903. General motherhouse, St. Jacut, Brittany, France; US provincial house, 5922 Blanco Rd., San Antonio, Tex. 78216. Educational, hospital, domestic work.

Sacred Heart of Jesus and of the Poor, Servants of the (Mexican), S.S.H.J.P.: Founded 1885, in Mexico; in US, 1907. General motherhouse, Apartado 92, Puebla, Pue., Mexico; US regional house, 237 Tobin Pl., El Paso, Tex. 79905.

Sacred Heart of Jesus for Reparation, Congregation of the Handmaids of the: Founded 1918, in Italy; in US, 1958. US address, Sunshine Park, R.D. 3, Steubenville, Ohio 43952.

Sacred Heart of Mary, Religious of the, R.S.H.M.: Founded 1848, in France; in US, 1877. Generalate, Rome, Italy. US provinces: 50 Wilson Park Dr., Tarrytown, N.Y. 10591; 8008 Loyola Blvd., Los Angeles, Calif. 90045.

Sacred Hearts, Religious of the Holy Union of the, S.U.S.C.: Founded 1826, in France; in US, 1886. Generalate, Rome, Italy. US provinces: 550 Rock St., Fall River, Mass. 02720; Main St., Groton, Mass. 01450. Varied ministries.

Sacred Hearts and of Perpetual Adoration,

Sisters of the, SS.CC.: Founded 1797, in France; in US, 1908. General motherhouse, Rome, Italy; US provincial house, 53 Ocean St., New Bedford, Mass. 02740. Varied ministries.

Sacred Hearts of Jesus and Mary, Sisters of the, S.H.J.M.: Established 1953, in US. General motherhouse, Essex, England; US address, 310 San Carlos Ave., El Cerrito, Calif. 94530.

Savior, Company of the, C.S.: Founded 1952, in Spain; in US, 1962. General motherhouse, Madrid, Spain; US foundation, 820 Clinton Ave., Bridgeport, Conn. 06608.

Savior, Sisters of the Divine, S.D.S.: Founded 1888, in Italy; in US, 1895. General motherhouse, Rome, Italy; US province, 4311 N. 100th St., Milwaukee, Wis. 53222. Educational, hospital work.

Social Service, Sisters of, S.S.S.: Founded 1908, in Hungary; in US, 1926. General motherhouse, 1120 Westchester Pl., Los Angeles, Calif. 90019.

Social Service, Sisters of, S.S.S.: Founded in Hungary, 1923. US address, 440 Linwood Ave., Buffalo, N.Y. 14209. Social work.

Teresa of Jesus, Society of St., S.T.J.: Founded 1876, in Spain; in US, 1910. General motherhouse, Rome, Italy; US provincial house, 154 Fair Ave., San Antonio, Tex. 78223.

Thomas of Villanova, Congregation of Sisters of St., S.S.T.V.: Founded 1661, in France; in US, 1948. General motherhouse, Neuilly-sur-Seine, France; US foundation W. Rocks Rd., Norwalk, Conn. 06851.

Trinity, Missionary Servants of the Most Blessed, M.S.B.T.: Founded 1912, in US, by Very Rev. Thomas A. Judge. General motherhouse, 3501 Solly St., Philadelphia, Pa. 19136. Educational, social work; health services.

Trinity, Sisters of the Most Holy, O.Ss.T.: Founded 1198, in Rome; in US, 1920. General motherhouse, Rome, Italy; US address, Immaculate Conception Province, 21320 Euclid Ave., Euclid, Ohio 44117. Educational work.

Ursula of the Blessed Virgin, Society of the Sisters of St., S.U.: Founded 1606, in France; in US, 1902. General motherhouse, France; US novitiate, Rhinebeck, N.Y. 12572. Educational work.

Ursuline Nuns (Roman Union), O.S.U.: Founded 1535, in Italy; in US, 1727. Generalate, Rome, Italy. US provinces: 323 E. 198th St., Bronx, N.Y. 10458; Crystal Heights Rd., Crystal City, Mo. 63019; 639 Angela Dr., Santa Rosa, Calif. 95401; 71 Lowder St., Dedham, Mass. 02026,

Ursuline Nuns of the Congregation of Paris, O.S.U.: Founded 1535, in Italy; in US, 1727, in New Orleans. US motherhouses: St. Martin, O. 45170; East and Miami Sts., Paola, Kans. 66071; 3115 Lexington Rd.,

Louisville, Ky. 40206; 2600 Lander Rd., Cleveland, O. 44124; Maple Mount, Ky. 42356; 2413 Collingwood Blvd., Toledo, O. 43620; 4250 Shields Rd., Canfield, O. 44406; 1339 E. McMillan St., Cincinnati, O. 45206.

Ursuline Nuns of the Congregation of Tildonk, Belgium, R.U.: Founded 1535, in Italy; in US, 1924. Generalate, Tildonk, Belgium; US address, 81-15 Utopia Parkway, Jamaica, N.Y. 11432. Educational, foreign mission work.

Ursuline Sisters, O.S.U.: Founded 1535, in Italy; in US, 1910. General motherhouse, Mount Calvary, Germany; US motherhouse, 1026 N. Douglas Ave., Belleville, Ill. 62221. Educational work.

Ursuline Sisters (Irish Ursuline Union), O.S.U.: General motherhouse, Blackrock, Cork, Ireland; US address, 1973 Torch Hill Rd., Columbus, Ga. 31903.

Venerini Sisters, Religious, M.P.V.: Founded 1685, in Italy; in US, 1909. General motherhouse, Rome, Italy; US provincialate; 23 Edward St., Worcester, Mass. 01605.

Victory Missionary Sisters, Our Lady of, O.L.V.M.: Founded 1922, in US. Motherhouse, Victory Noll, Box 109, Huntington, Ind. 46750. Educational, social work.

Vincent de Paul, Sisters: See Charity of St. Vincent de Paul, Sisters of.

Visitation Nuns, V.H.M.: Founded 1610, in France; in U.S. (Georgetown, D.C.), 1799. Contemplative, educational work. Two federations in U.S.

First Federation of North America. Major pontifical enclosure. Pres., Mother Mary Gabriella Muth, Monastery of the Visitation, 9001 Old Georgetown Rd., Bethesda, Md. 20014. Addresses of monasteries belonging to the federation: 2300 Springhill Ave., Mobile, Ala. 36607; 9001 Old Georgetown Rd., Bethesda, Md. 20014; 2002 Bancroft Pkwy., Wilmington, Del. 19806; 2209 E. Grace St., Richmond, Va. 23223; 5820 City Ave., Philadelphia, Pa. 19131; 1745 Parkside Blvd., Toledo, O. 43607; 2055 Ridgedale Dr., Snellville, Ga. 30278.

Second Federation of North America. Constitutional enclosure. Pres., Rev. Mother Anne Madeline Ernstmann, Visitation Monastery, 3200 S.W. Dash Point Rd., Federal Way, Wash. 98003. Addresses of monasteries belonging to the federation: 1500 35th St., Washington, D.C. 20007; 3020 N. Ballas Rd., St. Louis, Mo. 63131; 200 E. Second St., Frederick, Md. 21701; Mt. St. Chantal Monastery of the Visitation, Wheeling, W. Va. 26003; Ridge Blvd. and 89th St., Brooklyn, N.Y. 11209; 1600 Murdock Ave., Parkersburg, W. Va. 26101; 2000 Sixteenth Ave., Rock Island, Ill. 61201; 2475 Dodd Rd., Mendota Heights, St. Paul, Minn. 55120; Visitation Monastery, Georgetown, Ky. 40324; 3200 S.W. Dash Point Rd., Federal Way, Wash. 98003.

Visitation of the Congregation of the Immaculate Heart of Mary, Sisters of the, S.V.M.: Founded 1952, in US. Motherhouse, 900 Alta Vista St., Dubuque, Ia. 52001. Educational work, parish ministry.

Vocationist Sisters (Sisters of the Divine Vocations): Founded 1921, in Italy. General motherhouse, Naples, Italy; US foundation, Perpetual Help Nursery, 172 Broad St., Newark, N.J. 07104.

White Sisters: See Africa, Missionary Sisters of Our Lady of.

Wisdom, Daughters of, D.W.: Founded 1703, in France, by St. Louis Marie Grignon de Montfort; in US, 1904. General motherhouse, Vendee, France; US province, 385 S. Ocean Ave., Islip, N.Y. Education, health care, parish ministry, social services.

Xaverian Missionary Society of Mary, Inc., X.M.M.: Founded 1945, in Italy; in US, 1954. General motherhouse, Parma, Italy; US address, 242 Salisbury St., Worcester, Mass. 01609.

Xavier Mission Sisters (Catholic Mission Sisters of St. Francis Xavier), X.M.S.: Founded 1946, at Warren, Mich., by Cardinal Edward Mooney. General motherhouse, 37179 Moravian Dr., Mount Clemens, Mich. 48043. Educational, hospital, social work in missions.

ORGANIZATIONS OF RELIGIOUS

Men

Conference of Major Superiors of Men: An association of major superiors of religious institutes of men, founded in 1956 and established officially Mar. 23, 1960, by decree of the Congregation for Religious and Secular Institutes. Its purposes are to assist religious to fulfill their proper prophetic role in the Church and the world; to provide liaison opportunities among religious and with church officials; to exert Christian influence through its operations, and to serve as a national voice for the corporate views of superiors. Conference membership consists of 263 major superiors of institutes with a combined total of approximately 30,000 members. The principal officers are Rev. Ronald Carignan, O.M.I., president, and Rev. Donald P. Skwor, S.D.S., executive director. The national office is located at 8808 Cameron St., Silver Spring, Md. 20910.

National Assembly of Religious Brothers: Founded in 1972 as a grassroots organization open to members of all-brother institutes as well as mixed institutes of priests and brothers. It is a service organization for its members and those affected by their apostolates. The primary objectives of the NARB are: to publicize the unique vocations of brothers, to encourage the development of the spiritual life of all brothers; to promote increased awareness among brothers of their ministerial power for good; to provide a corporate voice for brothers in shaping the future of religious life; to heighten their concern with and involvement in the needs of the Church and society; and to further communication among brothers and provide liaison with various organizations of the Church. Membership in the assembly is open to brothers in the U.S. and Canada. Sacred Heart Brother Adrian Gaudin is president of the assembly. Brother Gerard Clark, C.SS.R., executive secretary, is located at 1 Liguori Drive, P.O. Box 26, Liguori, Mo. 63057.

Women

Association of Contemplative Sisters: Founded by nearly 140 representatives of 57 communities in the U.S. and Canada in August, 1969. Its principal purpose is development of the contemplative life-style for effective service to the Church. It has a membership of approximately 400. Sister Annamae Dannes, O.C.D., is president. The central office is located at 3176 Fairmount Blvd., Cleveland Heights, O. 44118.

Consortium Perfectae Caritatis: Named Association of Perfect Love after the Latin title of the Second Vatican Council's *Decree on the Appropriate Renewal of Religious Life,* and organized in March, 1971, at a meeting of nearly 150 sisters from 48 communities in the U.S. and Canada. Its purposes are to encourage the development of religious life in line with Vatican II guidelines and related directives, and to share experiences in the renewal of religious life. Sister Mary Elise, S.N.D., is executive director. The association is administered by a group of 14 superiors from 12 states and Canada. The mailing address is 13000 Auburn Rd., Chardon, Ohio 44024. Rev. James A. Viall is coordinator.

Las Hermanas: A national organization of Hispanic women formed in 1971 for the purpose of being "actively present to the ever changing needs" of Hispanics in the U.S. through programs of cultural awareness, leadership training, peace and justice concerns. The organization, with non Hispanic associates, is directed by a national coordinating team consisting of Olga Villa-Parra and Sisters Veronica Mendez, R.C.D., and Sylvia Sedillo, S.L. The address is P.O. Box 4274, Denver, Colo., 80204.

Leadership Conference of Women Religious: An association of major superiors of religious communities of women, with the purpose of promoting the spiritual and apostolic calling and works of sisterhoods in the U.S. Organized in the late 50s and approved by the Congregation for Religious and Secular Institutes June 13, 1962, it has a membership of approximately 700. Its original name, changed in 1971, was the Conference of Major Superiors of Women. With its formerly affiliated Sister Formation Conference, it inaugurated measures for the religious and professional development of sisters and has contributed to the renewal of religious life in this country. Sister Helen Flaherty, S.C., is president; Sister Lora Ann Quinonez, C.D.P., is executive director. The national secretariat is located at 8808 Cameron St., Silver Spring, Md. 20910.

National Assembly of Religious Women: Formed in 1970 and with the title, National Assembly of Women Religious, until August, 1982, a movement of feminist women committed to prophetic tasks of giving witness, raising awareness, and engaging in public action and advocacy for justice. Membership is both organizational and individual. Sister Marjorie Tuite, O.P., is national coordinator. Offices are located at 1307 S. Wabash Ave., Chicago, Ill. 60605.

National Black Sisters' Conference: Organized in August, 1968, for the purposes of determining priorities in service to black people, of promoting black vocations and the development of religious life in the unique black life-style, and to influence the formational and recruitment practices of white religious communities. Its members include 150 black sisters belonging to 123 religious communities. Sister Marie de Porres Taylor, S.N.J.M., is coordinator. The mailing address of the conference is 6226 Camden St., Oakland, Calif. 94605.

National Coalition of American Nuns: Organized under the leadership of Sister Margaret Traxler, S.S.N.D., in July, 1969, for efforts to secure recognition and development of the role of women in the Church and society, along with advocacy for social activism. Sister Donna Quinn, O.P., is president. Offices are located at 1307 S. Wabash Ave., Chicago, Ill 60605.

National Sisters' Vocation Conference: Formed in September, 1970, as a national organization dedicated to promoting understanding of the role of women, especially religious, in the Church through work in the vocation apostolate. It coordinates and provides informational and other services to persons and organizations in the vocation apostolate, and assists prospective candidates for religious life. Its membership includes approximately 1,200 women and men. Sister Gertrude Wemhoff, O.S.B., is executive director. The national office is located at 1307 S. Wabash Ave., Chicago, Ill. 60605.

Religious Formation Conference: Originally organized with the title of the Sister Formation Conference in 1953, for the purpose of promoting the spiritual and professional formation of sisters in the U.S. In 1976, the name was changed to Religious Formation

Conference to reflect openness to a membership including men and persons belonging to non-canonical religious groups. Sister Carol Ann Jokerst, C.C.V.I., is executive director. The national office is located at 1234 Massachusetts Ave. N.W., Washington, D.C. 20005.

Other Conferences

International Union of Superiors General (Women): Established in 1965, with approval of its statutes by the Congregation for Religious and Secular Institutes in 1967. Sister Regina Casey, M.S.C., is president.

Latin American Confederation of Religious: Established in 1959, with approval of its statutes by the Congregation for Religious and Secular Institutes in 1967. Father Mateo Perdia, C.P., is president.

National Conference of Vicars for Religious: Established in 1967 as a national organization of diocesan officials concerned with relations between their respective dioceses and religious communities engaged therein. A service and informational agency for vicars, it also carries on liaison with the Congregation for Religious and Secular Institutes, the National Conference of Catholic Bishops and other organizations concerned with religious. The president is Rev. Angelo Caligiuri, 100 S. Elmwood Ave., Buffalo, N.Y. 14202.

National Conferences: Conferences of religious superiors, generally separate for men and women, have been established in 19 countries in Europe, 14 in North and Central America, 10 in South America, 24 in Africa, and 20 in Asia and Oceania.

Union of Superiors General (Men): Established in 1957, with approval of its statutes by the Congregation for Religious and Secular Institutes in 1967. Father Vincent de Couesnongle, O.P., is president. Fathers John Vaughn, superior general of the Order of Friars Minor, and Paul Boyle, superior general of the Passionists, are American councillors of the union.

World Conference of Secular Institutes: Established in 1974.

Vocation Council

The National Catholic Vocation Council replaced the National Center for Church Vocations in 1977. The principal purpose of the council is to give the Church in the U.S. visible witness of the mutual collaboration of national vocation organizations in their effort to promote awareness and understanding of dedication to the Church, especially through the ordained ministry and vowed life. The council also services efforts of mutual concern and benefit to membership organizations in the recruitment and development of vocations to the priesthood, diaconate and vowed life.

Member organizations with representatives on the board of directors are: the National Sisters Vocation Conference, the National Conference of Diocesan Vocation Directors, the National Conference of Religious Vocation Directors of Men, Serra International, the Bishops' Committee on Vocations (National Conference of Catholic Bishops), the Leadership Conference of Women Religious and the Conference of Major Superiors of Men and the Conference of Secular Institutes.

Brother James Gaffney, C.F.C., is president; Sr. Gertrude Wemhoff, O.S.B., is chairperson of the administrative committee.

Offices are located at 1307 S. Wabash Ave., Chicago, Ill. 60605

SECULAR INSTITUTES

(Sources: Almanac survey; *Directory of Secular Institutes with Foundations in the U.S.A.,* published by the Publications Office, U.S. Catholic Conference; *Annuario Pontificio.*)

Secular institutes are societies of men and women living in the world who dedicate themselves by vow or promise to observe the evangelical counsels and to carry on apostolic works suitable to their talents and opportunities in the areas of their everyday life.

"Secular institutes are not religious communities but they carry with them in the world a profession of evangelical counsels which is genuine and complete, and recognized as such by the Church. This profession confers a consecration on men and women, laity and clergy, who reside in the world. For this reason they should chiefly strive for total self-dedication to God, one inspired by perfect charity. These institutes should preserve their proper and particular character, a secular one, so that they may everywhere measure up successfully to that apostolate which they were designed to exercise, and which is both in the world and, in a sense, of the world" (*Decree on the Appropriate Renewal of Religious Life,* No. 11; Second Vatican Council).

A secular institute reaches maturity in several stages. It begins as an association of the faithful, technically called a pious union, with the approval of a local bishop. Once it has proved its viability, he can give it the status of an institute of diocesan right, in accordance with norms and permission emanating from the Congregation for Religious and Secular Institutes. On issuance of a separate decree from this congregation, an institute of diocesan right becomes an institute of pontifical right.

Secular institutes, which originated in the latter part of the 18th century, were given full recognition and approval by Pius XII Feb. 2, 1947, in the apostolic constitution *Provida Mater Ecclesia.* On Mar. 25 of the same year a special commission for secular institutes was set up within the Congregation for Religious. Institutes were commended and confirmed by Pius XII in a motu proprio of Mar. 12, 1948, and were the subject of a special instruction issued a week later, Mar. 19, 1948.

The **United States Conference of Secular Institutes (CSI)** was established in October, 1972, following the organization of the World Conference of Secular Institutes in Rome. Its membership is open to all canonically erected secular institutes with members living in the United States. The conference was organized to offer secular institutes an opportunity to exchange experiences, to do research in order to help the Church carry out its mission, and to search for ways and means to make known the existence of secular institutes in the U.S. Address: c/o Claudette Cyr, president, 121 Greenwood St., Watertown, Conn. 06795.

Institutes in the U.S.

Caritas Christi: Originated in Marseilles, 1937; for women. Established as a secular institute of pontifical right Mar. 19, 1955. Address: P.O. Box 162, River Forest, Ill. 60305.

Company of St. Paul: Originated in Milan, Italy, 1920; for lay people and priests. Approved as a secular institute of pontifical right June 30, 1950. Address: 52 Davis Ave., White Plains, N.Y. 10605.

Company of St. Ursula, Daughters of St. Angela Merici ("The Angelines"): Founded in Brescia, Italy, 1535; for women. Approved as a secular institute of pontifical right 1958. Addresses: Lina Moser, President, Via Rosmini 128, 38100 Trento, Italy; D. Latz, P.O. Box 265, New Rochelle, N.Y. 10802.

DeSales Secular Institute: Founded in Vienna, Austria, 1940; for women. Pontifical right, 1964. Address: Rev. John Conmy, O.S.F.S., National Assistant, Childs, Md. 21916.

Diocesan Laborer Priests: Approved as a secular institute of pontifical right, 1952. The specific aim of the institute is the promotion, sustenance and cultivation of apostolic, religious and priestly vocations. Address: 3706 15th St. N.E., Washington, D.C. 20017.

Don Bosco Volunteers: Founded 1917; for women. Established as a secular institute of pontifical right Aug. 5, 1978. Address: Don Bosco Volunteers, 202 Union Ave., Paterson, N.J. 07502.

Handmaids of Divine Mercy: Founded in Bari, Italy, 1951; for women. Approved as an institute of pontifical right 1972. Address: Mary I. DiFonzo, 2410 Hughes Ave., Bronx, N.Y. 10458. International membership of 980.

Institute of Secular Missionaries: Founded in Vitoria, Spain, 1939; for women. Approved as a secular institute, 1955. Address: 2710 Ruberg Ave., Cincinnati, O. 45211, Att. E. Dilger.

Institute of the Heart of Jesus: Originated in France Feb. 2, 1791; restored Oct. 29, 1918; for diocesan priests and lay people. Received final approval from the Holy See as a secular institute of pontifical right Feb. 2, 1952. Rev. Jean Grebouval, superior general. Addresses: Central House, 202 Avenue du Maine, Paris 14me, France; U.S. address, Rev. John Lorenz, P.O. Box 4692, Des Moines, Iowa 50306. International membership of approximately 1,400.

Mission of Our Lady of Bethany: Founded in Plessis-Chevet, France, 1948; for women. Approved as an institute of diocesan right 1965. Address: Rev. Alfred J. Connick, 637 Cambridge St., Brighton, Mass. 02135.

Missionaries of the Kingship of Christ the King: Under this title are included three distinct and juridically separate institutes founded by Agostino Gemelli, O.F.M. (1878-1959).

(1) Women Missionaries of the Kingship of Christ — Founded in 1919, in Italy; definitively approved as an institute of pontifical rite 1953. Established in 15 countries. U.S. branch established 1950. Age at time of entrance, 21 to 40.

(2) Men Missionaries of the Kingship of Christ — Founded 1928, in Italy, as an institute of diocesan right. U.S. branch established 1962.

(3) Priest Missionaries of the Kingship of Christ — Established in U.S., 1954; approved as institute of pontifical right July 15, 1978. For diocesan priests.

Address: Rev. Stephen Hartdegen, O.F.M., Holy Name College, 14th and Shepherd Sts. N.E., Washington, D.C. 20017.

Oblate Missionaries of Mary Immaculate: Founded, 1952, and approved as a secular institute Feb. 2, 1962; for women. Addresses: Oblate Missionaries of Mary Immaculate, 91 Brookfield St., Lawrence, Mass. 01843. 7535 Boulevard Parent, Trois Rivieres, P. Q. G9A 5E1, Canada. International membership.

Rural Parish Workers of Christ the King: Originated in Cottleville, Mo., 1942; for women. An approved secular institute of the Archdiocese of St. Louis. Dedicated to the service of neighbor, especially in rural areas. Address: Box 300, Rt. 1, Cadet, Mo. 63630.

Schoenstatt Sisters of Mary: Originated in Schoenstatt, Germany, 1926; for women. Established as a secular institute of diocesan right May 20, 1948; of pontifical right Oct. 18, 1948. Addresses: Schoenstatt Sisters of Mary, W. 284 N. 698 Cherry Lane, Waukesha, Wis. 53186; House Schoenstatt, Star Rt. 1, Box 100, Rockport, Tex. 78382. International membership of more than 2,800.

Secular Institute of Pius X: Originated in Manchester, N.H., 1940; for priests and laymen. Approved as a secular institute, 1959 (first secular institute of diocesan right founded in the U.S. to be approved by the Holy See). Also admits married and unmarried men as associate members. Addresses: Lynchville Park, Goffstown, N.H. 03045. C.P. 1815, Quebec City, P.Q. G1K 7K7, Canada.

Society of Our Lady of the Way: Originated, 1936; for women. Approved as a secular institute of pontifical right Jan. 3, 1953. Addresses: 2701 14th Ave., San Francisco, Calif. 94127; 2339 N. Catalina St., Los Angeles, Calif. 90027; P.O. Box 412, Stamford, Conn. 06904; 2738 Noble Rd., No. 13B, Cleveland Heights, O. 44121. International membership, 300.

Teresian Institute: Founded in Spain 1911 by Pedro Poveda. Approved as an institute of pontifical right Jan. 11, 1924. Mailing Address: P.O. Box 34-3407, Coral Gables, Fla. 33114.

Voluntas Dei: Originated in Canada, 1958; for secular priests, laymen and couples. Approved as a secular institute May 6, 1965. Addresses: Institute Voluntas Dei, 7385, Blvd. Parent, Trois-Rivieres, Que., Canada G9A 5E1. Rev. Maurice Roy, Immaculate Conception Parish, Drawer A.F., Ajo, Ariz. 85321. International membership of approximately 210.

The *Annuario Pontificio* lists the following secular institutes of pontifical right which are not established in the U.S.:

For men: Christ the King; Institute of Our Lady of Life; Institute of Prado; Opus Dei; Priests of the Sacred Heart of Jesus.

For women: Alliance in Jesus through Mary; Apostles of the Sacred Heart; Catechists of Mary, Virgin and Mother; Catechists of the Sacred Heart of Jesus (Ukrainian); Cordimarian Filiation; Daughters of the Nativity of Mary; Daughters of the Queen of the Apostles; Daughters of the Sacred Heart; Evangelical Crusade; Faithful Servants of Jesus; Handmaids of Our Mother of Mercy; Institute of the Blessed Virgin Mary (della Strada); Institute of Notre Dame du Travail; Institute of Our Lady of Life; Institute of St. Boniface; Little Apostles of Charity; Life and Peace in Christ Jesus; Missionaries of Royal Priesthood; Missionaries of the Sick; Oblates of Christ the King; Oblates of the Sacred Heart of Jesus; Opus Dei; Servants of Jesus the Priest; Servite Secular Institute; Union of the Daughters of God; Workers of Divine Love; Workers of the Cross; Handmaids of Holy Church.

Associations

Association of Mary Immaculate: Founded 1963. Received diocesan approval Jan. 28, 1977. For mature men and women, widows and widowers; separate section for married couples. Training on cassette tape for blind or handicapped. Address: 8804 Arlington Expressway, Jacksonville, Fla. 32211.

Caritas: Originated in New Orleans, 1950; for women. Follow guidelines of secular institutes. Small self-supporting groups who live and work among the poor and oppressed; work in Louisiana and Guatemala. Address: Box 308, Abita Springs, La. 70420.

Daughters of Our Lady of Fatima: Originated in Lansdowne, Pa., 1949; for women. Received diocesan approval, Jan., 1952. Address: Fatima House, Rolling Hills Rd., Ottsville, Pa. 18942.

Focolare Movement: Inaugurated in Trent, Italy, in 1943, by Chiara Lubich and a small group of companions; for men and women. Approved as an association of the faithful, 1962. It is not a secular institute by statute; however, vows are observed by its totally dedicated core membership of 4,000 who live in small communities called Focolare (Italian word for "hearth") centers. There are 14 resident centers in the U.S. and two in Canada. GEN (New Generation) is the youth organization of the movement. An estimated 70,000 are affiliated with the movement in the U.S. and Canada; 3,000,000, worldwide. Publications include *Living City,* monthly; *GEN II* and *GEN III* for young people and children. Four week-long summer conventions, called "Mariapolis" ("City of Mary"), are held annually. Address for information: P.O. Box 496, New York, N.Y. 10021 (indicate men's or women's branch).

Institute of Apostolic Oblates: Founded in Rome, Italy, 1947; for women. Address: 2125 W. Walnut Ave., Fullerton, Calif. 92633 (provincial house).

Jesus Caritas — Fraternity of Priests: An international association of priests who strive to live in the spirit of Charles de Foucauld, combining an active life with a contemplative calling. U.S. address: Rev. Howard W. Calkins (National Responsible), St. Jerome Church, 230 Alexander Ave., Bronx, N.Y. 10454

Madonna House Apostolate: Originated in Toronto, Canada, 1930; for priests and lay persons. Diocesan pious union. Address: Madonna House, Combermere, Ontario, Canada KOJ ILO — Catherine Doherty (women), Jim Guinan (men), Rev. J. Callahan (priests). International membership and missions.

Pax Christi: Lay institute of men and women dedicated to witnessing to Christ, with special emphasis on service to the poor in Mississippi. Addresses: St. Francis Center, 708 Ave. I, Greenwood, Miss. 38930; LaVerna House, 2108 Altawoods Blvd., Jackson, Miss. 39204.

PRAISE FROM CHINA

The English-language *China Daily* praised three 17th-century Jesuit missionaries for their contributions to the sciences in China, according to a Vatican Radio report Mar. 3, 1982. The priests were mathematician Mateo Ricci and astronomers Johann Adam Schall and Ferdinandus Verbiest.

SECULAR ORDERS

Secular orders (commonly called third orders) are societies of the faithful living in the world who seek to deepen their Christian life and apostolic commitment in association with and according to the spirit of various religious institutes. The orders are called "third" because their foundation followed the establishment of the first (for men) and second (for women) religious orders with which they are associated.

Augustine, Third Order Secular of St.: Founded, 13th century; approved Nov. 7, 1400.

Carmel (The Lay Carmelite Order) (Calced): Founded, 13th century; approved by Pope Nicholas V, Oct. 7, 1452. Address: Aylesford, National Scapular Center, I-55 and Cass Ave. N. Darien, Ill. 60559. Approximately 16,500 members in U.S.

Carmelites, The Secular Order of Discalced (formerly the Third Order Secular of the Blessed Virgin Mary of Mt Carmel and of St. Teresa of Jesus): Rule based on the Carmelite reform established by St. Teresa and St. John of the Cross, 16th century; approved Mar. 23, 1594. Revised rule approved May 10, 1979. Office of National Secretariat, U.S.A.; P.O. Box 3079, San Jose, Calif. 95116. Approximately 3,500 members in U.S.

Dominican Laity: Founded in the 13th century. Addresses of provincial coordinators: 487 Michigan Ave. N.E., Washington, D.C. 20017; 1909 S. Ashland Ave., Chicago, Ill. 60608; 2390 Bush St., San Francisco, Calif. 94115, P.O. Box 3894, Little Rock, Ark. 72203.

Franciscan Order, Secular (SFO): Founded, 1209 by St. Francis of Assisi; approved Aug. 30, 1221. President: Miss Therese M. Devlin, 110 Shonnard Pl., Yonkers, N.Y. 10703. Approximately 780,000 throughout the world; 40,000 in U.S.

Mary, Third Order of: Founded, Dec. 8, 1850; rule approved by the Holy See, 1857. Addresses of provincial directors: 4408 — 8th St. N.E., Washington, D.C. 20017; 7 Harvard St., P.O. Box 66, Charlestown, Mass. 02129; 320 N. 20th Dr. W., Phoenix, Ariz. 85009. Approximately 14,000 in the world, 5,600 in U.S.

Mary, Third Order Secular of Servants of (Servite): Founded, 1233; approved, 1304. Address: Director of Third Order, 3401 S. Home Ave., Berwyn, Ill. 60402.

Mercy, Secular Third Order of Our Lady of (Mercedarian): Founded, 1219 by St. Peter Nolasco; approved the same year.

Norbert, Third Order of St.: Founded, 1122 by St. Norbert; approved by Pope Honorius II, 1126. Address: St. Norbert Abbey, De Pere, Wis. 54115.

Trinity, Third Order Secular of the Most Holy: Founded 1198; approved, 1219. Address: Trinitarian Provincial Offices, P.O. Box 5719, Baltimore, Md. 21208.

Oblates of St. Benedict are lay persons affiliated with a Benedictine abbey or monastery who strive to direct their lives, as circumstances permit, according to the spirit and Rule of St. Benedict.

NATIONAL SHRINE

The National Shrine of the Immaculate Conception is dedicated to the honor of the Blessed Virgin Mary, who was declared patroness of the United States in 1846.

The shrine project was launched in 1914; the site and foundation stone were blessed in 1920; the crypt, an underground church, was completed in 1926; the main church and superstructure were dedicated Nov. 20, 1959; more than 56 chapels and additional interior furnishings have been installed since the dedication. The shrine has a distinctive bell tower housing a 56-bell carillon.

The shrine is the seventh largest religious building in the world and the largest Catholic church in the Western Hemisphere, with normal seating and standing accommodations for 6,000 persons. The shrine contains some of the largest mosaics in the world.

Approximately one million persons visit the shrine each year. Open daily, it is located adjacent to the Catholic University of America, Michigan Ave. and Fourth St. N.E., Washington, D.C., 20017.

The shrine director is Msgr. Eugene G. Bilski.

CATHOLIC RIGHTS LEAGUE

The Catholic League for Religious and Civil Rights, founded in 1973, serves the Catholic community as an anti-defamation and civil-rights agency.

The league responds to defamation of Catholics and Catholicism in the media, and carries on educational activities in support of the religious and civil rights of Catholics in secular society.

It has a professional legal staff to defend in court the religious-freedom rights of Catholics and others. A research staff serves as a clearinghouse for information on public issues of concern to the Catholic community. Among the league's highest priorities are issues relating to the right to life and the right to freedom of choice in education.

The league, which has no official connection with the Church, is supported by contributions from its 30,000 members.

Father Virgil C. Blum, S.J., is president and founder of the league, which is headquartered at 1100 W. Wells St., Milwaukee, Wis. 53233. The league also has 15 local chapters across the country.

Speakers representing the league address groups which share its concern, interest and preoccupation with the defense and protection of civil and religious rights.

Missionary Activity of the Church

UNITED STATES FOREIGN MISSIONARIES

Data on U.S. foreign missionary personnel in the following tables were gathered by, and are reproduced with permission of, the United States Catholic Mission Association, 1233 Lawrence St. N.W., Washington, D.C. 20017.

For additional information about the Church in mission areas, see News Events and other Almanac entries.

Field Distribution, 1982

Under this and following headings, Alaska, Hawaii, etc., are considered abroad because they are outside the 48 contiguous states.

Africa: 956 (509 men, 447 women). Largest numbers in Tanzania, 174; Kenya, 161; Ghana, 103; Zambia, 78; Nigeria, 65.

Near East: 62 (39 men, 23 women). Largest numbers in Israel, 38; Egypt, 11; Lebanon, 9.

Far East: 1,501 (1,024 men, 477 women). Largest numbers in Philippines, 398; Japan, 327; Taiwan, 169; Korea, 138; India, 120; Hong Kong, 90.

Oceania: 673 (340 men, 333 women). Largest numbers in Hawaii, 223; Papua New Guinea, 206; Australia, 62; Mariana Islands, 48; Samoa, 34; Caroline Islands, 35.

Europe: 32 (17 men, 15 women). Largest numbers in Finland, 9; Sweden, 9; Denmark, 7.

North America: 319 (120 men, 199 women). Largest number in Alaska, 196.

Caribbean Islands: 522 (286 men, 236 women). Largest numbers in Puerto Rico, 231; Jamaica, 126; Haiti, 45.

Central America: 669 (401 men, 268 women). Largest numbers in Mexico, 212; Guatemala, 169.

South America: 1,511 (811 men, 700 women). Largest numbers in Brazil, 454; Peru, 429; Bolivia, 229; Chile, 178.

TOTAL: 6,245 (3,547 men, 2,698 women).

Men Religious, 1982

Eighty-eight mission-sending groups had 3,290 priests and brothers in overseas assignments.

Jesuits: 579 in 43 countries; largest group, 92 in the Philippines.

Maryknoll Fathers: 541 in 28 countries; largest group, 53 in Tanzania.

Franciscans (O.F.M.): 204 in 23 countries; largest group, 68 in Brazil.

Divine Word Missionaries: 156 in 13 countries; largest group, 53 in Papua New Guinea.

Redemptorists: 146 in 9 countries; largest group, 58 in Brazil.

Oblates of Mary Immaculate: 133 in 17 countries; largest group, 25 in Brazil.

Marianists: 132 in 15 countries; largest group, 42 in Hawaii.

Capuchins (O.F.M. Cap): 130 in 9 countries; largest group, 31 in Papua New Guinea.

Benedictines: 95 in 13 countries; largest group, 21 in Guatemala.

Columbans: 69 in 10 countries; largest group, 27 in the Philippines.

Holy Cross Fathers: 66 in 10 countries; largest group, 20 in Bangladesh.

Brothers of the Christian Schools: 66 in 11 countries; largest group, 27 in the Philippines.

Dominicans: 62 in 8 countries; largest group, 17 in Pakistan.

Holy Ghost Fathers: 59 in 7 countries; largest group, 25 in Tanzania.

Holy Cross Brothers: 53 in 6 countries; largest group, 19 in Brazil.

Passionists: 50 in 5 countries; largest group, 25 in the Philippines.

Conventual Franciscans (O.F.M. Conv): 49 in 8 countries; largest group, 15 in Zambia.

La Salette Missionaries: 44 in 6 countries; largest group, 14 in the Philippines.

Vincentians: 41 in 8 countries; largest group, 20 in Panama.

Marist Fathers: 38 in 10 countries; largest group, 12 in Hawaii.

Missionaries of the Sacred Heart: 30 in 4 countries; largest group, 23 in Papua New Guinea.

Augustinians: 29 in 3 countries; largest group, 19 in Peru.

White Fathers: 28 in 11 countries: largest group, 6 in Uganda.

Marist Brothers: 24 in 5 countries; largest group, 10 in Japan.

Missionhurst-CICM: 24 in 8 countries; largest group, 9 in the Dominican Republic.

Salesians: 24 in 9 countries; largest group, 8 in Canada.

Brothers of the Sacred Heart: 21 in 4 countries; largest group, 9 in Zambia.

Sixty-one other mission-sending institutes had 19 or less members in overseas assignments.

Diocesan Priests, 1982

One hundred and 78 diocesan priests from 79 dioceses were in overseas assignments in 1982.

The largest groups were from Boston (21 in 4 countries) and St. Louis (10 in 2 countries).

Fifty-three of the diocesan priests in overseas assignments were members of the

Missionary Society of St. James the Apostle, founded by Cardinal Richard J. Cushing of Boston in 1958. Its director is Rev. George F. Emerson, 24 Clark St., Boston, Mass. 02109.

Fourteen other diocesan priests in overseas assignments are working as Priest Associates with the Maryknoll Fathers, whose headquarters are in Maryknoll, New York 10545.

Sisters, 1982

Two hundred and 22 mission-sending groups had 2,560 sisters in overseas assignments.

Maryknoll Sisters: 406 in 24 countries; largest group, 57 in Hawaii.

School Sisters of Notre Dame: 101 in 17 countries; largest group, 16 in Puerto Rico.

Marists: 82 in 14 countries; largest group, 13 in Papua New Guinea.

Medical Mission Sisters: 64 in 18 countries; largest group, 15 in Ghana.

Sisters of Notre Dame de Namur: 64 in 10 countries; largest group, 17 in Kenya.

Daughters of Charity: 63 in 11 countries; largest group, 33 in Bolivia.

Sisters of St. Joseph (Carondelet): 58 in 3 countries; largest group, 28 in Hawaii.

Benedictines: 46 in 10 countries: largest group, 12 in Colombia.

Franciscan Missionaries of Mary: 43 in 16 countries; largest groups, 6 each in Australia, Ghana and Japan.

Sisters of the Holy Cross: 40 in 4 countries; largest group, 18 in Brazil.

Ursulines of the Roman Union: 40 in 11 countries; largest group, 8 in Thailand.

Servants of the Immaculate Heart of Mary (Philadelphia): 40 in 2 countries; larger group, 29 in Peru.

Franciscan Sisters of Allegany: 37 in 3 countries; largest group, 21 in Jamaica.

Society of the Sacred Heart: 31 in 7 countries; largest group, 15 in Japan.

Religious Sisters of Mercy of the Union in the U.S.A.: 30 in 9 countries; largest group, 13 in Jamaica.

Servants of the Holy Spirit: 30 in 7 countries; largest group, 11 in Ghana.

Sisters of the Holy Child Jesus: 25 in 6 countries; largest group, 10 in Nigeria.

Sisters of Notre Dame: 24 in 3 countries; largest group, 13 in India.

Little Sisters of the Poor: 24 in 12 countries; largest group, 5 in Hong Kong.

Sisters of the Third Franciscan Order, Minor Conventuals (Syracuse): 23 in 3 countries; largest group, 14 in Hawaii.

Sisters of the Assumption of the B.V.M.: 22 in 4 countries; largest group, 18 in Canada.

Sisters of St. Joseph (Brentwood): 21 in 2 countries; larger group, 20 in Puerto Rico.

Dominican Sisters (Adrian): 20 in 7 countries; largest group, 5 in Puerto Rico.

Adorers of the Blood of Christ: 20 in 5 countries; largest group, 6 in Liberia.

One hundred and 98 other mission-sending institutes had 19 or less members in overseas assignments.

Lay Volunteers, 1982

Two hundred and 17 lay volunteers of 21 sponsoring organizations were in overseas assignments in 1982.

Maryknoll Lay Missioners: 59 in 15 countries; largest group, 13 in Tanzania.

Jesuit Volunteer Corps: 53 in Alaska.

Lay Mission Helpers: 30 in 13 countries; largest group, 11 in Papua New Guinea.

Frontier Apostolate: 17 in Canada.

Catholic Medical Mission Board: 11 in 6 countries; largest group, 5 in Papua New Guinea. (This figure represents those whose term of service was for at least one year. In addition, 41 short-term volunteers served in 12 countries during the year.)

Milwaukee Latin American Office: 8 in 5 countries; largest group, 3 in Colombia.

Diocese of Davenport: 8 in 6 countries; largest groups, 2 each in Mexico and St. Lucia.

The other 14 sponsoring organizations had 5 members or less in overseas assignments.

U.S. MISSION ASSOCIATION

The United States Catholic Mission Association, juridically established Sept. 1, 1981, continues the activities and functions of the former U.S. Catholic Mission Council.

According to existing bylaws approved by the general assembly May 25, 1982, the USCMA is "open to all those who seek to promote global mission in community with others. It is envisioned to be an experience of the renewed Church, in which all members are equal. The methods of decision-making, of financial support, and of committee service reflect the underlying ecclesiology." The purpose of the association is the "promotion of global mission. Its primary focus is cross-cultural mission, with special emphasis on international justice."

Typical activities of the association are educational efforts related to the Church's teaching about its missionary nature, sponsorship of conferences on theological and pastoral foundations of missionary endeavor, liaison and cooperation with missionary bodies of other Christian churches, training programs and refresher courses for departing and returning missionaries, and general mission animation. The association is also responsible for gathering and publishing annual statistical data on U.S. missionary personnel overseas. It publishes the data in the annual, *Mission Handbook*. The association also publishes ten times a year *Mission Intercom*, a newsletter with brief information on the life and activities of the Church in the six continents.

Officers as of June 30, 1982, were: Sister

Mary Ann Dillon, R.S.M., president; Rev. Simon Smith, S.J., vice president; Rev. Anthony Bellagamba, I.M.C., executive director.

The office of the association is located at 1233 Lawrence St. N.E., Washington, D.C. 20017.

U.S. FOREIGN MISSIONARIES, 1960-1982

Year	Diocesan Priests	Religious Priests	Religious Brothers	Religious Sisters	Seminarians	Lay Persons	Total
1960	14	3018	575	2827	170	178	6782
1962	31	3172	720	2764	152	307	7146
1964	80	3438	782	3137	157	532	8126
1966	215	3731	901	3706	201	549	9303
1968	282	3727	869	4150	208	419	9655
1970	373	3117	666	3824	90	303	8373
1972+	246	3182	634	3121	97	376	7656
1973	237	3913*		3012		529	7691
1974	220	3084	639	2916	101	458	7418
1975	197	3023	669	2850	65	344	7148
1976	193	2961	691	2840	68	257	7010
1977	182	2882	630	2781	42	243	6760
1978	166	2830	610	2673	43	279	6601
1979	187	2800	592	2568	50	258	6455
1980	188	2750	592	2592	50	221	6393
1981	187	2702	584	2574	43	234	6324
1982	178	2668	578	2560	44	217	6245

+A corrected total for 1972 should read 7937, indicating losses of 436 from 1970 to 1972 and 246 from 1972 to 1973.
*Includes religious brothers and seminarians.

FIELD DISTRIBUTION BY AREAS, 1960-1982

Year	Africa	Far East	Near East	Oceania	Europe	N. Amer.	Carib. Is.	Cent. Amer.	S. Amer.	Total
1960	781	1959	111	986	203	337	991	433	981	6782
1962	901	2110	75	992	93	224	967	537	1247	7146
1964	1025	2332	122	846	69	220	1056	660	1796	8126
1966	1184	2453	142	953	38	211	1079	857	2386	9303
1968	1157	2470	128	1027	33	251	1198	936	2455	9655
1970	1141	2137	39	900	38	233	1067	738	2080	8373
1972	1107	1955	59	826	39	234	819	728	1889	7656
1973	1229	1962	54	811	40	253	796	763	1783	7691
1974	1121	1845	60	883	43	241	757	752	1716	7418
1975	1065	1814	71	808	37	252	698	734	1669	7148
1976	1042	1757	68	795	34	313	671	712	1618	7010
1977	1003	1659	62	784	34	296	629	702	1591	6760
1978	966	1601	57	769	34	339	593	705	1537	6601
1979	923	1562	65	743	37	332	562	686	1545	6455
1980	909	1576	65	711	35	294	548	699	1556	6393
1981	946	1529	70	696	36	315	511	693	1528	6324
1982	956	1501	62	673	32	319	522	669	1511	6245

HOME MISSIONS

The expression "home missions" is applied to places in the U.S. where the local church does not have its own resources, human and otherwise, which are needed to begin or, if begun, to survive and grow. These areas share the name "missions" with their counterparts in foreign lands because they too need outside help to provide the personnel and means for making the Church present and active there in carrying out its mission for the salvation of people.

Dioceses in the Southeast, the Southwest, and the Far West are most urgently in need of outside help to carry on the work of the Church. Millions of persons live in counties in which there are no resident priests. Many others live in rural areas beyond the reach and influence of a Catholic center. According to recent statistics compiled by the Glenmary Research Center, there are 545 priestless counties in the United States. Many states generally thought to be well off from a pastoral standpoint include areas in which the Catholic Church and the ministry of priests are virtually unknown.

About 20 per cent of the total U.S. population and less than three per cent of the Catholic population live within the boundaries of the 17 "most missionary" dioceses of the country. A "Survey of the Catholic Weakness" conducted by the National Catholic Rural Life Conference disclosed that the

Catholic Church ranked near the bottom of about 40 religious bodies in percentage of rural membership.

Mission Workers

A number of forces are at work to meet the pastoral needs of these missionary areas and to establish permanent churches and operating institutions where they are required. In many dioceses, one or more missions and stations are attended from established parishes and are gradually growing to independent status. Priests, brothers and sisters belonging to scores of religious institutes are engaged full-time in the home missions. Lay persons, some of them in affiliation with special groups and movements, are also involved.

The Society for the Propagation of the Faith, which conducts an annual collection for mission support in all parishes of the U.S., allocates 40 per cent of this sum for disbursement to home missions through the American Board of Catholic Missions.

The Catholic Church Extension Society provides one million dollars or more a year for the building of mission installations and related needs.

Special mission support is the purpose of the Commission for the Catholic Missions among the Colored People and the Indians.

Diocesan, parochial and high school mission societies frequently undertake projects in behalf of the home missions.

The **Glenmary Home Missioners**, founded by Father W. Howard Bishop in 1939, is the only home mission society established for the sole purpose of carrying out the pastoral ministry in small towns and the rural districts of the United States. With 75 priests and 29 professed brothers as of March 20, 1982, the Glenmary Missioners had 37 mission bases and 49 satellite missions in the archdioceses of Atlanta and Cincinnati, and in the dioceses of Birmingham, Charlotte, Covington, Dallas, Little Rock, Nashville, Jackson, Tulsa, Owensboro, Savannah, Richmond and Wheeling-Charleston. The Rev. Robert C. Berson is president. National headquarters are located in Fairfield, O. The mailing address is P.O. Box 46404, Cincinnati, O. 45246.

Black Missions

The Commission for Catholic Missions among the Colored People and the Indians reported the following (January, 1982), statistics for 86 dioceses and six religious communities to whom it supplied financial assistance: 993,000 Catholics; 658 churches; 860 priests; 141 predominantly black schools with 34,800 students; 255 integrated schools with 4,700 students.

Dioceses reporting the largest numbers of black Catholics were: Brooklyn, N.Y., 132,000; New Orleans, La., 85,000; Washington, D.C., 75,000; Lafayette, La., 58,000; New York, N.Y., 50,000; Baltimore, Md., 46,000; Galveston-Houston, 45,885; Philadelphia, Pa., 41,000; Detroit, Mich., 37,000; St. Louis, Mo., 30,650; San Diego, Calif., 28,000; Lake Charles, La., 20,000; Kansas City-St. Joseph, Mo., 18,000; Baton Rouge, La., 16,000; Rockville Centre, N.Y., 15,320; San Francisco, Calif., 14,300; Cleveland, O., 11,000; Newark, N.J., 10,000. The total black Catholic population of these 18 mainly urban dioceses numbered 733,155; they comprised nearly 74 per cent of the total black Catholic population of the 86 dioceses covered in the report.

The report noted that it was impossible to determine "whether, or to what extent, lapsed Catholics are included in a parish or diocesan report."

The commission report, which was limited in scope, did not cover all aspects of the Church's ministry to the black population, which was estimated to number more than 22 million. (See Index: Black Catholics.)

Indian Missions

The Commission for Catholic Missions among the Colored People and the Indians reported the following statistics (January, 1982) for 46 dioceses and one religious community to whom it supplied financial assistance: 264,000 Catholics, 346 churches and chapels, 268 priests, 23 elementary schools, four high schools.

The states with the largest number of missions and Catholic Indians are Arizona, New Mexico, North and South Dakota, Oklahoma and Montana, where almost two-thirds of the reservation Indians now live. Sixty-nine churches and chapels and four schools were maintained with 117 priests engaged in serving more than 163,000 Catholic Indians in these areas. Forty-five missions and three schools are located in the states of California, Minnesota, Wisconsin and Wyoming where 35 priests are serving the estimated 33,420 Catholic Indians there. Alaska has 45 mission churches and chapels and 35 priests to minister to approximately 27,000 Indians, Aleuts, Eskimos. In other states, the Commission reported, reservations were small; consequently only several schools and from one to five missions were maintained in most of them.

According to 1980 census reports, an estimated 376,000 of the total U.S. Indian population of 1,418,195 were living on federal reservations. An estimated 25,000 Catholic Indians were not on reservations.

Bishops Statement: The bishops of the United States, in a statement approved during a May 3 to 5, 1977, meeting in Chicago, urged American Catholics to increase their "understanding of the present needs, aspirations and values of the American Indian peoples." They recommended:

• that dioceses and Catholic organizations

make efforts to improve their ministry with American Indians;

• that church property adjacent to Indian lands or in the midst of urban Indian neighborhoods be made more available for use by Indian communities;

• that Catholic educational institutions examine textbooks and curricula, and promote programs in the appreciation of American Indian history, culture and spirituality;

• that special attention be given to government policy and legislation affecting Indians.

This special attention, the statement said, should focus on "advocacy of the speedy and equitable resolution of treaty and statute questions; protection of Indian land and resource rights; more adequate housing and delivery of social, education and health-care services; and increased levels of funding and technical assistance necessary to aid American Indians in achieving political and economic self-determination and full employment."

The bishops said, in conclusion: "We hope to fashion a renewed commitment to serve Indian peoples. In turn, their participation in and challenge to the Christian community will strengthen our common witness to Jesus and the gospel message."

Organizations

The Catholic Church Extension Society: This society was established for the purpose of preserving and extending the Church in the U.S. and its dependencies principally through the collection and disbursement of funds for missions. Since the time of its founding in 1905, approximately $86 million have been received and expended for this purpose. Disbursements in fiscal year 1981 were in excess of $5.7 million.

Works of the society are supervised by a board of governors consisting of twelve members: Cardinal John Cody, archbishop of Chicago, chancellor; Rev. Edward J. Slattery, president; five bishops or priests, and five laymen. Society headquarters are located at 35 E. Wacker Drive, Chicago, Ill. 60601.

Commission for Catholic Missions among the Colored People and the Indians: Organized in 1886, this commission provides financial support ($4,002,680 allocated in 1980-81 year to 127 dioceses) for religious works among Blacks and Indians in the United States. Funds are raised by an annual collection in all parishes of the country.

Cardinal John J. Krol is head of the board of directors. Msgr. Paul A. Lenz is secretary. Commission headquarters are located at 2021 H St. N.W., Washington, D.C. 20006.

Bureau of Catholic Indian Missions: Established in 1874 as the representative of Catholic Indian missions before the federal government and the public; made permanent organization in 1883 by Third Plenary Council of Baltimore. After a remarkable history of rendering important services to the Indian people, the bureau continues to represent the Catholic Church in the U.S. in her apostolate to the American Indian. Concerns are evangelization, catechesis, liturgy, family life, education, advocacy. Cardinal John Krol is president of the board; Msgr. Paul A. Lenz is secretary. Address: 2021 H St., Washington, D.C. 20006.

Rural Ministry Institute: The Edwin Vincent O'Hara Institute for Rural Ministry Education was founded in 1978 to provide training and other resource services for priests, seminarians religious and lay persons beginning or already involved in rural ministry. Brother David Andrews, C.S.C., is director. Address: 14th and Shepherd Sts. N.E., Washington, D.C. 20017.

Tekakwitha Conference: Established in 1939, the Conference includes active and former Catholic missionaries among Native American people and Native American people recognized as leaders in their respective communities. The primary focus is evangelization in these areas of concern: development of Native American ministry, catechesis, liturgy, family life, social justice ministry, education, ecumenical cooperation, urban ministry spirituality and vocations. The annual Conference serves as an opportunity for exchange of ideas, approaches and mutual support. Publications include a quarterly Newsletter and the annual Proceedings. President is Rev. Gilbert F. Hemauer, O.F.M. Cap. Address: 1818 Ninth Ave., South No. 5, Great Falls, Mont. 59405.

BLACK CATHOLICS

The National Office for Black Catholics, organized in August, 1970, is a central agency with the general purposes of promoting active and full participation by black Catholics in the Church and of making more effective the presence and ministry of the Church in the black community.

Its operations are in support of the aspirations and calls of black Catholics for a number of objectives, including the following:

• representation and voice for blacks among bishops and others with leadership and decision-making positions in the Church;

• vocational recruitment for the priesthood and religious life;

• recognition of the black heritage in liturgy, community life, theology and education.

James R. Henderson is executive director of the NOBC. The office is located at 1234 Massachusetts Ave. N.W., Washington, D.C. 20005.

Evangelization was one of the principal topics discussed at the biennial conference of the NOBC Aug. 4 to 7, 1982, in Houston. The theme of the gathering was "Spiriting the Good News: Black Catholics Furthering the

Movement through Network Development."

Father Giles Conwill, the keynote speaker, said that communication networks among all segments of the black community were needed to enhance unity among priests, religious and lay persons. "The black Catholic movement," he said, "can't be effective without all the elements being united."

He told attendants at the meeting that black Catholics had to deepen their knowledge and practice of the faith in order to be effective leaders in the Church. He added: "The first step toward effective evangelization would be the appointment of black bishops as ordinaries (heads of dioceses) and auxiliaries who can give direction, guidance and leadership to and for their people."

Meeting of Conferences

"Making a Way out of No Way" was the theme of another meeting — held in August, 1982, in Plymouth, Mich. — of representatives of the National Black Clergy Conference, the National Black Seminarians' Association and the National Black Sisters' Conference (see separate entry).

The purpose of the meeting was "to foster fraternity and sorority among black clergy and religious, and to provide members with resources for ministry and personal development," according to Father Edward Branch, president of the Clergy Conference and pastor of St. Benedict the Black Church and the Newman Center at Grambling State University, Grambling, La.

Statistics

In 1982, there were a million or more black Catholics in the U.S., comprising about four per cent of the total black population and two per cent of the Catholic population. Black priests and religious numbered, respectively, about 250 and 700. There were six black bishops: Bishop Joseph L. Howze, head of the Diocese of Biloxi, and Auxiliary Bishops Joseph A. Francis, S.V.D., of Newark, Eugene A. Marino, S.S.J., of Washingotn, Harold R. Perry, S.V.D., of New Orleans, James P. Lyke, O.F.M., of Cleveland, and Emerson Moore of New York.

Various dioceses have agencies like New York's Office of Black Ministry for pastoral and related service to the black community.

Josephite Pastoral Center

The Josephite Pastoral Center was established in September, 1968, as an educational and pastoral service agency for the Josephites in their mission work, specifically in the black community. St. Joseph's Society of the Sacred Heart, the sponsoring body, has about 185 priests and 20 brothers in 80 mostly southern parishes in 18 dioceses.

The staff of the center includes Father John G. Harfman, S.S.J., director, and Brother Damian Wilson, S.S.J., and Maria M. Lannon, associate directors. The center is located at St. Joseph Seminary, 1200 Varnum St. N.E., Washington, D.C. 20017.

HISPANICS

U.S. Census Bureau figures indicate that there were 14,605,883 persons of Hispanic origin in the United States in 1980. (Not counted were thousands of undocumented aliens in the country illegally.)

Between 1970 and 1980, there was a nationwide increase of 5,037,440 persons.

Regional increases for the same period were: Northeast, 709,381 for a total of 2,604,261; North Central, 228,144 for a total of 1,276,405; South, 1,707,365 for a total of 4,473,172; West, 2,884,291 for a total of 6,252,045.

Most persons of Hispanic origin in the United States have been baptized in the Catholic Church and comprise, probably, between 25 and 30 per cent of the Catholic population.

In the U.S., at the beginning of September, 1982, there were 14 Hispanic bishops (eight heads of dioceses and six auxiliaries, all named since 1970), 1,485 Hispanic priests, 450 Hispanic permanent deacons, 854 Hispanics in seminaries, and an estimated total of 724 Hispanic women religious.

Pastoral ministry to Hispanics varies, depending on differences among the people and the availability of personnel to carry it out.

The pattern in cities with large numbers of Spanish-speaking is built around special churches, centers or other agencies where pastoral and additional forms of service are provided in a manner suited to the needs, language and culture of the people. Services in some places are extensive and include legal advice, job placement, language instruction, recreational and social assistance, specialized counseling, replacement services. In many places, however, even where there are special ministries, the needs are generally greater than the means required to meet them.

Some of the urban dwellers have been absorbed into established parishes and routines of church life and activity. Many Spanish-speaking communities, especially those with transients, remain in need of special ministries.

An itinerant form of ministry best meets the needs of the thousands of migrant workers who follow the crops.

Special ministries for the Spanish-speaking have been in operation for a long time in dioceses of the Southwest. The total number of dioceses with such ministries is more than 75.

Pastoral care for Hispanics was the central concern of two national meetings, *encuentros,* held in 1972 and 1977. In line with recommendations made then, particular emphasis has since been focused on meetings and actions for increasing language capability among persons involved in ministry, awareness of Hispanic cultural elements in liturgy and practice, leadership development, and moves for the formation of basic Christian communities (*comunidades de base*). A task force for implementation is chaired by Archbishop Robert F. Sanchez of Santa Fe, N.M.

Agencies and Organizations

Secretariat for Hispanic Affairs: The national secretariat of the U.S. Catholic Conference, for service in promoting and coordinating pastoral ministry to the Spanish-speaking. Its basic orientation is toward integral evangelization, combining religious ministry with development efforts in programs geared to the culture and needs of Hispanics. Its concerns are urban and migrant Spanish-speaking people; communications and publications in line with secretariat purposes and the service of people; bilingual and bicultural religious and general education; liaison for and representation of Hispanics with church, civic and governmental agencies.

Paul Sedillo, Jr., is director of the national office at 1312 Massachusetts Ave. N.W., Washington, D.C. 20005.

The secretariat has working relationships with regional offices in the Northeast, Southeast, Midwest, Southwest, Far West and Northwest.

The Northeast regional office, officially the Northeast Pastoral Center for Hispanics, was established in 1976 and is supported by bishops in 14 states from Maine to Virginia. The executive director is Mario J. Paredes. The center is located at 1011 First Ave., New York, N.Y. 10022.

The Southeast regional office serves the entire South. Its South East Pastoral Institute offers courses in pastoral ministry, reaches out to communities throughout the region with its Evangelization Mobile Team and distributes audio-visual and print resources for Hispanic ministry. Father Mario Vizcaino, Sch. P., is director of the region and institute. The office is located at 2900 S.W. 87th Ave., Miami, Fla. 33165.

Five states of the Midwest are served by a Spanish Speaking Catholic Commission and the Midwest Hispanic Institute. The executive director of the commission is Estanislao Hernandez, located at P.O. Box 703 (Holy Cross Annex), Notre Dame, Ind. 46556. The institute, headed by Olga Villa-Parra, is located at St. Mary's College, Box 64, Notre Dame, Ind. 46556.

The territory assigned to the Southwest regional office, under reorganization, embraces Texas, Arkansas, New Mexico, Arizona and Colorado.

California and Nevada are served by the Far West office, which is a component of the California Catholic Conference. The regional director is Father Ricardo Chavez. The office

is located at 926 J St., Suite 1100, Sacramento Calif. 95814.

A two-year-old regional office serves the northwestern corner of the U.S. and Alaska. The director of the region is Sister Elisa Martinez. The office is located at 1623 N.W. 19th Ave., Portland, Ore. 97209.

In the Southwest, 55 Mexican-American priests organized **PADRES** in February, 1970, to help the Church identify more closely with the pastoral, social, economic and educational needs of the Spanish-speaking. The present membership exceeds 500, mainly in California, Texas, New Mexico and on the East Coast. PADRES is an acronym for the Spanish title, "Padres Asociados para Derechos Religiosos, Educativos y Sociales."

Leadership development of Hispanos is one of the principal concerns of PADRES, now a national organization with membership open to priests, brothers and deacons working in Hispanic ministry. Seminarians and others interested in working with the Hispanic community are eligible for honorary membership. Father Ramon Gaitan, O.A.R., is the national president. The national office is located at 3310 Garfield Ave., Kansas City. Kan. 66104.

An analogous organization of Chicano sisters, **Las Hermanas,** was organized in 1971 (see separate entry).

The Mexican American Cultural Center: Founded in 1972 as a pastoral institute with a variety of programs focused on the evangelization of Hispanics in the United States, particularly through lay leadership and liaison between North, Central and South America; named a center of liturgical research by the National Conference of Catholic Bishops.

Father Virgil Elizondo is president of the center, which is located at 3019 French Pl., P.O. Box 28185, San Antonio, Tex. 78228.

A National Resource Center for Hispanic Ministry, begun in 1981 at the Cultural Center by initiative of the U.S. Bishops' Committee on Hispanic Affairs, collects information on personnel and resources available to the Hispanic apostolate.

Miami Apostolate

The Spanish-Speaking Apostolate in metropolitan Miami is one of the most extensive in the country. It serves a population of well over 650,000 people — including Cubans who have established residence there since Fidel Castro rose to power Jan. 1, 1959; an increasing permanent Latin American population, and migrant workers.

Directly involved in the apostolate are 110 Spanish-speaking priests and 115 religious sisters. Spanish-speaking priests are assigned to 47 parishes. All pastoral programs of the archdiocese are duplicated in Spanish, and the social service agencies have Spanish-speaking personnel.

LEGAL STATUS OF CATHOLIC EDUCATION

The right of private schools to exist and operate in the United States is recognized in law. It was confirmed by the U.S. Supreme Court in 1925 when the tribunal ruled (Pierce v. Society of Sisters, see Church-State Decisions of the Supreme Court) that an Oregon state law requiring all children to attend public schools was unconstitutional.

Private schools are obliged to comply with the education laws in force in the various states regarding such matters as required basic curricula, periods of attendance, and standards for proper accreditation.

The special curricula and standards of private schools are determined by the schools themselves. Thus, in Catholic schools, the curricula include not only the subject matter required by state educational laws but also other fields of study, principally, education in the Catholic faith.

The Supreme Court has ruled that the First Amendment to the U.S. Constitution, in accordance with the No Establishment of Religion Clause of the First Amendment, prohibits direct federal and state aid from public funds to church-affiliated schools. (See several cases in Church-State Decisions of the Supreme Court.)

Public Aid

This prohibition does not extend to all child-benefit and public-purpose programs of aid to students of non-public elementary and secondary schools.

Statutes authorizing such programs have been ruled constitutional on the grounds that they:

• have a "secular legislative purpose";
• neither inhibit nor advance religion as a "principal or primary effect";
• do not foster "excessive government entanglement with religion."

Aid programs considered constitutional have provided bus transportation, textbook loans, school lunches and health services, and "secular, neutral or non-ideological services, facilities and materials provided in common to all school children," public and non-public.

The first major aid to education program in U.S. history containing provisions benefitting nonpublic school students was enacted by the 89th Congress and signed into law by President Lyndon B. Johnson Apr. 11, 1965. The Elementary and Secondary Education Act was designed to avoid the separation of Church and state impasse which had blocked all earlier aid proposals pertaining to nonpublic. and especially church-affiliated, schools. The objective of the program, under public control, is to serve the public purpose by aiding disadvantaged pupils in nonpublic as well as public schools.

With respect to college and university education in church-affiliated institutions, the Supreme Court has upheld the constitutionality of statutes providing student loans and, under the Federal Higher Education Facilities Act of 1963, construction loans and grants for secular-purpose facilities.

Catholic schools are exempt from real estate taxation in all of the states. Since Jan. 1, 1959, nonprofit parochial and private schools have also been exempt from several federal excise taxes.

Shared and Released Time

In a shared time program of education, students enrolled in Catholic or other church-related schools take some courses (e.g., religion, social studies, fine arts) in their own schools and others (e.g., science, mathematics, industrial arts) in public schools. Such a program has been given serious consideration in recent years by Catholic and other educators. Its constitutionality has not been seriously challenged, but practical problems — relating to teacher and student schedules, transportation, adjustment to new programs, and other factors — are knotty.

Several million children of elementary and high school age of all denominations have the opportunity of receiving religious instruction on released time. Under released time programs they are permitted to leave their public schools during school hours to attend religious instruction classes held off the public school premises. They are released at the request of their parents. Public school authorities merely provide for their dismissal, and take no part in the program.

NCEA

The National Catholic Educational Association, founded in 1904, is a voluntary organization of educational institutions and individuals concerned with Catholic education in the U.S. Its objectives are to promote and encourage the principles and ideals of Christian education and formation by suitable service and other activities.

The NCEA has 14,000 institutional and individual members. Its official publication is *Momentum.* Numerous service publications are issued to members.

Bishop John F. Cummins of Oakland, Calif., is chairman of the association. Msgr. John F. Meyers is president.

Headquarters are located at: 1077 30th St. N.W., Washington, D.C. 20007.

Other Educational Associations

National Association of Boards of Education: Founded in 1971 and made a department of the National Catholic Educational Association in 1973, to develop and promote policy-making boards for the advancement of Catholic education. Has a national membership of 1,307. Publishes *PolicyMaker* four times a year. Office: 1077 30th St. N.W., Washington, D.C. 20007.

National Forum of Catholic Parent Organizations: Founded in 1976 as a commission of the National Catholic Educational Association, to support and promote the role of parents as primary educators of their children. Has a national membership of 625 affiliates. Publishes *Parentcator* 5 five times a year. Office: 1077 30th St. N.W., Washington, D.C. 20007.

CATHOLIC SCHOOLS AND STUDENTS IN THE UNITED STATES

(Source: *The Official Catholic Directory, 1982;* figures as of Jan. 1, 1982. Archdioceses are indicated by an asterisk.)

Section, State Diocese	Univs. Colleges	Students	High Schools	Students	Elem. Schools	Students
NEW ENGLAND	26	58,247	123	67,599	529	145,352
Maine, Portland	1	460	3	1,003	22	5,711
New Hampshire, Manchester	5	4,876	6	2,634	21	6,479
Vermont, Burlington	3	2,687	3	1,271	11	2,905
Massachusetts	9	30,321	68	35,082	245	71,305
*Boston	4	20,303	51	24,281	162	47,902
Fall River	1	2,645	5	3,270	24	6,700
Springfield	1	606	4	3,256	35	10,493
Worcester	3	6,767	8	4,275	24	6,210
Rhode Island, Providence	2	7,935	13	7,147	64	18,135
Connecticut	6	11,968	30	20,462	166	40,817
*Hartford	3	1,878	15	11,199	97	23,408
Bridgeport	2	9,942	10	5,974	48	13,093
Norwich	1	148	5	3,289	21	4,316
MIDDLE ATLANTIC	62	164,091	364	243,466	2,118	670,296
New York	28	85,850	155	108,037	908	307,566
*New York	11	41,550	63	39,995	275	94,625
Albany	4	5,800	13	5,345	59	15,158
Brooklyn	2	19,606	21	25,556	176	88,991
Buffalo	6	13,292	21	9,094	144	32,312
Ogdensburg	1	313	3	1,041	26	5,217
Rochester	—	—	9	6,994	79	20,640
Rockville Centre	2	2,655	16	15,308	88	36,163
Syracuse	2	2,634	9	4,704	61	14,460
New Jersey	8	13,836	91	52,704	453	135,213
*Newark	4	11,520	45	22,625	204	58,001
Camden	—	—	11	8,100	67	20,173
Metuchen	—	—	9	5,205	52	15,347
Paterson	3	940	14	6,587	66	16,949
Trenton	1	1,376	12	10,187	64	24,743
Pennsylvania	26	64,405	118	82,725	757	227,517
*Philadelphia	10	32,283	51	49,567	283	116,818
Allentown	2	1,661	10	5,021	70	14,821
Altoona-Johnstown	2	2,155	3	1,846	39	7,750
Erie	3	6,132	10	4,268	56	14,782
Greensburg	2	1,956	2	1,403	48	8,956
Harrisburg	—	—	10	4,827	57	12,793
Pittsburgh	3	8,991	20	10,396	145	38,497
Scranton	4	11,227	12	5,397	59	13,100
SOUTH ATLANTIC	14	41,525	127	65,784	533	211,030
Delaware, Wilmington	—	—	8	5,183	29	11,103
Maryland, *Baltimore	4	10,364	25	13,104	87	29,006
District of Columbia, *Washington	3	21,480	25	11,648	83	25,168

Section, State Diocese	Univs. Colleges	Students	High Schools	Students	Elem. Schools	Students
Virginia	1	1,407	14	5,556	56	18,201
Arlington	1	1,407	4	2,714	28	9,983
Richmond	—	—	10	2,842	28	8,218
West Virginia, Wheeling-Charleston	1	1,050	9	2,237	36	6,088
North Carolina	2	1,217	3	1,217	34	8,073
Charlotte	2	1,217	2	982	15	4,156
Raleigh	—	—	1	235	19	3,917
South Carolina, Charleston	—	—	4	1,514	29	5,874
Georgia	—	—	7	3,846	29	9,490
*Atlanta	—'	—	2	1,737	13	4,525
Savannah	—	—	5	2,109	16	4,965
Florida	3	6,007	32	21,479	150	98,027
*Miami	2	4,855	17	12,115	64	25,642
Orlando	—	—	5	2,773	27	8,646
Pensacola-Tallahassee	—	—	1	709	10	2,829
St. Augustine	—	—	2	1,377	16	49,053
St. Petersburg	1	1,152	7	4,505	33	11,857
EAST NORTH CENTRAL	**51**	**131,796**	**312**	**205,364**	**2,155**	**600,825**
Ohio	11	29,244	88	58,317	521	167,479
*Cincinnati	4	19,958	22	17,530	121	40,133
Cleveland	3	5,807	26	20,619	169	63,506
Columbus	1	956	14	5,814	53	14,985
Steubenville	1	963	4	1,181	19	3,449
Toledo	1	640	16	8,638	95	27,778
Youngstown	1	920	6	4,535	64	17,628
Indiana	9	16,323	25	14,201	211	48,358
*Indianapolis	2	1,602	9	5,302	73	16,706
Evansville	—	—	5	2,012	30	4,893
Ft. Wayne-South Bend	5	12,423	5	3,470	44	11,940
Gary	1	1,316	4	2,974	42	11,337
Lafayette	1	982	2	443	22	3,482
Illinois	14	45,222	99	75,872	668	202,077
*Chicago	8	36,386	61	54,171	381	135,616
Belleville	1	1,072	4	2,352	54	9,044
Joliet	3	5,365	9	7,048	64	19,284
Peoria	—	—	8	3,836	58	12,660
Rockford	—	—	8	4,375	48	11,595
Springfield	2'	2,399	9	4,090	63	13,878
Michigan	8	18,707	67	38,169	340	95,628
*Detroit	5	13,274	45	24,600	165	57,165
Gaylord	—	—	5	1,077	20	3,746
Grand Rapids	1	3,442	4	2,967	46	9,297
Kalamazoo	1	545	3	1,188	21	4,419
Lansing	1	1,446	5	3,484	40	10,939
Marquette	—	—	1	72	12	2,536
Saginaw	—	—	4	4,781	36	7,526
Wisconsin	9	22,300	33	18,805	415	87,283
*Milwaukee	5	18,304	15	11,111	175	42,747
Green Bay	2	2,133	9	3,703	95	18,866
La Crosse	1	1,113	7	2,980	76	13,754
Madison	1	750	2	1,011	47	8,473
Superior	—	—	—	—	22	3,443
EAST SOUTH CENTRAL	**8**	**8,531**	**55**	**23,893**	**289**	**62,129**
Kentucky	5	6,025	29	13,313	160	31,696
*Louisville	3	3,836	11	7,846	79	17,449
Covington	1	1,299	13	3,832	53	9,244
Owensboro	1	890	5.	1,635	28	5,003
Tennessee	2	1,608	11	4,873	42	9,913
Memphis	1	1,329	6	2,563	16	4,332
Nashville	1	279	5	2,310	26	5,581

Section, State Diocese	Univs. Colleges	Students	High Schools	Students	Elem. Schools	Students
Alabama	1	898	5	2,934	50	12,358
*Mobile	1	898	3	1,760	27	7,208
Birmingham	—	—	2	1,174	23	5,150
Mississippi	—	—	10	2,773	37	8,162
Biloxi	—	—	5	1,658	17	3,627
Jackson	—	—	5	1,115	20	4,535
WEST NORTH CENTRAL	34	51,979	165	69,517	919	201,045
Minnesota	9	16,236	26	12,264	227	50,982
*St. Paul and Minneapolis	3	8,948	14	8,920	110	31,268
Crookston	—	—	2	321	11	1,762
Duluth	1	1,048	—	—	16	2,162
New Ulm	—	—	3	640	26	4,057
St. Cloud	3	4,214	3	959	37	6,722
Winona	2	2,026	4	1,424	27	5,011
Iowa	7	8,932	29	12,552	159	31,846
*Dubuque	3	3,853	11	5,109	60	14,931
Davenport	3	3,737	7	2,054	39	5,129
Des Moines	—	—	2	1,967	22	4,223
Sioux City	1	1,342	9	3,422	38	7,563
Missouri	7	19,000	46	25,266	286	69,544
*St. Louis	5	13,702	32	19,334	185	49,765
Jefferson City	—	—	2	897	36	5,988
Kansas City-St. Joseph	2	5,298	9	4,375	43	11,086
Springfield-Cape Girardeau	—	—	3	660	22	2,705
North Dakota	2	1,186	8	2,010	33	6,083
Bismarck	1	1,003	6	1,537	18	3,393
Fargo	1	183	2	473	15	2,690
South Dakota	2	905	5	1,609	27	4,940
Rapid City	—	—	2	428	3	754
Sioux Falls	2	905	3	1,181	24	4,186
Nebraska	1	897	34	9,749	97	18,886
*Omaha	1	897	21	7,218	64	13,786
Grand Island	—	—	7	1,140	9	994
Lincoln	—	—	6	1,391	24	4,106
Kansas	6	4,823	17	6,067	90	18,764
*Kansas City	3	2,740	7	3,185	38	8,900
Dodge City	1	627	—	—	12	1,737
Salina	1	758	6	1,076	12	2,059
Wichita	1	698	4	1,806	28	6.068
WEST SOUTH CENTRAL	12	22,220	125	50,541	520	158,246
Arkansas, Little Rock	—	—	6	2,125	34	5,518
Louisiana	4	8,158	64	28,950	200	82,357
*New Orleans	4	8,158	28	18,016	95	43,675
Alexandria-Shreveport	—	—	7	2,174	24	6,864
Baton Rouge	—	—	9	2,598	27	12,247
Houma-Thibodaux	—	—	3	1,291	12	4,959
Lafayette	—	—	15	4,081	33	11,511
Lake Charles	—	—	2	790	9	3,101
Oklahoma	1	342	5	2,227	31	6,910
*Oklahoma City	1	342	2	937	17	2,999
Tulsa	—	—	3	1,290	14	3,911
Texas	7	13,720	50	17,239	255	63,461
*San Antonio	4	6,492	15	4,017	56	15,832
Amarillo	—	—	2	172	12	2,195
Austin	1	2,474	1	233	15	3,256
Beaumont	—	—	2	694	10	2,066
Brownsville	—	—	2	775	8	2,083
Corpus Christi	—	—	4	1,458	30	5,435
Dallas	1	2,815	7	3,032	36	9,985
El Paso	—	—	3	1,199	19	4,429
Fort Worth	—	—	4	1,332	15	3,994
Galveston-Houston	1	1,939	10	4,327	50	13,256

Section, State Diocese	Univs. Colleges	Students	High Schools	Students	Elem. Schools	Students
Texas	7	13,720	50	17,239	255	63,461
San Angelo	—	—	—	—	4	930
Victoria	No separate statistics available.					
MOUNTAIN	5	6,753	36	14,483	190	47,733
Montana	2	2,571	5	1,334	22	3,973
Great Falls-Billings	1	1,201	3	668	18	3,250
Helena	1	1,370	2	666	4	723
Idaho, Boise	—	—	1	402	12	1,783
Wyoming, Cheyenne	—	—	1	133	7	1,413
Colorado	1	1,070	12	3,640	52	13,220
*Denver	1	1,070	9	3,196	42	11,692
Pueblo	—	—	3	444	10	1,528
New Mexico	2	3,112	5	1,796	31	7,758
*Santa Fe	2	3,112	3	1,641	22	5,678
Gallup	—	—	2	155	9	2,080
Arizona	—	—	8	4,688	46	14,107
Phoenix	—	—	6	3,452	26	8,816
Tucson	—	—	2	1,236	20	5,291
Utah, Salt Lake City	—	—	2	939	9	2,358
Nevada, Reno-Las Vegas	—	—	2	1,551	11	3,121
PACIFIC	23	47,595	158	92,505	780	229,200
Washington	4	8,860	12	7,315	84	20,321
*Seattle	2	5,067	9	5,880	58	15,034
Spokane	2	3,793	2	1,194	19	3,614
Yakima	—	—	1	241	7	1,673
Oregon	2	3,685	10	3,984	56	10,702
*Portland	2	3,685	9	3,873	52	10,022
Baker	—	—	1	111	4	680
California	16	32,974	126	76,756	607	187,003
*Los Angeles	5	8,387	57	35,925	234	75,616
*San Francisco	3	9,179	19	10,282	75	23,046
Fresno	—	—	2	1,443	25	6,727
Monterey	—	—	2	919	14	3,937
Oakland	4	3,430	11	6,600	57	15,632
Orange	1	125	5	4,020	36	13,885
Sacramento	—	—	9	4,229	42	11,479
San Bernardino	—	—	2	1,556	29	8,170
San Diego	1	4,791	6	3,314	42	13,270
San Jose	2	7,062	6	4,859	28	8,851
Santa Rosa	—	—	5	2,087	13	3,218
Stockton	—	—	2	1,522	12	3,172
Alaska	—	—	2	283	4	766
*Anchorage	—	—	—	—	2	266
Fairbanks	—	—	2	283	1	350
Juneau	—	—	—	—	1	150
Hawaii, Honolulu	1	2,076	8	4,167	29	10,408
EASTERN RITES	2	349	5	750	46	7,613
*Philadelphia	1	342	1	349	16	2,758
St. Nicholas	—	—	1	140	3	875
Stamford	1	7	3	261	9	944
*Pittsburgh	—	—	—	—	6	1,050
Parma	—	—	—	—	5	941
Passaic	—	—	—	—	7	1,045
Van Nuys	No separate statistics available.					
St. Maron	—	—	—	—	—	—
Newton	—	—	—	—	—	—
Armenians (Ap. Ex.)	No separate statistics available.					
Chaldeans (Ap. Ex.)	No separate statistics available.					
MILITARY ORDINARIATE	—	—	—	—	—	—
TOTALS 1982	237	533,086	1,470	833,902	8,079	2,333,469
TOTALS 1981	236	536,678	1,504	838,247	8,117	2,296,380
Totals 1972	260	428,853	1,815	961,996	9,206	3,105,417

SCHOOL STATISTICS

The status of Catholic educational institutions and programs in the United States at the beginning of 1982, 1981 and 1972 were reflected in figures (as of Jan. 1) reported by *The Official Catholic Directory, 1982.*

Colleges and Universities: 237 (1 more than in 1981 and 23 less than in 1972).

College and University Students: 533,086 (3,592 less than in 1981 and 104,233 more than in 1972).

High Schools: 1,470 (34 less than in 1981 and 345 less than in 1972).

High School Students: 833,902 (4,345 less than in 1981 and 128,094 less than in 1972).

Public High School Students Receiving Religious Instruction: 977,098 (14,186 more than in 1981 and 350,233 less than in 1972).

Elementary Schools: 8,079 (38 less than in 1981 and 1,127 less than in 1972).

Elementary School Students: 2,333,469 (37,089 more than in 1981 and 771,948 less than in 1972).

Public Elementary School Students Receiving Religious Instruction: 3,323,398 (104,195 less than in 1981 and 928,331 less than in 1972).

Teachers: 173,230 (2,254 more than in 1981 and 15,297 less than in 1972).

Lay Teachers: 129,014 (5,596 more than in 1981 and 24,778 more than in 1972).

Sisters: 36,066 (2,719 less than in 1981 and 34,598 less than in 1972).

Priests (Full-Time): 5,101 (436 less than in 1981 and 3,599 less than in 1972).

Brothers: 2,889 (128 less than in 1981 and 1,413 less than in 1972).

Scholastics: 160 (59 less than in 1981 and 465 less than in 1972).

TEACHER UNIONS

Catholic teacher unions organized in recent years include several in the Archdiocese of New York and locals in Philadelphia, Pittsburgh, Youngstown and Brooklyn. Several of them belong to the National Association of Catholic School Teachers, which has links with groups in Scranton, San Francisco, Los Angeles, Altoona-Johnstown, Kansas City, Mo., Cleveland and Louisville.

The purpose of the association is "to work with diocesan officials in an attempt to draw up acceptable guidelines that can be used by all parties to insure that the teachings of the Church are as applicable to the employer-employee relationship within the institutional Church as the Church has taught for so many years they are in the private and public sectors of industry." About 3,000 lay teachers belong to the New York Federation of Catholic Teachers, which broke relations in 1981 with the American Federation of Teachers.

Advocates of unionization argue with justification that teachers have a right to collective bargaining, that they deserve salaries and other contract provisions commensurate with their needs and the quality of their work, and that they need collective protection against authoritative and arbitrary actions by some administrators.

Bishops and school administrators have shown considerable reluctance to deal with unions. Fears have been expressed that union demands, financial and otherwise, might drive schools out of existence, change their character, or diminish control over them by the Church.

UNIVERSITIES AND COLLEGES IN THE UNITED STATES

(Sources: Almanac survey; *The Official Catholic Directory.*)

Listed below are institutions of higher learning established under Catholic auspices. Some of them are now independent.

Information includes: name of each institution; indication of male (m), female (w), coeducational (c) student body; name of founding group or group with which the institution is affiliated; year of foundation; number of students, in parentheses.

Albertus Magnus College (w): 700 Prospect St., New Haven, Conn. 06511. Dominican Sisters; 1925 (552).

Albuquerque, University of (c): St. Joseph Pl. N.W., Albuquerque, N.M. 87140. Sisters of St. Francis; 1920 (2,100).

Allentown College of St. Francis de Sales (c): Center Valley, Pa. 18034. Oblates of St. Francis de Sales; 1965 (925).

Alvernia College (c): Reading, Pa. 19607. Bernardine Sisters; 1958 (721).

Alverno College (w): 3401 S. 39th St. Milwaukee, Wis. 53215. School Sisters of St. Francis; 1936; independent (1,372).

Anna Maria College (c): Sunset Lane, Paxton, Mass. 01612. Sisters of St. Anne; 1946; independent (1,609).

Aquinas College (c): 1607 Robinson Rd. S.E., Grand Rapids, Mich. 49506. Sisters of St. Dominic; 1922 (2,400).

Assumption College (c): 500 Salisbury St., Worcester, Mass. 01609. Assumptionist Fathers; 1904 (2,664).

Avila College (c): 11901 Wornall Rd., Kansas City, Mo. 64145. Sisters of St. Joseph of Carondelet; 1916 (1,974).

Barat College (w): 700 E. Westleigh Rd., Lake Forest, Ill. 60045. Society of the Sacred Heart; 1919; independent (736).

Barry University (c): 11300 N.E. 2nd Ave., Miami, Fla. 33161. Dominican Sisters; 1940 (2,197).

Bellarmine College (c): 2000 Norris Pl., Louisville, Ky. 40205; Louisville archdiocese, 1950 (2,300).

Belmont Abbey College (c): Belmont, N.C. 28012. Benedictine Fathers; 1876 (855).

Benedictine College (c): Atchison, Kans. 66002. Benedictines, 1971 (1,082).

Biscayne College (c): 16400 N.W. 32nd Ave., Miami, Fla. 33054. Augustinian Fathers; 1962 (2,959).

Boston College (University Status) (c): Chestnut Hill, Mass. 02167. Jesuit Fathers; 1863 (14,166).

Brescia College (c): 120 W. 7th St., Owensboro, Ky. 42301. Ursuline Sisters; 1925 (890).

Briar Cliff College (c): W. 3303 Rebecca St., Sioux City, Ia. 51104. Sisters of St. Francis of the Holy Family; 1930 (1,342).

Cabrini College (c): Radnor, Pa. 19087. Missionary Srs. of Sacred Heart; 1957 (580).

Caldwell College (w): Caldwell, N.J. 07006. Dominican Sisters; 1939 (758).

Calumet College (c): 2400 New York Ave., Whiting, Ind. 46394. Society of the Precious Blood, 1951 (1,316).

Canisius College (c): 2001 Main St., Buffalo, N.Y. 14208. Jesuit Fathers; 1870; independent (4,079).

Cardinal Newman College (c): 7701 Florissant Rd., St. Louis, Mo. 63121. Catholic college with autonomous board of trustees; 1976.

Cardinal Stritch College (c): 6801 N. Yates Rd., Milwaukee, Wis. 53217. Sisters of St. Francis of Assisi; 1932; independent (1,120).

Carlow College (w): 3333 5th Ave., Pittsburgh, Pa. 15213. Sisters of Mercy; 1929 (1,013).

Carroll College (c): Helena, Mont. 59625. Diocesan Clergy; 1909 (1,370).

Catholic University of America, The (c): 620 Michigan Ave. N.E., Washington, D.C. 20064. Hierarchy of the United States; 1887. Pontifical University (7,750).

Catholic University of Puerto Rico (c): Ponce, P.R. Hierarchy of Puerto Rico; 1948; Pontifical University (10,771).

Chaminade University (c): 3140 Waialae Ave., Honolulu, Hawaii 96816. Marianists; 1955 (2,076).

Chestnut Hill College (w): Philadelphia, Pa. 19118. Sisters of St. Joseph; 1871 (989).

Christian Brothers College (c): 650 E. Parkway S., Memphis, Tenn. 38104. Brothers of the Christian Schools; 1871 (1,483).

Clarke College (c): 1550 Clarke Dr., Dubuque, Iowa 52001. Sisters of Charity, BVM; 1843 (850).

Creighton University (c): 2500 California St., Omaha, Neb. 68178. Jesuit Fathers; 1878 (5,600).

Dallas, University of (c): Irving, Tex. 75061. Private; 1956; independent (2,815).

Dayton, University of (c): 300 College Park Ave., Dayton, Ohio 45409. Marianists; 1850 (10,785).

De Paul University (c): 2323 N. Seminary Ave., Chicago, Ill. 60614. Vincentians; 1898 (13,300).

Detroit, University of (c): 4001 W. McNichols Rd. at Livernois, Detroit, Mich. 48221. Jesuit Fathers; 1877 (6,323).

Dominican College of Blauvelt (c): Orangeburg, N.Y. 10962. Dominican Sisters; 1952; independent (1,602).

Dominican College of San Rafael (c): San Rafael, Calif. 94901. Dominican Sisters; 1890; independent (694).

Duquesne University (c): 801 Bluff St., N.W., Pittsburgh, Pa. 15219. Holy Ghost Fathers; 1878 (6,628).

D'Youville College (c): 320 Porter Ave., Buffalo, N.Y. 14201. Grey Nuns of the Sacred Heart; 1908; independent (1,569).

Edgecliff College (c): 2220 Victory Pkwy., Cincinnati, Ohio 45206. Sisters of Mercy; 1935 (667).

Edgewood College (c): 855 Woodrow St., Madison, Wis. 53711. Dominican Sisters; 1927 (750).

Emmanuel College (w): 400 The Fenway, Boston, Mass. 02115. Sisters of Notre Dame de Namur; independent (1,067).

Fairfield University (c): Fairfield, Conn. 06430. Jesuit Fathers; 1942 (5,131).

Felician College (w): S. Main St., Lodi, N.J. 07644. Felician Sisters; 1942 (655). Coed in evening programs.

Fontbonne College (c): 6800 Wydown Blvd., St. Louis, Mo. 63105. Sisters of St. Joseph of Carondelet; 1917 (882).

Fordham University (c): Fordham Rd. and Third Ave., New York, N.Y. 10458. Society of Jesus (Jesuits); 1841; independent (14,800).

Fort Wright College (c): W. 4000 Randolph Rd., Spokane, Wash. 99204. Sisters of the Holy Names of Jesus and Mary; 1907 (389).

Gannon University (c): 109 W. 6th St., Erie, Pa. 16541. Diocese of Erie; 1944 (4,000).

Georgetown University (c): 37th and O Sts. N.W., Washington, D.C. 20057. Jesuit Fathers; 1789 (11,960).

Georgian Court College (w): Lakewood, N.J. 08701. Sisters of Mercy; 1908 (1,400). Coed in evening and graduate divisions.

Gonzaga University (c): Spokane, Wash. 99258. Jesuit Fathers; 1887 (3,404).

Great Falls, College of (c): 1301 20th St. S., Great Falls, Mont. 59405. Sisters of Providence; 1932 (1,234).

Gwynedd-Mercy College (c): Gwynedd Valley, Pa. 19437. Sisters of Mercy; 1948; independent (1,217).

Holy Cross, College of the (c): Worcester, Mass. 01610. Jesuit Fathers; 1843 (2,494).

Holy Family College (c): Grant and Frankford Aves., Philadelphia, Pa. 19114. Sisters of Holy Family of Nazareth; 1954 (1,438).

Holy Names College (c): 3500 Mountain Blvd., Oakland, Calif. 94619. Sisters of the Holy Names of Jesus and Mary; 1868 (678).

Illinois Benedictine College (c): Lisle, Ill.

60532. Benedictine Fathers of St. Procopius Abbey; 1887 (1,504).

Immaculata College (w): Immaculata, Pa. 19345. Sisters, Servants of the Immaculate Heart of Mary; 1920 (821).

Incarnate Word College (c): 4301 Broadway, San Antonio, Tex. 78209. Sisters of Charity of the Incarnate Word; 1881 (1,431).

Iona College (c): 715 North Ave., New Rochelle, N.Y. 10801. Congregation of Christian Brothers; 1940; independent (6,193).

John Carroll University (c): North Park and Miramar Blvds., Cleveland, Ohio. 44118. Jesuit Fathers; 1886 (3,890).

Kansas Newman College (formerly Sacred Heart College) (c): 3100 McCormick Ave., Wichita, Kans. 67213. Sisters Adorers of the Blood of Christ; 1933 (698).

King's College (c): Wilkes-Barre, Pa. 18711. Holy Cross Fathers; 1946 (2,343).

La Roche College (c): 9000 Babcock Blvd., Pittsburgh, Pa. 15237. Sisters of Divine Providence; 1963 (1,350)

La Salle College (c): 20th St. and Olney Ave., Philadelphia, Pa. 19141. Brothers of the Christian Schools; 1863 (7,420)

Le Moyne College (c): Syracuse, N.Y. 13214. Jesuit Fathers; 1946; independent (1,800).

Lewis University (c): Romeoville, Ill. 60441. Christian Brothers; 1930 (2,776).

Loras College (c): 1450 Alta Vista St., Dubuque, Ia. 52001. Archdiocese of Dubuque; 1839 (1,882).

Loyola College (c): 4501 N. Charles St., Baltimore, Md. 21210, Jesuits; 1852; combined with Mt. St. Agnes College, 1971 (6,211).

Loyola Marymount University (c): 7101 W. 80th St., Los Angeles, Calif. 90045. Society of Jesus; Religious of Sacred Heart of Mary, Sisters of St. Joseph of Orange; 1911 (6,359).

Loyola University (c): 6363 St. Charles Ave., New Orleans, La. 70118. Jesuit Fathers; 1904 (4,347).

Loyola University of Chicago (c): 820 N. Michigan Ave., Chicago, Ill. 60611. Jesuit Fathers; 1870 (16,140).

Madonna College (c): 36600 Schoolcraft Rd., Livonia, Mich. 48150. Felician Sisters; 1947 (3,385).

Manhattan College (c): 4513 Manhattan College Pkwy., New York, N.Y. 10471. Brothers of the Christian Schools; 1853; independent (5,000). Cooperative program with College of Mt. St. Vincent.

Manhattanville College (c): Purchase, N.Y. 10577. Society of the Sacred Heart; 1841; independent (2,047).

Marian College (c): Fond du Lac, Wis. 54935. Sisters of St. Agnes; 1936 (563).

Marian College (c): 3200 Cold Spring Rd., Indianapolis, Ind. 46222. Sisters of St. Francis (Oldenburg, Ind.); 1851 (879).

Marist College (c): Poughkeepsie, N.Y. 12601. Marist Brothers of the Schools; 1946; independent (1,899).

Marquette University (c): 615 N. 11th St., Milwaukee, Wis. 53233. Jesuit Fathers; 1881; independent (14,122).

Mary College (c): Bismarck, N.D. 58501. Benedictine Sisters; 1959 (1,003).

Marycrest College (c): 1607 W. 12th St., Davenport, Iowa 52804. Congregation of the Humility of Mary; 1939; independent (1,298).

Marygrove College (c): 8425 W. McNicholas Rd., Detroit, Mich. 48221. Sisters, Servants of the Immaculate Heart of Mary; 1910 (1,153).

Marylhurst Education Center (c): Marylhurst, Ore. 97036. Srs. of Holy Names of Jesus and Mary; 1893; independent (840).

Marymount College (w): Tarrytown, N.Y. 10591. Religious of the Sacred Heart of Mary; 1907; independent (1,244).

Marymount College of Kansas (c): Salina, Kans. 67401. Sisters of St. Joseph of Concordia; 1922 (758).

Marymount College of Virginia (w): 2807 N. Glebe Rd., Arlington, Va. 22007. Religious of the Sacred Heart of Mary; 1950; independent (1,407).

Marymount Manhattan College (w): 221 E. 71st St., New York, N.Y. 10021. Religious of the Sacred Heart of Mary; 1948; independent (2,275).

Maryville College (c): 13550 Conway Rd., St. Louis, Mo. 63141. Religious of the Sacred Heart; 1872; independent (1,688).

Marywood College (w): Scranton, Pa. 18509. Sisters, Servants of the Immaculate Heart of Mary; 1915 (3,191). Coed in graduate division.

Mater Dei College (c): Riverside Dr., Ogdensburg, N.Y. 13669. Sisters of St. Joseph; 1960 (300).

Mercy College of Detroit (c): 8200 W. Outer Dr., Detroit, Mich. 48219. Sisters of Mercy; 1941 (2,119).

Mercyhurst College (c): 501 E. 38th St., Erie, Pa. 16546. Sisters of Mercy; 1926 (1,441).

Merrimack College (c): North Andover, Mass. 01845. Augustinians; 1947 (2,205).

Misericordia (College Misericordia) (c): Dallas, Pa. 18612. Religious Sisters of Mercy of the Union; 1924 (1,176).

Molloy College (w): 1000 Hempstead Ave., Rockville Centre, N.Y. 11570. Dominican Sisters; 1955 (1,539).

Mount Marty College (c): Yankton, S.D. 57078. Benedictine Sisters; 1936 (553).

Mount Mary College (w): 2900 W. Menomonee River Pkwy., Milwaukee, Wis. 53222. School Sisters of Notre Dame; 1913 (1,127).

Mt. Mercy College (c): 1330 Elmhurst Dr. N.E., Cedar Rapids, Ia. 52402. Sisters of Mercy; 1928 (1,121).

Mt. St. Joseph on the Ohio, College of (w): Mt. St. Joseph, Ohio 45051. Sisters of Charity; 1920 (1,839).

Mt. St. Mary College (c): Newburgh, N.Y. 12550. Dominican Sisters; 1959; independent (1,015).

Mount St. Mary College (c): Emmitsburg, Md. 21727. Diocesan Clergy; 1808; independent (1,641).

Mt. St. Mary's College (w): 12001 Chalon Rd., Los Angeles, Calif. 90049 and 10 Chester Pl., Los Angeles, Calif. 90007 (Doheny Campus). Sisters of St. Joseph of Carondelet; 1925 (1,144). Coed in music, nursing and graduate programs.

Mt. St. Vincent, College of (c): Mt. St. Vincent-on-Hudson, New York, N.Y. 10471. Sisters of Charity; 1847; independent (1,200). Cooperative program with Manhattan College.

Mundelein College (w): 6363 N. Sheridan Rd., Chicago, Ill. 60660. Sisters of Charity of the Blessed Virgin Mary; 1929 (1,354).

Nazareth College (c): Nazareth, Mich. 49074. Sisters of St. Joseph; 1924; independent (540).

Nazareth College (c): East Ave., Rochester, N.Y. 14610. Sisters of St. Joseph of Rochester; 1924; independent (2,778).

Neumann College (formerly Our Lady of Angels) (c): Aston, Pa. 19014. Sisters of St. Francis; 1965 (786).

New Rochelle, College of (w): 29 Castle Pl., New Rochelle, N.Y. 10801 (main campus). Ursuline Nuns; 1904; independent (4,484). Coed in nursing, graduate, new resources divisions.

Niagara University (c): Niagara Univ., N.Y. 14109. Vincentian Fathers; 1856 (3,954).

Notre Dame, College of (c): Belmont, Calif. 94002. Sisters of Notre Dame de Namur; 1868; independent (1,420).

Notre Dame, University of (c): Notre Dame, Ind. 46556. Congregation of Holy Cross; 1842 (8,714).

Notre Dame College (w): 4545 College Rd., Cleveland, Ohio 44121. Sisters of. Notre Dame; 1922 (770).

Notre Dame College (w): Manchester, N.H. 03104. Sisters of the Holy Cross; 1950 (740).

Notre Dame of Maryland, College of (w): 4701 N. Charles St., Baltimore, Md. 21210. School Sisters of Notre Dame; 1873 (575).

Ohio Dominican College (c): Columbus, Ohio 43219. Dominican Sisters of St. Mary of the Springs; 1911 (956).

Our Lady of Holy Cross College (c): 4123 Woodland Dr., New Orleans, La. 70114. Congregation of Sisters Marianites of Holy Cross (758).

Our Lady of the Elms, College of (w): Chicopee, Mass. 01013. Sisters of St. Joseph; 1928 (606).

Our Lady of the Lake University of San Antonio (c): 411 S.W. 24th St., San Antonio, Tex. 78285. Sisters of Divine Providence; 1911 (1,695).

Portland, University of (c): 5000 N. Willamette Blvd., Portland, Ore. 97203. Holy Cross Fathers; 1901; independent (2,845).

Providence College (c): River Ave. and Eaton St., Providence, R.I. 02918. Dominican Friars; 1917 (3,400).

Quincy College (c): 1831 College Ave., Quincy, Ill. 62301. Franciscan Friars; 1859 (1,940).

Regis College (c): W. 50th Ave. and Lowell Blvd. Denver, Colo. 80221. Jesuit Fathers; 1887 (1,070).

Regis College (w): Weston, Mass. 02193. Sisters of St. Joseph; 1927; independent (1,179).

Rivier College (w): Nashua, N.H. 03060. Sisters of the Presentation of Mary; 1933; independent (2,035). Coed continuing education and graduate divisions.

Rockhurst College (c): 5225 Troost Ave., Kansas City, Mo. 64110. Jesuit Fathers; 1910 (3,324).

Rosary College (c): 7900 Division St., River Forest, Ill. 60305. Dominican Sisters; 1901 (1,692).

Rosemont College (w): Rosemont, Pa. 19010. Society of the Holy Child Jesus; 1921 (600).

Sacred Heart College (c): Belmont, N.C. 28012. Sisters of Mercy; 1935 (373).

Sacred Heart University (c): Fairfield (P.O. Bridgeport), Conn. 06604. Diocese of Bridgeport; 1963; independent (4,081).

St. Ambrose College (c): Davenport, Ia. 52803, Diocese of Davenport; 1882 (2,060).

Saint Anselm's College (c): Manchester N.H. 03102. Benedictine Monks; 1889 (1,901).

St. Basil's College (m): 195 Glenbrook Rd., Stamford, Conn. 06902. Byzantine-Ukrainian Rite Diocese of Stamford; 1939.

Saint Benedict, College of (w): St. Joseph, Minn. 56374. Benedictine Sisters; 1913 (2,189).

St. Bonaventure University (c): St. Bonaventure, N.Y. 14778. Franciscan Friars; 1856; independent (2,789).

St. Catherine, College of (w): 2004 Randolph St., St. Paul, Minn. 55105. Sisters of St. Joseph of Carondelet; 1905 (2,427).

St. Edward's University (c): Austin, Tex. 78704. Holy Cross Brothers; 1885; independent (2,474).

St. Elizabeth, College of (w): Convent Station, N.J. 07961. Sisters of Charity; 1899; independent (858).

St. Francis, College of (c): 500 N. Wilcox St., Joliet, Ill. 60435. Sisters of St. Francis of Mary Immaculate; 1925; independent (576).

St. Francis College (c): 180 Remsen St., Brooklyn, N.Y. 11201. Franciscan Brothers; 1884; private, independent in the Franciscsan tradition (2,882).

St. Francis College (c): 2701 Spring St., Fort Wayne, Ind. 46808. Sisters of St. Francis; 1890 (1,247).

St. Francis College (c): Loretto, Pa. 15940. Franciscan Fathers; 1847 (1,656).

St. John Fisher College (c): 3690 East Ave., Rochester, N.Y. 14618. Basilian Fathers; 1951; independent (1,700).

St. John's University (c): Grand Central and Utopia Pkwys., Jamaica, N.Y. 11439 (Queens Campus); 300 Howard Ave., Grymes Hill, Staten Island, N.Y. 10301 (Staten Island Campus). Vincentian Fathers; 1870 (18,490).

St. John's University (m): Collegeville, Minn. 56321. ·Benedictine Fathers; 1857 (2,009). Coed in graduate school.

St. Joseph College (w): 1678 Asylum Ave., West Hartford, Conn. 06117. Sisters of Mercy; 1932 (1,284). Coed in graduate school.

St. Joseph's College (c): N. Windham, Me. 04062. Sisters of Mercy; 1912 (460).

Saint Joseph's College (c): Rensselaer, Ind. 47978. Society of the Precious Blood; 1889 (982).

St. Joseph's College (c): 245 Clinton Ave., Brooklyn, N.Y. 11205 and 155 Roe Blvd., Patchogue, N.Y. 11772. Sisters of St. Joseph; 1916; independent (1,116).

St. Joseph's University (c): 5600 City Ave., Philadelphia, Pa. 19131. Jesuit Fathers; 1851 (5,587).

St. Joseph the Provider, College of (c): Clement Rd., Rutland, Vt. 05701. Sisters of St. Joseph; 1954; independent (154).

Saint Leo College (c): Saint Leo, Fla. 33574. Order of St. Benedict; 1889; independent (1,152).

St. Louis University (c): 221 N. Grand Blvd., St. Louis, Mo. 63103. Jesuit Fathers; 1818 (10,396).

Saint Martin's College (c): Lacey, Wash. 98503. Benedictine Monks; 1895 (761).

St. Mary, College of (w): 1901 S. 72nd St., Omaha, Neb. 68124. Sisters of Mercy; 1923; independent (897).

Saint Mary College (w): Leavenworth, Kans. 66048. Sisters of Charity of Leavenworth; 1923 (845).

St. Mary of the Plains College (c): Dodge City, Kans. 67801. Sisters of St. Joseph of Wichita; 1952 (627).

St. Mary-of-the-Woods College (w): St. Mary-of-the-Woods, Ind. 47876. Sisters of Providence; 1840 (770).

St. Mary's College (w): Notre Dame, Ind. 46556. Sisters of the Holy Cross; 1844 (1,853).

St. Mary's College (c): Orchard Lake, Mich. 48033. Secular Clergy; 1885 (240).

St. Mary's College (c): Moraga, Calif. 94575. Brothers of the Christian Schools; 1863 (2,648).

St. Mary's College (c): Winona, Minn. 55987. Brothers of the Christian Schools; 1912 (1,427).

St. Mary's Dominican College (w): 7214 St. Charles Ave., New Orleans, La. 70118. Dominican Sisters; 1910 (783).

St. Mary's University (c): One Camino Santa Maria, San Antonio, Tex. 78284. Society of Mary (Marianists); 1852 (3,268).

St. Michael's College (c): Winooski, Vt. 05404. Society of St. Edmund; 1904 (1,638).

St. Norbert College (c): De Pere, Wis. 54115. Norbertine Fathers; 1898; independent (1,733).

St. Peter's College (c): 2641 Kennedy Blvd., Jersey City, N.J. 07306. Jesuit Fathers; 1872 (4,053).

St. Rose, College of (c): 432 Western Ave., Albany, N.Y. 12203. Sisters of St. Joseph of Carondelet; 1920; independent (2,875).

St. Scholastica, College of (c): 1200 Kenwood Ave., Duluth, Minn. 55811. Benedictine Sisters; 1912 (1,048).

Saint Teresa, College of (w): Winona, Minn. 55987. Sisters of St. Francis; 1907 (609).

St. Thomas, College of (c): St. Paul, Minn. 55101. Archdiocese of St. Paul; 1885 (5,632).

St. Thomas, University of (c): 3812 Montrose Blvd., Houston, Tex. 77006. Basilian Fathers; 1947 (1,939).

St. Thomas Aquinas College (c): Sparkill, N.Y. 10976. Dominican Sisters of Sparkill; 1952; independent, corporate board of trustees (1,767).

St. Vincent College (m): Latrobe, Pa. 15650. Benedictine Fathers; 1846 (983).

St. Xavier College (c): 3700 W. 103rd St., Chicago, Ill. 60655. Sisters of Mercy; chartered 1847 (2,311).

Salve Regina — The Newport College (c): Ochre Point Ave., Newport, R.I. 02840. Sisters of Mercy; 1934 (1,960).

San Diego, University of (c): Alcala Park, San Diego, Calif. 92110. San Diego diocese and Religious of the Sacred Heart; 1949; independent (4,791).

San Francisco, University of (c): 2130 Fulton St., San Francisco, Calif. 94117. Jesuit Fathers; 1855 (7,065).

Santa Clara, University of (c): Santa Clara, Calif. 95053. Jesuit Fathers; 1851 (7,062).

Santa Fe, College of (c): Santa Fe, N. Mex. 87501. Brothers of the Christian Schools; 1947 (1,100).

Scranton, University of (c): Scranton, Pa. 18510. Society of Jesus; 1888 (4,517).

Seattle University (c): Broadway and East Madison, Seattle, Wash. 98122. Jesuit Fathers; 1891 (4,579).

Seton Hall University (c): South Orange, N.J. 07079. Diocesan Clergy; 1856 (10,346).

Seton Hill College (w): Greensburg, Pa. 15601. Sisters of Charity of Seton Hill; 1883 (727).

Siena College (c): Loudonville, N.Y. 12211. Franciscan Friars; 1937 (2,706).

Siena Heights College (c): Adrian, Mich.

49221. Dominican Sisters; 1919; independent (1,446).

Silver Lake College of Holy Family (c): 2406 S. Alverno Rd., Manitowoc, Wis. 54220. Franciscan Sisters of Christian Charity; 1935 (400).

Spalding College (c): 851 S. 4th St., Louisville, Ky. 40203. Sisters of Charity of Nazareth; 1814 (as Nazareth Academy); independent (1,005).

Spring Hill College (c): Mobile, Ala. 36608. Jesuit Fathers; 1830 (898).

Steubenville, University of (c): Steubenville, Ohio 43952. Franciscan Fathers; 1946 (963).

Stonehill College (c): North Easton, Mass. 02356. Holy Cross Fathers; 1948; independent (2,753).

Thomas More College (c): 2771 Turkey Foot Rd., Fort Mitchell, Covington, Ky. 41017. Diocese of Covington; 1921 (1,229).

Trinity College (w): Colchester Ave., Burlington, Vt. 05401. Sisters of Mercy; 1925 (869).

Trinity College (w): Michigan Ave. and Franklin St. N.E., Washington, D.C. 20017. Sisters of Notre Dame de Namur; 1897 (770). Coed in graduate school.

Ursuline College (w): 2550 Lander Rd., Cleveland, Ohio 44124. Ursuline Nuns; 1871 (1,147).

Villa Maria College (w): 2551 W. Lake Rd., Erie, Pa. 16505. Sisters of St. Joseph; 1925 (693).

Villanova University (c): Villanova, Pa. 19085. Order of St. Augustine; 1842 (10,341).

Viterbo College (c): La Crosse, Wis. 54601. Franciscan Sisters; 1890 (1,113).

Walsh College (c): 2020 Easton St. N.W., Canton, Ohio 44720. Brothers of Christian Instruction; 1958 (920).

Wheeling College (c): 316 Washington Ave., Wheeling, W. Va. 26003. Jesuit Fathers; 1954 (1,050).

Xavier University (c): Victory Pkwy. and Dana Ave., Cincinnati, Ohio 45207. Jesuit Fathers; 1831 (7,209).

Xavier University of Louisiana (c): 7325 Palmetto St., New Orleans, La. 70125. Sisters of Blessed Sacrament; 1925; lay religious administration board (2,237).

Catholic Junior Colleges

Ancilla Domini College (c): Donaldson, Ind. 46513. Ancilla Domini Sisters; 1937 (330).

Aquinas Junior College (c): Harding Rd., Nashville, Tenn. 37205. Dominican Sisters; 1961 (279).

Chatfield College (c): St. Martin, O. 45118. Ursulines (304).

Donnelly College (c): 1236 Sandusky Ave., Kansas City, Kans. 66102. Archdiocesan College; 1949 (710).

Don Bosco Technical Institute: 1151 San Gabriel Blvd., Rosemead, Calif. 91770. Salenians (315).

Elizabeth Seton College (c): 1061 N. Broadway, Yonkers, N.Y. 10701. Sisters of Charity; 1960; independent (1,472).

Harriman College (c): Harriman Heights Rd., Harriman, N.Y. 10926. Sisters of the Catholic Apostolate; 1956; independent (320).

Hilbert College (c): 5200 S. Park Ave., Hamburg, N.Y. 14075. Franciscan Sisters of St. Joseph; 1957; independent (607).

Holy Cross Junior College (c): Notre Dame, Ind. 46556. Brothers of Holy Cross; 1966 (265).

Lourdes College (c): Sylvania, Ohio 43560. Franciscan Srs.; 1958 (630).

Manor Junior College (w): Fox Chase Manor, Jenkintown, Pa. 19046. Sisters of St. Basil the Great; 1947 (342).

Maria College (c): 700 New Scotland Ave., Albany, N.Y. 12208. Sisters of Mercy; 1963 (512).

Maria Regina College (w): 1024 Court St., Syracuse, N.Y. 13208. Franciscan Sisters; 1963; independent (622).

Marymount Palos Verdes College (c): Rancho Palos Verdes, Calif. 90274. Religious of the Sacred Heart of Mary (449).

Mt. Aloysius Junior College (c): Cresson, Pa. 16630. Sisters of Mercy; 1939 (449).

Mt. St. Clare College (c): Bluff Blvd., and Springdale Dr., Clinton, Ia. 52732. Clinton Franciscans; 1928 (408). Four-year program in Business Administration (B.A.).

Presentation College (c): Aberdeen, S.D. 57401. Sisters of the Presentation; 1951 (325).

St. Catharine College (c); St. Catharine, Ky. 40061. Dominican Sisters; 1931 (243).

St. Gertrude, College of (c): Cottonwood, Ida. 83522. Benedictine Sisters.

St. Gregory's College (c): Shawnee, Okla. 74801. Benedictine Fathers; 1876 (341).

St. Mary's College of O'Fallon (c): 200 N. Main St., O'Fallon, Mo. 63366. Sisters of the Most Precious Blood; 1921 (643).

St. Mary's Junior College (c): 2500 S. 6th St., Minneapolis, Minn. 55454. Sisters of St. Joseph of Carondelet (789).

Springfield College in Illinois (c): 1500 N. Fifth St., Springfield, Ill. 62702. Ursuline Nuns; 1929 (441).

Trocaire College (c): 110 Red Jacket Pkwy., Buffalo, N.Y. 14220. Sisters of Mercy; 1958; independent (1,023).

Villa Julie College (c): Green Spring Valley Rd., Stevenson, Md. 21153. Sisters of Notre Dame de Namur; 1952; independent (870).

Villa Maria College of Buffalo (c): 240 Pine Ridge Rd., Buffalo, N.Y. 14225. Felician Srs.; 1960 (768).

Father Vincent D. Cushing, O.F.M., was elected in June, 1982, the first Catholic president of the Association of Theological Schools of the United States and Canada.

CAMPUS MINISTRY

"Campus ministry is a pastoral apostolate of service to the members of the entire college community through concern and care for persons, the proclamation of the Gospel, and the celebration of the liturgy," according to a set of guidelines drawn up by an eight-member commission of the National Catholic Educational Association. The general purpose of the ministry is to make the Church present and active in the academic community.

Ideally, according to the guidelines, elements of the ministry — carried on by teams of priests, men and women religious, and lay persons — include liturgical leadership; pastoral counseling; coordination of expressions and energies for religious life on campus; Christian witness on social and moral issues; objective and independent mediation between various groups on campus; participation in religious aspects of the work of the administration, faculty and students.

Status, Agencies

The dimensions and challenge of the campus ministry are evident from estimates that approximately 75 to 80 per cent of 2.4 million Catholics in colleges and universities are on non-Catholic public and private campuses. Serving them are about 1,200 full-time and 700 part-time campus ministry personnel.

The Office of Campus and Young Adult Ministry, under the Department of Education of the U.S. Catholic Conference, has responsibility for continuing support of ministry in this field. The office, headed by Father Joseph J. Kenna, is located at 1312 Massachusetts Ave. N.W., Washington, D.C. 20005.

The office has an advisory body, the National Committee of Diocesan Directors of Campus Ministry, composed of 30 elected and three ex officio members.

The autonomous Catholic Campus Ministry Association, is headquartered at 3700 West 103rd St., Chicago, Ill. 60655. Sister Margaret M. Ivers, I.B.V.M., is executive director.

DIOCESAN AND INTERDIOCESAN SEMINARIES

(Sources: Almanac survey; *Official Catholic Directory;* NC News Service.)

Information, according to states, includes names of archdioceses and dioceses, and names and addresses of seminaries. Types of seminaries, when not clear from titles, are indicated in most cases. Interdiocesan seminaries are generally conducted by religious orders for candidates for the priesthood from several dioceses. The list does not include houses of study only for members of religious communities. Archdioceses are indicated by an asterisk.

California: Los Angeles* — St. John's Seminary (major), 5012 E. Seminary Rd., Camarillo. 93010; St. John's College Seminary, 5118 E. Seminary Rd., Camarillo. 93010; Seminary of Our Lady, Queen of Angels (minor, high school), Box 1071, San Fernando. 91341.

San Diego — St. Francis Seminary (college residence), 1667 Santa Paula Dr., San Diego 92111.

San Francisco* — St. Patrick's Seminary (major), 320 Middlefield Rd., Menlo Park. 94025.

San Jose — St. Patrick's College, P.O. Box 151, Mountain View 94042.

Colorado: Denver* — St. Thomas Theological Seminary (major), 1300 S. Steele St., Denver 80210.

Connecticut: Hartford* — St. Thomas Seminary (minor), 467 Bloomfield Ave., Bloomfield. 06002.

Norwich — Holy Apostles College (delayed vocation seminary), 33 Prospect Hill Rd., Cromwell 06416.

Stamford Byzantine Rite — Ukrainian Catholic Seminary: St. Basil College (minor), 161 Glenbrook Rd., Stamford 06902; St. Basil's Preparatory School (minor), 39 Clovelly Rd., Stamford 06902.

District of Columbia: Washington* — Theological College, The Catholic University of America, 401 Michigan Ave., N.E. 20064.

Florida: Miami*, Pensacola-Tallahassee, St. Augustine, St. Petersburg — St. John Vianney College Seminary, 2900 S.W. 87th Ave., Miami 33165; St. Vincent de Paul Regional Seminary (major), Military Trail, P.O. Box 460, Boynton Beach. 33435.

Hawaii: Honolulu — St. Stephen's Seminary (college level), P.O. Box 699, Kaneohe. 96744.

Illinois: Belleville — St. Henry's Preparatory Seminary, 5901 W. Main St., Belleville 62223.

Chicago* — Quigley Preparatory Seminary (North), 103 East Chestnut St., Chicago 60611; Quigley Preparatory Seminary (South), 7740 South Western Ave., Chicago 60620; Niles College of Loyola University, 7135 N. Harlem Ave., Chicago 60631; St. Mary of the Lake Seminary, Mundelein. 60060.

Springfield — Immaculate Conception Seminary, 1903 E. Lake Dr., Springfield 62707.

Indiana: Indianapolis* — St. Meinrad Seminary, College and School of Theology (interdiocesan), St. Meinrad. 47577.

Iowa: Davenport — St. Ambrose College Seminary, 518 W. Locust St., Davenport 52803.

Dubuque* — Seminary of St. Pius X.

Loras College, Dubuque 52001.

Kansas: Kansas City* — Savior of the World Seminary (minor), 12601 Parallel Ave., Kansas City 66109.

Kentucky: Covington — Seminary of St. Pius X (interdiocesan), Erlanger. 41018.

Owensboro — St. Mark's School of Theology Seminary for Belated Vocations, South Union 42283.

Louisiana: New Orleans* — Notre Dame Seminary Graduate School of Theology, 2901 S. Carrollton Ave., New Orleans 70118; St. John Vianney Preparatory School, 3801 Monroe St., New Orleans 70118; St. Joseph Seminary College (interdiocesan), St. Benedict 70457.

Maryland: Baltimore* — St. Mary's Seminary and University, 5400 Roland Ave., Baltimore 21210; Mt. St. Mary's Seminary, Emmitsburg. 21727.

Massachusetts: Boston* — St. John's Seminary School of Theology, 127 Lake St., Brighton. 02135; St. John's Seminary, College of Liberal Arts, 197 Foster St., Brighton 02135; Pope John XXIII National Seminary, 558 South Ave., Weston. 02193.

Melkite Eparchy of Newton — St. Gregory the Theologian Seminary, 233 Grant Ave., Newton 02159; St. Basil's Seminary, 30 East St., Methuen 01844.

Michigan: Detroit* — Sacred Heart Seminary College, Inc., 2701 Chicago Blvd., Detroit 48206; Sts. Cyril and Methodius Seminary (independent institution primarily serving Polish-American community), Orchard Lake 48033; St. John's Provincial Seminary (major, for dioceses in Detroit province), 44011 Five Mile Rd., Plymouth. 48170.

Grand Rapids — St. Joseph's Minor Seminary, 600 Burton St., S.E., Grand Rapids 49507.

Minnesota: St. Cloud — School of Theology (St. John's Seminary), Collegeville. 56321.

St. Paul and Minneapolis* — St. Paul Seminary, 2260 Summit Ave., St. Paul. 55105; St. John Vianney College Seminary, 2115 Summit Ave., St. Paul. 55105.

Winona — Immaculate Heart of Mary Seminary, St. Mary's College, Winona 55987.

Missouri: Jefferson City — St. Thomas Aquinas Preparatory Seminary, 245 N. Levering Ave. Hannibal. 63401.

Kansas City-St. Joseph — St. John's Diocesan Seminary (high school), 2015 E. 72nd St. Kansas City. 64132.

St. Louis* — St. Louis Roman Catholic Theological Seminary (Kenrick Seminary), 7800 Kenrick Rd., St. Louis 63119; Cardinal Glennon College, 5200 Glennon Dr., St. Louis 63119; St. Louis Preparatory Seminary, 5200 Shrewsbury Ave., St. Louis 63119 (South), 3500 St. Catherine St., Florissant 63033 (North).

Montana: Helena — Diocesan Pre-Seminary Program, Carroll College, Helena 59601.

New Jersey: Newark* — Immaculate Conception Seminary (major), Darlington, Mahwah. 07430 (scheduled to be transferred to Seton Hall University by the end of 1983); Seton Hall University College Seminary of the Immaculate Conception, Divinity School, South Orange. 07079.

New Mexico: Gallup — Cristo Rey College and High School Seminary, 205 E. Wilson, Gallup 87301.

Santa Fe* — Immaculate Heart of Mary Seminary (college house of formation), Mt. Carmel Rd., Santa Fe 87501

New York: Brooklyn — Cathedral Preparatory Seminary of the Immaculate Conception, 555 Washington Ave., Brooklyn 11238; Cathedral Preparatory Seminary of the Immaculate Conception, 56-25 92nd St., Elmhurst. 11373; Cathedral College of the Immaculate Conception, 7200 Douglaston Parkway, Douglaston. 11362.

Buffalo — Christ the King Seminary (interdiocesan), 711 Knox Rd., East Aurora. 14052.

New York* — St. Joseph's Seminary (major), Dunwoodie, Yonkers. 10704: Cathedral Preparatory Seminary, 555 West End Ave., New York 10024.

Ogdensburg — Wadhams Hall, Riverside Dr., Ogdensburg 13669.

Rochester — Becket Hall College Seminary, 80 Fairport Rd., E. Rochester. 14445; St. Bernard's Seminary, 2260 Lake Ave., Rochester 14612.

Rockville Centre — Immaculate Conception Diocesan Seminary, Lloyd Harbor, Huntington, L.I. 11743; St. Pius X Preparatory Seminary, 1220 Front St., Uniondale, L.I. 11553.

St. Maron Diocese, Brooklyn — Our Lady of Lebanon Maronite Seminary, 7164 Alaska Ave. N.W., Washington, D.C. 20012.

Syracuse — Syracuse-Aquinas House, 702 Danforth St., Syracuse 13208.

North Dakota: Fargo — Cardinal Muench Seminary, 100 35th Ave. N.E., Fargo 58102.

Ohio: Cincinnati* — Mt. St. Mary's Seminary of the West, 6616 Beechmont Ave., Cincinnati. 45230 (division of the Athenaeum of Ohio).

Cleveland — St. Mary Seminary, 1227 Ansel Rd., Cleveland 44108; Borromeo College of Ohio, 28700 Euclid Ave. Wickliffe. 44092.

Columbus — Pontifical College Josephinum (interdiocesan), theologate and college, Columbus. 43085.

Toledo — Holy Spirit Seminary High School, 5201 Airport Highway, Toledo 43615.

Oregon: Portland* — Mt. Angel Seminary (college, pre-theology program, graduate school of theology), St. Benedict 97373; St. John Vianney House of Studies, 1538 Southwest Montgomery St., Portland 97201.

Pennsylvania: Allentown — Mary Immaculate Seminary (interdiocesan), Northampton 18067.

Erie — St. Mark's Seminary, 429 E. Grandview Blvd., Erie 16504.

Greensburg — St. Vincent Seminary (interdiocesan), Latrobe 15650.

Philadelphia* — Theological Seminary of St. Charles Borromeo, Overbrook. 19151.

Philadelphia Byzantine Rite (Ukrainians)* — St. Josaphat's Seminary, 201 Taylor St. N.E., Washington, D.C. 20017.

Pittsburgh Byzantine Rite (Ruthenians)* — Byzantine Catholic Seminary of Sts. Cyril and Methodius, 3605 Perrysville Ave., Pittsburgh. 15214.

Pittsburgh — St. Paul Seminary, 2900 Noblestown Rd. 15205.

Scranton — St. Pius X Seminary (college division), Dalton. 18414.

Rhode Island: Providence — Our Lady of Providence College Seminary, Warwick Neck Ave., Warwick. 02889.

Texas: Corpus Christi — Corpus Christi Minor Seminary, Rt. 1, Box 500. 78415.

Dallas — Holy Trinity Seminary (major), P.O. Box 3068, Irving. 75061.

El Paso — St. Charles Seminary High School, P.O. Box 17548, El Paso 79917.

Galveston-Houston — St. Mary's Seminary (major), 9845 Memorial Dr. Houston. 77024.

San Antonio* — The Assumption-St. John's Seminary (major), 2600 W. Woodlawn Ave., San Antonio 78284.

Washington: Spokane — Bishop White Seminary, E. 429 Sharp Ave., Spokane 99202.

West Virginia: Wheeling-Charleston — St. Joseph Preparatory Seminary, Rt. 6, Vienna. 26101; Seminary House of Studies (college residence), 1252 National Rd., Wheeling. 26003.

Wisconsin: Madison — Holy Name Seminary (High School), 3577 High Point Rd., Madison 53711.

Milwaukee* — St. Francis Seminary School of Pastoral Ministry, 3257 S. Lake Dr., Milwaukee 53207.

REPORT ON SEMINARIES

The Center for Applied Research in the Apostolate reported Dec. 2, 1981, a continuing decline in the number of students for the priesthood in the United States. The report was based on responses received from 400 "self-standing and collaborative seminaries and religious communities."

Declining Enrollment

The 1981-82 enrollment of students of theology was 3,819, considerably less — by 54 per cent — than the 8,325 reported for 1966-67, and 8.8 per cent less than the figure reported for 1980-81. Rates of decline from 1980-81 to 1981-82 were 7.8 and 11.7 per cent, respectively, for diocesan students and students belonging to religious communities.

Seminary college enrollment fell from 3,769 in 1980-81 to 3,580 in 1981-82, a loss of 5 per cent. The loss since 1966-67, when enrollment was 14,303, was 74 per cent.

High school seminary enrollment went down from 4,448 in 1980-81 to 4,117 in 1981-82, a loss of 7 per cent. The loss since 1966-67, when enrollment was 20,189, was 80 per cent.

Enrollment losses since 1966 were accompanied by declines in the number of diocesan seminaries, from 126 in that year to 86 in 1982. Comparative figures for seminaries of religious institutes were 481 and 217.

Changes

Institutions for the training of candidates for the priesthood have undergone change in recent years and now include not only traditional free-standing, residential seminaries with relatively self-sufficient faculties and resources, but also coalitions and consortiums of pooled faculties and non-academic houses and places of formation for students pursuing studies elsewhere in Catholic and/or secular colleges and universities.

The composition of student bodies in some academic programs has changed considerably with the enrollment of lay persons, including women, for the study of theology and preparation for various kinds of ministry in the Church. Between 1975 and 1979, there was a 35 per cent increase in the enrollment of nonseminarians in theological degree programs, according to a September, 1981, report.

Bishops' Program, Special Study

The academic, spiritual and pastoral preparation of students for the priesthood (diocesan and members of religious institutes) is subject to norms of the U.S. Bishops' Program of Priestly Formation. Approval of this program for the third time by the Congregation for Catholic Education was reported early in January, 1982.

Archbishop John R. Roach, president of the National Conference of Catholic Bishops, notified bishops in a letter dated Sept. 18, 1981, that the Holy See had ordered a comprehensive study of theological and college-level seminaries in this country. The purpose of the study is to determine how well seminaries are meeting the goals of academic, pastoral, liturgical and spiritual formation of candidates for the priesthood.

It was expected that the study would get under way in 1983, under the direction of Bishop John A. Marshall of Burlington, past chairman of the Bishops' Committee on Priestly Formation and former spiritual director of the North American College in Rome.

Bishop Marshall announced July 19,

1982, that the executive secretary for the project would be Father Donald Wuerl, former staff member of the Congregation for the Clergy and secretary to Cardinal John Wright from 1969 to 1979.

U.S. SEMINARIES AND STUDENTS, 1962-1982
(Source: *The Official Catholic Directory.*)

Year	Dioc. Seminaries	Total Dioc. Students	Religious Seminaries Scholasticates	Total Rel. Students	Total Seminarians
1962	98	23,662	447	22,657	46,319
1963	107	25,247	454	22,327	47,574
1964	112	26,701	459	22,049	48,750
1965	117	26,762	479	22,230	48,992
1966	126	26,252	481	21,862	48,114
1967	123	24,293	452	21,086	45,379
1968	124	22,232	437	17,604	39,836
1969	122	19,573	407	14,417	33,990
1970	118	17,317	383	11,589	28,906
1971	110	14,987	340	10,723	25,710
1972	106	13,554	326	9,409	22,963
1973	107	12,925	304	8,855	21,780
1974	109	11,765	293	7,583	19,348
1975	104	11,223	269	6,579	17,802
1976	102	11,015	269	6,232	17,247
1977	100	10,344	287	5,599	15,943
1978	98	9,560	278	5,438	14,998
1979	92	8,694	258	5,266	13,960
1980	92	8,552	252	4,674	13,226
1981	88	7,954	240	4,514	12,468
1982	86	7,625	217	4,020	11,645

PONTIFICAL UNIVERSITIES

(Principal source: *Annuario Pontificio.*)

These universities, listed according to country of location, have been canonically erected and authorized by the Sacred Congregation for Catholic Education to award degrees in stated fields of study.

New laws and norms governing ecclesiastical universities and faculties were promulgated in the apostolic constitution *Sapientia Christiana*, issued Apr. 15, 1979.

Argentina: Catholic University of S. Maria of Buenos Aires (June 16, 1960): Juncal 1912, Buenos Aires.

Belgium: Catholic University of Louvain (Dec. 9, 1425; 1834), with autonomous institutions for French- (Louvain) and Flemish- (Leuven) speaking: Place de l'Universite I, 1348 Louvain-La-Neuve (French); Naamsestraat 22B, 3000 Leuven (Flemish).

Brazil: Pontifical Catholic University of Rio de Janeiro (Jan. 20, 1947): Rua Marques de Sao Vicente 209, Rio de Janeiro, Est. de Guanabara.

Pontifical Catholic University of Rio Grande do Sul (Nov. 1, 1950): Praca Dom. Sebastiao 2, Porto Alegre, Estado do Rio Grande do Sul.

Pontifical Catholic University of Sao Paulo (Jan. 25, 1947): Rua Monte Alegre 984, Sao Paulo.

Pontifical University of Campinas (Sept. 8,

1956): Rua Marechal Deodoro 1099, Campinas, Sao Paulo.

Canada: Laval University (Mar. 15, 1876): Case Postale 460, Quebec G1K 7P4.

St. Paul University (formerly University of Ottawa) (Feb. 5, 1889): 223, Rue Main, Ottawa, K1S 1C4, Ontario.

University of Sherbrooke (Nov. 21, 1957): Chemin Ste.-Catherine, Cite Universitaire, Sherbrooke, Que. J1K 2R1.

Chile: Catholic University of Chile (June 21, 1888): Avenida Bernardo O'Higgins 340, Casilla 114D, Santiago de Chile.

Catholic University of Valparaiso (Nov. 1, 1961): Avenida Brasil 2950, Casilla 4059, Valparaiso.

Colombia: Bolivarian Pontifical Catholic University (Aug. 16, 1945): Calle 52, N. 43-53, Medellin.

Pontifical Xaverian University (July 31, 1937): Carrera 7, N. 40-62, Bogota D.E.

Cuba: Catholic University of St. Thomas of Villanueva (May 4, 1957): Avenida Quenta 16,660, Marianao, Havana. Taken over by the Castro government in May, 1961.

Ecuador: Catholic University of Ecuador (July 16, 1954): Doce de Octubre, N. 1076, Apartado 2184, Quito.

Ethiopia: University of Asmara (Sept. 8, 1960): Via Menelik II, 45, Post Office Box 1220, Asmara.

France: Catholic University of Lille (Nov. 18, 1875): Boulevard Vauban 60, 59046 Lille.

Catholic Faculties of Lyon (Nov. 22, 1875): 25, Rue du Plat, 69288 Lyon.

Catholic Institute of Paris (Aug. 11, 1875): 21, Rue d'Assas, 75270 Paris.

Catholic Institute of Toulouse (Nov. 15,1877): Rue de la Fonderie 31, 31068 Toulouse.

Catholic University of the West (Sept. 16, 1875): 3, Place Andre Leroy, B.P. 808, 49005 Angers.

Germany: Eichstatt Catholic University (Apr. 1, 1980): Ostenstrasse 26-28, D-8078, Eichstatt.

Guatemala: Rafael Landivar University (Oct. 18, 1961): 17 Calle 8-64, Z 10 Guatemala.

Ireland: St. Patrick's College (Mar. 29, 1896): Maynooth, Co. Kildare.

Italy: Catholic University of the Sacred Heart (Dec. 25, 1920): Largo Gemelli 1, 20123 Milan.

Japan: *Jochi Daigaku* (Sophia University) (Mar. 29, 1913): Chiyoda-Ku, Kioi-cho 7, Tokyo.

Lebanon: St. Joseph University of Beirut (Mar. 25, 1881): Rue de l'Universite St.-Joseph, Boite Postale 293, Beyrouth.

Netherlands: Nijmegen Roman Catholic University (June 29, 1923): Wilhelminasingel 13, Nijmegen.

Panama: University of S. Maria la Antigua (May 27, 1965): Apartado 2143, Panama 1.

Paraguay: Catholic University of Our Lady of the Assumption (Feb. 2, 1965): Comuneros e Independencia Nacional, Asuncion.

Peru: Catholic University of Peru (Sept. 30, 1942): Apartado 1761, Lima.

Philippine Islands: Pontifical University of Santo Tomas (Nov. 20, 1645): Espana Street, Manila.

Poland: Catholic University of Lublin (July 25, 1920): Aleje Raclawickie 14, Skr. Poczt. 279, 20-950, Lublin.

Portugal: Portuguese Catholic University (Nov. 1, 1967): Palma de Cima, 1600 Lisbon.

Puerto Rico: Catholic University of Puerto Rico (Aug. 15, 1972): Ponce, Puerto Rico 00731.

Spain: Catholic University of Navarra (Aug. 6, 1960): Ciudad Universitaria, Pamplona.

Pontifical University "Comillas" (Mar. 29, 1904): Canto Blanco, Apartado Postal 3082, Madrid 34.

Pontifical University of Salamanca (Sept. 25, 1940): Compania 1, Apartado 541, Salamanca.

University of Deusto (Aug. 10, 1963): Avenida de las Universidades, 28, Apartado 1, Bilbao.

Taiwan (China): Fu Jen Catholic University (Nov. 15, 1923, at Peking; reconstituted at Taipeh, Sept. 8, 1961): Hsinchuang, Taipeh Hsien.

United States: Catholic University of America (Mar. 7, 1889): Washington, D.C. 20064.

Georgetown University (Mar. 30, 1833): 37th and O Sts. N.W., Washington, D.C. 20057.

Niagara University (June 21, 1956): Niagara University, N.Y. 14109.

Venezuela: Catholic University "Andres Bello" (Sept. 29, 1963): Esquina Jesuitas, Apartado 422, Caracas.

ECCLESIASTICAL FACULTIES

(Source: *Annuario Pontificio*)

These faculties in Catholic seminaries and universities, listed according to country of location, have been canonically erected and authorized by the Sacred Congregation for Catholic Education to award degrees in stated fields of study. In addition to those listed here, there are other faculties of theology or philosophy in state universities and for members of certain religious orders only.

Argentina: Faculties of Philosophy and Theology, San Miguel (Sept. 8, 1932).

Australia: Institute of Theology, Sydney (Feb. 2, 1954).

Austria: Theological Faculty, Linz (Dec. 25, 1978).

Brazil: Ecclesiastical Faculty of Philosophy "John Paul II," Rio de Janeiro Aug. 6, 1981.

Canada: Pontifical Institute of Medieval Studies, Toronto (Oct. 18, 1939).

Dominican Faculty of Theology of Canada, Ottawa (1965; Nov. 15, 1975).

Regis College — Toronto Section of the Jesuit Faculty of Theology in Canada, Toronto (Feb. 17, 1956; Dec. 25, 1977).

College of Immaculate Conception — Montreal Section of Jesuit Faculties in Canada (Sept. 8, 1932).

France: Centre Sevres — Faculties of Theology and Philosophy of the Jesuits, Paris (Sept. 8, 1932).

Germany: Theological Faculty, Paderborn (June 11, 1966).

Theological Faculty of the Major Episcopal Seminary, Trier (Sept. 8, 1955)

Philosophical Faculty, Munich (1932; Oct. 25, 1971).

Theological-Philosophical Faculty, Frankfurt (1932; June 7, 1971).

Theological Faculty, Fulda (Dec. 22, 1978).

Great Britain: Heythrop College, University of London, London (Nov. 1, 1964). Theology, philosophy.

India: "Jnana Deepa" (Pontifical Athenaeum), Institute of Philosophy and Religion, Poona (July 27, 1926).

Pontificial Institute of Theology and Philosophy, Alwaye, Kerala (Feb. 24, 1972).

"Vidyajyoti," Institute of Religious Studies, Faculty of Theology, Delhi (1932; Dec. 9, 1974).

Dharmaran Pontifical Institute of Theology and Philosophy, Bangalore (Jan. 6, 1976).

St. Peter's Pontifical Institute of Theology, Bangalore (Jan. 6, 1976).

"Satya Nilayam," Institute of Philosophy and Culture. Faculty of Philosophy, Shembaganur (Sept. 8, 1932; Dec. 15, 1976).

Italy: Interregional Theological Faculty, Milan (Aug. 8, 1935).

Pontifical Theological Faculty of the Most Sacred Heart of Jesus, Cagliari, of the Pontifical Regional Seminary of Sardinia (July 5, 1927).

Pontifical Ambrosian Institute of Sacred Music, Milan (Mar. 12, 1940).

Theological Faculty of Sicily, Palermo (Dec. 8, 1980).

Theological Faculty of Southern Italy, Naples. Two sections: St. Thomas Aquinas Capodimonte (Oct. 31, 1941) and St. Louis Posillipo (Mar. 16, 1918). Pastoral Ignatian Institute, Messina (July 31, 1972).

Faculty of Philosophy "Aloisianum," Gallarate (1937; Mar. 20, 1974).

Ivory Coast: Catholic Institute of West Africa, Abidjan (Aug. 12, 1975).

Lebanon: University Centre for Religious and Ecclesiastical Sciences, Kaslik (Oct. 20, 1974).

Madagascar: Superior Institute of Theology, at the Regional Seminary of Antananarivo, Ambatoroka-Antananarivo (Apr. 21, 1960).

Malta: Faculty of Theology, Tal-Virtu (Nov. 22, 1769).

Peru: Pontifical and Civil Faculty of Theology, Lima (July 25, 1571).

Poland: Theological Faculty, Poznan (1969; pontifical designation, June 2, 1974).

Spain: Theological Faculty of Barcelona, of the Major Seminary of Barcelona and the College of St. Francis Borgia of San Cugat del Valles (Mar. 7, 1968).

Theological Faculty, Granada (1940; July 31, 1973).

Theological Faculty of the North, of the Metropolitan Seminary of Burgos and the Diocesan Seminary of Vitoria (Feb. 6, 1967).

Theological Faculty "San Vicente Ferrer," Valencia (Jan. 23, 1974).

Switzerland: Theological Faculty, Chur (Jan. 1, 1974).

Theological Faculty, Luzerne (Dec. 25, 1973).

United States: St. Mary's Seminary and University. School of Theology, Baltimore (May 1, 1822).

St. Mary of the Lake Faculty of Theology, Chicago (Sept. 30, 1929).

The Jesuit School of Theology, Berkeley, Calif. (Feb. 2, 1934, as "Alma College," Los Gatos, Calif.).

Vietnam: Theological Faculty of the Pontifical National Seminary of St. Pius X, Dalat (July 31, 1965). Activities suppressed.

The **Pontifical College Josephinum** (Theologate and College) at Columbus, Ohio, is a regional pontifical seminary. Established Sept. 1, 1888, it is immediately subject to the Holy See.

PONTIFICAL UNIVERSITIES AND INSTITUTES IN ROME
(Source: *Annuario Pontificio.*)

Pontifical Gregorian University (1552): Piazza della Pilotta, 4, 00187 Rome. Associated with the university are:

The **Pontifical Biblical Institute** (May 7, 1909): Via della Pilotta, 25, 00187 Rome.

The **Pontifical Institute of Oriental Studies** (Oct. 15, 1917): Piazza S. Maria Maggiore, 7, 00185 Rome.

Pontifical Lateran University (1773). Piazza S. Giovanni in Laterano, 4, 00184 Rome.

Pontifical Urban University (1627): Via Urban VIII, 16, 00165 Rome.

Pontifical University of St. Thomas Aquinas (**Angelicum**) (1580), of the Order of Preachers: Largo Angelicum, 1, 00184 Rome.

Pontifical University Salesianum (May 3, 1940; university designation May 24, 1973), of the Salesians of Don Bosco: Piazza dell' Ateneo Salesiano, 1, 00139 Rome. Associated with the university is the **Pontifical Institute of Higher Latin Studies** (Feb. 22, 1964).

Pontifical Athenaeum of St. Anselm (1687), of the Benedictines: Piazza dei Cavalieri di Malta, 5, 00153 Rome.

Pontifical Athenaeum Antonianum (of St. Anthony) (May 17, 1933), of the Order of Friars Minor: Via Merulana, 124, 00185 Rome.

Pontifical Institute of Sacred Music (1911; May 24, 1931): Piazza S. Agostino, 20-A, 00186, Rome.

Pontifical Institute of Christian Archeology (Dec. 11, 1925): Via Napoleone III, 1, 00185 Rome.

Pontifical Theological Faculty "St. Bonaventure" (Dec. 18, 1587), of the Order of Friars Minor Conventual: Via del Serafico, 1, 00142 Rome.

Pontifical Theological Faculty, Pontifical Institute of Spirituality "Teresianum" (1935), of the Discalced Carmelites: Piazza San Pancrazio, 5-A, 00152 Rome.

Pontifical Theological Faculty "Marianum" (1398), of the Servants of Mary: Viale Trente Aprile, 6, 00153 Rome.

Pontifical Institute of Arabic and Islamic Studies (1926), of the White Fathers: Piazza S. Apollinare, 49, 00186 Rome.

Pontifical Faculty of Educational Science "Auxilium" (June 27, 1970), of the Daughters of Mary, Help of Christians: Via di Selva Candida, 267, 00166 Rome.

Pontifical Institute "Regina Mundi" (1954): Lungotevere Tor di Nona, 7, 00186 Rome.

PONTIFICAL ACADEMY OF SCIENCES

(Sources: *Annuario Pontificio,* NC News Service. Membership as of Aug. 1, 1982.)

The Pontifical Academy of Sciences was constituted in its present form by Pius XI Oct. 28, 1936, in virtue of *In Multis Solaciis,* a document issued on his own initiative.

The academy is the only supranational body of its kind in the world, with a pope-selected, life-long membership of outstanding mathematicians and experimental scientists from many countries. The normal complement of members is 70; the total number, however, includes additional honorary and supernumerary members. Non-Catholics as well as Catholics belong to the academy.

Purposes of the academy are to honor pure science and its practitioners, to promote the freedom of pure science and to foster research.

The academy traces its origin to the *Linceorum Academia* (Academy of the Lynxes — its symbol) founded in Rome Aug. 17, 1603. Pius IX reorganized this body and gave it a new name — *Pontificia Accademia dei Nuovi Lincei* — in 1847. It was taken over by the Italian state in 1870 and called the *Accademia Nationale dei Lincei.* Leo XIII reconstituted it with a new charter in 1887. Pius XI designated the Vatican Gardens as the site of academy headquarters in 1922 and gave it its present title and status in 1936. Four years later he gave the title of Excellency to its members.

Scientists in the U.S. who presently hold membership in the Academy are: Edward Adelbert Doisy, professor emeritus of biochemistry at St. Louis University (May 29, 1948); Franco Rasetti, professor emeritus of physics at Johns Hopkins University, Baltimore, Md. (Oct. 28, 1936); George Speri-Sperti, president and director of the Institutum Divi Thomae in the Athanaeum of Ohio (Oct. 28, 1936); William Wilson Morgan, professor emeritus of astronomy at the University of Chicago (Sept. 24, 1964); Albert Szent-Gyorgyi, director of Institute for Muscle Research at the Marine Biological Laboratory, Woods Hole, Mass. (Apr. 10, 1970), Rita Levi-Montalcini, professor of biology at Washington University, St. Louis, Mo. (June 24, 1974); Severo Ochoa, professor emeritus, of the Roche Institute of Molecular Biology, Nutley, N.J. (June 24, 1974); Marshall Warren Nirenberg, professor of genetics and biochemistry at the National Institutes of Health, Bethesda, Md. (June 24, 1974); George Palade, professor of cellular biology at Yale University, New Haven, Conn. (Dec. 2, 1975); Victor Weisskopf, professor of physics at the Massachusetts Institute of Technology, Cambridge, Mass. (Dec. 2, 1975).

Appointed Apr. 17, 1978, were: David Baltimore, professor of biology, Har Gobind Khorana, professor of biochemistry, and Alexandar Rich, professor of biophysicis — all at the Massachusetts Institute of Technology, Cambridge, Mass.; Roger Walcott Sperry, professor of psychobiology, California Institute of Technology, Pasadena, Calif.

Christian Anfinsen, professor of biochemistry at the National Institutes of Health, Bethesda, Md., was appointed to the Academy May 13, 1981.

Deceased U.S. members of the Academy were: George D. Birkhoff, Alexis Carrel, Herbert Sidney Langfeld, Robert A. Millikan, Thomas H. Morgan, Theodore von Karman, Victor F. Hess, Peter Debye, Hugh Stott Taylor.

Other members of the Academy are listed below according to country of location; dates of their selection are given in parentheses.

Argentina: Luis F. Leloir (Apr. 22, 1968).

Austria: Hans Tuppy (Apr. 10, 1970).

Belgium: Christian de Duve (Apr. 10, 1970).

Brazil: Carlos Chagas (Aug. 18, 1961); Johanna Dobereiner (Apr. 17, 1978); Crodowaldo Pavan (Apr. 17, 1978).

Canada: Gerhard Herzberg (Sept. 24, 1964); Karel Wiesner (Apr. 17, 1978).

Chile: Hector Croxatto Rezzio (Dec. 2, 1975).

Denmark: Bengt Georg Stromgren (Dec. 2, 1975); Aage Bohr (Apr. 17, 1978).

France: Louis de Broglie (Apr. 5, 1955); Pierre Raphael Lepine (Sept. 24, 1964); Louis Leprince-Ringuet (Aug. 18, 1961); Jerome Lejeune (June 24, 1974); Andre Blanc-LaPierre (Apr. 17, 1978), Anatole Abragam (May 13, 1981), Andre Lichnerowicz (May 13, 1981), Bernard Pullman (May 13, 1981).

Germany: Rudolf L. Mossbauer (Apr. 10, 1970), Manfried Eigen (May 13, 1981).

Great Britain: Hermann Alexander Bruck (Apr. 5, 1955); Paul Adrien Dirac (Aug. 18, 1961); Alan Lloyd Hodgkin (Apr. 22, 1968); Alfred R. Ubbelohde (Apr. 22, 1968); Percy C. C. Garnham (Apr. 10, 1970); George Porter (June 24, 1974); Martin Ryle (Dec. 2, 1975); Max Ferdinand Perutz (May 13, 1981); Stanley Keith Runcorn (Sept. 13, 1981).

Hungary: Janos Zsentagothai (May 13, 1981).

India: Mambillikalathil Dovind Kumar Menon (May 13, 1981).

Israel: Michael Sela (Dec. 2, 1975).

Italy: Giovanni Battista Bonino (May 23, 1942); Bettolo Giovanni Battista Marini (Apr. 22, 1968); Giuseppe Colombo (Apr. 17, 1978); Giuseppe Moruzzi (Apr. 17, 1978); Giampietro Puppi (Apr. 17, 1978), Ennio De Giorgi (May 13, 1981), Abdus Salam (May 13, 1981).

Japan: Paul Sanichiro Mizushima (Aug. 18, 1961).

Kenya: Thomas R. Odhiambo (May 13, 1981).

Netherlands: Jan Hendrik Oort (Aug. 18, 1961).

New Zealand: Albert William Liley (Apr. 17, 1978).

Pakistan: Salimuzzaman Siddiqui (Sept. 24, 1964).

Peru: Alberto Hurtado (Aug. 18, 1961).

Poland: Karol Borsuk (Feb. 1, 1982).

Portugal: Antonio De Almeida (Apr. 8, 1961).

Spain: Manuel Lora Tomayo (Sept. 24, 1964).

Sweden: Sven Horstadius (Aug. 18, 1961).

Switzerland: John Carew Eccles (Apr. 8,

1961), Thomas Lambo (June 24, 1974), Werner Arber (May 13, 1981).

Vatican City: Daniel J. Kelly O'Connell, S.J. (Sept. 24, 1964).

Venezuela: Marcel Roche (Apr. 10, 1970).

Ex officio members: Rev. George V. Coyne, S.J., director of Vatican Observatory; Alfons Stickler, S.D.B., prefect of the Vatican Library; Msgr. Martino Giusti, prefect of the Secret Vatican Archives.

Honorary member: Silvio Ranzi, professor emeritus of biology and zoology of the University of Milan (May 13, 1981).

President: Carlos Chagas (Nov. 9, 1972).

NEW INTERNATIONAL ECONOMIC ORDER

The development of a new international economic order was the subject of an address Apr. 5, 1982, by Pope John Paul at a symposium organized by the Pontifical Commission for Justice and Peace. The symposium was entitled "From 'Rerum Novarum' to 'Laborem Exercens'" papal encyclicals on the social teaching of the Church.

The following excerpts are from the text circulated by the NC Documentary Service, Origins, July 1, 1982 (Vol. 12, No. 7).

I am pleased, . . . with the general theme of the symposium: "From *Rerum Novarum* to *Laborem Exercens:* Toward the Year 2000." On the eve of the third millennium, the world in fact finds itself facing new problems ... marked by questions, uncertainties and often even by powerlessness. Ideologies which at first glance and by reason of their very diffusion seemed bound to dominate minds in a lasting way, have completely succeeded only in giving proof of their limitations. They follow one another and are worn out, and continually give birth to the desire to find a more stable system of relations between men and nations.

New Possibilities

New possibilities are sighted on the horizon which can now no longer be conceived in restricted, uniquely national terms. If the problems which modern man must face cannot be understood except by realizing their world dimension, it will also be on the international scale, in many cases, that solutions will have to be sought. Rightly, therefore, a new international economic order is ever more frequently hoped for today. This order, overcoming the insufficient and inadequate models of the past, will assure mankind a just sharing in the goods of creation, with particular sensitivity for peoples in the process of development.

Man the Criterion

The social question is, and will always remain, "global," so to speak, from the moment it touches each human person in particular and all men together. It touches man in the depth of his nature and in his existence. Man himself, the dignity of his humanity, must constitute the profound inspiration and the dynamic strength for every search for adequate solutions to the problems of society. Man remains the decisive criterion for a world that wants to be built in justice and peace. From this global view of the human person, there must develop the principles of reflection, the norms of judgment about situations and structures, the directives for an action respectful of truth.

You know that the Church does not have direct competence for proposing technical solutions of an economic-political nature. However, she calls for a constant revision of all systems according to the criterion of the dignity of the human person. To this she calls the local churches, the Christian communities at various levels, the movements of apostolic and social action, pastors, teachers, researchers and, after all, every baptized person, according to his responsibility and the place he holds in society.

At the Service of Freedom

Allowing themselves to be guided by this fundamental criterion, false or partial systems, materialistic or economistic ideologies can be overcome. Thus it is that we make ourselves free for an objective examination of the social reality and for operative decisions aimed at the achievement of just solutions. Thus it is, above all, that we place ourselves at the service of true freedom rooted in God, to cooperate in his creative and redemptive work and to accomplish the salvation of mankind along the way marked out by Christ, true God and true man.

In proposing this doctrine of hers and in entrusting it to the active commitment of her children, the Church intends to serve the good of mankind, in sincere and positive collaboration with all men of good will, with all those in positions of responsibility, and with the institutions of international life.

Brothers and Sisters, in offering you my best wishes for fruitful work, I invoke upon you the constant assistance of God.

The National Conference of Catholic Charities: Established in 1910 to help advance and promote the charitable programs and activities of Catholic community and social service agencies in the United States. As the central and national organization for this purpose, it services member agencies and institutions by consultation, information and assistance in planning and evaluating social service programs under Catholic auspices.

The principal fields of service in which Catholic Charities agencies are engaged are family counseling, child welfare, services for unmarried mothers, community services, day care centers, neighborhood center programs, and care of the aged. Community organization and social action are also functions of Catholic Charities.

The NCCC conducts research with respect to service to the aging, community self-help programs, the institutional care of children, and other social service projects. It represents the Catholic philosophy of social service to government agencies and personnel, and to professional organizations in the field. Its publications include *Charities USA*, a monthly membership magazine, and *Social Thought*, a quarterly co-sponsored with the National School of Social Service of the Catholic University of America.

The NCCC membership includes 545 diocesan agencies and branches, 200 institutions and 3,000 individuals.

Rev. Thomas J. Harvey is executive director of the conference, with offices at 1346 Connecticut Ave. N.W., Washington, D.C. 20036.

The Society of St. Vincent de Paul, originally called the Conference of Charity: An association of Catholic laity devoted to personal service of the poor through the spiritual and corporal works of mercy. The first conference was formed at Paris in 1833 by Frederic Ozanam and his associates.

The first conference in the U.S. was organized in 1845 at St. Louis. There are now approximately 4,300 units of the society in this country, with a membership of about 34,000.

In the past 50 years, members of the society in this country have distributed among poor persons financial and other forms of assistance valued at approximately $320 million.

U.S. Vincentian councils and conferences participating in "twinning" programs assist their poorer counterparts abroad by sending them correspondence, information and financial aid on a continuing basis.

Under the society's revised regulations, women are being admitted to membership. Increasing emphasis is being given to stores and rehabilitation workshops of the society through which persons with marginal income can purchase refurbished goods at minimal cost. Handicapped persons are employed in renovating goods and store operations.

Amin A. de Tarrazi of Paris, France, is president of the Council General, the governing body of the society. There are approximately 750,000 members in the world.

The office of the U.S. Superior Council is located at 4140 Lindell Blvd., St. Louis, Mo. 63108.

Catholic Health Association of the United States, formerly Catholic Hospital Association: Founded in 1915, is a service organization for about 900 Catholic-sponsored health care facilities located throughout the United States.

The association is dedicated to the healing mission of the Church by promoting health of those who are sick or infirm because of age or disability; by respecting human dignity in the experience of sickness and death; and by fostering physical, psychological, emotional, spiritual and social well-being of people.

John E. Curley, Jr., is president. Executive offices are located at 4455 Woodson Rd., St. Louis, Mo. 63134.

The Official Catholic Directory, 1982, reported 635 Catholic general hospitals with 169,897 beds treating 36,723,368 patients; 75 special hospitals with 6,286 beds treating 445,205; and 121 nurses' schools with 20,027 students.

National Association of Catholic Chaplains: Founded in 1965. Membership is approximately 3,000.

Rev. Timothy J. Toohey is executive director. Address: 3257 S. Lake Dr., Milwaukee Wis. 53207.

BIRTHRIGHT

Birthright is a nondenominational guidance and referral service organization offering pregnant women alternatives to abortion, in line with the motto, "It is the right of every pregnant woman to give birth and the right of every child to be born."

Started by Mrs. Louise Summerhill of Toronto, Canada, in 1968, it has chapters in Canada, the United States, the United Kingdom, New Zealand, Australia and South Africa.

The executive director of Birthright, U.S.A., is Mrs. D. Cocciolone, 686 N. Broad St., Woodbury, N.J. 08096.

Birthright, although it has Catholics among its volunteers and draws some support from Catholic sources, insists on its original independent and nondenominational character. Birthright telephone numbers are listed in some local directories.

FACILITIES FOR RETIRED AND AGED PERSONS

(Sources: Almanac survey, *The Official Catholic Directory.*)

This list covers residence, health care and other facilities for the retired and aged under Catholic auspices. Information includes name, type of facility if not evident from the title, address, and total capacity (in parentheses); unless noted otherwise, facilities are for both men and women. Many facilities for the aged offer intermediate nursing care.

Alabama: Allen Memorial Home (Nursing Home), 735 S. Washington Ave., Mobile 36603 (94).

Good Samaritan Nursing Home, 1107 Voeglin Ave., Selma 36701 (26).

Sacred Heart Residence Little Sisters of the Poor, Box 6633, Mobile 36600 (115).

Villa Mercy (Skilled Nursing Facility, Hospice, Home Health Agency), P.O. Box 1096, Daphne 36526.

Arizona: Sacred Heart Home for the Aged, Little Sisters of the Poor, 1110 N. 16th St., Phoenix 85006 (128).

Villa Maria Geriatric Center (Skilled Nursing Facility and Apartments), 4310 E. Grant Rd., Tucson 85712 (93 beds, 50 apartments).

Arkansas: Benedictine Manor (Retirement Home), 2nd and Grand Sts., Hot Springs 71901 (100).

California: Casa Manana Inn, 3700 N. Sutter St., Stockton 95204 (175).

Cathedral Plaza, 1551 Third Ave., San Diego 92101 (221 apartments).

Catholic Women's Center (Residence for Retired Senior Women), 195 E. San Fernando St., San Jose 95112 (50).

Ellis Seniors Residence, 3263 First Ave., Sacramento 95817 (18).

Francis of Assisi Community, 148 Guerrero St., San Francisco 94103 (140); for elderly and handicapped.

Little Flower Haven (Residential Care Facility for Retired), 8585 La Mesa Blvd., La Mesa 92041 (93).

Little Sisters of the Poor, 300 Lake St., San Francisco 94118 (120).

Little Sisters of the Poor, Jeanne Jugan Residence, 2100 South Western Ave., San Pedro, Calif. 90732 (120).

Madonna Residence (Retirement Home for Women over 60), 1055 Pine St., San Francisco 94109 (46).

Marian Residence (Retirement Home), 124 S. College Dr., Santa Maria 93454 (58).

Nazareth House, 2121 N. 1st St., Fresno 93703 (80).

Nazareth House, 3333 Manning Ave., Los Angeles 90064 (107).

Nazareth House, 245 Nova Albion Way, Terra Linda, San Rafael 94903 (145).

Nazareth House Retirement Home, 6333 Rancho Mission Rd., San Diego 92108 (122).

Our Lady of Fatima Villa (Skilled Nursing Facility, Women), 20400 Saratoga/Los Gatos Rd., Saratoga 95070 (85).

Our Lady's Home, 3431 Foothill Blvd., Oakland 94601 (154).

St. Francis Home (Elderly and Retired Women), 1718 W. 6th St., Santa Ana 92703 (87).

Villa Scalabrini (Retirement Center), 10631 Vinedale St., Sun Valley 91352 (125).

Villa Siena (Residence and Intermediate Care), 1855 Miramonte Ave., Mountain View 94040 (50, residence; 20, intermediate care).

Colorado: Little Sisters of the Poor, 3629 W. 29th Ave., Denver 80211 (118).

St. Elizabeth Center (Retirement Home), 2825 W. 32nd Ave., Denver 80211 (187).

Connecticut: Augustana Homes, Simeon Rd., Bethel 06801.

Notre Dame Convalescent Home, 76 West Rocks Rd., Norwalk 06851 (60).

Regina Pacis Villa (Residence), RFD No. 1, Pomfret Center 06259 (16).

St. Joseph Guest Home (Women, Employed and Retired), 311 Greene St., New Haven 06511 (86).

St. Joseph's Home for the Aged, 88 Jackson St., Willimantic 06226 (37).

St. Joseph's Manor, Carmelite Srs. for Aged and Infirm, 6448 Main St., Trumbull 06611 (285).

St. Joseph's Residence, Little Sisters of the Poor, 1365 Enfield St., Enfield, Conn. 06082 (94)

St. Lucian's Home for the Aged, 532 Burritt St., New Britain 06053 (65).

St. Mary's Home (Residence and Health Care Facility), 291 Steele Rd., W. Hartford 06117 (177).

Villa Maria Rest Home for the Aged, West St., Thompson 06277 (30).

Delaware: Jeanne Jugan Residence, Little Sisters of the Poor, 185 Salem Church Rd., Newark 19713.

St. Patrick's House, Inc., 115 E. 14th St., Wilmington 19801 (14).

Florida: All Saints Home for the Aged, 2040 Riverside Ave., Jacksonville 32204 (57).

Carroll Manor, 3667 S. Miami Ave., Miami 33133

Casa Calderon, Inc., 800 W. Virginia St., Tallahassee 32304. Apartments (111).

Cor Jesu Retirement Center, 4918 N. Habana Ave., Tampa 33614 (75).

Haven of Our Lady of Peace (Residence and Health Care Facility), 5203 9th Ave., Pensacola 32504 (88).

Maria Manor Health Care Center, 10300 4th St. N., St. Petersburg 33702 (274).

Marian Towers, Inc. (Retirement Apartments), 17505 North Bay Rd., Miami Beach 33160.

Noreen McKeen Residence for Geriatric Care, 315 Flagler Dr. S., W. Palm Beach 33401.

Pennsylvania Retirement Residence, 208 Evernia St., W. Palm Beach 33401 (176).

St. Andrew Towers (Retirement Apartments), 2700 N.W. 99th Ave., Coral Springs 33065.

St. Dominic Gardens, 5849 N.W. 7th St., Miami 33126.

St. Elizabeth Gardens, Inc. (Retirement Apartments), 801 N.E. 33rd St., Pompano Beach 33064.

St. Joseph's Residence, 3485 N.W. 30th St., Ft. Lauderdale 33311.

Illinois: Addolorato Villa (Home for Aged), Highway 83, McHenry Rd., Wheeling 60090 (103).

Alvernia Manor (Residence), 1598 Main St., Lemont 60439 (56).

Carlyle Healthcare Center, 501 Clinton St., Carlyle 62231 (124).

Carmelite Carefree Village, 8419 Bailey Rd., Darien 60559 (96 units, 150 residents).

Cortland Manor Retirement Home, 1900 N. Karlow, Chicago 68639. (52).

Holy Family Villa (Residence and Health Care,), Lemont 60439 (102).

Huber Memorial Home (Women), 1000 30th St., Rock Island 61201 (16).

Jugan Terrace, Little Sisters of the Poor, 2300 N. Racine, Chicago 60614.

Little Sisters of the Poor Center for the Aging, 2325 N. Lakewood Ave., Chicago, Ill. 60614 (120).

Maryhaven, Inc. (Intermediate Care Facility), 1700 E. Lake Ave., Glenview 60025 (147).

Mayslake Village (Retirement Apartments), 1801 35th St., Oak Brook 60521 (630 Apartments).

Meredith Memorial Home, Public Square, Belleville 62220 (90).

Merkle-Knipprath Nursing Home, Rt. 1, Franciscan Brothers. Clifton 60927 (100).

Mother Theresa Home, 1270 Main St., Lemont 60439 (58).

Our Lady of Angels Retirement Home, 1201 Wyoming, Joliet 60435 (100).

Our Lady of the Snows Apartment Community (Retirement Apartment Community; Health Care Program), 9500 W. Ill., Rt. 15, Belleville 62223 (200).

Rosary Hill Home, 9000 W. 81st St., Justice 60458 (60).

St. Andrew Home, 7000 N. Newark Ave., Chicago 60648 (198).

St. Ann's Health Care Center, 770 State St., Chester 62233 (92).

St. Benedict Home, 6930 W. Touhy Ave., Niles 60648 (52).

St. Joseph's Home (Sheltered and Intermediate Care), 3306 S. 6th St. Rd., Springfield 62703 (121).

St. Joseph's Home, 2223 W. Heading Ave., Peoria 61604 (200).

St. Joseph's Home for the Aged, 649 E. Jefferson St., Freeport 61032 (109).

St. Joseph's Home for the Elderly, 80 W. Northwest Hwy., Palatine 60067 (135).

St. Joseph's Home of Chicago, Inc., 2650 N. Ridgeway Ave., Chicago 60647 (173).

St. Patrick's Residence (Sheltered and Intermediate Care; Skilled Nursing Facility), 22 E. Clinton St., Joliet 60431 (202).

Villa Saint Cyril (Residence), 1111 St. John's Ave., Highland Park 60035 (80).

Villa Scalabrini (Residence), 480 N. Wolf Rd., Northlake 60164 (249).

Indiana: Providence Retirement Home, 703 E. Spring St., New Albany 47150 (85).

Regina Pacis Home (Skilled Nursing and Intermediate Care Facility), 3900 Washington Ave., Evansville 47715 (154).

Sacred Heart Home (Comprehensive Nursing), R.R. 2, Avilla 46710 (130). LaVerna Terrace (for well elderly), same address (51 units).

St. Anne Home (Residence and Comprehensive Nursing), 1900 Randalia Dr., Ft. Wayne 46805 (154).

St. Anthony's Medical Center, Nursing Home, Main and Franciscan Rd., Crown Point 46307 (211).

St. Augustine Home for the Aged, Little Sisters of the Poor, 2345 W. 86th St., Indianapolis 46260 (120).

St. John's Home for the Aged, Little Sisters of the Poor, 1236 Lincoln Ave., Evansville 47714 (130).

St. Paul Hermitage, 501 N. 17th St., Beech Grove 46107 (105).

Iowa: The Alverno Health Care Facility, 849 13th Ave. N., Clinton 52732 (136).

Bishop Drumm Retirement Center, 5387 Winwood Dr., Des Moines 50324 (120 beds; 95 apartments).

Hallmar-Mercy Hospital (Home for the Aged), 701 Tenth St. S.E., Cedar Rapids 52403.

Holy Spirit Retirement Home (Nursing Home), 1701 W. 25th St., Sioux City 51103 (94).

Kahl Home for the Aged and Infirm (Intermediate Care Facility), 1101 W. 9th St., Davenport 52804 (125).

The Marian Home, 2400 6th Ave. North, Fort Dodge 50501 (97) and Marian Village (Apartments), 2320 6th Ave. North, Fort Dodge 50501.

Mary of the Angels Home (Women, Employed and Retired), 605 Bluff St., Dubuque 52001 (85).

Ritter Home for Retired Women, 1837 Sunnyside Ave., Burlington 52601 (6).

St. Anthony Nursing Home, 406 E. Anthony St., Carroll 51401 (80).

St. Francis Continuation Care and Nursing Home, Burlington 52601 (82).

Stonehill Care Center (Residence, Nursing Home), 3485 Windsor, Dubuque 52001 (250).

Kansas: Mt. Joseph (Intermediate Care Facility), 1110 W. 11, R.R. 1, Concordia 66901 (100).

St. John Rest Home (Intermediate Care Facility), 701 Seventh St., Victoria 67671 (60).

St. Joseph Home (Skilled Care Facility), 759 Vermont Ave., Kansas City 66101.

Villa Maria, Inc. (Intermediate Care Facility), 116 S. Central, Mulvane 67110 (66).

Kentucky: Cardome Residence for Women, Georgetown 40324 (30).

Carmel Home (Residence and Nursing Home), Old Hartford Rd., Owensboro 42301 (84).

Carmel Manor (Personal Care Home), Carmel Manor Rd., Ft. Thomas, 41075 (99).

Knottsville Personal Care Home, P.O. Box R. 1, Philpot 42366 (68).

Madonna Manor Nursing Home, 2344 Amsterdam Rd., Covington 41016 (38). (Cottages for Senior Citizens: 9, with 48 apartments.

St. Charles Nursing Home, 500 Farrell Dr., Covington 41011 (147).

St. Margaret of Cortona Home (Women, Personal Care Home), 1310 Leestown Pike, Lexington 40508 (24).

Taylor Manor Nursing Home, Versailles 40383 (82).

Louisiana: Bethany M.H.S. Health Care Center (Women), P.O. Box 2308, Lafayette 70501 (42).

Chateau de Notre Dame (Residence and Nursing Home), 2832 Burdette St., New Orleans 70125 (110 residential units, 180 nursing beds).

Christopher Inn Apartments, 2110 Royal St., New Orleans 70116.

Consolata Home (Nursing Home), 2319 E. Main St., New Iberia 70560.

Lafon Nursing Home of the Holy Family, 6900 Chef Menteur Hwy., New Orleans 70126 (171).

Mary-Joseph Residence for the Elderly, 4201 Woodland Dr., New Orleans 70114 (123).

Mater Dolorosa Adult Group Home, 1215 Dublin St., New Orleans 70118.

Metairie Manor, 4929 York St., Metairie 70001 (200 residential units).

Ollie Steele Burden Manor (Nursing Home), 4200 Essen Lane, Baton Rouge 70809 (60).

Our Lady of Prompt Succor Home (Nursing and Extended Care Facility), 751 E. Prudhomme Lane, Opelousas 70570.

St. Charles Nursing Home, P.O. Box 508, Newellton 71357.

St. Joseph's Home (Nursing Home), 2301 Sterlington Rd., Monroe 71201 (130).

St. Margaret's Daughters Nursing Home, (Women), 6220 Chartres St., New Orleans 70117 (110).

St. Martin Manor, 1501 N. Johnson St., New Orleans 70116 (140 residential units).

Wynhoven Apartments (Residence for Senior Citizens), 4600 - 10th St., Marrero 70072 (350).

Maine: Deering Pavilion (Apartments for Senior Citizens), 800 Forest Ave., Portland 04103 (200 units).

Marcotte Nursing Home, 100 Campus Ave., Lewiston 04240 (376).

Mt. St. Joseph (Nursing Home), Highwood St., Waterville 04901 (77).

St. Andre Health Care Facility, Inc. (Nursing Home), 407 Pool Rd., Biddeford 04005 (96).

St. Joseph's Manor, 1133 Washington Ave., Portland 04103 (200).

Seton Village, Inc., 1 Carver St., Waterville 04901 (140 housing units.)

Villa Muir, Home for Women, Bay View, Saco 04072 (15).

Maryland: Cardinal Shehan Center for the Aging, Inc., 2300 Dulaney Valley Rd., Towson 21204. Five services: 400-bed long-term care facility; 200 apartments for elderly; residence for elderly in urban area; outreach programs to elderly in homes; retirement residence for priests.

Carroll Manor (Residence and Nursing Home), 4922 La Salle Rd., Hyattsville 20782 (232).

Little Sisters of the Poor, St. Martin's Home (for the Aged), 601 Maiden Choice Lane, Baltimore 21228 (120).

Sacred Heart Home, 5805 Queens Chapel Rd., Hyattsville 20782 (102).

St. Joseph Nursing Home, 1222 Tugwell Dr., Baltimore 21228 (40).

Villa Rosa (Nursing Home), Lottsford Vista Rd., Mitchellville 20716 (99).

Massachusetts: Beaven-Kelly Home for Men (Rest Home), 1245 Main St., Brightside, Holyoke 01040 (55).

Catholic Memorial Home (Nursing Home), 2446 Highland Ave., Fall River 02720 (288).

Don Orione Nursing Home, 111 Orient Ave., East Boston 02128 (200). Adult day care center (30).

D'Youville Manor (Nursing Home), 981 Varnum St., Lowell 01854 (196). Day care program (20).

Jeanne Jugan Residence, Little Sisters of

the Poor (Nursing Home), 186 Highland Ave., Somerville 02143 (120).

Madonna Manor (Nursing Home), N. Washington St., N. Attleboro 02760 (121).

Marian Manor, Carmelite Sisters for the Aged and Infirm (Nursing Home), 130 Dorchester St., S. Boston, 02127 (376).

Marian Manor of Taunton Nursing Home, 33 Summer St., Taunton 02780 (83).

Maristhill Nursing Home, 66 Newton St., Waltham 02154 (120).

Mary Immaculate Nursing Home, Bennington St., Lawrence 01841 (250). Adult Day Health Care Center (30).

Mt. St. Vincent Nursing Home, Holy Family Rd., Holyoke 01040 (116).

Our Lady's Haven (Nursing Home), 71 Center St., Fairhaven 02719 (110).

The Protectory, Inc., 189 Maple St., Lawrence 01841. (111 units). The Second Protectory, Inc., 191 Maple St., Lawrence (106 units). Congregate Housing; Apartments.

Sacred Heart Nursing Home, 359 Summer St., New Bedford 02740 (215).

St. Francis Home for Aged, 37 Thorne St., Worcester 01604 (83). Adult Day Health Care (30).

St. Joseph Manor Nursing Home, 215 Thatcher St., Brockton 02402 (120).

St. Joseph's Manor (Rest Home, Women), 321 Centre St., Dorchester, Boston 02122 (95).

St. Luke's Home (Rest Home, Women), 85 Spring St., Springfield 01105 (92).

St. Patrick's Manor (Nursing Home), 863 Central St., Framingham 01701 (292).

Michigan: Bishop Noa Home for Senior Citizens, Escanaba 49829 (109).

Burtha M. Fisher Home, Little Sisters of the Poor (Residence and Nursing Home), 17550 Southfield Rd., Detroit 48235 (130).

Casa Maria (Residence), 600 Maple Vista, Imlay City 48444 (96).

Kundig Center (Residence), 3300 Jefferies Freeway, Detroit 48208 (180). Rooms and apartments.

Lourdes Nursing Home (Skilled Facility), 2300 Watkins Lake Rd., Pontiac 48054 (108).

Madonna Villa Senior Residence, 17825 Fifteen Mile Rd., Fraser, 48026 (90).

Marian Hall (Residence), 529 Detroit St., Flint 48502 (124).

Marian-Oakland West, 29250 W. Ten Mile Rd., Farmington Hills 48024 (100).

Marian Place (Residence), 408 W. Front St., Monroe 48161 (52).

Marycrest Manor (Skilled Nursing Facility), 15475 Middlebelt Rd., Livonia 48154 (55).

Marydale Center for Senior Citizens (Board and Apartments), 3147 Tenth Ave., Port Huron 48060 (74).

Maryhaven (Residence), 11350 Reeck Rd., Southgate 48195 (93).

St. Ann's Home, (Residence and Nursing Home), 2161 Leonard St. N.W., Grand Rapids 49504 (112).

St. Catherine Cooperative House for Elderly Women, 1641 Webb Ave., Detroit 48206.

St. Elizabeth Briarbank (Residence), P.O. Box O, 1315 N. Woodward Ave., Bloomfield Hills 48013 (55).

St. Francis Home (Nursing Home), 915 N. River Rd., Saginaw 48603 (100).

St. John Vianney Cooperative House for Men, 4806 Mt. Elliot, Detroit 48207 (30).

St. Joseph's Home for the Aged, 4800 Cadieux Rd., Detroit 48224 (104).

Stapleton Center (Residence), 9341 Agnes St., Detroit 48214 (65).

Villa Elizabeth (Nursing Home), 2100 Leonard St. N.E., Grand Rapids 49505 (136).

Villa Francesca (Residence, Women), 565 W. Long Lake Rd., Bloomfield Hills 48013 (18).

Villa Marie (Board and Apartments), 15131 Newburgh Rd., Livonia 48154.

Minnesota: Assumption Home, Cold Spring 56320 (68).

Bethany Home, Onamia 56359 (80).

Divine Providence Community Home (Intermediate Care), 700 Third Ave. N.W., Sleepy Eye 56085 (58).

Divine Providence Home (Skilled Nursing Home), Ivanhoe 56142 (51).

John Paul Apartments, Cold Spring 56320 (61). For elderly and handicapped.

Little Sisters of the Poor, Holy Family Residence (Skilled Nursing and Intermediate Care), 330 S. Exchange St., St. Paul 55102 (143).

Madonna Towers (Retirement Apartments and Nursing Home), 4001 19th Ave. N.W., Rochester 55901 (200).

Mary Rondorf Retirement Home, 222 N. 5th St., Staples 56479 (84).

Mother of Mercy Nursing Home, Albany 56307 (62).

Regina Nursing Home and Retirement Residence, Hastings 55033. Nursing home (61); retirement home (86).

Sacred Heart Hospice (Nursing Home), 1200 Twelfth St. S.W., Austin 55912 (59).

St. Ann's Residence, 330 E. 3rd St., Duluth 55805 (200).

St. Anne Hospice (Residence and Nursing Care), 1347 W. Broadway, Winona 55987 (121).

St. Benedict's Center (Nursing Home), 1810 Minnesota Blvd. S.E., St. Cloud 56301 (220).

St. Elizabeth's Hospital and Nursing Home, 1200-5th Grant Blvd., Wabasha 55981 (52).

St. Francis Home, Breckenridge 56520 (124).

St. Mary's Home (Nursing Home), 1925 Norfolk Ave., St. Paul 55116 (140).

St. Mary's Hospital and Nursing Home, Winsted 55395 (95).

St. Mary's Rehabilitation Center, 2512 S. 7th St., Minneapolis 55454 (240).

St. Mary's Villa (Nursing Home), Pierz 56364 (66).

St. Otto's Home (Nursing Home), Little Falls 56345 (159).

St. Therese Home (Residence and Health Care Facility) (302) and St. Therese Retirement Apartments (220), 8000 Bass Lake Rd., New Hope 55428.

St. William's Nursing Home, Parkers Prairie 56361 (61).

Villa of St. Francis Nursing Home, Morris 56267 (144).

Villa St. Vincent (Skilled Nursing Home and Residence), 516 Walsh St., Crookston 56726. Nursing home (80); residence (95).

Mississippi: Santa Maria Retirement Apartments, 305 E. Beach St., Biloxi, 39530.

Villa Maria Retirement Apartments, 921 Porter Ave., Ocean Springs 39564.

Missouri: The Alverne (Retirement Home), 1014 Locust St., St. Louis 63101 (251).

Cathedral Square Towers, 444 W. 12th St., Kansas City 64105. Apartments for elderly and handicapped.

Chariton Apartments (Retirement Apartments), 4249 Michigan Ave., St. Louis 63111 (122 units; 132 residents).

DePaul Community Health Center — St. Anne's Division (Nursing Home), 12349 DePaul Dr., Bridgeton 63044 (114).

LaVerna Heights Retirement Home (Women), 104 E. Park Ave., Savannah 64485 (40).

LaVerna Village Apartments, 1000-1005 Hall Ave., Savannah 64485 (20).

LaVerna Village Nursing Home, 904 Hall Ave., Savannah 64485 (120).

Little Sisters of the Poor, St. Alexis Home, 5331 Highland Ave., Kansas City 64110 (155).

Little Sisters of the Poor (Home for Aged), 3225 N. Florissant Ave., St. Louis 63107 (210).

Mary, Queen and Mother Center (Skilled-Intermediate Nursing Care), 7601 Watson Rd., St. Louis 63119 (220).

Mercy Villa (Nursing Home), Division of St. John's Regional Health Center, 1100 E. Montclair, Springfield 65807 (150).

Mother of Good Counsel Home (Nursing Home, Women), 6825 Natural Bridge Rd., Normandy, 63121.

Our Lady of Mercy Home (Residence and Nursing Home), 918-24 E. 9th St., Kansas City 64106 (153).

Our Lady of Mercy Country House, Box 451, R.R. No. 4, Liberty 64038 (39).

Price Memorial Skilled Nursing Facility Forby Rd., P.O. Box 476, Eureka 63025 (120.

St. Agnes Home for the Aged, 10341 Manchester Rd., Kirkwood 63122 (130).

St. Joseph Hill Nursing Care Facility (Men), Highway FF, Eureka 63025 (130).

St. Joseph's Home, 723 First Capitol Dr., St. Charles 63301 (101).

St. Joseph's Home for the Aged, 1306 W. Main St., Jefferson City 65101 (75).

Nebraska: Bergen Mercy Care Center (Health Care), 1870 S. 75th St., Omaha 68124 (250).

Madonna Professional Care Center, 2200 S. 52nd St., Lincoln 68506 (182).

Mt. Carmel Home, Keens' Memorial (Nursing Home), 412 W. 18th St., Kearney 68847 (76).

New Cassel Retirement Center, 900 N. 90th St., Omaha 68114. (156).

St. Joseph's Home (Residential Care), 320 E. Decatur St., West Point 68788 (48).

St. Joseph's Nursing Home, 401 N. 18th St., Norfolk 68701 (70).

St. Joseph's Villa, David City 68632. (65).

New Hampshire: Mount Carmel Nursing Home, 235 Myrtle St., Manchester 03104 (120).

St. Ann Home, 195 Dover Point Rd., Dover 03820 (53).

St. Francis Home (Nursing Home), Court St., Laconia 03246 (51).

St. Teresa Manor (Nursing Home), 519 Bridge St., Manchester 03104 (51).

St. Vincent de Paul Nursing Home, Providence Ave., Berlin 03570 (80).

New Jersey: Holy Family Residence (Women), 44 Rifle Camp Rd., P.O. Box 536, W. Paterson 07424 (64).

Little Sisters of the Poor, St. Joseph Home, 140 Shepherd Lane, Totowa 07512 (247).

Mater Dei Nursing Home, RD 3, Box 164, Rt. 40, P.O. Newfield 08344 (64).

Morris Hall, Home for the Aged (Residence and Skilled Nursing Home), 2361 Lawrenceville Rd., Lawrenceville 08648 (127).

Mount St. Andrew Villa (Residence), 55 W. Midland Ave., Paramus 07652 (59).

Our Lady's Residence (Nursing Home), Glendale and Clematis Aves., Pleasantville 08232 (104).

St. Ann's Home for the Aged (Skilled Nursing Home, Women), 198 Old Bergen Rd., Jersey City 07305 (106). Adult Medical Day Care.

St. Joseph's Home (Women), 240 Longhouse Dr., Hewitt 07421.

St. Joseph's Rest Home for Aged Women, 46 Preakness Ave., Paterson 07502 (30).

St. Joseph's Villa (Residence, Women), Peapack 07977 (18).

St. Mary's Catholic Home (Skilled Nursing Home), 1730 Kresson Rd., Cherry Hill 08003 (215).

Villa Maria (Residence and Infirmary, Women), 641 Somerset St., N. Plainfield 07061 (70).

New Mexico: Good Shepherd Manor (Residential Care for Aged Persons), Little Brothers of the Good Shepherd, P.O. Box 10248, Albuquerque 87114 (43).

New York: Bernardine Apartments, 417 Churchill Ave., Syracuse 13205.

Consolation Residence, 111 Beach Dr., West Islip 11795 (250).

Ferncliff Nursing Home, P.O. Box 386, River Rd., Rhinebeck 12572 (320).

Frances Schervier Home and Hospital, 2975 Independence Ave., New York 10463 (364).

The Heritage (Residence), 1450 Portland Ave., Rochester 14621.

Holy Family Home, 410 Mill St., Williamsville 14221 (90).

Little Sisters of the Poor, Jeanne Jugan Residence (Skilled Nursing and Health Related), 3200 Baychester Ave., Bronx 10475 (203).

Little Sisters of the Poor, Holy Family Home, 1740-84th St., Brooklyn 11214 (146).

Little Sisters of the Poor, Queen of Peace Residence, 110-30 221st St., Queens Village 11429 (202).

Madonna Home of Mercy Hospital (Nursing Home and Extended Care Facility) (140), and Mercy Hospital Health Related Facility (Residence) (58), Watertown 13601.

Madonna Residence, 1 Prospect Park W., Brooklyn, 11215 (290).

Mary Manning Walsh Home (Nursing Home), 1339 York Ave., New York 10021 (362).

Mercy General Hospital Nursing Home Unit, Tupper Lake 12986 (31).

Mt. Loretto Nursing Home, (Skilled Nursing Facility), R.D., 3, Amsterdam 12010 (82).

Nazareth Nursing Home, and Health Related Facility, 291 W. North St., Buffalo 14201 (122).

Our Lady of Hope Residence (Home for the Aged), Little Sisters of the Poor, 1 Jeanne Jugan Lane, Latham 12210 (250).

Ozanam Hall of Queens Nursing Home, Inc. (Skilled Nursing and Health-Related Facilities), 42-41 201st St., Bayside 11361 (432).

Providence Rest, 3304 Waterbury Ave., Bronx 10465 (200).

Resurrection Rest Home (Nursing Home and Health Related Facility, Women), Castleton 12033 (50).

Sacred Heart Home (Residence) 4520 Ransom Rd., Clarence 10431. Brothers of Mercy Nursing Home, 10570 Bergtold Rd., Clarence 14031. Brothers of Mercy Housing Co., Inc. (Apartments), 10500 Bergtold Rd., Clarence 14031.

Sacred Heart Nursing Home, 8 Mickle St., Plattsburgh 12901 (89).

St. Ann's Home (Nursing Home and Extended Care Facility), 1500 Portland Ave., Rochester 14621 (354).

St. Anthony's Home for the Aged, 5285 S. Park Ave., Hamburg 14075 (68).

St. Columban's on the Lake (Retirement Home), Silver Creek 14136 (50).

St. Elizabeth Home, 5539 Broadway, Lancaster 14086 (102).

St. Francis Home (Nursing and Health Related Facility), 147 Reist St., Williamsville 14221 (98).

St. Joseph's Guest Home, Missionary Sisters of St. Benedict,, 350 Cuba Hill Rd., Huntington 11743 (60).

St. Joseph's Home, Table Rock Sloatsburg 10974 (20).

St. Joseph's Home (Nursing Home), 420 Lafayette St., Ogdensburg 13669 (82).

St. Joseph's Nursing Home, 2535 Genesee St., Utica 13501 (120).

St. Joseph's Villa (Residence), 38 Prospect Ave., Catskill 12414 (60).

St. Luke Manor for Chronically Ill, 17 Wiard St., Batavia 14020 (20).

St. Mary's Manor, 515 Sixth St., Niagara Falls 14301 (119).

St. Patrick's Home for the Aged and Infirm, 66 Van Cortland Park S., Bronx 10463 (226).

St. Vincent's Home for the Aged, 319 Washington Ave., Dunkirk 14048 (36).

St. Zita's Home (Women), 143 W. 14th St., New York 10011 (46).

Teresian House, Washington Ave. Extension, Albany 12203 (300).

Uihlein Mercy Center (Nursing Home), Lake Placid 12946 (96).

North Carolina: Maryfield Nursing Home (116 beds) and Maryfield Acres (16 retirement homes), Greensboro Rd., High Point 27260 (115).

North Dakota: Holy Family Guest Home (Nursing Home), Carrington 58421 (38).

Manor St. Joseph Home for Aged and Infirm; Edgeley 58433 (40).

Marillac Manor (Retirement Apartments), 1016 N. 28th St., Bismarck 58501 (42 apartments).

St. Anne's Guest Home (Retirement), 524 N. 17th St., 813 Lewis Blvd., Grand Forks 58201 (56) Apartments (30).

St. Olav Guest (Retirement) Home, Powers Lake 58773 (20).

St. Vincent's Nursing Home, 1021 N. 26th St., Bismarck 58501 (94).

Ohio: Archbishop Leibold Home for the Aged, Little Sisters of the Poor, 476 Riddle Rd., Cincinnati 45220 (125).

Assumption Nursing Home, 550 W. Chalmers Ave., Youngstown 44511 (126).

Francesca Residence, 39 N. Portage Path, Akron 44303 (50).

Franciscan Terrace (Residence and Nursing Care), 100 Compton Rd., Cincinnati 45215 (160).

House of Loreto (Nursing Home), 2812 Harvard Ave. N.W., Canton 44709 (98).

Jennings Hall, Inc. (Intermediate Care Facility), 10204 Granger Rd., Garfield Heights 44125 (105).

Kirby Manor (Retirement Apartments), 11500 Detroit Ave., Cleveland 44102 (202 suites).

Little Sisters of the Poor, Sacred Heart Home, 4900 Navarre Ave., Oregon 43616 (158).

Little Sisters of the Poor, Sts. Joseph and Mary Home for Aged, 4291 Richmond Rd., Cleveland 44122 (140).

The Maria-Joseph Living Care Center, 4830 Salem Ave., Dayton 45416 (388).

Mount Alverna (Residence and Nursing Care for Aged), 6765 State Rd., Parma 44134 (200).

Mt. St. Joseph (Skilled Nursing Facility, Dual Certified), 21800 Chardon Rd., Cleveland 44117 (100).

Nazareth Towers, 300 E. Rich St., Columbus 43215. Hi-rise apartments for independent living.

St. Augustine Manor (Nursing Home), 7818 Detroit Ave., Cleveland 44102 (194).

St. Edward Nursing Home, 3131 Smith Rd., Akron 44313 (100).

St. Francis Home for the Aged, 182 St. Francis Ave., Tiffin 44883 (111).

St. Francis Rehabilitation Hospital and Nursing Home, 401 N. Broadway St., Green Springs 44836.

St. Joseph's Hospice (Nursing Home), 2308 Reno Dr., Louisville 44641 (100).

St. Margaret Hall (Residence and Nursing Facility), 1960 Madison Rd., Cincinnati 45206 (145).

St. Raphael Home (Nursing Home), 1550 Roxbury Rd., Columbus 43212 (80).

St. Rita's Home (Skilled Nursing Home), 880 Greenlawn Ave., Columbus 43223 (100).

St. Theresa Home for the Aged, 6760 Belkenton Pl., Cincinnati 45236 (120).

Schroder Manor (Residence and Skilled Nursing Care), Franciscan Sisters of the Poor, 1302 Millville Ave., Hamilton 45013 (85).

The Siena Home (Skilled Nursing Home), 235 W. Orchard Spring Dr., Dayton 45415 (99).

The Villa Sancta Anna Home for the Aged, 25000 Chagrin Blvd., Beachwood 44122 (68).

Oklahoma: Franciscan Villa, 17110 E. 51st St. S., Broken Arrow 74012. Intermediate nursing care (60); apartments (66).

St. Ann's Nursing Home, 3825 N.W. 19th St., Oklahoma City 73107 (82).

Oregon: Benedictine Nursing Center, S. Main St., Mt. Angel 97362 (127).

Maryville Nursing Home, 14645 S.W. Farmington, Beaverton 97007 (132).

Mt. St. Joseph's Residence and Extended Care Center, 3060 S.E. Stark St., Portland 97214 (317).

St. Catherine's Residence and Nursing Center, 3959 Sheridan Ave., North Bend 97459 (166).

St. Elizabeth's Nursing Home, 2365 4th St., Baker 97814 (93).

Pennsylvania: Ascension Manor I (Senior Citizen Housing), 911 N. Franklin St., Philadelphia 19123 (140 units).

Ascension Manor II (Senior Citizen Housing), 970 N. 7th St., Philadelphia 19123 (140 units).

Christ the King Manor, 1100 W. Long Ave., Du Bois 15801 (160).

Corpus Christi Residence, 7165 Churchland St., Pittsburgh 15206 (27).

Drueding Infirmary, 413 W. Master St., Philadelphia 19122 (52).

Garvey Manor (Nursing Home), Logan Blvd., Hollidaysburg, 16648 (150).

Holy Family Home, Little Sisters of the Poor, 5300 Chester Ave., Philadelphia 19143 (1600).

Holy Family Manor (Skilled Nursing Facility), 1200 Spring St., Bethlehem 18018 (200).

Holy Ghost Guest Home (Women), 4537 Wm. Flynn Hwy., Allison Park 15101 (15).

Immaculate Mary Home, (Skilled and Intermediate Nursing Care), Holme Circle and Welsh Rd., Philadelphia 19136 (300).

John XXIII Home, 2250 Shenango Freeway, Hermitage 16146 (100).

Little Flower Manor Nursing Home, 1201 Springfield Rd., Darby 19023 (122).

Little Flower Manor of Diocese of Scranton, (Long-Term Skilled Nursing and Intermediate Care Facility), 200 S. Meade St., Wilkes-Barre 18702.

Little Sisters of the Poor, 1028 Benton Ave. N.S., Pittsburgh 15212 (140).

Little Sisters of the Poor, Holy Family Residence, 2500 Adams Ave., Scranton 18509 (82).

Maria Joseph Manor, Danville 17821 (94).

Marian Manor (Residence and Nursing Care), 2695 Winchester Dr., Pittsburgh 15220 (172).

Mt. Trexler Skilled Nursing Unit of Sacred Heart Hospital, Limeport 18060 (65).

Redeemer Village, Huntingdon Pike, Huntingdon Valley 19006 (150 apartments).

Sacred Heart Manor (Nursing Home), 6445 Germantown Ave., Philadelphia 19119 (153).

St. Anne Home (Intermediate and Skilled Nursing Care), R.D. 2, Columbia 17512 (120).

St. Anne Home for the Elderly (Skilled Nursing Facility), 685 Angela Dr., Greensburg 15601 (125).

St. Basil's Home for Aged Women (Residential), Box 878, Uniontown 15401 (8).

St. Ignatius Nursing Home, 4401 Haverford Ave., Philadelphia 19104 (176).

St. John Neumann Nursing Home, 10400 Roosevelt Blvd. Philadelphia 19116 (196).

St. Joseph Home for the Aged, 1182 Holland Rd., Holland 18966 (96).

St. Joseph Home for the Aged (Skilled Nursing Facility), 5324 Penn Ave., Pittsburgh 15224 (150).

St. Joseph's House of Hospitality (Low Income Senior Citizen Residence for Men and Women), 1635 Bedford Ave., Pittsburgh 15219 (65).

St. Joseph Manor (Skilled Nursing Facility), 1616 Huntingdon Pike, Meadowbrook 19046 (250).

St. Joseph's Residence, 1111 S. Cascade St., New Castle 16101.

St. Leonard's Guest Home, 601 N. Montgomery St., Hollidaysburg 16648 (22).

St. Mary's Home of Erie, 607 E. 26th St., Erie 16504. Residential facility (110); geriatric nursing facility (196).

St. Mary's Manor for Sighted and Blind, 701 Lansdale Ave., Lansdale 19446 (160).

St. Mary's Villa (Nursing Home), Elmhurst 18416 (121).

Villa de Marillac Nursing Home, 5300 Stanton Ave., Pittsburgh 15206 (50).

Villa St. Teresa (Residence), 1215 Springfield Rd., Darby 19023 (53).

Villa Teresa (Nursing Home), 1051 Avila Rd., Harrisburg 17109 (178).

Vincentian Home for the Chronically Ill., Perrymont Rd., Pittsburgh 15237 (219).

Rhode Island: Jeanne Jugan Residence of the Little Sisters of the Poor, 964 Main St., Pawtucket 02860 (132).

L'Hospice St. Antoine (Home for Aged), 400 Mendon Rd., North Smithfield 02895 (244).

St. Clare Home for the Aged, 309 Spring St., Newport 02840 (44).

Scalabrini Villa (Convalescent, Rest — Nursing Home). 860 N. Quidnessett Rd., North Kingstown 02852 (70).

South Carolina: Carter-May Home, 1660 Ingram Rd., Charleston 29407 (12). Personal care home for elderly ladies.

South Dakota: Brady Memorial Home (Skilled Nursing Facility), 500 S. Ohlman St., Mitchell 57301 (60). Independent living units (2).

Maryhouse, Inc. (Skilled Nursing Facility), 717 E. Dakota, Pierre 57501 (82).

Mother Joseph Manor (Skilled Nursing Facility), 1002 North Jay St., Aberdeen 57401

(80). Apartment units (7). Adult day care program. Respite nursing care.

St. William's Home for the Aged (Intermediate Care, 60), and Angela Hall (Supervised Living, 15), 901 E. Virgil, Box 432, Milbank 57252.

Tekakwitha Nursing Home (Skilled and Intermediate Care). Sisseton 57262 (101).

Tennessee: Alexian Brothers Rest Home (Retired Men and Women), Signal Mountain 37377 (150).

Ave Maria Guild Home (Nursing Home), 2805 Charles Bryan Rd., Memphis 38134 (73).

Texas: Home for Aged Women-Men, 920 S. Oregon St., El Paso 79901 (24).

Mother of Perpetual Help Home (Intermediate Care Facility), 519 E. Madison Ave., Brownsville 78520 (39).

Mt. Carmel Home (Personal Care Home), 4130 S. Alameda St., Corpus Christi 78411 (92).

The Regis (Retirement Center), 400 Austin Ave., Waco 76701 (210).

The Retirement Residence, Inc., 2819 Rio Grande, Austin 78705 (100).

St. Ann's Home (Skilled Nursing Facility), P.O. Box 1179, Panhandle 79068 (52).

St. Anthony's Center (Skilled Nursing, Rehabilitation, Geriatric), 6301 Almeda Rd., Houston 77021 (372).

St. Benedict's Nursing Home, Alamo and Johnson Sts., San Antonio 78204 (197).

St. Dominic Residence Hall, 2401 E. Holcombe Blvd., Houston 77021.

St. Dominic Nursing Home, 6502 Grand Ave., Houston 77021 (120).

St. Elizabeth Nursing Home, 400 Austin Ave., Waco 76701 (179).

St. Francis Nursing Home (Home for Aged and Convalescents), 2717 N. Flores St., San Antonio 78212 (143).

St. Francis Village, Inc. (Retired and Elderly), Crowley. Mailing address — P.O. Box 16310, Ft. Worth 76133 (425).

St. Joseph Residence, 330 W. Pembroke St., Dallas 75208 (49).

San Juan Nursing Home (Skilled Care Facility), 300 N. Nebraska Ave., P.O. Box 1238, San Juan 78589 (52).

Utah: St. Joseph Villa (Skilled Nursing Home), 474 Westminster Ave., Salt Lake City 84115 (98).

Vermont: Loretto Home for Aged, 59 Meadow St., Rutland 05701 (54).

Michaud Memorial Manor (Home for Aged), Derby Line 05830 (24).

St. Joseph's Home for Aged, 243 N. Prospect St., Burlington 05401 (53).

Virginia: St. Francis Home, 2511 Wise St., Richmond 23225 (25).

St. Joseph's Home for the Aged, Little Sisters of the Poor, 1503 Michael Rd., Richmond 23229 (126).

Washington: Cathedral Plaza Apartments (Retirement Apartments), W. 1120 Sprague Ave., Spokane 99204 (150).

The Delaney, W. 242 Riverside Ave., Spokane 99201 (84).

The De Paul Retirement Apartments, 4831 35th Ave. S.W., Seattle 98126 (111 units).

Fahy Garden Apartments, W. 1403 Dean Ave., Spokane 99201 (31).

Fahy West Apartments, W. 1523 Dean Ave., Spokane 99201 (55).

The Josephinum (Retirement Home), 1902 2nd Ave., Seattle 98101 (228).

Mt. St. Vincent Nursing Center, 4831 35th Ave., S.W., Seattle 98126 (198).

The O'Malley, E. 707 Mission, Spokane 99202 (100).

St. Joseph Nursing Home, 1006 North H St., Aberdeen 98520 (33).

St. Joseph Care Center (Skilled Long-Term Care), West 20 — 90th Ave., Spokane 99204 (103). Adult day care center (35).

West Virginia: Knights of St. George Home, Wellsburg 26070 (44).

Welty Home for the Aged (Women), 21 Washington Ave., Wheeling 26003 (44).

Wisconsin: Alexian Village of Milwaukee (Retirement Community/Skiiled Nursing Home), 9301 N. 76th St., Milwaukee 53223 (197 apartments).

Bethany-St. Joseph Health Care Center, 2507 Shelby Rd., La Crosse 54601 (226).

Divine Savior Nursing Home, 715 W. Pleasant St., Portage 53901 (111).

Franciscan Villa of South Milwaukee, Inc. 3601 S. Chicago Ave., S. Milwaukee 53172 (150).

Hope Nursing Home, 439 Ashford Ave., Lomira 53048 (40).

McCormick Memorial Home for the Aged, 212 Iroquois St., Green Bay 54301 (70).

Marian Catholic Home, 3333 W. Highland Blvd., Milwaukee 53208 (360).

Maryhill Manor Nursing and Retirement Home, 973 Main St., Niagara 54151 (45).

Milwaukee Catholic Home, Inc., 2462 N. Prospect Ave., Milwaukee 53211 (185).

Nazareth House (Skilled Nursing Facility), Stoughton 53589 (100).

St. Ann Rest Home (Intermediate Care Facility, Women), 2020 S. Muskego Ave., Milwaukee 53204 (54).

St. Anne's Home for the Elderly (Aged Poor), 3800 N. 92nd St., Milwaukee 53222 (156).

St. Camillus Health Center (Skilled Nursing Home), 10100 W. Bluemound Rd., Wauwatosa 53226 (188).

St. Catherine Infirmary (Nursing Home), 5635 Erie St., Racine 53402 (40).

St. Elizabeth Home, 502 St. Lawrence Ave., Janesville 53545.

St. Elizabeth's Nursing Home (Women), 745 N. Brookfield Rd., Brookfield 53005 (16).

St. Francis Home, 700 West Ave. S., La Crosse 54601 (95).

St. Francis Home (Skilled Nursing Facility), 1800 New York Ave., Superior 54880 (192).

St. Francis Home (Skilled Nursing), 365 Gillett St., Fond du Lac 54935 (70).

St. Francis Manor (Retirement Residence), 3553 S. 41st St., Milwaukee 53221 (5).

St. Joan Antida Nursing Home (Women), 6640 W. Beloit Rd., W. Allis 53219 (76).

St. Joseph's Home, 705 Clyman St., Watertown 53094 (28).

St. Joseph's Home, 9244 29th Ave., Kenosha 53140 (89).

St. Joseph's Home, 5301 W. Lincoln Ave., W. Allis 53219 (124).

St. Joseph's Nursing Home, 464 S. St. Joseph Ave., Arcadia 54612 (72).

St. Joseph's Nursing Home, 2415 Cass St., La Crosse 54601 (62).

St. Joseph's Nursing Home, 400 Water Ave., Hillsboro 54634 (65).

St. Joseph Residence, Inc. (Nursing Home), 1925 Division St., New London 54961 (107).

St. Mary's Home for the Aged (Residence and Nursing Care), 2005 Division St., Manitowoc 54220 (172).

St. Mary's Nursing Home, 3516 W. Center St., Milwaukee 53210 (121).

St. Monica's Senior Citizens Home, 3920 N. Green Bay Rd., Racine 53404 (90).

St. Paul Home (Residence and Skilled Nursing Home), 509 W. Wisconsin Ave., Kaukauna 54130 (52).

Villa Clement (Nursing and Convalescent Center), 9047 W. Greenfield Ave., W. Allis 53214 (190).

Villa Loretto Nursing Home, Mount Calvary 53057 (52).

APPALACHIA COMMITTEE

The 600-member Catholic Committee of Appalachia consists of bishops, priests, religious and lay persons engaged in pastoral and social justice ministry in the 13-state region. Appalachia has been defined by Congress as including all of West Virginia and parts of Alabama, Georgia, Kentucky, Maryland, Mississippi, New York, North Carolina, Ohio, Pennsylvania, South Carolina, Tennessee and Virginia.

The committee is the Catholic Caucus of the Commission on Religion in Appalachia, an interfaith group.

Sister Honor Murphy, O.P., is executive director. Address: 31-A S. Third Ave., Prestonburg, Ky. 41653.

FACILITIES FOR HANDICAPPED CHILDREN AND ADULTS

Sources: Almanac survey; *Directory of Catholic Special Facilities and Programs for Handicapped Children and Adults,* published by the National Catholic Educational Association; *Official Catholic Directory.*

This listing covers facilities and programs with educational and training orientation. Information about other services for the handicapped can generally be obtained from the Catholic Charities Office or its equivalent (c/o Chancery Office) in any diocese. (See Index for listing of addresses of chancery offices in the U.S.)

Abbreviation code: b, boys; c, coeducational; d, day; g, girls; r, residential. Other information includes chronological age for admission. The number in parentheses at the end of an entry indicates total capacity or enrollment.

Deaf and Hard of Hearing

California: St. Joseph's Center for Deaf and Hard of Hearing (d,c; 3-14 yrs.), 4025 Grove St., Oakland 94609 (mailing address).

Illinois: Department of Vision and Hearing, Catholic Charities, 721 N. LaSalle St., Chicago 60610. Marian School for Hearing Impaired (at Most Holy Redeemer School) (d,c), 9536 S. Millard Ave., Evergreen Park 60642 (40).

Holy Trinity Day Classes for the Deaf (c; 3-14 yrs.) 1910 Taylor, Chicago 60612 (45).

Louisiana: Chinchuba Institute (r,d,c; 2-16 yrs.), P.O. Box 187, Marrero. 70072 (101).

Massachusetts: Boston School for the Deaf (r,d,c; 3-21 yrs.), 800 N. Main St., Randolph. 02368 (236).

Missouri: St. Joseph Institute for the Deaf (r,d,c; 3½-15 yrs.), 1483 82nd Blvd., University City, 63132 (150).

New York: Cleary School for the Deaf (d,c; infancy through high school), 301 Smithtown Blvd., Lake Ronkonkoma, L.I. 11779 (105).

St. Francis de Sales School for the Deaf (d,c; parent-infant programs through age 14), 260 Eastern Parkway, Brooklyn 11225.

St. Joseph's School for the Deaf (d,c; birth-13 yrs.), 1000 Hutchinson River Pkwy, Bronx. 10465 (230).

St. Mary's School for the Deaf (r,d,c; 3-21 yrs.), 2253 Main St., Buffalo. 14214 (260).

Ohio: St. Rita School for the Deaf (r,c; 4 yrs. and older), 1720 Glendale-Milford Rd., Cincinnati. 45215 (160).

Pennsylvania: Abp. Ryan Memorial Institute for Deaf (d,c; parent-infant programs through 8th grade), 3509 Spring Garden St., Philadelphia. 19104 (80).

De Paul Institute (d,c; birth-21 yrs.), Castlegate Ave., Pittsburgh. 15226 (132).

Wisconsin: St. John's School for the Deaf (r,d,c; 3-20 yrs.), 3680 S. Kinnickinnic Ave., Milwaukee. 53207 (125).

Emotionally And/Or Socially Maladjusted

This listing includes facilities for homeless and neglected as well as emotionally disturbed children and youth.

Arizona: Patterdell, 1820 W. Northern Ave., Phoenix. 85021.

Arkansas: St. Michael School, Monastery of Our Lady of Charity (c; grades kindergarten through 6th; day care), 1125 Malvern Ave., Hot Springs 71901.

California: Gracenter, Convent of the Good Shepherd (r, women), 501 Cambridge, San Francisco 94134 (9).

Hanna Boys Center (r; 10-15 yrs.), Box 100, Sonoma. 95476 (80).

Rancho San Antonio (r,b; 12-16 yrs.), 21000 Plummer St., Chatsworth. 91311 (118).

Stanford Lathrop Memorial Home and Group Homes, Sisters of Social Service, 800 N. Street, Sacramento 95814. Conduct six homes for boys and girls.

Colorado: Excelsior Youth Centers (r,g; 12-21 yrs.), 15151 E. Quincy Ave., Denver 80232 (74).

Mt. St. Vincent Home (r,c; 5-13 yrs.), 4159 Lowell Blvd., Denver. 80211 (45).

Connecticut: Highland Heights — St. Francis Home for Children (r,d,c; 8-12 yrs.), 651 Prospect St., New Haven. 06505 (38).

Mt. St. John (r,b; 11-16 yrs.), Kirtland St., Deep River. 06417 (75).

Delaware: Our Lady of Grace Home for Children (r,c; 6-12 yrs.), 487 Chestnut Hill Rd., Newark 19713 (28).

Florida: Boystown of Florida (r; 13-17 yrs.), 11400 SW 137th Ave., Miami 33186 (45).

Georgia: Village of St. Joseph (r,d,c; 6-16 yrs.), 2969 Butner Rd. S.W., Atlanta 30331 (40 r; 48 d).

Illinois: Guardian Angel (d,c; 5-15 yrs.), Plainfield at Theodore St., Joliet 60435.

Loyola Univ. of Chicago Child Guidance Center and Day School (c; pre-school to adolescence), 1043 Loyola Ave., Chicago 60626 (37).

St. Joseph Carondelet Child Center (r,b; 5-14 yrs.), 739 E. 35th St., Chicago. 60616 (40).

Indiana: Gibault School for Boys (r; 10-16 yrs.), 5901 Dixie Bee Rd., Terre Haute. 47802 (108).

Hoosier Boys Town (r; 10-16 yrs.), Schererville. 46375 (65).

Kentucky: Boys' Haven (r; 13 18 yrs.), 3201 Bardstown Rd., Louisville. 40205 (51).

Maryhurst School (r,g; 13-17 yrs.), 1015 Dorsey Lane, Louisville 40223 (42).

Our Lady of the Highlands (r,g; 13-17 yrs.), 938 Highland Ave., Ft. Thomas. 41075 (40).

Louisiana: Hope Haven — Madonna Manor School and Home (r,b; 6-17 yrs.), 1101 Barataria Blvd., Marrero 70072 (176).

Maison Marie Group Home (r,g; 13-18 yrs.), 3020 Independence St., Metairie 70002 (12).

Maryland: Christ Child Institute (r,d,c; 3-10½ yrs.), 4625 Edson Lane, Rockville. 20852 (28r, 15d).

Good Shepherd Center (r,d,g; 14-18 yrs.), 4100 Maple Ave., Baltimore. 21227 (90r, 15d).

Massachusetts: Cushing Hall (r,b; 11-14½ yrs.), 279 Tilden Rd., Scituate. 02066 (40). Diagnostic treatment center.

McAuley Nazareth Home for Boys (r; 6-12 yrs.), 77 Mulberry St., Leicester. 01524 (27).

Madonna Hall (r,g; 12-17 yrs.), Cushing Hill Dr., Marlboro 01752 (55).

Nazareth Child Care Center (r,d,c; 2-12 yrs.), 420 Pond St., Jamaica Plain, Mass. 02130 (112).

Our Lady of Providence Children's Center (r,d,c; 5-14 yrs.), 2112 Riverdale St., W. Springfield. 01089 (50). Diagnostic treatment program also.

St. Vincent Home (r,c), 2425 Highland Ave., Fall River 02720 (85).

Michigan: Barat House, Barat Human Services, League of Catholic Women (r,g; 13-17 yrs.), 5250 John R. St., Detroit. 48202 (24).

Boysville of Michigan, Inc. (r; 13-18 yrs.), 8744 Clinton-Macon Rd., Clinton. 49236 (180).

Don Bosco Hall (r,b; 13-17 years.), 10001 Petoskey Ave., Detroit. 48204 (38).

St. John's Home (r,c; 9-16 yrs.), 385 E. Leonard N.E., Grand Rapids 49503 (40).

St. Vincent Home for Children (r,c; 5-15 yrs.), 2800 W. Willow St., Lansing 48917 (38).

Villa Maria, Sisters of the Good Shepherd (r,g; 13-17 yrs.), 1315 Walker Ave. N.W., Grand Rapids. 49504 (30).

Vista Maria (r,d; 13-17 yrs.), 20651 W. Warren Ave., Dearborn Heights. 48127 (107 r; 20 d).

Minnesota: Busch Center (r,c; 10-18 yrs.), 1726 7th Ave. S., St. Cloud 56301 (20). Temporary emergency shelter care facility.

Home of the Good Shepherd, (r,g; 12-17 yrs.), 5100 Hodgson Rd., St. Paul. 55112 (48).

St. Cloud Children's Home (r,c; 12-16 yrs.), 1726 7th Ave. S., St. Cloud. 56301 (72).

St. James Children's Home (r,c), Woodland Hills, Duluth 55803 (120).

Tiffany House Group Home (c), 374 4th Ave. S., St. Cloud 56301 (11).

Missouri: Child Center of Our Lady (r,c; 4-12 yrs. — d,c; 4-17 yrs.), 7900 Natural Bridge Rd., St. Louis. 63121 (79).

Marillac Center for Children (r,d,c; 6-12 yrs.), 310 W. 106th St., Kansas City. 64114 (24 r; 70 d).

Marygrove (r,d,g; 13-17 yrs.), 2705 Mullanphy Lane, Florissant. 63031 (44).

Nebraska: Father Flanagan's Boys' Home (r; 10-18 yrs.), Boys Town, Nebr. 68010 (r, 390; d, 307).

Nevada: St. Yves School (r,g; 13-17 yrs.), 7000 North Jones Blvd., Las Vegas, 89106 (60).

New Jersey: Christopher House (c), 55 N. Clinton Ave., Trenton 08607. After care day center.

Collier Group Home (r,g; 13-18 yrs.), 47 Reckless Pl., Red Bank 07701.

Collier School (d,c; 13-18 yrs.), Wickatunk 07765.

Guidance Clinic of Catholic Welfare Bureau (c), 39 N. Clinton Ave., Trenton 08607. Psychiatric counseling for children and adults.

Mt. St. Joseph Children's Center (r,d,c; 6-12 yrs.), Shepherd Lane, Totowa 07512 (32).

New Jersey's Boystown (r; adolescents), 499 Belgrove Dr., Kearney 07032 (100).

New York: The Astor Home for Children (r,c; 5-12 yrs.), 36 Mill St., Rhinebeck 12572 (70). Group Homes (7-18 yrs.), 1200 Zarega Ave., Bronx 10462 (52). Child Guidance Clinics/Day Treatment (Rhinebeck, Poughkeepsie, Beacon, Bronx). Head start — Day Care (Poughkeepsie, Beacon, Hyde Park, Dover, Millerton).

Baker Hall (r,d,b; 10-18 yrs.), 150 Martin Rd., Lackawanna. 14218 (90).

LaSalle School (r,d; 12-18 yrs.), 391 Western Ave., Albany. 12203 (145). Also conducts group homes.

Madonna Heights Services (r,d,g; 11-17 yrs.), Burrs Lane, Huntington. 11743 (110). Also conducts group homes on Long Island and outpatient programs.

Saint Anne Institute (r,d,g; 12-18 yrs.), 160 N. Main Ave., Albany. 12206 (190).

St. Helena's Residence (r,g; 12-17 yrs.), 120 W. 60th St., New York. 10011 (20).

St. John's of Rockaway Beach (r,b; 10-18 yrs.), 144 Beach 111th St., Rockaway Park. 11694 (112). Also conducts group homes in Rockaway and Richmond Hill.

North Dakota: Home on the Range for Boys (r; 12-18 yrs.), Sentinel Butte. 58654 (36).

Ohio: Diocesan Child Guidance Center, Inc. (d,c; preschool) Outpatient counseling program (c; 2-18 yrs.), 840 W. State St., Columbus 43222.

Marycrest School for Girls (r,g; 13-18 yrs.), 7800 Brookside Rd., Independence. 44131 (70).

Parmadale/St. Anthony's Youth Services Village (r,c; 7-21 yrs.), 6753 State Rd., Parma 44134.

Rosemont School (r,g;d,c; 12-18 yrs.), 2440 Dawnlight Ave., Columbus 43211 (150).

Oregon: St. Mary's Home for Boys (r; 9-17 yrs.), 16535 S.W. Tualatin Valley Highway, Beaverton 97005 (43).

Pennsylvania: De LaSalle in Towne (d,b;

13-17 yrs.), 25 S. Van Pelt St., Philadelphia 19103 (100).

De LaSalle Vocational Day Treatment (b; 15-18 yrs.), P.O. Box 344 — Street Rd. and Bristol Pike, Bensalem 19020 (120).

Gannondale School for Girls (r; 12-17 yrs.), 4635 E. Lake Rd., Erie 16511 (57).

Harborcreek School for Boys (r; 10-17 yrs.), 5712 Iroquois Ave., Harborcreek 16421 (135). Also conducts group homes.

Lourdesmont Good Shepherd Adolescent Services (r,g;d,c; 13-17 yrs.), 537 Venard Rd., Clarks Summit 18411 (100).

Pauline Auberle Foundation, The Auberle Home for Boys (r,b; 13-18 yrs.), 1101 Hartman St., McKeesport 15132 (50).

St. Gabriel Hall (r,d,b; 12-17 yrs.), P.O. Box 13, Audobon 19407

St. Michael's School for Boys (r,b; 12-16 yrs.), Hoban Heights, Tunkhannock 18657 (120). Also conducts group homes.

Tennessee: DeNeuville Heights School for Girls (r; 12-18 yrs.), 3060 Baskin St., Memphis 38127 (52).

Texas: St. Joseph Youth Center (r,c; 12-17 yrs.), 901 S. Madison St., Dallas 75208 (48).

Washington: Morning Star Boys Ranch (Spokane Boys' Ranch, Inc.), (r,b; 9-18 yrs.), Box 781-A, Route 12, Spokane 99203 (55).

Wisconsin: Our Lady of Charity Center (r,c; 10-17 yrs.), 2640 West Point Rd., Green Bay 54303 (50).

St. Aemilian Child Care Center, Inc. (r,b; 6-12 yrs.), 8901 W. Capitol Dr., Milwaukee 53222 (57).

St. Charles Boys Home (r; 12-18 yrs.), 151 S. 84th St., Milwaukee 53214 (56).

St. Michael's Home for Children (r,c; 9-18 yrs.), 2902 East Ave. S., La Crosse 54601 (42).

Wyoming: St. Joseph's Children's Home (r,c; 6-18 yrs.), P.O. Box 1117, Torrington 82240 (48). Also conducts group home.

Developmentally Handicapped

This listing includes facilities for children and youth with learning disabilities and/or mental retardation.

Alabama: Father Walter Memorial Child Care Center (r,c; birth-12 yrs.), 2815 Forbes Dr., Montgomery 36199 (34). Skilled nursing facility.

California: Catholic Charities "Empower" Services to Developmentally Disabled Persons, 433 Jefferson St., Oakland 94607. Services include (in various locations): Evergreen Center (d; adults); Concord House (r; adults); C.O.R.E. (d; adults outreach program for homebound); Case Management (d; adults, children — social workers); Religious Nurture Program (d; adults, children).

Helpers of the Mentally Retarded, Inc., 2626 Fulton St., San Francisco 94118. Conducts three homes: Helpers Home for Girls (18 years and older), 2608 Fulton St. and 2626 Fulton St., San Francisco 94118; Helpers Home for Men (18 years and older), 2750 Fulton St., San Francisco 94118.

Kennedy Child Study Center (d,c; 5-13 yrs.), 1339 - 20th St., Santa Monica. 90404 (80). Also conducts a developmental nursery (18 mos.-3 yrs.) and a preschool for children from culturally deprived areas (3-5 yrs.).

St. Madeleine Sophie's Training Center (d,c; 18 yrs. and older), 2111 E. Madison Ave., El Cajon 92021 (102).

St. Vincent's (r,d,c; 8-18 yrs.), P.O. Drawer V, 4200 Calle Real, Santa Barbara 93102 (116).

Tierra del Sol (d,c; 18 yrs. and older), 9919 Sunland Blvd., Sunland 91040 (100).

Connecticut: Gengras Center (d,c; 6-21 yrs.), St. Joseph College, 1678 Asylum Ave., W. Hartford 06117 (70).

Special Education Department, Diocese of Bridgeport, 238 Jewett Ave., Bridgeport 06606.

Villa Maria Education Center (c), 159 Sky Meadow Dr., Stamford 06903 (31). For children with learning disabilities.

District of Columbia: Lt. Joseph P. Kennedy Jr. Institute (d,c; 5-20 yrs.), 801 Buchanan St. N.E., Washington 20017 (120). Also conducts group homes, continuing education and life skills training programs, contract employment and job placement.

St. Gertrude's School of Arts and Crafts (r,d,g; 6-18 yrs.), 4801 Sargent Rd. N.E., Washington 20017 (48).

Florida: Marian Center Services for Developmentally Handicapped and Mentally Retarded (r,d,c), 15701 Northwest 37th Ave., Opa Locka 33054. Offers variety of services.

Marian School for Exceptional Children (d,c; 6 mos.-5 yrs.), 326 Pine Terr., W. Palm Beach 33401.

Morning Star School (d,c; 4-12 yrs.), 725 Mickler Rd., Jacksonville 32211 (70).

Morning Star School (d,c; 3-12 yrs.), 954 Leigh Ave., Orlando 32804 (45).

Morning Star School (d,c; 6-13 yrs.), 4661 - 80th Ave., N., Pinellas Park 33565 (50).

Morning Star School (d,c; 6-13 yrs.), 302 E. Linebaugh Ave., Tampa 33612 (70).

Illinois: Bartlett Learning Center (r,d,c; 5-21 yrs.), 801 W. Bartlett Rd., Bartlett 60103 (138).

Good Shepherd Manor (permanent home for men; 18 yrs.), P.O. Box 260, Momence. 60954 (120).

Lt. Joseph P. Kennedy, Jr., School (r,b;d,c; 6-21 yrs.) and Job Training Center (c; 16 yrs. and older), 123rd and Wolf Rd., Palos Park. 60464 (101).

Misericordia Home South (r,c; 1 mo.-6 yrs.), 2916 W. 47th St., Chicago 60632 (122).

Misericordia Home North (r,c; 4-21 yrs.), 6300 North Ridge, Chicago (60).

Mt. St. Joseph (mentally handicapped women; 20-45 yrs.), Route 3, Box 365, Lake Zurich 60047 (160).

St. Francis School for Exceptional Children (r,c; 4-12 yrs.), 1209 S. Walnut Ave., Freeport 61032 (32).

St. Jude School (d,c; 5-18 yrs.), 2nd and Spring Ave., Aviston 62216 (30).

St. Mary of Providence (r,d,g; 4-21 yrs.), 4200 N. Austin Ave., Chicago 60634 (190).

St. Rose Center (d,c; 3-21 yrs.), 4911 S. Hoyne Ave., Chicago 60609 (60).

St. Vincent Residential School (c; 12 yrs. and older) (40), and St. Vincent Community Living Facility (adults) (20), and St. Vincent Supported Living Arrangement (adults) (60), 659 E. Jefferson St., Freeport 61032.

Special Education Program of the East St. Louis Deanery (d,c; 5-16 yrs.), 8213 Church Lane, East St. Louis 62203 (48).

Indiana: Marian Day School (d,c; 6-18 yrs.), 625 Bellemeade Ave., Evansville 47713 (45).

Providence House (r, men; 18 yrs. and up), 520 W. 9th St., Jasper 47546 (66).

St. Bavo Special Class (d,c; 6-15 yrs.), 512 W. 8th St., Mishawaka 46544 (12).

St. Mary Child Center School (d,c; 3-16 yrs.), 311 N. New Jersey St., Indianapolis 46204 (32). Developmentally Disabled.

Kansas: Holy Family Center (d,c; 6-21 yrs.), 619 S. Maize Rd., Wichita 67209 (65).

Lakemary Center, Inc. (r,d,c; 3-16 yrs.), 100 Lakemary Dr., Paola 66071 (72r,35d).

Kentucky: Msgr. Pitt Learning Center (d,c; 5 yrs. and older), 10715 Ward Ave., Louisville 40223 (74).

Ursuline Special Education Learning Center (d,c; 3½-14 yrs.), 3105 Lexington Rd., Louisville 40206 (50-56).

Louisiana: Department of Special Education, Archdiocese of New Orleans, 1522 Chippewa St., New Orleans 70130. Conducts day classes, a special day school, and a vocational rehabilitation center for the mentally retarded (300).

Holy Angels School (r,c; teen-age, 14 yrs. and older; nursery, 2 mo. to kindergarten age), 10450 Ellerbe Rd., Shreveport 71106 (237).

Padua House (r,c; birth-21 yrs.), 200 Beta St., Belle Chase 70037 (44).

Regina Caeli Center (d,c; 6-16 yrs.), 3903 Kingston, Lake Charles. 70605 (45).

St. Agnes Vocational Evaluation and Training Center (d,c), P.O. Box 53326, 715 East Blvd., Baton Rouge 70802 (140).

St. Mary Learning Center, St. Mary's Home (d,c; 6-18 yrs.), 601-A W. St. Mary, Lafayette 70506 (50).

St. Mary's Training School (r,c; 3-22 yrs.), P.O. Drawer 7768, Alexandria 71306 (150).

St. Michael Vocational Training Center (d,c; 16-21 yrs.), 1522 Chippewa St., New Orleans 70130.

Maryland: The Benedictine School for Exceptional Children (r,c; 6-16 yrs.), Ridgely

21660 (100). Also conducts Habilitation Center (r,c; 17 yrs. and older) (50).

Francis X. Gallagher Center (r), 2520 Pot Spring Rd., Timonium 21093 (54).

St. Elizabeth School for Special Education (d,c; 12 yrs. and older), 801 Argonne Dr., Baltimore 21218 (124).

St. Francis School for Special Education (d,c; 3-11 yrs.), 2226 Maryland Ave., Baltimore 21218 (60).

Massachusetts: Cardinal Cushing School and Training Center (r,d,c; 6-22 yrs.), Hanover 02339 (125 r; 100 d).

Mercy Centre for Developmental Disabilities (d,c; 3-22 yrs. and over), 25 West Chester St., Worcester 01605 (160).

Nazareth Hall (d,c; 7-14 yrs.), 887 Highland Ave., Fall River, 02720 (70).

Nazareth on the Cape (d,c; 6-15 yrs.), 261 South St., Hyannis 02601 (25).

St. Coletta Day School (d,c; 7-12 yrs., admission age), 85 Washington St., Braintree 02184 (150).

Michigan: Our Lady of Providence Center (r,d,g; 5-17 yrs., child caring; 18-26, adult foster care), 16115 Beck Rd., Northville. 48167 (100).

St. Louis Center and School (r,d,b; 6-18 yrs. child care; 18-26 yrs. adult foster care), 16195 Old U.S. 12, Chelsea 48118 (80).

Missouri: Department of Special Education, Archdiocese of St. Louis, 4472 Lindell Blvd., St. Louis. 63108. Conducts 27 special day classes (c; 5-16 yrs.).

Good Shepherd Manor (residential for developmentally disabled men; 16 yrs. and up), Little Brothers of the Good Shepherd, 3220 E. 23rd St., Kansas City 64127 (43).

Mt. Carmel Group Home (r,c; 16-21 yrs.), 8757 Annetta Ave., St. Louis 63147.

St. Joseph's Vocational Center (c; 15-21 yrs.), 5341 Emerson Ave., St. Louis 63120 (135).

St. Mary's Special School (r,c; 5-16 yrs.), 5341 Emerson Ave., St. Louis 63120 (138).

St. Peter's Special Classes (d,c; 5-21 yrs.), 314 W. High St., Jefferson City 65101 (45).

Universal Sheltered Workshop (c, adults), 6912 W. Florissant Ave., St. Louis 63136. Sheltered employment (80).

Nebraska: Madonna School for Exceptional Children (d,c; 5-21 yrs.), 2537 N. 62nd St., Omaha 68104 (65).

Villa Marie School (r,d,c; 7-16 yrs.), P. O. Box 80328, Waverly 68501 (25).

New Jersey: Archbishop Damiano School (d,c), 532 Delsea Dr., Westville Grove 08093.

Catholic Community Services, Multi-Service Center, 17 Mulberry St., Newark 07102.

Department of Special Education, Diocese of Camden, 1845 Haddon Ave., Camden 08108. Services include: Archbishop Damiano School (above), and full time programs at 6 Catholic Schools; adult evening classes (18-65 yrs.); religious education programs.

Department of Special Education, Diocese of Paterson. Murray House (r; adults), 389 Main St., Paterson 07501. Also conducts five other adult group homes and two adult opportunity centers.

Felician School for Exceptional Children (r,d,c; 2½-14 yrs.), 260 S. Main St., Lodi 07644 (120).

McAuley School for Exceptional Children (d,c; 5-9 yrs.), 1633 Rt. 22 at Terrill Rd., Plainfield-Watchung 07060 (40).

Marian Center (d,c; 7-14 yrs.), Delsea Dr. and Chestnut St., Vineland 08360 (30).

Mount Carmel Guild — Child Study Center Alhambra Pavilion (c; 6-12 yrs.), 31 Centre St., Newark 07102 (50).

Sr. Georgine Learning Center (d,c; 6-17 yrs.), 544 Chestnut Ave., Trenton 08611 (30).

New Mexico: St. Joseph's Manor (r,b; 14-29 yrs.), P.O. Box 610, Bernalillo 87004.

Little Brothers of the Good Shepherd, P.O. Box 610, Bernalillo 87004. Twenty-four-hour child care center for mentally and physically handicapped.

New York: Cantalician Center for Learning (d,c; birth-21 yrs.), 3233 Main St., Buffalo 14214 (250).

Cantalician Center Workshop (d,c; 18 yrs. and older), 129A Central Park Plaza, Buffalo 14214 (150). Also conducts a vocational evaluation and rehabilitation training program.

Catholic Charities, Diocese of Rockville Centre — Services for Retarded Adults, 50 N. Park Ave., Box X, Rockville Centre 11570. Conducts four residences for retarded adults.

Cobb Memorial School (r,c; 6-10 yrs.), Altamont 12009 (50).

Friends of L'Arche of Greater Syracuse, Inc. (r, adults), 1701 James St., Syracuse 13206 (12). Long-term facility following philosophy of Jean Vanier and L'Arche movement.

Maryhaven Vocational Rehabilitation Center (d,c; 18 yrs. and older), County Road 101, Box 600, Yaphank 11980 (265).

Mercy Home for Children (r,c), 273 Willoughby Ave., Brooklyn 11205.

St. Catherine Center for Children (r,c; birth to 12 yrs. and d,c; 3-12 yrs.), 30 N. Main St., Albany 12203 (140). Also conducts group home and specialized foster care programs.

St. Joseph School for Exceptional Children (r,d,c; 5-21 yrs.), 10807 Bennett Rd., Dunkirk 14048 (30). Residents must return home weekends and vacations.

School of the Holy Childhood (d,c; 5-21 yrs.), 1150 Buffalo Rd., Rochester 14624 (94). Adult program, 18-50 yrs.

Special Education Department, Diocese of Brooklyn (d,c; 3-18 yrs.), Office of Education, 345 Adams St., Brooklyn 11201 (235). Office for the Handicapped, Diocese of Brooklyn, 191 Joralemon St., Brooklyn 11201. Services include day care center and community residences for retarded adults.

Special Education Department, Archdiocese of New York, 1011 First Ave., New York 10022. Conducts 13 special day classes in 9 parish schools.

North Carolina: Holy Angels Nursery (r,c; birth to 12 yrs.), Belmont 28012 (66).

Ohio: Good Shepherd Manor (permanent care of men 18 years and older), P.O. Box 387, Wakefield 45687 (104).

Mary Immaculate School (d,c; 7-14 yrs.), 3837 Secor Rd., Toledo 43623 (60). For children with learning disabilities.

Marymount Rehabilitation Services (vocational rehabilitation; 16 yrs. and older), 12215 Granger Rd., Cleveland 44125.

MRS Industries (c; sheltered workshop), 4765 E. 131st St., Garfield Heights 44105.

Mt. Aloysius (r, men; 21 yrs. and over), Tile Plant Rd., New Lexington 43764 (100).

Our Lady of Angels Special School (d,c; 7-16 yrs.), 3570 Rocky River Dr., Cleveland 44111 (30).

Our Lady of the Elms Special School (d,c; 6-15 yrs.), 1230 W. Market St., Akron 44313 (74).

Rose Mary, The Johanna Graselli Rehabilitation and Education Center (r,c; 3-12 yrs.), 19350 Euclid Ave., Cleveland 44117 (40).

St. John's Villa (r,c,b, 6-14 yrs; g, 6-18 yrs., continued care, g, 18 yrs. and over), 620 Roswell Rd. N.W., Carrollton 44615 (221).

St. Joseph Center (d,c; 6-16 yrs.), 2346 W. 14th St., Cleveland 44113 (70).

Sheltered Workshop and Training Center (c; 16 yrs. and older), 1890 W. 22nd St., Cleveland 44113 (35).

Oregon: Emily School for Multi-Handicapped Children (d,c; 2½-5 yrs.), 830 N.E. 47th Ave., Portland 97213 (12).

Providence Children's Nursing Center (r; nursing care), 830 N. E. 47th Ave., Portland 97213 (54).

Pennsylvania: Clelian Heights School for Exceptional Children (r,d,c; 5-21 yrs.), R.D. 9, Box 607, Greensburg 15601 (100). Also conducts re-socialization program (r,d,c; 16-young adults).

Department of Special Education, Diocese of Pittsburgh, 162 Steuben St., Pittsburgh 15220. Conducts a program consisting of five special day classes.

Don Guanella School (r,d,b; 6-17 yrs.) and C. K. Center (r,c; adults, post-school age), Sproul Rd., Springfield 19064.

McGuire Memorial (r,d,c; infancy to 7 yrs.), 2119 Mercer Rd., New Brighton 15066 (99).

Mercy Day School: Center for Special Learning (d,c; 7-21 yrs.), 830 S. Woodward St., Allentown 18103 (80).

Our Lady of Confidence Day School (d,c;

5-18 yrs.), 10th and Lycoming Sts., Philadelphia 19140 (65b, 52g).

St. Anthony School for Exceptional Children (r,d,c; 6-16 yrs.), 13th St. and Hulton Rd., Oakmont 15139 (150).

St. Joseph Day School (c; 6-18 yrs.), 619 Mahantongo St., Pottsville 17901 (40).

St. Joseph's Center (r,c; birth-20 yrs.), 2010 Adams Ave., Scranton 18509 (85).

St. Katherine School (d,c; 4-18 yrs.), William Rd. and Bowman Ave., Philadelphia 19151 (150)

St. Mary of Providence Center (r,d,g; 6-14 yrs.), Elverson 19520 (120).

Tennessee: Madonna Day School for Retarded Children (d,c; 5-16), 4189 Leroy, Memphis 38108 (50).

St. Bernard School for Exceptional Children, (c; 4-8 yrs.), 2021 21st Ave. S., Nashville 37212 (25).

Texas: Notre Dame of Dallas Special School (d,c; 6-12 yrs.), Rt. 2, Box 4, Irving 75062. (108). Notre Dame Vocational Center, at same address, provides work-study program for exceptional young people over 16.

Virginia: St. Coletta School (d,c; 3-25 yrs.), 1305 N. Jackson St., Arlington 22201 (45).

St. Mary's Infant Home (r,c; 3 days-9 yrs.), 317 Chapel St., Norfolk 23504 (50).

Wisconsin: St. Coletta School (r,c), Jefferson 53549 (372). Offers the following programs:

a complete program of special education from kindergarten through elementary and advanced levels (r,d,c);

a work training center in preparation for job placement (r,c; 18-25 yrs.);

a residential care center (r,c; 45-85 yrs.);

a half-way house to give guidance and assist with problems (r; 18-24 yrs.);

sheltered workshop employment for the mentally retarded in a homelike environment (r,c; 25-45 yrs.).

St. Coletta Day School (c; 8-16 yrs.), 1725 N. 54th St., Milwaukee. 53208 (12).

Orthopedically Handicapped

Alabama: Father Purcell Memorial (r,c; birth to 14 yrs.), 2048 W. Fairview Ave., Montgomery 36108 (52). Skilled nursing home.

Kentucky: Redwood School and Rehabilitation Center (d,c; birth and up), 71 Orphanage Rd., Fort Mitchell 41017 (200).

Pennsylvania: St. Edmond's Home for Crippled Children (r,c; 2-10 yrs.)., 320 S. Roberts Rd., Rosemont 19010 (50).

Visually Handicapped

Illinois: Department of Vision and Hearing, Catholic Charities, 721 N. LaSalle St., Chicago 60610. Itinerant education services for visually impaired students attending regular Catholic elementary and high schools in Chicago archdiocese (30).

Maine: Visually Handicapped Services: 47 High St., Portland 04101; 41 Birch St., Biddeford 04005; 382 Sabattus St., Lewiston 04240; 95 Main St., Orono 04472; 224 Main St., Waterville. Itinerant teacher and other services.

New Jersey: St. Joseph's School for the Multiple Handicapped Blind (r,d,c; 3-21 yrs.), 253 Baldwin Ave., Jersey City 07306 (25).

New York: Catholic Charities Services for Visually Impaired, 272 Merrick Rd., Lynbrook 11563.

Catholic Guild for the Blind (itinerant teaching program, c; 5-17 yrs.), 345 Adams St., Brooklyn 11201.

Lavelle School for the Blind (r,d,c; 3-21 yrs.), 221st St. and Paulding Ave., Bronx 10469 (120).

Pennsylvania: St. Lucy Vision Program, Archdiocese of Philadelphia. St. Lucy Day School (d,c; 3½-14 yrs.), 929 S. Farragut St., Philadelphia. 19143 (30). Other programs services: parent-support group of VH children (0-5 yrs.); monitors VH services to parish schools and high schools; consultant service to religious education programs.

ORGANIZATIONS

(See separate article for a listing of facilities for the handicapped.)

Blind

The Carroll Center for the Blind (formerly the Catholic Guild for All the Blind): Located at 770 Centre St., Newton, Mass. 02158, the center conducts diagnostic evaluation and rehabilitation programs for blind people over 16 years of age, and maintains programs in community services for all ages, volunteer and special services, casework and counseling, low-vision training and professional training. It offers a large range of services for blind people who are not in residence, and maintains an office of public education and information. *AAR Review* is the quarterly publication of the center. The executive director is Rachel Rosenbaum.

Xavier Society for the Blind: The Society is located at 154 E. 23rd St., New York, 10010. Founded in 1900 by Rev. Joseph Stadelman, S.J., it is a center for publications for the blind and maintains a circulating library of approximately 7,000 volumes in Braille, large type and on tape. Its many publications include *The Catholic Review*, a monthly selection of articles of current interest from the Catholic press presented for the visually handicapped in Braille, on tape, and in large print. The director of Xavier is Rev. Anthony F. La Bau, S.J.

The Deaf

According to the National Catholic Office for the Deaf, there are approximately 95,000 Catholics among the total deaf population of

410,522. (The deaf were defined by the 1974 National Census of the Deaf Population as "those persons who could not hear and understand speech and who had lost — or never had — that ability prior to 19 years of age.) Reported statistics indicated: Students in Catholic schools for the deaf, 1,969; teachers, 570 (147 were religious). Personnel involved in out-of-school pastoral ministry to the deaf included: priests, 97 (35 full-time, 62 part-time); permanent deacons, 6 (part-time); sisters, 72 (27 full-time, 45 part-time); brothers, 3 (1 full-time, 2 part-time); lay people, 69 (4 full-time, 65 part-time).

Organizations involved in work for the deaf include the following.

International Catholic Deaf Association: Established by deaf adults in Toronto, Canada, in 1949, the association has more than 8,000 members in 121 chapters, mostly in the U.S. It is the only international lay association founded and controlled by deaf Catholic adults. It is affiliated with the World Federation of the Deaf. Home office address: 814 Thayer Ave., Silver Spring, Md. 20910. The ICDA publishes a monthly newsletter and *The Deaf Catholic,* a quarterly, and sponsors regional conferences, workshops and an annual convention.

National Catholic Office for the Deaf: Formally established in 1976, at Washington, D.C., to provide pastoral service to those who teach deaf children and adults, to the parents of deaf children, to pastors of deaf persons, and to organizations of the deaf. The office develops liturgical and religious education materials; organizes workshops, pastoral weeks, community weeks, leadership programs, cursillos; and serves as a clearinghouse for information concerning ministry to the deaf. It publishes *Listening,* a pastoral service for the hearing impaired, five times a year. The executive director is Sister Alverna Hollis, O.P. Address: 814 Thayer Ave., Silver Spring, Md. 20910.

Mentally Retarded

National Apostolate with Mentally Retarded Persons: Established in 1968, the apostolate has headquarters at Trinity College, P.O. Box 4588, Washington, D.C. 20017. It publishes the quarterly *NAMRP Journal* and a monthly newsletter, and has available a bibliography on the religious education of the retarded. Rev. William Finnegan is president of the apostolate; the executive director is Bro. Joseph Moloney, O.S.F.

Service Agencies

National Catholic Office for Persons with Disabilities: Established in 1982 to assist dioceses in developing pastoral services with handicapped persons. The executive director is Sister Rita Baum, S.S.J. Address: 1234 Massachusetts Avenue N.W., Washington, D.C. 20005.

Special Education Department, National Catholic Educational Association: Established in 1954 to coordinate under one agency information and service functions for all areas of special education under Catholic auspices. The executive director is Sr. Suzanne Hall, S.N.D. de N. Address: One Dupont Circle N.W., Suite 350, Washington, D.C. 20036.

OTHER SOCIAL SERVICES

Cancer Hospitals or Homes: The following homes or hospitals specialize in the care of cancer patients. They are listed according to state.

Penrose Cancer Hospital, Sisters of Charity of Cincinnati, 2215 N. Cascade Ave., Colorado Springs, Colo. 80907.

Our Lady of Perpetual Help Home, Servants of Relief for Incurable Cancer, 760 Washington St., S.W., Atlanta, Ga. 30315 (54).

Rose Hawthorne Lathrop Home, Servants of Relief for Incurable Cancer, 1600 Bay St., Fall River, Mass. 02724 (35).

Our Lady of Good Counsel Free Cancer Home, Servants of Relief for Incurable Cancer, 2076 St. Anthony Ave., St. Paul, Minn. 55104 (40).

Calvary Hospital, Inc., 1740-70 Eastchester Rd., Bronx, N.Y. 10461 (200). Sponsored by Catholic Charities, Department of Health and Hospitals, Archdiocese of New York.

St. Rose's Free Home for Incurable Cancer, Servants of Relief for Incurable Cancer, 71 Jackson St., New York, N.Y. 10002 (45).

Rosary Hill Home, Servants of Relief for Incurable Cancer, Hawthorne, N.Y. 10532 (72).

Holy Family Home, Servants of Relief for Incurable Cancer, 6707 State Rd., Parma, O. 44134 (50).

Sacred Heart Free Home for Incurable Cancer, Servants of Relief for Incurable Cancer, 1315 W. Hunting Park Ave., Philadelphia, Pa. 19140 (59).

Drug Abuse: Rehabilitation centers and outpatient clinics have been established in several dioceses. Facilities include:

Alpha House for Drug Rehabilitation (women) and Dismas House for Drug Rehabilitation (men), 396 Straight St., Paterson, N.J. 07501 (residential rehabilitation programs). Cedar Outpatient Clinic and Cedar Day Care Center, 101-105 Cedar St., Paterson, N.J. 07501 (outpatient services).

Bethesda Manor, 3290 N.W. 7th St., Miami, Fla. 33125. Residential program for detoxification and after-care for poly drug users including alcohol.

Daytop Village, Inc., 54 W. 40th St., New York, N.Y. 10018. Msgr. William B. O'Brien.

Five residential facilities and six outreach centers in New York.

New Hope Manor (live in therapeutic community for rehabilitation of female drug addicts), Graymoor, Garrison, N.Y. 10524.

St. Joseph's Hospital, L. E. Phillips Center for the Chemically Dependent, 2661 County Trunk I, Chippewa Falls, Wis. 54729 (46).

Alcoholics: Some priests and religious throughout the U.S. are committed in a special way to the personal rehabilitation and pastoral care of alcoholics through participation in Alcoholics Anonymous and other programs. Facilities for the rehabilitation of alcoholics include:

St. Christopher's Inn, Atonement Friars, Graymoor, Garrison, N.Y. 10524 (capacity, 180). Simple detoxification and recovery; males only, ages 18-70.

Matt Talbot Inn, 2270 Professor St., Cleveland, Ohio 44113 (capacity 23 men; Halfway House; residential treatment for male alcoholics).

Straight and Narrow Hospital for Alcoholism (20 beds), and Straight and Narrow Rehabilitation Center for Male Alcoholics (50 beds), 396 Straight St., Paterson, N.J. 07501. McNulty House for Male Alcoholics (10 beds), 101 Cedar St., Paterson, N.J. 07501. Straight and Narrow Alcohol Abuse Services (outpatient services), 896 E. 19th St., Paterson, N.J. 07501.

Sacred Heart Rehabilitation Center, Inc., 569 E. Elizabeth St., Detroit, Mich. 48201 (13 beds, detoxification; 60 beds, early treatment); 400 Stoddard Rd., Memphis, Mich. 48041 (123 beds, advance treatment). Both facilities serve male and female live-in clients.

Convicts: Priests serve as full- or part-time chaplains in penal and correctional institutions throughout the country. Limited efforts have been made to assist in the rehabilitation of released prisoners in Halfway House establishments.

Dining Rooms; Facilities for Homeless: Representative of places where meals are provided, and in some cases lodging and other services as well, are:

St. Anthony's Dining Room, 121 Golden Gate Ave., San Francisco, Calif. 94102. Founded in 1950 by Rev. Alfred Boeddeker, O.F.M. More than 14 million free meals have been served. Director, Rev. Floyd A. Lotito, O.F.M.

St. Vincent de Paul Free Dining Room, 675 23rd St., Oakland, Calif. 94604. Administered by Little Brothers of the Good Shepherd, under sponsorship of St. Vincent de Paul Society. Hot meals served at lunch time 7 days a week; clothing, lodging provided those in need.

Ozanam Inn, Little Brothers of the Good Shepherd, 843 Camp St., New Orleans, La. 70130. Under sponsorship of the St. Vincent de Paul Society.

St. Vincent's Dining Room, 505 W. 3rd St., Reno, Nev. 89503.

St. Vincent Dining Room, 650 S. Main St., Las Vegas, Nev. 89101.

Good Shepherd Refuge, Little Brothers of the Good Shepherd, 601 2nd St. S.W., Albuquerque, N.M. 87102.

Holy Name Centre for Homeless Men, Inc., 18 Bleeker St., New York, N.Y. 10012. A day shelter for alcoholic, homeless men. Provides social services and aid to transients and those in need. Affiliated with New York Catholic Charities.

St. Francis Inn, 2441 Kensington Ave., Philadelphia, Pa. 19125. Serves hot meals. Temporary shelter.

St. John's Hospice for Men, Little Brothers of the Good Shepherd, 1221 Race St., Philadelphia, Pa. 19107. Founded in 1963. Hot breakfast and dinner served to all in need; accommodations for 35 men for night shelter; clothing distributed daily to needy.

Camillus House, Little Brothers of the Good Shepherd, 726 N.E. First Ave., Miami, Fla. 33132. Food and shelter for needy men.

Temporary Shelters: Facilities for runaways, the abused, exploited and homeless include:

Anthony House, 246 2nd St., Jersey City, N.J. 07302. Under sponsorship of St. Anthony's Guild. For homeless women and children.

Covenant House, 460 W. 41st St., New York, N.Y. 10036. Non-sectarian. President, Rev. Bruce Ritter, O.F.M. Conv. Provides shelter and services for homeless, runaway and exploited youth under the age of 21, in New York. Toronto (Canada), Antigua and Guatemala.

Crescent House, 2929 S. Carrollton Ave., New Orleans, La. 70118. Temporary residence for abused women and their children.

The Dwelling Place, 409 W. 40th St., New York, N.Y. 10018. For homeless women.

Francis House, 1902 Cuming St., Omaha, Nebr. 68102. For homeless men.

The Good Shepherd Shelter, 1126 W. Grace St., Chicago, Ill. 60613. For abused women with children.

Good Shepherd Shelter, 2561 Venice Blvd., Los Angeles, Calif. 90019. For battered women with children.

Mercy Hospice, Sisters of Mercy, 334 S. 13th St., Philadelphia, Pa. 19107. Temporary shelter and relocation assistance for homeless women.

Mt. Carmel House, 471 G Pl., N.W., Washington, D.C. 20001. For homeless women.

Siena House of Hospitality, 804 N. 19th St., Omaha, Nebr. 68102. For homeless women.

Unwed Mothers: Residential and care services for unwed mothers are available in many dioceses.

There is great variety in retreat and renewal programs, with orientations ranging from the traditional to teen encounters. Central to all of them are celebration of the liturgy and deepening of a person's commitment to faith and witness in life.

Features of many of the forms are as follows.

Traditional Retreats: Centered around conferences and the direction of a retreat master; oriented to the personal needs of the retreatants; including such standard practices as participation in Mass, reception of the sacraments, private and group prayer, silence and meditation, discussions.

Team Retreat: Conducted by a team of several leaders or directors (priests, religious, lay persons) with division of subject matter and activities according to their special skills and the nature and needs of the group.

Closed Retreat: Involving withdrawal for a period of time — overnight, several days, a weekend — from everyday occupations and activities.

Open Retreat: Made without total disengagement from everyday involvements, on a part-time basis.

Private Retreat: By one person, on a kind of do-it-yourself basis with the one-to-one assistance of a director.

Special Groups: With formats and activities geared to particular groups; e.g., members of Alcoholics Anonymous, vocational groups and apostolic groups.

Marriage Encounters: Usually weekend periods of husband-wife reflection and dialogue; introduced into the U.S. from Spain in 1967.

Charismatic Renewal: Featuring elements of the movement of the same name; "Spirit-oriented"; communitarian and flexible, with spontaneous and shared prayer, personal testimonies of faith and witness.

Christian Community: Characterized by strong community thrust.

Teens Encounter Christ (TEC), SEARCH: Formats adapted to the mentality and needs of youth, involving experience of Christian faith and commitment in a community setting.

Christian Maturity Seminars: Similar to teen encounters in basic concept but different to suit persons of greater maturity.

Cursillo: see separate entry.

House of Prayer Experience: see separate entry.

Movement for a Better World: see separate entry.

Conference

Retreats International Inc.: The first organization for promoting retreats in the U.S. was started in 1904 in California. Its initial efforts and the gradual growth of the movement led to the formation in 1927 of the National Catholic Laymen's Retreat Conference, the forerunner of the men's division of Retreats International. The women's division developed from the National Laywomen's Retreat Movement which was founded in Chicago in 1936. The men's and women's divisions merged July 9, 1977. The services of the organization include an annual summer institute for retreat and pastoral ministry, regional conferences for retreat center leadership and area meetings of directors and key leadership in the retreat movement. The officers are: Auxiliary Bishop Robert Morneau of Green Bay, episcopal advisor; Mrs. Lucille Okenfuss, president; Rev. Thomas W. Gedeon, S.J., executive director. National office: 1112 Memorial Library, Notre Dame, Ind. 46556.

The freedom of the retreat apostolate in the U.S. contrasts significantly with conditions of the same apostolate in other countries. A case in point: The beating and arrest Aug. 20, 1981, in of Father Richardas Cherniauskas for conducting a retreat for young people near Moletai, Lithuania.

HOUSES OF RETREAT AND RENEWAL

(Principal sources: Almanac survey; *The Official Catholic Directory*.)

Abbreviation code: m, men; w, women; mc, married couples; y, youth. Houses and centers without code generally offer facilities to all groups. An asterisk after an abbreviation indicates that the facility is primarily for the group designated but that special groups are also accommodated. Houses furnish information concerning the types of programs they offer.

Alabama: Blessed Trinity Shrine Retreat, Holy Trinity 36859.

Visitation Sacred Heart Retreat House, 2300 Spring Hill Ave., Mobile 36607.

Alaska: Holy Spirit Retreat House, Star Route A, Box 2388, Anchorage 99507.

Arizona: Franciscan Renewal Center, Casa de Paz y Bien, 5802 E. Lincoln Dr., Box 220, Scottsdale 85252.

Mount Claret Cursillo Center, 4633 N. 54th St., Phoenix 85018.

Picture Rocks Retreat — A Christian Renewal Center, 7101 W. Picture Rocks Rd., Tucson 85704. Mailing address, Box 569, Cortaro 85230.

Spiritual Life Institute (individuals only), Nada Hermitage, Sedona 86336.

Arkansas: The Abbey Retreat (Coury House), Subiaco 72865.

California: Angela Center, 535 Angela Dr., Santa Rosa 95401.

Camp Mariastella (y*, families, ecumenical), Wrightwood 92397. Office, 1120

Westchester Pl., Los Angeles 90019.

Cenacle Retreat House 5340 Fair Oaks Blvd., Carmichael 95608.

Christ the King Retreat Center, Box 156, Citrus Heights 95610.

Christian Brothers Retreat House, 2233 Sulphur Springs Ave., St. Helena 94574.

Claretian Retreat Center, 1119 Westchester Pl., Los Angeles 90019.

El Carmelo Retreat House, 926 E. Highland Ave., Redlands 92373.

Holy Spirit Retreat Center, 4316 Lanai Rd., Encino 91436.

Immaculate Heart Retreat House, 3431 Waverly Dr., Los Angeles 90027. (Days of Recollection only.)

Jesuit Retreat House, P.O. Box 128, Los Altos 94022.

La Casa de Maria, 800 El Bosque Rd., Santa Barbara 93108.

Manresa Retreat House (m*), P.O. Box K, Azusa 91702.

Mary and Joseph Retreat Center, 5300 Crest Rd., Rancho Palos Verdes 90274.

Mater Dolorosa Retreat House (m*), 700 N. Sunnyside Ave., Sierra Madre 91024.

Mission San Miguel, San Miguel 93451.

Mount Mary Immaculate, 3254 Gloria Terr., Lafayette 94549.

Mt. Tabor Monastery, 17001 Tomki Rd., Redwood Valley 95470.

New Camaldoli Immaculate Heart Hermitage (m*, private), Big Sur 93920.

Old Mission San Luis Rey Retreat, P.O. Box 409, San Luis Rey 92068.

Poverello of Assisi Retreat House, 1519 Woodworth St., San Fernando 91340.

Sacred Heart Retreat House (w*), 920 E. Alhambra Rd., Alhambra 91801.

St. Andrew's Priory Retreat House, Valyermo 93563.

St. Anthony's Retreat House, 43816 Sierra Dr., Three Rivers 93271.

St. Charles Priory, Benet Hill, Oceanside 92054.

St. Clare's Retreat (w*), 2381 Laurel Glen Rd. Santa Cruz 95065.

St. Francis Retreat, P.O. Box 1070, San Juan Bautista 95045.

St. Joseph's Salesian Youth Center (St. Dominic Savio Retreat House) (y), 8301 Arroyo Dr., Rosemead 91770.

San Damiano Retreat, P.O. Box 767, Danville 94526.

Santa Sabina Center, 1520 Grand Ave., San Rafael 94901.

Serra Retreat, P.O. Box 127, Malibu 90265.

Vallombrosa Center (w*), 250 Oak Grove Ave., Menlo Park 94025.

Villa Maria del Mar, Santa Cruz. Mailing address, 2-1918 E. Cliff Dr., Santa Cruz 95062.

Colorado: Bethlehem Center, RR 1, Box 192, Broomfield 80020.

Convent of St. Walburga, 6717 S. Boulder Rd., Boulder 80303.

El Pomar Center, 1661 Mesa Ave., Colorado Springs 80906.

Sacred Heart Retreat House, Box 185, Sedalia 80135.

Connecticut: Cenacle Center for Meditation and Spiritual Renewal, Wadsworth St., P.O. Box 550, Middletown 06457.

Edmundite Apostolate and Conference Center, Enders Island, Mystic 06355.

Holy Family Retreat (m, mc*), 303 Tunxis Rd., West Hartford 06107.

Immaculata Retreat House, Route 32, Windham Rd., Willimantic 06226.

Mercy Center, 167 Neck Rd., Madison 06443.

Our Lady of Calvary Retreat (w*), Colton St., Farmington 06032.

Villa Maria Retreat House, 159 Sky Meadow Dr., Stamford 06903.

Delaware: St. Francis Renewal Center, 1901 Prior Rd., Wilmington 19809.

District of Columbia: Washington Retreat House (w*), 4000 Harewood Rd. N.E., Washington 20017.

Florida: Cenacle Retreat House, 1400 S. Dixie Highway, Lantana 33462.

Dominican Retreat House (Mary Queen of Apostles), 7275 S.W. 124th St., Kendall 33156.

Franciscan Center, 3010 Perry Ave., Tampa 33603.

Holy Name Priory, P.O. Drawer H, St. Leo 33574.

Our Lady of Florida Retreat House, 1300 US Hwy. No. 1, North Palm Beach 33408.

St. Leo's Abbey (m), St. Leo 33574.

Georgia: Ignatius House, 6700 Riverside Dr. N.W., Atlanta 30328.

Monastery of the Holy Spirit (m), 3780 Hwy. 212 S.W., Conyers 30207.

Idaho: Nazareth, 4450 N. Five Mile Rd., Boise 83704.

Illinois: Aylesford Carmelite Spiritual Center, I-55 at Cass Ave., N, Darien 60559.

Bellarmine Hall (m*), Box 268, Barrington 60010.

Bishop Lane Retreat House, R.R. 2, Box 214 A, Rockford 61102.

Cabrini Retreat Center, 9430 Golf Rd., Des Plaines 60016.

Cenacle Retreat House, 513 Fullerton Parkway, Chicago 60614.

Cenacle Retreat and Conference Center, P.O. Box 340, Warrenville 60555.

Childerley Retreat House, 506 McHenry Rd., Wheeling 60090.

Christian Life Center, 1209 W. Ogden Ave., La Grange Park 60525.

Divine Word International, Techny 60082.

Franciscan Apostolic Center, P.O. Box 42, Sangamon Ave., Springfield 67205.

King's House, N. 66th St., Belleville 62223.

King's House of Retreats, Box 165, Henry 61537.

La Salle Manor, Christian Brothers Retreat House, Plano 60545.

Longwood Cenacle, 11600 Longwood Dr., Chicago 60643.

National Shrine of Our Lady of the Snows, 9500 W. Illinois Route 15, Belleville 62223.

Our Lady of Angels Retreat and Renewal Center, 1901 E. 18th St., Quincy 62301.

Resurrection Center, 2710 S. Country Club Rd., Woodstock 60098.

Sacred Heart Center, 3000 Central Rd., Rolling Meadows 60008.

St. Francis Retreat, Mayslake, 1717 31st St., Oak Brook 60521.

St. Mary's Retreat House, P.O. Box 608, 1400 Main St., Lemont 60439.

Tolentine Center, 20300 Governors Highway, Olympia Fields 60461.

Viatorian Villa, 3015 N. Bayview Lane, McHenry 60050.

Villa Redeemer, Box 6, 1111 Milwaukee Ave., Glenview 60025.

Indiana: Alverna Center, 8140 Spring Mill Rd., Indianapolis 46260.

Crosier Center, 2620 E. Wallen Rd., Ft. Wayne 46825.

John XXIII Center, 407 W. McDonald St., Hartford City 47348.

Kordes Enrichment Center, R.R. 3, Box 200, Ferdinand 47532.

Lourdes Retreat House (m*), Box 156, Cedar Lake 46303.

Mount Saint Francis Retreat Center, Mount Saint Francis 47146.

Our Lady of Fatima Retreat House, 5353 E. 56th St., Indianapolis 46226.

Our Lady of Fatima Retreat Center, Box O, Notre Dame 46556.

St. Jude Guest House, St. Meinrad 47577.

St. Maur Theological Center, 4545 Northwestern Ave., Indianapolis 46208.

Sarto Retreat House, 4200 N. Kentucky Ave., Evansville 47711.

Seimetz Renewal Center, 1441 Hoffman St., Hammond 46327.

Solitude of St. Joseph, Notre Dame, Ind. 46556.

Iowa: American Martyrs Retreat House, 2209 N. Union Rd., Cedar Falls 50613.

Colfax Interfaith Spiritual Center, Box 37, Colfax, 50054.

Kansas: St. Augustine Retreat Center, A 3301 Parallel Parkway, Kansas City 66104.

Villa Christi Retreat House, 3033 W. Second St., Wichita 67203.

Kentucky: Marydale Retreat Center, 695 Donaldson Rd., Erlanger 41018.

Our Lady of Gethsemani (m, private), The Guestmaster, Abbey of Gethsemani, Trappist 40073.

Saint Thomas Center, 170 Crabbs Lane, Louisville 40206.

Louisiana: Abbey Christian Life Center, St. Joseph's Abbey, St. Benedict 70457.

Ave Maria Retreat House, Route 1, Box 0368 AB, Marrero 70072.

Cenacle Retreat House (w*), 5500 St. Mary St., P.O. Box 8115, Metairie 70011.

Manresa House of Retreats (m), P.O. Box 89, Convent 70723.

Maryhill Retreat House (Christian Life Center), 600 Maryhill Rd., Pineville 71360.

Our Lady of the Oaks Retreat House, P.O. Drawer D, Grand Coteau 70541.

Maine: St. Paul's Center, Oblate Fathers Retreat House (French-English), 136 State St., Augusta 04330.

Maryland: Bon Secours Spiritual Center, Marriottsville, Md. 21104.

CYO Retreat Center, P.O. Box 4235, 401 Randolph Rd., Silver Spring 20904.

CYO Retreat House (y*), 15523 York Rd.,Sparks 21152.

Christian Brothers Spiritual Center (y*), Rt. 85 South, Adamstown 21710.

Loyola Retreat House-on-Potomac, Faulkner 20632.

Manresa-on-Severn, P.O. Box 9, Annapolis 21404.

St. Joseph Spiritual Center, 3800 Frederick Ave., Baltimore 21229.

Massachusetts: Calvary Retreat Center, Passionist Community, 59 South St., Shrewsbury 01545.

Campion Renewal Center, 319 Concord Rd., Weston 02193.

Cenacle Retreat House, 200 Lake St., Brighton, Boston 02135.

Christian Formation Center, 475 River Rd., Andover 01810

Eastern Point Retreat House, Gonzaga Hall, Gloucester 01930.

Espousal Center, 554 Lexington St., Waltham 02154.

Esther House of Spiritual Renewal, Sisters of St. Anne, 783 Grove St., Worcester 01605.

Genesis Spiritual Life Center, 53 Mill St., Westfield 01085.

Glastonbury Abbey (Benedictine Monks), 16 Hull St., Hingham 02043.

Guest Retreat House (m*), St. Joseph's Abbey, Spencer 01562.

Holy Cross Fathers Retreat House, 490 Washington St., N. Easton 02356.

Jesuit Center, Sullivan Square, Charlestown, Boston 02129.

La Salette Center for Christian Living, 947 Park St., Attleboro 02703.

Loretto Retreat House, Jeffrey's Neck Rd., Ipswich 01938.

Marian Center (w*), 1365 Northampton St., Holyoke 01040.

Mater Dei Retreat House (boys), Old Groveland Rd., Bradford 01830.

Miramar Retreat House, Duxbury, 02332.

Mother of Sorrows Retreat House (m*), 110 Monastery Ave., W. Springfield 01089.

Mt. Carmel Christian Life Center, Oblong Rd., Williamstown 01267.

Sacred Heart Retreat House, Salesians of St. John Bosco, P.O. Box 271, Ipswich 01938.

St. Stephen Priory (Dominican), 20 Glen St., Box 370, Dover, Mass. 02030.

Salvatorian Center, 30 East St., Methuen 01844.

Michigan: Blessed Sacrament Retreat House, Sacramentine Sisters, Conway 49722.

Capuchin Retreat, Box 188, Washington 48094.

Colombiere Retreat/Conference Center, 9075 Big Lake Rd., Clarkston 48016.

Manresa Jesuit Retreat House, 1390 Quarton Rd., Bloomfield Hills 48013.

Mary Reparatrix Retreat Center (w*), 13600 Virgil, Detroit 48223.

Marygrove Center, Garden 49835.

Portiuncula in the Pines, 703 E. Main St., De Witt 48820.

Queen of Angels Retreat, Box 2026, 3400 S. Washington Blvd., Saginaw 48605.

St. Basil's Center, 3990 Giddings Rd., Pontiac 48057.

St. Clare Capuchin Retreat, 1975 N. River Rd., St. Clair 48079.

St. Lazare Retreat House, W. Spring Lake Rd., Spring Lake 49456.

St. Mary's Retreat House, 775 W. Drahner Rd., Oxford 48051.

St. Paul of the Cross Retreat House, 23333 Schoolcraft, Detroit 48223.

Minnesota: The Cenacle, 1221 Wayzata Blvd., Wayzata 55391.

Center for Spiritual Development, Box 538, 211 Tenth St., Bird Island 55310.

Christian Brothers Retreat Center, Rt. 2, Box 18, Marine-on-St. Croix 55047.

Christian Community Center, Assisi Heights, Box 4900, Rochester 55903.

The Dwelling Place, 216 3rd Ave. S., Sauk Rapids 56379.

Epiphany House of Prayer, 266 Summit Ave., St. Paul 55102.

Franciscan Retreats, Conventual Franciscan Friars, Prior Lake 55372.

Jesuit Retreat House (m), 8243 N. Demon-

treville Trail North, Lake Elmo 55109.

King's House of Retreats, 621 S. First Ave., Buffalo 55313.

Maryhill Retreat House, Society of Daughters of the Heart of Mary, 260 Summit Ave., St. Paul 55102.

Minneapolis Catholic Youth Center (y, mc), 2120 Park Ave. S., Minneapolis 55404.

Villa Maria Center, Frontenac 55026.

Welch Center (y), 605 N. Central Ave., Duluth 55807.

Missouri: Cenacle Retreat House, 900 S. Spoede Rd., St. Louis 63131.

Maria Fonte Solitude (private), P.O. Box 322, High Ridge 63049.

Marian Hall Retreat Center, Conception Seminary College, Conception 64433.

Marianist Apostolic Center, Glencoe 63038.

Our Lady of Assumption Abbey (m, w), Trappists, Rt. 5, Box 193, Ava 65608.

Our Lady of the Ozarks, P.O. Box 424, Carthage 64836.

Pallottine Renewal Center, R.R. 2, 15270 Old Halls Ferry Rd., Florissant 63034.

Passionist Retreat of Our Lady, Retreat House, Passionist Fathers and Brothers, 3036 Bellerive Dr., St. Louis 63121.

Queen of Heaven Solitude (private), Rt. 1, Box 107A, Marionville 65705.

St. Pius X Abbey, Abbey Rd., Pevely 63070.

The White House Retreat (m), 7400 Christopher Dr., St. Louis 63129.

Montana: Ursuline Retreat Center, 2300 Central Ave., Great Falls 59401.

Nebraska: Crosier Renewal Center, 223 E. 14th St., P.O. Box 789, Hastings 68901.

Good Counsel, R.R. 1, Box 110, Waverly 68462.

St. Columbans Foreign Mission Society, St. Columbans 68056.

New Hampshire: The Common - St. Joseph Monastery, Discalced Carmelite Friars, Peterborough 03458.

New Hampshire Monastery, Hundred Acres, New Boston 03070.

Oblate Fathers Retreat House, Rt. 3A, Lowell Rd., Hudson 03051.

St. Francis Retreat Center, 860 Central Rd., Rye Beach 03871.

New Jersey: Bethlehem Center for Prayer and Spiritual Growth (hermitage experience), Pleasant Hill Rd., Box 315, Chester 07930.

Blackwood Center, St. Pius X House, Box 216, Blackwood 08012.

Blessed Trinity Missionary Retreat Cenacle, 1190 Long Hill Rd., Stirling 07980.

Carmel Retreat House, 1071 Ramapo Valley Rd., Mahwah 07430.

Cenacle Retreat House, 411 River Rd., Highland Park 08904.

Franciscan Friars Retreat Center, St. Bonaventure Friary, 174 Ramsey St., Paterson 07501.

Good Shepherd Center, 74 Kahdena Rd., Morristown 07960.

Loyola House of Retreats, 161 James St., Morristown 07960.

Marianist Christian Family Living Center (families), Cape and Yale Ave., Cape May Point 08212.

Mt. St. John Academy, Gladstone, N.J. 07934.

Queen of Peace Retreat House, Route 206, Newton 07860.

St. Joseph's Villa (w), Srs. of St. John the Baptist, Peapack 07977.

San Alfonso Retreat House, 755 Ocean Ave., Long Branch 07740.

Villa Pauline Retreat and Guest House (w*), Hilltop Rd., Mendham 07945.

Xavier Center, Convent Station 07961.

New Mexico: Holy Cross Retreat House, P.O. Box 158, Mesilla Park 88047.

Our Lady of Guadalupe Monastery (families - pentecostal), Pecos 87552.

Our Lady Queen of Peace, 5825 Coors Rd. S.W., Albuquerque 87105.

New York: Bethany Retreat House, Route 208, Highland Mills 10930.

Bethlehem Retreat House (m*), Abbey of the Genesee, Piffard 14533.

Bishop Molloy Retreat House, 86-45 178th St., Jamaica, L.I. 11432.

Cabrini-on-the Hudson, West Park, N.Y. 12493.

Cardinal Spellman Retreat House, Passionist Fathers, 5801 Palisade Ave., Bronx (Riverdale) 10471.

Cenacle Center for Spiritual Renewal, Cenacle Rd., Lake Ronkonkoma 11779.

The Cenacle: Center for Spiritual Renewal, 693 East Ave., Rochester 14607.

Cenacle Retreat House, State Rd., P.O. Box 467, Bedford Village 10506.

Christ the King Retreat House, 500 Brookford Rd., Syracuse 13224.

Cormaria Retreat House, Sag Harbor, L.I. 11963.

Diocesan Cursillo Center (Spanish), 118 Congress St., Brooklyn 11201.

Dominican Retreat House, 1945 Union St., Schenectady 12309.

Don Bosco Retreat Center, Filor's Lane, West Haverstraw 10993.

Graymoor Christian Unity Center, Graymoor, Garrison 10524.

Jesuit Retreat House, North American Martyrs Shrine, Auriesville 12016.

Mary Reparatrix Retreat Center, 14 E. 29th St., New York 10016.

Monastery of the Precious Blood (w), Ft.

Hamilton Parkway and 54th St., Brooklyn 11219.

Mount Alvernia Retreat House, Wappingers Falls 12590.

Mount Manresa Retreat House, 239 Fingerboard Rd., Staten Island 10305.

Notre Dame Retreat House, Box 342, Foster Rd., Canandaigua 14424.

Queen of Apostles Retreat House, North Haven, Sag Harbor 11963.

Regina Maria Retreat House (w*), 77 Brinkerhoff St., Plattsburgh 12901.

Retreat House, Basilian Monastery, East Beach Rd., Glen Cove 11542.

St. Andrew's House, 89 A St. Andrew's Rd., Walden 12586.

St. Columban's Retreat House, P.O. Box 816, Derby 14047.

St. Gabriel Passionist Retreat House, 64 Burns Rd., P.O. Box P, Shelter Island 11965.

St. Ignatius Renewal Center, Diocese of Buffalo, 6969 Strickler Rd., Clarence Center 14032. Poustinia available.

St. Ignatius Retreat House, Searington Rd., Manhasset, L.I. 11030.

St. Joseph Center (Spanish Center), 523 W. 142nd St., New York 10031.

Stella Maris Retreat House and Center for Renewal, 130 E. Genesee St., Skaneateles 13152.

Stella Niagara Center of Renewal, 4421 Lower River Rd., Stella Niagara 14144.

Tagaste Monastery Retreat House (m, y), Suffern 10901.

North Carolina: Maryhurst Retreat House, P.O. Box 138, Pinehurst 28374.

North Dakota: Queen of Peace Retreat, Redemptorist Fathers, 1310 N. Broadway, Fargo 58102.

Ohio: Bergamo Conference Center, 4435 E. Patterson Rd., Dayton 45430.

Friarhurst Retreat House, 8136 Wooster Pike, Cincinnati 45227.

House of Prayer, 6832 Convent Blvd., Sylvania 43560.

Jesuit Renewal Center, 5361 S. Milford Rd., Milford 45150.

Jesuit Retreat House, 5629 State Rd., Cleveland 44134.

Loyola of the Lakes, 700 Killinger Rd., Clinton 44216.

Maria Stein Center, 2365 St. Johns Rd., Maria Stein 45860.

Men of Milford Retreat House (m*), Box 348, Milford 45150.

MSC Center, Rt. 4, Shelby 44875.

Our Lady of Consolation Renewal Center, 320 West St., Carey 43316.

Our Lady of the Pines, 1250 Tiffin St., Fremont 43420.

Sacred Heart, 3128 Logan Ave., Box 6074, Youngstown 44501.

St. Anthony Pilgrim House, 321 Clay St., Carey 43316. (Facilities only.)

St. Joseph Christian Life Center, 18485 Lake Shore Blvd., Cleveland 44119.

St. Joseph Renewal Center, 200 St. Francis Ave., Tiffin 44883.

Shrine Center for Renewal, Diocese of Columbus, 5277 E. Broad St., Columbus 43213.

Oklahoma: St. Gregory's Abbey, Shawnee 74801.

Oregon: Loyola Retreat House (Jesuit Center for Spiritual Renewal), 3220 S.E. 43rd St., Portland 97206.

Mt. Angel Abbey Guest-Retreat Center, St. Benedict 97373.

Our Lady of Peace Retreat (w*), 3600 S. W. 170th Ave., Beaverton 97005.

St. Benedict Lodge, 56630 N. Bank Rd., McKenzie Bridge 97401.

Shalom Prayer Center, Benedictine Sisters, Mt. Angel 97362.

Trappist Abbey Retreat (m*, private), P.O. Box 97, Lafayette 97127.

Pennsylvania: Byzantine Catholic Seminary (m), 3605 Perrysville Ave., Pittsburgh 15214.

Cenacle Retreat House (w*), 4721 Fifth Ave., Pittsburgh 15213.

Dominican Retreat House, Ashbourne Rd. and Juniper Ave., Elkins Park 19117.

Fatima House, Rolling Hills Rd., Ottsville 18942.

Jesuit Center for Spiritual Growth, Church Rd., Wernersville 19565.

Maria Wald Retreat House, Convent of the Precious Blood, New Holland Ave., Shillington 19607.

Marian Hall, St. Joseph Convent/Academy, R.D. 2, Columbia 17512.

Mercy Center, Box 370, Dallas 18612.

Mount St. Macrina Retreat Center, Mt. St. Macrina, Box 878, Uniontown 15401.

Our Lady of Fatima Center, Griffin Rd., Box 143, Elmhurst 18416.

St. Alphonsus Retreat House (m), Box 218, Tobyhanna 18466 (1,200).

St. Ann's Retreat House, Carrolltown Rd., Ebensburg 15931.

St. Emma Retreat House, 1001 Harvey St., Greensburg 15601.

St. Fidelis Seminary, Herman 16039.

St. Francis Retreat House, 3918 Chipman Rd., Easton 18042.

St. Francis Retreat House (w), Monocacy Manor, 395 Bridal Path Rd., Bethlehem 18017.

St. Gabriel's Retreat House (w), 631 Griffin Pond Rd., Clarks Summit 18411.

St. Joseph's-in-the-Hills (m*), Malvern 19355.

St. Paul of the Cross Retreat House, 148 Monastery Ave., Pittsburgh 15203.

Saint Raphaela Mary Retreat House, 616 Coopertown Rd., Haverford 19041.

St. Vincent Retreat House (m*, summer), Latrobe 15650.

Villa Maria Retreat Center, Box 208, Wernersville 19565.

Villa of Our Lady Retreat House (w, mc), Mt. Pocono 18344.

Rhode Island: Carmel Spiritual Center, 21 Battery St., Newport 02840.

Ephpheta House — A Center for Renewal, 10 Manville Hill Rd; mailing address, P.O. Box 1, Manville 02838.

Our Lady of Peace Spiritual Life Center, Ocean Rd., Narragansett 02882.

St. Dominic Savio Youth Center (y*), Broad Rock Rd., Box 67, Peace Dale 02883.

South Carolina: Springbank Christian Center, Dominican Retreat House, Kingstree 29556.

South Dakota: St. Martin's Community Retreat Center, R.R. 4, Box 253, Rapid City 57701.

Sioux Spiritual Center, Diocese of Rapid City, Plainview, 57771.

Tennessee: House of the Lord, 1306 Dellwood Ave., Memphis 38127.

House of the Lord, Rt. 4, Box 251, Paris 38242.

Texas: Catholic Renewal Center of North Texas, 4503 Bridge St., Ft. Worth 76103.

Cenacle Retreat House, 420 N. Kirkwood, Houston 77079.

Christian Holiday House and Renewal Center, Oblate Fathers, P.O. Box 635, Dickinson 77539.

Holy Name Retreat Center (m*), 430 Bunker Hill Rd., Houston 77024.

Montserrat Jesuit Retreat House, P.O. Box 398, Lake Dallas 75065.

Our Lady of the Pillar Christian Renewal Center, 2507 N.W. 36th St., San Antonio 78228.

Saint Joseph Retreat House (Casa San Jose), 127 Oblate Dr., San Antonio 78216.

San Juan Retreat House, ("El Rancho Alegre"), Diocese of Brownsville, P.O. Box 998, San Juan 78589.

Utah: Our Lady of the Holy Trinity Retreat House (m), Huntsville 84317.

Our Lady of the Mountains, 1794 Lake St., Ogden 84401.

Virginia: Dominican Retreat, 7103 Old Dominion Dr., McLean 22101.

Franciscan Center for Spiritual Renewal, Rt. 642, Box 825, Winchester 22601.

Holy Family Retreat House, Redemptorist Fathers, Box 3151, Hampton 23363.

Missionhurst Retreat Center, 4651 N. 25th St., Arlington 22207.

Spiritual Renewal Center (Genesis House), Rt. 2, Box 388 B, Richmond 23233.

Washington: Camp Field Retreat Center, P.O. Box 128, Leavenworth 98826.

Immaculate Heart Retreat House, Route 3, Box 653, Spokane 99203.

Redemptorist Palisades Retreat, P.O. Box 3739, Federal Way 98003.

St. Peter the Apostle Diocesan Retreat Center, Route 1, Box 86, Cowiche 98923.

Visitation Retreat Center (w), 3200 S.W. Dash Point Rd., Federal Way 98003.

West Virginia: Cenacle Retreat House, 1114 Virginia St. E., Charleston 25301.

St. Joseph Pastoral Center, Rt. 6, Vienna 26101.

Wisconsin: Cardoner Jesuit Retreat Center, 1501 S. Layton Blvd., Milwaukee 53215.

Holy Name Retreat House, Chambers Island; mailing address, 1825 Riverside Drive, P.O. Box 337, Green Bay 54305.

Jesuit Retreat House, 4800 Fahrnwald Rd., Oshkosh 54901.

Marynook — House of the Lord, 500 S. 12th St., Galesville 54630.

Monte Alverno Retreat House, 1000 N. Ballard Rd., Appleton 54911.

Mother of Perpetual Help, 1800 N. Timber Trail Lane, Oconomowoc 53066.

Retreat/Renewal Center, Notre Dame of the Lake, 700 W. Highland Rd., Mequon 53092.

St. Anthony Retreat Center, Marathon 54448.

St. Benedict Center (ecumenical retreat and conference center), Fox Bluff, P.O. Box 5070, Madison 53705.

St. Francis Friary and Retreat Center, 503 S. Browns Lake Dr., Burlington 53105.

St. Joseph's Retreat Center, Bailey's Harbor 54202.

St. Vincent Pallotti Center, Rt. 3, Box 61, Elkhorn 53121.

Schoenstatt Center, W. 284 N. 698 Cherry Lane, Waukesha 53186.

EVANGELIZATION

Evangelizers must understand culture and bring the "celebrations (of Christianity) into the cultures of other persons," declared Archbishop Jean Jadot in August, 1982, during the midwestern Fourth Annual Catholic Lay Celebration of Evangelization. Speaking in Minneapolis, he said: "We have more to do than to condemn what is around us today. We are called to restore a true Christian culture; and today, I am afraid, a Christian culture would be a counter-culture." Archbishop Jadot was apostolic delegate to the United States before becoming pro-prefect of the Vatican Secretariat for Non-Christians.

The keynoter of the celebration was Paulist Father Alvin Illig.

HOUSE OF PRAYER EXPERIENCE

(Source: Sister Ann E. Chester, I.H.M., 529 Stewart Rd., Monroe, Mich. 48202.)

The purpose of the House of Prayer Experience (HOPE) movement is to help active religious and priests and lay persons to acquire a contemporary style of contemplative life for renewal, inner growth and a more joyful personal and communal life in the light of the Gospel.

The starting point of participation in the movement is an extended period, from several weeks to several years, of concentration on intensive prayer with a community — a house of prayer experience. The result sought is an apostolic spirituality integrating prayer with action — especially for justice and peace.

Programs

The communities of houses of prayer consist of a relatively stable core of members with an authentic call to a deeper prayer life and of guests who come and go for shorter or longer periods of participation. The stability of the core group, while not a now-and-forever type of commitment, is such as to guarantee continuity in programs and the resources of experienced personnel in conducting them.

Program elements include the liturgy, meditation, scriptural reading and dialogue, shared prayer in the shared life of community, silence and solitude, search for new forms of prayer and for new adaptations of traditional forms — all against the background of existential conditions. The elements are oriented toward individual and personal needs and to various types of ministry, such as contemplative prayer itself and ministries concerned with a parish, the family, youth, inner-city pastoral work, spiritual development, the charismatic movement.

Houses

Two hundred and four listings were reported in the third *Annual Directory, Houses of Prayer*, released in the spring of 1979 by Clarity Publishing, Inc. (75 Champlain St., Albany, N.Y. 12204). Eighty-two of the houses were sponsored by more than 50 religious congregations of men and women, and 16 by dioceses. The 204 figure represented a 46 per cent increase in listings over those reported in 1978. Fifty-nine of the houses had programs focusing on the spiritual traditions of major religious orders. Houses of prayer or prayer study experience centers were located in 36 of the 50 states. There were also 13 Canadian listings.

Kresge House in Detroit, which provided services to the movement for 10 years, closed its door Aug. 31, 1980.

Lay Persons and Their Apostolate

SPECIAL AGENCIES

Some of the following agencies are engaged in carrying out programs of the United States Catholic Conference. Additional agencies are reported in other Almanac entries.

Religious Education/CCD (Confraternity of Christian Doctrine): Its objective is the religious education of persons from early childhood through adult life.

The modern expansion of Religious Education/CCD dates from publication of the encyclical letter *Acerbo Nimis* by Pope St. Pius X in 1905. His directive, that CCD programs be established in every parish, was incorporated in the Code of Canon Law and was reaffirmed by the Second Vatican Council in the *Decree on the Bishops' Pastoral Office in the Church.*

Religious Education/CCD programs are parish-based. Policies are developed by parish boards or commissions, and responsibility for administering programs rests ideally with a coordinator or director who is a trained professional in religious education.

On the diocesan level, Religious Education is coordinated by a director with a staff operating under the title of an office of religious education or a similar title. The diocesan office coordinates and acts as consultant to the work of local parish and regional programs; it conducts teacher-training courses, issues guidelines for unified programs, provides overall in-service aid and resources for local staffs and programs.

On the national level, Religious Education/CCD (formerly called the National Center for the Confraternity of Christian Doctrine, and since 1969 under the Department of Education, U.S. Catholic Conference) provides field and informational services along with representation for local diocesan programs and staffs. On the international level, it participates in programs which find their roots with the Vatican congregations that deal with religious education or catechesis.

Publications under the direction of Religious Education/CCD include *Living Light,* Catechetical Sunday materials and numerous other publications developed in conjunction with the National Conference of Diocesan Directors of Religious Education-CCD.

The Rev. David Beebe is representative for Religious Education/CCD in the Department of Education, U.S. Catholic Conference.

Offices are located at 1312 Massachusetts Ave. N.W., Washington, D.C. 20005.

National Council of Catholic Men: A federation of Catholic organizations through which Catholic men may be heard nationally on matters of common interest. NCCM is a constituent of the National Council of Catholic Laity.

The president is William H. Sandweg.

Offices are located at 4712 Randolph Dr., Annandale, Va. 22003.

National Council of Catholic Women: A federation of some 10,000 organizations of Catholic women in the U.S.; founded in 1920. NCCW unites Catholic organizations and individual Catholic women of the U.S., develops their leadership potential, assists them to act upon current issues in the Church and society, provides a medium through which Catholic women may speak and act upon matters of common interest, and relates to other national and international organizations in the solution of present-day problems. It is an affiliate of the World Union of Catholic Women's Organizations.

The official publication is *Catholic Woman,* issued 6 times a year.

The president is Mrs. Mary Meismer.

National office: 1312 Massachusetts Ave. N.W., Washington, D.C. 20005.

National Council of Catholic Laity: Formed in 1971 by the National Council of Catholic Men and the National Council of Catholic Women to provide direction and guidance to existing and new lay organizations. It sponsors conferences and is a contact agency for information about specialized groups in the Church. The publication is *NCCL News.*

The principal officers are Thomas Simmons, president; Isabelle Collora and David Bartkus, vice presidents.

The mailing address is P.O. Box 14525, Cincinnati, Ohio 45214.

National Catholic Rural Life Conference: Founded in 1923 through the efforts of Bishop Edwin V. O'Hara for the purpose of promoting the general welfare of rural people by a program of extensive services, publications and rural-related activities. Publications include the monthly *Catholic Rural Life.*

The conference has approximately 5,000 members among rural pastors, farmers, teachers, sociologists, economists, agricultural agents and officials. There are 127 officially appointed diocesan rural life directors.

Most Rev. Lawrence J. McNamara, bishop of Grand Island, Neb., is president. Mr. Gregory Cusack is executive director.

National headquarters are located at 4625 N.W. Beaver Dr., Des Moines, Ia. 50322.

Catholic Relief Services — USCC: The official overseas aid and development agency of American Catholics; it is a separately incorporated organization of the U.S. Catholic Conference.

CRS was founded in 1943 by the bishops of

the United States to help civilians in Europe and North Africa caught in the disruption and devastation of World War II.

Initially, CRS collected, purchased and shipped to war-torn countries huge quantities of food, clothing, medicines and other relief supplies which were distributed to hundreds of thousands of displaced persons, prisoners of war, bombed-out families, widows, orphans and other war victims.

As conditions in Europe improved in the late 1940s and early 1950s, the works conducted by CRS spread to other continents and areas — Asia, Africa and Latin America.

CRS staffs offices in 50 countries and has local representatives in another 35 countries. The agency works with local counterpart organizations to provide humanitarian assistance and emergency relief. Help is given strictly in response to need; race, creed, color and political affiliation are no consideration.

Although best known for its record of disaster response, compassionate aid to refugees and commitment to reconstruction and rehabilitation, CRS places primary focus on long-term development projects designed to help people to help themselves and to determine their own future.

Administrative funding for CRS comes from an annual collection, the Catholic Relief Services Annual Appeal (known variously as Bishops' Relief or American Catholic Overseas Aid Appeal), held during Lent in most of the 18,000 Catholic parishes of the U.S.

Major support is derived from private, individual donors through direct contributions and through a program of sacrificial giving called Operation Rice Bowl. Funds are also received from philanthropic foundations and humanitarian organizations in the U.S. and Europe. Clothing is collected each year, generally at Thanksgiving, for distribution overseas. More than 11 million pounds of used clothing, blankets and bolt goods are contributed annually through Catholic churches.

Assistance is received from the U.S. Government in several forms: foodstuffs available under Title II of Public Law 480, ocean-freight subsidies for government food and other privately generated relief supplies, and grants for both emergency programs and community development projects.

In 1981, the CRS global program in 70 countries employed 1,100 people and was valued at $350 million.

CRS headquarters are located at 1011 First Ave., New York, N.Y. 10022.

Family Life, USCC Department of Education: Established in 1931 as a central service agency for assisting, developing and coordinating family life programs throughout the United States.

It represents the family perspective to all aspects of church life; has responsibility for implementation of the Plan of Pastoral Action for Family Ministry and guidelines from the 1980 Synod of Bishops; handles communications and relations between the National Conference of Catholic Bishops and/or the U.S. Catholic Conference, government agencies, other churches and various movements and organizations outside the Church in marriage- and family-related issues.

Rev. Thomas F. Lynch is representative for family life in the Department of Education, U.S. Catholic Conference.

Headquarters are located at 1312 Massachusetts Ave. N.W., Washington, D.C. 20005.

SPECIAL APOSTOLATES AND GROUPS

Apostleship of the Sea: An international Catholic organization for the moral, social and spiritual welfare of seafarers and those involved in the maritime industry. It was founded in 1920 in Glasgow, Scotland, and formally approved by the Holy See in 1922. It is promoted and directed by the Pontifical Commission for Migrants and Tourism, Piazza San Calisto 16, Rome, Italy 00153. The U.S. unit is the Apostleship of the Sea in the United States, an affiliate of the NCCB-USCC, established in 1947. It serves 80 port chaplains in 73 U.S. ports on the seacoasts and the Great Lakes. Operations include a hospitality and welcoming program as well as counseling and spiritual services carried on by individual port chaplains through Catholic maritime clubs in Mobile, Ala.; Oakland, Wilmington and San Francisco, Calif.; Seattle, Wash.; New Orleans, La.; Miami, Fla. and interfaith clubs located in Milwaukee, Wis.; Newark and Port Elizabeth, N.J.; Houston, Galveston, Corpus Christi and Brownsville, Tex.; Pensacola, Fla.; Baltimore, Md. Recent developments have emphasized the interfaith cooperation on the port level in seamen's ministry. The episcopal promoter of the conference is Most Rev. Rene Gracida, P.O. Drawer 6068, Tallahassee, Fla. 32301. Rev. James E. Dillenburg is national director. Address of the national office is P.O. Box 12824, Pensacola, Fla. 32575. Also affiliated with the Apostleship of the Sea in the United States is the **National Catholic Conference for Seafarers.** The president is Rev. Rivers Patout, Houston International Seamen's Center, P.O. Box 9506, Houston, Tex. 77011.

Auxiliaries of Our Lady of the Cenacle (1878, France): An association of Catholic laywomen, under the direction of the Congregation of Our Lady of the Cenacle, who serve God through their own professions and life styles by means of vows. Members live a fully secular life consecrated according to the spirituality of the Cenacle and pursue individual apostolates. They number approximately 150 throughout the world. U.S. regional director: Sister Barbara Whittemore, r.c., 310 Cenacle Rd., Lake Ronkonkoma, N.Y. 11779.

Catholic Central Union of America (1855): One of the oldest Catholic lay organizations in the U.S., the Union is devoted to the development and vigor of Christian principles in personal, social, cultural, economic and civic life. It was the first society ever given an official mandate for Catholic Action by a committee of the American bishops, in 1936. The Central Bureau in St. Louis is the center for the separate but coordinated direction of the National Catholic Women's Union. The headquarters is also a publishing house (*Social Justice Review, The Catholic Woman's Journal,* other publications), a library of German-Americana and Catholic Americana, a clearinghouse for information, and a center for works of charity. Aid is given to the missions, and maintenance and direction are provided for St. Elizabeth's Settlement and Day Nursery in St. Louis. Union membership is approximately 12,000. Harvey J. Johnson is director of the Central Bureau located at 3835 Westminster Place, St. Louis, Mo. 63108. (See also: National Catholic Women's Union.)

Catholic Medical Mission Board (1928): Founded by Dr. Paluel Flagg and the Rev. Edward Garesche, S.J. Its purposes are to gather and ship medical supplies for the sick poor in mission lands, and to recruit and assign medical and paramedical personnel to overseas mission hospitals and dispensaries. Since its foundation, it has shipped approximately 45 million pounds of supplies. In 1981, more than $8.5 million in medicines were shipped to 1,711 mission distribution centers in 47 countries. Also in 1981, 44 medical volunteers were placed in 13 countries. Rev. Joseph J. Walter, S.J., is the director. Office: 10 W. 17th Street, New York, N.Y. 10011.

Center for Applied Research in the Apostolate (CARA): A research and development agency in the field of the Church's worldwide religious and social mission. Its purpose is to gather information for the use of decision-makers in evaluating the present status of the Church's mission of service and in planning programs of development toward greater effectiveness of its multiphased ministry in the future. CARA has research and planning programs focused on: church personnel (recruitment, selection training, utilization, effectiveness), overseas areas, diocesan planning, religious life, health care ministry, and other subjects. CARA was incorporated as a nonprofit corporation in the District of Columbia Aug. 5, 1964. Rev. Cassian J. Yuhaus, C.P., is president. Offices are located at 3700 Oakview Terrace, N.E., Washington, D.C. 20017.

Christian Family Movement (CFM) (1947): Originating in Chicago and having a membership of married couples and individuals, its purpose is to Christianize family life and create communities conducive to Christian family life. Since 1968, CFM in the U.S. has included couples from all Christian churches. The International Confederation of Christian Family Movements embraces a worldwide membership. National and international headquarters: Box 272, Ames, Iowa 50010. Spanish-speaking, CFM was organized in 1969 under the title **Movimiento Familiar Cristiano (MFC).** National spiritual director: Rev. Rafael Miranda, 8011 Williamatte, El Paso, Tex. 79907.

Christian Life Communities: Formerly known as Sodalities of Our Lady, they are groups of men and women, adults and youth, joined with other people involved in living their full Christian vocation and commitment in the world. The governing principles and operating norms of Sodalities, revised in the spirit of documents of the Second Vatican Council, were promulgated and approved by Pope Paul VI in 1971. The Spiritual Exercises of St. Ignatius remain a specific source and characteristic of the spirituality of the movement. Christian Life Communities are located in more than 50 countries; the U.S. Federation is comprised of approximately 150 communities. Eileen C. Burke is executive director. National office: 3721 Westminster Blvd., St. Louis, Mo. 63108. The World Federation office is located in Rome.

Cursillo Movement: An instrument of Christian renewal designed to form and stimulate persons to engage in apostolic action individually and in the organized apostolate, in accordance with the mission which individuals have to transform the environments in which they live into Christian environments. The movement originated in Spain, where the first cursillo was held near Palma, Mallorca, in 1949. It was introduced in the U.S. in 1957 and is functioning in more than 140 dioceses. The method of the movement involves a three-day weekend called a cursillo and a follow-up program known as the post-cursillo.

The weekend is an intensive experience in Christian community living centered on Christ and built around 15 talks (10 by laymen, five by priests), active participation in discussions and related activities, the celebration of the liturgy. The follow-up program focuses on small weekly reunions of three to five persons and larger group reunions, called ultreyas, in which participants share experiences and insights derived from their prayer life, study and apostolic action. The movement operates within the framework of diocesan and parish pastoral plans, and functions autonomously in each diocese under the direction of the bishop. Responsibility for growth and effectiveness rests with a diocesan leaders' school, a diocesan secretariat, or both. Most Rev. Joseph Green, former bishop of Reno, is episcopal advisor to the movement. Gerald P. Hughes is executive director of the National Cursillo Center, P.O. Box 210226, Dallas, Tex. 75211.

Frontier Apostolate (1956): Volunteers for a minimum of two years' service in their professional line (teachers, secretaries, houseparents, etc.) in the Diocese of Prince George, British Columbia, Canada. More than 2,600 have served since the start of the corps by Bishop Fergus O'Grady. There are about 150 men and women from 8 different countries actively engaged in works throughout the diocese. Address: Bishop O'Grady, College Rd., P.O. Box 7000, Prince George, B.C., Canada V2N 3Z2.

Grail, The (1921): An international movement of women concerned about the full development of all peoples, working in education, religious, social and cultural areas. Founded by Rev. Jacques van Ginneken, S.J., in The Netherlands, it was introduced in the U.S. in 1940. The Grail is at work in: Australia, Brazil, Canada, Costa Rica, Egypt, France, Germany, India, Italy, Kenya, The Netherlands, Nigeria, Philippines, Portugal, South Africa, Tanzania, Uganda, United States. U.S. headquarters: Grailville, Loveland, Ohio 45140. International Secretariat: Duisburger Strasse 470, 4330 Mulheim, West Germany.

Group Seven (1971): Started by the Glenmary Home Missioners to recruit Catholic men and women (married, single, religious, permanent deacon), 21 years of age and older for periods of two years or more in the U.S. home mission apostolate, particularly in the 17-state area of Appalachia, the South and Southeast. Members support themselves in their own profession or trade. They are given orientation and opportunity for ongoing mission training. Address: P.O. Box 1376, Wise, Va. 24293.

International Liaison, Inc. (1963): The U.S. Catholic Coordinating Center for Lay Volunteer Ministries, an affiliate of the U.S. Catholic Conference, is engaged in the promotion, recruiting and referral of lay volunteer personnel with church missions, interdenominational and private volunteer agencies throughout the U.S. The organization also assists mission agencies to facilitate participation by lay persons in ministries of the Church. Publications include *The Response,* an annual, and a quarterly newsletter. David J. Suley is the executive secretary. Office: 1234 Massachusetts Ave. N.W., Washington, D.C. 20005.

Jesuit Volunteer Corps (1956): Established by the Oregon Province of the Jesuits, for service to the poor and oppressed. Regional offices are located in Portland, Ore., Oakland, Calif., Houston, Tex., Detroit, Mich., and Philadelphia, Pa. There are 250 volunteers working among Eskimos, on Indian reservations and in inner-city areas. Address for information: P.O. Box 3928, Portland Ore. 97208.

Lay Mission-Helpers Association (1955): It trains and assigns men and women for work in overseas apostolates for periods of three years. Approximately 600 members of the association have served in overseas assignments since 1955. The Rev. Msgr. Lawrence O'Leary is director of the association. Headquarters: 1531 West Ninth St., Los Angeles, Calif. 90015.

The **Mission Doctors Association** recruits, trains and sends Catholic physicians and their families to mission hospitals and clinics throughout the world for tours of two to three years. Address: 1531 W. Ninth St., Los Angeles, Calif. 90015.

Legion of Mary (1921): Founded in Dublin, its purposes are the sanctification of its members and service to others. It is one of the largest lay organizations in the Church. U.S. address for information: The Legion of Mary, St. Louis Regional Senatus, Box 1313, St. Louis, Mo. 63188. The supreme governing body has offices at De Montfort House, North Brunswick St., Dublin 7, Ireland.

Movement for a Better World (1952): An international movement founded by Rev. Riccardo Lombardi, S.J. The U.S. promoting group, like its counterparts in other countries, conducts various types of renewal programs with a distinctive communitarian thrust for the purpose of motivating Christian witness and action for making a better world in accordance with the plan of God. Address for information: Sr. Mary Byrnes, 78 Grand St., Jersey City, N.J. 07302. The movement is a non-governmental organization with the United Nations and has a U.N. office at 777 U.N. Plaza, New York, N.Y. 10017.

Opus Dei: An association of Catholic faithful who strive to practice the Christian virtues, in their own states in life and through the exercise of their own professions or occupations in order to carry on an apostolate of witness to Christ. Since the purpose is strictly spiritual, members are free to hold the most diverse views on temporal matters, thus assuring a real pluralism of opinions in all cultural, economic, political and similar areas. Founded in Madrid in 1928 by Msgr. Josemaria Escriva de Balaguer (1902-1975), it received full approval from the Holy See June 16, 1950. Membership: more than 70,000 of 80 nationalities from all continents in separate branches for men and women. In the U.S., members of Opus Dei, along with nonmembers, conduct apostolic works corporately in major cities in the East, Midwest and on the West Coast. Elsewhere, Opus Dei members are engaged in universities, vocational institutes, training schools for farmers, and numerous other educational and charitable initiatives. An information office is located at 330 Riverside Dr., New York, N.Y. 10025. The legal names of the association in the U.S. are: Opus Dei; The Work of God, Inc.

Pax Christi (1948): International Catholic peace movement. Originated in Lourdes, France, as a union of French and German Catholics to symbolize a mutual effort to heal wounds inflicted by World War II, spread to Poland and Italy, and acquired its international title when it merged with the English organization Pax. A general secretariat is located at Antwerp, Belgium. **Pax Christi USA,** was founded in 1973 to establish peacemaking as a priority for the American Catholic Church, to work for disarmament, primacy of conscience, a just world order, education for peace, and alternatives to violence. A newsletter is published quarterly; membership, 5,000. Sr. Mary Evelyn Jegen, S.N.D., is national coordinator. Address: 3000 N. Mango Ave., Chicago, Ill. 60634.

Pax Romana — American Graduate and Professional Commission: The U.S. affiliate of Pax Romana, an international Catholic movement for intellectual and cultural affairs (see Catholic International Organizations). The president is Professor James E. Dougherty, St. Joseph University, Philadelphia, Pa. 19131. The Pax Romana representative to the United Nations is Professor W. Hilary Lee, Stevens Institute of Technology, Hoboken, N.J. 07030.

Regis College Lay Apostolate (1950): Founded by Sister Mary John Sullivan, C.S.J., it enlists college graduates for a year of teaching service in home and overseas missions. More than 250 lay apostles from Regis College and more than 400 from other colleges have served since the beginning of the program. Headquarters: Regis College, Weston, Mass. 02193

Southwest Volunteer Apostolate: Recruits and places volunteers for work among the Indians and Spanish-speaking of the Diocese of Gallup. Mailing address: P. O. Box 626, Gallup, N.M. 87301.

Center of Concern (1971): An independent, public-interest group engaged in analysis, education and advocacy relating to issues of global concern. Discussion is carried on within the framework of social justice. A newsletter, *Center Focus,* is published bimonthly. Peter J. Henriot, S.J., is director. Address: 3700 13th St. N.E., Washington, D.C. 20017.

CATHOLIC YOUTH ORGANIZATIONS

Boy Scouts in the Catholic Church: The National Catholic Committee on Scouting works with the Boy Scouts of America in developing the character and spiritual life of 600,000 members in units chartered to Catholic and non-Catholic organizations. *Boy's Life.* Committee Chairman, Henry B. Murphy, 149 N. Warren St., Trenton, N.J. 08608.

Camp Fire, Inc. (1910): 4601 Madison Ave., Kansas City, Mo. 64112. The Youth Activities representative of the USCC acts as advisor in matters pertaining to Catholic participation in the Camp Fire program. To help young people learn and grow in their individual ways through participation in enjoyable activities. Open to youth up to 21 years of age. Membership: approximately 500,000 (no exact statistics available on number of Catholics participating).

Catholic Forester Youth Program, Catholic Order of Foresters: 305 W. Madison Street, Chicago, Ill. 60606. To develop Christian leadership and promote the moral, intellectual, social and physical growth of its youth members. *Catholic Forester.* Membership: youth up to 16 years of age — about 25,000 in 776 local courts in U.S. the High Chief Ranger is John A. Gorski.

Catholic Youth Organization (CYO): Name of parish-centered diocesan Catholic youth programs throughout the country. CYO promotes a program of spiritual, social and physical activities. The original CYO was organized by Bishop Bernard Sheil of Chicago in 1930.

Columbian Squires (1925): P.O. Drawer 1670, New Haven, Conn. 06507. Junior organization of the Knights of Columbus. To train and develop leadership through active participation in a well-organized program of activities. Membership: 12- to 18-year-old Catholic boys. More than 20,000 in 1,000 circles (local units) active in the U.S., Canada, Puerto Rico, Mexico, Guam and the Philippines. *Squires Newsletter,* monthly.

Girl Scouts of the U.S.A.: 830 Third Ave., New York, N.Y. 10022. Girls from most archdioceses and dioceses in the U.S. and its possessions participate in Girl Scouting. The Youth Activities section, USCC, cooperates with Girl Scouts of the U.S.A. *Girl Scout Leader.* Membership: approximately three million (no exact statistics available on number of Catholic girls participating).

Holy Childhood Association (Pontifical Association of the Holy Childhood) (1843): 1720 Massachusetts Ave. N.W., Washington, D.C. 20036. The official children's mission-aid society of the Church; provides assistance to children in 94 mission countries. Furnishes mission education programs and materials to pupils in Catholic elementary schools and religious education programs. *It's Our World,* four times a year. National Director, Rev. Francis W. Wright, C.S.Sp.

Junior Catholic Daughters of the Americas: 10 W. 71st St., New York, N.Y. 10023. A major department of the Catholic Daughters of the Americas. To promote development of the whole person, service to others, spiritual growth. Membership: Juniors (11 to 18 years old); Juniorettes (6 to 10 years old).

Knights of the Altar (1937): P.O. Drawer 5476, Lakeland, Fla. 33803 (national office). Society for altar boys. *Young Heralds,* 6 times a year. Membership: 3,000 units in the U.S. and foreign countries.

National Catholic Forensic League (1952): To develop articulate Catholic leaders through an inter-diocesan program of speech and debate activities. *Newsletter,* quarterly. Membership: 600 schools; membership open to Catholic, private and public schools through the local diocesan league.

National Catholic Young Adult Ministry Association (1982): To strengthen the professional competence of those engaged in campus and young adult ministry. President, Rev. Paul Ojibway, S.A., 1925 Verendo, Los Angeles, Calif. 90027

National Christ Child Society Inc. (1887): 5151 Wisconsin Ave. N.W., Washington, D.C. 20016. Founder, Mary V. Merrick. A welfare organization for the care of underprivileged adults and children. Membership: approximately 10,000 adult and junior members in 29 cities in U.S. President, Mrs. John W. Wilson.

National Federation for Catholic Youth Ministry (1982): 3025 4th St. N.E., Washington, D.C. 20017. To foster the development of youth ministry in the United States through CYO and other expressions of ministry to, with, by and for youth. *Emmaus Newsletter,* quarterly. Executive Director, Mrs. Maggie Brown.

St. Dominic Savio Club (1950): Don Bosco, Filor's Lane, West Haverstraw, N.Y. 10993. To promote a program of spiritual, intellec-

tual and recreational activities. *Savio Notes,* six times a year. Membership: students in grades three through ten — more than 10,000 members in U.S., Canada and nine foreign countries.

Young Christian Students: 7436 W. Harrison, Forest Park, Ill. 60130. A student movement for Christian personal and social change. Membership: 500 in high schools and parishes.

Fraternities and Sororities

Alpha Delta Gamma (1924): P.O. Box 54321, Los Angeles, Calif. 90054. Fraternity. *Alphadelity.* Membership: 7,260 in 12 college chapters and 11 alumni associations.

Delta Epsilon Sigma (1939): College of Great Falls, Great Falls, Mont. 59405. National scholastic honor society for students, faculty and alumni of colleges and universities with a Catholic tradition. Membership: 26,500 in 100 chapters. Secretary, Dr. Charles M. Hepburn.

Kappa Gamma Pi (1926): A national Catholic college women's honor society for graduates who, in addition to academic excellence, have shown outstanding leadership in extracurricular activities. *Kappa Gamma Pi News,* quarterly. Membership: approximately 16,000 in 123 colleges; 40 alumnae chapters in metropolitan areas. President, Dr. Sally Ann Vonderbrink, 5747 Colerain Ave., Cincinnati, O. 45239.

Phi Kappa Theta: 332 Main St., Worcester, Mass. 01608. National collegiate fraternity with a Catholic heritage. Merger (1959) of Phi Kappa Fraternity, founded at Brown Univ. in 1889, and Theta Kappa Phi Fraternity, founded at Lehigh Univ. in 1919. *The Temple Magazine* quarterly, and newsletter, *The Sun.* Membership: 3,000 undergraduate and 36,000 alumni in 55 collegiate and 15 alumni chapters. Executive Director, Kirk Thomas.

ASSOCIATIONS, MOVEMENTS, SOCIETIES IN THE U.S.

(Principal source: Almanac survey.)
See Index for other associations, movements and societies covered elsewhere.

A

Academy of American Franciscan History (1944), Box 34440, West Bethesda, Md. 20817. Dir., Rev. John-Marie Cassese, O.F.M.

Academy of California Church History (1946), P.O. Box 1668, Fresno, Calif. 93717.

Albertus Magnus Guild (1953). Society of Christian scientists. Pres., Rev. William D. Sullivan, S.J., Boston College, Chestnut Hill, Mass. 02167.

American Benedictine Academy (1947). Scholarly Benedictine society. Pres., Rev. Colman Grabert, O.S.B., St. Meinrad Archabbey, St. Meinrad, Ind. 47577.

American Catholic Correctional Chaplains

Association (1952), 275 in 475 institutions. Pres., Rev. Kloman Riggie; Sec., Rev. Dismas Boeff, O.S.B., 2900 East Blvd., Cleveland, O. 44104.

American Catholic Historical Association (1919), Catholic University of America, Washington, D.C. 20064. *The Catholic Historical Review,* quarterly. Sec., Rev. Robert Trisco.

American Catholic Philosophical Association (1926), Catholic University of America, Washington, D.C. 20064; 1,500. *New Scholasticism,* quarterly, *Proceedings,* annually.

American Committee on Italian Migration (1952), 42 E. 23rd St., New York, N.Y. 10010; 6,000. *ACIM Newsletter* and *ACIM Nuova Via,* 6 times a year. Sec., Rev. Joseph A. Cogo, C.S.

Ancient Order of Hibernians in America, Inc. (1836); 120,000. *National Hibernian*

Digest, bimonthly. Nat. Pres., John P. Connolly; Nat. Sec., John W. Duffy, c/o P.O. Box 700, Riverdale Station, Bronx, N.Y. 10471.

Apostleship of Prayer (1849-France; 1861-U.S.): 114 E. 13th St., New York, N.Y. 10003. Promotes Daily Offering and Sacred Heart devotion.

Apostolate for Family Consecration (1975), The House of St. Joseph, Box 220, Kenosha, Wis. 53141; 26,000 members. Family reinforcement by transforming neighborhoods into God-centered communities Pres., Jerome F. Coniker.

Apostolate of Christian Action, (1956), P.O. Box 24, Fresno, Calif. 93707. *Divine Love,* quarterly.

Archconfraternity of Christian Mothers (**Christian Mothers**) (1881), 220 37th St., Pittsburgh, Pa. 15201; over 3,400 branches. Dir., Rev. Bertin Roll, O.F.M. Cap.

Archconfraternity of Our Lady of Perpetual Help and St. Alphonsus (1871), 526 59th St., Brooklyn, N.Y. 11220.

Archconfraternity of the Holy Ghost (1912), Holy Ghost Preparatory School, Bensalem, Pa. 19020 (U.S. headquarters). Nat. Dir., Very Rev. Henry J. Brown, C.S.Sp.

Association for Religious and Value Issues in Counseling (1962), division of American Personnel and Guidance Association. *Counseling and Values,* quarterly. Address, 2 Skyline Pl., Suite 400, 5203 Leesburg Pike, Falls Church, Va. 22041.

Association for Social Economics (formerly the Catholic Economic Association) (1941), De Paul University, 25 E. Jackson Blvd., Chicago, Ill. 60604; 1,200. *Review of Social Economy,* triannually.

Association for the Sociology of Religion (formerly the American Catholic Sociological Society) (1938), Loyola University of Chicago, 6525 N. Sheridan Rd., Chicago, Ill. 60626. *Sociological Analysis,* quarterly. Exec. Sec., Robert McNamara.

Association of Catholic Trade Unionists (1937), 58 Washington Square South, New York, N.Y. 10012. Exec. Sec., John C. Donohue.

Association of Marian Helpers (1946), Stockbridge, Mass. 01262; 750,000, mostly in U.S. *The Marian Helpers Bulletin,* quarterly.

Association of Romanian Catholics of America (1948), 4309 Olcott Ave., E. Chicago, Ind. 46312.

B

Blue Army of Our Lady of Fatima (1946), Washington, N.J. 07882; worldwide membership. *Soul,* bimonthly. U.S. Pres., Most Rev. Jerome Hastrich, bishop of Gallup, N. Mex.

C

Calix Society (1947), 7601 Wayzata Blvd., Minneapolis, Minn. 55426; 2,000 members in U.S. and Canada; *Chalice,* bimonthly. Association of Catholic alcoholics maintaining their sobriety through affiliation with and participation in Alcoholics Anonymous. Dir., R. D. Dickinson.

Campaign for Surplus Rosaries (1948) and the **Mid-America Rosary Museum** (1976), 1821 W. Short 17th St., North Little Rock, Ark. 72114. Collect rosaries and religious articles for free distribution to the poor throughout the world. Lay Internatl. Chairman, P. Marion Chudy, S.F.O.

Canon Law Society of America (1939), Catholic University, Washington, D.C. 20064. To further research and study in canon law; 1,600. Exec. Coord., Rev. James H. Provost.

Cardinal Mindszenty Foundation (CMF) (1958), P.O. Box 11321, St. Louis, Mo. 63105. To combat communism with knowledge and facts. Exec. Sec., Eleanor Schlafly.

Catholic Aid Association (1878), 49 W. Ninth St., St. Paul, Minn. 55102; 80,000. *Catholic Aid News,* monthly. Fraternal life insurance society. Pres., F. L. Spanier.

Catholic Alumni Clubs International (1957), To advance social, cultural and spiritual well-being of members. Membership limited to single Catholics with professional education; 7,000 in 50 clubs in U.S. International Pres., Jeanette Hess, Apt. 7, 396 Emerson Rd., Eggertsville, N.Y. 14226. International Chaplain, Rev. Peter Campbell, M.S.C., P.O. Box 6074, Youngstown, O. 44501.

Catholic Apostolate of Radio, Television and Advertising (1954), 1011 First Ave., New York, N.Y. 10022; 660 in New York City.

Catholic Biblical Association of America (1936), Catholic University of America, Washington, D.C. 20064; 947. *The Catholic Biblical Quarterly.* Pres., Rev. Philip King.

Catholic Big Brothers, Inc. (of Archdiocese of New York) (1911), 1011 First Ave., New York, N.Y. 10022; Newsletter, quarterly. To provide opportunities for male identification to fatherless boys, 7-15 years of age, through services of qualified adult male volunteers. Exec. Dir., Sr. Cecile Kaval, R.S.H.M.

Catholic Big Sisters, Inc. (of the Archdiocese of New York), 60 Lafayette St., New York, N.Y. 10013. Voluntary organization providing adjunctive services to Family Court, for girls up to 16 and boys up to 10 years of age. Dir., Hortense Baffa.

Catholic Commission on Intellectual and Cultural Affairs (CCICA) (1946), P.O. Box 21, Notre Dame, Ind. 46556; 268. Exec. Dir. Rev. Konrad Schaum.

Catholic Daughters of the Americas (1903), 10 W. 71st St., New York, N.Y. 10023; 170,000. *Share Magazine.* Nat. Regent, Miss Mary Murray.

Catholic Evidence Guild (1918, in England; 1931, in US), c/o 127 W. 31st St., New York, N.Y. 10001. Lay movement for spread of

Catholic truth by means of outdoor speaking.

Catholic Family Life Insurance (1868), 1572 E. Capitol Dr., Milwaukee, Wis. 53211; 48,000. *The Family Friend,* quarterly. Pres., David L. Springob.

Catholic Golden Age: National Headquarters, Scranton, Pa. 18503; 700,000. *CGA World Magazine,* bimonthly. Assist Catholics over 50 years of age in their religious and secular needs.

Catholic Guardian Society (1913), 1011 First Ave., New York, N.Y. 10022. Exec. Dir., James P. O'Neill.

Catholic Home Bureau for Dependent Children (1898), 1011 First Ave., New York, N.Y. 10022. Exec. Dir., Sr. Una McCormack.

Catholic Interracial Council of New York, Inc. (1934), 225 E. 52nd St., New York, N.Y. 10022. Sponsors programs and educational and research projects on racism, bigotry and discrimination, Newsletter, published periodically. Exec. Dir., John J. Garra.

Catholic Interracial Councils: See National Catholic Conference for Interracial Justice.

Catholic Knights of America (1877), 217 E. 8th St., Cincinnati, O. 45202; 12,600. *Catholic Knights of America Journal,* monthly. Fraternal insurance society.

Catholic Knights of St. George (1881), 709 Brighton Rd., Pittsburgh, Pa. 15233; 67,000. *Knight of St. George,* bimonthly. Fraternal insurance society. Pres., Joseph J. Miller.

Catholic Kolping Society of America (1923), 22515 Masonic Blvd., St. Clair Shores, Mich. 48082. *Kolping Banner,* monthly. International society concerned with spiritual, educational and physical development of members.

Catholic Lawyers' Guild. Organization usually on a diocesan basis, under different titles.

Catholic League (1943), 1200 N. Ashland Ave., Chicago, Ill. 60622. Exec. Dir., Most Rev. Alfred Abramowicz.

Catholic Library Association (1921), 461 W. Lancaster Avenue; Haverford, Pa., 19041; 3,162. *Catholic Library World,* monthly (Sept.-April), bimonthly (May-June, July-Aug.); *Catholic Periodical and Literature Index.* Pres., Kelly Fitzpatrick, Exec. Dir., Matthew R. Wilt.

Catholic Near East Welfare Association (Near East Missions) (1926), 1011 First Ave., New York, N.Y. 10022. *Near East Missions,* weekly column in 132 diocesan and four national newspapers. Aids missionary activity in 18 countries (under jurisdiction of the Sacred Congregation for the Oriental Church) in Europe, Africa and Asia, including the Holy Land. Nat. Sec., Rev. Msgr. John G. Nolan.

Catholic Negro-American Mission Board (1907), 2021 H. St. N.W., Washington, D.C. 20006.15,000. *Educating in Faith,* quarterly. Exec. Sec., Msgr. Paul A. Lenz.

Catholic One Parent Organization (COPO): To give widows and widowers an opportunity to meet others in the same situation, blending social and spiritual programs. Organized in various dioceses.

Catholic Order of Foresters (1883), 305 W. Madison St., Chicago, Ill. 60606; 167,000. *The Catholic Forester,* bimonthly. Fraternal insurance society. High Chief Ranger, John A. Gorski.

Catholic Pamphlet Society (1938), 2171 Fillmore Ave., Buffalo, N.Y. 14214. Parish pamphlet rack distributors. Dir., Rev. Msgr. Paul T. Cronin.

Catholic Peace Fellowship (1964), 339 Lafayette St., New York, N.Y. 10012; 6,500, *CPF Bulletin.* Peace education and action projects, development of the nonviolent tradition within the Catholic Church; draft counseling. Nat. Sec., Thomas C. Cornell.

Catholic Press Association of the U.S., Inc. (1911), 119 N. Park Ave., Rockville Centre, N.Y. 11570. *The Catholic Journalist* monthly; *Catholic Press Directory,* annually. Pres., Rev. Norman Muckerman, C.Ss.R. Exec. Dir., James A. Doyle.

Catholic Theological Society of America (1946), Office of Secretary, St. Mary of the Lake Seminary, Mundelein, Ill. 60060; 1,200. *Proceedings,* annually. Pres. (1982-83), Bernard Cooke.

Catholic Union of the Sick in America, Inc. (CUSA) (1947), 63 Wall St., New York, N.Y. 10005 (legal office); 1,200. Admin. Leader, Miss Anna Marie Sopko, 176 W. 8th St., Bayonne, N.J. 07002 (national central office).

Catholic War Veterans (1935), 2 Massachusetts Ave. N.W., Washington, D.C. 20001; 500 posts, *Catholic War Veteran,* bimonthly.

Catholic Worker Movement (1933), 36 E. First St., New York, N.Y. 10003. *The Catholic Worker,* 9 times a year. Lay apostolate founded by Peter Maurin and Dorothy Day; has Houses of Hospitality in 29 U.S. cities and several communal farms in various parts of the country. Promotes pacifism and anarchism in that it is decentralist, and believes in what the popes have termed the principle of subsidiarity, urging decentralization in the school system, community control, and in the economic field credit unions, cooperatives and unions of workers and mutual aid.

Catholic Workman (Katolicky Delnik) (1891), New Prague, Minn. 56071; 18,023. *Catholic Workman,* monthly. Fraternal and insurance society. Pres. Rudy G. Faimon.

Catholic Writers' Guild of America (1919), 65 East 89th St., New York, N.Y. 10028. Exec. Sec., Rev. Bernard J. McMahon.

Catholics United for the Faith (1968), 222 North Ave., Box S, New Rochelle, N.Y. 10801; 15,000 worldwide, *Lay Witness,* monthly. Lay apostolate founded in response to Vatican II's call to the laity. Pres., Mrs. Madeleine F. Stebbins.

Center for Pastoral Liturgy (1975), Catholic University of America, Washington, D.C. 20064. Concerned with promotion of pastoral-liturgical action in the U.S.; sponsors programs, publications, conferences, and workshops oriented toward the service of local churches. Dir., Rev. G. Thomas Ryan.

Central Association of the Miraculous Medal (1915), 475 E. Chelten Ave., Philadelphia, Pa. 19144. *Miraculous Medal,* quarterly. Dir., Rev. Robert P. Cawley, C.M.

Chaplains' Aid Association, Inc. (1917), 1011 First Ave., New York, N.Y. 10022. Pres., Most Rev. Philip J. Furlong.

Christopher Movement (1945), 12 E. 48th St., New York, N.Y. 10017. Without formal organization or meetings, the movement stimulates personal initiative and responsible action in line with Christian principles, particularly in the fields of education, government, industrial relations and communications. Christopher radio and TV programs are broadcast by more than 1,500 radio and TV stations; 700,000 copies of *Christopher News Notes* are distributed seven times a year without subscription fee; 110 weekly and 14 daily newspapers carry Christopher columns. Dir., Rev. John Catoir.

Citizens for Educational Freedom (1959): Nonsectarian group concerned with parents' right to educational choice by means of tuition tax credits and vouchers. National office: Suite 854 Washington Bldg., 15th St. and New York Ave. N.W., Washington, D.C. 20005.

Confraternity of Catholic Clergy (1976), 21-72 43rd St., Astoria, N.Y. 11105; *C.C.C. Newsletter,* bimonthly. To support priests by mutual prayer for personal holiness, loyalty to Pope and adherence to teaching of magisterium. Pres., Rev. Robert I. Bradley, S.J.

Confraternity of the Immaculate Conception of Our Lady of Lourdes (1874), Box 561, Notre Dame, Ind. 46556. Distributors of Lourdes water.

Confraternity of the Most Holy Rosary: See Rosary Altar Society.

Convert Movement Our Apostolate (CMOA) (1945), formerly Convert Makers of America, c/o Our Lady of Grace Rectory, 430 Avenue W, Brooklyn, N.Y. 11223. *Bulletin* quarterly. To train and assist lay persons on a parish level to discuss and present the Faith to interested persons on a one-to-one basis. Dir., Msgr. Erwin A. Juraschek.

Czech Catholic Union of Texas (K.J.T.) (1889), 214 Colorado St., La Grange, Tex. 78945; 16,535. *Nasinec,* weekly, and *K. J. T. News,* monthly. Fraternal and insurance society. Pres., Amos Pavlik.

D

Damien-Dutton Society for Leprosy Aid, Inc. (1944), 616 Bedford Ave., Bellmore, N.Y. 11710; 25,000. *Damien Dutton Call,* quarterly. Provides medicine, rehabilitation and research for conquest of leprosy. Pres., Howard E. Crouch, Dir., Sr. Mary Augustine, S.M.S.M.

Daughters of Isabella (1897), 375 Whitney Ave., New Haven, Conn. 06511; 120,000. International Regent, Mrs. Mary R. Bergman.

E

Edith Stein Guild, Inc. (1955), c/o Church of Our Lady of Victory, 60 William St., New York, N.Y. 10005. *ESG Newsletter.* Promotes Judaeo-Christian understanding and assists Jewish converts.

Enthronement of the Sacred Heart in the Home (1907), 3 Adams St., Fairhaven, Mass. 02719; over 2,500,000.

Eucharistic Guard for Nocturnal Adoration (1938), 800 North Country Club Rd., Tucson, Ariz. 85716.

Eymard League (1948), 194 E. 76 St., New York, N.Y. 10021; approximately 24,000. Dir., Rev. Ralph A. Lavigne, S.S.S.

F

Families for Christ (1977), 6026 W. Harwood Ave., Orlando, Fla., 32811; 8,000. Promote social reign of Christ. Pres., Albert Barone.

Families for Prayer (1982), 775 Madison Ave., Albany, N.Y. 12208. Dir., Rev. John J. Gurley, C.S.C.

Family Rosary Crusade (1942), and **Crusade for Family Prayer,** 773 Madison Ave., Albany, N.Y. 12208. Dir., Rev. Patrick Peyton, C.S.C.

Federation of Diocesan Liturgical Commissions (FDLC) (1969), 3033 4th St. N.E., Washington, D.C. 20017. Voluntary association of personnel from diocesan liturgical commissions of the U.S. The main purpose is promotion of the liturgy as the heart of Christian life, especially in the parish community. Exec. Sec., Rev. Thomas Richstatter, O.F.M.

Fellowship of Catholic Scholars (1977), Msgr. George A. Kelly, Newsletter editor, St. John's University, Jamaica, N.Y. 11439; 400 members. Interdisciplinary research and publications of Catholic scholars in accord with the magisterium of the Catholic Church. Pres., Rev. William Smith.

First Catholic Slovak Ladies' Association, USA (1892), 24950 Chagrin Blvd., Beachwood, Ohio 44122; 105,000. *Fraternally Yours,* monthly. Fraternal insurance society. Pres., Louise M. Yash.

First Catholic Slovak Union (Jednota) (1890), 3289 E. 55th St., Cleveland, Ohio 44127; 115,097. *Jednota,* weekly. Exec. Sec., Stephen F. Ungvarsky.

First Friday Clubs (1936). Organized on local basis; about 90 clubs in US, others elsewhere. Objectives are to spread devotion to the Sacred Heart, encourage members to receive Holy Communion on First Fridays and to meet at breakfast, luncheon or dinner for discussions of Catholic interest.

Franciscan Apostolate of the Way of the Cross (1949), 174 Ramsey St., Paterson, N.J. 07501. Stations Crucifix available on request. Dir., Rev. Cassian J. Kirk, O.F.M.

Friendship House (1938), 1746 W. Division, Chicago, Ill. 60622. *Community,* quarterly. Work for social justice through nonviolence and simple living; promote Catholic interracial apostolate.

G

Gabriel Richard Institute (1949), 2315 Orleans Ave., Detroit, Mich. 48207. Conducts Christopher leadership courses in 18 dioceses.

Gelasian Guild (1976), Association of Catholic attorneys working with the USCC; concerned with scholarly study of legal questions affecting Church-state relations. Pres., Rev. Charles Whelan, S.J., 106 W. 56th St., New York, N.Y. 10019.

Guard of Honor of the Immaculate Heart of Mary (1932), 135 West 31st St., New York, N.Y. 10001. An archconfraternity approved by the Holy See whose members cultivate devotion to the Blessed Virgin Mary, particularly through a daily Guard Hour of Prayer.

Guild of Catholic Lawyers (1928), Empire State Bldg., 350 Fifth Ave., Room 316, New York, N.Y. 10001; 600.

Guild of Our Lady of Ransom (1948), c/o St. Timothy's Rectory, 650 Nichols St., Norwood, Mass. 02062. Boston archdiocesan ministry for spiritual aid and rehabilitation of inmates of penal institutions. Exec. Dir. and Treas., Rev. Joseph P. McDermott.

Guild of St. Paul (1937), 601 Hill'n Dale, Lexington, Ky. 40503; 13,542; Nat. Spir. Dir., Rev. Msgr. Leonard Nienaber; Pres., Robert Parks.

H

Holy Name Society: Founded in 1274 by Blessed John Vercelli, master general of the Dominicans, to promote reverence for the Holy Name of Jesus; this is still the principal purpose of the society, which also develops lay apostolic programs in line with directives of the Second Vatican Council. Introduced in the U.S. by Dominican Father Charles H. McKenna in 1870-71, the society has about 5 million members on diocesan and parochial levels. With approval of the local bishop and pastor, women as well as men may be members.

Holy Name Society, National Association (NAHNS) (1970), 516 N. Front St., Minersville, Pa. 17954. Association of diocesan and parochial Holy Name Societies. Spir. Dir., Rev. James F. Lanergan, 140 Shawmut Ave., Boston, Mass. 02118. Exec. Sec., Stephen Andrusisian.

Hungarian Catholic League of America, Inc. (1945), 30 E. 30th St., New York, N.Y. 10016. Member of the National Catholic Resettlement Council. *Catholic Hungarian Sunday,* weekly. Pres., Rev. Msgr. John S. Sabo.

I

Institute on Religious Life (1974), 4200 N. Austin Ave., Chicago, Ill. 60634. *Consecrated Life,* semi-annually; *Religious Life,* 10 issues a year. To foster more effective understanding and implementation of teachings of the Church on religious life and promote growth in sanctity of all the faithful according to their state in life.

International Institute of the Heart of Jesus (1972), 7700 Blue Mound Rd., Milwaukee Wis. 53213 (corporate headquarters); 14 Borgo Angelico, 00193 Rome, Italy (executive offices). Promote awareness and appreciation of the mystery of the Heart of Christ and establish an international forum for the apostolate. Pres., Harry G. John.

Italian Catholic Federation of California, Central Council (1924), 1801 Van Ness Ave., San Francisco, Calif. 94109; 30,000; *Bollettino,* monthly. Sec., Robert Aquistapace.

J

John Carroll Society, The (1951), 1870 Wyoming Ave. N.W., Washington, D.C. 20009. Pres. Hon. Dr. James E. Boland.

Judean Society, Inc., The (1966), 1075 Space Park Way No. 336, Mt. View, Calif. 94043; over 800. International organization for divorced Catholic women. Self-help, mutual-help counseling groups. Foundress/Internatl., Dir., Frances A. Miller.

K

Knights of Peter Claver (1909), 554 Palmetto St., P.O. Box 204, Mobile, Ala. 36601; 17,000. *The Claverite,* biannually. Fraternal and aid society.

Knights of St. John, Supreme Commandery (1886), 6517 Charles Ave., Parma, O. 44129; Sup. Sec., Brig. Gen. Salvatore La Bianca.

Knights of the Immaculata (Militia Immaculatae, M.I.) (1917), National Center, 1600 W. Park Ave., Libertyville, Ill. 60048; canonically established with international headquarters in Rome. A pious association for evangelization and catechesis beginning with members' own inner renewal, through the intercession of the Blessed Virgin Mary.

L

Ladies of Charity of the United States, Association of (1960), 7806 Natural Bridge Rd., P.O. Box 5730, St. Louis, Mo. 63121; 40,000. International Association founded by St. Vincent de Paul in 1617. Pres., Mrs. Mary McNeill, 4240 Denny Ave., North Hollywood, Calif. 91602.

Lithuanian Groups: Ateitininkai, members of Lithuanian Catholic Federation Ateitis (1910), 9610 Singleton Dr., Bethesda, Md. 20817; to promote Catholic action and uphold Lithuanian heritage among youth; Pres., Joseph Laucka. Knights of Lithuania (1913), educational-fraternal organization. Pres., Loretta T. Stukas, 234 Sunlit Dr., Watchung, N.J. 07060. Lithuanian Catholic Alliance (1886), 73 S. Washington St., Wilkes-Barre, Pa. 18701; 147 branches; *Garsas,* monthly; fraternal insurance organization; Pres., Thomas E. Mack. Lithuanian Roman Catholic Federation of America (1906), umbrella organization for Lithuanian parishes and organizations; Pres., Saulius Kuprys, 4545 W. 63rd St., Chicago, Ill. 60629. Lithuanian Roman Catholic Priests' League (1909): religious-professional association; Pres., Albert Contons, 50 Orton-Marotta Way, Boston, Mass. 02127. Two organizations with offices at 351 Highland Blvd., Brooklyn, N.Y. 11207 — Lithuanian American Catholic Services (1975); religious, educational, research and service association; Exec. Dir., Rev. Casimir Pugevicius. Lithuanian Catholic Religious Aid, Inc. (1961); to assist persecuted Catholics in Lithuania; Pres., Most Rev. Vincent Brizgys.

Little Flower Mission League (1957), P.O. Box 25, Plaucheville, La. 71362. Sponsored by the Brothers of the Holy Eucharist.

Little Flower Society (1923), 11343 S. Michigan Ave., Chicago, Ill. 60628; 40,000, *Little Flower News,* monthly. Nat. Dir., Rev. Terrence Sempowski, O. Carm.

Liturgical Conference, The, 810 Rhode Island Ave. N.E., Washington, D.C. 20018. *Liturgy, Accent on Worship, Homily Service.* Education, research and publication programs for renewing and enriching Christian liturgical life. Ecumenical. Exec. Dir., Rachel Reeder.

Loyal Christian Benefit Association (1890), 305 W. 6th St., Erie, Pa. 16512; 56,623. *The Fraternal Leader,* bimonthly. Pres., Mrs. Catherine T. Kelly.

M

Marian Movement of Priests, Inc. Nat. Dir., Rev. Albert G. Roux, P.O. Box 8, St. Francis, Me. 04774.

Mariological Society of America (1949), Office of the Secretary, Marian Library, University of Dayton, Dayton, O. 45469: 300. *Marian Studies,* annually.

Markham Prayer Card Apostolate (Apostolate To Aid the Dying) (1931), Franciscan Sisters of the Poor, 60 Compton Rd., Cincinnati, Ohio 45215. Dir., Rev. Herman H. Kenning.

Maryheart Crusaders, The (1964), 22 Button St., Meriden, Conn. 06450; 2,000. *The Maryheart Crusader,* 4 times a year. To reunite fallen-away Catholics and promote religious education for adults. Pres., Louise D'Angelo.

Men of the Sacred Hearts (1964), Shrine of the Sacred Heart, Harleigh, Pa. 18225. Promote enthronement of Sacred Heart.

Missionary Association of Catholic Women (1916), 3521 W. National Ave., Milwaukee, Wis. 53215. Pres., Mrs. Elizabeth Schneider.

Missionary Cenacle Apostolate (MCA) (1909), 3501 Solly Ave., Philadelphia, Pa. 19136; 350. To foster spiritual and apostolic life of the laity through prayer, instruction, example and service.

Missionary Vehicle Association, Inc. (MIVA-America), 1233 Lawrence St. N.E., P.O. Box 29184, Washington, D.C. 20017. To raise funds to provide vehicles of all types to missionaries in need. Nat. Dir., Rev. Philip De Rea, M.S.C.

Morality in Media, Inc. (1962), 475 Riverside Dr., New York, N.Y. 10115; 50,000 members. Newsletter, 8 times a year *The Obscenity Law Reporter,* bimonthly. To stop traffic in pornography constitutionally and effectively, and promote principles of love, truth and taste in the media. A major project is the National Obscenity Law Center which provides legal information for prosecutors and other attorneys. Pres., Rev. Morton A. Hill, S.J.

N

National Alliance of Czech Catholics (1917), 2657-59 S. Lawndale Ave., Chicago, Ill. 60623; 450 parishes. Pres., Mr. Vaclav Hyvnar.

National Association of Church Personnel Administrators (1973), 100 E. 8th St., Cincinnati, O. 45202. Pres., Sr. Barbara Garland, S.C., Exec. Dir., Sr. Mary Ann Barnhorn, S.N.D.

National Association of Diocesan Ecumenical Officers, Pres., Rev. Alex J. Brunett, 17500 Farmington Rd., Livonia, Mich. 48152.

National Association of Pastoral Musicians (1976), 225 Sheridan St., N.W., Washington, D.C. 20011; 7,000. *Pastoral Music,* six times a year. For clergy and musicians. Pres. and Exec. Dir., Rev. Virgil C. Funk.

National Association of Priest Pilots (1964), Pres., Rev. John Hemann, 204 S. Jackson, Eagle Grove, Iowa 50533.

National Catholic Bandmasters' Association (1953), Box 523, Notre Dame University, Notre Dame, Ind. 46556. *The School Musician Magazine.*

National Catholic Cemetery Conference (1949), 710 N. River Rd., Des Plaines, Ill. 60016. *The Catholic Cemetery,* monthly. Pres., Rev. Nunzio J. Defoe.

National Catholic Conference for Interracial Justice (NCCIJ) (1960), 1200 Varnum St. N.E., Washington, D.C. 20017. National resource center and coordinator for Catholic interracial councils and individual members. Exec. Dir. Rev. Frederick M. Hinton.

National Catholic Development Conference (1968), 119 N. Park Ave., Rockville Centre, N.Y. 11570. Professional association of organizations and individuals engaged in raising funds for Catholic charitable activities.

Pres., Rev. Richard K. Knuge, S.M.; Exec. Dir., George T. Holloway.

National Catholic Disaster Relief Committee, 1346 Connecticut Ave. N.W., Suite 307, Washington, D.C. 20036.

National Catholic Pharmacists Guild of the United States (1962), 400 members; *The Catholic Pharmacist.* Pres., John P. Winkelmann, 1012 Surrey Hills Dr., St. Louis, Mo. 63117.

National Catholic Society of Foresters (1891), 35 E. Wacker, Chicago, Ill. 60601; 76,693; *National Catholic Forester,* quarterly. A fraternal insurance society. Pres., Mrs. Dolores M. Johnson.

National Catholic Stewardship Council (1962), 1 Columbia Place, Albany, N.Y. 12207. To promote the total concept of stewardship. Exec. Dir. Rev. James M. Mackey.

National Catholic Women's Union (1916), 3835 Westminster Pl., St. Louis, Mo. 63108; 15,200. *The Catholic Woman's Journal,* 10 times a year.

National Center for Urban Ethnic Affairs (1971): 1523 "O" St. N.W., Washington, D.C. 20005. To continue the expression of the Church's concern for problems of urban society. An affiliate of the USCC. Pres., Dr. John A. Kromkowski.

National Church Goods Association, 1114 Greenfield Lane, Mt. Prospect, Ill. 60056. Pres., Ted Cotter.

National Clergy Conference on Alcoholism, 3112-7th St. N.E., Washington, D.C. 20017. Exec. Dir., Rev. John F. X. O'Neill.

National Conference of Diocesan Vocation Directors (NCDVD) (1961), 1307 S. Wabash, Suite 350, Chicago, Ill. 60605. Coordinate diocesan awareness and discernment of vocations to the diocesan or religious priesthood and the religious life for both men and women. Provide information services. Exec. Dir., Rev. Timothy K. Johnson.

National Conference of Religious Vocations Directors of Men (NCRVDM), 1307 S. Wabash Ave., Suite 350, Chicago, Ill. 60605. *Call to Growth/Ministry, NCRVDM Newsletter,* quarterlies. Service organization for men and women religious assigned to vocational ministry. Exec. Dir., Rev. Steven Mudd, C.P.

National Federation of Catholic Physicians' Guilds (1927), 850 Elm Grove, Suite 11, Elm Grove, Wis. 53122; 6,700 in 88 autonomous guilds in U.S. and Canada, *Linacre Quarterly.* Pres., David P. Frelinger, M.D.

National Federation of Spiritual Directors (1972). Pres., Rev. Msgr. Henry F. Fawcett, St. Francis Seminary, 1667 Santa Paula Drive, San Diego, Calif. 92111.

National Guild of Catholic Psychiatrists, Inc. (1949). Integration of psychiatry and Roman Catholic theology. *The Bulletin.* Pres. (1981-1982), Louis M. Vuksinick, M.D. Mailing address: Exec. Sec., 120 Hill St., Whitinsville, Mass. 01588.

National Organization for Continuing Education of Roman Catholic Clergy, Inc. (1973). Membership, 130 dioceses, 71 religious provinces, 30 affiliated institutions. Pres., Rev. Edward Mahoney, 351 North Ave., Burlington, Vt. 05401. Exec. Dir., Rev. James Dunning, Catholic Theological Union, 5401 S. Cornell, Chicago, Ill. 60615 (national office).

Network (1971), 806 Rhode Island Ave. N.E., Washington, D.C. 20018. A Catholic social justice lobby.

Nocturnal Adoration Society of the United States (1882), 194 E. 76th St., New York, N.Y. 10021; 57,000 in 540 units.

North American Academy of Liturgy, c/o John Barry Ryan, Manhattan College, Bronx, N.Y. 10471. *Proceedings,* annually. Foster liturgical research, publication and dialogue on a scholarly level. Pres., Rev. John H. McKenna, C.M.

O

Order of the Alhambra (1904), 4200 Leeds Ave., Baltimore, Md. 21229. 11,000 in U.S. and Canada. Fraternal society dedicated to assisting retarded children. Supreme Commander, Sam Spatafore.

P

Paulist League (1924), 415 W. 59th St., New York, N.Y. 10019; 23,700. Dir., Rev. Robert A. O'Donnell, C.S.P.

Philangeli (Friends of the Angels) (1949 in England; 1956 in U.S.), Viatorian Fathers, 1115 E. Euclid St., Arlington Heights, Ill. 60004; approximately 750,000 in 60 countries. To encourage devotion to the angels.

Pious Union of Prayer (1898), St. Joseph's Home, P.O. Box 288, Jersey City, N.J. 07303; 51,000. *St. Joseph's Messenger and Advocate of the Blind,* quarterly.

Pious Union of the Holy Spirit (1900), 30 Gedney Park Dr., White Plains, N.Y. 10605. Pres., Rev. Jerome McHugh, O.F.M. Cap.

Pontifical Mission for Palestine (1949), c/o Catholic Near East Welfare Association, 1011 First Ave., New York, N.Y. 10022. Field offices in Beirut, Lebanon, Jerusalem and Amman, Jordan. The papal relief agency for 1.5 million Palestinian refugees in Lebanon, Syria, Jordan, and the Gaza Strip. Distributes food, clothing, other essentials; maintains medical clinics, orphanages, libraries, refugee camp schools and chapels, the Pontifical Mission Center for the Blind (Gaza), the Pontifical Mission Libraries (Jerusalem, Bethlehem, Nazareth), the Epheta Institute for Deaf-Mutes (Bethlehem). Pres., Rev. Msgr. John G. Nolan.

Pontifical Missionary Union in the USA (1936), 366 Fifth Ave., New York, N.Y. 10001. Pontifical organization to promote mission awareness among clergy, religious and candidates to priestly and religious life, and others engaged in pastoral ministry of the Church. Pres., Cardinal Terence Cooke, Nat. Dir., Rev. Msgr. William J. McCormack.

Priests' Eucharistic League (1887), 194 E. 76th St., New York, N.Y. 10021; 17,500. *Emmanuel,* monthly. Nat. Dir., Rev. Paul J. Bernier, S.S.S.

Pro Ecclesia Foundation (1970), 663 Fifth Ave., New York, N.Y. 10022. *Pro Ecclesia,* 10 times a year; other publications; Manhattan Cable-TV program. To answer attacks against Church and promote Church teachings. Pres., Dr. Timothy A. Mitchell.

Pro Maria Committee (1952), 22 Second Ave., Lowell, Mass. 01854. Promote devotion to Our Lady of Beauraing (See Index).

The Providence Association of the Ukrainian Catholics in America (Ukrainian Catholic Fraternal Benefit Society) (1912), 817 N. Franklin St., Philadelphia, Pa. 19123. *America* (Ukrainian-English).

R

Raskob Foundation for Catholic Activities, Inc. (1945), Kennett Pike and Montchanin Rd., P.O. Box 4019, Wilmington, Del. 19807. Exec. Vice Pres., Gerard S. Garey.

Reparation Society of the Immaculate Heart of Mary, Inc. (1946), 100 E. 20th St., Baltimore, Md. 21218. *Fatima Findings,* monthly. Dir. Rev. John Ryan, S.J.

Rosary Altar Society (Confraternity of the Most Holy Rosary) (1891, in US), 141 E. 65th St., New York, N.Y. 10021; 3,000,000. Prov. Dir., Rev. Flavian Morry, O.P.

Rosary League (1901), Franciscan Sisters of the Atonement, Graymoor, Garrison, N.Y. 10524.

S

Sacred Heart League, Walls, Miss. 38680; 700,000. Promote devotion to the Sacred Heart. Its program services include the Sacred Heart Auto League for careful, prayerful driving and the Apostolate of the Printed Word. Dir., Rev. Gregory Bezy, S.C.J.

St. Ansgar's Scandinavian Catholic League (1910), 40 W. 13th St., New York, N.Y. 10011; 1,000. *St. Ansgar's Bulletin,* annually.

St. Anthony's Guild (1924), Paterson, N.J. 07509. *Anthonian,* quarterly. Dir., Rev. Salvator Fink, O.F.M.

St. Jude League (1929), 221 W. Madison St., Chicago, Ill. 60606. *St. Jude Journal,* bimonthly. Dir., Rev. Mark J. Brummel, C.M.F.

St. Margaret of Scotland Guild, Inc. (1938), Graymoor, Garrison, N.Y. 10524; 2,200. Moderator, Bro. Pius MacIsaac, S.A.

St. Martin de Porres Guild (1935), 141 E. 65th St., New York, N.Y. 10021. Gen. Dir., Rev. Theodore Breslin, O.P.

St. Thomas Aquinas Foundation of the Dominican Fathers of the United States (STAF). Mod., Very Rev. Thomas H. McBrien, O.P.,

Providence College, Providence, R.I. 02918

Serra International (1938), 22 W. Monroe St., Chicago, Ill. 60603; 14,000 members in 466 clubs in 33 countries. *Serran,* bimonthly. Fosters vocations to the priesthood, and religious life, trains Catholic lay leadership. Formally aggregated to the Pontifical Society for Priestly Vocations, 1951. Pres., James E. Brennan.

Slovak Catholic Federation (1911): Founded by Rev. Joseph Murgas to promote and coordinate religious activities among Slovak Catholic fraternal societies, religious communities and Slovak ethnic parishes in their effort to address themselves to the special needs of Slovak Catholics in the U.S. and Canada. Pres., Rev. Joseph V. Adamec, 1515 Cass Ave., Bay City, Mich. 48706.

Slovak Catholic Sokol (1905), 205 Madison St., Passaic, N.J. 07055; 48,500. *Katolicky Sokol (Catholic Falcon),* weekly; *Priatel Dietok (Children's Friend),* semi-monthly.

Society for the Propagation of the Faith (1822), 366 Fifth Ave., New York, N.Y. 10001; established in 171 dioceses. General fund for ordinary and extraordinary subsidies for all mission diocese. *Mission,* 5 times a year; *Newsletter.* Is subject to Sacred Congregation for the Evangelization of Peoples. Nat. Dir., Rev. Msgr. William J. McCormack.

Society of St. Peter the Apostle (1898), 366 Fifth Ave., New York, N.Y. 10001; 171 dioceses. Church's central fund for support of seminaries, seminarians and novices in all mission dioceses. Nat. Dir., Rev. Msgr. William J. McCormack.

Spiritual Life Institute of America (1960), R.R. 3, Sedona, Arizona 86336. *Desert Call,* seasonal. An eremetical movement to foster the contemplative spirit in America. Founder, Rev. William McNamara, O.C.D. Second foundation: Primitive Wilderness Hermitage, Kemptville, Nova Scotia, Canada B0W 1Y0.

Stewardship Services, Inc., Suite 913, 1234 Massachusetts Ave. N.W., Washington, D.C. 20005. Non-profit membership organization that provides financial management consulting services for Catholic dioceses, congregations and institutions. Exec. Dir., Thomas J. Jenkins, Jr.

T

Theresians of America (1961), 5326 E. Pershing Ave., Scottsdale, Ariz. 85254; 5,000. Spiritual, intellectual and apostolic organization concerned with the vocation to Christian womanhood in both religious and lay states. Exec. Dir., Sr. Patricia Mullen.

U

United Societies of U.S.A. (1903), 613 Sinclair St., McKeesport, Pa. 15132; 4,066 members. *Prosvita-Enlightenment,* monthly newspaper.

United States Catholic Historical Society

(1884). 300. *Journal,* quarterly; and *Monograph Series,* annually. Exec. Sec., James J. Mahoney, St. Joseph's Seminary, Yonkers, N.Y. 10704.

W-Y

Western Catholic Union (1877), W.C.U. Bldg., 506-510 Maine St., Quincy, Ill. 62301; 27,351 members. *Western Catholic Union Record,* monthly.

Word of God Institute (1972), 487 Michigan Ave. N.E., Washington, D.C. 20017. For renewed biblical preaching, Bible sharing and evangelization. Dir., Rev. John Burke, O.P.

Young Ladies' Institute (1887), P.O. Box 99687, San Francisco, Calif. 94109. Grand Sec. Mrs. Sylvia Sharman.

Young Men's Institute (1883), 50 Oak St., San Francisco, Calif. 94102; 4,500. *Institute Journal,* bimonthly. Grand Sec., R. A. Bettencourt.

Knights of Columbus

The Knights of Columbus, which originated as a fraternal benefit society of Catholic men, was founded by Father Michael J. McGivney and chartered by the General Assembly of Connecticut Mar. 29, 1882.

In line with their general purpose to be of service to the Church, the Knights are active in many apostolic works and community programs.

Since January, 1947, the Knights have sponsored a program of Catholic advertising in secular publications with national circulation. This has brought some 6 million inquiries and led to more than 600,000 enrollments in courses in the Catholic faith. In recent years the Knights have broadened this program to include other media for spreading Christian and religious ideals. As a result substantial contributions have been made to support the work of the John LaFarge Institute in New York, the Catholic Communications Foundation in New York, and the Center for Applied Research in the Apostolate (CARA) in Washington. In 1975 the Knights also undertook funding of the up-link costs for telecasting papal ceremonies throughout the world via satellite.

K. of C. scholarship funds — two at the Catholic University of America, another for disbursement at other Catholic colleges in the U.S., one at Canadian colleges and others for the Philippines, Mexico and Puerto Rico — have provided college educations for some 1,500 students since 1914.

The order promotes youth activity through sponsorship of the Columbian Squires and through cooperation with other organized youth groups.

Recent programs undertaken by the Knights include: promotion of vocations to the priesthood and religious life; promotion of rosary devotion with free distribution of more than 250,000 rosaries a year; efforts to halt the increased killing of the unborn; assistance to the retarded and other disadvantaged people.

In 1980, local units of the Knights contributed more than $29 million to charitable and benevolent causes, and gave more than 9.2 million hours of community service.

K. of C. membership, as of Jan. 31, 1982, was 1,356,982 in 7,139 councils in the U.S., Canada, the Philippines, Cuba, Mexico, Puerto Rico, Panama, Guatemala, Guam and the Virgin Islands. Assets, as of Dec. 31, 1981, amounted to $1,049,870,443 and total insurance in force, $410,300,338.

The Knights' publication, *Columbia,* has the greatest circulation (over 1.3 million) of any Catholic monthly in North America.

Virgil C. Dechant is Supreme Knight.

International headquarters are located at One Columbus Plaza, New Haven, Conn. 06507.

100th Anniversary

Cardinal Agostino Casaroli, papal secretary of state, praised the Knights of Columbus for "knightly" service to humanity Aug. 3, 1982, and told the fraternal order that Pope John Paul held it in high esteem.

The papal representative to the 100th anniversary convention of the Knights said in a banquet address in Hartford, Conn., that the organization could be proud of its history as it looked ahead to even greater achievements in the future.

"As Catholics and as Americans, as Knights of Columbus," he said, "you have responsibilities which are quite special. The Holy Father does not doubt that you will face (these responsibilities) fully and directly."

Cardinal Casaroli's remarks were made in the keynote address at the organization's States Dinner.

Supreme Knight Virgil C. Dechant, noting the presence of more than 150 bishops and the speech to the Knights several hours earlier by President Reagan, said it was the greatest day in the history of the order.

Cardinal Casaroli also noted the presence of Reagan earlier in the day, saying it showed the esteem and appreciation of the President and others "for all that your association has done in the first 100 years of its existence." He said his own attendance at the convention showed how much the Pope and the Church esteemed the ideals and history of the organization.

Remarking that Father Michael McGivney, founder of the order, had first thought of calling it the "Sons of Columbus," Cardinal Casaroli indicated that calling its members "Knights" gave the organization a more compelling tone.

He also said the heritage of the Knights must be enriched with greater achievements.

CATHOLIC PRESS STATISTICS

The *1982 Catholic Press Directory*, published by the Catholic Press Association, reported a total of 531 periodicals in North America with a circulation of 27,110,060. There were 179 newspapers (four more than the number reported in the 1981 Directory) with a circulation of 5,770,518 (88,872 more). Magazines numbered 352 (an increase of 24) and had a circulation of 21,339,542 (819,381 more).

Newspapers

United States: 162; circulation, 5,525,483.

National newspapers, 10; circulation, 603,009.

Diocesan newspapers, 152; circulation, 4,922,474 (includes 6 diocesan editions of *Our Sunday Visitor* with a circulation of 71,992).

Canada: 12; circulation, 208,435.

National newspapers, 3; circulation, 79,314. (*Catholic Register,* weekly, 51,240; *L'Informateur Catholique,* twice a month, 20,000; *Catholic New Times,* biweekly, 8,074.)

West Indies, Others: 5 (diocesan); circulation, 36,600.

National newspapers in U.S. (Circulation figures are from the *1982 Catholic Press Directory,* unless indicated otherwise.) Weeklies: *Our Sunday Visitor,* 229,849; *National Catholic Register,* 74,256; *Catholic Twin Circle,* 69,846; *National Catholic Reporter,* 46,458; *El Visitante Dominical,* 42,600; *The Wanderer,* 41,400 (1980). Others: *Impact!,* 4 to 6 times a year, 40,000; *Bolletino,* monthly, 20,600; *P.A.D.R.E.S. National Bulletin,* quarterly.

Diocesan weekly newspapers in the U.S. with large circulations include: *Chicago Catholic,* 166,905; *Long Island Catholic* (Rockville

Centre), 152,392; *Catholic New York* (New York), 133,000; *Pittsburgh Catholic,* 121,500; *St. Louis Review,* 97,316; *The Tablet* (Brooklyn, N.Y.), 94,314; *Texas Catholic Herald* (Galveston-Houston), 91,000; *Catholic Voice* (Oakland, Calif.), 85,044;

Clarion Herald (New Orleans), 79,063; *Catholic Standard and Times* (Philadelphia), 78,564; *Denver Catholic Register,* 77,116; *The Evangelist* (Albany), 75,204; *The Monitor* (Trenton), 67,015; *Catholic Herald* (Milwaukee), 64,159; *The Pilot* (Boston), 60,031; *The Record* (Louisville), 58,479; *Catholic Witness* (Harrisburg), 58,000; *The Tidings* (Los Angeles), 56,117; *Florida Catholic* (Orlando), 56,258; *The Catholic Review* (Baltimore), 55,789; *Catholic Voice* (Omaha), 55,679.

The oldest Catholic newspaper in the United States is *The Pilot* of Boston, established in 1829 (under a different title).

Magazines

United States and Canada: 352; circulation, 21,339,542. English-language magazines, 323; circulation, 20,877,887. Other-language magazines, 29; circulation, 461,655. These statistics, from the *1982 Catholic Press Directory,* include *Sign* (circulation, 79,312) which ceased publication with its May, 1982 issue.

America (circulation, 35,000) and *Commonweal* (circulation, 18,212) are the only weekly and biweekly magazines, respectively, of general interest.

The monthly magazine with the largest circulation is *Columbia,* (1,275,331), the official organ of the Knights of Columbus.

General-interest monthly magazines with large circulations include: *Catholic Digest* (607,828); *Liguorian* (575,000); *St. Anthony's Messenger* (353,000); *U.S. Catholic* (49,881).

CATHOLIC NEWSPAPERS AND MAGAZINES IN THE U.S.

(Sources: *Catholic Press Directory, 1982*; Almanac survey; NC News Service.)

Abbreviation code: a, annual; bm, bimonthly; m, monthly; q, quarterly; w, weekly.

Circulation figures for some of these newspapers and magazines are given in the article, Catholic Press Statistics.

Newspapers

Advocate, The, w; 37 Evergreen Pl., E. Orange, N.J. 07018; Newark archdiocese.

Alive, m; 400 East Monroe, Phoenix, Ariz. 85004; Phoenix diocese.

America (Ukrainian-English), daily; 817 N. Franklin St., Philadelphia, Pa. 19123.

Anchor, The w; P.O. Box 7, Fall River, Mass. 02722; Fall River diocese.

Arizona Catholic Lifetime, biweekly; 64 W. Ochoa St., Tucson, Ariz. 85701; Tucson diocese.

Arlington Catholic Herald, w; 200 N. Glebe Rd., Suite 614, Arlington, Va. 22203; Arlington diocese.

Bayou Catholic, The, w; P.O. Box 9077, Houma, La. 70361; Houma-Thibodaux diocese.

Beacon, The, w; Box A, Pequannock, N.J. 07440; Paterson diocese.

Bishop's Bulletin, m; P.O. Box 665, Yankton, S. Dak. 57078.

Bolletino, m; 1801 Van Ness Ave., San Francisco, Calif. 94109; Central Council of Italian Catholic Federation.

Byzantine Catholic World, biweekly; 3643 Perrysville Ave., Pittsburgh, Pa. 15214; Pittsburgh Byzantine archdiocese.

Catholic Accent, w; P.O. Box 850, Greensburg, Pa. 15601; Greensburg diocese.

Catholic Advance, The, w; 424 N. Broadway, Wichita, Kans. 67202; Wichita diocese.

Catholic Banner, w; P.O. Box 818, Charleston, S.C. 29402; Charleston diocese.

Catholic Bulletin, w; 244 Dayton Ave., St. Paul, Minn. 55102; St. Paul and Minneapolis archdiocese.

Catholic Chronicle, biweekly; P.O. Box 1866, Toledo, O. 43603; Toledo diocese.

Catholic Commentary, w; P.O. Box 2239, Anchorage, Alaska 99510; one-page supplement in local newspaper; Anchorage archdiocese.

Catholic Commentator, The, w; P.O. Box 14746, Baton Rouge, La. 70808; Baton Rouge diocese.

Catholic Communicator, w; 202 Morningside Dr. S.E., Albuquerque, N.M. 87108. Santa Fe archdiocese.

Catholic Crosswinds, semi-monthly; 1001 N. Grand Ave., Pueblo, Colo. 81003; Pueblo diocese.

Catholic Exponent, biweekly; 315 Ohio One Bldg., Youngstown, O. 44503; Youngstown diocese.

Catholic Free Press, w; 47 Elm St., Worcester, Mass. 01609; Worcester diocese.

Catholic Herald, w; P.O. Box 26587, Milwaukee, Wis. 53226; Milwaukee archdiocese.

Catholic Herald — Madison Edition, w; P.O. Box 1176, Middleton, Wis. 53701.

Catholic Herald — Superior Edition, w; P.O. Box 310, Superior, Wis. 54880.

Catholic Herald, The, w; 5890 Newman Ct., Sacramento, Calif. 95819; Sacramento diocese.

Catholic Hungarian's Sunday, w; 1739 Mahoning Ave., Youngstown, O. 44509.

Catholic Key to the News, The, w; P.O. Box 1037, Kansas City, Mo. 64141; Kansas City-St. Joseph diocese.

Catholic Light, biweekly; 300 Wyoming Ave., Scranton, Pa. 18503; Scranton diocese.

Catholic Messenger, w; P.O. Box 939, Davenport, Ia. 52805; Davenport diocese.

Catholic Mirror, biweekly; 200 Jewett Bldg., Des Moines, Ia. 50309.

Catholic Missourian, w; P.O. Box 1107, Jefferson City, Mo. 65102; Jefferson City diocese.

Catholic New York, w; P.O. Box 5133, New York, N.Y. 10150; New York archdiocese.

Catholic Northwest Progress, w; 907 Terry Ave., Seattle, Wash. 98104; Seattle archdiocese.

Catholic Observer, biweekly; Box 1570, Springfield, Mass. 01101; Springfield diocese.

Catholic Post, The, w; P.O. Box 1722, Peoria, Ill. 61656; Peoria diocese.

Catholic Register, biweekly; Box 126-C, Logan Blvd., Hollidaysburg, Pa. 16648; Altoona-Johnstown diocese.

Catholic Review, w; 320 Cathedral St., Baltimore, Md. 21203; Baltimore archdiocese.

Catholic Sentinel, w; 2816 E. Burnside St., Portland, Ore. 97214; Portland archdiocese, Baker diocese.

Catholic Spirit, The, w; 161 Edgington Lane, Wheeling, W. Va. 26003; Wheeling-Charleston diocese.

Catholic Standard, w; 1711 N. St., N.W., Washington, D.C. 20036; Washington archdiocese.

Catholic Standard and Times, w; 222 N. 17th St., Philadelphia, Pa. 19103; Philadelphia archdiocese; Allentown diocese.

Catholic Star Herald, w; 1845 Haddon Ave., Camden, N.J. 08103; Camden diocese.

Catholic Sun, The, w; 257 E. Onondaga St., Syracuse, N.Y. 13202; Syracuse diocese.

Catholic Telegraph, w; 100 E. 8th St., Cincinnati, O. 45202; Cincinnati archdiocese.

Catholic Times, w; P.O. Box 636, Columbus, O. 43216; Columbus diocese.

Catholic Transcript, w; 785 Asylum Ave., Hartford, Conn. 06105; Hartford archdiocese, Bridgeport and Norwich dioceses.

Catholic Twin Circle, w; 1901 Avenue of the Stars, Suite 1511, Los Angeles, Calif. 90067.

Catholic Universe Bulletin, biweekly; 1027 Superior Ave. N.E., Cleveland, O. 44114; Cleveland diocese.

Catholic Virginian, w; 14 N. Laurel St., Box 26843, Richmond, Va. 23261; Richmond diocese.

Catholic Voice, The, w; 2918 Lakeshore Ave., Oakland, Calif. 94610; Oakland diocese.

Catholic Voice, The, w; P.O. Box 4010, Omaha, Nebr. 68104; Omaha archdiocese.

Catholic Week, w; P.O. Box 349, Mobile, Ala. 36601; Mobile diocese.

Catholic Weekly, The, w; P.O. Box 1405, Saginaw, Mich. 48605; Saginaw diocese.

Catholic Weekly, The, w; 1628 Lambden Rd., Flint, Mich. 48501; Lansing diocese.

Catholic Witness, The, w; P.O. Box 2555, Harrisburg, Pa. 17105; Harrisburg diocese.

Central California Register, biweekly; P.O. Box 1668, 1550 N. Fresno St., Fresno, Calif. 93717; Fresno diocese.

Central Washington Catholic, m; P.O. Box 505, Yakima, Wash. 98907. Yakima diocese.

Challenge, The, semimonthly; P.O. Box 14082, Jefferson Sta., Detroit, Mich. 48214. St. Maron diocese.

Chicago Catholic, The w; 155 E. Superior St., Chicago, Ill. 60611; Chicago archdiocese.

Church Today, biweekly; P.O. Box 7417, Alexandria, La. 71306; Alexandria-Shreveport diocese.

Church World, w; Industry Rd., Brunswick, Me. 04011; Portland diocese.

Clarion Herald, w; 523 Natchez St., New Orleans, La. 70130; New Orleans archdiocese.

Common Sense, w; 1325 Jefferson Ave., Memphis, Tenn. 38104; Memphis diocese.

Community, w; P.O. Box 10607, Jacksonville, Fla. 32207; one-page weekly in Sunday editions of two daily newspapers; Jacksonville diocese.

Compass, The, w; P.O. Box 909, Green Bay, Wis. 54305; Green Bay diocese.

Concern, 20 issues a year; 153 Ash St., Manchester, N.H. 03104; Manchester diocese.

Courier, The, biweekly; P.O. Box 949, Winona, Minn. 55987; Winona diocese.

Courier-Journal, w; 114 S. Union St., Rochester, N.Y. 14607; Rochester diocese.

Criterion, The, w; P.O. Box 174, Indianapolis, Ind. 46206; Indianapolis archdiocese.

Dakota Catholic Action, 9 times a year; P.O. Box 128, Wilton, N.D. 58579; Bismarck diocese.

Darbininkas (Lithuanian), w; 341 Highland Blvd., Brooklyn, N.Y. 11207; Lithuanian Franciscan Fathers.

Denver Catholic Register, w; P.O. Box 1620, Denver, Colo. 80201; Denver archdiocese.

Dialog, The, w; 1925 Delaware Ave., Wilmington, Del. 19899; Wilmington diocese.

Diocese of Orange Bulletin, m; Marywood Spirituality Center, 2811 E. Villa Real Dr., Orange, Calif. 92667.

Draugas (Lithuanian), daily; 4545 W. 63rd St., Chicago, Ill. 60629; Lithuanian Catholic Press Society.

East Texas Catholic, The, biweekly; P.O. Box 3948, Beaumont, Tex. 77704; Beaumont diocese.

Eastern Catholic Life, w; 101 Market St., Passaic, N.J. 07055; Passaic Byzantine eparchy.

Eastern Montana Catholic Register, w; P.O. Box 2107, Great Falls, Mont. 59403; Great Falls-Billings diocese.

Eastern Oklahoma Catholic, biweekly; Box 520, Tulsa, Okla. 74101; Tulsa diocese.

El Heraldo Catolico, bm; P.O. Box 19312, Sacramento, Calif. 95819; Sacramento diocese.

El Visitante de Puerto Rico (Spanish), w; Box 1967, San Juan, P.R. 00903; Bishops of Puerto Rico.

El Visitante Dominical (Spanish), w; P.O. Box 96, San Antonio, Tex. 78291; Missionary Society of Oblate Fathers of Texas, Inc.

Evangelist, The, w; 39 Philip St., Albany, N.Y. 12207; Albany diocese.

Florida Catholic, The, w; 321 Hillman Ave., P.O. Box 3551, Orlando, Fla. 32802; Orlando and St. Petersburg dioceses.

Gary Sunday Visitor, w; P.O. Box M-356, Gary, Ind. 46401; Gary diocese.

Georgia Bulletin, w; 680 W. Peachtree St. N.W., Atlanta, Ga. 30308; Atlanta archdiocese.

Globe, The, w; 1821 Jackson St., Sioux City, Ia. 51105; Sioux City diocese.

Guardian, The, w; P.O. Box 7417, Little Rock, Ark. 72217; Little Rock diocese.

Harmonizer, The (Edition O.S.V.), w; Cathedral Center, P.O. Box 11169, Fort Wayne, Ind. 46856; Fort Wayne-S. Bend diocese.

Hawaii Catholic Herald, w; 1184 Bishop St., Honolulu, H.I. 96813; Honolulu diocese.

Hlas Naroda (Voice of the Nation) (Czech-English), w; 2657-59 S. Lawndale Ave., Chicago. 60623.

Horizons, semimonthly; 1900 Carlton Rd., Parma, O. 44134; Parma diocese.

Idaho Register, w; P.O. Box 2835, Boise, Idaho 83701; Boise diocese.

Impact! 4 to 6 times a year; 1234 Massachusetts Ave. N.W. Suite 1004, Washington, D.C. 20005; National Office for Black Catholics.

Inland Catholic, The, w; P.O. Box 2788, San Bernardino, Calif. 92405. San Bernardino diocese.

Inland Register, w; P.O. Box 48, Spokane, Wash. 99210; Spokane diocese.

Inside Passage, w; 419 6th St., Juneau, Alaska 99801; Juneau diocese.

Intermountain Catholic, The, w; P.O. Box 2489, Salt Lake City, Utah 84110; Salt Lake City diocese.

Jednota (Slovak-Eng.), w; Jednota and Rosedale Aves., Middletown, Pa. 17057; First Catholic Slovak Union.

Joliet Catholic Explorer, w; St. Charles Borromeo Pastoral Center, Rt. 53 and Airport Rd., Romeoville, Ill. 60441. Joliet diocese.

Lafayette Sunday Visitor, w; P.O. Box 5808, Lafayette, Ind. 47903; Lafayette diocese.

Lake Shore Visitor, w; P.O. Box 4047, Erie, Pa. 16512; Erie diocese.

Leaven, The, w; 2220 Central, Kansas City, Kans. 66110; Kansas City archdiocese.

Long Island Catholic, The, w; P.O. Box 700, Hempstead, N.Y. 11551; Rockville Centre diocese.

Message, The, w; P.O. Box 4169, Evansville, Ind. 47711; Evansville diocese.

Messenger, The, w; 224 W. Lincoln St., Belleville, Ill. 62221; Belleville diocese.

Messenger, The, w; P.O. Box 268, Covington, Ky. 41012; Covington diocese.

Michigan Catholic, The, w; 2701 Chicago

Blvd., Detroit, Mich. 48206; Detroit archdiocese.

Mirror, The, biweekly; M.P.O. Box 847, Springfield, Mo. 65801; Springfield-Cape Girardeau diocese.

Mississippi Today, w; P.O. Box 2130, Jackson, Miss. 39205; Jackson and Biloxi dioceses.

Monitor, The, w; 441 Church St., San Francisco, Calif. 94114; San Francisco archdiocese, Stockton and Santa Rosa dioceses.

Monitor, The, w; 139 N. Warren St., Trenton, N.J. 08607; Trenton diocese.

Morning Star, The, w; P.O. Box 3223, Lafayette, La. 70502; Lafayette diocese.

Narod Polski (Polish-Eng.) semi-monthly; 984 Milwaukee Ave., Chicago, Ill. 60622.

Nasa Nada (Eng.-Croatian), m; 4848 S. Ellis Ave., Chicago, Ill. 60615; Croatian Catholic Union.

National Catholic Register, w; 1901 Avenue of the Stars, Suite 1511, Los Angeles, Calif. 90067.

National Catholic Reporter, The, w; P.O. Box 281, Kansas City, Mo. 64141.

New Earth, The, m (Oct-June); P.O. Box 1750, Fargo, N.D. 58107; Fargo diocese.

New Star, The, w; 2208 W. Chicago Ave., Chicago, Ill. 60622; St. Nicholas of Chicago Ukrainian diocese.

North Carolina Catholic, w; 300 Cardinal Gibbons Dr., Raleigh, N.C. 27606 and 1524 E. Morehead St., Charlotte, N.C. 28207; Raleigh and Charlotte dioceses.

North Country Catholic, w; Box 326, Ogdensburg, N.Y. 13669; Ogdensburg diocese.

Northwestern Kansas Register, w; P.O. Box 958, Salina, Kans. 67401; Salina diocese.

Nuevo Amanecer, m; P.O. Box 155, Brooklyn, N.Y. 11243; for Hispanic Catholic community of Brooklyn diocese.

Observer, The, w; P.O. Box 2079, Monterey, Calif. 93940; Monterey diocese.

Observer, The, biweekly; 921 W. State St., Rockford, Ill. 61102; Rockford diocese.

One Voice, w; P.O. Box 10822, Birmingham, Ala. 35202; Birmingham diocese.

Our Northland Diocese, 22 issues annually; P.O. Box 610, Crookston, Minn. 56716; Crookston diocese.

Our Sunday Visitor, w; 200 Noll Plaza, Huntington, Ind. 46750; national edition and official publication for 6 dioceses.

Outlook, m (Sept.-June); 215 W. 4th St., Duluth, Minn. 55806; Duluth diocese.

P.A.D.R.E.S. National Bulletin, q; 3310 Garfield Ave., Kansas City, Kans. 66104.

Pilot, The, w; 49 Franklin St., Boston, Mass. 02110; Boston archdiocese.

Pittsburgh Catholic, The, w; 110 Third

Ave., Pittsburgh, Pa. 15222; Pittsburgh diocese.

Polish American Journal, m; 413 Cedar Ave., Scranton, Pa. 18505.

Proclaimer, w; P.O. Box 2824, Kalamazoo, Mich. 49003; Kalamazoo diocese.

Record, The, w; 433 S. 5th St., Louisville, Ky. 40202; Louisville archdiocese.

Redwood Crozier, The, w; Santa Rosa, Calif., diocese; first issue scheduled, June 28, 1982.

St. Cloud Visitor, w; 810 Germain St., St. Cloud, Minn. 56301; St. Cloud diocese.

St. Joseph's-Blatt (German-Eng.), m; St. Benedict, Ore. 97373; Manfred F. Ellenberger.

St. Louis Review, w; 462 N. Taylor Ave., St. Louis, Mo. 63108; St. Louis archdiocese.

Shlakh — The Way, w; 805 N. Franklin St., Philadelphia, Pa. 19123; Philadelphia archeparchy. Stamford and Chicago eparchies.

Sooner Catholic, The, biweekly; P.O. Box 32180, Oklahoma City, Okla. 73123; Oklahoma City archdiocese.

South Texas Catholic, w; P.O. Box 2584, Corpus Christi, Tex. 78403; Corpus Christi diocese.

Southern Catholic, The, m; 855 W. Carolina St., Tallahassee; Pensacola-Tallahassee diocese.

Southern Cross, The, w; P.O. Box 81869, San Diego, Calif. 92138; San Diego diocese.

Southern Cross, The, w; 601 E. 6th St., Waynesboro, Ga. 30830; Savannah diocese.

Southern Nebraska Register, w; P.O. Box 80329, Lincoln, Nebr. 68501; Lincoln diocese.

Southwest Kansas Register, w; P.O. Box 1317, Dodge City, Kans. 67801; Dodge City diocese.

Steubenville Register, w; P.O. Box 160, Steubenville, O. 43952; Steubenville diocese.

Tablet, w; 1 Hanson Pl., Brooklyn, N.Y. 11243; Brooklyn diocese.

Tennessee Register, The, w; 2400 21st Ave. S., Nashville, Tenn. 37212; Nashville diocese.

Texas Catholic, w; 3915 Lemmon Ave., Dallas, Tex. 75219; Dallas and Fort Worth dioceses.

Texas Catholic Herald, The, w; 1700 San Jacinto St., Houston, Tex. 77002; Galveston-Houston diocese.

Tidings, The, w; 1530 W. 9th St., Los Angeles, Calif. 90015; Los Angeles archdiocese.

Time and Eternity, w; 514 E. Lawrence St., Springfield, Ill. 62703; Springfield diocese.

Times-Review, The, w; P.O. Box 937, La Crosse, Wis. 54601; La Crosse diocese.

Today's Catholic, w; P.O. Box 12429, San Antonio, Tex. 78212; San Antonio archdiocese.

Upper Peninsula Catholic, w; P.O. Box 548, Marquette, Mich. 49855; Marquette diocese.

Valley Catholic Witness, 208 Iris, McAllen, Tex. 78501; one page every other week in three area newspapers; Brownsville diocese.

Vermont Catholic Tribune, biweekly; 351 North Ave., Burlington, Vt. 05401; Burlington diocese.

Visitor, The, w; 184 Broad St., Providence, R.I. 02903; Providence diocese.

Voice, The, w; 6201 Biscayne Blvd., Miami, Fla. 33138; Miami archdiocese.

Voice of the Southwest, w; P.O. Box 7, San Fidel, N. Mex. 87049; Gallup diocese.

Wanderer, The, w; 201 Ohio St., St. Paul, Minn. 55107.

WestMont Word, biweekly; P.O. Box 1729, Helena, Mont. 59624; Helena diocese.

West Nebraska Register, w; P.O. Box 608, Grand Island, Nebr. 68801; Grand Island diocese.

West River Catholic, m; P.O. Box 678, Rapid City, S. Dak. 57709; Rapid City diocese.

West Texas Angelus, biweekly; 116 S. Oakes, San Angelo, Tex. 76903; San Angelo diocese.

West Texas Catholic, w; 1800 N. Spring, Amarillo, Tex. 79107; Amarillo diocese.

Western Michigan Catholic, w; 650 Burton S.E., Grand Rapids, Mich. 49507; Grand Rapids diocese.

Western New York Catholic Visitor, m; 100 S. Elmwood Ave., Buffalo, N.Y. 14202; Buffalo diocese.

Witness, The, w; 1229 Mt. Loretta, Dubuque, Ia. 52001; Dubuque archdiocese.

Wyoming Register, w; P.O. Box 1308, Cheyenne, Wyo. 82001.

Magazines, Other Periodicals

ADRIS Newsletter, q; Department of Theology, Fordham University, Bronx, N.Y. 10458. Association for the Development of Religious Information Services.

AIM (Aids in Ministry), q; 1800 W. Winnemac Ave., Chicago, Ill. 60640.

Alaskan Shepherd, 6 times a year; 1312 Peger Rd., Fairbanks, Alaska 99701.

America, w; 106 W. 56th St., New York, N.Y. 10019.

American Benedictine Review, St. Benedict's Abbey, Atchison, Kans. 66002.

American Midland Naturalist, q; Notre Dame, Ind. 46556.

Americas, The, q; Box 34440, W. Bethesda, Md. 20817; Academy of American Franciscan History.

Amerikanski Slovenec (Slovenian), w; 6117 St. Clair Ave., Cleveland, O. 44103; Slovenian Catholic Union.

Angel Guardian Home Quarterly, The, q; 6301 12th Ave., Brooklyn, N.Y. 11219.

Anthonian, q; Paterson, N.J. 07509; St. Anthony's Guild.

Anthropological Quarterly, q; 620 Michigan Ave. N.E., Washington, D.C. 20064.

Apostolate of Our Lady, m; Carey, O. 43316; Our Lady of Consolation National Shrine.

Apostolate of the Little Flower, bm; P.O. Box 5280, 906 Kentucky Ave., San Antonio, Tex. 78201; Discalced Carmelite Fathers.

Archeparchal Bulletin, q; 815 N. Franklin St., Philadelphia, Pa. 19123.

Atchison Benedictine Community News (ABC News), bm; Mount St. Scholastica Convent, Atchison, Kans. 66002.

Ateitis (The Future) (Lithuanian), m; 7235 S. Sacramento Ave., Chicago, Ill. 60629; for youth.

Ave Maria (Polish), 6 times a year; 600 Doat St., Buffalo, N.Y. 14211; Felician Srs.

Benedictine Orient, bm; 2400 Maple Ave., Lisle, Ill. 60532.

Benedictines, semiannually; Mt. St. Scholastica, Atchison, Kans. 66002.

Bernardine Bulletin, The, semiannually; 647 Spring Mill Rd., Villanova, Pa. 19085; Bernardine Srs..

Best Sellers, m; Univ. of Scranton, Scranton, Pa. 18510.

Better World, q; Belford, N.J. 07718; Mary Productions Guild.

Bible Today, The, bm; Liturgical Press, Collegeville, Minn. 56321.

BLUEPRINT for Social Justice, 10 times a year; Institute of Human Relations, Loyola University, New Orleans, La. 70118.

Bringing Religion Home, m; 221 W. Madison St., Chicago, Ill. 60606.

Brothers' Newsletter, q; Passionist Monastery, P.O. Box 150, West Springfield, Mass. 01089; National Assembly of Religious Brothers.

Call Board, The, 5 times a year; 1501 Broadway, Suite 2400, New York, N.Y. 10036; Catholic Actors' Guild.

Camillian: Journal of the National Association of Catholic Chaplains, q; 325 S. Lake Dr., Milwaukee, Wis. 53207; National Association of Catholic Chaplains.

Catechist, The, m (exc. Dec., June-Aug.); 2451 E. River Rd., Dayton, O. 45439.

Catholic Aid News, m; 49 W. 9th St., St. Paul, Minn. 55102.

Catholic Biblical Quarterly, q; Catholic University of America, Washington, D.C. 20064; Catholic Biblical Assn.

Catholic Cemetery, The, m; 710 N. River Rd., Des Plaines, Ill. 60016; National Catholic Cemetery Conference.

Catholic Digest, The, m; P.O. Box 43090, St. Paul, Minn. 55164.

Catholic Forester Magazine, bm; 305 W. Madison St., Chicago, Ill. 60606; Catholic Order of Foresters.

CGA World Magazine, bm; National

Headquarters, Cahtolic Golden Age, Scranton, Pa. 18503.

Catholic Historical Review, q; 620 Michigan Ave. N.E., Washington, D.C. 20064; American Catholic Historical Assn.

CHA in Washington, The, m; 4455 Woodson Rd., St. Louis, Mo. 63134; Catholic Health Association.

Catholic Journalist, The, m; 119 N. Park Ave., Rockville Centre, N.Y. 11570; Catholic Press Association.

C.K. of A. Journal, m; 217 E. 8th St., Cincinnati, O. 45202; Catholic Knights of America.

C.L. of C. Index, m; 2770 E. Main St., Columbus, O. 43209.

Catholic Lawyer, q; St. John's University, Jamaica, N.Y. 11439; St. Thomas More Institute for Legal Research.

Catholic League Newsletter, m; 1100 W. Wells St., Milwaukee, Wis. 53233; Catholic League for Religious and Civil Rights.

Catholic Library World, 10 times a year; 461 W. Lancaster Ave., Haverford, Pa. 19041; Catholic Library Association.

Catholic Life Magazine, m (exc. July-Aug.); 35750 Moravian Dr., Fraser, Mich. 48026; PIME Missionaries.

Catholic Mind, The, m (exc. July-Aug.); 106 W. 56th St., New York, N.Y. 10019.

Catholic Near East Magazine, q; 1011 First Ave., New York, N.Y. 10022; Catholic Near East Welfare Assn.

Catholic Periodical and Literature Index, bm; 461 W. Lancaster Ave., Haverford, Pa. 19041; Catholic Library Association.

Catholic Pharmacist, q; 1012 Surrey Hills Dr., St. Louis, Mo. 63117; National Catholic Pharmacists Guild.

Catholic Press Directory, a; 119 N. Park Ave. Rockville Centre, N.Y. 11570; Catholic Press Assn.

Catholic Quote, m; Valparaiso, Nebr. 68065; Rev. Jerome Pokorny.

CRS News, q; 1011 First Ave., New York, N.Y. 10022. Catholic Relief Services.

Catholic Review (Braille), m; 154 E. 23rd St., New York, N.Y. 10010; Xavier Society for the Blind.

Catholic Rural Life, m; 4625 N.W. Beaver Dr., Des Moines, Ia. 50322; National Catholic Rural Life Conference.

Catholic Trends, biweekly; 1312 Massachusetts Ave. N.W. Washington, D.C. 20005; NC News Service.

Catholic University of America Law Review, q; Washington, D.C. 20064.

Catholic Update, m; 1615 Republic St., Cincinnati, O. 45210.

Catholic War Veteran, bm; 2 Massachusetts Ave. N.W., Washington, D.C. 20001.

Catholic Woman, bm; 1312 Massachusetts Ave. N.W., Washington, D.C. 20005. National Council of Catholic Women.

Catholic Woman's Journal, 10 times a year;

3835 Westminster Pl., St. Louis, Mo. 63108; National Catholic Women's Union.

Catholic Worker, 9 times a year; 36 E. First St., New York, N.Y. 10003.

Catholic Workman, m; 112½ E. Main, New Prague, Minn. 56071.

Catholic Youth Ministry, 10 times a year; 22 Willow St., Mystic, Conn. 06355.

Charities USA, m; 1346 Connecticut Ave. N.W., Washington, D.C. 20036; National Conference of Catholic Charities.

Chicago Studies, 3 times a year; P.O. Box 665, Mundelein, Ill. 60060.

Christian Life Communities Harvest, 6 times a year; 3721 Westminster Pl., St. Louis, Mo. 63108; National Federation of Christian Life Communities.

Christian Renewal News, P.O. Box 467, La Puente, Calif. 91747. Apostolate of Christian Renewal.

Christopher News Notes, 7 times a year; 12 E. 48th St., New York, N.Y. 10017; The Christophers, Inc.

City of God, The, 3 times a year; 4545 Northwestern Ave., Indianapolis, Ind. 46208; St. Maur Theological Center.

Classical Bulletin, 6 times a year; 221 N. Grand Blvd., St. Louis, Mo. 63103.

Claverite, The, biannually; 554 Palmetto St., P.O. Box 204, Mobile, Ala. 36601; Knights of Peter Claver.

Columban Mission, m (exc. June, Aug.); St. Columbans, Nebr. 68056; Columban Fathers.

Columbia, m; One Columbus Plaza, New Haven, Conn. 06507; Knights of Columbus.

Columbian, The, w; 188 W. Randolph St., Chicago, Ill. 60601.

Comboni Missions, 6 times a year; 8108 Beechmont Ave., Cincinnati, O. 45230.

Commitment, q; 1200 Varnum St. N.E., Washington, D.C. 20017; National Catholic Conference for Interracial Justice.

Commonweal, biweekly; 232 Madison Ave., New York, N.Y. 10016.

Communio — International Catholic Review, q; Gonzaga University, Spokane, Wash. 99202.

Community, q; 1746 W. Division St., Chicago, Ill. 60622; Friendship House.

Consecrated Life, semi-annually; 4200 N. Austin Ave., Chicago, Ill. 60634; Institute on Religious Life. English edition of *Informationes,* official publication of Sacred Congregation for Religious and Secular Institutes.

Consolata, 6 times a year; P.O. Box C, Somerset, N.J. 08873.

Contact, 10 times a year; 123-15 14 Ave., College Point, N.Y. 11356; Sisters of St. Dominic.

Contemplative Review, q; Beckley Hill, Barre, Vt. 05641; Association of Contemplative Sisters.

Context, 22 issues a year; 221 W. Madison St., Chicago, Ill. 60606.

Cord, The, m; P.O. Drawer F, St. Bonaventure, N.Y. 14778.

Counseling and Values, q; 2 Skyline Place, Suite 400, 5203 Leesburg Pike, Falls Church, Va. 22041; Association for Religious and Value Issues in Counseling.

Cross Currents, q; Mercy College, 555 Broadway, Dobbs Ferry, N.Y. 10522.

Crossroads Radio Centre, bm; 1089 Elm St., W. Springfield, Mass. 01089.

Crusader's Almanac, The, biannually; 1400 Quincy St. N.E., Washington, D.C. 20017; Commissariat of the Holy Land.

CRUX of the News, w; 75 Champlain St., Albany, N.Y. 12204.

Damien-Dutton Call, q; 616 Bedford Ave., Bellmore, N.Y. 11710.

Damien Report, The, m; 131 Kuulei Rd., Kailua, H.I. 96734.

Daystar, a; 172 Foster St., Brighton, Mass. 02135; Franciscan Missionary Sisters for Africa.

Deaf Blind Weekly, The (Braille), w; 154 E. 23rd St., New York, N.Y. 10010; Xavier Society for the Blind.

Desert Call, q; SLIA-Nada, R.R. 3, Sedona, Ariz. 86336; Spiritual Life Institute of America.

Diakonia, 3 times a year; Fordham Univ., Bronx, N.Y. 10458; John XXIII Center for Eastern Christian Studies.

Dimensions, m; 119 N. Park Ave., Rockville Centre, N.Y. 11570; National Catholic Development Conference.

Divine Love, q; P.O. Box 24, Fresno, Calif. 93707.

Divine Word Messenger, semiannually; Bay St. Louis, Miss. 39520.

Divine Word Missionaries, q; Techny, Ill. 60082.

Ecumenical Trends, m (exc. July-Aug.); Graymoor Ecumenical Institute, Garrison, N.Y. 10524.

Ecumenist, The, 6 times a year; Paulist Press, 545 Island Rd., Ramsey, N.J. 07446.

Educating in Faith, q; 2021 H St. N.W., Washington, D.C. 20006. Catholic Negro-American Mission Board.

Emmanuel, m (bm July-Aug.); 194 E. 76th St., New York, N.Y. 10021; Blessed Sacrament Fathers.

Emmaus Letter, q; 1312 Massachusetts Ave. N.W., Washington, D.C. 20005. National CYO Federation.

Encounter, 2 times a year; 200 Lake St., Boston, Mass. 02135; Religious of the Cenacle.

Envoy, bm; Office of Public Relations, Catholic University of America, Washington, D.C. 20064.

Extension, m; 35 E. Wacker Dr., Suite 400, Chicago, Ill. 60601; Catholic Church Extension Society.

Family, m; 50 St. Paul's Ave., Boston, Mass. 02130; Daughters of St. Paul.

Family Festivals, bm; Resource Publications, 7291 Cornoado Dr., San Jose, Calif. 95129.

Family Friend, q; P.O. Box 11563, Milwaukee, Wis. 53211; Catholic Family Life Insurance.

Fatima Findings, m; 100 E. 20th St., Baltimore, Md. 21218; Reparation Society of the Immaculate Heart of Mary.

Fellowship of Catholic Scholars Newsletter, q; St. John's University, Jamaica, N.Y. 11439.

Fiat, The, q; P.O. Box 382, Cohoes, N.Y. 12047; Apostolate of Suffering.

Filipino Catholic Newsmagazine, semimonthly; 114 E. 2nd St., Los Angeles, Calif. 90012; Filipino Catholic Publications, Inc.

Franciscan Herald, m; 1434 W. 51st St., Chicago, Ill. 60609.

F.M.A. Focus, q; 274-280 W. Lincoln Ave., Mt. Vernon, N.Y. 10550; Franciscan Mission Associates.

Franciscan Reporter, q; 3140 Meramec St., St. Louis, Mo. 63138.

Franciscan Studies, a; St. Bonaventure, N.Y. 14778; Franciscan Institute.

Fraternal Leader, bm; 305 W. 6th St., Erie, Pa. 16512; Loyal Christian Benefit Association.

Fund Raising Forum, m; 119 N. Park Ave., Rockville Centre, N.Y. 11570; National Catholic Development Conference.

Garsas (Lithuanian-English), m; 341 Highland Blvd., Brooklyn, N.Y. 11207; Lithuanian Roman Catholic Alliance of America.

Generation, m; 221 W. Madison St., Chicago, Ill. 60606.

Glenmary's Challenge, q; P.O. Box 46404, Cincinnati, O. 45246; Glenmary Home Missioners.

God's Word Today, m; P.O. Box 7705, Ann Arbor, Mich. 48107.

Good Shepherd (Slovak and English), a; 425 W. 12th Ave., Gary, Ind. 46407; Slovak Catholic Federation of America.

Goose Corn, 10 issues a year; 221 W. Madison St., Chicago, Ill. 60606.

Harmony, 4 or 5 times a year; 8300 Morganford Rd., St. Louis, Mo. 63123; Benedictine Srs. of Perpetual Adoration.

Holy Name Newsletter, m (exc. July and Dec.); P.O. Box 4033, Rocky Mount, N.C. 27801; National Association of the Holy Name Society.

Homiletic and Pastoral Review, m; 86 Riverside Dr., New York, N.Y. 10024.

Horizons: Journal of the College Theology Society, biannual; Villanova University, Villanova, Pa. 19085.

Hospital Progress, m; 4455 Woodson Rd.,

St. Louis, Mo. 63134; Catholic Health Association.

Human Development, q; Jesuit Educational Center, 130 John St., New York, N.Y. 10038.

Human Life Issues, q; St. John's University. Collegeville, Minn. 56321; Human Life Center.

I.C. Good News, q; Loyola Center, 5600 City Ave., Philadelphia, Pa. 19131; North City Catholic Conference, Inc.

Immaculata, m; 1600 W. Park Ave., Libertyville, Ill. 60048; Franciscan Fathers.

In-Formation, 8 times a year; 1234 Massachusetts Ave., N.W., Washington, D.C. 20005; Religious Formation Conference.

Institute Journal, bm; 50 Oak St., San Francisco, Calif. 94102; Young Men's Institute.

Integrity, m; 6243 S. Fairfield Ave., Chicago, Ill. 60629; Rev. L. Dudley Day, O.S.A.

Interface, q; 1312 Massachusetts Ave. N.W., Washington, D.C. 20005; Bishops' Committee for Ecumenical and Interreligious Affairs.

International Philosophical Quarterly; Fordham University, Bronx, N.Y. 10458.

International Review — Natural Family Planning, q; St. John's University, Collegeville, Minn. 56321.

It's Our World, 4 times a year; 800 Allegheny Ave., Pittsburgh, Pa. 15233; Holy Childhood Association.

Jesuit, The, q; 39 E. 83rd St., New York, N.Y. 10028.

Jesuit Blackrobe, q; 3601 W. Fond du Lac Ave., Milwaukee, Wis. 53216.

Jesuit Bulletin, 4 times a year; 4511 W. Pine Blvd., St. Louis, Mo. 63108; Jesuit Seminary Aid Association.

Josephite Harvest, The, q; 1130 N. Calvert St., Baltimore, Md. 21202; Josephite Missionaries.

Jurist, The, semiannually; Catholic University of America, Washington, D.C. 20064; School of Canon Law.

Katolicky Sokol (Catholic Falcon) (Slovak-English), w; 205 Madison St., Passaic, N.J. 07055; Slovak Catholic Sokol.

Kinship, q; P.O. Box 39188, Cincinnati, O. 45229; Glenmary Sisters.

KIT — Keeping in Touch, m; 1820 Mt. Elliott Ave., Detroit, Mich. 48207; Capuchin Province of St. Joseph.

Knights of St. John, q; 6517 Charles Ave., Cleveland, O. 44129.

Kolping Banner, m; 115-14 227th St., Cambria Heights., N.Y. 11411; Catholic Kolping Society.

Laivas (Lithuanian), m; 4545 W. 63rd St., Chicago, Ill. 60629.

Land of Cotton, q; 2048 W. Fairview Ave.,

Montgomery, Ala. 39196; City of St. Jude. Mobile diocese.

Law Briefs, m; 1312 Massachusetts Ave. N.W., Washington, D.C. 20005; Office of General Counsel, USCC.

Law Reports, m; 4455 Woodson Rd., St. Louis, Mo. 63134.

Leaven, q; Convent of the Holy Spirit, Techny, Ill. 60082.

Leaves, bm; 23715 Ann Arbor Trail, Dearborn Heights, Mich. 48127; Mariannhill Fathers.

Let's Pray Together, w; 773 Madison Ave., Albany, N.Y. 12208; Families for Prayer.

Letter from St. Paul Newsletter, 8-10 times a year; 955 Lake Dr., St. Paul, Minn. 55120; National Marriage Encounter.

Liguorian, m; 1 Liguori Rd., Liguori, Mo. 63057; Redemptorist Fathers.

Linacre Quarterly, q; 850 Elm Grove Rd., Elm Grove, Wis. 53122; Federation of Catholic Physicians Guilds.

Listening, 5 times a year; 814 Thayer Ave., Silver Spring, Md. 20910. National Catholic Office for the Deaf.

Liturgy, q; 810 Rhode Island Ave. N.E. Washington, D.C. 20018.

Living Light, The, q; 11 Park Place, New York, N.Y. 10007; Department of Education, USCC.

Marian Helpers Bulletin, q; Stockbridge, Mass. 01262; Association of Marian Helpers and of the Congregation of Marian Fathers.

Marriage and Family Living, m; Abbey Press, St. Meinrad, Ind. 47577.

Marriage Encounter, m; 955 Lake Dr., St. Paul, Minn. 55120; National Marriage Encounter.

Mary Magazine and Aylesford News, bm; Cass Ave. N. at I-55, P.O. Box 65, Darien Ill. 60559; Carmelite Fathers.

Maryknoll, m; Maryknoll, N.Y. 10545; Catholic Foreign Mission Society.

Master's Work, q; Convent of Holy Spirit, Techny, Ill. 60082; Holy Spirit Missionary Sisters.

Media and Values, q; 1962 S. Shenandoah, Los Angeles, Calif. 90034; National Sisters Communication Service.

Medical Mission News, bm; 10 W. 17th St., New York, N.Y. 10011; Catholic Medical Mission Board, Inc.

Medical Mission Sisters News, 4 times a year; 8400 Pine Road, Philadelphia, Pa. 19111.

Men of Malvern, bm; Malvern, Pa. 19355; Laymen's Retreat League of Philadelphia.

Messenger, The, m; 16010 Detroit Ave., Lakewood, O. 44107.

Messenger of St. Joseph's Union, The, 108 Bedell St., Staten Island, N.Y. 10309.

MHS Review (Franciscanews), q; 232 S. Home Ave., Pittsburgh, Pa. 15202.

Mid-America, 3 times a year; Loyola University, Chicago, Ill. 60626.

Miesiecznik Franciszkanski (Polish), m; 165 E. Pulaski St., Pulaski, Wis. 54162; Franciscan Fathers.

Migration Today, 5 times a year; 209 Flagg Pl., Staten Island, N.Y. 10304; Center for Migration Studies.

Miraculous Medal, The, q; 475 E. Chelten Ave., Philadelphia, Pa. 19144; Central Association of the Miraculous Medal.

Mission, 5 times a year; 366 Fifth Ave., New York, N.Y. 10001; Society for Propagation of the Faith.

Mission, bm; 1663 Bristol Pike, Bensalem, Pa. 19020; Sisters of the Blessed Sacrament.

Mission Helper, The, q; 1001 W. Joppa Rd., Baltimore, Md. 21204; Mission Helpers of the Sacred Heart.

Missionhurst, 6 times a year; 4651 N. 25th St., Arlington, Va. 22207; Immaculate Heart of Mary Mission Society, Inc.

Mission Intercom, 10 times a year; 1233 Lawrence St., N.E., Washington, D.C. 20017; U.S. Catholic Mission Council.

Missionaries of Africa Report, bm; 1622 21st St. N.W., Washington, D.C. 20009; Society of Missionaries of Africa (White Fathers).

Modern Liturgy, 8 times a year; Resource Publications, 7291 Coronado Dr., San Jose, Calif. 95129.

Modern Schoolman, The, q; 3700 W. Pine Blvd., St. Louis, Mo. 63108; St. Louis University.

Momentum, 4 times a year; Suite 350, One Dupont Circle, Washington, D.C. 20036; National Catholic Educational Asssociation.

Mother Cabrini Messenger, bm; 434 W. Deming Pl., Chicago, Ill. 60614; Mother Cabrini League.

MSC Spotlite, q; 305 S. Lake St., Aurora, Ill. 60507; Missionaries of the Sacred Heart.

My Daily Visitor, bm; 200 Noll Plaza, Huntington, Ind. 46750; Our Sunday Visitor, Inc.

My Friend, 10 times a year; 50 St. Paul's Ave., Jamaica Plain, Boston, Mass. 02130; for children.

NAWR Trends, m (Sept.-June); 1307 S. Wabash Ave., Chicago, Ill. 60605.

National Catholic Forester, q; 35 E. Wacker Dr., Chicago, Ill. 60601.

National Jesuit News, m; St. Joseph's University, Philadelphia, Pa. 19131.

National Service Committee Newsletter, 8-12 times a year; 237 N. Michigan St., South Bend, Ind. 46601; Catholic Charismatic Renewal.

Network Quarterly; Newsletter, bm; 806 Rhode Island Ave. N.E., Washington, D.C. 20018; Network.

New Catholic World, bm; 545 Island Rd., Ramsey, N.J. 07446.

New Covenant, m; P.O. Box 8617, Ann Arbor, Mich. 48107; Catholic Charismatic Renewal.

New Scholasticism, q; 715 Memorial; Library, Notre Dame, Ind. 46556. American Catholic Philosophical Association.

News/Views, 5 times a year; 1307 S. Wabash Ave., Chicago, Ill. 60605; National Sisters Vocation Conference.

News and Views, q; 3900 Westminster Pl.; St. Louis, Mo. 63108; Sacred Heart Program.

Newsletter, The, 4 times a year; 1234 Massachusetts Ave. N.W., Washington, D.C. 20005; International Liaison for Lay Volunteer Service.

Newsletter of the Bureau of Catholic Indian Missions, 6 times a year; 2021 H St. N.W., Washington, D.C. 20006.

North American Voice of Fatima, m; 1023 Swann Rd., Youngstown, N.Y. 14174.

Notre Dame Magazine, 5 times a year; Notre Dame Univ., Notre Dame, Ind. 46556.

Nursing Sisters Today, q; 310 Prospect Park W., Brooklyn, N.Y. 11215; Congregation of Infant Jesus.

Oblate World and Voice of Hope, bm; 350 Jamaica Way, Boston, Mass. 02130; Oblates of Mary Immaculate.

Origins, 48 times a year; 1312 Massachusetts Ave., N.W., Washington, D.C. 20005; NC News Service.

Our Lady of the Snows Newsletter, bm; 15 S. 59th St., Belleville, Ill. 62223; Shrine of Our Lady of the Snows.

Our Lady's Digest, bm; Box 777, Twin Lakes, Wis. 53181; La Salette Fathers.

Our Lady's Missionary, m; 315 Topsfield Rd., Ipswich, Mass. 01938; La Salette Fathers.

Pacer, bm; 500 17th Ave., Seattle, Wash. 98124; Providence Medical Center.

Padres' Trail, 4 times a year; St. Michael's Mission, St. Michael, Ariz. 86511; Franciscan Fathers.

Paraclete, 4 times a year; P.O. Box 2000, Wheaton, Md. 20902; Holy Ghost Fathers.

Parish Communication, 10 times a year, 22 Willow St., Mystic, Conn. 06355.

Parish Ministry, 6 times a year; 299 Elizabeth St., New York, N.Y. 10012; National Conference of Catholic Bishops' Parish Project.

Parish Visitor, q; 25 Elm St., Oneonta, N.Y. 13820; Parish Visitors of Mary Immaculate.

Pastoral Life, m; Route 224, Canfield, Ohio 44406; Society of St. Paul.

Pastoral Music, 6 times a year; 225 Sheridan St., N.W. Washington, D.C. 20011; National Association of Pastoral Musicians.

Paulist Fathers News, 6 times a year; 415 W. 59th St., New York, N.Y. 10019.

People of God Messenger, 10 times a year; 202 Morningside Dr. S.E., Albuquerque,

N.M. 87108; Santa Fe archdiocesan office of communications.

Perpetual Help World, q; 294 E. 150th St., Bronx, N.Y. 10451; Redemptorists.

Philosophy Today, q; Carthagena Station, Celina, Ohio 45822.

Pilgrim, q; Jesuit Fathers, Auriesville, N.Y. 12016; Shrine of North American Martyrs.

Pope Speaks, The, q; Our Sunday Visitor, Inc., 200 Noll Plaza, Huntington, Ind. 46750.

Priatel Dietok (Children's Friend) (Slovak), semi-monthly; 205 Madison St., Passaic, N.J. 07055; Slovak Catholic Sokol.

Priest, The, 11 times a year; 200 Noll Plaza, Huntington, Ind. 46750; Our Sunday Visitor, Inc.

Probe, bm (Sept.-June); 1307 S. Wabash Ave., Chicago, Ill. 60605; NAWR.

Professional Placement Newsnotes, bm; 10 W. 17th St., New York, N.Y. 10011; Catholic Medical Mission Board, Inc.

Program Supplement, 18 times a year; Columbus Plaza, New Haven, Conn. 06507; Knights of Columbus.

Provincial Annals, irregularly; Holy Name Province, Order of Friars Minor, 135 West 31st St., New York, N.Y. 10001.

Quarterly, The, 2021 H St. N.W., Washington, D.C. 20006; Commission for Catholic Missions Among the Colored People and the Indians.

Queen; bm; 26 S. Saxon Ave., Bay Shore, N.Y. 11706; Montfort Fathers.

Reign of the Sacred Heart, m; Hales Corners, Wis. 53130.

Religion Teacher's Journal, m (Sept.-May); P.O. Box 180, Mystic, Conn. 06355.

Religious Book Review, q; 1210 King St., Wilmington, Del. 19801.

Religious Life, m (bm, May-Aug.); 4200 N. Austin Ave., Chicago, Ill. 60634; Institute on Religious Life.

Renascence, q; Marquette University, Milwaukee, Wis. 53233.

Respect Life Report, m; 1312 Massachusetts Ave. N.W., Washington, D.C. 20005; Committee for Pro-Life Activities, NCCB.

Response, The, annual; 1234 Massachusetts Ave. N.W., Washington, D.C. 20005; International Liaison.

Review for Religious, bm; Room 428, 3601 Lindell Blvd., St. Louis, Mo. 63108.

Review of Politics, q; Box B, Notre Dame, Ind. 46556.

Review of Social Economy, 3 times a year; 25 E. Jackson Blvd., Chicago, Ill. 60604; Association for Social Economics.

Revista Maryknoll (Spanish-English), m; Maryknoll, N.Y. 10545; Catholic Foreign Mission Society of America.

Roze Maryi (Polish), m; Eden Hill, Stockbridge, Mass. 01262; Marian Fathers.

Sacred Music, q; 548 Lafond Ave., St. Paul, Minn. 55103.

St. Anthony Messenger, m; 1615 Republic St., Cincinnati, O. 45210; Franciscan Fathers.

St. Anthony's Newsletter, m; Mt. St. Francis, Ind. 47146.

St. Joseph's Messenger and Advocate of the Blind, q; St. Joseph Home, P.O. Box 288, Jersey City, N.J. 07303.

Salesian Bulletin, bm; 148 Main St., New Rochelle, N.Y. 10802; Salesian Fathers.

Salesian Missions, q; 148 Main St., New Rochelle, N.Y. 10802; Salesians of St. John Bosco.

Salt, m; 221 W. Madison St., Chicago, Ill. 60606; Claretians.

Salvatorian Newsletter, The, q; Society of the Divine Savior, Salvatorian Center, Wis. 53062.

Sandal Prints, bm; 1820 Mt. Elliott Ave., Detroit, Mich. 48207; Capuchin Fathers.

Scalabrinians, 3 times a year; 209 Flagg Pl., Staten Island, N.Y. 10304.

School Guide, a; 80 W. Broad St., Mt. Vernon, N.Y. 10552.

School Sister, The, q; Notre Dame of the Lake, Mequon, Wis. 53092; Sisters of Notre Dame.

SCRC Vision, The, m; 5730 W. Manchester Ave., Los Angeles, Calif. 90045; Southern California Renewal Communities.

Scripture in Church, 4 times a year; P.O. Box 9, Northport, N.Y. 11768.

Second Spring, bm; 121 Golden Gate Ave., San Francisco, Calif. 94102; Adult Benevolent Association.

Serenity, q; 601 Maiden Choice Lane, Baltimore, Md. 21228; Little Sisters of the Poor.

Serran, The, bm; 22 W. Monroe St., Chicago, Ill. 60603; Serra International.

Share, 1312 Massachusetts Ave. N.W., Washington, D.C. 20005; Dept. of Communications, USCC.

Share, q; 16 Acorn Dr., Annapolis, Md. 21401; Catholic Daughters of the Americas.

Share the Word, m; 3031 Fourth St. N.E., Washington, D.C. 20017; Paulist Catholic Evangelist Center.

Shepherd's Call, The, q; 901 Thirteenth St., N.W., Albuquerque, N.M. 87103; Brothers of Good Shepherd.

Silent Advocate, bm; St. Rita School for the Deaf, 1720 Glendale-Milford Rd., Cincinnati, O. 45215.

Sister Miriam Teresa League of Prayer Bulletin, q; League Headquarters, Convent Station, N.J. 07961.

SC News, m (Sept.-May); 4400 Churchman Ave., Louisville, Ky. 40215; Sisters of Charity of Nazareth.

Sisters Today, m (exc. July-Aug.); Liturgical Press, Collegeville, Minn. 56321.

Social Justice Review, bm; 3835 Westminster Pl., St. Louis, Mo. 63108; Catholic Central Union of America.

Social Thought, q; 1346 Connecticut Ave. N.W., Washington, D.C. 20036; National Conference of Catholic Charities.

Sons of Mary Missionary Society, q; 567 Salem End Rd., Framingham, Mass. 01701.

Sophia, m; P.O. Box 265, Newton Center, Mass. 02159; Newton Melkite eparchy.

Soul, bm; Mountain View Rd., Washington, N.J. 07882; Blue Army.

Southern Jesuits, The, 3 times a year; 211 Pere Marquette Bldg., New Orleans, La. 70112.

Spectrum, q; 1011 First Ave., New York, N.Y. 10022; Catholic Relief Services.

Spirit, biannually; Seton Hall University, South Orange, N.J. 07079; poetry magazine.

Spirit and Life, 6 times a year; 8300 Morganford Rd., St. Louis, Mo. 63123; Benedictine Srs. of Perpetual Adoration.

Spirit and the Bride, The, 10 times a year; 4140 Lindell Blvd., St. Louis, Mo. 63108; Catholic Charismatic Renewal Office.

Spiritual Book News, 8 times a year; Notre Dame, Ind. 46556.

Spiritual Life, q; 2131 Lincoln Rd. N.E., Washington, D.C. 20002; Discalced Carmelites.

Spirituality Today (formerly Cross and Crown), q; 1909 S. Ashland Ave., Chicago, Ill. 60608, Dominican Fathers.

Squires Newsletter, m; Columbus Plaza, New Haven, Conn. 06507; Columbian Squires.

Star, 10 times a year; 18 W. Bijou, Colorado Springs, Colo. 80903.

Strain Forward, 11 times a year; 50 St. Paul's Avenue, Jamaica Plain, Boston, Mass. 02130; Daughters of St. Paul.

Studies in Formative Spirituality, 3 times a year; Institute of Formative Spirituality, Duquesne Univ., Pittsburgh, Pa. 15219.

Studies in the Spirituality of Jesuits, 5 times a year; 3700 W. Pine Blvd., St. Louis, Mo. 63108.

Sword, semiannually; 29 N. Broadway, Joliet, Ill. 60435.

Tekakwitha Conference Newsletter, q; 1818 Ninth Ave. So. No. 5, Great Falls, Mont. 59405.

Theological Studies, q; Georgetown Univ., 37th and O Sts., N.W., Washington, D.C. 20057.

Theology Digest, q; 3634 Lindell Blvd., St. Louis, Mo. 63108.

Theresian, News, The, 6 times a year; 5326 E. Pershing Ave., Scottsdale, Ariz. 85254.

Thirsting for Justice, q; 1312 Massachusetts Ave. N.W. Washington, D.C. 20005, Campaign for Human Development.

This Week, w; 135 W. 31st St., New York, N.Y. 10001; Franciscan Communication Office, Holy Name Province.

Thomist, The, q; 487 Michigan Ave. N.E.,

Washington, D.C. 20017; Dominican Fathers.

Thought, q; Fordham University Press, Box L, Bronx, N.Y. 10458; Fordham University.

Today's Catholic Teacher, m (Sept.-May); 2451 E. River Rd., Suite 200, Dayton, O. 45439.

Today's Parish, m (Sept.-May); P.O. Box 180, Mystic, Conn. 06355.

To Him She Leads, q; Michigan Ave. and 4th St. E., Washington, D.C.; National Shrine of the Immaculate Conception.

Topic, semi-annually; 151 Thompson St., New York, N.Y. 10012. Secular Franciscan Order, Province of Immaculate Conception.

Trinity Missions, q; P.O. Box 7130, Silver Springs, Md. 20907.

Ultreya Magazine, m; 4500 W. Davis St., Dallas, Tex. 75211. Cursillo Movement.

L'Union (French), 5 times a year; 1 Social St., Woonsocket, R.I. 02895.

UNIREA, The Union (Romanian and English), m; 4309 Olcott Ave., East Chicago, Ind. 46312.

U.S. Catholic, m; 221 W. Madison St., Chicago, Ill. 60606; Claretian Fathers.

Venture, 26 times during school year; 2451 E. River Rd., Dayton, O. 45439, Pflaum Press. Intermediate grades.

Vision, 3 times a year; P.O. Box 28185, San Antonio, Tex. 78228. Mexican American Cultural Center.

Visions, 26 times during school year; 2451 E. River Rd., Dayton, O. 45439; Pflaum Press.

Vox Regis Alumni Newsletter, 3 times a year; 711 Knox Rd., East Aurora, N.Y. 14052; Christ the King Seminary.

Waif's Messenger, m; P.O. Drawer X, Chicago, Ill. 60690; Mission of Our Lady of Mercy.

Way — of St. Francis, 10 times a year; 109 Golden Gate Ave., San Francisco, Calif. 94102; Franciscan Fathers of California, Inc.

Western Catholic Union Record, m; 906 W.C.U. Bldg., Quincy, Ill. 62301; Western Catholic Union.

Westfriars, m; 2011 38th Ave., Oakland, Calif. 94601; St. Barbara Province, Order of Friars Minor.

Wheeling College Chronicle, 4 times a year; 316 Washington Ave., Wheeling, W. Va. 26003.

Word of God, w; 2187 Victory Blvd., Staten Island, N.Y. 10314; Society of St. Paul.

Working for Boys, q; Box A, Danvers, Mass. 01923; Xaverian Brothers.

Worldwide Family Spirit, ten times a year; 1097 Jefferson Ave., Akron, Ohio 44313, Worldwide Marriage Encounter.

Worship, 6 times a year; St. John's Abbey,

Collegeville, Minn. 56321. North American Academy of Liturgy.

Xaverian Missions Newsletter, 101 Summer St., Holliston, Mass. 01746; Xaverian Missionary Fathers.

Your Edmundite Missions Newsletter, bm; 1428 Broad St., Selma, Ala. 36701; Southern Missions of Society of St. Edmund.

Zeal, q; St. Elizabeth Mission Society of the Sisters of St. Francis, N. Main St., Allegany, N.Y. 14706.

Foreign Catholic Periodicals

Principal source: Catholic Almanac survey. Included are English-language Catholic periodicals published outside the U.S.

African Ecclesial Review (AFER), bm; Gaba Publications, P.O. Box 908, Eldoret, Kenya.

Australasian Catholic Record, q; St. Patrick's Seminary, Manly, New South Wales, Australia.

Christ to the World, bm; Via di Propaganda 1-C, 00187, Rome, Italy.

Clergy Review, m; 48 Great Peter St., London, SW1P 2HB, England.

Doctrine and Life, m, and **Supplement to Doctrine and Life,** bm; Dominican Publications, St. Saviour's, Dublin 1, Ireland.

Downside Review, q; Newman Bookshop, 87 St. Aldates, Oxford, England.

Dublin Review, q; 14 Howick Place, London, S.W. 1, England.

East Asian Pastoral Review, q; East Asian Pastoral Institute, P.O. Box 1815, Manila, Philippines.

Eastern Churches Review, semi-annual; 9 Alfred St., Oxford, England.

Faith Today, 10 times a year; Dominican Publications, St. Saviour's, Dublin 1, Ireland.

Furrow, m; St. Patrick's College, Maynooth, Ireland.

Heythrop Journal q; Heythrop College, 11 Cavendish Sq., London W1M, OAN, England (Editorial Office).

Irish Biblical Studies, q; Union Theological College, Belfast BT7 1JT, N. Ireland.

Irish Theological Quarterly, q; St. Patrick's College, Maynooth, Ireland.

L'Osservatore Romano, w; Vatican City.

Louvain Studies, semi-annual; Naamsestraat 100 B-3000, Louvain, Belgium.

Lumen Vitae, q; International Center for Studies in Religious Education, 184, rue Washington, 1050 Brussels, Belgium.

Maynooth Review, q; St. Patrick's College, Maynooth, Ireland.

Mediaeval Studies, annual; Pontifical Institute of Mediaeval Studies, 59 Queen's Park Crescent East, Toronto, Ont., Canada M5S 2C4.

Month, m; 114 Mount St., London, W1Y, 6AH, England.

Music and Liturgy, q; Bamsthorn, Ockham Rd., North, West Horsley, Leatherhead, Surrey, England.

New Blackfriars, m; edited by English Dominicans, Blackfriars, Oxford, England.

One in Christ, q; Turvey Abbey, Turvey, Beds. MK43 8DE, England.

Recusant History, biannual; Catholic Record Society, 114 Mount St., London, W1Y 6AH, England.

Religion and Society, q; Christian Institute for the Study of Religion and Society, 17 Miller Rd., P.O. Box 4600, Bangalore 560 046, India.

Social Studies, q; St. Patrick's College, Maynooth, Ireland.

Studies in Religion/Sciences Religieuses (bilingual), q; Wilfrid Laurier University Press, Waterloo, Ont., Canada N2L 3C5.

Sursum Corda—Lift Up Your Hearts, bm; Box 79, Box Hill, Victoria, Australia 3128.

Tablet, The w; 48 Great Peter St., SW1P 2HB, London, England.

Teilhard Review, The, 3 times a year; The Teilhard Centre for the Future of Man, 23 Kensington Square, London W8 5 HN, England.

Theology, bm; S.P.C.K. Holy Trinity Church, Marylebone Rd., London, NW1 4DU, England.

Way, The, q; and **Supplements to The Way,** triannual: 39 Fitzjohn's Ave., London NW3 5JT, England.

Catholic News Agencies

(Sources: International Catholic Union of the Press, Geneva; Catholic Press Association, U.S.)

Argentina: Agencia Informativa Catolica Argentina (AICA), Rodriguez Pena 846, 4⁰ Casilla de Correo Central 2886, Buenos Aires.

Austria: Katholische Presse-Agentur (Kathpress), Singerstrasse 6.2, 1010 Vienna 1.

Belgium: Centre d'Information de Presse (CIP), 1 Bd. Charlemagne, 1041 Bruxelles (Brussels).

Germany: Katholische Nachrichten Agentur (KNA), Adenauer Allee 134, 5300 Bonn 1.

Great Britain: Catholic Information Office of England and Wales (CIOEW), 74, Gallows Hill Lane, Abbots Langley, Herts WD5 OB2.

Greece: Agence TYPOS Rue Acharnon 246, Athenes 815.

Hong Kong: UCA-News, P.O. Box 9791, Hong Kong.

Hungary: Magyar Kurir, Karolyi w 4-8, Postafiok 41, Budapest V.

India: South Asia Religious News (SARNews), P.O. Box 4228, New Delhi 110.048.

Italy: Agenzia Stampa Catholica Associata

(ASCA), v. uffici del Vicario 30, I-00186 Rome.

Spain: Prensa Asociada (PA), Alfonso XI, 4—Apartado 14530, Madrid 14.

Switzerland: Katholische Internationale Presse-Agentur (KIPA), Case Postale 1054 CH 1701, Fribourg.

Centre International de Reportages et d'Information Culturelle (CIRIC), 10, av. de la Gare-des-Eaux Vives, CH-1207 Geneva.

United States of America: NC News Service (NC), 1312 Massachusetts Ave. N.W., Washington, D.C. 20005.

Yugoslavia: Aktusinosti Krscanska Sadasnjost (AKSA), Marulicev TRG 14, Zagreb p.p. 02-748.

Zaire: Documentation et Information Africaine (DIA), B.P. 2598, Kinshasa I.

Missions: Agenzia Internationale Fides (AIF), Palazzo di Propagande Fide, Via di Propaganda I-c, 00187 Rome, Italy.

Agencies distributing news related to Catholicism as well as other news are:

France: Agence France Presse (AFP), 13 Place de la Bourse, Paris 2e.

Italy: Agenzia Nazionale Stampa Associata (ANSA), Via Propaganda 27, Rome.

United States of America: Religious News Service (RNS), 43 W. 57th St., New York, N.Y. 10019.

U.S. Press Services

National Catholic News Service (NC), established in 1920, provides a worldwide daily news report by wire throughout the U.S. and into Canada, Europe and Australia, and by mail to other subscribers, serving Catholic publications and broadcasters including Vatican Radio, and institutional subscribers in more than 40 countries. NC also provides feature and photo services and a weekly religious education package, "Know Your Faith." It publishes "Origins," a weekly documentary service, and "Catholic Trends," a fortnightly newsletter. NC maintains a full-time bureau in Rome. It is a division of the United States Catholic Conference, with offices at 1312

Massachusetts Ave. N.W., Washington, D.C. 20005. The director and editor-in-chief is Richard W. Daw.

Religious News Service (RNS) provides domestic and foreign Catholic and other religious news in daily photos and features; "The Religious News Reporter," a weekly 15-minute radio and/or TV package; "The Week in Religion," a feature. RNS was inaugurated in 1933 by the National Conference of Christians and Jews as an independent news agency. Its offices are located at 43 W. 57th St., New York, N.Y. 10019.

Eastern Rite Information Service (ER), for Eastern Church news; 2208 W. Chicago Ave., Chicago, Ill. 60622.

Spanish-Language Service: A weekly news summary, *Resumen Semanal de Noticias,* provided by NC News Service, is used by a number of diocesan newspapers. Some papers carry features of their own in Spanish.

Books

The Official Catholic Directory, annual, P. J. Kenedy and Sons, 866 Third Ave., New York, N.Y. 10022. First edition, 1817.

The Catholic Almanac, annual; Our Sunday Visitor, Inc., 200 Noll Plaza, Huntington, Ind. 46750, publisher; editorial offices, 620 Route 3, Clifton, N.J. 07013. First edition, 1904.

The American Catholic Who's Who, biennial; 1312 Massachusetts Ave., N.W., Washington, D.C. 20005. First volume, 1934-35.

BOOK CLUBS

Catholic Book Club (1928), 106 W. 56th St., New York, N.Y. 10019. Sponsors the Campion Award.

Catholic Digest Book Club (1954), Catholic Digest Magazine, P.O. Box 43090, St. Paul, Minn. 55164.

Herald Book Club (1958), Franciscan Herald Press, 1434 W. 51st St., Chicago, Ill. 60609.

Thomas More Book Club (1939), Thomas More Association, 225 W. Huron St., Chicago, Ill. 60610.

CATHOLIC WRITERS' MARKET

(Source: Almanac survey.)

Editors call the following suggestions to the attention of writers:

Manuscripts should be typewritten, double-spaced, on one side of the page.

Writers should know the editorial policy, purpose and style of the publication to which they submit manuscripts. Sample copies may easily be obtained, often for the mere cost of postage. Some editors suggest that writers send outlines of proposed material, in order to facilitate editorial decision and direction. "Timely" copy should be submitted considerably in advance of the date of proposed publication; some editors advise a period of

three months. Authors are urged to avoid sermonizing. Writers should not expect extensive criticism of their work, although they should profit from advice and direction when these are given. Editors are not required to state their reasons for rejecting manuscripts. Replies regarding the acceptance or rejection of copy are usually made within a few weeks.

All writers should send to editors stamped, self-addressed envelopes for the return of material. Those who write to Canadian editors may use international reply coupons, not U.S. stamps.

Payment is made on acceptance or publication. Rates are sometimes variable because of the reputation of the writer, the quality and length of the manuscript, the amount of editorial work required for its final preparation.

America: 106 W. 56th St., New York, N.Y. 10019. Ed., Rev. Joseph A O'Hare, S.J. Weekly, circulation 37,000; $21 per year.

ARTICLES on important public issues evaluated scientifically and morally; serious and authenticated articles on family life, education, religion, and social and political issues with ethical or religious implications; occasionally, "thought" pieces; 1,000-2,000 words — 3¢ a word. VERSE, short and modern, befitting a Catholic publication but not necessarily religious—$7.50 and up. No fiction.

Annals of St. Anne de Beaupre, The: P.O. Box 1000, St. Anne de Beaupre, Que., Canada G0A 3C0. Ed., Rev. Roch Achard, C.Ss.R. Monthly, circulation 65,000; $5 per year.

FICTION: Stories of general Catholic interest, preferably with slant on devotion to St. Anne; 1,500-1,600 words — 1½-2¢ a word. ARTICLES of solid general interest to Catholics: on aspects of devotion to St. Anne, relative to history of the devotion in North America or elsewhere; on educational or social problems, or situations that should be of concern to all — especially Christians: 1,200-1,500 words — 4¢ a word, Payment on acceptance.

BLUEPRINT for Social Justice: Institute for Human Relations, Loyola University, New Orleans, La. 70118. Ed., John J. Mawhinney, S.J. Ten times a year, circulation 4,500; sent free on request.

ARTICLES on current social-justice issues; length, about 2,000 words.

Catechist: 2451 E. River Rd., Dayton, O. 45439. Ed., Patricia Fischer. Monthly August through April (exc. Dec.), circulation 41,988; $11.95 per year.

ARTICLES of interest to teachers of religion in parochial schools and CCD programs: 1,200-1,800 words — rate varies. PHOTOGRAPHS, black and white — rate varies. Payment on publication.

Catholic Digest: P.O. Box 43090, St. Paul, Minn. 55164. Ed., Henry Lexau. Monthly, circulation 603,027; $8.97 per year.

ARTICLES of close-to-home interest for average Catholic — rates vary; most frequent payments are $200 for originals, $100 for reprints; payment on acceptance. FILLERS, short features and jokes — rates vary; payment on publication. Cover pictures — $150. No fiction or verse. No queries necessary.

Columban Mission: St. Columbans, Nebr. 68056. Ed., Rev. Richard Steinhilber. Monthly (exc. June, Aug.); circulation 228,975; $3 per year.

ARTICLES mostly from missions or staff written; occasionally accept feature or factual articles on social and religious aspects of Asian and Latin American life; 2,000 words

— $100 and up. PHOTOGRAPHS of Asian and Latin American subjects and photo stories — $10 each.

Columbia: Columbus Plaza, New Haven, Conn. 06507. Ed., Elmer Von Feldt. Monthly, circulation 1,311,274; $3 per year. Official organ of the Knights of Columbus.

ARTICLES dealing with current events, social problems, Catholic apostolic activities: 2,500-3,500 words (must be accompanied by glossy photos) — $400 to $500. FICTION, Christian viewpoint: up to 3,000 words — up to $400. SATIRE: 1,000 words — $200. CARTOONS, pungent, wordless humor — $25. COVERS — $750.

Commonweal: 232 Madison Ave., New York, N.Y. 10016. Ed., James O'Gara. Biweekly, circulation 20,000; $24 per year.

ARTICLES, political, religious and literary subjects: 1,000-3,000 words — 2¢ a word. VERSE, serious poetry of high literary merit — about 40¢ a line.

Crusader's Almanac: Franciscan Monastery, 1400 Quincy St. N.E., Washington, D.C. 20017. Ed., Rev. Bartholomew Bengisser, O.F.M. Biannually, circulation 85,000; $1 per year.

ARTICLES about the Holy Land, Bible and Crusades given preference — 1¢ a word.

Emmanuel: 194 E. 76th Street, New York, N.Y. 10021. Editor-in-Chief, Rev. Paul J. Bernier, S.S.S. Monthly, bimonthly July-Aug., circulation 9,300; $15 per year.

ARTICLES, spirituality for those in Church ministry, Eucharistic, pastoral, theological, Scriptural: 2,000-3,000 words — $40-$50.

Family Festivals: 23 Madison Dr., Laurel Springs, N.J. 08021. Ed., Sam Macintosh. Bimonthly, circulation, 9,000; $16 per year.

ARTICLES, examples of family ritual or customs; 500-1,000 words — 3¢ a word. BOOK REVIEWS — $1 plus book. All material should be queried (send S.A.S.E. if reply expected.) Writers' guidelines available with S.A.S.E. Sample copies, $2.50 each.

Franciscan Herald: 1434 W. 51st St., Chicago, Ill. 60609. Monthly, circulation 8,000; $11 per year.

ARTICLES concerning St. Francis of Assisi and related subjects; application of Gospel principles to living Catholicism today; 2,000 words — $35. BOOK REVIEWS related to Franciscan topics — $10.

Hospital Progress: 4455 Woodson Rd., St. Louis, Mo. 63134. Ed., C. S. Boyer. Monthly, circulation 14,000; $25 per year (U.S. and Canada); $30 (foreign).

Official journal of the Catholic Health Association of the United States.

ARTICLES, health-care oriented; administrative procedures and theories; hospital departmental services: 1,500-3,000 words — $1 per column inch. BOOK REVIEWS, hospital oriented — payment by agreement.

Immaculata: 1600 W. Park Ave., Libertyville, Ill. 60048. Ed., Rev. Bernard M. Geiger, O.F.M. Conv. Ten issues a year, circulation 19,000; $10 per year.

Official publication of Knights of the Immaculata.

ARTICLES: seasonal, following liturgical calendar of the Church; conversion stories, profiles of saints; analyses of contemporary Catholic events; 700-1,200 words — $35 and up. POETRY, 8-40 lines — payment varies. PHOTOS, DRAWINGS, CARTOONS with accompanying article or separately — $10 to $30. BOOK REVIEWS — $15 to $35. Query preferred. Payment on publication.

Institute Journal: 50 Oak St., San Francisco, Calif. 94102. Ed., Thomas P. Brady. Bimonthly, $1 per year.

FICTION — no fixed rate. PHOTOGRAPHS — $15.

Josephite Harvest, The: 1130 N. Calvert St., Baltimore, Md. 21202. Ed., Rev. Earle A. Newman, S.S.J. Quarterly; circulation 40,000; $2 per year.

ARTICLES concerning apostolate of Catholic Church in U.S. to the black community.

Liguorian: One Liguori Dr., Liguori, Mo. 63057. Ed., Norman J. Muckerman, C.SS.R. Monthly, circulation over 570,000; $6 per year.

FICTION concerning current situations; stories with a Christian influence yet without maudlin sentimentality; 1,500-2,000 words — 7-10¢ a word. ARTICLES on family, Scripture, liturgy; material for older readers and those under 21 needed; 1,500-2,000 words — 7-10¢ a word. POETRY, 10 lines or less — $10. ILLUSTRATIONS and BOOK REVIEWS on assignment only.

Living Light, The: Editorial offices, Department of Education, 1312 Massachusetts Ave. N.W., Washington D.C. 20005. Quarterly, circulation 4,000; $12 per year.

ARTICLES on religious education, catechetics, Scripture: under 3,000 words — 3¢ per word.

Marian Helpers Bulletin: Eden Hill, Stockbridge, Mass. 01262. Ed., Rev. Walter F. Pelczynski, M.I.C. Quarterly, circulation over 750,000; $1 per year. Overstocked at present.

Marriage and Family Living: St. Meinrad, Ind. 47577. Ed., Ila M. Stabile. Monthly, circulation 60,000; $12.50 per year.

ARTICLES: (1) aimed at enriching the husband-wife and parent-child relationship by expanding religious and psychological insights or sensitivity: 1,000-2,000 words; (2) informative, aimed at helping couple cope, in practical ways, with problems of modern living: maximum 2,000 words; (3) personal essays relating amusing and/or heartwarming incidents that point up the human side of marriage and family life: maximum 1,500

words — 7¢ a word. PHOTOS: 8x11 b & w glossies, color transparencies — $10 minimum. 4-color cover photo — $150; b & w cover photo — $50; 2-page spread in contents — $35; 1-page in contents — $30. Photos of couples especially desired. Model releases required.

Buys North American serial rights only. Report on submissions in 3 to 4 weeks. Sample copy available for 50¢. Payment on acceptance.

Maryknoll: Maryknoll, N.Y. 10545. Ed., Moises Sandoval. Monthly, circulation more than 300,000; $1 per year.

ARTICLES must apply in some way to the hopes and aspirations, the culture, the problems and challenges of peoples in Asia, Africa and Latin America: 1,000-1,500 words — average payment, $100. Outline wanted before submission of material. PHOTOS: More interested in photo stories than in individual black and whites and color transparencies. Photo stories — up to $150, black and white; up to $200, color. Individual photos — $20, black and white; $35, color. Transparencies returned after use. Query to be made before sending photos.

Messenger of the Sacred Heart, The: 833 Broadview Ave., Toronto, Ont., Canada, M4K 2P9. Ed., Rev. F. J. Power, S.J. Monthly, circulation 23,000; $5 per year.

FICTION: stories which appeal to men, written with humor—good family reading: maximum, 2,000 words — 2¢ a word. ARTICLES of Catholic interest: 2,500 words — 2¢ a word. Payment upon acceptance.

Miraculous Medal, The: 475 E. Chelten Ave., Philadelphia, Pa. 19144. Ed., Rev. Robert P. Cawley, C.M. Quarterly, circulation 100,000.

FICTION, of general interest. Catholic in principle: 1,500-2,000 words — 2¢ a word and up. VERSE, religious in theme or turn; preferably about Our Lady: maximum 20 lines — 50¢ a line and up. Payment on acceptance. No articles.

Modern Liturgy: 7291 Coronado Dr., San Jose, Calif. 95129. Ed. William Burns. Nine issues a year, circulation, 15,000; $24 per year.

FICTION: parables, fantasy, fables; 1,000 words — 3¢ a word. ARTICLES: how-to, sample services, skills for liturgical artists; 1,200 words — 3¢ a word. POETRY, up to 50 lines — $10. BOOK REVIEWS appropriate for liturgy or religious education — $1 plus book.

Writers' guidelines available, send S.A.S.E.; or, for $3, a recent issue of magazine.

My Daily Visitor: Noll Plaza, Huntington, Ind. 46750. Mng. Ed., Patrick R Moran. Bimonthly, circulation 19,000; $6.75 per year.

A pocket-sized booklet of reflections for each day of the month.

MATERIAL: Daily reflections based on

spiritual meditation, the feast of the day or the liturgical season: maximum 165 words per page (each day's reflection is printed on a separate page) — $100 for series of reflections.

New Catholic World: 545 Island Rd., Ramsey, N.J. 07446. Mng. Ed., Robert Heyer. Bimonthly, circulation 14,000; $9 per year. Thematic issues.

ARTICLES, related to themes of issue (query editor): about 1,800-2,000 words. Rates of payment supplied.

Our Family: Box 249,Dept. ©, Battleford, Sask., Canada SOM OEO. Ed., Rev. Albert Lalonde, O.M.I. Monthly, circulation 13,200; $7 per year; $10 in U.S.

FICTION, adult only; stories that reflect lives, problems and concerns of audience; anything true to human nature; no sentimentality or blatant moralizing; stories with "woven in" Christian message: 1,000-3,000 words — 3¢ to 5¢ a word. ARTICLES related to family living; religion, education, social, biographical, marriage, courtship, domestic, institutional: 1,000-3,000 words — 3¢ to 5¢ a word. POETRY, in the market for many more poems; should deal with man in search for himself, for God, for others, for love, for meaning in life, for commitment: 8-30 lines — $3-$10. PHOTOS — purchased with manuscript as package (extra payment for photos); also in search of individual photos for editorial use. FILLERS — anecdotes of inspirational value, straight exposition, short humor. Writers' guide and photo specification sheet available on request (free). A sample copy is available for $1.50. Usually buys first North American serial rights; will consider purchasing second or reprint rights.

Our Sunday Visitor Magazine: Noll Plaza, Huntington, Ind. 46750. Ed., Rev. Vincent J. Giese. Weekly, circulation 320,000; $16 per year.

ARTICLES, no limitation on subjects other than those imposed by good taste and orthodoxy. Picture and text stories, profiles of individuals and organizations; articles that reflect moral, cultural, historical, social, economic and certain political concerns about the U.S. and the world; articles on current problems. Practical, factual and anecdotal material is sought: 750-1,000 words — $75-$100, usual payment. Queries are preferred to unsolicited completed manuscripts. PHOTO-GRAPHS, picture stories preferred rather than individual photos. Picture stories (color) — $100 and up.No fiction or poetry.

Parish Family Digest: Noll Plaza, Huntington, Ind. 46750. Ed., Patrick R. Moran. Bimonthly, circulation 140,000.

ARTICLES of timely interest to the young and growing Catholic family as a unit of the Catholic parish — personality profiles, interviews, social concerns, education, humor, inspiration and family and parish-family interrelationships; 1,000 words or less — 5¢ a

word. REPRINTS — $25. CARTOONS — $10 each for exclusives. FILLERS — $5 each for exclusives based on personal experience.

Pastoral Music: 225 Sheridan St. N.W., Washington, D.C. 20011. Ed. Daniel Connors. Bimonthly, circulation 8,000; $18 per year.

FICTION and ARTICLES — 4¢ a word.

Priest, The: 200 Noll Plaza, Huntington, Ind. 46750. Ed., Rev. Vincent J. Giese. Eleven issues a year, circulation 10,000; $16.50 per year.

ARTICLES of benefit to priests and seminarians in any of the following areas: priestly spirituality, contemporary theology, liturgy, apostolate and ministry, pastoral notes, Scripture. Controversial subject matter acceptable provided it does not go beyond the realm of orthodoxy or respect for authority or demands of fraternal charity: 6-15 double-spaced pages — $25 to $100 (about $6 per manuscript page).

Queen of All Hearts: 40 S. Saxon Ave., Bay Shore, N.Y. 11706. Ed., Rev. James McMillan, S.M.M.; Mng. Ed., Rev. Roger M. Charest S.M.M. Bimonthly; circulation 8,500; $8 per year (U.S.), $9 (Canada and foreign).

FICTION: short stories, preferably with a Marian theme: 1,000-2,000 words. ARTICLES that bring out the importance of devotion to Payment varies. VERSE with Marian theme — payment, two years' subscription. No artwork or fillers.

Religion Teacher's Journal: Twenty-Third Publications, P.O. Box 180, Mystic, Conn. 06355. Ed., Gwen Costello. Seven issues a year, circulation 40,000; $12 per year.

FICTION about teachers relating to children, children and liturgical seasons; maximum length, 7 typewritten, double-spaced pages — $100 maximum. ARTICLES on catechesis, methods, theology, sample programs, how-to ideas, etc.; length and rates same as above. ILLUSTRATIONS, black and white — $15 each; covers/color slides — $25.

Review for Religious: Room 428, 3601 Lindell Blvd., St. Louis, Mo. 63108. Ed., D.F.X. Meenan, S.J. Bimonthly, circulation 18,990; $9 per year.

ARTICLES, of interest to religious: 3,000-6,000 words — $6 per printed page.

St. Anthony Messenger: 1615 Republic St., Cincinnati, O. 45210. Ed., Rev. Norman Perry, O.F.M. Monthly, circulation 360,000; $10 per year.

FICTION: Written out of a totally Christian background, illuminating the truth of human nature for adults. No preachiness, sentimentality. FACT ARTICLES: 3,000-3,500 words. Outstanding personalities (must be based on personal interview). Information and comment on major movements in the Church: application of Christian faith to daily life; real-life solutions in the areas of a) family life, education; b) personal living (labor, leisure, art, psychology, spirituality). Human interest narrative. Humor. Photos and picture stories. Query letters welcome.

St. Joseph's Messenger and Advocate of the Blind: St. Joseph's Home, P.O. Box 288, Jersey City, N.J. 07303. Ed., Sr. Ursula Maphet, C.S.J. Quarterly, circulation 51,000; $2 per year.

FICTION, and ARTICLES, contemporary, mainstream themes, 500-1,500 words — 1¢ to 3¢ a word.

Salesian Missions: 148 Main St., New Rochelle, New York 10802. Ed., Rev. Edward J. Cappelletti, S.D.B. Quarterly, circulation 1,000,000; $1 per year.

ARTICLES: mission interest; pertaining to Salesian Society, life, spirit and educational system of St. John Bosco; adolescent interest and education — 5¢ a word and up. PHOTOGRAPHS — $6. Suggest queries before submitting material. Payment on acceptance. Early report.

Social Justice Review: 3835 Westminster Pl., St. Louis, Mo. 63108. Ed., Harvey J. Johnson. Bimonthly, circulation 1,276; $12 per year.

ARTICLES: research, editorial and review: 2,000-4,000 words — $4 per column. No fiction.

Spiritual Life: 2131 Lincoln Rd., N.E., Washington, D.C. 20002. Ed., Rev. Christopher Latimer, O.C.D. Quarterly, circulation 18,000; $6 per year.

ARTICLES, must follow scope of magazine: 3,000-5,000 words — rate varies. Sample copy and instructions for writers sent upon request.

Spirituality Today: 1909 S. Ashland Ave., Chicago, Ill. 60608. Ed., Rev. Christopher Kiesling, O.P. Quarterly, circulation 5,000; $7 per year.

ARTICLES concerning any phase of the spiritual life: minimum 3,000-4,000 words — 1¢ a word. No fiction or poetry.

Today's Catholic Teacher: 2451 E. River Rd., Suite 200, Dayton, O. 45439. Monthly Sept. through May (exc. Dec.), circulation 60,000; $10.95 per year.

ARTICLES of professional and personal

interest to teachers, administrators, pastors, parish councils and school board members concerning Catholic schools and CCD programs: 600-800 words, 1,500-3,000 words — $15-$75. Premium payment for superior content and writing presentation. Black and white photos helpful. Payment on publication.

Today's Parish: Twenty-Third Publications, P.O. Box 180, Mystic, Conn. 06355. Ed., Carol Clark. Seven issues a year, circulation 20,000; $14 per year.

ARTICLES, 1,200-1,500 words — $60 to $100. PHOTOS — $15.

WAY — of St. Francis: 109 Golden Gate Ave. San Francisco, Calif. 94102. Ed., Simon Scanlon, O.F. M. Ten times a year, circulation 8,000; $5 per year.

ARTICLES, in keeping with the purpose of the magazine, to bear effective witness to the ideals and aims of the Order of St. Francis: to view the world through Christian eyes; to point up the relationship between abstract belief and concrete action in the modern world: 1,500-2,200 words — $30 to $50. PHOTOGRAPHS: bought with articles.

Working for Boys: Box A, Danvers, Mass. 01923. Ed., Brother Alphonsus Dwyer, C.F.X. (Mss. to Bro. Alois, C.F.X., Assoc. Ed., St. John's High School, Shrewsbury, Mass, 01545.) Quarterly, circulation 16,000; $1 per year.

FICTION, preferably seasonal: 800-1,000 words — 4¢ a word. ARTICLES, preferably seasonal: All Souls, Christmas, Easter, Summer: 800-1,000 words — 4¢ a word. VERSE, seasonal, 4-16 lines — 25¢-50¢ a line.

Worship: St. John's Abbey, Collegeville, Minn. 56321. Ed., Rev. Aelred Tegels, O.S.B. Bimonthly, circulation 6,784; $14 per year.

ARTICLES related to the engagement of the magazine in ongoing study of both the theoretical and pastoral dimensions of liturgy; examines historical traditions of worship in their doctrinal context, the experience of worship in Christian churches, the findings of contemporary theology, psychology, communications, cultural anthropology, and sociology insofar as they have a bearing on public worship: 5,000-8,000 words. No fiction or poetry.

RADIO, TELEVISION, THEATRE

Radio and Television

Christopher Radio Program: 15-minute interview-discussion series, "Christopher Closeup," weekly, on 242 stations; a one-minute "Christopher Thought for Today," daily, on 1,828 stations. Address: 12 E. 48th St., New York, N.Y. 10017.

Christopher TV Series, "Christopher Closeup": Originated in 1951. Half-hour and quarter-hour interviews in color, weekly, on 67 commercial stations, 118 American Forces

Network outlets, CBN and PTL syndicate stations and 24 cable systems, Address; 12 E. 48th St., New York, N.Y. 10017.

Crossroads (Radio): Originated in 1954 as the Hour of the Crucified, produced by the Passionist Priests and Brothers. Weekly, on nearly 130 stations. Address: 1089 Elm St., West Springfield, Mass. 01089.

Directions (TV): Originated in 1960, this weekly half-hour program is a news-oriented approach to reporting social, moral and religious issues within a Catholic context. The Department of Communication, NCCB/USCC, cooperates in the production of some 15 segments a year, in addition to interfaith and seasonal specials; carried at variable dates on more than 80 stations (ABC).

For Our Times (TV): Originated in April 1979, this weekly half-hour series produced by CBS in a unique joint cooperative consultation with the Department of Communication, NCCB/USCC, the National Council of Churches and the New York Board of Rabbis focuses on the ethical and social challenges confronting American society today. Format: documentary and studio discussion (CBS).

Guideline (Radio): Produced in cooperation with the Department of Communication, NCCB/USCC. Weekly program designed to set forth the teachings of the Catholic Church and to discuss issues the Church faces in the contemporary world; heard on approximately 65 stations (NBC).

On This Rock (Radio): Originated in 1941, produced in cooperation with the Department of Communication, NCCB/USCC. A 15-minute weekly program currently employing a youth-oriented music and commentary format; heard on more than 950 stations (ABC).

Sacred Heart Program (Radio, TV): Originated in 1939, operated by the Jesuits. Produces three radio programs and one 15-minute TV program weekly. Address: 3900 Westminster Place, St. Louis, Mo. 63108.

Religious Specials (TV): The Department of Communication, NCCB/USCC, cooperates in the production of four one-hour Catholic specials a year and occasional seasonal or tri-faith presentations. These programs offer a varied format: film, dramatizations, panel discussions, music and commentary, etc. Catholic portions are telecast on approximately 140 stations (NBC).

Theatre

Catholic University Drama Department: Established in 1937. Offers degree courses in theatre arts, produces five plays a year in The Hartke Theatre. Affiliated with National Players and Olney Theatre. Chairman of the department, William H. Graham. Address: Catholic University of America, Washington, D.C. 20064.

National Players: An operation of University Players, a non-profit organization affiliated with the Drama Department of the Catholic University. It originated in 1949 and is the oldest classical touring company in the U.S.

Olney Theatre Corporation: A non-profit organization affiliated with the Drama Department of Catholic University. It operates Olney Theatre, Olney, Md., an Équity theatre designated the State Summer Theatre of Maryland in 1978.

Catholic Actors' Guild of America, Inc.: Established in 1914 to provide material and spiritual assistance to people in the theatre. Has more than 500 members; publishes *The Call Board* bimonthly. Address: 1501 Broadway, Suite 2400, New York, N.Y. 10036.

Communications Services

Cross Current Communications: Dedicated to producing quality Catholic TV programming covering all phases of movements and personalities in the contemporary Church. "Crossfire" documentary series. Address: 3220 Geronimo Dr., Oxnard, Calif. 93033.

Eternal Word Television Network, Inc., 5817 Old Leeds Rd., Birmingham, Ala. 35210. Mother M. Angelica, P.C.P.A., foundress.

Father Justin Rosary Hour: Station F — Box 217, Buffalo, N.Y. 14212.

Father Peyton's Family Theater Productions: Films for TV, for sale and rental. Address: 7201 Sunset Blvd., Hollywood, Calif. 90046.

Franciscan Communications: An audio-visual media center dedicated to the production of public service broadcasting material and audio-visual media for religious education. Creators and producers of TeleSPOTS and AudioSPOTS, 10- to 60-second public service messages for radio and TV; TeleKETICS films and media kits, filmstrips, slide programs, video cassettes, phonograph records and tapes, for religious, moral and value education. Address: 1229 South Santee St., Los Angeles, Calif. 90015.

Mary Productions "Airtime": Originated in 1950. Offers royalty-free scripts for stage, film, radio and tape production. Audio and video tapes of lives of the saints and historical characters. Address: Mary Productions Guild, 58 Lenison Ave., Belford, N.J. 07718.

Oblate Centro de Comunicación, Oblates of Mary Immaculate: National Hispanic communications center. Produces TV and radio programs; publishes religious educational books, audio-visual materials and a weekly Spanish newspaper; organizes annual San Antonio Cine Festival, International Latino Film Festival. Address: P.O. Box 96, San Antonio, Tex. 78291.

Passionist Communications Center, 117 Harmon Ave., Pelham, N.Y. 10803. Sunday Mass on TV.

Paulist Communications: Contracts with dioceses and parishes to provide public service programs free to radio stations and scripts to priest-broadcasters; contacts stations for dioceses. Address: 2257 Barry Ave., Los Angeles, Calif. 90064.

Paulist Productions: Producers and distributors of the INSIGHT Film Series (available for TV at no charge), and educational film series. Purchase and rental information available. Address: P.O. Box 1057, Pacific Palisades, Calif. 90272.

Catholic Telecommunications Network of America (CTNA): 95 Madison Avenue, Suite 804, New York, N.Y. 10016.

Catholic Television Network (CTN): Instructional TV operations have been established in the following archdioceses and dioceses. Archdioceses are indicated by an asterisk.

Boston,* Mass.: Rev. James Hawker, Director, 468 Beacon St. 02115.

Brooklyn, N.Y.: Rev. Michael J. Dempsey, Director, 1712 10th Ave., 11215.

Chicago,* Ill.: Mr. Charles E. Hinds, Executive Director, One N. Wacker Dr. 60606.

Los Angeles,* Calif.: Mr. Steven J. Gorski, 1520 W. Ninth St. 90015.

New York,* N.Y.: Sr. M. Irene Fugazy, Director, Seminary Ave., Yonkers, N.Y. 10704.

Rockville Centre, N.Y.: Rev. Thomas Hartman, Director, 1345 Admiral Lane, Uniondale, N.Y. 11553.

San Francisco,* Calif.: Mr. Thomas A. Combellick, 324 Middlefield Rd., Menlo Park, Calif. 94025.

Unda-USA: A national professional Catholic association for broadcasters and allied communicators organized in 1972. It suc-

ceeded the Catholic Broadcasters Association of America which in 1948 had replaced the Catholic Forum of the Air organized in 1938. It is a member of the international Catholic association for radio and television known as Unda (the Latin word for "wave," symbolic of air waves of communication). Subgroups include Catholic Television Network, the Association of Catholic Radio and Television Syndicators, and the Association of Diocesan Directors. Unda-USA publishes a newsletter six times a year for members, sponsors an annual general assembly and presents the Gabriel Awards annually for excellence in broadcasting. President, Rev. John Geaney, C.S.P., 320 Cathedral St., Baltimore, Md. 21201. National office: 3035 Fourth St. N.E., Washington, D.C. 20017.

The Catholic Communications Foundation (CCF) was established by the Catholic Fraternal Benefit Societies in 1966 to lend support and assistance to development of the broadcasting apostolate of the Church. The CCF, promotes the development of diocesan communications capabilities and funds a scholarship program at the Annual Institute for Religious Communications. CCF officers include Bishop Anthony G. Bosco, chairman of the board. Address: Suite 198, Box 9000, Carlsbad, Calif. 92008.

DIOCESAN COMMUNICATIONS OFFICES, DIRECTORS

(Sources: *1982 Directory of Catholic Communications Personnel,* published by the Office of Public Affairs, USCC; *Official Catholic Directory;* NC News Service. Archdioceses are designated by an asterisk.)

Alabama: Birmingham — Rev. Martin Muller (Communications), Box 6147, Birmingham 35209.

Mobile* — Rev. Robert L. Anderson, S.J. (Ed., *The Catholic Week),* 400 Government St., Mobile 36601.

Alaska: Anchorage* — Bro. Charles P. McBride, C.S.C. (Communications), P.O. Box 2239, Anchorage 99510.

Fairbanks — Rev. Vincent G. Wissman, C.S.P. (Radio-TV), P.O. Box 55091, North Pole 99705. Rev. James Poole, S.J., Box 101, Nome 99762.

Juneau — Miss Carol Crater (Ed., *Inside Passage),* 419 Sixth St., Juneau 99801.

Arizona: Phoenix — Mr. Thomas Altt (Acting Dir., Communications), Rev. John S. Banahan (Radio-TV), 400 E. Monroe St., Phoenix 85004.

Tucson — Mr. Robert Nordmeyer (Ed., *Arizona Catholic Lifetime),* 64 W. Ochoa St., Tucson 85701.

Arkansas: Little Rock — Mr. William W. O'Donnell (Assoc. Dir., Communications), 2500 N. Tyler St., Little Rock 72217.

California: Fresno — Mr. Joseph Jasmin (Information), Box 4273, Fresno 93744.

Los Angeles* — Msgr. Joseph Pollard

(Communications), Sr. Gail Tenney, O.S.F., Mr. Steven Gorski (ETV), 1530 W. 9th St., Los Angeles 90015.

Monterey — Rev. Dennis M. Gilbert (Communications Commission), Old Mission, 941 Chorro, P.O. Box 1483, San Luis Obispo 93406; Rev. Felix Migliazzo (Ed., *The Observer),* Box 2079, Monterey 93940.

Oakland — Mrs. Reggie Finney (Public Relations), Dan Morris (Ed., *The Catholic Voice),* 2900 Lakeshore Ave., Oakland 94610.

Orange — Mr. Thomas A. Fuentes (Communications), P.O. Box 2590, Newport Beach 92663.

Sacramento — Rev. Brendan Considine (Communications and Media), P.O. Box 235, Folsom 95630.

San Bernardino — Dan E. Pitre (Ed., *Inland Catholic),* P.O. Box 2788, San Bernardino 92405.

San Diego — Rev. George A. Byrne (Communications), Box 80428, San Diego 92138.

San Francisco* — Rev. Michael Reis (Producer, Creative Services), Rev. Harry Schlitt (Director, Archdiocesan Communications Center), Mr. Jack Kelly (Radio-TV), 2655 Van Ness Ave., San Francisco 94109; Rev. Miles O'Brien Riley (Director, Information), 441 Church St., San Francisco 94114.

San Jose — Arlene Goetze (Communications), 7600 Y St. Joseph Ave., Los Altos 94022.

Santa Rosa — Msgr. Walter J. Tappe

(Communications), P.O. Box 1297, Santa Rosa 95403.

Stockton — Yvonne Goodman (Communications), Box 4237, Stockton 95204.

Colorado: Denver* — Rev. C. B. Woodrich (Information), 200 Josephine St., Denver 80206.

Pueblo — Ms. Geraldine Carrigan (Communications; Ed., *Catholic Crosswinds*), 1001 N. Grand Ave., Pueblo 81003.

Connecticut: Bridgeport — Rev. Nicholas V. Grieco (Communications), 238 Jewett Ave., Bridgeport 06606; Rev. Alfred J. Sienkiewicz (Radio-TV), 385 Scofieldtown Rd., Stamford 06903.

Hartford* — Rev. Edmund S. Nadolny (Radio-TV), 785 Asylum Ave., Hartford 06105.

Norwich — Jacqueline M. Keller (Communications), 201 Hickory St., Norwich 06360.

Stamford (Ukrainian Diocese) — Rev. Lew Lubynsky, 303 Eddy Glover Blvd., New Britain 06053.

Delaware: Wilmington — Mr. F. Eugene Donnelly (Secretary, Communications), Box 2030, Wilmington 19899.

District of Columbia: Washington* — Rev. Maurice T. Fox (Delegate, Communications), Mr. Jay Cormier (Director, Communications), Box 29260, Washington 20017.

Florida: Miami* — Rev. Donald Connolly (Communications), Marjorie Donohue (Public Information), 6301 Biscayne Blvd., Miami 33138. Rev. Jose P. Nickse (Radio-TV), 6200 N.E. 4th Ct., Miami 33138.

Orlando — Sister Estelle Scully, S.P. (Communications), Box 3551, Orlando 32802.

Pensacola-Tallahassee — Mr. Gerald Butterfield (Communications), 855 W. Carolina St., Tallahassee 32304.

St. Augustine — Sr. Carol Stovall, S.S.J. (Communications), Box 10607, Jacksonville 32207. Msgr. R. Joseph James (Radio-TV), 1649 Kingsley Ave., Orange Park 32073.

St. Petersburg — Rev. Desmond Daly, P.O. Box 18081, Tampa 33679.

Georgia: Atlanta* — Rev. Msgr. Noel C. Burtenshaw (Communications), 680 W. Peachtree St. N.W., Atlanta 30308.

Savannah — Rev. Joseph Stranc (Communications), 12 W. Jones Ave., Statesboro 30458. Mrs. Gillian Brown (Information), P.O. Box 8789, Savannah 31412.

Hawaii: Honolulu — Msgr. Francis A. Marzen, 1184 Bishop St., Honolulu 96813.

Idaho: Boise — Rev. David L. Riffle (Communications Center), 6003 Overland, Boise 83709.

Illinois: Belleville — Rev. Richard G. Mohr (Communications), 220 W. Lincoln St., Belleville 62221.

Chicago* — Mr. Peter Foote (Communications), P.O. Box 1979, Chicago 60690. Rev.

James Moriarty (Radio-TV), One N. Wacker Dr., Suite 1100, Chicago 60606.

Joliet — Rev. William F. Irwin (Communications), St. Charles Borromeo Pastoral Center, Rt. 53 and Airport Rd., Romeoville 60441.

Peoria — Mr. Robert England (Communications), 1301 N.E. Glendale,, Peoria 61603.

Rockford — Msgr. Thomas G. Doran, Chancellor, 1245 N. Court St., Rockford 61101.

St. Nicholas in Chicago for Ukrainians — Msgr. Jaroslav Swyschuk (Eastern Rite Information Bureau), 2208 W. Chicago Ave., Chicago 60622.

Springfield — Rev. Richard L. Paynic (Ed., *Time and Eternity*), Rev. Neal Dee (Radio-TV), 514 E. Lawrence, Springfield 62703.

Indiana: Evansville — Rev. Joseph L. Ziliak (Information), P.O. Box 4169, Evansville 47711.

Fort Wayne-South Bend — Mr. Lou Jacquet (Ed., *The Harmonizer*), P.O. Box 11169, Ft. Wayne 46856.

Gary — Rev. John F. Morales (Communications), P.O. Box M474, Gary 46401.

Indianapolis* — Mr. Charles J. Schisla (Communications), 136 W. Georgia St., Indianapolis 46225.

Lafayette — Office of Information. 3104 W. County Rd., 100 North, Kokomo 46901.

Iowa: Davenport — Rev. Francis C. Henricksen (Communications), Box 939, Davenport 52805.

Des Moines — Sr. Mira Mosle, B.V.M. (Communications), 2910 Grand Ave., Box 1816, Des Moines 50306.

Dubuque* — Sr. Carol Hoverman (Communications), 1229 Mt. Loretta Ave. Dubuque 52001.

Sioux City — Mr. Joe Maher (Ed., *The Globe*), 1821 Jackson St., Sioux City 51105; Msgr. Frank Brady (Radio-TV), 1212 Morningside Ave., Sioux City 51106.

Kansas: Dodge City — Rev. Daniel V. Heim, Our Lady of Guadalupe Church, 805 Avenue J, Dodge City 67801.

Kansas City* — Rev. William Maher (Ed., *The Leaven*), Box 2329, Kansas City 66110.

Salina — Msgr. Raymond Menard (Information), Box 958, Salina 67401.

Wichita — Rev. Arthur A. Busch (Communications), 424 N. Broadway, Wichita 67202.

Kentucky: Covington — Sr. Colleen Winston, O.S.B. (Communications), Box 192, Covington 41012.

Louisville* — Rev. John H. Morgan, 1305 W. Market St., Louisville 40203.

Owensboro — Msgr. George Hancock (Information), 4003 Frederica St., Owensboro 42301; Rev. Leonard Reisz (Radio-TV), 1001 W. 7th St., Owensboro 42301.

Louisiana: Alexandria-Shreveport — Mr.

Al Nassif (Information), Box 7417, Alexandria 71306.

Baton Rouge — Mr. Thomas Barbarie (Ed., *Catholic Commentator*), Box 14746, Baton Rouge 70898.

Houma-Thibodaux — Mr. Louis Aguirre (Communications, Ed., *The Bayou Catholic*), P.O. Box 9077, Houma 70361.

Lafayette — Rev. David Primeaux (Communications), Glenn Norwood (Radio-TV), Box 3223, Lafayette 70502.

Lake Charles — Mr. Truman Stacey (Diocesan News), 1100 16th St., Lake Charles 70601.

New Orleans* — Mr. Thomas M. Finney (Communications, Public Relations), 7887 Walmsley Ave., New Orleans 70125.

Maine: Portland — Mr. Clarence F. McKay (Communications), 510 Ocean Ave., Portland 04103.

Maryland: Baltimore* — Rev. John Geaney, C.S.P. (Communications), 320 Cathedral St., Baltimore 21201.

Massachusetts: Boston* — Rev. Peter V. Conley (Communications), 49 Franklin St., Boston 02110; Rev. Francis T. McFarland (Radio-TV), 55 Chapel St., Newton 02160.

Fall River — Rev. John F. Moore (Communications), 410 Highland Ave., Fall River 02722; Rev. John F. Hogan, (TV), 494 Slocum Rd., N. Dartmouth 02747.

Springfield — Msgr. David P. Welch (Ed., *Catholic Observer*), Box 1570, Springfield 01101; Rev. John P. Moore, C.P. (Radio-TV), 1089 Elm St., W. Springfield 01089.

Worcester — Rev. John W. Barrett (Communications), 49 Elm St., Worcester 01609.

Melkite Eparchy of Newton — Rev. Ronald Golini (Communications), P.O. Box 265, Newton 02159.

Michigan: Detroit* — Rev. Patrick Halfpenny (Communications), 305 Michigan Ave., Detroit 48226.

Gaylord — Betty J. Ballou (Communications), 202 W. Mitchell Ave., Gaylord 49735.

Grand Rapids — Rev. John J. Giammona, 267 Sheldon Ave. S.E., Grand Rapids 49503.

Kalamazoo — Mr. Paul Leonard (Communications), 215 N. Westnedge Ave., Kalamazoo 49005.

Lansing — Director of Communications, 300 W. Ottawa St., Lansing 48933.

Marquette — Gregory B. Bell (Communications), Box 550, Marquette 49855.

Saginaw — Director of Communications, 5800 Weiss St., Saginaw 48603.

Minnesota: Crookston — Rev. Richard Boyd (Information), Rev. Gerald Noesen (Radio-TV), Box 610, Crookston 56716.

Duluth — Pat Winter (Information), 215 W. 4th St., Duluth 55806.

New Ulm — Rev. Dennis Labat (Communications), 1400 Chancery Dr., New Ulm 56073.

St. Cloud — Ms. Rosemary Borgert (Infor-

mation), 810 St. Germain St., Box 1068, St. Cloud 56302.

St. Paul and Minneapolis* — Ms. Joan Bernet (Communications), 226 Summit Ave., St. Paul 55102.

Winona — Communications, Box 588, Winona 55987.

Mississippi: Biloxi — Mary Wimberly (Assoc. Ed., *Mississippi Today*), P.O. Box 1189, Biloxi 39533.

Jackson — Mrs. Janna Avalon (Ed., *Mississippi Today*), Box 2130, Jackson 39205.

Missouri: Jefferson City — Mr. Mark Saucier (Communications), Box 417, Jefferson City 65101.

Kansas City-St. Joseph — Rev. John C. Weiss (Communications), 1357 N.E. 42nd Terr., Kansas City 64116.

St. Louis* — Msgr. Edward O'Donnell (Information), 4445 Lindell Blvd., St. Louis 63108; Mr. Ronald Coleman (Public Relations), 2249 S. Brentwood Blvd., St. Louis 63144. Rev. Joseph M. O'Brien (Radio-TV), 4140 Lindell Blvd., St. Louis 63108.

Springfield-Cape Girardeau — Mrs. Marilyn Vydra (Communications), Mr. Dale Moore (Creative Services), 200 McDaniel Bldg., Springfield 65806.

Montana: Great Falls-Billings — Box 2107, Great Falls 59403.

Helena — Rev. Robert J. O'Donnell (Chancellor, Communications), Box 1729, Helena 59624.

Nebraska: Grand Island — Director of Communications, P.O. Box 1531, Grand Island 68801.

Lincoln — Rev. James D. Dawson (Information), Box 80328, Lincoln 68501.

Omaha* — Rev. Mel Rempe (Communications), 100 N. 62nd St., Omaha 68132.

Nevada: Reno-Las Vegas — Msgr. Thomas Meger, Chancellor, Box 1211, Reno 89504; Mr. Gerard E. Sherry (Information), 953 Sahara Ave., Las Vegas 89104.

New Hampshire: Manchester — Mr. Thomas Mierzwinski (Communications), Rev. John Poirier (Radio-TV), 153 Ash St., Manchester 03105.

New Jersey: Camden — Msgr. Charles Giglio (Information), Box 709, Camden 08101.

Newark* — Michael S. McGraw (Information, Public Affairs), 31 Mulberry St., Newark 07102.

Passaic (Byzantine Rite Eparchy) — Rev. Nicholas Alishofski, (Ed., *Eastern Catholic Life*), 101 Market St., Passaic 07055.

Paterson — Sister Pat Kowalski, O.S.M. (Communications), Box 17, Pequannock, N.J. 07440.

Trenton — Sr. Rosemary Jeffries, R.S.M. (Communications), 701 Lawrenceville Rd., Trenton 08648.

New Mexico: Gallup — Rev. Cormac Antram, O.F.M. (Communications, Radio-TV), P.O. Box 39, Tohatchi 87325.

Santa Fe* — Rev. Albert Gallegos (Communications-Media), 202 Morningside Dr. S.E., Albuquerque 87108.

New York: Albany — Rev. Michael Farano (Information), 465 State St., Albany 12206.

Brooklyn — Mr. Frank DeRosa (Information), Box C, Brooklyn 11202.

Buffalo — Rev. Msgr. Robert E. Nesslin (Communications), 100 S. Elmwood Dr., Buffalo 14202.

New York* — Rev. Edwin F. O'Brien (Communications), Rev. Peter J. Madori (Radio-TV Project Coordinator), Rev. Lester S. Avestruz, O.S.A. (Spanish Media), 1011 First Ave., New York, N.Y. 10022. Sr. Irene Fugazy (Instructional TV), Seminary Ave., Yonkers, 10704.

Ogdensburg — Rev. David W. Stinebrickner (Information), 622 Washington St., Ogdensburg 13669; Rev. Donald Kramberg (Radio-TV), Wadhams Hall, RFD No. 4, Ogdensburg 13669.

Rochester — Rev. Charles J. Latus (Information), 1150 Buffalo Rd., Rochester 14624.

Rockville Centre — Rev. Msgr. Daniel S. Hamilton (Information), Box 700, Hempstead 11551; Rev. Thomas J. Hartman (Radio-TV), 1345 Admiral Lane, Uniondale 11553.

St. Maron Diocese (Maronite Rite) — Rev. Richard Saad, 836 8th St. S., Birmingham, Ala. 35205.

Syracuse — Mr. Ron Smith (Communications), 240 E. Onondaga St., Syracuse 13202.

North Carolina: Charlotte — Ms. Mary C. Coyne (Asst. Ed., *North Carolina Catholic*), 1524 E. Moorehead St., Charlotte 28207.

Raleigh — Rev. Joseph G. Vetter (Communications), 300 Cardinal Gibbons Dr., Raleigh 27606.

North Dakota: Bismarck — Rev. John J. Owens, Box 128, Wilton 58579.

Fargo — Deacon Matt Lanz (Ed., *The New Earth*), Box 1750, Fargo 58107.

Ohio: Cincinnati* — Mr. Daniel J. Kane (Communications), Rev. Theodore Kosse (Radio-TV), 100 E. 8th St., Cincinnati 45202.

Cleveland — Rev. Frank P. Kosem (Delegate, Communications), Mr. J. Jerome Lackamp (Radio-TV), Mr. Patrick DiSalvatore (Public Relations), 1027 Superior Ave., Cleveland 44114.

Columbus — Rev. James P. Hanley (Vicar, Communications), Mr. Richard J. Hatem (Radio-TV), Sr. Mary LaVernne, O.S.F. (Public Relations, Information), 197 E. Gay St., Columbus 43215.

Parma (Byzantine Rite Eparchy) — Rev. Donald Petyo, 5500 W. 54th St., Parma 44129.

Steubenville — Rev. Msgr. James C. Marshall, Box 969, Steubenville 43952.

Toledo — Mr. Jim Richards (Communications), 2544 Parkwood Ave., Toledo 43610.

Youngstown — Rev. Bernard Bonnot (Communications), Miss Jean M. Nero (Public/Media Relations), Mr. Michael Bacon (Radio-TV), 144 W. Wood St., Youngstown 44503.

Oklahoma: Oklahoma City* — Rev. David F. Monahan (Communications), Box 32180, Oklahoma City 73123.

Tulsa — Rev. Dennis C. Dorney, Chancellor, 820 S. Boulder St., Box 2009, Tulsa 74101.

Oregon: Baker — Rev. Joseph B. Hayes, Sacred Heart Church, 815 High St., Klameth Falls 97601.

Portland* — Robert Riler (Communications), 2838 E. Burnside St., Portland 97214.

Pennsylvania: Allentown — Rev. Stanley T. Sosnowski (Information), 202 N. 17th St., Box F, Allentown 18105.

Altoona-Johnstown — Msgr. Philip Saylor (Information), Box 413 Logan Blvd., Hollidaysburg 16648.

Erie — Rev. Thomas McSweeney (Communications), Gannon University, 703 Peach St. Erie 16541.

Greensburg — Mrs. Alice Laurich (Communications), Box 850, Greensburg 15601.

Harrisburg — Sr. Arlene Ronollo, S.S.J. (Communications), 4800 Union Deposit Rd., Box 3557, Harrisburg 17105.

Philadelphia* — Msgr. Charles Mynaugh (Communications), 222 North 17th St., Philadelphia 19103.

Philadelphia* (Ukrainian) — Rev. Ronald Popivchak, Box 126, Bridgeport 19405.

Pittsburgh* (Byzantine Rite) — Msgr. Edward V. Rosack (Information), 624 Park Rd., Ambridge 15003; Most Rev. John M. Bilock (Radio-TV), 54 Riverview Ave., Pittsburgh 15214.

Pittsburgh — Rev. Ronald P. Lengwin (Communications), 111 Boulevard of the Allies, Pittsburgh 15222.

Scranton — Rev. Joseph P. Gilgallon, 300 Wyoming Ave., Scranton 18503.

Rhode Island: Providence — Marianne Postiglione, R.S.M. (Communications), One Cathedral Square, Providence 02903. Gilles D. Dery (Media Center), 200 High Service Ave. N. Providence 02904.

South Carolina: Charleston — Dr. Paul C. Beach (Communications), Box 818, Charleston 29402.

South Dakota: Rapid City — Mr. Brian T. Olszewski, Box 678, Rapid City 57709.

Sioux Falls — Rev. Leonard Thury, Holy Family Catholic Church, 321 E. 3rd St., Mitchell 57301; Rev. Thomas J. Ryan, 509 Capital, Yankton 57078.

Tennessee: Memphis — Msgr. Paul W. Clunan (Communications), 203 S. White Station Rd., Memphis 38117.

Nashville — Mr. Joseph A. Sweat (Com-

634   Communications Offices

munications, Public Relations), 2400 21st Ave. S., Nashville 37212.

Texas: Amarillo — Terri Goodman (Information), 1800 N. Spring St., Box 5644, Amarillo 79107.

Austin — Rev. Guy Gurath, Box 13327, Austin 78711.

Beaumont — Rev. James Vanderholt (Communications), P.O. Box 3948, Beaumont 77704.

Brownsville — Sr. Mildred McGovern, S.C.N., Box 547, Brownsville 78520.

Corpus Christi — Joseph Michael Feist (Public Information), Sr. Janie Barrera (Communications Coordinator), Rev. Robert E. Freeman (Communications), 620 Lipan St., Corpus Christi 78401.

Dallas — Deacon Steve Landregan (Communications), Patricia Hasbrouck (ETV), 3915 Lemmon Ave., Dallas 75219.

El Paso — Mr. Andrew Sparke (Parochial Schools TV), 1101 Birch St., El Paso 79930.

Fort Worth — Rev. Reynold Matus, St. Vincent de Paul Church, 5819 W. Pleasant Ridge Rd., Arlington 76016.

Galveston-Houston — Msgr. John L. Fos, 1700 San Jacinto St., Box 1878, Houston 77001; Byron Higgins (Radio-TV), Box 907, Houston 77001.

San Angelo — Rev. Maurice J. Voity (Communications), Box 1829, San Angelo 76902.

San Antonio* — Rev. John W. Yanta (Communications), Box 12429, San Antonio 78212.

Utah: Salt Lake City — Sr. Margaret Andre Stechschulte, O.P. (Media and Communication), 27C St., Salt Lake City 84103.

Vermont: Burlington — Rev. Joseph T. Sullivan (Communications), 351 North Ave., Burlington 05401.

Virginia: Arlington — Ellen McCloskey (Communications), 200 N. Glebe Rd., Arlington 22203.

Richmond — Mr. Bob Edwards (Communications), 811 Cathedral Pl., Richmond 23220.

Washington: Seattle* — Dr. Maury Sheridan, 907 Terry Ave., Seattle 98104.

Spokane — Rev. Michael J. Savelesky (Communications), Box 1453, Spokane 99210.

Yakima — Rev. P. J. Auve, Pastoral Office, Box 505, Yakima 98907.

West Virginia: Wheeling-Charleston — Rev. Victor Seidel, S.T., Box 230, Wheeling 26003.

Wisconsin: Green Bay — Mr. Tony Kuick (Communications), Box 66, Green Bay 54305.

La Crosse — Rev. Bernard McGarty (Communications), Box 69, La Crosse 54601.

Madison — Maureen Quinn Hartin (Communications), 3577 High Point Rd., Rt. 2, Madison 53711.

Milwaukee* — Sr. Mary Luke Baldwin, S.S.N.D. (Communications), 345 N. 95th, Box 2018, Milwaukee 53201.

Superior — Rev. Robert Urban (Information), 1512 N. 12th St., Superior 54880.

Wyoming: Cheyenne — Rev. Roy Lansing (Information), P.O. Box 1387, Cheyenne 82001.

Catholic Communications Northwest: Regional communications center serving dioceses in Alaska, Idaho, Montana, Oregon and Washington. Executive Director, Dr. Maury Sheridan, 907 Terry Ave., Seattle, Wash. 98104.

Delaware Valley Catholic Office for Television and Radio: Interdiocesan agency of the Archdiocese of Philadelphia and the dioceses of Camden and Trenton, N.J. Address: 222 North 17th St., Philadelphia, Pa. 19103.

Other Communications Offices

American Social Communications Conference: Rev. Aloysius Svobodny, O.M.I., executive secretary, 104 N. Mississippi River Blvd., St. Paul, Minn. 55104.

Center for Communications Ministry (formerly the National Sisters Communications Service): A mass communications consulting and resource agency serving religious orders of men and women. Publishes *Media and Values,* a quarterly review of trends in contemporary communications. Sister Elizabeth Thoman, C.H.M., executive director, 1962 S. Shenandoah, Los Angeles, Calif. 90034.

International Mission Radio Association: Rev. Jude Bradley, O.S.B., treasurer-administrator, St. Paul's Abbey, Newton, N.J. 07860.

Jesuits in Communication in North America (JESCOM): Rev. Donald R. Campion, S.J., executive secretary, Suite 402, 1717 Massachusetts Ave., N.W., Washington, D.C. 20005.

Maryknoll Media Relations: Rev. Paul Newpower, M.M., director, Maryknoll Fathers and Brothers, Maryknoll, N.Y. 10545.

National Franciscan Communications Conference: Rev. James J. Gardiner, S.A., president, Graymoor, Garrison, N.Y. 10524.

National Office

The National Catholic Office for Information (NCOI), successor to the NCWC Bureau of Information, serves as the official spokesman for both the United States Catholic Conference and the National Conference of Catholic Bishops in relating to the news media. The NCOI is part of the NCCB USCC Office for Public Affairs.

The office also provides services and coordination for diocesan information offices.

William Ryan is director of the office, which is located at 1312 Massachusetts Ave. N.W., Washington, D.C. 20005.

Honors and Awards

Pontifical Orders

The Pontifical Orders of Knighthood are secular orders of merit whose membership depends directly on the pope. Details regarding the various orders are handled by a special agency in the Secretariat of Briefs, an office in the Papal Secretariat of State.

Supreme Order of Christ (Militia of Our Lord Jesus Christ): The highest of the five pontifical orders of knighthood, the Supreme Order of Christ was approved Mar. 14, 1319, by John XXII as a continuation in Portugal of the suppressed Order of Templars. Members were religious with vows and a rule of life until the order lost its religious character toward the end of the 15th century. Since that time it has existed as an order of merit. Paul VI, in 1966, restricted awards of the order to Christian heads of state.

Order of the Golden Spur (Golden Militia): Although the original founder is not certainly known, this order is one of the oldest knighthoods. Indiscriminate bestowal and inheritance diminished its prestige, however, and in 1841 Gregory XVI replaced it with the Order of St. Sylvester and gave it the title of Golden Militia. In 1905 St. Pius X restored the Order of the Golden Spur in its own right, separating it from the Order of St. Sylvester. Paul VI, in 1966, restricted awards of the order to Christian heads of state.

Order of Pius IX: Founded by Pius IX June 17, 1847, the order is awarded for outstanding services for the Church and society, and may be given to non-Catholics as well as Catholics. The title to nobility formerly attached to membership was abolished by Pius XII in 1939. In 1957 Pius XII instituted the Class of the Grand Collar as the highest category of the order; in 1966, Paul VI restricted this award to heads of state "in solemn circumstances." The other three classes are of Knights of the Grand Cross, Knight Commanders with and without emblem, and Knights. The new class was created to avoid difficulties in presenting papal honors to Christian or non-Christian leaders of high merit.

Order of St. Gregory the Great: First established by Gregory XVI in 1831 to honor citizens of the Papal States, the order is conferred on persons who are distinguished for personal character and reputation, and for notable accomplishment. The order has civil and military divisions, and three classes of knights.

Order of St. Sylvester: Instituted Oct. 31, 1841, by Gregory XVI to absorb the Order of the Golden Spur, this order was divided into two by St. Pius X in 1905, one retaining the name of St. Sylvester and the other assuming the title of Golden Militia. Membership consists of three degrees: Knights of the Grand Cross, Knight Commanders with and without emblem, and Knights.

Ecclesiastical Order

Order of the Holy Sepulchre: Critical opinion is divided regarding various details of the history of the order. It is certain, however, that these knights first appeared in the Holy Land and were in existence at the end of the 11th century. Some assign earlier dates or origin, claiming as founders St. James the Apostle, first bishop of Jerusalem, and St. Helena, builder of the Basilica of the Holy Sepulchre. Others hold that Godfrey of Bouillon instituted the order in 1099 and that it took its name from the Holy Sepulchre where its members were knighted.

The order lost a great deal of prestige after the fall of the Latin Kingdom of Jerusalem and the consequent departure of the knights from the Holy Land. It was united with the Knights of St. John in 1489, came under the grand mastership of Alexander VI in 1496 and shortly thereafter was split into three national divisions, German, French and Spanish. Pius IX re-established the Latin patriarchate of Jerusalem in 1847 and gave the patriarch the faculty of conferring the order of knighthood. This right had been held by the Franciscan custos following the appointment of the Friars as guardians of the Holy Land in 1342. Three classes of membership were designated in 1868. Leo XIII later instituted the Cross of Honor (which does not confer knighthood) in three classes — gold, silver and bronze — and also the Dames of the Holy Sepulchre. From 1907 to 1928 the pope was grand master, an office now held by a cardinal. Revised statutes for the order went into effect in 1949, 1962 and 1967. The 1949 constitution enjoined the knights "to revive in modern form the spirit and ideal of the Crusades with the weapons of faith, the apostolate, and Christian charity."

The Order of the Holy Sepulchre now has five classes: 12 Knights of the Collar and four degrees, with separate divisions of each for men and women — Grand Cross, Commanders with Plaque, Commanders and Knights. Three honorary decorations are awarded, vis., Palm of the Order, Cross of Merit (which may be bestowed on non-Catholics), and the Pilgrim's Shell.

Investiture ceremonies combine a profession of faith with the ancient ritual of knighthood dubbing. Candidates do not take monastic vows but pledge an upright Christian life and loyalty to the pope.

The grand master of the order is Cardinal Maximilien de Furstenberg.

There are four lieutenancies of the order in the United States.

Order of Malta

The Sovereign Military Hospitaller Order of St. John of Jerusalem of Rhodes and of Malta traces its origin to a group of men who maintained a Christian hospital in the Holy Land in the 11th century. The group was approved as a religious order — the Hospitallers of St. John — by Paschal II in 1113.

The order, while continuing its service to the poor, principally in hospital work, assumed military duties in the twelfth century and included knights, chaplains and sergeants-at-arms among its members. All the knights were professed monks with the vows of poverty, chastity and obedience. Headquarters were located in the Holy Land until the last decade of the 13th century and on Rhodes after 1308 (whence the title, Knights of Rhodes).

After establishing itself on Rhodes, the order became a sovereign power like the sea republics of Italy and the Hanseatic cities of Germany, flying its own flag, coining its own money, floating its own navy, and maintaining diplomatic relations with many nations.

The order was forced to abandon Rhodes in 1522 after the third siege of the island by the Turks under Sultan Suliman I. Eight years later, the Knights were given the island of Malta, where they remained as a bastion of Christianity until near the end of the 18th century. Headquarters have been located in Rome since 1834.

The title of Grand Master of the Order, in abeyance for some time, was restored by Leo XIII in 1879. A more precise definition of both the religious and the sovereign status of the order was embodied in a new constitution of 1961 and a code issued in 1966.

Religious aspects of the order are subject to regulation by the Holy See. At the same time the sovereignty of the order, which is based on international law, is recognized by the Holy See and by 42 countries with which full diplomatic relations are maintained.

The four main classifications of members are: Knights of Justice, who are religious with the vows of poverty, chastity and obedience; Knights of Obedience, who make a solemn promise to strive for Christian perfection; Knights of Honor and Devotion and of Grace and Devotion — all of noble lineage; and Knights of Magistral Grace. There are also chaplains, Dames and Donats of the order.

The order, with five grand priories, three sub-priories and 37 national associations, is devoted to hospital and charitable work of all kinds in some 77 countries.

The Grand Master, who is the sovereign head of the order, has the title of Most Eminent Highness with the rank of Cardinal. He must be of noble lineage and under solemn vows for a minimum period of 10 years.

The present Grand Master is Fra' Angelo de Mojana di Cologna, a lawyer of Milan, who was elected for life May 8, 1962, by the Council of State.

The address of headquarters of the order is Via Condotti, 68, Palazzo Malta, 00187 Roma, Italia.

Papal Medals

Pro Ecclesia et Pontifice: This decoration ("For the Church and the Pontiff") had its origin in 1888 as a token of the golden sacerdotal jubilee of Leo XIII; he bestowed it on those who had assisted in the observance of his jubilee and on persons responsible for the success of the Vatican Exposition. The medal bears the likeness of Leo XIII on one side; on the other, the tiara, the papal keys, and the words *Pro Ecclesia et Pontifice*. Originally, the medal was issued in gold, silver or bronze. It is awarded in recognition of service to the Church and the papacy.

Benemerenti: Several medals ("To a well-deserving person") have been conferred by popes for exceptional accomplishment and service. The medals, which are made of gold, silver or bronze, bear the likeness and name of the reigning pope on one side; on the other, a laurel crown and the letter "B."

These two medals may be given by the pope to both men and women. Their bestowal does not convey any title or honor of knighthood.

AMERICAN CATHOLIC AWARDS

Aquinas Medal, by the American Catholic Philosophical Association for outstanding outstanding contributions to the field of Catholic philosophy.

Jacques Maritain (1951), Etienne Gilson (1952), Gerald Smith, S.J. (1955), Gerald B. Phelan (1959), Rudolf Allers (1960), James A. McWilliams, S.J. (1961) Charles De Koninck (1964), James Collins (1965).

Martin C. D'Arcy (1967), Dr. Josef Pieper (1968), Leo R. Ward (1969), Bernard Lonergan, S.J. (1970), Henry B. Veatch (1971),

Joseph Owens, C.SS.R. (1972), A. Hilary Armstrong (1973), Cornelio Fabro (1974), Anton Pegis (1975), Mortimer J. Adler (1976), Frederick C. Copleston (1977), Fernand Van Steenberghen (1978), John Paul II (1979), W. Norris Clarke, S.J. (1980), Ernan McMullin (1981), G.E.M. Anscombe (1982).

Bellarmine Medal (1955), by Bellarmine College (Louisville, Ky.), to persons in national or international affairs who, in controversial matters, exemplify the characteristics of St. Robert Bellarmine in charity, justice and temperateness.

Jefferson Caffery (1955), Gen. Carlos Romulo (1956), U.S. Rep. John W. McCormack (1957), Frank M. Folsom (1958), Robert D. Murphy (1959), James P. Mitchell (1960), Frederick H. Boland (1961); Gen. Alfred M. Gruenther (1962), Henry Cabot Lodge (1963), R. Sargent Shriver (1964), Irene Dunne (1965), Sen. Everett M. Dirksen (1966), Nicholas Katzenbach (1967), Danny Thomas (1968), J. Irwin Miller (1969), Theodore M. Hesburgh, C.S.C. (1970), Sen. John Sherman Cooper (1971), (no award, 1972), Dr. William B. Walsh (1973), Most Rev. Fulton J. Sheen (1974), William F. Buckley, Jr. (1977), Rev. Jesse L. Jackson (1979), Mother Teresa of Calcutta (1981).

Berakah Award (1976), by the North American Academy of the Liturgy, to recognize distinguished contribution to the professional work of liturgy by a liturgist or person of an allied vocation.

Aidan Kavanagh, O.S.B. (1976), Godfrey Diekmann, O.S.B. (1977), Massey Hamilton Shepherd (1978), Rev. Frederick McManus, (1979), Horton Davies (1980), Frank Kacmarcik (1981), Robert W. Hovda (1982).

Borromeo Award (1960), by Carroll College (Helena, Mont.), for zeal, courage and devotion in the spirit of St. Charles Borromeo.

William D. Murray (1960), Robert E. Sullivan (1961), Vincent H. Walsh (1962), Leo V. Kelly (1963), Joseph A. Kimmet (1964), Dr. W. E. Long (1965), Frank E. Blair (1968), Gough, Booth, Shanahan and Johnson (1971), Egon E. Mallman, S.J. (1973), Christian Brothers of Ireland (1974), Most Rev. Raymond Hunthausen (1975), Dominican Sisters of Spokane, Wash., of the Province of the Immaculate Heart of Mary (1976), Rev. Emmett Shea (1977), Most Rev. Eldon B. Schuster (1978), Rev. Paul B. Kirchen (1979). Sister Alice Ann Byrne, O.P. (1980), Sheila McShane and Rev. James Hazelton (1981).

Brent Award (1976), by the Diocese of Arlington, Va., for distinguished service to fellowman.

Dr. Mildred F. Jefferson (1976), Most Rev. John J. Russell (1977), U.S. Rep. Henry J. Hyde and William B. Ball, Esq. (1978), Mrs. Hazel Hagarty (1979), Mother Mary Claudia, I.H.M. (1980), Dr. Josephina Magno (1981).

Campion Award (1955), by the Catholic Book Club for distinguished service in Catholic letters.

Jacques Maritain (1955), Helen C. White (1956), Paul Horgan (1957), James Brodrick, S.J. (1958), Sister M. Madeleva (1959), Frank J. Sheed and Maisie Ward (1960), John La Farge, S.J. (1961), Harold C. Gardiner, S.J. (1962);

T. S. Eliot (1963), Barbara Ward (1964), Msgr. John T. Ellis (1965), John Courtney Murray, S.J. (1966), Phyllis McGinley (1967),

Dr. George N. Shuster (1968), G. B. Harrison (1970), Walter and Jean Kerr (1971), Karl Rahner, S.J. (1974), John J. Delaney (1976).

Cardinal Gibbons Medal (1949) by the Alumni Association of the Catholic University of America for distinguished and meritorious service to the Church, the United States or the Catholic University.

Carlton J. H. Hayes (1949), Gen. Carlos P. Romulo (1950), Fulton Oursler (1951), Most Rev. Fulton J. Sheen (1953), J. Edgar Hoover (1954), Gen. J. Lawton Collins (1955), U.S. Sen. John F. Kennedy and Ignatius Smith, O.P. (1956), Most Rev. Bryan J. McEntegart (1957), Thomas E. Murray (1958);

Gen. Alfred M. Gruenther (1959), Karl F. Herzfeld (1960), Charles G. Fenwick (1961), Luke E. Hart (1962), John W. McCormack (1963), John A. McCone (1964), R. Sargent Shriver (1965), Hon. Earl Warren (1966), James J. Norris (1967), Danny Thomas (1968), Theodore Hesburgh, C.S.C. (1969), Dr. Carroll Hochwalt (1970), Most Rev. James E. Walsh (1971), Cardinal Patrick O'Boyle (1972), Helen Hayes (1973), Sen. Mike Mansfield (1974), Judge John J. Sirica (1975), Cardinal Lawrence Shehan (1976), Benjamin T. Rome (1977), Dr. Clarence C. Walton (1978), Cardinal Terence Cooke (1979), Peter Grace (1980), Msgr. John Tracy Ellis (1981).

Cardinal Spellman Award (1947), by the Catholic Theological Society for outstanding achievement in the field of theology.

Revs. Francis J. Connell, C.SS.R., Emmanuel Doronzo, O.M.I., Gerald Yelle, S.S., William R. O'Connor, John C. Murray, S.J. (1947); Eugene Burke, C.S.P. (1948), Bernard J. J. Lonergan, S.J. (1949), John C. Murray, S.J. (1950), Msgr. William R. O'Connor (1951), Emmanuel Doronzo, O.M.I. (1952), Gerald Kelly, S.J. (1953), Francis J. Connell, C.SS.R. (1954), Edmond D. Benard (1955), John C. Ford, S.J. (1956);

Gerard Yelle, S.S. (1957), Msgr. Joseph C. Fenton (1958), Juniper Carol, O.F.M. (1959), Rev. John Quasten (1960), Cyril C. Vollert, S.J. (1961), Walter J. Burghardt, S.J. (1962), Rev. Francis Dvornik (1963), Barnabas Ahern, C.P. (1964), Godfrey Diekmann, O.S.B. (1965), Paul K. Meagher, O.P. (1966), John L. McKenzie, S.J. (1967), Dr. Martin R. P. McGuire (1968), Richard A. McCormick, S.J. (1969), Avery Dulles, S.J. (1970), Raymond E. Brown, S.S. (1971).

For recipients after 1971, see John Courtney Murray Award.

Catholic Action Medal (1934), by St. Bonaventure University (St. Bonaventure, N.Y.).

Alfred E. Smith (1934), Michael Williams (1935), Joseph Scott (1936), Patrick Scanlan (1937), George J. Gillespie (1938), William F Montavon (1939), John J. Craig (1940), John S. Burke (1941), Dr. George Speri Sperti (1942), Francis P. Matthews (1943);

Jefferson Caffery (1944), John A. Coleman (1945), David Goldstein (1946), Clement Lane (1947), Paul W. Weber (1948), Bruce M. Mohler (1949), Edward M. O'Connor (1950), Richard F. Pattee (1951), James M. O'Neill (1952), John E. Swift (1953);

Frank M. Folsom (1954), Walter L. McGuiness (1955), Carlton J. H. Hayes (1956), Thomas E. Murray (1957), Paul V. Murray (1958), Dr. John L. Madden (1959), Christopher H. Dawson (1960), Stephen Kuttner (1961), Charles De Koninck (1962), Lt. Gen. G. Trudeau (1963), Frank J. Sheed (1964), Danny Thomas (1965), Walter and Jean Kerr (1966), Sir Hugh Stott Taylor (1967), Maurice Lavanoux (1968).

The Catholic University of America Patronal Medal (1974), by the University for outstanding contributions to the Catholic Church and in promoting interest and devotion to Mary, patroness of the University.

Most Rev. Fulton J. Sheen (1974), Sister M. Claudia Honsberger, I.H.M. (1975), Rev. Theodore A. Koehler (1976), Rev. Ross MacKenzie, Presbyterian clergyman (1977), (No award, 1978), Cardinal John J. Carberry, Mother Teresa (1979) Rev. Patrick J. Peyton, C.S.C. (1980), Virgil C. Dechant (1981).

Cecilia Medal (1952), by the Music Department of Boys Town (Nebr.) for outstanding work in liturgical music.

Winifred T. Flanagan (1952), Dom Francis Missia (1953), Omer Westendorf (1954), Dom Ermin Vitry (1955), William A. Reilly (1956), Flor Peeters (1957), Roger Wagner (1958), Most Rev. Gerald T. Bergan (1959), Francis T. Brunner, C.SS.R. (1960), Jean Langlois (1961);

James B. Welch (1962), W. Ripley Dorr (1963), C. Alexander Peloquin (1964), Dr. Louise Cuyler (1965), Dr. Eugene Selhorst (1966), Dr. Paul Manz (1967), Myron J. Roberts (1968), Norman T. Letter (1969), Rev. Elmer Pfeil (1969), Rev. Richard Schuler (1970), Frank Szynski (1979), Evelyn Letter (1980).

Christian Culture Award (1941), by Assumption University (Canada) to outstanding lay exponents of Christian ideals.

Sigrid Undset (1941), Jacques Maritain (1942), Philip Murray (1943), Frank J. Sheed (1944), Arnold M. Walter (1945), Henry Ford II (1946), George S. Sperti (1947), Richard Pattee (1948), Etienne Gilson (1949), Paul Doyon (1950), Christopher Dawson (1951), John C.H. Wu (1952);

Charles Malik (1953), Ivan Mestrovic (1954), F. W. Foerster (1955), Paul Martin (1956), Robert Speaight (1947), Allen Tate (1958), Barbara Ward (1959), John Cogley (1960), Peter Drucker (1961), Benjamin E. Mays (1962), John Quincy Adams (1963);

William Foxwell Albright (1964), Dr. Karl Stern (1965), John Howard Griffin (1966), Edith K. Peterkin (1967), Dr. Mircea Eliade

(1968), Dr. James D. Collins (1969), Dorothy Day (1970), Dr. Marshall McLuhan (1971), James M. Cameron (1972), Jean Vanier (1973), Robert J. Kreyche (1974), John T. Noonan, Jr. (1975), Dorothy Donnelly (1976), William Kurelek (1977), Anthony Walsh (1978), Malcolm Muggeridge (1979), Conrad W. Baars, M.D. (1980), Rosemary Haughton (1981), Roy Bonisteel (1982).

Collegian Award (1949), by "The Collegian," weekly student newspaper of La Salle College (Phila.), for public service in the field of communications.

Ed Sullivan (1949), Morley Cassidy (1950), Bob Considine (1951), Red Smith (1952), George Sokolsky (1953), Edward R. Murrow (1954), David Lawrence (1955), Jim Bishop (1956), Richard W. Slocum (1957), Chet Huntley (1958);

John C. O'Brien (1959), Walter Cronkite (1960), David Brinkley (1961), James Reston (1962), Charles Collingwood (1963), Art Buchwald (1964), Nancy Dickerson (1965), Charles Schulz (1966), Sandy Grady (1967), Harrison E. Salisbury (1968), Ralph W. Howard (1969), (not awarded 1970-77), Lawrence M. O'Rourke (1978).

Damien-Dutton Award (1953), by the Damien-Dutton Society for service toward conquest of leprosy or for the promotion of better understanding of social problems connected with the disease.

Stanley Stein (1953), Joseph Sweeney, M.M. (1954), Sister Marie Suzanne (1955), Dr. Perry Burgess (1956), John Farrow (1957), Dr. H. Windsor Wade (1958), Sister Hilary Ross (1959), Msgr. Louis J. Mendelis (1960), Dr. Kensuke Mitsuda (1961), Pierre d'Orgeval, SS.CC. (1962);

Eunice Weaver (1963), Dr. Robert Cochrane (1964), John F. Kennedy, posthumously (1965), The Peace Corps (1966), Dr. Howard A. Rusk (1967), Dr. Frans Hemerijckx (1968), Dr. Victor G. Heiser (1969), Dr. Dharmendra (1970), Dr. Chapman H. Binford (1971), Dr. Patricia Smith (1972), Dr. Jacinto Convit (1973), Dr. Jose N. Rodriguez (1974), Dr. Oliver Hasselblad (1975), Dr. Yoshio Yoshie (1976), Drs. Paul and Margaret Brand (1977), Dr. Fernando Latapi (1978), Dr. Stanley Browne (1979) Robert Watelet (1980), American Leprosy Missions (1981).

The De La Salle Medal, by Manhattan College, for significant contribution to the moral, cultural or educational life of the nation.

John F. Brosnan (1951), Cardinal Francis Spellman (1952), Most Rev. Joseph P. Donahue (1953), Most Rev. Edwin V. O'Hara, posthumously (1956), Sr. Mary Emil, I.H.M. (1957), Msgr. Joseph E. Schieder (1958), Very Rev. Bro. Bertrand, O.S.F. (1959), Dr. Roy J. Deferrari (1960).

John Courtney Murray, S.J. (1961), Bro. Clair Stanislaus, F.S.C. (1962), Most Rev.

Bryan J. McEntegart (1963), Sr. M. Rose Eileen, C.S.C. (1964), Mother Kathryn Sullivan, R.S.C.J. (1965), Bro. Bernard Peter, F.S.C. (1966), Dr. William Hughes Mulligan (1967), C. Alfred Koob, O. Praem. (1968), Theodore M. Hesburgh, C.S.C. (1970), Most Rev. Edwin B. Broder ick (1971), Very Rev. Bro. Charles Henry, F.S.C. (1972), Mary Shea Giordano (1973), Dorothy Day (1974), Henry Viscardi, Jr. (1975), Sister Elinor R. Ford, O.P. (1976), John D. de Butts (1977), Thomas A. Murphy (1978), Gabriel Hauge (1979), Irving S. Shapiro (1980), Maurice F. Granville (1981), Frank T. Cary (1982).

Edith Stein Award (1955), by the Edith Stein Guild for service toward better understanding between Christians and Jews.

Sister Noemi de Sion (1956), Authur B. Klyber, C.SS.R. (1957), Rev. John M. Oesterreicher (1958), John J. O'Connor (1959), Victor J. Donovan, C.P. (1960), Jacques and Raissa Maritain (1961), Gerard E. Sherry (1962), Mother Kathryn Sullivan, R.S.C.J. (1963), Paulist Press (1964), Rev. Edward N. Flannery (1965), Mother Katherine Hargrove, R.S.C.J. (1966), Gregory Baum, O.S.A. (1967), Sr. Rose Albert Thering (1968), Msgr. Vincent O. Genova (1969), Dr. Joseph Lichten (1970), Philip Scharper (1971), Rabbi Marc Tanenbaum (1972), Leon Paul (1973).

Emmanuel D'Alzon Medal (1954), by Assumptionists to persons exemplifying the ideals of their founder.

Jacques Maritain (1954), Michael F. Doyle (1955), Cardinal Richard J. Cushing (1956), Mother Mary St. Elizabeth (1956), Most Rev. John J. Wright (1959), Paolino Gerli (1960), Most Rev. Honoré van Waeyenbergh (1961), J. Peter Grace (1963), Danny Thomas (1967), Miss Mary Dowd, posthumously (1970), Most Rev. Bernard J. Flanagan (1974), Mother Helene-Marie Bories, S.A., and Cardinal Johannes Willebrands (1980).

Father McKenna Award (1950), by the national headquarters of the Holy Name Society, for outstanding service to the society's ideals.

Msgr. John J. Murphy, Msgr. Henry J. Watterson, Msgr. Frederic J. Allchin (1950), Eustace Struckhoff, O.F.M., Msgr. Joseph A. McCaffrey, Msgr. Francis P. Connelly, Rev. Raymond E. Jones, Msgr. Joseph E. Maguire, Msgr. Edward J. Kelly, Msgr. J. Frederick Kriebs, Rev. Thomas E. O'Connell, Very Rev. Charles L. Elslander, Rev. Joseph J. Heim, Msgr. F. Borgias Lehr (1951);

Rev. Francis J. Hannegan (1954), Rev. Charles A. Hoot, Rev. Louis A. Hinnebusch, O.P., Rev. John O. Purcell, Rev. Paul M. Lackner (1955), Msgr. F. J. Timoney (1958), Rev. Thomas F. McNicholas (1960), James A. Quinn, O.P., and Rev. John C. Griffith (1961), Msgr. Joseph A. Aughney (1962),

Msgr. Cornelius P. Higgins (1963), Msgr. Charles P. Mynaugh (1964), Msgr. Charles P. Muth, Rev. Patrick J. Foley (1971), Rev. Msgr. Robert T. Kickham (1973), Rev. John D. Malone, O.P. (1975), Rev. John Bendix (1977), Msgr. Joseph Coughlin (1979), John Brendan Larnen, O.P. (1980).

Fidelitas Medal (1949), by Orchard Lake Schools (Sts. Cyril and Methodius Seminary, St. Mary's College, St. Mary's Preparatory), to an outstanding American Catholic of Polish descent for fidelity in serving God and country.

Msgr. Lucian Bojnowski (1949), Msgr. Adalbert Zadala (1950), Msgr. John Gulcz (1951), Joseph Kania (1952), Msgr. Francis Karabasz (1953), Rev. Valentine Biczysko (1954), Dr. Edwin Dobski (1955), Very Rev. Justin Figas, O.F.M. Conv. (1956), Hon. Arthur Koscinski (1957), Miss Adela Lagodzinska (1958), Msgr. Casimir Piejda (1959), Msgr. Ladislaus Sikora (1960), Msgr. Vincent Borkowicz (1961), Msgr. Ladislaus Nowakowski (1962), Msgr. Peter Walkowiak (1963), Charles Rozmarek (1964), Rev. Simon Kilar (1965);

Mother Mary Alexander (1966), Msgr. Francis Kowalczyk (1967), Cardinal John J. Krol (1968), Sen. Edmund S. Muskie (1969), Msgr. Peter Adamski (1970), Joseph Pranica (1971), Hon. Frank G. Schemanske (1972), Mrs. Dora Alska (1973), Benjamin Stefanski (1974), Robert Goralski (1975), Aloysius Mazewski (1976), Msgr. John Wodarski (1977), Dr. Zbigniew Brzezinski (1978), Msgr. Alexander Cendrowski (1979), Stanley (Bobby) Vinton, Jr. (1980), Rev. Anthony Iwuc (1981), Frank C. Padzieski (1982).

Franciscan International Award (1958), by the Conventual Franciscans (Prior Lake, Minn.) for outstanding contributions to the development of life.

Mr. and Mrs. Ignatius A. O'Shaughnessy (1959), Archbishop William O. Brady (1960), Lawrence Welk (1961), Charles Kellstad (1962), Dr. Finn J. Larsen (1963), Dr. Charles W. Mayo (1964), Ara Parseghian (1965), F. K. Weyerhaueser (1966);

Alcoholics Anonymous (1967), James T. Griffin (1968), George S. Harris (1969), Baroness Catherine DeHueck Doherty (1970), Harry Reasoner (1971), Dr. Billy Graham (1972), Dr. and Mrs. John C. Willke (1973), Gov. Patrick J. Lucey (1974), Joe and Jan Rigert (1975), Dr. B. F. Pearson (1976), Francis S. MacNutt, O.P. (1977), Dr. Mildred F. Jefferson (1978), Bruce Ritter, O.F.M. Conv. (1979), John E. McCarthy (1980), William B. Wasson, O.F.M. (1981), Lorand and Anna Andahazy (1982).

George M. Cohan Award (1970), by the Catholic Actors Guild of America, Inc., for outstanding contribution to Church and the arts.

Gilbert V. Hartke, O.P. (1970), Ruby

Keeler (1971), Frances Fuller and Worthington Miner (1972), Patsy Kelly (1973), Earl Wilson (1974), Kate Smith (1975), Hildegarde (1976), Jack O'Brian (1977), Bishop Edwin B. Broderick (1978), Claudette Colbert (1979), Frederick O'Neal (1980), William J. O'Malley (1982).

Good Samaritan Award (1968), by the National Catholic Development Conference to recognize the concern for one's fellowman exemplified by the Good Samaritan.

Bishop Edward E. Swanstrom (1968), Berard Scarborough, O.F.M. (1969), Bishop Joseph B. Whelan, C.S.Sp. (1970), Mother Teresa (1971), Bishop Michael R. Dempsey (1972), Msgr. Ralph W. Beiting (1973), Rev. Daniel Egan, S.A. (1974), Dr. Isabel S. Dumont and Joan Mulder (1975), Msgr. Clement H. Kern (1976), Sister Maria Rosa Leggol, S.S.S.F. (1977), Bruce Ritter, O.F.M. Conv. (1978), Rev. William Wasson (1979), Mother Anna Dengel, S.C.M.M., M.D. (1980), Staff of Calvary Hospital (1981).

Hoey Awards (1942), by the Catholic Interracial Council of New York (225 E. 52nd St., New York, N.Y. 10022). Presented annually to persons who have worked to promote social and interracial justice.

Frank A. Hall and Edward La Salle (1942), Philip Murray and Ralph H. Metcalfe (1943), Mrs. Edward V. Morrell and John L. Yancey (1944), Paul D. Williams and Richard Barthe (1945), Richard Reid and Charles L. Rawlings (1946), Julian J. Reiss and Clarence T. Hunter (1947), Mrs. Anna McGarry and Ferdinand L. Rousseve (1948), John J. O'Connor and M. C. Clarke (1949), J. Howard McGrath and Lou Montgomery (1950), Mrs. Roger L. Putnam and Francis M. Hammond (1951);

Charles F. Vatterot, Jr., and Joseph J. Yancey (1952), Joseph J. Morrow and John B. King (1953), Mrs. Gladys D. Woods and Collins J. Seitz (1954), Millard F. Everett and Dr. James W. Hose (1955), Frank M. Folsom and Paul G. King (1956), George Meany and James W. Dorsey (1957), James T. Harris and Robert S. Shriver, Jr. (1958), Percy H. Steele, Jr., and John P. Nelson (1959);

William Duffy, Jr., and George A. Moore (1960), Ralph Fenton and Mrs. Osma Spurlock (1961), Benjamin Muse and Dr. Eugene T. Reed (1962), James T. Carey and Percy H. Williams (1963), Arthur J. Holland and Frederick O'Neal (1964), Gerard E. Sherry and James R. Dumpson (1965), Jane M. Hoey and Mrs. Roy Wilkins (1966), Dr. Frank Horne and Lt. Gov. Malcolm Wilson (1967), E. H. Molisani and John Strachan (1968);

Harold E. McGannon and Hulan E. Jack (1969), George P. McManus, Alfred B. Del Bello, Maceo A. Thomas and Cleo Joseph L. Froix, M.D. (1970), Most Rev. Francis J. Mugavero and Most Rev. Harold R. Perry

(1971), Joseph F. Crangle and Alen E. Pinado (1972), Meade H. Esposito and Robert B. Boyd (1973), Hon. Harold A. Stevens and Thomas Van Arsdale (1974), Hon. Kenneth E. Sherwood, Joseph Trerotola (1975), William M. Ellinghaus and Hon. Lucille Rose (1976), Hon. Carlos Romero Barcelo and Lena Horne (1977), J. Peter Grace and Hon. Basil A. Paterson (1978), Helen Hayes, Felisa Rincon de Gautier and Cecil E. Ward (1979), Maureen O'Sullivan, Jack John Olivero, Peter J. Ottley (1980), James Joy, Jr., Elizabeth McCann, Mollie Moon (1981).

Honor et Veritas Award (1959), by the Catholic War Veterans to outstanding Americans.

Cardinal Francis J. Spellman (1960), Gen. Douglas MacArthur (1961), U. S. Sen. Thomas J. Dodd (1962), Gen. William Westmoreland (1966), Dean Rusk (1967), Col. Martin T. Riley (1968), Theodore M. Hesburgh, C.S.C. (1969), Kenneth D. Wells (1970), Danny Thomas (1971), Thomas V. Cuite (1972), Lawrence Welk (1973), Congressman Melvin Price (1975), Thomas Gleason (1980).

Howard R. Marraro Prize (1973), by the American Catholic Historical Association for a book on Italian history or Italo-American history or relations.

Eric W. Cochrane (1974), Silvano Tomasi (1975), Sarah Rubin Blanshei (1977), Paul F. Grendler (1978), David R. Coffin (1979), Richard Krautheimer (1980), Felix Gilbert (1981).

Insignis Medal (1951), by Fordham University for extraordinary distinction in the service of God and humanity.

Dr. Carlos Espinosa Davila, Arthur H. Hayes (1955), Pierre Harmel, Victor Andres Belaunde (1956), M. E. Michelet (1957), Daniel Linehan, S.J., Dr. Victor F. Hess (1958), Dr. George N. Shuster, John H. Tully, Albert Conway (1959), Charles F. Vatterot, Cardinal Agagianian, Charles Norman and Lucy W. Shaffer, David C. Cronin, S.J. (1960);

Cardinal Spellman (1961), Edward P. Gilleran (1962), Joseph A. Martino, William J. Tracy (1963), Brother James M. Kenny, S.J., and Austin Ripley (1966), Vincent T. Lombardi (1967), Melkite Patriarch Maximos V Hakim of Antioch (1968), Joseph and Marian Kaiser (1970), Joseph P. Routh (1973), Edgar Debany and Cardinal Sergio Pignedoli (1975), Eugene J. O'Brien, S.J. (1980), Archbishop Carlo Martini (1981).

John Courtney Murray Award (1972), by the Catholic Theological Society for distinguished achievement in theology Originated in 1947 as the Cardinal Spellman Award.

Rev. Charles E. Curran (1972), Bernard Lonergan, S.J. (1973), George A. Tavard, A.A. (1974), Rev. Carl Peter (1975), Rev. Richard P. McBrien (1976), Frederick E.

Crowe (1977), Edward J. Kilmartin, S.J. (1978), Bernard Cooke (1979), David Tracy (1980), Rev. Gerald Sloyan (1981), Rev. George J. Dyer (1982).

John Gilmary Shea Prize (1944), by the American Catholic Historical Association for scholarly works on the history of the Catholic Church broadly considered.

Carlton J. H. Hayes (1946), John H. Kennedy (1950), George W. Pare (1951), Rev. Philip Hughes (1954), Annabelle M. Melville (1955), Rev. John Tracy Ellis (1956), Rev. Thomas J. McAvoy, C.S.C. (1957), Rev. John M. Daley, S.J. (1958), Rev. Robert A. Graham, S.J. (1959);

Rev. Maynard Geiger, O.F.M. (1960), Rev. John C. Murray, S.J. (1961), Francis Dvornik (1962), Oscar Halecki (1963), Helen C. White (1964), John T. Noonan (1965), Rev. Robert I. Burns, S.J. (1966 and 1967), Rev. Edward S. Surtz, S.J. (1968), Robert Brentano (1969), David M. Kennedy (1970), Jaroslav Pelikan (1971), John T. Noonan (1972), Robert E. Quirk (1973), Bro. Thomas W. Spalding, C.F.X. (1974), Jay P. Dolan (1975), Emmet Larkin (1976), Timothy Tackett (1977), Charles W. Jones (1978), Kenneth M. Setton (1979), Richard Krautheimer (1980), John W. Boyer (1981).

John La Farge Memorial Award for Interracial Justice (1965), by the Catholic Interracial Council of New York. Presented annually to a leading citizen of the community regardless of race, color or creed for promoting social and interracial justice.

Cardinal Francis J. Spellman (1965), U.S. Sen. Jacob K. Javits (1966), Gov. Nelson Rockefeller (1967), George F. Meany (1968), Whitney M. Young, Jr. (1969), Harry Van Arsdale, Jr. (1970), John V. Lindsay (1971), Earl W. Brydges (1972), Louis K. Lefkowitz (1973), Arthur Levitt (1974), Robert F. Wagner (1975), Gustave L. Levy (1976), Cardinal Terence Cooke (1977), E. Howard Molisani (1978), Gov. Hugh L. Carey (1979), Sen. Daniel Patrick Moynihan, Hazel Dukes (1980), Hon. Edward Regan, Bayard Rustin (1981), Hon. William A. Shea, Frederick O'Neal (1982).

King Award (1971), by the U.S. Catholic Historical Society for significant contribution in the study of the history of the Catholic Church in t he U.S.

Jeremiah F. O'Sullivan (1971), Oskar Halecki (1972), Ross J. S. Hoffman (1973), Jcseph G. E. Hopkins (1974), Victor L. Ridυεr (1975), Elisa A. Carrillo (1976).

Laetare Medal (1883), by the University of Notre Dame for distinguished accomplishment for Church or nation by an American Catholic.

John Gilmary Shea (1883), Patrick J. Keeley (1884), Eliza Allen Starr (1885), Gen. John Newton (1886), Edward Preuss (1887), Patrick V. Hickey (1888), Anna Hansen Dorsey (1889), William J. Onahan (1890), Daniel Dougherty (1891), Henry F. Brownson (1892);

Patrick Donahoe (1893), Augustin Daly (1894), Mrs. Mary A. Sadlier (1895), Gen. William S. Rosecrans (1896), Dr. Thomas A. Emmet (1897), Timothy E. Howard (1898), Mary G. Caldwell (1899), John Creighton (1900), William B. Cockran (1901), Dr. John B. Murphy (1902);

Charles J. Bonaparte (1903), Richard C. Kerens (1904), Thomas B. Fitzpatrick (1905), Dr. Francis Quinlan (1906), Katherine E. Conway (1907), James C. Monaghan (1908), Frances Tiernan (Christian Reid) (1909), Maurice F. Egan (1910), Agnes Repplier (1911), Thomas M. Mulry (1912);

Charles G. Herbermann (1913), Edward Douglass White (1914), Mary V. Merrick (1915), Dr. James J. Walsh (1916), Admiral William S. Benson (1917), Joseph Scott (1918), George Duval (1919), Dr. Lawrence F. Flick (1920), Elizabeth Nourse (1921), Charles P. Neil (1922);

Walter G. Smith (1923), Charles D. Maginnis (1924), Dr. Edward F. Zahm (1925), Edward N. Hurley (1926), Margaret Anglin (1927), John J. Spalding (1928), Alfred E. Smith (1929), Frederick P. Kenkel (1930), James J. Phelan (1931), Dr. Stephen J. Maher (1932);

John McCormack (1933), Genevieve Garvan Brady (1934), Frank Spearman (1935), Richard Reid (1936), Jeremiah Ford (1937), Dr. Irvin Abell (1938), Josephine Brownson (1939), Gen. Hugh A. Drum (1940), William T. Walsh (1941), Helen C. White (1942);

Thomas F. Woodlock (1943), Anne O'Hare McCormick (1944), G. Howland Shaw (1945), Carlton J. H. Hayes (1946), William B. Bruce (1947), Frank C. Walker (1948), Irene Dunne (Mrs. Francis Griffin) (1949), Gen. Joseph L. Collins (1950), John H. Phelan (1951), Thomas E. Murray (1952);

I. A. O'Shaughnessy (1953), Jefferson Caffery (1954), George Meany (1955), Gen. Alfred M. Gruenther (1956), Clare Boothe Luce (1957), Frank M. Folsom (1958), Robert D. Murphy (1959), George N. Shuster (1960), Pres. John F. Kennedy (1961), Dr. Francis J. Braceland (1962);

Adm. George W. Anderson, Jr. (1963), Phyllis McGinley (1964), Frederick D. Rossini (1965), Mr. and Mrs. Patrick F. Crowley (1966), J. Peter Grace (1967), R. Sargent Shriver (1968), Justice William J. Brennan, Jr. (1969), Dr. William B. Walsh (1970), Walter and Jean Kerr (1971), Dorothy Day (1972), Rev. John A. O'Brien (1973), James A. Farley (1974), Sister Ann Ida Gannon, B.V.M. (1975), Paul Horgan (1976), Sen. Mike Mansfield (1977), Msgr. John Tracy Ellis (1978), Helen Hayes (1979), Rep. Thomas P. O'Neill, Jr. (1980), Edmund S. Muskie

(1981), Cardinal John Francis Dearden (1982).

Lumen Christi Award (1978) by the Catholic Church Extension Society to persons making an outstanding contribution in service to the American home missions.

Miss Florence Kaster (1978), Miss Joan Mulder and Isabel Dumont, M.D. (1979), Sr. Ida Brasseur, S.S.A. (1980), Msgr. Joseph G. Cassidy (1981), Bishop Sidney M. Metzger (1982).

Marianist Award (1949), by the University of Dayton for outstanding service in America to the Mother of God (until 1966); for outstanding contributions to mankind (from 1967).

Juniper Carol, O.F.M. (1950), Daniel A. Lord, S.J. (1951), Patrick J. Peyton, C.S.C. (1952) , Roger Brien, S.G.G. (1953), Emil Neubert, S.M. (1954), Joseph A. Skelly, C.M. (1955), Frank Duff (1956), Eugene F. Kennedy and John McShain (1957), Winifred A. Feely (1958), Abp. John F. Noll (1959), Eamon R. Carroll, O. Carm. (1960), Coley Taylor (1961), Abbe Rene Laurentin (1963), Philip C. Hoelle, S.M. (1964), Cyril O. Vollert, S.J. (1965), Eduardo Frei Montalvo (1967).

Marian Library Medal (1953), by the Marian Library of the University of Dayton. Awarded annually (until 1967) to encourage books in English on the Blessed Virgin Mary. Awarded every four years (from 1971), at the time of an International Mariological Congress, to a scholar for Mariological studies.

Most Rev. Fulton J. Sheen (1953), Msgr. John S. Kennedy (1954), Rev. William G. Most (1955), Ruth Cranston (1956), Juniper Carol, O.F.M. (1957), Donald C. Sharkey and Joseph Debergh, O.M.I. (1958), Edward O'Connor, C.S.C. (1959), John J. Delaney (1960), Sister Mary Pierre, S.M. (1961), Marion A. Habig, O.F.M. (1962), Titus F. Cranny, S.A. (1963), Hilda C. Graef (1964), Edward Schillebeeckx, O.P. (1965), Cyril Vollert, S.J. (1966), Thomas O'Meara, O.P. (1967).

Charles Balic, O. F. M. (1971), Giuseppe M. Besutti (1975), Sergio Alvarez Campos, O.F.M. (1979).

Mater et Magistra Award (1963), by the College of Mt. St. Joseph on the Ohio to women for social action in the pattern and spirit of the encyclical *Mater et Magistra.*

Jane Hoey (1964), Mary Dolan (1965), Mrs. Anne Fremantle (1966), Margaret Mealey (1967), Mrs. Arthur L. Zepf, Sr. (1968), Alice R. May (1969), Mother Teresa (1974).

Mendel Medal (1928), by Villanova University for scientists.

Dr. John A. Kolmer (1929), Dr. Albert F. Zahm (1930), Dr. Karl F. Herzfeld (1931), Dr. Francis P. Garvan (1932), Dr. Hugh Stott Taylor (1933), Abbe Georges Lemaitre (1934), Dr. Francis Owen Rice (1935), Rev. Julius A. Nieuwland, C.S.C. (1936), Pierre Teilhard de Chardin, S.J. (1937), Dr. Thomas Parran (1938);

Rev. John M. Cooper (1939), Dr. Peter J. W. Debye (1940), Dr. Eugene M. K. Geiling (1941), Dr. Joseph A. Becker (1942), Dr. George Speri Sperti (1943), Dr. John C. Hubbard (1946), Frank N. Piasecki (1954), James B. Macelwane, S.J. (1955), Dr. William J. Thaler (1960), Dr. James A. Shannon (1961), Maj. Robert M. White (1963), Dr. Charles A. Hufnagel (1965), Dr. Alfred M. Bongiovanni (1968).

Msgr. John P. Monaghan Social Action Award by the Assn. of Catholic Trade Unionists; originally (1948), the Quadragesimo Anno Medal.

John Quincy Adams (1948), Brother Justin, F.S.C. (1949), Joseph Bierne (1950), Rev. Raymond A. McGowan (1951), Philip Murray (1952), Charles M. Halloran (1953), U.S. Sen. Robert F. Wagner, Sr. (1954), Rev. John P. Monaghan (1955), John C. Cort (1956), Msgr. Joseph F. Connolly (1957);

George Meany (1958), Robert F. Kennedy (1959), Thomas Carey (1960), James B. Carey (1961), Rev. Joseph Hammond (1966), Paul Jennings (1967), Matthew Guinan (1968), David Sullivan (1969), Vincent McDonnell (1970).

The O'Neil D'Amour Award (1976), by the National Association of Boards of Education/NCEA, for outstanding contribution of statewide, regional, national or international significance to the Catholic board movement.

Rev. Msgr. Olin J. Murdick (1977), Rev. Gerald A. Gettelfinger (1980), Sr. Mary Benet McKinney, O.S.B. (1981), Bishop William B. Friend (1982).

O'Reilly-Conway Medal (1979), by *The Pilot,* Boston archdiocesan newspaper, for distinctive contributions to journalism.

Anthony LaCamera (1979), Elliot Norton (1980), Frank Reynolds (1981), Ruth Mehrtens Galvin (1982).

Peace Award (1950), by the Secular Franciscan Order.

Myron C. Taylor (1950), John Foster Dulles (1951), John W. McCormack (1952), John C. Wu (1953), Ralph Bunche (1954), John R. Gariepy (1956), Most Rev. Richard J. Cushing (1957), Patrick McGeehan, Sr. (1958), Victor Andres Belaunde (1959), J. Edgar Hoover (1960), George K. Hunton (1961);

Mrs. Lester Auberlin (1962), Rev. Martin Luther King (1963), Most Rev. John J. Wright (1964), Pope Paul VI (1965), Cardinal Wyszynski (1966), Bishop Fred Pierce Corson (1967), Robert F. Kennedy, posthumously (1968), Msgr. Robert Fox (1969), Bishop James Walsh, M.M. (1970), Jean Vanier (1972), Mother Teresa of Calcutta (1974),

Dom Helder Camara (1975), Archbishop Joseph L. Bernardin (1976), Jose Francisco Garcia Bauer (1977), Manuella Mattioli (1978), Dorothy Day (1979), Pres. Anwar Sadat (1980).

Peter Guilday Prize (1972), by the American Catholic Historical Association for articles accepted by the editors of the *Catholic Historical Review* which are the first scholarly publications of their authors.

James P. Gaffey (1972), B. Robert Kreiser (1974), J. Dean O'Donnell, Jr. (1976), Mark A. Gabbert (1977), Virginia W. Leonard (1978), Vincent J. McNally (1980).

Pius XII Marian Award (1955), by the Montfort Missionaries for promotion of the devotion of consecration to the Immaculate Heart of Mary.

Denis M. McAuliffe, O.P. (1955), James M. Keane, O.S.M. (1956), Rev. John Cantwell (1957), Marie Delicia Unson (1958), Rev. Herman J. Vincent of St. Henry's Parish, Bridge City, Tex., and parishioners of St. Helen's Mission, Orangefield, Tex. (1959), Leo Dillon (1960), De Montfort Groups of Detroit, Mich., and Rev. Thomas Kerwin, their spiritual director (1961), Frank Duff (1965), Mr. and Mrs. Thomas F. Larkin, Jr. (1973).

Poverello Medal (1949), by The College of Steubenville (Ohio), "in recognition of great benefactions to humanity, exemplifying in our age the Christ-like spirit of charity which filled the life of St. Francis of Assisi."

Alcoholics Anonymous Fellowship (1949), Edward F. Hutton (1950), the Court of Last Resort, New York, N.Y. (1951), The Lions International (1952), Variety Clubs International (1953), Llewellyn J. Scott (1954), Dr. Jonas E. Salk and Associates (1955), Mother Anna Dengel (1956), Catherine de Hueck Doherty (1957), D. M. Hamill (1958);

Daniel W. Egan, T.O.R. (1959, posthumously), Mrs. Emma C. Zeis (1960), Donald H. McGannon (1961), Jane Wyatt (1962), Birgit Nilsson (1963), Arthur Joseph Rooney (1964), Joe E. Brown (1965), Project Hope (1966), Lena F. Edwards, M.D. (1967), VISTA (1968), Jack Twyman (1969), The Salvation Army (1970), Most Rev. John K. Mussio (1971), Bro. George J. Hungerman, F.M.S.I., M.D. (1972), The Dismas Committee of the St. Vincent de Paul Society (1973) U.S. Sen Mark O. Hatfield (1974), Sr. Mary Agatha, O.S.F., and Rev Kevin R. Keelan, T.O.R. (1975), Mother Teresa of Calcutta (1976), Dorothy Day (1977), Leon Jaworski (1978), Bishop Bernard J. Topel (1979), International Shrine Association (1980-81), Rev. Bruce Ritter, O.F.M. Conv. (1981-82).

Regina Medal (1959), by the Catholic Library Association for outstanding contributions to children's literature.

Eleanor Farjeon (1959), Anne Carroll Moore (1960), Padraic Colum (1961),

Frederick G. Melcher (1962), Anne Nolan Clark (1963), May Hill Arbuthnot (1964), Ruth Sawyer Durand (1965), Leo Politi (1966), Bertha Mahony Miller (1967), Marguerite de Angeli (1968), Lois Lenski (1969), Ingri and Edgar Parin d'Aulaire (1970), Tasha Tudor (1971), Meindert DeJong (1972), Frances Clarke Sayers (1973), Robert McCloskey (1974), Lynd Ward and May McNeer (1975), Virginia Haviland (1976), Marcia Brown (1977), Scott O'Dell (1978), Morton Schindel (1979), Beverly Cleary (1980), Augusta Baker (1981), Theodore Seuss Geisel (Dr. Seuss) (1982).

St. Bonaventue University Justice and Peace Medal (1981), by St. Bonaventure University (St. Bonaventure, N.Y.).

Bishop Thomas J. Gumbleton (1981), Eileen Egan (1982).

St. Francis de Sales Award (1959), by the Catholic Press Association for distinguished contribution to Catholic journalism.

Dale Francis (1959), Frank A. Hall (1960), John C. Murray, S.J. (1961), Albert J. Nevins, M.M. (1962), Floyd Anderson (1963), Rev. Patrick O'Connor (1964), John Cogley (1965), Joseph Breig (1966), John Reedy, C.S.C. (1967), Bishop James P. Shannon (1968), no award (1969), Msgr. Robert G. Peters (1970), Francis A. Fink (1971), Jeremy Harrington, O.F.M. (1972), Robert E. Burns (1973), Gerard E. Sherry (1974), John B. Sheerin, C.S.P. (1975), Lillian R. Block (1976), A.E.P. Wall (1977), Donald Thorman, posthumously (1978), Walter J. Burghardt, S.J. (1979), Thurston Davis, S.J. (1980), John F. Fink (1981), Allen C. Bradley, posthumously (1982).

St. Francis Xavier Medal (1954), by Xavier University (Cincinnati) to persons exemplifying the spirit of St. Francis Xavier.

Most Rev. Fulton J. Sheen, Rev. Leo Kampsen, Msgr. Frederick G. Hochwalt (1954), James Keller, M.M. (1955), Gen. Carlos P. Romulo (1956), Stan Musial, Aloysius A. Breen, S.J., Edwin G. Becker (1957), Msgr. (Maj. Gen.) Patrick J. Ryan, Msgr. (Maj. Gen.) Terrence P. Finnegan, Msgr. (Rear Adm.) George A. Rosso (1958);

T. L. Bouscaren, S.J. and Dr. Thomas A. Dooley (1959), Neal Ahern and Celestine J. Steiner, S.J. (1960), Philip J. Scharper (1961), Charles Dismas Clark, S.J. (1962), Pres. John F. Kennedy (posthumously) and J. Paul Spaeth (1963), James B. Donovan (1964), Charles H. Keating, Jr. (1965), Frank Blair (1967), Martin H. Work (1968), Lt. Col. William A. Anders and Archbishop Karl J. Alter (1969), Bishop James E. Walsh, M.M. (1970), Lawrence Welk, Rev. Msgr. Ralph W. Beiting (1971), Paul L. O'Connor, S.J. (1972), James F. Maguire, S.J., Edward P. VonderHaar (posthumously) (1973), G. Milton Wurzelbacher (1974), D. J. O'Conor (posthumously) (1975), Bishop John K. Mussio

(1977), C. Robert Beirne and George H. Brueggeman (1978), Msgr. Robert Sherry and Rev. Emerson Colaw (1979), Msgr. George Higgins (1980), Archbishop Joseph L. Bernardin (1981).

St. Vincent de Paul Medal (1948), by St. John's University (Jamaica, N.Y.), for outstanding service to Catholic charities.

Francis D. McGarey (1948), John A. Coleman (1949), Aloysius L. Fitzpatrick (1950), Frank J. Lewis (1951), Howard W. Fitzpatrick (1952), Richard F. Mulroy (1953), Harry J. Kirk (1954), Bernard J. Keating (1955), John M. Nolan (1956), John R. Gariepy (1957);

Charles E. McCarthy (1958), Frederick V. Goess (1959), Maurice J. Costello, M.D. (1960), Thomas F. Hanley (1961), John J. Lynch (1962), William H. Walters (1963), George E. Heneghan (1964), James A. Quigney (1965), Henry J. Shields (1966);

Eugene McGovern (1967), George J. Krygier (1968), James A. Cousins (1969), Edward T. Reilly (1970), T. Raber Taylor (1971), Luke J. Smith (1972), William C. Rohrkemper (1973), Edward V. Murtaugh (1974), Frank V. Buckley (1975), Martin J. Loftus (1976), John F. Coppinger (1977), Howard E. Halaska (1978), Ronald T. Y. Choo (1979), John J. Stanton (1980), Allan L Hicks (1981).

Serra Award of the Americas (1947), by the Academy of American Franciscan History for service to Inter-American good will.

Sumner Welles (1947), Pablo Martinez del Rio (1948), Dr. Herbert E. Bolton (1949), Gabriela Mistral (1950), Carlos E. Castaneda (1951), Victor A. Belaunde (1952), Clarence Haring (1953), Alceu Amoroso Lima (1954), France V. Scholes (1956);

Silvio Zavala (1957), John Tate Lanning (1958), John Basadre (1959), Arthur Preston Whitaker (1960), Marcel Bataillon (1961), Javier Malagon y Barcelo (1962), Dr. George P. Hammond (1964), Augustin Millares Carlo (1970), Max Savelle (1976), Miguel Leon-Portilla (1978).

Signum Fidei Medal (1942), by the Alumni Association of La Salle College (Phila.) for noteworthy contributions to the advancement of humanitarian principles in keeping with Christian tradition.

Brother E. Anselm, F.S.C. (1942), Karl H. Rogers (1943), Very Rev. Edward V. Stanford, O.S.A. (1944), Mrs. Edward V. Morrell (1945), Cardinal Dennis Dougherty (1946), Max Jordan (1947), John J. Sullivan (1948), Dr. Louis H. Clerf (1949), Most Rev. Gerald P. O'Hara (1950), Most Rev. Fulton J. Sheen (1951);

John H. Harris (1952), James Keller, M.M. (1953), John M. Haffert (1954), Dr. Francis J. Braceland (1955), Matthew H. McCloskey (1956), Henry Viscardi, Jr. (1957), no award (1958), Dr. Joseph J. Toland, Jr. (1959), Luke

E. Hart (1960), Joseph E. McCafferty (1961);

Martin H. Work (1962), R. Sargent Shriver (1963), Mother M. Benedict, M.D. (1964), Sen. Eugene McCarthy (1965), William B. Ball (1966), Frank Folsom (1967), Rev. Leon H. Sullivan (1968), Rev. William J. Finley (1969);

Dr. James W. Turpin (1970), Lisa A. Richette, Esq. (1971), Rev. Melvin Floyd (1972), Elwood E. Kieser, C.S.P. (1973), Msgr. Philip J. Dowling (1974), James C. Giuffre, M.D. (1975), Most Rev. Bernard J. Topel (1976), Mildred Jefferson, M.D. (1977), Judge Genevieve Blatt (1978), Rita Ungaro Schiavone (1979), Rev. Aloysius Schwartz (1980), Sister Mary Luke, O.P. (1981), William and Helene Sample (1982).

Soteriological Award (1967), by the Confraternity of the Passion (Third Order of the Passionists, Corpus Christi Residence, 80 David St., South River, N.J. 08882), for outstanding exemplification of sharing in the Passion of Christ in contemporary society.

Most Rev. Cuthbert M. O'Gara, C.P. (1967), Mrs. Martin Luther King, Jr. (1968), Veronica's Veil Players (1969), Mother Mary Teresa Benedetti, C.P. (1970), Dr. Billy Graham (1971), Mrs. Florence Kuhn (1972), Rev. Martin J. Tooker, C.P. (1973), Mrs. Mary Sloan (1974), Aileen Leary (1975), Marie Gallagher (1976), Grete Faber and Georgianna Wendt (1977), Regina Adamecz (1979), Connie Dawson (1980).

Stella Maris Medal (1960), by Mary Manse College (Toledo, O.) for service.

Alice R. May (1960), Emma Endres Kountz (1961), Elizabeth M. Zepf (1962), Judge Geraldine F. Macelwane (1963), Ven. Mother Mary Adelaide, O.S.F. (1964), Marian Rejent, M.D. (1966), Mrs. Irene Hubbard McCarthy (1967), Sr. Ruth Hickey, S.G.M. (1969), Mrs. Ella Phillips Stewart (1970), Sr. M. Lawrence Wilson (1971), Mrs. Carol Pietrykowski (1972), Miss Rita O'Grady (1973), Mildred L. Bayer, R.N. (1975).

Sword of Loyola (1964), by Loyola University of Chicago to person or persons exemplifying Ignatius of Loyola's courage, dedication and service.

J. Edgar Hoover (1964), Col. James McDivitt and Maxime A. Faget (1965), Lt. Dieter Dengler (1966), Brig. Gen. David Sarnoff (1967), Capt. Edward V. Rickenbacker (1968), Dr. Thomas O. Paine and William A. Anders (1969), Most Rev. Fulton J. Sheen (1970), Helen Hayes (1971), James F. Maguire, S.J. (1972), Mr. and Mrs. Foster G. McGaw (1973), John F. Smith, Jr. (1974), Bob Newhart (1975), Arthur Fiedler (1976), Mildred F. Jefferson, M.D. (1977), Rev. Vincent T. O'Keefe, S.J. (1978), George S. Halas (1979), Cardinal John Cody (1980), Mrs. John W. Clarke (1981).

U.S. Catholic Award (1978), by editors o₁

U.S. *Catholic* magazine for furthering the cause of women in the Church.

Sr. Agnes Cunningham, S.S.C.M. (1978), Sr. Marjorie Tuite, O.P. (1979), Sr. M. Theresa Kane, R.S.M. (1980), Most Revs. Raymond G. Hunthausen, Rembert G. Weakland, Charles A. Buswell, Michael F. McAuliffe, William E. McManus (1981), Mrs. Patricia C. Crowley (1982).

Vercelli Medal (1947), by the Holy Name Society for distinguished service to ideals of the society.

William Bruce, Paul M. Brennan, Joseph Scott, Stephen Barry, Patrick Kennedy (1947), R. W. Hoogstraet (1948), William H. Collins (1949), Ward D. Hopkins (1950), Charles A. Burkholder, James C. Connell, James T. Vocelle, Edwin J. Allen, Fred A. Muth, Austin J. Roche, Michael Lawlor (1951), Michael L. Roche (1953), Maurice J. O'Sullivan, Lucien T. Vivien, Jr. (1954);

John A. Lee, Sr., Daniel M. Hamill, Clarence F. Boggan, Louis J. Euler, Henry J. McGreevy, Ralph F. Nunlist (1955), James J. McDonnell (1957), Joseph J. Wilson (1958), William J. Meehan (1959), Paul Meade (1960), William T. Tavares (1961), David M. Martin (1962), Bert M. Walz (1963), Herbert Michelbrook (1964), Alfred A. McGarraghy (1965), Frank J. Beuerlein (1968), Humbert J. Campana (1970), Richard Asmus (1971), Charles J. Little (1973), William J. Burke, Jr. (1974), Stephen Andrusisian (1975), James P. Bailey (1976), Lanaux Marston (1977), Louis C. Fink (1979), J. Earl Knott, Jr. (1980).

CHRISTOPHER AWARDS

Christopher Awards were presented Feb. 25, 1982, in New York City to writers, directors and producers for their work in books, motion pictures and television.

Award winners were selected on the basis of works which embodied artistic and technical excellence and which had received a significant degree of public acceptance as well as affirming the highest value of the human spirit.

The award is a bronze medallion which bears the Christopher motto: "Better to light one candle than to curse the darkness."

Books

Asking for Trouble: The Autobiography of a Banned Journalist, Donald Woods; Atheneum.

The Fragile Curtain, Karen Burton Mains; David C. Cook Publishing Co.

A Miracle to Believe In, Barry Neil Kaufman; Doubleday.

Pioneer Women: Voices from the Kansas Frontier, Joanna L. Stratton; Simon and Shuster.

Refusenik: Trapped in the Soviet Union, Mark Ya. Azbel; Houghton Mifflin.

Righteous Gentile: The Story of Raoul Wallenberg, Missing Hero of the Holocaust, John Bierman; Viking Press.

Within the Whirlwind, Eugenia Ginzburg, translated by Ian Boland; Harcourt Brace Jovanovich (Helen and Kurt Wolff Book).

Books for Young People

My Mom Travels a Lot, Caroline Feller Bauer, illustrated by Nancy Winslow Parker; Picture Book (Frederick Warne).

Even If I Did Something Awful, Barbara Shook Hazen, illustrated by Nancy Kincade; Atheneum; ages 6-9.

A Gift of Mirrorvax, Malcolm MacCloud; Atheneum; ages 10-14.

The Islanders, John Rowe Townsend; Lippincott; young adult.

Motion Pictures

"The Boat Is Full," Quartet/Films Inc. George Reinhart, Markus Imhoof.

"Chariots of Fire," Ladd Company and Warner Bros. Dodi Fayed, David Puttnam, Hugh Hudson, Colin Welland.

"Gallipoli," Paramount. Francis O'Brien, Robert Stigwood Patricia Lovell, Peter Weir, David Williamson.

"Heartland," Levitt-Pickman. Annick Smith, Michael Hausman, Beth Ferris, Richard Pearce.

Television Specials

"Bill," CBS. Alan Landsburg, Mel Stuart, Anthony Page, Corey Blechman.

"Bitter Harvest," NBC. Charles Fries, Tony Ganz, Roger Young, Richard Friedenberg.

"Close Harmony," WNET/PBS. Nigel Noble.

"The Color of Friendship: An ABC Afterschool Special," ABC. Diana Kerew, Patrick McCormick, Stan Lathan, Johnny Dawkins.

"Crisis at Central High," CBS. Richard Levinson, William Link, Freyda Rothstein, David Susskind, Robert A. Papazian, Lamont Johnson.

"Family Reunion," NBC. Lucy Jarvis, Fielder Cook, Allan Sloane.

"James Cagney: That Yankee Doodle Dandy," PBS. Ron Devillier, Brian Donegan, Richard Schickel.

"A Long Way Home," ABC. Alan Landsburg, Tom Kuhn, Linda Otto, Robert Markowitz, Dennis Nemec.

"The Marva Collins Story," CBS. Marian Rees, Conrad Holzgang, Peter Levin, Clifford Campion.

"Miracle on Ice," ABC. Frank von Zerneck, Robert Greenwald. Steven H. Stern, Lionel Chetwynd.

"The Patricia Neal Story," CBS. Lawrence Schiller, Don Silverman, Anthony Harvey, Anthony Page, Robert Anderson.

"The Pride of Jesse Hallam," CBS. Frank Konigsberg, Sam Manners, Gary Nelson, Suzanne Clauser.

Special Awards

"Today," NBC — for 30 years of five-day-a-week reporting on the nation and the world.

James Cagney — for his singular contribution to the dramatic arts.

SCIENCE AND THE CHURCH

Following are excerpts from an address delivered by Pope John Paul June 15, 1982, during a visit to the European Center for Nuclear Research in Geneva, Switzerland.

These excerpts are from the text circulated by the NC Documentary Service, Origins, July 15, 1982 (Vol. 12, No. 8).

There was a time when certain men of science were tempted to shut themselves up in an attitude imbued with "scientism." This was a philosophical choice rather than a scientific attitude, with a wish to disregard other forms of knowledge. If such was the case, those times seem to have gone by; the majority of scientists admit that the natural sciences cover only part of reality, with their method based on experimentation and on reproduction of results; or, rather, they reach it only under a certain aspect. Philosophy, art, religion — religion, above all, which is aware of being linked with a transcendent revelation — perceive other aspects of the reality of the universe, of man, above all.

Science and Faith

The Church well maintains the specific distinction between scientific and religious knowledge and their methods. She is likewise sure of their being complementary to each other and of their having a profound harmony around the one same God, the Creator and Redeemer of man. The Church wishes to remove all misunderstanding about this point. She respects the science of nature in its order. Natural science is not a threat in her eyes, but rather a more thoroughgoing manifestation of the Creator-God. She rejoices at the progress of science, and so ... she encourages your research carried out in the spirit we have mentioned. She admits in any case that contemporary scientific culture calls for maturer faith in Christians, openness to the language of and the questions raised by scientists, a sense of the orders of knowledge and differing approaches to truth. In a word, she desires that the dialogue between science and faith may enter upon an ever more positive stage — even though it has experienced tensions in history — and be intensified at all levels.

Love of truth, sought in humility, is one of the great values capable of uniting men of today across the various cultures. Scientific culture is not opposed to humanist culture or to mystical culture. All authentic culture is openness to the essential, and there is no truth that cannot become universal. So it is that I quite recently decided to set up a Pontifical Council for Culture at Rome. I was well aware in doing so of this fundamental reality uniting all mankind, and I explicitly willed that the council shall be open to all researchers and research centers.

Applications of Research

You will permit me to mention some possible applications of your research, even though they go beyond your task, your responsibilities and the purpose of the center. History shows us that the discovery of new phenomena leads in time to prodigious applications of them, often completely unexpected applications. There can be no doubt that your countries, the governments and technicians of your countries, follow your research with all the more interest the more they count on making intense use of it in the more or less long term. And what utilization might be foreseen of the structure of the atom and possible disintegration of it?

Men will be able to draw out the best and worst — the best for the service of man and his development in applications that might concern his health, his food resources, his energy resources, the protection of nature — and the worst, involving destruction of the biological equilibrium, dangerous radioactivity and, above all, engines of destruction, already terribly dangerous by their power and number.

Concern of the Church

The Church has spoken often enough of the danger of atomic weapons. I myself have taken a good number of initiatives in this regard. But, as I reminded members of the Pontifical Academy of Sciences Nov. 14, 1980, even as regards the peaceful use of nuclear energy, the Church, together with all men of good will, wishes that all consequences be exactly examined — regarding radioactive impact, for example, and genetics, pollution of the environment, disposal of nuclear waste — that strict guarantees be established and information be commensurate with these problems.

This does not come under your direct responsibility. But you see what is at stake better than others do. Consequently, it is particularly incumbent on you to promote information in these domains, above all in regard to those in charge of technical applications, and to insist that the results of science — so marvelous in themselves — will never be turned against man at the technological level and will always be employed only for the good of humanity by people inspired by the greatest love for mankind.

DEATHS SEPTEMBER, 1981, TO SEPTEMBER, 1982

Bartholome, Bishop Peter W., 89, June 17, 1982, near Ward Springs, Minn; bishop of St. Cloud from 1953 to 1968.

Bell, Bishop Alden J., 78, Aug. 28, 1982, Sacramento, Calif.; bishop of Sacramento from 1962 to 1979.

Betancourt, Romulo, 73, Sept. 28, 1981, New York, N.Y.; Venezuelan statesman; introduced democratic reforms during his two terms as president (1945-48; 1959-64); settled church-state issues with the Vatican.

Blanchette, Bishop Romeo R., 69, Jan. 10, 1982, Joliet, Ill.; bishop of Joliet from 1966 to 1979, when he retired because of amyotrophic lateral sclerosis (Lou Gehrig's disease).

Boekenfoehr, Bishop John, O.M.I., 79, Aug. 10, 1982, Cornwall, Ont., Canada; U.S.-born bishop of Kimberley, South Africa, from 1953 to 1974.

Bradley, Allen C., 68, Dec. 14, 1981, Springfield, N.J.; Catholic Press Association postal specialist; awarded its 1982 St. Francis de Sales Award posthumously; long-time office manager of *The Advocate,* Newark archdiocesan paper.

Breig, Joseph A., 76, Feb. 6, 1982, Orlando, Fla., while attending Mass; editor and columnist for the Catholic press for more than 30 years.

Buckley, Rev. Joseph W., S.M., 76, Sept. 11, 1981, New Orleans, La.; superior general of the Marists, from 1961 to 1970.

Bugnini, Archbishop Annibale, 69, July 3, 1982, Rome, Italy; influential figure in the liturgical reform of the Second Vatican Council; papal pro-nuncio to Iran from 1976; tried, unsuccessfully, to mediate release of 52 U.S. hostages.

Cavanaugh, Rev. Francis P., C.S.C., 82, June 4, 1982, Notre Dame, Ind.; educator.

Clancy, Rev. William, C.O., 59, Jan. 6, 1982, Pittsburgh, Pa.; journalist; associate editor of *Commonweal,* 1952-56; religion editor of *Newsweek,* 1956-57; founded *Worldview,* monthly journal of the Council of Religion and International Affairs; ordained priest in 1964; provost, from 1968, of Pittsburgh Oratory which he helped found.

Cody, Cardinal John P., 74, Apr. 25, 1982, Chicago, Ill.; archbishop of Chicago from 1965; cardinal from 1967; episcopal career marked with achievements and controversy; noted as an able administrator; as apostolic administrator (1962-64) and later archbishop (1964-65) of New Orleans, he gained national attention for carrying out integration of Catholic schools in the archdiocese; in Chicago, he was charged by some priests with lack of communication and consultation; his last year was troubled by unsubstantiated charges that he had misused Church funds.

Considine, Rev. John J., M.M., 84, May 4, 1982, Maryknoll, N.Y.; editor, author, promoter of mission activities; organized the USCC Latin America Bureau (1960); director (1926-34) of *Fides,* news service of the missions which he founded at the request of the Congregation for the Propagation of the Faith; founded the Papal Volunteers for Latin America; appointed advisor to the Peace Corps by President Kennedy.

Dahood, Rev. Mitchell J., S.J., 60, Mar. 8, 1982, Rome, Italy; American biblical scholar; professor at the Pontifical Biblical Institute, Rome, from 1956.

Donahue, Bishop Stephen J., 88, Aug. 17, 1982, New York, N.Y.; auxiliary bishop of New York from 1934 to 1969.

Dunkerley, Sister Dorothea, O.S.U., 84, Dec. 30, 1981, New Rochelle, N.Y.; educator; first woman president of the College of New Rochelle, 1950-57.

Durant, Will, 96, Nov. 7, 1981, Los Angeles, Calif.; Pulitzer Prize-winning historian and philosopher; left the Church as young man; reconciled before his death.

Felici, Cardinal Pericle, 70, Mar. 22, 1982, Foggia, Italy; noted Latin scholar and expert in canon law; headed the Apostolic Signatura, the Church's highest court, and the Commission for the Revision of the Code of Canon Law which completed its work of revision in 1981; a central figure in the Second Vatican Council; cardinal from 1967.

Finn, Msgr. Charles A., 104, Mar. 7, 1982, Boston, Mass.; believed the oldest priest in U.S.; priest for 79 years.

Frei, Eduardo, 71, Jan. 22, 1982, Santiago, Chile; Christian Democratic Party president of Chile, 1964-70.

Graner, Archbishop Lawrence L., C.S.C., 81; Apr. 21, 1982, Notre Dame, Ind.; bishop (1947) and first archbishop of Dacca, Bangladesh from 1950 to 1966.

Green, Bishop Michael Joseph, 64, Aug. 30, 1982, Pontiac, Mich.; bishop of Reno from 1967 to 1974, when he resigned.

Guilfoyle, Bishop Merlin J., 73, Nov. 20, 1981, Stockton, Calif.; bishop of Stockton from 1969 to 1979; columnist for the Catholic press while auxiliary bishop of San Francisco, from 1950 to 1969.

Hagarty, John L. (Jack), 78, Mar. 23, 1982, Washington, D.C.; retired Georgetown University head football coach; teams under his direction won 23 consecutive games, 1938-40.

Hennessy, Rev. David, A.A., 68, Mar. 23, 1982, Charlotte, N.C.; Catholic chaplain of Ringling Brothers and Barnum and Bailey Circus and other U.S. circuses.

Hervas y Benet, Bishop Juan, 77, June 6, 1982, Felanix, Spain; one of the founders and the first national moderator of the Cursillo Movement.

Issenmann, Bishop Clarence G., 75, July 29, 1982, Cleveland, O.; promoted professionalism and freedom in the Catholic press; bishop of Cleveland from 1966 to 1974.

Jordan, Archbishop Anthony, O.M.I., 80, Mar. 4, 1982, Edmonton, Canada; archbishop of Edmonton from 1964 to 1973.

Karasiewicz, Rev. Joseph, 59, Dec. 13, 1981, Detroit, Mich.; parish priest who gained national attention in 1980 when he led an unsuccessful protest against demolition of a parish church and neighborhood to make way for a General Motors plant.

Kearney, Rev. Vincent S., S.J., 68, Sept. 8, 1981, New York, N.Y.; associate editor of *America;* authority on Arab-Israeli relations.

Kelly, Msgr. Francis W., 71, Jan. 9, 1982, Oceanside, Calif; U.S. Navy chaplain; "Father Foxhole" of World War II, who was mentioned frequently in *Guadacanal Diary;* awarded the Purple Heart and Legion of Merit.

Kugelman, Rev. Richard, C.P., 72, Oct. 13, 1981, West Palm Beach, Fla.; scripture scholar; member of the board of translators of the *New American Bible.*

Luoni, Archbishop Silvio, 61, Apr. 12, 1982, Busto Arsizio, Italy; in the Vatican diplomatic service from 1953.

McCormick, Rev. John, S.S., 77, Oct. 13, 1981, Catonsville, Md.; rector of the Theological College of Catholic University of America, 1949-68; leader in post-conciliar seminary reform in the U.S.

Nold, Bishop Wendelin J., 81, Oct. 1, 1981, Houston, Tex.; bishop of Galveston-Houston from 1950 to 1975.

Palmer, Rev. Paul F., S.J., 73, Feb. 14, 1982, New York, N.Y.; theologian, author.

Parent, Archbishop Charles-Eugene, 80, June 3, 1982, Rimouski, Canada; archbishop of Rimouski from 1951 to 1967.

Price, Jo-Ann (Mrs. Harry W. Baehr), 57, July 15, 1982, Brooklyn, N.Y.; journalist; prize-winning religion reporter of the *New York Herald Tribune,* 1951-65; New York correspondent for NC News Service from 1973.

Ray, Lt. Col., Charles, 43, Jan. 18, 1982, Paris, France; military attache at the U.S. Embassy in Paris; assassinated.

Rocco, Archbishop Carmine, 70, May 12, 1982; Vatican diplomat since 1961; nuncio to Brazil from 1973.

Roncalli, Giuseppe, 87, Nov. 17, 1981, Sotto il Monte, Italy; youngest and only survivor of Pope John XXIII's 13 brothers and sisters.

Rudloff, Rev. Leo A., O.S.B., 80, Aug. 17, 1982, Weston, Vt.; promoted Jewish-Christian relations; abbot of Dormition Abbey, Jerusalem, 1953-68.

Scheele, Sister Augustine, O.S.F., 85, Mar. 13, 1982, Milwaukee, Wis.; educator; president of Alverno College, 1948-68.

Seper, Cardinal Franjo, 76, Dec. 30, 1981, Rome, Italy; Yugoslavian cardinal; prefect of the Sacred Congregation for the Doctrine of the Faith from 1968 to November, 1981; one of the first non-Italians to hold a key post in the Roman Curia; cardinal from 1965; during his tenure as prefect, the congregatino censured Hans Kung, examined the work of Edward Schillebeeckx, and was involved in efforts to reconcile Archbishop Lefebvre.

Sheed, Frank, 84, Nov. 20, 1981, Jersey City, N.J.; author; lecturer; street preacher; pioneer in the modern Catholic lay apostolate; with his wife Maisie Ward (died 1975) founded Sheed and Ward in 1926, a major Catholic publishing house for nearly 50 years; works include *Theology and Sanity, Society and Sanity.*

Sisson, Sister Mary Elise, S.S.S., 84, July 21, 1982, Meadowbrook, Pa.; music educator; promoted black musical talent.

Slattery, Rev. William M., C.M., 87, Aug. 10, 1982, Philadelphia, Pa.; superior general of the Vincentians and Daughters of Charity, 1947-68, the first American to hold the post.

Smith, Walter Wellesley (Red), 76, Jan. 15, 1982, Stamford, Conn.; sportswriter for the *New York Herald Tribune* and, from 1971, the *New York Times;* awarded the Pulitzer Prize in 1976.

Sullivan, Bishop Joseph V., 63, Sept. 4, 1982, Baton Rouge, La.; bishop of Baton Rouge from 1974.

Swain, Germaine, July 10, 1982, San Francisco, Calif; journalist; Secular Franciscan; NC News Service Hong Kong correspondent, 1960-74; active in charitable works.

Tennelly, Rev. John B., S.S., 91, Oct. 18, 1981, Catonsville, Md.; director of the Bureau of Catholic Indian Missions and Commission for Catholic Missions among Colored People and Indians from 1936 to 1976, when he retired.

Unger, Rev. Dominic, O.F.M. Cap., 75, July 11, 1982, Hays, Kans.; theologian; fellow of the Pontifical Marian Academy.

Walsh, Sister Mary Rosalia, M.H.S.H., 85, Jan. 21, 1982, Towson, Md.; pioneer of religious education in U.S.; author; sister of Bishop James E. Walsh, M.M. (died 1981).

Walsh, Rev. Michael P., S.J., 70, Apr. 23, 1982, Boston, Mass.; educator; president of Fordham University, 1969-72, during time of financial crisis; balanced the budget.

Ward, Rev. William J., O.S.F.S., 76, Oct. 11, 1981, Philadelphia, Pa.; superior general of the Oblates of St. Francis de Sales from 1970.

Weldon, Bishop Christopher J., 76, Mar. 19, 1982, Springfield, Mass.; bishop of Springfield from 1950 to 1977.

Wey, Alexander J., 84, Nov. 17, 1981, Cleveland, O.; journalist; pioneer in development of the Catholic Press Association.

Zebrowski, Brother Zeon, O.F.M. Conv., 90, Apr. 24, 1982, Tokyo, Japan; Polish missionary in Japan for 52 years; arrived there in 1930 with St. Maximilian Kolbe.